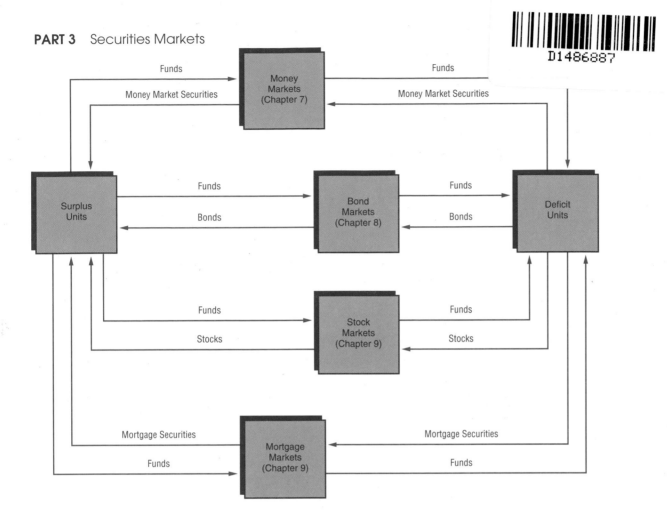

THIRD EDITION

FINANCIAL MARKETS AND INSTITUTIONS

THIRD EDITION

FINANCIAL MARKETS AND INSTITUTIONS

JEFF MADURA

Florida Altantic University

WEST PUBLISHING COMPANY

Minneapolis/Saint Paul   New York   Los Angeles   San Francisco

Copyediting: Jan Krygier
Composition: Parkwood Composition
Artwork: Publication Services
Interior Design: John Edeen
Cover Design: Caroline Vaaler, Three Fish Design
Cover Photo: Manhattan, NY, by Kunio Owaki/The Stock Market

WEST'S COMMITMENT TO THE ENVIRONMENT

In 1906, West Publishing Company began recycling materials left over from the production of books. This began a tradition of efficient and responsible use of resources. Today, up to 95 percent of our legal books and 70 percent of our college and school texts are printed on recycled, acid-free stock. West also recycles nearly 22 million pounds of scrap paper annually—the equivalent of 181,717 trees. Since the 1960s, West has devised ways to capture and recycle waste inks, solvents, oils, and vapors created in the printing process. We also recycle plastics of all kinds, wood, glass, corrugated cardboard, and batteries, and have eliminated the use of Styrofoam book packaging. We at West are proud of the longevity and the scope of our commitment to the environment.

Production, Prepress, Printing and Binding by West Publishing Company.

British Library Cataloguing-in-Publication Data. A catalogue record for this book is available from the British Library.

Library of Congress Cataloging-in-Publication Data

Madura, Jeff.
    Financial markets and institutions / Jeff Madura. — 3rd ed.
       p.   cm.
    Includes index.
    ISBN 0-314-04160-5 (hard)
    1. Financial institutions.   2. Capital market.   3. Money market.
  I. Title.
  HG173.M26   1995
  332—dc20   94-17238
                                                                  CIP

To Mary

ABOUT THE AUTHOR

Jeff Madura is Sun Bank Professor of Finance at Florida Atlantic University. He has written several textbooks, including *International Financial Management.* His research, on topics of banking and financial markets, has been published in numerous journals, including *Journal of Financial and Quantitative Analysis, Journal of Money, Credit and Banking, Journal of Banking and Finance, Applied Financial Economics, Journal of Risk and Insurance, Journal of Financial Research,* and *Journal of Financial Services Research.* He has received awards for excellence in teaching and research, and has served as a consultant for commercial banks, securities firms, and other corporations.

BRIEF CONTENTS

PART 1   **OVERVIEW OF THE FINANCIAL ENVIRONMENT**   1

CHAPTER 1   **ROLE OF FINANCIAL MARKETS AND INSTITUTIONS**   3
CHAPTER 2   **DETERMINATION OF INTEREST RATES**   23
CHAPTER 3   **RELATIONSHIPS BETWEEN INTEREST RATES AND SECURITY PRICES**   47
CHAPTER 4   **STRUCTURE OF INTEREST RATES**   73

PART 2   **THE FED AND MONETARY POLICY**   111

CHAPTER 5   **FUNCTIONS OF THE FED**   113
CHAPTER 6   **MONETARY THEORY AND POLICY**   137

PART 3   **SECURITIES MARKETS**   173

CHAPTER 7   **MONEY MARKETS**   175
CHAPTER 8   **BOND MARKETS**   199
CHAPTER 9   **MORTGAGE MARKETS**   227
CHAPTER 10   **STOCK MARKETS**   249

PART 4   **DERIVATIVE SECURITIES MARKETS**   289

CHAPTER 11   **FINANCIAL FUTURES MARKETS**   291
CHAPTER 12   **OPTIONS MARKETS**   319
CHAPTER 13   **INTEREST RATE SWAP MARKETS**   355
CHAPTER 14   **FOREIGN EXCHANGE DERIVATIVE MARKETS**   391

PART 5   **COMMERCIAL BANKING**   419

CHAPTER 15   **COMMERCIAL BANK SOURCES AND USES OF FUNDS**   421
CHAPTER 16   **BANK REGULATION**   443

CHAPTER 17 **BANK MANAGEMENT** 475

CHAPTER 18 **BANK PERFORMANCE** 511

CHAPTER 19 **INTERNATIONAL BANKING** 535

PART 6 **NONBANK FINANCIAL INSTITUTIONS** 561

CHAPTER 20 **SAVINGS INSTITUTIONS** 563

CHAPTER 21 **CREDIT UNIONS** 595

CHAPTER 22 **FINANCE COMPANIES** 611

CHAPTER 23 **MUTUAL FUNDS** 627

CHAPTER 24 **SECURITIES FIRMS** 655

CHAPTER 25 **PENSION FUNDS** 677

CHAPTER 26 **INSURANCE COMPANIES** 695

CONTENTS

PREFACE   xxvii

PART 1   OVERVIEW OF THE FINANCIAL ENVIRONMENT   1

CHAPTER 1   ROLE OF FINANCIAL MARKETS AND INSTITUTIONS   3

Overview of Financial Markets   4
Primary versus Secondary Markets   4
Money versus Capital Markets   4
Organized versus Over-the-Counter Markets   4
Financial Market Efficiency   5
Securities Traded in Financial Markets   5
Financial Market Regulation   7
Financial Market Globalization   7
Role of Financial Institutions in Financial Markets   8
Role of Depository Institutions   8
Role of Nondepository Financial Institutions   9
Illustration of Financial Institution Roles   11
Comparison of Financial Institutions   12
Summary   13
Questions   14
WSJ Case Application   16
Projects   17
References   20

CHAPTER 2   DETERMINATION OF INTEREST RATES   23

Loanable Funds Theory   23
Household Demand for Loanable Funds   23
Business Demand for Loanable Funds   24
Government Demand for Loanable Funds   25
Foreign Demand for Loanable Funds   26
Aggregate Demand for Loanable Funds   27
Supply of Loanable Funds   27
Equilibrium Interest Rate   29
Changes in the Equilibrium Interest Rate   31

The Fisher Effect   33
Key Issues Regarding Interest Rates   34
  Impact of Inflation on Interest Rates   34
  Impact of a Government Budget Deficit on Interest Rates   35
  Impact of Foreign Interest Rates   36
Evaluation of Interest Rates Over Time   37
Forecasting Interest Rates   38
Summary   41
Questions   41
WSJ Case Application   44
Projects   46
References   46

CHAPTER 3   **RELATIONSHIPS BETWEEN INTEREST RATES AND SECURITY PRICES**   47

Bond Valuation   47
  Valuation of Bonds with Semiannual Payments   50
  Use of Annuity Tables for Valuation   52
Impact of Interest Rate Movements on Bond Prices   53
  Relationships Between Coupon Rate, Required Return and
    Bond Price   53
  Implications for Financial Institutions   57
Bond Price Sensitivity   57
  Influence of Maturity on Bond Price Sensitivity   57
  Influence of Coupons on Bond Price Sensitivity   58
Bond Price Elasticity   58
Duration   59
  Duration of a Portfolio   60
Forecasting Bond Prices   61
Forecasting Bond Yields   62
Forecasting Bond Portfolio Values   64
Forecasting Bond Portfolio Returns   65
Summary   66
Questions   67
Problems   68
Project   70
WSJ Case Application   71
References   72

CHAPTER 4   **STRUCTURE OF INTEREST RATES**   73

Factors Affecting Yields Among Securities   73
  Default Risk   74
  Liquidity   75
  Tax Status   76
  Term to Maturity   78
  Special Provisions   79
Explaining Actual Yield Differentials   80

Estimating the Appropriate Yield   82
A Closer Look at the Term Structure   83
  Pure Expectations Theory   84
  Liquidity Premium Theory   90
  Segmented Markets Theory   91
  Integrating the Theories on the Term Structure   93
  Use of the Yield Curve   94
  Impact of Debt Management on the Term Structure   97
  Historical Review of the Term Structure Relationship   99
International Structure of Interest Rates   100
Summary   100
Questions   101
Problems   103
WSJ Case Application   104
Projects   106
References   108
Integrative Problem: Interest Rate Forecasts and Investment Decisions   109

P A R T   2   THE FED AND MONETARY POLICY   111

C H A P T E R   5   FUNCTIONS OF THE FED   113

Organization of the Fed   113
  Federal Reserve District Banks   114
  Member Banks   114
  Board of Governors   115
  Federal Open Market Committee (FOMC)   116
  Advisory Committees   116
  Integration of Federal Reserve Components   117
Monetary Policy Tools   117
  Open Market Operations   118
  Adjusting the Discount Rate   121
  Adjusting the Reserve Requirement Ratio   121
  Comparison of Monetary Policy Tools   124
Impact of Technical Factors on Reserves   125
Fed Control of Money Supply   125
  Fed Emphasis on Money Supply Rather than Interest Rates   126
Recent Money Supply Target Shooting   126
Monetary Control Act of 1980   127
Global Monetary Policy   130
Summary   132
Questions   133
WSJ Case Application   134
Project   135
References   135

C H A P T E R 6   **MONETARY THEORY AND POLICY**   137

Monetary Theory   137
  Pure Keynesian Theory   137
  Quantity Theory and the Monetarist Approach   141
  Theory of Rational Explanations   143
  Integrating Monetary Theories   144
Trade-Off Faced by the Fed   145
Lags in Monetary Policy   148
Assessing the Impact of Monetary Policy   148
  Forecasting Money Supply Movements   149
  Forecasting the Impact of Monetary Policy on the Economy   154
Integrating Monetary and Fiscal Policies   154
  History   154
  Monetizing the Debt   158
  Market Reaction to Integrated Policies   159
Global Effects on U.S. Monetary Policy   160
Summary   164
Questions   164
Project   166
WSJ Case Application   167
References   168
Integrative Problem: Fed Watching   170

P A R T 3   **SECURITY MARKETS**   173

C H A P T E R 7   **MONEY MARKETS**   175

Money Market Securities   175
  Treasury Bills   176
  Commercial Paper   179
  Negotiable Certificates of Deposit (NCDs)   183
  Repurchase Agreements   183
  Federal Funds   184
  Banker's Acceptances   186
Institutional Use of Money Markets   188
Interaction Among Money Market Yields   190
Globalization of Money Markets   191
  Eurodollar Deposits and Euronotes   192
  Euro-Commercial Paper   194
  Performance of International Money Market Securities   194
  International Integration of Money Markets   195
Summary   195
Questions   195
Problems   196
WSJ Case Application   197
Project   198

CHAPTER 8   **BOND MARKETS**   199

Treasury Bonds   199
   Treasury Bond Quotations   200
   Stripped Bonds   201
Municipal Bonds   201
Corporate Bonds   203
   Characteristics of Corporate Bonds   203
   Bond Financing for Leveraged Buyouts   204
   Low- and Zero-Coupon Bonds   208
   Variable-Rate Bonds   208
   Convertible Bonds   208
Evaluating Bond Risk   210
   Interest Rate Risk   210
   Default Risk   212
Interaction Among Bond Yields   213
Bond Portfolio Management   214
Institutional Use of Bond Markets   215
Globalization of Bond Markets   216
   Eurobond Market   217
   Tax Effects   218
   Impact of Exchange Rates on Returns of Foreign Bonds   218
   Diversifying Bonds Internationally   219
Summary   220
Questions   220
Problem   223
WSJ Case Application   224
Projects   225
References   226

CHAPTER 9   **MORTGAGE MARKETS**   227

Background on Mortgages   227
Residential Mortgage Characteristics   227
   Insured versus Conventional Mortgages   228
   Fixed-Rate versus Adjustable-Rate Mortgages   229
   Determination of Mortgage Rates   230
   Mortgage Maturities   230
Creative Mortgage Financing   232
   Graduated-Payment Mortgage (GPM)   232
   Growing-Equity Mortgage   233
   Second Mortgage   233
   Shared-Appreciation Mortgage   234
Risk from Holding Mortgages   234
Secondary Mortgage Market Activities   234
   Use of Mortgage-Backed Securities   236
   Mortgage-Backed Securities for Small Investors   238
Institutional Use of Mortgage Markets   240
Globalization of Mortgage Markets   242
Summary   243

Questions 243
WSJ Application 245
Project 246
References 247

CHAPTER 10   **STOCK MARKETS** 249

Background on Common Stock 249
   Voting Rights 249
   Purchasing Stock on Margin 250
Background on Preferred Stock 251
Public Placement of Stock 251
   Shelf-Registration 253
Stock Exchanges 255
   Regulation of Stock Exchange Trading 256
Institutional Use of Stock Markets 257
   Program Trading 258
Stock Valuation Models 260
   Capital Asset Pricing Model 260
   Arbitrage Pricing Model 261
Determinants of Stock Price Movements 262
   Economic Factors 262
   Other Factors 263
   Evidence on Factors Affecting Stock Prices 264
Corporate Search for Undervalued Stock 265
   Managerial Assessment of the Firm's Own Stock 267
   Search for Overvalued Stocks 267
Stock Market Efficiency 268
   Test of the Efficient Market Hypothesis 269
Globalization of Stock Markets 270
   Investing in Foreign Markets 272
   Integration among Stock Markets 273
Summary 276
Questions 276
Problems 278
WSJ Case Application 279
Project 280
References 281
Appendix 10: Evaluation of Stock Performance 283
Integrative Problem: Asset Allocation 286

PART 4   **DERIVATIVE SECURITY MARKETS** 289

CHAPTER 11   **FINANCIAL FUTURES MARKETS** 291

Background on Financial Futures 291
   Steps Involved in Trading Futures 292
   Purpose of Trading Financial Futures 293

Interpreting Financial Future Tables   293
Valuation of Financial Futures   295
Speculating with Interest Rate Futures   295
Closing out the Futures Position   297
Hedging with Interest Rate Futures   298
    Using Interest Rate Futures to Create a Short Hedge   298
    Using Interest Rate Futures to Create a Long Hedge   301
    Hedging Net Exposure   301
    Cross-Hedging   301
    Hedging Assets Subject to Prepayment   303
Bond Index Futures   303
Stock Index Futures   304
    Speculating with Stock Index Futures   305
    Hedging with Stock Index Futures   305
    Dynamic Asset Allocation with Stock Index Futures   306
    Prices of Stock Index Futures Versus Underlying Stocks   306
    Arbitrage with Stock Index Futures   307
    Circuit Breakers on Stock Index Futures   307
Institutional Use of Futures Markets   310
Globalization of Futures Markets   311
    Non-U.S. Participation in U.S. Futures Contracts   311
    Foreign Stock Index Futures   311
    Currency Futures Contracts   312
Summary   312
Questions   313
Problems   315
WSJ Case Application   316
Projects   318
References   318

CHAPTER 12   **OPTIONS MARKETS**   319

Background on Stock Options   319
Speculating with Stock Options   320
    Speculating with Call Options   320
    Speculating with Put Options   323
Determinants of Stock Option Premiums   325
    Determinants of Call Option Premiums   325
    Determinants of Put Option Premiums   328
Hedging with Stock Options   330
    Hedging with Call Options   330
    Hedging with Put Options   332
Stock Index Options   332
    Hedging with Stock Index Options   332
    Dynamic Asset Allocation with Stock Index Options   334
Options on Futures Contracts   335
    Speculating with Options on Futures   335
    Hedging with Options on Futures   338
Institutional Use of Options Markets   339

Globalization of Options Markets   339
  Currency Options Contracts   341
Summary   341
Questions   342
Problems   343
WSJ Case Application   346
Projects   347
References   348
Appendix 12: Option Valuation   350

CHAPTER 13   **INTEREST RATE SWAP MARKETS**   355

Background   355
Participation by Financial Institutions   357
Types of Interest Rate Swaps   358
  Plain Vanilla Swaps   358
  Forward Swaps   361
  Callable Swaps   363
  Putable Swaps   363
  Extendable Swaps   365
  Zero-Coupon-for-Floating Swaps   367
  Rate-Capped Swaps   367
  Equity Swaps   368
  Other Types of Swaps   370
Risks of Interest Rate Swaps   370
  Basis Risk   370
  Credit Risk   371
  Sovereign Risk   372
Pricing Interest Rate Swaps   372
  Prevailing Market Interest Rates   372
  Availability of Counterparties   372
  Credit and Sovereign Risk   372
Applications of Interest Rate Swaps   373
  Application to Financial Institutions   373
  Application to Bond Issuers   373
Interest Rate Caps, Floors, and Collars   376
  Interest Rate Caps   376
  Interest Rate Floors   378
  Interest Rate Collars   378
Globalization of Swap Markets   380
  Currency Swaps   381
  Risks of Currency Swaps   383
Summary   384
Questions   384
Problems   386
WSJ Case Application   387
Project   388
References   388

CHAPTER 14   **FOREIGN EXCHANGE DERIVATIVE MARKETS**   391

Background on Foreign Exchange Markets   391
Exchange Rate Quotations   392
Types of Exchange Rate Systems   392
Exchange Rate Mechanism (ERM) Crisis   394
Factors Affecting Exchange Rate Movements   396
Differential Inflation Rates   396
Differential Interest Rates   397
Government Intervention   397
Speculation in Foreign Exchange Markets   398
Movements in Exchange Rates   399
Foreign Exchange Derivatives   399
Forward Contracts   401
Currency Futures Contracts   402
Currency Swaps   402
Currency Options Contracts   402
Use of Foreign Exchange Derivatives for Speculating   403
International Arbitrage   405
Locational Arbitrage   405
Covered Interest Arbitrage   407
Institutional Use of Foreign Exchange Markets   408
Summary   410
Questions   410
Problems   411
Project   413
WSJ Case Application   414
References   415
Integrative Problem: Choosing Among Derivative Securities   417

PART 5   **COMMERCIAL BANKING**   419

CHAPTER 15   **COMMERCIAL BANK SOURCES AND USE OF FUNDS**   421

Bank Sources of Funds   421
Transaction Deposits   422
Savings Deposits   422
Time Deposits   423
Money Market Deposit Accounts   423
Federal Funds Purchased   423
Borrowing from the Federal Reserve Banks   425
Repurchase Agreements   425
Eurodollar Borrowings   426
Bonds Issued by the Bank   426
Bank Capital   426
Summary of Bank Sources of Funds   426

Uses of Funds by Banks   426
Cash   427
Bank Loans   427
Investment in Securities   432
Federal Funds Sold   432
Repurchase Agreements   433
Eurodollar Loans   433
Fixed Assets   434
Summary of Bank Uses of Funds   434
Off-balance Sheet Activities   435
Loan Commitments   435
Standby Letters of Credit   435
Forward Contracts   435
Swap Contracts   436
Summary   436
Questions   436
WSJ Case Application   438
Project   440
References   440
Appendix 15: Electronic Funds Transfer   441

CHAPTER 16   **BANK REGULATION**   443

Regulatory Structure   443
Regulation of Bank Ownership   444
Balance Sheet Regulations   445
Regulation of Deposit Insurance   445
Regulation of Loans   446
Regulation of Other Assets   446
Regulation of Capital   446
Off-Balance-Sheet Regulations   447
Interest Rate Regulations   447
Deposit Rate Regulations   447
Loan Rate Regulations   449
Geographic Regulations   449
Intrastate Regulations   449
Interstate Regulations   449
Circumventing Interstate Barriers   452
Regulation on Nonbanking Activities   453
Bank Provision of Securities Services   453
Bank Provision of Insurance Services   456
Nonbank Provision of Banking Services   457
How Regulators Monitor Banks   457
Capital Adequacy   458
Asset Quality   458
Management   458
Earnings   459
Liquidity   459
Rating Bank Characteristics   459

Corrective Action by Regulators   460
Funding the Closure of Failing Banks   460
The "Too-Big-to-Fail" Issue   464
Argument for Government Rescue   465
Argument Against Government Rescue   466
Proposals for Government Rescue   466
Summary   467
Questions   467
WSJ Case Application   469
Projects   471
References   471
Appendix 16: Summary of DIDMCA and the Garn-St Germain Act   472

CHAPTER 17   **BANK MANAGEMENT**   475

Managing Liquidity   476
Use of Securitization to Boost Liquidity   476
Managing Interest Rate Risk   476
Methods to Assess Interest Rate Risk   477
Methods to Reduce Interest Rate Risk   482
Managing Exposure to Default Risk   484
Measuring Default Risk   485
Diversifying Default Risk   486
Bank Capital Management   489
Management Based on Forecasts   491
Bank Restructuring to Manage Risks   492
Bank Acquisitions   493
Integrated Bank Management   495
Examples of Bank Mismanagement   498
Franklin National Bank   498
First Pennsylvania Bank   499
Penn Square Bank   499
Continental Illinois Bank   499
Bank of New England   500
Implications of Bank Mismanagement   500
Summary   500
Questions   501
Problems   502
WSJ Case Application   505
Project   506
References   507

CHAPTER 18   **BANK PERFORMANCE**   511

Performance Evaluation of Banks   511
Interest Income and Expenses   512
Noninterest Income and Expenses   513
Return on Assets and Equity   517
Risk Evaluation of Banks   520

How to Evaluate a Bank's Performance   522
   Examination of Return on Assets (ROA)   522
   Information Used in Evaluating Bank Performance   524
Bank Failures   528
   Reasons for Bank Failure   528
Summary   529
Questions   530
Problem   531
WSJ Case Application   532
Projects   533
References   534

CHAPTER 19   **INTERNATIONAL BANKING**   535

Bank Migration to Foreign Countries   535
Global Bank Regulations   536
   Uniform Global Regulations   537
Global Bank Competition   539
   Competition for Investment Banking Services   540
Impact of Eastern European Reform   541
Risks of a Eurobank   542
   Default Risk   542
   Exchange Rate Risk   542
   Interest Rate Risk   543
   Combining All Types of Risk   543
International Debt Crisis   544
   Reducing Bank Exposure to LDC Debt   545
   Use of the Brady Plan to Reduce LDC Debt Exposure   547
Country Risk Assessment   548
   Economic Indicators   548
   Debt Management   548
   Political Factors   549
   Structural Factors   549
   Overall Rating   549
   Country Risk Ratings   549
Summary   551
Questions   553
WSJ Case Application   554
Project   556
References   556
Integrative Problem: Forecasting Bank Performance   557

PART 6   **NONBANK FINANCIAL INSTITUTIONS**   561

CHAPTER 20   **SAVINGS INSTITUTIONS**   563

Background on Savings Institutions   563
   Ownership   563
   Savings Banks   564

Sources of Funds   564
  Deposits   565
  Borrowed Funds   565
  Capital   565
Uses of Funds   566
  Cash   566
  Mortgages   566
  Mortgage-backed Securities   566
  Other Securities   567
  Consumer and Commercial Loans   567
  Other Uses of Funds   567
Allocation of Sources and Uses of Funds   569
Regulation of Savings Institutions   569
  Geographic Regulations   570
  Product Regulations   570
Exposure to Risk   570
  Liquidity Risk   570
  Default Risk   571
  Interest Rate Risk   571
Management of Interest Rate Risk   572
  Adjustable-Rate Mortgages (ARMs)   573
  Interest Rate Futures Contracts   574
  Interest Rate Swaps   574
  Interest Rate Caps   576
  Conclusions About Interest Rate Risk   577
Interaction with Other Financial Institutions   577
Participation in Financial Markets   578
Performance of Savings Institutions   579
Savings and Loan Crisis   580
  Reasons for Failure   580
  Provisions of the FIRREA   583
  Creation of the RTC   583
  Financing the Bailout   584
  Potential Impact of the Bailout   584
  Performance Since the FIRREA   585
Future Outlook for Savings Institutions   585
Savings Institutions in Other Countries   587
Summary   588
Questions   590
Problem   590
WSJ Case Application   591
Projects   592
References   593

CHAPTER 21   **CREDIT UNIONS**   595

Background of Credit Unions   595
  Ownership of Credit Unions   595
  Objectives of Credit Unions   595
  Size of Credit Unions   596
  Advantages and Disadvantages of Credit Unions   597

Sources of Credit Union Funds   597
Uses of Credit Union Funds   599
Regulation of Credit Unions   600
Insurance for Credit Unions   602
Credit Union Exposure to Risk   602
   Liquidity Risk   602
   Default Risk   603
   Interest Rate Risk   604
Performance of Credit Unions   604
Summary   606
Questions   606
WSJ Case Application   607
References   609

CHAPTER 22   **FINANCE COMPANIES**   611

Types of Finance Companies   611
Sources of Finance Company Funds   612
   Loans from Banks   612
   Commercial Paper   612
   Deposits   612
   Bonds   613
   Capital   613
   Relative Importance of Fund Sources   613
Uses of Finance Company Funds   614
   Consumer Loans   614
   Business Loans   615
   Leasing   615
   Real Estate Loans   615
   Relative Importance of Uses of Funds   615
Regulation of Finance Companies   615
Risks Faced by Finance Companies   616
   Liquidity Risk   616
   Interest Rate Risk   617
   Default Risk   617
Performance of Finance Companies   617
Captive Finance Subsidiaries   620
Interaction with Other Financial Institutions   620
Participation in Financial Markets   621
Multinational Finance Companies   622
Summary   622
Questions   622
WSJ Case Application   624
Project   625
References   626

CHAPTER 23   **MUTUAL FUNDS**   627

Background on Mutual Funds   627
   Estimating the Net Asset Value   628

Mutual Fund Classifications   628
Load versus No-Load Mutual Funds   629
Management of Mutual Funds   629
Open-End versus Closed-End Funds   630
Returns and Risks of Mutual Funds   630
Stock and Bond Mutual Funds   630
Growth Funds   631
Capital Appreciation Funds   631
Income Funds   631
Growth and Income Funds   632
Tax-free Funds   632
High Yield (Junk Bond) Funds   632
International and Global Funds   632
Asset Allocation Funds   634
Specialty Funds   634
Growth and Size of Mutual Funds   634
Relative Performance of Mutual Funds   635
Regulation and Taxation of Mutual Funds   637
Background on Money Market Funds   638
Money Market Fund Characteristics   640
Asset Composition   640
Maturity   640
Risk   642
Management of Money Market Funds   644
Regulation and Taxation of Money Market Funds   645
Real Estate Investment Trusts   646
Interaction with Other Financial Institutions   646
Use of Financial Markets   647
Globalization through Mutual Funds   648
Summary   649
Questions   650
WSJ Case Application   652
Projects   653
References   653

CHAPTER 24   **SECURITIES FIRMS**   655

Regulation of Securities Firms   655
Investment Banking Services   656
How Investment Banking Firms Facilitate LBOs   656
How Investment Banking Firms Facilitate Arbitrage   658
How Investment Banking Firms Facilitate New Stock Issues   660
How Investment Banking Firms Facilitate New Bond Issues   662
Brokerage Services   663
Market Orders   663
Limit Orders   663
Short Selling   664
Full-Service Versus Discount Brokerage Services   664
Allocation of Revenue Sources   664
Risks of Securities Firms   665
Market Risk   665

Interest Rate Risk   666
Credit Risk   666
Exchange Rate Risk   666
Interaction with Other Financial Institutions   666
Participation in Financial Markets   666
Globalization of Securities Firms   668
Summary   671
Questions   672
WSJ Case Application   674
Project   675
References   676

CHAPTER 25   **PENSION FUNDS**   677

Background on Pension Funds   677
Types of Private Pension Plans   678
Underfunded Pensions   678
Pension Fund Management   680
Management of Insured Versus Trust Portfolios   680
Management of Private Versus Public Pension Portfolios   681
Corporate Control by Pension Plans   682
Management of Interest Rate Risk   682
Performance Evaluation of Pension Portfolios   683
Performance of Pension Portfolio Managers   684
Pension Regulations   684
The Pension Benefit Guarantee Corporation   685
Accounting Regulations   686
Interaction with Other Financial Institutions   687
Participation in Financial Markets   687
Foreign Investment by Pension Funds   688
Summary   689
Questions   690
WSJ Case Application   691
References   693

CHAPTER 26   **INSURANCE COMPANIES**   695

Background   695
Types of Life Insurance Policies   696
Whole-Life Insurance   696
Term Insurance   696
Variable Life Insurance   696
Universal Life Insurance   696
Group Plans   697
Provision of Health Care Insurance   697
Sources and Uses of Funds   697
Government Securities   698
Corporate Securities   699
Mortgages   699

Real Estate   699
Policy Loans   700
Exposure to Risk   702
Interest Rate Risk   702
Default Risk   702
Liquidity Risk   702
Asset Management   703
Property and Casualty Insurance   705
Reinsurance   706
Regulation of Insurance Companies   707
Performance Evaluation of Insurance Companies   708
Interaction with Other Financial Institutions   710
Participation in Financial Markets   712
Multinational Insurance Companies   712
Summary   714
Questions   714
WSJ Case Application   716
Project   718
References   718
**Integrative Problem: Assessing the Influence of Economic Conditions Across
    Nonbank Financial Institutions**   719
Financial Data Bank   F–1
Glossary   G–1
Index   I–1

PREFACE

Business news is increasingly dominated by events relating to financial markets and institutions. In the early 1990s, several related events occurred which have significantly changed the financial environment. These include:

- reform of the commercial banking industry
- continuing efforts to revive savings institutions
- interstate expansion of all types of financial services
- the expansion of financial services offered by financial institutions
- the use of special techniques to hedge a security portfolio's risk
- the increasing international integration of financial markets

This text provides a conceptual framework that can be used to understand how recent events have affected the financial environment. Each type of financial market is described with a focus on its utilization by financial institutions, its internationalization, and recent events that have affected it. Each type of financial institution is described with a focus on its regulatory aspects, management, use of financial markets, and performance.

This text is suitable for both undergraduate and masters level courses in financial markets, financial institutions, or the combination of markets and institutions. Some courses may attempt to maximize the comprehension level by assigning the more difficult questions and problems, the case problem, and the projects in each chapter, and the "Integrative Problem" at the end of each part. In addition, selected articles summarized in the "Applied Research" boxes (discussed shortly) could be assigned as required reading, as they help reinforce the concepts presented.

ORGANIZATION OF THE TEXT

This text is organized as follows. Part One (Chapters 1 to 4) introduces the key financial markets and financial institutions, explains interest rate movements in the financial markets, and describes the impact that interest rates (and other factors) can have on security prices. Part Two (Chapters 5 and 6) describes the functions of the Federal Reserve System and how the Fed influences interest rates and other economic conditions with its monetary policy. Part Three (Chapters 7 through 10) covers the major security markets, while Part Four (Chapters 11 through 14) covers the derivative security markets. Each chapter in these two parts focuses on a particular market. The integration of each market with other markets is stressed throughout these chapters. Part Five (Chapters 15 to 19) concentrates on commercial banking, while Part Six (Chapters 20 to 26) covers all other types of financial institutions.

Courses that emphasize financial markets would focus on the first four parts (Chapters 1–14). Some commercial banking chapters would still likely be assigned. Courses that emphasize financial institutions would focus on Parts One, Two, Five, and Six, although some background on securities markets (Part Three) could be helpful. Finally, some courses that are designed to emphasize financial markets and institutions may attempt to focus on particular markets and institutions, depending on other available courses. For example, if a course on derivative securities is commonly offered, Part Four of this text may be ignored. Alternatively, if an available Investments course provides a thorough background on various types of securities, Part Three can be avoided. A final alternative is to use most of the class time on the conceptual problems, and allow students to read the more factual chapters on their own. In general, Parts One, Two, Four, and Five are more conceptual and, therefore, may require more attention in the classroom. The chapters on Securities Markets (Part Three) and on Nonbank Financial Institutions (Part Six) generally require less attention in the classroom.

Regardless of the sequence of chapters desired, it is highly recommended that the *Wall Street Journal* Case be assigned in each chapter, along with selected "Questions." The Case can serve as a focal point for class discussion.

COVERAGE OF MAJOR CONCEPTS AND EVENTS

Numerous concepts relating to recent events and current trends in financial markets are discussed throughout the chapters, including:

- regulatory reform in the banking industry
- the use of junk bonds to finance acquisitions
- the measurement and use of duration
- the use of interest rate swaps and currency swaps by bond portfolio managers
- the use of collateralized mortgage obligations (CMOs) and real estate mortgage investment conduits (REMICs) in the mortgage markets
- the use of portfolio insurance strategies to reduce risk
- government rescues of failing banks
- bank strategies for reducing exposure to the debt of less developed countries
- the savings and loan crisis
- the increasing importance of mutual funds
- the underfunding of pension funds

Each chapter is self-contained so professors can use classroom time to focus on the more complex concepts and rely on the text to cover the other concepts. Chapters can be rearranged without a loss in continuity.

APPROACH OF THE TEXT

The approach of the text is to reinforce the key concepts in the following ways:

1. OPENING DIAGRAM: A diagram is provided at the beginning of each part to illustrate in general terms how the key concepts to be covered in that part are related. This offers some intuition about the organization of chapters in that part.
2. OBJECTIVES: The key concepts are identified within a bulleted list of the objectives at the beginning of the chapter.
3. EMPHASIS: The key concepts are thoroughly described in the chapter.
4. "POINT OF INTEREST" BOXES: The "Point of Interest" boxes within chapters offer additional insight on these concepts, as they explain how various techniques are used by practitioners.
5. "APPLIED RESEARCH" BOXES: The "Applied Research" boxes within chapters summarize recent research findings on the key concepts and theories presented.
6. SUMMARY: The key concepts are summarized at the end of the chapter in a bulleted list that corresponds to the list of objectives at the beginning of the chapter.
7. END OF CHAPTER QUESTIONS AND PROBLEMS: Many of the Questions and Problems at the end of each chapter test the students knowledge of the key concepts.
8. CASE APPLICATION: The "Case Application" at the end of each chapter provides a Wall Street Journal article that illustrates how the chapter's key concepts apply to real world situations. Questions at the end of the WSJ Case test the student's understanding of how the key concepts are used in practice.
9. PROJECTS: At the end of each chapter, projects are recommended for students who wish to more thoroughly understand one or more of the key concepts. A data bank provided in the back of the text can be used for some of the projects.
10. INTEGRATIVE PROBLEM: The Integrative Problem at the end of each part integrates the key concepts across chapters within that part.

The concepts in each chapter can be reinforced by one or more of the text's features. Each professor has his or her own method to help students get the most out of the text. Each professor's use of the features will vary with the level of students and the focus of the course. A course that focuses mostly on financial markets may emphasize projects such as taking positions in securities and derivative instruments, and other related projects that involve *The Wall Street Journal.* Conversely, a course that focuses on financial institutions may emphasize projects such as reviewing recent annual reports to fully understand how a particular financial institution's performance is affected by its policies, industry regulations, and economic conditions.

CHANGES IN THIS EDITION _____

- All chapters have been updated to incorporate recent trends and events.
- The chapters have been revised to place more emphasis on the key concepts, while removing other, less useful, material.
- Where appropriate, major regulatory changes that affect various financial markets and institutions are discussed.
- The chapters on financial institutions explain recent strategies these institutions have implemented to expand their lines of business.
- A Case has been included at the end of every chapter that tests one's ability to link chapter concepts with realistic situations extracted from *The Wall Street Journal.*
- The chapters on the Federal Reserve System (Chapter 5) and Monetary Policy (Chapter 6) have been moved to just before the chapters on the various financial markets.
- The two chapters on Bank Regulation have been consolidated into one chapter.
- The chapter on Monetary Theory and Policy (Chapter 6) uses the loanble funds framework (from Chapter 2) to explain how money supply adjustments affect interest rates. This allows for a consistent foundation to develop interest rate theories.
- The "Foreign Exchange Derivatives Markets" chapter has been substantially revised to focus on the use of derivatives for speculating and hedging.
- The chapter on Bank Management (Chapter 17) has been revised to incorporate portfolio theory and bank restructuring decisions.
- Acetate transparencies are now available.
- Several new "Point of Interest" and "Applied Research" boxes have been added to incorporate recent developments.
- Many of the key conceptual relationships discussed are supported by graphs containing the most recent data available.
- The "Global Aspects" sections have been expanded in many chapters to incorporate the continuing globalization of financial markets.

ACKNOWLEDGEMENTS _____

The motivation to write this textbook was primarily due to encouragement by E. Joe Nosari (Florida State University). Several professors helped to develop the text outline and offered suggestions on the coverage of concepts in the first three editions of this text. They are acknowledged as follows in alphabetical order:

Ibrahim Affaneh
Indiana University of Pennsylvania

Henry C. F. Arnold
Seton Hall University

James C. Baker
Kent State University

Gerald Bierwag
Florida International University

Carol Billingham
Central Michigan University

Randy Billingsley
Virginia Tech University

Rita M. Biswas
State University of New York at
    Albany

Paul J. Bolster
Northeastern University

Sarah Bryant
George Washington University

William Carner
University of Missouri—Columbia

C. Steven Cole
University of North Texas

M. Cary Collins
University of Tennessee

Wayne C. Curtis
Troy State University

Steven Dobson
University of Houston

Richard J. Dowen
Northern Illinois University

James Felton
Central Michigan

Stuart Fletcher
Appalachian State University

Clifford L. Fry
University of Houston

Edward K. Gill
California State—Chic.

Claire G. Gilmore
St. Joseph's University

Owen Gregory
University of Illinois—Chicago

John Halloran
University of Notre Dame

Gerald A. Hanweck
George Mason University

Hildegard R. Hendrickson
Seattle University

Jerry M. Hood
Loyola University—New Orleans

Paul Hsueh
University of Central Florida

Carl D. Hudson
Auburn University

John S. Jahera, Jr.
Auburn University

Mel Jameson
University of Nevada

Shane Johnson
Bowling Green State University

Richard H. Keehn
University of Wisconsin—Parkside

James B. Kehr
Miami University of Ohio

George Kutner
Marquette University

Robert Lamy
Wake Forest University

David J. Leahigh
King's College

Morgan Lynge, Jr.
University of Illinois

Judy E. Maese
New Mexico State University

Robert W. McLeod
University of Alabama

James McNulty
Florida Atlantic University

Charles Meiburg
University of Virginia

Jose Mercado-Mendez
Central Missouri State University

Neil Murphy
Virginia Commonwealth University

Dale Osborne
University of Texas—Dallas

Coleen Pantalone
Northeastern University

D. Anthony Plath
University of North Carolina—
    Charlotte

Rose Prasad
Central Michigan University

Alan Reichert
Cleveland State University

Kenneth L. Rhoda
LaSalle University

Lawrence C. Rose
San Jose State University

Jack Rubens
Bryant College

Robert Schweitzer
University of Delaware

Ahmad Sorhabian
California State Polytechnic
    University—Pomona

S. R. Stansell
East Carolina University

Harry J. Turtle
University of Manitoba

Geraldo M. Vasconcellos
Lehigh University

Michael C. Walker
University of Cincinnati

Colin Young
Bentley College

Several others offered suggestions for clarification, including Stephen Borde (University of Central Florida), Michael Suerth (Interstate National Corporation), Alan Tucker (Pace University), and Emilio Zarruk (Florida Atlantic University).

This text also benefited from the research departments of several Federal Reserve district banks, the Federal National Mortgage Association, the National Credit Union Administration, the U.S. League of Savings Institutions, the American Council of Life Insurance, the Investment Company Institute, and the Chicago Mercantile Exchange.

Editors Esther Craig and John Szilagyi at West Publishing Company were helpful in all stages of the book writing process. A special thanks is due to production editors, Brenda Owens and Laura Nelson at West for their efforts to ensure a quality final product.

Finally, I wish to thank my parents, Arthur and Irene Madura, and my wife, Mary, for their moral support. Without their influence, this textbook would not exist.

PART 1

OVERVIEW OF THE FINANCIAL ENVIRONMENT

Part One focuses on the flow of funds across financial markets, interest rates, and security prices. Chapter 1 introduces the key financial markets and the financial institutions that participate in those markets. Chapter 2 explains how changes in the flow of funds affect interest rates. Chapter 3 explains how interest rate movements influence security prices. Chapter 4 identifies factors other than interest rates that influence security prices. Participants in financial markets use this information to value securities and make investment decisions.

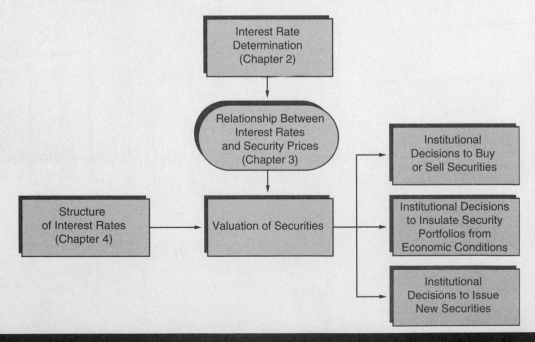

CHAPTER 1

ROLE OF FINANCIAL MARKETS AND INSTITUTIONS

Households, corporations, and governments frequently use financial markets to invest excess funds or to borrow funds. A **financial market** is a market in which financial assets (securities) such as stocks and bonds can be purchased or sold. One party transfers funds in financial markets by purchasing financial assets previously held by another party.

Financial markets play a crucial role in helping individuals, corporations, and government agencies obtain financing. They allow individuals to obtain home mortgages and automobile loans. They allow corporations to obtain long-term financing for expansion, or to obtain short-term financing when experiencing a temporary shortage of funds. They also enable government agencies to borrow funds. Most large expenditures in the economy are financed with funds obtained in financial markets.

Financial markets also play a crucial role in helping individuals or corporations invest in financial assets. They offer alternative investment opportunities for individuals or corporations with excess funds. This chapter provides a background on financial markets and the financial institutions that participate in them.

The specific objectives of this chapter are to:

- describe the types of financial markets that accommodate various transactions,
- describe the role of financial institutions within financial markets, and
- identify the types of financial institutions that facilitate transactions in financial markets.

OVERVIEW OF FINANCIAL MARKETS

The main participants in financial market transactions are households, businesses (including financial institutions), and governments that purchase or sell financial assets. Those participants that provide funds are called **surplus units,** while participants that enter financial markets to obtain funds are called **deficit units.** The federal government commonly acts as a deficit unit. The Treasury finances the budget deficit by issuing Treasury securities. The main providers of funds are households. Foreign investors also commonly invest in U.S. Treasury securities, as does the Federal Reserve System (the Fed). The Fed plays a major role in the financial markets because it controls the U.S. money supply and participates in the regulation of depository institutions.

Many participants in the financial markets simultaneously act as surplus and deficit units. For example, a business may sell new securities and use some of the proceeds to establish a checking account. Thus, funds are obtained from one type of financial market and used in another.

Primary Versus Secondary Markets

New securities are issued in **primary markets,** while existing securities are resold in **secondary markets.** Primary market transactions provide funds to the initial issuer of securities; secondary market transactions do not. Some securities have a more active secondary market and are therefore more marketable than others. This is an important feature for financial market participants to know about if they plan to sell security holdings prior to maturity. The issuance of new corporate stock or new Treasury securities represents a primary market transaction, while the sale of existing corporate stock or Treasury security holdings by any businesses or individuals represents a secondary market transaction.

Money Versus Capital Markets

Financial markets that facilitate the flow of short-term funds (with maturities of less than one year) are known as **money markets,** while those that facilitate the flow of long-term funds are known as **capital markets.** Securities with a maturity of one year or less are called **money market securities,** whereas securities with a maturity of more than one year are called **capital market securities.** Common stocks are classified as capital market securities, because they have no defined maturity. Money market securities generally have a higher degree of **liquidity** (can be liquidated easily without a loss of value). However, capital market securities are typically expected to generate a higher annualized return to investors.

Organized Versus Over-the-Counter Markets

Some secondary stock market transactions occur at an **organized exchange,** which is a visible marketplace for secondary market transactions. The New York Stock Exchange and American Stock Exchange are organized exchanges for secondary stock market transactions. Other financial market transactions occur in the **over-the-counter (OTC) market,** which is a telecommunications network.

FINANCIAL MARKET EFFICIENCY

When particular securities are perceived to be undervalued by the market, their prices increase in response to demand. Overvalued securities are sold by investors, and their prices decrease. Because securities have market-determined prices, their favorable or unfavorable characteristics as perceived by the market are reflected in their prices. When security prices fully reflect all available information, the markets for these securities are said to be efficient. When markets are inefficient, investors can use available information ignored by the market in order to earn abnormally high returns on their investments.

Even if markets are efficient, this does not imply that individual or institutional investors should ignore the various investment instruments available. Investors differ with respect to the default risk they are willing to incur, the desired liquidity of securities, and their tax status, making some types of securities preferable to some investors but not to others.

Some securities that are not as safe and liquid as desired may still be considered if the potential return is sufficiently high. Investors normally attempt to balance the objective of high return with their particular preference for low default risk and adequate liquidity. When financial markets are efficient, any relevant information pertaining to risk will be reflected in the prices of securities.

As time passes, new information about economic conditions and corporate performance becomes available. Investors quickly attempt to assess how this information will influence the values of securities. As investors buy or sell securities in response to this information, the security prices reach a new equilibrium. Some information has an immediate impact on security prices because market participants take positions in securities as soon as the information is released. For example, because participants in the bond markets react immediately to money supply announcements, bond prices adjust immediately to these announcements.

Announcements that do not contain any new valuable information will not elicit a market response. In some cases, market participants take their position in anticipation of a particular announcement. If the announcement was fully anticipated, there will be no response in the equilibrium price of securities to the announcement.

SECURITIES TRADED IN FINANCIAL MARKETS

The securities traded in financial markets can be classified as either equity or debt securities. **Equity securities** (common stock and preferred stock) represent ownership in a business. **Debt securities** represent IOUs; investors who purchase these securities are creditors. While equity securities typically have no maturity, debt securities have maturities ranging form one day to twenty years or longer. The use of debt securities has increased significantly in recent years. From 1980 to 1989, the total amount of debt outstanding in the United States more than doubled. This can be attributed to looser credit standards, huge government budget deficits, the desire by some corporations to finance their expenditures with debt, and the corporate need for borrowed funds to finance takeovers. However, in the early 1990s, there was greater emphasis on the use of equity securities, as some corporations reduced their debt levels.

Exhibit 1.1 identifies some of the more commonly traded securities, discussed in more detail in later chapters. Markets have been developed for each of the securities identified in Exhibit 1.1, allowing surplus units to transfer funds to deficit units by purchasing the securities.

EXHIBIT 1.1 Summary of Popular Securities

MONEY MARKET SECURITIES	ISSUED BY	COMMON INVESTORS	COMMON MATURITIES	SECONDARY MARKET ACTIVITY
Treasury bills	Federal government	Households and firms	13 weeks, 26 weeks, 1 year	High
Retail CDs	Banks and savings institutions	Households	7 days to 5 years or longer	Nonexistent
NCDs	Large banks and savings institutions	Firms	2 weeks to 1 year	Moderate
Commercial paper	Bank holding companies, finance companies, and other companies	Firms	1 day to 270 days	Low
Eurodollar deposits	Banks located outside the U.S.	Firms and governments	1 day to 1 year	Nonexistent
Banker's acceptances	Banks (exporting firms can sell the acceptances at a discount to obtain funds)	Firms	30 days to 270 days	High
Federal funds	Depository institutions	Depository institutions	1 day to 7 days	Nonexistent
Repurchase agreements	Nonfinancial firms and financial institutions	Nonfinancial firms and financial institutions	1 day to 15 days	Nonexistent
CAPITAL MARKET SECURITIES				
Treasury notes and bonds	Federal government	Households and firms	3 to 30 years	High
Municipal bonds	State and local governments	Households and firms	10 to 30 years	Moderate
Corporate bonds	Firms	Households and firms	10 to 30 years	Moderate
Equity securities	Firms	Households and firms	No maturity	High (for stocks of large firms)

FINANCIAL MARKET REGULATION

Securities markets are regulated in various ways. Many regulations were enacted in response to fraudulent practices before the Great Depression. The Securities Act of 1933, for example, was intended to ensure complete disclosure of relevant financial information on publicly offered securities and prevent fraudulent practices in selling these securities. The Securities Exchange Act of 1934 extended the disclosure requirements to secondary market issues. It also declared illegal a variety of deceptive practices, such as misleading financial statements and trading strategies designed to manipulate the market price. In addition, it established the Securities and Exchange Commission (SEC) to oversee the securities markets, and the SEC has implemented additional laws over time. Securities laws do not prevent investors from making poor investment decisions but only attempt to ensure full disclosure of information and thus protect against fraud.

Some recent securities regulations have been imposed to reduce market volatility. Because the disruptions may reflect overreactions to rumors, so-called **circuit breakers** are now used to temporarily halt the trading of some securities or contracts.

In addition to the markets themselves, financial institutions participating in these markets are also regulated. Some regulations apply to all financial institutions, while others are applicable only to a specific type. Details on regulations are provided throughout the text.

The performance of various financial institutions is linked to regulation. A common dilemma in regulating any type of financial institution is imposing enough regulation to ensure safety without imposing so much regulation that would reduce competition and efficiency.

FINANCIAL MARKET GLOBALIZATION

Until recently, certain barriers in foreign securities markets have historically limited international security transactions. One barrier was a lack of information about the foreign companies represented by the securities and the tax liability applicable to income earned form these transactions. Another was the excessive cost of executing international transactions. Information on foreign companies is now more accessible, and some financial institutions have created various opportunities for investors to invest in foreign securities without incurring excessive transaction costs. Consequently, the volume of international security transactions has greatly increased.

Although financial markets around the world have become more internationally integrated, the most pronounced changes have occurred in Europe. In the late 1980s and early 1990s, numerous regulations were eliminated, and others were standardized across European countries. This encouraged the expansion of financial services across borders. Deregulatory momentum increased in the early 1990s as governments in Eastern Europe allowed for **privatization,** in which government-owned firms were sold to individuals. In addition, stocks of firms were allowed to be publicly traded.

Because of more integrated financial markets, U.S. market movements may have a greater impact on foreign market movements, and vice versa. Because interest rates are influenced by the supply of and demand for available funds, they are now more susceptible to foreign lending or borrowing acitivities. As an example, the U.S. financial markets have become a popular choice for foreign investment. U.S. interest rates would likely have been higher during the mid and late 1980s without this foreign inflow of funds. Yet U.S. interest rates are now more susceptible to potential withdrawal of foreign funds.

ROLE OF FINANCIAL INSTITUTIONS IN FINANCIAL MARKETS

If financial markets were **perfect,** all information about any securities for sale in primary and secondary markets would be continuously and freely available to investors (including the creditworthiness of the security issuer). In addition, all information identifying investors interested in purchasing securities as well as investors planning to sell securities would be freely available. Furthermore, all securities for sale could be broken down (or unbundled) into any size desired by investors, and security transaction costs would be nonexistent. Under these conditions, financial intermediaries would not be necessary.

Because markets are **imperfect,** securities buyers and sellers do not have full access to information and cannot always break down securities to the precise size they desire. Financial institutions are needed to resolve the problems caused by market imperfections. They receive requests from surplus and deficit units on what securities are to be purchased or sold, and they use this information to match up buyers and sellers of securities. Because the amount of a specific security to be sold will not always equal the amount desired by investors, financial institutions sometimes unbundle the securities by spreading them across several investors until the entire amount is sold. Without financial institutions, the information and transaction costs of financial market transactions would be excessive.

Role of Depository Institutions

A major type of financial intermediary is the depository institution, which accepts deposits from surplus units and provides credit to deficit units through loans and purchases of securities. Depository institutions are popular financial institutions for the following reasons.

- They offer deposit accounts that can accommodate the amount and liquidity characteristics desired by most surplus units.
- They repackage funds received from deposits to provide loans of the size and maturity desired by deficit units.
- They accept the risk on loans provided.
- They have more expertise than individual surplus units to evaluate the creditworthiness of deficit units.
- They diversify their loans among numerous deficit units and can absorb defaulted loans better than individual surplus units could.

To appreciate these advantages, consider the flow of funds from surplus units to deficit units if depository institutions did not exist. Each surplus unit would have to identify a deficit unit desiring to borrow the precise amount of funds available for the precise time period in which funds would be available. Furthermore, each surplus unit would have to perform the credit evaluation and incur the risk of default. Under these conditions, many surplus units would likely hold their funds rather than channel them to deficit units. Thus, the flow of funds from surplus units to deficit units would be disrupted.

When a depository institution offers a loan, it is acting as a creditor, just as if it had purchased a debt security. Yet, the more personalized loan agreement is less marketable in the secondary market than a debt security, because detailed loan provisions on a loan can differ significantly among loans. Any potential investors would need to review all provisions before purchasing loans in the secondary market.

A more specific description of each depository institution's role in the financial markets follows.

COMMERCIAL BANKS.   In aggregate, commercial banks are the most dominant financial institution. They serve surplus units by offering a wide variety of deposit accounts, and they transfer deposited funds to deficit units by providing direct loans or purchasing securities. Commercial banks serve both the private and public sectors, as their deposit and lending services are utilized by households, businesses, and government agencies.

SAVINGS INSTITUTIONS.   Like commercial banks, savings and loan associations (S&Ls) offer deposit accounts to surplus units and then channel these deposits to deficit units. However, S&Ls have concentrated on residential mortgage loans, while commercial banks have concentrated on commercial loans. This difference in the allocation of funds has caused the performance of commercial banks and S&Ls to differ significantly over time. Recent deregulatory provisions, though, have permitted S&Ls more flexibility as to how they allocate their funds, causing their functions to become more similar to those of commercial banks. Although S&Ls can be owned by shareholders, most are mutual (depositor owned).

Savings banks are similar to savings and loan associations, except that they have more diversified uses of funds. However, the difference in uses of funds has narrowed over time. Like S&Ls, most savings banks are mutual.

CREDIT UNIONS.   Credit unions differ from commercial banks and savings institutions in that (1) they are nonprofit and (2) they restrict their business to the credit union members, who share a common bond (such as a common employer or union). Because of the common bond characteristic, credit unions tend to be much smaller than other depository institutions. They use most of their funds to provide loans to their members.

Role of Nondepository Financial Institutions

Some financial institutions generate funds from sources other than deposits but also play a major role in financial intermediation. These institutions are briefly described here.

FINANCE COMPANIES.   Most finance companies obtain funds by issuing securities, then lend the funds to individuals and small businesses. The functions of finance companies overlap the functions of depository institutions, yet each type of institution concentrates on a particular segment of the financial markets (explained in the chapters devoted to these institutions).

MUTUAL FUNDS. Mutual funds sell shares to surplus units and use the funds received to purchase a portfolio of securities. Some mutual funds concentrate their investment in capital market securities, such as stocks or bonds. Others, known as **money market mutual funds,** concentrate in money market securities. The minimum denomination of the types of securities purchased by mutual funds is typically greater than the savings of an individual surplus unit. By purchasing shares of mutual funds and money market mutual funds, small savers are able to invest in a diversified portfolio of securities with a relatively small amount of funds.

SECURITIES FIRMS. Securities firms provide a wide variety of functions in financial markets. Some securities firms use their information resources to act as a **broker,** executing securities transactions between two parties. Many financial transactions are standardized to a degree. For example, stock transactions are normally in multiples of 100 shares. To expedite the securities trading process, the delivery procedure for each security transaction is also somewhat standard.

Brokers charge a fee for executing transactions. The fee is reflected in the difference (or **spread**) between their **bid** and **ask** quotes. The markup as a percentage of the transaction amount will likely be greater for less common transactions, as more time is needed to match up buyers and sellers. It will also likely be greater for transactions of relatively small amounts in order to provide adequate compensation for the time involved in executing the transaction.

Some securities firms place newly issued securities for corporations; this task differs from traditional brokerage activities because it involves the primary market. Securities firms commonly **underwrite** the securities, meaning they guarantee the issuer a specific price for the securities to be placed.

Furthermore, securities firms often act as **dealers,** making a market in specific securities by adjusting their inventory of securities. While a broker's income is mostly based on the markup, the dealer's income is influenced by the performance of the security portfolio maintained. Some dealers also provide brokerage services and therefore earn income from both types of activities.

Certain financial institutions represent both securities firms and mutual funds. For example, Merrill Lynch provides brokerage services, underwrites securities, acts as a dealer for securities, and manages various mutual funds.

PENSION FUNDS. Many corporations and government agencies offer pension plans to their employees in which funds are periodically contributed by the employees, their employers, or both. The funds contributed are invested in securities until they are withdrawn (upon retirement) by the employees. Investments by pension funds provide financing for deficit units.

INSURANCE COMPANIES. Insurance companies receive premiums in exchange for insurance policies payable upon death, illness, or accidents and use the funds to purchase a variety of securities. In this way, they finance the needs of deficit units.

Because insurance companies, pension funds, and some mutual funds are major investors in stocks, they can have some influence over the management of publicly traded firms. In recent years, many large institutional investors have publicly criticized the management of specific firms, which has resulted in corporate restructuring, or even the firing of executives in some cases. Thus, institutional investors not only provide financial support to companies but exercise some degree of corporate control over them. By serving as activist shareholders, they can help ensure that managers of publicly held corporations are making decisions that are in the best interests of the shareholders.

Illustration of Financial Institution Roles

The role of financial institutions in facilitating the flow of funds from individual surplus units to deficit units is illustrated in Exhibit 1.2. Surplus units are shown on the left side of the exhibit, while deficit units are shown on the right side. Three different flows of funds from surplus units to deficit units are illustrated in Exhibit 1.2. One set of flows represents deposits from surplus units that are transformed by depository institutions into loans for deficit units. A second set of flows represents purchases of securities (commercial paper) issued by finance companies that are transformed into finance company loans for deficit units. A third set of flows reflects the purchases of shares issued by mutual funds, which are used by the mutual funds to purchase securities of deficit units.

In addition to the funding provided by surplus units, the deficit units also receive funding from insurance companies and pension funds. Because insurance companies and pension funds purchase massive amounts of stocks and bonds, they finance much of the expenditures made by large deficit units, such as corporations and government agencies.

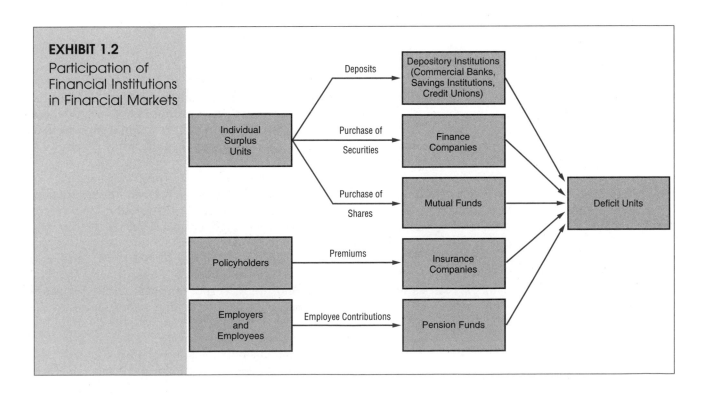

EXHIBIT 1.2
Participation of Financial Institutions in Financial Markets

POINT OF INTEREST

IMPACT OF THE STOCK MARKET CRASH OF OCTOBER 1987 ON FINANCIAL INSTITUTIONS

Because of their different characteristics, financial institutions react differently to any given economic event. However, all were adversely affected by the stock market crash of October 1987. The market value of stock portfolios managed by insurance companies and pension funds declined substantially as a result of the crash. The value of most stock mutual funds declined. However, some of the securities firms that manage these funds were not as severely affected, because the investors shifted funds from stocks into bonds and money market securities, thereby generating much brokerage activity. Nevertheless, investment banking activity declined overall because the low market prices of stock discouraged corporations from issuing new stock. The stock market crash even affected those depository institutions that did not maintain stock portfolios. It generated a pessimistic outlook on the economy that led to a decline in the demand for loans and a higher percentage of loan defaults, causing a consequent decline in stock prices of depository institutions.

Securities firms are not shown in Exhibit 1.2, but play a very important role in facilitating the flow of funds. Many of the transactions between the financial institutions and deficit units are executed by securities firms. Furthermore, some funds flow directly from surplus units to deficit units as a result of security transactions, with securities firms serving as brokers.

COMPARISON OF FINANCIAL INSTITUTIONS

The relative importance of various financial institutions has changed considerably over time. Although commercial bank assets as a proportion of total financial institution assets has decreased, commercial banks still maintain more assets in aggregate than other types of financial institutions. Mutual fund assets have grown at the fastest pace.

Exhibit 1.3 summarizes the main sources and uses of funds for each type of financial institution. Households with savings are served by the depository institutions. Households with deficient funds are served by depository institutions and finance companies. Large corporations and governments that issue securities obtain financing from all types of financial institutions.

In the 1960s and 1970s, financial institutions were highly specialized, and therefore were confronted with little competition across industries. Commercial banks served as the key lender of short-term corporate funds, while securities firms helped corporations obtain long-term funds. Savings institutions specialized in mortgages, while insurance companies focused their investment in bonds.

There was also very little competition in obtaining funds. Deposits provided by surplus units to commercial banks and savings institutions were heavily regulated to prevent competition. However, the development of mutual funds in

EXHIBIT 1.3   Summary of Institutional Sources and Uses of Funds

FINANCIAL INSTITUTIONS	MAIN SOURCES OF FUNDS	MAIN USES OF FUNDS
Commercial banks	Deposits from households, businesses, and government agencies	Purchases of government and corporate securities; loans to businesses and households
Savings institutions	Deposits from households, businesses, and government agencies	Purchases of government and corporate securities; mortgages and other loans to households; some loans to businesses
Credit unions	Deposits from credit union members	Loans to credit union members
Finance companies	Securities sold to households and businesses	Loans to households and businesses
Mutual funds	Shares sold to households, businesses, and government agencies	Purchases of long-term government and corporate securities
Money market funds	Shares sold to households, businesses, and government agencies	Purchases of short-term government and corporate securities
Pension funds	Employer/employee contributions	Purchases of long-term government and corporate securities
Insurance companies	Insurance premiums and earnings from investments	Purchases of long-term government and corporate securities

the 1970s created competition for funds held by surplus units. Deregulation of deposit rates in the early 1980s provided additional competition for these funds. Furthermore, savings institutions, insurance companies, and other financial institution were given more flexibility by regulators on their use of funds in the 1980s. The momentum for additional flexibility continued in the 1990s. Today, many financial institutions are offering a greater variety of products and services to diversify their business. As a consequence, their services overlap more and competition has increased. Because there are different regulatory agencies for different types of financial institutions, coordination among these regulators is important, but it is difficult to maintain. While these regulators are considering requests by some financial institutions to offer various services, other financial institutions are exploiting regulatory loopholes and challenging the regulators to stop them. Meanwhile, still other financial institutions are entering geographic areas that were previously off limits. Differential regulations can cause some financial institutions to have a comparative advantage over others.

SUMMARY

- Financial markets facilitate the transfer of funds from surplus units to deficit units. Because funding needs vary among deficit units, various financial markets have been established. The primary market allows for the issuance of new securities, while the secondary market allows for the sale of existing securities. Money markets facilitate the sale of short-term securities, while capital markets facilitate the sale of long-term securities.

- Depository and nondepository institutions help to finance the needs of deficit units. Depository institutions can serve as effective intermediaries within financial markets because they have greater information on possible sources and uses of funds, they are capable of assessing the creditworthiness of borrowers, and they can repackage deposited funds in sizes and maturities desired by borrowers.

  Nondepository institutions are major purchasers of securities, and therefore provide funding to deficit units.

- The main depository institutions are commercial banks, savings institutions, and credit unions. The main nondepository institutions are finance companies, mutual funds, pension funds, and insurance companies.

QUESTIONS

1. Explain the meaning of surplus units and deficits units. Provide an example of each.

2. Distinguish between primary and secondary markets.

3. Distinguish between money and capital markets.

4. Distinguish between perfect and imperfect security markets.

5. Explain why the existence of imperfect markets creates a need for financial institutions.

6. Explain the meaning of efficient markets. Why might we expect markets to be efficient most of the time?

7. In recent years, several securities firms have been guilty of using inside information when purchasing securities, thereby achieving returns well above the norm (even when accounting for risk). Does this suggest that the security markets are not efficient? Explain.

8. What was the purpose of the Securities Act of 1933? What was the purpose of the Securities Exchange Act of 1934? Do these laws prevent investors from making poor investment decisions? Explain.

9. If barriers to international securities markets are reduced, will a country's interest rate be more or less susceptible to foreign lending or borrowing activities? Explain.

10. In what way could the international flow of funds explain the decline in U.S. interest rates?

11. Distinguish between the functions of a broker and those of a dealer and explain how each is compensated.

12. Why is it necessary for securities to be somewhat standardized?

13. What are the functions of securities firms?

14. Explain why some financial flows of funds cannot occur through the sale of standardized securities.

15. If securities were not standardized, how would this affect the volume of financial transactions conducted by brokers?

16. Commercial banks use some funds to purchase securities and other funds to make loans. Why are securities more marketable than loans in the secondary market?

17. How have the asset compositions of savings and loan associations differed from commercial banks? Explain why and how this distinction may change over time.

18. With regard to the profit motive, how are credit unions different from other financial institutions?

19. Compare the main sources and uses of funds for finance companies, insurance companies, and pension funds.

20. What is the function of a mutual fund? Why are mutual funds popular among investors?

21. How does a money market mutual fund differ from a stock or bond mutual fund?

22. Classify the types of financial institutions mentioned in this chapter as either depository or nondepository. Explain the general difference between depository and nondepository institution sources of funds.

23. It is often stated that all types of financial institutions have begun to offer services that were previously offered only by certain types. Consequently, many financial institutions are becoming more similar in terms of their operations. Yet, the performance levels still differ significantly among types of financial institutions. Why?

24. Look in a recent business periodical for news about a recent financial transaction that involves two financial institutions. For this transaction, determine the following:
    a. How is each institution's balance sheet affected?
    b. Will either institution receive immediate income from the transaction?
    c. Who is the ultimate user of funds?
    d. Who is the ultimate source of funds?

25. Which types of financial institutions do you deal with? Explain whether you are acting as a surplus unit or a deficit unit in your relationship with each financial institution.

26. Explain how the privatization of companies in Europe can lead to the development of new securities markets.

Companies' Earnings Surged 61% As Economy Grew at a Rapid Pace

A *Wall Street Journal* News Roundup

Corporate profits, fueled by strong economic growth and continued cost-cutting, turned in another sharp rise in the fourth quarter. For the period, 674 major corporations reported net income surged a cumulative 61% from the 1992 quarter, according to a *Wall Street Journal* Survey. The result compared with a 24% gain in the third quarter.

After-tax profits from continuing operations also jumped in the latest quarter, with a gain of 38%; in the third quarter the rise was 31%.

Analysts had been looking for a sizable earnings gain, since the Commerce Department had reported that the gross domestic product rose at an annual rate of 5.9% in the period, sharply higher than the 2.9% rate in the third quarter. But the actual results far exceeded expectations.

Although economists don't see the economy continuing to grow at the swift pace of the fourth quarter, they do look for real GDP growth of more than 3% this year, up from the 2.9% rate for 1993. The effects of the January earthquake in California and the wretched weather in most parts of the country, they believe, will be more than offset by gains later on.

"Profits should be surprisingly robust," says Edward Yardeni of C. J. Lawrence. "The efforts made by corporate America to become lean and mean will pay off in a big way."

The corporate downsizing is leading to sharp increases in productivity, or output per man-hour. Stephen S. Roach, of Morgan Stanley & Co., says, "Productivity in the quarter surged at a 4.2% an-nual rate, fully one percentage point faster than we were expecting. That's the second quarter in a row of 4% gains, a welcome turnaround from the 1% average decline in the first half of 1993."

Yet another factor aiding profits is lower interest costs. "Profits have been boosted by a $21 billion drop in net interest payments since the third quarter of 1991," Mr. Yardeni says. "Our forecast of still-lower long-term interest rates suggests interest costs could fall further."

Most analysts expect inflation to remain subdued in 1994, a situation that should contribute to profit gains. The Federal Reserve's recent increase in the federal funds rate, the fee banks charge on overnight loans to one another, lifted optimism that the inflation rate this year will remain a bit below 3%.

Banks continued to report impressive earnings, benefiting from wide margins between lending rates and the banks' own cost of funds. They were also helped by lower loan-loss provisions, continued cost-cutting and increased lending.

For big banks, trading profits continued to be strong, particularly at J. P. Morgan and Bankers Trust New York. Bankers Trust reported a record $449 million in trading revenue, while Morgan's was $606 million, up sharply from $200 million a year earlier.

For most banks, which continue to rely on lending for a major portion of their revenue, net interest margins slipped somewhat in the latest period but remained at historically wide levels.

Thrifts generally posted a solid quarter, buoyed by low interest rates and the improving economy. H. F. Ahmanson's results reflected a sharp drop in nonperforming assets, to 1.89% of total assets, their lowest level since January 1991. Golden West's earnings, though down slightly, were a bit above analysts' expectations. Great Western, in the midst of what some analysts say is an overdue campaign to cut costs and clean up its portfolio, drove down its level of bad assets to 2.09% from an extremely high 5.12% a year earlier.

In the brokerage industry, it was hard not to make money on Wall Street in the fourth quarter. In general, trading, money management and sales of securities were profitable businesses for securities firms as the industry's three-year-old boom rolled on.

Powering the industry's profit surge was, in the U.S., record issuance of new stocks and bonds and, in the overseas markets, double-digit and even triple-digit gains in stocks and bonds. Moreover, many firms reported that commission income rose 20% or more, as individual investors continued to seek securities that offer richer yields than the standard bank certificate of deposit.

SOURCE: The Wall Street Journal (February 22,1994): p.A11. Reprinted by permission of *The Wall Street Journal* © 1994 Dow Jones & Company, Inc. All rights reserved worldwide.

Continued

CASE APPLICATION: RECENT PERFORMANCE OF FINANCIAL INSTITUTIONS

Continued

QUESTIONS

1. Why do you think the Federal Reserve (the central bank of the U.S.) can substantially influence the performance of firms?

2. Banks benefited from increased lending during the quarter that was evaluated. How is the increased lending related to the Federal Reserve actions?

3. Banks and thrifts (savings institutions) also benefited during the quarter from wide margins between lending rates and their cost of funds. Explain how the Federal Reserve might influence the margin. If interest rates decline, wouldn't lending rates and the cost of funds to depository institutions decline by the same amount?

4. The securities firms (in the brokerage industry) experienced favorable performance over the quarter, but for different reasons than the commercial banks or savings institutions. What economic conditions would have caused the securities firms to perform well? Is their performance linked in any way with the Federal Reserve actions?

PROJECTS

1. **Obtaining Information on Financial Institutions**
    a. Throughout the semester, various financial institutions will be discussed. Order an annual report from (1) a commercial bank, (2) a savings and loan association, and (3) a life insurance company. The annual reports will allow you to relate the theory provided in related chapters to the particular financial institution of concern. In addition, your professor may assign projects on financial institutions that require an annual report. You should request the annual reports immediately so that they will arrive by the time you need them.
    b. Order a prospectus for a stock mutual fund, a bond mutual fund, a money market mutual fund, and an international mutual fund. This information will reinforce the discussion later in the semester on these types of funds. Toll-free phone numbers are usually available for requesting a prospectus. Call the 1-800 directory assistance number to obtain phone numbers of the investment companies sponsoring the mutual funds in which you are interested.

2. **Taking Positions in Investment Instruments**
    Throughout the semester, a variety of investment instruments will be explained. By following the price of various investment instruments, you will more fully understand how prices respond to events that occur throughout the semester. Use the most recent issue of the *Wall Street Journal (WSJ)* to make the following investment decisions. (Near the end of the semester, you will be asked to close out your fictitious investment positions in order to determine your return or yield on each investment.) Write your decisions in your notebook. Exhibit A provides an outline you can use to fill in your notebook.

EXHIBIT A Outline to Follow for Your Notebook

a. NYSE Stock: name of stock _____
                                       purchase price of stock _____
                                       dividend _____

b. AMEX Stock: name of stock _____
                                         purchase price of stock _____
                                       dividend _____

c. NASDAQ Stock: name of stock _____
                                       purchase price of stock _____
                                       dividend _____

d. BOND MUTUAL FUND: name of company _____
                                       name of specific mutual fund _____
                                       offer (purchase) price _____

e. STOCK MUTUAL FUND: name of company _____
                                       name of specific mutual fund _____
                                       offer (purchase) price _____

f. INTERNATIONAL FUND: name of company _____
                                       name of specific mutual fund _____
                                       offer (purchase) price _____

g. CALL OPTION: name of stock for call option purchased _____
                                       strike price _____
                                       expiration date (month) _____
                                       premium paid per share _____

h. PUT OPTION: name of stock for put option purchased _____
                                         strike price _____
                                       expiration date (month) _____
                                       premium paid per share _____

i. FUTURES CONTRACT: financial futures contract purchased _____
                                       settle (closing) price _____
                                       expiration date (month) _____

---

    a. Look up the section "New York Stock Exchange (NYSE) Stocks" (listed in the index on the front page of *WSJ*). Choose one stock that you would like to invest in. Write down the dividend and the closing stock price.

    b. Look up the section "American Stock Exchange (AMEX) Stocks" (listed in the index on the front page of *WSJ*). Choose one stock that you would like to invest in. Write down the dividend and the closing stock price.

    c. Look up the section "Nasdaq National Market Issues." Choose one stock that you would like to invest in. Write down the dividend and the closing stock price.

    d. Look up the section "Mutual Fund Quotations" (listed as "Mutual Funds" in the index on the front page of *WSJ*). Choose one bond mutual fund (usually designated with the word *Bond* or *Income* in the name of the fund). Write down the name of the fund. Write down the offer price (your purchase price) and the name of the company offering the fund (shown in bold letters).

e. Using the "Mutual Fund Quotations, " choose one stock fund (often referred to as "Growth" or "Equity"). Write down the offer price and the name of the company offering the fund.

f. Using the "Mutual Fund Quotations," choose one international mutual fund (usually designated with "intl" or "foreign" within the name of the fund). Write down the offer price along with the name of the company offering the fund.

g. Look up the section "Listed Options" and choose a call option for a stock whose price you expect to rise that has an expiration date slightly beyond the end of your semester. Pick a strike price that is close to the prevailing stock price and write down the corresponding option premium quoted, along with the expiration date, strike price, and stock of concern. Your professor may elaborate on this part in class.

h. Using the section "Listed Options," choose a put option for a stock whose price you expect to decline that has an expiration date slightly beyond the end of your semester. Pick a strike price that is close to the prevailing stock price and write down the corresponding option premium quoted, along with the expiration date, strike price, and stock of concern. Your professor may elaborate on this part in class.

i. Look up the section "Future Prices" in *WSJ*. Find the futures quotes on "Treasury Bonds (CBT)" and on the "S&P 500 Index (CME)." If you believe that Treasury bond prices will rise by a greater percentage than stock prices in general over your investment horizon, you should choose the Treasury bond futures. Use a settlement month (in the first column under the heading) slightly beyond the end of your semester. Write down the "settle" price (in the fifth column) that corresponds with that month.

If you believe that stock prices will generally rise by a greater percentage than Treasury bond prices over your investment horizon, you should choose the S&P 500 Index futures. Use a settlement month slightly beyond the end of your semester. Write down the "settle" price (in the fifth column) that corresponds with that month.

3. **Measuring Your Investment Performance**
   Near the end of the semester (on a date specified by your professor), you will close out your investment positions. On the date you close out your positions, determine the existing prices of all the instruments you invested in. Using this information along with your purchase price, determine the return on each investment instrument. Use the following guidelines for calculating the returns on your investments.

   a. The return on the stock can be determined as:

$$\frac{(\text{selling price} - \text{purchase price}) + (\text{dividend}/4)}{\text{purchase price}}$$

It is assumed here that one quarterly dividend is paid.

If you wish to annualize your results, multiply your return times 12/N, where N represents the number of months in which the investment was held.

This guideline also applies to the computation of returns for all investment instruments discussed here.

b. See Part a.

c. See Part a.

d. The return on the mutual fund can be determined as

$$\frac{\text{NAV} - \text{purchase price}}{\text{purchase price}}$$

where NAV represents net asset value. Some funds may offer shares as dividends, which would not be accounted for in this estimation of return. Yet, this computation can at least be used to assess the general performance of the fund over the semester.

If your fund does have a load fee, you may wish to calculate the return ignoring the fee, just to determine how the fund itself performed. Of course, the result would overstate your actual return on load funds because it ignores the load fee you would have paid.

e. See Part d.

f. See Part d.

g. If the existing price of the stock is above the strike price, the return on your call option position can be determined as

$$\frac{\text{existing stock price} - \text{call option strike price} - \text{call option premium}}{\text{call option premium}}$$

If the existing price of the stock is below the strike price so that the option expires without being exercised, the return on the options position is -100 percent.

h. If the existing price of the stock is below the stroke price, the return on your put option can be determined as

$$\frac{\text{put option strike price} - \text{existing stock price} - \text{put option premium}}{\text{put option premium}}$$

If the existing price of the stock is above the strike price so that the option is not exercised by the expiration date, the return on the put option position would be -100 percent.

i. Assuming that you sell the identical futures contract as the one you purchased at the beginning of the semester, the difference between the selling price and buying price represents the profit (or loss) that will occur on the settlement date. The return could be determined as the profit (or loss) per unit as a percentage of the initial investment, where the initial investment represents a margin deposit. Assume your margin deposit is 50 percent of the buying price. Using this assumption, it is possible to lose more than 100 percent of your initial investment.

REFERENCES

Benston, George J., and Clifford W. Smith, Jr. "A Transaction Cost Approach to the Theory of Financial Intermediation." *Journal of Finance* (May 1976): 215–232.

Black, Harold A., and Robert L. Schweitzer. "Did Regulatory Actions Discourage Consumer Demand for Treasury Bills?" *Journal of Banking and Finance* (February 1993): 19–26.

Brooks, Robert, "Investment Decision Making With Derivative Securities." *Financial Review* (November 1989): 511–528.

Bryan, Lowell. "The Credit Bomb in Our Financial System." *Harvard Business Review* (January–February 1987): 45–51.

Davidson, Lawrence S., and Richard T. Froyen. "Monetary Policy and Stock Returns: Are Stock Markets Efficient?" *Review,* Federal Reserve Bank of St. Louis (March 1982): 3–12.

Franke, Gunter. "Costless Signaling in Financial Markets." *Journal of Finance* (September 1987): 809–822.

Hahn, Thomas K. "Commercial Paper." *Economic Quarterly,* Federal Reserve Bank of Richmond, Spring 1993, pp. 45–67.

Herring, Richard, and Prashant Vankudre. "Growth Opportunities and Risk–Taking by Financial Intermediaries." *Journal of Finance* (July 1987): 583–600.

Pardee, Scott. "Internationalization of Finance Markets." *Economic Review,* Federal Reserve Bank of Kansas City (February 1987): 3–7.

Stanhouse, Bryan E. "Credit Evaluation, Information Production, and Financial Intermediation." *Journal of Financial Services Research* (September 1993): 217–233.

DETERMINATION OF INTEREST RATES

Interest rate movements affect the policies and performance of all types of financial institutions. For this reason, it is critical for managers of financial institutions to understand why interest rates change, how their movements affect performance, and how to manage according to anticipated movements.

The specific objectives of this chapter are to:

- explain how the loanable funds theory can be used to understand why interest rates change,
- identify the most relevant factors that affect interest rate movements, and
- explain how to forecast interest rates.

LOANABLE FUNDS THEORY

The **loanable funds theory,** commonly used to explain interest rate movements, suggests that the market interest rate is determined by the factors that control the supply of and demand for loanable funds. "Demand for loanable funds" is a widely used phrase in financial markets pertaining to the borrowing activities of households, businesses, and governments. The common sectors that demand loanable funds are identified and described here. Then the sectors that supply loanable funds to the markets are described. Finally, the demand and supply concepts are integrated to explain interest rate movements.

Household Demand for Loanable Funds

Households commonly demand loanable funds to finance housing expenditures. In addition, they finance the purchases of automobiles and household items, which results in installment debt. As the aggregate level of household income rises over time, so does installment debt. The level of installment debt as a percentage of disposable income has been increasing since 1983. It is generally low in recessionary periods.

If households could be surveyed at any given point in time to indicate the quantity of loanable funds they would demand at various interest rate levels, there would be an inverse relationship between the interest rate and the quantity of loanable funds demanded. This simply implies that at any point in time, households would demand a greater quantity of loanable funds at lower rates of interest.

A hypothetical household demand for loanable funds schedule is shown in Exhibit 2.1. This schedule depicts the amount of funds that would be demanded at various possible interest rates for a given point in time. Various events can cause household borrowing preferences to change and therefore shift the demand schedule. For example, if tax rates on household income are expected to significantly decrease in the future, households might believe that they can more easily afford future loan repayments and thus be willing to borrow more funds. For any interest rate, the quantity of loanable funds demanded by households would be greater as a result of the tax law adjustment. This represents an outward shift in the demand schedule.

Business Demand for Loanable Funds

Businesses demand loanable funds to invest in long-term (fixed) and short-term assets. The quantity of funds demanded by businesses depends on the number of business projects to be implemented. Businesses evaluate a project by comparing the present value of its cash flows to its initial investment, as follows:

$$NPV = -INV + \sum_{t=1}^{n} \frac{CF_t}{(1 + i)^t}$$

where

NPV = net present value of project

INV = initial investment

CF_t = cash flow in period t

i = required rate of return on project

Projects with a positive net present value (NPV) are accepted because the present value of their benefits outweighs the costs. The required return to implement any given project will be lower if interest rates are lower. Consequently, more projects will have positive NPVs, and a greater amount of financing is required. This implies that businesses will demand a greater quantity of loanable funds when interest rates are lower, as illustrated in Exhibit 2.2.

In addition to long-term assets, businesses also invest in short-term assets (such as accounts receivable and inventory) in order to support ongoing operations. Any demand for funds resulting from this type of investment is positively related to the number of projects implemented and thus inversely related to the interest rate. The opportunity cost of investing in short-term assets is higher when interest rates are higher. Therefore, firms generally attempt to support

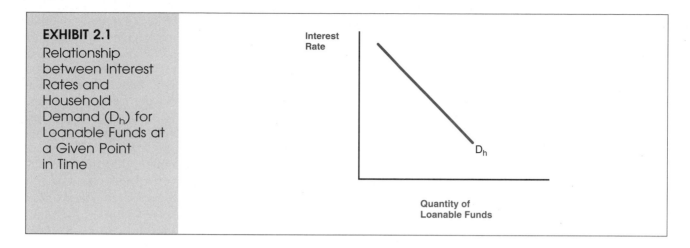

EXHIBIT 2.1

Relationship between Interest Rates and Household Demand (D_h) for Loanable Funds at a Given Point in Time

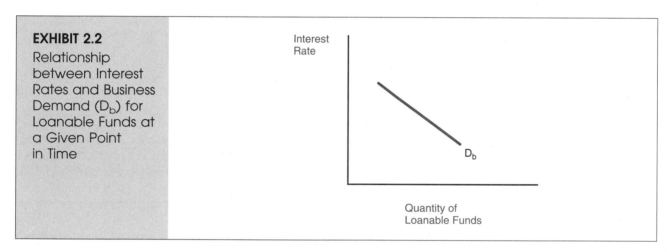

EXHIBIT 2.2

Relationship between Interest Rates and Business Demand (D_b) for Loanable Funds at a Given Point in Time

ongoing operations with fewer funds during periods of high interest rates. This is another reason that a firm's total demand for loanable funds is inversely related to interest rates at any point in time. Although the demand for loanable funds by some businesses may be more sensitive than others to interest rates, all businesses are likely to demand more funds if interest rates are lower at a given point in time.

The business demand-for-loanable-funds schedule can shift in reaction to any events that affect business borrowing preferences. For example, if economic conditions become more favorable, the expected cash flows on various proposed projects will increase. More proposed projects will have expected returns that exceed a particular required rate of return (sometimes called hurdle rate). There will be additional acceptable projects as a result of more favorable economic forecasts, causing an increased demand for loanable funds.

Government Demand for Loanable Funds

Whenever a government's planned expenditures cannot be completely covered by its incoming revenues from taxes and other sources, it demands loanable funds. Municipal (state and local) governments issue municipal bonds to obtain funds, while the federal government and its agencies issue Treasury securities and federal agency securities. These securities represent government debt.

Federal government expenditure and tax policies are generally thought to be independent of interest rates. Thus, the federal government demand for funds is said to be **interest-inelastic,** or insensitive to interest rates. However, municipal governments sometimes postpone proposed expenditures if the cost of financing is too high, implying that their demand for loanable funds is somewhat sensitive to interest rates.

Like the household and business demand, the government demand for loanable funds can shift in response to various events. For example, assume the federal government demand-for-loanable-funds schedule is D_{G1} in Exhibit 2.3. Assume that new bills were passed that caused a net increase in the deficit of $20 billion. The federal government demand for loanable funds would increase by that amount. The new demand schedule, D_{G2} in the exhibit, would shift inward if the government budget deficit were reduced.

Foreign Demand for Loanable Funds

The demand for loanable funds in a given market also includes foreign demand by foreign governments or corporations. For example, the British government may obtain financing by issuing British Treasury securities to U.S. investors, representing a British demand for U.S. funds. Because foreign financial transactions are becoming so common, they can have a significant impact on the demand for loanable funds in any given country. A foreign country's demand for U.S. funds is influenced by the differential between its interest rates and U.S. rates (along with other factors). Other things being equal, a larger quantity of U.S. funds would be demanded by foreign governments and corporations if their domestic interest rates were high relative to U.S. rates. Therefore, for a given set of foreign interest rates, the quantity of U.S. loanable funds demanded by foreign governments or firms will be inversely related to U.S. interest rates.

The foreign demand schedule can shift in response to economic conditions. For example, assume the original foreign demand schedule is D_{f1} in Exhibit 2.4.

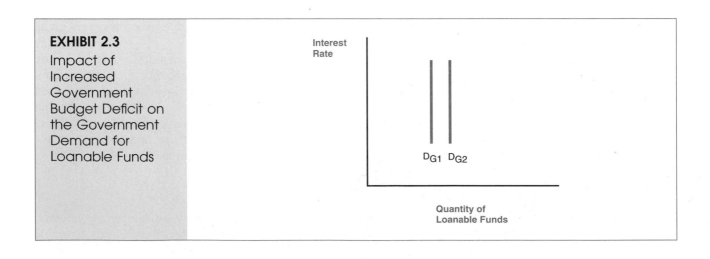

EXHIBIT 2.3

Impact of Increased Government Budget Deficit on the Government Demand for Loanable Funds

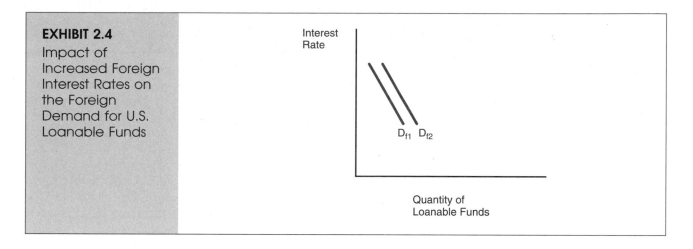

EXHIBIT 2.4
Impact of Increased Foreign Interest Rates on the Foreign Demand for U.S. Loanable Funds

If foreign interest rates rise, foreign firms and governments would likely increase their demand for U.S. funds, as represented by a shift from D_{f1} to D_{f2}.

Aggregate Demand for Loanable Funds

The aggregate demand for loanable funds is the sum of the quantities demanded by the separate sectors at any given interest rate, as shown in Exhibit 2.5. Because most of these sectors are likely to demand a larger quantity of funds at lower interest rates (other things being equal), the aggregate demand for loanable funds is inversely related to interest rates at any point in time. If the demand schedule of any sector should change, the aggregate demand schedule will be affected as well.

Supply of Loanable Funds

Supply of loanable funds is a commonly used term to represent funds provided to financial markets by savers. The household sector is the largest supplier, but loanable funds are also supplied by some government units that temporarily generate more tax revenues than they spend or by some businesses whose cash inflows exceed outflows. Households as a group, however, represent a net supplier of loanable funds, whereas governments and businesses are net demanders of loanable funds.

Suppliers of loanable funds are willing to supply more funds if the interest rate (reward for supplying funds) is higher, other things being equal (Exhibit 2.6). A supply of loanable funds exists even at a very low interest rate because some households choose to postpone consumption until later years, even when the reward (interest rate) for saving is low.

Foreign households, governments, and corporations commonly supply funds to their domestic markets by purchasing domestic securities. In addition, they have been a major creditor to the U.S. government by purchasing large amounts of Treasury securities. The large foreign supply of funds to the U.S. market is partially attributed to the high saving rates of foreign households. Exhibit 2.7 compares the personal saving rate of households in the United States to those of

EXHIBIT 2.5 Determination of the Aggregate Demand Schedule for Loanable Funds

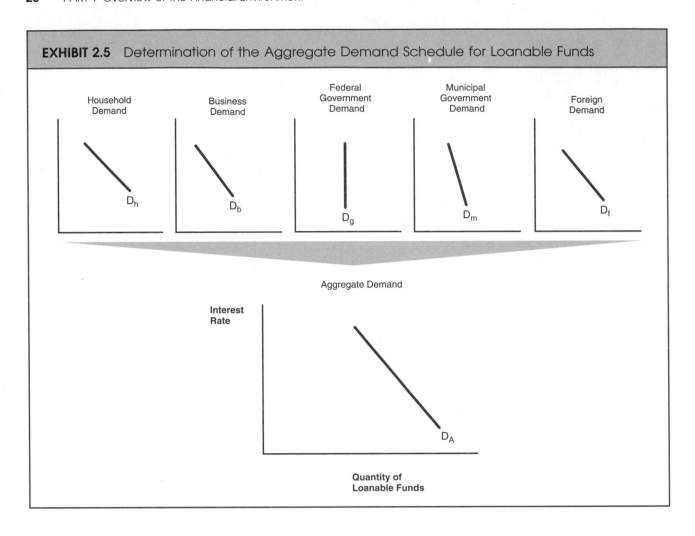

three major foreign countries. Percentages for the United Kingdom and Germany are about twice the U.S. percentage, and Japan's about four times as great.

The supply of loanable funds in the United States is also influenced by the monetary policy implemented by the Federal Reserve System. The Fed controls the amount of reserves held by depository institutions and can influence the amount of savings that can be converted into loanable funds.

Note that the attention given to financial institutions in this section has been minimal. Although financial institutions play a critical intermediary role in channeling funds, they do not represent the ultimate suppliers of funds. Any change in the financial institution's supply of funds results only from a change in habits by the ultimate suppliers—the households, businesses, or governments.

The aggregate supply schedule of loanable funds represents the combination of all sector supply schedules along with the supply of funds provided by the Fed's monetary policy. The steep slope of the aggregate supply schedule in Exhibit 2.6 indicates that it is interest-inelastic, or somewhat insensitive to interest rates. The quantity of loanable funds demanded is normally expected to be more sensitive to interest rates than the quantity of loanable funds supplied.

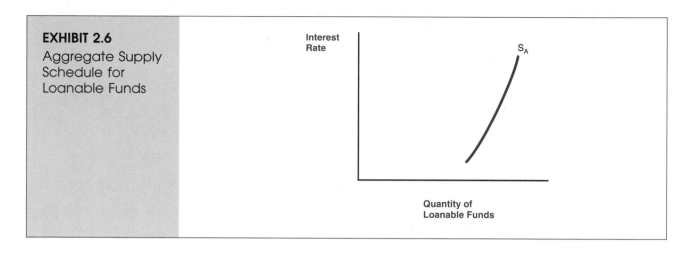

EXHIBIT 2.6
Aggregate Supply
Schedule for
Loanable Funds

EXHIBIT 2.7	Personal Saving Rates in the United States and Other Industrial Countries (Percentage of Disposable Income)		
United States	**Japan**	**United Kingdom**	**Germany**
5.4%	22.3%	11.2%	12.6%

Equilibrium Interest Rate

An understanding of equilibrium interest rates is necessary to assess how various events can affect interest rates. Because activities in financial institutions and markets revolve around interest rate projections, the concept of equilibrium interest rates is applicable to all remaining chapters of the text. It is presented first from an algebraic perspective and then from a graphical perspective. Following this presentation, several examples are offered to reinforce the concept.

ALGEBRAIC PRESENTATION. The equilibrium interest rate is that which equates the aggregate demand for funds with the aggregate supply of loanable funds. The aggregate demand for funds (D_A) can be written as

$$D_A = D_h + D_b + D_G + D_m + D_f$$

where D_h = gross household demand for loanable funds

D_b = gross business demand for loanable funds

D_G = gross federal government demand for loanable funds

D_m = gross municipal government demand for loanable funds

D_f = gross foreign demand for loanable funds

The aggregate supply of funds (S_A) can be written as

$$S_A = S_h + S_b + S_G + S_m + S_f$$

where S_h = gross household supply of loanable funds

S_b = gross business supply of loanable funds

S_G = gross federal government supply of loanable funds

S_m = gross municipal government supply of loanable funds

S_f = gross foreign supply of loanable funds

In equilibrium, $D_A = S_A$. If the aggregate demand for loanable funds increases without a corresponding increase in aggregate supply, there will be a shortage of loanable funds. Interest rates will rise until an additional supply of loanable funds is available to accommodate the excess demand. If the gross supply of loanable funds increases without a corresponding increase in gross demand, there will be a surplus of loanable funds. Interest rates will fall until the quantity of funds supplied no longer exceeds the quantity of funds demanded.

In many cases, both supply and demand for loanable funds are changing. Given an initial equilibrium situation, the equilibrium interest rate should rise when $D_A > S_A$ and fall when $D_A < S_A$.

GRAPHICAL PRESENTATION. When combining the aggregate demand and aggregate supply schedules of loanable funds (refer to Exhibits 2.5 and 2.6), it is possible to compare the total amount of funds that would be demanded to the total amount of funds that would be supplied at any particular interest rate. Exhibit 2.8 illustrates the combined demand and supply schedules. At the equilibrium interest rate of i_e, the supply of loanable funds is equal to the demand for loanable funds.

At any interest rate above i_e, there is a surplus of loanable funds. Some potential suppliers of funds would be unable to successfully supply their funds at the prevailing interest rate. Once the market interest rate is lowered to i_e, the quantity of funds supplied is sufficiently reduced and the quantity of funds de-

EXHIBIT 2.8
Interest Rate
Equilibrium

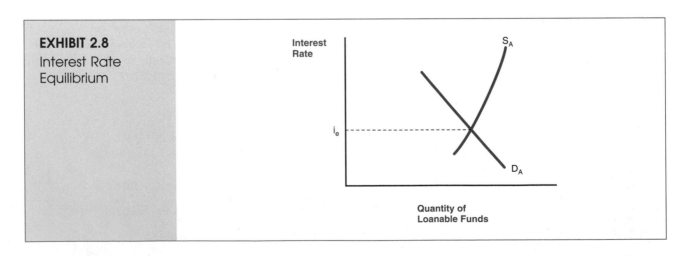

manded is sufficiently increased such that there is no longer a surplus of funds. When a disequilibrium situation exists, market forces should cause an adjustment in interest rates until equilibrium is achieved.

If the prevailing interest rate is below i_e, there will be a shortage of loanable funds. Borrowers will not be able to obtain all the funds that they desire at that rate. Because of the shortage of funds, the interest rate will increase, causing two reactions. First, more savers will enter the market to supply loanable funds, now that the reward (interest rate) is higher. Second, some potential borrowers will decide not to demand loanable funds at the higher interest rate. Once the interest rate rises to i_e, the quantity of loanable funds supplied has increased and quantity of loanable funds demanded has decreased to the extent that a shortage no longer exists. An equilibrium position is achieved once again.

Changes in the Equilibrium Interest Rate

The equilibrium interest rate changes over time because of changes in the demand and supply schedules of loanable funds. Examples illustrating the adjustment in the equilibrium interest rate follow.

Assume that as a result of more optimistic economic projections, most businesses increase their planned expenditures for expansion, which translates into a greater amount of additional borrowing. The aggregate demand schedule would shift outward (to the right). The supply of loanable funds schedule may also shift, but it is more difficult to know how it should shift. It is possible that the increased expansion by businesses could lead to more income for construction crews, and so forth, who service the expansion. Thus, the quantity of savings—and therefore of loanable funds supplied at any possible interest rate—could increase, causing an outward shift in the supply schedule. Yet, there is no assurance that the volume of savings will truly increase. Even if a shift were to occur, it would likely be of a smaller magnitude than the shift in the demand schedule.

In summary, the expected impact of the increased expansion by businesses is an outward shift in the demand schedule and no obvious change in the supply schedule (Exhibit 2.9). The shift in the aggregate demand schedule to D_{A2} in the exhibit causes an increase in the equilibrium interest rate to i_{e2}.

EXHIBIT 2.9
Impact of
Increased
Expansion by Firms

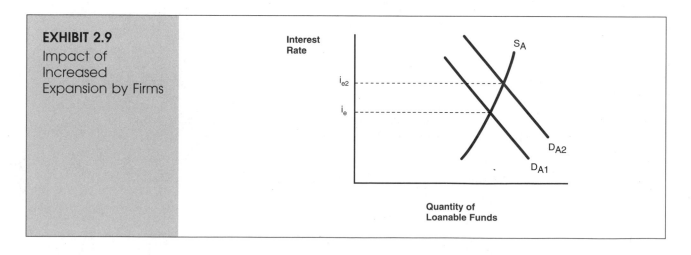

In reality, there are no published comprehensive schedules that measure the quantity of funds to be supplied or demanded at every possible interest rate. However, one could still access the expected impact of a particular event without even knowing the specific numbers that correspond to these schedules. Any event that causes an outward shift in the demand schedule should force interest rates up (as long as the supply schedule is not forced out by an equal or greater degree). Though it is difficult to predict the precise change in the interest rate due to a particular event, an ability to assess the direction of supply or demand schedule shifts can at least help one understand why interest rates changed in a specific direction.

As a second example, consider how a slowdown in the economy would affect the demand and supply schedules of loanable funds and the equilibrium interest rate. The demand schedule would shift inward (to the left), reflecting less demand for loanable funds at any possible interest rate. The supply schedule could possibly shift a little, but it is questionable which way it would shift. One could argue that a slowdown should cause increased saving at any possible interest rate as households prepared for the possibility of being laid off. Yet, the gradual reduction in labor income that occurs during an economic slowdown could reduce households' ability to save. Historical data support this latter expectation. Any shift that did occur would likely be minor relative to the shift in the demand schedule. Therefore, the equilibrium interest rate is expected to decrease, as illustrated in Exhibit 2.10.

Up to this point, the focus has been on shifts in the demand for loanable funds. In some cases, the supply of loanable funds may be significantly affected, which would also cause an adjustment in the equilibrium interest rate. For example, assume that the Social Security system is deteriorating and that households anticipate that they will not receive any funds from it in the future. This may increase their desire to save. Graphically, such a scenario would represent an outward shift in the supply schedule. It is even possible that the demand schedule could shift inward because some households may also attempt to borrow less (although we shall assume no change in our demand schedule here). Exhibit 2.11 illustrates the shifts in the supply schedule. As a result of this shift, the equilibrium interest rate would decrease.

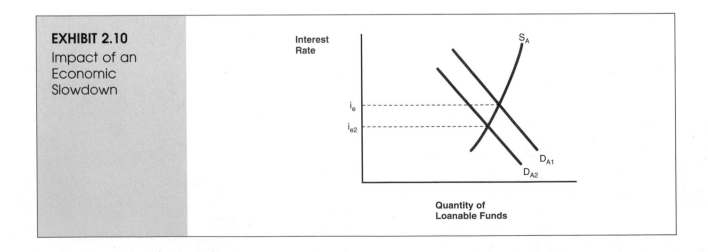

EXHIBIT 2.10

Impact of an Economic Slowdown

EXHIBIT 2.11

Impact of an Increased Desire by Households to Save for Retirement

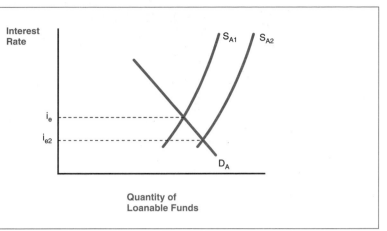

THE FISHER EFFECT

More than 50 years ago, Irving Fisher proposed a theory of interest rate determination that is still widely used today. It does not contradict the loanable funds theory but simply offers an additional explanation for interest rate movements. Fisher proposed that nominal interest payments compensate savers in two ways. First, they compensate for a saver's reduced purchasing power. Second, they provide an additional premium to savers for foregoing present consumption. Savers are willing to forego consumption only if they receive a premium on their savings above the anticipated rate of inflation, as shown in the following equation:

$$i_n = E(I) + i_r$$

where i_n = nominal or quoted rate of interest

$E(I)$ = expected inflation rate

i_r = real rate of interest

This relationship between interest rates and expected inflation is often referred to as the **Fisher effect.** The difference between the nominal interest rate and the expected inflation rate is the real return to a saver after adjusting for the reduced purchasing power over the time period of concern. It is referred to as the **real rate of interest,** because, unlike the nominal rate of interest, it adjusts for the expected rate of inflation. The preceding equation can be rearranged to express the real rate of interest as

$$i_r = i_n - E(I)$$

If the normal interest rate was equal to the expected inflation rate, the real interest rate would be zero. Savings would accumulate interest at the same rate that prices are expected to increase, so that the purchasing power of savings would remain stable.

If today's expected inflation can be measured along with today's nominal interest rate, the **ex ante** real interest rate can be estimated. The term *ex ante* means before the fact. Our discussion focuses on expected inflation rather than actual inflation, because it is expected inflation that influences the habits of savers and borrowers more than actual inflation.

Because the expected inflation rate is difficult to estimate, the ex ante real interest rate is difficult to measure. The actual inflation rate that has occurred can serve as an imperfect substitute for the expected inflation when monitoring the real interest rate over time. If the actual inflation rate is used, the **ex post** (after the fact) real interest rate is measured.

Exhibit 2.12 illustrates the ex post real interest rate over the 1970–1993 period. In some periods it was negative, implying that inflation exceeded the nominal interest rate. This was especially true during the 1973–1975 period when oil prices increased substantially, igniting inflation. If investors had been aware before the fact that inflation was going to be so high, they would have required higher nominal interest rates on their savings. Alternatively, they would have saved fewer funds, knowing that the purchasing power of their savings was decreasing.

Notice from Exhibit 2.12 that the ex post real interest rate has been relatively high in recent years. Thus, the realized rate of inflation may have been lower than anticipated, perhaps because oil prices declined to a greater degree than anticipated.

When the inflation rate is higher than anticipated, the ex post real rate of interest is less than desired for savers. Borrowers benefit, because they were able to borrow at a lower nominal interest rate than would have been offered if inflation had been accurately forecasted. When the inflation rate is lower than anticipated, the ex post real rate of interest is higher than expected for savers, and borrowers are adversely affected.

Throughout the text, the term *interest rate* will be used to represent the nominal, or quoted, rate of interest. Keep in mind, however, that because of inflation, purchasing power is not necessarily increasing during periods of rising interest rates. If one is more concerned with changes in purchasing power, real interest rates should be assessed rather than nominal interest rates.

Key Issues Regarding Interest Rates

As will be demonstrated throughout the text, interest rate movements are a major concern to all financial institutions and markets. They can affect decision making, performance, and the growth of any particular financial institution. Three of the more common issues regarding interest rates are (1) how a change in expected inflation affects interest rates, (2) how a government budget deficit affects interest rates, and (3) how foreign interest rate movements can affect U.S. interest rates. A discussion of these issues follows.

Impact of Inflation on Interest Rates

The Fisher effect and loanable funds theory can be used to assess how inflationary expectations could affect nominal interest rates. According to the Fisher effect, expectations of higher inflation cause savers to require a higher nominal

EXHIBIT 2.12 Ex Post Real Interest Rates over Time

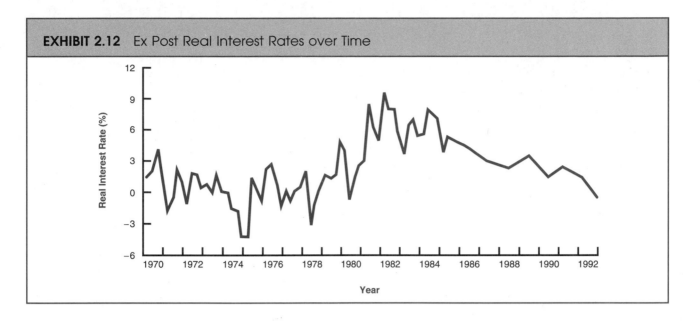

interest rate on savings, because this is the only way that they can maintain the existing real rate of interest.

According to loanable funds theory, expectations of higher inflation cause an increase in the demand for loanable funds, as households and businesses are motivated to increase their expenditures before prices increase. For this same reason, households and businesses are less willing to save. The shifts in the supply and demand schedules cause a shortage of funds at the prevailing nominal interest rates—and therefore force an increase in the equilibrium interest rate. Although the Fisher effect and loanable funds theory provide different explanations for the same result, they are closely related. The reason for the shift in the demand and supply of loanable funds suggested by loanable funds theory is based on the saver's desire to maintain the existing real rate of interest (as suggested by the Fisher effect).

Impact of a Budget Deficit on Interest Rates

Consider how an increase in the federal government deficit would affect interest rates, assuming no other changes in habits by consumers and firms. A higher federal government deficit increases the quantity of loanable funds demanded at any prevailing interest rate, causing an outward shift in the demand schedule. Assuming no offsetting increase in the supply schedule, interest rates will rise. Given a certain amount of loanable funds supplied to the market (through savings), excessive government demand for these funds tends to "crowd out" the private demand (by consumers and corporations) for funds. The federal government may be willing to pay whatever is necessary to borrow these funds, while the private sector may not. This impact is known as the **crowding-out effect.** Exhibit 2.13 illustrates the flow of funds between the federal government and the private sector.

There is a counterargument that the supply schedule might shift outward if the government creates more jobs by spending more funds than it collects from

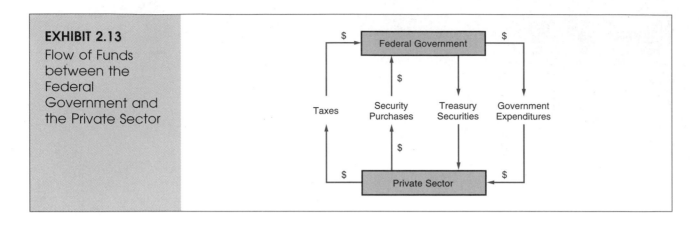

EXHIBIT 2.13
Flow of Funds between the Federal Government and the Private Sector

the public (this is what causes the deficit in the first place). If this were to occur, the deficit might not necessarily place upward pressure on interest rates. Much research has investigated this issue and, in general, has shown that higher deficits place upward pressure on interest rates.

Impact of Foreign Interest Rates

GLOBAL ASPECTS

The large flow of funds between countries causes interest rates in any given country to become more susceptible to interest rate movements in other countries. To illustrate the influence of foreign markets, consider the efforts to reunify East and West Germany in 1989 and 1990. The corporate demand for funds increased in response to economic expansion, which placed upward pressure on German interest rates. The new opportunities in Germany encouraged German and U.S. investors to invest funds there. Consequently, the supply of loanable funds provided by U.S. and German investors to the U.S. declined, placing upward pressure on U.S. interest rates.

During 1990, Japanese interest rates also increased in response to efforts by the Japanese government to dampen inflationary pressure. This encouraged Japanese investors to keep their funds in Japan rather than invest in the U.S., which contributed to the reduced supply of loanable funds in the United States. In essence, the upward pressure on Japanese interest rates placed upward pressure on U.S. interest rates.

The Single European Act of 1987 mandated that barriers on capital flows between many European countries be phased out by 1992. This caused a greater integration of interest rates between European countries, so that a given country's interest rates became even more susceptible to interest rate movements of other countries.

In 1992, the German government maintained relatively high interest rates to slow inflationary pressure (by reducing economic growth). Investors from other European countries attempted to capitalize on the high interest rates in Germany. As funds flowed from other European countries to Germany, there was upward pressure on interest rates across these countries.

Although many cross-border barriers to international capital flows have been removed, one remaining barrier is exchange rate risk. If a country's currency is expected to weaken, it may not attract funds even if its interest rate is high.

EFFECT OF THE BUDGET DEFICIT ON INTEREST RATES

The impact of federal deficits on interest rates has been debated for several years. While it is generally suggested that an increase in the federal government deficit places upward pressure on interest rates, some studies have found little or no relationship between the size of the federal deficit and interest rates.

A recent study by Hoelscher reassessed the relationship between deficits and long-term interest rates over the period from 1953 to 1984. Several regression models were applied to test the relationship, each model specifying a particular measure of the deficit. The analysis found a positive and significant relationship between the size of the deficit and long-term interest rates.

For example, one model determined that each $100 billion of the federal deficit is predicted to increase long-term interest rates by 142 basis points (1.42%). While the various models utilized by Hoelscher generated different results, there was a significant positive relationship, regardless of the way in which the federal deficit was defined.

Investors from other countries are adversely affected if the currency denominating their investment weakens. Because the exchange rate effect can more than offset a higher interest rate, exchange rate risk can discourage investors from capitalizing on higher foreign interest rates. For this reason, interest rates will not necessarily be the same across countries, even if there are no other barriers. Nevertheless, the removal of barriers has encouraged more international investment, which allows funds to be used wherever they are expected to benefit investors the most.

EVALUATION OF INTEREST RATES OVER TIME

Now that the more important determinants of interest rates have been identified, we can review interest rates over time and explain why they moved as they did. Exhibit 2.14 illustrates nominal interest rates over the past several years. One-year Treasury bill rates were used as a proxy for interest rates here. Although other securities had different rates, their rate movements were somewhat similar to those of Treasury bills. The rise in interest rates in 1973 was partially due to higher expected inflation (ignited by oil price hikes), which caused a strong demand for loanable funds. In late 1973 and 1974, the economy slowed down and a recession occurred. This led to a reduced demand for loanable funds by businesses because future expansion plans were postponed. In addition, household demand for loanable funds also decreased as spending habits adjusted during the recession. Consequently, interest rates fell. During the 1978–79 period, interest rates increased as a result of high inflation, strong economic growth, and therefore strong demand for loanable funds. In 1980 a mild recession occurred, which reduced the demand for loanable funds and thus reduced interest rates. A quick reversal in interest rates occurred in 1981 as the economy strengthened, only to turn back down in 1982 because of a severe recession. Interest rates remained low during the mid-1980s as oil prices decreased and inflationary expectations subsided. In the late 1980s, U.S. interest rates increased slightly, partially because of the influence of German reunification. In the 1990s, interest rates declined as a recession caused a substantial decline in the demand for loanable funds.

The supply of loanable funds is also a critical factor that can help explain movements in interest rates. During the mid-1970s, the Federal Reserve System substantially increased the money supply, which placed downward pressure on interest rates during that period. However, it is commonly believed that such excessive growth in the money supply could have caused expectations of higher inflation (as will be thoroughly explained in later chapters), which contributed to the strong demand for loanable funds (and rising interest rates) over the late 1970s. This discussion shows how the factors identified in this chapter can be useful for explaining interest rate movements over time.

FORECASTING INTEREST RATES

Exhibit 2.15 summarizes the key factors that are evaluated when forecasting interest rates. With an understanding of how each factor affects interest rates, it is possible to forecast how interest rates may change in the future. When forecasting household demand for loanable funds, it may be necessary to assess consumer credit data to determine the borrowing capacity of households. Seasonal factors (such as Christmas or summer vacations) could also be important, as well as the expected unemployment rate and a host of other factors that affect the earning power of households. The potential supply of loanable funds provided by households may be determined in the same manner.

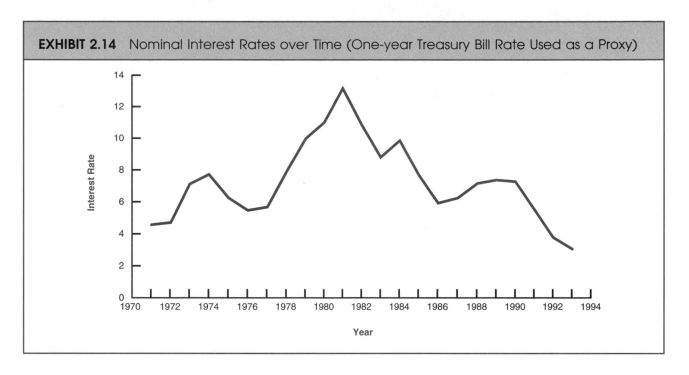

EXHIBIT 2.14 Nominal Interest Rates over Time (One-year Treasury Bill Rate Used as a Proxy)

Business demand for loanable funds can be forecasted by assessing future plans for corporate expansion and the future state of the economy. Federal government demand for loanable funds could be influenced by the future state of the economy because it affects tax revenues to be received and the amount of unemployment compensation to be paid out, factors that affect the size of the government deficit. The Federal Reserve System's money supply targets may be assessed by reviewing public statements about the Fed's future objectives, although those statements are somewhat vague.

Interest rates are commonly forecasted with the use of regression analysis, as illustrated with the following example. Assume that Fighting Irish, Inc., a diversified financial services company, needs to forecast interest rates one quarter ahead. It identifies and compiles historical data on factors that may influence each sector's demand. It then applies regression analysis to the historical data in order to estimate the sensitivity of each sector's demand to each factor. This sensitivity is measured by the estimated regression coefficients. Next, the factors are forecasted and used along with the estimated regression coefficients to forecast the sector's future demand for loanable funds. These forecasts can be combined to estimate the aggregate demand for loanable funds simply by replicating the procedure. The resulting projections are then used to forecast net demand:

$$ND_A = D_A - S_A$$
$$= [D_h + D_b + D_G + D_m + D_f] - [S_h + S_b + S_G + S_m + S_f]$$

If the forecasted level of ND_A is positive or negative, a disequilibrium will exist temporarily. If positive, it will be corrected by an upward adjustment in interest rates. If negative, it will be corrected by a downward adjustment. The degree of adjustment is positively correlated with the forecasted magnitude of ND_A.

EXHIBIT 2.15 Framework for Forecasting Interest Rates

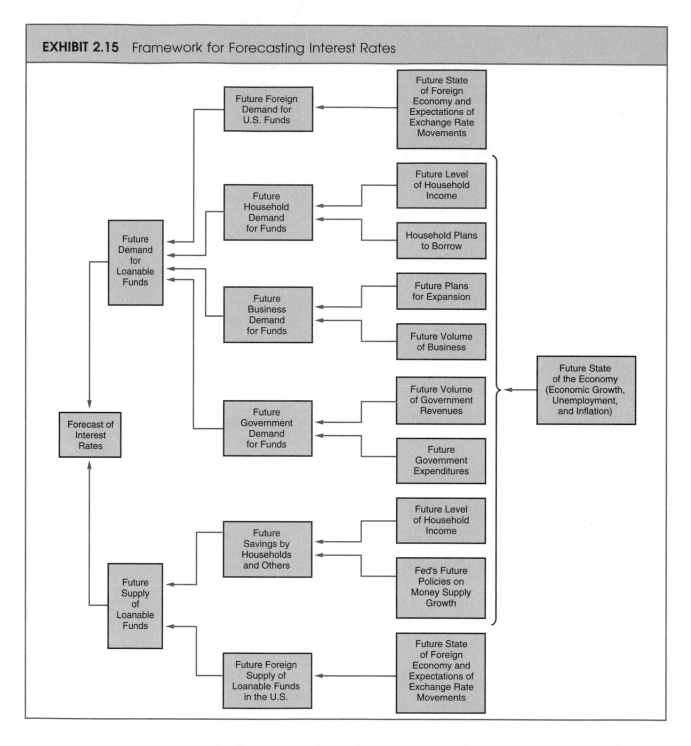

The limitations of any forecasting procedure can be recognized from the preceding example. First, it is difficult to properly include all relevant factors in a regression model. Some subjective factors such as inflationary expectations are difficult to quantify. In addition, the sensitivity of each sector to factors can change over time. Therefore, the estimated regression coefficients may misspecify the actual sensitivity of each sector's demand or supply to each factor over the forecasted period. Furthermore, forecasts of the factors that influence demand and supply are needed for the forecasted period. If these forecasts are inaccurate, the ND_A forecast will be, too, even if the regression coefficients were accurately estimated.

To illustrate the difficulty in forecasting interest rates, consider how U.S. interest rates will be affected by the simultaneous existence of a higher government deficit, increased growth in the money supply, and increased foreign funds into the United States. There is no clear-cut answer. One can, however, make an educated guess by estimating the individual impact of each event on interest rates and then combining the expected impacts of all these events. Because the impact of some events may be greater than that of others, it is necessary to measure not only the direction but also the magnitude of each impact.

To verify which factors should be considered when forecasting interest rates, obtain a recent business periodical article that provides interest rate projections by various economists and consultants. Interest rate projections by top economists are typically dependent on the following factors: the Fed's money supply growth, the state of the economy, inflation, the federal budget deficit, tax reform, and oil prices. Even though economists consider similar factors, they develop different interest rate projections because of their diverse forecasts of these factors and the relative influence the factors have on interest rates.

SUMMARY

- The loanable funds framework shows how the equilibrium interest rate is dependent on the aggregate supply of available funds and the aggregate demand for funds. As conditions cause the aggregate supply or demand schedules to change, interest rates gravitate toward a new equilibrium.

- The more relevant factors that affect interest rate movements are changes in economic growth, inflation, the budget deficit, foreign interest rates, and money supply. These factors can have a strong impact on the aggregate supply of funds or on the aggregate demand for funds, and therefore affect the equilibrium interest rate.

- Given that the equilibrium interest rate is determined by supply and demand conditions, changes in the interest rate can be forecasted by forecasting changes in the supply of loanable funds or in the demand for loanable funds. Thus, the factors that influence the supply and demand for funds must be forecasted in order to forecast interest rates.

QUESTIONS

1. Explain why interest rates changed as they did over the past year.

2. Explain what is meant by interest elasticity.

3. Would you expect federal government demand for loanable funds to be more or less interest-elastic than household demand for loanable funds? Why?

4. If the federal government planned to expand the space program, how might this affect interest rates?

5. Explain why interest rates tend to decrease during recessionary periods.

6. Obtain or develop forecasts of economic growth and inflation. Use this information to forecast interest rates one year from now.

7. Jayhawk Forecasting Services analyzed several factors that could affect future interest rates. Most factors were expected to place downward pressure on interest rates. Jayhawk also felt that although the annual budget deficit was to be cut by 40 percent from the previous year, it would still be very large. Thus, it believed that the deficit's impact would more than offset the other effects and therefore forecasted interest rates to increase by 2 percent. Comment on Jayhawk's logic.

8. Should increasing money supply growth place upward or downward pressure on interest rates? Justify your answer.

9. Consider a scenario where inflation is low and is not expected to rise in the future. In addition, assume that the Fed substantially increases the money supply. Explain how this would likely affect interest rates.

10. What is the logic behind the Fisher effect's implied positive relationship between expected inflation and nominal interest rates?

11. What is the difference between the ex ante and ex post real rate of interest?

12. Estimate the ex post real rate of interest over the past year.

13. Review historical interest rates to determine how they react to recessionary periods. Explain this reaction.

14. Why do forecasts of interest rates differ among experts?

15. During the stock market crash in October 1987, interest rates declined. Use the loanable funds framework discussed in this chapter to explain why.

16. If foreign investors expected that the U.S. dollar's value would weaken over the next few years, how might this affect (a) the foreign supply of funds to the U.S. markets and (b) U.S. interest rates? Explain.

17. A well-known economist recently suggested that lower interest rates will stimulate the economy. Yet, this chapter implied that a strong economy can cause high interest rates. Do these concepts conflict? Explain.

18. Assume that if the U.S. dollar strengthens, it can place downward pressure on U.S. inflation. Based on this information, how might expectations of a strong dollar affect the demand for loanable funds in the United States and U.S. interest rates? Is there any reason to think that expectations of a strong dollar could also affect the supply of loanable funds? Explain.

19. If financial market participants overestimate inflation in a particular period, will ex post real interest rates be relatively high or low? Explain.

20. Why might you expect interest rate movements of various industrialized countries to be more highly correlated in recent years than in earlier years?

21. In November 1989, the wall separating East and West Germany was removed. Some analysts say that this event led to an increase in German and U.S. interest rates. Offer a possible explanation as to why this event could cause an increase in German and U.S. interest rates.

22. In August 1990, the Persian Gulf crisis occurred, resulting in some significant reactions in financial markets. Why would the crisis be expected to place upward pressure on U.S. interest rates? Why might some investors expect the crisis to place downward pressure on U.S. interest rates?

Big Deficit Cut Could Sharply Reduce Rates

Constance Mitchell, New York

If President Clinton keeps his promise to slash the nation's massive budget deficit, how much would interest rates drop?

Many economists believe that cutting the federal deficit by $100 billion or more would bring yields on long-term bonds down sharply—perhaps by as much as a full percentage point. And that would pave the way for cheaper mortgages for homeowners and lower borrowing costs for businesses.

"The deficit is costing us significantly in terms of long-term interest rates," says David Wyss, an economist at Data Resources Inc., a Boston economic consulting firm. Allen Sinai, chief economist at Boston Co. agrees. "The expectations of permanently high federal deficits has in my view been worth as much as a couple of percentage points in long-term interest rates," he says.

But to get long-term rates down, the Clinton administration would have to make major—and permanent—cuts in the federal deficit, which is expected to reach $300 billion this year.

Data Resources, Boston Co. and WEFA Group in Bala Cynwyd, Pa.— three of the nation's leading economic consultants—each plugged hypothetical deficit cuts into the computer models they use to predict the behavior of the U.S. economy. All came to similar conclusions.

If the government cut the federal deficit by $100 billion, they say, the yield on the benchmark 30-year Treasury

bond, now at 7.29%, would fall to between 6.4% and 6.6%.

If the Clinton administration really takes an ax to the deficit and whacks out $200 billion, long-term Treasury bond yields would plummet even further—to low as 5.75%. That's lower than the yield on 30-year bonds has ever been since the Treasury resumed issuing 30-year bonds in 1978.

"If you reduce Uncle Sam's presence in the credit markets, then there is a good bond market rally lurking out there," says Donald Straszhelm, chief economist at Merrill Lynch & Co. That's because prices of existing bonds rise as interest rates decline.

Despite the nation's growing budget deficit, the Federal Reserve has been successful in driving down short-term interest rates over the past three years, as the economy weakened and inflation faded. Yields on three-month Treasury bills, for example, have plunged five percentage points to about 3% now from 8% in 1990. But long-term interest rates have been much more stubborn, falling less than 1¾ percentage points since 1990. And one of the major reasons for that is the ballooning federal budget deficit, say economists.

Lower long-term interest rates would be good news for consumers and for the U.S. government, the nation's biggest debtor. Take a look at home-mortgage rates, which closely track the yields on long-term Treasury notes and bonds.

Suppose the Clinton financial team can cut the deficit enough to drive long-term interest rates down by one percentage point. And suppose that produced a decline in the rate on a 30-year mortgage to, say, 7% from 8%. That would reduce the annual payments on a $100,000 home loan to about $7,980 from $8,808, for a saving of over $800 a year.

Uncle Sam would win, too. A decline of one percentage point in the yield on 30-year Treasury bonds, to 6.3%, would save the government more than $400 million annually in interest payments on any new bonds that it sells, and several billion dollars over the life of the issue. (That assumes that the government sells $40 billion of 30-year bonds, the same amount it sold in 1992.)

The White House budget office estimates that a sustained one percentage point decline in interest rates across the board would save the government more than $13 billion in the first year.

With the deficit currently projected to reach close to $300 billion this year, an immediate cut of $100 billion seems unlikely. Nevertheless, economists say big cuts in the deficit are probably necessary before long-term interest rates can come down substantially.

The deficit, they say, keeps long-term interest rates high for two major reasons. First, the huge supply of bonds the government must sell to finance the growing deficit is beginning to test investor de-

Continued

CASE APPLICATION: EFFECT OF THE BUDGET DEFICIT ON INTEREST RATES

Continued

mand. In recent quarters, the government has been selling between $10 billion and $12 billion each of 30-year bonds and 10-year notes. In 1984, the size of the 30-year bond sales were just $5 billion each quarter and the 10-year note sales were about $5.5 billion.

"If you believe in the law of supply and demand, then you have to believe that government borrowing sends interest rates upward," said Data Resources' Mr. Wyss. "You can argue over how much the deficit affects interest rates, but it's clear that it does raise interest rates."

Secondly, the rapidly rising deficit has raised concern among some investors that the nation's debt problem could some day become unmanageable and trigger an inflation crisis. They note that the nation's borrowing needs are growing much faster than the deficit, partly because the Treasury not only borrows to finance the current deficit, but it also must refinance "or refund" older maturing debt. Last year, when the deficit was about $297 billion, the government borrowed more than $500 billion from investors, a large portion of which was used to refund older debt.

"What so many people don't see is the monster called the refunding dilemma," says Ron Ryan, president of Ryan Labs Inc., a bond market research firm. "The refundings now are larger than almost any deficit we have ever had in any year and it's snowballing." Anxiety about the government's heavy debt burden makes investors demand a "risk" premium when they buy government bonds.

Says Mr. Sinai: "If one looks at the history of nations around the world, those that have accumulated huge deficits have eventually inflated their way out of their debtor position." He points to several heavily indebted Latin Amer-

ican countries that tried to cure their debt woes by allowing their economies to overheat. In theory, a fast-rising economy would create extra tax revenues, which over a few years would help wipe out big deficits. But in practice, such strategies have often led to staggering levels of inflation. Some investors fear that the U.S. could one day resort to such a strategy of hyperinflation, even though many observers in Washington doubt that the Federal Reserve would ever let that happen.

Economists who compare "real" interest rates, which are rates adjusted for inflation, also feel that the deficit is keeping long-term interest rates unusually high.

"If you look at where real long-term interest rates are now, and compare them to earlier periods of time, you can see that there is a premium built into current rates," says Bruce Steinberg, manager of macroeconomic analysis at Merrill Lynch. And that premium, he says, "must reflect excesses in federal government borrowing."

Looking back three or four decades, interest rates on long-term bonds have been 2.5 percentage points to three percentage points above inflation. So if inflation was running at 2%, yields on long-term bonds would be 5% or lower. But even though inflation is currently running at between 2% and 3%, yields on 30-year Treasury bonds are 7.29%. That has many economists convinced that something other than inflation—the federal deficit—is putting upward pressure on long-term interest rates.

There are a few skeptics who say it's nearly impossible to forecast how much interest rates would fall if the deficit were reduced. Robert Giordano, chief economist at Goldman, Sachs & Co., says, "It's very hard for somebody to dem-

onstrate statistically that the budget deficit has kept yields a lot higher than they otherwise would be."

Mr. Giordano notes that yields on long-term bonds have declined over the past three years from a high of 9% in mid-1990, even as the budget deficit continued to expand. The reason: slower economic growth and the easing of inflation.

Still, even Mr. Giordano believes that if the deficit were cut, long-term interest rates would fall. That's because the economy would weaken due to the decline in government spending.

QUESTIONS

1. Why do many *Wall Street Journal* articles (like this one) focus on potential changes in interest rates?

2. Explain the comment from the firm Data Resources that "the deficit is costing us significantly in terms of long-term interest rates."

3. Explain how the weak economy and low inflation had offset the pressure of the budget deficit on interest rates, using the demand and supply loanable funds in your explanation.

4. Explain the comment from Merrill Lynch that real long-term interest rates contain a premium that reflects the excesses in federal government borrowing.

PROJECTS

1. **Forecasting Interest Rates**
    Review the "Credit Markets" section of the *Wall Street Journal* (listed in the index of the front page) for the past five days. Use this section to determine the factors likely to have the largest impact on future interest rate movements. Then create your own forecasts as to whether interest rates will increase or decrease from now until the end of this school term, based on your assessment of any factors that affect interest rates. Explain your forecast.

2. **Assessing the Accuracy of Interest Rate Forecasts**
    Find a business periodical at least one year old that provided interest rate projections one year ahead.
    a. Determine how far off the projected rates were from actual rates.
    b. Offer some reasons why the actual rates turned out to be lower or higher than what was projected.

REFERENCES

Belongia, Michael T. "Predicting Interest Rates: A Comparison of Professional and Market-Based Forecasts." *Review,* Federal Reserve Bank of St. Louis (March 1987): 9–15.

Ceccheti, Stephen G. "High Real Interest Rates: Can They Be Explained?" *Economic Review* (September–October 1986): 31–41.

Cook, Timothy, and Thomas Hahn. "The Information Content of Discount Rate Announcements and Their Effect on Market Interest Rates." *Journal of Money, Credit and Banking* (May 1988): 167–180.

DeFina, Robert H. "The Link between Savings and Interest Rates: A Key Element in the Tax Policy Debate." *Business Review,* Federal Reserve Bank of Philadelphia (November–December 1984): 15–21.

Hendershott, Patric H., and Joe Peek. "Treasury Bill Rates in the 1970s and 1980s," *Journal of Money, Credit, and Banking* (May 1992): 195–214.

Hoelscher, Gregory. "New Evidence on Deficits and Interest Rates." *Journal of Money, Credit, and Banking* (February 1986): 1–17, 2.

Kopcke, Richard W. "The Determinants of Investment Spending." *New England Economic Review,* Federal Reserve Bank of Boston (July–August 1985): 19–34.

Miller, Preston J. "Budget Deficit Mythology." *Quarterly Review,* Federal Reserve Bank of Minneapolis (Fall 1983): 1–13.

Tatom, John A. "A Perspective on the Federal Deficit Problem." *Review,* Federal Reserve Bank of St. Louis (June–July 1986): 5–17.

Taylor, Herbert. "Interest Rates: How Much Does Expected Inflation Matter." *Business Review,* Federal Reserve Bank of Philadelphia (July–August 1982): 3–12.

Webster, Charles E., Jr. "The Effects of Deficits on Interest Rates." *Economic Review,* Federal Reserve Bank of Kansas City (May 1983): 19–28.

CHAPTER 3

RELATIONSHIPS BETWEEN INTEREST RATES AND SECURITY PRICES

The values of debt securities such as bonds and mortgages can change significantly in response to interest rate movements. Thus, the values are closely monitored by financial institutions that consider buying or selling these securities.

The specific objectives of this chapter are to:

- demonstrate how prices of bonds (and other debt securities) are valued and are influenced by interest rate movements,
- explain how the sensitivity of bond prices to interest rates is dependent on particular bond characteristics,
- demonstrate how bond prices can be forecasted, and
- demonstrate how bond portfolio values can be forecasted.

BOND VALUATION

Bond valuation is conceptually similar to the valuation of capital budgeting projects, businesses, or even real estate. The appropriate price reflects the present value of cash flows to be received. The discount rate selected to compute present value is critical to accurate valuation. Exhibit 3.1 shows the wide range of present value results yielded by different discount rates, for a $10,000 payment in 10 years. The appropriate discount rate for valuing any asset is the yield that could be earned on alternative investments with similar risk and maturity.

The market price of a bond is determined by not only the size but also the timing of the payments made to bondholders. Funds received sooner can be reinvested to earn additional returns. Thus, a dollar to be received soon has a

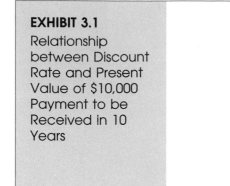

EXHIBIT 3.1

Relationship between Discount Rate and Present Value of $10,000 Payment to be Received in 10 Years

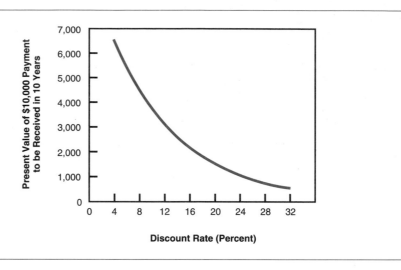

higher present value than one to be received later. The impact of maturity on the present value of a $10,000 payment is shown in Exhibit 3.2, assuming that a return of 10 percent could be earned on available funds. The $10,000 payment has a present value of $8,264 if it is to be paid in two years. This implies that if $8,264 were invested today and earned 10 percent annually, it would be worth $10,000 in two years. Exhibit 3.2 also shows that a $10,000 payment made 20 years from now has a present value of only $1,486, and a $10,000 payment made 50 years from now has a present value of only $85 (based on the 10 percent discount rate).

The current price of a bond should be the present value of its remaining cash flows. The present value (PV) of a bond is

$$\text{PV of bond} = \frac{C}{(1 + i)^1} + \frac{C}{(1 + i)^2} + \cdots \frac{C + P}{(1 + i)^n}$$

where

C = coupon payment provided in each period

P = par value

i = interest rate per period used to discount the bond

n = number of periods to maturity

Consider a bond that has a par value of $1,000, pays $100 at the end of each year in coupon payments, and has three years remaining until maturity. Assume that the prevailing annualized yield on other bonds with similar characteristics is 12 percent. In this case, the appropriate price of the bond can be determined as follows. The future cash flows to investors who would purchase this bond are $100 in Year 1, $100 in Year 2, and $1,100 (computed as $100 in coupon payments plus $1,000 par value) in Year 3. The appropriate market price of the bond is its present value:

$$\begin{aligned} \text{PV of bond} &= \$100/(1 + .12)^1 + \$100/(1 + .12)^2 + \$1,100/(1 + .12)^3 \\ &= \$89.29 + \$79.72 + \$782.96 \\ &= \$951.97 \end{aligned}$$

EXHIBIT 3.2
Relationship between Time of Payment and Present Value of Payment

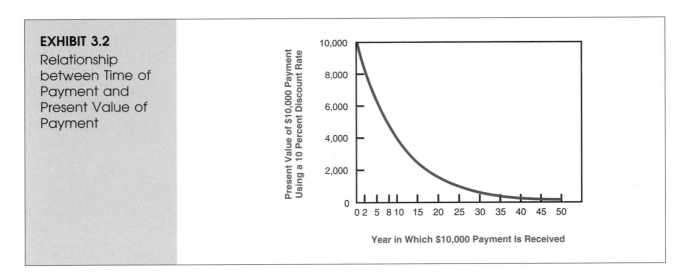

EXHIBIT 3.3
Valuation of a Three-Year Bond

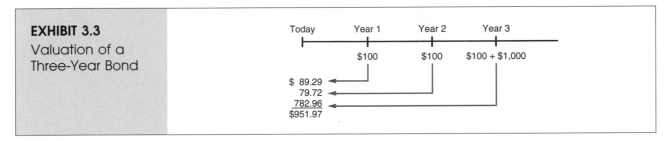

This valuation procedure is illustrated in Exhibit 3.3. Because it was assumed that investors required a 12 percent return, i equals 12 percent for this example. At the price of $951.97, the bondholders purchasing this bond would receive a 12 percent annualized return.

Bond valuation can be simplified with a present-value table, as is shown in Exhibit 3.4. Each **present value interest factor (PVIF)** in this exhibit represents the present value of $1 for a specified period (n) and interest rate. Coupon payments and the par value can be multiplied by their respective PVIFs to determine the present value of the bond. For example, the present value of the bond just described is reestimated as follows, using the table in Exhibit 3.4:

$$\text{PV of bond} = \$100 \,(\text{PVIF}_{i=12\%, n=1}) + \$100 \,(\text{PVIF}_{i=12\%, n=2}) + \$1,100 \,(\text{PVIF}_{i=12\%, n=3})$$

$$= \$100 \,(.8929) \quad + \$100 \,(.7972) \quad + \$1,100 \,(.7118)$$

$$= \$89.29 \quad + \$79.72 \quad + \$782.98$$

$$= \$951.99$$

The slightly different answer is due to rounding.

Because fixed-rate mortgages offer a fixed stream of payments like bonds, they can be valued in a manner similar to bonds. Thus, the concepts described in this chapter for bonds also apply to the valuation of mortgages.

EXHIBIT 3.4 Present Value Interest Factors (PVIF)

Period n	1%	2%	3%	4%	5%	6%	7%	8%	9%	10%	11%	12%
1	.9901	.9804	.9709	.9615	.9524	.9434	.9346	.9259	.9174	.9091	.9009	.8929
2	.9803	.9612	.9426	.9246	.9070	.8900	.8734	.8573	.8417	.8264	.8116	.7972
3	.9706	.9423	.9151	.8890	.8638	.8396	.8163	.7938	.7722	.7513	.7312	.7118
4	.9610	.9238	.8885	.8548	.8227	.7921	.7629	.7350	.7084	.6830	.6587	.6355
5	.9515	.9057	.8626	.8219	.7835	.7473	.7130	.6806	.6499	.6209	.5935	.5674
6	.9420	.8880	.8375	.7903	.7462	.7050	.6663	.6302	.5963	.5645	.5346	.5066
7	.9327	.8706	.8131	.7599	.7107	.6651	.6227	.5835	.5470	.5132	.4817	.4523
8	.9235	.8535	.7894	.7307	.6768	.6274	.5820	.5403	.5019	.4665	.4339	.4039
9	.9143	.8368	.7664	.7026	.6446	.5919	.5439	.5002	.4604	.4241	.3909	.3606
10	.9053	.8203	.7441	.6756	.6139	.5584	.5083	.4632	.4224	.3856	.3522	.3220
11	.8963	.8043	.7224	.6496	.5847	.5268	.4751	.4289	.3875	.3505	.3173	.2875
12	.8874	.7885	.7014	.6246	.5568	.4970	.4440	.3971	.3555	.3186	.2858	.2567
13	.8787	.7730	.6810	.6006	.5303	.4688	.4150	.3677	.3262	.2897	.2575	.2292
14	.8700	.7579	.6611	.5775	.5051	.4423	.3878	.3405	.2992	.2633	.2320	.2046
15	.8613	.7430	.6419	.5553	.4810	.4173	.3624	.3152	.2745	.2394	.2090	.1827
16	.8528	.7284	.6232	.5339	.4581	.3936	.3387	.2919	.2519	.2176	.1883	.1631
17	.8444	.7142	.6050	.5134	.4363	.3714	.3166	.2703	.2311	.1978	.1696	.1456
18	.8360	.7002	.5874	.4936	.4155	.3503	.2959	.2502	.2120	.1799	.1528	.1300
19	.8277	.6864	.5703	.4746	.3957	.3305	.2765	.2317	.1945	.1635	.1377	.1161
20	.8195	.6730	.5537	.4564	.3769	.3118	.2584	.2145	.1784	.1486	.1240	.1037
21	.8114	.6598	.5375	.4388	.3589	.2942	.2415	.1987	.1637	.1351	.1117	.0926
22	.8034	.6468	.5219	.4220	.3418	.2775	.2257	.1839	.1502	.1228	.1007	.0826
23	.7954	.6342	.5067	.4057	.3256	.2618	.2109	.1700	.1378	.1117	.0907	.0738
24	.7876	.6217	.4919	.3901	.3101	.2470	.1971	.1577	.1264	.1015	.0817	.0659
25	.7798	.6095	.4776	.3751	.2953	.2330	.1842	.1460	.1160	.0923	.0736	.0588
26	.7720	.5976	.4637	.3607	.2812	.2198	.1722	.1352	.1064	.0839	.0663	.0525
27	.7644	.5859	.4502	.3468	.2678	.2074	.1609	.1252	.0976	.0763	.0597	.0469
28	.7568	.5744	.4371	.3335	.2551	.1956	.1504	.1159	.0895	.0693	.0538	.0419
29	.7493	.5631	.4243	.3207	.2429	.1846	.1406	.1073	.0822	.0630	.0485	.0374
30	.7419	.5521	.4120	.3083	.2314	.1741	.1314	.0994	.0754	.0573	.0437	.0334
35	.7059	.5000	.3554	.2534	.1813	.1301	.0937	.0676	.0490	.0356	.0259	.0189
40	.6717	.4529	.3066	.2083	.1420	.0972	.0668	.0460	.0318	.0221	.0154	.0107
45	.6391	.4102	.2644	.1712	.1113	.0727	.0476	.0313	.0207	.0137	.0091	.0061
50	.6080	.3715	.2281	.1407	.0872	.0543	.0339	.0213	.0134	.0085	.0054	.0035

Valuation of Bonds with Semiannual Payments

In reality, most bonds have semiannual payments. The present value of such bonds can be computed as follows. First, the annualized coupon should be split in half because two payments are made per year. Second, the annual discount rate should be divided by 2 to reflect two six-month periods per year. Third, the

EXHIBIT 3.4 Present Value Interest Factors (PVIF) (Continued)

Period n	13%	14%	15%	16%	17%	18%	19%	20%	25%	30%	35%	40%	50%
1	.8850	.8772	.8696	.8621	.8547	.8475	.8403	.8333	.8000	.7692	.7407	.7143	.6667
2	.7831	.7695	.7561	.7432	.7305	.7182	.7062	.6944	.6400	.5917	.5487	.5102	.4444
3	.6931	.6750	.6575	.6407	.6244	.6086	.5934	.5787	.5120	.4552	.4064	.3644	.2963
4	.6133	.5921	.5718	.5523	.5337	.5158	.4987	.4823	.4096	.3501	.3011	.2603	.1975
5	.5428	.5194	.4972	.4761	.4561	.4371	.4190	.4019	.3277	.2693	.2230	.1859	.1317
6	.4803	.4556	.4323	.4104	.3898	.3704	.3521	.3349	.2621	.2072	.1652	.1328	.0878
7	.4251	.3996	.3759	.3538	.3332	.3139	.2959	.2791	.2097	.1594	.1224	.0949	.0585
8	.3762	.3506	.3269	.3050	.2848	.2660	.2487	.2326	.1678	.1226	.0906	.0678	.0390
9	.3329	.3075	.2843	.2630	.2434	.2255	.2090	.1938	.1342	.0943	.0671	.0484	.0260
10	.2946	.2697	.2472	.2267	.2080	.1911	.1756	.1615	.1074	.0725	.0497	.0346	.0173
11	.2607	.2366	.2149	.1954	.1778	.1619	.1476	.1346	.0859	.0558	.0368	.0247	.0116
12	.2307	.2076	.1869	.1685	.1520	.1372	.1240	.1122	.0687	.0429	.0273	.0176	.0077
13	.2042	.1821	.1625	.1452	.1299	.1163	.1042	.0935	.0550	.0330	.0202	.0126	.0051
14	.1807	.1597	.1413	.1252	.1110	.0985	.0876	.0779	.0440	.0254	.0150	.0090	.0034
15	.1599	.1401	.1229	.1079	.0949	.0835	.0736	.0649	.0352	.0195	.0111	.0064	.0023
16	.1415	.1229	.1069	.0930	.0811	.0708	.0618	.0541	.0281	.0150	.0082	.0046	.0015
17	.1252	.1078	.0929	.0802	.0693	.0600	.0520	.0451	.0225	.0116	.0061	.0033	.0010
18	.1108	.0946	.0808	.0691	.0592	.0508	.0437	.0376	.0180	.0089	.0045	.0023	.0007
19	.0981	.0829	.0703	.0596	.0506	.0431	.0367	.0313	.0144	.0068	.0033	.0017	.0005
20	.0868	.0728	.0611	.0514	.0443	.0365	.0308	.0261	.0115	.0053	.0025	.0012	.0003
21	.0768	.0638	.0531	.0443	.0370	.0309	.0259	.0217	.0092	.0040	.0018	.0009	.0002
22	.0680	.0560	.0462	.0382	.0316	.0262	.0218	.0181	.0074	.0031	.0014	.0006	.0001
23	.0601	.0491	.0402	.0329	.0270	.0222	.0183	.0151	.0059	.0024	.0010	.0004	.0001
24	.0532	.0431	.0349	.0284	.0231	.0188	.0154	.0126	.0047	.0018	.0007	.0003	.0001
25	.0471	.0378	.0304	.0245	.0197	.0160	.0129	.0105	.0038	.0014	.0006	.0002	.0000
26	.0417	.0331	.0264	.0211	.0169	.0135	.0109	.0087	.0030	.0011	.0004	.0002	.0000
27	.0369	.0291	.0230	.0182	.0144	.0115	.0091	.0073	.0024	.0008	.0003	.0001	.0000
28	.0326	.0255	.0200	.0157	.0123	.0097	.0077	.0061	.0019	.0006	.0002	.0001	.0000
29	.0289	.0224	.0174	.0135	.0105	.0082	.0064	.0051	.0015	.0005	.0002	.0001	.0000
30	.0256	.0196	.0151	.0116	.0090	.0070	.0054	.0042	.0012	.0004	.0001	.0000	.0000
35	.0139	.0102	.0075	.0055	.0041	.0030	.0023	.0017	.0004	.0001	.0000	.0000	.0000
40	.0075	.0053	.0037	.0026	.0019	.0013	.0010	.0007	.0001	.0000	.0000	.0000	.0000
45	.0041	.0027	.0019	.0013	.0009	.0006	.0004	.0003	.0000	.0000	.0000	.0000	.0000
50	.0022	.0014	.0009	.0006	.0004	.0003	.0002	.0001	.0000	.0000	.0000	.0000	.0000

number of periods should be doubled to reflect two times the number of annual periods. Incorporating these adjustments, the present value is determined as follows:

$$\text{PV of bond with semiannual payments} = \frac{C/2}{(1 + i/2)^1} + \frac{C/2}{(1 + i/2)^2} + \cdots \frac{C/2 + P}{(1 + i/2)^{2n}}$$

where $C/2$ is the semiannual coupon payment (one-half of what the annual coupon payment would have been) and $i/2$ is the periodic discount rate used to discount the bond. The last part of the equation shows $2n$ in the denominator exponent to reflect the doubling of periods.

To illustrate the use of bond valuation with semiannual payments, consider the previous example of a bond with $1,000 par value, a 10 percent coupon rate, and three years to maturity. Assuming a 12 percent required return, the present value would be computed as follows:

$$
\begin{aligned}
\text{PV of bond} &= \frac{\$50}{(1.06)^1} + \frac{\$50}{(1.06)^2} + \frac{\$50}{(1.06)^3} + \frac{\$50}{(1.06)^4} + \frac{\$50}{(1.06)^5} + \frac{\$50 + \$1,000}{(1.06)^6} \\
&= \$47.17 + \$44.50 + \$41.98 + \$39.60 + \$37.36 + \$740.21 \\
&= \$950.82
\end{aligned}
$$

This example could also have been worked using PVIF tables.[1]

The remaining examples assume annual coupon payments so that we can focus on the concepts presented without concern about adjusting annual payments.

Use of Annuity Tables for Valuation

Any bond can be valued by separating its payments into two components:

$$\text{PV of bond} = \text{PV of coupon payments} + \text{PV of principal payment}$$

A bond's coupon payments represent an **annuity,** or an even stream of payments over a given period of time. The present value of any annuity can be determined by multiplying the annuity amount times the appropriate **present value interest factor of an annuity (PVIFA)**. The table in Exhibit 3.5 can be used to identify the appropriate PVIFA. To illustrate, recall the example of the 10 percent coupon bond with annual coupon payments, a $1,000 par value, and three years to maturity. The PVIFA for this example is $\text{PVIFA}_{i=12\%,\,n=3} = 2.4018$, as shown in Exhibit 3.5. This is used to determine the present value of the coupon payments:

$$
\begin{aligned}
\text{PV of coupon payments} &= C\,(\text{PVIFA}_{i=12\%,n=3}) \\
&= \$100\,(2.4018) \\
&= \$240.18
\end{aligned}
$$

---

[1]Technically, the semiannual rate of 6 percent is overstated. For a required rate of 12 percent per year, the precise six-month rate would be 5.83 percent. With the compounding effect, that would generate interest on interest; this semiannual rate over two periods would achieve a 12 percent return. Because the approximate semiannual rate of 6 percent is higher than the precise rate, the present value of the bond is slightly understated.

The present value of the principal must also be determined:

$$\text{PV of principal} = \frac{\$1,000}{(1.12)^3} \text{ or } \$1,000 \ (\text{PVIF}_{i=12\%, n=3})$$

$$= \$1,000 \ (.7118)$$

$$= \$711.80$$

When the PV of coupon payments is combined with the principal, the bond's present value is about $951.98 (computed as $240.18 + $711.80).

The use of PVIFA tables is especially efficient for valuing long-term bonds. For example, determine the present value of bonds with an 8 percent coupon rate, a par value of $100,000, and 20 years to maturity, using a 14 percent required rate of return:

$$\text{PV of bonds} = \text{PV of coupon payments} + \text{PV of principal}$$

$$= \$8,000 \ (\text{PVIFA}_{i=14\%, n=20}) + \$100,000 \ (\text{PVIF}_{i=14\%, n=20})$$

$$= \$8,000 \ (6.6231) + \$100,000 \ (.0728)$$

$$= \$52,985 + \$7,280$$

$$= \$60,265$$

This implies that investors requiring a 14 percent return would pay no more than $60,265 for these bonds.

IMPACT OF INTEREST RATES ON BOND PRICES

When interest rates rise, the prices of existing bonds decrease. The reason is that higher interest rates cause investors to require higher rates of return, which reduces the present value (and therefore market price) of existing bonds. When interest rates decrease, the required rate of return by investors decreases, and the present values of bonds increase. The inverse relationship between interest rates and prices of existing bonds is a simple but critical concept for all investors. Because interest rates are volatile, so are bond prices. Investors frequently forecast interest rates in order to determine how the required rate of return on bonds will change and, therefore, how bond prices will change.

The relationship between interest rates and bond prices carries important implications for various financial institutions such as commercial banks, savings institutions, and insurance companies that invest in bonds. When interest rates rise, the market value of their bond portfolios decreases, and the converse is true.

Relationships Between Coupon Rate, Required Return, and Bond Price

Bonds that sell at a price below their par value are called **discount bonds.** The larger the investor's required rate of return relative to the coupon rate, the larger will be the discount of a bond with a particular par value. As an extreme example, consider a **zero-coupon bond** (which has no coupon payments) with three

EXHIBIT 3.5 Present Value Interest Factors for an Annuity (PVIFA)

Period n	1%	2%	3%	4%	5%	6%	7%	8%	9%	10%	11%	12%
1	0.9901	0.9804	0.9709	0.9615	0.9524	0.9434	0.9346	0.9259	0.9174	0.9091	0.9009	0.8929
2	1.9704	1.9416	1.9135	1.8861	1.8594	1.8334	1.8080	1.7833	1.7591	1.7355	1.7125	1.6901
3	2.9410	2.8839	2.8286	2.7751	2.7232	2.6730	2.6243	2.5771	2.5313	2.4869	2.4437	2.4018
4	3.9020	3.8077	3.7171	3.6299	3.5460	3.4651	3.3872	3.3121	3.2397	3.1899	3.1024	3.0373
5	4.8534	4.7135	4.5797	4.4518	4.3295	4.2124	4.1002	3.9927	3.8897	3.7908	3.6959	3.6048
6	5.7955	5.6014	5.4172	5.2421	5.0757	4.9173	4.7665	4.6229	4.4859	4.3553	4.2305	4.1114
7	6.7282	6.4720	6.2303	6.0021	5.7864	5.5824	5.3893	5.2064	5.0330	4.8684	4.7122	4.5638
8	7.6517	7.3255	7.0197	6.7327	6.4632	6.2098	5.9713	5.7466	5.5348	5.3349	5.1461	4.9676
9	8.5660	8.1622	7.7861	7.4353	7.1078	6.8017	6.5152	6.2469	5.9952	5.7590	5.5370	5.3282
10	9.4713	8.9826	8.5302	8.1109	7.7217	7.3601	7.0236	6.7101	6.4177	6.1446	5.8892	5.6502
11	10.368	9.7868	9.2526	8.7605	8.3064	7.8869	7.4987	7.1390	6.8052	6.4951	6.2065	5.9377
12	11.255	10.575	9.9540	9.3851	8.8633	8.3838	7.9427	7.5361	7.1607	6.8137	6.4924	6.1944
13	12.134	11.348	10.635	9.9856	9.3936	8.8527	8.3577	7.9038	7.4869	7.1034	6.7499	6.4235
14	13.004	12.106	11.296	10.563	9.8986	9.2950	8.7455	8.2442	7.7862	7.3667	6.9819	6.6282
15	13.865	12.849	11.938	11.118	10.380	9.7122	9.1079	8.5595	8.0607	7.6061	7.1909	6.8109
16	14.718	13.578	12.561	11.652	10.838	10.106	9.4466	8.8514	8.3126	7.8237	7.3792	6.9740
17	15.562	14.292	13.166	12.166	11.274	10.477	9.7632	9.1216	8.5436	8.0216	7.5488	7.1196
18	16.398	14.992	13.754	12.659	11.690	10.828	10.059	9.3719	8.7556	8.2014	7.7016	7.2497
19	17.226	15.678	14.324	13.134	12.085	11.158	10.336	9.6036	8.9501	8.3649	7.8393	7.3658
20	18.046	16.351	14.877	13.590	12.462	11.470	10.594	9.8181	9.1285	8.5136	7.9633	7.4694
21	18.857	17.011	15.415	14.029	12.821	11.764	10.836	10.017	9.2922	8.6487	8.0751	7.5620
22	19.660	17.658	15.937	14.451	13.163	12.042	11.061	10.201	9.4424	8.7715	8.1757	7.6446
23	20.456	18.292	16.444	14.857	13.489	12.303	11.272	10.371	9.5802	8.8832	8.2664	7.7184
24	21.243	18.914	16.936	15.247	13.799	12.550	11.469	10.529	9.7066	8.9847	8.3481	7.7843
25	22.023	19.523	17.413	15.622	14.094	12.783	11.654	10.675	9.8226	9.0770	8.4217	7.8431
26	22.795	20.121	17.877	15.983	14.375	13.003	11.826	10.810	9.9290	9.1609	8.4881	7.8957
27	23.560	20.707	18.327	16.330	14.643	13.211	11.987	10.935	10.027	9.2372	8.5478	7.9426
28	24.316	21.281	18.764	16.663	14.898	13.406	12.137	11.051	10.116	9.3066	8.6016	7.9844
29	25.066	21.844	19.188	16.984	15.141	13.591	12.278	11.158	10.198	9.3696	8.6501	8.0218
30	25.808	22.396	19.600	17.292	15.372	13.765	12.408	11.258	10.274	9.4269	8.6938	8.0552
35	29.409	24.999	21.487	18.665	16.374	14.498	12.948	11.655	10.567	9.6442	8.8552	8.1755
40	32.835	27.355	23.115	19.793	17.159	15.046	13.332	11.925	10.757	9.7791	8.9511	8.2438
45	36.095	29.490	24.519	20.720	17.774	15.456	13.606	12.108	10.881	9.8628	9.0079	8.2825
50	39.196	31.424	25.730	21.482	18.256	15.762	13.801	12.233	10.962	9.9148	9.0417	8.3045

years remaining to maturity and $1,000 par value. Assume the investor's required rate of return on the bond is 13 percent. The appropriate price of this bond can be determined by the present value of its future cash flows:

$$\text{PV of bond} = \$0/(1 + .13)^1 + \$0/(1 + .13)^2 + \$1,000/(1 + .13)^3$$
$$= \$0 + \$0 + \$693.05$$
$$= \$693.05$$

EXHIBIT 3.5   Present Value Interest Factors for an Annuity (PVIFA) (Continued)

Period n	13%	14%	15%	16%	17%	18%	19%	20%	25%	30%	35%	40%	50%
1	0.8850	0.8772	0.8696	0.8621	0.8547	0.8475	0.8403	0.8333	0.8000	0.7692	0.7407	0.7143	0.6667
2	1.6681	1.6467	1.6257	1.6052	1.5852	1.5656	1.5465	1.5278	1.4400	1.3609	1.2894	1.2245	1.1111
3	2.3612	2.3216	2.2832	2.2459	2.2096	2.1743	2.1399	2.1065	1.9520	1.8161	1.6959	1.5889	1.4074
4	2.9745	2.9137	2.8550	2.7982	2.7432	2.6901	2.6386	2.5887	2.3616	2.1662	1.9969	1.8492	1.6049
5	3.5172	3.4331	3.3522	3.2743	3.1993	3.1272	3.0576	2.9906	2.6893	2.4356	2.2200	2.0352	1.7366
6	3.9975	3.8887	3.7845	3.6847	3.5892	3.4976	3.4098	3.3255	2.9514	2.6427	2.3852	2.1880	1.8244
7	4.4226	4.2883	4.1604	4.0386	3.9224	3.8115	3.7057	3.6046	3.1611	2.8021	2.5075	2.2628	1.8829
8	4.7988	4.6389	4.4873	4.3436	4.2072	4.0776	3.9544	3.8372	3.3289	2.9247	2.5982	2.3306	1.9220
9	5.1317	4.9464	4.7716	4.6065	4.4506	4.3030	4.1633	4.0310	3.4631	3.0190	2.6653	2.3790	1.9480
10	5.4262	5.2161	5.0188	4.8332	4.6585	4.4941	4.3389	4.1925	3.5705	3.0915	2.7150	2.4136	1.9653
11	5.6869	5.4527	5.2337	5.0286	4.8364	4.6560	4.4865	4.3271	3.6564	3.1473	2.7519	2.4383	1.9769
12	5.9176	5.6603	5.4206	5.1971	4.9884	4.7932	4.6105	4.4392	3.7251	3.1903	2.7792	2.4559	1.9846
13	6.1218	5.8424	5.5831	5.3423	5.1183	4.9095	4.7147	4.5327	3.7801	3.2233	2.7994	2.4685	1.9897
14	6.3025	6.0021	5.7245	5.4675	5.2293	5.0081	4.8023	4.6106	3.8241	3.2487	2.8144	2.4775	1.9931
15	6.4624	6.1422	5.8474	5.5755	5.3242	5.0916	4.8759	4.6755	3.8593	3.2682	2.8255	2.4839	1.9954
16	6.6039	6.2651	5.9542	5.6685	5.4053	5.1624	4.9377	4.7296	3.8874	3.2832	2.8337	2.4885	1.9970
17	6.7291	6.3729	6.0472	5.7487	5.4746	5.2223	4.9897	4.7746	3.9099	3.2948	2.8398	2.4918	1.9980
18	6.8399	6.4674	6.1280	5.8178	5.5339	5.2732	5.0333	4.8122	3.9279	3.3037	2.8443	2.4941	1.9986
19	6.9380	6.5504	6.1982	5.8775	5.5845	5.3162	5.0700	4.8435	3.9424	3.3105	2.8476	2.4958	1.9991
20	7.0248	6.6231	6.2593	5.9288	5.6278	5.3527	5.1009	4.8696	3.9539	3.3158	2.8501	2.4970	1.9994
21	7.1016	6.6870	6.3125	5.9731	5.6648	5.3837	5.1268	4.8913	3.9631	3.3198	2.8519	2.4979	1.9996
22	7.1695	6.7429	6.3587	6.0113	5.6964	5.4099	5.1486	4.9094	3.9705	3.3230	2.8533	2.4985	1.9997
23	7.2297	6.7921	6.3988	6.0442	5.7234	5.4321	5.1668	4.9245	3.9764	3.3254	2.8543	2.2989	1.9998
24	7.2829	6.8351	6.4338	6.0726	5.7465	5.4509	5.1822	4.9371	3.9811	3.3272	2.8550	2.4992	1.9999
25	7.3300	6.8729	6.4641	6.0971	5.7662	5.4669	5.1951	4.9476	3.9849	3.3286	2.8556	2.4994	1.9999
26	7.3717	6.9061	6.4906	6.1182	5.7831	5.4804	5.2060	4.9563	3.9879	3.3297	2.8560	2.4996	1.9999
27	7.4086	6.9352	6.5135	6.1364	5.7975	5.4919	5.2151	4.9636	3.9903	3.3305	2.8563	2.4997	2.0000
28	7.4412	6.9607	6.5335	6.1520	5.8099	5.5016	5.2228	4.9697	3.9923	3.3312	2.8565	2.4998	2.0000
29	7.4701	6.9830	6.5509	6.1656	5.8204	5.5098	5.2292	4.9747	3.9938	3.3317	2.8567	2.4999	2.0000
30	7.4957	7.0027	6.5660	6.1772	5.8294	5.5168	5.2347	4.9789	3.9950	3.3321	2.8568	2.4999	2.0000
35	7.5856	7.0700	6.6166	6.2153	5.8582	5.5386	5.2512	4.9915	3.9984	3.3330	2.8571	2.5000	2.0000
40	7.6344	7.1050	6.6418	6.2335	5.8713	5.5482	5.2582	4.9966	3.9995	3.3332	2.8571	2.5000	2.0000
45	7.6609	7.1232	6.6543	6.2421	5.8773	5.5523	5.2611	4.9986	3.9998	3.3333	2.8571	2.5000	2.0000
50	7.6752	7.1327	6.6605	6.2463	5.8801	5.5541	5.2623	4.9995	3.9999	3.3333	2.8571	2.5000	2.0000

This very low price of the bond is necessary to generate a 13 percent annualized return to investors. If the bond offered coupon payments, the price would have been higher because those coupon payments would provide part of the return required by investors. Consider another bond with similar par value and maturity that offers a 13 percent coupon rate. The appropriate price of the bond would now be

$$\text{PV of bond} = \$130/(1 + .13)^1 + \$130/(1 + .13)^2 + \$1,130/(1 + .13)^3$$
$$= \$115.04 + \$101.81 + \$783.15$$
$$= \$1,000$$

Notice that the price of this bond is exactly equal to its par value. This is because the entire compensation required by investors is provided by the coupon payments.

Finally, consider a bond with a similar par value and term to maturity that offers a coupon rate of 15 percent, which is above the investor's required rate of return. The appropriate price of this bond as determined by its present value is

$$\text{PV of bond} = \$150/(1 + .13)^1 + \$150/(1 + .13)^2 + \$1,150/(1 + .13)^3$$
$$= \$132.74 + \$117.47 + \$797.01$$
$$= \$1,047.22$$

The price of this bond exceeds its par value because coupon payments are large enough to offset that and still provide a 13 percent annualized return.

From the examples provided, the following relationships should now be clear. First, if the coupon rate of a bond is below the investor's required rate of return, the present value of the bond (and therefore the price of the bond) should be below the par value. Second, if the coupon rate equals the investor's required rate of return, the price of the bond should be the same as the par value. Finally, if the coupon rate of a bond is above the investor's required rate of return, the price of the bond should be above the par value. These relationships are shown in Exhibit 3.6 for a bond with a 10 percent coupon and a par value of $1,000. If investors required a return of 5 percent and desired a 10-year maturity, they would be willing to pay $1,390 for this bond. If they required a return of 10 percent on this same bond, they would be willing to pay $1,000. If they required a 15 percent return, they would be willing to pay only $745. The relationships described here hold for any bond, regardless of its maturity.

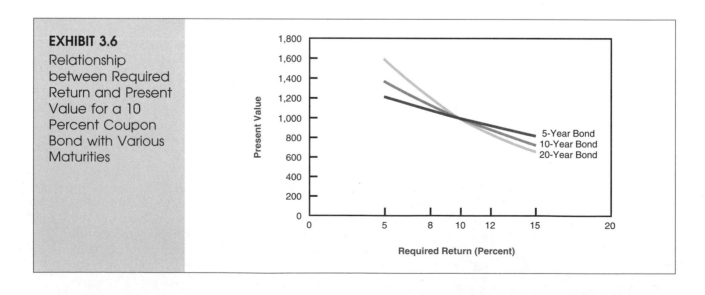

EXHIBIT 3.6

Relationship between Required Return and Present Value for a 10 Percent Coupon Bond with Various Maturities

Implications for Financial Institutions

The impact of interest rate movements on a financial institution depends on how the institution's asset and liability portfolios are structured, as illustrated in Exhibit 3.7. Financial institutions with interest rate-sensitive liabilities that invest heavily in bonds are exposed to interest rate risk. Many financial institutions attempt to adjust the size of their bond portfolio according to their expectations about future interest rates. The expected return is higher when using unevenly matched rate sensitivities because the mismatch allows an institution to take advantage of the effects of interest rate expectations. When rates are expected to rise, bonds can be sold and the proceeds used to purchase short-term securities, whose market values are less influenced by interest rate movements. When rates are expected to fall, the bond portfolio can be expanded in order to capitalize on the expectations. An aggressive approach offers greater potential for high return but also exposes investors to more risk when their expectations are wrong.

Fixed-rate mortgages generate periodic fixed payments, similar to bonds. Thus, the preceding comments apply to financial institutions such as savings institutions that hold mortgage portfolios. A primary reason for financial problems of savings institutions in the late 1970s was the rise in interest rates, which reduced the market value of their mortgage portfolios. This is a classic example of **interest rate risk,** or the risk that the market value of assets will decline in response to interest rate movements.

BOND PRICE SENSITIVITY

The sensitivity of bond prices to interest rate movements is dependent on the bond's time to maturity and the coupon rate of the bond. The influence of these two bond characteristics on bond price sensitivity is explained next.

Influence of Maturity on Bond Price Sensitivity

As interest rates (and therefore required rates of return) decrease, long-term bond prices (as measured by their present value) increase by a greater degree than

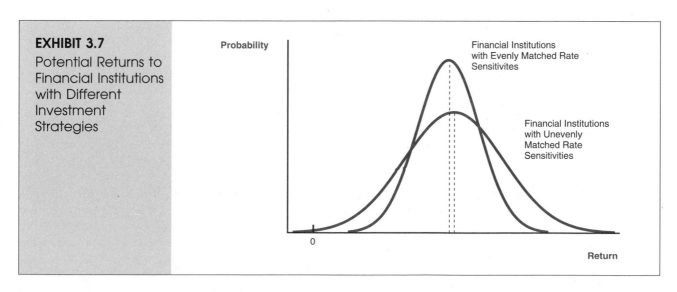

EXHIBIT 3.7
Potential Returns to Financial Institutions with Different Investment Strategies

short-term bonds, because the long-term bonds will continue to offer the same coupon rate over a longer period of time than short-term bonds. Of course, if interest rates increase, prices of the long-term bonds would decline by a greater degree.

Influence of Coupons on Bond Price Sensitivity

The prices of bonds with relatively low coupon payments are also somewhat more sensitive to interest rate movements than those with higher payments. Exhibit 3.8 compares price sensitivity of 10-year bonds with $1,000 par value and four different coupon rates: 0 percent, 5 percent, 10 percent, and 15 percent. Initially, the required rate of return (i) on the bonds is assumed to be 10 percent. The price of each bond would therefore be the present value of its future cash flows, discounted at 10 percent. The initial price of each bond is shown in Column 2. The top panel shows the effect of a decline in interest rates that reduces the investor's required return to 8 percent. The prices of the bonds based on an 8 percent required return are shown in Column 3. The percentage change in the price of each bond resulting from the interest rate movements is shown in Column 4. Notice that the percentage change is highest for the zero coupon bond and lower for bonds with higher coupon rates.

BOND PRICE ELASTICITY

The sensitivity of bond prices (BP) to changes in the required rate of return (i) is commonly measured by the **bond price elasticity (BP^e)**, which is estimated as

$$BP^e = \frac{\text{percent change in } BP}{\text{percent change in } i}$$

If the required rate of return is assumed to change from 10 percent to 8 percent, the bond price of the zero coupon bonds will rise from $386 to $463. Thus, the bond price elasticity (BP^e) is

$$BP^e = \frac{\dfrac{\$463 - \$386}{\$386}}{\dfrac{8\% - 10\%}{10\%}}$$

$$= \frac{+\ 19.9\%}{-\ 20\%}$$

$$= -\ .997$$

This implies that for each one percent change in interest rates, bond prices change by 0.997 percent in the opposite direction. The price elasticity for each bond is estimated in Exhibit 3.8 according to the assumed change in the required rate of return. The elasticities confirm that prices of bonds with higher coupon rates are less sensitive to interest rate movements.

The estimated bond price elasticity for any particular bond may vary
an adjustment in required rates of return, as illustrated in the lower par
Exhibit 3.8. Note, however, that the prices of bonds with relatively low cou
rates are more sensitive regardless of the change in required rates of returi

Also notice from Exhibit 3.8 that the price sensitivity of any particular bond
is greater for declining interest rates than rising interest rates. The bond price
elasticity is negative in all cases, reflecting the inverse relationship between interest rate movements and bond price movements.

Financial institutions frequently assess the price sensitivity of their existing
bond holdings to possible interest rate movements. If their bond portfolio contains a relatively large portion of zero- or low-coupon bonds, they will be more
favorably affected by declining interest rates. Of course, they would also be more
unfavorably affected by rising rates. Financial institutions can reduce the sensitivity of their bond portfolio to interest rate movements by concentrating on
high-coupon bonds.

DURATION

An alternative measure of bond price sensitivity is the bond's **duration,** which
is a measurement of the life of the bond on a present value basis. The longer a

---

EXHIBIT 3.8 Sensitivity of 10-Year Bonds with Different Coupon Rates to Interest Rate Changes

EFFECTS OF A DECLINE IN THE REQUIRED RATE OF RETURN

(1) Bonds with a Coupon Rate of:	(2) Initial Price of Bonds (When $i=10\%$)	(3) Price of Bonds when $i=8\%$	(4) $=[(3)-(2)]/(2)$ Percentage Change in Bond Price	(5) Percentage Change in i	(6) $=(4)/(5)$ Bond Price Elasticity (BP^e)
0%	$ 386	$ 463	+19.9%	−20.0%	−.997
5	693	799	+15.3	−20.0	−.765
10	1,000	1,134	+13.4	−20.0	−.670
15	1,307	1,470	+12.5	−20.0	−.624

EFFECTS OF AN INCREASE IN THE REQUIRED RATE OF RETURN

(1) Bonds with a Coupon Rate of:	(2) Initial Price of Bonds (When $i=10\%$)	(3) Price of Bonds when $i=12\%$	(4) $=[(3)-(2)]/(2)$ Percentage Change in Bond Price	(5) Percentage Change in i	(6) $=(4)/(5)$ Bond Price Elasticity (BP^e)
0%	$ 386	$ 322	−16.6%	+20.0%	−.830
5	693	605	−12.7	+20.0	−.635
10	1,000	887	−11.3	+20.0	−.565
15	1,307	1,170	−10.5	+20.0	−.525

bond's duration, the greater is its sensitivity to interest rate changes. A commonly used measure of a bond's duration (DUR) is:

$$DUR = \frac{\sum\limits_{t=1}^{n} \dfrac{C_t(t)}{(1 + i)^t}}{\sum\limits_{t=1}^{n} \dfrac{C_t}{(1 + i)^t}}$$

where C_t = the coupon or principal payments generated by the bond

   t = the time at which the payments are provided

   i = the bond's yield to maturity

The numerator of the duration formula represents the present value of future payments, weighted by the time interval until the payments occur. The longer the intervals until payments are made, the larger will be the numerator, and the larger will be the duration. The denominator of the duration formula represents the discounted future cash flows resulting from the bond, which is the present value of the bond.

As an example, the duration of a bond with $1,000 par value and a 7 percent coupon rate, three years remaining to maturity, and a 9 percent yield to maturity is:

$$DUR = \frac{\dfrac{\$70}{(1.09)^1} + \dfrac{\$70(2)}{(1.09)^2} + \dfrac{\$1070(3)}{(1.09)^3}}{\dfrac{\$70}{(1.09)^1} + \dfrac{\$70}{(1.09)^2} + \dfrac{\$1070}{(1.09)^3}}$$

$$= 2.80 \text{ years}$$

By comparison, the duration of a zero-coupon bond with a similar par value and yield to maturity is:

$$DUR = \frac{\dfrac{\$1,000(3)}{(1.09)^3}}{\dfrac{(\$1,000}{(1.09)^3}}$$

$$= 3 \text{ years.}$$

The duration of a zero-coupon bond is always equal to the bond's term to maturity. The duration of any coupon bond is always less than the bond's term to maturity, because some of the payments occur at intervals prior to maturity.

Duration of a Portfolio

Bond portfolio managers commonly attempt to **immunize** their portfolio, or insulate their portfolio from the effects of interest rate movements. A first step in this process is to determine the sensitivity of their portfolio to interest rate movements. Once the duration of each individual bond is measured, the bond portfolio's duration (DUR_p) can be estimated as

$$DUR_P = \sum_{j=1}^{m} w_j\, DUR_j$$

where m represents the number of bonds in the portfolio, w_j is bond j's market value as a percentage of the portfolio market value, and DUR_j is bond j's duration. In other words, the duration of a bond portfolio is the weighted average of bond durations, weighted according to relative market value. Financial institutions concerned with interest rate risk may compare their asset duration to their liability duration. Assuming that the value of earning assets is approximately equal to liabilities, the difference between their durations can be used to assess the impact of interest rate movements. A positive difference means that the market value of the institution's assets is more rate sensitive than the market value of its liabilities. Thus, during a period of rising interest rates, the market value of the assets would be reduced by a greater degree than that of liabilities. The institution's real net worth (market value of net worth) would therefore decrease.

FORECASTING BOND PRICES

To illustrate how a financial institution can assess the potential impact of interest rate movements on their bond holdings, assume that Longhorn Savings and Loan recently purchased Treasury bonds in the secondary market with a total par value of $40 million. The bonds will mature in five years and have an annual coupon rate of 10 percent. Longhorn is attempting to forecast the market value of these bonds two years from now because it may sell the bonds at that time. Therefore, it must forecast the investor's required rate of return and use that as the discount rate to determine the present value of the bond's cash flows over the final three years of its life. The computed present value would represent the forecasted price two years from now.

To continue with our example, assume the investor's required rate of return two years from now is expected to be 12 percent. This rate would be used to discount the periodic cash flows over the remaining three years. Given coupon payments of $4 million per year (10% × $40 million) and a par value of $40 million, the predicted present value is determined:

$$
\begin{aligned}
\text{PV of bonds two years from now} &= \frac{\$4{,}000{,}000}{(1.12)^1} + \frac{\$4{,}000{,}000}{(1.12)^2} + \frac{\$44{,}000{,}000}{(1.12)^3} \\
&= \$3{,}571{,}429 + \$3{,}188{,}775 + \$31{,}318{,}331 \\
&= \$38{,}078{,}535
\end{aligned}
$$

An illustration of this exercise is provided in Exhibit 3.9, using a time line. The market value of the bonds two years ahead is forecasted to be slightly more than $38 million. This is the amount Longhorn expects to receive if it sells the bonds then.

EXHIBIT 3.9
Forecasting the
Market Value of
Bonds

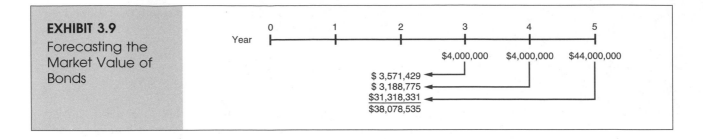

As a second example, assume that Aggie Insurance Company recently purchased corporate bonds in the secondary market with a par value of $20 million, a coupon rate of 14 percent (with annual coupon payments), and three years until maturity. The firm desires to forecast the market value of these bonds in one year because it may consider selling the bonds at that time. It expects the investor's required rate of return on similar investments to be 11 percent in one year. Using this information, it discounts the bond's cash flows ($2.8 million in annual coupon payments and a par value of $20 million) over the final two years at 11 percent to determine their present value (and therefore market value) one year from now:

$$
\begin{array}{l}
\text{PV of bonds} \\
\text{one year} \\
\text{from now}
\end{array}
= \frac{\$2,800,000}{(1.11)^1} + \frac{\$22,800,000}{(1.11)^2}
$$

$$= \$2,522,522 + \$18,504,991$$

$$= \$21,027,513$$

Thus, the market value of the bonds is expected to be slightly more than $21 million one year from now.

FORECASTING BOND YIELDS

The **yield to maturity** can be determined by solving for the discount rate at which the present value of future payments (coupon payments and par value) to the bondholder would equal the bond's current price. The trial-and-error method can be used by applying a discount rate and computing the present value of the payments stream. If the computed present value is higher than the current bond price, the computation should be repeated using a higher discount rate. Conversely, if the computed present value is lower than the current bond price, try a lower discount rate. Computer programs and bond tables are also available to determine the yield to maturity.

If bonds are held to maturity, the yield is known. However, if they are sold prior to maturity, the yield is not known until the time of sale. Investors can, however, attempt to forecast the yield with the methods just demonstrated, in which the forecasted required rate of return is used to forecast the market value (and therefore selling price) of the bonds. This selling price can then be incorporated within the cash flow estimates to determine the discount rate at which the present value of cash flows equals the investor's initial purchase price. Suppose that Wildcat Bank purchases bonds with the following characteristics:

- Par value = $30 million
- Coupon rate = 15% (annual payments)
- Remaining time to maturity = 5 years
- Purchase price of bonds = $29 million

The bank plans to sell the bonds in four years. The investor's required rate of return on similar securities is expected to be 13 percent at that time. Given this information, Wildcat forecasts its annualized bond yield over the four-year period in the following manner.

The first step is to forecast the present value (or market price) of the bonds four years from now. To do this, the remaining cash flows (one final coupon payment of $4.5 million plus the par value of $30 million) over the fifth and final year should be discounted (at the forecasted required rate of return of 13 percent) back to the fourth year when the bonds are to be sold:

$$\text{PV of bonds four years from now} = \frac{\$34,500,000}{(1.13)^1}$$

$$= \$30,530,973$$

This predicted present value as of four years from now serves as the predicted selling price in four years.

The next step is to incorporate the forecasted selling price at the end of the bond portfolio's cash flow stream. Then the discount rate that equates the present value of the cash flow stream to the price at which the bonds were purchased will represent the annualized yield. In our example, Wildcat Bank's cash flows are coupon payments of $4.5 million over each of the four years it holds the bonds; the fourth year's cash flows should also include the forecasted selling price of $30,530,973 and therefore sum to $35,030,973. Recall that Wildcat Bank purchased the bonds for $29 million. Given this information, the equation to solve for the discount rate (i) is

$$\$29 \text{ million} = \frac{\$4,500,000}{(1 + i)^1} + \frac{\$4,500,000}{(1 + i)^2} + \frac{\$4,500,000}{(1 + i)^3} + \frac{\$35,030,973}{(1 + i)^4}$$

The trial-and-error method can be used to determine the discount rate if a computer program is not available. The use of PVIF and PVIFA tables can expedite the process. With a discount rate of 17 percent, the present value would be

$$\text{PV of bonds using a 17\% discount rate} = \frac{\$4,500,000}{(1.17)^1} + \frac{\$4,500,000}{(1.17)^2} + \frac{\$4,500,000}{\cdot(1.17)^3} + \frac{\$35,030,973}{(1.17)^4}$$

$$= \$3,846,154 + \$3,287,311 + \$2,809,667 + \$18,694,280$$

$$= \$28,637,412$$

This present value is slightly less than the initial purchase price. Thus, the discount rate at which the present value of expected cash flows equals the purchase price is just slightly less than 17 percent. Consequently, Wildcat Bank's expected return on the bonds is just short of 17 percent.

It should be recognized that the process for determining the yield to maturity assumes that any payments received prior to the end of the holding period can be reinvested at the yield to maturity. If, for example, the payments could only be reinvested at a lower rate, the yield to maturity would overstate the actual return to the investor over the entire holding period.

With a computer program, the financial institution could easily create a distribution of forecasted yields based on various forecasts for the required rate of return four years from now. Without a computer, the process illustrated here would need to be completed for each forecast of the required rate of return. The computer actually follows the same steps but can more quickly make the computations.

Financial institutions that forecast bond yields must first forecast interest rates for the point in time at which they plan to sell their bonds. These forecasted rates can be used along with information about the securities to predict the required rate of return that will exist for the securities of concern. The predicted required rate of return is applied to cash flows beyond the time of sale to forecast the present value (or selling price) of the bonds at the time of sale. The forecasted selling price is then incorporated when estimating cash flows over the investment horizon. Finally, the yield to maturity on the bonds is determined by solving for the discount rate that equates these cash flows to the initial purchase price. The accuracy of the forecasted yield depends on the accuracy of the forecasted selling price of the bonds, which in turn depends on the accuracy of the forecasted required rate of return for the time of the sale.

FORECASTING BOND PORTFOLIO VALUES

Financial institutions can quantitatively measure the impact of possible interest rate movements on the market value of their bond portfolio by separately assessing the impact on each type of bond and then consolidating the individual impacts. Assume that Seminole Financial Inc. has a portfolio of bonds with the required return (i) on each type of bond as shown in the upper portion of Exhibit 3.10. Interest rates are expected to increase, causing an anticipated increase of one percent in the required return of each type of bond. Assuming no adjustment in the portfolio, Seminole's anticipated bond portfolio position is displayed in the lower portion of Exhibit 3.10.

The anticipated market value of each type of bond in the exhibit was determined by discounting the remaining year's cash flows beyond one year by the anticipated required return. The market value of the portfolio is expected to decline by more than $12 million as a result of the anticipated increase in interest rates.

This simplified example assumed a portfolio of only three types of bonds. In reality, a financial institution may have several types of bonds, with several maturities for each type of bond. Computer programs are widely available for assessing the market value of the portfolio. The financial institution gives the computer program input on the cash flow trends of all bond holdings and the

EXHIBIT 3.10   Measurements and Forecasts of Bond Portfolio Market Value

PRESENT BOND PORTFOLIO POSITION OF SEMINOLE FINANCIAL INC.

Type of Bonds	Present i	Par Value	Years to Maturity	Present Market Value of Bonds
9% coupon Treasury bonds	9%	$ 40,000,000	4	$ 40,000,000
14% coupon corporate bonds	12%	100,000,000	5	107,207,200
10% coupon gov't agency bonds	10%	150,000,000	8	150,000,000
		290,000,000		297,207,200

FORECASTED BOND PORTFOLIO POSITION OF SEMINOLE FINANCIAL INC.

Type of Bonds	Forecasted i	Par Value	Years to Maturity as of One Year from Now	Forecasted Market Value of Bonds in One Year
9% coupon Treasury bonds	10%	$ 40,000,000	3	$ 39,004,840
14% coupon corporate bonds	13%	100,000,000	4	102,973,000
10% coupon gov't agency bonds	11%	150,000,000	7	142,938,000
		290,000,000		284,915,840

anticipated required rates of return for each bond at the future time of concern. The computer uses the anticipated rates to estimate the present value of cash flows at that future time. These present values are then consolidated to determine the forecasted value of the bond portfolio.

The key variable in forecasting the bond portfolio's market value is the anticipated required return for each type of bond. The prevailing interest rates on short-term securities are commonly more volatile than rates on longer-term securities, so the required returns on bonds with three or four years to maturity may change to a greater degree than the longer-term bonds. In addition, as economic conditions change, the required returns of some risky securities could change even if the general level of interest rates remains stable.

FORECASTING BOND PORTFOLIO RETURNS

Financial institutions measure their overall bond portfolio returns in various ways. One way is to account not only for coupon payments but also for the change in market value over the holding period of concern. The market value at the beginning of the holding period is perceived as the initial investment. The market value at the end of that period is perceived as the price at which the bonds would have been sold. Even if the bonds are retained, the measurement of return requires an estimated market value at the end of the period. Finally, the coupon payments must be accounted for as well. The measurement of a bond portfolio's return is no different than the measurement of an individual bond's return. Mathematically, the bond portfolio return can be determined by solving for i in the following equation:

$$MVP = \sum_{t=1}^{n} \frac{C_t}{(1 + i)^t} + \frac{MVP_n}{(1 + i)^n}$$

where MVP = today's market value of the bond portfolio

C_t = coupon payments received at the end of period t

MVP_n = market value of the bond portfolio at the end of the investment period of concern

i = the discount rate that equates the present value of coupon payments and the future portfolio market value to today's portfolio market value

To illustrate, recall that Seminole Financial Inc. forecasted its bond portfolio value for one year ahead. Its annual coupon payments (C) sum to $32,600,000 (computed by multiplying the coupon rate of each type of bond by the respective par value). Using this information, along with today's MVP and the forecasted MVP (called MVP_n), its annual return is determined by solving for i as follows:

$$MVP = \frac{C_1 + MVP_n}{(1 + i)^1}$$

$$\$297{,}207{,}200 = \frac{\$32{,}600{,}000 + \$284{,}915{,}840}{(1 + i)^1}$$

$$\$297{,}207{,}200 = \frac{\$317{,}515{,}840}{(1 + i)^1}$$

The discount rate (or i) is estimated to be about 7 percent. (Work this yourself for verification.) Therefore, the bond portfolio is expected to generate an annual return of about 7 percent over the one-year investment horizon. The computations to determine the bond portfolio return can be tedious, but financial institutions use computer programs. If this type of program is linked with another program to forecast future bond prices, a financial institution can input forecasted required returns for each type of bond and let the computer determine projections of the bond portfolio's future market value and its return over a specified investment horizon.

SUMMARY

- The value of a debt security (such as bonds) is the present value of future cash flows generated by that security, using a discount rate that reflects the investor's required rate of return. As market interest rates rise, the required rate of return by investors increases. The discounted value of bond payments declines when the higher discount rate is applied. Thus, the present value of a bond declines, which forces the bond price to decline.

- Bond prices are more sensitive to interest rate movements for bonds that have a longer time to maturity, other things being equal. Prices of bonds with relatively low coupon payments are more sensitive to interest rate movements.

■ Bond prices can be forecasted for a particular point in time by forecasting the required rate of return on the bond at that time (which is primarily dependent on interest rates). The forecasted required rate of return can be used to discount the firm's remaining cash flows beyond that point to determine the present value (price) of the bond for that point in time.

■ The value of a bond portfolio is a weighted average of individual bonds. Thus, the bond portfolio's value can be forecasted by consolidating the forecasts of the individual bonds within the portfolio.

QUESTIONS

1. Based on your forecast of interest rates, would you recommend that investors purchase bonds today? Explain.

2. As interest rates decrease, explain the impact on
    a. An investor's required rate of return.
    b. The present value of existing bonds.
    c. The prices of existing bonds.

3. Why is the relationship between interest rates and security prices important to financial institutions?

4. Determine the direction of bond prices over the past year and explain the reason for it.

5. How would a financial institution with a large bond portfolio be affected by falling interest rates? Would it be affected more than a financial institution with a greater concentration of bonds (and less short-term securities)? Explain.

6. How is a financial institution with a large portfolio of fixed-rate mortgages affected by rising interest rates? Explain.

7. If a bond's coupon rate is above its required rate of return, would its price be above or below its par value? Explain.

8. Is the price of a long-term bond more or less sensitive to a change in interest rates than the price of a short-term security? Why?

9. Why does the required rate of return for a particular bond change over time?

10. Assume that inflation is expected to decline in the near future. How could this affect future bond prices? Would you recommend that financial institutions increase or decrease their concentration in long-term bonds based on this expectation? Explain.

11. Explain the concept of bond price elasticity. Would bond price elasticity suggest a higher price sensitivity for zero-coupon bonds or high-coupon bonds that are offering the same yield to maturity? Why? What does this suggest about the market value volatility of mutual funds containing zero-coupon Treasury bonds versus high-coupon Treasury bonds?

12. You anticipate that a well-respected analyst will make the following projections: (1) U.S. inflation will decline, and (2) foreign investors expect the dollar to strengthen consistently over the long run. The market has not yet responded to this information, but it will once the news is announced. You plan to purchase either (1) 10-year bonds, (2) 20-year zero-coupon bonds, or (3) one-year securities. Assume you only have funds available for one year. Assume that before the news is announced, each investment had the same expected return for a one-year horizon. If your goal is to maximize return (you do not place a premium on risk), which investment would you choose? Explain.

13. If you had known in October 1989 that the wall separating East and West Germany was going to be torn down, would you have recommended that German investors sell their bond holdings or buy more bonds? Explain.

14. During the Persian Gulf crisis in August 1990, bond prices in many countries declined. Why do you think bond prices declined? Would you expect bond prices to decline more in Japan or in the United Kingdom as a result of the crisis? Explain.

PROBLEMS

1. Assume the following information for an existing bond that provides annual coupon payments:

> Par value = $1,000
> Coupon rate = 11%
> Maturity = 4 years
> Required rate of return by investors = 11%

a. What is the present value of the bond?
b. If the required rate of return by investors were 14 percent instead of 11 percent, what would be the present value of the bond?
c. If the required rate of return by investors were 9 percent, what would be the present value of the bond?

2. Assume the following information for existing zero coupon bonds:

> Par value = $100,000
> Maturity = 3 years
> Required rate of return by investors = 12%

How much should investors be willing to pay for these bonds?

3. Assume that you require a 14 percent return on a zero-coupon bond with a par value of $1,000 and six years to maturity. What is the price you should be willing to pay for this bond?

4. Bulldog Bank has just purchased bonds for $106 million that have a par value of $100 million, three years remaining to maturity, and an annual coupon rate of 14 percent. It expects the required rate of return on these bonds to be 12 percent one year from now.
a. At what price could Bulldog Bank sell these bonds for one year from now?

    b. What is the expected annualized yield on the bonds over the next year, assuming they are to be sold in one year?

5. Sun Devil Savings has just purchased bonds for $38 million that have a par value of $40 million, five years remaining to maturity, and a coupon rate of 12 percent. It expects the required rate of return on these bonds to be 10 percent two years from now.
    a. At what price could Sun Devil Savings sell these bonds for two years from now?
    b. What is the expected annualized yield on the bonds over the next two years, assuming they are to be sold in two years?
    c. If the anticipated required rate of return of 10 percent in two years is overestimated, how would the actual selling price differ from the forecasted price? How would the actual annualized yield over the next two years differ from the forecasted yield?

6. Spartan Insurance Company plans to purchase bonds today that have four years remaining to maturity, a par value of $60 million, and a coupon rate of 10 percent. Spartan expects that in three years, the required rate of return on these bonds by investors in the market will be 9 percent. It plans to sell the bonds at that time. What is the expected price it will sell these bonds for in three years?

7. Gator Company plans to purchase either (1) zero-coupon bonds that have 10 years to maturity, a par value of $100 million, and a purchase price of $40 million, or (2) bonds with similar default risk that have five years to maturity, a 9 percent coupon rate, a par value of $40 million, and a purchase price of $40 million.

    Gator can invest $40 million for five years. Assume that the market's required return in five years is forecasted to be 11 percent. Which alternative would offer Gator a higher expected return (or yield) over the five-year investment horizon?

8. The portfolio manager of Panther Company has excess cash that is to be invested for four years. He can purchase four-year Treasury notes that offer a 9 percent yield. Alternatively, he can purchase new 20-year Treasury bonds for $2.9 million that offer a par value of $3 million and an 11 percent coupon rate with annual payments. The manager expects that the required return on these same 20-year bonds will be 12 percent four years from now.
    a. What is the forecasted market value of the 20-year bonds in four years?
    b. Which investment is expected to provide a higher yield over the four-year period?

9. Doran Investment Company manages a broad portfolio with this composition:

	Par Value	Present Market Value	Years Remaining to Maturity
Zero-coupon bonds	$200,000,000	$ 63,720,000	12
8% Treasury bonds	300,000,000	290,000,000	8
11% corporate bonds	400,000,000	380,000,000	10
		733,720,000	

It expects that in four years, investors in the market will require an 8 percent return on the zero-coupon bonds, a 7 percent return on the Treasury bonds, and a 9 percent return on the corporate bonds. Estimate the market value of the bond portfolio four years from now.

PROJECT

1. **Comparing Bond Price Sensitivity Among Bonds with Different Coupon Characteristics**

    Use a recent business periodical to determine the prices of Treasury bonds with a 10-year maturity and three different coupon rate characteristics: a relatively high coupon rate, a relatively low coupon rate, and a zero-coupon rate. Determine the percentage change in the price that would occur for each bond if interest rates rose by one percentage point. What if interest rates decreased by two percentage points? Based on your results, which type of bond was most sensitive to a change in interest rates? Which type was least sensitive? Explain the results.

Longer-Term Treasurys Break Losing Streak As Greenspan Reassures Investors on Inflation

By Leslie Scism and Thomas D. Lauricella, New York

Ending a five-session losing streak, prices of longer-term U.S. Treasury notes and bonds eked out moderate gains in quiet trading yesterday.

Corporate debt securities generally edged up in price alongside Treasurys, but owners of many **R.H. Macy & Co.** bonds took it on the chin. The retailer's unsecured debt traded down dramatically on news that the company has been negotiating a reorganization plan with **Fidelity Investments** and General Electric Capital, a unit of **General Electric Co.** Macy previously was negotiating with bondholders, and the fact that it switched allies raised prospects that a "cram down" plan could be in the works. (In a cram down, an unpalatable reorganization plan is forced upon creditors with the least amount of clout.) Late yesterday, a federal bankruptcy judge appointed a mediator to help negotiate a settlement, and prices recovered slightly.

Macy's 14.5% senior subordinated debentures maturing in 1998 were bid as low as 37.5 yesterday, down from 45 on Friday, when the market closed early in advance of the Presidents Day weekend. As the market closed yesterday, those securities were bid at 40.5, down 4.5 points from Friday. Among disappointed holders are many small investors who had rushed to snap the bonds up in the hope that **Federated Department Stores** Inc.'s recent investment in Macy's secured debt signaled the beginning of a bidding war.

The yield on the benchmark 30-year Treasury fell to 6.60% yesterday. That's down from 6.62% Friday. Its price, which moves inversely to yield, ended at 95 13/32, up 5/16, or $3.125 for a bond with a $1,000 face amount. The big price driver was Congressional testimony by Federal Reserve Chairman Alan Greenspan. In his semiannual talk before a House Banking subcommittee yesterday morning, he said the Fed is likely to continue boosting short-term interest rates, but he played down fears that inflationary pressures are now present. Instead, he emphasized signs that inflation is well under control, such as muted wage increases.

"Prior to his speech, many investors thought the Fed's earlier action [to increase the federal-funds rate] confirmed inflationary expectations," said Alan Kral, a portfolio manager for Trevor Stewart Burton & Jacobsen Inc. Trevor Stewart is a money-management firm with $1 billion in assets and has recently been buying longer-term Treasury debt. "Hopefully, the idea gets across now that the Fed is trying to knock down expectations before they get started," Mr. Kral said.

While talking tough on inflation, the Fed chairman provided no clues as to the timing of the next Fed tightening. His hints of future interest-rate hikes kept pressure on the prices of shorter-term Treasury maturities. Those are the securities most affected by a Fed tightening. The benchmark two-year note ended slightly down in price, while the three-year note ended unchanged.

At the same time, longer-term issues attracted scattered buying as traders and investors were reassured by Mr. Greenspan's anti-inflation stance. "We saw good interest in [securities maturing in] five years and out, and we couldn't sell anything that was under five years," said John Costas, manager of government-securities trading at CS First Boston Inc. "Greenspan sent a solid message, saying that the Fed's tightening is a rational approach and that its goal is to truly be pre-emptive."

Even some of the few remaining bond bulls are hesitant about declaring that a rally—however modest—is in the works. "Some of the bounce [yesterday] reflects the virulence of the sell-off at the end of last week, which, after all, was not based on any economic news of importance," said John Lipsky, chief economist for Salomon Brothers Inc. "But it's going to take more action by the Fed to convince investors [among other things] that they don't face a resurgence of inflationary pressures as the economy uses up its cushion of excess capacity." Mr. Lipsky believes yields on the 30-year bond will fall back below 6% later this year, provided that growth remains moderate, inflation is stable and fiscal policy is restrictive, among other things.

Ed Labenski, president of IDS Fixed-Income Advisors, Minneapolis, noted that some of yesterday's buying likely was the "completion of the digestion of the last [30-year bond] auction. Some

Continued

CASE APPLICATION: BOND MARKET RESPONSES TO ECONOMIC INFORMATION

Continued

people bought, panicked, sold and now the debt is finding a more permanent home.'' He anticipates that more-telling Treasury price movements will be determined by employment numbers to be released March 4 and the producer price index on March 15.

With Mr. Greenspan's testimony now history, many traders' attention is now focused on this week's auctions. The Treasury is slated to sell $17 billion of two-year notes and $11 billion of five-year notes. In when-issued trading late yesterday, the two-year note yielded 4.58%, and the five-year note yielded 5.50%. . . .

Corporate & Junk Bonds

R.H. Macy bonds saw active trading in an otherwise mostly quiet day in the corporate debt market.

Early yesterday, Macy bonds plummeted in price by about eight points—or $80 for a bond with a $1,000 face value—on the report in The Wall Street Journal that the retailer, which is in bank-

ruptcy proceedings, has been negotiating a reorganization plan with Fidelity Investments and General Electric Capital. Such a plan likely would call for full repayment of bank-debt holders Federated Department Stores, **Prudential Insurance Co. of America** and Fidelity. That would probably leave little value for the bondholders, making the possibility of ''a cram-down plan at least plausible,'' said Max Holmes, high-yield strategist at Salomon Brothers. . . .

Trading in the investment-grade market was light with spreads over Treasurys widening by 0.01 to 0.02 percentage point, traders said. . . .

Generally, trading in the junk bond market was light, with prices down by about 1/4 point.

SOURCE: *The Wall Street Journal* (February 23, 1994): p. CZ0. Reprinted by permission of *The Wall Street Journal* © 1994 Dow Jones & Company, Inc. All rights reserved worldwide.

QUESTIONS

1. Interpret the statement that "bond investors are no longer giving the growing economy the benefit of the doubt about inflation."

2. Explain how the Federal Reserve actions earlier in the month are used to rationalize the decline in bond prices.

3. Why do you think bond market participants pay so much attention to speeches by Alan Greenspan or other Federal Reserve board members.

4. Why would the "flood of Treasury securities slated to be sold" influence the actions of bond market participants?

REFERENCES

Bierwag, G. O., George G. Kaufman, Cynthia M. Latta, and Gordon Roberts. "Duration: Response to Critics." *Journal of Portfolio Management* (Winter 1987): 48–52.

Gatti, James F. "Risk and Return on Corporate Bonds: A Synthesis." *Quarterly Review of Economics and Business* (Summer 1983): 53–70.

Lewellen, Wilbur G., and Douglas R. Emery. "On the Matter of Parity Among Financial Obligations." *Journal of Finance* (March 1981): 97–111.

Maloney, Kevin J., and Jess B. Yawitz. "Interest Rate Risk, Immunization, and Duration." *Journal of Portfolio Management* (Spring 1986): 41–48.

McConnell, John J., and Gary G. Schlarbaum. "Returns, Risks, and Pricing of Income Bonds, 1956–76." *Journal of Business* (January 1981): 33–57.

CHAPTER 4

STRUCTURE OF INTEREST RATES

Yields offered by debt securities at a given point in time have a particular structure. Some types of debt securities always offer a higher yield than others. Individual and institutional investors must understand why quoted yields vary, so that they can determine whether the extra yield on a given security outweighs any unfavorable characteristics. Financial managers of corporations or government agencies in need of funds must understand why quoted yields of debt securities vary, so that they can estimate the yield they would have to offer in order to sell new debt securities.

The specific objectives of this chapter are to:

- describe how characteristics of debt securities cause their yields to vary,
- demonstrate how to estimate the appropriate yield for any particular debt security, and
- explain the theories behind the term structure of interest rates (relationship between the term of maturity and yield of securities).

FACTORS AFFECTING YIELDS AMONG SECURITIES _____

Debt securities offer different yields because they exhibit different characteristics that influence the yield to be offered. In general, securities with unfavorable characteristics will offer higher yields to entice investors. Yet, some debt securities

USING *THE WALL STREET JOURNAL*

WSJ
YIELDS ACROSS SECURITIES

Yield quotations of different types of securities are disclosed each day in *The Wall Street Journal*, as shown here. The yields can be compared to reinforce how premiums are required to compensate for various characteristics. For example, the difference in yields between the long-term ("10+yr") Treasury bonds and high quality ("High Qlty") corporate bonds is attributed to the safety, liquidity, and the relative tax advantage of Treasury securities. The difference in yields between the long-term high quality and medium quality corporate bonds is primarily attributed to default risk differentials. The difference between the municipal (government obligation, ("G.O.") and corporate bond yields is mainly attributed to the tax advantage of municipal bonds.

SOURCE: *The Wall Street Journal*, August 1, 1994, p. C20. Reprinted by permission of *The Wall Street Journal*, © Dow Jones & Company, Inc. All rights reserved worldwide.

YIELD COMPARISONS

Based on Merrill Lynch Bond Indexes, priced as of midafternoon Eastern time.

		7/29	7/28	−52 Week− High	Low
Corp.-Govt. Master		6.97%	7.15%	7.29%	5.19%
Treasury	1-10yr	6.32	6.51	6.64	4.23
	10+ yr	7.54	7.70	7.90	6.01
Agencies	1-10yr	6.92	7.08	7.19	5.03
	10+ yr	7.81	7.95	8.05	6.40
Corporate					
	1-10 yr High Qlty	7.19	7.37	7.52	5.32
	Med Qlty	7.52	7.72	7.88	5.76
	10+yr High Qlty	8.02	8.16	8.34	6.93
	Med Qlty	8.50	8.63	8.81	7.29
Yankee bonds(1)		7.78	7.94	8.09	6.27
Current-coupon mortgages (2)					
GNMA 8.00%		8.13	8.32	8.59	6.07
FNMA 8.00%		8.04	8.24	8.49	6.10
FHLMC7.50%		8.02	8.26	8.51	6.10
High-yield corporates		10.67	10.72	10.79	9.25
New tax-exempts					
10-yr G.O. (AA)		5.40	5.52	5.97	4.56
20-yr G.O. (AA)		5.82	5.94	6.69	4.91
30-yr revenue (A)		6.19	6.34	6.71	5.30

Note: High quality rated AAA-AA; medium quality A-BBB/Baa; high yield, BB/Ba-C.

(1) Dollar-denominated, SEC-registered bonds of foreign issuers sold in the U.S. (2) Reflects the 52-week high and low of mortgage-backed securities indexes rather than the individual securities shown.

---

have favorable features as well. The yields on debt securities are affected by the following characteristics:

- Default risk
- Liquidity
- Tax status
- Term to maturity
- Special provisions

Default Risk

Because most securities are subject to the risk of default, investors must consider the creditworthiness of the security issuer. Although investors always have the option of purchasing risk-free Treasury securities, they may prefer some other securities if the yield compensates them for the risk. Thus, if all other characteristics besides default risk are equal, securities with a higher degree of risk would have to offer higher yields to be chosen. Default risk is especially relevant for longer-term securities that expose creditors to the possibility of default for a longer time.

Default risk premiums of one percent, two percent, or more may not seem significant. But for corporations borrowing $10 million through the issuance of

EXHIBIT 4.1   Rating Classification by Rating Agencies

Description of Security	RATINGS ASSIGNED BY:	
	Moody's	Standard and Poor's
Highest quality	Aaa	AAA
High quality	Aa	AA
High-medium quality	A	A
Medium quality	Baa	BBB
Medium-low quality	Ba	BB
Low quality (speculative)	B	B
Poor quality	Caa	CCC
Very poor quality	Ca	CC
Lowest quality (in default)	C	DDD,D

bonds, an extra percentage point as a premium reflects $100,000 in additional interest expenses per year.

Investors who do not necessarily desire to assess the creditworthiness of corporations that issue bonds can benefit from bond ratings provided by rating agencies. These ratings are based on a financial assessment of the issuing corporation. The higher the rating, the lower the perceived default risk. As time passes, economic conditions can change, and the perceived default risk of a corporation can change as well. Thus, bonds previously issued by a firm could be rated at one level, while a subsequent issue from the same firm could be rated at a different level. The ratings could also differ if the collateral provisions differ among the bonds.

The most popular rating agencies are Moody's Investor Service and Standard and Poor's Corporation. A summary of their rating classification schedules is provided in Exhibit 4.1. Moody's ratings range from Aaa for highest quality to C for lowest quality, while Standard and Poor's range from AAA to D. Because different methods are used by these rating agencies to assess creditworthiness of firms and state governments, a particular bond could be assigned a different rating by each agency; however, differences are usually small.

Some financial institutions such as commercial banks are required by law to invest only in **investment-grade bonds,** which are rated as Baa or better by Moody's and BBB or better by Standard and Poor's. This requirement is intended to limit the portfolio risk of the financial institutions.

Liquidity

Investors prefer securities that are **liquid,** meaning that they could be easily converted to cash without a loss in value. Thus, if all other characteristics were equal, securities with lower liquidity would have to offer a higher yield to be preferred. Securities with a short-term maturity or an active secondary market

IMPACT OF THE STOCK MARKET CRASH OF OCTOBER 1987 ON DEFAULT RISK PREMIUMS

During the stock market crash on October 19, 1987, the bond market rallied. Many investors who liquidated their stock holdings purchased bonds, placing upward pressure on the prices of existing bonds. There was also a shift in the risk perception of bonds, as shown in the exhibit below. The risk perception can be measured by a bond's risk premium (the difference between the bond's yield and a risk-free Treasury bond with the same maturity). Notice from the exhibit how the risk premium on both Baa and AAA bonds increased by almost a full percentage point between October 16 and October 22. The significant jump in the risk premium suggests that investors changed their risk perception of these bonds.

SOURCE: *Chicago Fed Letter*, December 1987.

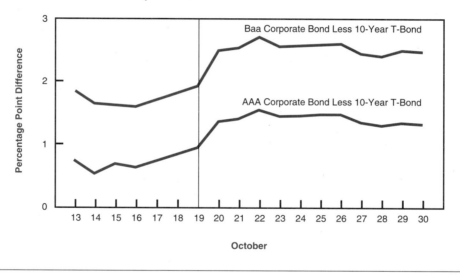

have higher liquidity. For investors who will not need their funds until the securities mature, lower liquidity is tolerable. Other investors, however, are willing to accept a lower return in exchange for a high degree of liquidity.

Tax Status

Investors are more concerned with after-tax income than before-tax income earned on securities. If all other characteristics are similar, taxable securities would have to offer a higher before-tax yield to investors than tax-exempt securities to be preferred. The extra compensation required on such taxable securities depends on the tax rates of individual and institutional investors. Investors in high tax brackets benefit most from tax-exempt securities.

When assessing the expected yields of various securities, it is common to convert them into an after-tax form, as follows:

$$Y_{at} = Y_{bt} (1 - T)$$

where

Y_{at} = after-tax yield

Y_{bt} = before-tax yield

T = investor's marginal tax rate

Investors retain only a percentage $(1 - T)$ of the before-tax yield once taxes are paid. Consider a taxable security that offers a before-tax yield of 14 percent. When converted into after-tax terms, the yield will be reduced by the tax percentage. The precise after-tax yield is dependent on the tax rate (T). If the tax rate of the investor is 20 percent, the after-tax yield will be

$$Y_{at} = Y_{bt} (1 - T)$$

$$= 14\% (1 - .2)$$

$$= 11.2\%$$

Exhibit 4.2 presents after-tax yields based on a variety of tax rates and before-tax yields. For example, a taxable security with a before-tax yield of 6 percent will generate an after-tax yield of 5.4 percent to an investor in the 10 percent tax bracket, 4.8 percent to an investor in the 20 percent tax bracket, and so on. This exhibit shows why investors in high tax brackets are attracted to tax-exempt securities.

In some cases, investors wish to determine the before-tax yield necessary to match the after-tax yield of a tax-exempt security. This can be done by rearranging the terms of the previous equation:

$$Y_{bt} = \frac{Y_{at}}{(1 - T)}$$

EXHIBIT 4.2 After-Tax Yields Based on Various Tax Rates and Before-Tax Yields

	BEFORE-TAX YIELD:							
Tax Rate	**6%**	**8%**	**10%**	**12%**	**14%**	**16%**	**18%**	**20%**
10%	5.40%	7.20%	9.00%	10.80%	12.60%	14.40%	16.20%	18.00%
15	5.10	6.80	8.50	10.20	11.90	13.60	15.30	17.00
20	4.80	6.40	8.00	9.60	11.20	12.80	14.40	16.00
28	4.32	5.76	7.20	8.64	10.08	11.52	12.96	14.40
34	3.96	5.28	6.60	7.92	9.24	10.56	11.88	13.20

EXHIBIT 4.3 Comparison of Maturity and Yield of Government Securities as of August 5, 1994	
MATURITY	**ANNUALIZED YIELD**
1 Month	3.80%
3 Months	4.20
6 Months	4.76
1 Year	5.21
2 Years	5.94
3 Years	6.31
4 Years	6.68
5 Years	7.33
10 Years	7.41
15 Years	7.64
20 Years	7.65

Suppose that a firm in the 20 percent tax bracket is aware of a tax-exempt security that is paying a yield of 8 percent. To match this after-tax yield, taxable securities must offer a before-tax yield of

$$Y_{bt} = \frac{Y_{at}}{(1 - T)} = \frac{8\%}{(1 - .2)} = 10\%$$

State taxes should be considered along with federal taxes in determining the after-tax yield. Treasury securities are exempt from state income tax, and municipal securities are sometimes exempt as well.[1] Because states impose different income tax rates, a particular security's after-tax yield may vary with the location of the investor.

Term to Maturity

Maturity differs among securities and is another reason that security yields differ. The **term structure of interest rates** defines the relationship between maturity and annualized yield, holding other factors such as risk constant.

Any available business periodical can be used to determine the annualized yields of Treasury securities with different terms to maturity. The annualized yields for federal government securities of varied maturities are listed in Exhibit 4.3. A graphic comparison of these maturities and annualized yields is provided in Exhibit 4.4. The connection of points plotted in that exhibit is commonly referred to as a **yield curve.** Because this yield curve is upward sloping, it indicates

---

[1]The interest income on so-called tax-free municipal bonds is exempt from federal income tax. Yet, the interest on some municipal bonds is subject to federal income tax. Capital gains income is subject to federal income tax. In addition, most states charge income tax on interest from municipal bonds issued in other states.

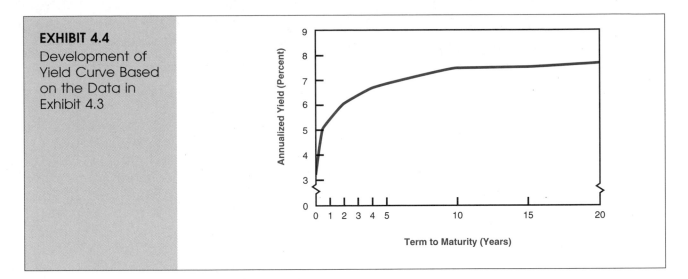

EXHIBIT 4.4
Development of Yield Curve Based on the Data in Exhibit 4.3

that the Treasury securities with longer maturities offered higher annualized yields. A downward sloping curve implies the opposite, and a horizontal yield curve implies that annualized yields are similar for securities with different maturities.

The term structure of interest rates shown in Exhibit 4.4 shows that securities that are similar in all ways except their term to maturity may offer different yields. Because the demand and supply conditions for securities may vary among maturities, so may the price (and therefore yield) of securities. A comprehensive explanation of the term structure of interest rates is provided later in this chapter.

Special Provisions

If a security offers any special provision to investors, its yield may be influenced. One type of provision, called a **call feature,** allows the issuer of the bonds to buy the bonds back before maturity at a specified price. As an example, Florida Power & Light had issued bonds with a 16 percent yield in 1981. By 1986, interest rates had dropped substantially, so the call feature was used to retire its 1981 bonds and new bonds were issued at a yield of about 9.9 percent. The result was an interest savings of about 6.1 percent, or $61,000 per million dollars borrowed on an annual basis.

Because a call feature could force investors to sell their bonds sooner than they would like, investors may require extra compensation to purchase them, especially during those periods when interest rates are expected to decrease, making it more likely that the bonds will be called. Thus, the yield on callable bonds should be higher than on noncallable bonds, other things being equal.

Another special provision of bonds that can affect the yield is a **convertibility clause,** which allows investors to convert the bond into a specified number of common stock shares. If the market price of the bonds declines, investors who wish to dispose of the bonds have an alternative to selling them in the market. For this reason, investors will accept a lower yield on securities that contain the convertibility feature, other things being equal.

EXHIBIT 4.5 Yield Comparison of Securities with Identical (three-month) Maturities Over Time

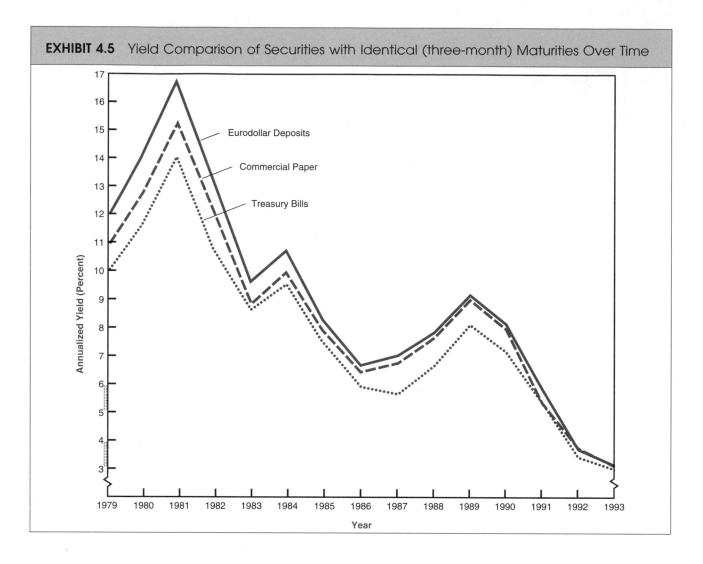

EXPLAINING ACTUAL YIELD DIFFERENTIALS

The differentials in yields among money market securities can be explained by the characteristics just described. Commercial paper rates are typically just slightly higher than T-bill (Treasury bill) rates, as investors require a slightly higher return to compensate for default risk and less liquidity. Eurodollar deposit rates are higher than yields on other money market securities with the same maturity because of their lower degree of liquidity and higher degree of default risk during that period.

Exhibit 4.5 illustrates the annualized yields of each money market security (with a three-month maturity). Although these yields are quite volatile from year to year, their respective differences do not normally change much over time. The difference between yields on T-bills and other risky securities was noticeably higher during the recessionary phase in the early 1980s, primarily because of higher default risk during that period.

EVALUATION OF THE TERM STRUCTURE THEORIES

An abundance of research has been conducted on the term structure of interest rates, offering insight into the various theories. Research by Meiselman and others has found that interest rate expectations have a strong influence on the term structure of interest rates. To assess whether other factors are also influential, the forecasting accuracy of the implied forward rates has been evaluated. Accurate forward rates would imply that the market can effectively assess future interest rates and that the expectations theory is, by itself, a proper explanation for the term structure of interest rates. Research has found, however, that forward rates generally are not accurate. To know whether this inaccuracy implies the existence of other factors that affect the term structure of interest rates, the forecasting errors must be more closely evalu-

ated. Presence of a systematic bias is evident, which may suggest that other factors are relevant. The liquidity premium, for example, could cause consistent positive forecasting errors, meaning forward rates tend to overestimate future interest rates. Research by Kessel found evidence of this.

Some research has also analyzed liquidity premiums. Some studies found that the size of liquidity premiums varies inversely with interest rate levels. However, research by Kessel and others found the opposite relationship. The difference in research results can be attributed to different sample periods examined and/or different research methodologies.

Although it is difficult to determine whether the term structure of interest rates has been influenced by

segmented market forces, some research has been conducted on this topic. A study by Elliot and Echols examined Treasury security data for a variety of maturities and found discontinuities in the yield-maturity relationship. The researchers suggest that the reason could be distinctly different supply and demand conditions for particular maturity segments.

Although the results of research differ, there is some evidence that expectations theory, liquidity preference theory, and segmented markets theory all have some validity. Thus, if the term structure is used to assess the market's expectations of future interest rates, investors should first net out the liquidity premium and any unique market conditions for various maturity segments.

Market forces cause the yields of all securities to move in the same direction. To illustrate, assume the Treasury experiences a large increase in the budget deficit and issues a large number of T-bills to finance the increased deficit. This action creates a large supply of T-bills in the market, placing downward pressure on the price and upward pressure on the T-bill yield. As the yield begins to rise, it approaches the yield of other short-term securities. Businesses and individual investors are now encouraged to purchase T-bills rather than these risky securities because they can achieve about the same yield while avoiding default risk. The switch to T-bills lowers demand for risky securities, thereby placing downward pressure on their price and upward pressure on their yields. Thus, the risk premium on risky securities would not disappear completely.

With regard to capital market securities, municipal bonds have the lowest before-tax yield, yet their after-tax yield is typically above that of Treasury bonds from the perspective of high-tax bracket investors. Treasury bonds are expected to offer the lowest yield because they are free from default risk and can easily be liquidated in the secondary market. Investors prefer municipal or corporate bonds over Treasury bonds only if the after-tax yield is sufficiently higher to compensate for default risk and a lower degree of liquidity.

EXHIBIT 4.6 Yield Differentials of Corporate Bonds

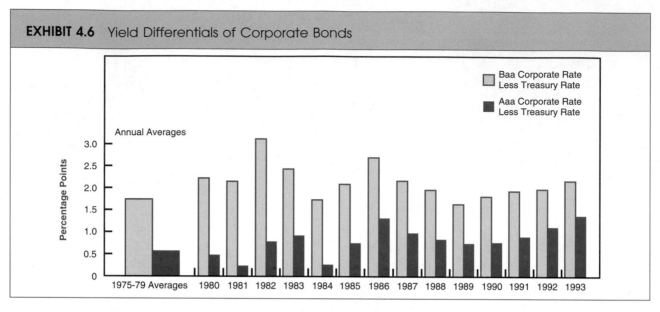

Note: Chart shows yield to maturity on seasoned corporate and Treasury debt with 10 years to maturity.
SOURCE: Moody's Bond Survey, and *FRBNY Quarterly Review* (Spring 1990), p. 17, updated by author.

To assess how capital market security yields can vary because of default risk, Exhibit 4.6 illustrates yields of corporate bonds in two different risk classes. The yield differentials among capital market securities can change over time as perceptions of risk change.

ESTIMATING THE APPROPRIATE YIELD

The discussion up to this point suggests that the appropriate yield to be offered on a security is based on the risk-free rate for the corresponding maturity, with adjustments to capture various characteristics. This model is specified below:

$$Y_n = R_{f,n} + DP + LP + TA + CALLP + COND$$

where Y_n = yield of an n-day security

$R_{f,n}$ = yield of an n-day Treasury (risk-free) security

DP = default premium to compensate for default risk

LP = liquidity premium to compensate for less liquidity

TA = adjustment due to the difference in tax status

$CALLP$ = call feature premium to compensate for the possibility that the security will be called

$COND$ = convertibility discount

These are the characteristics identified earlier that explain yield differentials among securities. Although maturity is another characteristic that can affect the yield, it is not included here because it is controlled for by matching the maturity of the risk-free security to that of the security of concern. For example, if the three-month T-bill's annualized rate were 8 percent and a corporation planned to issue 90-day commercial paper, it would need to determine the default premium (*DP*) and liquidity (*LP*) to offer on its commercial paper to make it as attractive to investors as a three-month (13-week) T-bill. The federal tax status on commercial paper is the same as on T-bills. Yet, income earned from investing in commercial paper is subject to state taxes, whereas income earned from investing in T-bills is not. Investors may require a premium for this reason alone if they reside in a location where state and local income taxes apply.

Assume that the corporation believed that a 0.7 percent default risk premium, a 0.2 percent liquidity premium, and a 0.3 percent tax adjustment were necessary to sell its commercial paper to investors. Because call and convertibility features are applicable only to bonds, they can be ignored here. The appropriate yield to be offered on the commercial paper is

$$Y_n = R_{f,n} + DP + LP + TA$$
$$= 8\% + .7\% + .2\% + .3\%$$
$$= 9.2\%$$

As time passes, the appropriate commercial paper rate would change, perhaps because of changes in the risk-free rate, default premium, liquidity premium, and tax adjustment.

Some corporations may postpone plans to issue commercial paper until the economy improves and the required premium for default risk is reduced. Yet even then, the market rate of commercial paper may increase if interest rates increase. For example, if over time the default risk premium decreases from 0.7 percent to 0.5 percent but $R_{f,n}$ increases from 8 percent to 8.7 percent, the appropriate yield to be offered on commercial paper (assuming no change in the previously assumed liquidity and tax adjustment premiums) would be

$$Y_n = R_{f,n} + DP + LP + TA$$
$$= 8.7\% + .5\% + .2\% + .3\%$$
$$= 9.7\%$$

The strategy to postpone issuing commercial paper would backfire in this example. Even though the default premium decreased by 0.2 percent, the general level of interest rates rose by 0.7 percent, so the net change in the commercial paper rate is + 0.5 percent. This example shows that the increase in a security's yield over time does not necessarily mean the default premium has increased.

The assessment of yields as described here could also be applied to long-term securities. If, for example, a firm desired to issue a 20-year corporate bond, it could identify the field of a new 20-year Treasury bond and add on the premiums for default risk, liquidity risk, and so on, to determine the yield at which it could sell corporate bonds.

A CLOSER LOOK AT THE TERM STRUCTURE

Of all the factors that affect the yields offered on debt securities, the factor that is most difficult to understand is the term to maturity. For this reason, a more comprehensive explanation of the relationship between term to maturity and annualized yield (referred to as the term structure of interest rates) is necessary.

Various theories have been used to explain the relationship between maturity and annualized yield of securities, including the pure expectations theory, liquidity premium theory, and segmented markets theory. Each of these theories is explained here.

Pure Expectations Theory

According to the pure expectations theory, the term structure of interest rates (as reflected in the shape of the yield curve) is determined solely by expectations of future interest rates. To understand how interest rate expectations may influence the yield curve, assume that investors who plan to purchase securities must decide between short-term and long-term securities. Assume that the annualized yields of short-term and long-term securities are similar; that is, the yield curve is flat. If investors begin to believe that interest rates will rise, they will invest mostly in short-term securities so that they can soon reinvest their funds at higher yields after interest rates increase. When investors flood the short-term market and avoid the long-term market, they may cause the yield curve to adjust as shown in Exhibit 4.7. The strong demand by investors for short-term securities will force prices up and annualized yields down. Meanwhile, the lack of demand for long-term securities forces prices down and annualized yields up.

Even though the annualized short-term yields become lower than annualized long-term yields, investors in short-term securities are satisfied, because they expect interest rates to rise. They will make up for the lower short-term yield when these securities mature, and they reinvest at a higher rate (if interest rates rise) at maturity.

Assuming that the borrowers who plan to issue securities also expect interest rates to increase, they would prefer to lock in the present interest rate over a long period of time. Thus, borrowers would generally prefer to issue long-term securities rather than short-term securities. This results in a large supply of long-term securities for sale and a relatively small supply of short-term securities. Consequently, there is downward pressure on the equilibrium price of long-term

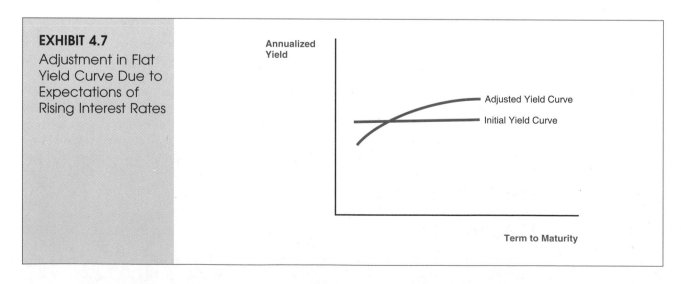

EXHIBIT 4.7

Adjustment in Flat Yield Curve Due to Expectations of Rising Interest Rates

WSJ

USING *THE WALL STREET JOURNAL*

YIELD CURVE

A graph illustrating the yield curve is typically shown in the "Credit Markets" section of *The Wall Street Journal*. Annualized yields of Treasury securities are shown for terms to maturity ranging from three months to 30 years. Yield curves are shown for three different points in time to illustrate how the yield curve has changed recently.

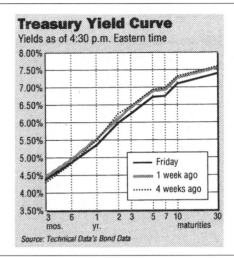

securities (due to large supply of long-term securities issued) and upward pressure on the price of short-term securities (due to the small supply of short-term securities issued). The yields of the respective securities would move inversely with the price movements. The pressure on the yield curve from such borrowing activities is similar to that caused by the investing activities. Overall, the expectation of higher interest rates changes the demand for securities and the supply of securities issued in different maturity markets, which forces the shape of the yield curve to pivot upward (counterclockwise).

Consider how the yield curve would be affected if both investors and borrowers expected interest rates to decrease in the future. Investors would prefer to invest in long-term securities rather than short-term securities, because they could lock in today's interest rate before interest rates fall. Borrowers would prefer to issue short-term securities so that as these securities mature, new securities could be issued at a lower interest rate.

Based on the expectation of lower interest rates in the future, demand by investors will be low for short-term securities and high for long-term securities. The amount issued by borrowers will be small for long-term securities and large for short-term securities. This will place downward pressure on short-term security prices and upward pressure on short-term yields. The shortage of long-term securities for sale will place upward pressure on their prices and downward pressure on long-term yields. Overall, the expectation of lower interest rates causes the shape of the yield curve to pivot downward (clockwise). Exhibit 4.8 summarizes the impact of interest rate expectations on the slope of the yield curve.

Algebraic Presentation. Investors monitor the yield curve to determine the rates that exist for securities with various maturities. They can purchase either a security with a maturity that matches their investment horizon or a security with a shorter term and reinvest the proceeds at maturity. If a particular investment

EXHIBIT 4.8   Impact of Expected Interest Rate Changes on Slope of the Yield Curve

	IMPACT OF EXPECTED INCREASE IN INTEREST RATES	IMPACT OF EXPECTED DECREASE IN INTEREST RATES
Demand for short-term securities by investors	Upward pressure	Downward pressure
Supply of short-term securities issued by borrowers	Downward pressure	Upward pressure
Price of short-term securities	Upward pressure	Downward pressure
Yield on short-term securities	Downward pressure	Upward pressure
Demand for long-term securities by investors	Downward pressure	Upward pressure
Supply of long-term securities issued by borrowers	Upward pressure	Downward pressure
Price of long-term securities	Downward pressure	Upward pressure
Yield on long-term securities	Upward pressure	Downward pressure
Shape of yield curve	Upward slope	Downward slope

strategy is expected to generate a higher return over the investment horizon, investors may use that strategy. This could affect the prices and yields of securities with different maturities, realigning the rates so that the expected return over the entire investment horizon would be similar, regardless of the strategy used. If investors were indifferent to security maturities, they would want the return of any security to equal the compounded yield of consecutive investments in shorter-term securities. That is, a two-year security should offer a return that is similar to the anticipated return from investing in two consecutive one-year securities. A four-year security should offer a return that is competitive with the expected return from investing in two consecutive two-year securities or four consecutive one-year securities, and so on.

To illustrate these equalities, consider the relationship between interest rates on a two-year security and a one-year security as follows:

$$(1 + {}_t i_2)^2 = (1 + {}_t i_1)(1 + {}_{t+1} r_1)$$

where

$\quad {}_t i_2 =$ the known annualized interest rate of a two-year security as of time t

$\quad {}_t i_1 =$ the known annualized interest rate of a one-year security as of time t

$\quad {}_{t+1} r_1 =$ the one-year interest rate that is anticipated as of time $t+1$ (one year ahead)

The term i represents a quoted rate, which is therefore known, whereas r represents a rate to be quoted at some point in the future, which is therefore uncertain. The left side of the equation represents the compounded yield to investors who purchase a two-year security, while the right side of the equation represents the anticipated compounded yield from purchasing a one-year security and reinvesting the proceeds in a new one-year security at the end of one year. If time t is today, $_{t+1}r_1$ can be estimated by rearranging terms.

$$1 + {}_{t+1}r_1 = \frac{(1 + {}_ti_2)^2}{(1 + {}_ti_1)}$$

$$_{t+1}r_1 = \frac{(1 + {}_ti_2)^2}{(1 + {}_ti_1)} - 1$$

The term $_{t+1}r_1$, referred to as the **forward rate,** is commonly estimated in order to represent the market's forecast of the future interest rate. As a numerical example, assume that as of today (time t) the annualized two-year interest rate is 10 percent, while the one-year interest is 8 percent. The forward rate is estimated as follows:

$$_{t+1}r_1 = \frac{(1 + .10)^2}{(1 + .08)} - 1$$

$$= .1203704$$

Conceptually, this rate implies that one year from now, a one-year interest rate must equal about 12.037 percent in order for consecutive investments in two one-year securities to generate a return similar to that of a two-year investment. If the actual one-year rate beginning one year from now (at period $t+1$) is above (below) 12.037 percent, the return from two consecutive one-year investments will exceed (be less than) the return on a two-year investment.

The forward rate is sometimes used as an approximation of the market's consensus interest rate forecast, because if the market had a different perception, demand and supply of today's existing two-year and one-year securities would adjust to capitalize on this information. Of course, there is no guarantee that the forward rate will forecast the future interest rate with perfect accuracy.

The greater the difference between the implied one-year forward rate and today's one-year interest rate, the greater the expected change in the one-year interest rate. If the term structure of interest rates is solely influenced by expectations of future interest rates, the following relationships hold.

SCENARIO	STRUCTURE OF YIELD CURVE	EXPECTATIONS ABOUT THE FUTURE INTEREST RATE
1. $_{t+1}r_1 > {}_ti_1$	Upward slope	Higher than today's rate
2. $_{t+1}r_1 = {}_ti_1$	Flat	Same as today's rate
3. $_{t+1}r_1 < {}_ti_1$	Downward slope	Lower than today's rate

Forward rates can be determined for various maturities. The relationships described here can be applied when assessing the change in the interest rate of a security with any particular maturity.

The previous example can be expanded to solve for other forward rates. For example, the equality specified by the pure expectations theory for a three-year horizon is

$$(1 + {}_t i_3)^3 = (1 + {}_t i_1)(1 + {}_{t+1} r_1)(1 + {}_{t+2} r_1)$$

where ${}_t i_3$ = the annualized interest rate on a three-year security
                    as of time t,

        ${}_{t+2} r_1$ = the one-year interest rate that is anticipated
                    as of time $t+2$ (two years).

All other terms were already defined. By rearranging terms, we can isolate the forward rate of a one-year security beginning two years from now:

$$1 + {}_{t+2} r_1 = \frac{(1 + {}_t i_3)^3}{(1 + {}_t i_1)(1 + {}_{t+1} r_1)}$$

$$_{t+2} r_1 = \frac{(1 + {}_t i_3)^3}{(1 + {}_t i_1)(1 + {}_{t+1} r_1)} - 1$$

If the one-year forward rate beginning one year from now (${}_{t+1} r_1$) has already been estimated, this estimate along with actual one-year and three-year interest rates can be used to estimate the one-year forward rate two years from now. Recall that our previous example assumed ${}_t i_1 = 8$ percent, and ${}_{t+1} r_1$ was estimated to be about 12.037 percent. Assume that a three-year security has an annualized interest rate of 11 percent (${}_t i_3 = 11$ percent). Given this information, the one-year forward rate two years from now is

$$_{t+2} r_1 = \frac{(1 + {}_t i_3)^3}{(1 + {}_t i_1)(1 + {}_{t+1} r_1)} - 1$$

$$= \frac{(1 + .11)^3}{(1 + .08)(1 + .12037)} - 1$$

$$= \frac{1.367631}{1.21} - 1$$

$$= 13.02736\%$$

Thus, the market anticipates a one-year interest rate of 13.02736 percent as of two years from now.

The yield curve can also be used to forecast annualized interest rates for periods other than one year. For example, the information provided in the last example could be used to determine the two-year forward rate beginning one year from now.

According to the pure expectations theory, a one-year investment followed by a two-year investment should offer the same annualized yield over the three-year horizon as a three-year security that could be purchased today. This equality is shown as follows:

$$(1 + {}_t i_3)^3 = (1 + {}_t i_1)(1 + {}_{t+1} r_2)^2$$

where ${}_{t+1} r_2$ = the annual interest rate of a two-year security anticipated
                    as of time $t+1$

By rearranging terms, $_{t+1}r_2$ can be isolated:

$$(1 + {}_{t+1}r_2)^2 = \frac{(1 + {}_t i_3)^3}{(1 + {}_t i_1)}$$

Recall that today's annualized yields for one-year and three-year securities are 8 percent and 11 percent, respectively. With this information, $_{t+1}r_2$ is estimated as follows:

$$
\begin{aligned}
(1 + {}_{t+1}r_2)^2 &= \frac{(1 + {}_t i_3)^3}{(1 + {}_t i_1)} \\
&= \frac{(1 + .11)^3}{(1 + .08)} \\
&= 1.266325 \\
(1 + {}_{t+1}r_2) &= \sqrt{1.266325} \\
&= 1.1253 \\
{}_{t+1}r_2 &= .1253
\end{aligned}
$$

Thus, the market anticipates an annualized interest rate of about 12.53 percent for two-year securities beginning one year from now.

Pure expectations theory is based on the premise that the forward rates are unbiased estimators of future interest rates. If forward rates are biased, investors could attempt to capitalize on the bias. To illustrate, our previous numerical example determined the one-year forward rate beginning one year ahead to be about 12.037 percent. If the forward rate was thought to contain an upward bias, the expected one-year interest rate beginning one year ahead would be less than 12.037 percent. Therefore, investors with funds available for two years would earn a higher yield by purchasing two-year securities rather than purchasing one-year securities for two consecutive years. Their actions would cause an increase in the price of two-year securities and a decrease in that of one-year securities. The yields of the securities would move inversely with the price movements. The attempt by investors to capitalize on the forward rate bias would essentially eliminate the bias.

If forward rates are unbiased estimators of future interest rates, financial market efficiency is supported, and the information implied by market rates about the forward rate cannot be used to generate abnormal returns. As new information develops, investor preferences would change, yields would adjust, and the implied forward rate would adjust as well.

If a long-term rate is expected to equal a geometric average of consecutive short-term rates covering the same time horizon (as is suggested by pure expectations theory), long-term rates would likely be more stable than short-term rates. As expectations about consecutive short-term rates change over time, the average of these rates is less volatile than the individual short-term rates. Thus, long-term rates are much more stable than short-term rates.

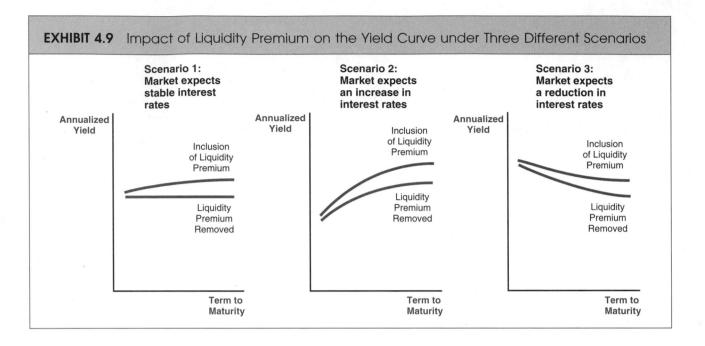

EXHIBIT 4.9 Impact of Liquidity Premium on the Yield Curve under Three Different Scenarios

Liquidity Premium Theory

Some investors may prefer to own short-term rather than long-term securities because a shorter maturity represents greater liquidity. In this case, they may be willing to hold long-term securities only if compensated with a premium for the lower degree of liquidity. Although long-term securities can be liquidated prior to maturity, their prices are more sensitive to interest rate movements. Short-term securities are normally considered to be more liquid because they are more likely to be converted to cash without a loss in value.

The preference for the more liquid short-term securities places upward pressure on the slope of a yield curve. Liquidity may be a more critical factor to investors at particular points in time, and the liquidity premium will change over time accordingly. As it does, so will the yield curve. This is the **liquidity premium theory.**

Exhibit 4.9 combines the simultaneous existence of expectations theory and a liquidity premium. Each graph shows different interest rate expectations by the market. Regardless of the interest rate forecast, the yield curve is affected in a somewhat similar manner by the liquidity premium.

When expectations theory is combined with the liquidity theory, the yield on a security will not necessarily be equal to the yield from consecutive investments in shorter-term securities over the same investment horizon. For example, the yield on a two-year security can be determined as

$$(1 + {}_t i_2)^2 = (1 + {}_t i_1)(1 + {}_{t+1} r_1) + L_2$$

where L_2 represents the liquidity premium on a two-year security. The yield generated from the two-year security should exceed the yield from consecutive investments in one-year securities by a premium that compensates the investor for less liquidity. The relationship between the liquidity premium and term to maturity can be expressed as follows:

$$0 < L_1 < L_2 < L_3 < \ldots < L_{20}$$

where the subscript represents years to maturity. This implies that the liquidity premium would be more influential on the difference between annualized interest rates on one-year and twenty-year securities than on the difference between one-year and two-year securities.

If liquidity influences the yield curve, the forward rate overestimates the market's expectation of the future interest rate. A more appropriate formula for the forward rate would account for the liquidity premium. Reconsider the example where $i_1 = 8\%$, and $i_2 = 10\%$. Assume that the liquidity premium on a two-year security is 0.5 percent. The forward rate is

$$_{t+1}r_1 = \frac{(1 + {_t}i_2)^2}{(1 + {_t}i_1)} - 1 - [L_2/(1 + i_1)]$$

$$_{t+1}r_1 = \frac{(1.10)^2}{1.08} - 1 - [.005/(1 + .08)]$$

$$= .11574$$

The one-year forward rate as it was estimated earlier (12.037 percent) should overstate the market's expected interest rate, because a liquidity premium is also included in the longer-term security's interest rate. Forecasts of future interest rates implied by a yield curve are adjusted slightly lower when accounting for the liquidity premium.

Even with the existence of a liquidity premium, yield curves could still be used to interpret interest rate expectations. A flat yield curve would be interpreted as the market's expecting a slight decrease in interest rates (without the effect of the liquidity premium, the yield curve would have had a slight downward slope). A slight upward slope would be interpreted as no expected change in interest rates because if the liquidity premium were removed, this yield curve would be flat.

Segmented Markets Theory

According to **segmented markets theory,** investors and borrowers choose securities with maturities that satisfy their forecasted cash needs. For example, pension funds and life insurance companies may generally prefer long-term investments that coincide with their long-term liabilities. Commercial banks may prefer more short-term investments to coincide with their short-term liabilities. If investors and borrowers participate only in the maturity market that satisfies their particular needs, markets are segmented. That is, the shifting by investors (or borrowers) from the long-term market to the short-term market or vice versa would occur only if the timing of their cash needs changed. According to segmented markets theory, the choice of long-term versus short-term maturities is predetermined according to need rather than expectations of future interest rates.

Assume that most investors have funds available to invest for only a short period of time and therefore desire to invest primarily in short-term securities.

Also assume that most borrowers need funds for a long period of time and therefore desire to issue mostly long-term securities. The result would be upward pressure on the price and downward pressure on the yield of short-term securities. In addition, there would be downward pressure on the price and upward pressure on the yield of long-term securities. Overall, the scenario described would create an upward-sloping yield curve.

Now consider the opposite scenario in which most investors wish to invest their funds for a long period of time, while most borrowers need funds for only a short period of time. According to segmented markets theory, there would be downward pressure on the price and upward pressure on the yield of short-term securities. In addition, there would be upward pressure on the price and downward pressure on the yield of long-term securities. Exhibit 4.10 illustrates how the segmented markets theory can explain the shape of the yield curve at any point in time. If there was more balance in the investor's demand and borrower's supply of securities issued between the short-term and long-term markets, the yields of short- and long-term securities would be more similar.

Our example separated the maturity markets into just short-term and long-term. In reality, several maturity markets may exist. Within the short-term market, some investors may prefer maturities of one month or less, while others prefer maturities of one to three months. Regardless of how many maturity markets exist, the yields of securities with various maturities should be somewhat influenced by the desires of investors and borrowers to participate in the maturity market that best satisfies their needs.

The segmented markets theory has support because some participants are likely to choose a maturity based on their needs. A corporation that needs additional funds for 30 days would not consider issuing long-term bonds for such

EXHIBIT 4.10 Impact of Different Scenarios on Yield Curve According to Segmented Markets Theory		
	IMPACT OF SCENARIO 1: (INVESTORS HAVE MOSTLY SHORT-TERM FUNDS AVAILABLE; BORROWERS WANT LONG-TERM FUNDS)	**IMPACT OF SCENARIO 2: (INVESTORS HAVE MOSTLY LONG-TERM FUNDS AVAILABLE; BORROWERS WANT SHORT-TERM FUNDS)**
Demand for short-term securities by investors	Upward pressure	Downward pressure
Supply of short-term securities issued by borrowers	Downward pressure	Upward pressure
Price of short-term securities	Upward pressure	Downward pressure
Yield on short-term securities	Downward pressure	Upward pressure
Demand for long-term securities by investors	Downward pressure	Upward pressure
Supply of long-term securities issued by borrowers	Upward pressure	Downward pressure
Price of long-term securities	Downward pressure	Upward pressure
Yield of long-term securities	Upward pressure	Downward pressure
Shape of yield curve	Upward slope	Downward slope

a purpose. Savers with short-term funds are restricted from some long-term investments, such as 10-year certificates of deposit that cannot be easily liquidated. Note that this theory of segmented markets conflicts with the general presumption of the pure expectations theory that maturity markets are perfect substitutes for one another.

A limitation of the segmented markets theory is that some borrowers and savers have the flexibility to choose among various maturity markets. For example, corporations that need long-term funds may initially obtain short-term financing if they expect interest rates to decline. Investors with long-term funds may make short-term investments if they expect interest rates to rise. Some investors with short-term funds available may be willing to purchase long-term securities that have an active secondary market.

Some financial institutions focus on a particular maturity market, while others are more flexible. Commercial banks obtain most of their funds in short-term markets but spread their investments into short-, medium-, and long-term markets. Savings institutions have historically focused on attracting short-term funds and lending funds for long-term periods.

If maturity markets were completely segmented, an adjustment in the interest rate in one market would have no impact on other markets. Yet, there is clear evidence that interest rates among maturity markets move closely in tandem over time, proving there is some interaction among markets, which implies that funds are being transferred across markets.

Although markets are not completely segmented, the preference of particular maturities can affect the prices and yields of securities with different maturities and therefore affect the yield curve's shape. Therefore, the segmented markets theory appears to be a partial explanation for the yield curve's shape, not the sole explanation.

A more flexible perspective of the segmented markets theory, referred to as **preferred habitat theory,** offers a compromising explanation for the term structure of interest rates. This theory suggests that although investors and borrowers may normally concentrate on a particular natural maturity market, certain events may cause them to wander from it. For example, commercial banks that obtain mostly short-term funds may select investments with short-term maturities as a natural habitat. However, if they wish to benefit from an anticipated decline in interest rates, they may select medium- and long-term maturities instead. Preferred habitat theory acknowledges that natural maturity markets may influence the yield curve but recognizes that interest rate expectations could entice market participants to stray from preferred maturities.

Integrating the Theories on the Term Structure

To illustrate how all three theories can simultaneously affect the yield curve, assume the following conditions:

1. Investors and borrowers who select security maturities based on anticipated interest rate movements currently expect interest rates to rise.
2. Most borrowers are in need of long-term funds, while most investors have only short-term funds to invest.
3. Investors prefer more liquidity to less.

The first condition, related to expectations theory, suggests the existence of an upward-sloping yield curve, other things being equal. This is shown in Exhibit 4.11 as curve E. The segmented markets information (condition 2) also favors the upward-sloping yield curve. When conditions 1 and 2 are considered simultaneously, the appropriate yield curve may look like curve E + S. The third condition relating to liquidity would then place a higher premium on the longer-term securities because of their lower degree of liquidity. When this condition is included with the first two, the yield curve may look like curve E + S + L.

In our example, all conditions placed upward pressure on long-term yields relative to short-term yields. In reality, there will sometimes be offsetting conditions, as one condition places downward pressure on the slope of the yield curve while the others place upward pressure on the slope. For example, if condition 1 were revised to suggest the expectation of lower interest rates in the future, this condition by itself would result in a downward-sloping yield curve. When combined with the other conditions that favor an upward-sloping curve, it would create a partial offsetting effect. This yield curve would exhibit a downward slope if the effect of the interest rate expectations dominated the combined liquidity premium and segmented markets effects. Conversely, an upward slope would exist if the liquidity premium and segmented markets effects dominated the effects of interest rate expectations.

Use of the Term Structure

At any point in time, the shape of the yield curve can be used to assess the general expectations of investors and borrowers about future interest rates. Recall from expectations theory that an upward-sloping yield curve generally results from the expectation of higher interest rates, while a downward sloping yield curve generally results from the expectation of lower interest rates. However, the expectations about future interest rates must be interpreted cautiously, because liquidity and specific maturity preferences could influence the yield curve's shape. It is generally believed, though, that interest rate expectations are a major contributing factor to the yield curve's shape, and the curve's shape should pro-

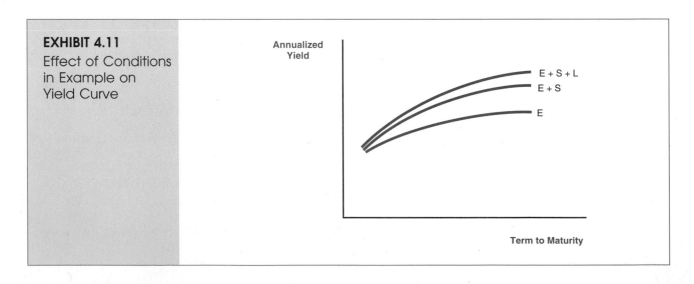

EXHIBIT 4.11

Effect of Conditions in Example on Yield Curve

POINT OF INTEREST

IMPACT OF THE STOCK MARKET CRASH OF OCTOBER 1987 ON TERM STRUCTURE OF INTEREST RATES

During the stock market crash of October 1987, many investors liquidated their stock holdings and purchased money market securities. The result was an abrupt decline in money market yields. Because securities with longer maturities were not affected as much, the term structure of interest rates was affected. To illustrate the shift in the term structure, the exhibit below shows a trend in the difference between the 30-year Treasury bond and a 3-month Treasury bill over the period of October 13 to 30. The exhibit suggests that the upward slope of the yield curve must have become steeper over this period. According to expectations theory, such results would imply that investors expected interest rates to rise in the future. The fact that some investors substituted money market securities for capital market securities (stock) during this period suggests that markets are not entirely segmented.

SOURCE: *Chicago Fed Letter*, December 1987.

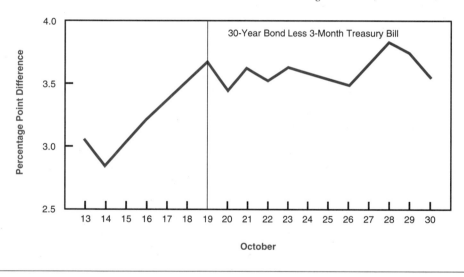

vide a reasonable indication (especially if the liquidity premium effect is accounted for) of the market's expectations about future interest rates.

Some analysts believe that flat or inverted yield curves indicate a recession in the near future. The rationale is that given a positive liquidity premium, such yield curves reflect the expectation of lower interest rates. This is commonly associated with expectations of a reduced demand for loanable funds, which could result in a recession. Exhibit 4.12 shows the differential between 10-year and 3-month Treasury securities over time. A differential close to zero reflects a flat yield curve, while a negative differential reflects an inverted yield curve. Each time the yield curve became flat or inverted, a recession occurred shortly thereafter.

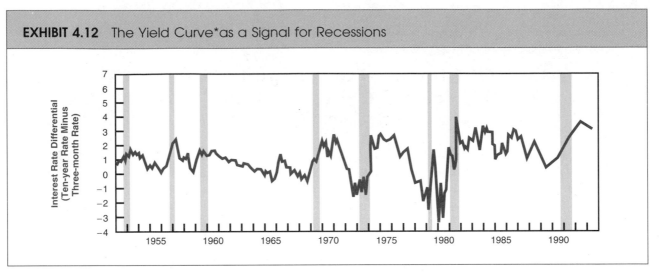

EXHIBIT 4.12   The Yield Curve*as a Signal for Recessions

*The general shape of the yield curve is measured as the differential between annualized 10-year and 3-month interest rates. Recessionary periods are shaded.
SOURCE: *FRBSF Weekly Letter,* March 10, 1989, updated by author.

Although investors can use the yield curve to interpret the market's consensus expectation of future interest rates, they may have their own interest rate projections. By comparing their projections to those implied by the yield curve, they can attempt to capitalize on the difference. For example, if an upward-sloping yield curve exists, suggesting a market expectation of increasing rates, investors expecting stable interest rates could benefit from investing in long-term securities. From their perspective, long-term securities are undervalued because they reflect the market's expectation of higher interest rates. Strategies such as this are effective only if the investor can consistently forecast better than the market.

If the yield curve is upward sloping, some investors may attempt to benefit from the higher yields on longer-term securities, even when they have funds for only a short period of time. The secondary market allows investors the opportunity to attempt this strategy, referred to as **riding the yield curve.** Consider an upward-sloping yield curve such that some one-year securities offer an annualized yield of 7 percent while 10-year bonds can be purchased at par value and offer a coupon rate of 12 percent. An investor with funds available for one year may decide to purchase the bonds and sell them in the secondary market after one year. The investor earns 5 percent more than what was possible on the one-year securities, if the bonds can be sold for what they were purchased for after one year. The risk of this strategy is the uncertainty of the price at which the security can be sold in the near future. If the upward-sloping yield is interpreted as the market's consensus of higher interest rates in the future, the price of a security would be expected to decrease in the future. In this case, investors are justified in purchasing a long-term security for a short-term period only if they believe the consensus forecast interpreted from the yield curve is incorrect. Although the market's forecast implied by the yield curve often differs from the interest rate that actually occurs, it is difficult to know in advance whether the market will overestimate or underestimate the future interest rate.

The yield curve is commonly monitored by financial institutions whose liability maturities are distinctly different from their asset maturities. Consider a bank that obtains much of its funds through short-term deposits and uses the funds to provide long-term loans or purchase long-term securities. An upward-sloping yield curve is favorable to the bank because annualized short-term deposit rates are significantly lower than annualized long-term investment rates. The bank's spread is higher than it would be if the yield curve were flat. Some commercial banks may attempt to capitalize on an upward-sloping yield curve by pursuing a greater proportion of short-term deposits and long-term investments. Yet, if the bank believes that the upward slope of the yield curve indicates higher interest rates in the future (as reflected in the expectations theory), it will expect its cost of liabilities to increase over time, as future deposits would be obtained at higher interest rates. Any long-term loans previously provided at a fixed rate would represent a relatively low return in the future if interest rates increase.

The yield curve is also useful for firms that plan to issue bonds. By assessing the prevailing rates on securities for various maturities, firms can estimate the rates to be paid on bonds with different maturities. This may enable them to decide the maturity for the bonds they issue.

Impact of Debt Management on Term Structure

Debt management represents the decisions by the Treasury to finance the deficit. These decision can have a significant influence on economic variables monitored by financial market participants. The Treasury must determine the composition of short-term versus long-term debt, which can affect the term structure of interest rates and therefore the relative desirability of various securities. The composition can also affect the level of investment and therefore aggregate demand. For example, if the Treasury uses a relatively large proportion of long-term debt, this would place upward pressure on long-term yields. Because long-term investment is sensitive to long-term financing rates, corporations may reduce their investment in fixed assets. Conversely, if the Treasury uses mostly short-term securities to finance its deficit, long-term interest rates may be relatively low, thereby stimulating corporate investment in fixed assets.

In May 1993, the U.S. Treasury enacted a new policy to reduce its offerings of 30-year bonds, while increasing its offering of short-term securities. This change in the Treasury's financing strategy was expected to reduce financing costs. At the time of the decision, the yield curve exhibited a steep upward slope, as annualized interest rates on short-term Treasury securities were 3 to 4 percentage points lower than annualized interest rates on long-term Treasury securities. Thus, if interest rates were to remain steady, the annual savings in financing expenses to the Treasury (and therefore to taxpayers) would be $35 million on every $1 billion borrowed.

The shift from borrowing more short-term funds and fewer long-term funds was expected to place upward pressure on short-term interest rates and downward pressure on the long-term interest rates, as shown in Exhibit 4.13. The top left graph represents the market for short-term funds while the top right graph represents the market for long-term funds. Although there are numerous maturity markets, the focus on only two markets is sufficient to make a point here. In the short-term market, the equilibrium short-term interest rate is determined by the supply and demand schedules for short-term funds, which were initially S_{s1} and D_{s1} respectively. In the long-term market, the equilibrium long-term interest rate is determined by the supply and demand schedules for long-term

EXHIBIT 4.13   Potential Impact of Treasury Shift from Long-term to Short-term Financing

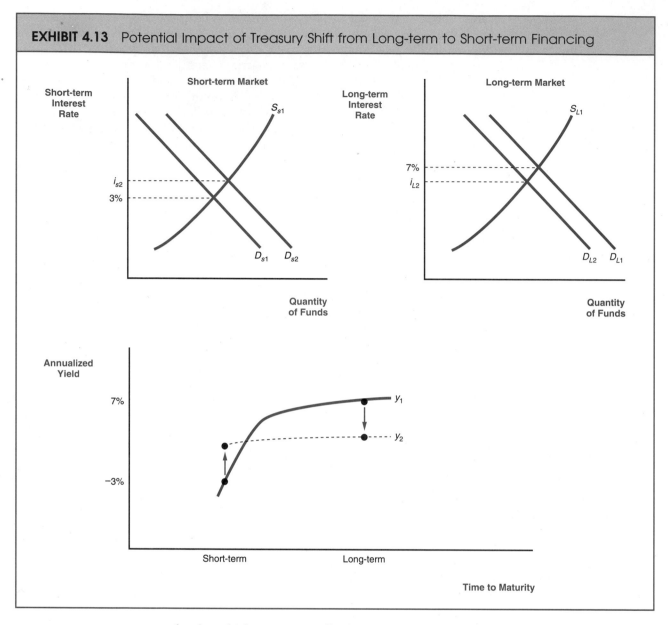

funds, which were initially S_{L1} and D_{L1} respectively. The shift in government policy causes the demand schedule for short-term funds to shift outward to D_{s2} and the demand schedules for long-term funds to shift inward from D_{L1} to D_{L2}. Consequently, the short-term interest rate rises from 3 percent to i_{s2}, while the long-term interest rate declines from 7 percent to i_{L2}. This effect would cause a flatter yield curve, (from the yield curve called y_1 in the lower graph of Exhibit 4.13 to the yield curve called y_2). The corporate cost of financing long-term projects would be reduced, and may therefore result in increased corporate spending. For this reason, the Treasury expected that the change in policy could stimulate the economy. However, recognize that as equilibrium long-term and short-term interest rates begin to change as shown in Exhibit 4.13, some investors may shift from the long-term market to the short-term market as short-term interest rates become more attractive. This reflects a shift in the supply schedules for short-term and long-term markets, which could partially offset the shift in the demand schedules caused by the Treasury's policy change.

Some analysts expressed fear that the emphasis on short-term financing would actually increase the Treasury's financing costs. If interest rates increased over time, the emphasis on short-term financing could backfire as the short-term securities mature, and new financing would be necessary at the prevailing interest rates.

Historical Review of the Term Structure

The specific shape of the yield curve changes over time, as illustrated in Exhibit 4.14. Notice that the slope of each yield curve is more pronounced for maturities

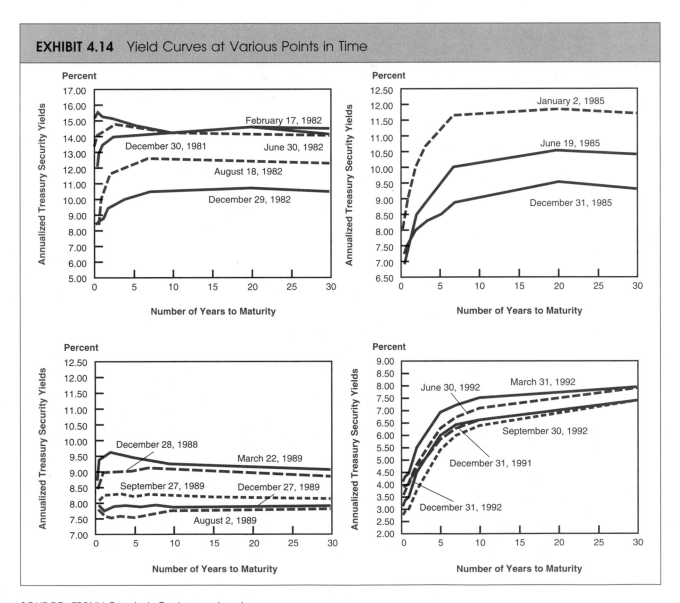

EXHIBIT 4.14   Yield Curves at Various Points in Time

SOURCE: *FRBNY Quarterly Review,* various issues.

up to five years and then levels off somewhat for longer maturities. Yield curves are not always upward sloping. In the late 1970s and early 1980s, securities with shorter maturities commonly offered higher annualized yields because of the very high interest rates of that period combined with the expectation that rates would decrease. Although the upward slope has generally persisted since 1982, the degree of slope has changed. In 1985, when nominal interest rates were relatively low, the upward slope became quite pronounced, perhaps because of expectations that interest rates would increase in the future. By the late 1980s, the yield curve was somewhat flat. In the early 1990s, when nominal interest rates were again very low, the yield curve exhibited a steep upward slope.

INTERNATIONAL STRUCTURE OF INTEREST RATES

GLOBAL ASPECTS

Interest rate movements across countries tend to be positively correlated as a result of internationally integrated financial markets. Yet the actual interest rates may vary significantly across countries at a given point in time. The differential between interest rates of risky securities between any two countries is usually similar to the differential between the risk-free rates of those countries. This implies that the differential in interest rates is primarily attributed to general supply-and-demand conditions across countries rather than differences in default premiums, liquidity premiums, or other factors unique to the individual securities.

Because forward rates reflect the market's expectations of future interest rates, the term structure of interest rates for various countries should be monitored for the following reasons. First, with the integration of financial markets, movements in one country's interest rate can affect interest rates in other countries. Thus, some investors may estimate the forward rate in a foreign country to predict the foreign interest rate, which in turn may affect domestic interest rates. Second, foreign securities and some domestic securities are influenced by foreign economies, which are dependent on foreign interest rates. If the foreign forward rates can be used to forecast foreign interest rates, they can enhance forecasts of foreign economies. Because exchange rates are also influenced by foreign interest rates, exchange rate projections may be more accurate when using foreign forward rates to forecast foreign interest rates.

If the real rate of interest was fixed, inflation rates for future periods could be predicted for any country in which the forward rate could be estimated. Recall that the nominal interest rate consists of an expected inflation rate plus a real rate of interest. Because the forward rate represents an expected nominal interest rate for a future period, it also represents an expected inflation rate plus a real rate of interest in that period. The expected inflation in that period is estimated as the difference between the forward rate and the real rate of interest.

SUMMARY

- Quoted yields of debt securities at a given point vary for the following reasons. First, securities with higher default risk must offer a higher yield. Second, securities that are less liquid must offer a higher yield. Third, taxable securities must offer a higher before-tax yield than tax-exempt securities. Fourth, securities with longer maturities offer a different yield (not consistently higher or lower) than securities with shorter maturities. Fifth, securities with a call provision offer a higher yield, while securities with a convertibility clause offer a lower yield.

- The appropriate yield for any particular debt security can be estimated by first determining the risk-free Treasury security rate on a debt security with a similar maturity. Then, adjustments can be made according to the default risk, liquidity, tax status, and other provisions.

- The term structure of interest rates can be explained by three theories. First, pure expectations theory suggests that the shape of the yield curve is dictated by interest rate expectations. Under expectations of rising interest rates, investors prefer securities with short-term maturities, and borrowers prefer securities with long-term maturities, resulting in an upward-sloping yield curve. Under expectations of declining interest rates, investors prefer securities with long-term securities, and borrowers prefer securities with short-term securities, resulting in a downward-sloping yield curve.

  Second, the liquidity premium theory suggests that if a shorter maturity reflects greater liquidity, it should not have to offer as high a yield as securities with longer terms to maturity.

  Third, the segmented markets theory suggests that there are different needs of investors or borrowers, which cause the demand and supply conditions to vary across different maturities; that is, there is a segmented market for each term to maturity, which causes yields to vary among these maturity markets.

  When consolidating the theories, the term structure of interest rates is dependent on interest rate expectations, investor preferences for liquidity, and unique needs of investors and borrowers in each maturity market.

QUESTIONS

1. Identify the relevant characteristics of any security that can affect the security's yield.
2. What effect does a high default risk have on securities?
3. Discuss the relationship between the yield and liquidity of securities.
4. Do high-tax or low-tax bracket investors benefit more from tax-exempt securities? Why?
5. Do municipal bonds or corporate bonds offer a higher before-tax yield at a given point in time? Why? Which has the higher after-tax yield?
6. If taxes did not exist, would Treasury bonds offer a higher or lower yield than municipal bonds with the same maturity? Why?
7. Explain how a yield curve would shift in response to a sudden expectation of rising interest rates, according to the pure expectations theory.
8. What is the meaning of the forward rate in the context of the term structure of interest rates?

9. Why might forward rates consistently overestimate future interest rates? How could such a bias be avoided?

10. Assume there is a sudden expectation of lower interest rates in the future. What would be the effect on the shape of the yield curve? Explain.

11. Explain the liquidity premium theory.

12. If liquidity and interest rate expectations are both important for explaining the shape of a yield curve, what does a flat yield curve indicate about the market's perception of future interest rates?

13. If a downward-sloping yield curve is mainly attributed to segmented markets theory, what does that suggest about the demand and supply of funds in the short-term and long-term maturity markets?

14. If the segmented markets theory causes an upward-sloping yield curve, what does this imply?

15. If markets are not completely segmented, should we dismiss the segmented markets theory as even a partial explanation for the term structure of interest rates? Explain.

16. Explain the preferred habitat theory.

17. What factors influence the shape of the yield curve?

18. Describe how financial market participants use the yield curve.

19. Would yields be higher for callable bonds or noncallable bonds that are similar in all other respects? Why?

20. How could the Treasury's decision to finance its deficit with mostly long-term funds affect the term structure of interest rates? If short-term and long-term markets are segmented, would the Treasury's decision have a more or less pronounced impact on the term structure? Explain.

21. The lifting of the Iron Curtain in November 1989 was anticipated to result in an increase in the number of new businesses. Long-term funds were needed to support such a trend. How would this event affect the slope of the yield curve?

22. Assume that the yield curves in the United States, France, and Japan were flat. If the U.S. yield curve were to suddenly become positively sloped, do you think the yield curves in France and Japan would be affected? If so, how?

23. Assume the yield curve exhibited a slight downward slope. An event then occurred that caused the short-term yields offered on new securities to increase and long-term yields offered on new securities to decrease. Assume that the shift in the yield curve was due to changes in interest rate expectations.
    a. Did the event cause higher or lower forecasted future interest rates than the forecasted future rates implied by the yield curve prior to the event?
    b. Based on the shift in the yield curve, did investors increase or reduce their demand for short-term securities?
    c. Based on the shift in the yield curve, did investors increase or reduce their demand for long-term securities?

PROBLEMS

1. **a.** Assume that as of today, the annualized two-year interest rate is 13 percent, while the one-year interest rate is 12 percent. Use only this information to estimate the one-year forward rate.

   b. Assume that the liquidity premium on a two-year security is 0.3 percent. Use this information to reestimate the one-year forward rate.

2. Assume that as of today, the annualized interest rate on a three-year security is 10 percent, while the annualized interest rate on a two-year security is 7 percent. Use only this information to estimate the one-year forward rate two years from now.

3. If $_t i_1 > {}_t i_2$, what is the market consensus forecast about the one-year forward rate one year from now? Is this rate above or below today's one-year interest rate? Explain.

Gimmick of Refinancing U.S. Debt

Bruce Bartlett

The economic types around President Clinton are proposing an amazing "free lunch": It is possible, they argue, to reduce the budget deficit and stimulate the economy at the same time simply by changing the way the Treasury Department finances the national debt. The proposal—that the government cut back on long-term borrowings and move into shorter-term securities—was endorsed by President Clinton during the campaign. More recently, Laura Tyson, the newly appointed chairman of the Council of Economic Advisers, has backed it, as has the Democratic Study Group (DSG) in Congress, which just issued a paper on the subject.

At present, the Treasury funds the national debt through a mix of securities: bills with very short maturities (less than one year), notes with medium maturities (two to 10 years) and bonds with long maturities (10 to 30 years). As of Sept. 30, 1992, 34.2% of the privately held public debt outstanding matures in less than one year, 36.6% matures in one to five years, 12.5% matures in five to 10 years, and 16.6% matures in 10 years or more.

The DSG proposal criticizes current Treasury practice on the ground that interest rates on long-term securities are very high compared with those on short-term securities. The yield is about 3% on three-month Treasury bills, for example, but close to 7.25% on 30-year Treasury bonds. Consequently, it is argued, the federal government could save billions of dollars by financing its debt through short-term securities rather than long-term bonds. The DSG report estimates that if interest rates remain unchanged from current levels, the government would achieve a saving of $27.8 billion over two years by selling only three-month bills and no notes or bonds.

Disruptive to Financial Markets

There may well be some merit in shifting a portion of Treasury borrowing toward shorter-term securities—the Bush Treasury in fact made a move in that direction. But any effort to do all—or nearly all—of Treasury borrowing through three-month bills would be highly disruptive to financial markets and probably cost the government more in the long run.

For one thing, short-term rates would rise for supply-and-demand reasons: When the government floods the market with shorter-term instruments, it has to offer the buyer a more attractive product. Higher rates would in turn reduce the government's savings. This shift to shorter-term borrowing would also create hardship for insurance companies, pension funds and other entities that need Treasury securities of various maturities to match their assets and liabilities. For them there is no adequate private-sector alternative.

Most important, though, interest rates cannot be assumed to remain at today's relatively low level. In 1981, yields on the Treasury's 30-year bond rose to more than 14%. Just a few years earlier they had been in the 7% range, as they are today.

Had the Treasury funded all its debt at the short end in the 1970s, it would have paid a horrendous price when the general level of interest rates rose sharply in the early 1980s. Largely because a large portion of the debt was funded through longer-term securities, the burden of interest payments was held down.

The assumptions behind such proposals have additional problems. It is risky to assume, as the DSG report does, that the "normal" yield curve slopes upward (i.e., higher rates on longer-term securities). As Sidney Homer notes in his "History of Interest Rates," throughout the entire 19th century and up until 1930, the "normal" yield curve sloped downward, with higher rates on short-term securities and lower rates on long-term. And this situation is not unprecedented in recent years as well. Ask Germany, which currently has an inverted yield curve.

In short, today's 7.25% 30-year bond may appear to be a bargain in a few years if interest rates rise once again. Certainly the homeowners who are refinancing 30-year mortgages believe this to be the case. Despite the fact that interest rates on adjustable-rate mortgages (ARMs) are several percentage points lower than on fixed-rate mortgages, most people still prefer the latter. The reason is simple: Although they pay more in the short-run, most people believe that the risk is largely on the upside. Thus they prefer to lock in today's interest rates even when cheaper ARMs are available.

Continued

CASE APPLICATION: FINANCING DECISIONS BASED ON THE YIELD CURVE

Continued

The same is true of the federal government. Although a higher short-term cost may be paid for financing across all maturities, the Treasury has consistently maintained that in the long run this lowers the overall cost of financing the debt. Were it just an issue of saving interest on the public debt, nothing more would have to be said. However, the authors of the DSG paper—and other refinancing advocates—go on to argue that shifting Treasury financing toward shorter-term securities would lower long-term interest rates throughout the economy. They argue that even if short-term rates increased, the policy would be stimulative because long-term rates are said to be more important for investment.

The DSG cites the results of a study by Benjamin Friedman of Harvard indicating that such a shift in Treasury borrowing would lower long-term interest rates and increase real gross domestic product and real investment spending. However, in the study, long-term Treasury rates fall less than short-term Treasury rates rise, and private-sector interest rates on corporate bonds fall much less than rates on Treasury securities. Lowering the rate on Treasury securities doesn't necessarily mean other rates will fall as well.

In Prof. Friedman's simulation, which is based largely on data from the 1970s, all other things are equal, especially monetary policy. The study also assumes that interest rates are set almost entirely by supply and demand, whereas most economists believe that inflationary expectations are the key element in the determination of long-term rates. In fact, what the yield curve really measures is inflationary expectations.

Prof. Friedman's analysis is at odds with the experience of the 1960s. Back then, some readers may recall, the Federal Reserve pursued a policy of "twisting" the yield curve.

Operation Twist came about during the Kennedy administration, when the administration pressured the Fed to abandon its policy of conducting monetary policy through the purchase and sale of Treasury bills only. The administration's goal was to raise short-term interest rates, in order to maintain the exchange value of the dollar, and simultaneously to lower long-term rates, in order to stimulate domestic investment. This was to be accomplished by having the Fed buy fewer short-term securities and more long-term securities, with the goal of twisting or flattening the yield curve—exactly what the refinancers propose today.

To be sure, Operation Twist was never carried out with any vigor by the Fed. Indeed, the Fed's holding of long-term Treasury securities increased only very modestly in the early 1960s. The Treasury for its part failed to cooperate, continuing to issue large amounts of long-term securities and negating the Fed's actions.

Nevertheless, there were a number of studies of Operation Twist, all of which concluded that the policy had no effect on the rate structure whatsoever. Many of the criticisms are relevant to the DSG proposal.

If arbitragers know what the government is trying to accomplish, they can easily frustrate it by doing the reverse: borrowing long (selling bonds) and lending short (buying bills).

Decline in Growth

Because inventories and consumer durables are commonly financed with short-term borrowing, any rise in short-term interest rates, even if offset by a decline in long-term rates, will tend to cause consumers to defer major purchases and firms to cut back on inventory investment. This will cause growth to decline at least in the short-term.

Other work shows that any attempts to manipulate the yield curve are fruitless for another reason: Long- and short-term interest rates tend to rise and fall together over time (see chart). The same forces that largely determine the level of interest rates—the rate of return on capital, the supply of private saving, the overall level of government borrowing, etc.—affect all parts of the maturity spectrum.

Any new Operation Twist would require concerted action by both the Treasury and the Fed to achieve success. However, given the independence of the Fed, such cooperation is difficult to ensure. It is a pipe dream to think that we can costlessly stimulate the economy and lower the government's interest cost simultaneously simply by altering the Treasury's financing methods. If such a policy is to be pursued, it should be pursued modestly.

SOURCE: The Wall Street Journal (January 29, 1993): p. A14. Reprinted by permission of *The Wall Street Journal* © 1993 Dow Jones & Company, Inc. All rights reserved worldwide.

QUESTIONS

1. Would the refinancing of U.S. debt maturities be more seriously considered when the yield curve is flat or when it has a steep upward slope? Why?

2. If the Treasury focuses more on short-term financing when an upward sloping yield curve exists, what conditions could cause this strategy to backfire?

3. The Fed's "Operation Twist" strategy did not twist the yield curve. What forces might prevent the Fed from converting an upward sloping yield curve into a downward sloping yield curve within a given period?

4. If maturity markets were segmented, do you believe "Operation Twist" would have been more succesful? Explain.

PROJECTS

1. **Explaining Today's Yield Differentials**
   a. Using the most recent issue of *The Wall Street Journal*, review the section called "Money Rates" (listed on the index in the front page). Determine the following interest rates:

Federal funds rate	= _____
Commercial paper rate (with shortest maturity)	= _____
Certificates of deposit (one-month maturity)	= _____
Banker's acceptances (30-day maturity)	= _____
London Interbank Offered Rates (LIBOR) (one-month maturity)	= _____
Treasury bills (13-week maturity)	= _____

   b. Rank the securities from highest interest rate to lowest and provide a brief explanation for the differences in yields among these securities.
   c. Using the most recent issue of *The Wall Street Journal*, review the "Yield Comparison Table" (sometimes listed in the section entitled "Credit Markets"). Use the table to report the following yields:

Type	Maturity	Yield
Treasury	10-year	_____
Corporate: High-quality	10-year	_____
Corporate: Medium-quality	10-year	_____

   If default risk is the only reason for the yield differentials, what is the default risk premium on the corporate high-quality bonds? On the medium-quality bonds?

   During the 1982 recession, high-quality corporate bonds offered a yield of 0.79 percent above Treasury bonds, and medium-quality bonds offered a yield of about 3.11 percent above Treasury bonds. How do these yield differentials compare to the differentials today? Explain the reason for the change in yield differentials.

   d. Using the same table from *The Wall Street Journal*, determine the yield on tax-exempt bonds with a 10-year maturity.

Complete the following table:

Marginal Tax Bracket of Investors	Before-tax yield that would be necessary to achieve existing after-tax yield of tax-exempt bonds.	If the tax-exempt bonds have the same risk and other features as high-quality corporate bonds, which type of bond is preferable for investors in each tax bracket?
10%		
15%		
20%		
28%		
34%		

2. **Examining Recent Adjustments in Default Risk**

   Using the most recent issue of *The Wall Street Journal*, review the section called "Credit Ratings." Report any changes in credit ratings, and for each change explain the following:

   a. What was the reason given for the change in credit ratings? How does this reason relate to default risk?

   b. How will the change in ratings influence the market price of these securities?

   c. How will the change in ratings influence the yield to be earned by investors who previously invested in these securities and are about to sell them?

   d. How will the change in ratings influence the expected yield to be earned by investors who now invest in these securities?

3. **Determining and Interpreting Today's Term Structure**

   a. Using the most recent issue of *The Wall Street Journal*, review the table called "Treasury Bonds, Notes & Bills" (listed in the index on the front page as "Treasury Issues"). Use the table to determine the yields for the various maturities:

Term to Maturity	Annualized Yield
1 year	
2 years	
3 years	

   Assuming that the differences in these yields are solely because of interest rate expectations, determine the one-year forward rate as of one year from now and the one-year forward rate as of two years from now.

    b. Within *The Wall Street Journal*, a "Treasury Yield Curve" is provided. Use this curve to describe the market's expectations about future interest rates. If a liquidity premium exists, how would this affect your perception of the market's expectations?

REFERENCES

Abken, Peter A. "Inflation and the Yield Curve." *Economic Review*, Federal Reserve Bank of Kansas City (May/June 1993): 13–31.
    . "Innovations in Modeling the Term Structure of Interest Rates." *Economic Review*, Federal Reserve Bank of Atlanta (July/August 1990): 2–27.

Cornell, Bradford. "Measuring the Term Premium: An Empirical Note." *Journal of Economics and Business* (February 1990): 89–92.

Elliot, J. W., and M. E. Echols. "Market Segmentation, Speculative Behavior, and the Term Structure of Interest Rates." *Review of Economics and Statistics* (February 1976): 40–49.

Fama, Eugene F. "The Information in the Term Structure." *Journal of Financial Economics* (December 1984): 509–528.
    . "Term, Structure Forecasts of Interest Rates, Inflation, and Real Returns." *Journal of Monetary Economics* (January 1990): 59–76.

Froot, Kenneth A. "New Hope for the Expectations Hypothesis of the Term Structure of Interest Rates." *The Journal of Finance* (June 1989): 283–305.

Garner, C. Alan. "The Yield Curve and Inflation Expectations." *Economic Review*, Federal Reserve Bank of Kansas City (September–October 1987): 3–14.

Goh, Jeremy C., and Louis H. Ederington. "Is a Bond Rating Downgrade Bad News, Good News or No News for Stockholders?" *Journal of Finance* (December 1993): 2001–2008.

Heuson, Andrea J. "The Term Premia Relationship Implicit in the Term Structure of Treasury Bills." *The Journal of Financial Research* (Spring 1988): 13–20.

Hilliard, Jimmy E., and Susan D. Jordan. "Hedging Interest Rate Risk Under Term Structure Effects: An Application to Financial Institutions." *Journal of Financial Research* (Winter 1992): 355–368.

Kessel, Reuben A. *The Cyclical Behavior of Term Structure of Interest Rates*. Occasional Paper 91. New York: National Bureau of Economic Research.

Meiselman, David. *The Term Structure of Interest Rates*. Englewood Cliffs, NJ: Prentice-Hall, 1962.

Mishkin, Frederic S. "What Does the Term Structure Tell Us About Future Inflation?" *Journal of Monetary Economics* (January 1990): 77–96.

Mougoue, Mbodja. "The Term Structure of Interest Rates as a Cointegrated System: Empirical Evidence from the Eurocurrency Market." *Journal of Financial Research* (Fall 1992): 285–296.

Russell, Steven. "Understanding the Term Structure of Interest Rates: The Expectations Theory." *Review*, Federal Reserve Bank of St. Louis (July/August 1992): 36–50.

INTEREST RATE FORECASTS AND INVESTMENT DECISIONS _____

This problem requires an understanding of how economic conditions affect interest rates and bond prices (Chapters 2, 3, and 4).

Your task is to use information about existing economic conditions to determine whether to increase or decrease the average maturity on your bond portfolio. Your bond portfolio consists of 80 percent U.S. bonds and 20 percent French bonds. Because you maintain a portfolio of Treasury bonds only, you focus on interest rate risk rather than credit risk. You will rely on your own economic forecasts—not those of the rest of the world—to make your decisions. Your main concern is the performance of your bond portfolio over the next year. The following information is available to you:

1. Over the past six months, U.S. interest rates have declined while French interest rates have increased.
2. The U.S. economy has weakened over the past year, while the French economy has improved.
3. The U.S. savings rate (proportion of income saved) is expected to decrease slightly over the next year, while the French savings rate will remain stable.
4. You believe the central banks in the United States and in France are not expected to implement any policy that would have a significant impact on interest rates.
5. You expect the U.S. economy to strengthen considerably over the next year but still be weaker than it was two years ago. You expect the French economy to remain stable.
6. You expect the U.S. annual budget deficit to increase slightly from last year but be significantly less than the average annual budget deficit over the past five years. You expect the French budget deficit to be about the same as last year.
7. You expect the U.S. inflation rate to rise slightly, although it is still not expected to reach the relatively high levels of two years ago. You expect the French inflation rate to decline.
8. Based on some events last week, the dollar is expected by most economists and investors around the world (including yourself) to weaken against the French franc and other foreign currencies over the next year. This expectation was already accounted for in your forecasts of inflation and economic growth.

9. The yield curve in the United States presently exhibits a consistent downward slope. The yield curve in France presently exhibits an upward slope. You believe that the liquidity premium on securities is quite small.

QUESTIONS

a. Using the information available to you, recommend whether the average time to maturity on your U.S. bond portfolio should be increased, reduced, or kept as is. Defend your recommendation.

b. Using the information available to you, recommend whether the average time to maturity on your French bond portfolio should be increased, reduced, or kept as is. Defend your recommendation.

PART 2

THE FED AND MONETARY POLICY

The chapters in Part Two explain how the Federal Reserve System (the Fed) affects economic conditions. Because the policies implemented by the Fed can influence securities prices, they are closely monitored by financial market participants. The Fed's policies are assessed by market participants to value securities and make investment decisions.

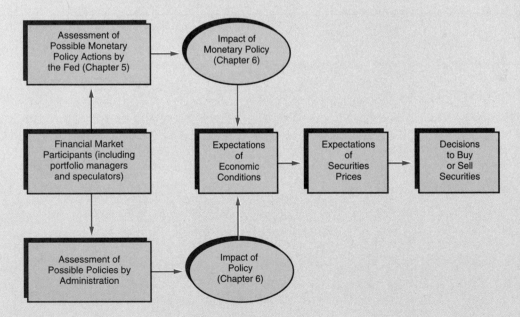

CHAPTER 5

FUNCTIONS OF THE FED

The Federal Reserve System (the Fed), as the central bank of the United States, has the responsibility of conducting national monetary policy. Such policy influences interest rates and other economic variables that determine the prices of securities. Participants in the financial markets therefore closely monitor the Fed's monetary policy. It is important that they understand how the Fed's actions may influence security prices, so that they can manage their security portfolios in response to the Fed's policies.

The specific objectives of this chapter are to:

- identify the key components of the Fed that dictate monetary policy,
- describe the tools used by the Fed to influence monetary policy, and
- explain how bank regulation in the early 1980s affected monetary policy.

ORGANIZATION OF THE FED

In 1791 the First Bank of the United States was created to oversee the commercial banking system and attempt to maintain a stable economy. Because its 20-year charter was not renewed by Congress, First Bank was terminated in 1811. A major criticism of this central bank was that is interfered with the development of the banking system and economic growth. Its termination, however, reduced public confidence in the banking system. In 1816 the Second Bank of the United States was established, and because its 20-year charter also was not renewed by Congress, it was terminated in 1836.

During the late 1800s and early 1900s, several banking panics occurred, culminating with a major crisis in 1907. This motivated another attempt to establish a central bank. Accordingly, in 1913 the Federal Reserve Act was passed, establishing reserve requirements for those commercial banks that desired to become members. It also specified 12 districts across the United States as well as a city in each district where a Federal Reserve district bank was to be established. Each district bank had the ability to buy and sell government securities, which could affect the money supply (as will be explained later in this chapter). Each district bank focused on its particular district, without much concern for other districts. Over time, a more centralized system was organized, where money supply decisions were assigned to a particular group of individuals rather than across 12 district banks.

The Fed earns most of its income in the form of interest on its holdings of U.S. government securities (to be discussed shortly). It also earns some income from providing services to financial institutions. Most of its income is transferred to the Treasury.

The Fed as it exists today has five major components:

- Federal Reserve district banks
- Member banks
- Board of Governors
- Federal Open Market Committee (FOMC)
- Advisory committees

Federal Reserve District Banks

The 12 Federal Reserve districts are identified in Exhibit 5.1, along with the city where each district bank is located and the district branches. The New York district bank is considered the most important because many large banks are located in this district. Commercial banks that become members of the Fed are required to purchase stock in their **Federal Reserve district bank.** This stock, which is not traded in a secondary market, pays a maximum dividend of 6 percent annually.

Each Fed district bank has nine directors. Six of them are elected by member banks in that district. Of these six directors, three are professional bankers and three are businesspeople. Besides these six directors, three other directors are appointed by the Board of Governors (to be discussed shortly). The nine directors appoint the president of their Fed district bank.

Fed district banks facilitate operations within the banking system by clearing checks, replacing old currency, and providing loans (through the discount window) to depository institutions in need of funds. They also collect economic data and conduct research projects on commercial banking and economic trends.

Member Banks

Commercial banks can elect to become member banks if they meet specific requirements of the Board of Governors. All national banks (chartered by the Comptroller of the Currency) are required to be members of the Fed, while other banks (chartered by their respective states) are not. Member banks currently represent about 35 percent of all banks, and about 70 percent of all bank deposits are in these member banks.

EXHIBIT 5.1   Locations of Federal Reserve District Banks and Branches

SOURCE: *Federal Reserve Bulletin.*

Board of Governors

The **Board of Governors** (sometimes called the Federal Reserve Board) is made up of seven individual members with offices in Washington, D.C. Each member is appointed by the president of the United States (and confirmed by the Senate) and serves a nonrenewable 14-year term. Such a long term is thought to reduce political pressure on these members and thus encourage the development of policies that will benefit the U.S. economy over the long run. Each member's starting terms have been staggered so that one term expires in every even-numbered year.

One of the seven board members is selected by the president to be Federal Reserve chairman for a four-year term, which may be renewed. The chairman has no more voting power than any other member, but may have more influence. As an example, Paul Volcker, who served as chairman from 1979 to 1987, was very persuasive.

The board has two main roles: (1) regulating commercial banks and (2) controlling monetary policy. It supervises and regulates commercial banks that are members of the Fed and bank holding companies. It oversees the operation of the 12 Federal Reserve districts banks in their provision of services to depository institutions and their supervision of specific commercial banks. It also establishes regulations in consumer finance. It was previously responsible for determining ceiling interest rates on bank deposits; those ceilings were completely phased out by 1986 as a result of the Depository Institutions Deregulation and Monetary Control Act of 1980. The Board continues to participate in the supervision of member banks and in setting credit controls, such as margin requirements (percentage of a purchase of securities that must be paid with nonborrowed funds).

With regard to monetary policy, the Board has direct control in two monetary policy tools and participates in the control of a third tool. First, it has the power to revise reserve requirements imposed on depository institutions. Second, it authorizes changes in the **discount rate,** or the interest rate charged on Fed district bank loans to depository institutions. Any changes in the discount rate or reserve requirements can affect the money supply level, as explained later in the chapter. The Board can also control money supply by participating in the decisions of the Federal Open Market Committee, discussed next.

Federal Open Market Committee (FOMC)

The **Federal Open Market Committee (FOMC)** is made up of the seven members in the Board of Governors plus presidents of five Fed district banks (the New York district bank plus four of the other eleven Fed district banks as determined on a rotating basis). Presidents of the seven remaining Fed district banks typically participate in the FOMC meetings but are not allowed to vote on policy decisions. The chairman of the Board of Governors serves as chairman of the FOMC.

The main goals of the FOMC are to promote high employment, economic growth, and price stability. Achievement of these goals would stabilize financial markets, interest rates, foreign exchange values, and so on. Because the FOMC may not be able to achieve all of its main goals simultaneously, it may concentrate on resolving a particular economic problem.

The FOMC attempts to achieve its goals through control of the money supply. It meets about every six weeks to review economic conditions and determine appropriate monetary policy to improve economic conditions and prevent potential adverse conditions from erupting. Its decision will be forwarded to what is called the **Trading Desk** (or the **Open Market Desk)** at the New York Fed district bank. It is here that open market operations, or the Fed's trading of government securities, are carried out. The specific manner by which this trading affects money supply is discussed later in the chapter.

Advisory Committees

The Federal Advisory Council consists of one member from each Federal Reserve district. Each district's member is elected each year by the board of directors of the respective district bank. The council meets in Washington, D.C., at least four times a year and makes recommendations to the Fed about economic and banking-related issues.

The Consumer Advisory Council is made up of 30 members, representing the financial institutions industry and its consumers. This committee normally meets with the board four times a year to discuss consumer-related issues.

The Thrift Institutions Advisory Council is made up of representatives of savings banks, savings and loan associations, and credit unions. Its purpose is to offer views on issues specifically related to these types of institutions.

Integration of Federal Reserve Components

Exhibit 5.2 shows the relationships between the various components of the Federal Reserve System. The advisory committee advises the board, while the board oversees operations of the district banks. The board and representatives of the district banks make up the FOMC.

MONETARY POLICY TOOLS

Changes in money supply can have a major impact on economic conditions. Financial market participants closely monitor the Fed's actions so that they can anticipate how the money supply will be affected. This information is then used to forecast economic conditions and securities prices. The relationship between the money supply and economic conditions is discussed in detail in the following chapter. First, it is important to realize *how* the Fed controls the money supply.

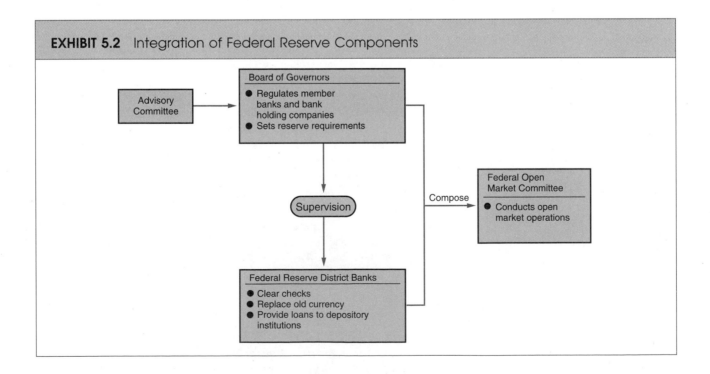

EXHIBIT 5.2 Integration of Federal Reserve Components

The Fed can use three monetary policy tools to either increase or decrease the money supply:

- Open market operations
- Adjusting the discount rate
- Adjusting the reserve requirement ratio

Open Market Operations

Members of the FOMC meet eight times a year. At each meeting, the target money supply growth level is determined. This level is influenced by existing economic conditions. The FOMC's decision on the target money supply level is forwarded to the Trading Desk (at the New York Federal Reserve district bank) through a statement called the **policy directive.** The FOMC objectives are specified in the form of a target range, such as an annualized growth rate of 3 percent to 5 percent in the money supply over the next few months, rather than one specific money supply level. The FOMC may also specify a desired target range for the federal funds rate, even though this rate is not set by the Fed. The manager of the Trading Desk uses the policy directive as a guideline to instruct traders on the amount of government securities to buy or sell.

The Fed's buying and selling of government securities (through the Trading Desk) is referred to as **open market operations,** and represents the most common means by which the Fed controls the money supply. Even though the Trading Desk only receives a policy directive from the FOMC eight times a year, it continuously uses open market operations in response to ongoing changes in bank deposit levels in order to maintain money supply within the specified target range.

FED PURCHASE OF SECURITIES. When traders at the Trading Desk are instructed to purchase a specified dollar amount of securities, they call government securities dealers. The dealers provide a list of securities for sale that gives the denomination and maturity of each as well as the **ask quote** presented by the dealer (the price at which the dealer is willing to sell the security). From this list, the traders attempt to purchase those that are most attractive (lowest prices for whatever maturities are desired) until they have purchased the amount requested by the manager of the Trading Desk. The accounting department of the New York district bank then notifies the government bond department to receive and pay for those securities.

When the Fed purchases securities through the government securities dealers, the commercial banks that handle securities transactions for the dealers will be credited this amount on their reserve accounts maintained at the Fed. Consequently, total reserves of commercial banks will increase by the dollar amount of securities purchased by the Fed. Exhibit 5.3 shows this adjustment for a deal in which the Trading Desk paid $1 billion for securities. The increase of $1 billion in reserves represents demand deposits of $1 billion for government securities dealers.

The Fed's purchase of government securities has a different impact than another institution's purchase, because it results in additional bank reserves and increases the ability of banks to make loans and create new deposits. An increase in reserves can allow for a net increase in deposit balances and therefore an increase in money supply. Conversely, the purchase of government securities by someone other than the Fed results in offsetting reserve positions at commercial banks.

FED SALE OF SECURITIES.   If the Trading Desk is instructed to decrease the money supply, its traders can sell government securities (obtained from previous purchases) to government securities dealers. The securities would be sold to the dealers that submitted the highest bids. As the dealers pay for the securities, the reserve balances that their clearing banks maintain at the Fed would be reduced.

The balance sheet effects of this event are shown in Exhibit 5.4, assuming that the total sale amounted to $1 billion. As the clearing banks of the dealers pay for the government securities, their level of reserves is reduced. In addition, the demand deposit accounts of government securities dealers are reduced.

FED USE OF REPURCHASE AGREEMENTS.   If the Fed desires to just temporarily increase the aggregate level of bank reserves, the Trading Desk may use **repurchase agreements.** It would purchase Treasury securities from government securities dealers with an agreement to sell back the securities at a specified date in the near future. Initially, the reserve level would rise as the securities were sold; it would then be reduced when the dealers repurchased the securities. Repurchase agreements are used by the Trading Desk during holidays and other such periods to correct temporary imbalances in the level of bank reserves. To correct a temporary excess of reserves, it sells some of its Treasury securities holdings to securities dealers and agrees to repurchase them at a specified future date.

HOW OPEN MARKET OPERATIONS AFFECT INTEREST RATES.   Even though most interest rates are market-determined, the Fed can have a strong influence on these rates by controlling the supply of loanable funds. When the Fed uses open market operations to increase bank reserves, banks have more funds that can be loaned out. This can influence various market-determined interest rates. First,

---

EXHIBIT 5.3   Impact of a Fed Purchase of Government Securities

FEDERAL RESERVE BANK OF NEW YORK

Assets	Liabilities
+ $1 billion in Treasury securities	+ $1 billion in reserve accounts of the security dealers' clearing bank

THE DEALERS' CLEARING BANKS

Assets	Liabilities
+ $1 billion in reserve accounts at the Fed	+ $1 billion in demand deposits of dealers

---

EXHIBIT 5.4 Impact of a Fed Sale of Government Securities

FEDERAL RESERVE BANK OF NEW YORK

Assets	Liabilities
− $1 billion in Treasury securities	− $1 billion in reserve accounts of the security dealers' clearing bank

THE DEALERS' CLEARING BANKS

Assets	Liabilities
− $1 billion in reserve accounts at the Fed	− $1 billion in demand deposits of dealers

---

the federal funds rate (interest rate on loans between banks) may decline as some banks have a larger supply of excess reserves to lend out in the federal funds market. Second, banks with excess reserves may offer new loans at a lower interest rate in order to make use of these funds. Third, these banks may also lower interest rates offered on deposits because they have more than adequate funds to conduct existing operations.

As bank deposit rates decline, households with available funds may search for alternative investments such as Treasury securities or other debt securities. As more funds are invested in these securities, the yields will decline. Thus, open market operations used to increase bank reserves not only influence bank deposit and loan rates, but the yields on other debt securities as well. The reduction in yields on debt securities implies a lower cost of borrowing for the issuers of new debt securities. This can encourage potential borrowers (including corporations and individuals) to borrow and make expenditures that they might not have made if interest rates were higher.

If open market operations were used to reduce bank reserves, the opposite effects would be anticipated. More banks would have deficient reserves, and fewer banks would have any excess reserves. Thus, there would be upward pressure on the federal funds rate, on the loan rates charged to individuals or firms, and on the rates offered to bank depositors. As bank deposit rates rise, some investors may be encouraged to create bank deposits rather than invest in other debt securities. This activity would cause a reduction in the amount of funds available for these debt instruments, thereby increasing the yield offered on the instruments. More specific details about how money supply adjustments can affect interest rates and economic conditions are provided in the following chapter.

DYNAMIC VERSUS DEFENSIVE OPEN MARKET OPERATIONS. The intent of open market operations can be classified as either **dynamic** or **defensive.** Dynamic operations are implemented to increase or decrease the level of reserves; defensive operations offset the impact of other conditions that affect the level of reserves. For example, if the Fed expects a large inflow of cash into commercial banks, it could offset this inflow by selling some of its Treasury security holdings.

Adjusting the Discount Rate

The discount window of the Fed offers depository institutions three types of credit. Adjustment credit is offered for short-term liquidity problems, seasonal credit for a seasonal liquidity squeeze, and extended credit for severe liquidity problems that will not be resolved in the near future. Any type of credit extended by the Fed represents an increase in reserves at depository institutions, as shown in Exhibit 5.5. If, on the other hand, depository institutions borrow from one another, there is simply a transfer of funds among institutions, and the total level of reserves is not increased.

To increase money supply, the Fed (specifically the Board of Governors) could authorize a reduction in the discount rate. This would encourage depository institutions that are short on funds to borrow from the Fed rather than from other sources such as the federal funds market. To decrease money supply, it could attempt to discourage use of the discount window by increasing the discount rate. Depository institutions in need of short-term funds would likely obtain funding from alternative sources. As existing discount window loans were repaid to the Fed while new loans were obtained from sources other than the discount window, there would be a decrease in the level of reserves.

Because the federal funds rate is market-determined, it tends to move in line with other market-determined interest rates and changes on a continuous basis. The discount rate remains constant until it is adjusted by the Fed. In the early 1990s, the Fed reduced the discount rate six times. The Fed may reduce the discount rate to keep it in line with other interest rates or as an attempt to reduce other interest rates.

Adjusting the Reserve Requirement Ratio

Depository institutions are subject to a **reserve requirement ratio,** which is the proportion of their deposit accounts that must be held as reserves. This ratio is set by the Board of Governors. Depository institutions have historically been forced to maintain between 8 and 12 percent of their transactions accounts (such

---

EXHIBIT 5.5 Effect of Increased Use of Discount Window

FEDERAL RESERVE BANK

Assets	Liabilities
Increase in loans provided	Increase in the reserve accounts at depository institutions

DEPOSITORY INSTITUTIONS

Assets	Liabilities
Increase in reserves maintained at the Fed	Increase in loan payables due

REACTION OF THE FED TO THE STOCK MARKET CRASH IN 1987

On October 19, 1987, the Dow Jones Industrial Index declined by more than 500 points, the largest decline in history. The Federal Reserve System took action to prevent further adverse effects. On the morning after the crash, the Fed issued a statement that it was prepared to provide liquidity to the financial markets. It became actively involved in open market operations to ensure adequate liquidity. Because it was concerned that economic growth would be adversely affected by the crash, the Fed loosened money supply.

The Fed also monitored bank deposit balances to ensure that the crash did not cause runs on bank deposits. It monitored credit relationships between commercial banks and securities firms because such relationships can change abruptly during a financial crisis. In general, the financial fears that caused the crash did not escalate, and financial markets stabilized shortly after the crash. The calming of the markets may have been partially because of the Fed's efforts to ensure adequate liquidity and restore confidence in the financial system.

as checking accounts) and a smaller proportion of their other savings accounts as required reserves, which cannot be used to earn interest.

Because the reserve requirement ratio affects the degree to which money supply can change, it is sometimes modified by the Board of Governors to adjust the money supply. When the Board of Governors reduces the reserve requirement ratio, it increases the proportion of a bank's deposits that can be lent out by depository institutions. As the funds loaned out are spent, a portion of them will return to the depository institutions in the form of new deposits. The lower the reserve requirement ratio, the greater the lending capacity of depository institutions, so any initial change in bank reserves can cause a larger change in money supply.

During the 1980s, the reserve requirement ratio on some types of time deposits was removed by the Board of Governors. In December 1990, the reserve requirement ratio on negotiable certificates of deposit was removed. In 1992, the reserve requirement ratio on transactions accounts was reduced from 12 percent to 10 percent.

HOW RESERVE REQUIREMENT ADJUSTMENTS AFFECT MONEY GROWTH. To illustrate how adjustments in the reserve requirement ratio can affect money supply growth, a simplified example follows. Assume the following information:

Assumption 1. Banks obtain all their funds from demand deposits and use all funds except required reserves to make loans.

Assumption 2. The public does not store any cash; any funds withdrawn from banks are spent, and any funds received are deposited in banks.

Assumption 3. The reserve requirement ratio on demand deposits is 10 percent.

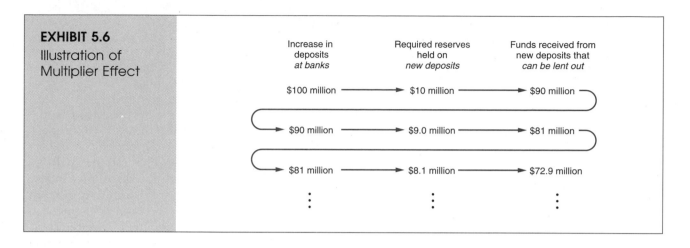

EXHIBIT 5.6
Illustration of
Multiplier Effect

Increase in deposits *at banks*	Required reserves held on *new deposits*	Funds received from new deposits that *can be lent out*
$100 million	$10 million	$90 million
$90 million	$9.0 million	$81 million
$81 million	$8.1 million	$72.9 million

Based on these assumptions, 10 percent of all bank deposits are maintained as required reserves, and the other 90 percent are loaned out (zero excess reserves). Now assume that the Fed initially uses open market operations by purchasing $100 million worth of Treasury securities.

As the Treasury securities dealers sell securities to the Fed, their deposit balances at commercial banks increase by $100 million. Banks maintain 10 percent of the $100 million, or $10 million, as required reserves and lend out the rest. As the $90 million lent out is spent, it returns to banks as new demand deposit accounts (by whoever receives the funds that were spent). Banks maintain 10 percent, or $9 million, of these new deposits as required reserves and lend out the remainder ($81 million). Because of this cycle, the initial increase in demand deposits (money) multiplies into a much larger amount. Exhibit 5.6 summarizes this cycle. This cycle will not continue forever. Every time the funds lent out return to a bank, a portion (10 percent) is retained as required reserves. Thus, the amount of new deposits created is less for each round. Under the previous assumptions, the initial money supply injection of $100 million would multiply by 1/(reserve requirement ratio), or 1/.10, to equal 10, so that the total change in money supply once the cycle is complete is $100 million × 10 = $1 billion.

The simplified example demonstrates that an initial injection of funds will multiply into a larger amount. The reserve requirement controls the amount of loanable funds that can be created from new deposits. A higher reserve requirement ratio causes an initial injection of funds to multiply by a smaller amount. Conversely, a lower reserve requirement ratio causes it to multiply by a greater amount. In this way, the Fed can adjust money supply growth by adjusting the reserve requirement ratio.

Our example exaggerates the amount by which money multiplies. Consumers sometimes hold cash, and banks sometimes hold excess reserves, contradicting the assumptions of banks holding only demand deposits and zero excess reserves. Consequently, major leakages occur, and money does not multiply to the extent shown in the example. The money multiplier can change over time because of changes in the excess reserve level and in consumer preferences of demand deposits versus time deposits (which are not included in the most narrow definition of money). This complicates the task of forecasting how an initial adjustment in bank reserves will ultimately affect the money supply level.

Comparison of Monetary Policy Tools

Exhibit 5.7 compares the ways that monetary policy tools increase or decrease money supply growth. The Fed does not need to simultaneously use all three tools. In fact, it typically chooses to use open market operations, although it does have the option of using the other tools if necessary.

The frequent use of open market operations as a monetary policy tool is due mainly to its convenience and the disadvantages of using the alternative tools. An adjustment in the discount rate will affect the money supply only if depository institutions respond (borrow more or less from the Fed than normal) because of the adjustment. In addition, borrowings through the discount window are for a very short term, so that any adjustment in reserves resulting from an increase or decrease in loans from the Fed is only temporary. An adjustment in the reserve requirement ratio can cause erratic shifts in money supply. Thus, there is a higher probability of missing the target money supply level when using the reserve requirement ratio.

Open market operations do not suffer from these limitations. In addition, open market operations can be used without signaling the Fed's intentions and can easily be reversed without the public's knowing. A reverse adjustment in the reserve requirement ratio or the discount rate, however, could cause more concern by the public and reduce the Fed's credibility.

Because the rate by which injected funds will multiply is uncertain (even when leaving the reserve requirement ratio unchanged), open market operations are not guaranteed to accomplish the money growth target. Even so, they can be continuously used over time to manipulate the money supply toward the desired money supply target.

EXHIBIT 5.7   Comparison of Monetary Policy Tools

MONETARY POLICY TOOL	TO INCREASE MONEY SUPPLY GROWTH	TO DECREASE MONEY SUPPLY GROWTH
Open market operations	Fed should (through the Trading Desk) purchase government securities in the secondary market.	Fed should (through the Trading Desk) sell government securities in the secondary market.
Adjusting the discount rate	Fed should lower the discount rate to encourage borrowing through the discount window.	Fed should raise the discount rate to discourage borrowing through the discount window.
Adjusting reserve requirements	Fed should lower the reserve requirement ratio to cause money to multiply at a higher rate.	Fed should raise the reserve requirement ratio to cause money to multiply at a lower rate.

IMPACT OF TECHNICAL FACTORS ON RESERVES

Even if the Fed does not intervene, the volume of reserves can change as a result of so-called technical factors, such as currency in circulation and Federal Reserve float. When the amount of currency in circulation increases (such as during the holiday season), the corresponding increase in net deposit withdrawals reduces reserves. When it decreases, the net addition to deposits increases reserves. Federal Reserve float is the amount of checks credited to banks' reserves that have not yet been collected. A rise in float causes an increase in bank reserves, and a decrease in float causes a reduction in bank reserves.

A staff at the Federal Reserve Bank of New York along with a staff at the Board of Governors in Washington, D.C., provides daily forecasts of how technical factors such as these will affect the level of reserves. Because these factors affect the reserve level, the Fed must account for such influences when implementing monetary policy. The manager of the Trading Desk incorporates the expected impact of technical factors on reserves into the instructions to traders. If the policy directive calls for growth in reserves but technical factors are expected to increase reserves, the instructions would reflect a smaller injection of reserves than if the technical factors were ignored. Conversely, if technical factors are expected to reduce reserves, the instructions would reflect a larger injection of reserves to offset the impact of technical factors.

FED CONTROL OF MONEY SUPPLY

When the Fed manipulates money supply to influence economic variables, it must decide what form of money to manipulate. The optimal form of money should (1) be controllable by the Fed and (2) have a predictable impact on economic variables when adjusted by the Fed. The most narrow form of money, known as **M1,** includes currency held by the public and checking deposits (such as demand deposits, NOW accounts, and automatic transfer balances) at depository institutions. Although M1 has received the most attention in recent years, it does not include all funds that can be used for transactions purposes. For example, checks can be written against a **money market deposit account (MMDA)** offered by depository institutions or against a money market mutual fund. In addition, funds can easily be withdrawn from savings accounts to make transactions. For this reason, a broader measure of money, called **M2,** also deserves consideration. It includes everything in M1 as well as savings accounts and small time deposits, MMDAs, and some other items. Another measure of money, called **M3,** includes everything in M2 as well as large time deposits and other items. Although there are even a few other broader measures of money, M1, M2, and M3 receive the most attention. A comparison of M1, M2, and M3 is provided in Exhibit 5.8.

During the deregulation phase (early 1980s) in the depository institutions industry, various new deposit accounts were created, and consumers were switching among accounts. The transfer of funds from demand deposit accounts to MMDAs caused a reduction in M1, even without the Fed's taking any action to reduce it. A transfer of funds from savings into NOW accounts, for example, would cause an increase in M1 simply because of a change in consumer habits rather than monetary policy actions. The M1 measure became quite volatile over

---

EXHIBIT 5.8   Comparison of Money Supply Measures

MONEY SUPPLY MEASURE

M1 = currency + checking deposits

M2 = M1 + savings deposits, MMDAs, overnight repurchase agreements, Eurodollars, noninstitutional money market mutual funds, and small time
deposits

M3 = M2 + institutional money market mutual funds, large time deposits, and
repurchase agreements and Eurodollars lasting more than one day

---

this period and was difficult for the Fed to control. The broader M2 measure
was not as sensitive to the consumer's change of habits, because most deposit
accounts are included under M2. Even though individual components of M2
(such as MMDAs and NOW accounts) were affected by deregulation, the overall
level of M2 was not.

Fed Emphasis on Money Supply

In the 1970s the Fed attempted to simultaneously control the money supply and
interest rates within specified target ranges. It used the federal funds rate as its
representative interest rate to control, which in turn can influence other interest
rates. Simultaneous control of the money supply and federal funds rate is not
always possible. Consider Exhibit 5.9 which shows hypothetical target ranges for
the money supply growth and federal funds rate. Notice that both variables are
near the upper boundary of their respective ranges. If the Fed desires to maintain
the federal funds rate within its range, it would likely inject more funds into the
economy (increase money supply growth). However, this will force the money
supply growth above its upper boundary. If it instead maintains money supply
growth within its range, it may be unable to prevent the federal funds rate from
rising above its upper boundary.

The Fed recognized that it could not simultaneously control both variables
and as of October 1979 chose to focus primarily on money supply. Though it
continued to monitor the federal funds rate, it did not feel compelled to maintain
it within a narrow range. Exhibit 5.10 shows how the federal funds rate range
was widened as of October 1979. The increased emphasis on the money supply
was intended to achieve a more stable economy over the long run.

Recent Money Supply Target Shooting

To illustrate the Fed's ability to control the money supply, Exhibit 5.11 shows
target growth boundaries for M2 and M3. The Fed normally has better control
of M2 or M3 than M1. In the early 1990s, low interest rates in the U.S. encouraged
individuals to withdraw deposits from banks and invest in common stock. Thus,
the M2 and M3 levels were significantly affected by the behavior of depositors.

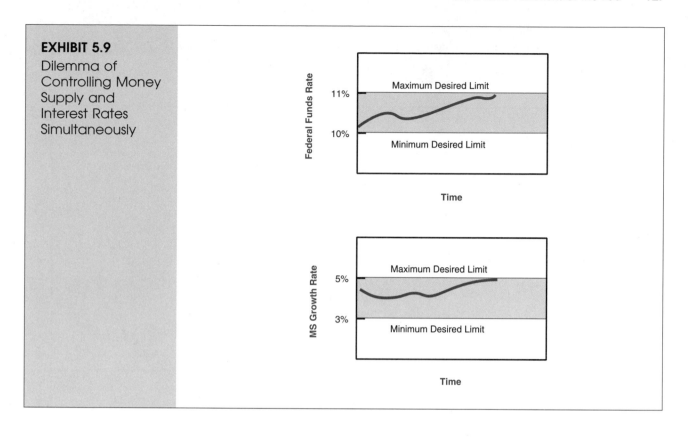

EXHIBIT 5.9

Dilemma of Controlling Money Supply and Interest Rates Simultaneously

Exhibit 5.11 shows that the M2 and M3 levels were sometimes growing at a low rate, and were below the minimum target range set by the Fed.

The Fed has both short-term and long-term target ranges for money supply. Even though it may overshoot or undershoot its short-term targets, its long-term targets have been hit with some success. Of course, this does not guarantee that the monetary growth will influence the economy as expected, yet it at least suggests that the Fed is capable of controlling long-term growth of money supply within ranges.

MONETARY CONTROL ACT OF 1980

In 1980 the Depository Institutions Deregulation and Monetary Control Act (DIDMCA) was passed. Commonly referred to as the Monetary Control Act, it had two key objectives. First, it was intended to deregulate some aspects of the depository institutions industry (discussed in the chapters on depository institutions). Second, it was intended to enhance the Fed's ability to control the money supply.

Before DIDMCA, member banks of the Federal Reserve were subject to its reserve requirements, while nonmember banks were subject to the reserve requirements of their respective states. Nonmember banks were often at an advantage in that they could typically maintain their required reserves in some interest-bearing form (such as in the form of Treasury securities). A member bank's required

EXHIBIT 5.10   Adjustment in Federal Funds Rate Target Range When Fed Shifted Emphasis on Money Supply

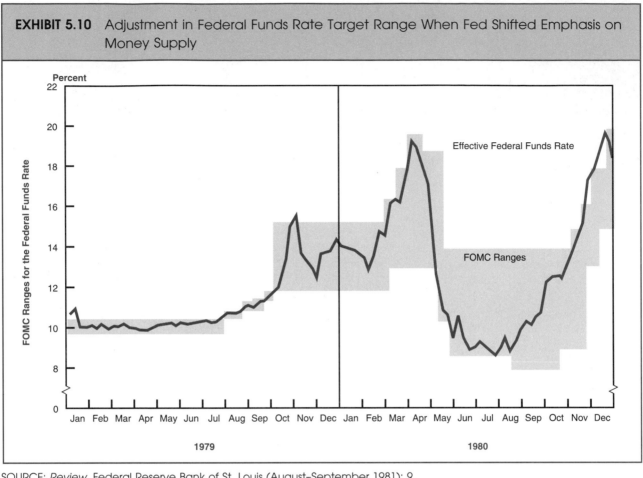

SOURCE: *Review,* Federal Reserve Bank of St. Louis (August–September 1981): 9.

reserves could only be held as balances at the Fed or vault cash and therefore could not earn interest. This disadvantage to member banks became more pronounced in the 1970s, when interest rates were generally higher than in previous years. The opportunity cost of tying up funds in a noninterest-bearing form increased. As a result, some member banks dropped their membership.

As Fed memberships decreased, so did the Fed's ability to control the money supply through reserve requirement adjustments, because it could adjust reserve requirements only of *member* banks to manipulate money supply. The Monetary Control Act mandates that all depository institutions be subject to the same reserve requirements imposed by the Fed. The reserve requirements were reduced relative to what the Fed previously required, but all required reserves were still to be held in a noninterest-bearing form. The revised reserve requirements were phased in over an eight-year period.

A related provision of the Monetary Control Act is that all depository institutions must report their deposit levels promptly to the Fed. This improves the Fed's knowledge of the current level of deposits in the banking system at any point in time. In the past, the Fed may have underestimated the prevailing money supply at times and thus increased the money supply above the level desired. With the improved reporting system, it should have a better feel for the prevailing money supply level and therefore make better adjustments.

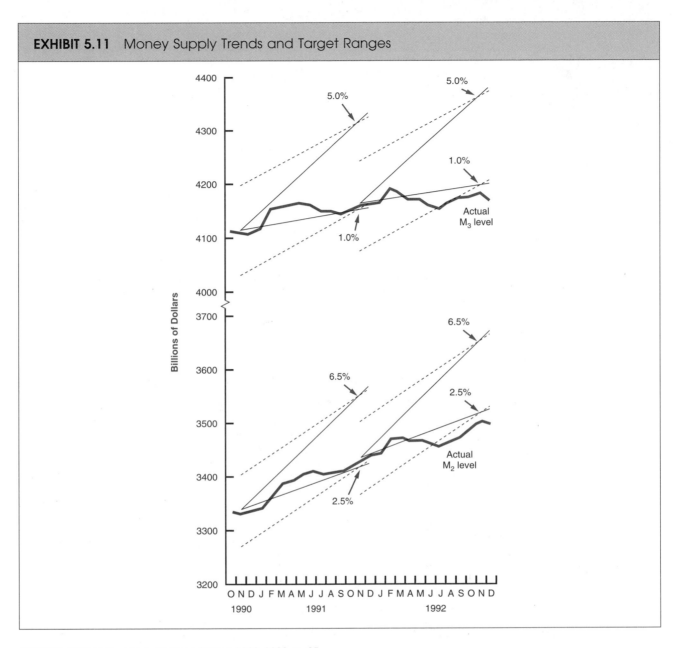

EXHIBIT 5.11   Money Supply Trends and Target Ranges

SOURCE: *FRBNY Quarterly Review,* Spring 1992–1993, p. 95.

In addition to reserve requirement and reporting laws, the Monetary Control Act allows all depository institutions that offer transaction accounts (such as demand deposits or NOW accounts) access to the discount window. Previously, only member banks were allowed access. This provision provides the Fed additional control over the money supply, because more institutions will have access to the discount window. However, the Fed does not frequently use the discount-window technique to control money supply.

USING *THE WALL STREET JOURNAL*

FED INFORMATION

The Wall Street Journal (WSJ) provides the following information related to this chapter on a daily basis:

- Three measures of the money supply (M1, M2, M3) over the last month.
- Borrowings from the Fed by member banks over the last month.
- Excess reserves of member banks over the last month.

This information is contained in a section called "Federal Reserve Data" and is used to assess future policy actions of the Fed.

The "Credit Markets" section also typically discusses the Fed's latest policies or potential policies in the future.

Statistics to be released each week on the money supply and other economic indicators are identified every Monday in *The Wall Street Journal*. The previous level of each economic indicator is provided, along with a forecast for the level that will be announced in the current week. The three most popular measures of money (M1, M2, and M3) are included in this report.

SOURCE: *The Wall Street Journal,* August 8, 1994, p. C2. Reprinted by permission of *The Wall Street Journal,* © Dow Jones & Company, Inc. All rights reserved worldwide.

Tracking the Economy — Aug. 8, 1994

Key statistics scheduled to be released this week:

ECONOMIC INDICATOR	PERIOD	RELEASE DATE	PREVIOUS ACTUAL	TECHNICAL DATA CONSENSUS FORECAST
Initial Jobless Claims	Week to Aug. 6	Thursday	319,000	329,000
Producer Prices	July	Thursday	Unchanged	+0.4%
Retail Sales	July	Thursday	+0.6%	Unchanged
Money Supply: M2	Week to Aug. 1	Thursday	+$5.8 billion	+$1.5 billion
Consumer Prices	July	Friday	+0.3%	+0.4%
Business Inventories	June	Friday	+1.1%	+0.2%

Source: Technical Data

GLOBAL MONETARY POLICY

GLOBAL ASPECTS

Each country has its own central bank that conducts monetary policy. The central banks of industrialized countries tend to have somewhat similar goals, which essentially reflect price stability (low inflation) and economic growth (low unemployment). However, the resources and conditions vary among countries, which may cause some central banks to focus on one particular economic goal.

Like the Fed, central banks of other industrialized countries use open market operations, reserve requirement adjustments, and adjustments in the interest rate they charge on loans to banks as monetary policy tools. The monetary policy

APPLIED RESEARCH

RESEARCH CONDUCTED BY THE FED

The Board of Governors and the 12 Federal Reserve district banks conduct comprehensive research on bank performance, bank regulation, monetary policy, and other related topics. Many research articles by the research departments of the district banks are listed as references at the end of each chapter in this text. More information about research publications available can be obtained by writing to the Board of Governors and the Fed district banks. Addresses are listed below.

Board of Governors of the Federal Reserve System
Publications Services
Washington, DC 20551
(202) 452-3244

FRB Atlanta
Research Department,
Publications Unit
104 Marietta Street
Atlanta, GA 30303-2713
(404) 521-8788

FRB Boston
Bank and Public Services
Department
600 Atlantic Avenue
Boston, MA 02106
(617) 973-3459

FRB Chicago
Public Information Center
230 South LaSalle Street
Chicago, IL 60690
(312) 322-5112

FRB Cleveland
Public Information Center
P.O. Box 6387
Cleveland, OH 44101
(216) 579-2048

FRB Dallas
Public Affairs Department
Station K
Dallas, TX 75222
(214) 651-6289

FRB Kansas City
Public Affairs Department
925 Grand Avenue
Kansas City, MO 64198
(816) 881-2402

FRB Minneapolis
Office of Public Information
250 Marquette Avenue
Minneapolis, MN 55480
(612) 340-2446

FRB New York
Public Information Department
33 Liberty Street
New York, NY 10045
(212) 791-6134

FRB Philadelphia
Public Information Department
P.O. Box 66
Philadelphia, PA 19105
(215) 574-6115

FRB Richmond
Public Service Department
P.O. Box 27622
Richmond, VA 23261
(804) 643-1250

FRB St. Louis
Bank Relations and
Public Information Department
P.O. Box 442
St. Louis, MO 63166
(314) 444-8421

FRB San Francisco
Public Information Department
P.O. Box 7702
San Francisco, CA 94120
(415) 974-3234

tools are generally used as a means of affecting local market interest rates in order to influence economic conditions.

Because country economies are integrated, the Fed must consider the present economic conditions of other major countries when assessing the U.S. economy. The Fed may be most effective if it coordinates its activities with central banks of other countries. Such coordination is commonly used by central banks when the banks intervene in the foreign exchange market. However, the coordination of monetary policies may be difficult because of conflicts of interest.

Countries in the European Community have considered promoting policy coordination by developing a European central bank, sometimes referred to as the Euro-Fed. However, the appropriate monetary policy in a European country undergoing expansion would be inappropriate for a different country experiencing recession. Plans have been proposed to coordinate European central bank policies to bring about a convergence in the economies of the European community. This would make it much easier for individual members of a central bank to agree on suitable monetary policy.

A more extreme proposal for central bank coordination is a single monetary policy for all industrialized European countries. In 1991, the Maastricht treaty called for the goal of a single European currency by 1999.

A single European currency would create a single money supply throughout Europe, rather than a separate money supply for each currency. Thus, European monetary policy would be consolidated, as any effects on the supply of money would affect all European countries using that one currency as their form of money.

A major concern of a single European currency is based on the concept of a single European monetary policy. Each country's government may prefer to implement its own monetary policy. Under a uniform currency arrangement, each country has only partial input to the European monetary policy that would be implemented on all European countries, including its own. The system would be analogous to that used in the U.S., where there is a single currency across states. Just as the monetary policy in the U.S. cannot be separated across different states, European monetary policy with a single European currency cannot be separated across European countries. Although country governments may disagree on the ideal monetary policy to enhance their local economies, they would all have to agree on a single European monetary policy. Any given policy used in a particular period may benefit some countries while adversely affecting others.

SUMMARY

- The key components of the Federal Reserve System are the Board of Governors and the Federal Open Market Committee. The Board of Governors of the Federal Reserve System determines the discount rate, or interest rate charged on loans from the Fed to depository institutions. It also determines the reserve requirements on account balances at depository institutions.

  The Federal Open Market Committee (FOMC) of the Federal Reserve System determines the money supply target range that is most appropriate for affecting interest rates and other economic conditions.

- The three main tools used by the Fed to conduct monetary policy are open market operations, the discount rate, and the reserve requirement ratio. Open market operations represent the Fed's buying and selling of securities, as a means of adjusting money supply. Securities are purchased by the Fed as a means of increasing the money supply and are sold by the Fed as a means of reducing the money supply.

  The discount rate can be raised by the Fed as a restrictive monetary policy to discourage bank borrowing from the Fed to depository institutions. Conversely, it can be reduced by the Fed as an expansionary policy to encourage more bank borrowing from the Fed.

  The reserve requirement ratio can be raised by the Fed as a restrictive monetary policy to reduce the degree to which money multiplies. Conversely, it can be reduced by the Fed as an expansionary monetary policy to increase the degree to which money multiplies.

■ In 1980, DIDMCA was passed, which imposed uniform reserve requirements across all depository institutions. Thus, the reserve requirement became a more powerful monetary policy tool because it affected more depository institutions. DIDMCA also allowed all depository institutions with transaction accounts access to the discount window. This increased the potential power of the discount rate as a monetary policy tool.

QUESTIONS

1. Briefly describe the origination of the Federal Reserve System.

2. Describe the functions of the Fed district banks.

3. What are the main goals of the Federal Open Market Committee? How does it attempt to achieve these goals?

4. Explain how the Fed increases the money supply through open market operations.

5. What is the policy directive, and who carries it out?

6. How is the money supply adjusted through the discount window?

7. How is money supply growth affected by an increase in the reserve requirement ratio?

8. What are the disadvantages of using the discount window or reserve requirement ratio to adjust the money supply?

9. Describe the characteristics that would be desirable for a measure of money to be manipulated by the Fed.

10. Explain the dilemma of attempting to simultaneously control money supply and the federal funds rate.

11. What are the two key objectives of the Monetary Control Act?

12. Have the reserve requirement revisions of the Monetary Control Act improved the Fed's ability to manipulate the money supply? Explain.

13. How does the Monetary Control Act help the Fed avoid improper adjustments of the money supply?

The Fed May Decide It's Time to Tighten

Lindley H. Clark, Jr., New York

Dec. 20 1993
P. A1
New York

When the Federal Open Market Committee meets tomorrow to set the Federal Reserve's monetary policy for the months ahead, it is likely to decide on a bias toward restraint.

The committee, at its May and July policy meetings, decided on a similar bias but backed away from taking any restrictive actions. The federal funds rate, the fee the bank charges on very short-term loans to commercial banks, remained firmly locked at 3%, and the money supply continued to expand briskly. There has been no change in the Fed's policy stance since September 1992, when the funds rate was reduced to its present level.

In view of the current economic environment, it may be time for a change. *The economy is developing considerable momentum. Final demand is catching up with production, comments Eugene Sherman of M.A. Schapiro & Co. The second and third quarters of this year saw reasonably strong personal-consumption expenditures, housing sales and business-equipment investment. But industrial production, housing starts and construction did not increase as rapidly. Therefore, inventories and the flow of goods to market were depleted. Business now has to expand output to catch up.*

So it isn't surprising that the employment data in recent months have been very encouraging. Nonfarm payrolls in November showed fairly strong growth for the third straight month, and total civilian employment posted a very large gain in November for the second month in a row. At the moment, this hardly seems to be the "jobless recovery" that many people were talking about a few months ago, although much of the job market remains weak.

So far, most economists think that the improving economic numbers suggest only a continuation of moderate growth through 1994, with some analysts basing such forecasts at least partly on a belief that the Fed won't sit on its hands all year. The 51 analysts interviewed monthly by Blue Chip Economic Indicators, a Secona, Ariz., newsletter, on the average expect inflation-adjusted gross domestic product to grow 2.9% next year, almost unchanged from the 2.8% gain they see for this year. And they look for the consumer price index to rise 2.9% in 1994, a bit less than this year's 3.0%.

That sort of outlook—modest growth and modest inflation—hardly indicates an obvious need for monetary tightening. Moreover, the Fed is under pressure from the Clinton administration and Congress to keep interest rates down and money abundant. The House Banking Committee continues to snipe at the central bank, contending that monetary policy somehow would be improved if the presidents of the regional Fed banks were appointed by President Clinton instead of by the directors of the individual banks.

However, as Nobel laureate Milton Friedman says, monetary policy works its way through the economy with "long and variable lags." An accommodative policy has been supporting the economy through the current recovery, and the economy is looking stronger. As former Fed Chairman William McChesney Martin once said, the Fed's task often is to take the punch bowl away just as the party is getting good.

Earlier this year, Fed Chairman Alan Greenspan argued that the inflation-adjusted federal funds rate must be pushed into positive territory if inflation is to be kept under control. With the funds rate and the consumer price index both around 3%, as they have been for several months, the real funds rate is zero, which is dangerous territory. The last time real short-term rates were negative, recalls David Jones of Aubrey G. Lanston & Co., was in the 1970s, when inflation pressures soared.

In theory, businessmen and consumers could learn to cope with 1970s-style inflation if they knew it would be stable. If they were sure inflation would always be 10%, prices and wages could be geared to that so they would rise automatically. But it's at least as hard to keep inflation constant at 10% as it is to keep it stable at 2% or zero. And the constant changes that would be required to gear an economy to 10% would be mind-boggling.

But how do you hit, say, a constant zero? In a recent speech, Jerry L. Jordan, president of the Cleveland Federal Reserve Bank, argued that the Fed should

Continued

CASE APPLICATION: SETTING MONETARY POLICY

Continued

aim at such a target by setting an explicit objective for the consumer price index. Attaining such an objective wouldn't be easy, but the effort alone would enhance the Fed's credibility. If the Fed should deviate from its goal, the public would know that the bank intended to get back on track.

Realistically, Mr. Jordan suggests that the Fed target a specific CPI level for the year 2000 and then conduct monetary policy to keep the CPI fluctuating around a trend line leading to that goal. Once the goal was attained, policy would be conducted to keep the CPI near that target.

There is some indication that the Federal Reserve may already have moved to a less accommodative policy. The monetary base, consisting of bank reserves and currency in circulation, had grown at double-digit rates through most of this year, but from Oct. 13 to Dec. 9, it grew only 5.9%.

Although a few economists expect the Fed to raise the funds rate almost immediately, the majority predict that it will wait until the first quarter of 1994. The economy grew strongly in last year's fourth quarter and then slowed sharply in the first three months of this year. Few analysts expect a repeat, but they would like to be sure.

SOURCE: *The Wall Street Journal* (December 20, 1993): p. A1. Reprinted by permission of *The Wall Street Journal* © 1993 Dow Jones & Company, Inc. All rights reserved worldwide.

QUESTIONS

1. Why are recent economic indicators discussed within the assessment of what the Fed's future monetary policy will be? Isn't the Fed more concerned about future economic conditions?

2. Offer your interpretation of the comment by a former Fed chairman who said that "the Fed's task is to take the punch bowl away just as the party is getting good." How does that relate to the main theme of the article?

3. Alan Greenspan thought it was necessary to push "real" (inflation-adjusted) short-term interest rates into positive territory. It was mentioned that the last time real short-term rates were negative, inflationary pressure soared. Explain why inflation may increase when real short-term interest rates are negative.

PROJECT

1. **Assessing Revisions in FOMC Money Supply Targets**
   Review recent articles in the *Federal Reserve Bulletin* or the *FRBNY Quarterly Review* to determine whether money supply targets have been recently revised by the FOMC. What explanation is given for revisions?

REFERENCES

Batten, Dallas S., and Daniel L. Thornton. "M_1 and M_2: Which Is the Better Monetary Target?" *Review*, Federal Reserve Bank of St. Louis (June–July 1983): 36–42.

Broaddus, J. Alfred. "Central Banking: Then and Now." *Economic Quarterly*, Federal Reserve Bank of Richmond (Spring 1993): 1–11.

Grier, Kevin B., and Mark J. Perry. "The Effect of Money Shocks on Interest Rates in the Presence of Constitutional Hetereskedasticity." *Journal of Finance* (September 1993): 1445–1455.

Hakes, David R. "The Objectives and Priorities of Monetary Policy Under Different Federal Reserve Chairmen." *Journal of Money, Credit, and Banking* (August 1990): 327–337.

Havrilesky, Thomas. "The Influence of Federal Advisory Council on Monetary Policy." *Journal of Money, Credit, and Banking* (February 1990): 37–50.

Higgins, Bryan. "Policy Implications of Recent M2 Behavior." *Economic Review*, Federal Reserve Bank of Kansas City (3rd Quarter 1992): 21–36.

McNees, Stephen K. "The Discount Rate: The Other Monetary Policy Tool." *New England Economic Review* (July/August 1993): 3–22.

Mitchell, Karlyn, and Douglas K. Pearce. "Discount Window Borrowing Across Federal Reserve Districts: Evidence Under Contemporaneous Reserve Accounting." *Journal of Banking and Finance* (August 1992): 771–790.

Sellon, Gordon H. "The Instruments of Monetary Policy." *Economic Review*, Federal Reserve Bank of Kansas City (May 1984): 3–20.

Thornton, Daniel L. "Targeting M2: The Issue of Monetary Control." *Review*, Federal Reserve Bank of St. Louis (July/August 1992): 23–34.

Wagster, John. "The Information Content of Discount Rate Announcements Revisited." *Journal of Money, Credit, and Banking* (February 1993): 132–137.

CHAPTER 6

MONETARY THEORY AND POLICY

The previous chapter discussed the Fed and how it controls money supply, information essential to financial market participants. It is just as important for participants to know how changes in money supply affect the economy, which is the subject of this chapter.

The specific objectives of this chapter are to:

- describe the well-known theories about monetary policy,
- explain the tradeoffs involved in monetary policy, and
- describe how financial market participants monitor and forecast the Fed's policies.

MONETARY THEORY

The type of monetary policy implemented by the Fed depends on the economic philosophies of the FOMC members. Some of the more well-known theories that can influence the Fed's policies are described here.

Pure Keynesian Theory

One of the most popular theories that can influence Fed policy is the **Keynesian theory,** which was developed by John Maynard Keynes, a British economist. To do justice to explaining this theory would require an entire text. The Keynesian theory suggests how the Fed can affect the interaction between the demand for money and the supply of money to affect interest rates, the aggregate level of spending, and therefore economic growth.

The general points of Keynesian theory can be explained by using the loanable funds framework described in Chapter 2. Recall that the interaction of the supply of loanable funds available and the demand for loanable funds determines the interest rate charged on loanable funds. Much of the demand for loanable funds is by households, corporations, and government agencies that need to borrow money. Recall that the demand schedule indicates the quantity of funds that would be demanded (at that time) at various possible interest rates. This schedule is downward sloping because many potential borrowers would borrow a larger quantity of funds at lower interest rates.

The supply schedule of loanable funds indicates the quantity of funds that would be supplied (at that time) at various possible interest rates. This schedule is upward sloping because suppliers of funds tend to supply a larger amount of funds when the interest rate is higher. Assume that as of today, the demand and supply schedules for loanable funds are represented as D_1 and S_1 in the left graph of Exhibit 6.1. Based on these schedules, the equilibrium interest rate would be i_1. The right graph of Exhibit 6.1 represents the typical relationship between the interest rate on loanable funds and the level of business investment as of today. The relation is inverse because corporations are more willing to expand when interest rates are relatively low. Given today's equilibrium interest rate of i_1, the level of business investment is B_1.

Assume that the economy is presently weak, and the Fed desires to increase the level of spending as a means of stimulating the economy. The Fed can use open market operations by purchasing Treasury securities from various financial institutions in the secondary market. As the financial institutions that sell their Treasury securities receive payment from the Fed, their account balances increase, without any offsetting decrease in the account balances of any other financial institutions. Thus, there is a net increase in deposit accounts (money),

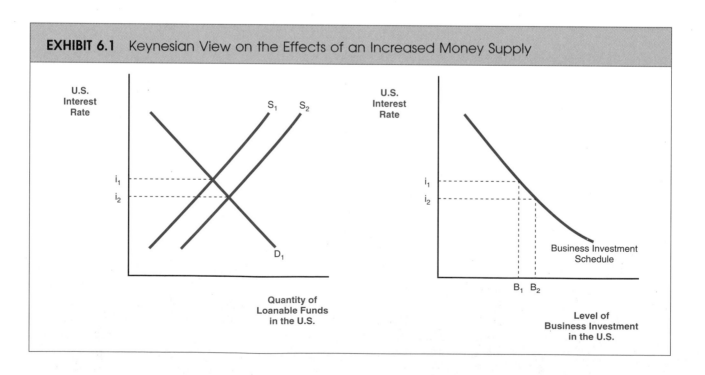

EXHIBIT 6.1   Keynesian View on the Effects of an Increased Money Supply

which converts to an increase in the quantity of loanable funds. Assume that the Fed's action resulted in an increase of $5 billion in loanable funds. The quantity of loanable funds supplied would now be $5 billion higher at any possible interest rate level. This means that the supply schedule for loanable funds shifts outward to S_2 in Exhibit 6.1. The difference between S_2 and S_1 is that S_2 incorporates the additional $5 billion of loanable funds as a result of the Fed's actions.

Given the shift in the supply schedule for loanable funds, the quantity of loanable funds supplied exceeds the quantity of loanable funds demanded at the interest rate level i_1. Thus, the new interest rate will decline to i_2, because the quantities of loanable funds supplied and demanded are equal to that level.

The lower interest rate level causes an increase in the level of business investment from B_1 to B_2. The increase in business investment represents new business spending that was triggered by lower interest rates, which reduced the corporate cost of financing new projects.

The Keynesian philosophy advocates an active role of the federal government in correcting economic problems. It conflicts with the classical theory that production (supply) creates its own demand and gained support during the Great Depression when the existing level of production had clearly exceeded demand, causing massive layoffs. Under such conditions, the Keynesian theory would have prescribed stimulative federal government policies, such as high monetary growth.

If excessive inflation is the main concern, the pure Keynesian philosophy would still focus on aggregate spending as the variable that must be adjusted. A portion of the high inflation is possibly due to excessive spending that is pulling up prices, commonly referred to as **demand-pull inflation.** The Keynesian approach would prescribe a federal government policy to reduce aggregate spending. More specifically, the Fed could use open market operations by selling some of its holdings of Treasury securities in the secondary market. As financial institutions make payments to purchase these Treasury securities, their account balances decrease, without any offsetting increase in the account balances of any other financial institutions. Thus, there is a net decrease in deposit accounts (money), which results in a net decrease in the quantity of loanable funds. Assume that the Fed's action caused a decrease of $5 billion in loanable funds. The quantity of loanable funds supplied would now be $5 billion lower at any possible interest rate level. This reflects an inward shift in the supply schedule from S_1 to S_2, as shown in Exhibit 6. 2.

Given the inward shift in the supply schedule for loanable funds, the quantity of loanable funds demanded exceeds the quantity of loanable funds supplied at the original interest rate level (i_1). Thus, the interest rate will increase to i_2, because the quantities of loanable funds supplied and demanded are equal at that level.

The higher interest rate level causes a decrease in the level of business investment from B_1 to B_2. The decline in business investment is attributed to the increased corporate cost of financing new projects. As economic growth is slowed by the reduction in business investment, inflationary pressure may be reduced. Thus, the reduction in money supply is an indirect means by which the Fed may reduce inflation.

Exhibit 6.3 summarizes the Keynesian view of how the Fed (as the central bank of the U.S.) can affect economic conditions through its influence on the level of bank reserves. The top part of the exhibit illustrates a stimulative

EXHIBIT 6.2 Keynesian View on the Effects of a Reduced Money Supply

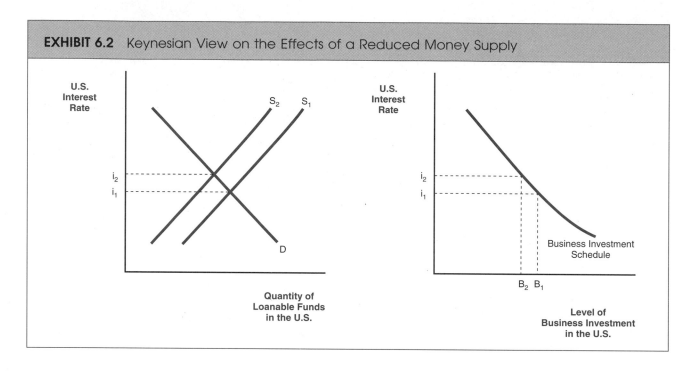

EXHIBIT 6.3

Summary of the Keynesian View on How Monetary Policy Affects Economic Conditions

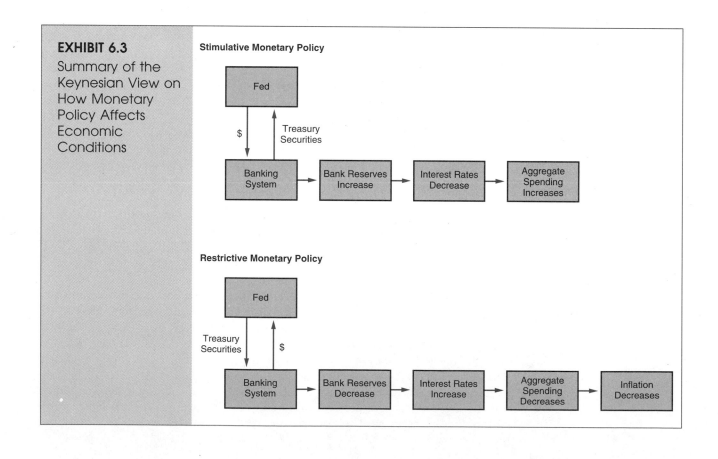

monetary policy intended to boost economic growth, while the bottom part of the exhibit illustrates a restrictive monetary policy intended to reduce inflation.

EFFECTS OF A CREDIT CRUNCH ON A STIMULATIVE POLICY.   The economic impact of monetary policy (as explained with the Keynesian view) may be dependent on the willingness of banks to lend funds. Even if the Fed increases the level of bank reserves during a weak economy, banks may be unwilling to extend credit to some potential borrowers, which results in a *credit crunch.* It could be argued that if banks do not lend out the newly created funds that result from the Fed's increase in bank reserves, the economy will not be stimulated. Yet the perception that banks will not lend out sufficient funds is caused by the effects of a weak economy on loan repayment probability. Banks provide loans only after confirming that the borrower's future cash flows will be adequate to make loan repayments. During a weak economy, the future cash flows of many potential borrowers are more uncertain, causing a reduction in loan applications (demand for loans) and in the number of qualified loan applicants.

Banks and other lending institutions have a responsibility to their depositors, shareholders, and regulators to avoid loans that are likely to default. Because default risk rises during a weak economy, some potential borrowers will be unable to obtain loans. Others may only qualify if they pay high-risk premiums to cover their default risk. Thus, it is possible that the effects of monetary policy can be limited if potential borrowers do not qualify or are unwilling to incur the high-risk premiums. Yet, because borrowers with very low risk should not be affected by the credit crunch, they may respond to the lower cost of funds that results from lower interest rates. A stimulative monetary policy will be more effective if there are sufficient qualified borrowers that will borrow more funds once interest rates are reduced.

A credit crunch could even occur during a period when a restrictive monetary policy is implemented. As money supply is reduced, and interest rates are increased, some potential borrowers may be unable to obtain loans because the interest payments would be too high. This magnifies the effects of a restrictive monetary policy, because the higher interest rates not only discourage some potential borrowers from obtaining loans, but also prevent others from obtaining loans.

Overall, a credit crunch may partially offset the desired effects of a stimulative monetary policy and magnify the effects of a restrictive monetary policy. Yet, assuming the Fed recognizes the possible influence of the credit crunch, it could modify the specific money supply targets to offset any distortions caused by such a crunch.

Quantity Theory and the Monetarist Approach

The quantity theory is applicable to monetary policy because it suggests a particular relationship between money supply and the degree of economic activity. It is based on the so-called equation of exchange, as follows:

$$MV = PQ$$

where M = amount of money in the economy
V = velocity of money
P = weighted average price of goods and services in the economy
Q = quantity of goods and services sold

Velocity represents the average number of times each dollar changes hands per year. The right side of the equation of exchange represents the total value of goods and services produced. If velocity is constant, a given adjustment in money supply will produce a predictable change in the total value of goods and services. Thus, a direct relationship between money supply and gross national product is evident.

An early form of the theory assumed Q constant in the short run, which implied a direct relationship between money supply and prices. If the money supply is increased, the average price level will increase. However, the assumption of a stable quantity is not realistic today. The original quantity theory has been revised by the **Monetarists** into what is referred to as the **modern quantity theory of money.** Milton Friedman and others relaxed the stable-quantity assumption to suggest that a given increase in money supply leads to a predictable increase in the value of goods and services produced.

Because velocity represents the ratio of money stock to nominal output, it is affected by any factor that influences this ratio. Income patterns can affect velocity because they influence the amount of money held by households. Factors that increase the ratio of money holdings to income of households reduce velocity, while factors that reduce this ratio increase velocity. Households maintain more money if their income is received less frequently. Credit cards can reduce the need to hold money balances. Expectations of high inflation encourage households to hold balances of less money, thereby increasing velocity. Yet, Friedman has found that velocity changes in a predictable manner and is not related to fluctuations in money supply. Therefore, the equation of exchange can be applied to assess how money can affect aggregate spending.

The Monetarist approach advocates a stable, low growth in the money supply. It may be criticized for being too passive, but its supporters contend that it allows economic problems to resolve themselves without causing additional problems. Suppose the United States experiences a recession. While the typical Keynesian monetary policy prescription would be high money growth, Monetarists would avoid a loose money policy on the grounds that it tends to ignite inflationary expectations, which can increase the demand for money and place upward pressure on interest rates. The Monetarist cure for the recession would not call for any revision in the existing monetary policy. Instead, Monetarists would expect the stagnant economy to reduce corporate and household borrowing and thus result in lower interest rates. Once interest rates are reduced to a low enough level, they will encourage borrowing and therefore stimulate economic growth. Because the Monetarist approach to achieve lower interest rates does not require an increase in money supply growth, inflationary expectations should not be ignited as they might be under the Keynesian approach.

A major limitation of the Monetarist approach is the timing involved in improving the economy. Is the public willing to suffer while the recession cures itself, or would it prefer a more active (Keynesian) approach to quickly resolve the recession, even though other economic problems might arise as a result?

While recognizing the strong impact of money supply fluctuations on the economy, Monetarists do not believe money growth should be actively adjusted. Instead they believe in accepting a natural rate of unemployment, and they criticize the government for trying to achieve a lower than natural rate at the price of inflation, especially because the lower rate is unlikely to prevail in the long run. Friedman has found that the impact of money supply growth on economic

MONETARIST PROPOSAL TO STABILIZE MONEY SUPPLY GROWTH

A strong form of Monetarism would be to set the money supply growth level at a particular rate and permanently maintain it at that rate. This is often referred to as the **fixed money supply rule.** If implemented, this would have significant implications for financial markets. There would no longer be a need for financial market participants to monitor the Fed, because the Fed's importance would be greatly reduced. Instead, the focus could shift to all the other factors that affect economic conditions. Because the Fed would not be able to revise monetary policy, it could not be blamed for a poor economy. The fiscal policymaking group would be solely responsible for the state of the economy.

There are some concerns about a fixed money supply rule. First, what form of money supply should be controlled at a fixed-growth rate? Second, what is the appropriate rate? The decision must be an arbitrary one which, if proved wrong over the years, could be harmful.

In addition, a severe problem could arise in the future that would require a change in monetary policy, yet change would be prohibited by a fixed money supply rule. Finally, a fixed money supply rule would increase the power of the fiscal policy side, which is more politically motivated. The existing power of the Fed allows more of a long-run concern about economic conditions than would be the case if all power were held by the fiscal side.

A compromise may be to employ a fixed money supply rule that is subject to adjustment if it is not working well. However, this dampens the advantages of a fixed rule. The financial markets would again have to follow the Fed and forecast when the rule might be revised, because any revision would have an impact on the economy. This compromise essentially represents the system as it is today, where a money supply target is set but is changed periodically at the discretion of the Fed.

growth has a long lag time and is uncertain, which is why he advocates a constant rate of monetary growth.

A major difference in the beliefs of Keynesians and Monetarists is the perceived relative importance of inflation and unemployment. Keynesians tend to focus on maintaining low unemployment and are therefore more willing to tolerate any inflation that results from stimulative monetary policies. Monetarists are more concerned about maintaining low inflation and are therefore more willing to tolerate what they refer to as a natural rate of unemployment.

Theory of Rational Expectations

The **theory of rational expectations** implies that the public accounts for all existing information when forming its expectations. As applied to a monetary policy, this theory suggests that households and business, having witnessed historical effects of monetary policy actions, will use this information to forecast the impact of an existing policy and act accordingly. For example, if the Fed uses a loose monetary policy to stimulate the economy, households will respond by increasing their spending as they anticipate that higher inflation will result from the policy. In addition, businesses will increase their investment in machinery

EXHIBIT 6.4

Effects of an Increased Money Supply According to the Monetarist Approach and Rational Expectations Theory

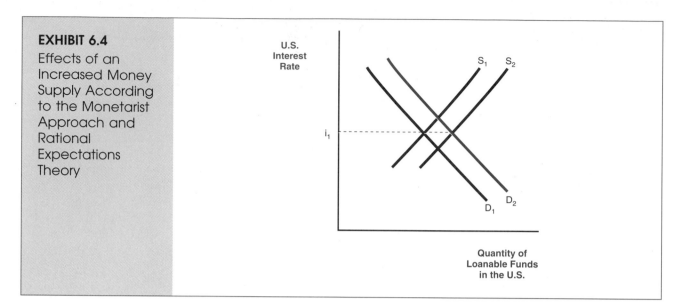

and equipment in an attempt to beat impending higher costs of borrowing. Further, participants in the labor market will negotiate for higher wages to compensate for higher anticipated inflation, and the level of savings will be reduced while the level of borrowing will increase. These forces will offset the impact of an increase in money supply. Therefore, the policy will not affect interest rates or economic growth. In general, rational expectations supports the contention by Friedman and some other Monetarists that changes in monetary policy are unlikely to have any sustained positive impact on the economy.

The criticism of the Keynesian theory according to the Monetarist approach and rational expectations theory is illustrated in Exhibit 6.4. The curves drawn in black reflect the Keynesian view on how a stimulative monetary policy (increased money supply) can place downward pressure on interest rates. In fact, these curves are the same as those shown in Exhibit 6.1. A key criticism of the Keynesian view is that the quantity of loanable funds demanded is presumed to remain unchanged by the adjustment in money supply. Proponents of the Monetarist approach and rational expectations theory would suggest that the increased money supply would increase inflationary expectations, which would cause a higher demand for loanable funds at any possible interest rate. This reflects an outward shift in the demand schedule for loanable funds, as is illustrated by the D_2 curve in Exhibit 6.4. The outward shift in the demand schedule can completely offset the outward shift in the supply schedule, so that the interest rate is not reduced at all. Thus, the level of business investment would not be affected by the Fed's adjustment in the money supply, and the general level of spending in the economy would remain as it was. Under these conditions, the adjustment in money supply is not effective in stimulating economic growth.

Integrating Monetary Theories

The FOMC as a whole is not thought to be pure Keynesian or pure Monetarist. FOMC members adjust monetary growth targets when they see fit (in line with the Keynesian philosophy) but are quite aware of the potential adverse consequence of excessive money supply growth (as suggested by Monetarists). If a stimulative boost is needed and if severe inflation does not appear to be a potential consequence, a loose money policy may be implemented. However, if inflation is a major concern, the Fed must weight the costs and benefits of a stimulative monetary policy.

The decisions by the FOMC members may also be influenced by the political party that appointed them. Recent research by Puckett found that dissenting votes by FOMC members appointed by Democratic U.S. presidents were in favor of looser monetary policy, while those members appointed by Republican U.S. presidents were in favor of tighter monetary policy. The dissenting votes by presidents of the Federal Reserve district banks were similar to those of members appointed by Republican presidents.

It is important for financial market participants to keep track of the FOMC member personalities over time. As members of the FOMC are replaced, there can be a shift in the overall philosophy of the FOMC, which can result in a different monetary policy.

TRADE-OFF FACED BY THE FED

The Fed monitors economic variables, such as inflation, unemployment, and gross national product (GNP), over time. Although it does not have direct control over these variables, it can attempt to influence them by manipulating the money supply.

Ideally, the Fed would like to maintain low inflation, steady GNP growth, and low unemployment. Because GNP growth can lead to low unemployment, these two goals may be achieved simultaneously. Yet it has often been suggested that low inflation and low unemployment cannot be consistently maintained. For more than 200 years, economists have recognized a possible trade-off between the two. In 1958, in an article that became famous, Professor A. W. Phillips compared the annual percentage change in average unemployment rate and wages in the United Kingdom from 1861 to 1913. His research confirmed a negative relationship between the two variables. This relationship suggested that government policies designed to cure unemployment appear to place upward pressure on wages. In addition, government policies designed to cure inflation can cause more unemployment. This negative relationship came to be known as the **Phillips curve.** The concept provided a new framework for the central bank and the Administration to determine government policies.

Research on the U.S. inflation and unemployment data revealed that the relationship was frequently changing. Shifts in the Phillips curve were attributed to unionization, changing productivity, and, more recently, changing expectations about inflation.

When inflation is higher than the Fed deems acceptable, the Fed may consider implementing a tight-money policy to reduce economic growth. As economic growth slows, producers cannot as easily raise their prices and still maintain sales volume. Similarly, workers are not in demand and do not have much bargaining power on wages. Thus, the use of tight money to slow economic growth can reduce the inflation rate. A possible cost of the lower inflation rate is higher unemployment. If the economy becomes stagnant because of the tight-money policy, sales decrease, inventories accumulate, and firms may reduce their work force to reduce production.

EXHIBIT 6.5
Trade-off between Reducing Inflation and Unemployment

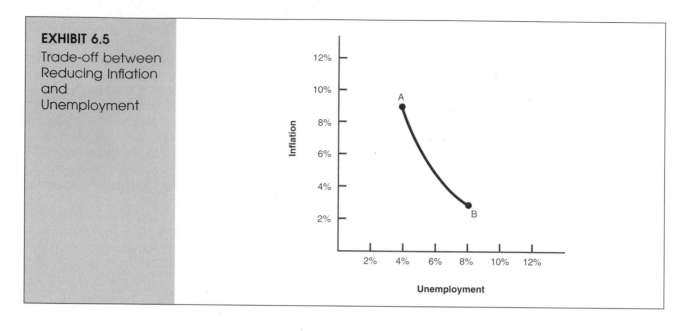

Given that a loose-money policy can reduce unemployment while a tight-money policy can reduce inflation, the Fed must determine whether unemployment or inflation is a more serious problem. It may not be able to cure both problems simultaneously. In fact, it may not be able to fully eliminate either problem. While a loose-money policy can stimulate the economy, it does not guarantee that unskilled workers will be hired. While a tight-money policy can reduce inflation caused by excessive spending, it cannot reduce inflation caused by such factors as an agreement among the oil cartel to keep oil prices high.

The Fed has sometimes been criticized for using quick-fix policies that cause more volatile business cycles. In other words, it may remedy one problem but cause a new one. The 1982 recession was a case where it tried to avoid that mistake. Afraid that inflation would result from stimulating the economy with a loose-money policy, the Fed was initially unwilling to allow excessive growth in the money supply.

To illustrate the trade-off involved, consider a situation where because of specific cost factors (higher energy and insurance costs, etc.), inflation will be at least 3 percent. This amount of inflation will exist no matter what type of monetary policy the Fed implements. Also assume that because of the number of unskilled workers and people between jobs, the unemployment rate will be at least 4 percent. A loose-money policy sufficiently stimulates the economy to maintain unemployment at that minimum level of 4 percent. However, such a stimulative policy may also cause additional inflation beyond the 3 percent level. Or a tight-money policy could maintain inflation at the 3 percent minimum, but unemployment would likely rise above the 4 percent minimum.

This trade-off is illustrated in Exhibit 6.5. Here the Fed can use a very stimulative (loose-money) policy that is expected to result in point A (9 percent inflation and 4 percent unemployment). Alternatively, it can use a very restrictive (tight-money) policy that is expected to result in point B (3 percent inflation and

8 percent unemployment). Or it can enact a more compromising policy that would result in some point along the curve extending from point A to point B.

Historical inflation and unemployment rates on a yearly basis show that when one of these problems worsens, the other does not automatically improve. Both variables can rise or fall over time. Yet this does not refute the trade-off faced by the Fed. It simply means that some outside factors have affected inflation or unemployment or both. To illustrate, recall that the Fed could have achieved point A, point B, or somewhere along the curve connecting these points during a particular time period. Now assume that oil prices have substantially increased and several product liability lawsuits have occurred. These events will affect consumer prices such that the minimum inflation rate would be, say, 6 percent. In addition, assume that various training centers for unskilled workers have been closed down, leaving a higher number of unskilled workers. This forces the minimum unemployment rate to 6 percent. Now the Fed's trade-off position has changed. The Fed's new set of possibilities is shown as curve CD in Exhibit 6.6. Note that the points reflected on curve CD are not as desirable as the points along curve AB that were previously attainable. No matter what type of monetary policy the Fed uses, both the inflation and the unemployment rates will be higher than in the previous time period. Yet this is not the fault of the Fed. In fact, the Fed is still faced with a trade-off between point C (11 percent inflation, 6 percent unemployment), point D (6 percent inflation, 10 percent unemployment), and somewhere within those points along curve CD.

A classic example of the trade-off confronting the Fed was the crisis in the Persian Gulf during the summer of 1990. There were numerous indications of a possible recession in the United States, encouraging the Fed to use a loose-money policy. However, the abrupt increase in oil prices at that time placed upward pressure on U.S. inflation. Thus, the Fed was less willing to use a

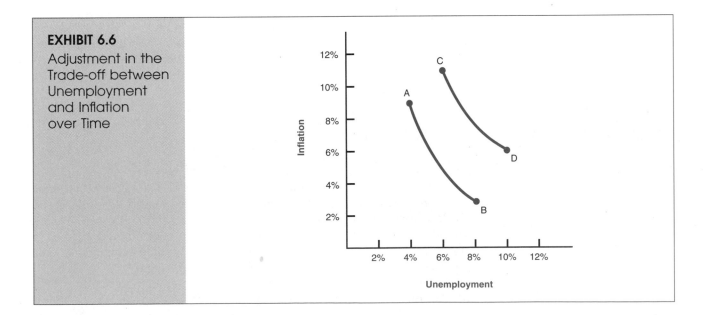

EXHIBIT 6.6

Adjustment in the Trade-off between Unemployment and Inflation over Time loose-money policy, because of the additional inflationary pressure that would result from it.

LAGS IN MONETARY POLICY

One of the main reasons that monetary policy is so complex is the lag between the time an economic problem arises and the time it will take for an adjustment in money supply growth to solve it. Three specific lags are involved. First, there is a lag between the time the problem arises and the time it is recognized—a **recognition lag.** Most economic problems are initially revealed by statistics, not actual observation. Because economic statistics are reported on only a periodic basis, they will not immediately signal a problem. For example, the unemployment rate is reported on a monthly basis. A sudden increase in unemployment may not be detected until the end of the month when statistics reveal the problem. And even though most economic variables are updated monthly, the recognition lag could still be longer than one month. For example, if unemployment increases slightly each month for two straight months, the Fed may not necessarily act on this information, because the information may not appear to be significant. Only after a few more months of steadily increasing unemployment might the Fed recognize that a serious problem exists. In such a case, the recognition lag may be four months or longer.

The time from which a serious problem is recognized until the time the Fed implements a policy to resolve it is known as the **implementation lag.** Then, even after the Fed implements a policy, there will be an **impact lag** until it has its full impact on the economy. For example, an adjustment in money supply growth may have an immediate impact to some degree on the economy, but its full impact may not be manifested until a year or so after the adjustment.

These lags hinder the Fed's control of the economy. Suppose the Fed uses a loose-money policy to stimulate the economy and reduce unemployment. By the time the implemented monetary policy begins to take effect, the unemployment rate may have already reversed itself as a result of some other outside factors (such as a weakened dollar that increased foreign demand for U.S. goods and created U.S. jobs). Thus, a problem of more concern may now be inflation (because the economy is heating up again) which may be further ignited by the loose-money policy. If not for monetary policy lags, implemented policies would have a higher rate of success.

ASSESSING THE IMPACT OF MONETARY POLICY

Financial market participants will not all necessarily react to monetary policy in the same manner, because they trade different securities. The expected or actual impact of monetary policy on long-term mortgage rates may differ from corporate and municipal bond rates, money market rates, and stock prices. Exhibit 6.7 shows the various components of the financial environment that are affected by monetary policy. This exhibit implies that the most influential economic variable on the performance for many financial markets is interest rates.

Even financial market participants that trade the same securities may react differently to the monetary policy, because they may have different expectations

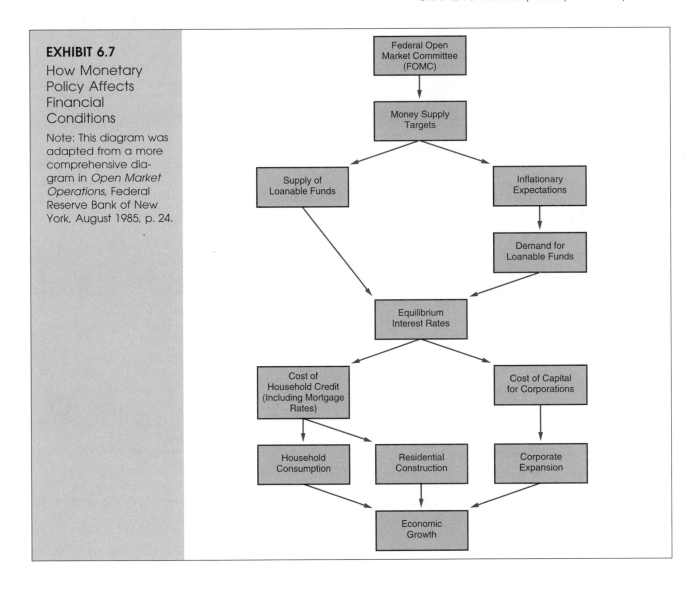

EXHIBIT 6.7

How Monetary Policy Affects Financial Conditions

Note: This diagram was adapted from a more comprehensive diagram in *Open Market Operations*, Federal Reserve Bank of New York, August 1985, p. 24.

about the impact of monetary policy on economic variables. They have only limited success in forecasting economic variables because of the difficulty in forecasting (1) money supply movements and (2) how future money supply movements will affect interest rates. Each of these forecasting aspects is discussed in the following subsections.

Forecasting Money Supply Movements

Business periodicals will from time to time specify the weekly ranges of M_1 and M_2 based on the Fed's most recent disclosure of its target range. The Fed is less concerned about meeting its targets on a weekly basis than about meeting its long-term targets. Yet, some financial participants compare the actual money supply levels with weekly ranges that can be estimated from the Fed's longer term target ranges. Weekly ranges represent the path that the Fed would follow over time if it were to move toward its targets at a constant rate. For example, if the target growth range is specified as 4 percent to 6 percent annually, the money supply should grow at a weekly rate of between 4%/52 and 6%/52 (given 52 weeks per year). If the Fed consistently over- or undershoots these weekly ranges, it may desire to offset that at some point in the future.

When the actual money supply is not within the target range, it could be because of a change in the Fed's range that has not yet been publicly announced. The Fed may be meeting its new targets, while financial market participants believe it plans to adjust money to meet its previously announced range. Normally, the Fed attempts to avoid revising target ranges, because if it changes them too often, it may lose some credibility. Persistent changes might suggest that it is unsure of how money supply fluctuations affect the economy.

In some periods, the Fed is more willing than usual to let the money supply wander outside its target range. For example, during the initial stage of deregulated deposit accounts in 1982–1984, the Fed was less concerned than usual when the reported money supply was above its target range. It felt that the reported money supply level may have been distorted and focused its policy actions on whatever would improve the economy rather than on meeting its money supply targets.

Any changes in the Fed's monetary policy plans are publicized about 45 days later in the *Federal Reserve Bulletin.* These plans are often vague, which makes the interpretation difficult. In addition, statistical measures of the money supply are not completely up-to-date. Thus, financial market participants cannot confirm from any changes in these money supply statistics whether the Fed has recently adjusted its money supply targets. Given the lack of information, financial market participants sometimes guess at the Fed's monetary policy plans and make their decisions according to this guess. Some participants may take a passive approach and presume that the most recently publicized money supply targets set by the Fed are still intact. Other participants may have reason to suspect that the Fed recently revised its money supply targets.

MARKET REACTION TO REPORTED MONEY SUPPLY LEVELS.   On every Thursday afternoon, the most up-to-date money supply figures are released. Financial market participants will often use these newly released figures to predict how the Fed will adjust money supply in the future and therefore how interest rates and security prices may be influenced. Consider the role of bond portfolio managers who work for financial institutions. When they expect interest rates to rise, they should also expect that the values of their current holdings of bonds will decrease and may therefore reduce their bond holdings in favor of short-term securities. They could replenish their bond portfolio once interest rates increase and prices of existing bonds decline.

As an example, Exhibit 6.8 shows movements in the money supply (MS) over time. The dotted lines form the Fed's most recently disclosed money supply target range. This range was disclosed in Week 1. The range specifies money supply growth of between 3 percent and 6 percent on an annualized basis. In Weeks 1 through 5, the Fed managed to control money supply within its target. In Week 6, bond portfolio managers were awaiting the release of the money supply figures. If the reported money supply is near point A, this suggests that the Fed overshot its target range and may tighten money supply in the near

EXHIBIT 6.8
Possible Money
Supply Movements
over Time

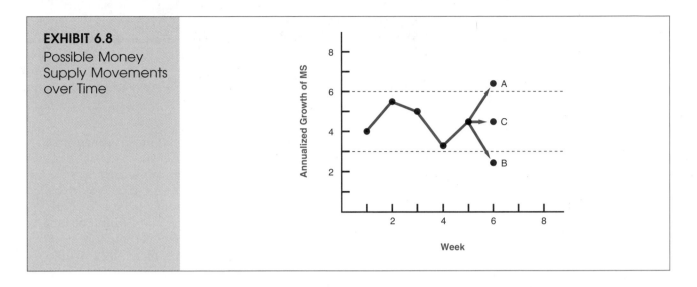

future to push it back within the target range. Given the expectation of the Fed's pursuing a tight-money policy, bond portfolio managers may expect higher interest rates in the near future and thus sell some of their bonds before prices decline.

As a second possibility, the reported money supply level may be near point B, which would suggest that the Fed undershot its target range. If so, the Fed may loosen money supply in the near future to push it back within the target range. Given the expectation of a future loose-money policy, bond portfolio managers may expect lower interest rates in the near future (assuming that the loose money does not ignite inflationary expectations) and thus purchase more bonds now. Some portfolio managers may wait until the Fed is consistently above or below its range before they anticipate a concerted Fed effort to move back within the range.

As a third possibility, the reported money supply level may be near point C, which would suggest that the Fed has remained within its target range. This does not offer much of a hint as to whether the Fed will tighten or loosen money supply in the future. Thus, bond portfolio managers may react less to this scenario than to the previous two.

Because all bond portfolio managers receive the report on money supply at the same time, they may not be able to capitalize as easily on the information. For example, if the reported money supply leads all of them to expect higher interest rates, they will all try to simultaneously sell some of their bonds. Consequently, there could be a large amount of bonds for sale but very little demand for the bonds, which would immediately force the price of these bonds down. When the reported money supply leads bond portfolio managers to expect lower interest rates, managers will all try to purchase more bonds, which could immediately force the market price of bonds up.

ANTICIPATING REPORTED MONEY SUPPLY LEVELS. Bond portfolio managers recognize that it is difficult to capitalize on a money supply report unless they react before other bond portfolio managers do. The only way this could be done is to forecast what the money supply announcements will be on each Thursday

---

POINT OF INTEREST

SHOULD THE FED ANNOUNCE ITS MONETARY POLICY IMMEDIATELY?

Financial market participants would prefer that any revision in the Fed's money supply target range be announced immediately. They would also prefer that all matters regarding monetary policy be disclosed immediately, because then they could make decisions based on more accurate information. There would be less guessing, and movements in securities prices might be less volatile. Guessing often causes overreaction in the financial markets and thus more volatile securities price movements.

The Fed might reply that if it immediately disclosed its monetary policy plans, securities prices would be more volatile. Under the current situation, where there is less information disclosed and financial market participants are more uncertain of the future, there are usually some buyers and some sellers of all securities, because there is disagreement about which way interest rates and securities prices will move. If everyone had accurate information about the Fed's plans, there would be a more pronounced movement into or out of certain securities, and the prices would be very sensitive to such volatile movements. If prices of securities were more volatile, their perceived risk would be greater, and the public would have less confidence in holding securities. The Fed might further argue that much of whatever impact it does have on interest rates is completed by the time the financial markets are aware of the Fed's intentions.

In 1993, House Banking Chairman Henry Gonzalez stated that the results of 11 of 34 Fed policy meetings over the period 1989–1993 were leaked to the public. He suggested that because the information is often leaked, the Fed should immediately announce its policy decisions. Fed chairman Alan Greenspan replied that the early release of Fed policy would cause more volatile movements in security prices.

At this time, it is difficult to conclude which argument has more support. This issue will surely continue to be debated in the future.

---

afternoon. As an example, reconsider Exhibit 6.8 and assume that you are a bond portfolio manager assessing the situation during Week 6. On Wednesday, the day before the money supply figures are released, you have completed your assessment. You believe that the Fed has overshot its money supply targets and will therefore tighten money supply in the near future to get back within its range. This would lead to higher interest rates and lower bond prices in the future. Based on your expectations, you sell your bonds on Wednesday. If your expectation is correct, you will be able to sell some of your bonds at a higher price on Wednesday than if you had waited until after the money supply was reported on Thursday. Assume that you sold $1 million worth of bonds on Wednesday, and on Thursday, after the money supply was reported, bond prices fell by 2 percent. In this case, you would receive $20,000 more than if you had waited until after the money supply was reported to sell your bonds. This is an example of the potential benefits of correctly forecasting the money supply figure before it is released.

Various consulting firms forecast the money supply level based on information from a sample of banks and then sell their forecasts to bond portfolio managers. Some bond portfolio managers purchase these forecasts, because the fee is small relative to the potential return that can be generated if the right strategy (buy versus sell) is implemented. Others are more doubtful of the accuracy of these forecasts, so they either develop their own or simply wait until the money supply figure is reported.

Even if forecasts of the reported money supply could be perfected, bond portfolio managers might incorrectly guess the Fed's future monetary policy plans. For example, if the most recently reported money supply showed that the Fed had overshot its money supply target range, it would be rational for financial market participants to expect the Fed to push the money supply back within its initially established range. However, the money supply might be within a newly established but not yet publicized target range.

MARKET REACTION TO DISCOUNT RATE ADJUSTMENTS.   Besides the comparison of the most recently reported (or anticipated) money figures to the money supply growth targets, financial market participants have other methods of forecasting future money supply movements. One of the more common methods is to monitor actual or potential changes in the discount rate by the Fed. A change in the discount rate is often thought to signal a change in money supply targets. A decrease in the discount rate may signal a stimulative monetary policy designed to reduce interest rates. An increase in the discount rate may signal a tight-money policy designed to increase interest rates. It is not the revision in the discount rate, but the potentially revised money supply targets accompanying this revision that are so important.

Some discount rate adjustments are policy related while others are technical (intended to bring the discount rate in line with other market rates). Because the Fed normally does not announce whether the adjustment is policy related or technical, financial market participants must interpret each adjustment themselves.

Because a change in the discount rate is often thought to signal the Fed's future monetary policy, financial market participants attempt to predict when the Fed will change the discount rate and by how much. If they can accurately forecast a future adjustment, they can take advantageous positions in securities prior to the actual adjustment.

Some critics contend that the financial markets often overreact to discount rate revisions, because a revision may indicate nothing about the future course of monetary policy and economic conditions. This is because the Fed commonly revises the discount rate to move it back in line with other interest rates. In such situations, there may be no adjustment in money supply targets; and a change in the discount rate without any other adjustments is not likely to significantly affect the economy.

Since 1980, discount rate changes have commonly preceded market interest rate movements in the same direction. Thus, market participants are often justified in interpreting discount rate adjustments as a signal about future interest rate movements, regardless of whether the Fed planned such movements.

In 1989 a former director of Federal Reserve Bank of New York was convicted of leaking confidential information about likely changes in the discount rate to a securities firm before the information was publicized. This confirms that some securities firms believe that discount rate announcements can influence securities prices.

Forecasting the Impact of Monetary Policy

Even if financial market participants could correctly anticipate changes in money supply movements, they might not be able to predict future economic conditions. The historical relationship between money supply and economic variables has not remained perfectly stable over time. Some adjustments in the money supply caused by the behavior of depositors can distort the relationship between money supply levels and economic growth. For example, during the period 1992–1993 interest rates declined and some individuals withdrew their deposits to invest in stocks. Consequently, the money supply level (as measured by M_2) decreased even though the funds were still invested within the U.S. This type of reduction in money supply may not have the same effect on the economy as if the funds were pulled out of the economy by the Fed. Thus, the relationship between the money supply and economic growth is affected.

IMPACT OF MONETARY POLICY ACROSS FINANCIAL MARKETS. Because monetary policy can have a strong influence on interest rates and economic growth, it affects the securities traded in all financial markets. The type of influence monetary policy can have on each financial market is summarized in Exhibit 6.9. Some institutions hire economists to focus on assessing monetary policy so that they can determine how their various securities portfolios will be affected.

INTEGRATING MONETARY AND FISCAL POLICIES

Although the Fed has the power to make decisions without the approval of the presidential administration, the Fed's monetary policy is commonly influenced by the administration's fiscal policies. In some situations, the Fed and the administration have used complementary policies to resolve economic problems. In other situations, they have used conflicting policies. A brief history of their solutions to economic problems is provided below. Given the unstable relationship between money supply and economic conditions, financial market participants must attempt to incorporate the potential impact of any external forces on that relationship.

History

The presidential administration has historically been most concerned with the objective of maintaining strong economic growth and low unemployment. The Fed generally shared the same concern in the early 1970s. A year before President Nixon's reelection in 1972, the economy was somewhat stagnant, and inflation was higher than in previous years. The Nixon Administration and the Fed combined their power to resolve their problems. The administration enforced wage-price controls (although many exceptions were allowed) to limit inflation, while the Fed used a stimulative monetary policy to reduce unemployment. Although such a stimulative policy can normally lead to higher inflation, the wage-price controls temporarily prevented inflationary consequences. By the 1972 presidential reelection, economic conditions had improved, which was a primary reason for Nixon's victory. Yet, when wage-price controls were lifted in 1973, inflation increased.

EXHIBIT 6.9 Impact of Monetary Policy across Financial Markets

TYPE OF FINANCIAL MARKET	RELEVANT FACTORS INFLUENCED BY MONETARY POLICY	KEY INSTITUTIONAL PARTICIPANTS
Money Market	Interest Rates: ■ Affect the secondary market values of existing money market securities. ■ Affect yields on newly issued money market securities: Economic Growth: ■ Affects the risk premium on money market securities.	Commercial banks, savings institutions, credit unions, money market funds, insurance companies, finance companies, pension funds.
Bond Market	Interest Rates: ■ Affect the secondary market values of existing bonds. ■ Affect the yields offered on newly issued bonds. Economic Growth: ■ Affects the risk premium on corporate and municipal bonds.	Commercial banks, savings institutions, bond mutual funds, insurance companies, finance companies, pension funds.
Mortgage Market	Interest Rates: ■ Affect the demand for housing and therefore the demand for mortgages. ■ Affect the secondary market values of existing mortgages. ■ Affect the interest rates on new mortgages. Economic Growth: ■ Affects the demand for housing and therefore the demand for mortgages. ■ Affects the risk premium on mortgages.	Commercial banks, savings institutions, credit unions, insurance companies, pension funds.
Stock Market	Interest Rates: ■ Affect the required return on stocks and therefore the market values of stocks. Economic Growth: ■ Affects projections for corporate earnings and therefore stock values.	Stock mutual funds, insurance companies, pension funds.
Futures Market	Interest Rates: ■ Affects the values of bond futures contracts, including Treasury bond futures and bond index futures. ■ Affects the required return on stocks and therefore the market values of stocks, which in turn influence the value of stock index futures.	Institutions that consider hedging their bond or stock portfolios with financial futures, such as commercial banks, savings institutions, mutual funds, insurance companies, finance companies, and pension funds.

Continued

EXHIBIT 6.9 Impact of Monetary Policy across Financial Markets (Continued)

TYPE OF FINANCIAL MARKET	RELEVANT FACTORS INFLUENCED BY MONETARY POLICY	KEY INSTITUTIONAL PARTICIPANTS
Futures Market *Continued*	**Economic Growth:** ■ Affects projections for corporate earnings and the stock market, which in turn influences the value of stock index futures.	
Stock Options	**Interest Rates:** ■ Affect the required return on stocks and therefore the market values of stocks, which in turn influence option prices. **Economic Growth:** ■ Affects projections for corporate earnings and therefore stock values, which in turn influence option prices.	Institutions that are active in the stock market, including stock mutual funds, insurance companies, pension funds, and securities firms.
Currency Options	**Interest Rates:** ■ Affect the demand for currencies and therefore the values of currencies, which in turn affect currency option prices. **Economic Growth:** ■ Affects the demand for currencies and therefore the values of currencies, which in turn affect currency options prices.	Institutions that invest in securities denominated in foreign currencies, such as commercial banks, international mutual funds, insurance companies, and pension funds.
Interest Rate Swap	**Interest Rates:** ■ Affect the performance of interest rate swaps.	Institutions that invest in bonds, and hedge interest rate risk.
Currency Swap	**Interest Rates:** ■ Affect the values of currencies, which in turn affect the performance of currency swaps. **Economic Growth:** ■ Affects the values of currencies, which in turn affect the performance of currency swaps.	Institutions that are exposed to exchange rate risk.
Foreign Exchange	**Interest Rates:** ■ Affect the demand for currencies and therefore the values of currencies, which in turn affect currency option prices.	Institutions that are exposed to exchange rate risk.

By 1980, inflation was close to 10 percent annually, and unemployment was also high. At that time, the administration attempted to stimulate the economy by reducing tax rates. Yet, the Fed used a relatively tight monetary policy to reduce inflation. As expected, the tight-money policy slowed economic growth and effectively reduced inflation. Although the Fed was given partial credit for lowering inflation, it was also criticized for causing the 1982 recession and for not resolving the 1982 recession as quickly as it could have. However, had the Fed used a stimulative policy to eliminate the recession, inflation could have reignited.

The Fed's increased concern for inflation during the early 1980s relative to the 1970s was partially attributed to the appointment of Paul Volcker as chairman in 1979. Volcker was a strong believer in reducing the inflationary spiral that continued throughout the 1970s. Financial market participants who understood Volcker's beliefs may have been able to forecast the Fed's anti-inflationary monetary policy during the early 1980s.

The Fed and the administration sometimes differ on whether economic growth (and unemployment) or inflation deserves the most attention. Some of their most intense arguments occurred during the recessionary periods preceding the 1984 presidential election. The frequent arguments during that period are summarized below with the following hypothetical conversation:

Administration: We are receiving all the criticism from the farmers, auto workers, etc., who are out of work. If you would loosen money supply, interest rates would decline, spending would increase, and jobs would be created.

Fed: First of all, we are receiving as much criticism from the unemployed as you are. Second, if you didn't create such a large federal deficit, interest rates would already be lower, and you wouldn't have to rely on a loose monetary policy to stimulate the economy.

Administration: We are currently trying to reduce our budget deficit. In the meantime, your sole concern to reduce inflation is causing millions of people to be unemployed and is therefore reducing our tax revenues and increasing our deficit.

Fed: If we don't attempt to reduce inflation, who will? You are more interested in the next election, and you believe that higher unemployment causes more lost votes than higher inflation would cause. If we allow excessive growth in the money supply now, the long-term consequences of higher inflation could be devastating. We have witnessed how sustained inflation can force interest rates up, possibly leading to a stagnant economy over time. Thus, the ultimate result could be both high unemployment and inflation if we don't reduce inflation now.

Administration: We agree that excessive growth in the money supply can lead to continued inflation. But you have been too tight with money lately. Do you think the public is satisfied with your tight-money policy?

Fed:	The public may not understand that although our policy is painful now, it will benefit them over the long run.
Administration:	Do you think that unemployed people are going to believe that?
Fed:	Probably not. And you certainly don't make it any easier by claiming that it is our fault that they are unemployed.
Administration:	So when are you going to loosen up in order to end this severe recession?
Fed:	When it appears that loosening up will not reignite inflation.
Administration:	How long are you willing to wait for such conditions, while millions of people are without jobs?
Fed:	As long as necessary!

To conclude this argument, the Fed did loosen the money supply in 1983, causing a significant decline in interest rates. The economy subsequently improved, and inflation remained low. Some critics use these results as evidence to claim that the Fed could have loosened the money supply earlier to more quickly eliminate the recession without reigniting inflation. Others suggest that the Fed's policy worked only because it was implemented after inflation had fully subsided. Finally, others claim that the Fed purposely maintained a relatively tight monetary policy to demonstrate that it makes its own decisions and will not surrender to pressure by any presidential administration.

A somewhat similar argument between the Fed and the administration occurred during the 1992 presidential election. Again, the Fed seemed determined to fight inflation, while the administration appeared to be more concerned with the unemployment level.

Monetizing the Debt

An ongoing dilemma faced by the Fed is whether to help finance the federal budget deficit that has been created from fiscal policy. To illustrate, consider an example in which the administration decides to implement a new fiscal policy that will result in a larger federal deficit than what was originally expected. The Fed must first assess the potential impact that this new fiscal policy will have on the economy. A likely concern of the Fed is the possibility of a crowding-out effect, in which excessive borrowing by the Treasury crowds out other potential borrowers (such as households or corporations) in competing for whatever loanable funds are available. This can cause higher interest rates and therefore may restrict economic growth. The Fed may counter by loosening money supply, which might offset the increased demand for loanable funds by the federal government. This action is known as **monetizing the debt,** as the Fed is partially financing the federal deficit. Exhibit 6.10 illustrates how this works. As the Treasury issues new Treasury securities in the primary market to finance the deficit, there may be upward pressure on interest rates. The Fed could offset this pressure by using open market operations to purchase Treasury securities (from government securities dealers) in the secondary market. Before the Fed monetizes the debt, it may first monitor how the additional borrowing by the Treasury is affecting interest rates. If there is no significant change in interest rates, the Fed may decide not to intervene.

When the Fed purchases Treasury securities, the Treasury must repurchase the securities at maturity just as if an individual or a firm owned them. Thus,

EXHIBIT 6.10
Monetization of
Debt by the Fed

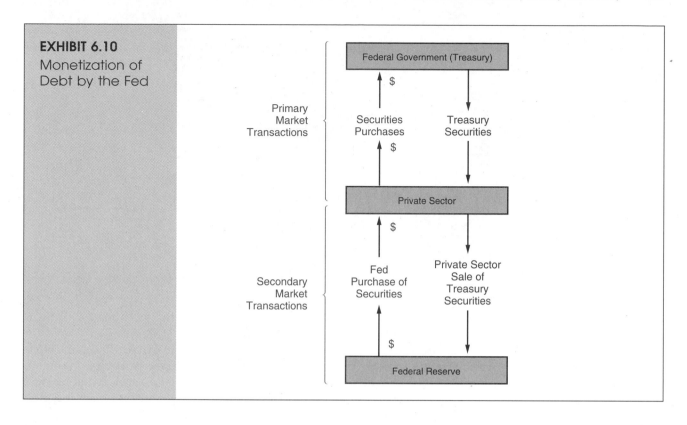

Treasury securities held by the Fed still reflect debt from the Treasury's per-spective. However, the Treasury may sometimes prefer that the Fed monetize the debt, because if it does not, interest rates could rise and reduce economic growth.

The Fed may have preferred not to monetize the debt, because such a strat-egy requires higher money supply growth, which could ignite inflation. How-ever, if the Fed does not monetize the debt, there may be a greater likelihood of a weak economy.

Market Reaction to Integrated Policies

Financial market participants must consider the potential policies of both the administration (fiscal) and the Fed (monetary) when assessing future economic conditions. Exhibit 6.11 provides a broad overview of how the participants mon-itor monetary and fiscal policy actions. The participants forecast the type of mon-etary and fiscal policies that will be implemented and then determine how these anticipated policies will affect future economic conditions. For example, they must forecast shifts in the supply of and demand for loanable funds, which requires a forecast of the factors that affect such funds. The supply of loanable funds can be affected by the Fed's adjustment of the money supply or any changes in tax policies by the administration. The demand for loanable funds is affected by any change in inflationary expectations, which can be influenced by fluctuations in money supply or aggregate spending. In addition, the demand for loanable funds is affected by government expenditures. Tax revisions could

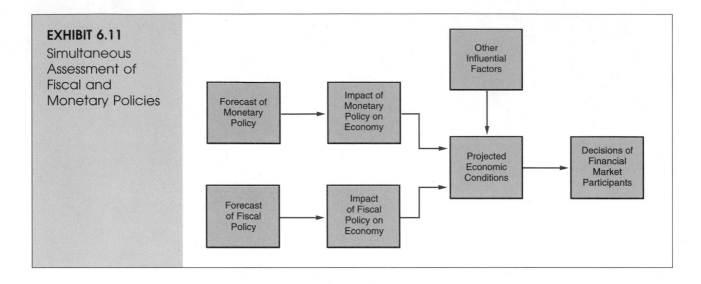

EXHIBIT 6.11
Simultaneous Assessment of Fiscal and Monetary Policies

also affect the demand for loanable funds if they affect the incentive for firms or individuals to borrow.

Once forecasts of the supply of and demand for loanable funds are completed, interest rate movements can be forecasted. Interest rate projections are necessary to forecast the aggregate demand for goods and services, which will influence the level of economic growth, the unemployment rate, and inflation rate. Other factors not directly related to government policies, such as oil prices and labor contract situations, also have an impact on the economic variables, and these, too, have to be considered.

GLOBAL EFFECTS ON MONETARY POLICY

GLOBAL ASPECTS

Financial market participants must recognize that the type of monetary policy to be implemented by the Fed is somewhat dependent on various international factors. For example, a weak dollar can stimulate U.S. exports, discourage U.S. imports, and therefore stimulate the U.S. economy. In addition, it tends to exert inflationary pressure in the United States. Thus, the Fed would be less likely to use a stimulative monetary policy when the dollar is weak. For example, a weak dollar in 1992 prevented the Fed from using a stimulative monetary policy, as the Fed was concerned about inflationary pressure. A strong dollar tends to reduce inflationary pressure but also dampen the U.S. economy. Therefore, the Fed is more likely to use a stimulative policy during a strong-dollar period.

International flows of funds can also affect the Fed's monetary policy. If there is upward pressure on U.S. interest rates that can be offset by foreign inflows of funds, the Fed may not feel compelled to use a loose-money policy. However, if foreign investors reduce their investment in U.S. securities, the Fed may be forced to intervene to prevent interest rates from rising.

The Fed's policies may depend partly on foreign economies. For example, in the late 1980s and early 1990s, U.S. government officials requested that governments of other industrialized countries stimulate their respective economies. If, over time, these foreign governments comply, there will be an indirect stimulus

MONETARY POLICY IN THE SOVIET UNION

As an international example of how excessive monetary growth can affect inflation, consider the situation in the Soviet Union, which was separated into several Soviet republics. The exhibit here shows the relationship between the broad money growth level and the inflation rate over the period 1992–1993 for 13 of these republics. The exhibit shows a strong positive relationship between excess money growth and inflation. At one extreme, Estonia and Latvia had money growth and inflation levels of less than 10 percent. At the other extreme, Ukraine experienced a money growth rate of about 1,500 percent and an inflation rate of about 1,500 percent.

SOURCE: *International Economic Conditions,* Federal Reserve Bank of St. Louis, February 1994.

to the United States through a greater demand for U.S. exports. Consequently, the Fed may not need to use a stimulative monetary policy. Of course, foreign governments may not comply with U.S. requests, just as the U.S. government policies do not necessarily comply with foreign government requests. But the point of this discussion is that because economies are integrated, one country's monetary policy may depend partly on government policies in other countries.

Given the international integration in money and capital markets, a government's budget deficit can affect interest rates of various countries. This concept, referred to as **global crowding out,** is illustrated in Exhibit 6.12. An increase in the U.S. budget deficit causes an outward shift in the federal government demand for U.S. funds and therefore in the aggregate demand for U.S. funds (from D_1 to D_2). This crowding out effect forces the interest rate in the United States to increase from i_1 to i_2 if the supply curve (S) is unchanged. As U.S. rates rise, they attract funds from investors in other countries, such as Germany and Japan. As foreign investors use more of their funds to invest in U.S. securities, the supply of available funds in their respective countries declines. Consequently,

EXHIBIT 6.12 Illustration of Global Crowding Out

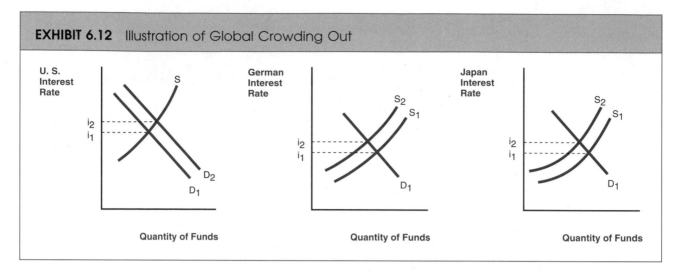

there is upward pressure on non-U.S. interest rates as well. The impact will be most pronounced on those countries whose investors would most likely be attracted to the higher U.S. interest rates. The possibility of global crowding out has caused national governments to criticize one another for large federal budget deficits.

Effects of international economic integration are shown in Exhibit 6.13. Each of the four countries tend to experience its highest inflation rate (1980, 1981) or highest unemployment rate (1983) at the same time as the others. Each country also experienced its lowest inflation rate (1986) and lowest unemployment rate (1979) at the same time as the others. The similarity in the economic conditions over time suggests that financial market participants must consider economies of other countries when assessing their own.

European Monetary Policy

European countries have considered using more policy coordination among their central banks, and have even considered creating a single European currency, which would allow for a single European monetary policy. Although this would be a major step toward integrating European economies, there are some major philosophical differences between European countries that may prevent a more coordinated central bank effort. To illustrate, consider the situation in 1992 when the German government focused on controlling inflation and implemented a tight monetary policy. This increased German interest rates and attracted money from other European countries. Because exchange rates between European currencies were tied (within narrow boundaries), European investors capitalized on the high German interest rates without much concern about exchange rate risk. The flow of funds out of other European countries reduced the supply of funds in these countries. Consequently, interest rates increased in these countries as well at a time when their respective governments were attempting to lower interest rates in order to stimulate their economies. The end result was less aggregate spending throughout European countries because of the increase in interest rates. Such a result was especially undesirable during 1992, because some European countries were in the midst of a recession.

EXHIBIT 6.13   Comparison of Inflation and Unemployment Rates in Four Major Countries

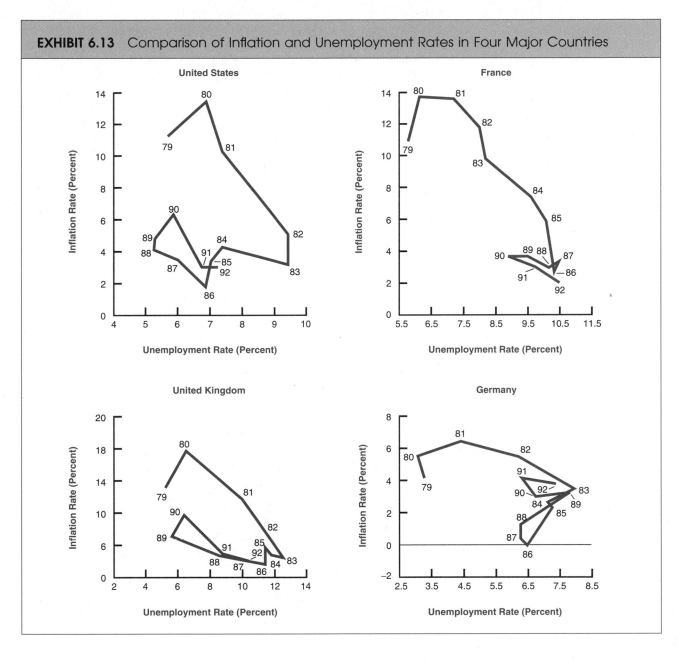

This example illustrates the degree to which European economies are integrated as a result of the exchange rate mechanism (ERM) that links European currency values. When exchange rates are tied, a high interest rate in one country has a strong influence on interest rates in other countries. Funds will flow to the country with a more attractive interest rate, which reduces the supply of funds in the other countries and places upward pressure on their interest rates. The flow of funds should continue until the interest rate differential has been eliminated or reduced. This process will not necessarily apply to countries not participating in the ERM because the exchange rate risk may discourage the flow of funds to the countries with relatively high interest rates. However, because the ERM requires central banks to maintain the exchange rates between currencies within specified boundaries, investors moving funds among the participating European countries are less concerned about exchange rate risk.

In 1993, the boundaries applied within the ERM were widened, allowing more fluctuation in exchange rates between European currencies. This may discourage money flows to the European country with the highest interest rate because there is more exchange rate risk. Yet, it also causes more segmented European economies, and reduces the likelihood of increased coordination among European monetary policies.

SUMMARY

- The Keynesian theory suggests how the Fed can affect the interaction between demand for money and the supply of money, which affects interest rates, aggregate spending, and economic growth. As the Fed increases the money supply, interest rates should decline, which results in more aggregate spending (because of cheaper financing rates) and higher economic growth. As the Fed decreases the money supply, interest rates should increase, which results in less aggregate spending (because of higher financing rates), lower economic growth, and lower inflation.

- The Monetarist approach suggests that excess growth in the money supply can cause inflationary expectations. Therefore, expansionary monetary policy by the Fed may have limited effects because increasing the money supply may also result in an increased demand for money (in response to higher inflationary expectations). Thus, interest rates may not necessarily be controlled by the Fed's adjustment in money supply, and the impact of monetary policy on aggregate spending is questionable.

- A stimulative monetary policy is likely to increase economic growth, but may also cause higher inflation. A restrictive monetary policy is likely to reduce inflation, but may also reduce economic growth. Thus, the Fed faces a trade-off when implementing monetary policy. Given a possible trade-off, the Fed tends to assess whether the potential benefits of any proposed monetary policy outweigh the potential adverse effects.

- Financial market participants attempt to forecast the Fed's future monetary policies and the effects of these policies on economic conditions. Using this information, they can determine how their security holdings would be affected, and can adjust their security portfolios accordingly.

QUESTIONS

1. How does the Fed's monetary policy affect economic conditions?

2. Describe the economic trade-off faced by the Fed in achieving its economic goals.

3. What is a criticism of using quick-fix policies?

4. When does the Fed use a loose-money policy and when does it use a tight-money policy?

5. Briefly summarize the pure Keynesian philosophy and identify the key variable considered.

6. Briefly summarize the Monetarist approach.

7. Why might the Fed have difficulty in controlling the economy in the manner desired? Be specific.

8. What is the recognition lag? Explain why it occurs.

9. When does the implementation lag occur?

10. Assume that the Fed's primary goal is to cure inflation. How can it use open market operations to achieve its goal? What is a possible adverse effect of this action by the Fed (even if it achieves its goal)?

11. When it was announced on June 2, 1987, that Paul Volcker would resign as chairman of the Federal Reserve, the dollar weakened substantially. Why do you think this may have occurred?

12. Why do financial market participants closely monitor money supply movements?

13. Why do financial market participants that monitor monetary policy have only limited success in forecasting economic variables?

14. If a change in the discount rate is not likely to directly affect market interest rates, why do financial markets sometimes react to such a change?

15. Why would the Fed try to avoid frequent changes in the money supply?

16. Explain why an increase in the money supply can affect interest rates in different ways. Incorporate the potential impact of the money supply on the supply of loanable funds and demand for loanable funds when answering this question.

17. What other factors might be considered by financial market participants that are assessing whether an increase in money supply growth will affect inflation?

18. How do financial market participants use the up-to-date money supply figures released every Thursday afternoon?

19. Describe how portfolio managers in the bond market may react if the Fed overshoots its target range.

20. Why would financial markets react less to money supply announcements during a recessionary period?

21. Why did financial markets react less to money supply announcements during the period of deregulation when new types of deposits were introduced by depository institutions?

22. Explain how some bond portfolio managers attempt to capitalize on their projections of money supply announcements.

23. Do you think the Fed used a monetary policy in the early 1980s that was too tight? Explain.

24. Is the Fed independent of the presidential administration? Explain.

25. Explain the meaning of monetizing the debt. How can this action improve economic conditions? What is the risk involved?

26. Assess the economic situation today. Is the administration more concerned with reducing unemployment or inflation? Does the Fed have a similar opinion? If not, is the administration publicly criticizing the Fed? Is the Fed publicly criticizing the administration? Explain.

27. Why might a foreign country's government policies be closely monitored by investors in other countries, even if the investors plan no investments in that country?

28. What is global crowding out?

PROJECT

1. Market Assessment of Fed Policy
   Review the "Credit Markets" section of *The Wall Street Journal* (listed in the index on the first page) over the past five days. Summarize the market assessments of the Fed on each day. Also summarize the market's expectations about future interest rates. Are these expectations primarily because of the Fed's monetary policy or because of other factors? The following table can be used for your analysis:

	MARKET ASSESSMENT OF THE FED	MARKET EXPECTATIONS OF FUTURE INTEREST RATES	ARE THE MARKET'S INTEREST RATE EXPECTATIONS DUE TO FED POLICY?
1 day ago			
2 days ago			
3 days ago			
4 days ago			
5 days ago			

Fed Is Likely to Lift Rates, Greenspan Says

Timing, Amount of Increase Depend on the Markets' Inflation Expectations

David Wessel, Washington

Federal Reserve Chairman Alan Greenspan told Congress that the Fed is likely to continue boosting short-term interest rates—but how much and how soon depends on expectations about inflation.

Inflation-adjusted "short-term rates are more likely to have to rise than fall from here. I cannot, however, tell you when any such rise would occur," Mr. Greenspan told a House banking subcommittee two weeks after the Fed's first move to raise interest rates in five years.

While acknowledging financial markets' anxiety that "a strengthening economy is sowing the seeds of an acceleration of prices later this year," the chairman of the nation's central bank used his semiannual report to Congress to try to persuade markets that they don't have much to worry about. "Overall cost and price pressures still appear to remain damped," he said.

Stock and bond prices climbed amid investor relief that Mr. Greenspan delivered no unpleasant surprises in his testimony. The Dow Jones Industrial Average jumped 24.20 points, to 3911.66.

"History . . . tells us that inflation requires financial tinder, which, at the moment, as I see it, is lacking," Mr. Greenspan said. Wages don't seem to be accelerating, he said. Advances in productivity, or output per hour of work, are holding down labor costs. The money supply, broadly defined, is growing slowly," he added.

Moreover, he played down fears that the U.S. economy is growing so fast that it threatens to overheat. Although its "forward momentum remains intact," the Los Angeles earthquake and the severe winter weather have slowed the economy, and an uptick in claims for unemployment benefits suggests "a somewhat less buoyant degree of activity," the Fed chief said.

The central bank, Mr. Greenspan vowed, won't wait until inflation actually shows itself before raising interest rates again. Instead, it is watching reflections of market expectations for inflation—particularly the price of gold, exchange rates and the relationship between long- and short-term interest rates.

Responding to a question from Rep. John LaFalce (D., N.Y.), Mr. Greenspan underscored the significance of changes in the price of gold, saying it is "a reasonably good indicator amongst others of what inflation expectations are doing. . . . It's not a perfect indicator, but it is a very good indicator."

With money-supply measures no longer providing a useful guide for the Fed, Mr. Greenspan added, "we are seeking anything which gives us insight into the process, and what history does tell us is that gold is a useful indicator thereof." Former Fed Gov. Wayne Angell, long an advocate of tracking gold prices, smiled and nodded from his seat in the audience.

Gold prices surged late last year as the U.S. economy rebounded, and haven't moved much this year.

Fed policy makers expect consumer-price inflation of about 3% this year, "a shade higher" than last year's 2.7%, according to a report Mr. Greenspan submitted with his testimony. The report also said that a poor 1993 harvest has left some crops scarce, a repeat of last year's decline in energy prices is unlikely, and "competitive pressure damping wage and price increases will be less strong and less pervasive than they have been recently."

President Clinton told reporters he was encouraged by Mr. Greenspan's testimony, citing the Fed chairman's view that conditions for economic growth are better than they have been for decades and that there isn't any sign of an increase in inflation. The president refused to talk about short-term interest rates, however.

'Insurance' Move

Mr. Greenspan described the Fed's move to raise short-term interest rates earlier this month as "low-cost insurance" against the risk of "a future destabilizing build-up of inflationary pressures." He said the central bank had been holding interest rates "abnormally low" in response to the unusual drive of consumers and businesses to pay down debt. With that phase of the economic expansion past, the Fed no longer had any reason to continue holding rates so slow, he said.

Neither Democratic nor Republican members of the subcommittee were convinced. "Inflation is frozen in its tracks," said Rep. Paul Kanjorksi (D., Pa.), chairman of the subcommittee. Fed critic Rep. Henry Gonzalez (D., Texas),

Continued

CASE APPLICATION: MONETARY POLICY DECISIONS

Continued

chairman of the full committee, didn't attend.

Mr. Greenspan in the past has pointed to the Fed's goal of setting short-term rates at levels that will encourage the bond market to keep long-term interest rates low. But as Mr. Kanjorksi and others noted repeatedly, long-term rates have risen since the Fed's Feb. 4 move. Put on the defensive, Mr. Greenspan said that short- and long-term interest rates tend to move together and suggested that the test of monetary policy is whether long-term rates rise less than they otherwise would; he didn't say how that can be determined.

Other Items Noted

In other matters, Mr. Greenspan and the report he submitted said:

■ Fed officials expect the economy to grow a moderate 3% to 3 1/4% this year, but at best they expect only a slight decrease in the unemployment rate from the 6.7% reported for January.

■ The Fed's unusual public announcement of its Feb. 4 decision to raise interest rates wasn't intended as a precedent, but the central bank does plan changes in its disclosure policies, which are to be announced in the future.

■ The signals from money-supply measures, once crucial to Fed thinking, have been "effectively jammed" by changes in financial markets and the unusual nature of the current business cycle. Thus, the Fed continues to largely disregard them.

■ The Fed has deliberately lengthened the maturity of its portfolio of Treasury securities to 3.2 years from 3.0 years in 1992 by buying longer-term debt. At the beginning of the 1980s, the average maturity of the central bank's portfolio was greater than four years and it declined steadily until 1991, when it reached 2.9 years. Some economists have urged the Fed to buy more longer-term securities to help reduce long-term interest rates.

SOURCE: *The Wall Street Journal* (February 23, 1994): p. A2. Reprinted by permission of *The Wall Street Journal* © 1994 Dow Jones & Company, Inc. All rights reserved worldwide.

QUESTIONS

1. Alan Greenspan, Federal Reserve chairman, stated that the Fed will not wait until inflation actually shows itself before raising interest rates again. Interpret this statement.

2. Explain why gold prices may be a reasonable indicator of future inflation. Why doesn't the Fed simply enact monetary policy based on actual inflation rates?

3. Why were farm and energy prices assessed within Alan Greenspan's discussion?

4. Explain why the Fed's lengthening of maturities on its portfolio of Treasury securities could affect the yield curve. Why would economists prefer that the Fed focus on long-term interest rates rather than short-term interest rates?

REFERENCES

Broaddus, J. Alfred. "Central Banking: Then and Now." *Economic Quarterly*, Federal Reserve Bank of Richmond (Spring 1993), pp. 1–11.

Deaves, Richard. "Money Supply Announcements and Market Reactions in an Open Economy." *Journal of Money, Credit, and Banking* (May 1990): 154–164.

Furlong, Frederick T. "International Dimensions of U.S. Economic Policy in the 1980s." *Economic Review*, Federal Reserve Bank of San Francisco (Spring 1989): 3–16.

Glick, Reuven, and Michael Hutchinson. "Economic Integration and Fiscal Policy Transmission: Implications for Europe in 1992 and Beyond." *Economic Review*, Federal Reserve Bank of San Francisco (Spring 1990): 17–28.

Grier, Kevin B., and Mark J. Perry. "The Effect of Money Shocks on Interest Rates in the Presence of Conditional Hetereskedasticity." *Journal of Finance* (September 1993): 1445–1455.

Hetzel, Robert L. "Central Banks' Independence in Historical Perspective: A Review Essay." *Journal of Monetary Economics* (January 1990): 165–176.

Higgins, Bryan. "Policy Implications of Recent M2 Behavior." *Economic Review*, Federal Reserve Bank of Kansas City (3rd Quarter 1992): 21–36.

McNees, Stephen K. "The Discount Rate: The Other Monetary Policy Tool." *New England Economic Review* (July/August 1993): 3–22.

Mitchell, Karlyn, and Douglas K. Pearce. "Discount Window Borrowing Across Federal Reserve Districts: Evidence Under Contemporaneous Reserve Accounting." *Journal of Banking and Finance* (August 1992): 771–790.

Puckett, Richard H. "Federal Open Market Committee Structure and Decisions." *Journal of Monetary Economics* 14, no. 1 (1984): 97–104.

Roley, V. Vance, and Carl E. Walsh. "Unanticipated Money and Interest Rates." *American Economic Review* (May 1984): 49–54.

Roth, Howard. "Effects of Financial Deregulation on Monetary Policy." *Economic Review*, Federal Reserve Bank of Kansas City (March 1988): 17–29.

Schirm, David C., Richard G. Sheehan, and Michael G. Ferri. "Financial Market Responses to Treasury Debt Announcements." *Journal of Money, Credit, and Banking* (August 1989): 394–400.

Strongin, Steven, and Vefa Tarhan. "Money Supply Announcements and the Market's Perception of Federal Reserve Policy." *Journal of Money, Credit, and Banking* (May 1990): 135–153.

Thornton, Daniel L. "The Discount Rate and Market Interest Rates: Theory and Evidence." *Review*, Federal Reserve Bank of St. Louis (August–September 1986): 5–21.

Urich, Thomas J. "The Information Content of Weekly Money Supply Announcements." *Journal of Monetary Economics* (July 1982): 73–88.

Wagster, John. "The Information Content of Discount Rate Announcements Revisited." *Journal of Money, Credit, and Banking* (February 1993): 132–137.

FED WATCHING

This problem requires an understanding of the Fed (Chapter 5) and monetary policy (Chapter 6). It also requires an understanding of how economic conditions affect interest rates and securities prices (Chapters 2, 3, and 4).

Like many other investors, you are a "Fed watcher," who constantly monitors any actions taken by the Fed to revise monetary policy. You believe that there are three key factors affecting the interest rates. Assume that the most important factor is the Fed's monetary policy. The second most important factor is the state of the economy, which influences the demand for loanable funds. The third factor is the level of inflation, which also influences the demand for loanable funds. Because monetary policy can affect interest rates, it affects economic growth as well. By controlling monetary policy, the Fed influences the prices of all types of securities.

The following information is available:

- Economic growth has been consistently strong over the past few years but is beginning to slow down.
- Unemployment is as low as it has been in the past decade but has risen slightly over the past two quarters.
- Inflation has been about 5 percent per year for the past few years.
- The dollar has been strong.
- Oil prices have been very low.

Yesterday, an event occurred that you believe will cause much higher oil prices in the United States and a weaker U.S. economy in the near future. You plan to determine whether the Fed will respond to the economic problems that are likely to develop.

You reviewed previous situations of economic slowdowns caused by a decline in the aggregate demand for goods and services in the past and found that each economic slow down precipitated a loose-money policy by the Fed. Inflation was 3 percent or less in each of the previous economic slowdowns. Interest rates generally declined in response to these policies, and the U.S. economy improved.

Assume that the philosophy of the Fed regarding monetary policy is to maintain economic growth and low inflation. There does not appear to be any major fiscal policy forthcoming that will have a major effect on the economy. The future economy is up to the Fed. The present policy of the Fed is a 2 percent annual growth rate in the money supply. You believe that the economy is headed toward a recession unless the Fed uses a very stimulative monetary policy, such as a 10 percent annual growth rate in the money supply.

A general consensus of economists is that the Fed will revise its monetary policy to stimulate the economy for three reasons: (1) it recognizes the potential costs of higher unemployment if a recession occurs, (2) it consistently used a stimulative policy in the past to prevent recessions, and (3) the administration has been pressuring the Fed to use a stimulative monetary policy. Although you consider the opinions of the economists, you plan to make your own assessment of the Fed's future policy. Two quarters ago, the gross national product (GNP) declined by one percent. Last quarter, the GNP declined again by one percent. Thus, there is a clear evidence that the economy has recently slowed down.

QUESTIONS

a. Do you think that the Fed will use a stimulative monetary policy at this point? Explain.

b. You maintain a large portfolio of U.S. bonds. Your opinion is that if the Fed does not revise its monetary policy, the U.S. economy will continue to decline. If the Fed stimulates the economy at this point, you believe that you would be better off with stocks than with bonds. Based on this information, do you think you should switch to stocks? Explain.

PART 3

SECURITY MARKETS

Part Three focuses on how four types of security markets facilitate the flow of funds from surplus units to deficit units. Chapter 7 focuses on money markets for investors and borrowers trading short-term securities. Chapters 8 and 9 focus on bond markets and mortgage markets, respectively, for investors and borrowers trading long-term securities. Chapter 10 focuses on stock markets, which normally involves long-term investors. Because some financial market participants trade securities in all of these markets, there is much interaction between these markets, as emphasized throughout the chapters.

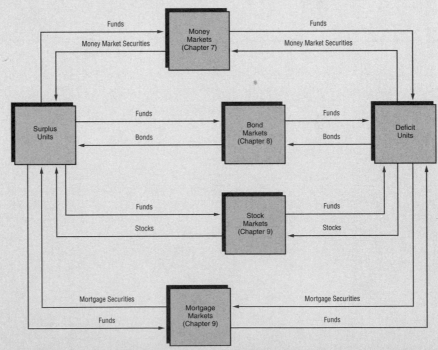

CHAPTER 7

MONEY MARKETS

Money markets are used to facilitate the transfer of short-term funds from individuals, corporations, or governments with excess funds to those with deficient funds. Even investors who focus on long-term securities tend to maintain some money market securities for liquidity.

The specific objectives of this chapter are to:

- provide a background on the most popular money market securities,
- explain how money markets are used by institutional investors, and
- explain how money markets have become globalized.

MONEY MARKET SECURITIES

Securities with maturities within one year are referred to as **money market securities.** They are issued by corporations and governments to obtain short-term funds. They are originally issued within the **primary market,** which is a telecommunications network whereby investors can be informed that new securities are for sale. Generally, the issuer has no obligation to repurchase securities until maturity, yet investors who purchase them before maturity may be able to sell them through the **secondary market.** Money market securities that have an active secondary market are preferred, because they allow investors more flexibility.

The more popular money market securities are:

- Treasury bills
- Commercial paper

- Negotiable certificates of deposit
- Repurchase agreements
- Federal funds
- Banker's acceptances

Each of these instruments is described in turn.

Treasury Bills

When the U.S. government needs to borrow funds, the U.S. Treasury frequently issues short-term securities known as Treasury bills (or T-bills). These are sold weekly through an auction. One-year T-bills are issued on a monthly basis. The par value (amount received by investors at maturity) of T-bills is a minimum of $10,000 in multiples of $5,000 thereafter. T-bills are attractive to investors because they are backed by the federal government and therefore are virtually free of default risk. Another attractive feature of T-bills is their liquidity, due to their short maturity and strong secondary market. Existing Treasury bills can be sold in the secondary market through government securities dealers, who profit by purchasing the bills at a slightly lower price than they sell them for.

TREASURY BILL AUCTION.   The primary Treasury bill market is an auction by mail. Investors submit bids on the Treasury bill applications for the maturity of their choice. An example of a 26-week Treasury bill application is shown in Exhibit 7.1. Investors have an option to bid competitively or noncompetitively. Competitive bids must be received by Federal Reserve banks by Monday 1:00 P.M. Eastern time of each week and are then wired to the Treasury. The Treasury has a specified amount of funds that it plans to borrow during the 26-week period, and this dictates the amount of Treasury bill bids it will accept. After accounting for noncompetitive bids, it accepts the highest competitive bids first and works its way down until it has generated the amount of funds from competitive bids that it needs. Any bids that are below that cutoff point are not accepted.

To ensure that their bid will be accepted, investors can use a noncompetitive bid. The price they will pay (per $1,000 par value) is the weighted average price paid by all competitive bidders whose bids were accepted. Because noncompetitive bidders do not know this amount in advance, they write a check for the par value of the Treasury bills they have requested. Once the auction results are completed, the Treasury sends a check back to them that represents the difference between par value and the final price.

Noncompetitive bidders are limited to purchasing Treasury bills with a maximum par value of $1 million per auction. Consequently, large corporations typically make competitive bids so they can purchase larger amounts.

Applications to purchase a Treasury bill can be obtained at no charge from a Federal Reserve district or branch bank. Alternatively, investors can ask a broker or a commercial bank to obtain and send in the application for them. The fee charged for this service normally ranges from $25 to $75. This fee can have a significant impact on the yield to an investor who purchases a Treasury bill with a $10,000 par value. For larger denominations, such as $100,000, the yield is less sensitive to a fee.

The results of the weekly auction of 13-week and 26-week Treasury bills are summarized in major daily newspapers each Tuesday. Some of the more com-

EXHIBIT 7.1 Example of a Treasury Bill Application

FORM PD F 5176-2
(February 1990)

TREASURY
DIRECT ®

OMB No. 1535-0069
Expires: 09-30-92

TENDER FOR 26-WEEK TREASURY BILL

TENDER INFORMATION AMOUNT OF TENDER: $ _____	FOR DEPARTMENT USE

BID TYPE (Check One)   ☐ NONCOMPETITIVE   ☐ COMPETITIVE AT . %

ACCOUNT NUMBER   ___ - ___ - ___ .

TENDER NUMBER
912794

INVESTOR INFORMATION

ACCOUNT NAME

CUSIP

ISSUE DATE

RECEIVED BY

DATE RECEIVED

ADDRESS

EXT REG   ☐

FOREIGN   ☐

BACKUP   ☐

REVIEW   ☐

CITY   STATE   ZIP CODE

TAXPAYER IDENTIFICATION NUMBER

CLASS   ☐

1ST NAMED
OWNER   ___ - ___ -   **OR**   ___ -
SOCIAL SECURITY NUMBER   EMPLOYER IDENTIFICATION NUMBER

TELEPHONE NUMBERS

WORK ( ) ___ - ___   HOME ( ) ___ - ___

PAYMENT ATTACHED

TOTAL PAYMENT: $ _____

NUMBERS

CASH (01): $ _____   CHECKS (02/03): $ _____

SECURITIES (05): $ _____ $ _____

OTHER (06): $ _____ $ _____

DIRECT DEPOSIT INFORMATION

ROUTING NUMBER

FINANCIAL INSTITUTION NAME

ACCOUNT NUMBER

ACCOUNT NAME

ACCOUNT TYPE   ☐ CHECKING
(Check One)
☐ SAVINGS

AUTOMATIC REINVESTMENT

1   2   3   4   Circle the number of sequential 26-week reinvestments you want to schedule at this time

AUTHORIZATION   For the notice required under the Privacy and Paperwork Reduction Acts, see the accompanying instructions.

I submit this tender pursuant to the provisions of Department of the Treasury Circulars, Public Debt Series Nos. 1-86 and 2-86 and the public announcement issued by the Department of the Treasury.

Under penalties of perjury, I certify that the number shown on this form is my correct taxpayer identification number and that I am not subject to backup withholding because (1) I have not been notified that I am subject to backup withholding as a result of a failure to report all interest or dividends, or (2) the Internal Revenue Service has notified me that I am no longer subject to backup withholding. I further certify that all other information provided on this form is true, correct and complete.

_____   _____
SIGNATURE   DATE
SEE INSTRUCTIONS FOR PRIVACY ACT AND PAPERWORK REDUCTION ACT NOTICE

★U.S.GPO:1991-0-522-194/40123

monly reported statistics are the dollar amount of applications and Treasury securities sold, the average price of the accepted competitive bids, and the coupon equivalent (annualized yield) for investors who paid the average price.

The results of a recent Treasury bill auction are shown in Exhibit 7.2. At each auction, the prices paid for six-month T-bills are significantly lower than prices paid for three-month T-bills because the investment term is longer. The lower price results in a higher unannualized yield that compensates investors for their longer term investment.

ESTIMATING THE YIELD. T-bills do not offer coupon payments but are sold at a discount from par value. Their yield is influenced by the difference between the selling price and purchase price. If an investor purchases a newly issued T-bill and holds it until maturity, the return is based on the difference between the par value and the purchase price. If the T-bill is sold prior to maturity, the return is based on the difference between the price for which the bill was sold in the secondary market and the purchase price.

The annualized yield from investing in a T-bill (Y_T) can be determined as

$$Y_T = \frac{SP - PP}{PP} \times \frac{365}{n}$$

where

SP = selling price

PP = purchase price

n = number of days of the investment (holding period)

Assume that an investor purchases a T-bill with a six-month (182-day) maturity and $10,000 par value for $9,600. If this T-bill is held to maturity, its yield is

$$Y_T = \frac{\$10,000 - \$9,600}{\$9,600} \times \frac{365}{182} = 8.36\%$$

If the T-bill is sold prior to maturity, the selling price and therefore the yield are dependent on market conditions at the time of the sale. Suppose the investor

---

EXHIBIT 7.2 Example of Treasury Bill Auction Results

	13-WEEK TREASURY BILL AUCTION	26-WEEK TREASURY BILL AUCTION
Applications	$27,368,770,000	$28,091,585,000
Accepted Bids	$10,007,520,000	$10,035,955,000
Average Price of Accepted Bids (Per $100 Par Value)	$98.620	$97.128
Coupon Equivalent (Yield)	5.63%	5.91%

SOURCE: *The Wall Street Journal.* See *The Wall Street Journal* on any Tuesday for the information pertaining to Monday's Treasury Bill auction.

plans to sell the T-bill after 120 days and forecasts a selling price of $9,820 at that time. The expected annualized yield based on this forecast is

$$Y_T = \frac{\$9,820 - \$9,600}{\$9,600} \times \frac{365}{120} = 6.97\%$$

The higher the forecasted selling price, the higher the expected annualized yield.

Business periodicals frequently quote the T-bill discount (or T-bill rate) along with the T-bill yield. The T-bill discount (D_T) represents the percent discount of the purchase price from par value (*par*) for newly issued T-bills and is computed as

$$D_T = \frac{par - PP}{par} \times \frac{360}{n}$$

A 360-day year is used to compute the T-bill discount. Using the information from the previous example, the T-bill discount is

$$D_T = \frac{\$10,000 - \$9,600}{\$10,000} \times \frac{360}{182} = 7.91\%$$

For a newly issued T-bill that is held to maturity, the T-bill yield will always be higher than the discount. The difference occurs because the purchase price is the denominator of the yield equation, while the par value is the denominator of the T-bill discount equation, and the par value will always exceed the purchase price of a newly issued T-bill. In addition, the yield formula uses a 365-day year versus a 360-day year for the discount computation.

Commercial Paper

Commercial paper is a short-term debt instrument issued only by well-known, creditworthy firms and is typically unsecured. It is normally issued to provide liquidity or finance a firm's investment in inventory and accounts receivable. The issuance of commercial paper is an alternative to short-term bank loans.

The minimum denomination of commercial paper is usually $100,000. The typical denominations are in multiples of $1 million. Maturities are normally between 20 and 45 days but can be as short as one day or as long as 270 days. The 270-day maximum is due to a Securities and Exchange Commission (SEC) ruling that paper with a maturity exceeding 270 days must be registered.

An active secondary market for commercial paper does not exist. However, it is sometimes possible to sell the paper back to the dealer who initially helped to place it. In most cases, commercial paper is held until maturity by investors. Financial institutions such as finance companies and bank holding companies are major issuers of commercial paper. Exhibit 7.3 shows the growth in the use of commercial paper over the last 10 years. The exhibit also shows that much of the commercial paper has been issued by financial institutions. In recent years, nonfinancial corporations have increased their reliance on commercial paper as a source of short-term funds.

RATINGS. In 1970 Penn Central Transportation Company defaulted on $82 million of commercial paper. Since that time, corporations have found that it is

EXHIBIT 7.3 Comparison of U.S. Commercial Paper Outstanding by Issuer

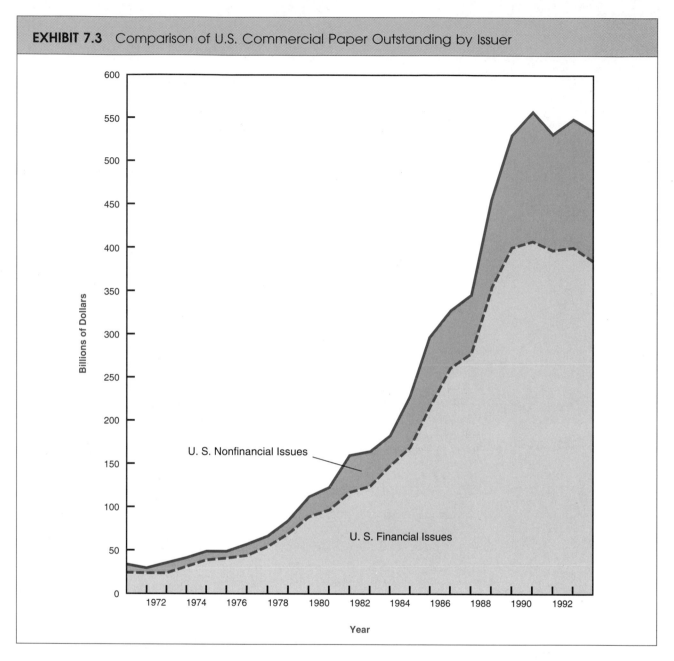

SOURCE: Board of Governors of the Federal Reserve System, *Flow of Funds; FRBNY Quarterly Review* (Autumn 1987): 25; and *Federal Reserve Bulletin.*

easier to place commercial paper if they have it rated. Companies such as Moody's Investors Service, Standard & Poor's Corporation, and Fitch Investor Service perform this service. Some potential investors rely on the ratings as a measure of default risk, while other potential investors prefer to assess the risk themselves. The ratings have been reasonable indicators of financial problems. For example, ratings on firms such as Wang Laboratories, Lomas Financial, and Drexel Burnham indicated high risk well before these firms defaulted on their commercial paper.

A higher risk classification can increase a corporation's commercial paper rate by as much as 150 basis points (1.5 percent). The difference reached 150 basis points during some recessions but has been less than 50 basis points over other periods.

From 1970 to 1988 there were only a few major defaults on commercial paper. However, in 1989 several major issuers defaulted, including Wang Labs, Lomas Financial, and Drexel Burnham Lambert. All of these issues were rated highly until the default. These defaults led to a growing number of commercial paper issues (called **junk commercial paper**) that were rated low or not rated at all.

PLACEMENT. Some firms place commercial paper directly with investors. Others use commercial paper dealers, at a cost of usually one-eighth of one percent of the face value. This transaction cost is generally less than it would cost to create a department within the firm to place commercial paper directly. Those companies that frequently issue commercial paper may reduce expenses by creating such a department. Most nonfinancial companies prefer to use commercial paper dealers rather than in-house resources to place their commercial paper. Their liquidity needs, and therefore their commercial paper issues, are cyclical, so an in-house direct-placement department would not be efficiently used throughout the year. Finance companies typically maintain an in-house department because they frequently borrow in this manner regardless of the business cycle.

A comparison of the directly-placed and dealer-placed commercial paper issued by financial firms (Exhibit 7.4) shows that the amounts of both types have consistently increased since 1970s, with the exception of the recessionary periods in 1982 and in the early 1990s.

BACKING COMMERCIAL PAPER. Issuers of commercial paper typically maintain backup lines of credit in case they cannot roll over (reissue) commercial paper at a reasonable rate. Such an event could occur if their assigned rating was lowered. A backup line of credit provided by a commercial bank allows the company the right (but not the obligation) to borrow a specified maximum amount of funds over a specified period of time. The fee for the line can either be a direct percentage of the total accessible credit (such as 0.5 percent) or be in the form of required compensating balances (such as 10 percent of the line).

ESTIMATING THE YIELD. At a given point in time, the yield on commercial paper is slightly higher than the yield on a T-bill with the same maturity, because commercial paper carries some default risk and is less liquid. Like T-bills, commercial paper is sold at a discount from par value. The nominal return to investors who retain the paper until maturity is the difference between the price paid for the paper and the par value. Thus, the yield received by a commercial paper investor can be determined in a manner similar to the T-bill yield, although a 360-day year is usually used. For example, if an investor purchases 30-day commercial paper with a par value of $1,000,000 for a price of $990,000, the yield ($Y_{cp}$) is

$$Y_{cp} = \frac{\$1,000,000 - \$990,000}{\$990,000} \times \frac{360}{30}$$

$$= 12.12\%$$

EXHIBIT 7.4   Comparison of U.S. Commercial Paper Outstanding by Type of Placement

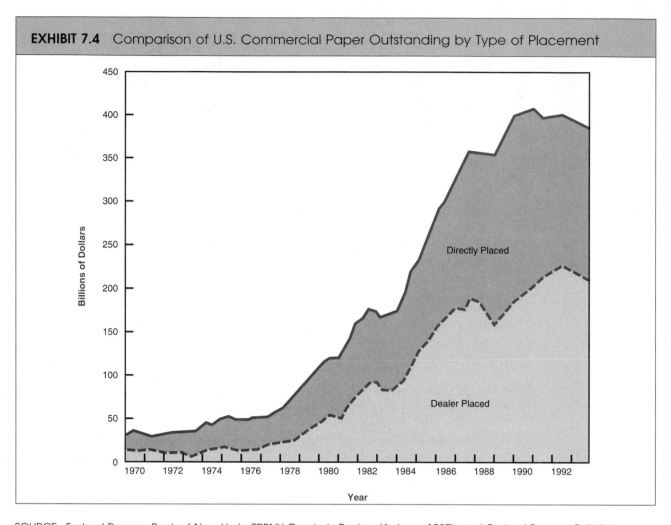

SOURCE: Federal Reserve Bank of New York, *FRBNY Quarterly Review* (Autumn 1987); and *Federal Reserve Bulletin.*

When a firm plans to issue commercial paper, the price (and therefore yield) to investors is uncertain. Thus, the cost of borrowing funds is uncertain until the paper is issued. Consider the case of a firm that plans to issue 90-day commercial paper with a par value of $5,000,000. It expects to sell the commercial paper for $4,850,000. The yield it expects to pay investors (its cost of borrowing) is estimated to be

$$
\begin{aligned}
Y_{cp} &= \frac{par - PP}{PP} \times \frac{360}{n} \\
&= \frac{\$5,000,000 - \$4,850,000}{\$4,850,000} \times \frac{360}{90} \\
&= 12.37\%
\end{aligned}
$$

When firms sell their commercial paper at a lower (higher) price than projected, their cost of raising funds will be higher (lower) than what they initially anticipated. For example, if the firm initially sold the commercial paper for $4,865,000, the cost of borrowing would have been about 11.1 percent (check the math as an exercise).

Ignoring transaction costs, the cost of borrowing with commercial paper is equal to the yield earned by investors holding the paper until maturity. The cost of borrowing can be adjusted for transaction costs (charged by the commercial paper dealers) by subtracting the nominal transaction fees from the price received.

Some corporations prefer to issue commercial paper rather than borrow from a bank because it is usually a cheaper source of funds. Yet, even the large credit-worthy corporations that are able to issue commercial paper normally obtain some short-term loans from commercial banks in order to maintain a business relationship with them.

Negotiable Certificates of Deposit (NCDs)

The **negotiable certificate of deposit (NCD)** is issued by large commercial banks and other depository institutions as a short-term source of funds. Its minimum denomination is $100,000, although a $1 million denomination is more common. Nonfinancial corporations often purchase NCDs. Although NCD denominations are typically too large for individual investors, they are sometimes purchased by money market funds that have pooled individual investors' funds. Thus, the existence of money market funds allows individuals to be indirect investors in NCDs, making a more active NCD market.

Maturities on NCDs normally range from two weeks to one year. A secondary market for NCDs exists, providing investors with some liquidity. However, institutions prefer not to have their newly issued NCDs compete with their previously issued NCDs that are being resold in the secondary market. The oversupply of NCDs for sale can force them to sell their newly issued NCDs at a lower price.

PLACEMENT. Some issuers place their NCDs directly; others use a correspondent institution that specializes in placing NCDs. Another alternative is to sell NCDs to securities dealers, who in turn resell them. A portion of unusually large issues is commonly sold to NCD dealers. However, NCDs can normally be sold to investors directly at a higher price.

MEASUREMENT OF THE PREMIUM. NCDs must offer a premium above the Treasury bill yield to compensate for less liquidity and safety. The premiums are generally higher during recessionary periods. The premiums also reflect the market's perception about the safety of the financial system. For example, the premiums were higher in 1984 relative to other recent nonrecessionary years, because of the financial problems of Continental Illinois Bank and the heightened risk perception in the banking industry.

Repurchase Agreements

A repurchase agreement (or repo) represents the sale of securities by one party to another with an agreement to repurchase the securities at a specified date and price. In essence, the repo transaction represents a loan backed by the securities.

If the borrower defaults on the loan, the lender has claim to the securities. Most repo transactions use government securities, although some involve other securities such as commercial paper or NCDs. A **reverse repo** refers to the purchase of securities by one party from another with an agreement to sell them. Thus, a repo and reverse repo can represent the same transaction but from different perspectives. These two terms are sometimes used interchangeably, so a description of a repo transaction may actually reflect a reverse repo.

Repo transactions are negotiated through a telecommunications network. Dealers and repo brokers act as financial intermediaries to create repos for firms with deficient and excess funds, receiving a commission for their services.

When the borrowing firm can find a counterparty to the repo transaction, it avoids the transaction fee involved in having a government securities dealer find the counterparty. Some companies that commonly engage in repo transactions have an in-house department for finding counterparties and executing the transactions. These same companies that borrow through repos may, from time to time, serve as the lender. That is, they purchase the government securities and agree to sell them back in the near future. Because the cash flow of any large company changes on a daily basis, it is not unusual for a firm to act as an investor one day (when it has excess funds) and a borrower the next (when it has a cash shortage).

Financial institutions such as banks, savings and loan associations, and money market funds often participate in repurchase agreements. Many nonfinancial institutions are active participants as well. The dollar volume of repos has more than tripled in the past eight years. Transaction amounts are usually for $10 million or more. The most common maturities are from one day to fifteen days and for one, three, and six months. A secondary market for repos does not exist. Some firms in need of funds will set the maturity on a repo to be the minimum time period for which they need temporary financing. If they still need funds when the repo is about to mature, they will borrow additional funds through new repos and use these funds to fulfill their obligation on maturing repos.

ESTIMATING THE YIELD.   The repo rate is determined by the difference between the initial selling price of the securities and the agreed-upon repurchase price, annualized with a 360-day year. For example, securities initially purchased by an investor at a price (*PP*) of $9,852,217, with an agreement to sell them back at a price (*SP*) of $10,000,000 at the end of a 60-day period, offer a yield (or repo rate) of

$$
\begin{aligned}
\text{Repo Rate} &= \frac{SP - PP}{PP} \times \frac{360}{n} \\
&= \frac{\$10,000,000 - \$9,852,217}{\$9,852,217} \times \frac{360}{60} \\
&= 9\%
\end{aligned}
$$

Federal Funds

The federal funds market allows depository institutions to effectively lend or borrow short-term funds from each other at the so-called **federal funds rate.** As

EXHIBIT 7.5 Comparison of the Federal Funds Rate and Treasury Bill Rate

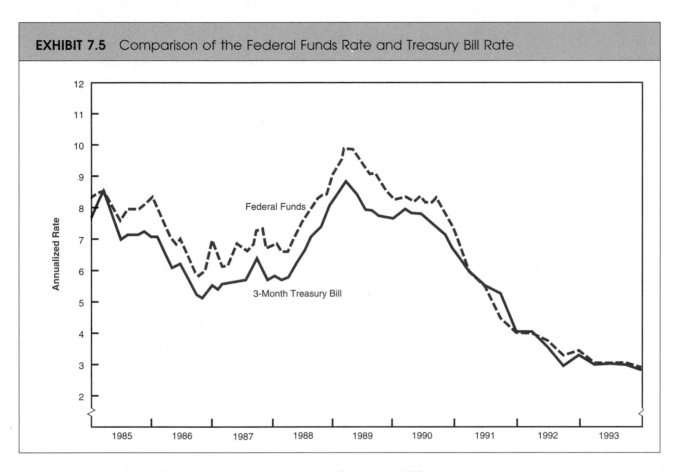

SOURCE: *Monetary Trends,* Federal Reserve Bank of St. Louis (December 1990), updated by author.

shown in Exhibit 7.5, the federal funds rate is normally slightly higher than the Treasury bill rate at any point in time. The negotiations between two depository institutions may take place directly over the telephone or may occur through a federal funds broker. Once a loan transaction is agreed upon, the lending institution can instruct its district Federal Reserve bank to debit its reserve account and to credit the borrowing institution's reserve account by the amount of the loan. If the loan is for just one day, it will likely be based on an oral agreement between the parties, especially if the institutions commonly do business with each other.

Commercial banks are the most active participants in the federal funds market. Federal funds brokers serve as financial intermediaries in the market, matching up institutions that wish to sell (lend) funds with those that wish to purchase (borrow) them. The brokers receive a commission for their service. The transactions are negotiated through a telecommunications network that links federal funds brokers with the participating institutions. Most loan transactions are for $5 million or more and usually have a one- to seven-day maturity (although the loans may often be extended by the lender if the borrower desires more time).

The importance of lending between depository institutions can be realized by measuring the volume of interbank loans on commercial bank balance sheets over time. The interbank loan volume outstanding now exceeds $200 billion.

Banker's Acceptances

A **banker's acceptance** represents a bank accepting responsibility for a future payment. It is commonly used for international trade transactions. Exporters often prefer that banks act as guarantor before sending goods to importers whose credit rating is not known. The bank therefore facilitates international trade by stamping ACCEPTED on a draft, which obligates payment at a specified point in time. In turn, the importer will pay the bank what is owed to the exporter along with a fee to the bank for guaranteeing the payment.

Exporters can hold the banker's acceptance until the date at which payment is to be made, yet they frequently sell the acceptance before then at a discount to obtain cash immediately. The investor who purchases the acceptance then receives the payment guaranteed by the bank in the future. The investor's return on a banker's acceptance, like that of commercial paper, is derived from the difference between the discounted price paid for the acceptance and the amount to be received in the future. Maturities on banker's acceptances often range from 30 to 270 days. Because there is a possibility of banks' defaulting on payment, investors are exposed to a slight degree of default risk. Thus, they deserve a return above the T-bill yield as compensation.

Because acceptances are often discounted and sold by the exporting firm prior to maturity, an active secondary market exists. Dealers match up companies that wish to sell acceptances with other companies that wish to purchase them. The bid price of dealers is less than their ask price, which creates their **spread,** or their reward for doing business. The spread is normally between one-eighth and seven-eighths of one percent.

STEPS INVOLVED IN BANKER'S ACCEPTANCES. The sequence of steps involved in a banker's acceptance is illustrated in Exhibit 7.6. To understand the sequence of steps, consider the example of a U.S. importer of Japanese goods. First, the importer places a purchase order for the goods (Step 1). If the Japanese exporter is unfamiliar with the U.S. importer, it may demand payment before delivery of goods, which the U.S. importer may be unwilling to make. A compromise may be reached through the creation of a banker's acceptance. The importer requests its bank to issue a **letter of credit (L/C)** on its behalf (Step 2). The L/C represents a commitment by that bank to back the payment owed to the Japanese exporter. Then the L/C is presented to the exporter's bank (Step 3), which informs the exporter that the L/C has been received (Step 4). The exporter than sends the goods to the importer (Step 5) and sends the shipping documents to its bank (Step 6), which passes them along to the importer's bank (Step 7). At this point, the banker's acceptance is created, which obligates the importer's bank to make payment to the holder of the banker's acceptance at a specified future date. The banker's acceptance may be sold to the money market investor at a discount. Potential purchasers of acceptances are short-term investors. When the acceptance matures, the importer pays its bank, which in turn pays the money market investor who presents the acceptance.

The creation of a banker's acceptance allows the importer to receive goods from an exporter without sending immediate payment. The selling of the acceptance creates financing for the exporter. Even though banker's acceptances are often created to facilitate international transactions, they are not limited to money market investors with international experience. Investors who purchase accep-

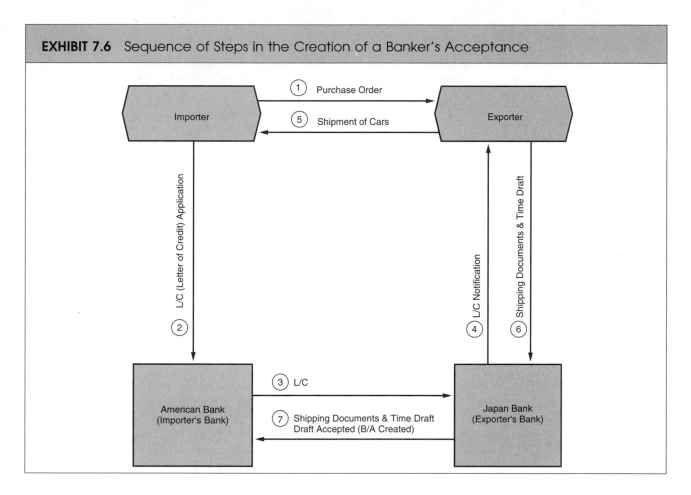

EXHIBIT 7.6 Sequence of Steps in the Creation of a Banker's Acceptance

SOURCE: Adapted from *Instruments of the Money Market,* Federal Reserve Bank of Richmond, Sixth Edition, p. 127. For a more comprehensive explanation, see this source.

tances are more concerned with the credit of the bank that guarantees payment than with the credit of the exporter or importer. For this reason, the default risk on a banker's acceptance is somewhat similar to that of NCDs issued by commercial banks. Yet, because acceptances have the backing of the bank as well as the importing firm, they may be perceived as having slightly less default risk than NCDs.

POPULARITY OF BANKER'S ACCEPTANCES.   Although acceptances are initially created by banks, they are perceived by some other firms as a potential source of funds. Firms that receive the acceptance as a result of exporting goods or that purchase the acceptance in the market shortly after it has been created can sell the acceptance in the market whenever they need funds.

Exhibit 7.7 shows the trend in banker's acceptances outstanding. Although the dollar volume is large, it is considerably less than that of commercial paper or repurchase agreements. As long as the commercial banks that create acceptances are favorably perceived by investors, the secondary market for acceptances should continue to be active.

EXHIBIT 7.7 Volume of Banker's Acceptances Outstanding over Time

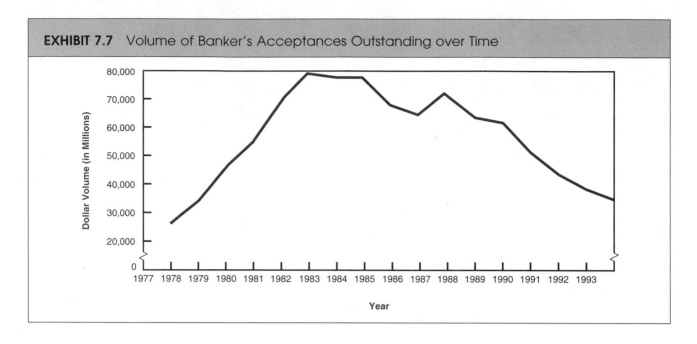

INSTITUTIONAL USE OF MONEY MARKETS

The institutional use of money market securities is summarized in Exhibit 7.8. Financial institutions purchase money market securities in order to simultaneously earn a return and maintain adequate liquidity. They issue money market securities when experiencing a temporary shortage of cash. Because money markets serve businesses, the average transaction size is very large and is typically executed through a telecommunications network.

Money market securities can be used to enhance liquidity in two ways. First, newly issued securities generate cash. The institutions that issue new securities have created a short-term liability in order to boost their cash balance. Second, institutions that previously purchased money market securities will generate cash upon liquidation of the securities. In this case, one type of asset (the security) is replaced by another (cash).

Most financial institutions maintain sufficient liquidity by holding either some securities that have very active secondary markets or securities with short-term maturities. Treasury bills are the most popular money market instrument because of their marketability, safety, and short-term maturity. Although Treasury bills are purchased through an auction, other money market instruments are commonly purchased through dealers or specialized brokers. For example, commercial paper is purchased through commercial paper dealers or directly from the issuer, NCDs are usually purchased through brokers specializing in NCDs, federal funds are purchased (borrowed) through federal funds brokers, and repurchase agreements are purchased through repo dealers.

Financial institutions whose future cash inflows and outflows are more uncertain will generally maintain additional money market instruments for liquidity. For this reason, depository institutions such as commercial banks allocate a greater portion of their asset portfolio to money market instruments than pension funds.

EXHIBIT 7.8 Institutional Use of Money Markets

TYPE OF FINANCIAL INSTITUTION	PARTICIPATION IN THE MONEY MARKETS
Commercial banks and savings institutions	■ Bank holding companies issue commercial paper. ■ Some banks and savings institutions issue NCDs, borrow or lend funds in the federal funds market, engage in repurchase agreements, and purchase Treasury bills. ■ Commercial banks create banker's acceptances. ■ Commercial banks provide backup lines of credit to corporations that issue commercial paper.
Finance companies	■ Issue large amounts of commercial paper.
Money market mutual funds	■ Use proceeds from shares sold to invest in Treasury bills, commercial paper, NCDs, repurchase agreements, and banker's acceptances.
Insurance companies	■ May maintain a portion of its investment portfolio as money market securities for liquidity.
Pension funds	■ May maintain a portion of its investment portfolio as money market securities that may be liquidated when portfolio managers desire to increase their investment in bonds or stocks.

Financial institutions that purchase money market securities are acting as a creditor to the initial issuer of the securities. For example, when they hold Treasury bills, they are creditors to the Treasury. Yet, the Treasury bill transactions in the secondary market commonly reflect a flow of funds between two nongovernment institutions. Treasury bills represent a source of funds for those financial institutions that liquidate some of their Treasury bill holdings. In fact, this is the main reason that Treasury bills are held by financial institutions. Other money market instruments are also purchased by financial institutions to provide liquidity, including federal funds (purchased by depository institutions), repurchase agreements (purchased by depository institutions and money market funds), banker's acceptances, and CDs (purchased by money market funds).

Some financial institutions issue their own money market instruments to obtain cash. For example, depository institutions issue CDs, while bank holding companies and finance companies issue commercial paper. Depository institutions also obtain funds through the use of repurchase agreements or in the federal funds market.

Many money market transactions involve two financial institutions. For example, a federal funds transaction involves two depository institutions. Money market funds commonly purchase CDs from banks and savings institutions. Repurchase agreements are frequently negotiated between two commercial banks.

MONEY MARKET RATES

A table in *The Wall Street Journal* called "Money Rates" provides the interest rates on a wide variety of money market securities. The name of the rate or security is listed in bold. For securities with several common maturities, the rate on each maturity is disclosed.

MONEY RATES

Thursday, August 4, 1994

The key U.S. and foreign annual interest rates below are a guide to general levels but don't always represent actual transactions.

PRIME RATE: 7¼%. The base rate on corporate loans posted by at least 75% of the nation's 30 largest banks.

FEDERAL FUNDS: 4 5/16% high, 4 3/16% low, 4 3/16% near closing bid, 4 5/16% offered. Reserves traded among commercial banks for overnight use in amounts of $1 million or more. Source: Prebon Yamane (U.S.A.) Inc.

DISCOUNT RATE: 3½%. The charge on loans to depository institutions by the Federal Reserve Banks.

CALL MONEY: 6%. The charge on loans to brokers on stock exchange collateral. Source: Dow Jones Telerate Inc.

COMMERCIAL PAPER placed directly by General Electric Capital Corp.: 4.35% 30 to 59 days; 4.48% 60 to 89 days; 4.58% 90 to 119 days; 4.62% 120 to 179 days; 4.90% 180 to 239 days; 5.12% 240 to 270 days.

COMMERCIAL PAPER: High-grade unsecured notes sold through dealers by major corporations: 4.43% 30 days; 4.58% 60 days; 4.68% 90 days.

CERTIFICATES OF DEPOSIT: 3.68% one month; 3.84% two months; 4.04% three months; 4.48% six months; 4.88% one year. Average of top rates paid by major New York banks on primary new issues of negotiable C.D.s, usually on amounts of $1 million and more. The minimum unit is $100,000. Typical rates in the secondary market: 4.35% one month; 4.60% three months; 4.98% six months.

BANKERS ACCEPTANCES: 4.33% 30 days; 4.46% 60 days; 4.53% 90 days; 4.62% 120 days; 4.80% 150 days; 4.86% 180 days.

LONDON LATE EURODOLLARS: 4½% - 4⅜% one month; 4⅝% - 4¾% two months; 4¾% - 4⅝% three months; 4⅞% - 4¾% four months; 5 1/16% - 4 15/16% five months; 5⅛% - 5% six months.

LONDON INTERBANK OFFERED RATES (LIBOR): 4½% one month; 4¾% three months; 5⅛% six months; 5⅜% one year. The average of interbank offered rates for dollar deposits in the London market based on quotations at five major banks. Effective rate for contracts entered into two days from date appearing at top of this column.

FOREIGN PRIME RATES: Canada 7.25%; Germany 4.98%; Japan 3%; Switzerland 7.50%; Britain 5.25%. These rate indications aren't directly comparable; lending practices vary widely by location.

TREASURY BILLS: Results of the Monday, August 1, 1994, auction of short-term U.S. government bills, sold at a discount from face value in units of $10,000 to $1 million: 4.35% 13 weeks; 4.75% 26 weeks.

FEDERAL HOME LOAN MORTGAGE CORP. (Freddie Mac): Posted yields on 30-year mortgage commitments. Delivery within 30 days 8.45%, 60 days 8.53%, standard conventional fixed-rate mortgages; 5.625%, 2% rate capped one-year adjustable rate mortgages. Source: Dow Jones Telerate Inc.

FEDERAL NATIONAL MORTGAGE ASSOCIATION (Fannie Mae): Posted yields on 30 year mortgage commitments (priced at par) for delivery within 30 days 8.39%, 60 days 8.48%, standard conventional fixed rate-mortgages; 6.65%, 6/2 rate capped one-year adjustable rate mortgages. Source: Dow Jones Telerate Inc.

MERRILL LYNCH READY ASSETS TRUST: 3.76%. Annualized average rate of return after expenses for the past 30 days; not a forecast of future returns.

Offered rates of negotiable, bank-backed business credit instruments typically financing an import order.

INTERACTION AMONG MONEY MARKET YIELDS

Companies investing in money markets closely monitor the yields on the various instruments. Because the instruments serve as reasonable substitutes for each other, the investing companies may exchange instruments to achieve a more attractive yield. This causes yields among these instruments to be somewhat similar. If a disparity in yields arises, companies will avoid the low-yield instruments in favor of the high-yield instruments. This places upward pressure on yields of the low-yield security and downward pressure on the high-yield securities, causing realignment.

During periods of heightened uncertainty about the economy, there is a shift from risky money market securities to Treasury securities. This so-called flight to quality creates a greater differential between yields, as risky money market securities must provide a larger premium to attract investors.

Exhibit 7.9 shows the yields of money market securities over time. The high degree of correlation among security yields is obvious. T-bills consistently offer slightly lower yields than the other securities because they are very liquid and free from default risk.

EXHIBIT 7.9 Money Market Yields (Averages, Annualized)

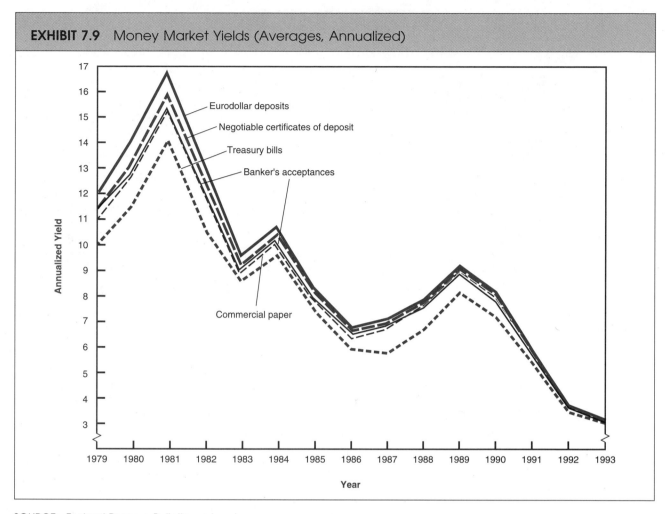

SOURCE: *Federal Reserve Bulletin,* various issues.

GLOBALIZATION OF MONEY MARKETS

GLOBAL ASPECTS

Market interest rates vary among countries, as shown in Exhibit 7.10. The interest rate differentials occur because geographic markets are somewhat segmented. However, because many markets are accessible to foreign investors and borrowers, interest rate differentials have encouraged international money market transactions. The growth in such transactions is also attributed to tax differences among countries, speculation on exchange rate movements, and a reduction in government barriers that were previously imposed on foreign investment in securities. U.S. Treasury bills and commercial paper are very accessible to foreign investors. In addition, securities such as Eurodollar deposits, Euronotes, and Euro-commercial paper are widely traded throughout the international money markets, as discussed in the following subsections.

INTEREST RATE LINKAGE BETWEEN THE UNITED STATES AND PACIFIC BASIN COUNTRIES

Countries in the Pacific Basin, such as Hong Kong, Singapore, Japan, and Taiwan, have loosened their restrictions on international financial transactions. Consequently, financial markets have become more globally integrated. A recent study by Glick evaluated the linkage between Pacific Basin real rates of interest and U.S. real rates of interest. Glick found that the linkage between the Pacific Basin and the United States is somewhat similar to the linkage between European countries and the United States. This suggests not only that financial market conditions in the United States can affect real interest rates in Pacific Basin countries but also that conditions in Pacific Basin countries can affect real interest rates in the United States.

The relationship between the U.S. and Pacific Basin real interest rates is not perfect, because remaining restrictions and transactions costs discourage some financial flows between these countries. Nevertheless, the results of this study suggest that in forecasting U.S. real interest rates, analysts must monitor conditions in other countries that may affect fund flows to the United States.

Eurodollar Deposits and Euronotes

As corporations outside the United States (especially in Europe) increased international trade transactions in U.S. dollars, the U.S. dollar deposits in non-U.S. banks (called **Eurodollar certificates of deposit** or Eurodollar CDs) grew. Furthermore, because interest rate ceilings were historically imposed on dollar deposits in U.S. banks, corporations with large dollar balances often deposited their funds overseas to receive a higher yield.

Eurodollar CD volume has grown substantially over time, as a significant portion of international trade and investment transactions involves the U.S. dollar as a medium of exchange. Some firms overseas receive U.S. dollars as payment for exports and invest in Eurodollar CDs. Because these firms may expect to need dollars to pay for future imports, they retain dollar-denominated deposits rather than convert dollars to their home currency.

In the so-called **Eurodollar market,** banks channel the deposited funds to other firms that need to borrow them in the form of Eurodollar loans. The deposit and loan transactions in Eurodollars are typically $1 million or more per transaction, so only governments and large corporations participate in this market. Because transactions amounts are large, investors in the market avoid some costs associated with the continuous small transactions that occur in retail-oriented markets. In addition, Eurodollar CDs are not subject to reserve requirements, which means that banks can lend out 100 percent of the deposits that arrive. For these reasons, the spread between the rate banks pay on large Eurodollar deposits and what they charge on Eurodollar loans is relatively small. This allows attractive interest rates for both depositors and borrowers in the Eurodollar market. The rates offered on Eurodollar deposits are slightly higher than rates offered on negotiable certificates of deposit.

A secondary market for Eurodollar CDs exists, allowing the initial investors to liquidate their investment if necessary. The growth in Eurodollar volume has made the secondary market more active.

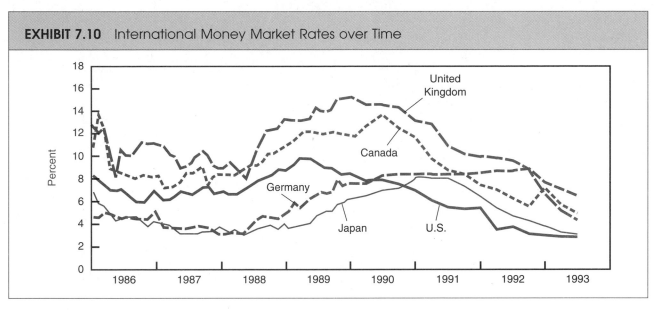

EXHIBIT 7.10 International Money Market Rates over Time

SOURCE: Federal Reserve Bank of St. Louis and International Monetary Fund.

Investors in fixed-rate Eurodollar CDs are adversely affected by rising market interest rates, while issuers of these CDs are adversely affected by decreasing rates. To deal with this interest rate risk, **Eurodollar floating-rate CDs** (called FRCDs) have been used in recent years. The rate adjusts periodically to the London Interbank Offer Rate (LIBOR), which is the interest rate charged on interbank dollar loans. As with other floating-rate instruments, the rate on FRCDs ensures that the borrower's cost and investor's return reflect prevailing market interest rates.

Over time, the volume of deposits and loans denominated in other foreign currencies has also grown because of an increased international trade, increased flows of funds among subsidiaries of multinational corporations, and existing differences among country regulations on bank deposit rates. Consequently, the so-called **Eurocurrency market** was developed, made up of several banks (called **Eurobanks)** that accept large deposits and provide large loans in foreign currencies. These same banks also make up the **Eurocredit market,** which is mainly distinguished from the Eurocurrency market by the longer maturities on loans.

The Eurobanks participating in the Eurocurrency market are located not only in Europe but also in the Bahamas, Canada, Japan, Hong Kong, and some other countries. Since 1978, Eurocurrency deposits at commercial banks have quadrupled. Over this time period, the value of dollar deposits has represented between 70 percent and 80 percent of the market value of all Eurocurrency deposits. In recent years, the percentage has declined slightly, because of the growth in nondollar Eurocurrency deposits.

Short-term **Euronotes** are issued in bearer form, with common maturities of one, three, and six months. The typical investors in Euronotes often include the Eurobanks that are hired to place the paper. These Euronotes are sometimes underwritten, thereby guaranteeing the issuer a specific price. In addition, the underwriters may even guarantee a price at which the notes can be rolled over (reissued at maturity). The Euronotes described here differ from the traditional meaning of medium-term loans provided by Eurobanks.

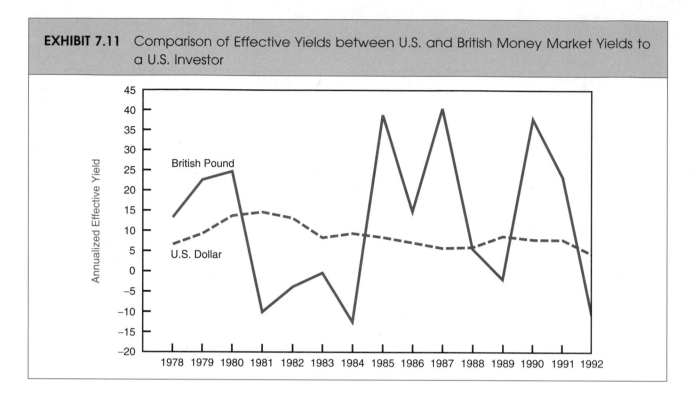

EXHIBIT 7.11 Comparison of Effective Yields between U.S. and British Money Market Yields to a U.S. Investor

Euro-Commercial Paper

Euro-commercial paper (Euro-CP) is issued without the backing of a banking syndicate. Maturities can be tailored to satisfy investors. Dealers that place commercial paper have created a secondary market by being willing to purchase existing Euro-CP before maturity. The Euro-CP market is used by large corporations that wish to hedge future cash inflows in a particular foreign currency. For example, if a U.S. corporation expects to receive three million marks as payment for goods in three months, it may borrow marks today and convert them to dollars to support U.S. operations. The marks to be received in three months can then be used to repay the loan. If the German interest rates are lower than the U.S. interest rates, this strategy allows the U.S. corporation to reduce its financing cost without being exposed to exchange rate risk.

The Euro-CP rate is typically between 50 and 100 basis points above LIBOR. Euro-CP is sold by dealers, at a transaction cost ranging between 5 and 10 basis points of the face value. This market is tiny compared to the U.S. commercial paper market. Yet, some non-U.S. companies can more easily place their paper here, where they have a household name.

Performance of International Securities

The performance of international money market securities could be assessed over time by measuring the effective yield, which incorporates exchange rate movements. For example, the effective yield for a U.S. investor that invests in British money market securities is shown in Exhibit 7.11. The effective yield was generally higher than the alternative domestic yields during the periods 1978–1980 and 1985–1987 and 1990–1991 as a result of the strengthened pound during those periods. Conversely, the effective yield on British money market securities was negative during the period 1981–1984 in 1989, and in 1992, when the pound depreciated. Most investors would not invest in foreign money market securities every period but would choose to do so only when the foreign currency is expected to appreciate. The results displayed in Exhibit 7.11 show the high potential yields and the risk from investing in foreign money market securities. The risk could be reduced somewhat by spreading the investment across securities denominated in several currencies.

International Integration of Money Markets

The large flows of short-term funds between countries cause interest rates in any given country to become more susceptible to interest rate movements in other countries. To illustrate the influence of foreign markets, consider the efforts to reunify East and West Germany in 1989 and 1990. The corporate demand for funds increased in response to economic expansion, which placed upward pressure on German interest rates. The new opportunities in Germany encouraged German and U.S. investors to invest funds there. Consequently, the supply of loanable funds in the U.S. provided by U.S. and German investors declined, placing temporary upward pressure on U.S. interest rates.

The Single European Act of 1987 mandated that barriers on capital flows between Western European countries be phased out by 1992. This caused a greater integration of interest rates between European countries, so that a given country's interest rates become even more susceptible to interest rate movements of other countries.

SUMMARY

- The main money market securities are Treasury bills, commercial paper, NCDs, repurchase agreements, federal funds, and banker's acceptances. These securities vary according to the issuer. Consequently, their perceived degree of default risk can vary. They also have different degrees of liquidity. Therefore, the quoted yields at any given point in time vary among money market securities.

- Financial institutions manage their liquidity by participating in money markets. They may issue money market securities when they experience cash shortages and need to boost liquidity. They can also sell holdings of money market securities to obtain cash.

- Interest rates vary among countries. Some investors are attracted to high interest rates in foreign countries, which causes funds to flow to those countries. Consequently, money markets have become globally integrated. Investments in foreign money market securities are subject to exchange rate risk, because the foreign currency denominating the securities could depreciate over time.

QUESTIONS

1. Explain how the Treasury uses the primary market to obtain adequate funding.

2. How can investors using the primary Treasury bill market be assured that their bid will be accepted?

3. Why do large corporations typically make competitive bids rather than non-competitive bids for Treasury bills?

4. Describe the activity in the secondary Treasury bill market. How can this degree of activity benefit investors in Treasury bills?

5. Who issues commercial paper?

6. Why do some firms create a department that can directly place commercial paper? What criteria affect the decision to create such a department?

7. Why are ratings assigned by rating agencies on commercial paper?

8. What types of financial institutions issue commercial paper?

9. Explain how investors' preferences for commercial paper will change during a recession. How should this reaction affect the difference between commercial paper rates and Treasury bill rates during recessionary periods?

10. How can small investors participate in the investment of negotiable certificates of deposit (NCDs)?

11. Based on what you know about repurchase agreements, would you expect them to have a lower or higher annualized yield than commercial paper? Why?

12. What is the use of a banker's acceptance to (a) exporting firms, (b) importing firms, (c) commercial banks, and (d) investors?

13. Explain how money markets can accommodate the desired cash positions of institutions.

14. Why might Treasury bills sometimes be considered as a potential source of funds to a financial institution?

PROBLEMS

1. Assume an investor purchased a six-month T-bill with $10,000 par for $9,000 and sold it 90 days later for $9,100. What is the yield?

2. Newly issued three-month T-bills with a par value of $10,000 sold for $9,700. Compute the T-bill discount.

3. Assume an investor purchased six-month commercial paper with a face value of $1,000,000 for $940,000. What is the yield?

4. Stanford Corporation arranged a repurchase agreement in which it purchased securities for $4,900,000 and will sell the securities back for $5,000,000 in 40 days. What is the yield (or repo rate) to Stanford Corporation?

Nervous Strategists No Longer Believe 'Cash Is Trash'

John R. Dorfman

Wall Street strategists are getting nervous.

Many of them think the long bond-market is over, and say it's time to sell some bonds. But, nervous about the stock market, they don't suggest that investors plow the proceeds into stocks.

Instead, they urge investors to raise cash. That's remarkable at a time when the yields on cash investments (ultra-safe vehicles like Treasury bills, money-market funds and bank accounts) are the lowest in a generation, about 3%. It's as if a food critic were to recommend a soft drink knowing full well it has no fizz.

The average cash level recommended by strategists at a dozen brokerage houses tracked by *The Wall Street Journal* has climbed to 14.25% of assets, the highest in three years. And the average bond allocation has fallen to 28.75%, the lowest since December 1989.

For stocks, the strategists on average recommend an allocation of 57%, a shade above normal. But many of them say they aren't wildly bullish on stocks; they are just reacting to a lack of attractive alternatives.

To be sure, PaineWebber Inc. and Kidder Peabody & Co. are sticking with the cash-is-trash philosophy that served their clients well in 1992 and so far in 1993. But nine of the 12 firms in the Journal survey recommend 15% cash or more. A 10% cash holding is often considered normal.

Performance vs. Prudence

"It's not that I *want* to have cash," says Rao Chalasani of Kemper Securities Inc., whose 30% cash position is among the highest. "I'm balancing performance against prudence."

He's not alone in feeling cautious. Since Dec. 31, Bill Dodge of Dean Witter Reynolds Inc., Raymond Worseck of A.G. Edwards & Sons Inc., and Charles Clough of Merrill Lynch & Co. have raised their recommended cash allocations at least five percentage points.

The quarterly study estimates how investors would do by following the strategists' asset-allocation advice. The study is conducted with help from Wilshire Associates of Santa Monica, Calif., and Economics Office of Hanover, N.H.

Robin Carpenter, president of Economics Office, points out that Greg Smith of Prudential Securities Inc. and Mr. Dodge of Dean Witter have the best bond-market timing records in the study. Mr. Smith currently has only 15% in bonds and Mr. Dodge only 25%.

Unusual Returns

In the study's latest snapshot, the strategists were closely bunched because stocks and bonds have given roughly equal returns. Few people expect that unusual state of affairs to last, though: All investments are not created equal.

Here's a rundown on what some leading strategists are saying. They are listed in order of 12-month performance.

PaineWebber. Strategist Edward Kerschner, the leader for the quarter and 12-month period ended in March, expects stocks to provide a return of about 8% to 10% this year, including dividends. "That's half of what you got in the '80s, but this ain't the '80s," Mr. Kerschner says.

That return is still "better than bonds, and triple the return on cash," he says. Accordingly, his blend is 69% stocks, 30% bonds and only 1% cash. "I think the risk of a correction (market decline) is low," Mr. Kerschner says. "You'd have to have a big rate pickup or an economic collapse, which seems very unlikely."

Kidder Peabody. "For the first time in a while, we see some real dramatic currents in the market, a lot of them stirred up by President Clinton," says strategist Easton Ragsdale. Still, he recommends 70% stocks. "It's not that stocks look so attractive, but fixed income looks less attractive," and cash worse yet, he explains. Kidder's economists expect interest rates to stay put about where they are. If so, bonds won't rise or fall much in value. Therefore, "you look at the yields themselves," says Mr. Ragsdale. With 30-year Treasury bonds yielding 6.74%, "the yield differential supports bonds over cash."

Shearson Lehman Brothers Inc. Shearson's strategist, Michael Sherman, resigned this month to join Leon Cooperman's Omega Advisors Inc. as a money manager. During the past six

Continued

CASE APPLICATION: RELIANCE ON MONEY MARKETS

Continued

years, Mr. Sherman guided investors who followed his advice to an estimated gain of 118.4%, second-best in the study. Concerned about high stock valuations, he cut stocks five points to 50% on Dec. 21, and has been carrying 15% in cash.

Dean Witter. The bond rally is probably over, says Mr. Dodge. He says Mr. Clinton's economic plan contains "less deficit reduction than meets the eye," inflation is accelerating a bit, and the economy is stronger than winter weather made it look. He says he believes rates on 30-year Treasury bonds will inch up to 7.25% or 7.5% by late fall. That's why he has sliced his bond allocation 10 percentage points, to the current 25%.

Goldman, Sachs & Co. Co-strategists Steven Einhorn and Abby Cohen chopped their stock allocation 15 percentage points last quarter, to 60%. We have "a suspended bull," says Mr. Einhorn. "We have a stuck kind of market, with a safety net provided by the fundamentals and a ceiling provided by Washington." Mr. Einhorn expresses concern about "antibusiness sentiment" in remarks by President Clinton; he also sees "uncertainty with respect to the budget package, health-care reform, and corporate tax rates."

Merrill Lynch. Mr. Clough clipped five percentage points off his stock position last quarter, and is holding bonds at 30%, a bit below normal for him. "I don't think the markets are going to do much of anything" in the next few months, Mr. Clough says. In his view, the important thing is to focus on industrial companies, especially those that are downsizing, and to avoid consumer growth stocks that "are losing pricing and profit strength."

Prudential Securities. Mr. Smith is the study's leader for the past five years (up 100.1%) and since inception (up 125.3% since Jan. 1, 1987). He has sliced his bond allocation four times this year, to the current 15%. "I think the rally in the government (bond) market has been overdone," he says, though he still likes junk bonds and tax-exempt municipals. Stocks, he thinks, will beat bonds—if you pick the right stocks. "I think it will look like a bear market in the old leadership, drugs and consumer-product companies," Mr. Smith says. He sees strength in auto stocks, capital-goods markers and airlines.

Kemper Securities. Mr. Chalasani has cut bonds back to 20%, the lowest figure he can remember. Warning signs for the bond market, he says, include a perking up in the economy, indications that inflation is no longer on the wane, a declining dollar, and a gentle rise in the price of gold. Things look better for stocks, he says, but he's worried by high valuations and uncertainty about what will be coming out of Washington this year.

A. G. Edwards. The biggest bond allocation, 40%, belongs to Mr. Worseck, who could fairly be accused of excessive devotion to bonds in the past. Be that as it may, Mr. Worseck says, people today are itching to buy bonds to escape from low-yielding bank accounts. So the bond rally could run on for quite a while yet.

Besides, he says, bond bulls do have some good arguments. Inflation fears are overblown, and Mr. Clinton's deficit-reduction program should slow the economy by 1995, keeping interest rates low.

SOURCE: *The Wall Street Journal* (April 22, 1993): p. C1. Reprinted by permission of *The Wall Street Journal* © 1993 Dow Jones & Company, Inc. All rights reserved worldwide.

QUESTIONS

1. Why would securities firms such as Salomon Brothers, Dean Witter, and Shearson Lehman recommend that investors maintain 15 percent of their money as cash (money market securities) when such an investment is earning about 3 percent annually?

2. PaineWebber recommended that only 1 percent of an investor's funds be allocated toward cash, while other securities firms recommended higher proportions. What causes the disparity among recommendations?

3. Why might the recommended allocation toward cash (money market securities) change over time, even if the expected performance of stocks or bonds was stable?

PROJECT

1. **Assessing Default Risk Premiums over Time**
   Using the data bank, measure the difference between the annualized yields of three-month commercial paper and three-month Treasury bills over time. Compare this differential to the degree of economic growth (as measured by GNP growth) over time. Explain the relationship that you find.

BOND MARKETS

Bonds are debt obligations issued by governments or corporations with long-term maturities. Bond markets are needed to facilitate the flow of long-term funds from surplus units to deficit units.

The specific objectives of this chapter are to:

- provide a background on bonds,
- explain the risks of bonds,
- explain how bond markets are used by institutional investors, and
- explain how bond markets have become globalized.

Bonds are often classified according to the type of issuer:

- Treasury bonds issued by the Treasury
- Municipal bonds issued by state and local governments
- Corporate bonds issued by corporations

A discussion of each type of bond follows.

TREASURY BONDS

The U.S. Treasury commonly issues Treasury notes or Treasury bonds to finance federal government expenditures. The minimum denomination for Treasury notes or bonds is $1,000. The key difference between a note and a bond is that note maturities are usually less than 10 years, while bond maturities are 10 years or more. An active secondary market allows investors to sell Treasury notes or

THE SALOMON BROTHERS SCANDAL

During each Treasury bond offering, bond dealers purchase Treasury bonds and then redistribute them to clients (other financial institutions) that wish to purchase them. During a 1990 Treasury bond auction, Salomon Brothers purchased 65 percent of the Treasury bonds issued. This proportion exceeded the 35 percent maximum that was allowed for any single bond dealer. Some other bond dealers had made commitments to sell Treasury bonds to their clients (financial institutions), but were unable to obtain a sufficient amount because Salomon Brothers dominated the auction. The other dealers had to obtain the Treasury bonds from Salomon Brothers in order to fulfill their commitments. Because Salomon Brothers controlled most of the auction, it was able to charge high prices for the Treasury bonds desired by other bond dealers.

There was some concern that such activity could discourage investors from obtaining Treasury bonds if there is a market perception that bond prices are manipulated. If the lack of trust in the auction process could reduce the demand for Treasury bonds, it would raise the yields that the Treasury needs to offer to sell the bonds, which ultimately increases the cost to taxpayers.

In the summer of 1991, the Securities and Exchange Commission (SEC) and the Justice Department reviewed Salomon Brothers' involvement in the Treasury auction process. On August 18, 1991, the Treasury Department temporarily barred Salomon Brothers from bidding in Treasury securities for clients. In May 1992, Salomon Brothers paid fines of $190 million to the SEC and Justice Department. It also created a reserve fund of $100 million to cover claims from civil lawsuits.

bonds prior to maturity. The typical fee charged by discount brokers on Treasury bond transactions valued at $10,000 is typically between $40 and $70.

The yield from holding a Treasury bond, as with other bonds, depends on the coupon rate and on the difference between the purchase price and selling price. (Examples of bond yield calculations were provided in Chapter 3.) Investors in Treasury notes and bonds receive semiannual interest payments from the Treasury. Although the interest is taxed by the federal government as ordinary income, it is exempt from state and local taxes, if any exist. Domestic and foreign firms and individuals are common investors in Treasury notes and bonds.

Treasury Bond Quotations

The Treasury bond quotations in newspapers are typically listed in order of maturity, as shown in Exhibit 8.1 for just three bond quotes. The coupon rate, shown in the first column, will vary substantially among bonds, because bonds that were issued when interest rates were high (such as in the early 1980s) will have higher coupon rates than when interest rates were low (such as in the early 1990s).

If the bond contains a call feature allowing the issuer to repurchase the bonds prior to maturity, it is specified beside the maturity date in the second column. For example, the second and third bonds in Exhibit 8.1 mature in the year 2008

EXHIBIT 8.1 Example of Bond Price Quotations

RATE	MATURITY DATE	BID	ASKED	BID CHANGE	YIELD
10.75	Aug. 2005	120-17	120-23	+07	8.37%
8.38	Aug. 2003-08	100-09	100-15	+11	8.32
8.75	Nov. 2003-08	103-05	103-11	+10	8.34

but can be called from the year 2003 thereafter. The bid price (what a buyer is willing to pay) and asked price (what a holder of a bond is willing to sell the bond for) are quoted in hundreds of dollars, with fractions expressed as thirty-seconds of a dollar. For example, if the first bond had a face value of $100,000, its asked price would be $120,719. The price of this bond is much higher than the other two bonds shown, primarily because it offers a higher coupon rate. However, its yield to maturity is similar to the others (see last column in Exhibit 8.1). From an investor's point of view, the coupon rate advantage over the other two bonds is essentially offset by the high price to be paid for that bond.

Stripped Bonds

The cash flows of bonds are commonly transformed—stripped by securities firms—so that one security represents the principal payment only while a second security represents the interest payments. For example, consider a 10-year Treasury bond with a par value of $100,000 that has a 12 percent coupon rate and semiannual coupon payments. This bond could be stripped into a principal-only (PO) security that will provide $100,000 upon maturity and an interest-only (IO) security that will provide 20 semiannual payments of $6,000 each.

Investors who desire a lump-sum payment in the distant future may prefer the principal-only part, while investors desiring periodic cash inflows may prefer the interest-only part. Because the cash flows of the underlying securities are different, so are the degrees of interest rate sensitivity.

A market for Treasury strips was originally created by securities firms in the early 1980s. Merrill Lynch created the Treasury Investment Growth Receipts (TIGRs), in which it purchased Treasury securities and then stripped them to create principal-only securities and interest-only securities. Other securities firms also began to create their own version of these so-called **stripped securities.** In 1985, the Treasury created the STRIPS program, in which it exchanges stripped securities for underlying Treasury securities.

MUNICIPAL BONDS

Like the federal government, state and local governments frequently spend more than the revenues they receive. To finance the difference, they issue **municipal bonds,** most of which can be classified as either **general obligation bonds** or **revenue bonds.** Payments on general obligation bonds are supported by the municipal government's ability to tax, whereas payments on revenue bonds must be generated by revenues of the project (tollway, toll bridge, state college dormitory, etc.) for which the bonds were issued. If insufficient revenues are generated, revenue bonds could default, as happened in the summer of 1983 with bonds issued by the Washington Public Power Supply System (called "WHOOPS") to finance the construction of two nuclear power plants. Because the project's costs became higher than expected, the plants were never completed and the Washington Public Power Supply System defaulted on the bonds.

Revenue bonds and general obligation bonds typically promise interest payments on a semiannual basis. Common purchasers of these bonds include financial and nonfinancial institutions as well as individuals. The minimum denomination of municipal bonds is typically $5,000. A secondary market exists for them, although it is less active than the one for Treasury bonds. One of the most attractive features of municipal bonds is that the interest income such bonds provide is normally exempt from federal taxes and in some cases is exempt from state and local taxes.

The volume of state and local government bonds issued is displayed in Exhibit 8.2. Revenue bonds have consistently dominated since 1975. The total

EXHIBIT 8.2   Dollar Volume of State and Local Government Securities Issued (in millions of $)

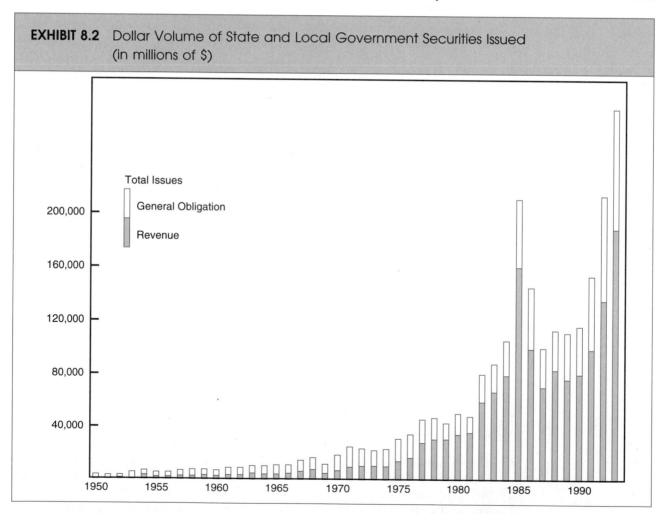

SOURCE: *Federal Reserve Bulletin.*

amount of bond financing by state and local governments has generally increased over time. It was relatively high in 1985 because of concern by state and local governments that tax reform would repeal the tax-exempt status of newly issued bonds, requiring them to offer a higher before-tax yield. In anticipation, they issued a particularly large volume of bonds.

The Tax Reform Act of 1986 limited the use of tax-exempt bonds. Consequently, state and local governments desiring to finance projects (such as housing and airports) that were not purely for government purposes were sometimes forced to sell taxable bonds (called taxable munis).

CORPORATE BONDS

When corporations need to borrow for long-term periods, they issue **corporate bonds,** which usually promise the owner interest on a semianual basis. The minimum denomination is $1,000. The degree of secondary market activity varies; some large corporations have a much larger amount of bonds outstanding in the market, which increases secondary market activity and the bond's liquidity. Common purchasers of corporate bonds include many financial and some nonfinancial institutions as well as individuals. The fee charged by discount brokers on corporate bond transactions valued at $10,000 is typically between $40 and $80. Although most corporate bonds have maturities between 10 and 30 years, corporations such as Boeing, Ford, and Texaco have recently issued 50-year bonds. These bonds can be attractive to insurance companies that are attempting to match their long-term policy obligations. In 1993, Coca-Cola Co. and Walt Disney Co. issued 100-year bonds.

Characteristics of Corporate Bonds

Corporate bonds can be described according to a variety of characteristics. The bond **indenture** is a legal document specifying the rights and obligations of both the issuing firm and the bondholders. It is very comprehensive (normally several hundred pages) and is designed to address all matters related to the bond issue (collateral, payment dates, default provisions, call provisions, etc.).

Federal law requires that for each bond issue of significant size a **trustee** be appointed to represent the bondholders in all matters concerning the bond issue. This includes monitoring the issuing firm's activities to ensure compliance with the terms of the indenture. If the terms of the indenture are violated, the trustee initiates legal action against the issuing firm and represents the bondholders in that action. Bank trust departments are frequently hired to perform the duties of trustee.

SINKING-FUND PROVISION. Bond indentures frequently include a **sinking-fund provision,** or a requirement that the firm retire a certain amount of the bond issue each year. This provision is considered to be an advantage to the remaining bondholders, because it reduces the payments necessary at maturity.

Specific sinking-fund provisions can vary significantly among bond issues. For example, a bond with 20 years until maturity could have a provision to retire 5 percent of the bond issue each year. Or it could have a requirement to retire 5 percent each year beginning in the fifth year, with the remaining amount to be retired at maturity. The actual mechanics of bond retirement are carried out by the trustee.

PROTECTIVE COVENANTS.   Bond indentures normally place on the issuing firm restrictions that are designed to protect the bondholders from being exposed to increasing risk during the investment period. These so-called protective covenants frequently limit the amount of dividends and corporate officers' salaries the firm can pay and also restrict the amount of additional debt the firm can issue. Other financial policies may be restricted as well.

CALL PROVISIONS.   Most bonds include a provision allowing the firm to call the bonds. A **call provision** normally requires the firm to pay a price above par value when it calls its bonds. The difference between the bond's par value and call price is the **call premium.** There are two principal uses of a call provision. First, if market interest rates decline after a bond issue has been sold, the firm might end up paying a higher rate of interest than the prevailing rate for a long period of time. Under these circumstances, the firm may consider selling a new issue of bonds with a lower interest rate and using the proceeds to retire the previous issue by calling the old bonds.

The second principal use of the call provision is to retire bonds as required by a sinking-fund provision. Many bonds have two different call prices: a lower price for calling the bonds to meet sinking-fund requirements and a higher price if the firm calls the bond for any other reason.

A call provision is normally viewed as a disadvantage to bondholders because it can disrupt their investment plans and reduce their investment returns. As a result, firms must pay slightly higher rates of interest on bonds that are callable, other things being equal.

BOND COLLATERAL.   Bonds can be classified according to whether they are secured by collateral and by the nature of that collateral. Usually it is a mortgage on real property (land and buildings). A **first mortgage bond** has first claim on the specified assets. A **chattel mortgage bond** is secured by personal property.

Bonds unsecured by specific property are called **debentures** (backed only by the general credit of the issuing firm). These bonds are normally issued by large, financially sound firms whose ability to service the debt is not in question. Debentures that have claims against the firm's assets that are junior to the claims of both mortgage bonds and regular debentures are called **subordinated debentures.** Owners of these debentures receive nothing until the claims of mortgage bondholders, regular debenture owners, and secured short-term creditors have been satisfied. The main providers of subordinated debt are pension funds and insurance companies.

Bond Financing for Leveraged Buyouts

A leveraged buyout (LBO) is typically financed with senior debt (such as debentures and collateralized loans) and subordinated debt. The senior debt accounts for 50 percent to 60 percent of LBO-financing on the average.

The LBO activity in the late 1980s more than doubled that in the early 1960s. In 1988, there were more than 100 LBOs in which a publicly held firm was taken private. The premium paid when repurchasing shares to execute the LBO typi-

How bond rating downgrades may increase stock prices

It may seem obvious that a bond rating downgrade would reduce the value of a firm by conveying negative news about it. However, recent research by Goh and Ederington suggest that the effects of a credit downgrade are dependent on the underlying reason for the downgrade. The authors explain that a credit downgrade that is attributed to deteriorated financial prospects of the firm should cause a negative impact on the firm's stock price. However, a credit downgrade that is attributed to a high degree of financial leverage can possibly improve the stock price, even if

bondholders are adversely affected. A higher degree of financial leverage can be beneficial to stockholders because it offers potentially higher returns on the equity invested. There is a higher degree of risk associated with high financial leverage, but the higher risk is partially borne by the bondholders, even if they do not share in the potential for higher returns. In essence, a credit downgrade could cause a so-called wealth transfer from bondholders to stockholders.

The authors compiled a list of credit downgrades, and separated

them according to whether they were driven by deteriorated financial prospects for the firm or increased financial leverage. They found that a credit downgrade caused a negative effect on the firm's stock price when it was driven by deteriorated financial prospects. Conversely, a credit downgrade driven by higher financial leverage had a favorable effect on the firm's stock price. This supports the hypothesis that the downgrades driven by higher financial leverage may cause a wealth transfer to stockholders.

cally ranges between 30 percent and 40 percent above the prevailing market price. This suggests that the investors conducting the LBO believed that the firm was substantially undervalued when it was publicly held. By reducing the equity interest of the firm down to a small group of people (possibly the management and other employees), managerial efficiency of the firm is expected to increase. The costs of monitoring management to ensure that management's decisions are in the best interests of the shareholders are negligible when management owns all of the stock.

Although LBOs may possibly enhance managerial efficiency, they have raised a concern about the corporate debt level. During the 1980s, corporate debt of U.S. firms increased substantially. Because many U.S. firms are now operating with a higher degree of financial leverage, they may be more likely to fail if economic conditions deteriorate. The impact of the recession in the early 1990s on corporate performance may have been more pronounced because of the high degree of financial leverage.

In the early 1990s, some firms reversed their financial leverage position after engaging in LBOs. That is, they reissued stock to reduce their degree of financial leverage.

Junk Bonds

Corporate bonds are assigned quality ratings by credit rating agencies, based on their perceived degree of default risk. Those bonds that are perceived to have high risk are referred to as **junk bonds.** During the 1980s, junk bonds became popular as firms desired debt financing to finance acquisitions. These firms were attempting to expand without issuing new stock, so that profits could ultimately be distributed to existing shareholders. Some of the firms planning to use debt financing were perceived to have high risk, especially given the high proportion of debt in their capital structure. Although their newly issued bonds were assigned a low-grade ("junk") quality rating, numerous financial institutions were willing to purchase these bonds because of the relatively high yield offered.

The market value of junk bonds outstanding is approximately $225 billion, which represents about 25 percent of the value of all corporate bonds and about 5 percent of the value of all bonds (including Treasury and municipal bonds). About one-third of all junk bonds were once rated higher but have been downgraded below the investment-grade levels. The remaining two-thirds were considered to be below investment-grade quality as they were initially issued. About two-thirds of all junk bond issues are used to finance takeovers (including LBOs). Some junk bond issues are used by firms to revise their capital structure (the proceeds from issuing bonds are used to repurchase stock, thereby increasing the proportion of debt in the capital structure).

The primary investors in junk bonds are life insurance companies and pension funds. In addition, some mutual funds maintain portfolios of junk bonds. Individuals represent about one-tenth of all investors in the junk bond market. Some issuers of junk bonds are attempting to attract more individual investors by lowering denominations to $1,000. Also, some mutual funds allow investors to invest in a diversified portfolio of junk bonds with a small investment.

Junk bonds offer high yields to compensate investors for the high risk. As the market's perception of economic conditions changed, so does the premium. Exhibit 8.3 shows how the junk bond premium increased during 1989 in response to increased concern about the economy.

PERFORMANCE. Junk bonds are generally perceived to offer high returns with high risk. During the mid-1980s, junk bond defaults were relatively infrequent, which may have renewed public interest in them and encouraged corporations to issue more.

The recent performance of junk bonds has not been as favorable. After the stockmarket crash of October 1987, the market became more concerned about

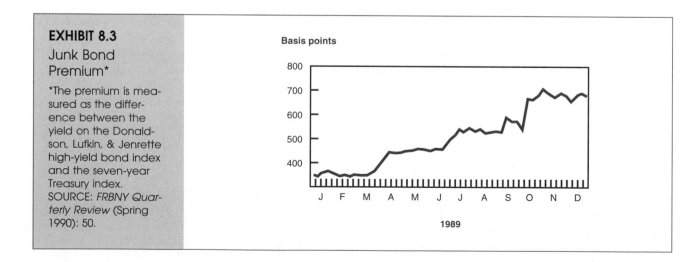

EXHIBIT 8.3

Junk Bond Premium*

*The premium is measured as the difference between the yield on the Donaldson, Lufkin, & Jenrette high-yield bond index and the seven-year Treasury index.
SOURCE: *FRBNY Quarterly Review* (Spring 1990): 50.

Basis points

1989

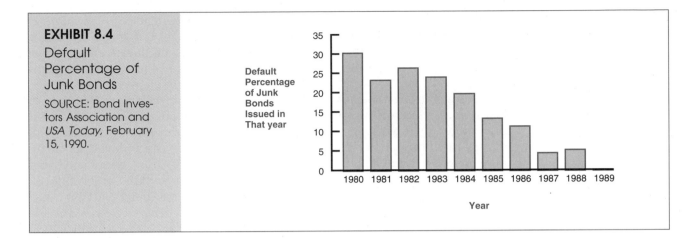

EXHIBIT 8.4

Default Percentage of Junk Bonds

SOURCE: Bond Investors Association and *USA Today*, February 15, 1990.

the risk of junk bonds. Issuers had to lower the price to compensate for the higher perceived risk. The junk bond market received another blow in the late 1980s, as insider trading charges were filed against Drexel Burnham Lambert Inc., the main dealer in the market, for violating various regulations.

Exhibit 8.4 shows the percentage of junk bonds issued in a particular year that were in default by 1990. The older the junk bonds, the higher the default percentage.

In 1989, high-rated corporate bonds experienced a yield of 12.5 percent, while junk bonds experienced a return of −0.09 percent. In 1990, defaults of junk bonds amounted to $24.6 billion, almost 9 percent of the value of all junk bonds outstanding.

In 1990, the popularity of junk bonds declined as a result of three key factors. First, there were allegations of insider trading against some participants in the junk bond market. Second, the financial problems of a few major issuers of junk bonds scared some investors away. Third, the financial problems in the thrift industry caused regulators to more closely regulate investments by thrifts. The Financial Institutions Reform Recovery and Enforcement Act (FIRREA) mandated that savings institutions liquidate their investments in junk bonds. Because savings institutions controlled about 7 percent of the junk bond market, there was additional downward pressure on prices. Although these institutions were given five years to liquidate the junk bonds to alleviate some downward pressure on junk bond prices, many of them liquidated these bonds within a few months after the Act was implemented.

CONTAGION EFFECTS. Investors may be systematically discouraged from investment in junk bonds by specific adverse information, which means the junk bond market is susceptible to **contagion effects.** For example, over the two weeks after Ivan Boesky admitted insider trading violations, prices of junk bonds declined because of reduced investor demand. Information about any specific firm's inability to service its junk bond debt could also signal future problems for most highly leveraged firms and therefore cause a decline in prices of all junk bonds.

In September 1989, Campeau Corporation was experiencing financial problems and had to obtain a $250 million loan to make interest payments on its junk bonds. Investors feared that other issuers of junk bonds might experience similar problems and reduced their demand for the bonds, causing a decline in junk bond prices.

Drexel Burnham Lambert's filing for bankruptcy in February 1990 caused investors to shift from junk bonds to risk-free Treasury bonds. Consequently, the price differential between the two types of bonds widened, and, therefore, so did the yield differential. That is, junk bonds were attractive to investors only if they offered a greater premium than before. In March 1990, Columbia Savings and Loan announced its plans to divest its $3.5 billion portfolio of junk bonds, causing another shift by investors from junk bonds to risk-free bonds.

Many firms that issue junk bonds have excessive debt service payments and may possibly experience cash flow deficiencies if sales are less than anticipated. Thus, they are all susceptible to a single underlying event, such as an economic downturn. Furthermore, the media attention about a single well-known firm that may be unable to service its junk bond payments can cause increased concern (whether justified or not) about other highly leveraged firms. Such concern could encourage investors to sell holdings of junk bonds or discourage other investors from purchasing junk bonds.

Low- and Zero-Coupon Bonds

In the early 1980s, firms began issuing bonds with coupons roughly half the size of the prevailing rate and later with zero coupons. These **low-coupon** or **zero-coupon bonds** are therefore issued at a deep discount from par value. Investors are taxed annually on the amount of interest earned, even though much or all of the interest will not be received until maturity. The amount of interest taxed is the amortized discount (the gain at maturity is prorated over the life of the bond). Low- and zero-coupon corporate bonds are purchased mainly for tax-exempt investment accounts (pension funds, individual retirement accounts, etc.).

To the issuing firm, these bonds have the advantage of requiring low or no cash outflow during their life. Additionally, the firm is permitted to deduct the amortized discount as interest expense for federal income tax purposes, even though it does not pay interest. This adds to the firm's cash flow. Finally, the demand for low- and zero-coupon bonds has been great enough that firms can, in most cases, issue them at a lower cost than regular bonds.

Variable-Rate Bonds

The highly volatile interest rates experienced during the 1970s inspired the development of **variable-rate bonds,** which affect the investor and borrower as follows: (1) they allow investors to benefit from rising market interest rates over time, and (2) they allow issuers of bonds to benefit from declining rates over time.

Convertible Bonds

Another type of bond, known as the **convertible bond,** allows investors to exchange a bond for a stated number of shares of the firm's common stock. This conversion feature offers investors the potential for high returns if the price of

WSJ | USING *THE WALL STREET JOURNAL*

BOND INFORMATION

The Wall Street Journal (WSJ) provides the following information related to this chapter on a daily basis:

- Price quotations on corporate bonds traded on the New York Stock Exchange and American Stock Exchange (see "NYSE/Amex Bonds").
- Price quotations on Treasury bonds and notes, and on bonds issued by other government agencies (see "Treas./Gov't. Issues").
- A section called "Credit Markets" describes recent price trends in debt markets, and explains major changes in the prices. It also provides a yield curve based on Treasury securities with different maturities.
- A section called "New Securities Issues" identifies firms that issued new debt securities.

- A "Bond Data Bank" contains bond price information on bonds of various types of issuers (example shown here). It also provides information on international bonds issued by foreign governments and on Eurodollar bonds. Percentage changes in the bond prices are shown since the previous day, since the beginning of the year, and over a 12-month period. This table can be used to compare price changes across different types of bonds.

SOURCE: *The Wall Street Journal*, August 4, 1994, p. C19. Reprinted by permission of *The Wall Street Journal*. © Dow Jones & Company, Inc. All rights reserved worldwide.

BOND MARKET DATA BANK 8/4/94

MAJOR INDEXES

HIGH	LOW (12 MOS)		CLOSE	NET CHG	% CHG	12-MO CHG		% CHG	FROM 12/31		% CHG
U.S. TREASURY SECURITIES		(Lehman Brothers indexes)									
4158.35	3966.84	Intermediate	4077.62	− 3.26	− 0.08	+	42.35 +	1.05	− 39.09	−	0.95
5766.90	4960.69	Long-term	5192.29	− 11.45	− 0.22	−	196.33 −	3.64	− 320.34	−	5.81
1668.45	1368.35	Long-term(price)	1415.35	− 3.41	− 0.24	−	164.18 −	10.39	− 155.77	−	9.91
4514.72	4199.01	Composite	4335.42	− 4.78	− 0.11	−	8.96 −	0.21	− 102.04	−	2.30
U.S. CORPORATE DEBT ISSUES		(Merrill Lynch)									
709.45	656.43	Corporate Master	680.97	+ 0.48	+ 0.07	+	2.57 +	0.38	− 16.76	−	2.40
518.52	487.79	1-10 Yr Maturities	504.62	+ 0.23	+ 0.05	+	7.29 +	1.47	− 6.74	−	1.32
546.54	493.69	10+ Yr Maturities	514.90	+ 0.51	+ 0.10	−	3.69 −	0.71	− 18.91	−	3.54
332.37	309.91	High Yield	323.96	+ 0.20	+ 0.06	+	14.04 +	4.53	− 0.98	−	0.30
522.98	477.83	Yankee Bonds	494.76	+ 0.43	+ 0.09	−	3.01 −	0.60	− 16.71	−	3.27
TAX-EXEMPT SECURITIES		(Bond Buyer; Merrill Lynch: Dec. 31, 1986 = 100)									
106-18	88-2	Bond Buyer Municipal	92-15	+ -1	+ 0.03	−	9-19 −	9.40	− 11-21	−	11.19
108.32	100.33	7-12 yr G.O.	104.47	− 0.07	− 0.07	+	1.97 +	1.92	− 2.50	−	2.34
109.89	97.44	12-22 yr G.O.	104.38	− 0.05	− 0.05	+	0.93 +	0.90	− 4.16	−	3.83
108.19	96.33	22+ yr Revenue	101.65	− 0.34	− 0.33	+	2.16 −	2.08	− 5.01	−	4.70
MORTGAGE-BACKED SECURITIES		(current coupon; Merrill Lynch: Dec. 31, 1986 = 100)									
216.20	197.64	Ginnie Mae(GNMA)	205.14	− 0.02	− 0.01	+	2.93 +	1.45	− 6.51	−	3.08
214.73	197.82	Fannie Mae(FNMA)	205.18	− 0.08	− 0.04	+	0.93 +	0.46	− 5.31	−	2.52
130.84	120.58	Freddie Mac(FHLMC)	124.93	− 0.05	− 0.04	+	0.64 +	0.51	− 3.17	−	2.47
CONVERTIBLE BONDS		(Merrill Lynch: Dec. 31, 1986 = 100)									
189.40	177.60	Investment Grade	183.78	− 0.34	− 0.18	+	0.79 +	0.43	− 3.55	−	1.90
210.43	189.61	High Yield	192.97	+ 0.04	+ 0.02	−	0.15 −	0.08	− 11.84	−	5.78

the firm's common stock rises. Investors are therefore willing to accept a lower rate of interest on these bonds, which allows the firm to obtain financing at a lower cost.

EVALUATING BOND RISK

When investors consider bonds, they assess not only the expected yield but also the various types of risk, as explained here.

Interest Rate Risk

The precise impact of interest rate movements on a bond's market value depends on the cash flow characteristics of the bond. The prices of bonds with longer terms to maturity are more susceptible to interest rate movements. In addition, prices of low-coupon or zero-coupon bonds are more susceptible to interest rate movements.

Because interest rates have been more volatile in the past two decades, the yields on Treasury bonds have been more volatile as well. The volatility was especially high in the late 1970s and early 1980s, as interest rates were very unsteady during that period.

Given the increased interest rate risk, bond portfolio managers allocate much of their time predicting interest rates. Their investment decision are based on the forecasted movements in interest rates. Any factors that are expected to influence interest rates are often used to explain why bond prices rise or fall. Some of the more critical factors follow.

IMPACT OF MONEY SUPPLY GROWTH. When money supply growth is increased by the Federal Reserve System, two reactions are possible. First, the increased money supply may result in an increased supply of loanable funds. If demand for loanable funds is not affected, the increased money supply should place downward pressure on interest rates, causing bond portfolio managers to expect an increase in bond prices and thus purchase bonds based on such expectations. An alternative reaction is to expect that the increased money supply growth will lead to a higher level of inflation. A historical positive relationship between money supply growth and inflation substantiates this expectation. On this basis, bond portfolio managers may expect a large increase in the demand for loanable funds (as a result of inflationary expectations), causing an increase in interest rates and lower bond prices. Such forecasts would encourage immediate sales of long-term bonds.

IMPACT OF OIL PRICES. Oil prices have a major impact on a variety of wholesale and consumer prices. Bond portfolio managers therefore forecast oil prices and their potential impact on inflation in order to forecast interest rates. A forecast of lower oil prices results in expectations of lower interest rates, causing bond portfolio managers to purchase more bonds. A forecast of high oil prices results in expectations of higher interest rates, causing bond portfolio managers to sell some of their bond holdings. As a recent example, the Persian Gulf crisis in the summer of 1990 caused an abrupt increase in the price of oil and an upward revision in inflationary expectations. Bond prices plunged in response to adverse information about the Persian Gulf crisis.

EVENT RISK FOR RJR NABISCO

As reported in *Mergers and Acquisitions,* the $24.7 billion leveraged buyout in 1988 by Kohlberg Kravis Roberts, Inc. (KKR), of RJR Nabisco, Inc., not only was the largest LBO ever but also ranks as one of the largest acquisitions. The equity investment by KKR was only about $1.4 billion, less than 6 percent of the purchase price. Drexel Burnham Lambert, Inc., and Merrill Lynch & Company also had a small equity investment in the buyout.

The debt financing was composed of long-term bank loans, short-term loans that were to be repaid once some of RJR's assets were sold, and bonds. More than $5 billion of debt was supplied by Japanese banks.

Before the acquisition, RJR's long-term debt was less than its shareholders' equity. After the acquisition, RJR's long-term debt was more than 12 times its shareholders' equity. Annual interest expenses were expected to be more than five times what they were before the acquisition. Thus, there was a need for additional cash

flow to accommodate the substantial increase in financial leverage. In 1988, RJR's cash flows totaled $1.8 billion, which was not expected to be sufficient to meet interest payments on debt. In May, RJR attempted to sell various businesses to improve its cash position.

It is of interest to note that RJR issued stock to reduce its degree of financial leverage in 1990 and again in 1991. The original market price was $5 per share, which was similar to the price KKR paid for the shares in 1988. Yet, within a few months, the price almost doubled. Many other firms with excessive financial leverage resulting from a previous LBO also reissued stock in the early 1990s. They typically used some of the proceeds from the stock issuance to retire some outstanding debt, thereby reducing their periodic interest payments on debt. This process is more feasible for firms that could issue shares of stock for high prices, because the proceeds would retire a larger amount of outstanding debt.

IMPACT OF THE DOLLAR.   To the extent that fluctuations in the dollar affect interest rates, they affect U.S. bond prices. Holding other things equal, expectations of a weaker dollar are likely to increase inflationary expectations because they increase the prices of imported supplies. Such expectations also price foreign competitors out of the market, allowing U.S. firms to increase their prices. Thus, U.S. interest rates are expected to rise and bond prices are expected to decrease when the dollar is expected to weaken. Foreign investors expecting dollar depreciation are less willing to hold U.S. bonds, because the coupon payments will convert to less of their home currency in that event, and this could cause an immediate net sale of bonds, placing further downward pressure on bond prices.

Expectations of a strong dollar should have the opposite results. A stronger dollar reduces the prices paid for foreign supplies, thus lowering retail prices. In addition, because a stronger dollar makes the prices of foreign products more attractive, domestic firms must maintain low prices in order to compete. Consequently, low inflation, and therefore low interest rates, are expected, and bond portfolio managers are likely to purchase more bonds.

SIMULTANEOUS IMPACT OF ALL FACTORS.   If investors could correctly predict the interest rate for a certain point in time, they could predict with a high degree of accuracy how bond prices would be affected at that time. However, they are

PERCEIVED RELIABILITY OF BOND RATINGS

A recent study by Ederington, Yawitz, and Roberts examines the informational content of bond ratings. Some of the more relevant results of the study are summarized below:

1. When market participants evaluate a bond issue's creditworthiness, they consider recent financial information about the company of concern above and beyond the information embedded within the ratings by Moody's or Standard & Poor's.

2. When compared for reliability, neither Moody's nor Standard & Poor's ratings were found to be clearly superior to the other.

3. When existing bonds have not been rated for a long period of time, market participants tend to place more emphasis on publicly available financial information and less on the ratings assigned by ratings agencies. This suggests that a rating is perceived to be more reliable for assessing the short-term creditworthiness of the bond issue than the long-term creditworthiness. Perhaps ratings would be consistently emphasized by market participants if they were updated more frequently by the rating agencies.

limited in their ability to forecast interest rates by two main factors. First, it is impossible to accurately predict all changes in all factors (such as money supply, oil prices, and the dollar value) that influence inflation and therefore interest rates. Second, even if these factors could be predicted with perfect accuracy, their impact on interest rates cannot. To deal with the uncertainty, bond portfolio managers often develop a variety of possible interest rate scenarios for a future point in time and estimate bond prices for each scenario. In this way, they can create a probability distribution of forecasted bond prices that can be used to help them decide whether to buy or sell bonds.

Default Risk

Bond portfolio managers also monitor factors that reduce the bond issuer's ability to meet its payment obligations. At one extreme, Treasury bonds are normally perceived to have zero default risk, because they are backed by the federal government. However, municipal and corporate bonds are exposed to default risk. Small investors frequently rely on bond ratings provided by rating agencies such as Moody's or Standard & Poor's as a measure of default risk. Since 1976 the number of downgrades has exceeded the number of upgrades. The difference was most pronounced during the 1982 recession and in the early 1990s when several corporations were perceived to have an excessive amount of debt.

Bond portfolio managers who trade millions of dollars of bonds on a daily basis may both monitor bond ratings and conduct their own evaluation of the bonds. Their own evaluation would include an assessment of the bond issuer's financial ratios over time. Ratios that compare cash flow to interest owed would be most useful. Historical financial ratios are not necessarily proper indicators of the future, so bond portfolio managers may attempt to forecast the bond issuer's future earnings and cash flow and determine from that whether the debt payments can be covered.

EVENT RISK.   Bonds are susceptible to **event risk,** which typically reflects an increase in the perceived risk of default resulting from a corporate restructuring of debt or a takeover. Consider a firm whose management engages in a leveraged buyout by using newly borrowed funds to repurchase outstanding shares of stock. The result is a much higher degree of financial leverage for the firm and a higher probability of bankruptcy. The prices of bonds existing before the LBO attempt will decline in response to the higher risk. Although those investors that have an equity interest in the firm can benefit from the higher financial leverage, bondholders become exposed to more risk without any corresponding increase in potential return. To illustrate the potential bond price reaction to an LBO attempt, consider the case of RJR Nabisco, Inc., which experienced the largest LBO ever. In the fall of 1988, when management of RJR proposed the LBO, bond prices declined by 20 percent.

Bondholders began to more aggressively defend against event risk. Some institutional investors that maintain large bond portfolios sued firms that initiated LBOs. As an example, Metropolitan Life Insurance Company and Jefferson Pilot Life Insurance Company filed a suit charging RJR Nabisco's management with violating its fiduciary responsibility to its existing bondholders when it initiated an LBO. Bondholders can also defend against event risk by specifying in protective covenants a limit on the amount of additional bonds the firm can issue in the future.

INTERACTION AMONG BOND YIELDS

Yields among bonds can vary according to such factors as default risk, marketability, and tax status. Yet, the differential remains somewhat stable over time because investors will switch to bonds that are perceived as more favorable. For example, if the Treasury issues an unusually large number of Treasury bonds in the primary market, such a large supply places downward pressure on the market price and upward pressure on the market yield of these bonds. Consequently, holders of corporate bonds with default risk may then switch to Treasury bonds, because such bonds can achieve almost the same yield without being exposed to default risk. This tendency places downward pressure on the Treasury bond yields and upward pressure on corporate bonds, restoring the yield differential between the two. Thus, because some investors perceive various bonds as substitutes, their buy and sell decisions will stabilize yield differentials among the bonds.

Exhibit 8.5 compares yields on various types of bonds over time. The yields among securities are highly correlated. Notice that the difference between the corporate Baa and corporate Aaa bond yields widens during the poor economic periods of the early 1930s, 1973–1974, and 1982, when investors required a higher default risk premium.

Yield differentials among bonds can change when investors perceive a characteristic of a particular type of bond to be more or less favorable than before. For example, if interest rates suddenly decline, those existing bonds that have a call feature are more likely to be called. Thus, bonds containing the call feature will sell only if the price is lowered. This implies that the yield differential adjusts to the changing perception of the factor that caused the differential.

EXHIBIT 8.5   Comparison of Bond Yields

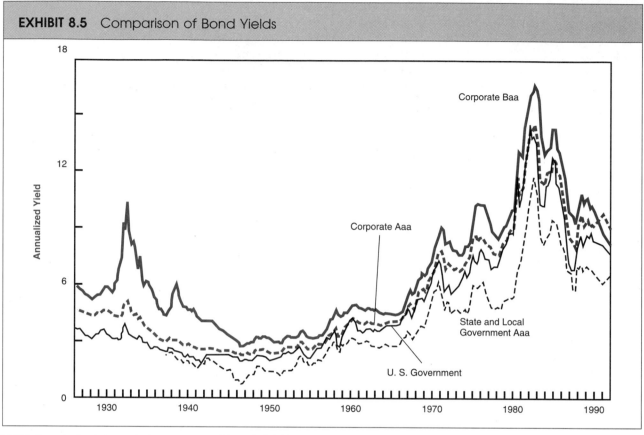

NOTE: Trends depict quarterly averages of bond yields.
SOURCE: *Federal Reserve Bulletin.*

BOND PORTFOLIO MANAGEMENT

Some bond portfolio managers will actively restructure their portfolio in anticipation of economic conditions. If they expect favorable economic conditions, they
will increase their holdings of bonds with higher default risk. When the economic
outlook is more pessimistic, they will shift toward bonds with low or no default
risk. Others take a more passive approach in which their mix of bonds with
different degrees of risk remains somewhat constant (except in unusual
circumstances).

If bond portfolio managers anticipate lower interest rates, they may attempt
to benefit from that by replacing short-maturity bonds with long-maturity bonds,
or high-coupon bonds with low- or zero-coupon bonds. If they anticipate higher
interest rates, they may concentrate on short-maturity and/or high-coupon
bonds. In addition, they may temporarily liquidate part of their bond portfolio
and use the proceeds to invest in money market securities. When their expectations of future interest rates change, they can liquidate the money market securities and invest in more bonds.

A more passive strategy would be to diversify among bonds that exhibit
varied degrees of sensitivity to interest rate movements. Such a mix might even

be permanently maintained. Although this strategy would have a lower potential return than an actively managed bond portfolio, it would not be as adversely affected if interest rates moved in the opposite direction of what was expected. Furthermore, transaction costs would be much lower.

INSTITUTIONAL USE OF BOND MARKETS

All financial institutions participate in the bond markets, as summarized in Exhibit 8.6. Commercial banks, bond mutual funds, insurance companies, and pension funds are dominant participants in the bond market activity on any given day. A financial institution's investment decisions will often simultaneously affect bond market and other financial market activity. For example, an institution's anticipation of higher interest rates may cause a sale of its bond holdings and a purchase of either money market securities or stocks. Conversely, expectations of lower interest rates may encourage financial institutions to shift investment from their money market security and/or stock portfolios to their bond portfolio.

EXHIBIT 8.6 Participation of Financial Institutions in Bond Markets

FINANCIAL INSTITUTION	PARTICIPATION IN BOND MARKETS
Commercial banks and savings and loan associations (S&Ls)	■ Purchase bonds for their asset portfolio. ■ Sometimes place municipal bonds for municipalities. ■ Sometimes issue bonds as a source of secondary capital.
Finance companies	■ Commonly issue bonds as a source of long-term funds.
Mutual funds	■ Use funds received from the sale of shares to purchase bonds; some bond mutual funds specialize in particular types of bonds, while others invest in all types.
Brokerage firms	■ Facilitate bond trading by matching up buyers and sellers of bonds in the secondary market.
Investment banking firms	■ Place newly issued bonds for governments and corporations; they may underwrite the bonds and therefore assume the risk of market price uncertainty or place the bonds on a best-efforts basis in which they do not guarantee a price for the issuer.
Insurance companies	■ Purchase bonds for their asset portfolio.
Pension funds	■ Purchase bonds for their asset portfolio.

BENEFITS FROM DIVERSIFYING AMONG BONDS

Because the market values of bonds are inversely related to interest rate movements, it may seem that diversification among bonds would not reduce risk. However, a study by McEnally and Boardman found that a bond portfolio's risk (as measured by variance of returns) can be substantially reduced by diversifying. This study estimated the mean variance of a set of one-bond, two-bond, three-bond, ... forty-bond portfolios. The general relationship between the mean variance and number of bonds in the portfolio is shown in the exhibit below. As the number of bonds in the portfolio was increased, the mean variance of the bond portfolio declined. The degree of risk reduction became smaller as the number increased.

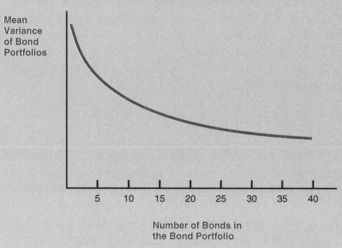

Mean Variance of Bond Portfolios

Number of Bonds in the Bond Portfolio

GLOBALIZATION OF BOND MARKETS

GLOBAL ASPECTS

Bond markets have become increasingly integrated among countries. Exhibit 8.7 shows that foreign purchases and sales of U.S. bonds increased substantially in recent years. The value of foreign transactions during the early 1990s was more than seven times the value of transactions during the period 1982–1984.

The increased volume in the foreign trading of U.S. securities exists partially because U.S. corporations are issuing more securities in foreign markets. In addition, mutual funds containing U.S. securities are accessible to foreign investors. Furthermore, primary dealers of U.S. Treasury notes and bonds have opened offices in London, Tokyo, and other foreign cities to accommodate the foreign demand for these securities.

U.S. Treasury bonds are traded 24 hours a day around the world. When the U.S. markets close, markets in Hong Kong and Tokyo are opening. As these markets close, Western Europe markets are opening. The U.S. market opens as markets in London and other European cities are closing. Thus, the prices of U.S. Treasury bonds at the time the U.S. market opens may differ substantially from the previous day's closing price.

EXHIBIT 8.7 Foreign Trading of U.S. Bonds (in Billions of Dollars)

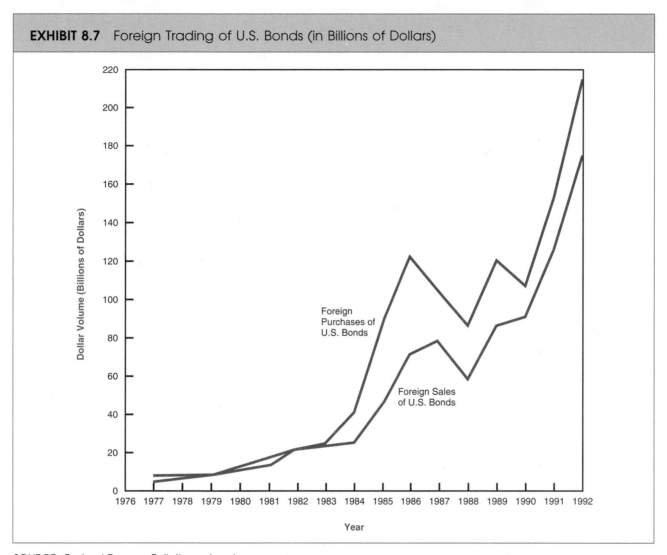

SOURCE: *Federal Reserve Bulletin,* various issues.

In recent years, low-quality bonds have been issued globally by governments and large corporations. These bonds have been referred to as **global junk bonds.** The demand for these bonds has been high as some institutional investors are attracted to their high yields. For example, corporate bonds have been issued by Klabin (Brazil) and Cementos Mexicanos (Mexico), while government bonds have been issued by Brazil, Mexico, Venezuela, the Czech Republic, and Spain.

Eurobond Market

In 1963 U.S.-based corporations were limited to the amount of funds they could borrow in the United States for overseas operations. Consequently, these corporations began to issue bonds in the so-called Eurobond market, where bonds denominated in various currencies were placed. The U.S. dollar is used the most, denominating 70 percent to 75 percent of the Eurobonds.

Non-U.S. investors who desire dollar-denominated bonds may use the Eurobond market if they prefer the bearer form to the registered form of corporate bonds issued in the United States. Alternatively, they may use the Eurobond market because they are more familiar with bond placements within their own country.

An underwriting syndicate of investment banks participates in the Eurobond market by placing the bonds issued. It normally underwrites the bonds, guaranteeing a particular value to be received by the issuer. Thus, the syndicate is exposed to underwriting risk, or the risk that it will be unable to sell the bonds above the price that it guaranteed the issuer.

The issuer of Eurobonds can choose the currency in which the bonds should be denominated. The issuer's periodic coupon payments and repayment of principal will normally be in this currency. Moreover, the financing cost from issuing bonds depends on the currency chosen. In some cases, a firm may denominate the bonds in a currency with a low interest rate and use earnings generated by one of its subsidiaries to cover the payments. For example, the coupon rate on a Eurobond denominated in Swiss francs may be 5 percentage points lower than a dollar-denominated bond. A U.S. firm may consider issuing Swiss franc-denominated bonds and converting the francs to dollars for use in the United States. Then it could instruct a subsidiary in Switzerland to cover the periodic coupon payments with earnings that the subsidiary generates. In this way, a lower financing rate would be achieved without exposure to exchange rate risk.

Tax Effects

Before 1984, foreign investors who directly purchased U.S.-placed bonds were subject to a 30 percent withholding tax. A variety of tax treaties between the United States and other countries caused this withholding tax to affect investors in some countries more than others. Because of the withholding tax, many U.S. bonds were issued in the Eurobond market through financing subsidiaries in the Netherlands Antilles. A tax treaty allowed interest payments from Antilles subsidiaries of U.S.-based corporations to non-U.S. investors to be exempt from the withholding tax, and U.S. firms that used this method of financing were able to sell their bonds at a higher price. Thus, they obtained funds at a relatively low cost. Some U.S. firms did not use this financing method, because there was a cost of establishing a financing subsidiary in the Netherlands Antilles, and because they knew that this method of circumventing the withholding tax might be prohibited by the U.S. government at some point in the future.

In July 1984 the U.S. government abolished the withholding tax and allowed U.S. corporations to issue bearer bonds directly to non-U.S. investors. This caused a large increase in the volume of bonds sold to non-U.S. investors.

Impact of Exchange Rates on Foreign Bonds

Financial institutions often consider purchasing foreign securities whose expected returns are higher than expected returns on domestic securities. For example, U.S. life insurance companies or pension funds may consider the purchase of bonds denominated in British pounds (£) if the yield is higher than U.S. bond yields. However, the yield will be affected by exchange rate fluctuations. Consider a U.S. financial institution's purchase of bonds with a par value of £2 mil-

EXHIBIT 8.8 Dollar Cash Flows Generated from a Foreign Bond under Three Scenarios

SCENARIO I (STABLE POUND)	YEAR					
	1	2	3	4	5	6
Forecasted value of pound	$1.50	$1.50	$1.50	$1.50	$1.50	$1.50
Forecasted dollar cash flows	$300,000	$300,000	$300,000	$300,000	$300,000	$3,300,000
SCENARIO II (WEAK POUND)						
Forecasted value of pound	$1.48	$1.46	$1.44	$1.40	$1.36	$1.30
Forecasted dollar cash flows	$296,000	$292,000	$288,000	$280,000	$272,000	$2,860,000
SCENARIO III (STRONG POUND)						
Forecasted value of pound	$1.53	$1.56	$1.60	$1.63	$1.66	$1.70
Forecasted dollar cash flows	$306,000	$312,000	$320,000	$326,000	$332,000	$3,740,000

lion, a 10 percent coupon rate (payable at the end of each year), presently priced at par value, and with six years remaining until maturity. Consider how the dollar cash flows to be generated from the investment will differ under the three scenarios shown in Exhibit 8.8. The cash flows in the last year also account for the principal payment. The sensitivity of dollar cash flows to the pound's value is obvious.

From the perspective of the investing institution, the most attractive foreign bonds offer a high coupon rate and are denominated in a currency that strengthens over the investment horizon. Although the coupon rates of some bonds are fixed, the future value of any foreign currency is uncertain. Thus, there is a risk that currency will depreciate and more than offset any coupon rate advantage.

Diversifying Bonds Internationally

Financial institutions may attempt to reduce their exchange rate risk by diversifying among foreign securities denominated in various foreign currencies. In this way, a smaller proportion of their foreign security holdings will be exposed to the depreciation of any particular foreign currency. Because the movements of many foreign currency values are highly correlated, U.S. investors may reduce exchange rate risk only slightly when diversifying among European securities. For this reason, U.S. financial institutions commonly attempt to purchase securities across continents rather than within a single continent, as a review of the foreign securities purchased by pension funds, life insurance companies, or most international mutual funds would show.

Institutional investors also diversify their bond portfolio internationally in order to reduce exposure to interest rate risk. If all bonds were from a single country, the values of all bonds in the portfolio would be systematically affected by interest rate movements in that country. International diversification of bonds reduces the sensitivity of the overall bond portfolio to any single country's interest rate movements.

Another key reason for international diversification is the reduction of credit (default) risk. The investment in bonds issued by corporations from a single country can expose investors to a relatively high degree of credit risk. The credit risk of corporations is highly dependent on economic conditions. Shifts in credit risk will likely be systematically related to the country's economic conditions. Because economic cycles differ across countries, there is less chance of a systematic increase in the credit risk of internationally diversified bonds.

SUMMARY

- Bonds can be classified in three categories according to the type of issuer: Treasury bonds, municipal bonds, and corporate bonds. The issuers are perceived to have different levels of default risk. In addition, the bonds have different degrees of liquidity and different provisions. Thus, quoted yields at a given point in time vary across bonds.

- Because bond prices are inversely related to interest rate risk, investors monitor the factors that can affect interest rates, such as money supply, oil prices, and the strength of the U.S. dollar.

  Bond prices may also change in response to changes in perceived default risk, which can be driven by economic conditions. Default risk can also increase when the issuer of the bond enacts a risky policy, such as increased financial leverage.

- Many institutional investors, such as commercial banks, insurance companies, pension funds, and bond mutual funds, are major investors in bonds. The holdings of bonds are adjusted by these institutional investors in response to expectations of future interest rates.

- Bond yields vary among countries. Investors are attracted to high bond yields in foreign countries, causing funds to flow to those countries. Consequently, bond markets have become globally integrated. Investments in foreign bonds are subject to exchange rate risk, because the foreign currency denominating the bonds could depreciate over time.

QUESTIONS

1. What is a bond indenture?
2. What is the function of a trustee, as related to bond issues?

3. Explain the use of a sinking-fund provision. How can it reduce the risk of investors?

4. What are protective covenants?

5. Explain the call provision of bonds. How can it affect the price of a bond?

6. Explain the common types of collateral for bonds.

7. What are debentures? How do they differ from subordinated debentures?

8. What are the advantages and disadvantages to a firm that issues low- or zero-coupon bonds?

9. Are variable-rate bonds attractive to investors who expect interest rates to decrease? Explain.

10. Why can convertible bonds be issued by firms at a higher price than other bonds?

11. Explain how bond prices may be affected by money supply growth, oil prices, and the expected value of the dollar.

12. Explain why a passive strategy in bond portfolio management would result in lower transaction costs than a more aggressive strategy.

13. Assume that oil-producing countries have agreed to reduce their oil production by 30 percent. How would bond prices be affected by this announcement? Explain.

14. Assume that the bond market participants suddenly expect the Fed to substantially increase money supply.
    a. Assuming no threat of inflation, how would bond prices be affected by this expectation?
    b. Assuming that inflation may result, how would bond prices be affected?

15. During the 1990s, the trade deficit figures have been closely monitored by bond portfolio managers.
    a. When the trade deficit figure was higher than anticipated, bond prices typically declined. Explain why this reaction may have occurred.
    b. In some cases, the trade deficit figure was very large, but the bond markets did not respond to the announcement of it. Assuming that no other information offset its impact, explain why the bond markets may not have responded to the announcement.

16. Assume that the bond yields in Japan rise. How might U.S. bond yields be affected? Why?

17. Assume that the Japanese government announces plans to impose a special high tax on income earned by Japanese investors who have purchased non-Japanese bonds. How might this announcement affect U.S. bond prices immediately, even before the plan is finalized?

18. Assume that news is announced that causes bond portfolio managers to suddenly expect much higher economic growth. How might bond prices be affected by this expectation? Explain.

19. Assume that news is announced that causes bond portfolio managers to suddenly anticipate a recession. How might bond prices be affected? Explain.

20. A U.S. insurance company chose to purchase British 20-year Treasury bonds instead of U.S. 20-year Treasury bonds because the coupon rate was 2 percent higher on the British bonds. Assume that the insurance company sold the bonds after five years. Its yield over the five-year period was substantially less than the yield it would have received on the U.S. bonds over the same five-year period. Assume that the U.S. insurance company had hedged its exchange rate exposure. Given that the lower yield was not because of default risk or exchange rate risk, explain how the British bonds could possibly generate a lower yield than the U.S. bonds. (Assume that either type of bond could have been purchased at the par value.)

21. Explain how the Financial Institutions Reform, Recovery, and Enforcement Act (FIRREA) could have affected the market value of junk bonds.

22. Explain why news of the financial problems of Campeau Corporation could cause the prices of junk bonds issued by other firms to decrease, even when those firms had no business relationships with Campeau.

23. An insurance company purchased bonds issued by Hartnett Company two years ago. Today, Hartnett Company began to issue junk bonds and use the funds to repurchase most of its existing stock. Why might the market value of those bonds held by the insurance company be affected by this action?

24. The pension fund manager of Utterback Co. (a U.S. firm) chose to purchase German 20-year Treasury bonds instead of U.S. 20-year Treasury bonds. The coupon rate was 2 percent lower on the German bonds. Assume that the manager sold the bonds after five years. The yield over the five-year period was substantially more than the yield it would have received on the U.S. bonds over the same five-year period. Assume that the manager had hedged any exchange rate exposure. Explain how the German bonds could possibly generate a higher yield than the U.S. bonds. (Assume that the price of either bond was initially equal to its respective par value.) Be specific.

25. On January 17, 1991, bond prices soared in the United States in response to an attack by a group of countries on missile installations in Iraq. Explain the reason for the large increase in bond prices.

26. In January 1993, when President Clinton's proposed program of increased taxes was released, bond prices increased. Explain why.

27. From 1952 to 1992, the average annual total return on bonds (including the percentage change in the bond prices) was about 8 percent, when a Republican president was in office, versus about zero percent when a Democratic president was in office. Offer some political arguments that may have caused this differential.

PROBLEM

1. Cardinal Company, a U.S.-based insurance company, considers purchasing bonds denominated in Canadian dollars, with a maturity of six years, a par value of C$50 million, and a coupon rate of 12 percent. The bonds can be purchased at par by Cardinal and would be sold four years from now. The current exchange rate of the Canadian dollar is $.80. Cardinal expects that the required return by Canadian investors on these bonds four years from now will be 9 percent. If Cardinal purchases the bonds, it will sell them in the Canadian secondary market four years from now. The following exchange rates are forecast as follows:

YEAR	EXCHANGE RATE OF C$
1	$.80
2	.77
3	.74
4	.72
5	.68
6	.66

    a. Determine the expected U.S. dollar cash flows to Cardinal over the next four years. Refer to Chapter 3 to determine the present value of a bond.
    b. Does Cardinal expect to be favorably or adversely affected by the interest rate risk? Explain.
    c. Does Cardinal expect to be favorably or adversely affected by exchange rate risk? Explain.

Bond Bulls See Danger, Turn Bearish
Fed's Rate Increase, Inflation Jitters Spur Emotional Sell-Off

Thomas T. Vogel Jr., New York

The bond bulls are running scared lately and investors are getting trampled.

So even if bond prices bounce back from their recent emotional sell-off, the longer-term outlook is cloudy, analysts say. And some pros believe things are going to get worse before they get better.

Yields on long-term Treasury bonds surged to 6.62% Friday, their highest since July. The bond market closed early at 2 p.m. EST. That hastily arranged closing fueled some talk—strongly denied by bond dealers—that the dealers had fled the field in order to cut their losses.

No matter why the bond market closed early, it is clear that bond investors are no longer giving the growing U.S. economy the benefit of the doubt about inflation. Inflation is bad news for bond investors because it makes an investment with a fixed rate of return less attractive.

Investors had thought that despite the economy's growth, inflation was remaining in check. But now investors are worried that inflationary pressures are increasing, even though most economists say the opposite.

The market is readjusting to a change in psychology," commented John Costas, head of government trading at CS First Boston Inc. Most Wall Street traders "have never seen [such bearish sentiment] before," he said.

"It's a bear market. People have stopped the denial process and are selling," said Paul McCulley, chief economist at UBS Securities Inc. . . .

What sparked all the selling was the Fed's move earlier this month to raise the federal-funds rate, which banks charge each other on overnight loans, to 3.25% from 3%. The move was supposed to nip inflationary pressures in the bud. And it may very well have. But instead of inspiring confidence in bond investors that the Fed is in fact fighting inflation before it becomes a problem, the rate boost has investors wondering when the next rate increase will be and whether bond yields can stay where they are much longer.

More so than at any other time in the past year, the bond market will be closely listening to what Fed Chairman Alan Greenspan has to say about all this. He is scheduled to deliver his semiannual Humphrey-Hawkins testimony before a House Banking subcommittee this morning.

There are several signs that things are likely to get worse before they get better. One is the Dow Jones Utility Average, widely seen as a contrary indicator of trends in long-term bond yields. It measures the stock-price changes of 11 electric utilities and four natural-gas companies; many analysts believe it anticipates major changes in interest-rate cycles. That's because utilities tend to pay high dividends and often attract the kind of conservative, yield-oriented investors who also buy bonds. When investors expect bond yields to rise, they sell off utility stocks, betting that a rise in bond yields will make these stocks less valuable.

For much of last year, the utility stock-price average rose in advance of a precipitous drop in long-term bond yields to 5.79% in October. For much of this year, however, the utility average has been falling. Since the start of the year, it has dropped 18.52 points, to 208.54 as of Friday, the lowest point in 22 months.

Another omen is the revisions many analysts on Wall Street are making to their rosy forecasts for interest rates this year. The day the Federal Reserve raised short-term interest rates, Goldman, Sachs & Co.'s director of economic research, Robert Giordano, was predicting another drop in long-term interest rates to the levels seen last year. But on Friday, Mr. Giordano told the Dow Jones News Service that he wouldn't be surprised if the 30-year bond yield rose to 7%.

The technical research department at Smith Barney Shearson Inc. sent a report entitled "Bond Alert!" to clients on Friday. The report said that "with a higher probability of additional risk, we strongly recommend that investors [in the bond market] who have not taken protective measures do so immediately." The report warns of the possibility of long-term rates rising to anywhere between 6.90% and 7.30%.

Another concern is a flood of Treasury securities slated to be sold this week. The Treasury is scheduled to sell $17 billion of two-year notes tomorrow and $11 billion of five-year notes Thursday.

Many on Wall Street believe that part of what weighed down the market last week was primary dealers unloading large holdings of unsold three-year and 10-year notes and 30-year bonds from

Continued

CASE APPLICATION: PRICE MOVEMENTS AMONG BONDS

Continued

the Treasury's huge quarterly refunding the week before. With investors worried about interest rates, Wall Street may force the government to push yields substantially higher to make underwriting the two auctions worthwhile.

Many on Wall Street think the sell-off has been overdone. One of them is Ms. Kenworthy of Dreyfus. "Some of this is an overreaction," she said. "We all need to do a reality check." If investors think the Federal Reserve is getting set to raise short-term interest another 1 to 1.5 percentage points to fight inflation, they "should be cashing out" of the bond market, she said. "But I don't believe that is happening," she said. "There is not enough incipient inflation to warrant that kind of tightening.

The price of 30-year bonds has dropped too far and they represent "good value," Ms. Kenworthy says. But she

adds: "You have to be pretty stout-hearted to jump in there now when the market psychology is so nasty." Moreover she recommends that investors in junk bonds watch their holdings carefully. "With stocks selling off, [junk bonds] might be subject to somewhat of a correction," she said. Junk bonds often trade like stocks because their prices are very sensitive to changes in the health of a company.

SOURCE: *The Wall Street Journal,* February 22, 1994, p. C1. Reprinted by permission of *The Wall Street Journal* © 1994 Dow Jones & Company, Inc. All rights reserved worldwide.

QUESTIONS

1. Explain why Alan Greenspan's message in his discussion with

a House Banking subcommittee that inflation is under control could affect bond prices.

2. Explain why the bond prices of R.H. Macy & Co. declined.

3. The president of IDS Fixed-Income Advisors stated that more signals about future bond price movements will be provided in the upcoming employment and producer price indexes. If the employment index shows a favorable increase, how do you think Treasury bond prices would respond? Would junk bonds respond in the same manner? How would a rise in the producer price index affect Treasury and junk bonds?

PROJECTS

1. **Impact of Treasury Financing on Bond Prices**
   The Treasury will periodically issue new bonds to finance its deficit. Review recent issues of *The Wall Street Journal* or check its index in your library to find a recent article on such financing. Does the article suggest that financial markets are expecting upward pressure on interest rates as a result of the Treasury financing? Is the Fed expected to intervene in order to reduce the potential impact on interest rates (according to the article)? What happened to prices of existing bonds when the Treasury announced its intentions to issue new bonds?

2. **Assessing Default Risk Premiums over Time**
   Using the data bank, measure the difference between the annualized yields of corporate Baa bonds and Treasury bonds over time. Compare this differential to the degree of economic growth (as measured by GNP growth) over time. Explain the relationship that you find.

REFERENCES

Altman, Edward I. "The Convertible Debt Market: Are Returns Worth the Risk?" *Financial Analysts Journal* (July–August, 1989): 23–80.

Altman, Edward I., and Scott A. Nammacher. "The Default Rate Experience on High-Yield Corporate Debt." *Financial Analysts Journal* (July–August 1985): 25–42.

Becketti, Sean. "The Role of Stripped Securities in Portfolio Management." *Economic Review,* Federal Reserve Bank of Kansas City (May 1988): 20–31.

———. "The Truth About Junk Bonds." *Economic Review,* Federal Reserve Bank of Kansas City (July/August 1990): 45–54.

Eberhart, Allan C., and Richard J. Sweeney. "Does the Bond Market Predict Bankruptcy Settlement?" *Journal of Finance* (July 1992): 943–980.

Ederington, Louis, Jess Yawitz, and Brian Roberts. "The Informational Content of Bond Ratings." *Journal of Financial Research* (Fall 1987): 211–226.

Goh, Jeremy C. and Louis H. Ederington. "Is a Bond Rating Downgrade Bad News, Good News, or No News for Stockholders?" *Journal of Finance* (December 1993): 2001–2008.

Jegadeesh, Narasimhan. "Treasury Auction Bids and the Salamon Squeeze." *Journal of Finance* (September 1993): 1403–1419.

Ma, Christopher K., and Garry M. Weed. "Fact and Fancy of Takeover Junk Bonds." *Journal of Portfolio Management* (Fall 1986): 34–37.

McEnally, Richard W., and Calvin M. Boardman. "Aspects of Corporate Bond Portfolio Diversification." *Journal of Financial Research* (Spring 1979): 27–36.

Rosengren, Eric S. "Defaults of Original Issue High-Yield Convertible Bonds." *Journal of Finance* (March 1993): 345–362.

———. "The Case for Junk Bonds." *New England Economic Review,* Federal Reserve Bank of Boston (May/June 1990): 40–49.

Smith, Donald J., and Robert A. Taggart, Jr. "Bond Market Innovations and Financial Intermediation." *Business Horizons* (November/December 1989): 24–33.

Spivey, Michael F. "The Cost of Including a Call Provision in Municipal Debt Contracts." *Journal of Financial Research* (Fall 1989): 203–216.

MORTGAGE MARKETS

Mortgages are securities used to finance housing purchases, originated by various financial institutions, such as savings institutions and mortgage companies. A secondary mortgage market accommodates originators of mortgages that desire to sell their mortgages prior to maturity. Both the origination process and the secondary market activities for mortgages have become much more complex in recent years.

The specific objectives of this chapter are to:

- describe the characteristics of residential mortgages,
- describe the common types of creative mortgage financing, and
- explain how mortgage-backed securities are used.

BACKGROUND ON MORTGAGES

Exhibit 9.1 discloses the mortgage debt outstanding over time by type of property. The majority of mortgage debt outstanding is on one- to four-family properties, while commercial properties are a distant second. The level of mortgage debt has generally risen over time, although not at a constant rate. The effects of the mild recession in 1980 and severe recession in 1982 on mortgage debt are obvious. Families tend to avoid housing purchases that would increase their debt during recessionary periods. Because residential mortgages (one- to four-family and multifamily) dominate the mortgage market, they receive the most attention in this chapter.

RESIDENTIAL MORTGAGE CHARACTERISTICS

When financial institutions originate residential mortgages, the mortgage contract created should specify whether the mortgage is federally insured, the

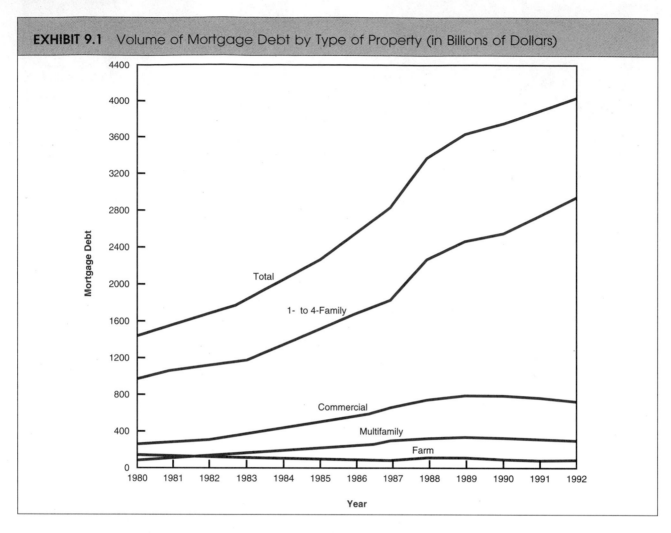

EXHIBIT 9.1 Volume of Mortgage Debt by Type of Property (in Billions of Dollars)

SOURCE: *Federal Reserve Bulletin.*

amount of the loan, whether the interest rate is fixed or adjustable, the interest rate to be charged, the maturity, and other special provisions that may vary among contracts. Over time, financial institutions have become more aware of the specific borrowing preferences of those who purchase residential housing. Yet, each family requesting a mortgage may have a different preference for the loan structure.

Insured Versus Conventional Mortgages

Mortgages are often classified as federally insured or conventional. Federally insured mortgages guarantee loan repayment to the lending financial institution, thereby covering it against the possibility of default by the borrower. An insurance fee of 0.5 percent of the loan amount is applied to cover the cost of insuring the mortgage. The guarantor can be either the Federal Housing Administration (FHA) or the Veterans Administration (VA). Borrowers applying for FHA and

VA mortgage loans from a financial institution must meet various requirements specified by those government agencies in order to qualify. In addition, the maximum mortgage amount is limited by law (although the limit varies among states to account for cost of housing differences). The volume of FHA loans has consistently exceeded that of VA loans since 1960. Both types of mortgages have become increasingly popular over the past 30 years.

Conventional mortgages are also provided by financial institutions. Although they are not federally insured, they can be privately insured so that the lending financial institutions can still avoid exposure to default risk. The insurance premium paid for such private insurance would likely be passed on to the borrowers. They can choose to incur the default risk themselves and avoid the insurance fee. Yet, most participants in the secondary mortgage market will purchase only those conventional mortgages that are privately insured (unless the mortgage's loan-to-value ratio is less than 80 percent).

Fixed-Rate Versus Adjustable-Rate Mortgages

One of the most important provisions in the mortgage contract is the interest rate. It can be specified as a fixed rate or can allow for periodic rate adjustments over time. The **fixed-rate mortgage** locks in the borrower's interest rate over the life of the mortgage. Thus, the periodic interest payment received by the lending financial institution is constant, regardless of how market interest rates change over time. Financial institutions that hold fixed-rate mortgages in their asset portfolio are exposed to interest rate risk, because they commonly use funds obtained from short-term customer deposits to make long-term mortgage loans. If interest rates increase over time, the financial institution's cost of obtaining funds (from deposits) will increase. Yet, the return on its fixed-rate mortgage loans will be unaffected, causing its profit margin to decrease.

Borrowers with fixed-rate mortgages do not suffer from the effects of rising interest rates, but they also fail to benefit from declining rates. Although they could attempt to refinance (obtain a new mortgage to replace the existing mortgage) at the lower prevailing market interest rate, transaction costs (such as closing costs and an origination fee) would be incurred.

In contrast to the fixed-rate mortgage, the **adjustable-rate mortgage (ARM)** allows the mortgage interest rate to adjust to market conditions. Its contract will specify a precise formula for this adjustment. The formula and the frequency of adjustment can vary among mortgage contracts. A common ARM uses a one-year adjustment, with the interest rate tied to the average Treasury bill rate over the previous year (for example, the average T-bill rate plus 2 percent may be specified).

Because the interest rate of the ARM moves with prevailing interest rates, financial institutions can stabilize their profit margin. If their cost of funds rises, so does their return on mortgage loans. For this reason, ARMs have become very popular over time.

Most ARMs specify a maximum allowable fluctuation in the mortgage rate per year and over the mortgage life, regardless of what happens to market interest rates. These so-called caps are commonly 2 percent per year and 5 percent for the mortgage lifetime. To the extent that market interest rates move outside these boundaries, the financial institution's profit margin on ARMs could be affected by interest rate fluctuations. Yet, this interest rate risk is significantly less than that of fixed-rate mortgages.

Although the ARM reduces the uncertainty about the financial institution's profit margin, it creates uncertainty for the borrower, whose future mortgage payments will depend on future interest rates. Because some home purchasers prefer fixed-rate mortgages, lending institutions continue to offer them.

Some ARMs now contain an option clause that allows mortgage holders to switch to a fixed-rate within a specified period, such as one to five years after the mortgage is originated (the specific provisions vary).

Determination of Mortgage Rates

The mortgage rate quoted by a financial institution depends primarily on the prevailing market interest rates for similar mortgages, which in turn is influenced by the market cost of funds. Thus, the average market rate for a particular type of mortgage is used as a base and then is adjusted according to various factors. For example, if local competitors are offering lower rates than the national market, the rate may have to be adjusted downward. (Indeed, some institutions use just the local area as a more appropriate market rate than the national average.)

In addition to considering a market rate, the lending institution should evaluate its flow of funds. If it has excess funds available to finance mortgages, it may reduce its mortgage rate slightly to attract more mortgage applications. The risk of the mortgage applicant does not have much impact on the mortgage rate, although it is evaluated to determine whether the mortgage application should be approved.

Exhibit 9.2 illustrates how mortgage rates have changed over time, following the pattern of long-term Treasury security rates. The rates have a premium that compensates the mortgage holder for the additional credit risk and lower degree of marketability.

Another factor that affects the mortgage rate is whether the mortgage specifies a fixed or adjustable interest rate. Mortgage lenders normally charge a higher initial interest rate on the fixed-rate mortgage to compensate for incurring more interest rate risk. The difference is usually between 1.5 percent and 3 percent.

Mortgage Maturities

During the 1970s, mortgages typically were originated with a 30-year maturity. However, the 15-year mortgage has recently become very popular because of the potential savings in total interest expenses. Exhibit 9.3 compares the payments necessary for 15- and 30-year mortgages based on various mortgage loan amounts and an 11 percent rate. For example, a $100,000 mortgage at 11 percent requires monthly payments (excluding taxes and insurance) of $952.32 over 30 years. The same mortgage would require monthly payments of $1,136.60 over 15 years, totaling $204,588 versus $342,835. The reduction in total payments on mortgages with shorter lives is due to the more rapid amortization and consequent lower cumulative interest. Although mortgages with shorter lives can reduce total payments, their higher monthly payments represent an opportunity cost, as the additional funds could have been put to some other use. Yet, many borrowers believe that this disadvantage is outweighed by favorable features.

From the perspective of the lending financial institution, there is a lower degree of interest rate risk on a 15-year fixed-rate mortgage than on a 30-year

EXHIBIT 9.2 Comparison of Mortgage Rates to Other Rates Over Time

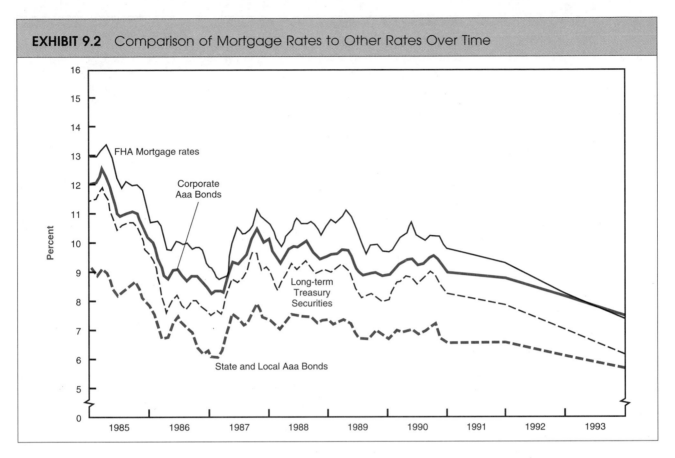

SOURCE: Data from the Federal Reserve Bank of St. Louis.

fixed-rate mortgage, because the former exists for only half the period of the latter. Accordingly, financial institutions generally charge a lower interest rate on 15-year loans than on 30-year loans, other provisions being equal.

An alternative to mortgages with 15- and 30-year maturities is the **balloon-payment mortgage,** which requires interest payments for a three- to five-year period. At the end of this period, full payment of the principal (the balloon payment) is required. Because principal payments are not made until maturity, the monthly payments are lower. Realistically, most borrowers have not saved enough funds to pay off the mortgage in three to five years, so the balloon payment in effect forces them to request new mortgages and therefore subjects them to refinancing risk.

AMORTIZING MORTGAGES. Given the maturity and interest rate on a mortgage, the **amortization schedule** can be developed to determine monthly payments broken down into principal and interest. During the early years of a mortgage, most of the payment reflects interest. Over time, as some of the principal has been paid off, the interest proportion decreases.

The lending institution that holds a fixed-rate mortgage will receive a fixed amount of equal periodic payments over a specified period of time. The amount depends on the principal amount of the mortgage, the interest rate, and the

EXHIBIT 9.3	Comparison of Payments Necessary for 15- and 30-Year Mortgages (Based on an Interest Rate of 11 Percent)			
	APPROXIMATE MONTHLY PAYMENT FOR A:		APPROXIMATE TOTAL PAYMENTS FOR A:	
Amount of Mortgage	15-year Mortgage	30-year Mortgage	15-year Mortgage	30-year Mortgage
$ 50,000	$ 568.30	$ 476.17	$102,294	$171,421
75,000	852.45	717.48	153,441	258,293
100,000	1,136.60	952.32	204,588	342,835
200,000	2,273,20	1,913.26	409,176	688,774

maturity. If insurance and taxes are to be included in the mortgage payment, then they, too, influence the amount. As an example, consider a 30-year (360 months) $100,000 mortgage that specifies an annual interest rate of 11 percent. To focus on the mortgage principal and interest payments, insurance and taxes are not included in this example. A breakdown of monthly principal versus monthly interest paid is shown in Exhibit 9.4. Note the larger proportion of interest paid in the earlier years and of principal paid in the later years. Computer programs are widely available to determine the amortization schedule for any type of mortgage.

CREATIVE MORTGAGE FINANCING

Various methods of creative financing have been developed to make housing more affordable, including

- Graduated-payment mortgage
- Growing-equity mortgage
- Second mortgage
- Shared-appreciation mortgage

Although these methods are the most common, several other innovative techniques exist. Moreover, as the needs and preferences of borrowers change over time, additional methods of creative financing are likely to emerge.

Graduated-Payment Mortgage (GPM)

The **graduated-payment mortgage (GPM)** allows borrowers to initially make small payments on the mortgage; the payments are increased on a graduated basis over the first 5 to 10 years; payments then level off from there. GPMs are tailored for families who anticipate higher income and thus the ability to make larger monthly mortgage payments as time passes. In a sense, they are delaying part of their mortgage payment.

EXHIBIT 9.4 Example of Amortization Schedule for Selected Years (Based on a 30-Year $100,000 Mortgage at 11 Percent)

PAYMENT NUMBER	PAYMENT OF INTEREST	PAYMENT OF PRINCIPAL	TOTAL PAYMENT	REMAINING LOAN BALANCE
1	$916.67	$ 35.65	$952.32	$99,964.35
2	916.34	35.98	952.32	99,928.37
.	.	.	.	.
.	.	.	.	.
.	.	.	.	.
.	.	.	.	.
.	.	.	.	.
100	864.34	87.98	952.32	94,202.62
101	863.53	88.80	952.32	94,113,82
.	.	.	.	.
.	.	.	.	.
.	.	.	.	.
.	.	.	.	.
200	733.18	219.14	952.32	79,764.19
201	731.17	221.16	952.32	79,543.03
.	.	.	.	.
.	.	.	.	.
.	.	.	.	.
.	.	.	.	.
300	406.55	545.77	952.32	43,804.89
301	401.54	550.78	952.32	43,254.12
.	.	.	.	.
.	.	.	.	.
.	.	.	.	.
359	17.30	935.02	952.32	951.73
360	8.72	943.60	952.32	-0-

Growing-Equity Mortgage

A **growing-equity mortgage** is similar to the GPM in that the initial monthly payments are low and increase over time. Unlike the GPM, however, the payments never level off but continue to increase (typically by about 4 percent per year) throughout the life of the loan. With such an accelerated payment schedule, the entire mortgage may be paid off in 15 years or less.

Second Mortgage

A second mortgage can be used in conjunction with the primary or first mortgage. Financial institutions may place a limit on the first mortgage amount based on the borrower's income. Other financial institutions may consider offering a second mortgage, with a maturity shorter than on the first mortgage. In addition, the interest rate on the second mortgage is higher because the second mortgage is behind the existing first mortgage in priority claim against the property in the event of default. The higher interest rate reflects greater compensation as a result of higher risk to providers of second mortgages.

Sellers of homes sometimes offer buyers a second mortgage. This is especially common if the old mortgage is assumable and if the selling price of the home is much higher than the remaining balance on the first mortgage. Through offering a second mortgage, the seller can make the house more affordable and therefore more marketable. The specific interest rate and maturity terms are negotiated between the seller and the buyer.

Shared-Appreciation Mortgage

A **shared-appreciation mortgage** allows a home purchaser to obtain a mortgage at a below-market interest rate. In return, the lender providing the attractive loan rate will share in the price appreciation of the home. The precise percentage of appreciation allocated to the lender is negotiated at the origination of the mortgage.

RISK FROM HOLDING MORTGAGES

Financial institutions that hold mortgages in their asset portfolio are exposed to two types of risk. First, they incur interest rate risk, or the sensitivity of earnings (and net worth) to interest rate fluctuations. Because mortgages are long-term in nature and deposits are commonly short-term, this interest rate risk is a primary concern. Of course, institutions with this type of balance sheet structure are not just adversely affected by rising interest rates; they also benefit from declining rates. Yet, the favorable impact is somewhat dampened, as a large proportion of mortgages are refinanced when interest rates decrease.

The second risk of mortgages is possible late payments or even default, referred to as credit or default risk. The default rate on mortgages has generally increased over the past 25 years. The most pronounced increases occur in recessionary periods, such as 1974 and 1982. There is some concern that although ARMs reduce interest rate risk, they may increase credit risk, as borrowers may be unable to make mortgage payments during periods of increasing interest rates. Yet, lending financial institutions can obtain insurance to cover against default risk if they are willing to pay the insurance premiums.

SECONDARY MORTGAGE MARKET ACTIVITIES

Financial institutions that originate mortgages sometimes sell them if they are short of cash. In addition, they may prefer to reduce their holdings of fixed-rate mortgages if interest rates are expected to increase. Some financial institutions such as mortgage companies may simply desire to service mortgages (originate them, process payments, etc.), but not finance them. They periodically pool their recently originated mortgages together and sell them but commonly continue to

COMPENSATION IN MORTGAGE BANKING

Mortgage companies specialize in originating mortgages. The services offered are somewhat similar across mortgage companies. Thus, it is human resources that tend to diminish one mortgage company from another through the service, competency, and efficiency of their employees. Because the employees of mortgage companies can significantly influence performance, they are commonly compensated through a bonus system. The base salary is low but is complemented with an attractive bonus package. In this way, inefficient loan officers are encouraged to seek employment elsewhere.

Bonuses to loan officers of mortgage banks can be provided for developing customer relationships, and by developing special knowledge of the services offered and marketing skills. New loan officers are typically encouraged to focus on developing knowledge, while the veteran loan officers focus more on customer relationships.

Compensation schemes tend to incorporate quality control to discourage loan officers from initiating relationships with high-risk customers just to generate business. For this reason, flat-rate commissions on business volume have been eliminated by many mortgage companies.

Given recent innovations in mortgage banking on mortgage provisions, employees must be encouraged to monitor techniques used by the competition and to ensure that the mortgage services are advanced to accommodate customer needs. Overall, compensation systems for mortgage banks are aligning compensation with efforts that maximize the value of the firm.

---

service them. For all these reasons, a secondary market for mortgages is desirable. It is not, however, as active as the secondary markets for other capital market instruments (such as stocks and bonds), because differing mortgage characteristics cannot be standardized as easily. In addition, the amount of each mortgage is small. Compare this to a financial institution's holdings of a corporation's bonds, which may represent an amount of $20 million or more. If it were to sell these bonds, a potential purchaser would need only one credit evaluation before making its decision. Although a potential purchaser could buy a group of mortgages, it would need to evaluate the credit on each mortgage involved. If the mortgages were insured against default risk, this credit check would not be necessary. The selling of a group of mortgages in the secondary market is still difficult because the mortgages may have different interest rates, maturities, and so forth, complicating the evaluation process. However, mortgages with similar characteristics can be pooled to offer a more standardized product.

The financial institutions that ultimately finance mortgages may differ from the institutions that service them. Suppose USA Savings and Loan originates and services mortgages for a few years, then sells the mortgages to Safety Insurance Company but continues to service them. The borrowers continue to send their monthly mortgage payments to USA Savings and Loan, even though USA no longer holds claim to the mortgages. USA processes the payments and charges the new holder of the mortgages (Safety Insurance Company) a fee for the processing. It deducts this fee from the mortgage payments received and sends the remainder to Safety Insurance Company.

The secondary market for mortgages has been enhanced as a result of **securitization,** which involves the pooling and repackaging of loans into securities. The securities are then sold to investors, who become the owners of the loans represented by those securities. This process allows for the sale of smaller mortgage loans that could not be easily sold in the secondary market on an individual basis. When several small mortgage loans are packaged together, they become more attractive to the large institutional investors that focus on large transactions. Securitization removes the loans from the balance sheet of the financial institution that provided them. Consequently, securitization can reduce a financial institution's exposure to default risk or interest rate risk.

Use of Mortgage-Backed Securities

As an alternative to selling their mortgages outright in the secondary market, financial institutions can issue mortgage-backed securities, a method whereby a security is created that is backed by mortgage loans.

Mortgage-backed securities come in various forms; the more common are **mortgage pass-through securities.** A group of mortgages held by a trustee of the issuing institution serves as collateral for these securities. The interest and principal payments on the mortgages are sent to the financial institution, which then transfers (passes through) the payments to the owners of the mortgage-backed securities after deducting fees for servicing and for guaranteeing payments to the owners. This process allows the savings institutions and banks that originate mortgages to adjust their balance sheets. Thus, they can earn fees from servicing the mortgages while avoiding exposure to interest rate risk and credit risk.

The issuance of pass-through securities can reduce the financial institution's exposure to interest rate risk because it ties the payments received from mortgages to the payments sent to security owners. To the extent that the financial institutions use pass-through securities to finance mortgages holdings, they can insulate their profit margin from interest rate fluctuations. The interest and principal payments to owners of pass-through securities can vary over time. For example, if a higher-than-normal proportion of the mortgages backing the securities are prepaid in a specific period, the payments received by the financial institution will be passed through (after deducting a servicing fee) to the security owners.

Five of the more common types of mortgage pass-through securities are

- Ginnie Mae
- Fannie Mae
- Publicly issued
- Participation certificates
- Collateralized mortgage obligations (CMOs)

Each type is described in turn.

GINNE MAE MORTGAGE-BACKED SECURITIES.   Financial institutions issue securities that are backed by FHA and VA mortgages. The Government National Mortgage Association (GNMA), frequently referred to as Ginnie Mae, guarantees timely payment of principal and interest to investors who purchase these securities. The funds received from their sale are used to finance the mortgages. All mortgages pooled together to back Ginnie Mae pass-throughs must have the same interest rate. The interest rate received by purchasers of the pass-throughs is slightly less (typically 50 basis points) than that rate. This difference reflects a fee to the financial institution servicing the loan and to GNMA for guaranteeing full payment of interest and principal to the security purchasers. The outstanding balance of GNMA pass-throughs has grown substantially in recent years.

FANNIE MAE MORTGAGE-BACKED SECURITIES. The Federal National Mortgage Association (FNMA), commonly referred to as Fannie Mae, issues mortgage-backed securities and uses the funds to purchase mortgages. In essence, Fannie Mae channels funds from investors to financial institutions that desire to sell their mortgages. These financial institutions may continue to service the mortgages and would earn a fee for this service, while Fannie Mae receives a fee for guaranteeing timely payment of principal and interest to the holders of the mortgage-backed securities. The mortgage payments on mortgages backing these securities are sent to the financial institutions that service the mortgages. The payments are channeled through to the purchasers of mortgage-backed securities, which may be collateralized by conventional or federally insured mortgages.

Some mortgage-backed securities issued by Fannie Mae are stripped by separating the principal and interest payments streams and selling them as separate securities. For investors who purchase these securities, the timing of the payments is uncertain, as many mortgages are prepaid when interest rates decline so that they can be refinanced at lower interest rates.

PUBLICLY ISSUED PASS-THROUGH SECURITIES (PIPs). Another type of pass-through security, called PIP, is similar to GNMA mortgage-backed securities, except that it is backed by conventional rather than FHA or VA mortgages. The mortgages backing the securities are insured through private insurance companies.

PARTICIPATION CERTIFICATES (PCs). The Federal Home Loan Mortgage Association, called Freddie Mac, sells **participation certificates (PCs)** and uses the proceeds to finance the origination of conventional mortgages from financial institutions. This provides another outlet (in addition to Fannie Mae) for savings institutions and savings banks that desire to sell their conventional mortgages in the secondary market.

COLLATERALIZED MORTGAGE OBLIGATIONS (CMOs). In 1983 **collateralized mortgage obligations (CMOs)** were developed. They have semiannual interest payments, unlike other mortgage-backed securities that have monthly payments. The CMOs that represent a particular mortgage pool are segmented into classes (or tranches). The first class has the quickest payback. Any repaid principal is initially sent to owners of the first-class CMOs until the total principal amount representing that class is fully repaid. Then any further principal payments are sent to owners of the second-class CMOs until the total principal amount representing that class is fully repaid. This process continues until principal payments are made to owners of the last-class CMOs. CMO issues commonly have between 3 and 10 classes. Individual CMOs have a maximum average life of 10 years.

The attractive feature of CMOs is that investors can choose a class that will fit their maturity desires. Even though investors are still uncertain as to when the securities will mature, they have a better feel for the maturity structure than with other pass-through securities. Investors who purchase third-class CMOs know that they will not receive any principal payments until the first- and second-class CMO owners are completely paid off.

One concern about CMOs is the speed of payback in response to lower interest rates. When interest rates decline, mortgages are prepaid, which accelerates the payments back to the holders of CMOs. This forces investors to reinvest their funds elsewhere under the prevailing (low interest rate) conditions. During the period 1991–1993, massive mortgage prepayments caused the accelerated payments on CMOs as described above. Given the uncertainty about CMOs' maturity (because of the possible prepayment), determining the market valuation of CMOs is very difficult.

CMOs are sometimes segmented into "interest-only" (IO) and "principal-only" (PO) classes. Investors in interest-only CMOs receive only interest payments that are paid in on the underlying mortgages. When mortgages are prepaid, the interest payments on the underlying mortgages are terminated, and so are payments to investors in interest-only CMOs. For example, mortgage prepayments may cut off the interest rate payments on the CMO after a few years, even though these payments were initially expected to last five years or more. Consequently, investors in these CMOs could lose 50 percent or more of their initial investment. The relatively high yields offered on interest-only CMOs is attributed to their high degree of risk.

Because investors in the principal-only CMO receive principal payments only, they generally receive payments further into the future. Even though the payments to these investors represent principal, the maturity is uncertain because of possible prepayment of the underlying mortgages. For these investors, accelerated prepayment of mortgages is beneficial because they receive their complete payments earlier than expected.

Although CMOs can be a useful investment, their risks must be recognized. Coastal States Life Insurance Co. invested much of its available funds in CMOs and failed in 1992 as the market value of its CMOs declined. Insurance regulators are now closely monitoring insurance companies that may have excessive exposure in CMOs. In addition, many mutual funds that invest in CMOs are reassessing their potential risk. Just as loans to less developed countries and high-yield (junk) bonds received more attention after their performance declined, CMOs are now receiving much more attention. Given their popularity in recent years and the difficulty in measuring the market value of CMOs, regulators are concerned that a pronounced decline in CMO values could have a severe effect on many financial institutions.

Mortgage-Backed Securities for Small Investors

Pass-through securities have been historically restricted to large investors. Ginnie Mae pass-throughs, for example, come in minimum denominations of $25,000, with $5,000 increments above. In recent years, however, unit trusts have been created that allow small investors to participate. For example, a portfolio of Ginnie Mae pass-through securities is sold in $1,000 pieces. Each piece represents a tiny fraction of the overall portfolio of securities. These unit trusts have become

FANNIE MAE's BATTLE AGAINST INTEREST RATE RISK

Fannie Mae has historically made a secondary market for mortgages. It was created in 1938 with the intent of purchasing government-guaranteed mortgages from financial institutions that desired to sell them. Since it reorganized into a privately owned corporation in 1968, it also has purchased conventional mortgage loans. To finance its purchases, Fannie Mae issues short-term notes as well as intermediate and long-term securities to investors. It pays slightly lower interest rates on the securities it issues than the rates received on the mortgages it buys. Its asset-portfolio profits are generated from this interest rate spread. Fannie Mae's action result in a transfer of funds from investors to those financial institutions that are selling mortgages. Fannie Mae holds the mortgages, and the investors hold the debt securities it issues.

In 1981 and 1982 Fannie Mae experienced losses of more than $100 million, primarily because the average lifetime of mortgages purchased exceeded that of the securities it issued. Consequently, its cost of funds was more sensitive to interest rate movements than its return on mortgages. When interest rates increased, the cost of funds increased, but its return on mortgages remained somewhat stable, and its interest margin became negative.

To reduce its exposure to interest rate risk, Fannie Mae now commonly buys adjustable-rate mortgages. The return generated by these mortgages moves in tandem with interest rate fluctuations. In addition, Fannie Mae now buys 15-year mortgages and second mortgages, which have shorter maturities than the traditional 30-year mortgages. The market values of these mortgages are less sensitive than 30-year mortgages to interest rate movements. Fannie Mae also increased the maturities on the securities it issues to make them more similar to the maturities of its mortgage holdings. Now that its return on mortgages and its cost of funds are similarly sensitive to interest rate changes, its interest rate spread has been somewhat stable in recent years. Fannie Mae is now more capable of insulating itself against interest rate fluctuations.

very popular in recent years. The composition of the portfolio is not adjusted over time.

Some mutual funds offer Ginnie Mae funds, which, like the unit trusts, represent a portfolio of GNMA pass-through securities. Unlike the unit trust, the composition of the mutual fund's portfolio can be actively managed (adjusted) by the securities firm over time. As would be expected, the market values of Ginnie Mae unit trusts and mutual funds are inversely related to interest rate movements. The Ginnie Mae unit trust is more sensitive to increasing interest rates because its composition cannot be adjusted. A mutual fund can modify the Ginnie Mae portfolio composition (shift to shorter term maturities) if it anticipates increasing interest rates. Some mutual funds also invest in Fannie Mae mortgage-backed securities and PCs (participation certificates), allowing the small investor access to them.

Pass-through securities are attractive because they can be purchased in the secondary market without purchasing the servicing of the mortgages that back them. In addition, the holders of pass-throughs are insured in the event of

MORTGAGE MARKET INFORMATION

The Wall Street Journal provides the following information related to this chapter on a daily basis:

- Price quotations on mortgage-based securities and on collateralized mortgage obligations.

- Reports on recent performance and new issuances of mortgage-backed securities, contained in the "Credit Markets" section.

---

default. Furthermore, pass-throughs are very liquid and can be used as collateral for repurchase agreements. Yet, the performance of pass-throughs is susceptible to the borrower's prepayment habits. Prepayments increase when market interest rates fall below the mortgage rates, because of the high frequency of refinancing at those times, and decrease when market interest rates exceed mortgage rates. Thus, the maturities of pass-throughs will be shorter during the former periods and longer during the latter.

A new instrument called the real estate mortgage conduit (REMIC) was created as a result of the Tax Reform Act of 1986. Although the REMIC allows financial institutions to sell mortgage assets and issue mortgage-backed securities, it is not a taxable entity when used as a conduit for passing mortgage payments to holders of mortgage-backed securities. REMICs enhance the security backing of mortgages because of their favorable tax features.

INSTITUTIONAL USE OF MORTGAGES

Financial institutions such as savings institutions and commercial banks originate and service mortgages. Yet, other financial institutions also participate by investing in mortgages. Exhibit 9.5 provides a breakdown of financial institutions that purchase and hold mortgages. The financial institutions identified here hold in aggregate about 43 percent of the entire dollar amount of all mortgages. Government agencies such as the Government National Mortgage Association (GNMA) and Federal National Mortgage Association (FNMA) hold a large proportion of the mortgages not held by the financial institutions described above.

Exhibit 9.6 classifies the mortgages of the financial institutions into four types of borrower categories. The savings institutions dominate the one- to four-family and multifamily markets. They also participate in commercial mortgages, but to a lesser degree. They have continually increased their participation in commercial mortgages in recent years, however. Commercial banks dominate the commercial mortgage market, with life insurance companies behind them. Commercial banks also heavily participate in residential mortgages but are far behind savings institutions in that market.

Another type of financial institution that participates in the mortgage business is the mortgage company. Because it quickly sells the mortgages it origi-

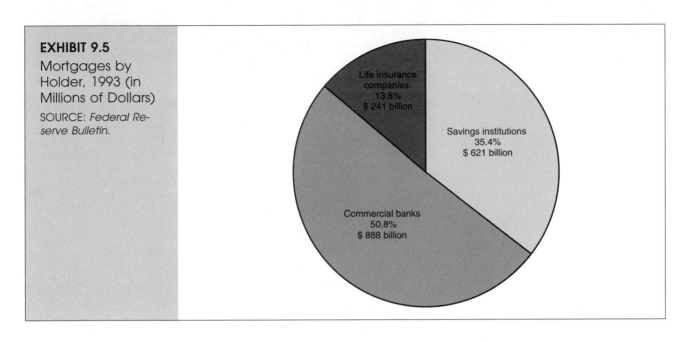

EXHIBIT 9.5
Mortgages by Holder, 1993 (in Millions of Dollars)

SOURCE: *Federal Reserve Bulletin.*

Life insurance companies
13.8%
$ 241 billion

Savings institutions
35.4%
$ 621 billion

Commercial banks
50.8%
$ 888 billion

nates, it does not maintain a large mortgage portfolio. The majority of its earnings are generated from origination and servicing fees. Because mortgage companies do not typically finance mortgages themselves, they are not as exposed to interest rate risk as other financial institutions.

As mortgage companies originate mortgages, they pool them together and then sell the entire pool at once. When a mortgage is originated, it has market value similar to the face value. As market interest rates change, though, the market value of the mortgage changes. Investors are willing to pay more for a given fixed-rate mortgage if market interest rates are lower, because that mortgage offers locked-in payments. Conversely, investors would pay less for such mortgages if market interest rates are higher at the time. The mortgage company's concern is that market interest rates might increase from the time the mortgage is originated until it is sold. Even though mortgage companies tend to sell the mortgages they originate within a short period of time, just a small change

EXHIBIT 9.6 Mortgage Holdings among Financial Institutions, 1993 (in Billions of Dollars)

| | MORTGAGES ALLOCATED TO: | | | | |
	1- to 4-Family	Multifamily	Commercial	Farm	Total
Savings institutions	$486	$67	$ 66	$10	$619
Commercial banks	508	38	322	19	887
Life insurance companies	10	27	196	8	241

SOURCE: *Federal Reserve Bulletin.*

EXHIBIT 9.7   Institutional Use of Mortgage Markets

TYPE OF FINANCIAL INSTITUTION	PARTICIPATION IN MORTGAGE MARKETS
Commercial banks and savings institutions	■ Originate commercial and residential mortgages and service mortgages and maintain mortgages within their investment portfolios. ■ Issue mortgage-backed securities to finance some of their mortgage holdings. ■ Purchase mortgage-based securities.
Credit unions and finance companies	■ Originate mortgages and maintain mortgages within their investment portfolios.
Mutual funds	■ Have sold shares and used the proceeds to construct portfolios of mortgage pass-through securities.
Brokerage firms	■ Serve as financial intermediaries between sellers and buyers of mortgages in the secondary market.
Investment banking firms	■ Offer instruments to help institutional investors in mortgages hedge against interest rate risk.
Insurance companies	■ Commonly purchase mortgages in the secondary market.

in interest rates over this period can significantly affect the value of the mortgages.

A summary of the institutional use of mortgage markets is provided in Exhibit 9.7. Most institutional participation could be broadly classified as either (1) originating and servicing or (2) financing. Commercial banks and savings institutions are the primary originators of mortgages. These institutions, along with credit unions, finance companies, mutual funds, and insurance companies, help finance mortgages by maintaining them in their investment portfolios.

Some institutional participation in mortgage markets represents neither origination nor financing of mortgages. Brokerage firms participate by matching up sellers and buyers of mortgages in the secondary market. Investment banking firms participate by helping institutional investors hedge their mortgage holdings against interest rate risk. They offer interest rate swaps to these institutions, which provide a stream of variable-rate payments in exchange for fixed-rate payments.

GLOBALIZATION OF MORTGAGE MARKETS

Mortgage market activity is not confined within a single country. For example, non-U.S. financial institutions hold mortgages on U.S. property, and vice versa.

GLOBAL ASPECTS Large U.S. banks often maintain mortgage-banking subsidiaries in foreign countries. In addition, the use of interest rate swaps to hedge mortgages in the U.S. often involves a non-U.S. counterpart. Although investment banking firms may serve as the financial intermediary, they commonly search for a non-U.S. financial institution that desires to swap variable-rate payments in exchange for fixed-rate payments.

Participants in mortgage markets closely follow international economic conditions because of the potential impact on interest rates. Bond- and mortgage-portfolio decisions are highly influenced by announcements related to the value of the dollar. In general, any announcements that imply a potentially weaker dollar tend to cause expectations of higher U.S. inflation and therefore higher U.S. interest rates. The demand for fixed-rate mortgages would likely decline in response to such announcements. Announcements that imply a potentially stronger dollar tend to cause the opposite expectations and effects. However, it is difficult to show evidence of these relationships, because expectations do not always occur and often change from one day to the next.

SUMMARY

- Residential mortgages can be characterized by whether they are federally insured, the type of interest rate used (fixed or floating), and the maturity. Quoted interest rates on mortgages vary at a given point in time, depending on these characteristics.

- Popular methods of creative mortgage financing include graduated-payment mortgage, growing-equity mortgage, second mortgage, and shared-appreciation mortgage. These methods may enable borrowers to obtain adequate financing.

- Mortgage pass-through securities represent mortgages serviced by the financial institutions that originated them, but are held by other investors. Five of the more popular types of mortgage pass-through securities are Ginnie Mae, Fannie Mae, publicly issued, participation certificates, and collateralized mortgage obligations (CMOs).

QUESTIONS

1. Distinguish between FHA and conventional mortgages.

2. Explain how mortgage lenders can be affected by interest rate movements. Also explain how they can insulate against interest rate movements.

3. Explain how caps on adjustable-rate mortgages can affect a financial institution's exposure to interest rate risk.

4. What is the general relationship between mortgage rates and long-term government security rates?

5. How does the initial rate on adjustable rate mortgages differ from the rate on fixed-rate mortgages? Why?

6. Why is the 15-year mortgage attractive to homeowners?

7. Is the interest rate risk to the financial institution higher for a 15-year or a 30-year mortgage? Why?

8. Explain the use of a balloon-payment mortgage. Why might a financial institution prefer to offer this type of mortgage?

9. Describe the graduated-payment mortgage. What type of homeowners would prefer this type of mortgage?

10. Describe the growing-equity mortgage. How does it differ from a graduated-payment mortgage?

11. Why are second mortgages offered by some home sellers?

12. Describe the shared-appreciation mortgage.

13. Mortgage lenders with fixed-rate mortgages should benefit when interest rates decline, yet research has shown that such a favorable impact is dampened. By what?

14. Describe the trend in mortgage delinquencies over the past several years.

15. Explain why some financial institutions prefer to sell the mortgages they originate.

16. Compare the secondary market activity for mortgages to the other capital market instruments (such as stocks and bonds). Provide a general explanation for the difference in the activity level.

17. Describe how mortgage pass-through securities are used. How can the use of pass-through securities reduce a financial institution's interest rate risk?

18. Describe how collateralized mortgage obligations (CMOs) are used and why they have been popular.

19. Explain how the maturity on pass-through securities can be affected by interest rate movements.

20. What type of financial institution finances the majority of one- to four-family mortgages? What type of financial institution finances the majority of commercial mortgages?

21. Explain how the mortgage company's degree of exposure to interest rate risk differs from other financial institutions.

22. Explain Fannie Mae's participation in the mortgage market. Explain why Fannie Mae experienced losses in 1981 and 1982. How has Fannie Mae reduced its exposure to interest rate risk in recent years?

The CMO Return You See May Not Be What You Get

Barbara Donnelly

Last year, Ed Glynn heard a radio advertisement for a triple-A "government-guaranteed" investment that would pay 9% a year for 15 years.

"It sounded great," says the retired New Jersey car-wash owner. Convinced he was getting the equivalent of "a long-term Treasury bond that would pay 9% for 15 years," Mr. Glynn says he invested $52,000 in so-called "collateralized mortgage obligations," or CMOs.

But nine months later, his "long-term" investment was abruptly retired. Mr. Glynn was handed back his money, minus a $2,000 premium he had paid above the CMOs' face value, and forced into the uncomfortable position of trying to reinvest that cast at a time when interest rates have plunged. "I had no idea I would get my money back so soon," he says.

A lot of individuals—and even many sophisticated institutional investors—are finding themselves in the same boat these days, as falling interest rates continue to wreak havoc in the huge but little-understood CMO market.

Implicit Guarantee

CMOs are "derivative" securities created out of traditional mortgage-backed bonds, primarily those issued by the Federal National Mortgage Association and the Federal Home Loan Mortgage Corp. CMOs do come with the same triple-A credit rating as the mortgage-backed bonds underlying them, and, at least implicitly, their face value is guaranteed by the U.S. government.

As with other mortgage securities, however, investors can be hit hard at a time of falling interest rates. That's because when rates fall, homeowners typically rush to refinance—taking out new loans at lower rates and prepaying their old mortgages. Those prepayments are then passed on to investors in securities backed by the mortgages.

With the latest drop in interest rates, prepayment fears are soaring. Refinancing activity—a leading indicator of CMO prepayments—has jumped to 3½ times its early-July level, matching last January's record rate, according to the Mortgage Bankers Association. By autumn, prepayments are expected to exceed even last spring's torrid pace, dealers say.

Dumping by Investors

Lower rates have particularly sticky consequences for certain types of CMOs. And with rates at the lowest levels ever seen in the 15-year history of the mortgage-backed market, CMOs that just two months ago were viewed as relatively safe from prepayment are now being dumped by investors afraid of being caught short, like Mr. Glynn, by an unexpected return of principal.

"It's kind of a dicey time in CMO land right now," says Andrew Stone, senior managing director of mortgage-backed securities at Daiwa Securities America Inc. "A lot of clients are very nervous and don't know what to do, so many are moving into Treasury bonds to wait it out."

Because of quirky features that make it impossible to nail down a CMO's real maturity or yield, valuing these bonds "is much more a question of subjective interpretation," says Rodger Shay, vice president at Shay Investment Services Inc., an institutional bond boutique. With prepayment rates in such transition, "there's a lot of confusion over the outlook for CMOs, and pricing is very messy" throughout this $550 billion market, he adds.

CMOs are created through the financial equivalent of genetic engineering. Issuers take the interest and principal payments from traditional mortgage-backed securities and reshape them into dozens of separate CMO offspring, or "tranches," each with its own maturity, interest-rate and seniority within the CMO's overall structure.

The idea is to transform normal mortgage-backed securities into a wide array of securities with something to appeal to everyone, from the most conservative to the most venturesome investor. To achieve this, different CMO tranches are allotted different shares of the prepayment risk of the underlying mortgage security; in general, the higher a CMO tranche's risk, the higher its yield.

For example, "interest-only" CMOs—which, as their name suggests, receive only the interest payments on the mortgage collateral that backs CMOs—

Continued

CASE APPLICATION: RETURN AND RISK OF CMOs

Continued

"have just gotten killed," says Daiwa's Mr. Stone. IO prices have plummeted as much as 35% in the past four weeks, and "although we expect IOs will come back into favor, it won't be before more pain—things will get worse before they get better," he says.

Unlike other CMO tranches, IOs don't repay any principal when they retire. Instead, those payments go to holders of "principal-only," or PO, tranches that offset the IOs. The problem is, when lower interest rates cause homeowners to pay off their old mortgages and refinance at lower rates, the mortgage collateral that backs the IOs evaporates. When that happens, the IO's interest payments are cut off and IO holders lose all the money they invested.

Because of that risk, IO yields tend to be very high, making them popular with insurance companies, mutual funds and other yield-hungry institutions. But the risk also makes IOs super-sensitive to falling interest rates.

Investors in most other types of CMOs don't risk losing their principal, just getting it back earlier than they planned—minus any premium they may have paid above the CMO's face value. But "for someone who invested long term at an 8% yield to fund college tuition, it's definitely a problem if you get your money back in six months and have to do it all over again at a much lower yield," says Shay Investment's Mr. Shay.

Since all parts of a CMO deal must add up to the total risk of the underlying mortgage collateral, the prepayment risk that's siphoned off one type of tranche is by necessity dumped into other tranches. For example, IOs and POs offset one another.

The type that Mr. Glynn bought is known as a "companion" CMO, a security whose high yields have made it a hot seller with small investors in the past couple of years. But "companions" are also highly volatile because they are designed to act as shock-absorbers for "planned amortization class" CMOs, or PACs. Companions shield PACs from early redemption, getting more than their share of prepayments when refinancings soar and less than their share when refinancings dry up.

The high prepayments have come back to haunt investors in companions—particularly companions that are priced at a premium above their face value, such as those Mr. Glynn owned. Indeed, the refinancing rush of last winter and spring vaporized many such companions, leaving their investors in the lurch. If prepayments rise as expected, more and more companions will begin to disappear.

Meanwhile, with fewer companions around to absorb prepayment shock, even some PACs aren't as safe as they used to be. That's because "when the companions are chewed through, PACs with the thinnest protection become the new companions," says Mr. Shay. In CMO lingo, the PAC gets "busted."

As a result, even some PAC investors are finding themselves exposed for the first time to the shock of early redemption. "Busted PACs are definitely a recent feature of the market," says Daiwa's Mr. Stone.

SOURCE: *The Wall Street Journal,* August 3, 1992, p. C11. Reprinted by permission of *The Wall Street Journal* © 1992 Dow Jones & Company Inc. All rights reserved worldwide.

QUESTIONS

1. Explain interest-only (IO) collateralized mortgage obligations (CMOs), and why they can be risky.

2. Why is it difficult to estimate the proper value of CMOs?

3. Explain the principal-only (PO) CMOs, and their risk.

PROJECT

1. **Assessing Mortgage Rates**

    In the "Money Rates" section of *The Wall Street Journal (WSJ)*, rates on conventional fixed-rate mortgages are quoted (see "Federal Home Loan Mortgage Corporation"). Obtain data on a mortgage rate and the 30-year Treasury bond rate (quoted in the section of *WSJ* called "Yield Comparisons") for the beginning of each of the past six months. Describe any movements in the mortgage rates over this six-month period. Have mortgage rates changed because of a general change in market interest rates, a change in the risk perception of mortgages, or both? Explain.

REFERENCES

Anderson, Gary A., Joel R. Barber, and Chun Hao Chang. "Prepayment Risk and the Duration of Default-Free Mortgage-Backed Securities." *Journal of Financial Research* (Spring 1993): 1–9.

Furlong, Frederick T. "Savings and Loan Asset Composition and the Mortgage Market." *Economic Review*, Federal Reserve Bank of San Francisco (Summer 1985): 14–24.

Goldberg, Lawrence, and Andrea Heuson. "Fixed Versus Variable Rate Financing: The Influence of Borrower, Lender, and Market Characteristics." *Journal of Financial Services Research* (May 1992): 49–60.

Green, Jerry, and John B. Shoven. "The Effects of Interest Rates on Mortgage Prepayments." *Journal of Money, Credit, and Banking* (February 1986): 41–59.

Kau, James, Donald Keenan, Walter Muller III, and James Epperson. "The Valuation and Securitization of Commercial and Multifamily Mortgages." *Journal of Banking and Finance* (September 1987): 525–546.

Stutzer, Michael J., and William Roberds. "Adjustable Rate Mortgages: Increasing Efficiency More Than Housing Activity." *Quarterly Review*, Federal Reserve Bank of Minneapolis (Summer 1985): 10–20.

CHAPTER 10

Stock Markets

Stock is frequently traded among individuals and financial institutions. Its value changes significantly in response to economic conditions. Consequently, participants in the stock market closely monitor the factors that affect stock prices.

The specific objectives of this chapter are to:

- describe how stock exchanges facilitate the trading of stock,
- describe how stock markets are used by financial institutions,
- describe valuation models used to value stock, and
- identify the economic factors that affect stock prices.

BACKGROUND ON COMMON STOCK

Common stock is a certificate representing partial ownership in a corporation. Like debt securities, common stock is issued by firms to obtain funds. However, the purchaser of stock becomes part owner, rather than just a creditor. Although the issuing corporation is not obligated to repurchase this stock at any time in the future, shareholders can sell it to other investors within the secondary market.

Voting Rights

The ownership of common stock entitles shareholders to a number of rights not available to other individuals. Normally, only the owners of common stock are permitted to vote on certain key matters concerning the firm. Among those key matters are the election of the board of directors, authorization to issue new shares of common stock, approval of amendments to the corporate charter, and adoption of by-laws. Many investors assign their vote to management through the use of a proxy. Many other shareholders simply fail to vote at all. As a result, management normally receives the majority of the votes and can elect its own candidates as directors. If investors become dissatisfied with the firm's performance, they can compete with management in the solicitation of proxy votes in what is known as a proxy fight. If the dissident shareholders can gain enough votes, they can elect one or more directors who share their views. In this case, shareholders are truly exercising their control.

As a classic example of the influence of a proxy, the directors of UAL were forced to sell the parent company of United Airlines to its employees. If they had not agreed to this, they could have been replaced through a proxy campaign led by Coniston Partners of New York, which owned about 12 percent of UAL. Even when managers win a proxy contest, they usually leave a company within three years after the contest.

Institutional investors such as pension funds, mutual funds, and insurance companies sometimes hold a large proportion of a corporation's stock and can influence corporate policies through proxy contests. In the 1990s, several firms promised significant concessions to their institutional investors, including the placement of major shareholders on their boards of directors.

Purchasing Stock on Margin

Investors can purchase stock on margin (with borrowed funds) by signing up for a margin account with their broker. The margin limit is 50 percent, meaning they can use as much as 50 percent borrowed funds (from the brokerage firm) to purchase stocks. Over short-term periods, the return on stocks (R) purchased on margin can be estimated as follows:

$$R = \frac{SP - INV - LOAN + D}{INV}$$

where

SP = selling price

INV = initial investment by investor, not including borrowed funds

$LOAN$ = loan payments paid on borrowed funds, including both principal and interest

D = dividend payments

Consider a stock priced at $40 that pays an annual dividend of $1 per share. Investors purchase the stock on margin, paying $20 per share and borrowing the remainder from the brokerage firm at 10 percent annual interest. If, after one year, the stock is sold at a price of $60 per share, the return on the stock would be

$$R = \frac{\$60 - \$20 - \$22 + 1}{\$20}$$

$$= \frac{\$19}{\$20}$$

$$= 95\%$$

The brokerage firm has the right to demand more collateral (more cash or stocks) or to sell the stock if the stock price declines by a specified amount. Investors must respond to this **margin call.** During the stock market crash in October 1987, those who did not have cash available to respond to the margin call sold their stock, causing additional downward pressure on stock prices.

Margin requirements are enforced to restrict the amount of credit extended to customers by stock brokers. They were originally imposed in 1934, following a period of volatile market swings, to discourage excessive speculation and ensure greater stability.

The ability of increased margin requirements to stabilize stock price movements is dependent on whether such requirements can discourage excessive speculation. Although margin requirements have been changed only 22 times in the United States, they have been changed about 100 times in Japan over the past 35 years. A recent study by Hardouvelis and Peristiani found a strong negative relationship between the change in margin requirements and the volatility of the Japanese stock market. The authors' findings imply that the Federal Reserve may be able to stabilize U.S. stock market movements by increasing margin requirements in the United States.

BACKGROUND ON PREFERRED STOCK

Preferred stock represents an equity interest in a firm but usually does not allow for significant voting rights. Preferred shareholders technically share the ownership of the firm with common shareholders and are therefore compensated only when earnings have been generated. Therefore, if the firm does not have sufficient earnings from which to pay the preferred stock dividends, it may omit the dividend without fear of being forced into bankruptcy. A cumulative provision on most preferred stock prevents dividends from being paid on common stock until all preferred stock dividends (both current and those previously omitted) have been paid. Yet, the owners of preferred stock do not normally participate in the profits of the firm beyond the stated fixed annual dividend. All profits above those needed to pay dividends on preferred stock belong to the owners of common stock.

Because the payment of dividends on preferred stock can be omitted, firms assume less risk when they issue it than when they issue bonds. However, if a firm omits the payment of preferred stock dividends, it may be unable to raise new capital until the omitted dividends have been paid, because investors will be reluctant to make new investments in a firm unable to compensate its existing sources of capital.

From a cost perspective, preferred stock is a less desirable source of capital than bonds. Because there is no legal requirement for a firm to pay preferred stock dividends, investors must be enticed to assume the risk involved by receiving higher dividends. In addition, preferred stock dividends are technically compensation to owners of the firm. Therefore, payment of dividends is not a tax-deductible expense to the firm, whereas interest on bonds is tax deductible. Because preferred stock normally has no maturity, it presents a permanent source of financing.

PUBLIC PLACEMENT OF STOCK

Stock offerings are classified as initial public offerings or secondary offerings. An **initial public offering** (IPO) represents a first-time offering of shares by a specific firm to the public. As a privately-held firm expands, it may need more funds than it can obtain through borrowing, and therefore considers an IPO. An investment banking firm (IBF) will normally be hired to recommend the amount of stock to issue and the asking price for the stock. It will also attempt to place the shares with investors. As time passes, the firm may decide to issue additional stock and again hire a securities firm for advice and placement of new shares. Because firms considering IPOs are not well known to investors, they must provide detailed financial statements to describe their financial condition for potential investors.

IPOs tend to occur more frequently during bullish stock market periods, when potential investors are more interested in purchasing new stocks. They also occur more frequently when other investment opportunities are not as attractive. As an example, in 1993 the stock market was bullish, and low interest rates discouraged investors from investing in interest-bearing instruments (such as bonds). Consequently, investor demand for new stocks was strong. Firms were more willing to engage in IPOs during this period because they were confident that they could sell all of their shares. In the first six months of 1993, there were about 325 IPOs, which set a record.

A **secondary stock offering** represents a new stock offering by a specific firm that already has stock outstanding. The firm will likely hire an investment banking firm to sell its shares. Because the firm has shares in the market already, it can monitor the market price when anticipating the price at which it can sell new shares. However, if it floods the market with more shares than investors are willing to purchase, it can cause a decline in the equilibrium price of all of its shares.

Firms tend to monitor stock market movements when deciding when to engage in a secondary stock offering. They are more willing to issue new stock when the market price of their outstanding shares is relatively high. Thus, some firms are viewed as "market-timers," because they time their secondary stock offering to correspond with bullish stock market conditions.

Exhibit 10.1 shows the dollar value of publicly placed common and preferred stock over time. In general, the volume of stock issued has increased. However, many firms used excessive debt in place of stock during the late 1980s, which caused the volume of publicly placed stock to decline.

Changes in the corporate financing with new equity are illustrated in Exhibit 10.2. The net equity issuance per year is measured as the value of new equity offerings minus the value of equity removed through acquisitions or stock repurchases. The net equity issuance was negative and large in the 1980s, especially following the 1987 stock market crash. Low stock prices in the late 1980s caused many firms to repurchase some of their stock, and discouraged them from issuing new stock. In the early 1990s, the net equity issuance was positive, as many firms took advantage of the bullish stock market to issue new stock at higher prices.

Corporations sometimes focus their sales of stock toward a particular group of people, such as their existing shareholders, giving them **preemptive rights** (first priority) to purchase the new stock. By placing newly issued stock with existing shareholders, the firm avoids diluting ownership. Preemptive rights are exercised by purchasing new shares during the subscription period (which normally lasts a month or less) at the price specified by the rights. Alternatively, the rights can be sold to someone else.

EXHIBIT 10.1 Value of Publicly Placed Stock

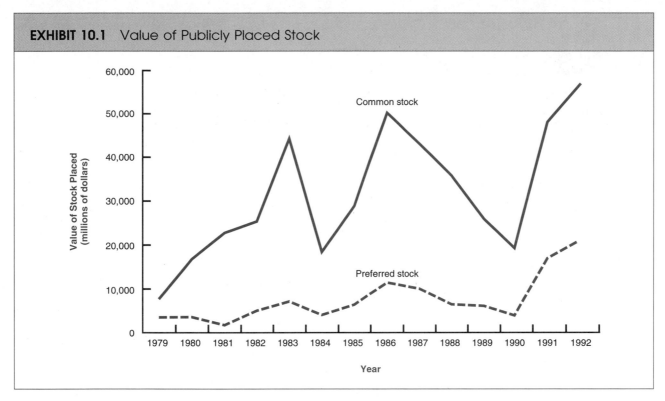

SOURCE: *Federal Reserve Bulletin,* various issues.

Shelf-Registration

Because of a 1982 Securities and Exchange Commission (SEC) rule, corporations can publicly place securities without the time lag often caused by registering with the SEC. This so-called **shelf-registration** fulfills SEC requirements up to two years before issuing new securities. The registration statement contains financing plans over the upcoming two years. The securities are, in a sense,

EXHIBIT 10.2 Net Equity Issuance by U.S. Industrial Firms

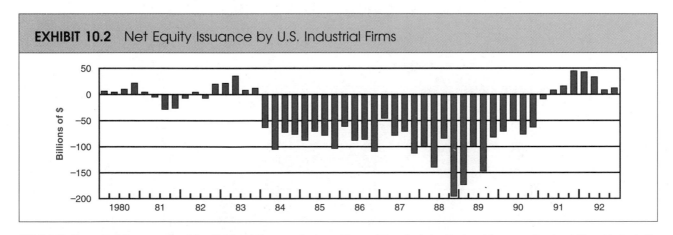

SOURCES: Board of Governors of the Federal Reserve System, Flow of Funds data; Federal Reserve Bank of New York staff estimates; and *FRBNY Quarterly Review,* Winter 1992–1993, p. 6.

WSJ | USING *THE WALL STREET JOURNAL*

STOCK INFORMATION

The Wall Street Journal (WSJ) provides the following information related to this chapter on a daily basis:

- Price quotations on stocks traded on various exchanges.
- A section called "Foreign Markets" discloses share price information for foreign stocks of many different countries.
- A section called "Heard on the Street" describes rumors or expectations about particular stocks.
- A section called "World Markets" discloses the stock index prices of these markets.
- A section called "Abreast of the Market" describes recent trends in the market, forecasts by economists, and trends in economic activity.

- Summary information on stock market trading is provided, including most active issues, number of issues traded, number of advances and declines, biggest percentage gainers and losers, and a breakdown of the trading volume on the NYSE every half hour.
- A section called "New Securities Issues" identifies firms that issued new stocks or debt securities.
- The stock market data bank, which summarizes general market movements, is shown here. The change in the index is measured relative to the previous trading day and to the year-end price.

SOURCE: *The Wall Street Journal*, August 4, 1994, P. C2. Reprinted by permission of *The Wall Street Journal*, © 1994 Dow Jones & Company, Inc. All rights reserved worldwide.

STOCK MARKET DATA BANK — 8/4/94

MAJOR INDEXES

HIGH	LOW (†365 DAY)		CLOSE	NET CHG	% CHG	†365 DAY CHG	% CHG	FROM 12/31	% CHG
DOW JONES AVERAGES									
3978.36	3537.24	30 Industrials	x3765.79	− 26.87	− 0.71	+ 216.82	+ 6.11	+ 11.70	+ 0.31
1862.29	1546.02	20 Transportation	x1604.28	− 8.05	− 0.50	+ 11.41	+ 0.72	− 158.04	− 8.97
256.46	176.71	15 Utilities	x191.34	− 0.66	− 0.34	− 60.70	− 24.08	− 37.96	− 16.55
1447.06	1263.56	65 Composite	x1310.90	− 7.80	− 0.59	− 5.24	− 0.40	− 70.13	− 5.08
456.27	416.31	Equity Mkt. Index	433.68	− 2.68	− 0.61	+ 7.63	+ 1.79	− 8.51	− 1.92
NEW YORK STOCK EXCHANGE									
267.71	243.14	Composite	253.27	− 1.31	− 0.51	+ 4.73	+ 1.90	− 5.81	− 2.24
327.93	294.33	Industrials	311.56	− 1.87	− 0.60	+ 17.19	+ 5.84	− 3.70	− 1.17
246.95	199.04	Utilities	213.02	− 0.66	− 0.31	− 21.85	− 9.30	− 16.90	− 7.35
285.03	235.16	Transportation	246.81	− 1.11	− 0.45	+ 0.47	+ 0.19	− 23.67	− 8.75
233.33	200.75	Finance	213.13	− 0.70	− 0.33	− 9.79	− 4.39	− 3.69	− 1.70
STANDARD & POOR'S INDEXES									
482.00	438.92	500 Index	458.40	− 3.05	− 0.66	+ 10.27	+ 2.29	− 8.05	− 1.73
560.59	506.38	Industrials	533.36	− 3.95	− 0.74	+ 26.79	+ 5.29	− 6.83	− 1.26
453.63	372.17	Transportation	388.29	− 3.05	− 0.78	− 4.29	− 1.09	− 37.31	− 8.77
189.49	148.69	Utilities	160.45	− 0.58	− 0.36	− 17.71	− 9.94	− 12.13	− 7.03
48.40	41.39	Financials	45.08	− 0.19	− 0.42	− 1.35	− 2.91	+ 0.81	+ 1.83
184.79	162.44	400 MidCap	170.79	− 0.47	− 0.27	+ 2.23	+ 1.32	− 8.59	− 4.79
NASDAQ									
803.93	693.79	Composite	720.18	− 3.51	− 0.49	+ 4.68	+ 0.65	− 56.62	− 7.29
851.80	703.27	Industrials	722.56	− 2.94	− 0.41	− 7.51	− 1.03	− 83.28	− 10.33
956.91	858.96	Insurance	900.51	− 8.94	− 0.98	− 2.96	− 0.33	− 20.08	− 2.18
771.94	649.39	Banks	766.30	− 3.35	− 0.44	+ 115.02	+ 17.66	+ 76.87	+ 11.15
356.61	307.55	Nat. Mkt. Comp.	319.82	− 1.59	− 0.49	+ 3.47	+ 1.10	− 23.79	− 6.92
342.72	282.87	Nat. Mkt. Indus.	291.34	− 1.22	− 0.42	− 0.59	− 0.20	− 31.42	− 9.73
OTHERS									
487.89	422.67	Amex	441.35	+ 0.76	+ 0.17	+ 5.82	+ 1.34	− 35.80	− 7.50
305.87	273.73	Value-Line(geom.)	283.00	− 0.83	− 0.29	+ 3.51	+ 1.26	− 12.28	− 4.16
271.08	238.22	Russell 2000	244.81	− 0.95	− 0.39	+ 6.59	+ 2.77	− 13.78	− 5.33
4804.31	4373.58	Wilshire 5000	4532.65	− 23.10	− 0.51	+ 80.82	+ 1.82	− 125.18	− 2.69

†-Based on comparable trading day in preceding year.

shelved until the firm needs to issue them. Shelf-registrations allow firms quick access to funds without repeatedly being slowed by the registration process, enabling those corporations anticipating higher market interest rates to quickly lock in their financing costs. Although this is beneficial to issuing corporations, potential purchasers must realize that the information disclosed in the registration may not accurately reflect the firm's financial status over the two-year shelf period, because it is not continually updated.

Stock Exchanges

In addition to the primary markets where stocks are initially placed, secondary markets exist to facilitate the trading of existing stocks. Brokerage firms serve as financial intermediaries between buyers and sellers of stock in the secondary market. Brokers receive the orders from the customers and pass the orders on to the exchange through a telecommunications network. The orders are frequently executed a few seconds later. Full-service brokers offer advice to customers on stocks to buy or sell, while discount brokers only execute the transactions desired by the customers. For a transaction involving 100 shares, the fee may be about 4 percent of the transaction amount when using a full-service broker versus about 1 percent when using a discount broker. The fees charged by brokers for larger transactions are relatively low when measured in proportion to the transaction amount.

Organized Exchanges

Organized stock exchanges are used to execute secondary market transactions. The more popular organized stock exchanges are the New York Stock Exchange, the American Stock Exchange, the Midwest Stock Exchange, and the Pacific Stock Exchange. The New York Stock Exchange is by far the largest, controlling 80 percent of the volume of all organized exchange transactions in the United States. More than 2,300 different stocks are traded on this exchange. The firms listed on the New York Stock Exchange are typically much larger than those listed on the other exchanges. Each of the exchanges has a trading floor where the buying and selling of securities takes place.

Individuals or firms that purchase a seat on the stock exchange are provided the right to trade securities there. (The term *seat* is somewhat misleading because all trading is carried out by individuals standing in groups.) Each brokerage firm must own a seat on the exchange so that it can purchase or sell the securities requested by its clients. The price of a seat on the New York Stock Exchange has ranged from $200,000 to more than $1 million in recent years.

The trading that takes place on the floor of an organized exchange resembles an auction. Those members of the exchange attempting to sell a client's stock strive to obtain the highest price possible, while members purchasing stock for their clients aim for the lowest price possible. When members of the floor of the exchange announce the sale of a certain number of shares of a certain stock, they receive bids for that stock by other members. They either accept the highest bid or hold the stock until an acceptable bid is offered. Any member of the organized exchange can act both as a seller and a buyer.

Over-the-Counter Market

Stocks not listed on the organized exchanges are traded in the **over-the-counter** (OTC) market. Like the organized exchanges, the over-the-counter market also facilitates secondary market transactions. Unlike the organized exchanges, the OTC market does not have a trading floor. Instead, the buy and sell orders are completed through a telecommunications network. Because there is no trading floor, it is not necessary to buy a seat to trade within this exchange. However, it is necessary to register with the SEC.

Many stocks in the over-the-counter market are served by the **National Association of Securities Dealers Automatic Quotations (NASDAQ)**, which is an electronic quotation system that provides immediate price quotations. Firms that wish to have their prices quoted by the NASDAQ must meet specific requirements on the minimum assets, capital, and number of shareholders. There are about 5,000 stocks traded on the NASDAQ. Most of the stocks represent relatively small firms. However, stocks of some very large firms, including Apple Computer, Intel, and MCI Communications, are also traded. In 1982, about 32 percent of share transactions were executed through the NASDAQ; by 1992, the proportion had increased to 47 percent. Transactions costs as a percentage of the investment tend to be higher on the NASDAQ than on the NYSE or ASE.

Role of Specialists, Floor Traders, and Market-makers

Transactions on the New York and American stock exchanges are facilitated by specialists and floor brokers. **Specialists** take positions in specific stocks, and stand ready to buy or sell these stocks. **Floor brokers** execute stock transactions for their clients. Transactions on the NASDAQ are facilitated by so-called **market-makers,** who stand ready to buy or sell specific stocks in response to customer orders made through a telecommunications network. Thus, market-makers serve the NASDAQ in a manner similar to how specialists serve the New York and American stock exchanges.

Recently, much attention has been given to **market microstructure,** which represents the process by which securities such as stocks are traded. For a stock market to work effectively, it must be liquid, meaning that stocks can be sold immediately at minimal transactions costs. In a liquid market, the **bid** price that brokers are willing to pay for a stock should be just slightly less than the **ask** price at which they would sell the stock.

The liquidity of the stock market is enhanced by market-makers (or specialists), who are required to make a market at all times in an effort to stabilize prices.

Regulation of Stock Exchange Trading

The Securities Exchange Acts of 1933 and 1934 were created to prevent unfair or unethical trading practices on the security exchanges. These acts gave the SEC authority to monitor the exchanges and required listed companies to file a registration statement and financial reports with the SEC and the exchanges. In addition, directors and major shareholders of firms were required to file monthly reports on any changes in stock holdings.

INSTITUTIONAL USE OF STOCK MARKETS

Exhibit 10.3 summarizes the participation of various types of financial institutions in the stock market. Some of these institutions finance their growth by issuing stock. Insurance companies, pension funds, and stock mutual funds are common purchasers of newly issued stock in the primary markets on a daily basis. Their performance is highly dependent on the returns generated by their stock portfolios.

Many stock market transactions involve two financial institutions. For example, an insurance company may purchase the newly issued stocks of a commercial bank. If the insurance company someday sells this stock in the secondary market, a mutual fund or pension fund may possibly act as the purchaser. Because some financial institutions hold large amounts of stock, their collective sales or purchases of stocks can significantly affect stock market prices.

The high volume of trading of secondary stock market activity is attributed to institutional buying and selling. Thus, financial institutions increase the marketability of stocks by creating such an active secondary market.

EXHIBIT 10.3 Institutional Use of Stock Markets

TYPE OF FINANCIAL INSTITUTION	PARTICIPATION IN STOCK MARKETS
Commercial banks	■ Issue stock to boost their capital base. ■ Manage trust funds that usually contain stocks.
Stock-owned savings institutions	■ Issue stock to boost their capital base.
Savings banks	■ Invest in stocks for their investment portfolios.
Finance companies	■ Issue stock to boost their capital base.
Stock mutual funds	■ Use the proceeds from selling shares to invest in stocks.
Securities firms	■ Issue stock to boost their capital base. ■ Place new issues of stock. ■ Offer advice to corporations that consider acquiring the stock from other companies. ■ Execute buy and sell orders of investors.
Insurance companies	■ Issue stock to boost their capital base. ■ Invest a large proportion of their premiums in the stock market.
Pension funds	■ Invest a large proportion of pension fund contributions in the stock market.

Program Trading

Program trading has been defined by the New York Stock Exchange (NYSE) as the simultaneous buying and selling of a portfolio of at least 15 different stocks valued at more than $1 million. This is a narrow definition, as the term is sometimes used in other contexts. The most common program traders are securities firms, such as Salomon Brothers, Morgan Stanley & Company, and Bear Stearns & Company. They conduct the trades for their own accounts or for other institutional investors such as pension funds, mutual funds, and insurance companies. The term *program* refers to the use of computers in what is known as the Designated Order Turnaround (DOT) system at the NYSE, which allows traders to send orders to many trading posts at the exchange.

In the late 1980s, about 20 million shares per day were traded as a result of program trading. About 75 percent of these shares were on the NYSE, while 5 percent of the shares were traded on other U.S. markets and 20 percent were traded on non-U.S. markets. In the early 1990s, program trading activity increased. During a typical week, some of the participating securities firms may trade 20 or 30 million shares to conduct program trading.

Program trading is commonly used to reduce the susceptibility of a stock portfolio to stock market movements. For example, one form of program trading is to sell numerous stocks that become "overpriced" (based on a particular model used to value those stocks). Program trading can also refer to the purchase of numerous stocks that become "underpriced."

Program trading can be combined with the trading of stock index futures to create **portfolio insurance.** This involves the use of futures or options contracts on a stock index. A decline in the market would result in a gain on the futures or options position, which can offset the reduced market value of the stock portfolio. The use of futures to create portfolio insurance is described in Chapter 11, while the use of options is described in Chapter 12.

IMPACT OF PROGRAM TRADING ON STOCK VOLATILITY.   Program trading is commonly cited as the reason for the decline or rise in the stock market. The underlying reason for a large amount of program trading, however, is that institutional investors believe that numerous stocks are over- or undervalued. Although program trading can cause share prices to reach a new equilibrium more rapidly, it does not necessarily imply that it causes more volatility in the stock market. A recent study by Furbush assessed the relationship between the intensity of program trading and stock price volatility. Furbush assessed five-minute intervals of stock index prices and stock index futures prices during the week of the October 1987 crash. He found that greater declines in stock prices are not systematically associated with more intense program trading.

A study by Roll compared the magnitude of the October 1987 crash for markets using program trading versus markets in other countries. Roll found that the average share price decline of markets using program trading averaged 21 percent versus a 28 percent decline for other countries. Thus, is does not appear that program trading caused more pronounced losses during the crash.

Some critics have suggested that program trading instigated the crash. Roll found, however, that many Asian stock markets where program trading does not exist plunged several hours before the opening of the U.S. market on Black Monday (October 19, 1987).

IMPACT OF THE OCTOBER 1987 STOCK MARKET CRASH ON FINANCIAL MARKETS

On October 19, 1987, the Dow Jones Industrial Average declined to 1738.42 from 2246.74 on the previous trading day. This represents a 22.6 percent decline, significantly exceeding the 12.8 percent one-day decline on October 28, 1929. Various financial markets and institutions were affected by the stock market crash:

- Most foreign stock markets experienced a somewhat similar downturn as the U.S. market.
- Many investors who sold stocks placed their funds in short-term money market securities; consequently, yields on newly issued commercial paper Treasury bills and bank CDs declined.
- Other investors who sold stocks placed their funds in other capital market securities, such as bonds and mortgages; consequently, prices of existing bonds increased.
- The market value of assets in insurance companies and pension funds was substantially reduced because of their large holdings of stocks. Investment companies that held stock in their own accounts were also adversely affected. Investment companies that manage stock mutual funds were forced to sell stocks in the funds in order to cover redemptions by fund shareholders. Investors who sold stock mutual fund shares often placed their money in other mutual funds managed by the same investment company (such as bond funds and money market funds).
- The underwriting activity of investment banking firms declined as corporations postponed new issues of stock (because the market price per share of stock was so low).
- Interest in acquisitions increased, as many companies were perceived as bargains, with their stock prices so low.
- Interest in leveraged buyouts increased as managers and other investors were more able to retire a company's stock and convert it into a privately held company. However, leveraged buyouts often necessitate a large amount of financing. Creditors were more skeptical after the crash and less willing to provide funds needed for leveraged buyouts.

Brokerage firms sustained huge losses on their own security holdings. However, these losses were at least partially offset by fees earned from a high volume of securities transactions and from advisory fees on mergers and acquisitions during the fourth quarter of 1987.

One of the key differences between the stock market crash of October 1987 and the crash in 1929 was the effect on bank deposits. In 1929 the reduced public confidence caused not only a liquidation of stocks but massive deposit withdrawals as well. This did not occur in 1987, because of the deposit insurance of up to $100,000 per bank account. In addition, borrowing margins on stocks were limited to 50 percent in 1987 versus 78 percent in 1929. Furthermore, a much larger percentage of investors were margin buyers in 1929 than in 1987.

Share volume on the New York Stock Exchange exceeded 600 million shares on the day of the crash, which was almost twice the previous record of trading volume on a given day. Share volume for the week was 2.3 billion shares. Because of the huge increase in trading volume, brokerage firms were unable to keep up with the processing of orders. The New York and American stock exchanges closed early so that the processing of orders could catch up. The trading of some stocks stopped because of the imbalances of orders. Although the markets calmed shortly after, the crash caused some concern about the capabilities, risk, and regulations of stock markets.

STOCK VALUATION MODELS _____

One of the first models on pricing assets was developed by John B. Williams in 1931. This model is still applicable today. Williams stated that the price of a stock should reflect the present value of the stock's future dividends, or:

$$\text{Price} = \sum_{t=1}^{\infty} \frac{D_t}{(1+k)^t}$$

where
$$t = \text{period}$$
$$D = \text{dividend}$$
$$k = \text{discount rate}$$

The model can account for uncertainty by allowing D_t to be revised in response to revised expectations about a firm's cash flows, or allowing k to be revised in response to changes in the required rate of return by investors. The model serves as a useful framework for stock valuation, but because forecasting future dividends (or corporate cash flows) into infinity is difficult, other models have also been considered.

Capital Asset Pricing Model

Because the returns on stocks are uncertain, they are commonly assessed in terms of a probability distribution. When assessing multiple periods, risk-averse investors should prefer that their overall investment generate high returns and low variability in returns, as variability serves as a proxy for risk. Given this objective, investors can consider constructing a stock portfolio, because combinations of stocks can achieve lower variability in returns without necessarily reducing the expected return.

For large portfolios, the risk contribution of a single stock is the covariance of its returns with the returns of other stocks in the portfolio. Diversification across stocks with low covariances tends to reduce the overall variability of the portfolio. Research by Sharpe showed that under specific assumptions, individuals would invest in (1) a market portfolio consisting of all assets and (2) risk-free assets (such as Treasury securities). Investors could achieve their desired balance of risk and potential return by properly allocating funds between these two types of assets. Those investors that are more averse to risk would invest in a greater proportion of funds in risk-free securities.

The contributions of Sharpe and others led to the development of the **capital asset pricing model (CAPM)**, which suggests that the return of an asset (R_j) is influenced by the prevailing risk-free rate (R_f), the market return (R_m), and the covariance between the R_j and R_m as follows:

$$R_j = R_f + B_j(R_m - R_f)$$

where B_j represents the **beta** and is measured as $\text{COV}(R_j, R_m)/\text{VAR}(R_m)$. This model implies that given a specific R_f and R_m, investors will require a higher return on an asset that has a higher beta. A higher beta reflects a higher covariance between the asset's returns and market returns, which contributes more risk to the portfolio of assets held by the investor.

APPLIED RESEARCH

Is beta dead?

The capital asset pricing model (CAPM) suggests that the return of a particular stock is positively related to its beta (a measure of systematic risk). However, a recent study by Fama and French has found that beta was unrelated to the return on stocks over the period 1963–1990. This study tests numerous forms of a model in which the average stock return of a firm over a specified period is hypothesized to be a function of three variables: (1) the firm's systematic risk (as measured by beta), (2) size (as measured by the market value of equity), and (3) the book value of the firm's equity in proportion to the firm's market value of equity. Fama and French found that stock returns (1) were not significantly related to beta, (2) were inversely related to the firm's size, and (3) were positively related to the ratio of book value of equity to market value of equity. One implication that might be drawn is that the size and ratio of book value to market value should be considered in any pricing model used to explain why stock returns vary among firms. A larger implication is that the stock returns are not influenced by their

respective betas. This has much relevance given that many investment models used by practitioners are based on a positive relation between stock returns and risk. In essence, the study is suggesting that investors are not being rewarded (with higher returns) when incurring higher degrees of systematic risk.

Because the two additional variables in the model may indirectly measure the firm's risk, the results of Fama and French do not necessarily refute the risk-return relationship. It is possible that investors are rewarded when investing in stocks with higher risk, but that risk is captured within the size of the firm rather than within the firm's beta.

Given the importance of the relation between stock returns and beta, a recent study by Chan and Lakonishok reassessed this relation. They found that the relation varied with the time period that was used, which implies that it is difficult to make implications about the future based on the findings in any specific period. They found that there was a strong positive relation between the stock returns and betas across firms until 1982, but no significant relation between returns and beta over

the period 1982–1990. They suggest that the results over the 1982–1990 period may be an exception, and will not necessarily be indicative of the future. Thus, they conclude that although it is appropriate to question whether beta is the driving force behind stock returns, it may be premature to pronounce beta dead.

Furthermore, if beta is a stable measure of the firm's sensitivity to market movements, it would still be useful for determining which stocks are more feasible investments when the stock market is expected to perform well. Thus, a firm's beta should still be monitored by investors.

Chan and Lakonishok assessed the 10 worst months for the U.S. stock market in order to compare the returns of firms with relatively high betas versus firms with relatively low betas. They found that firms with the highest betas performed much worse than firms with low betas in those periods. They also found that high-beta firms outperformed low-beta firms during market upswings. These results support the measurement of beta as an indicator of the firm's response to market upswings or downswings.

The CAPM is based on the premise that the only type of risk relevant to investors is systematic (nondiversifiable) risk as measured by beta. Those risks that are firm-specific can be diversified away. The CAPM has been given much attention by researchers. Although it has been criticized for having some limitations in application, it is commonly used in conjunction with other, more subjective methods in assessing whether particular stocks are over- or undervalued.

Arbitrage Pricing Model

An alternative pricing model is based on the **arbitrage pricing theory (APT)**. The APT differs from the CAPM in that it suggests that a stock's prices can be influenced by a set of factors in addition to the market. The factors may possibly reflect economic growth, inflation, and other variables that could systematically influence asset prices. The following model is based on the APT:

$$E(R) = B_0 + \sum_{i=1}^{n} B_i F_i + u_j$$

where

$$E(R) = \text{expected return of asset}$$

$$B_0 = \text{a constant}$$

$$F_1 \dots F_n = \text{values of factors 1 to } n$$

$$B_i = \text{sensitivity of the asset return to particular factor}$$

$$u_j = \text{residual term}$$

The model suggests that in equilibrium, expected returns on assets are linearly related to the covariance between asset returns and the factors. This is distinctly different from the CAPM, wherein expected returns are linearly related to the covariance between asset returns and the market. The appeal of the APT is that it allows for factors (such as industry effects) other than the market to influence the expected returns of assets.

DETERMINANTS OF STOCK PRICE MOVEMENTS

Stock prices are driven by two types of factors: (1) economic factors and (2) other unrelated factors.

Economic Factors

A firm's value should reflect the present value of its future cash flows. Because earnings are a primary component of corporate cash flows, it is understandable that many investors use forecasted earnings to determine whether a firm's stock is over- or undervalued. Numerous economic factors that influence corporate earnings are closely monitored, including inflation, interest rates, growth in the gross national product, consumer trends, and the shifts in the balance of trade. Because fiscal and monetary policies imposed by governments affect these factors, they are also continually monitored by investors.

IMPACT OF INTEREST RATES.   One of the most prominent economic forces driving stock market prices is the risk-free interest rate. Investors should consider purchasing a risky asset only if they expect to be compensated with a risk premium for the risk incurred. Given a choice of risk-free Treasury securities or stocks, stocks should be considered only if they are appropriately priced to reflect a sufficiently high expected return above the risk-free rate. The relation between interest rates and stock prices is not constant over time. However, most of the largest stock market declines have occurred in periods when interest rates increased substantially.

IMPACT OF THE DOLLAR.   The value of the dollar can affect U.S. stock prices for a variety of reasons. First, foreign investors tend to purchase U.S. stocks when the dollar is weak and sell them when it is near its peak. Thus, the foreign demand for any given U.S. stock may be higher when the dollar is expected to strengthen, other things being equal. Also, stock prices are affected by the impact of the dollar's changing value on cash flows. Stock prices of U.S. firms primarily involved in exporting could be favorably affected by a weak dollar and adversely affected by a strong dollar. U.S. importing firms could be affected in the opposite manner.

Stock prices of U.S. companies may also be affected by exchange rates if stock market participants measure performance by reported earnings. A multinational corporation's consolidated reported earnings would be affected by exchange rate fluctuations even if the company's cash flows were not affected. A weaker dollar tends to inflate the reported earnings of a U.S.-based company's foreign subsidiaries. Some analysts would argue that any effect of exchange rate movements on financial statements is irrelevant unless cash flows were also affected.

The changing value of the dollar can also affect stock prices by affecting expectations of economic factors that influence the firm's performance. For example, if a weak dollar stimulates the U.S. economy, it may enhance the value of a U.S. firm whose sales are dependent on the U.S. economy. A strong dollar could adversely affect such a firm if it dampens U.S. economic growth.

Because inflation affects some firms, a weak dollar value could indirectly affect a firm's stock by placing upward pressure on inflation. A strong dollar would have the opposite indirect impact.

Some companies attempt to insulate the exposure of their stock price to the changing value of the dollar, while other companies purposely remain exposed with the intent to benefit from it.

Other Factors

Any underlying forces that can cause institutional investors as a group to buy or sell shares should have an influence on stock prices. These forces would typically reflect expectations about economic conditions. However, some investment decisions by institutional investors occur for other reasons. Because many portfolio managers are evaluated over the calendar year, they tend to invest in the riskier small stocks at the beginning of the year and shift to larger (more stable) companies near the end of the year to lock in their gains. This tendency places upward pressure on small stocks in January of every year, causing a so-called January effect. Some studies have found that most of the annual stock market gains occur in January. As investors discovered the January effect, they began to take more positions in stocks in the prior month. This has placed upward pressure on stocks in mid-December, forcing the January effect to begin in December.

NOISE TRADING. If irrational or uninformed investors take stock positions that affect the demand for particular stocks, prices of these stocks may be affected. In recent years, a theory known as **noise trading** has been used to explain why stock prices are not always driven by fundamental factors. There are many uninformed investors whose buy or sell positions push the stock's price away from its fundamental value. In essence, the stock price is distorted as a result of the "noise" caused by uninformed investors (called **"noise traders"**). Given the uncertainty about a stock's fundamental value, informed investors may be unwilling to capitalize on the discrepancy. Consequently, a market "correction" may not necessarily occur.

If informed (knowledgeable) investors have superior information, transactions between market-makers and informed investors will benefit informed traders at the expense of market-makers. However, transactions involving unknowledgeable investors (with little or inferior information) may benefit market-makers.

Market-makers can attempt to protect themselves by setting a wide spread between their bid and ask prices. The greater the market-maker's uncertainty about specific stocks, the wider would be the spread set on those stocks. If informed investors did not have superior information, market-makers would be less concerned about losing on transactions, and would be able to set smaller spreads. Thus, the size of the spread should be smaller in stock markets that are more informationally efficient. In such markets, prices of existing stocks should reflect all information, and informed investors would not have an advantage. Stocks that have relatively little trading are normally subject to greater price volatility. Thus, the spreads on these stocks are wider to reflect the higher degree of uncertainty.

TRENDS. A nonfundamental factor sometimes used to make investment decisions is the trend of recent stock prices (referred to as **technical analysis)**. The rationale behind technical analysis is that if trends are repetitive, investors can take positions in stocks as they recognize the particular trend occurring. Technical analysis is often criticized by investors who focus solely on fundamental factors for making investment decisions. Nevertheless, many investors rely on their charts of historical stock price movements when deciding on stocks to buy or sell.

To the extent that numerous investors use historical trends and psychology to make investment decisions, these factors could also help explain the variation in stock market movements. Consider the coincidental relationship between the winner of the Super Bowl and the performance of the stock market during that year. In 1978, Leonard Koppett, a sports writer for the *New York Times*, reported that a victory by a team from the National Football League (NFL) was followed by an up year in the stock market, while a victory by an American Football League (AFL) team was followed by a down year. A study by Dyl and Schatzberg assessed the market performance following Super Bowls after 1978. The authors of the study found that the differential performance has become even more pronounced since this coincidental relationship was detected, as if investors actually began to use Super Bowl results to make investment decisions. Dyl and Schatzberg state:

> When Leonard Koppett discovered and reported the phenomenon in 1978, this "knowledge" became a part of the set of information available to investors in general. If investors subsequently used this "knowledge" in making investment decisions, their behavior might perpetuate the Super Bowl stock market relationship.

This example illustrates how some tendencies, even without rationale, may influence stock market movements.

Evidence on Factors Affecting Stock Prices

Although fundamental factors influence stock prices, they do not fully account for stock price movements. A well-known study by Schiller suggests that because stock prices are supposed to reflect a weighted average of discounted dividends, they should actually be less volatile than dividends. Schiller acknowledges, however, that stock prices are 5 to 13 times more volatile than what would be expected if they reflected the present value of future dividends. Schiller attempts to reconcile the differences between theory and reality (see *The Economist,* June 2, 1990, p. 81) by suggesting that there are two types of investors: (1) smart-money investors who value stock prices based on new relevant information and trade accordingly and (2) noise traders, who are influenced by fads and fashions (including historical price trends). Stocks can exhibit excessive volatility because their prices are partially driven by fads and fashions, which may be unrelated to the present value of future dividends.

A recent study by Roll confirms that stock prices are driven by other forces in addition to fundamental factors. Roll found that only about one-third of the variation in stock returns can be explained by systematic economic forces. A related study by Cutler, Poteba, and Summers reassessed this issue by considering the influence of major news announcements not accounted for in Roll's study. Even after accounting for this information, most of the variation in stock returns could not be explained. The study suggests that movements in stock prices may be partially attributed to investor reliance on other investors for stock market valuation. Many investors make decisions without their own assessment of a firm's value, but in response to an adjustment in the stock price that may signal other investors' valuations. This can cause an overreaction in stock prices to new information.

As evidence of stock market overreactions, the magnitudes of the largest daily declines in the stock market were much greater than what would be expected, based on the economic information disclosed on those days. This evidence confirms that market prices are sometimes driven by more than fundamental factors. Regulators are concerned about the potential magnitude of stock market declines because of the possible impact on the economy. Consider the possible effects on spending when the market value of stock portfolios of retired people declines by more than 20 percent on a single day.

CORPORATE SEARCH FOR UNDERVALUED STOCK

Firms whose shares are perceived by other firms to be undervalued become targets. Potential acquiring firms consider purchasing the target if the present value of the target's expected future cash flows generated exceeds the acquisition price.

Several common reasons exist for considering an acquisition. First, the combination of two firms may reduce redundancy in some operations and allow for synergistic benefits. In such a case, the value of the combination exceeds the sum of separate entities. Second, an acquisition may capitalize on tax shields that would not be applicable for the individual entities. Third, an acquisition may allow for the replacement of inefficient management and therefore improve the firm's operations. Fourth, an acquisition may create a more diversified set of operations so that the corporation is less reliant on conditions of any particular industry. This may reduce the perceived probability of bankruptcy and reduce the corporation's cost of funds.

To the extent that investors anticipate such benefits to be realized, they should respond favorably to an acquisition. Much research has been conducted

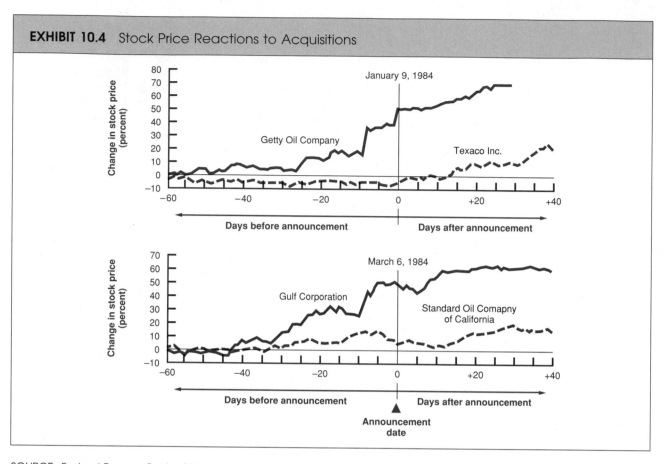

EXHIBIT 10.4   Stock Price Reactions to Acquisitions

SOURCE: *Federal Reserve Bank of New York Quarterly Review* (Spring 1984): 28.

to determine how investors react. In general, the studies have found a large positive share price reaction of target firms. However, the share prices of acquiring firms were not favorably affected. In fact, some of the studies detected a negative share price reaction for acquiring firms (see, for example, the study by Asquith).

Examples of the stock price reaction to acquisitions are illustrated in Exhibit 10.4. The top graph illustrates Texaco's acquisition of Getty Oil Company, while the lower graph illustrates the acquisition by Standard Oil of Gulf Corporation. In both cases, the share price reaction was much more favorable for the target than the acquiring firm.

The lack of a favorable market reaction to acquiring firms suggests that the market does not anticipate acquiring firms to benefit from the acquisition. In some cases, the initial motive for the acquisition may be suspect. For example, some investors may believe that the motive of the acquiring firm's managers is growth, which may lead to more power and higher salaries for them. Even if investors believe that a motive is valid, they may not expect the firm to follow through on what needs to be done. For example, there is some evidence that firms engaging in acquisitions to reduce repetitive operations of two units never eliminate the redundancy, perhaps because of the potential low morale that results from layoffs.

Managerial Assessment of the Firm's Own Stock

A firm's stock price is monitored not only by other corporations but also by the firm's own managers. If management perceives the stock to be overvalued, it may issue additional stock to capitalize on the situation. Numerous academic studies have found that new stock issues by firms elicit an unfavorable share price response, which may reflect the market's interpretation of a new issue that the stock is overvalued.

Management may also consider repurchasing existing shares in the secondary market when it believes the stock is undervalued. For example, several firms repurchased shares just after the October 1987 stock market crash, as if the post-crash prices were too low. In general, studies have found evidence of a favorable stock price response to stock repurchase announcements, which implies that the announcement signals the management's perception that the share price is undervalued. The market responds favorably to this signal.

LEVERAGED BUYOUTS. Another reason that managers may monitor their firm's stock price is their own potential investment opportunities. If managers believe the stock price is undervalued, they may consider forming a group to purchase the stock as a means of buying their firm. This strategy normally requires substantial borrowed funds by the group, which is why it is commonly referred to as a **leveraged buyout** (LBO). The LBO was commonly used for acquisitions in the 1980s. Even when the stock of a firm is appropriately priced to reflect the firm's future cash flows, a group of employees may believe that they could restructure the firm's operations to improve cash flows. Thus, the prevailing stock price may be perceived as undervalued from their perspective and motivate them to engage in an LBO.

The use of debt to retire a company's stock creates a very highly leveraged capital structure. One favorable aspect of such a revised capital structure is that the ownership of the firm is normally reduced to a small group of people, who may be managers of the firm. Thus, there is less likelihood of so-called agency costs that occur when managers act in their own self-interests instead of the firm's. However, a major concern of LBOs is that the firm will experience cash flow problems over time because of the high periodic debt payments that result from the high degree of financial leverage. The firm financed in this way has a high potential return but is risky.

Some firms that had engaged in LBOs issue new stock after improving the firm's performance. This process is referred to as a **reverse leveraged buyout** (reverse LBO). Although the LBO may have been used to purchase all the stock of a firm that has not achieved its potential performance (causing its stock to be priced low), the reverse LBO is normally desirable when the stock can be sold at a high price. In essence, the owners hope to issue new stock at a much higher price than they paid for it when enacting the LBO. The volume of IPOs and reverse LBOs is illustrated in Exhibit 10.5. The volume of initial public offerings (IPOs) and reverse LBOs was relatively low in the late 1980s, as stock prices were low shortly after the 1987 stock market crash. However, the volume increased during the bullish stock market period in the early 1990s.

Search for Overvalued Stocks

Some institutional or individual investors capitalize on a stock that is perceived to be overvalued by using a strategy called **short-selling,** which involves

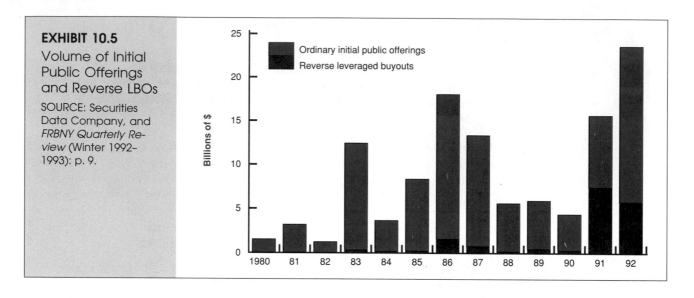

EXHIBIT 10.5
Volume of Initial Public Offerings and Reverse LBOs

SOURCE: Securities Data Company, and *FRBNY Quarterly Review* (Winter 1992–1993): p. 9.

borrowing the stock owned by someone else and selling it in the market. The short seller is required to pay the dividends that were to be paid to the person who loaned the stock. The short seller will purchase stock in the market after the stock's price has fallen, and provide the stock to the person who loaned the stock. The actions described above are facilitated by brokerage firms. The short seller's profit is the difference between the original sell price and the price paid for the stock, after subtracting any dividend payments made to the party from whom the stock was borrowed. The risk to the short seller is that the stock's price may not necessarily decrease as expected. Thus, the short seller may end up purchasing stock at a higher price than the original selling price.

Stock Market Efficiency

If stock markets are efficient, the prices of stocks at any point in time should fully reflect all available information. As investors must attempt to capitalize on new information that is not already accounted for, stock prices should adjust immediately. Investors commonly over- or underreact to information. This does not mean markets are inefficient unless the reaction is biased (consistently over- or underreacting). In this case, investors who recognized the bias would be able to earn abnormally high risk-adjusted returns.

Efficient markets can be classified into three forms: weak, semistrong, and strong. **Weak-form efficiency** suggests that security prices reflect all market-related data, such as historical security price movements and volume of securities trades. Thus, investors will not be able to earn abnormal returns on a trading strategy that is solely based on past price movements.

Semistrong-form efficiency suggests that security prices fully reflect all public information. The difference between public information and market-related information is that public information also includes announcements by firms, economic news or events, and political news or events. Market-related information is a subset of public information. Thus, if semistrong-form efficiency holds, weak-form efficiency must hold as well. Yet weak-form efficiency could possibly hold, while semistrong-form efficiency does not. In this case, investors could earn abnormal returns by using the relevant information that was not immediately accounted for by the market.

Strong-form efficiency suggests that security prices fully reflect all information, including private or insider information. If strong-form efficiency holds, semistrong-form efficiency must hold as well. However, semistrong-form efficiency could hold, while strong-form efficiency does not, if insider information leads to abnormal returns.

Tests of the Efficient Market Hypothesis

Weak-form efficiency has been tested by searching for a nonrandom pattern in security prices. If the future change in price is related to recent changes, historical price movements could be used to earn abnormal returns. In general, studies have found that historical price changes are independent over time. Therefore, historical information is already reflected by today's price and cannot be used to earn abnormal profits. Even for those cases where some dependence was detected, the transaction costs were expected to offset any excess return earned.

There is some evidence that stocks have performed better in specific time periods. For example, small stocks have performed unusually well in the month of January ("January effect"). Second, stocks have historically performed better on Fridays than on Mondays ("weekend effect"). Third, stocks have historically performed well on the trading days just before holidays ("holiday effect"). To the extent that a given pattern continues and can be used by investors to earn abnormal returns, market inefficiencies exist. In most cases, there is no clear evidence that such patterns persist once they are recognized by the investment community.

Semistrong-form efficiency has been tested by assessing how security returns adjust to particular announcements. One type of announcement is related specifically to the firm, such as an announced dividend increase, acquisition, or stock split. Another type of announcement is economy related, such as an announced decline in the Fed's discount rate. In general, security prices immediately reflected the information from the announcements. That is, the securities were not consistently over- or undervalued. Consequently, abnormal returns could not consistently be achieved. This is especially true when considering transaction costs.

Tests of strong-form efficiency are difficult, because the inside information used is not publicly available and cannot be properly tested. Nevertheless, many forms of insider trading could easily result in abnormally high returns. For example, there is clear evidence that share prices of target firms rise substantially as the acquisition is announced. If insiders purchased stock of targets prior to others, they would normally achieve abnormally high returns. Insiders are discouraged from using this information because it is illegal, not because markets are strong-form efficient.

There is some evidence of unusual profits when investing in initial public offerings (IPOs). Yet, this type of investment is unique in that the stock was not previously available to investors. A recent study by Chalk and Pearry assessed returns on stocks just after IPOs. On the first day, returns averaged more than

20 percent, which was clearly abnormal. The second day the mean return was much lower but still about one percent above the overall stock market return. On subsequent days the returns were lower. Thus, it appeared that abnormally high returns occurred only during the first two days.

The authors also compared stocks in different price groups to determine whether the market reaction to IPOs depended on price level. The return on the first day was abnormally high, regardless of the price group, but especially for stocks priced at $1 per share or less. The returns on low-priced stocks averaged more than 55 percent on the first day of the IPO. Because transactions costs are higher for low-priced stocks, the high returns of newly issued low-priced stocks are overstated. Yet even when accounting for these transaction costs, the authors found that the low-priced stocks generated abnormally high returns on the first day.

Other studies have also found that IPOs were initially underpriced, with returns averaging as much as 48 percent over the first week after the stock was issued (see the article by Saunders for a review of all the studies). One of the primary reasons for the underpricing is the inability of corporations issuing the stock to convey their financial condition to investors. Consequently, shares are sold at relatively low prices, so that initial purchasers are beneficiaries at the expense of the corporations.

Another possible reason for underpricing is that the investment banking firms underwriting an IPO intentionally underprice to ensure that the entire issue can be placed. In addition, underwriters are required to exercise due diligence in ensuring the accuracy of the information that they provide to investors about the corporation. Thus, underwriters are encouraged to err on the low side when setting a price for IPOs.

Some analysts might contend that given imperfect information about IPOs, investors will participate only if prices are low. Thus, the potential return must be high enough to compensate for the lack of information about these corporations and the risk incurred. Using this argument, the underpricing does not imply market inefficiencies but rather reflects the high degree of uncertainty.

GLOBALIZATION OF STOCK MARKETS

GLOBAL ASPECTS

Stock markets are becoming globalized in the sense that firms in need of funds can tap foreign markets, and investors can purchase foreign stocks. In recent years, many firms have obtained funds from foreign markets through international stock offerings. This strategy may represent an effort by the firm to enhance its global image. Alternatively, it may enable the firm to more easily place the entire issue of new stock among investors, as the issuing firm is tapping a larger poor of potential investors.

International stock offerings are used by U.S. firms as well as non-U.S. firms. Although some large non-U.S. firms have developed a market for their stock in the U.S., others are unwilling to do so because of Securities and Exchange Commission (SEC) regulations. The SEC requires that any firms desiring to list their stock on a U.S. stock exchange must provide financial statements that satisfy U.S. accounting standards, and are therefore compatible with financial statements of U.S. firms. This requirement creates an expense to non-U.S. firms that can be

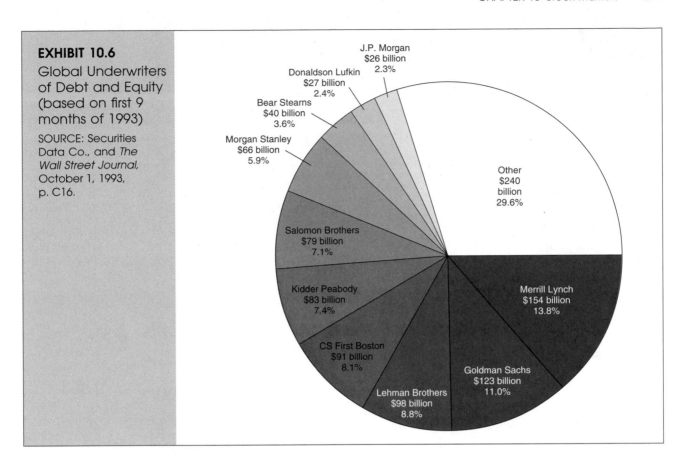

EXHIBIT 10.6

Global Underwriters of Debt and Equity (based on first 9 months of 1993)

SOURCE: Securities Data Co., and *The Wall Street Journal,* October 1, 1993, p. C16.

J.P. Morgan
$26 billion
2.3%

Donaldson Lufkin
$27 billion
2.4%

Bear Stearns
$40 billion
3.6%

Morgan Stanley
$66 billion
5.9%

Salomon Brothers
$79 billion
7.1%

Kidder Peabody
$83 billion
7.4%

CS First Boston
$91 billion
8.1%

Lehman Brothers
$98 billion
8.8%

Goldman Sachs
$123 billion
11.0%

Merrill Lynch
$154 billion
13.8%

Other
$240
billion
29.6%

avoided if they choose not to list on U.S. exchanges. Thus, some non-U.S. firms develop markets for their stock in other foreign markets instead of the U.S.

In order to allow European investors easy access to all European Stocks, the development of a centralized stock exchange has been considered. However, European stock exchanges are now creating a cross-listing system called **Eurolist,** that will allow investors of one country to easily purchase shares of large firms based in other participating countries. The ultimate goal is to allow any publicly traded firm based in the European Community to list its stock on all other European stock exchanges without having to prepare a separate application or a prospectus in the language of each stock exchange. Under these conditions, cross-border trading of stocks would be less costly, and there would be no need to create one centralized stock exchange for all European firms.

Investment banks facilitate the international placement of new stock through one or more syndicates across countries. Many investment banks and commercial banks based in the U.S. provide underwriting and other investment banking services in foreign countries. In fact, the top 10 global underwriters of debt and equity securities (which are listed in Exhibit 10.6) have their headquarters located in the U.S.

The ability of investment banks to place new shares in foreign markets is somewhat dependent on the stock's perceived liquidity in that market. A secondary market for the stock must be established in foreign markets to enhance

EXHIBIT 10.7   Foreign Trading of U.S. Stocks (in Billions of Dollars)

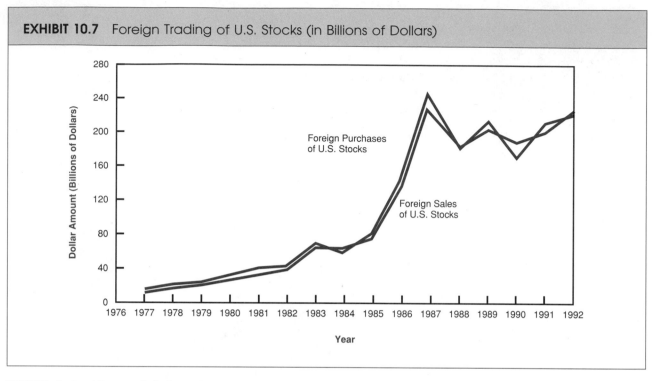

SOURCE: *Federal Reserve Bulletin,* various issues.

liquidity and make newly issued stocks more attractive. Listing stock on a foreign stock exchange not only enhances the stock's liquidity but also may increase the firm's perceived financial standing when the exchange approves the listing application. It can also protect a firm against hostile takeovers because it disperses ownership and makes it more difficult for other firms to gain a controlling interest. There are some costs of listing on a foreign exchange, such as translating an annual report in a foreign currency and making financial statements compatible with the accounting standards used in that country.

The degree to which stock trading is becoming internationalized is illustrated in Exhibit 10.7, which shows the volume of U.S. stocks purchased and sold by foreign investors. The volume of trading in the late 1980s and 1990s was much larger than in earlier years.

Investing in Foreign Markets

In recent years, barriers to foreign stock markets have been removed, thereby allowing investors new investment opportunities. In addition, new stock markets are being developed in China, Hungary, Jamaica, Poland, Venezuela, and many other countries. Foreign stocks are often appealing to investors because of the potential for high returns. For example, stock prices in Argentina, Chile, Hong Kong, Mexico, an Venezuela increased by more than 200 percent on average over the 1988–1993 period.

Some foreign stock markets are relatively new and small, and are possibly not as efficient as the U.S. stock market. Thus, investors may be attracted to these markets if some stocks may be undervalued. However, because some of these markets are small, they may be susceptible to manipulation by large traders. Furthermore, insider trading is more prevalent in many foreign markets, because of a lack of enforcement. In general, large institutional investors and insiders based in the foreign markets may have some advantages.

Although international stocks can generate high returns, they also may exhibit high risk. Some of the smaller stock markets are often referred to as casinos because of the wild gyrations in gains and losses and the panic trading that occurs. On a single day in December 1989, the volume of shares traded on the Taiwan stock exchange was 1.1 billion, which was 921 million more shares than what was traded on the New York Stock Exchange (NYSE) on the same day. This differential is especially amazing when considering that there were only 186 stocks listed on the Taiwan stock exchange at that time.

The smaller markets experience large price swings because of two characteristics. First, the small number of shares for some firms allows large trades to jolt the equilibrium price. Second, valid financial information about firms is sometimes lacking, causing investors to trade according to rumors. Information from continual rumors causes more volatile trading patterns than factual data.

Investment in foreign stocks is subject to exchange rate risk because foreign stocks are denominated in foreign currencies. When the currency denominating a foreign stock depreciates over the investment period, the returns to investors holding foreign stocks are reduced.

METHODS USED TO INVEST IN FOREIGN STOCKS. Investors can easily invest in stocks of foreign companies that are listed on the local stock exchanges. However, this set of stocks is quite limited. Foreign stocks not listed on local stock exchanges can be purchased through some full-service brokerage firms that have offices in foreign countries. However, the transaction costs incurred from purchasing foreign stocks in this manner are high.

An alternative means of investing in foreign stocks is by purchasing **American depository receipts (ADRs)**, which are certificates representing ownership of foreign stocks. ADRs are attractive to U.S. investors for the following reasons. First, they are closely followed by U.S. investment analysts. Second, companies represented by ADRs are required by the Securities and Exchange Commission (SEC) to file financial statements consistent with the generally accepted accounting principles in the United States. These statements may not be available for other non-U.S. companies. Third, reliable quotes on ADR prices are consistently available, with existing currency values factored in to translate the price into dollars. However, although ADRs have advantages, there is only a limited amount to select from. Also, the ADR market is less active than other stock markets. Consequently, ADRs are less liquid than most listed U.S. stocks.

Another method for investing in foreign stocks is to purchase shares of **international mutual funds,** which are portfolios of international stocks created and managed by various financial institutions. Thus, individuals can diversify across international stocks by investing in a single international mutual fund. Some international mutual funds focus on a specific foreign country, while others contain stocks across several countries or even several continents.

Integration among Stock Markets

Stock price movements among international stock markets may be somewhat related because some underlying economic factors reflecting the world's general

USING *THE WALL STREET JOURNAL*

GLOBAL STOCK MARKET QUOTATIONS

The recent performance of various stock markets is summarized each day in *The Wall Street Journal*, as shown here. For each stock market, the summary table provides the percentage change from the previous trading day, from one year ago, and from the beginning of the year. This table can be used to confirm that stock markets generally move in the same direction, but by different degrees. Much of the information in the indexes are from the U.S. perspective, meaning that they account for exchange rate adjustments over the period of concern. Notice that the table also summarizes the performance of a world stock index, which represents a weighted composite of various stock markets.

SOURCE: Reprinted by permission of *The Wall Street Journal* © 1994, Dow Jones & Company, Inc. All rights reserved worldwide.

DOW JONES WORLD STOCK INDEX

Monday, August 22, 1994

REGION/ COUNTRY	DJ EQUITY MARKET INDEX LOCAL CURRENCY	PCT. CHG.	IN U.S. DOLLARS								
			CLOSING INDEX	CHG.	PCT. CHG.	12-MO HIGH	12-MO LOW	12-MO CHG.	PCT. CHG.	FROM 12/31	PCT. CHG.
Americas			110.79	− 0.20	− 0.18	115.99	105.21	+ 1.11	+ 1.01	− 1.39	− 1.23
Canada	114.04	− 0.03	95.81	+ 0.10	+ 0.10	107.30	88.37	+ 2.94	+ 3.17	− 4.54	− 4.53
Mexico	194.02	+ 1.71	178.46	+ 4.10	+ 2.35	203.25	124.51	+ 45.57	+ 34.29	− 4.42	− 2.42
U.S.	437.48	− 0.26	437.48	− 1.16	− 0.26	456.27	416.31	+ 3.97	+ 0.92	− 4.71	− 1.07
Europe			119.72	+ 0.03	+ 0.03	122.60	106.36	+ 12.15	+ 11.30	+ 3.64	+ 3.13
Austria	110.89	− 1.17	110.12	− 0.72	− 0.65	111.50	93.56	+ 13.39	+ 13.84	+ 5.30	+ 5.06
Belgium	122.55	− 0.65	121.95	− 0.03	− 0.03	123.06	98.83	+ 17.77	+ 17.06	+ 10.41	+ 9.33
Denmark	104.74	− 0.96	102.47	− 0.27	− 0.26	107.35	85.32	+ 14.44	+ 16.40	+ 6.75	+ 7.05
Finland	231.56	+ 0.70	192.44	+ 3.36	+ 1.78	192.44	117.96	+ 59.91	+ 45.20	+ 53.77	+ 38.78
France	118.56	− 1.35	117.20	− 0.92	− 0.78	124.46	106.71	+ 7.00	+ 6.35	− 0.59	− 0.50
Germany	127.02	− 1.02	125.91	− 0.30	− 0.24	126.25	104.08	+ 19.54	+ 18.37	+ 6.97	+ 5.86
Ireland	142.51	− 0.25	118.67	+ 0.26	+ 0.22	125.99	97.84	+ 15.05	+ 14.52	+ 6.71	+ 6.00
Italy	155.17	+ 2.64	123.18	+ 3.92	+ 3.29	143.55	81.75	+ 12.52	+ 11.31	+ 24.07	+ 24.29
Netherlands	137.23	− 0.79	134.77	− 0.11	− 0.08	135.53	114.62	+ 19.57	+ 16.98	+ 9.03	+ 7.18
Norway	135.40	− 0.38	120.39	+ 0.36	+ 0.30	121.30	95.85	+ 21.12	+ 21.28	+ 17.11	+ 16.57
Spain	126.10	− 0.81	95.72	− 0.07	− 0.07	106.94	87.92	+ 5.21	+ 5.76	+ 0.84	+ 0.88
Sweden	154.32	− 0.38	113.49	+ 1.83	+ 1.64	122.77	94.26	+ 11.03	+ 10.77	+ 9.42	+ 9.05
Switzerland	152.81	− 0.88	160.85	− 0.50	− 0.31	172.92	131.44	+ 27.85	+ 20.94	+ 2.58	+ 1.63
United Kingdom	133.70	− 0.56	111.33	− 0.10	− 0.09	118.15	100.94	+ 6.87	+ 6.57	− 0.97	− 0.87
Asia/Pacific			127.83	+ 0.43	+ 0.34	128.84	98.67	+ 9.31	+ 7.86	+ 21.07	+ 19.74
Australia	120.94	+ 0.25	116.63	− 0.45	− 0.38	128.45	95.15	+ 16.63	+ 16.63	+ 3.34	+ 2.95
Hong Kong	214.87	+ 0.44	216.09	+ 0.96	+ 0.45	279.65	163.69	+ 46.31	+ 27.27	− 54.27	− 20.07
Indonesia	207.55	− 0.53	191.43	− 1.01	− 0.53	248.28	168.11	+ 18.29	+ 10.56	− 42.49	− 18.17
Japan	96.76	− 0.36	123.41	+ 0.50	+ 0.41	125.50	91.51	+ 6.58	+ 5.63	+ 27.70	+ 28.94
Malaysia	240.09	+ 0.67	256.17	+ 1.41	+ 0.55	284.09	176.10	+ 80.07	+ 45.47	− 13.82	− 5.12
New Zealand	141.92	+ 0.08	157.32	+ 0.27	+ 0.17	172.58	132.55	+ 18.10	+ 13.00	+ 5.80	+ 3.83
Singapore	159.85	− 1.46	172.58	− 2.44	− 1.39	184.75	132.48	+ 39.01	+ 29.20	− 6.64	− 3.71
Thailand	242.58	− 0.08	229.21	0.00	0.00	256.46	130.50	+ 93.46	+ 68.84	− 14.69	− 6.02
Asia/Pacific (ex. Japan)			174.42	+ 0.13	+ 0.08	199.98	134.44	+ 37.76	+ 27.63	− 19.18	− 9.90
World (ex. U.S.)			123.66	+ 0.31	+ 0.25	124.02	102.52	+ 9.93	+ 8.73	+ 13.14	+ 11.88
DJ WORLD STOCK INDEX			118.74	+ 0.08	+ 0.07	119.04	105.71	+ 6.58	+ 5.86	+ 7.66	+ 6.90

Indexes based on 6/30/82=100 for U.S., 12/31/91=100 for World.   ©1994 Dow Jones & Co. Inc., All Rights Reserved

financial condition may systematically affect all markets. To the degree that one country's economy can influence the economies of other countries, expectations about economies across countries may be somewhat similar. Thus, stock markets across countries may respond to some of the same expectations. Integration is an important concept because of its implications about benefits from interna-

EXHIBIT 10.8 Impact of the Crash on Four Stock Markets

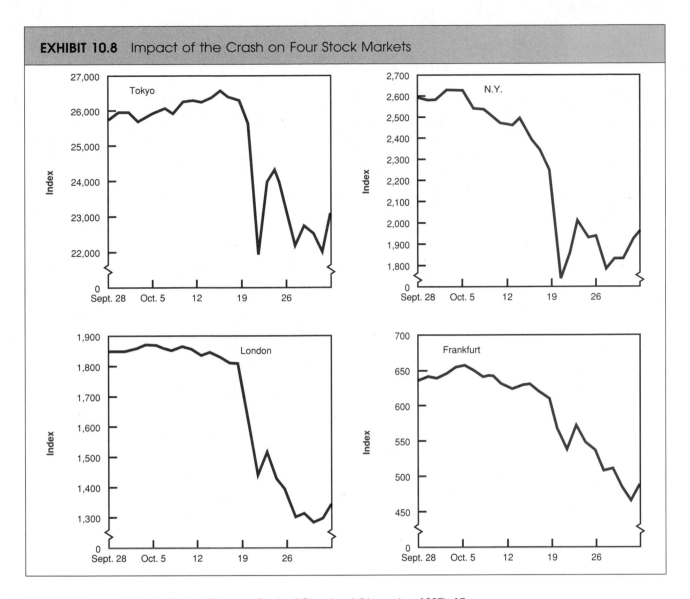

SOURCE: *Economic Trends,* Federal Reserve Bank of Cleveland (November 1987): 17.

tional diversification. A high degree of integration implies that stock returns of different countries would be affected by common factors. Therefore, the returns of stocks from various countries would move in tandem, allowing only modest benefits from international diversification.

INTEGRATION OF MARKETS DURING THE 1987 CRASH. Exhibit 10.8 compares the U.S. stock market movements to three foreign stock markets during October 1987. Although the U.S. market suffered a major decline, the other three markets were severely affected as well. The high correlation among country stock markets during the crash suggests that the underlying cause of the crash systematically affected all markets. Many institutional investors buy and sell stocks on numerous stock exchanges. As they anticipated a worldwide decline in stock prices, they liquidated some stocks from all markets rather than from just the U.S. market.

SUMMARY

- Organized stock exchanges are used to facilitate secondary market transactions. Members of the exchanges trade stock for their own accounts or for their clients. An over-the-counter exchange also exists, whereby stock transactions are executed through a telecommunications network.

- Some financial institutions obtain funding by issuing new stock in the stock markets. However, the dominant form of institutional participation in the stock market is in the secondary market, where financial institutions purchase and sell stock. Stock mutual funds, pension funds, and insurance companies are the major institutional investors in the stock market. Securities firms serve as brokers by matching up buyers and sellers in the stock market.

- Various models are used to value stocks. One popular model measures the present value of future expected dividends. A second model, known as the capital asset pricing model (CAPM), suggests that the return on a stock can vary from other stocks because of its degree of systematic risk. A third model, known as the arbitrage pricing model, suggests that return on a stock can vary from other stocks because it is dependent on the stock's systematic risk, as well as other factors (such as industry effects).

- Stock prices can be influenced by economic factors such as interest rates, economic growth, inflation, and the strength of the dollar. Other factors that change expectations of economic conditions can also affect stock prices.

QUESTIONS

1. Explain the rights of common shareholders that are not available to other individuals.

2. What is the danger of issuing too much stock?

3. Explain why a firm is normally perceived to exhibit higher risk after experiencing a leveraged buyout (LBO).

4. In the movie *Wall Street,* Bud Fox is a broker who conducts trades for Gordan Gekko's firm. Gekko purchases shares of firms he believes are undervalued. Various parts of the movie offer excellent examples of concepts discussed in this chapter.
   a. Bud Fox makes the comment to Gordon Gekko that a firm's break-up value is twice its market price. What is Fox suggesting in this statement? How would employees of the firm respond to Fox's statement?
   b. Once Bud Fox informs Gordon Gekko that Mr. Wildman is secretly planning to acquire a target firm in Pennsylvania, Gekko tells Bud to buy a large amount of this stock. Why?
   c. Gordon Gekko states, "Wonder why [mutual] fund managers can't beat the S&P 500? Because they are sheep." What is Gekko's point? How does it relate to market efficiency?

5. Explain the role of investment banking firms during a public placement of stock.

6. Are organized stock exchanges used to place newly issued stock? Explain.

7. Explain the difference between weak-form, semistrong-form, and strong-form efficient market hypotheses. Which hypothesis is most difficult to test? Which is most likely to be rejected?

8. Explain how to test weak-form efficiency in the stock market.

9. At the time a management group of RJR Nabisco initially considered engaging in an LBO, RJR's stock price was less than $70 per share. Ultimately, RJR was acquired by the firm Kohlberg, Kravis, and Roberts (KKR) for about $108 per share. Does the large discrepancy between the stock price before an acquisition was considered versus after the acquisition mean that RJR's stock price was initially undervalued? If so, does this imply that the market was inefficient?

10. A consulting firm was hired to determine whether a particular trading strategy could generate abnormal returns. The strategy involved taking positions based on recent historical movements in stock prices. The strategy did not achieve abnormal returns. Consequently, the consulting firm concluded that the stock market is weak-form efficient. Do you agree? Explain.

11. How do you think the U.S. stock prices would react to expectations of a weak dollar, assuming that inflation was not a major concern? What if inflation was a major concern?

12. If you expected the dollar to strengthen, would you expect stock returns of U.S. exporting companies or importing companies to be higher? Why?

13. Would foreign investors find U.S. stocks more attractive if they expected the dollar to strengthen or weaken? Explain.

14. How have international mutual funds (IMFs) increased the degree of international integration of capital markets among countries?

15. Describe the pattern in the volume of foreign investment in U.S. stocks.

16. Explain ADRs.

17. In the 1990s, many stock portfolio managers closely monitored the U.S. trade deficit figures. When the trade deficit was announced to be higher than expected, the stock market often declined significantly.

    a. Why might the market react in such a manner, even when the trade figures announced have already occurred?
    b. In some periods, the announced trade deficit was large, but the market did not respond. Offer a possible explanation for this lack of response.

18. Stock prices seem to be more volatile since the crash than they were before the crash. Why? Do you think it is because economic conditions are more volatile, or because investors now react more than before to financial news?

19. Briefly describe the conclusion reached by Furbush and by Roll from their studies of the relationship between the intensity of program trading and the magnitude of the declines in stock prices during the stock market crash.

20. Assume that the expected inflation has just been revised upward by the market. Would the required return by investors who invest in stocks be affected? Explain.

PROBLEMS

1. Assume that Vogl stock is priced at $50 per share and pays a dividend of $1 per share. Investors purchased the stock on margin, paying $30 per share and borrowing the remainder from the brokerage firm at 10 percent annualized. If, after one year, the stock is sold at a price of $60 per share, what is the return to the investors?

2. Assume that Duever stock is priced at $80 per share and pays a dividend of $2 per share. Investors purchased the stock on margin, paying $50 per share and borrowing the remainder from the brokerage firm at 12 percent annualized. If, after one year, the stock is sold at a price of $90 per share, what is the return to the investors?

3. Assume the following information over a five-year period:
   - Average risk-free rate = 6%
   - Average return for Crane stock = 11%
   - Average return for Load stock = 14%
   - Standard deviation of Crane stock returns = 2%
   - Standard deviation of Load stock returns = 4%
   - Beta of Crane stock = 0.8
   - Beta of Load stock = 1.1

   Using the information in appendix 10, determine which stock has higher risk-adjusted returns when using the Sharpe Index. Which stock has higher risk-adjusted returns when using the Treynor Index? Show your work.

4. Assume Mess stock has a beta of 1.2. If the risk-free rate is 7 percent and the market return is 10 percent, what is the expected return on Mess stock?

CASE APPLICATION: STOCK MARKET RESPONSE TO ECONOMIC NEWS

Long-Awaited Correction Is Under Way, Some Argue

Steven E. Levingston

Stock market investors got a severe case of the jitters last week. The Dow Jones Industrial Average shot higher in early trading on several days, only to plummet later in those sessions. Although the industrial average ended the week just marginally lower and barely more than 2% below its all-time high, some analysts are now proclaiming that the long-awaited stockmarket correction has arrived.

The culprit for the market's downturn, these analysts say, is the recent rise in both short and long-term interest rates and fears that further increases are coming.

More sanguine forecasters argue, however, that given the health of the economy and the low starting point for the rise in rates, a full-blown correction isn't yet in the cards. And certainly the bull market remains intact, they contend.

Outlook for Rates

Among the pessimists, Joseph McAlinden, market strategist at Dillon Read, says the latest market declines reflect investors' realization that interest rates have been rising for three months and will continue to climb.

"I've been saying for some time that I expect a 15% correction on the Dow from its high," says Mr. McAlinden. "You never really know when these things begin, but at this point the evidence is pretty overwhelming we're into it."

Mr. McAlinden notes that long-term interest rates hit their low in October and have been climbing ever since. He says that inflation tends to hit its low roughly about four months after long rates, suggesting that last week's reassuring report on consumer prices may have been the low for inflation. With inflation rising, according to Mr. McAlinden's scenario, interest rates will climb, too, roiling the stock market. He sees the correction lasting until the 1994 fourth quarter.

Market's Vulnerability

"Stocks are even more vulnerable to the prospect of rising rates because the stock market's climb has been driven for so long by falling rates," he says.

Gail Dudack, market strategist at S. G. Warburg, is predicting a 10% decline in stock prices. She has been lowering her holdings of stock slightly since late December and now has 10% of her portfolio in cash. Last week's stock market performance only confirmed her view that the correction is under way.

"Everybody has been talking about us being in the best of all worlds and so much of that has been factored into the market," she says. "That has left investors wide open for disappointment."

Ms. Dudack argues that cash coming into the market isn't likely to remain at the high levels of recent years. As cash infusions into stocks moderate, there will be less fuel to drive prices higher. "The public has more stocks as a percentage of their portfolios than they've

had in 20 years and that cycle is maturing," she says.

Smaller Drop Is Predicted

A. C. Moore, portfolio manager and strategist at Argus Investment Management in Santa Barbara, Calif., sees a downturn of smaller proportions, amounting to no more than a 6% decline from the Dow's high. Mr. Moore sees evidence of the decline in several technical indicators, among them the poor ratio of stocks hitting new highs to those failing to new lows.

He remains upbeat about the overall trend in stock prices, partly because of the interest-rate environment. He is less worried than many analysts that the stock market will crack because of further boosts in short-term interest rates.

"The Federal Reserve has been more stimulative over the last several years than it has ever been since World War II," Mr. Moore says. "So there's a lot of room for the Fed to increase rates without threatening the attractiveness of common stocks."

It may be premature to proclaim the start of a stock market correction, says Joseph Battipaglia, chief investment strategist at Gruntal & Co. He contends that as long as short-term interest rates rise gradually the market can continue to climb. But another Fed rate boost following closely on the last would further rattle the stock market, he says.

Continued

CASE APPLICATION: STOCK MARKET RESPONSE TO ECONOMIC NEWS

Continued

"The question is whether or not the Fed moves again soon," he asserts. "If it's sooner rather than later, that suggests the Fed has uncovered some inflation problem that it's trying to correct."

But Mr. Battipaglia believes the inflation worries are overdone. Indeed, even with the concerns on Friday, gold and oil prices fell, suggesting inflation may not be the bogeyman pessimists fear. Mr. Battipaglia expects stock prices to resume their upward trend, with the Dow industrials breaking through the 4000 level this year. "Our strategy is to remain invested," he says. "This bull market is not over."

Nothing to Worry About

The current stock market jitters are nothing more than the usual experience after a Fed rate increase and nothing to worry about, says Don Hays, director of investment strategy at Wheat, First Securities/Butcher & Singer in Richmond, Va. Mr. Hays argues that it was expected that after the rate increase most analysts

would begin predicting higher inflation, higher interest rates and a sharp correction.

"All this has encouraged my enthusiasm for stocks, not diminished it," Mr. Hays says. "Within the next week or two the stock market will get back on a persistent uptrend based on improving earnings."

Mr. Hays dismisses the doomsayers announcing the start of a correction. "This isn't a correction; it's a pause maybe," he says. "When you have monetary conditions like this you never have a correction of more than 4% and this is barely 2%."

Edward Yardeni, chief economist at C. J. Lawrence, urges investors to keep their eye on the economic fundamentals. He says the sterling consumer price report last week combined with the recovery's continued strength add up to a strong positive environment for stocks.

"This, too, will pass—the fundamentals will eventually win out," Mr. Yardeni adds. "In the long term, I'm still very bullish. The Dow will be going over

4000 within months and moving higher from there." . . .

QUESTIONS

1. Interpret the statement that the "stock market's climb has been driven for so long by falling [interest] rates."

2. Explain why the Federal Reserve actions are linked with the expectations of future stock prices.

3. A market strategist of S. G. Warburg stated that cash infusion into stocks will moderate, causing less upward pressure on stock prices. Explain the economic conditions that caused this opinion.

PROJECT

1. **Assessing Stock Market Movements**
   Review the section "Abreast of the Market" in *The Wall Street Journal* (listed in the index on the first page) for the past five trading days. For each day, explain whether the market went up or down and identify the factors contributing to the change.

	DID THE STOCK MARKET RISE OR FALL? BY HOW MUCH?	REASONS GIVEN FOR THE RISE OR FALL IN THE STOCK MARKET
1 day ago		
2 days ago		
3 days ago		
4 days ago		
5 days ago		

REFERENCES

Asquith, Paul. "Merger Bids, Uncertainty, and Stockholder Returns." *Journal of Financial Economics* (April 1983): 51–83.

Barrett, W. Brian, Andrea Heuson, Robert Kolb, and Gabriele Schropp. "The Adjustment of Stock Prices to Completely Unanticipated Events." *Financial Review* (November 1987): 345–354.

Benesh, Gary, and Robert Pari. "Performance of Stocks Recommended on the Basis of Insider Trading Activity." *Financial Review* (February 1987): 145–158.

Carter, Richard, and Steven Manaster. "Initial Public Offerings and Underwriter Reputation." *Journal of Finance* (September 1990): 1045–1068.

Chalk, Andrew J., and John W. Pearry III. "Initial Public Offerings: Daily Returns, Offering Types and the Price Effect." *Financial Analysts Journal* (September–October 1987): 65–69.

Chan, Louis K. C., and Josef Lakonishok. "Are the Reports of Beta's Death Premature?" *Journal of Portfolio Management* (Summer 1993): 51–62.

Cho, D. Chinhyung, and William Taylor. "The Seasonal Stability of the Factor Structure of Stock Returns." *Journal of Finance* (December 1987): 1195–1212.

Cutler, David M., Jams M. Poterba, and Lawrence H. Summers. "What Moves Stock Prices?" *Journal of Portfolio Management* (Spring 1989): 4–12.

DeBondt, Werner F. M., and Richard Thaler. "Further Evidence on Investor Overreaction and Stock Market Seasonability." *Journal of Finance* (July 1987): 557–581.

Dyl, Edward A., and John D. Schatzberg. "Did Joe Montana Save the Stock Market?" *Financial Analysts Journal* (September–October 1989): 4–5.

Edelman, Richard B., and H. Kent Baker. "Liquidity and Stock Exchange Listing." *Financial Review* (May 1990): 231–250.

Fama, Eugene F., and Kenneth R. French. "The Cross-Section of Expected Stock Returns." *Journal of Finance* (June 1992): 427–465.

Furbush, Dean. "Program Trading and Price Movement: Evidence from the October 1987 Market Crash." *Financial Management* (Autumn 1989): 68–83.

Gerard, Bruno, and Nanda Vikram. "Trading and Manipulation Around Seasoned Equity Offerings." *Journal of Finance* (March 1993): 213–245.

Hardouvelis, Gikas, and Steve Peristiani. "Do Margin Requirements Matter? Evidence from U.S. and Japanese Stock Markets." *FRBNY Quarterly Review* (Winter 1989–90): 16–34.

Hasbrouck, Joel, and George Sofianos. "The Trades of Market Makers: An Empirical Analysis of NYSE Specialists." *Journal of Finance* (December 1993): 1565–1593.

Kim, Moon. "Macro-Economic Factors and Stock Returns." *Journal of Financial Research* (Summer 1987): 87–98.

Lintner, John. "The Valuation of Risk Assets and Selection of Risky Investments in Stock Portfolios and Capital Budgets." *Review of Economics and Statistics* (February 1965): 13–37.

Madura, Jeff. "Influence of Foreign Markets on Multinational Stocks: Implications for Investors." *International Review of Economics and Business* (October–November 1989): 1009–1018.

⸻. "International Portfolio Construction." *Journal of Business Research* (Spring 1985): 87–95.

Madura, Jeff, and Wm. R. McDaniel. "Impact of the 1987 Crash on Gains from International Diversification." *Journal of International Finance* (Fall 1989): 23–35.

Madura, Jeff, and Wallace Reiff. "A Hedge Strategy for International Portfolios." *Journal of Portfolio Management* (Fall 1985): 70–74.

Markowitz, Harry. "Portfolio Selection." *Journal of Finance* (March 1952): 77–91.

Mossin, Jan. "Equilibrium in a Capital Asset Market." *Econometrica* (October 1966): 768–783.

Netter, Jeffry M., and Mark L. Mitchell. "Stock Repurchase Announcements and Insider Transactions after the October 1987 Stock Market Crash." *Financial Management* (Autumn 1989): 84–96.

Roll, Richard. "R^2." *Journal of Finance* (July 1988): 541–566.

Roll, Richard. "The International Crash of October 1987." *Financial Analysts Journal* (October 1988): 19–35.

Rozeff, Michael, and Mir A. Zaman. "Market Efficiency and Insider Trading: New Evidence." *Journal of Business* (January 1988): 25–44.

Saunders, Anthony. "Why Are So Many New Stock Issues Underpriced?" *Business Review*, Federal Reserve Bank of Philadelphia (March/April 1990): 3–12.

Schiller, Robert. "Do Stock Prices Move Too Much to Be Justified by Subsequent Dividends?" *American Economic Review* (June 1981): 421–436.

Schwert, G. William. "Why Does Stock Market Volatility Change Over Time?" *Journal of Finance* (December 1989): 1115–1159.

Shanken, Jay. "The Current State of the Arbitrage Pricing Theory." *Journal of Finance* (September 1992): 1569–1574.

Sharpe, William F. "Capital Asset Prices: A Theory of Market Equilibrium under Conditions of Risk." *Journal of Finance* (September 1964): 425–442.

Thomas, Lee R. III. "Currency Risks in International Equity Portfolios." *Financial Analysts Journal* (March/April 1988): 68–70.

EVALUATION OF STOCK PERFORMANCE

The performance of individual stocks or particular stock portfolios can be assessed by measuring their risk-adjusted returns. One common proxy for risk is the beta, which measures sensitivity of the stock's returns to market returns. This can be computed from historical data using the following regression model:

$$R_j = B_0 + B_1 R_m + u$$

where
R_j = return of stock j

R_m = market return

B_0 = intercept

B_1 = regression coefficient that serves as an estimate of beta

u = error term

An alternative risk measure of a stock is the standard deviation of the stock's historical returns. Both forms of risk measure the variability of stocks. The beta accounts only for the variability that is systematically related to market returns, often referred to as **systematic risk.** This measure of risk would be most appropriate if any unsystematic variability were diversified away. The standard deviation measures total variability of a stock's returns.

Once a stock's risk is measured, its risk-adjusted returns can be determined by consolidating the return and the risk measurement. There are two commonly used techniques to measure risk-adjusted returns:

- Sharpe Index (reward-to-variability ratio)
- Treynor Index (reward-to-systematic risk ratio)

SHARPE INDEX

If total variability is thought to be the appropriate measure of risk, a stock's risk-adjusted returns can be determined by the reward-to-variability ratio (also called the **Sharpe Index**), computed as

$$\text{Sharpe Index} = \frac{\overline{R} - \overline{R}_f}{\sigma}$$

where

$\overline{R}$ = average return on the stock

$\overline{R}_f$ = average risk-free rate

σ = standard deviation of the stock's returns

The higher the stock's mean return is relative to the mean risk-free rate and the lower the standard deviation, the higher the Sharpe Index. This index measures the excess return above the risk-free rate per unit of risk.

Assume the following information for two stocks:

- Average return for Sooner stock = 16%
- Average return for Longhorn stock = 14%
- Average risk-free rate = 10%
- Standard deviation of Sooner stock returns = 15%
- Standard deviation of Longhorn stock returns = 8%

$$\text{Sharpe Index for Sooner stock} = \frac{16\% - 10\%}{15\%}$$

$$= .40$$

$$\text{Sharpe Index for Longhorn stock} = \frac{14\% - 10\%}{8\%}$$

$$= .50$$

Even though Sooner stock had a higher average percentage return, Longhorn stock had a higher performance because of its lower risk. If a stock had an average return that was less than the average risk-free rate, the Sharpe index for that stock would be negative.

TREYNOR INDEX

If beta is thought to be the most appropriate type of risk, a stock's risk-adjusted returns can be determined by the **Treynor Index,** computed as

$$\text{Treynor Index} = \frac{\overline{R} - \overline{R}_f}{B}$$

where B = the stock's beta. The Treynor Index is similar to the Sharpe Index, except that it uses beta rather than standard deviation to measure the stock's risk. The higher the Treynor Index, the higher the return relative to the risk-free rate, per unit of risk.

Reconsider the information provided earlier on Sooner stock and Longhorn stock. Using this information, and assuming that Sooner's stock beta = 1.2 while Longhorn's beta = 1.0, the Treynor Index is computed for each stock as follows:

$$\text{Treynor Index for Sooner stock} = \frac{16\% - 10\%}{1.2}$$

$$= .05$$

$$\text{Treynor Index for Longhorn stock} = \frac{14\% - 10\%}{1.0}$$
$$= .04$$

Based on the Treynor Index, Sooner stock had higher performance. The choice of the fund with higher performance depends on the preferred measure of risk and therefore on the preferred index. In some cases, the indexes will lead to the same results. As with the Sharpe Index, the Treynor Index is negative for a stock whose average return is less than the average risk-free rate.

ASSET ALLOCATION_____

This problem requires an understanding of how economic conditions influence interest rates and security prices (Chapters 2, 3, 4, 7, 8, and 10).

As a personal financial planner, one of your tasks is to prescribe the allocation of available funds across money market securities, bonds, and stocks. Your philosophy is to take positions in securities that will benefit most from your forecasted changes in economic conditions. As a result of a recent event in Japan, you expect that in the next month Japanese investors will reduce their investment in U.S. Treasury securities, as they will instead invest most of their funds in Japanese securities. This shift in funds is expected to persist for at least a few years. You believe this single event will have a major effect on economic factors in the United States, such as interest rates, exchange rates, and economic growth within the next month. Because the prices of securities in the United States are affected by these economic factors, you must determine how to revise your prescribed allocation of funds across securities.

QUESTIONS

a. How will U.S. interest rates be directly affected by the event (holding other factors equal)?

b. How will economic growth in the United States be affected by the event? How might this influence the values of securities?

c. Assume that day-to-day exchange rate movements are dictated primarily by the flow of funds between countries, especially international bond and money market transactions. How will exchange rates be affected by possible changes in the international flow of funds that are caused by the event?

d. Using your answer to (a) only, explain how prices of U.S. money market securities, bonds, and stocks would be affected.

e. Now use your answer to (b) along with your answer to (a) to assess the impact on security prices. Would prices of risky securities be affected more or less than those of risk-free securities with a similar maturity? Why?

f. Based on your answer to (c), explain how the impact of the event on corporate performance could vary across U.S. firms.

g. Assume that for diversification purposes, you prescribe that at least 20 percent of an investor's funds should be allocated to money market securities, to bonds, and to stocks. That allows you to allocate the remaining 40 percent however you desire across those securities. Based on all the information you have about the event, prescribe the proper allocation of funds across the three types of U.S. securities. (Assume that the entire investment will be concentrated in U.S. securities.) Defend your prescription.

h. Would you recommend high-risk or low-risk money market securities? Would you recommend high-risk or low-risk bonds? Why?

i. What types of stocks would you recommend? Why?

j. Assume that you would consider recommending as much as 20 percent of the funds to be invested in foreign securities. Revise your prescription to include foreign securities if you desire (identify the type of security and the country).

k. If the event of concern increased the demand instead of reducing the supply of loanable funds in the United States, would the assessment of future interest rates be different? What about the general assessment of economic conditions? What about the general assessment of bond prices? What about the general assessment of stock prices?

PART 4

DERIVATIVE SECURITY MARKETS

Derivatives are financial contracts whose values are derived from the values of underlying assets. They are widely used to speculate on future expectations or to reduce a security portfolio's risk. The chapters in Part Four focus on derivative security markets. Each of these chapters explains how institutional portfolio managers and speculators use these markets. Many financial market participants simultaneously use all these markets, as is emphasized throughout the chapters.

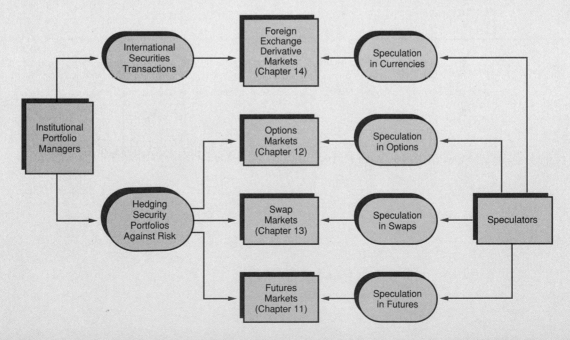

CHAPTER 11

FINANCIAL FUTURES MARKETS

In recent years, financial futures markets have received much attention because of their potential to generate large returns to speculators and their high degree of risk. However, these markets can also be used to reduce the risk of financial institutions and other corporations.

The specific objectives of this chapter are to:

- explain how financial futures contracts are valued,
- explain how interest rate futures contracts are used to speculate or hedge, based on anticipated interest rate movements,
- explain how stock index futures contracts are used to speculate or hedge, based on anticipated stock price movements, and
- describe how financial institutions participate in the financial futures markets.

BACKGROUND ON FINANCIAL FUTURES

A **financial futures contract** is a standardized agreement to deliver or receive a specified amount of a specified financial instrument at a specified price and date. The buyer of a financial futures contract buys the financial instrument, while the seller of a financial futures contract delivers the instrument for the specified price. Financial futures contracts are traded on organized exchanges, which establish and enforce rules for such trading.

The operations of financial futures exchanges are regulated by the Commodity Futures Trading Commission (CFTC). The CFTC approves futures contracts before they can be listed by futures exchanges, and imposes laws to prevent unfair trading practices.

Many of the popular financial futures contracts are on debt securities such as Treasury bills, Treasury notes, Treasury bonds, and Eurodollar CDs. These contracts are referred to as **interest rate futures.** Alternatively, there are also financial futures contracts on stock indexes, which are referred to as **stock index futures.** For each type of contract, the settlement dates at which delivery would occur are in March, June, September, and December. Most financial futures contracts in the U.S. are traded on the Chicago Board of Trade or the Chicago Mercantile Exchange.

Only the members of a futures exchange can engage in futures transactions on the exchange floor, unless such privileges have been leased to someone else. The purchase of a seat on the exchange entitles membership. The price of a seat on any exchange fluctuates over time, in accordance with the demand for seats and supply of seats for sale.

Members of a futures exchange can be classified as either **commission brokers** (also called floor brokers) or **floor traders.** Floor brokers execute orders for their customers. Many of them are employees of brokerage firms, while others work independently. Floor traders (also called **locals**) trade futures contracts for their own account.

Steps Involved in Trading Futures

Customers who desire to buy or sell futures contracts call brokerage firms that execute futures transactions. Accounts are opened for these customers at the brokerage firms. Customers are required by the futures exchange to establish a margin deposit with their respective brokers before the transaction can be executed. This so-called **initial margin** is typically between 5 percent and 18 percent of a futures contract's full value. Brokers commonly require margin requirements above those established by the exchanges. As the futures contract price changes on a daily basis, its value is "marked to market," or revised to reflect the prevailing conditions. When the contract's value moves in an unfavorable direction, participants in futures contracts receive a **margin call** from the broker, requiring additional margin money to satisfy what is called the **maintenance margin.** These margin requirements reduce the risk that participants will later default on their obligations.

Orders requested by customers are communicated to telephone stations located near the trading floor of the futures exchange. The floor brokers accommodate these orders. Each type of financial futures contract is traded in a particular location on the trading floor. The floor brokers make their offers to trade by open outcry, in which they specify the quantity of contracts they wish to buy or sell. Other floor brokers and traders interested in trading the particular type of futures contract can respond to the open outcry. For every buyer of a futures contract, there is a corresponding seller. A futures exchange facilitates the trading process but does not take buy or sell positions on the futures contracts. When an agreement between two traders on the trading floor is reached, each trader documents the specifics of the agreement (including the price), and the information is transmitted to the customers.

If there are more traders with buy offers than sell offers for a particular financial futures contract, the futures price will rise until this imbalance is removed. Price changes on financial futures contracts are indicated on quotation tickers.

A clearinghouse facilitates the trading process by recording all transactions and guaranteeing timely payments on futures contracts. This precludes the need for a purchaser of a futures contract to check the creditworthiness of the contract seller. In fact, purchasers of contracts do not even know who the sellers are, and vice versa. The clearinghouse also supervises the delivery of contracts as of settlement date.

Purpose of Trading Financial Futures

Financial futures are traded to either speculate on prices of securities or hedge existing exposure to security price movements. The **speculators** in financial futures markets take positions to profit from expected changes in price of futures contracts over time. Other participants, referred to as **hedgers,** take positions to reduce their exposure to future movements in interest rates or stock prices.

Many hedgers who maintain large portfolios of stocks or bonds take a futures position to hedge their risk. Speculators commonly take the opposite position and therefore serve as the counterparty on many futures transactions. Thus, speculators provide liquidity to the futures market.

Speculators in futures can be classified according to their methods. **Day traders** normally close out their futures positions on the same day that the positions were initiated. They attempt to capitalize on price movements during a single day. Conversely, **position traders** maintain the futures positions that they initiate for longer periods of time (for weeks or months) and therefore attempt to capitalize on expected price movements over a longer time horizon.

INTERPRETING FINANCIAL FUTURES TABLES

Prices of interest rate futures contracts vary from day to day and are reported in the financial pages of newspapers. *The Wall Street Journal* provides a comprehensive summary of trading activity on various financial futures contracts. Assume the information in Exhibit 11.1 is disclosed on a particular day in May 1997, which refers to the previous trading day. From this exhibit, the futures contract specifying delivery of the Treasury bills for June opened at 94.00 (per $100 par value). The highest trading price for the day was 94.26, while the low was 94.00, with a closing price (settle price in Column 5) of 94.20 at the end of the day. The change in Column 6 reflects the difference between settle price and the quoted settle price on the previous trading day. The reported discount in Column 7 is based on the settle price and represents the percentage difference between the purchase price and par value. The change in the discount in Column 8 represents the difference between quoted discount and the discount on the previous day. The open interest in Column 9 represents the number of outstanding futures contracts for the settlement date of concern.

Exhibit 11.1 provides information for T-bill futures contracts with four different settlement months. Once the June settlement date passes, the other months would be moved up one row in the table, and information on T-bill futures with a settlement date for the following June would be shown in the fourth row.

EXHIBIT 11.1 Example of Treasury Bill Futures Quotations

TREASURY BILL FUTURES

	(1)	(2)	(3)	(4)	(5)	(6)	(7)	(8)	(9)
							Discount		
		Open	High	Low	Settle	Change	Settle	Change	Open Interest
June 1997		94.00	94.26	94.00	94.20	+.30	5.80	−.30	16,000
Sept 1997		93.80	94.05	93.80	94.05	+.28	5.95	−.28	2,519
Dec 1997		93.62	93.79	93.62	93.75	+.24	6.25	−.24	287
March 1998		93.45	93.60	93.45	93.60	+.23	6.40	−.23	206

Futures on Treasury bonds and notes are also available and can be used for hedging portfolio positions or for speculation. Specific characteristics of these contracts are disclosed in Exhibit 11.2. Both Treasury bond and note futures traded on the Chicago Board of Trade (CBT) represent a face value of $100,000, which is substantially less than the $1,000,000 face value of securities underlying the T-bill futures contracts.

EXHIBIT 11.2 Characteristics of Treasury Bond and Note Futures Traded on the Chicago Board of Trade (CBT)

CHARACTERISTIC OF FUTURES CONTRACT	U.S. TREASURY BOND FUTURES	U.S. TREASURY NOTE FUTURES
Size	$100,000 face value.	$100,000 face value.
Deliverable grade	U.S. Treasury bonds maturing at least 15 years from date of delivery if not callable; coupon rate is 8%.	U.S. Treasury notes maturing at least 6½ years but not more than 10 years from the first day of the delivery month; coupon rate is 8%.
Price quotation	In points ($1,000) and thirty-seconds of a point.	In points ($1,000) and thirty-seconds of a point.
Minimum price fluctutation	One thirty-second (1/32) of a point, or $31.25 per contract.	One thirty-second (1/32) of a point, or $31.25 per contract.
Daily trading limits	Three points ($3,000) per contract above or below the previous day's settlement price.	Three points ($3,000) per contract above or below the previous day's settlement price.
Settlement months	March, June, September, December.	March, June, September, December.

VALUATION OF FINANCIAL FUTURES

As the market price of the financial asset represented by the financial futures contract changes, so will the value of the contract. For example, if the prices of Treasury bonds rise, the value of an existing Treasury bond futures contract should rise because the contract has locked in the price at which Treasury bonds can be purchased.

The price of any financial futures contract generally reflects the expected price of the underlying security (or index) as of the settlement date. Thus, any factors that influence that expected value should influence the current prices of financial futures. A primary factor is the current price of the underlying security (or index), which normally serves as a somewhat useful indicator of the future price. In addition, some information about economic or market conditions may influence the futures price even if it does not affect the current price. For example, a particular regulatory event anticipated six months from now could possibly affect the futures price even if it does not affect the price of the underlying security. Thus, the futures price is mainly a function of the prevailing price of the underlying security plus an expected adjustment in that price by the settlement date. Changes in the futures price should occur in response to either changes in the prevailing price or changes in the expected adjustment in that price by the settlement date.

Another factor that influences the futures price is the opportunity cost (or benefits) involved in a futures contract rather than owning the underlying security. An investor who purchases stock index futures rather than the stocks themselves does not receive the dividends. By itself, this factor would cause the stock index futures to be priced lower than the stocks themselves. However, the investor's initial investment is much smaller when purchasing the stock index futures, which may allow the investor to generate interest income on the remaining funds. By itself, this factor would cause the stock index futures to be priced higher than the stocks themselves. When considering both factors, the effects are somewhat offsetting.

SPECULATING WITH INTEREST RATE FUTURES

The use of interest rate futures for speculating can be explained with the following example. In February, Jim Sanders forecasts that interest rates will decrease over the next month. If his expectation is correct, the market value of Treasury bills should increase. Sanders calls a broker and requests the purchase of a Treasury bill futures contract. Assume that the price of the T-bill futures contract purchased was 94.00 (a 6 percent discount), and the price of T-bills as of the March settlement date is 94.90 (a 5.1 percent discount). Sanders could accept delivery of the T-bills and sell them for more than he purchased them for. Because T-bill futures represent $1 million of par value, the nominal profit from this speculative strategy is:

Selling Price	$949,000	(94.90% of $1,000,000)
− Purchase Price	− $940,000	(94.00% of $1,000,000)
= Profit	$9,000	(0.90% of $1,000,000)

In this example, Sanders benefited from his speculative strategy because interest rates declined from the time the futures position was taken until the settlement date. If interest rates had risen over this period, the price of T-bills as of the settlement date would have been below 94.00 (reflecting a discount above 6 percent), and Sanders would have incurred a loss. For example, if the price of T-bills as of the March settlement date was 92.50 (representing a discount of 7.5 percent), the nominal profit from this speculative strategy is:

Selling Price	$925,000	(92.50% of $1,000,000)
− Purchase Price	− $940,000	(94.00% of $1,000,000)
= Profit	$15,000	(1.50% of $1,000,000)

If Sanders had, as of February, anticipated that interest rates would rise by March, he would have sold a Treasury bill futures contract with a March settlement date, obligating him to provide Treasury bills to the purchaser as of the delivery date. If Treasury bill prices had actually declined by March, Sanders would have been able to obtain Treasury bills at a lower market price in March than what he was obligated to sell those bills for. Again, there is always the risk that interest rates (and therefore Treasury bill prices) will move contrary to expectations. In such an event, Sanders would have paid a higher market price for the Treasury bills than what he could sell them for.

The potential payoffs from trading futures contracts are illustrated in Exhibit 11.3. The left graph represents a purchaser of futures, while the right graph represents a seller of futures. The S labeled on each graph represents the initial price at which a futures position is created. The points along the horizontal axis represent the market value of the securities represented by futures contract as of the delivery date. The maximum possible loss when purchasing futures is the amount to be paid for the securities, yet this loss would occur only if the market value of the securities became zero. The amount of gain (or loss) to a speculator

EXHIBIT 11.3 Potential Payoffs from Speculating in Financial Futures

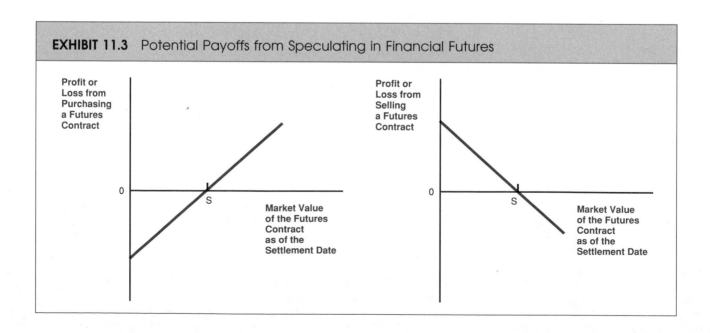

who initially purchased futures would equal the loss (or gain) to a speculator who initially sold futures on the same date (assuming zero transaction costs).

CLOSING OUT THE FUTURES POSITION

Most buyers and sellers of financial futures contracts do not actually make or accept delivery of the financial instrument, but rather offset their positions by the settlement date. For example, speculators who purchased Treasury bond futures contracts could sell similar futures contracts by the settlement date. Because they now own a contract to receive and a contract to deliver, the obligations net out. The gain or loss from involvement in the futures positions depends on the futures price at the time of the purchase versus the futures price at the time of the sale. If the price of the securities represented by the futures contract has risen over the period of concern, speculators who initially purchased Treasury bond futures would likely have paid a lower futures price than what they can sell the futures contract for. Thus, a positive gain would have resulted, and the size of the gain would depend on the degree of movement in prices of the securities underlying the contract.

Consider an opposite situation (referred to as a "short" position) where the sale of futures was followed by a purchase of futures a few months later in order to offset the initial short position. If security prices rose over this period, the earlier contract to sell futures would be priced lower than the later contract to purchase futures. Thus, a loss would have been incurred.

As an example of taking an offsetting position, assume the futures contract on Treasury bonds was purchased by a speculator at a price of 90–00. One month later, the same futures contract is sold in order to close out the position. At this time, the futures contract specifies 92–10, or 92 and 10/32nds percent of the par value as the price. Given that the futures contract on Treasury bonds specifies a par value of $100,000, the nominal profit is:

Selling Price	$92,312	(92 and 10/32% of $100,000)
− Purchase Price	− $90,000	(90.00% of $100,000)
= Profit	$2,312	(2 and 10/32% of $100,000)

If the initial position was a sale of the futures contract, a purchase of that same type of contract would close out the position. For example, assume a speculator took an initial short position. Using the numbers in the previous example, a loss of $2,312 (ignoring transaction costs) would result from closing out the short position one month later. A position would be closed out at a loss by participants who expect that a larger loss will occur if the position is not closed out. If the short position is not closed out before the settlement date, the investor assuming that position is obligated to deliver the securities underlying the futures contract at that time.

It has been estimated that only 2 percent of all futures contracts actually involve delivery, yet this does not reduce the effectiveness of futures contracts for speculation or hedging. Because the contract prices move with the financial instrument representing the contract, an offsetting position at the settlement date generates the same gain or loss as if the instrument were delivered.

HEDGING WITH INTEREST RATE FUTURES

Financial institutions can classify their assets and liabilities by the sensitivity of their market value to interest rate movements. The difference between their volume of rate-sensitive assets and rate-sensitive liabilities represents their exposure to interest rate risk. Over the long run, they may attempt to restructure their assets or liabilities to balance the degree of rate sensitivity. Yet, restructuring the balance sheet takes time. In the short run, they may consider using financial futures to hedge their exposure to interest rate movements. A variety of financial institutions use financial futures to hedge their interest rate risk, including mortgage companies, securities dealers, commercial banks, savings institutions, pension funds, and insurance companies.

As financial institutions were adversely affected by rising interest rates in 1980, they began to use Treasury bond futures to hedge against interest rate risk. During the late 1980s and early 1990s, Treasury bond futures became even more popular for hedging.

Using Interest Rate Futures to Create a Short Hedge

The most common use of interest rate futures by financial institutions is the **short hedge,** as explained by the following example. Consider a commercial bank that currently holds a large amount of corporate bonds and long-term fixed-rate commercial loans, and its primary source of funds has been short-term deposits. The bank will be adversely affected if interest rates rise in the near future because its liabilities are more rate-sensitive than its assets. Although the bank believes that its bonds are a reasonable long-term investment, it anticipates that interest rates will rise temporarily. Therefore, it hedges against the interest rate risk by selling futures on securities that have characteristics similar to the securities it is hedging, so that the future prices will change in tandem with these securities. One possible strategy is to sell Treasury bond futures because the price movements of Treasury bonds are highly correlated with movements in corporate bond prices.

If interest rates rise as expected, the market value of existing corporate bonds held by the bank will decline. Yet, this could be offset by the favorable impact of the futures position. The bank locked in the price at which it could sell Treasury bonds. It can purchase Treasury bonds at a lower price just prior to settlement of the futures contract (because the value of bonds would have decreased) and profit from fulfilling its futures contract obligation. Alternatively, it could offset its short position by purchasing futures contracts similar to the type that it sold earlier.

If interest rates decrease over this period, the market value of Treasury bonds will increase and the bank will be forced to purchase the bonds at a higher price than it could sell them for. Yet, the market value of its corporate bonds will increase, thereby offsetting the loss incured on the futures position.

NUMERICAL EXAMPLE.   Assume that Charlotte Insurance Company plans to satisfy cash needs in six months by selling its U.S. Treasury bond holdings for $5 million at that time. It is concerned that interest rates might increase over the next three months, which would reduce the market value of bonds by the time they are sold. To hedge against this possibility, Charlotte plans to sell U.S. Treasury bond futures. It sells 50 Treasury bond futures contracts with a par value of $5 million ($100,000 per contract) for 98–16 (or 98 and 16/32% of par value).

Suppose that the actual price of the futures contract declined to 94–16 because of an increase in interest rates. Charlotte can close out its short futures position by purchasing contracts identical to those that it has sold. If it purchases 50 Treasury bond futures contracts at the prevailing price of 94–16, its profit per futures contract would be:

Selling Price	$98,500	(98.50% of $100,000)
− Purchase Price	− $94,500	(94.50% of $100,000)
= Profit	$4,000	(4.00% of $100,000)

Given that Charlotte had a position in 50 futures contracts, its total profit from its position would be $200,000 ($4,000 per contract × 50 contracts). This gain on the futures contract position would help offset the reduced market value of Charlotte's bond holdings.

If interest rates rise by a greater degree over the six-month period, the market value of Treasury bond holdings will decrease further. However, the price of Treasury bond futures contracts will also decrease by a greater degree, creating a larger gain from the short position in Treasury bond futures. If interest rates decrease, the futures prices will rise, causing a loss on the futures position. But this will be offset by a gain in the market value of Treasury bond holdings.

This example presumes that the **basis,** or difference between the price of a security and the price of a futures contract, remains the same. In reality, the price of the security may fluctuate more or less than the futures contract used to hedge it. If so, a perfect offset will not result when hedging a given face value amount of securities with the same face value amount of futures contracts.

RESEARCH.   A recent study by Morris simulated the results from hedging a Treasury bond portfolio. The so-called hedged portfolio in Exhibit 11.4 reflects the market value of the Treasury bond portfolio combined with a short position in Treasury bond futures. Conversely, there is no futures position taken for the unhedged portfolio. This exhibit shows that the value of the hedged portfolio is much more stable than that of the unhedged portfolio.

CONCLUSIONS ABOUT A SHORT HEDGE.   When one considers both the rising and declining interest rate scenarios, the advantages and disadvantages of interest rate futures are obvious. Interest rate futures can hedge against adverse events but also hedge against favorable events. Exhibit 11.5 compares two probability distributions of returns generated by a financial institution whose liabilities are more rate-sensitive than its assets. If the institution hedges its exposure to interest rate risk, its probability distribution of returns is narrower than if it does not hedge. The return from hedging would have been higher than without hedging if interest rates increased (see left portion of graph) but lower if interest rates decreased (see right portion of graph).

A financial institution that hedges with interest rate futures is less sensitive to economic events. Thus, financial institutions that frequently use interest rate futures may be able to reduce the variability of their earnings over time, which

EXHIBIT 11.4 Comparison of Treasury Bond Portfolios: Unhedged Versus Hedged with Treasury Bond Futures

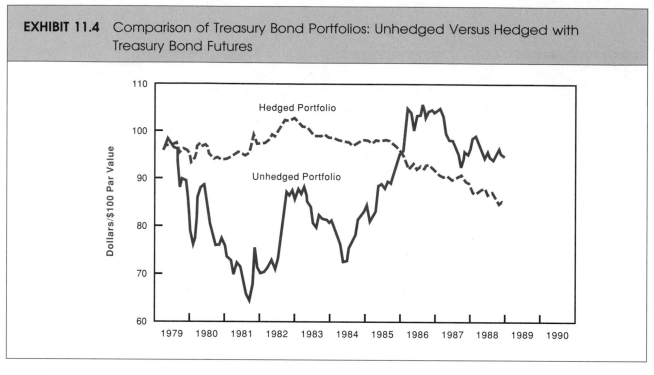

NOTE: The bond portfolio is an equally weighted portfolio of the 30-year U.S. Treasury bond that matures in November 2007 and the 10-year U.S. Treasury bond that matures in May 1989. The hedged price is the price of the minimum risk hedged portfolio of bonds using the nearest futures contract with at least one month until expiration.

SOURCE: *Financial Market Volatility and the Economy,* Federal Reserve Bank of Kansas City (1990): 143.

EXHIBIT 11.5

Comparison of Probability Distributions of Returns: Hedged Versus Unhedged Positions

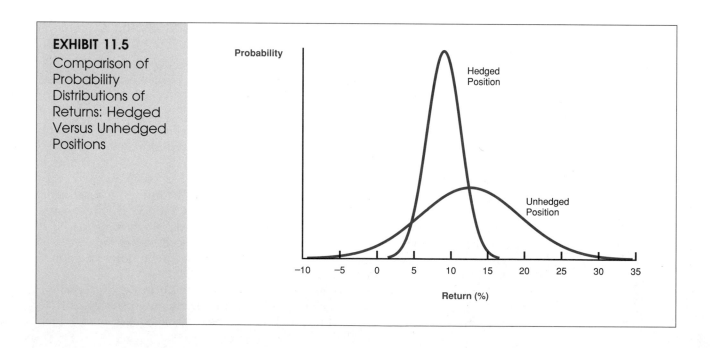

reflects a lower degree of risk. Yet, it should be recognized that hedging will not likely remove all uncertainty, because it is virtually impossible to perfectly hedge the sensitivity of all cash flows to interest rate movements.

Using Interest Rate Futures to Create a Long Hedge

Some financial institutions use a **long hedge** to reduce exposure to the possibility of declining interest rates. Consider government securities dealers who plan to purchase long-term bonds in a few months. If the dealers are concerned that prices of these securities will rise before the time of their purchases, they may purchase Treasury bond futures contracts. These contracts lock in the price at which Treasury bonds can be purchased, regardless of what happens to market rates prior to the actual purchase of the bonds.

As another example, consider a bank that has obtained a large amount of its funds from large CDs with a maturity of five years. Also assume that most of its assets represent loans with rates that adjust every six months. This bank would be adversely affected by a decline in interest rates because interest earned on assets would be more sensitive than interest paid on liabilities. To hedge against the possibility of lower interest rates, the bank could purchase Treasury bill futures to lock in the price on Treasury bills at a specified future date. If interest rates decline, the gain on the futures position could partially offset any reduction in the bank's earnings due to the reduction in interest rates.

Hedging Net Exposure

Because interest rate futures contracts result in transactions costs, they should be used only to hedge **net exposure,** which reflects the difference between asset and liability positions. Consider a bank that has $300 million in long-term assets and $220 million worth of long-term fixed-rate liabilities. If interest rates rise, the market value of long-term assets will decline, while the bank benefits from the fixed rate on the $220 million in long-term liabilities. Thus, the net exposure is only $80 million (assuming that the long-term assets and liabilities are similarly affected by rising interest rates). The financial institution should therefore focus on hedging its net exposure of $80 million by creating a short hedge.

Cross-Hedging

Although the concept of using interest rate futures is logical, the actual implementation is difficult. In many situations, the characteristics of the assets being hedged differ from the assets represented by the futures contract. Because the impact of changing interest rates on the prices of the two types of assets may differ, a perfect offsetting effect is unlikely. Thus, the bond portfolio of the financial institution is still somewhat exposed to interest rate movements. This exposure is referred to as **basis risk.**

To deal with this problem, financial institutions attempt to identify an asset represented by futures contracts whose market value moves closely in tandem with that of the assets they want to hedge. Their use of a futures contract on one financial instrument to hedge their position in a different financial instrument is known as **cross-hedging.** The effectiveness of a cross-hedge depends on the degree of correlation between the market values of the two financial instruments.

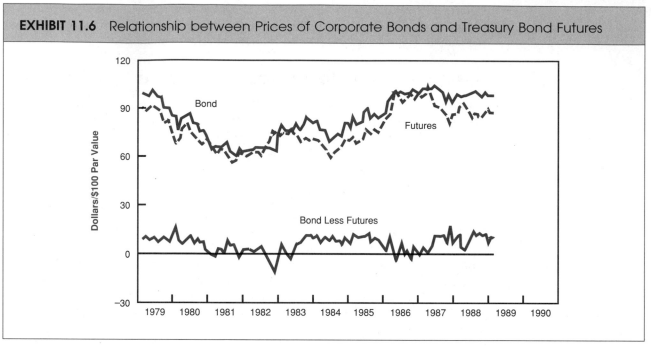

EXHIBIT 11.6 Relationship between Prices of Corporate Bonds and Treasury Bond Futures

NOTE: Corporate bond is an A-rated 9.50 percent 30-year bond of a U.S. industrial firm. The futures price is the price of the nearest Chicago Board of Trade Treasury bond future with at least one month until expiration.

SOURCE: *Financial Market Volatility and the Economy,* Federal Reserve Bank of Kansas City (1990): 142.

If the price of the underlying security of the futures contract moves closely in tandem with the security hedged, the futures contract can provide an effective hedge.

To illustrate how cross-hedging works, consider the use of Treasury bond futures to hedge portfolios of corporate bonds. The price movements in a corporate bond portfolio and Treasury bond futures are illustrated in Exhibit 11.6. The price movements of the Treasury bond futures are highly correlated with the corporate bond portfolio.

Although both Treasury bonds and corporate bonds may be similarly sensitive to interest rate movements (assuming their maturities and coupon payment structures are similar), corporate bond prices are affected by economic conditions that influence the probability of default. For example, news that signals the possibility of a recession could cause investors to shift from corporate bonds to Treasury bonds. During this transition, the market value of an institution's corporate bond portfolio may decline, while Treasury bond prices are rising. Thus, the sale of Treasury bond futures to hedge against the expected temporary decline in the market value of a corporate bond portfolio would not have been effective.

Even when the futures contract is highly correlated with the portfolio being hedged, the value of the futures contract may change by a higher or lower percentage than the portfolio's market value. If the futures contract value is less volatile than the portfolio value, hedging will require a greater amount of principal represented by the futures contracts. For example, assume that for every percentage movement in the portfolio, the price of the futures contract changes by 0.8 percent. In this case, the value of futures contracts to fully hedge the portfolio would be 1.25 times the principal of the portfolio (computed as 1 divided by 0.8). Over time, this so-called hedge ratio will change, forcing the portfolio manager to adjust by liquidating some of the futures contracts.

Hedging Assets Subject to Prepayment

A problem arises when the assets to be hedged may be prepaid earlier than their designated maturity. Suppose a commercial bank sells Treasury bond futures in order to hedge its holdings of corporate bonds, and just after the futures position is created, the bonds are called by the corporation that initially issued them. If interest rates subsequently decline, the bank would incur a loss from its futures position without a corresponding gain from its bond position (because the bonds were called earlier).

As a second example, consider a savings and loan association with large holdings of long-term fixed-rate mortgages that are mostly financed by short-term funds. It sells Treasury bond futures to hedge against the possibility of rising interest rates; then, after the futures position is established, interest rates decline, and many of the existing mortgages are prepaid by homeowners. The savings and loan association would incur a loss from its futures position without a corresponding gain from its fixed-rate mortgage position (because the mortgages were prepaid).

BOND INDEX FUTURES

A bond index futures contract allows for the buying and selling of a bond index for a specified price at a specified date. For financial institutions that trade in municipal bonds, the Chicago Board of Trade offers **Municipal Bond Index (MBI) futures.** The index is based on the **Bond Buyer Index** of 40 actively traded general obligation and revenue bonds. The specific characteristics of MBI futures are disclosed in Exhibit 11.7. Because MBI futures are based on an index rather than on the bonds themselves, there is no physical exchange of bonds. Instead, these futures contracts are settled in cash. Bond index futures represent another form of interest rate futures.

Consider an insurance company that will be receiving large cash flows in the near future. Although it plans to use some of the incoming funds to purchase municipal bonds, it is concerned that because of the likely downward trend in interest rates, municipal bond prices may increase before it can purchase them. Thus, it purchases MBI futures. If the company's expectation is correct, the futures position will generate a gain, which can be used to pay for the higher priced bonds once it has sufficient funds. Conversely, if bond prices fall, the company will incur a loss from its futures position.

As a second example, consider an investment banking firm that has agreed to underwrite bonds for various municipalities. Assume that the firm expects the market prices of bonds to decline in the near future. Such an event could reduce underwriting profits if the market price falls before these bonds are sold. To hedge this risk, the firm could sell MBI futures. The futures position would generate a gain and offset the reduced underwriting profits if its expectations are correct.

EXHIBIT 11.7 Characteristics of Municipal Bond Index Futures	
CHARACTERISTIC OF FUTURES CONTRACT	**MUNICIPAL BOND INDEX FUTURES**
Trading unit	1,000 times the Bond Buyer Municipal Bond Index. A price of 90–00 represents a contract size of $90,000.
Price quotation	In points and thirty-seconds of a point.
Minimum price fluctuation	One thirty-second ($1/32$) of a point, or $31.25 per contract.
Daily trading limits	Three points ($3,000) per contract above or below the previous day's settlement price.
Settlement months	March, June, September, and December.
Settlement procedure	Municipal Bond Index futures settle in cash on the last day of trading. The settlement price is based on the Bond Buyer Municipal Bond Index value of that day.

STOCK INDEX FUTURES

A stock index futures contract allows for the buying and selling of a stock index for a specified price at a specified date. Futures are available for various stock indexes. For example, there is a futures contract on the S&P 500 index, which represents a composite of 500 large corporations. The purchase of an S&P 500 futures contract obligates the purchaser to purchase the S&P 500 index at a specified settlement date for a specified amount. Thus, participants who expect the stock market to perform well before the settlement date may consider purchasing S&P 500 index futures. Conversely, participants who expect the stock market to perform poorly before the settlement date may consider selling S&P 500 index futures.

Stock index futures contracts have four settlement dates in a given year—the third Friday in March, June, September, and December. The securities underlying the stock index futures contracts are not deliverable; settlement occurs through a cash payment. On the settlement date, the futures contract is valued according to the quoted stock index. The net gain or loss on the stock index futures contract is the difference between the futures price when the initial position was created and the value of the contract as of the settlement date.

As with other financial futures contracts, stock index futures can be closed out before the settlement date by taking an offsetting position. For example, if an S&P 500 futures contract with a December settlement date was purchased in September, this position could be closed out in November by selling a S&P 500 futures contract with the same December settlement date. When a position is closed out prior to the settlement date, the net gain or loss on the stock index futures contract is the difference between the futures price when the position was created and the futures price when the position was closed out.

Some speculators prefer to trade stock index futures rather than actual stocks because of smaller transaction costs. The commission cost of a purchase and subsequent sale of S&P 500 futures contracts is substantially less than the equivalent stocks contained in the S&P 500.

DO STOCK INDEX FUTURES INCREASE STOCK MARKET VOLATILITY?

A recent study by Edwards attempted to determine whether the trading of stock index futures increases stock market volatility. For much of the period in which stock index futures have existed (since 1982), stock market volatility was found to be relatively low. Edwards concludes that the stock index futures trading is not likely to be the primary cause of the recent increase in stock market volatility. While he acknowledges that there is no clear explanation for the higher degree of stock market volatility, he suggests that it may be because of the large U.S. balance of trade deficit, the substantial decline in the value of the dollar, and the large federal budget deficit. These are the same factors that contributed to the stock market crash in October 1987. The volatility in the stock market was even higher for several months after the crash than during the months before the crash. Perhaps this increase in volatility is the result of the crash itself and simply reflects more frequent transactions into and out of the stock markets.

Speculating with Stock Index Futures

Assume Boulder Insurance Company plans to purchase a variety of stocks for its stock portfolio in December, once cash inflows are received. Although it does not have cash to purchase the stocks immediately, it is anticipating a large jump in stock market prices before December. Given this situation, it decides to purchase S&P 500 index futures. The futures price on the S&P 500 index with a December settlement date is 400. The value of an S&P 500 futures contract is $500 times the index. Because the S&P 500 futures prices should move with the stock market, it will rise over time if the company's expectations are correct. Assume that the S&P 500 index rose to 460 on the settlement date.

In this example, the nominal profit on the S&P 500 index futures would be:

Selling Price	$230,000	(Index value of 460 × $500)
− Purchase Price	− $200,000	(Index value of 400 × $500)
= Profit	$30,000	

Thus, Boulder Insurance Company was able to capitalize on its expectations even though it did not have sufficient cash to purchase stock. If the stock prices had decreased over the period of concern, the S&P 500 futures index would have decreased, and Boulder Insurance Company would have incurred a loss on its futures position.

Hedging with Stock Index Futures

Stock index futures are also commonly used to hedge the market risk of an existing stock portfolio. For example, assume that a stock mutual fund expects the stock market to decline temporarily, causing a temporary decline in its stock portfolio. The selling of its stocks with the intent to repurchase them in the near future would result in excessive transaction costs. A more efficient solution is to sell stock index futures. If its stock portfolio was similar to the S&P 500 index, it could sell futures contracts on that index. If the stock market declined as expected, the mutual fund would generate a gain when closing out the stock index futures position, which would somewhat offset the loss on its stock portfolio.

This hedge would be more effective if their portfolio was diversified like an S&P 500 index. The value of a less diversified stock portfolio would be less correlated with the S&P 500 index, so that a gain from selling index futures may not completely offset the loss in the portfolio during a market downturn. Assuming that the stock portfolio moves in tandem with the S&P 500, a full hedge would involve the sale of the amount of futures contracts whose combined underlying value is equal to the market value of the stock portfolio being hedged.

Dynamic Asset Allocation with Stock Index Futures

Institutional investors are increasingly using **dynamic asset allocation,** which reflects switching between risky and low-risk investment positions over time in response to changing expectations. This strategy allows managers to increase the exposure of their portfolios when they expect favorable market conditions, and reduce their exposure when they expect unfavorable market conditions. Stock portfolio managers can purchase stock index futures when they anticipate favorable market movements, which creates more pronounced effects of market conditions. Conversely, they can sell stock index futures when they anticipate unfavorable market movements to reduce the effects that market conditions will have on their stock portfolios. As expectations change frequently, portfolio managers commonly alter their degree of exposure. Stock index futures allows the portfolio managers to alter their risk-return position without restructuring their existing stock portfolios. This method of dynamic asset allocation avoids the substantial transaction costs that would be associated with restructuring the stock portfolios.

Prices of Stock Index Futures Versus Stocks

The prices of index futures and the stocks representing the index could differ to some degree. To understand why, consider a situation in which many institutional investors anticipate a temporary decline in stock prices. Because the decline is expected to be only temporary, the investors prefer not to liquidate their stock portfolios. As a form of portfolio insurance, they sell stock index futures so that any decline in the market value of their stock portfolio would be offset by a gain on their futures position. The actions of numerous institutional investors to sell index futures instead of selling stocks to prepare for a market decline can cause the index futures price to be below the prevailing stock prices.

In some cases, index futures prices may exceed the prices of stocks that the index comprises. As favorable information about the stock market becomes available, investors can buy either stock index futures or the actual stocks that make up the index. The purchase of futures can take place immediately with a small up-front payment. The purchase of actual stocks may take longer because of the time needed to select specific stocks. In addition, a larger up-front investment is necessary. This explains why the price of stock index futures may more quickly reflect investor expectations about the market than stock prices.

Recent studies have found a high degree of correlation between the stock index futures and the index itself. Price movements in the stock index sometimes lag behind movement in the stock index futures by up to 45 minutes. This confirms that the stock index futures more rapidly reflect new information that can influence expectations about the stock market. Even though the index futures price movements frequently preceded stock index movements, the relationship was not consistent enough to develop an exploitable trading strategy in which positions in a stock index are taken based on the most recent movement in the futures index.

Arbitrage with Stock Index Futures

Recall from the previous chapter that program trading has been narrowly defined by the NYSE to reflect the simultaneous buying and selling of at least 15 different stocks valued at more than $1 million. Program trading is commonly used in conjunction with the trading of stock index futures contracts in a strategy known as **index arbitrage.** Securities firms act as **arbitrageurs** by capitalizing on discrepancies between prices of index futures and stocks. Index arbitrage involves the buying or selling of stock index futures with a simultaneous opposite position in the stocks that the index comprises. The index arbitrage is instigated when prices of stock index futures differs significantly from the stocks that are represented by the index. For example, if the index futures contract is priced high relative to the stocks representing the index, an arbitrageur may consider purchasing the stocks and simultaneously selling stock index futures. Alternatively, if the index futures are priced low relative to the stocks representing the index, an arbitrageur may purchase index futures and simultaneously sell stocks. An arbitrage profit is attainable if the price differential exceeds the costs incurred from trading in both markets.

Index arbitrage does not cause the price discrepancy between the two markets, but rather responds to it. The arbitrageur's ability to detect price discrepancies between stock and futures markets is enhanced by computers. Roughly 50 percent of all program trading activity is for the purpose of index arbitrage.

Some critics suggest that the index arbitrage activity of purchasing index futures while selling stocks adversely affects stock prices. However, if index futures did not exist, institutional investors could not have used portfolio insurance. In this case, a general expectation of a temporary market decline would more likely encourage the sales of stocks to prepare for the decline, which would even accelerate the drop in prices. In 1990, the Securities and Exchange Commission approved a proposal to limit index arbitrage when the Dow Jones Industrial Average rises or falls by 50 points.

Circuit Breakers on Stock Index Futures

The 1987 stock market crash led to recommendations by a presidential task force to recommend **circuit breakers** to prevent further crashes. Circuit breakers are trading restrictions imposed on specific stocks or stock indexes. In October 1988, the NYSE imposed circuit breakers on stocks. For example, if the Dow Jones Industrial Average stock index declines by 250 points below the previous day's closing price, the NYSE prohibits trading for one hour. In addition, the Chicago Mercantile Exchange (CME) imposed circuit breakers on the S&P 500 futures contract. If the price of this contract declines by 12 points below the previous day's closing price, the CME prohibits trading at lower prices for a half hour. A second circuit breaker on this contract is tripped if the contract declines by 30 points below the previous day's closing price. (See the study by Morris for additional details on circuit breakers.)

By prohibiting trading for short time periods, the exchanges may allow investors to determine whether any previous rumors were true and to work out credit arrangements if they received a margin call. If prices are still perceived to be too high as the markets are reopened, the prices will decline further. Thus, circuit breakers do not guarantee that prices will turn upward. Yet, they may be able to prevent large declines in prices that would be attributed to panic selling rather than to fundamental forces.

The first test for the circuit breakers was on October 13, 1989, when stocks declined by about 5 percent on average. The price trend of stocks and index futures for this day is illustrated in Exhibit 11.8. At 2:07 P.M., the first circuit breaker tripped as the S&P futures contract declined by 12 points below the previous day's closing price. The stocks were not, however, subject to that circuit breaker, and their prices continued their decline while index futures trading was halted. When the index futures market was reopened, the index futures price dropped sharply, then increased for a few minutes, and then declined until 2:45 P.M., at which time it was 30 points below the previous day's close. Consequently, the second breaker was imposed. Since the Dow Jones Industrial Av-

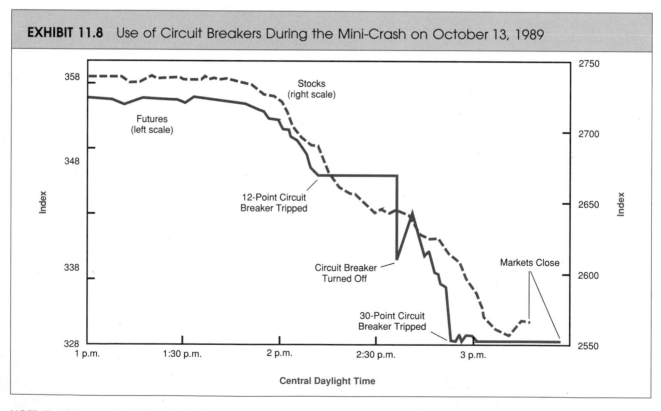

EXHIBIT 11.8 Use of Circuit Breakers During the Mini-Crash on October 13, 1989

NOTE: The futures price is the minute-by-minute average of the December 1989 S&P 500 stock index futures contract traded at the Chicago Mercantile Exchange. The stock price is the minute-by-minute average of the Dow Jones Industrial Average.

SOURCE: *Economic Review,* Federal Reserve Bank of Kansas City (March/April 1990): 39.

WSJ USING *THE WALL STREET JOURNAL*

FINANCIAL FUTURES QUOTATIONS

The Wall Street Journal provides quotations on various stock and interest rate index futures contracts, as shown here. The most popular index futures contract is the S&P 500 index futures. The most popular interest rate futures contracts are Treasury bond futures and Treasury note futures. For each type of futures contract, there are various settlement dates, one date for each row. For each settlement date, the open, high, low, and settle (closing) prices are quoted across the row. The change ("chg") in the futures price from the previous day is also disclosed in the row, along with the high and low prices since that futures contract became available, and the open interest (number of existing contracts that have not been offset).

INDEX

S&P 500 INDEX (CME) $500 times index

	Open	High	Low	Settle	Chg	High	Low	Open Interest
Sept	461.40	461.70	458.25	458.35	− 3.10	485.20	436.75	194,392
Dec	463.70	463.70	460.55	460.70	− 3.15	487.10	438.85	15,542
Mr95	....	....	464.00	− 3.05	479.00	441.45	2,872	
June	....	....	467.45	− 3.05	472.70	449.50	1,354	

Est vol 45,870; vol Wed 41,071; open int 214,160, −1,078.
Indx prelim High 461.49; Low 458.40; Close 458.40 −3.06

S&P MIDCAP 400 (CME) $500 times index
Sept 171.90 172.25 170.55 170.65 − 1.25 186.70 161.50 11,991
Est vol 548; vol Wed 437; open int 12,091, −36.
The index: High 171.44; Low 170.33; Close 170.79 −.47

NIKKEI 225 STOCK AVERAGE (CME) −$5 times index
Sept 20680. 20785. 20670. 20700. + 75.0 21775. 16240. 22,391
Est vol 855; vol Wed 906; open int 22,866, +214.
The index: High 20700.94; Low 20565.21; Close 20676.84 +44.11

GSCI (CME) −$250 times GSCI nearby prem.
Aug 181.20 181.80 179.80 n.a. n.a. 184.80 167.00 1,655
Oct 181.30 181.40 180.50 181.00 + .10 184.40 171.90 3,889
Est vol 2,457; vol Wed 2,248; open int 6,190, +16.
The index: High 182.02; Low 179.59; Close 180.95 +.33

MAJOR MARKET INDEX (CME) −$500 times index
Aug 388.00 388.00 385.40 385.40 − 2.70 388.55 369.90 3,007
Sept 387.40 387.40 385.70 385.70 − 2.65 399.35 360.55 107
Dec .... 387.30 − 2.70 400.45 361.75 187
Est vol 104; vol Wed 46; open int 3,301, +1.
The index: High 388.52; Low 385.73; Close 385.73 −2.79

NYSE COMPOSITE INDEX (NYFE) −500 times index
Sept 254.55 254.65 252.90 252.95 − 1.75 267.90 241.00 3,578
Dec 255.55 255.55 253.95 253.90 − 1.75 264.50 244.15 286
Est vol 1,713; vol Wed 1,503; open int 3,974, +13.
The index: High 254.58; Low 253.26; Close 253.27 −1.31

KR-CRB INDEX (NYFE) −500 times index
Sept 232.10 233.50 231.60 233.50 + .95 241.50 221.10 2,166
Dec 233.75 235.25 233.70 235.35 + .95 241.00 225.00 1,711
Mr95 236.70 236.95 236.70 237.20 + .95 242.75 228.70 959
May .... 238.70 + .95 240.75 238.75 655
Est vol 242; vol Wed 436; open int 5,491, +71.
The index: High 232.75; Low 231.06; Close 232.45 +.96

CAC-40 STOCK INDEX (MATIF) − FFr 200 per index pt.
Aug 2130. 2132. 2097. 2102. − 25. 1958. 1878. 24,878
Sept 2137. 2138. 2107. 2109. − 26 2127. 1863.5 26,807
Dec 2166. 2166. 2166. 2138. − 26. 2195. 1987. 7,870
Mr95 2178. 2178. 2178. 2166. − 25. 2190.5 1946. 4,199
Est vol 19,927; vol Wed 15,247; open int 63,754, +996.

FT−SE 100 INDEX (LIFFE) −£25 per index point
Sept 3184. 3188. 3157. 3158. − 17.0 3550. 2852. 55,478
Dec 3190. 3190. 3190. 3171. − 17.0 3190. 2965. 3,915
Est vol 9,503; vol Wed 8,206; open int 59,393, −1,207.

ALL ORDINARIES SHARE PRICE INDEX (SFE)
A$25 times index
Sept 2079. 2107. 2071. 2103. + 19. 2330. 1704. 76,088
Dec 2095. 2095. 2095. 2114. + 19. 2300. 1940. 3,062
Mr95 .... 2135. + 19. 2242. 1974. 1,775
June 2125. 2125. 2125. 2153. + 19. 2145. 1990. 3,386
Est vol 4,691; vol Wed 5,063; open int 84,311, +2,400.
The index: High 2083.5; Low 2064.3; Close 2083.5 +11.2

INTEREST RATE

T-BONDS (CBT)
$100,000; points and 64ths of 100%

Strike	Calls—Settle			Puts—Settle		
Price	Sep	Dec	Mar	Sep	Dec	Mar
103	1-63	....	....	0-29	....	....
104	1-19	2-18	2-41	0-49	2-30	3-36
105	0-48	....	....	1-15	....	....
106	0-24	1-26	1-54	1-54	3-37	4-46
107	0-11	....	....	2-40	....	....
108	0-04	0-51	1-14	3-34	4-61	6-03

Est. vol. 85,000;
Wed vol. 44,115 calls; 30,589 puts
Op. int. Wed 448,558 calls; 354,452 puts

T-NOTES (CBT)
$100,000; points and 64ths of 100%

Strike	Calls—Settle			Puts—Settle		
Price	Sep	Dec	Mar	Sep	Dec	Mar
103	2-19	2-30	....	0-09	1-19	....
104	1-31	1-56	....	0-21	1-44	....
105	0-53	1-23	....	0-43	2-10	....
106	0-26	0-60	....	1-16	2-47	....
107	0-09	0-40	....	1-63	....	....
108	0-03	0-25	....	3-54	....	....

Est vol 32,500   Wed 11,542 calls 18,-663 puts
Op int Wed   117,459 calls 163,020 puts

MUNICIPAL BOND INDEX (CBT)
$100,000; pts. & 64ths of 100%

Strike	Calls—Settle			Puts—Settle		
Price	Aug	Sep	Oct	Aug	Sep	Oct
90	....	2-45	....	....	0-39	....
91	1-32	2-01	....	....	....	....
92	0-48	1-26	....	....	....	....
93	0-19	0-59	....	....	1-52	....

Est vol 50   Wed 50 calls 0 puts
Op int Wed   1,006 calls 671 puts

5 YR TREAS NOTES (CBT)
$100,000; points and 64ths of 100%

Strike	Calls—Settle			Puts—Settle		
Price	Sep	Dec	Mar	Sep	Dec	Mar
10350	1-30	1-34	....	0-09	0-63	....
10400	1-03	1-16	....	0-14	1-13	....
10450	0-46	1-00	....	0-25	....	....
10500	0-28	0-50	....	0-39	....	....
10550	0-16	0-38	....	0-59	....	....
10600	0-08	0-29	....	1-19	....	....

Est vol 15,000   Wed 3,609 calls 25,-427 puts
Op int Wed   54,531 calls 99,315 puts

EURODOLLAR (CME)
$ million; pts. of 100%

Strike	Calls—Settle			Puts—Settle		
Price	Sep	Dec	Mar	Sep	Dec	Mar
9450	0.48	0.18	0.19	0.02	0.37	0.61
9475	0.27	0.09	0.12	0.06	0.52	0.78
9500	0.10	0.03	0.07	0.14	0.70	0.98
9525	0.03	0.01	0.04	0.32	0.94	1.20
9550	0.01	.0004	0.02	0.55	1.19	1.43
9575	.0004	.0004	0.01	0.79	1.44	1.68

Est. vol. 142,652;
Wed vol. 35,455 calls; 60,420 puts
Op. int. Wed 933,853 calls; 952,572 puts

LIBOR − 1 Mo. (CME)
$3 million; pts. of 100%

Strike	Calls—Settle			Puts—Settle		
Price	Aug	Sep	Oct	Aug	Sep	Oct
9500	0.42	0.25	0.18	.0004	0.05	0.17
9525	0.19	0.09	0.07	0.02	0.14	0.31
9550	0.03	0.03	0.03	0.11	0.33	0.52
9575	.0004	.0004	....	0.33	0.55	....

erage did not decline by 250 points on this day, the NYSE circuit breaker was not imposed.

On July 23, 1990, the circuit breakers were tested once again. Stock market prices plunged in the morning, causing the imposition of a circuit breaker on stock index futures. Meanwhile, the NYSE asked members to temporarily stop index arbitrage trades. The pessimism subsided shortly thereafter. Some traders acknowledged that the market decline could have been much more pronounced without the use of circuit breakers on this day.

INSTITUTIONAL USE OF FUTURES MARKETS

Exhibit 11.9 summarizes the manner by which various types of financial institutions participate in futures markets. Financial institutions generally use futures contracts to reduce risk, as has already been illustrated by several examples. Some commercial banks and savings institutions use a short hedge to protect against a possible increase in interest rates. Some bond mutual funds, pension funds, and life insurance companies take short positions in interest rate futures to insulate their bond portfolios from a possible increase in interest rates. Stock

EXHIBIT 11.9 Institutional Use of Futures Markets

TYPE OF FINANCIAL INSTITUTION	PARTICIPATION IN FUTURES MARKETS
Commercial banks	■ Take positions in futures contracts to hedge against interest rate risk.
Savings institutions	■ Take positions in futures contracts to hedge against interest rate risk.
Securities firms	■ Execute futures transactions for individuals and firms. ■ Take positions in futures to hedge their own portfolios against stock market or interest rate movements.
Mutual funds	■ Take positions in futures contracts to speculate on future stock market or interest rate movements. ■ Take positions in futures contracts to hedge their portfolios against stock market or interest rate movements.
Pension funds	■ Take positions in futures contracts to hedge their portfolios against stock market or interest rate movements.
Insurance companies	■ Take positions in futures contracts to hedge their portfolios against stock market or interest rate movements.

mutual funds, pension funds, and insurance companies take short positions in stock index futures to partially insulate their respective stock portfolios from adverse stock market movements.

GLOBALIZATION OF FUTURES MARKETS

The trading of financial futures involves the assessment of international financial market conditions. The foreign flow of funds into and out of the United States can affect interest rates and therefore the market value of Treasury bonds, corporate bonds, mortgages, and other long-term debt securities. Portfolio managers assess international flows of funds to forecast changes in interest rate movements, which in turn affect the value of their respective portfolios. Even speculators assess the international flows of funds to forecast interest rates so that they can determine whether to take short or long futures positions.

Non-U.S. Participation in U.S. Futures Contracts

Financial futures contracts on U.S. securities are commonly traded by non-U.S. financial institutions that maintain holdings of U.S. securities. These institutions use financial futures to reduce their exposure to U.S. stock market or interest rate movements. The Chicago Board of Trade has allowed more access to non-U.S. customers by expanding the trading hours of the exchange to cover various time zones.

Foreign Stock Index Futures

Foreign stock index futures have been created to either speculate on or hedge against potential movements in foreign stock markets. Expectations of a strong foreign stock market would encourage purchasing futures contracts on the representative index. Conversely, if firms expected a decline in the foreign market, they would consider selling futures on the representative index. In addition, financial institutions with substantial investment in a particular foreign stock market could hedge against a temporary decline in that market by selling foreign stock index futures.

Some of the more popular foreign stock index futures contracts are identified in Exhibit 11.10. Numerous other foreign stock index futures contracts have recently been created. In fact, futures exchanges have recently been established in Ireland, France, Spain, and Italy. Financial institutions around the world can use futures contracts to hedge against temporary declines in their asset portfolios. Speculators can take long or short positions to speculate on a particular market with a relatively small initial investment. Financial futures on debt instruments (such as futures on German government bonds) are also offered by the numerous exchanges in non-U.S. markets, including the London International Financial Futures Exchange (LIFFE), Singapore International Monetary Exchange (SEMEX), and Sydney Futures Exchange (SFE).

Technology in electronic trading of futures contracts is allowing for an internationally integrated futures market. Globex is a round-the-world electronic trading network that has been used by the Chicago Board of Trade. It allows for trading of financial futures contracts even when the trading floor is closed.

EXHIBIT 11.10 Popular Foreign Stock Index Futures Contracts	
NAME OF STOCK FUTURES INDEX	**DESCRIPTION**
Nikkei 225	225 Japanese stocks
Toronto 35	35 stocks on Toronto stock exchange
Financial Times-Stock Exchange 100	100 stocks on London stock exchange
Barclays share price	40 stocks on New Zealand stock exchange
Hang Seng	33 stocks on Hong Kong stock exchange
Osaka	50 Japanese stocks
All ordinaries share price	307 Australian stocks

Currency Futures Contracts

A futures contract on a foreign currency is a standardized agreement to deliver or receive a specified amount of a specified foreign currency at a specified price (exchange rate) and date. The settlement months are March, June, September, and December. Some companies act as hedgers in the currency futures market by purchasing futures on currencies that they will need in the future to cover payables or by selling futures on currencies that they will receive in the future. Speculators in the currency futures market may purchase futures on a foreign currency that they expect to strengthen against the U.S. dollar or sell futures on currencies that they expect to weaken against the U.S. dollar.

Purchasers of **currency futures contracts** can hold the contract until the settlement date and accept delivery of the foreign currency at that time or can close out their long position prior to the settlement date by selling the identical type and number of contracts before then. If they close out their long position, their gain or loss is determined by the futures price when they created a long position versus the futures price at the time the position was closed out. Sellers of currency futures contracts either decide to deliver the foreign currency at the settlement date or close out their position by purchasing the identical type and number of contracts prior to the settlement date. Currency futures contracts are discussed in more detail in Chapter 14.

SUMMARY

- A financial futures contract is a standardized agreement to deliver or receive a specified amount of a specified financial instrument at a specified price and date. As the market value of the underlying instrument changes, so will the value of the financial futures contract. As the market value of the underlying instrument rises, there is a greater demand for the futures contract that has locked in the price of the instrument.

- An interest rate futures contract locks in the price to be paid for a specified debt instrument. Speculators who expect interest rates to decline can purchase interest rate futures contracts, because the market value of the underlying debt instrument should rise. Speculators who expect interest rates to rise can sell interest rate futures contracts, because the market value of the underlying debt instrument should decrease.

  Interest rate futures contracts can be sold by financial institutions (or other firms) that desire to hedge against rising interest rates. These contracts can be purchased by financial institutions that desire to hedge against declining interest rates. If interest rates move in the direction that was anticipated, the financial institutions will gain from their futures position, which can partially offset any adverse effects of the interest rate movements on their normal operations.

- Stock index futures contracts can be purchased by speculators who expect stock prices to increase, or sold by speculators who expect stock prices to decrease. Stock index futures can be sold by financial institutions who expect a temporary decline in stock prices and wish to hedge their stock portfolios.

- Depository institutions such as commercial banks and savings institutions commonly sell interest rate futures contracts to hedge against a possible increase in interest rates. Bond mutual funds, pension funds, and insurance companies also sell interest rate futures contracts to hedge their bond portfolios against a possible increase in interest rates.

  Stock mutual funds, pension funds, and insurance companies frequently sell stock index futures contracts to hedge their stock portfolios against a possible temporary decrease in stock prices.

QUESTIONS

1. Describe the general characteristics of a futures contract.

2. How does a clearinghouse facilitate the trading of financial futures contracts?

3. How does the price of a financial futures contract change as the market price of the security it represents changes? Why?

4. Explain why some futures contracts may be more suitable than others for hedging exposure to interest rate risk.

5. Would speculators buy or sell Treasury bond futures contracts if they expected interest rates to increase? Explain.

6. What is the maximum loss to a purchaser of a futures contract?

7. Explain how purchasers of financial futures contracts can offset their position. How is their gain or loss determined?

8. Explain how sellers of financial futures contracts can offset their position. How is their gain or loss determined?

9. Assume a financial institution had a larger amount of rate-sensitive assets than rate-sensitive liabilities. Would it likely be more adversely affected by an increase or decrease in interest rates? Should it purchase or sell interest rate futures contracts in order to hedge its exposure?

10. Assume a financial institution had a larger amount of rate-sensitive liabilities than assets. Would it likely be more adversely affected by an increase or decrease in interest rates? Should it purchase or sell interest rate futures contracts in order to hedge its exposure?

11. Why do some financial institutions remain exposed to interest rate risk, even when they believe that the use of interest rate futures could reduce their exposure?

12. Explain the difference between a long hedge and a short hedge used by financial institutions. When is a long hedge more appropriate than a short hedge?

13. Explain how the probability distribution of a financial institution's returns is affected when it uses interest rate futures to hedge. What does this imply about its risk?

14. Describe the act of cross-hedging. What determines the effectiveness of a cross-hedge?

15. How might a savings association use Treasury bond futures to hedge its fixed-rate mortgage portfolio (assuming that its main source of funds is short-term deposits)? Explain how prepayments on mortgages can limit the effectiveness of the hedge.

16. Describe stock index futures. How could they be used by a financial institution that is anticipating a jump in stock prices but does not yet have sufficient funds to purchase large amounts of stock?

17. Why would a pension fund or insurance company even consider selling stock index futures?

18. Blue Devil Savings & Loan Association has a large portion of 10-year fixed-rate mortgages and obtains most of its funds from short-term deposits. It uses the yield curve to assess the market's anticipation of future interest rates. It believes that expectations of future interest rates are the major force in affecting the yield curve. Assume that an upward-sloping yield curve exists with a steep slope. Based on this information, should Blue Devil consider using financial futures as a hedging technique? Explain.

19. Explain why stock index futures may more quickly reflect investor expectations about the market than stock prices.

20. Explain how index arbitrage may be used.

21. Explain the use of circuit breakers.

22. Elon Savings and Loan Association has a large portion of 30-year mortgages with floating interest rates that adjust on an annual basis and obtains most of its funds by issuing 5-year certificates of deposit. It uses the yield curve to assess the market's anticipation of future interest rates. It believes that expectations of future interest rates are the major force in affecting the yield

curve. Assume that a downward-sloping yield curve exists with a steep slope. Based on this information, should Elon consider using financial futures as a hedging technique? Explain.

PROBLEMS

1. Spratt Company purchased Treasury bill futures contracts when the quoted price was 93.50. When this position was closed out, the quoted price was 94.75. Determine the profit or loss per contract, ignoring transaction costs.

2. Suerth Investments Inc. purchased Treasury bill futures contracts when the quoted price was 95.00. When this position was closed out, the quoted price was 93.60. Determine the profit or loss per contract, ignoring transaction costs.

3. Toland Company sold Treasury bill futures contracts when the quoted price was 94.00. When this position was closed out, the quoted price was 93.20. Determine the profit or loss per contract, ignoring transaction costs.

4. Rude Dynamics Inc. sold Treasury bill futures contracts when the quoted price was 93.26. When this position was closed out, the quoted price was 93.90. Determine the profit or loss per contract, ignoring transaction costs.

5. Egan Company purchased a futures contract on Treasury bonds that specified a price of 91–00. When the position was closed out, the price of the Treasury bond futures contract was 90–10. Determine the profit or loss, ignoring transaction costs.

6. R. C. Clark sold a futures contract on Treasury bonds that specified a price of 92–10. When the position was closed out, the price of the Treasury bond futures contract was 93–00. Determine the profit or loss, ignoring transaction costs.

7. Marks Insurance Company sold S&P 500 stock index futures that specified an index of 490. When the position was closed out, the index specified by the futures contract was 520. Determine the profit or loss, ignoring transaction costs.

Portfolio Surprise: Many Americans Run Hidden Financial Risk From 'Derivatives'

Exotic Investment Contracts Increasingly Permeate Pension, Mutual Funds

Barbara Donnelly Granito and
Craig Torres

When the securities first showed up in a brokerage-firm confirmation statement for the account of an elderly widow, John S. Leech recalls thinking they looked "odd."

"I'm accustomed to looking at confirmation statements, and I didn't understand what it was," says Mr. Leech, a Smith Barney broker in Fort Lauderdale, Fla., who was serving not as the widow's broker but as trustee of her $500,000 portfolio. The securities—some 20% of the portfolio—were listed as triple-A-rated bonds issued by a quasi-federal-government agency. There weren't any obvious risks.

But risky they were. While most bond prices were rising, the value of these securities plummeted about 50% in just seven months, wiping out 10% of the widow's portfolio. Mr. Leech, who is battling with lawyers to recoup the loss from her independent investment adviser, didn't realize the securities were a form of "derivatives"—strange, hybrid investments that look like one thing and act like another. Once used solely by sophisticated financial institutions, derivatives have mushroomed in the past decade and are surfacing in the investment mainstream.

Broad Exposure

Many Americans are far more involved in derivatives than they realize. Their pension funds, mutual funds and insurance companies are knee-deep in the market, and wading in further.

"Most buyers of fixed-income mutual funds, for example, already own derivatives indirectly, whether they know it or not," says Kenneth Sullivan, who heads the derivative-products group at Republic National Bank of New York. Fixed-income, or bond, funds in the U.S. have some 12 million individual shareholders and $673 billion of assets.

What are derivatives, exactly? Though some of them resemble ordinary investments, they really are financial arrangements rather than securities. Their values are derived from changes in one or more underlying variables, such as stock markets here and abroad, interest rates, currencies and commodity prices. Some are standardized contracts, such as futures and options on stock indexes and Treasury securities listed on exchanges. But most are customized contracts traded privately among consenting investors.

Several Risks

The riskiness of derivatives depends not only on how they are used but on what safeguards funds have in place to limit potential glitches. In private deals, the main risk is that the party on the other side of the transaction won't live up to the bargain. And because derivatives transaction may involve several markets, problems in one corner of the playing field can rock other markets as well.

A case in point: The last big derivative fad on Wall Street was the mid-1980s boom in "portfolio insurance."

That hedging strategy aimed to profit from market declines through craftily timed selling of Standard & Poor's index futures. It worked like a graduated stop-loss order: Whenever the market dropped by a certain amount, futures would be sold, and if the market continued to fall, more futures would be sold, so that the investor would be wholly out of the market if prices fell to a predetermined level. Thus, portfolio insurance effectively created a put option—the right, without obligation, to sell an asset at a set price over a specified period.

That was fine in theory, but the market crash of 1987 showed how things can go awry when such bets lurking in derivatives markets spring out on an unsuspecting public. In October of that year, declining stock prices triggered the strategy, and the effect was akin to yelling "Fire!" in a crowded theater. The sudden sale of billions of dollars worth of S&P futures so startled investors that everyone rushed to the exit at once; sellers couldn't find enough buyers, and what followed was trading gridlock as prices plunged.

A Vast Market

But portfolio insurance, at its peak, involved no more than about $200 billion—far less than the $5 trillion market capitalization of all U.S. exchange-listed and over-the-counter stocks. By contrast, the Federal Reserve estimates that the banks it regulates alone hold some $7

Continued

CASE APPLICATION: MANAGING PORTFOLIOS WITH THE USE OF FUTURES CONTRACTS

Continued

trillion of privately negotiated derivatives. Exchange-listed derivatives add up to another $4.5 trillion of contracts world-wide. In addition, about a third of the $1.2 trillion mortgage-backed securities market consists of mortgage derivatives. . . .

Even presumably sophisticated investors can get trapped. Merrill Lynch & Co. lost $250 million in trading related to principal-only mortgage securities several years ago. In early 1992, J. P. Morgan & Co. dropped $50 million on interest-only mortgage derivatives. In the first two months of 1993, Salomon Inc. lost $250 million, understood to be mainly in mortgage derivatives. Also this year, Showa Shell Seikiyu K.K., a Japanese oil company, admitted to losing some $1.59 billion from trading currency derivatives, and last month, Nippon Steel Chemical Co., a unit of Nippon Steel Corp., reported losing $135.4 million in currency derivatives.

So, are derivatives bad for investors? In many respects, they can be good for investors. Derivatives give money managers enormous flexibility in mixing and matching features of stocks, bonds, currencies, commodities and other assets. Derivatives also can reduce the cost of administering a portfolio and enable managers to buy and sell big positions without distorting prices. And they enable managers to rev up or scale back their portfolios' risk exposure in unprecedented ways. Some use this capability conservatively, others aggressively. Investment funds' derivatives strategies range from plain-Jane hedging to bare-faced speculation.

"I don't think the risk should be attributed to derivatives themselves; they're just the way to accomplish it," says Thomas Lucey, chief of institutional management at Putnam Investments. "If you give a 16-year-old a high-powered Porsche and he gets in an accident, do you blame the Porsche?"

Stepped-Up Leverage

However, too many Porsches may be roaring down the investment highway at once. Many derivatives allow dealers and investors to make huge market bets without paying full price; indeed, no money at all changes hands in some derivatives trades. That is one way derivatives reduce investors' costs, but it also means "they create a lot of leverage in the system," says Frank Rabinovitch, managing director at Pacific Investment Management Co., which runs $46 billion of pension and mutual funds. "It's why we're extra careful about" whom the firm trades derivatives with in private transactions.

No wonder, considering the firm's exposure. Futures, options and other derivative positions amount to 35% to 45% of its flagship $3.4 billion Total Return mutual fund—and that is not counting the 20% in mortgage-security derivatives. "That's about consistent with our [pension] accounts," Mr. Rabinovitch says.

Investors can use derivatives both to shuck risks they don't want and to bet more boldly on risks they do want. For instance, opportunities for traditional stock pickers, such as James Craig, manager of the $8 billion Janus Fund, are no longer restricted by national boundaries now that they can hedge currency risks.

Like most other big mutual funds, Janus has changed its prospectus to allow use of currency contracts and other derivatives. So, last fall, Mr. Craig was able to protect his largest investment, 90,000 shares of Swiss drug maker Roche Holding AG, from a drop in the Swiss franc.

It was a shrewd move. From October to February, the Swiss franc fell 18.2%; the hedge saved Janus Fund about $26 million. Of course, if the Swiss franc had risen instead, the hedge would have cut the fund's return on the Roche investment. But that is not the point. "The currency decision isn't what I'm here to do for a living—I'm here to pick stocks," he says.

SOURCE: *The Wall Street Journal* (August 10, 1993): p. A1. Reprinted by permission of *The Wall Street Journal* © 1993. Dow Jones & Company, Inc. All rights reserved worldwide.

QUESTIONS

1. Explain why there were heavy sales of stock index futures contracts in October 1987, when the stock market crash occurred.

2. It is suggested that derivatives such as financial futures contracts allow money managers to protect their positions without distorting prices. Explain.

3. Many stock portfolio managers have used stock index futures to reduce risk while others have used them to increase potential return (and increase risk). Create a short example of how a manager could use them to increase the portfolio's potential return (and risk).

4. How would a mutual fund such as Janus Fund, which sometimes invests in foreign stocks, use currency futures to hedge its exchange rate risk?

PROJECTS

1. **Assessing Changes in Futures Prices**
   Use *The Wall Street Journal* to determine the recent futures prices on Treasury bonds and on the S&P 500 index. Also obtain the futures prices that existed six weeks ago. Then complete the following table.

	Recent Futures Price	Futures Price 6 weeks ago	Profit or Loss on a Long Position over This 6-Week Period	Reason for Change in the Futures Price
Treasury Bonds				
S&P 500 Index				

2. **Developing a Futures Trading Strategy**
   Using the data bank, assess interest rate movements to determine whether the direction of movement in a period can be accurately forecasted by using information about the previous period (or periods). Explain.

REFERENCES

Castelino, Mark G. "Basis Volatility: Implications for Hedging," *Journal of Financial Research* (Summer 1989): 157–172.

Edwards, Franklin R. "Does Futures Trading Increase Stock Market Volatility?" *Financial Analysts Journal* (January–February 1988): 63–69.

Furbush, Dean. "Program Trading and Price Movement: Evidence from the October 1987 Market Crash." *Financial Management* (Autumn 1989): 68–83.

Grossman, Sanford. "Program Trading and Market Volatility: A Report on Interday Relationships." *Financial Analysts Journal* (July–August 1988): 18–28.

Hill, Joanne M. "Program Trading of Equities: Renegade or Mainstream?" *Business Horizons* (November–December 1989): 47–55.

Kawaller, Ira G., and Paul D. Koch, and Timothy W. Koch. "Intraday Market Behavior and the Extent of Feedback Between the S&P 500 Future Prices and the S&P 500 Index." *Journal of Financial Research* (Summer 1993): 107–121.

————. "The Relationship between the S&P 500 Index and S&P 500 Index Futures Prices." *Economic Review,* Federal Reserve Bank of Atlanta (May/June 1988): 2–10.

Kleindon, Allan W., and Robert E. Whaley. "On Market? Stocks, Futures, and Options During October 1987." *Journal of Finance* (July 1992): 851–877.

Koch, Paul D. "Reexamining Intraday Simultaneity in Stock Index Future Markets." *Journal of Banking and Finance* (December 1993): 1191–1205.

Morris, Charles S. "Coordinating Circuit Breakers in Stock and Futures Markets." *Economic Review,* Federal Reserve Bank of Kansas City (March/April 1990): 35–48.

————. "Managing Interest Rate Risk with Interest Rate Futures." *Economic Review,* Federal Reserve Bank of Kansas City (March 1989): 3–20.

————. "Managing Stock Market Risk with Stock Index Futures." *Economic Review,* Federal Reserve Bank of Kansas City (June 1989): 3–16.

Thosar, Satish, and Lenos Trigeorgis. "Stock Volatility and Program Trading: Theory and Evidence." *Journal of Applied Corporate Finance* (Winter 1990): 91–96.

CHAPTER 12

OPTIONS MARKETS

Stock options can be used by speculators to benefit from their expectations. They can also be used by financial institutions to reduce their risk.

The specific objectives of this chapter are to:

- explain how stock options are used to speculate,
- explain why stock option premiums vary, and
- explain how options are used by financial institutions to hedge their security portfolios.

BACKGROUND ON STOCK OPTIONS

Options are classified as calls or puts. A **call option** grants the owner the right to purchase a specified financial instrument for a specified price (called the **exercise price** or **strike price)** within a specified period of time. There are two major differences between purchasing an option and purchasing a futures contract. First, the option requires that a premium be paid in addition to the price of the financial instrument. Second, owners of options can choose to let the option expire on the so-called expiration date, without exercising it. That is, call options grant a right, but not an obligation, to purchase a specified financial instrument. The seller (sometimes called the **writer)** of a call option is obligated to provide the specified financial instrument at the price specified by the option contract if the owner exercises the option. Sellers of the call options receive an up-front fee (the premium) from the purchaser as compensation.

A call option is often referred to as **in the money** when the market price of the underlying security exceeds the exercise price, as **at the money** when it is equal to the exercise price, and as **out of the money** when it is below the exercise price.

The second type of option is known as a **put option.** It grants the owner the right to sell a specified financial instrument for a specified price within a specified period of time. As with call options, owners pay a premium to obtain put options. They can exercise the options at any time up to the expiration date but are not obligated to do so.

A put option is often referred to as "in the money" when the market price of the underlying security is below the exercise price, "at the money" when it is equal, and "out of the money" when it exceeds the exercise price.

Call and put options specify 100 shares for the stocks to which they are assigned. Premiums paid for call and put options are determined on the trading floor of exchanges through competitive open outcry between exchange members. The premium for a particular option changes over time as it becomes more or less desirable to traders.

Option contracts are guaranteed by a clearinghouse to ensure that option writers fulfill their obligations. Participants can close out their option positions by making an offsetting transaction. For example, purchasers of an option can offset their positions at any point in time by selling an identical option. The gain or loss is determined by the premium paid when purchasing the option versus the premium received when selling an identical option. Sellers of options can close out their positions at any point in time by purchasing an identical option.

In addition to the "American-style" stock options just described, "European-style" stock options are also available. Although "American-style" stock options can be exercised at any time until the expiration date, the "European-style" stock options can only be exercised just before expiration.

SPECULATING WITH STOCK OPTIONS

Stock options are frequently traded by investors who are attempting to capitalize on their expectations. The decision to speculate by trading call options versus put options depends on the speculator's expectations.

Speculating with Call Options

To illustrate how call options can be used to speculate, consider Pat Jackson, who expects Steelco stock to increase from its current price of $113 per share but does not want to tie up her available funds by investing in stocks. She purchases a call option on Steelco with an exercise price of $115 for a premium of $4 per share. Before the option's expiration date, Steelco's price rises to $121. At that time, Jackson exercises her option, purchasing shares at $115 per share. She then immediately sells those shares at the market price of $121 per share. Her net gain on this transaction is measured below:

Amount received when selling shares	$121 per share
− Amount paid for shares	− $115 per share
− Amount paid for the call option	− $4 per share
= Net gain	$2 per share, or $200 for one contract.

If the price of Steelco stock had not risen above $115 before the option's expiration date, Jackson would have let the option expire. Her net loss would have been the $4 per share she initially paid for the option, or $400 for one option contract.

The potential gains or losses from this call option are shown in the top portion of Exhibit 12.1, based on the assumptions that (1) the call option is exercised on the expiration date, if at all, and (2) if the call option is exercised, the shares received are immediately sold. Exhibit 12.1 shows that the maximum loss when purchasing this option is the premium of $4 per share. For stock prices between $115 and $119, the option is exercised, and the purchaser of a call option incurs a net loss of less than $4 per share. The stock price of $119 is a break-even point, because the gain from exercising the option exactly offsets the premium paid for it. At stock prices above $119, a net gain would be realized.

The lower portion of Exhibit 12.1 shows the net gain or loss to a writer of the same call option, assuming that the writer obtains the stock only when the option is exercised. Under this condition, the call option writer's net gain (loss) is the call option purchaser's net loss (gain), assuming zero transaction costs. The maximum gain to the writer of a call option is the premium received.

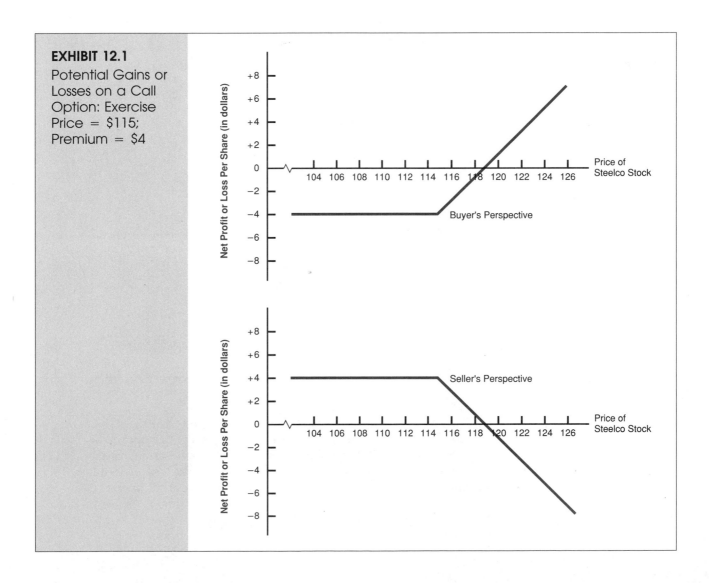

EXHIBIT 12.1

Potential Gains or Losses on a Call Option: Exercise Price = $115; Premium = $4

Quotations of options on numerous stocks are disclosed in *The Wall Street Journal* as shown here. The name of the stock is identified in bold in the left column. The exercise ("strike") price is shown in the second column, with the expiration month in the third column. The next two columns disclose the volume of existing contracts and the most recently quoted premium for a call option with that exercise price and expiration date. The remaining two columns disclose the volume of existing contracts and the most recently quoted premium for a put option with that exercise price and expiration date.

Notice that there are several exercise price and expiration alternatives available for some stocks. Each row under a given stock represents a unique combination of exercise price and expiration date. The number directly under the name of the stock is the most recent market price of that stock.

LISTED OPTIONS QUOTATIONS

Option/Strike	Exp.	Call Vol.	Call Last	Put Vol.	Put Last
AGCO 40	Oct	...	...	30	13/16
A M R 55	Sep	...	...	31	11/8
55¾ 60	Sep	248	7/16	5	37/8
55¾ 60	Oct	31	11/8	...	...
55¾ 60	Nov	140	13/4	10	51/8
A S A 45	Sep	78	19/16	73	1/2
46⅛ 45	Oct	...	...	75	11/16
46⅛ 45	Nov	78	27/8	40	13/8
46⅛ 50	Oct	47	1/2	...	...
46⅛ 50	Nov	153	7/8	72	41/2
46⅛ 50	Feb	40	17/8	40	55/8
AST Rs 15	Sep	24	23/8	48	5/16
17 17½	Sep	115	3/4	30	11/4
17 17½	Oct	10	13/16	115	15/8
17 17½	Nov	41	13/4	53	17/8
17 20	Sep	112	1/8	18	3
17 20	Nov	40	7/8	...	...
AT&T 45	Oct	...	...	60	1/8
53 50	Sep	...	...	66	1/4
53 55	Sep	77	5/16	...	...
53 55	Oct	174	3/4	23	211/16
53 55	Jan	113	15/8	30	31/8
53 60	Oct	60	1/8	...	...
53 60	Jan	329	1/2	...	...
Abbt L 30	Sep	41	7/8	24	1/2
30½ 30	Nov	32	15/8	34	11/8
30½ 35	Feb	98	3/4	5	51/8
Aclaim 17½	Sep	30	17/8	35	9/16
19 20	Sep	145	3/4	...	...
19 22½	Oct	38	1/2	...	...
Actava 7½	Dec	230	41/4	...	...
Acuson 10	Oct	40	31/8	...	...
13⅛ 10	Jan	40	33/4	...	...
13⅛ 15	Jan	31	1	...	...
Adaptc 20	Sep	20	11/8	60	7/8
A M D 22½	Oct	10	61/2	70	3/16
28¾ 25	Oct	34	43/8	34	5/8
28¾ 30	Sep	208	3/8	24	15/8
28¾ 30	Oct	151	13/8	50	23/4
28¾ 30	Jan	125	215/16	...	...
Advnta 35	Oct	104	15/16	...	...
AdvanB 30	Jan	...	21/8	...	...
Aetna 55		...	...	...	11/8

Option/Strike	Exp.	Call Vol.	Call Last	Put Vol.	Put Last
BestBuy 22½	Sep	40	9	...	...
30⅜ 22½	Dec	...	...	40	3/4
30⅜ 25	Sep	57	61/8	964	3/8
30⅜ 25	Oct	60	67/8	121	3/4
30⅜ 25	Dec	40	77/8	...	...
30⅜ 27½	Sep	52	41/2	387	11/16
30⅜ 30	Sep	878	21/2	1042	111/16
30⅜ 30	Oct	15	31/2	62	21/2
30⅜ 30	Dec	22	43/8	35	27/8
30⅜ 32½	Sep	549	13/16	399	27/8
30⅜ 35	Sep	137	5/8	324	41/2
30⅜ 35	Oct	128	13/8	...	...
30⅜ 35	Dec	56	21/2	20	53/4
30⅜ 37½	Sep	60	1/4	...	...
Beth S 17½	Jan	10	41/4	50	9/16
20½ 20	Sep	30	11/4	...	...
20½ 20	Oct	515	13/4	...	...
20½ 22½	Jan	45	11/4	...	...
Bevrly 12½	Sep	40	13/4	...	...
13½ 15	Dec	50	5/8	10	113/4
Biogen 45	Sep	60	43/8	30	13/8
47¹⁵⁄₁₆ 45	Oct	58	6	302	31/8
47¹⁵⁄₁₆ 50	Sep	3	15/8	32	33/4
47¹⁵⁄₁₆ 50	Oct	43	33/8	...	...
47¹⁵⁄₁₆ 50	Apr	63	81/8	...	...
Biomet 10	Oct	36	1	...	...
10⁷⁄₁₆ 10	Apr	37	11/2	...	...
10⁷⁄₁₆ 12½	Oct	40	3/16	...	...
10⁷⁄₁₆ 12½	Jan	61	3/8	...	...
BirStl 25	Oct	50	11/2	...	...
Blk Dk 22½	Nov	127	7/8	...	...
Blkbst 25	Sep	55	21/2	30	3/16
27⅛ 30	Sep	361	1/8	2	211/16
27¼ 30	Oct	48	3/8	20	3
27¼ 30	Dec	56	7/8	...	...
Boeing 40	Sep	30	41/8	9	1/8
44⅛ 40	Nov	41	47/8	5	3/8
44⅛ 40	Feb	...	...	48	1
44⅛ 45	Sep	136	9/16	852	13/8
44⅛ 45	Oct	71	1	70	13/4
44⅛ 45	Nov	178	17/16	55	21/2
44⅛		30	23/8	6	27/8

Several call options are available for a given stock, and the risk-return potential will vary among them. Assume that three types of call options were available on Steelco stock with a similar expiration date, as described in Exhibit 12.2. The potential gains or losses per unit for each option are also shown in Exhibit 12.2, assuming that the option is exercised on the expiration date, if at all. It is also assumed that if the speculators exercise the call option, they immediately sell the stock. The comparison of different options for a given stock illustrates the various risk-return trade-offs from which speculators can choose.

EXHIBIT 12.2
Potential Gains or Losses for Three Call Options (Buyer's Perspective)

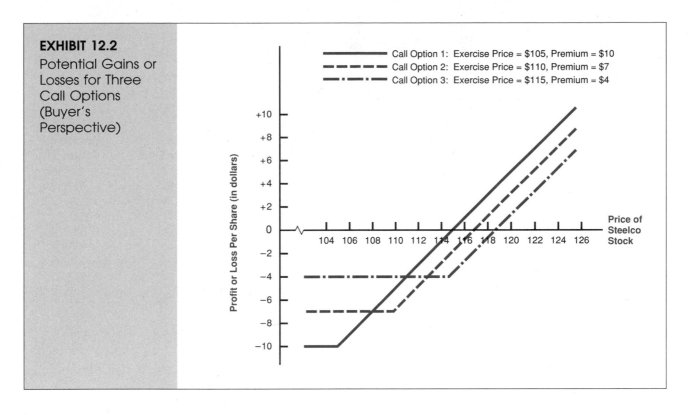

Purchasers of call options would normally be most interested in returns (profit as a percentage of the initial investment) under various scenarios. For this purpose, the contingency graph can be revised to reflect returns for each possible price per share of the underlying stock. The first step is to convert the profit per unit into a return for each possible price, as shown in Exhibit 12.3. For example, for the stock price of $116, Call Option 1 generates a return of 10 percent ($1 per share profit as a percentage of the $10 premium paid), Call Option 2 generates a loss of about 14 percent ($1 per share loss as a percentage of the $7 premium paid), and Call Option 3 generates a loss of 75 percent ($3 per share loss as a percentage of the $4 premium paid).

The data can be transformed into a contingency graph as shown in Exhibit 12.4. This graph illustrates how the potential losses from Call Option 1 are relatively low, but potential returns in the event of a high stock price are also relatively low. Conversely, the potential losses for Call Option 3 are relatively high, but potential returns in the event of a high stock price are also relatively high.

Speculating with Put Options

If speculators had expected the price of Steelco stock to decrease, they might have considered purchasing a put option. For example, assume that a put option on Steelco was available with an exercise price of $110 and with a premium of $2. If the price of Steelco stock falls below $110, speculators could purchase the stock and then exercise their put options to benefit from the transaction. However, they would need to make at least $2 per share on this transaction in order

EXHIBIT 12.3 Potential Returns on Three Different Call Options

Price of Steelco	OPTION 1: EX. PRICE = $105 PREMIUM = $10		OPTION 2: EX. PRICE = $110 PREMIUM = $7		OPTION 3: EX. PRICE = $115 PREMIUM = $4	
	Profit Per Unit	Percentage Return	Profit Per Unit	Percentage Return	Profit Per Unit	Percentage Return
$104	−$10	−100%	−$7	−100%	−$4	−100%
106	− 9	− 90	− 7	−100	− 4	−100
108	− 7	− 70	− 7	−100	− 4	−100
110	− 5	− 50	− 7	−100	− 4	−100
112	− 3	− 30	− 5	− 71	− 4	−100
114	− 1	− 10	− 3	− 43	− 4	−100
116	1	10	− 1	− 14	− 3	− 75
118	3	30	1	14	− 1	− 25
120	5	50	3	43	1	25
122	7	70	5	71	3	75
124	9	90	7	100	5	125
126	11	110	9	129	7	175

EXHIBIT 12.4

Potential Returns for Three Call Options (Buyer's Perspective)

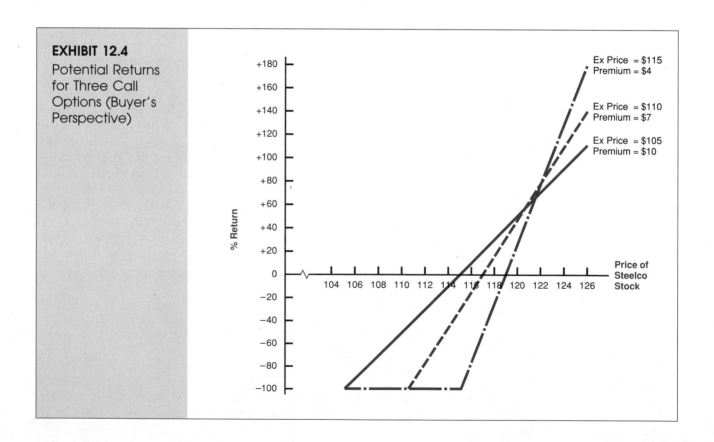

to fully recover the premium paid for the option. If the speculators exercised the option when the market price was $104, their net gain is measured as follows:

Amount received when selling shares	$110 per share
− Amount paid for shares	− $104 per share
− Amount paid for the put option	− $ 2 per share
= Net gain	$ 4 per share

The potential gains or losses from the put option described here are shown in the top portion of Exhibit 12.5, based on the assumptions that (1) the put option is exercised on the expiration date, if at all, and (2) the shares would be purchased just before the put option is exercised. Exhibit 12.5 shows that the maximum loss when purchasing this option is $2 per share. For stock prices between $108 and $110, the purchaser of a put option incurs a net loss of less than $2 per share. The stock price of $108 is a break-even point, because the gain from exercising the put option would exactly offset the $2 per share premium.

The lower portion of Exhibit 12.5 shows the net gain or loss to a writer of the same put option, assuming that the writer sells the stock received as the put option is exercised. Under this condition, the put option writer's net gain (loss) is the put option purchaser's net loss (gain), assuming zero transaction costs. The maximum gain to the writer of a put option is the premium received. As with call options, there are normally several put options available for a given stock, and the potential gains or losses will vary among them.

DETERMINANTS OF STOCK OPTION PREMIUMS

Stock option premiums are determined by market forces. Any characteristic of an option that results in many willing buyers but few willing sellers will place upward pressure on the option premium. Thus, the option premium must be sufficiently high to equalize the demand by buyers and the supply that sellers are willing to sell. This generalization applies to call options and put options. The specific characteristics that affect the demand and supply conditions, and therefore affect the option premiums, are described below.

Determinants of Call Option Premiums

Call option premiums are affected primarily by the following factors:

- Market price of the underlying instrument (relative to option's exercise price)
- Volatility of the underlying instrument
- Time to maturity of the call option

INFLUENCE OF THE MARKET PRICE. The greater the existing market price of the underlying financial instrument relative to the exercise price, the higher the call option premium, other things being equal. A financial instrument's value has a higher probability of increasing well above the exercise price if it is already close to or above the exercise price. Thus, one would be willing to pay a higher premium for a call option on that instrument.

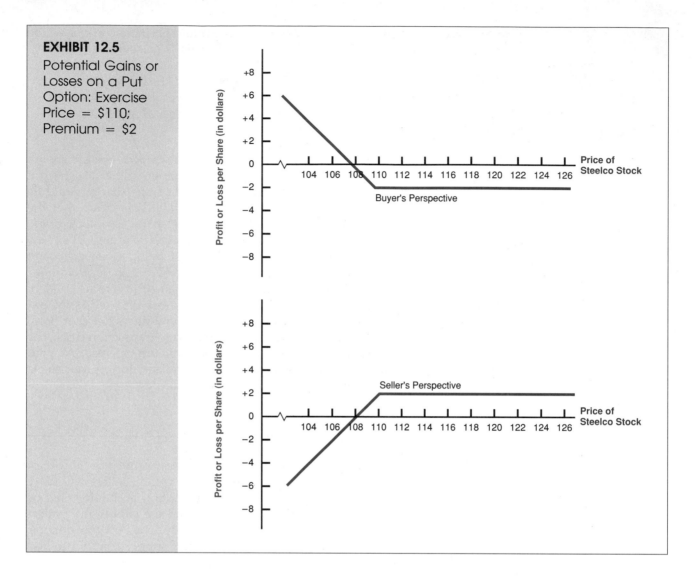

EXHIBIT 12.5

Potential Gains or Losses on a Put Option: Exercise Price = $110; Premium = $2

The influence of the market price of an instrument (relative to the exercise price) on the call option premium can also be understood by comparing options with different exercise prices on the same instrument at a given point in time. For example, consider the data shown in Exhibit 12.6 for IBM call options quoted on April 10, 1994, with a similar expiration date. The premium for the call option with the $45 exercise price was more than $7.00 higher than the premium for the option with the $60 exercise price. This example confirms that a higher premium is required to lock in a lower exercise price on call options.

INFLUENCE OF THE INSTRUMENT'S VOLATILITY. The greater the volatility of the underlying financial instrument, the higher the call option premium, other things being equal. There is a higher probability of an instrument's price increasing well above the exercise price if the instrument is volatile. Thus, one would be willing to pay a higher premium for a call option on that instrument. To illus-

WSJ

USING *THE WALL STREET JOURNAL*

LONG-TERM OPTION QUOTATIONS

Quotations for long-term options (called "LEAPS") are disclosed in *The Wall Street Journal,* as shown here. For each stock identified in the left column, one or more exercise ("strike") prices are disclosed (see the second column). The expiration date ("exp.") is in the third column. The next two columns indicate the volume of contracts that have been traded for the call option on that stock and the most recent premium paid for the call option. The remaining two columns indicate the volume of contracts that have been traded for the put option in that stock and the most recent premium paid for the put option.

SOURCE: *The Wall Street Journal,* August 8, 1994, P. C12. Reprinted by permission of *The Wall Street Journal,* © 1994. Dow Jones & Company, Inc. All rights reserved worldwide.

LEAPS — LONG TERM OPTIONS

Option/	Strike	Exp.	Call Vol.	Call Last	Put Vol.	Put Last
ABarck	17½	Jan 96	29	7½	...	...
22⅛	25	Jan 96	65	3⅝	...	...
22⅛	30	Jan 96	20	2 1/16	...	...
AT&T	45	Jan 96	...	...	40	1¼
54⅛	55	Jan 96	9	5¾	10	4⅞
54⅛	60	Jan 96	30	3⅝	10	7⅞
54⅛	70	Jan 96	10	1 5/16	...	...
AbtLab	30	Jan 96	20	2⅝	...	...
27½	35	Jan 96	43	1⅛	...	...
AirTch	30	Jan 96	15	2⅞	...	...
AmExpr	30	Jan 96	100	3	...	...
Amgen	40	Jan 96	13	15½	...	...
50 13/16	55	Jan 97	45	9½	...	...
Anheus	60	Jan 96	...	...	105	8⅝
AppleC	40	Jan 96	13	4½	...	...
BellAt	50	Jan 96	12	10¼	1	2¼
Boeing	40	Jan 96	27	8⅜	...	...
45⅛	45	Jan 96	450	5½	5	3⅞
45⅛	50	Jan 95	200	6½	...	...
45⅛	50	Jan 96	200	3⅝	...	...
45⅛	55	Jan 96	15	2¼	...	...
BorInt	10	Jan 96	100	5	...	...
12⅝	25	Jan 96	20	1¼	...	...
BrMySq	50	Jan 96	23	7	10	3
53⅞	60	Jan 96	19	2⅜	...	...
53⅞	70	Jan 96	11	¾	...	...
Caterp	80	Jan 96	...	...	30	2⅜
Chiron	35	Jan 96	100	27⅝	...	...
58½	50	Jan 96	...	...	20	5⅞
Chrysl	30	Jan 96	40	17¾	...	...
45⅞	50	Jan 96	10	6½	3	7½
45⅞	60	Jan 96	10	3	...	...
Cisco	15	Jan 96	26	8½	...	...
CocaCl	30	Jan 96	...	...	10	½
43⅝	30	Jan 97	...	...	20	¾
43⅝	40	Jan 96	40	7¼	...	...
43⅝	50	Jan 96	10	2⅝	...	...
ColGas	35	Jan 97	20	5¾	...	...
Compaq	38⅜	Jan 96	58	6	...	...
33⅝	40	Jan 96	80	5	...	...
33⅝	45	Jan 96	20	3¾	...	...
Digital	15	Jan 97	10	9⅜	...	...
20⅜	20	Jan 97	12	7	...	...
20⅜	30	Jan 96	18	2 9/16	5	10¼
Disney	30	Jan 97	...	...	40	1⅛
42¼	40	Jan 97	...	...	20	3¾
42¼	50	Jan 97	25	6	10	9
DuPont	55	Jan 96	11	9⅛	...	...
EKodak	45	Jan 97	30	9⅜	...	...
FedNMt	100	Jan 97	20	7¾	...	...
Ford	25	Jan 97	615	8¼	10	2⅛
FordM	25	Jan 96	10	7	...	...
29¾	32½	Jan 96	60	3¼	5	5
GTE	30	Jan 96	10	3⅞	...	...
32⅜	35	Jan 96	52	1⅞	12	4¾
GenEl	30	Jan 97	...	...	120	½
49⅛	55	Jan 96	12	3	...	...
Glaxo	15	Jan 96	20	4½	50	1¼
18⅝	20	Jan 96	22	2⅛	...	...
18⅝	20	Jan 97	...	...	20	4⅜
18⅝	25	Jan 96	10	13/16	...	...
GnMotr	40	Jan 96	10	14⅛	...	...
50¼	45	Jan 96	10	11⅛	2	3⅜
50¼	60	Jan 96	17	4¼	...	...
50¼	60	Jan 97	46	7¼	10	13⅛
50¼	65	Jan 96	11	3	...	...
50¼	70	Jan 96	18	2⅛	...	...
Hmstke	12½	Jan 97	...	...	24	1⅝
17⅞	22½	Jan 97	15	4⅛	...	...
Homstk	25	Jan 96	10	2 1/16	...	...
IBM	50	Jan 96	5	16½	70	2
62½	60	Jan 96	64	10⅝	9	5⅜
62½	70	Jan 96	15	6	12	10½
IntPap	80	Jan 96	13	6½	...	...
Intel	40	Jan 96	15	21¼	...	...
58⅛	65	Jan 96	13	7½	...	...
JohnJn	45	Jan 97	1	9½	81	3½
47⅞	50	Jan 96	7	4⅛	15	5
K mart	15	Jan 96	22	3⅛	2	1⅞
16⅜	20	Jan 96	10	1⅛	...	...
MCI	25	Jan 96	15	3¼	...	...
MMM	45	Jan 97	...	...	20	2⅛
Magnal	55	Jan 96	...	...	15	17¼
McDonld	22½	Jan 96	...	...	30	1
26¼	32½	Jan 96	16	1 11/16	...	...
Merck	25	Jan 96	...	...	32	1 3/16
29⅞	25	Jan 97	10	7¾	15	1¾
29⅞	30	Jan 96	48	3¾	17	3
29⅞	30	Jan 97	22	5⅛	27	3¾
29⅞	35	Jan 96	21	2	...	...
29⅞	40	Jan 96	60	⅞	...	...
Micsft	32½	Jan 96	20	22½	...	...
52½	40	Jan 96	10	17	...	...
52½	47½	Jan 96	...	...	10	3½
52½	50	Jan 96	13	10⅜	...	...
52½	55	Jan 96	21	7⅞	...	...
52½	57½	Jan 96	26	6⅝	...	...
Motorla	50	Jan 96	20	10⅞	4	4⅞
52⅝	60	Jan 96	10	6	...	...
NatnsBk	55	Jan 96	110	6⅛	140	5
Novell	15	Jan 96	10	4⅞	...	...
NwbNwk	25	Jan 96	13	10⅝	...	...
Nynex	40	Jan 96	15	3¼	...	...
OcciPet	17½	Jan 96	...	...	30	9/16
Oracle	20	Jan 96	80	19⅞	...	...
PepsiC	30	Jan 96	3	4⅝	10	2⅜
31	35	Jan 96	17	2⅜	...	...
31	40	Jan 96	43	1⅜	...	...
PhilMr	40	Jan 96	30	15⅜	...	...
55⅛	50	Jan 96	240	8½	200	4⅛
55⅛	60	Jan 96	46	4⅛	5	9¼
55⅛	60	Jan 97	20	6	...	...
55⅛	80	Jan 96	10	11/16	...	...
PlacrD	15	Jan 96	20	7¼	...	...
20¼	20	Jan 96	12	4½	...	...
ProctG	50	Jan 96	...	...	40	2⅞
RJR Nb	7½	Jan 96	20	1	...	...
6¼	10	Jan 96	10	½	...	...
Salomn	35	Jan 97	35	13⅜	...	...
43	60	Jan 96	10	1 15/16	...	...
SchrPl	55	Jan 96	200	14¾	...	...
65¾	70	Jan 96	...	...	30	7¼
SnapBv	12½	Jan 96	...	...	30	2
SunMic	35	Jan 96	20	1⅞	...	...
TelMex	40	Jan 96	15	25	...	...
63	45	Jan 96	...	...	20	2
63	55	Jan 96	380	15¼	13	4⅞
63	65	Jan 96	28	9⅝	7	9⅛
63	85	Jan 96	315	4⅛	...	...
TexInd	80	Jan 96	...	...	26	11⅞
34⅞	100	Jan 96	75	7½	...	...
TexInst	60	Jan 97	52	29⅛	...	...
79⅛	70	Jan 97	...	...	54	9¼
Travelr	45	Jan 96	15	1¾	...	...
US Surg	20	Jan 96	2	6½	20	3
22¼	25	Jan 97	13	5¾	...	...
Unisys	10	Jan 96	45	1 9/16	...	...
Unocal	25	Jan 96	...	...	50	1½
28¼	30	Jan 96	20	3	...	...
Upjohn	30	Jan 96	...	...	11	2¾
WalMrt	20	Jan 96	250	6⅜	...	...
24½	25	Jan 96	...	...	60	2½
24½	30	Jan 96	104	1¾	10	6
WarnL	80	Jan 97	...	...	20	11⅛
Wellflt	20	Jan 96	14	5¾	...	...
Wolwth	12½	Jan 97	50	5¼	...	...
WstgEl	10	Jan 96	15	3⅜	...	...
11¾	10	Jan 97	45	4⅛	10	1⅛
11¾	12½	Jan 97	10	2⅞	20	2⅛
11¾	15	Jan 96	16	1¼	...	...

EXHIBIT 12.6 Relationship between Exercise Price and Call Option Premium on IBM Stock

EXERCISE PRICE	PREMIUM FOR JULY EXPIRATION DATE
45	$8^1/_2$
50	$5^1/_4$
55	$2^3/_4$
60	$1^1/_4$
65	$^9/_{16}$

trate, call options on small stocks normally have higher premiums than call options on large stocks because small stocks are typically more volatile.

INFLUENCE OF THE CALL OPTION'S TIME TO MATURITY. The longer the call option's time to maturity, the higher the call option premium, other things being equal. A longer time period until expiration allows the owner of the option more time to exercise the option. Thus, there is a higher probability that the instrument's price will move well above the exercise price before the option expires.

The relationship between the time to maturity and the call option premium is illustrated in Exhibit 12.7 for IBM call options quoted on April 10, 1994, with a similar exercise price. The premium was $6.62 per share for the call option with an October expiration month versus $2.87 per share for the call option with an April expiration month. The difference reflects the additional time in which the October call option can be exercised.

Determinants of Put Option Premiums

The premium paid on a put option is dependent on the same factors that affect the premium paid on a call option. However, the direction of influence varies for one of the factors, as explained below.

EXHIBIT 12.7 Relationship between Time to Maturity and Call Option Premium on IBM Stock

EXPIRATION DATE	PREMIUM FOR OPTION WITH A $50 EXERCISE PRICE
April	$2^7/_8$
May	$3^7/_8$
July	$5^1/_4$
October	$6^5/_8$

INFLUENCE OF THE MARKET PRICE. The higher the existing market price of the underlying financial instrument relative to the exercise price, the lower the put option premium, other things being equal. A financial instrument's value has a higher probability of decreasing well below the exercise price if it is already close to or below the exercise price. Thus, one would be willing to pay a higher premium for a put option on that instrument. This influence on the put option premium differs from the influence on the call option premium, because a lower market price is preferable from the perspective of put option purchasers.

The influence of the market price of an instrument (relative to the exercise price) on the put option premium can also be understood by comparing options with different exercise prices on the same instrument at a given point in time. For example, consider the data shown in Exhibit 12.8 for IBM put options with a similar expiration date quoted on April 10, 1994. The premium for the put option with the $60 exercise price was more than $7.00 per share higher than the premium for the option with the $45 exercise price. The difference reflects the more favorable price at which the stock can be sold when holding the put option with the higher exercise price.

INFLUENCE OF THE INSTRUMENT'S VOLATILITY. The greater the volatility of the underlying financial instrument, the higher the put option premium, other things being equal. This relationship also held for call option premiums. There is a higher probability of an instrument's price deviating far from the exercise price if the instrument is volatile. One would be willing to pay a higher premium for a put option on that instrument, because its market price is more likely to decline well below the option's exercise price.

INFLUENCE OF THE PUT OPTION'S TIME TO MATURITY. The longer the time to maturity, the higher the put option premium, other things being equal. This relationship also held for put option premiums. A longer time period until expiration allows the owner of the option more time to exercise the option. Thus, there is a higher probability that the instrument's price will move well below the exercise price before the option expires.

The relationship between the time to maturity and the put option premium is shown in Exhibit 12.9 for IBM put options with a similar exercise price quoted on April 10, 1994. The premium was $3.38 per share for the put option with an October expiration month versus $.35 per share for the put option with an April expiration month. The difference reflects the additional time in which the put option with the October expiration date can be exercised.

EXHIBIT 12.8	Relationship between Exercise Price and Put Option Premium on IBM Stock	
EXERCISE PRICE	**PREMIUM FOR JUNE EXPIRATION DATE**
$45	$13/16$
50	$2^5/16$
55	$4^5/8$
60	$8^1/2$

EXHIBIT 12.9 Relationship between Time to Maturity and Put Option Premium on IBM Stock	
EXPIRATION DATE	**PREMIUM FOR A $50 EXERCISE PRICE**
April	$5/16$
May	$1^5/16$
June	$2^5/16$
October	$3^3/8$

HEDGING WITH STOCK OPTIONS

Call and put options on selected stocks and stock indexes are commonly used for hedging against possible stock price movements. Financial institutions such as mutual funds, insurance companies, and pension funds manage large stock portfolios and are the most common users of options for hedging.

Hedging With Call Options

To illustrate how call options are used to hedge, consider a case in which Portland Pension Fund purchases a substantial amount of Steelco stock. Assume it is somewhat concerned that the stock may perform poorly over the next few months. The sale of a call option on Steelco stock can hedge against such a potential loss. This is known as a **covered call,** because the option is covered, or backed, by stocks already owned.

If the market price of Steelco stock rises, the call option will likely be exercised, and Portland Pension Fund will fulfill its obligation by selling its Steelco stock to the purchaser of the call option at the exercise price. Conversely, if the market price of Steelco stock declines, the option will not be exercised. Consequently, Portland would not have to sell its Steelco stock, and the premium received from selling the call option would represent a gain that could partially offset the decline in the price of the stock. In this case, although the market value of the institution's stock portfolio is adversely affected, it is at least partially offset by the premium received from selling the call option.

NUMERICAL EXAMPLE. The logic of covered call writing to hedge can be reinforced by extending the previous example with specific assumptions. Assume that Portland Pension Fund purchased Steelco stock at the market price of $112 per share. To hedge against a temporary decline in Steelco's stock price, Portland sold call options on Steelco stock with an exercise price of $110 per share for a premium of $5 per share. The net profit to Portland Pension Fund when using covered call writing is represented by the dashed line in Exhibit 12.10 for various possible scenarios. For comparison purposes, the profit earned by Portland Pension Fund if it did not use covered call writing but sold the stock on the option's expiration date is also illustrated (see the solid diagonal line) for various possible scenarios in Exhibit 12.10. Notice how the results from covered call writing are

EXHIBIT 12.10   Risk-Return Trade-off from Covered Call Writing

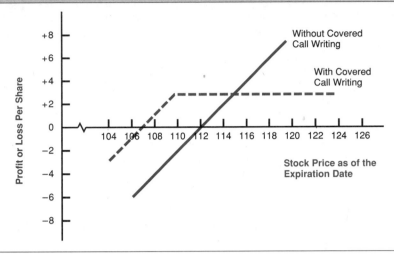

EXPLANATION OF PROFIT PER SHARE FROM COVERED CALL WRITING

MARKET PRICE OF STEELCO AS OF THE EXPIRATION DATE	PRICE AT WHICH PORTLAND PENSION FUND SELLS STEELCO STOCK		PREMIUM RECEIVED FROM WRITING THE CALL OPTION		PRICE PAID FOR STEELCO STOCK		PROFIT OR LOSS PER SHARE
$104	$104	+	$5	−	$112	=	−$3
105	105	+	5	−	112	=	− 2
106	106	+	5	−	112	=	− 1
107	107	+	5	−	112	=	0
108	108	+	5	−	112	=	1
109	109	+	5	−	112	=	2
110	110	+	5	−	112	=	3
111	110	+	5	−	112	=	3
112	110	+	5	−	112	=	3
113	110	+	5	−	112	=	3
114	110	+	5	−	112	=	3
115	110	+	5	−	112	=	3
116	110	+	5	−	112	=	3
117	110	+	5	−	112	=	3
118	110	+	5	−	112	=	3
119	110	+	5	−	112	=	3
120	110	+	5	−	112	=	3

not as bad as without covered call writing when the stock performs poorly, but not as good when the stock performs well.

The table below the graph in Exhibit 12.10 explains the profit or loss per share from covered call writing. At any price above $110 per share as of the expiration date, the call option would be exercised, and Portland would have to sell its holdings of Steelco stock at the exercise price of $110 per share to the purchaser of the call option. The net gain to Portland would be $3 per share, determined as the premium of $5 per share, received when writing the option, minus the $2 per share difference between the price paid for the Steelco stock and the price at which the stock is sold. When comparing the profit or loss per scenario with versus without covered call writing, it is clear that covered call writing limits the upside potential return on stocks but also reduces the risk.

Hedging With Put Options

Put options on stock are also used to hedge stock positions. To illustrate, reconsider the example in which Portland Pension Fund was concerned about the possible temporary decline in the price of Steelco stock. Portland could hedge against a temporary decline in Steelco's stock price by purchasing put options on that stock. In the event that Steelco's stock price declines, Portland would likely generate a gain on its option position, which would help offset the reduction in the stock's price. If Steelco's stock price does not decline, Portland would not exercise its put option. The use of put options to hedge is more typical for situations in which there is a concern of just a temporary decline in a stock's value. If portfolio managers were more concerned about the long-term performance of the stock, they would likely sell the stock itself rather than hedge the position.

STOCK INDEX OPTIONS

A **stock index option** provides the right to trade a specified stock index at a specified price by a specified expiration date. Call options on stock indexes allow the right to purchase the index while put options on stock indexes allow the right to sell the index.

Options are offered on the S&P 100 index, the S&P 500 index, the Major Market Index (20 stocks that attempt to mirror movements in the overall market), the Value Line index (1,700 stocks), the National OTC index (100 stocks traded in the Over-the-Counter market), and the NYSE Composite (all stocks traded on the New York Stock Exchange). Options are also offered on some industry indexes, such as a computer technology index and an institutional index. If and when the index option is exercised, the cash payment is equal to a specified dollar amount multiplied by the difference between the index level and the exercise price.

Options on indexes have become popular for speculating on general movements in the stock market overall. Speculators who anticipate a sharp increase in stock market prices overall may consider purchasing call options on one of the aforementioned market indexes. Conversely, speculators who anticipate a stock market decline may consider purchasing put options on these indexes.

Hedging With Stock Index Options

Financial institutions such as insurance companies and pension funds maintain large stock portfolios whose values are driven by general market movements. If the stock portfolio is broad enough, any changes in its value will likely be highly correlated with the market movements. For this reason, portfolio managers consider purchasing put options on a stock index to protect against stock market

USING *THE WALL STREET JOURNAL*

STOCK INDEX OPTION QUOTATIONS

Quotations for various stock index options are disclosed in *The Wall Street Journal,* as shown here. Some of the more popular index options are the S&P 100 index and the S&P 500 index. Options are also available on a Japanese stock index. For each option, the expiration month is shown in the first column. The exercise ("Strike") price is disclosed in the second column, followed by the letter "c" (for call option) or "p" (for put option). The volume of contracts traded on the day ("vol.") for that specific option is also disclosed, along with the premium that was last quoted ("last"). The "net chg." represents the change in the price from the previous trading day, while "open int." represents the open interest, or amount of contracts outstanding on that particular option.

SOURCE: *The Wall Street Journal,* August 5, 1994, P. C13. Reprinted by permission of *The Wall Street Journal,* © 1994. Dow Jones & Company, Inc. All rights reserved worldwide.

INDEX OPTIONS TRADING

Thursday, August 4, 1994

Volume, last, net change and open interest for all contracts. Volume figures are unofficial. Open interest reflects previous trading day. p-Put c—Call

CHICAGO

NASDAQ-100(NDX)

Strike	Vol.	Last	Net Chg.	Open Int.
Sep 330p	3	15/16	− 1 11/16	1,585
Oct 330p	750	2	...	...
Sep 340c	75	32½	− 4	435
Aug 355c	50	13½	− 3½	855
Aug 355p	10	1⅛	+ ⅝	611
Aug 360c	199	9½	− 2½	1,868
Aug 360c	123	2¼	+ 1	294
Sep 360p	151	4½	+ ½	4,371
Aug 365c	293	5¼	− 4½	1,052
Aug 365p	364	4	+ 1½	980
Oct 365p	2,400	9½	− 1¾	1
Aug 370c	393	2¾	− 2½	1,129
Aug 370p	193	5¾	+ 2¼	924
Sep 370c	100	7	− 1⅞	323
Sep 370p	12	8⅛	+ 1¼	132
Aug 375c	159	1½	− 1¼	1,050
Aug 375p	38	7½	+ 1	180
Aug 380p	255	12½	+ 2¼	1,261
Oct 380c	2,500	5¾	− 3½	204
Sep 390p	1	20¼	+ 3	363

Call vol. ....3,794 Open Int........ 20,300
Put vol.........4,300 Open Int........32,003

RUSSELL 2000(RUT)

Strike	Vol.	Last	Net Chg.	Open Int.
Aug 240c	4	⅞	+ 7/16	1,289
Aug 245c	8	2	− 9/16	297
Aug 245p	12	2	+ ⅝	752
Sep 245p	10	3⅞	+ ⅜	1,982
Sep 250c	50	1⅞	− 6¾	1,762
Sep 250p	75	7	+ 1⅞	6,362

Call vol. ....58 Open Int.........8,484
Put vol. ....401 Open Int........21,752

S & P 100 INDEX(OEX)

Strike	Vol.	Last	Net Chg.	Open Int.
Sep 370p	31	5/16	...	5,844
Oct 370p	100	11/16	+ 1/16	4,839
Nov 370p	30	1¼	...	513
Aug 375p	650	⅛	...	5,350
Oct 375p	520	1	+ ¼	196
Aug 380p	20	⅛	...	10,416
Sep 380p	1	7/16	...	5,876
Oct 380p	28	1¼	+ 3/16	2,126
Aug 385p	40	⅛	...	11,990
Sep 385p	182	⅝	+ ⅛	4,604

S & P 500 INDEX-AM(SPX)

Strike	Vol.	Last	Net Chg.	Open Int.
Sep 350c	?	110⅝	+ 6⅞	1,496
Sep 350p	1,540	1/16	...	9,641
Aug 410p	80	1/16	− 1/16	4,822
Aug 420p	40	⅛	...	5,910
Aug 425p	189	⅛	...	9,600
Aug 430p	5	¼	...	20,119
Sep 430p	1,010	11/16	+ 1/16	31,464
Oct 430p	7	2⅞	+ ½	1,537
Aug 435p	5	¼	...	14,163
Sep 435p	16	1¼	− 1/16	14,332
Aug 440c	1	19	− 2⅞	4,006
Aug 440p	1,809	½	+ 1/16	17,837
Sep 440p	1,553	2⅛	+ ⅜	52,145
Oct 440p	2	3½	...	983
Aug 445c	101	14⅜	− ⅜	13,038
Sep 445p	2,425	⅞	+ ⅜	26,284
Aug 445p	1,063	3	+ 15/16	21,761
Aug 450c	160	10⅛	− 1	17,576
Sep 450c	2,790	1 11/16	+ 1/16	26,145
Sep 450c	336	12⅜	− 2	34,685
Sep 450p	3,976	3¾	+ ⅞	56,629
Oct 450p	249	6½	+ 1⅜	7,766
Aug 455c	561	5⅝	− 2⅛	16,395
Aug 455c	4,310	2¾	+ 1⅛	19,585
Sep 455c	200	8¾	− 1⅞	32,553
Sep 455p	1,078	5⅛	+ 1⅛	20,289
Oct 455p	33	7⅜	+ 1	1,028
Aug 460c	3,990	2 13/16	− 15/16	22,764
Aug 460p	5,751	4⅞	+ 2	14,357
Sep 460c	1,690	5¼	− 1½	20,763
Sep 460p	1,218	7⅛	+ 1½	15,660
Oct 460c	300	10¼	− ⅛	5,489
Oct 460p	555	8⅝	+ ½	6,615
Aug 465c	10,407	15/16	− 9/16	43,186
Aug 465p	1,021	7⅞	+ 2⅛	5,837
Sep 465c	826	3¼	− 1	12,270
Sep 465p	139	9⅝	+ 1¾	3,352
Oct 465c	103	7	...	1,594
Oct 465p	104	11½	+ 1⅛	32
Aug 470c	8,532	⅛	− ¼	30,146
Aug 470p	30	11⅞	+ 2¾	3,494
Sep 470c	1,170	1 11/16	− ½	20,505
Sep 470p	20	12¾	+ 1⅞	6,893
Oct 470c	1,000	4⅜	− ⅝	3,286
Aug 475c	1,725	⅛	− 1/16	26,563
Aug 475p	3	16¼	+ 1⅞	1,482
Sep 475c	2,380	1	+ ¼	55,423
Sep 475p	50	16⅝	+ 1	14,614
Oct 475p	5	17¾	+ 2	3
Aug 480c	700	1/16	...	16,443
Sep 480c	10	⅜	− 1/16	24,875

AMERICAN

HONG KONG INDEX(HKO)

Strike	Vol.	Last	Net Chg.	Open Int.
Sep 180p	3	3½	+ ⅝	290
Aug 195p	50	5¾	+ ¼	151

Call vol. .... 0 Open Int..........4,326
Put vol.............53 Open Int...........3,737

INSTITUTIONAL-AM(XII)

Strike	Vol.	Last	Net Chg.	Open Int.
Sep 400c	25	5/16	− 11/16	98
Aug 445p	5	9/16	− ⅝	27
Aug 450p	10	15/16	− 3/16	281
Aug 465c	25	1⅛	− 1 11/16	1,189
Oct 465p	25	11⅜	− 2⅝	100
Oct 470p	50	14	+ 2	75

Call vol. ....25 Open Int.......... 36,527
Put vol. .... 115 Open Int........ 16,784

JAPAN INDEX(JPN)

Strike	Vol.	Last	Net Chg.	Open Int.
Aug 200c	2	10¼	+ ⅝	98
Aug 205c	3	6	− ¼	1,873
Sep 205c	2	7¾	+ ¼	583
Aug 210c	10	2⅝	+ ½	793
Sep 210p	150	4⅜	− ⅞	385
Sep 215c	20	2 7/16	− 9/16	305
Aug 220c	15	⅛	+ 1/16	491
Aug 220p	1	10⅜	− 5½	14
Aug 220c	11	1¼	− ¼	797

Call vol. .... 251 Open Int........ 27,853
Put vol. .... 581 Open Int........ 26,748

MAJOR MARKET(XMI)

Strike	Vol.	Last	Net Chg.	Open Int.
Oct 360p	3	2 3/16	+ 1/16	20
Aug 365p	20	¼	...	328
Aug 365p	4	15/16	− 3/16	60
Aug 370c	4	17¾	+ 1½	33
Oct 370p	6	3½	− ⅝	78
Aug 375c	327	⅞	+ ¼	1,334
Sep 375p	5	2⅜	+ ⅛	403
Aug 380c	1	7½	− 1⅝	924
Aug 380p	339	1¾	+ ¾	1,948
Sep 380p	5	3⅛	...	555
Aug 385c	15	4⅜	− ⅛	404
Aug 385p	79	3¼	+ 1¼	875
Sep 385c	30	5⅛	+ ⅜	30
Oct 385c	9	9¾	+ 3⅛	10

declines. The put options should be purchased on the stock index that most closely mirrors the portfolio to be hedged. If the stock market experiences a severe downturn, the market value of the portfolio declines. Yet, the put options on the stock index will generate a gain because the value of the index would be less than the exercise price. The greater the market downturn, the greater is the decline in the market value of the portfolio, but the greater is the gain from holding put options on a stock index. Thus, the overall impact on the firm is minimized because of this offsetting effect.

If the stock market rises, the put options on the stock index will not be exercised. Thus, there would have been a cost of purchasing the options that is not recovered. This situation is similar to purchasing other forms of insurance, but not using them. Some portfolio managers may still believe the options were worthwhile for temporary protection against downside risk.

HEDGING WITH LONG-TERM STOCK INDEX OPTIONS. In the early 1990s, **long-term equity anticipations** (LEAPs) were created for option market participants who wanted options with longer terms until expiration. For example, LEAPs on the S&P 100 and S&P 500 indexes were available, with expiration dates extending at least two years ahead. Each of these indexes is revised to 1/10 its normal size when applying LEAPs. This results in smaller premiums, which makes the LEAPs more affordable to smaller investors.

The transaction costs in hedging over a long period are lower than the costs of continually repurchasing short-term put options each time the options expire or are exercised. Furthermore, the costs of continually repurchasing put options are uncertain, whereas the costs of purchasing a put option on a long-term index option are known immediately.

Dynamic Asset Allocation With Stock Index Options

Dynamic asset allocation involves the switching between risky and low-risk investment positions over time in response to changing expectations. Stock index options are used by some portfolio managers as a tool for dynamic asset allocation. For example, stock portfolio managers can purchase call options on a stock index when they anticipate favorable market movements, which creates more pronounced effects of market conditions. They are essentially using stock index options to increase their exposure to stock market conditions. Conversely, they can purchase put options on a stock index when they anticipate unfavorable market movements to reduce the effects that market conditions will have on their stock portfolios.

Because stock options are available with various exercise prices, portfolio managers can select an exercise price that satisfies the degree of protection desired. For example, assume an existing stock index was quite similar to the existing stock portfolio, and assume the portfolio managers wanted to protect against a loss beyond 5 percent. If the prevailing level of the index was 400, the managers could purchase put options that have an exercise price of 380, because that level is 5 percent lower than 400. If the index declined to a level below 380, the option would be exercised and the gain from exercising the option would partially offset the reduction in the stock portfolio's market value.

This strategy represents a form of insurance, where the premium paid for the put option is similar to an insurance premium. Because the index would have to decline by 5 percent before the option would possibly be exercised, this reflects a type of "deductible" that is common in insurance policies. If portfolio managers desired to protect against even smaller losses, they could purchase a put option that specifies a higher exercise price on the index, such as 390. However, the premium paid for the option would be larger for the extra protection. In other words, the cost of the portfolio insurance would be higher because of the smaller "deductible" desired.

Another form of dynamic asset allocation is for portfolio managers to sell (write) call options on stock indexes in periods when they expect the stock market to be very stable. This strategy does not create a perfect hedge but can enhance the portfolio performance in periods when the stock prices are stagnant or decreasing.

Portfolio managers can adjust the risk-return profile of their investment position by using stock index options rather than restructuring their existing stock portfolios. This form of dynamic asset allocation avoids the substantial transaction costs associated with restructuring the stock portfolios.

OPTIONS ON FUTURES CONTRACTS

In recent years, the concept of options has been applied to the concept of futures contracts to create options on futures contracts (sometimes referred to as "futures options"). An option on a particular futures contract allows one the right (but not an obligation) to purchase or sell that futures contract for a specified price within a specified period of time. Thus, options on futures grant the power to take the futures position if favorable conditions occur but the flexibility to avoid the futures position (by letting the option expire) if unfavorable conditions occur. Like other options, a premium is paid by one who wishes to purchase options on futures.

Options are available on stock index futures. They are used for speculating on expected stock market movements or hedging against adverse market conditions. Individuals and financial institutions use them in a manner similar to how stock index options are used.

Options are also available on interest rate futures, such as Treasury note futures or Treasury bond futures. The settlement dates of the underlying futures contracts are usually a few weeks after the expiration date of the corresponding options contracts.

A call option on interest rate futures grants the right to purchase a futures contract at a specified price within a specified period of time. A put option on financial futures grants the right (again, not an obligation) to sell a particular financial futures contract at a specified price within a specified period of time. Because interest rate futures contracts can hedge interest rate risk, options on interest rate futures might be considered by any financial institution that is exposed to this risk, including savings institutions, commercial banks, life insurance companies, and pension funds.

Speculating With Options on Futures

Speculators who anticipate a decline in interest rates may consider purchasing a call option on Treasury bond futures. If their expectations are correct, the market

WSJ
USING *THE WALL STREET JOURNAL*
OPTIONS ON FUTURES QUOTATIONS

Quotations of options on futures are disclosed in *The Wall Street Journal*. The exercise ("strike") price of the futures contract is specified in the left column. The premiums for various expiration months of the call options on the futures contracts are disclosed in the next three columns, while premiums for various expiration months of put options on the futures contracts are disclosed in the following three columns.

The expiration month of each option occurs shortly before the settlement date of the corresponding futures contract.

SOURCE: *The Wall Street Journal*, August 23, 1994, P. C15. Reprinted by permission of *The Wall Street Journal*, © 1994 Dow Jones & Company, Inc. All rights reserved worldwide.

FUTURES OPTIONS PRICES

INTEREST RATE

T-BONDS (CBT)
$100,000; points and 64ths of 100%

Strike	Calls-Settle			Puts-Settle		
Price	Oct	Dec	Mar	Oct	Dec	Mar
99	....	....	0-28	....	....	....
100	2-04	2-55	....	0-46	1-33	2-37
101	1-29	....	....	1-07	....	....
102	0-61	1-49	2-14	1-39	2-26	3-37
103	0-37	....	....	2-15	....	....
104	0-19	1-00	1-30	2-61	3-41	4-50

Est. vol. 70,000;
Fri vol. 48,019 calls; 61,339 puts
Op. int. Fri 200,807 calls; 155,595 puts

T-NOTES (CBT)
$100,000; points and 64ths of 100%

Strike	Calls-Settle			Puts-Settle		
Price	Oct	Nov	Dec	Oct	Nov	Dec
101	....	....	....	0-18	....	0-51
102	....	2-09	0-32	....	....	1-07
103	0-60	....	1-36	0-56	....	1-34
104	0-31	....	1-05	1-29	....	2-03
105	0-14	....	0-44	2-12	....	2-40
106	0-05	....	0-27	....	....	3-23

Est vol 18,400 Fri 14,691 calls 28,530 puts
Op int Fri 49,484 calls 65,1958 puts

MUNICIPAL BOND INDEX (CBT)
$100,000; pts. & 64ths of 100%

Strike	Calls-Settle			Puts-Settle		
Price	Sep	Oct	Nov	Sep	Oct	Nov
88	2-29	....	....	0-18	....	....
89	1-44	....	....	0-32	....	....
90	1-02	....	....	0-53	....	....
91	0-38	....	....	....	....	....
92	0-18	....	....	....	....	....
93	0-09	....	....	2-59	....	....

Est vol 1 Fri 0 calls 0 puts
Op int Fri 927 calls 671 puts

5 YR TREAS NOTES (CBT)
$100,000; points and 64ths of 100%

Strike	Calls-Settle			Puts-Settle		
Price	Oct	Nov	Dec	Oct	Nov	Dec
10300	0-47	....	1-09	0-32	....	0-58
10350	....	....	0-56	0-48	....	1-09
10400	0-18	....	0-43	1-03	....	1-27
10450	0-10	....	0-31	....	....	....
10500	....	....	0-22	....	....	....
10550	....	....	0-14	....	....	....

Est vol 1,000 Fri 2,341 calls 5,739 puts
Op int Fri 13,416 calls 14,323 puts

EURODOLLAR (CME)
$ million; pts. of 100%

Strike	Calls-Settle			Puts-Settle		
Price	Sep	Dec	Mar	Sep	Dec	Mar
9450	0.38	0.08	0.10	.0004	0.37	0.66
9475	0.15	0.03	0.05	0.02	0.57	0.85
9500	0.01	0.01	0.02	0.13	0.80	1.07
9525	.0004	.0004	.0004	0.37	1.05	1.32
9550	.0004	.0004	.0004	0.62	1.30	1.57
9575	.0004	.0004	.0004	0.87	1.55	1.82

Est. vol. 54,792;
Fri vol. 22,677 calls; 28,732 puts
Op. int. Fri 933,167 calls; 982,314 puts

INDEX

S&P 500 STOCK INDEX (CME)
$500 times premium

Strike	Calls-Settle			Puts-Settle		
Price	Sep	Oct	Nov	Sep	Oct	Nov
455	10.35	14.80	....	2.60	4.55	....
460	6.65	11.10	....	3.85	5.80	....
465	3.55	7.75	10.00	5.75	7.40	....
470	1.50	4.95	....	8.70	9.55	....
475	0.50	2.85	....	12.65	....	....
480	0.15	1.45	....	17.30	....	....

Est vol 15,406 Fri 15,027 calls 42,404 puts
Op int Fri 69,217 calls 114,061 puts

GSCI (CME)
$250 times GSCI nearby Prem.

Strike	Calls-Settle			Puts-Settle		
Price	Sep	Oct	Nov	Sep	Oct	Nov
169	....	....	....	....	....	....
170	....	....	....	....	....	....
171	....	....	....	....	....	....
172	....	3.00	....	....	4.20	....
173	....	....	....	....	....	....
174	0.60	....	....	....	3.80	....

Est vol 200 Fri 0 calls 1 puts
Op int Fri 2,178 calls 2,179 puts

value of Treasury bonds would rise, and the price of a Treasury bond futures contract would rise as well. The speculators could exercise their option to purchase futures at the exercise price, which would be lower than the value of the futures contract. They could then sell futures (to create an offsetting position) at a higher price than the price at which they purchased futures. If interest rates had risen, the speculators would likely let their options expire, and their loss would be the premium paid for the call options on futures. Thus, their loss from purchasing options on futures is more limited than if they simply purchased futures contracts.

Some speculators who expect interest rates to remain stable or decline may be willing to sell a put option on Treasury bond futures. If their expectations are correct, the price of a futures contract will likely rise, and the put option will not be exercised. Therefore, sellers of the put option would earn the premium charged.

Speculators who anticipate an increase in interest rates may consider purchasing a put option on Treasury bond futures. If their expectations are correct, the market value of Treasury bonds would decline, and the price of a Treasury bond futures contract would decline as well. The speculators could exercise their option to sell futures at the exercise price, which would be higher than the value of the futures contract. They could then purchase futures (to create an offsetting position) at a lower price than the price at which they sold futures. If interest rates had declined, the speculators would likely let the options expire, and their loss would be the premium paid for the put options on futures.

Some speculators who anticipate an increase in interest rates may be willing to sell a call option on Treasury bond futures. If their expectations are correct, the price of the futures contract will likely decline, and the call option will not be exercised.

NUMERICAL EXAMPLES. To reinforce the concept of speculating with options on futures, consider an example in which a student expects interest rates to decline and purchases a call option on Treasury bond futures. The exercise price on Treasury bond futures is 94–32 (94 and 32/64 percent of $100,000, or $94,500). The call option is purchased at a premium of 2–00 (or 2 percent of $100,000), which equals $2,000. Assume that as a result of a decline in interest rates, the price of the Treasury bond futures contract rises over time, and is valued at $99–00 ($99,000) shortly before the option's expiration date. At this time, the student decides to exercise the option, and closes out the position by selling an identical futures contract. The student's net gain from this speculative strategy is:

Selling Price of T-Bond Futures	$99,000	(99.00% of $100,000)
− Purchase Price of T-Bond Futures	− $94,500	(94.50% of $100,000)
− Call Option Premium Paid	− $ 2,000	(2.00% of $100,000)
= Net Gain to Purchaser of Call Option on Futures	$ 2,500	(2.50% of $100,000)

This net gain of $2,500 represents a return on investment of 125% for the speculator.

Now consider what would have happened to a speculator who had the opposite expectation over this period, and sold a call option on Treasury bond futures. Assume that a professor sold the call option purchased by the student, and would be obligated to purchase the futures contract at the time the option was exercised. The professor's net gain from this speculative strategy is:

Selling Price of T-Bond Futures	$94,500	(94.50% of $100,000)
− Purchase Price of T-Bond Futures	− $99,000	(99.00% of $100,000)
+ Call Option Premium Received	+ $ 2,000	(2.00% of $100,000)
= Net Gain to Seller of Call Option on Futures	− $ 2,500	(−2.50% of $100,000)

In the absence of transaction costs, the professor's loss is equal to the student's gain. If the Treasury bond futures price had remained lower than the exercise price of 94–32 ($94,500) until the expiration date, the option would not have been exercised; the net gain from purchasing the call option on Treasury bond futures would have been −$2,000 (the premium paid for the option) while the net gain from selling the call option would have been $2,000.

As an alternative example, assume a student expects interest rates to increase and purchases a put option on Treasury bond futures. Assume the exercise price on Treasury bond futures is 97–00 ($97,000) and the premium paid for the put option is 3–00 ($3,000). Assume that as a result of increasing interest rates, the price of the Treasury bond futures contract declines over time, and is valued at 89–00 ($89,000) shortly before the option's expiration date. At this time, the student decides to exercise the option, and closes out the position by purchasing an identical futures contract. The student's net gain from this speculative strategy is:

Selling Price of T-Bond Futures	$97,000	(97.00% of $100,000)
− Purchase Price of T-Bond Futures	− $89,000	(89.00% of $100,000)
− Put Option Premium Paid	− $ 3,000	(3.00% of $100,000)
= Net Gain to Purchaser of Put Option on Futures	$ 5,000	(5.00% of $100,000)

This net gain of $5,000 represents a return on investment of about 167 percent for the student.

The person who sold the put option on Treasury bond futures to the student in this example would have incurred a loss of $5,000, assuming that the position was closed out (by selling an identical futures contract) on the same date that the student's position was closed out.

If the Treasury bond futures price had remained above the exercise price of 97–00 until the expiration date, the option would not have been exercised, and the net gain to the student who purchased the put option would have been −$3,000 (the premium paid for the put option).

Hedging with Options on Futures

Options on futures contracts are also used to hedge against risk. To illustrate, assume that Emory Savings and Loan Association has a large number of long-term fixed-rate mortgages that are mainly supported by short-term funds, and would therefore be adversely affected by rising interest rates. It was shown in the previous chapter that the sales of Treasury bond futures could partially offset the adverse effect of rising interest rates in such a situation. Recall that if interest rates were to decline, the potential increase in Emory's interest rate spread (difference between interest revenues and expenses) would be partially offset by the loss on the futures contract.

One potential limitation of selling interest rate futures to hedge mortgages is that the mortgages may be prepaid by households. If interest rates decline and most fixed-rate mortgages are prepaid, an S&L will incur a loss on the futures position without an offsetting gain on its spread. To protect against this risk, Emory could purchase put options on Treasury bond futures. Assume that Emory purchased put options on Treasury bond futures with an exercise price of 98–00 ($98,000) for a premium of 2–00 ($2,000) per contract. The initial Treasury bond futures price was 99–00 at the time. First, assume a scenario in which interest rates rise, causing the Treasury bond futures price to decline to 91–00. In this scenario, Emory would exercise its right to sell Treasury bond futures,

EXHIBIT 12.11   Results from Hedging with Put Options on Treasury Bond Futures

	SCENARIO 1: • INTEREST RATES RISE • T-BOND FUTURES PRICE DECLINES TO 91-00	SCENARIO 2: • INTEREST RATES DECLINE • T-BOND FUTURES PRICE INCREASES TO 104-00
Effect on Emory's spread	Spread is reduced	Spread is increased, but mortgage prepayments may occur
Effect on T-Bond Futures Price	Futures price decreases	Futures price increases
Decision on exercising the put option	Exercise put option	Do not exercise put option
Selling price of T-Bond futures	$98,000	Not sold
− Purchase price of T-Bond futures	−$91,000	Not purchased
−Price paid for put option	−$ 2,000	−$2,000
=Net gain per option	$ 5,000	−$2,000

and offset its position by purchasing identical futures contracts, generating a net gain of $5,000 per contract, as shown in Exhibit 12.11. The gain on the futures position would help offset the reduction in Emory's spread that occurred because of higher interest rates.

Now consider a second scenario in which interest rates decline, causing the Treasury bond futures price to rise to 104–00. In this scenario, Emory would not exercise the put options on Treasury bond futures because the futures position would result in a loss.

This example shows how a put option on futures offers more flexibility than simply selling futures. However, a premium must be paid for the put option. Financial institutions that wish to hedge interest rate risk should compare the possible outcomes from using interest rate futures versus put options on interest rate futures in order to hedge interest rate risk.

INSTITUTIONAL USE OF OPTIONS MARKETS

Exhibit 12.12 summarizes the uses of options by various types of financial institutions, some of which the previous examples have illustrated. Although options positions are sometimes taken by financial institutions for speculative purposes, they are more commonly intended for hedging. Savings institutions and bond mutual funds use options on interest rate futures to hedge interest rate risk. Stock mutual funds, insurance companies, and pension funds use stock index options and options on stock index futures to hedge their stock portfolios.

GLOBALIZATION OF OPTIONS MARKETS

The globalization of stock markets has resulted in the need for a globalized market in stock options. Options on stock indexes representing various countries are

EXHIBIT 12.12 Institutional Use of Options Markets

TYPE OF FINANCIAL INSTITUTION	PARTICIPATION IN OPTIONS MARKETS
Commercial banks	■ Sometimes offer currency options to businesses.
Savings institutions	■ Sometimes take positions in options on futures contracts to hedge interest rate risk.
Mutual funds	■ Stock mutual funds take positions in stock index options to hedge against a possible decline in prices of stocks within their portfolios. ■ Stock mutual funds sometimes take speculative positions in stock index options in an attempt to increase their returns. ■ Bond mutual funds sometimes take positions in options on futures to hedge interest rate risk.
Securities firms	■ Serve as a broker by executing stock option transactions for individuals and businesses.
Pension funds	■ Take positions in stock index options to hedge against a possible decline in prices of stocks within their portfolio. ■ Take positions in options on futures contracts to hedge their bond portfolios against interest rate movements.
Insurance companies	■ Take positions in stock index options to hedge against a possible decline in prices of stocks within their portfolio. ■ Take positions in options on futures contracts to hedge their bond portfolios against interest rate movements.

GLOBAL ASPECTS

now available. Options exchanges have been established in numerous non-U.S. countries, including Australia, Austria, Belgium, France, Germany, and Singapore. U.S. portfolio managers that maintain large holdings of stocks from specific countries are heavily exposed to the conditions of those corresponding markets. Rather than liquidate the portfolio of foreign stocks to protect against a possible temporary decline, the managers can purchase put options on the foreign stock index of concern. Portfolio managers residing in these countries could also use this strategy to hedge their stock portfolios.

Portfolio managers desiring to capitalize on the expectation of temporary favorable movements in foreign markets can purchase call options on the corresponding stock indexes. Thus, the existence of options on foreign stock indexes allows portfolio managers to hedge or speculate based on forecasts of foreign market conditions. The trading of options on foreign stock indexes avoids the transaction costs associated with buying and selling large portfolios of foreign stocks.

Currency Options Contracts

A **currency call option** provides the right to purchase a specified currency for a specified price within a specified period of time. Corporations involved in international business transactions use currency call options to hedge future payables. If the exchange rate at the time payables are due exceeds the exercise price, corporations can exercise their options and purchase the currency at the exercise price. Conversely, if the prevailing exchange rate is lower than the exercise price, corporations can purchase the currency at the prevailing exchange rate and let the options expire.

Speculators purchase call options on currencies that they expect to strengthen against the dollar. If the foreign currency strengthens as expected, they can exercise their call options to purchase the currency at the exercise price and then sell the currency at the prevailing exchange rate.

A **currency put option** provides the right to sell a specified currency for a specified price within a specified period of time. Corporations involved in international business transactions may purchase put options to hedge future receivables. If the exchange rate at the time they receive payment in a foreign currency is less than the exercise price, they can exercise their option by selling the currency at the exercise price. Conversely, if the prevailing exchange rate is higher than the exercise price, they can sell the currency at the prevailing exchange rate and let the options expire.

Speculators purchase put options on currencies they expect to weaken against the dollar. If the foreign currency weakens as expected, the speculators can purchase the currency at the prevailing spot rate and exercise their put options to sell the currency at the exercise price.

For every buyer of a currency call or put option, there must be a seller (or writer). A writer of a call option is obligated to sell the specified currency at the specified strike price if the option is exercised. A writer of a put option is obligated to purchase the specified currency at the specified strike price if the option is exercised. Speculators may be willing to write call options on foreign currencies that they expect to weaken against the dollar or write put options on those they expect to strengthen against the dollar. If a currency option expires without being exercised, the writer keeps the up-front premium received. Currency options are discussed in more detail in Chapter 14.

SUMMARY

- Speculators purchase call options on stocks whose prices are expected to rise and purchase put options on those expected to decrease. They purchase call options on interest rate futures contracts when they expect interest rates to decrease. They buy currency call options when they expect foreign currencies to strengthen and currency put options when they expect foreign currencies to weaken.

- The premium of a stock option is influenced by the characteristics of the option and underlying stock that can affect the potential gains. First, the higher the market price of the stock relative to the exercise price, the higher the premium. Second, the higher the stock's volatility, the higher the premium. Third, the longer term until expiration, the higher the premium.

For put options, the higher the market price of the stock relative to the exercise price, the lower the premium. The volatility of the underlying stock and the term to expiration are related to the put option premium in the same manner as the call option premium.

■ Options markets are widely used by financial institutions to hedge positions. If the institutions desire to hedge against rising interest rates, they may purchase put options on financial futures. Financial institutions such as pension funds and insurance companies can use stock options to hedge their stock portfolios. To hedge against a potential short-term decline in stock prices, they may purchase put options or sell call options. By accommodating the hedging needs of financial institutions, options markets can reduce the risk of these institutions and enhance the public's confidence in the financial system.

QUESTIONS

1. Describe the general differences between a call option and a futures contract.

2. How are call options used by speculators? Describe the conditions in which their strategy would backfire.

3. How are put options used by speculators? Describe the conditions in which their strategy would backfire.

4. Describe the maximum loss that could occur for a purchaser of a call option.

5. Under what conditions would speculators sell a call option?

6. What is the risk to speculators who sell put options?

7. Identify the factors affecting the premium paid on a call option. Describe how each factor affects the size of the premium.

8. Identify the factors affecting the premium paid on a put option. Describe how each factor affects the size of the premium.

9. How can financial institutions with stock portfolios use stock options when they expect stock prices to rise substantially but do not yet have sufficient funds to purchase more stock?

10. Why would a financial institution holding ABC stock consider buying a put option on this stock rather than simply sell the stock?

11. Describe a call option on interest rate futures. How does it differ from purchasing a futures contract?

12. Describe a put option on interest rate futures. How does it differ from selling a futures contract?

13. Assume a savings institution had a large number of fixed-rate mortgages and obtained most of its funds from short-term deposits. How could it use options on interest rate futures to hedge its exposure to interest rate movements? Would futures or options on futures be more appropriate if the institution was concerned that interest rates would decrease, causing a large number of mortgage prepayments?

14. Three S&Ls have identical balance sheet compositions, emphasizing short-term deposits, and long-term fixed-rate mortgages. The S&Ls took the following positions three years ago:

Name of S&L	Position
La Crosse	Sold financial futures.
Stevens Point	Purchased put options on interest rate futures.
Whitewater	Did not take any position in futures.

Assume that interest rates declined consistently over the past three years. Which of the three S&Ls would have achieved the best performance based on this information? Explain.

PROBLEMS

1. A call option on Illinois stock specifies an exercise price of $38. Today's price of the stock is $40. The premium on the call option is $5. Assume the option will not be exercised until maturity, if at all. Complete the following table:

Assumed Stock Price at the Time the Call Option Is About to Expire	Net Profit or Loss per Share to be Earned by the Writer (Seller) of the Call Option
$37	
39	
41	
43	
45	
48	

2. A call option on Michigan stock specifies an exercise price of $55. Today's price of the stock is $54 per share. The premium on the call option is $3. Assume the option will not be exercised until maturity, if at all. Complete the following table for a speculator who purchases the call option:

Assumed Stock Price at the Time the Call Option is About to Expire	Net Profit or Loss per Share to be Earned by the Speculator
$50	
52	
54	
56	
58	
60	
62	

3. A put option on Iowa stock specifies an exercise price of $71. Today's price of the stock is $68. The premium on the put option is $8. Assume the option will not be exercised until maturity, if at all. Complete the following table

for a speculator who purchases the put option (and currently does not own the stock):

Assumed Stock Price at the Time the Put Option Is About to Expire	Net Profit or Loss per Share to be Earned by the Speculator
$60	
64	
68	
70	
72	
74	
76	

4. A put option on Indiana stock specifies an exercise price of $23. Today's price of the stock is $24. The premium on the put option is $3. Assume the option will not be exercised until maturity, if at all. Complete the following table:

Assumed Stock Price at the Time the Put Option Is About to Expire	Net Profit or Loss per Share to be Earned by the Writer (or Seller) of the Put Option
$20	
21	
22	
23	
24	
25	
26	

5a. Assume that Evanston Insurance Inc. has purchased shares of stock E at $50 per share. It will sell the stock in six months. It considers using a strategy of covered call writing to partially hedge its position in this stock. The exercise price is $53, the expiration date is six months, and the premium on the call option is $2. Complete the following table:

Possible Price of Stock E in 6 Months	Profit or Loss per Share if a Covered Call Strategy Is Used	Profit or Loss per Share if a Covered Call Strategy Is Not Used
$47		
50		
52		
55		
57		
60		

5b. Assume that each of the six stock prices in the first column in the table has an equal probability of occurring. Compare the probability distribution of the profits (or losses) per share when using covered call writing versus not using it. Would you recommend covered call writing in this example? Explain.

6. Purdue Savings and Loan Association purchased a put option on Treasury bond futures with a September delivery date and an exercise price of 91–16. Assume the put option has a premium of 1–32. Assume that the price of the Treasury bond futures decreases to 88–16. Should Purdue exercise the option or let the option expire? What is Purdue's net gain or loss after accounting for the premium paid on the option?

7. Wisconsin Inc. purchased a call option on Treasury bond futures at a premium of 2–00. The exercise price is 92–08. If the price of the Treasury bond futures rises to 93–08, should Wisconsin Inc. exercise the call option or let it expire? What is Wisconsin's net gain or loss after accounting for the premium paid on the option?

8. DePaul Insurance Company purchased a call option on an S&P 500 futures contract. The option premium is quoted as $6. The exercise price is $430. Assume the index on the futures contract becomes $440. Should DePaul exercise the call option or let it expire? What is the net gain or loss to DePaul after accounting for the premium paid for the option?

9. Assume that Coral Inc. has purchased shares of stock M at $28 per share. Coral will sell the stock in six months. It considers using a strategy of covered call writing to partially hedge its position in this stock. The exercise price is $32, the expiration date is six months, and the premium on the call option is $2.50. Complete the following table:

Possible Price of Stock M in 6 Months	Profit or Loss per Share if a Covered Call Strategy Is Used
$25	
28	
33	
36	

10. Smart Savings Bank desired to hedge its interest rate risk. It was considering two possibilities: (1) sell Treasury bond futures at a price of 94–00, or (2) purchase a put option on Treasury bond futures. At the time, the price of Treasury bond futures was 95–00. The face value of Treasury bond futures was $100,000. The put option premium was 2–00, and the exercise price was 94–00. Just before the option expired, the Treasury bond futures price was 91–00, and Smart Savings Bank would exercise the put option at that time, if at all. This is also the time at which it would offset its futures position, if it had sold futures. Determine the net gain to Smart Savings Bank if it had sold Treasury bond futures versus if it had purchased a put option on Treasury bond futures. Which alternative would have been more favorable, based on the situation that occurred?

Stock-Options Industry Seeks to End Slide by Selling to Individual Investors

Jeffrey Taylor

The stock-options industry is selling itself to individual investors as never before. But not everyone is buying.

"We tend to discourage that type of investing," says Walter Roberts, manager of a Dean Witter Reynolds branch office in Wayzata, Minn. "Over the long term, I have very rarely seen anybody be profitable by trading options."

In a nutshell, Mr. Robert's sentiments sum up the problem the options industry has faced since the 1987 crash, when thousands of overly aggressive investors were devastated in the nation's options markets. Since then, the options business has been in a slump, which many in the industry blame on a single, speculative strategy popular before the crash.

To capitalize on the stock market's huge gains in the mid-1980s, many investors had taken to selling "put" options contracts that entitled their buyers to sell stocks for high prices if the market plunged. And if the market rose instead, the puts expired worthless and their sellers pocketed the money they had collected for selling them.

'In Lust With the Strategy'

"With the market going crazy on the upside, anybody who wrote puts, especially index puts, kept on making money, basically free money," says Harrison Roth, chief options strategist for Cowen & Co. "So they fell in lust with the strategy, and increased their commitment to an unreasonable size."

Then, on Oct. 19, 1987, when the Dow Jones Industrial Average plunged more than 500 points, many of the investors who had fallen into this habit were wiped out. The cataclysm gave people "the wrong impression of options, as dangerous and speculative, if not immoral," Mr. Roth says.

This impression, to some degree, persists today. While stock trading volume has returned to precrash levels, options volume hasn't. Stock-options volume is on a pace to reach 125 million contracts by year end, according to Options Clearing Corp., which clears trades for all U.S. options markets. That would be up about 20% from 1992, but still nearly 24% less than the 164 million options trades in 1987.

The main reason for this year's increase, market strategists say, is stock market uncertainty. With the Dow Jones industrials near 3600 and opinions sharply divided about where the average will go from here, many investors are learning to use options in conservative ways—to protect, or hedge, their stock market profits, or in low-risk strategies aimed at augmenting the returns of their stock portfolios.

"There is a great deal of nervousness in the market," says John Platt, vice president for options at Raymond James & Co. "The popularity of buying options to protect positions has been increasing in the past year or so."

To capitalize on this trend, the options industry is mounting a marketing drive aimed at toning up the image of options and wooing back individual in-

vestors to the U.S.'s four big options exchanges. Its message: Options don't have to be speculative.

Certain options strategies have regained currency, in part because big brokerage firms such as Merrill Lynch are stepping up their efforts to teach investors about them.

Perhaps most popular in today's uncertain stock market is the technique of hedging a portfolio of stocks by *buying* put options. These options confer the right to sell stocks for prespecified prices. For investors worried about a stock market correction, the strategy amounts to locking in gains in a portfolio.

Strategy's Cost

The cost of the strategy is the "premium," or fee, an investor pays for the option, plus the broker's commission. For blue-chip stocks, options premiums usually run a few hundred dollars apiece; each option confers the right to sell 100 shares.

"It's similar to buying fire insurance for your house," says William Floersch, vice chairman of the Chicago Board Options Exchange and head of a market-making firm there. "You have to pay a premium for it, but you can sleep nights knowing that you're protected."

For example, an investor with a relatively stable, $250,000 portfolio of blue-chip stocks might choose to hedge by buying put options on the Standard

Continued

CASE APPLICATION: USING OPTIONS FOR PORTFOLIO MANAGEMENT

Continued

& Poor's 500 index of large-capitalization stocks. It would cost about $1,800, says Cowen & Co.'s Mr. Roth, to use these options to hedge, for three months, the entire portfolio against a 150-point drop in the industrials.

If a correction of that magnitude occurred, the gain in the value of the options would offset the loss in the stocks. If it didn't, most or all of the $1,800 cost of the options would be lost.

Hedges can also be structured over a longer period of time, or for more specialized stock portfolios. "Probably the most important thing is to find the stock index that most closely matches your portfolio," Mr. Roth says. "There are 31 different indexes: 15 are broad-based, and 16 are sector indexes that track particular industrial sectors, such as biotechnology, banks or gold and silver."

Another low-risk method of using options is called "covered call writing," in which an investor buys stock and then sells "call" options on it. These options entitle someone else to buy the stock, if its price rises, for the price at which the investor bought it. Meanwhile, the investor collects premiums on the options.

Brokers sometimes use this strategy to augment returns in a relatively stable portfolio, selling call options on stocks that aren't likely to reach the level at which the buyer of the options gains the right to purchase the shares.

"We've always been very supportive of covered call writing, trying to get some incremental return, as opposed to just outright holding of the shares themselves," says William J. Kehoe, a vice president for options at Merrill Lynch.

The Options Industry Council is running investor seminars and circulating videos that describe these and other basic options strategies, both to hedge stock market profits and to enhance stock returns with relatively little risk.

The council is also trying to inform individual investors about the variety of options that trade today, including stock-index options that track particular industrial sectors of the market and options called "leaps" that allow investors to take long-term market positions.

"Sure, people can speculate with options," says Mr. Roth. "But you can also do things with options that you can't do in other markets, and that is to hedge your holdings, whether in an individual sector or a broad position in the market."

1. Explain why the writers of put options on stocks were devastated by the October 1987 stock market crash.

2. Portfolio managers sometimes use stock index options to hedge against a temporary market downturn. Explain how they would select among index options to hedge their portfolio. Why do you think the options position would not completely insulate against a market downturn?

3. Explain how portfolio managers can use covered call writing to hedge stocks against a market downturn. Explain how the results of hedging with covered call writing differ from purchasing put options on the stocks.

SOURCE: *The Wall Street Journal* October 12, 1993, p. C1. Reprinted by permission of *The Wall Street Journal* © 1993 Dow Jones & Company, Inc. All rights reserved worldwide.

PROJECTS

1a. Obtain the stock options data just before and after the stock market crash of October 19, 1987, for a particular stock you are interested in (or assigned by your professor). Complete the following:

Name of Company _____

Exercise Price of Call Option _____

Call Option Premium as of October 16, 1987 (use the October 19, 1987 issue of *The Wall Street Journal*) _____

Put Option Premium as of October 16, 1987 (use the October 19, 1987 issue of *The Wall Street Journal*) _____

Call Option Premium as of October 19, 1987 (use the October 20, 1987 issue of *The Wall Street Journal*) _____

Put Option Premium as of October 19, 1987 (use the October 20, 1987 issue of *The Wall Street Journal*) _____

1b. What was the percentage change in the call option premium? What was the percentage change in the put option premium?

2a. Obtain recent stock options data for a particular stock you are interested in. Use a recent issue of *The Wall Street Journal* to complete the following table (use the same expiration month for all quoted premiums):

Name of Stock	Exercise Price	Premium on Call Option	Premium on Put Option

2b. Explain the relationship between the option's exercise price and (1) the call option premium and (2) the put option premium.

3a. Obtain recent stock options data for a particular stock you are interested in. Use a recent issue of *The Wall Street Journal* to complete the following table (use the same exercise price for all quoted premiums):

Name of Stock _____

Expiration Month	Premium on Call Option	Premium on Put Option

3b. Explain the relationship between the option's time to maturity and (1) the call option premium and (2) the put option premium.

4a. Obtain recent stock options data for a particular stock you are interested in. Using the *The Wall Street Journal*, complete the following table:

Name of Stock _____

	Recently Quoted Premium for a Particular Exercise Price and Expiration Month	Quoted Premium for That Same Exercise Price and Expiration Month as of One Month Ago
Call option		
Put option		

4b. Explain why the call option premium increased or decreased. Determine the percentage change in the premium. Do the same for the put option premium.

REFERENCES

Aggarwal, Raj, and Edward Gruca. "Intraday Trading Patterns in the Equity Options Market." *Journal of Financial Research* (Winter 1993): 285–297.

Black, Fisher, and Myron Scholes. "The Pricing of Options and Corporate Liabilities." *Journal of Political Economy* (May–June 1973): 637–654.

———. "The Valuation of Option Contracts and a Test of Market Efficiency." *Journal of Finance* (May 1972): 399–417.

Chan, Kalok, Y. Peter Chung, and Herb Johnson. "Why Option Prices Lag Stock Prices: A Testing-based Explanation." *Journal of Finance* (December 1993): 1957–1967.

Detemple, Jerome, and Philippe Jorion. "Option Listing and Stock Retrns." *Journal of Banking and Finance* (October 1990): 781–801.

Longstaff, Francis A. "Pricing Options With Extendible Maturities: Analysis and Applications." *Journal of Finance* (July 1990): 935–958.

Smith, Clifford W., Jr. "Option Pricing: A Review." *Journal of Financial Economics* (January–March 1976): 3–51.

Vihj, Anand M. "Liquidity of the CBOE Equity Options." *Journal of Finance* (September 1990): 1157–1180.

Option Valuation

In 1973 Black and Scholes devised an option-pricing model that motivated further research on option valuation pricing that continues to this day. Their formula for the value of a call option (V) is

$$V = SN(d_1) - Xe^{-R_fT}N(d_2)$$

where $\quad S$ = stock price

$N(d_1)$ and $N(d_2)$ = probabilities from the cumulative normal distribution evaluated at d_1 and d_2

X = exercise price of the call option

e = base e antilog or 2.7183

R_f = risk-free rate of return for one year

T = time to maturity of the call option expressed as a fraction of a year

The terms $N(d_1)$ and $N(d_2)$ deserve further elaboration. N represents a cumulative probability for a unit normal variable, where

$$d_1 = \frac{\ln(S/X) + R_fT}{\sigma\sqrt{T}} + \frac{1}{2}\sigma\sqrt{T}$$

where $\ln(S/X)$ represents the natural logarithm and σ represents the standard deviation of the continuously compounded rate of return on the underlying stock, and

$$d_2 = d_1 - \sigma\sqrt{T}$$

Some of the key assumptions underlying the Black-Scholes option-pricing model are

- The risk-free rate is known and constant over the life of the option.
- The probability distribution of stock prices is lognormal.
- The variability of a stock's return is constant.
- The option is to be exercised at maturity, if at all.
- There are not transaction costs involved in trading options.
- Tax rates are similar for all participants who trade options.
- The stock of concern does not pay cash dividends.

Several variants of the Black-Scholes model have been developed to account for alternative assumptions, such as that stocks do pay dividends.

To illustrate the application of the Black-Scholes option-pricing model, assume the following information:

- Current stock price is $72.
- Exercise price of the American call option is $70.
- Annual risk-free rate of interest is 7 percent.
- Time to maturity of the call option is one-half of the year.
- Standard deviation of the continuously compounded rate of return on stock is .10.

First, d_1 must be determined, as follows:

$$d_1 = \frac{\ln\left(\frac{S}{X}\right) + R_f T}{\sigma\sqrt{T}} + \frac{1}{2}\sigma\sqrt{T}$$

$$= \frac{\ln(72/70) + .07(.50)}{.10\sqrt{.50}} + \frac{1}{2}(.10)(\sqrt{.50})$$

$$= .8934 + .0353$$

$$= .9287$$

$$d_2 = d_1 - \sigma\sqrt{T}$$

$$= .9287 - .10\sqrt{.50}$$

$$= .8580$$

Using a table that identifies the area under the standard normal distribution function (see Exhibit 12A.1), the cumulative probability can be determined. Because $d_1 = .9287$, the cumulative probability from zero to .9287 is about .3231 (from Exhibit 12A.1, using interpolation). Because the cumulative probability for a unit normal variable from minus infinity to zero is .50, the cumulative probability from minus infinity to .9287 is .50 + .3231 = .8231.

For d_2, the cumulative probability from zero to .8580 is .3042. Therefore, the cumulative probability from minus infinity to .8580 is .50 + .3042 = .8042.

Now that $N(d_1)$ and $N(d_2)$ have been estimated, the call option value can be estimated:

$$V = SN(d_1) - Xe^{-R_f T} N(d_2)$$

$$= \$72 \, (.8231) - \$70 \, (2.7183)^{-.07(.50)} \, (.8042)$$

$$= \$59.26 - \$54.36$$

$$= \$4.90$$

Various computer programs are available to expedite the estimation of option values. As the characteristics represented by the pricing formula change, the

EXHIBIT 12A.1 Cumulative Probabilities of the Standard Normal Distribution Function

d	0.00	0.01	0.02	0.03	0.04	0.05	0.06	0.07	0.08	0.09
0.0	0.0000	0.0040	0.0080	0.0120	0.0160	0.0199	0.0239	0.0279	0.0319	0.0359
0.1	0.0398	0.0438	0.0478	0.0517	0.0557	0.0596	0.0636	0.0675	0.0714	0.0753
0.2	0.0793	0.0832	0.0871	0.0910	0.0948	0.0987	0.1026	0.1064	0.1103	0.1141
0.3	0.1179	0.1217	0.1255	0.1293	0.1331	0.1368	0.1406	0.1443	0.1480	0.1517
0.4	0.1554	0.1591	0.1628	0.1664	0.1700	0.1736	0.1772	0.1808	0.1844	0.1879
0.5	0.1915	0.1950	0.1985	0.2019	0.2054	0.2088	0.2123	0.2157	0.2190	0.2224
0.6	0.2257	0.2291	0.2324	0.2357	0.2389	0.2422	0.2454	0.2486	0.2517	0.2549
0.7	0.2580	0.2611	0.2642	0.2673	0.2704	0.2734	0.2764	0.2794	0.2823	0.2852
0.8	0.2881	0.2910	0.2939	0.2967	0.2995	0.3023	0.3051	0.3078	0.3106	0.3133
0.9	0.3159	0.3186	0.3213	0.3238	0.3264	0.3289	0.3315	0.3340	0.3365	0.3389
1.0	0.3413	0.3438	0.3461	0.3485	0.3508	0.3531	0.3554	0.3577	0.3599	0.3621
1.1	0.3643	0.3665	0.3686	0.3708	0.3729	0.3749	0.3770	0.3790	0.3810	0.3830
1.2	0.3849	0.3869	0.3888	0.3907	0.3925	0.3944	0.3962	0.3980	0.3997	0.4015
1.3	0.4032	0.4049	0.4066	0.4082	0.4099	0.4115	0.4131	0.4147	0.4162	0.4177
1.4	0.4192	0.4207	0.4222	0.4236	0.4251	0.4265	0.4279	0.4292	0.4306	0.4319
1.5	0.4332	0.4345	0.4357	0.4370	0.4382	0.4394	0.4406	0.4418	0.4429	0.4441
1.6	0.4452	0.4463	0.4474	0.4484	0.4495	0.4505	0.4515	0.4525	0.4535	0.4545
1.7	0.4554	0.4564	0.4573	0.4582	0.4591	0.4599	0.4608	0.4616	0.4625	0.4633
1.8	0.4641	0.4649	0.4656	0.4664	0.4671	0.4678	0.4686	0.4693	0.4699	0.4706
1.9	0.4713	0.4719	0.4726	0.4732	0.4738	0.4744	0.4750	0.4756	0.4761	0.4767
2.0	0.4773	0.4778	0.4783	0.4788	0.4793	0.4798	0.4803	0.4808	0.4812	0.4817
2.1	0.4821	0.4826	0.4830	0.4834	0.4838	0.4842	0.4846	0.4850	0.4854	0.4857
2.2	0.4861	0.4866	0.4830	0.4871	0.4875	0.4878	0.4881	0.4884	0.4887	0.4890
2.3	0.4893	0.4896	0.4898	0.4901	0.4904	0.4906	0.4909	0.4911	0.4913	0.4916
2.4	0.4918	0.4920	0.4922	0.4925	0.4927	0.4929	0.4931	0.4932	0.4934	0.4936
2.5	0.4938	0.4940	0.4941	0.4943	0.4945	0.4946	0.4948	0.4949	0.4951	0.4952
2.6	0.4953	0.4955	0.4956	0.4957	0.4959	0.4960	0.4961	0.4962	0.4963	0.4964
2.7	0.4965	0.4966	0.4967	0.4968	0.4969	0.4970	0.4971	0.4972	0.4973	0.4974
2.8	0.4974	0.4975	0.4976	0.4977	0.4977	0.4978	0.4979	0.4979	0.4980	0.4981
2.9	0.4981	0.4982	0.4982	0.4982	0.4984	0.4984	0.4985	0.4985	0.4986	0.4986
3.0	0.4987	0.4987	0.4987	0.4988	0.4988	0.4989	0.4989	0.4989	0.4990	0.4990

option value would change as well. The following relationships hold when all other factors are constant:

- The higher the stock price, the higher the call option value.
- The higher the exercise price, the lower the call option value.
- The higher the standard deviation of the return on the stock, the higher the call option value.
- The greater the time to maturity, the higher the call option value.
- The higher the risk-free rate, the higher the call option value.

These relationships can be verified by reviewing the call option pricing formula. The value of any particular call option can change as a result of (1) a change in the underlying stock's price, (2) a change in the perceived volatility of the stock by investors, (3) a decline in the remaining time to maturity on the option, and (4) a change in the prevailing risk-free rate.

Some research has found that the Black-Scholes model undervalues some options and overvalues others. While a variety of alternative option-pricing models have been developed, none has been found to properly value all options. Nevertheless, their accuracy rate is high enough to make them useful; and, in addition to valuing options, they can be used for assessing the market's perception of a particular stock's risk. By using today's option price, exercise price, the underlying stock's price, the risk-free rate, and the remaining time to maturity, the so-called implied standard deviation can be determined to assess the market's perception of the stock's volatility. For example, the implied standard deviations just after the stock market crash of 1987 were much higher than those a year or so before the crash, indicating an increase in investors' risk perception of stocks.

CHAPTER 13

INTEREST RATE SWAP MARKETS

Many firms have inflow and outflow payments that are not equally sensitive to interest rate patterns. Consequently, they are exposed to interest rate risk. Markets for interest rate swaps have been established to mitigate these risks.

The specific objectives of this chapter are to:

- describe the types of interest rate swaps that are available,
- describe the risks of interest rate swaps,
- identify other interest rate derivative instruments that are commonly used, and
- describe how the interest rate swap markets have become globalized.

BACKGROUND

An **interest rate swap** is an arrangement whereby one party exchanges one set of interest payments for another. The most common arrangement involves an exchange of fixed-rate interest payments for floating-rate interest payments over time. Provisions of an interest rate swap include

- The notional principal value upon which the interest rates are applied to determine the interest payments involved.
- The fixed interest rate.
- The formula and type of index used to determine the floating-rate.
- The frequency of payments, such as every six months, or every year.
- The lifetime of the swap.

For example, a swap arrangement may involve an exchange of 11 percent fixed-rate payments for floating payments of the prevailing one-year Treasury bill rate

355

+ one percent, based on $30 million of notional principal, at the end of each of the next seven years. Other money market rates are sometimes used instead of the Treasury bill rate to index the interest rate.

Although each participant in the swap agreement owes the other participant at each payment date, the amounts owed are typically netted out so that only the net payment is made. If a firm owes 11 percent of $30 million (the notional principal) but is supposed to receive 10 percent of $30 million on a given payment date, it will send a net payment of 1 percent of the $30 million, or $300,000.

The market for swaps is facilitated by "over-the-counter" trading rather than trading on an organized exchange. Given the uniqueness of the provisions detailed in each swap arrangement, swaps are less standardized than other derivative instruments such as futures or options. Thus, a telecommunications network is more appropriate than an exchange to work out specific provisions of swaps.

The popularity of interest rate swaps grew in the early 1980s in response to the effects of large fluctuations in interest rate movements on corporations. Although some manufacturing companies were exposed to interest rate movements, financial institutions were exposed to a greater degree and became the primary users of interest rate swaps. By the mid-1980s, the volume of interest rate swaps was in the hundreds of billions of dollars. Initially, only those institutions wishing to swap payments on amounts of $10 million or more engaged in interest rate swaps. However, in recent years, swaps have been conducted on smaller amounts as well. The increasing popularity in the interest rate swap market is illustrated in Exhibit 13.1.

Financial institutions such as savings institutions and commercial banks in the United States traditionally had more interest rate-sensitive liabilities than assets and therefore were adversely affected by increasing interest rates. Conversely, some financial institutions in other countries (such as some commercial banks in Europe) had access to long-term fixed-rate funding but used funds primarily for floating-rate loans. These institutions were adversely affected by declining interest rates.

The two types of financial institutions described in the preceding paragraph could engage in an interest rate swap with each other to reduce their exposure to interest rate risk. Specifically, the U.S. financial institutions could agree to send fixed-rate interest payments to the European financial institutions in exchange for floating-rate payments. This type of arrangement is illustrated in Exhibit 13.2. In the event of rising interest rates, U.S. financial institutions receive higher interest payments from the floating-rate portion of the swap agreement, which helps to offset the rising cost of obtaining deposits. In the event of declining interest rates, the European financial institution provides lower interest payments in the swap arrangement, which helps to offset the lower interest payments received on its floating-rate loans.

In our example, the U.S. financial institution forgoes the potential benefits from a decline in interest rates, while the European financial institution forgoes the potential benefits from an increase in interest rates. The interest rate swap is enabling each institution to offset any gains or losses that result specifically from interest rate movements. Consequently, as interest rate swaps reduce interest rate risk, they can also reduce potential returns. Most financial institutions that anticipated interest rates to move in a favorable direction would not hedge their positions. Interest rate swaps are primarily used by financial institutions that would be adversely affected by the expected movement in interest rates.

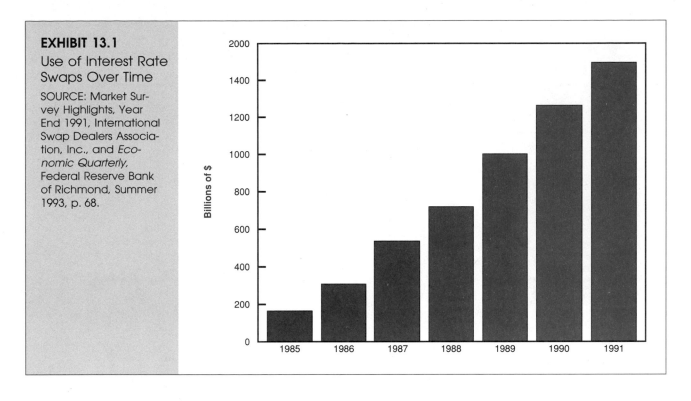

EXHIBIT 13.1
Use of Interest Rate Swaps Over Time

SOURCE: Market Survey Highlights, Year End 1991, International Swap Dealers Association, Inc., and *Economic Quarterly*, Federal Reserve Bank of Richmond, Summer 1993, p. 68.

A primary reason for the popularity in interest rate swaps is the existence of market imperfections. If the parties involved in a swap could easily access funds from various markets without having to pay a premium, they would not need to engage in swaps. Using our previous example, a U.S. financial institution could access long-term funds directly from the European market, while the European institution could access short-term funds directly from the U.S. depositors. However, a lack of information about foreign institutions and convenience encourages individual depositors to place deposits locally. Consequently, swaps are necessary for some financial institutions to obtain the maturities or rate sensitivities on funds that they desire.

PARTICIPATION BY FINANCIAL INSTITUTIONS

Financial institutions participate in the swap markets in various ways, as summarized in Exhibit 13.3. Financial institutions such as commercial banks, savings institutions, insurance companies, and pension funds that are exposed to interest rate movements commonly engage in swaps to reduce interest rate risk.

A second form of participation in the swap market is acting as an intermediary. Some commercial banks and securities firms serve in this capacity by matching up firms and facilitating the swap arrangement. Financial institutions that serve as intermediaries for swaps charge fees for their services. They may even provide credit guarantees (for a fee) to each party in the event that the counterparty does not fulfill its obligation. Under these circumstances, the parties engaged in swap agreements would assess the creditworthiness of the

EXHIBIT 13.2 Illustration of an Interest Rate Swap

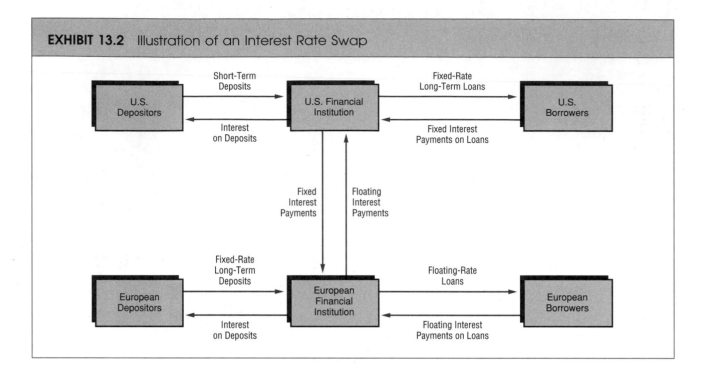

intermediary that is backing the swap obligations. For this reason, participants in the swap market prefer intermediaries that have a high credit rating.

A third form of participation is acting as a dealer in swaps, whereby the financial institution will take the counterparty position in order to serve a client. In such a case, the financial institution may be exposing itself to interest rate risk unless it has recently taken the opposite position as a counterparty for another swap agreement.

TYPES OF INTEREST RATE SWAPS

In response to diverse needs among firms, a variety of interest rate swaps have been created. Some of the more commonly used swaps are

- Plain vanilla swaps
- Forward swaps
- Callable swaps
- Putable swaps
- Extendable swaps
- Zero-coupon-for-floating swaps
- Rate-capped swaps
- Equity swaps

Plain Vanilla Swaps

The **plain vanilla swap** involves the periodic exchange of fixed-rate payments for floating-rate payments and is sometimes referred to as a fixed-for-floating

---

EXHIBIT 13.3   Participation of Financial Institutions in Swap Markets

FINANCIAL INSTITUTION	PARTICIPATION IN SWAP MARKETS
Commercial banks	■ Engage in swaps to reduce interest rate risk. ■ Serve as an intermediary by matching up two parties in a swap. ■ Serve as a dealer, in which the counterparty position is taken to accommodate a party that desires to engage in a swap.
Savings and loan associations and savings banks.	■ Engage in swaps to reduce interest rate risk.
Finance companies	■ Engage in swaps to reduce interest rate risk.
Securities firms	■ Serve as an intermediary by matching up two parties in a swap. ■ Serve as a dealer, in which the counterparty position is taken to accommodate a party that desires to engage in a swap.
Insurance companies	■ Engage in swaps to reduce interest rate risk.
Pension funds	■ Engage in swaps to reduce interest rate risk.

---

swap. This type of swap was used in the example involving the U.S. and European institutions.

Exhibit 13.4 illustrates the exchange of payments under different interest rate scenarios when using a plain vanilla swap. Although infinite possible interest rate scenarios exist, only two scenarios are considered: (1) a consistent rise in market interest rates and (2) a consistent decline in market interest rates. A graph of these two scenarios will help illustrate how the U.S. institution is affected by each type of interest rate swap to be discussed.

Exhibit 13.4 and the exhibits that follow are presented from the U.S. financial institution's perspective. When ignoring transaction costs, the graphs could easily be transformed for the European institution's perspective. The interest payments by the U.S. institution represent the receipts of the European institution, while the receipts of the U.S. institution represent the payments by the European institution.

Keep in mind that the U.S. institution in our example has rate-sensitive liabilities and rate-insensitive assets. Therefore, an unhedged institution is unfavorably affected by rising interest rates and favorably affected by declining interest rates. With these effects in mind, it will be easy to compare the hedging effectiveness of each type of interest rate swap. Some types of interest rate swaps will better offset any unfavorable effects of interest rate movements on the U.S. institution. However, those swaps would also offset to a greater degree any favorable effects. Other types of interest rate swaps are not as effective as a hedge but allow more flexibility to benefit from favorable interest rate movements.

NUMERICAL EXAMPLE.   Bank of Orlando has negotiated a plain vanilla swap in which it will exchange fixed payments of 9 percent for floating payments equal

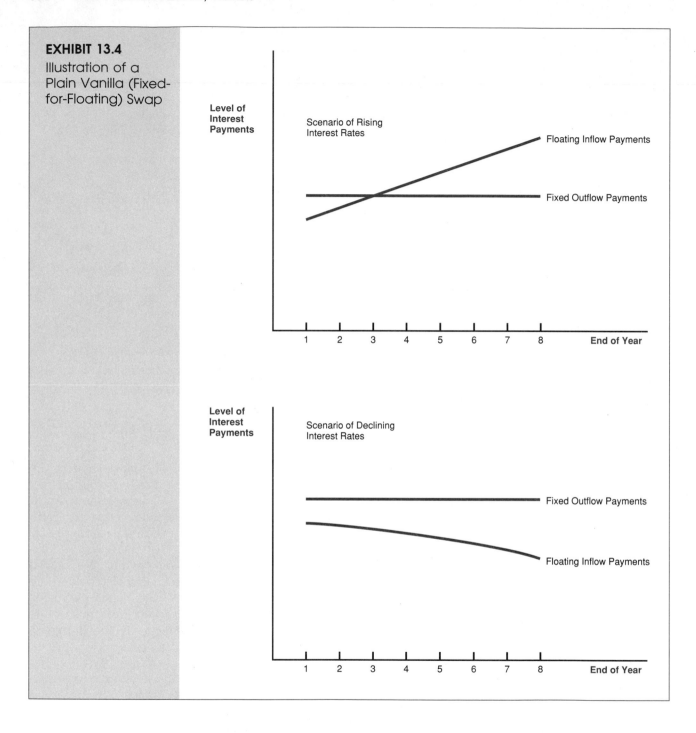

EXHIBIT 13.4

Illustration of a Plain Vanilla (Fixed-for-Floating) Swap

to LIBOR + 1 percent at the end of each of the next five years. LIBOR represents the London Interbank Offer Rate, or the interest rate charged on loans between European banks. The LIBOR varies among currencies; for swap examples involving U.S. firms, the LIBOR on U.S. dollars would normally be used. Assume the notional principal is $100 million.

Two scenarios are disclosed for LIBOR in Exhibit 13.5. The first scenario (in the top panel of Exhibit 13.5) reflects rising U.S. interest rates, which would cause LIBOR to increase. The second scenario (in the lower panel) reflects declining U.S. interest rates, which would cause LIBOR to decrease. The swap differential derived for each scenario represents the fixed interest rate paid minus the floating interest rate received. The net dollar amount to be transferred as a result of the swap is determined by multiplying the swap differential by the notional principal.

Forward Swaps

A **forward swap** involves an exchange of interest payments that does not begin until a specified future point in time. For example, consider a U.S. financial institution that is currently insulated against interest rate risk. Assume that three

EXHIBIT 13.5 Possible Effects of a Plain Vanilla Swap Agreement (Fixed Rate of 9 Percent in Exchange of Floating Rate of LIBOR + 1 Percent)

	YEAR				
SCENARIO I	1	2	3	4	5
LIBOR	7.0%	7.5%	8.5%	9.5%	10.0%
Floating Rate Received	8.0%	8.5%	9.5%	10.5%	11.0%
Fixed Rate Paid	9.0%	9.0%	9.0%	9.0%	9.0%
Swap Differential	−1.0%	−0.5%	0.5%	1.5%	2.0%
Net Dollar Amount Received Based on Notional Value of $100 Million	−$1,000,000	−$500,000	+$500,000	+$1,500,000	+$2,000,000

	YEAR				
SCENARIO II	1	2	3	4	5
LIBOR	6.5%	6.0%	5.0%	4.5%	4.0%
Floating Rate Received	7.5%	7.0%	6.0%	5.5%	5.0%
Fixed Rate Paid	9.0%	9.0%	9.0%	9.0%	9.0%
Swap Differential	−1.5%	−2.0%	−3.0%	−3.5%	−4.0%
Net Dollar Amount Transferred on a Notional Value of $100 Million	−$1,500,000	−$2,000,000	−$3,000,000	−$3,500,000	−$4,000,000

years from now, the institution plans to increase its proportion of fixed-rate loans (in response to consumer demand for these loans) and reduce its proportion of floating-rate loans. To prevent the adverse effects of rising interest rates after that point in time, it may want to engage in interest rate swaps. It could immediately arrange for a forward swap that will begin three years from now. The forward swap allows the institution to lock in the terms of the arrangement today, even though the swap period is delayed (see Exhibit 13.6).

EXHIBIT 13.6
Illustration of a Forward Swap

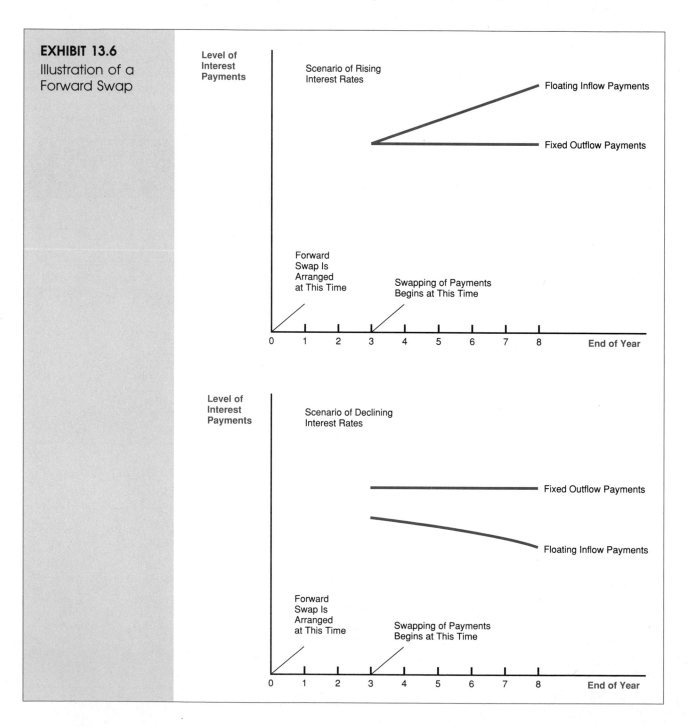

Although the financial institution could have waited before arranging for a swap, it may prefer a forward swap to lock in the terms of the swap arrangement at the prevailing interest rates. To illustrate, assume the U.S. financial institution expects interest rates to be higher three years from now than they are today. If the institution waits until then to negotiate a swap arrangement, the fixed interest rate specified in the arrangement will likely be higher at that time.

A forward interest rate swap may allow the institution to negotiate a fixed rate today that is less than the expected fixed rate on a swap negotiated in the future. Because the institution will be exchanging fixed payments for floating-rate payments, it wants to minimize the fixed rate used for the swap agreement.

The fixed rate negotiated on a forward swap will not necessarily be the same as the fixed rate negotiated on a swap that begins immediately. The pricing conditions on any swap are based on expected interest rates over the swap lifetime.

Like any interest rate swap, forward swaps involve two parties. Our example of a forward swap involves a U.S. institution that expects interest rates to rise and wants to immediately lock in the fixed rate that it would pay when the swap period begins. The party that takes the opposite position in the forward swap would likely be an institution that will be adversely affected by declining interest rates (such as the European institution described earlier) and expects interest rates to decline by the time the swap period begins. This institution would prefer to lock in the prevailing fixed rate, because that rate is expected to be higher than the applicable fixed rate when the swap period begins. Because this institution would be receiving the fixed interest payments, it wishes to maximize the fixed rate specified in the swap arrangement.

Callable Swaps

Another use of an interest rate swap is through **swap options** (or swaptions). A **callable swap** provides the party making the fixed payments with the right to terminate the swap prior to its maturity. It allows the fixed-rate payer to avoid exchanging future interest payments if it desires.

As an example, consider the U.S. institution that wanted to swap fixed interest payments for floating interest payments to reduce any adverse effects of rising interest rates. If interest rates decline, the interest rate swap arrangement offsets the potential favorable effects on this institution. A callable swap could allow the institution to terminate the swap in the event that interest rates decline (see Exhibit 13.7).

The disadvantage of a callable swap is that the party given the right to terminate the swap pays a premium that is reflected in a higher fixed interest rate than what the party would pay without the call feature. The party may also incur a termination fee in the event that it exercises its right to terminate the swap arrangement.

Putable Swaps

A **putable swap** provides the party making the floating-rate payments with a right to terminate the swap. To illustrate, reconsider the European institution that wanted to exchange floating-rate payments for fixed-rate payments to reduce adverse effects of declining interest rates. If interest rates rise, the interest rate swap arrangement offsets the potential favorable effects on the financial

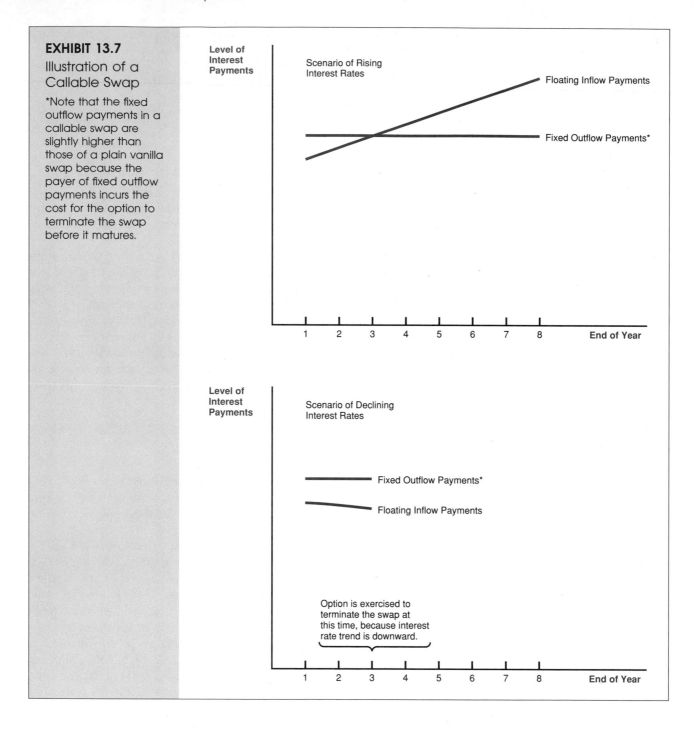

EXHIBIT 13.7

Illustration of a Callable Swap

*Note that the fixed outflow payments in a callable swap are slightly higher than those of a plain vanilla swap because the payer of fixed outflow payments incurs the cost for the option to terminate the swap before it matures.

institution. A putable swap could allow the institution to terminate the swap in the event that interest rates rise (see Exhibit 13.8). As with callable swaps, the party given the right to terminate the swap pays a premium. For putable swaps, the premium is reflected in a higher floating rate than what would be paid without the put feature. The party may also incur a termination fee in the event that it exercises its right to terminate the swap arrangement.

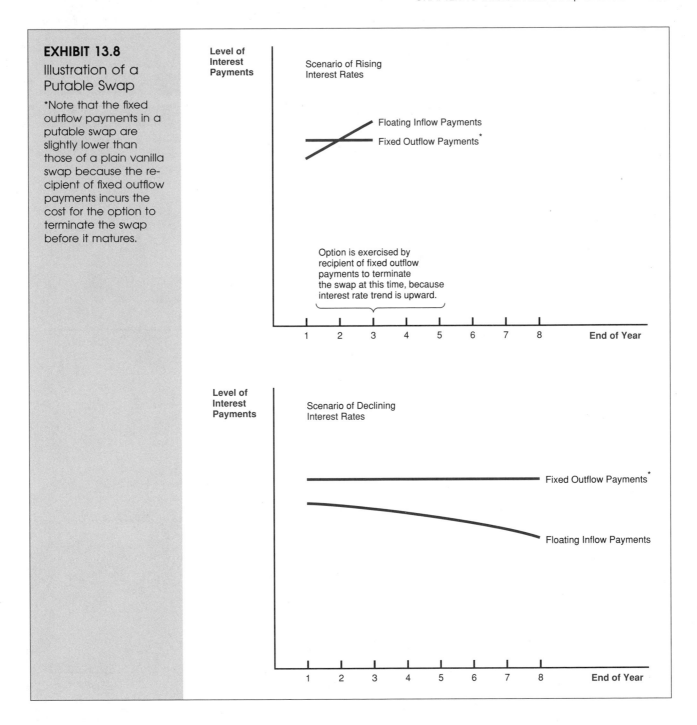

EXHIBIT 13.8

Illustration of a Putable Swap

*Note that the fixed outflow payments in a putable swap are slightly lower than those of a plain vanilla swap because the recipient of fixed outflow payments incurs the cost for the option to terminate the swap before it matures.

Extendable Swaps

An **extendable swap** contains an extendable feature that allows the fixed-for-floating party to extend the swap period. Consider a U.S. financial institution that negotiates a fixed-for-floating swap for eight years. Assume that interest rates increased over this time period as expected. If the institution believes

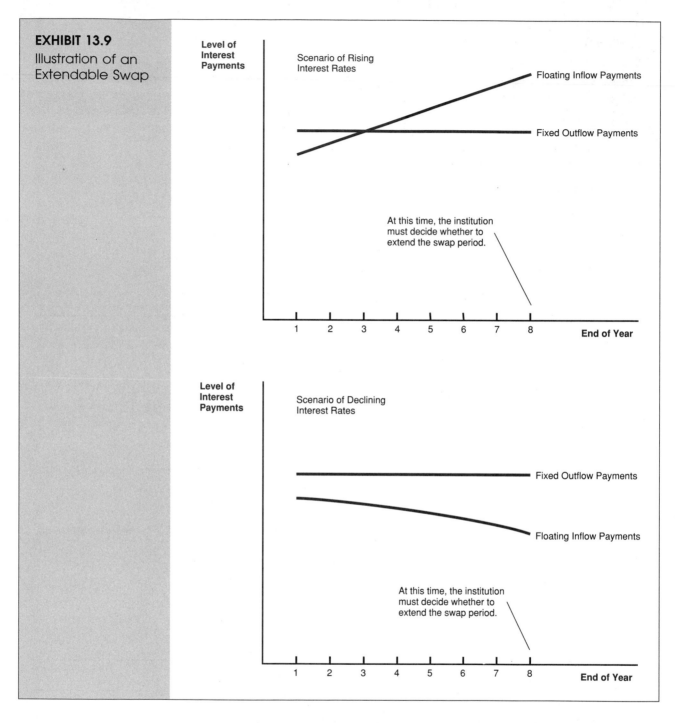

EXHIBIT 13.9
Illustration of an Extendable Swap

interest rates will continue to rise, it may prefer to extend the swap period (see Exhibit 13.9). Although it could create a new swap, the terms would reflect the current economic conditions. A new swap would typically involve an exchange of fixed payments at the prevailing higher interest rate for floating payments. The U.S. financial institution would prefer to extend the previous swap agreement that calls for fixed payments at a lower interest rate, because the interest rates were lower at the time that the swap was created. The U.S. financial institution has additional flexibility because of the extendable feature.

The terms of an extendable swap reflect a price paid for the extendability feature. That is, the interest rates specified in the swap agreement allowing for an extension are not as favorable to the U.S. financial institution as they would have been without the feature. In addition, if the institution does extend the swap period, it may have to pay an extra fee.

Zero-Coupon-for-Floating Swaps

Another special type of interest rate swap is the **zero-coupon-for-floating swap.** The fixed-rate payer makes a single payment at the maturity date of the swap agreement, while the floating-rate payer makes periodic payments throughout the swap period. For example, consider a financial institution that primarily attracts short-term deposits and currently has large holdings of zero-coupon bonds that it purchased several years ago. At the time it purchased the bonds, it expected interest rates to decline. Now it has become concerned that interest rates will rise over time, which will not only increase its cost of funds but also reduce the market value of the bonds. This financial institution could request a swap period that matches the maturity of its bond holdings. If interest rates rise over the period of concern, the institution would benefit from the swap arrangement, thereby offsetting any adverse effects on the institution's cost of funds. The other party in this type of transaction could possibly be a firm that expects interest rates to decline (see Exhibit 13.10). Such a firm would be willing to provide floating-rate payments based on this expectation, because the payments would decline over time, while the single payment to be received at the end of the swap period is fixed.

Rate-Capped Swaps

A **rate-capped swap** involves the exchange of fixed-rate payments for floating-rate payments, whereby the floating payments are capped. Reconsider the example in which a U.S. financial institution arranges a swap with a European institution to exchange fixed payments for floating payments. The European institution may want to limit its possible payments by setting a cap or ceiling on the interest rate it must pay. It may, for example, want to set a cap at 13 percent so that it knows what its maximum payments would be. The floating-rate payer pays an up-front fee to the fixed-rate payer for this feature.

Consider the perspective of a fixed-rate payer (the U.S. financial institution) involved in a rate-capped swap. The size of potential floating payments to be received is now limited by the cap, which may reduce the effectiveness of the swap in hedging the firm's interest rate risk. If interest rates rise above the cap, the floating payments received will not move in tandem with the interest the institution will pay depositors for funds (see Exhibit 13.11). However, the institution might believe that interest rates will not exceed a specified level and would therefore be willing to allow for a cap. If interest rates exceed the cap, the U.S. institution will receive fewer payments than if a cap did not exist. However, these forgone payments could possibly be offset by the up-front fee received for allowing a cap.

Equity Swaps

An **equity swap** involves the exchange of interest payments for payments linked to the degree of change in a stock index. For example, an equity swap arrangement could allow a company to swap a fixed interest rate of 7 percent in

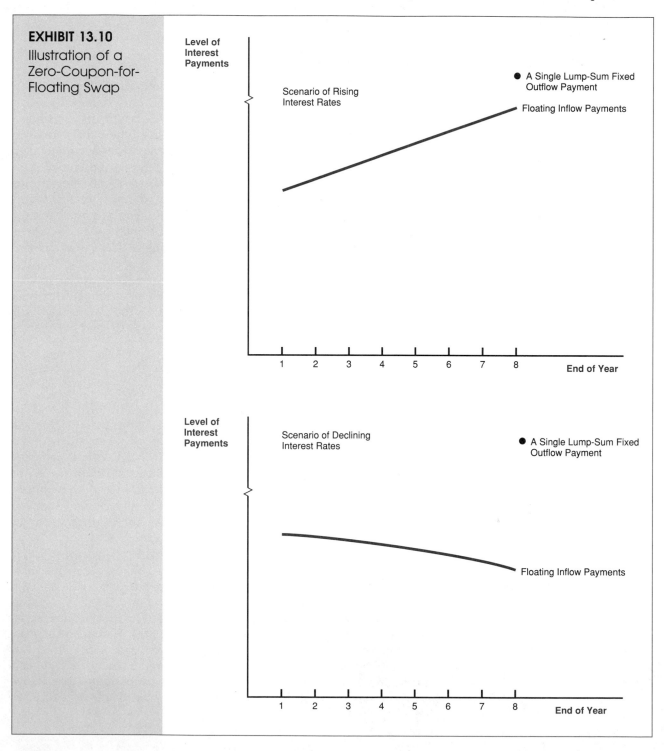

EXHIBIT 13.10

Illustration of a Zero-Coupon-for-Floating Swap

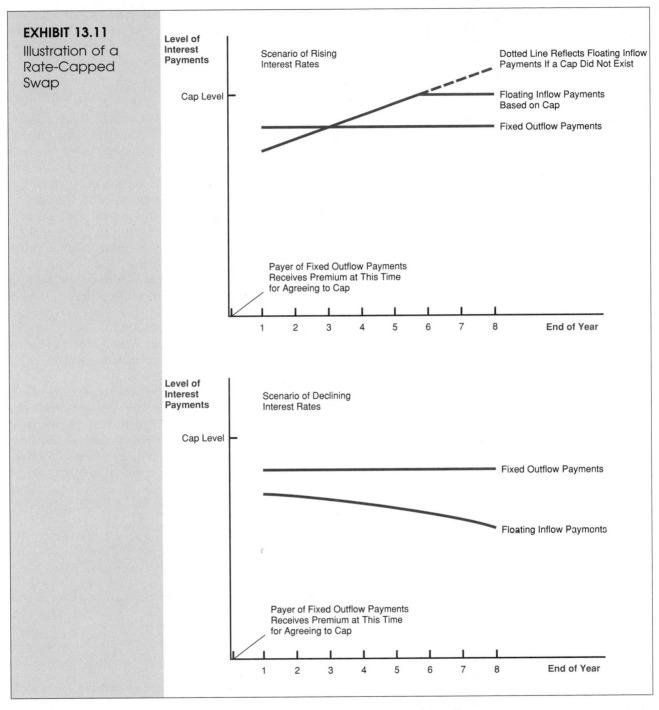

EXHIBIT 13.11
Illustration of a Rate-Capped Swap

exchange for the rate of appreciation on the S&P 500 index each year over a four-year period. If the stock index appreciated by 9 percent over the year, the differential is 2 percent (9 percent received minus 7 percent paid), which would be multiplied by the notional principal to determine the dollar amount received. If the stock index appreciated by less than 7 percent, the company would have to make a net payment. This type of swap arrangement may be appropriate for portfolio managers of insurance companies or pension funds that are managing stocks and bonds. The swap would enhance their investment performance in bullish stock market periods without requiring the managers to change their existing allocation of stocks and bonds.

Other Types of Swaps

A variety of other swaps are also available, and additional types will be created to accommodate future needs by firms. Some swaps have recently been used by firms for tax purposes. As an example, consider a firm that has expiring tax loss carryforwards from previous years. To utilize the carryforwards before they expire, a firm may engage in a swap that calls for receipt of a large up-front payment with somewhat less favorable terms over time. The firm may realize an immediate gain on the swap, with possible losses in future years. The tax loss carryforwards from previous years can be applied to the immediate gain from the swap to offset any taxes on the immediate gain. Any future losses realized from future payments due to the swap agreement may be used to offset future gains from other operations.

As a second example, consider a firm that expects future losses but will realize large gains from operations in this year. The firm could take the opposite position to that described in the previous example. That is, it would arrange for a swap in which it makes an immediate large payment, and it receives somewhat favorable terms on future payments. This firm will incur a tax loss on the swap this year, which can be used to offset some of its gains from other operations to reduce its tax liability.

In some cases, interest rate swaps are combined with the issuance of bonds to achieve lower costs of debt. Corporate borrowers may be able to borrow at a more attractive interest rate when using floating-rate debt than fixed-rate debt. Yet, if they wanted fixed payments on their debt, they could swap fixed-rate payments for floating-rate payments and use the floating-rate payments received to cover their coupon payments. Alternatively, some corporations may prefer borrowing at a floating rate but have an advantage of borrowing at a fixed rate. These corporations can issue fixed-rate bonds and then swap floating-rate payments in exchange for fixed-rate payments.

RISKS OF INTEREST RATE SWAPS

There are several types of risk to consider when engaging in interest rate swaps. Three of the more common types of risks are basis risk, credit risk, and sovereign risk.

Basis Risk

The interest rate of the index used for an interest rate swap will not necessarily move perfectly in tandem with the floating-rate instruments of the parties involved in the swap. For example, the index used on a swap may rise by 0.7 percent over a particular period, while the cost of deposits to a U.S. financial institution rises by 1.0 percent over the same period. The net effect is that the higher interest rate payments received from the swap agreement do not fully offset the increase in the cost of funds. This so-called basis risk prevents the interest rate swap from completely eliminating the financial institution's exposure to interest rate risk.

THE BRITISH SWAP CONTROVERSY

In the late 1980s, many municipalities in the United Kingdom engaged in interest rate swaps by agreeing to exchange floating-rate payments in exchange for fixed-rate payments. British interest rates increased after this period. This placed a financial burden on the municipalities. Some of the municipalities discontinued their payments, shifting the burden to British banks which were counterparties of these swaps. These banks were owed the equivalent of about $1 billion in payments. Although the banks argued that the municipalities are obligated to honor the swap contracts, the British government declared, in May 1991, that it would not intervene in the controversy. Consequently, the banks were forced to appeal to the court system for help in retrieving the funds owed to them. The event carries major implications for the swap markets in the United Kingdom, because it suggests that parties must use the court system to ensure that swap obligations are honored. Some banks are no longer settling their swap transactions with other banks. Some municipalities have claims against other municipalities and against other banks. It will likely take several years to resolve the situation through the court system.

Credit Risk

There is risk that a firm involved in an interest rate swap may not meet its payment obligations. However, this credit risk is not overwhelming for the following reasons. As soon as the firm recognizes that it has not received the interest payments it is owed, it will discontinue its payments to the other party. The potential loss is a set of net payments that would have been received (based on the differential in swap rates) over time. In some cases, a financial intermediary that matched up the two parties incurs the credit risk by providing a guarantee (for a fee). If so, the parties engaged in the swap do not need to be concerned with the credit risk, assuming that the financial intermediary will be able to cover any guarantees promised.

CONCERNS ABOUT A SWAP CREDIT CRISIS. The willingness of large banks and securities firms to provide guarantees has increased the popularity of interest rate swaps, but has also raised concerns about widespread adverse effects if any of these intermediaries cannot meet their obligations. If a large bank that has taken numerous swap positions and guaranteed many other swap positions fails, there could be several defaults on swap payments. Such an event could cause cash flow problems for other swap participants, and force them to default on some payment obligations they have on swaps or other financial agreements. Given how globally integrated the swap network is, defaults by a single large financial intermediary could be transmitted throughout the world.

Because of such concerns, various regulators have considered methods of reducing credit risk in the market. For example, bank regulators have considered forcing banks to maintain more capital if they provide numerous guarantees on swap payments. In addition, proposals have been made to create a regulatory agency that would oversee the swap market and minimize credit risk. Other proposals require more complete disclosure of swap positions and guarantees created by financial intermediaries. Given the large growth in swaps, the concerns about credit risk in the market will continue to receive much attention.

Sovereign Risk

Sovereign risk reflects potential adverse effects resulting from a country's political conditions. Various political conditions could prevent the counterparty from meeting its obligation in the swap agreement. For example, a counterparty could be taken over by the government, who then decides not to meet its payment obligations. Alternatively, the government could impose foreign exchange controls that prohibit the counterparty from making its payments.

Sovereign risk differs from credit risk because it is dependent on the financial status of the government rather than the counterparty itself. A counterparty could have very low credit risk but conceivably be perceived as having high sovereign risk because of its government. It does not have control over some restrictions that are imposed by its government.

PRICING INTEREST RATE SWAPS

The setting of specific interest rates for an interest rate swap is referred to as pricing the swap. The pricing is influenced by several factors, including prevailing market interest rates, availability of counterparties, and credit and sovereign risk.

Prevailing Market Interest Rates

The fixed interest rate specified in a swap is influenced by supply and demand conditions for funds with the appropriate maturity. For example, the plain vanilla (fixed-for-floating) interest rate swap would have specified a much higher fixed interest rate if structured in 1980 (when interest rates were near their peak) than in 1994 (when interest rates were significantly lower). In general, the interest rates specified in a swap agreement will reflect the prevailing interest rates at the time of the agreement.

Availability of Counterparties

Swap pricing is also determined by the availability of counterparties. If there were numerous counterparties available for a particular swap desired, a party would possibly be able to negotiate a more attractive deal. For example, consider a U.S. financial institution that wants a fixed-for-floating swap. If there are several European institutions that are willing to serve as the counterparty, the U.S. institution might be able to negotiate a slightly lower fixed rate.

The availability of counterparties can change in response to economic conditions. For example, in a period where interest rates are expected to rise, many institutions would want a fixed-for-floating swap but few institutions would be willing to serve as the counterparty. The fixed rate specified on interest rate swaps would be higher under these conditions than if many financial institutions expected interest rates to decline.

Credit and Sovereign Risk

A party involved in an interest rate swap must assess the probability of default by the counterparty. For example, a U.S. financial institution wanting a fixed-for-floating swap would likely require a lower fixed rate applied to its outflow payments if the credit risk or sovereign risk of the counterparty was high. However, if a well-respected financial intermediary guaranteed payments by the counterparty, the fixed rate would be higher.

APPLICATIONS OF INTEREST RATE SWAPS

The following examples of two common applications may enhance one's understanding of the effects of an interest rate swap.

Application to Financial Institutions

Many financial institutions use interest rate swaps to reduce their interest rate risk. Consider the traditional savings institution whose liabilities are more rate sensitive than its assets. Exhibit 13.12 illustrates how an interest rate swap can hedge interest rate risk for such an institution. This exhibit is similar to Exhibit 13.4, except that it also shows the interest costs and revenues earned from normal operations. When interest rates rise, the floating inflow payments move in tandem with the rising cost of funds, thereby maintaining a stable spread. When interest rates fall, the floating-rate payments decline, but so does the cost of funds.

If the savings institution does not use an interest rate swap, its interest spread is the difference between the inflow payments on the fixed-rate mortgages and its cost of funds (see Exhibit 13.13, focusing only on the colored lines). For the scenario of rising interest rates (top graph in Exhibit 13.13), the institution experiences a negative spread once interest rates rise. For the scenario of declining interest rates (bottom graph in Exhibit 13.13), the spread remains positive and grows over time.

If the institution hedges, the interest spread can be measured as the sum of two differentials. First, there is a consistent positive difference between the floating inflow payments and the cost of funds. In addition, there is a consistent positive difference between the inflow payments on the fixed-rate mortgages and the fixed outflow payments resulting from the swap.

The interest spread when remaining unhedged versus using interest rate swaps is shown in Exhibit 13.13. In a period of rising interest rates (top graph), the swap results in a more favorable interest rate spread. However, in a period of declining interest rates (bottom graph), the use of a swap prevents the institution from receiving a larger spread over time. This exhibit illustrates how an interest rate swap affects an institution's risk-return tradeoff.

Application to Bond Issuers

Some companies that issue bonds use interest rate swaps to reconfigure the future bond payments to a more preferable structure. As an example, consider two firms that want to issue bonds:

- Quality Company is a highly rated firm that prefers to borrow at a variable rate.
- Risky Company is a low-rated firm that prefers to borrow at a fixed rate. Assume the rates these companies would pay for issuing either variable-rate or fixed-rate Eurobonds are as follows:

	FIXED-RATE BOND	VARIABLE-RATE BOND
Quality Company	9%	LIBOR + 1/2%
Risky Company	10 1/2%	LIBOR + 1%

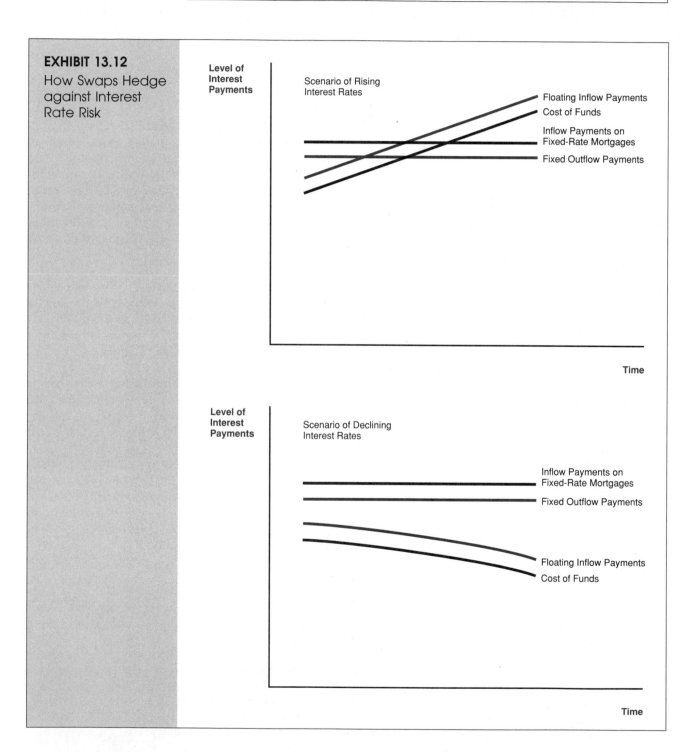

EXHIBIT 13.12

How Swaps Hedge against Interest Rate Risk

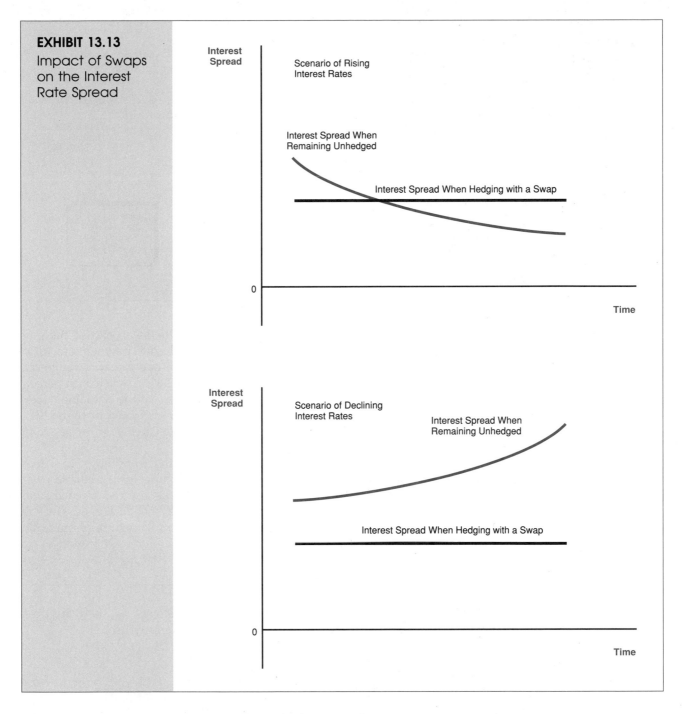

EXHIBIT 13.13
Impact of Swaps on the Interest Rate Spread

Based on the information given, Quality Company has a comparative advantage when issuing either fixed-rate or variable-rate bonds, but its advantage is greater when issuing fixed-rate bonds. Quality Company could issue fixed-rate bonds while Risky Company issues variable-rate bonds. Quality could provide variable-rate payments to Risky in exchange for fixed-rate payments.

Assume that Quality negotiated with Risky to provide variable-rate payments at LIBOR plus $1/2$ percent in exchange for fixed-rate payments of $9 1/2$ percent. This interest rate swap is shown in Exhibit 13.14. Quality Company

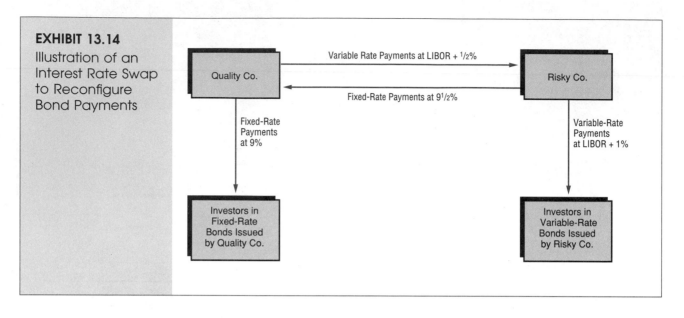

EXHIBIT 13.14
Illustration of an Interest Rate Swap to Reconfigure Bond Payments

benefits, because its fixed-rate payments received on the swap exceed the payments owed to bondholders by ½ percent. Its variable-rate payments to Risky Company are the same as what it would have paid if it had issued variable-rate bonds. Risky is receiving LIBOR plus ½ percent on the swap, which is ½ percent less than what it must pay on its variable-rate bonds. Yet, it is making fixed payments of 9½ percent, which is one percent less than it would have paid if it had issued fixed-rate bonds. Overall, it saves ½ percent per year on financing costs.

Two limitations of the swap just described are worth mentioning. First, there is a cost of time and resources associated with searching for a suitable swap candidate and negotiating the swap terms. Second, there is a risk to each swap participant that the counterparty could default on payments. For this reason, financial intermediaries may match up participants and sometimes assume the default risk involved (for a fee).

INTEREST RATE CAPS, FLOORS, AND COLLARS

In addition to the more traditional forms of interest rate swaps, there are three other interest rate derivative instruments that are commonly used:

- interest rate caps,
- interest rate floors,
- interest rate collars.

These instruments are normally classified separately from interest rate swaps, but do result in interest payments between participants. Each of these instruments can be used by financial institutions to capitalize on expected interest rate movements or to hedge their interest rate risk.

Interest Rate Caps

An **interest rate cap** offers payments in periods when a specified interest rate index exceeds a specified ceiling (cap) interest rate. The payments will be based on the amount by which the interest rate exceeds the ceiling, multiplied by the notional principal specified in the agreement. A fee is paid up-front to purchase an interest rate cap, and the lifetime of a cap commonly ranges between 3 and 8 years.

The typical purchaser of an interest rate cap is a financial institution that is adversely affected by rising interest rates. If interest rates rise, the payments received from the interest rate cap agreement will help offset any adverse effects.

The seller of an interest rate cap receives the fee paid up-front, and is obligated to provide periodic payments when the prevailing interest rates exceed the ceiling rate specified in the agreement. The typical seller of an interest rate cap is a financial institution that expects interest rates to remain stable or decline.

Large commercial banks and securities firms serve as dealers for interest rate caps, in which they act as the counterparty on the transaction. They also serve as brokers, matching up participants that wish to purchase or sell interest rate caps. They may even guarantee (for a fee) the interest payments that are to be paid to the purchaser of the interest rate cap over time.

NUMERICAL EXAMPLE. Assume that Buffalo Savings Bank purchases a five-year cap for a fee of 4 percent of notional principal valued at $60 million (so the fee is $2.4 million), with an interest rate ceiling of 10 percent. The agreement specifies LIBOR as the index used to represent the prevailing market interest rate.

Assume that LIBOR moved over the next five years as is shown in Exhibit 13.15. Based on the movements in LIBOR, Buffalo Savings Bank received payments in three of the five years. The amount received by Buffalo in any year is based on the percentage points above the 10 percent ceiling multiplied by the notional principal. For example, in Year 1 the payment is zero because LIBOR was below the ceiling rate. However, in Year 2, LIBOR exceeded the ceiling by 1%, thereby resulting in a payment of $600,000 (1% × $60 million) to Buffalo Savings Bank. To the extent that Buffalo's performance is adversely affected by high interest rates, the interest rate cap creates a partial hedge by providing payments to Buffalo that are proportionately related to the interest rate level.

EXHIBIT 13.15   Illustration of an Interest Rate Cap

		END OF YEAR:				
	0	**1**	**2**	**3**	**4**	**5**
LIBOR		6%	11%	13%	12%	7%
Interest Rate Ceiling		10%	10%	10%	10%	10%
LIBOR's Percentage Points Above the Ceiling		0%	1%	3%	2%	0%
Payments Received (Based on $60 million of notional principal)		$0	$600,000	$1,800,000	$1,200,000	$0
Fee Paid	$2,400,000					

The seller of the interest rate cap in this example would have had the opposite payments of those shown for the purchaser in Exhibit 13.15.

Interest rate caps can be devised to meet various risk-return profiles. For example, Buffalo Savings Bank could have purchased an interest rate cap with a ceiling rate of 9 percent to generate payments whenever interest rates exceeded that ceiling. However, the fee paid up-front for this interest rate cap would be higher.

Interest Rate Floors

An **interest rate floor** offers payments in periods when a specified interest rate index falls below a specified floor rate. The payments will be based on the amount by which the interest rate falls below the floor rate, multiplied by the notional principal specified in the agreement. A fee is paid up-front to purchase an interest rate floor, and the lifetime of the floor commonly ranges between 3 and 8 years. The interest rate floor can be used to hedge against lower interest rates in the same manner that the interest rate cap hedges against higher interest rates. Any financial institution that purchases an interest rate floor would receive payments if interest rates decline below the floor, which would help offset any adverse interest rate effects.

The seller of an interest rate floor receives the fee paid up-front, and is obligated to provide periodic payments when the interest rate on a specified money market instrument falls below the floor rate specified in the agreement. The typical seller of an interest rate floor is a financial institution that expects interest rates to remain stable or rise. Large commercial banks or securities firms serve as dealers and/or brokers of interest rate floors, just as they do for interest rate swaps or caps.

NUMERICAL EXAMPLE. Assume that Toland Finance Co. purchases a five-year interest rate floor for a fee of 4 percent of notional principal valued at $60 million (so the fee is $2.4 million), with an interest rate floor of 8 percent. The agreement specifies LIBOR as the index used to represent the prevailing interest rate.

Assume that LIBOR moved over the next five years as is shown in Exhibit 13.16. Based on the movements in LIBOR, Toland received payments in two of the five years. The dollar amount received by Toland in any year is based on the percentage points below the 8% floor multiplied by the notional principal. For example, in Year 1, LIBOR was 2% less than the interest rate floor, resulting in a payment of $1,200,000 (2% of $60 million) to Toland Finance Co. The seller of the interest rate floor in this example would have had the opposite payments of those shown for the purchaser in Exhibit 13.16.

Interest Rate Collars

An **interest rate collar** represents the purchase of an interest rate cap with a simultaneous sale of an interest rate floor. In its simplest form, the fee received up-front from selling the interest rate floor to one party can be used to pay the fee for purchasing the interest rate cap from another party. Any financial institution that desires to hedge against the possibility of rising interest rates can purchase an interest rate collar. The hedge results from the interest rate cap, which will generate payments to the institution if interest rates rise above the interest rate ceiling.

EXHIBIT 13.16   Illustration of an Interest Rate Floor

	END OF YEAR:					
	0	1	2	3	4	5
LIBOR		6%	11%	13%	12%	7%
Interest Rate Floor		8%	8%	8%	8%	8%
LIBOR's Percentage Points Below the Floor		2%	0%	0%	0%	1%
Payments Received (Based on $60 million of notional principal)		$1,200,000	$0	$0	$0	$600,000
Fee Paid	$2,400,000					

Because the collar also involves the sale of an interest rate floor, this obligates the financial institution to make payments if the interest rates decline below the floor. Yet, if interest rates rise as expected, the interest rates would remain above the floor, so that the financial institution would not have to make payments.

NUMERICAL EXAMPLE. Assume that Pittsburgh Bank's performance is inversely related to interest rates. It anticipates that interest rates will rise over the next several years, and decides to hedge its interest rate risk by purchasing a five-year interest rate collar, with LIBOR as the index used to represent the prevailing interest rate. The interest rate cap specifies a fee of 4 percent of notional principal valued at $60 million (so the fee is $2.4 million), with an interest rate ceiling of 10 percent. The interest rate floor specifies a fee of 4 percent of notional principal valued at $60 million, and an interest rate floor of 8 percent.

Assume that LIBOR moved over the next five years as is shown in Exhibit 13.17. Based on the movements in LIBOR, the payments received from purchasing the interest rate cap and the payments made from selling the interest rate floor are derived separately over each of the five years. Because the fee received from selling the interest rate floor was equal to the fee paid for the interest rate cap, the initial fees offset. The net payments received by Pittsburgh Bank as a result of purchasing the collar are equal to the payments received from the interest rate cap minus payments made as a result of the interest rate floor. In the years when interest rates were relatively high, the net payments received by Pittsburgh Bank were positive.

This example illustrates how the collar can generate payments when interest rates are high, which may offset the adverse effects of high interest rates on the bank's normal operations. Although the net payments were negative in those years when interest rates were low, the performance of the bank's normal operations should have been strong when interest rates were low. Like many other hedging strategies, the interest rate collar reduces the sensitivity of the financial institution's performance to interest rate movements.

EXHIBIT 13.17 Illustration of an Interest Rate Collar (Combined Purchase of Interest Rate Cap and Sale of Interest Rate Floor)

		END OF YEAR:				
		0	1	2	3	4	5
	LIBOR		6%	11%	13%	12%	7%
Purchase of Interest Rate Cap:	Interest Rate Ceiling		10%	10%	10%	10%	10%
	LIBOR's % Points Above the Ceiling		0%	1%	3%	2%	0%
	Payments Received		$0	$600,000	$1,800,000	$1,200,000	$0
	Fee Paid	$2,400,000					
Sale of Interest Rate Floor:	Interest Rate Floor		8%	8%	8%	8%	8%
	LIBOR's % Points Below the Floor		2%	0%	0%	0%	1%
	Payments Made		$1,200,000	$0	$0	$0	$600,000
	Fee Received	$2,400,000					
	Fee Received Minus Fee Paid	$0					
	Payments Received Minus Payments Made		−$1,200,000	+$600,000	+$1,800,000	+$1,200,000	−$600,000

GLOBALIZATION OF SWAP MARKETS

GLOBAL ASPECTS

The market for interest rate swaps is not restricted to the U.S. As mentioned earlier, European financial institutions commonly have opposite exposure to interest rate risk and therefore take swap positions counter to the positions desired by U.S. financial institutions. Manufacturing corporations from various countries that are exposed to interest rate risk also engage in interest rate swaps.

Exhibit 13.18 discloses the interest rate swaps outstanding (as measured by notional principal) per currency. This exhibit shows that dollar-denominated interest rate swaps represent about half the value of all interest rate swaps outstanding. The Japanese yen is the second most popular currency used to denominate interest rate swaps. Much of the remaining interest rate swaps outstanding are denominated in European currencies. Exhibit 13.18 illustrates how

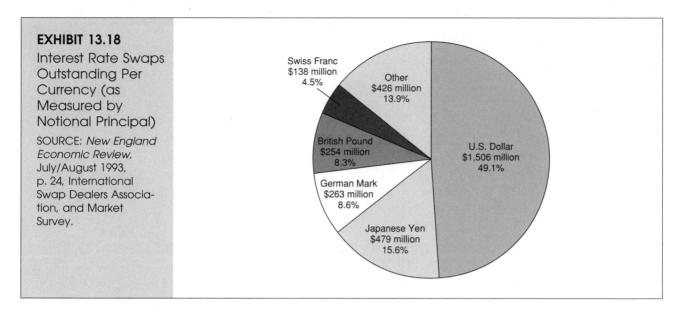

EXHIBIT 13.18

Interest Rate Swaps Outstanding Per Currency (as Measured by Notional Principal)

SOURCE: *New England Economic Review,* July/August 1993, p. 24, International Swap Dealers Association, and Market Survey.

interest rate swaps are not only popular in the U.S., but in other industrialized countries as well.

Given that swap participants are from various countries, the banks and securities firms that serve as intermediaries have a globalized network of subsidiaries. In this way, they can link participants from various countries. One obvious barrier to the global swap market is the lack of information participants have about other participants based in other countries. Thus, concerns about credit risk may discourage some participants from engaging in swaps. Yet this barrier is reduced when international banks and securities firms that serve as intermediaries are willing to back the payments that are supposed to occur in accordance with the provisions of the swap agreement.

Currency Swaps

A **currency swap** is an arrangement whereby currencies are exchanged at specified exchange rates and at specified intervals. It is essentially a combination of currency future contracts, although most futures contracts are not available for periods in the distant future. Currency swaps are commonly used by firms to hedge their exposure to exchange rate fluctuations. For example, consider a U.S. firm that expects to receive 2 million British pounds (£) in each of the next four years. It may want to lock in the exchange rate at which it can sell British pounds over the next four years. A currency swap would specify the exchange rate at which the £ 2 million could be exchanged in each year. To simplify the example, assume the exchange rate specified by a swap is $1.70 (which is the spot exchange rate at the time of the swap arrangement), so that the firm will receive $3.4 million (£ 2 million × $1.70 per £) in each of the four years. Conversely, if the firm does not engage in a currency swap, the dollar amount received will depend on the spot exchange rate at the time the pounds are converted to dollars.

The impact of the currency swap is illustrated in Exhibit 13.19. This exhibit also shows the payments that would have been received under two alternative

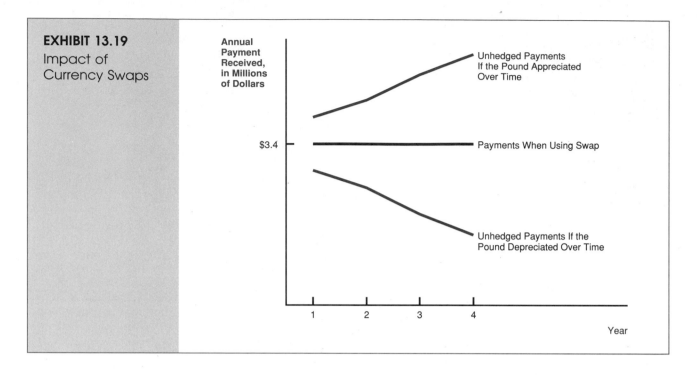

EXHIBIT 13.19
Impact of
Currency Swaps

scenarios if a currency swap had not been arranged. Note that the payments received from the swap would have been less favorable than the unhedged strategy if the pound appreciated against the dollar over that period. However, the payments received from the swap would have been more favorable than the unhedged strategy if the pound depreciated against the dollar over that period. The currency swap arrangement reduces the firm's exposure to changes in the pound's value.

The large commercial banks that serve as financial intermediaries sometimes take positions. That is, they may agree to swap currencies with a firm rather than simply search for a suitable swap candidate.

As with interest rate swaps, the currency swap has several variations. Some currency swap arrangements may allow one of the parties an option to terminate the contract. That party would incur a premium for the option, which could either be charged up-front or be reflected within the exchange rates specified in the swap arrangement.

USING CURRENCY SWAPS TO HEDGE BOND PAYMENTS.   Although currency swaps are commonly used to hedge payments on international trade, they may also be used in conjunction with bond issues to hedge foreign cash flows. Consider, for example, a U.S. firm called Philly Company that wants to issue a German mark-denominated bond (because it could make payments with mark inflows to be generated from ongoing operations). However, assume that this firm is not well-known to investors that would consider purchasing mark-denominated bonds. Also, consider a firm called Windy Company that wants to issue dollar-denominated bonds because its inflow payments are mostly in dollars. However, it is not well-known to the investors that would purchase these bonds. If Philly is known within the dollar-denominated market, while Windy is known within the

EXHIBIT 13.20
Illustration of a
Currency Swap

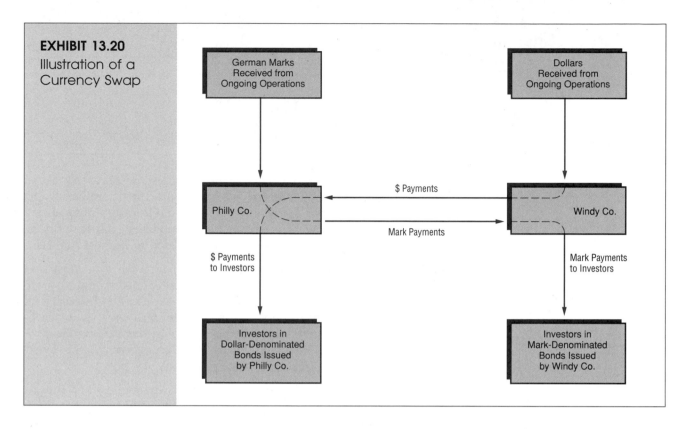

mark-denominated market, the following transactions would be appropriate. Philly could issue dollar-denominated bonds, while Windy issues mark-denominated bonds. Philly could exchange marks for dollars to make its bond payments. Windy would receive marks in exchange for dollars to make its bond payments. This type of currency swap is illustrated in Exhibit 13.20.

Risks of Currency Swaps

The same types of risk applicable to interest rate swaps may also apply to currency swaps. First, basis risk could exist if the firm could not obtain a currency swap on the currency it was exposed to and used a related currency instead. For example, consider a U.S. firm with cash inflows in Italian lire that could not find a counterparty to enact a swap in lire. The firm may enact a swap in German marks, because movements in the mark and the lire against the dollar are highly correlated. To be specific, the firm would enact a currency swap to exchange marks for dollars. As it received lire, it would convert them to marks and then exchange the marks for dollars as specified by the swap arrangement. However, because the exchange rate between lire and marks is not constant, basis risk exists.

A second type of risk of currency swaps is credit risk, which reflects the possibility that the counterparty defaults on its obligation. The potential loss is somewhat limited, however, because one party can discontinue exchanging its currency if it no longer receives currency from the counterparty.

A third type of risk is sovereign risk, which reflects the possibility of a country's restricting the convertibility of a particular currency. In this case, a party involved in a swap arrangement may not be able to fulfill its obligation because its government prohibits the convertibility of a local currency to another currency. This scenario would be less likely in countries that encourage free trade of goods and securities across borders.

SUMMARY

- Various types of interest rate swaps are used to reduce interest rate risk. Some of the more popular types of interest rate swaps are plain vanilla swaps, forward swaps, callable swaps, putable swaps, extendable swaps, rate-capped swaps, and equity swaps. Each type of swap accommodates a particular need for financial institutions or other firms that are exposed to interest rate risk.

- When engaging in interest rate swaps, the participants can be exposed to basis risk, credit risk, and sovereign risk. Basis risk prevents the interest rate swap from completely eliminating the swap user's exposure to interest rate risk. Credit risk reflects the possibility that the counterparty on a swap agreement may not meet its payment obligations. Sovereign risk reflects the possibility that political conditions could prevent the counterparty in a swap agreement from meeting its payment obligations.

- In addition to the traditional forms of interest rate swaps, three other interest rate derivative instruments commonly used to hedge interest rate risk include interest rate caps, interest rate floors, and interest rate collars. Interest rate caps offer payments when a specified interest rate index exceeds the interest rate ceiling (cap), and therefore can hedge against rising interest rates. Interest rate floors offer payments when a specified interest rate index falls below a specified interest rate floor, and can be used to hedge against declining interest rates. An interest rate collar reflects the purchase of an interest rate cap with a simultaneous sale of an interest rate floor, and is used to hedge against rising interest rates.

- The interest rate swap market has become globalized in the sense that financial institutions from various countries participate. Interest rate swaps are available in a variety of currencies.

QUESTIONS

1. Assume Bowling Green Savings & Loan uses short-term deposits to fund fixed-rate mortgages. Explain how Bowling Green can use interest rate swaps to hedge its interest rate risk.

2. Why would savings institutions avoid the use of interest rate swaps, even when they are highly exposed to interest rate risk?

3. Explain the possible roles of securities firms in the swap market.

4. Explain the types of cash flow characteristics that would cause a firm to hedge interest rate risk by swapping floating-rate payments for fixed payments.

5. Assume that Rider Company negotiates a forward swap that is to begin two years from now, in which it will swap fixed payments for floating-rate payments. If, over the next two years, interest rates rise substantially, explain the effect on Rider. That is, would Rider have been better off by using a forward swap than by simply waiting two years before negotiating the swap? Explain.

6. Explain the advantage of a swap option to a financial institution that wants to swap fixed payments for floating payments.

7. Back Bay Insurance Company negotiated a callable swap involving fixed payments in exchange for floating payments. Assume that interest rates decline consistently up until the swap maturity date. Do you think Back Bay would have possibly terminated the swap prior to maturity? Explain.

8. Chelsea Finance Company receives floating inflow payments from its provision of floating-rate loans. Its outflow payments are fixed because of its recent issuance of long-term bonds. Chelsea is somewhat concerned that interest rates will decline in the future. Yet, it does not want to hedge its interest rate risk, because it believes interest rates may increase. Recommend a solution to Chelsea's dilemma.

9. Bull and Finch, Inc., wants a fixed-for-floating swap. It expects interest rates to rise far above the fixed rate that it would have to pay and remain very high until the swap maturity date. Should it consider negotiating for a rate-capped swap with the cap set at two percentage points above the fixed rate? Explain.

10. Comiskey Savings provides fixed-rate mortgages of various maturities, depending on what customers want. It obtains most of its funds from issuing certificates of deposit with maturities ranging from one month to five years. Comiskey has decided to engage in a fixed-for-floating swap to hedge its interest rate risk. Is Comiskey exposed to basis risk?

11. Shea Savings negotiated a fixed-for-floating swap with a reputable firm in South America that has an exceptional credit rating. Shea was very confident that a default on inflow payments would not occur because of the very low credit risk of the South American firm. Do you agree? Explain.

12. North Pier Company entered into a two-year swap agreement which would provide fixed-rate payments for floating-rate payments. Over the next two years, interest rates declined. Based on these conditions, did North Pier Company benefit from the swap?

13. Explain how an equity swap could allow Marathon Insurance Co. to capitalize on expectations of a strong stock market performance over the next year without altering its existing portfolio mix of stocks and bonds.

14. Explain how the failure of a large commercial bank could cause a worldwide swap credit crisis.

15. Markus Company purchases supplies from France once a year. Would it have been favorably affected it if had established a currency swap arrangement when the dollar strengthened? What if it had established a currency swap arrangement when the dollar generally weakened?

16. Explain basis risk as related to a currency swap.

17. Give an example of how sovereign risk is related to currency swaps.

18. Explain why some companies that issue bonds engage in interest rate swaps in financial markets. Why do they not simply issue bonds that require the type of payments (fixed or variable) that they prefer to make?

19. Explain why some companies that issue bonds engage in currency swaps. Why do they not simply issue bonds in the currency that they would prefer to use for making payments?

PROBLEMS

1. Cleveland Insurance Co. has just negotiated a three-year plain vanilla swap in which it will exchange fixed payments of 8 percent for floating payments of LIBOR + 1 percent. The notional principal is $50 million. LIBOR is expected to be 7 percent, 9 percent, and 10 percent at the end of each of the next three years.
   a. Determine the net dollar amount to be received (or paid) by Cleveland per year.
   b. Determine the dollar amount to be received (or paid) by the counterparty on this interest rate swap per year based on the forecasts of LIBOR assumed above.

2. Assume that Northbrook Bank purchases a four-year cap for a fee of 3 percent of notional principal valued at $100 million, with an interest rate ceiling of 9 percent, and LIBOR as the index representing the market interest rate. Assume that LIBOR is expected to be 8%, 10%, 12%, and 13% at the end of each of the next four years.
   a. Determine the initial fee paid, and also determine the expected payments to be received by Northbrook if LIBOR moves as forecasted.
   b. Determine the dollar amount to be received (or paid) by the seller of the interest rate cap based on the forecasts of LIBOR assumed above.

3. Assume that Iowa City Bank purchases a three-year interest rate floor for a fee of 2 percent of notional principal valued at $80 million, with an interest rate floor of 6 percent, and LIBOR representing the interest rate index. The bank expects LIBOR to be 6 percent, 5 percent, and 4 percent respectively at the end of each of the next three years.
   a. Determine the initial fee paid, and also determine the expected payments to be received by Iowa City if LIBOR moves as forecasted.
   b. Determine the dollar amounts to be received (or paid) by the seller of the interest rate based on the forecasts of LIBOR assessed above.

4. Assume that Ward Bank has just purchased a three-year interest rate collar, with LIBOR as the interest rate index. The interest rate cap specifies a fee of 2 percent of notional principal valued at $100 million, and an interest rate ceiling of 9 percent. The interest rate floor specifies a fee of 3 percent of notional principal valued at $100 million, and an interest rate floor of 7 percent. Assume that LIBOR is expected to be 6 percent, 10 percent, and 11 percent respectively at the end of each of the next three years. Determine the net fees paid, and also determine the expected *net* payments to be received as a result of purchasing the interest rate collar.

CASE APPLICATION: RISK WITHIN THE SWAP MARKETS

Lawmakers Question Agencies' Ability To Regulate the Derivatives Market

Kenneth H. Bacon, Washington

Members of the House Banking Committee expressed skepticism about the ability of federal agencies to regulate the fast-growing derivatives market and suggested that new laws may be necessary.

Officials from six financial regulatory agencies voiced confidence that they're on top of the increasingly popular products and have adequate regulatory authority. Derivatives are financial instruments that banks, brokers and their customers used to defray the risk of changes in interest rates, stock prices, foreign-exchange rates and commodities prices.

'Deja Vu, All Over Again'

But members of the banking panel reminded the regulators that they had heard the same assurances a decade ago as thrifts and banks were changing in response to the deregulation of interest rates. "Oh my God, this is deja vu all over again," said Rep. Marge Roukema (R., N.J.). "We're still paying for the S&L debacle."

Rep. Jim Leach of Iowa, the panel's ranking Republican, said, "There is no escaping the circumstance that derivative activities in the '90s must be examined in the context of the decade of the '80s, when America overleveraged itself with junk bonds, junk real estate and junk S&Ls." Rep. Joseph Kennedy (D., Mass.) added, "I think the basic concern is that this is simply another Wall Street-developed house of cards."

Yesterday's hearing was the panel's first on the use of derivatives by banks; legislation, if any, will be a long time coming. But several members mentioned areas where they believe legislation may be necessary. Committee Chairman Henry Gonzalez (D., Texas) noted "the absence of standardized and adequate disclosure of bank derivative activities" and said Congress should mandate improved disclosure.

Impact on Earnings

The comptroller of the currency, Eugene Ludwig, agreed that current reporting requirements aren't adequate. He said that regulators are looking at ways to require banks and other dealers in derivatives to reveal more information about the impact of their activities on their earnings. This will lead to "increasing market scrutiny of derivatives activity," he said.

Rep. Leach said that derivatives activities by banks and brokers are regulated at the federal level, but that insurance companies, which also participate in the booming market, are largely exempt from federal scrutiny. "Maybe Congress should address that issue, and I suspect it might," Mr. Leach said. Insurance companies are regulated primarily by state agencies.

Rep. Richard Baker (R., La.) suggests that stop-trading orders, or "circuit breakers," should be used during periods of unusual turbulence in the derivatives markets. Such a move would expand the use of circuit breakers, which exchanges

currently use to regulate the large over-the-counter market for derivatives.

Theoretical Risk

Members of the panel repeatedly mentioned the complexity and size of the derivatives market. Mr. Gonzalez said the theoretical risk of loss that some big banks face exceeds their capital several times over. According to figures supplied by the comptroller of the currency, Chemical Banking Corp. is the largest bank dealer in derivatives with $2.11 trillion of the instruments outstanding. The bank's "worst case" exposure to loss is $31.89 billion, or 2.68 times its capital.

Bankers Trust New York Corp., the second-largest bank dealer with $1.8 trillion of derivatives, faces a theoretical exposure that is nearly six times its capital, the figures show. Mr. Ludwig stressed that losses of this size could occur only in the highly unlikely case that all customers defaulted on their obligations. Even if this happened, the amount of loss could well be overstated. . . .

The financial industry is generally united behind the position that the current combination of self-regulation and government supervision provides enough protection against widespread losses from derivatives. There is a fear that legislation would slow the development of products that are marketed primarily as ways to hedge and reduce risk.

Andrew Hove, chairman of the Federal Deposit Insurance Corp., said there

Continued

CASE APPLICATION: RISK WITHIN THE SWAP MARKETS

Continued

is a considerable amount of self-policing, because institutions won't make commitments with parties that lack financial strength. ''The combination of sound institution management, market forces and appropriate regulatory supervision under existing guidelines sharply reduces the likelihood'' of significant damage to the banking industry, he said.

SOURCE: *The Wall Street Journal,* October 29, 1993, p. A4. Reprinted by permission of *The Wall Street Journal,* © 1993 Dow Jones & Company, Inc. All rights reserved worldwide.

QUESTIONS

1. The swaps market has been described as "another Wall Street-developed house of cards." What do you think this phrase means? Why is the swaps market a concern to regulators?

2. Chemical Banking Corp. was cited as the largest bank dealer in derivatives, with $2.11 trillion of the instruments outstanding, and "worst case" exposure loss of $31.89 billion. What type of requirements do you think could be imposed on swap arrangements that would limit the risk on a bank?

3. Commercial banks, securities firms, and other financial institutions can serve as swap dealers. What problems exist when attempting to regulate the swaps market whose participants represent various types of financial institutions?

PROJECT

1. **Assessing the Performance of Interest Rate Swaps**
   Using the data bank, determine whether a firm whose liabilities were more rate sensitive than its assets would have been favorably affected by using a fixed-for-floating swap over a period specified by your professor.

REFERENCES

Arak, Marcelle, Arturo Estrella, Laurie Goodman, and Andrew Silver. "Interest Rate Swaps: An Alternative Explanation." *Financial Management* (Summer 1988): 12–18.

Brown, Keith C., and Donald J. Smith. "Forward Swaps, Swap Options, and the Management of Callable Debt." *Journal of Applied Corporate Finance* (Winter 1990): 59–68.

————. "Recent Innovations in Interest Rate Risk Management and the Reintermediation of Commercial Banking." *Financial Management* (Winter 1988): 45–58.

Einzig, Robert. "Swaps at Transamerica: Analysis and Applications." *Journal of Applied Corporate Finance* (Winter 1990): 48–58.

Goodman, Laurie S. "The Use of Interest Rate Swaps in Managing Corporate Liabilities." *Journal of Applied Corporate Finance* (Winter 1990): 35–47.

Jordon, James V., and Robert J. Mackay. "The New Regulation of Hybrid Debt Instruments." *Journal of Applied Corporate Finance* (Winter 1990): 72–84.

Kawaller, Ira G. "Interest Rate Swaps Versus Eurodollar Strips." *Financial Analysts Journal* (September–October 1989): 55–61.

Litzenberger, Robert H. "Swaps: Plain and Fanciful." *Journal of Finance* (July 1992): 831–850.

McNulty, James E. "The Pricing of Interest Rate Swaps." *Journal of Financial Services Research* (March 1990): 53–63.

Rendleman, Richard. "How Risks Are Shared in Interest Rate Swaps." *Journal of Financial Services Research* (February 1993): 5–34.

Simons, Katerina. "Measuring Credit Risk in Interest Rate Swaps." *New England Economic Review* (November/December 1989): 29–37.

Stapleton, R. C., and M. G. Subrahmanyam. "The Analysis and Valuation of Interest Rate Options." *Journal of Banking and Finance* (December 1993): 1079–1095.

Titman, Sheridan. "Interest Rate Swaps and Corporate Financing Choices." *Journal of Finance* (September 1992): 1503–1516.

Wall, Larry D., and John J. Pringle. "Alternative Explanations of Interest Rate Swaps: A Theoretical and Empirical Analysis." *Financial Management* (Summer 1989): 59–73.

CHAPTER 14

FOREIGN EXCHANGE DERIVATIVE MARKETS

In recent years, various derivative instruments have been created to manage or capitalize on exchange rate movements. These so-called **foreign exchange derivatives** (or ``forex'' derivatives) include forward contracts, currency futures contracts, currency swaps, and currency options. Foreign exchange derivatives account for about half of the daily foreign exchange transaction volume.

The potential benefits from using foreign exchange derivatives are dependent on the expected exchange rate movements. Thus, it is necessary to understand why exchange rates change over time before exploring the use of foreign exchange derivatives.

The specific objectives of this chapter are to:

- explain how various factors affect exchange rates,
- describe how foreign exchange derivatives can be used to hedge exchange rate risk, and
- describe how foreign exchange derivatives can be used to capitalize on expected exchange rate movements.

BACKGROUND ON FOREIGN EXCHANGE MARKETS

As international trade and investing have increased over time, so has the need to exchange currencies. Foreign exchange markets represent a global telecommunications network among the large commercial banks that serve as financial intermediaries for such exchange. These banks are located in New York, Tokyo, Hong Kong, Singapore, Frankfurt, Zurich, and London. Foreign exchange transactions at these banks have been increasing over time.

At any point in time, the price at which banks will buy a currency (bid price) is slightly lower than the price at which they will sell it (ask price). As with markets for other commodities and securities, the market for foreign currencies is more efficient because of financial intermediaries (commercial banks). Otherwise, individual buyers and sellers of currency would be unable to identify counterparties to accommodate their needs.

Exchange Rate Quotations

Exhibit 14.1 shows the approximate foreign exchange rates of the major currencies that existed as of August 28, 1994. These exchange rates are listed in any major newspaper on a daily basis. Directly across from the currency name (in the second column) is the **spot exchange rate** for immediate delivery. The exchange rates in this column define the value of a foreign currency in terms of U.S. dollars. The exchange rates in the third column are expressed as the number of units per dollar. According to the foreign exchange table, the British pound's value is $1.535, which implies that .651 pound equals $1. The German mark is worth $.6345, which implies that 1.576 marks equal $1. Each exchange rate in the third column is simply the reciprocal of what is shown in the second column.

For widely used currencies such as the British pound and German mark, **forward rates** are available and are listed just below the respective spot rates. The use of forward exchange rates is described later in the chapter.

Types of Exchange Rate Systems

From 1944 to 1971, the exchange rate at which one currency could be exchanged for another was maintained by governments within one percent of a specified rate. This period was known as the **Bretton Woods era,** because the agreement among country representations occurred at the Bretton Woods Conference. The manner by which governments were able to control exchange rates is discussed later in the chapter.

By 1971 the U.S. dollar was clearly overvalued. That is, its value was maintained only by central bank intervention. In 1971 an agreement among all major countries (known as the **Smithsonian Agreement)** allowed for devaluation of the dollar. In addition, the Smithsonian Agreement called for a widening of the boundaries from 1 percent to $2^{1}/_{4}$ percent around each currency's set value. Governments intervened in the foreign exchange market whenever exchange rates threatened to wander outside the boundaries.

In 1973, the boundaries were eliminated. Since then, the exchange rates of major currencies have been floating without any government-imposed boundaries. Yet, governments may still intervene in the foreign exchange market in order to influence the market value of their currency. A system whereby exchange rates are market-determined without boundaries but subject to government intervention is called a **dirty float.** This can be distinguished from a **freely floating** system, in which the foreign exchange market is totally free from government intervention. Governments continue to intervene in the foreign exchange market from time to time.

Some currencies are still pegged to another currency or a unit of account and maintained within specified boundaries. For example, many European cur-

EXHIBIT 14.1   Foreign Exchange Rate Quotations (August 28, 1994)

COUNTRY (CURRENCY)	U.S. $ EQUIV.	CURRENCY PER U.S. $
Australia (Dollar)	.744	1.34
Austria (Schilling)	.089	11.15
Belgium (Franc)	.031	32.5
Brazil (Real)	1.130	.89
Britain (Pound)	1.535	.651
30-Day Forward	1.534	.652
90-Day Forward	1.532	.653
180-Day Forward	1.530	.654
Canada (Dollar)	.730	1.369
30-Day Forward	.729	1.370
90-Day Forward	.729	1.371
180-Day Forward	.728	1.373
Colombia (Peso)	.001225	816.00
Denmark (Krone)	.160	6.24
France (Franc)	.1849	5.410
30-Day Forward	.1848	5.411
90-Day Forward	.1846	5.417
180-Day Forward	.1844	5.424
Germany (Mark)	.6345	1.576
30-Day Forward	.6344	1.576
90-Day Forward	.6343	1.577
180-Day Forward	.6350	1.574
Greece (Drachma)	.0042	238.00
Hong Kong (Dollar)	.1294	7.727
Italy (Lira)	.00063	1585.00
Japan (Yen)	.01005	99.53
30-Day Forward	.01007	99.30
90-Day Forward	.01011	98.88
180-Day Forward	.01019	98.12
Mexico (Peso)	.2956	3.382
Netherlands (Guilder)	.5652	1.769
New Zealand (Dollar)	.6027	1.659
Norway (Krone)	.1445	6.913
Singapore (Dollar)	.6668	3.74
Spain (Peseta)	.00765	130.68
Sweden (Krona)	.1295	7.72
Switzerland (Franc)	.7524	1.329
SDR	1.4496	.6898
ECU	1.2100	. . . .

rencies are part of the so-called **exchange rate mechanism** (ERM), in which they are pegged to a multi-currency unit of account known as the **European Currency Unit (ECU)**. Because these currencies are pegged to the same unit of account, they are essentially pegged to each other. Governments intervene to ensure that exchange rates between these currencies are maintained within the established boundaries.

During the 1980s, the boundaries surrounding the exchange rates were 2.25 percent above and below a specified exchange rate between each pair of European currencies. However, in the early 1990s central banks were unable to maintain exchange rates between European currencies within these boundaries. Consequently, the boundaries were widened substantially in 1993.

Exchange Rate Mechanism (ERM) Crisis

The exchange rate mechanism experienced severe problems in the fall of 1992, as economic conditions and goals varied among European countries. The German government focused on controlling inflation and implemented a tight monetary policy, which increased German interest rates. Money flowed out of other European countries into Germany to capitalize on the relatively high German interest rates. Because exchange rates between European currencies were tied (within boundaries), European investors could capitalize on the high German interest rates without much concern about exchange rate risk. The flow of funds out of other European countries reduced the supply of funds in these countries. Consequently, interest rates increased in these countries as well at a time when their respective governments were attempting to lower interest rates in order to stimulate their economies. The end result was less aggregate spending in countries because of the increase in interest rates. Such a result was especially undesirable during 1992, because some European countries were in the midst of a recession.

This example illustrates the degree to which European economies are integrated as a result of the ERM. When exchange rates are tied, a high interest rate in one country has a strong influence on interest rates in the other countries. Funds will flow to the country with a more attractive interest rate, which reduces the supply of funds in the other countries and places upward pressure on their interest rates. The flow of funds should continue until the interest rate differential has been eliminated or reduced. This process will not necessarily apply to countries outside the ERM because the exchange rate risk may discourage the flow of funds to the countries with relatively high interest rates. However, because the ERM requires central banks to maintain the exchange rates between currencies within specified boundaries, investors moving funds among the participating European countries are less concerned about exchange rate risk.

In the fall of 1992, the central banks of European countries attempted to maintain exchange rates through direct intervention in the foreign exchange markets. They also attempted to increase interest rates, which would discourage investors from investing in German marks to capitalize on high German interest rates. However, this form of intervention was conflicting with the goals of stimulating European economies. In an attempt to stabilize the ERM, the central banks of some European countries were prevented from lowering interest rates to stimulate their economies.

Tensions rose in Europe during this period as countries were forced to maintain higher interest rates in response to German's desire to maintain higher interest rates. The German government was more concerned about inflation and less concerned about unemployment because its economy was relatively strong. However, other European governments were more concerned about stimulating their economies to reduce their high unemployment levels. As the German restrictive monetary policy indirectly caused higher interest rates throughout Eu-

POINT OF INTEREST

PROPOSAL FOR A SINGLE EUROPEAN CURRENCY

In 1991, the Maastricht treaty proposed the goal of a single European currency by the year 1999. One major advantage of a single European currency is the complete elimination of exchange rate risk between European currencies, which could encourage more trade and capital flows across European borders. There is some exchange rate risk within the exchange rate mechanism (ERM) because exchange rates can move within boundaries, and exchange rates between European currencies may be realigned by the European governments. If there was a single currency, realignment would not be a possibility. In addition, foreign exchange transaction costs associated with transactions between European countries would be eliminated. The goal of a single European currency is consistent with the goal of the Single European Act to remove trade barriers between European borders, because exchange rate risk is an implicit trade barrier. A single European currency would result in a single money supply throughout Europe, rather than a separate money supply for each currency. Thus, European monetary policy would be consolidated, as any ef-

fects on the supply of money would affect all European countries using that one currency as their form of money.

A major concern of having a single European currency is based on the concept of a single European monetary policy. Each country's government may prefer to implement its own monetary policy. It would have to adapt to a system in which it has only partial input to the European monetary policy that would be implemented in all European countries, including its own. The system would be analogous to that used in the U.S., where there is a single currency across states. Just as the monetary policy in the U.S. cannot be separated across different states, European monetary policy with a single European currency cannot be separated across European countries. Although country governments may disagree on the ideal monetary policy to enhance their local economies, they would all have to agree on a single European monetary policy. Any given policy used in a particular period may enhance some countries and adversely affect others.

rope, the other European countries pressured the German government to use a more stimulative monetary policy.

In October 1992, the British and Italian governments suspended their participation in the ERM, because their own goals for a stronger economy could not be satisfied if their interest rates were to be so highly influenced by the German interest rates. By suspending participation in the ERM, the currencies were no longer tied to the German mark and other European currencies. Therefore, even if interest rates were higher in some European countries, funds in Great Britain and in Italy would not necessarily flow to those countries because of exchange rate risk. In this way, the British and Italian interest rates would not be more dependent on local conditions than the conditions of other European countries. Ireland, Finland, Norway, and Sweden were also adversely affected by the ERM crisis. They discontinued their efforts to maintain the exchange rate alignment by lowering their interest rates and devaluing their currencies relative to the German mark.

Factors Affecting Exchange Rates _____

The value of a currency adjusts to changes in demand and supply conditions, moving toward equilibrium. In equilibrium, there is no excess or deficiency of that currency. For example, a large increase in the U.S. demand for German goods and German securities would result in an increased demand for German marks. Because the demand for marks would then exceed the supply of marks for sale, the market makers (commercial banks) would experience a shortage of marks and would respond by increasing the quoted price of marks. Therefore, the mark would **appreciate,** or increase in value.

As a second example, assume that German corporations begin to purchase more U.S. goods and that German investors purchase more U.S. securities. These actions reflect an increased sale of marks in exchange for dollars, causing a surplus of marks in the market. The value of the mark would therefore **depreciate,** or decline, in order to once again achieve equilibrium. In reality, both the demand for marks and the supply of marks for sale can change simultaneously. The adjustment in the exchange rate will depend on the direction and magnitude of these changes.

Supply and demand for a currency are influenced by a variety of factors, including (1) differential inflation rates, (2) differential interest rates, and (3) government intervention. These factors are discussed in the following subsections.

Differential Inflation Rates

Begin with an equilibrium situation and consider what would happen to the U.S. demand for marks and the supply of German marks for sale if U.S. inflation suddenly became much higher than German inflation. The U.S. demand for German goods would increase, reflecting an increased U.S. demand for German marks. In addition, the supply of marks to be sold for dollars would decline as the German desire for U.S. goods decreased. Both forces would place upward pressure on the value of the mark.

Under the reverse situation, where German inflation suddenly becomes much higher than U.S. inflation, the U.S. demand for marks would decrease, while the supply of marks for sale would increase, placing downward pressure on the value of the mark.

A well-known theory regarding the relationship between inflation and exchange rates, **purchasing power parity (PPP)**, suggests that the exchange rate will, on average, change by a percentage that reflects the inflation differential between the two countries of concern. For example, assume an initial equilibrium situation where the British pound's spot rate is $1.60, U.S. inflation is 3 percent, and British inflation is also 3 percent. If U.S. inflation suddenly increased to 5 percent, the British pound would appreciate against the dollar by approximately 2 percent according to PPP. The rationale is that the United States would increase its demand for British goods as a result of the higher U.S. prices, placing upward pressure on the pound's value. Once the pound appreciated by 2 percent, the purchasing power of U.S. consumers would be the same whether the consumers purchased U.S. goods or British goods. Although the U.S. goods would have risen in price by a higher percentage, the British goods would then be just as expensive to U.S. consumers because of the pound's appreciation. Thus, a new equilibrium exchange rate results from the change in U.S. inflation.

In reality, exchange rates do not always change as suggested by the PPP theory. The other factors that influence exchange rates (discussed next) can distort the PPP relationship. Thus, all these factors must be considered when assessing why an exchange rate has changed. Furthermore, forecasts of future exchange rates must account for the potential direction and magnitude of changes in all factors that affect exchange rates.

Differential Interest Rates

Consider what would happen to the U.S. demand for marks and the supply of marks for sale if U.S. interest rates were to suddenly become much higher than German interest rates. The demand by U.S. investors for German interest-bearing securities would decrease, as these securities would become less attractive. In addition, the supply of marks to be sold in exchange for dollars would increase as German investors increased their purchases of U.S. interest-bearing securities. Both forces would place downward pressure on the mark's value. Under the reverse situation, opposite forces would occur, resulting in upward pressure on the mark's value. In general, the currency of the country with a higher increase (or smaller decrease) in interest rates is expected to appreciate, other factors held constant.

Government Intervention

Central banks commonly consider adjusting a currency's value to influence economic conditions. For example, the U.S. central bank may wish to weaken the dollar to attract more demand for its exports, which can stimulate its economy. However, a weaker dollar can also reduce foreign competition (by raising the prices of foreign goods to U.S. consumers), which may cause U.S. inflation. Alternatively, the U.S. central bank may prefer to strengthen the dollar to intensify foreign competition, which can reduce U.S. inflation.

A country's government can intervene in the foreign exchange market to affect a currency's value. Direct intervention occurs when a country's central bank (such as the Federal Reserve Bank for the United States or the Bank of England for Great Britain) sells some of its currency reserves for a different currency. For example, if the Federal Reserve Bank desired to weaken the dollar, it could sell some of its dollar reserves in exchange for foreign currencies. In essence, it would thereby increase the U.S. demand for foreign currencies in the foreign exchange market, which could cause those currencies to appreciate against the dollar. To strengthen the dollar, it could sell some of its foreign currency reserves in exchange for dollars.

As an indirect method of intervention, the government could influence those factors (such as inflation or interest rates) that affect a currency's value. Alternatively, it could place restrictions on international trade or on international investments. For example, if the U.S. government imposed trade restrictions on U.S. imports, this would limit the U.S. demand for foreign currencies and would place downward pressure on those currencies' values.

Central bank intervention can be overwhelmed by market forces, however, and therefore may not always succeed in reversing exchange rate movements, yet it may significantly affect the foreign exchange markets in two ways. First, it may slow the momentum of exchange rate movements. Second, it may cause commercial banks and other corporations to reassess their foreign exchange strategies if they believe the central banks will continue intervention.

In September 1985 central banks of the five major industrial powers (the Group of Five) developed an intervention strategy to weaken the U.S. dollar value. Within two weeks, the dollar depreciated by 13 percent against the Japanese yen and 9 percent against the German mark. Each country's central bank sold $1 billion or more during this intervention period. This amount seems insignificant in light of the massive daily volume of foreign exchange transactions. Yet, foreign exchange traders suggest that skill and timing are more important than the amount spent during the intervention process. If central banks work together and use proper timing, they can have a more lasting impact on currency values than if they do not. Many intervention efforts prior to September 1985 just temporarily jolted the markets, only to have exchange rates continue their pattern the following day. However, the intervention in September 1985 was the beginning of the dollar's reversal. Although the transactions were not sufficient for a long-term reversal, they may have affected the strategies of the market participants, leading to a sustained weakening of the dollar.

In 1991, the Federal Reserve System was faced with an interesting dilemma. The dollar had weakened considerably against most other major currencies. The dollar's weakness was primarily attributed to low U.S. interest rates relative to foreign interest rates. In order to stimulate the sagging U.S. economy, the Federal Reserve had pushed interest rates lower with a loose monetary policy (including a decrease in its discount rate). Meanwhile, Bundesbank (the German central bank) had raised interest rates in Germany to halt any momentum in inflation caused by a strong economy. The changes in interest rates caused some global investors to shift their investments from the U.S. to Germany. In February 1991, when the dollar reached an all-time low against the mark, central banks used marks and other currencies to purchase U.S. dollars in the foreign exchange market. This attempt of direct intervention was overwhelmed by market forces resulting from interest rate differentials, which were partially attributed to the central banks. Thus, the dollar continued to decline despite the direct intervention. The lesson from this example is that direct intervention in the foreign exchange market cannot usually offset exchange rate movements that are caused by economic conditions. The central banks would have been more successful in boosting the dollar's value if they raised U.S. interest rates and lowered foreign interest rates. Yet, this would have conflicted with their initial objectives of stimulating the U.S. economy and slowing German inflation.

SPECULATION IN FOREIGN EXCHANGE MARKETS

Many commercial banks take positions in currencies to capitalize on expected exchange rate movements. For example, if a commercial bank expects the mark to depreciate against the dollar, it may take a *short* position in marks and a *long* position in dollars. That is, it will first borrow marks from another bank, then exchange the marks for dollars to provide a short-term dollar loan to a bank that needs dollars. When the loan period is over, it receives dollars back with interest, converts them back to marks, and pays off its debt in marks with interest. If the dollar strengthens over this period, the bank receives more marks per dollar than the number of marks needed to purchase each dollar in the first place. As a numerical example, assume the following information:

- Interest rate on borrowed marks (DM) is 6 percent annualized.
- Interest rate on dollars loaned out is 7 percent annualized.
- Spot rate is 2 marks per dollar (one mark = $.50).
- Expected spot rate in six days is 2.05 marks per dollar.
- Bank can borrow DM20 million.

The following steps can be taken to determine the profit from "shorting" marks and "going long" on dollars:

Step 1. Borrow DM20 million marks and convert to $10 million (at $.50 per mark).

Step 2. Invest the $10 million for one week at 7 percent annualized or (.11667 percent over six days), which will generate $10,011,667.

Step 3. After six days, convert the $10,011,667 into marks at the spot rate that exists at that time. Based on the expected rate of 2.05 marks per dollar, the dollars would convert to DM20,523,917.

Step 4. Pay back the loan of DM20 million plus interest of 6 percent annualized (.1 percent over six days), which equals DM20,020,000.

The result is that the bank earned DM503,917 profit over a six-day period. Although potential profits are attractive, the speculative performance will depend on the uncertain future spot rate at the time the short and long positions are closed out.

MOVEMENTS IN EXCHANGE RATES

The foreign exchange market has received much attention in recent years because of the degree to which currency movements can affect a firm's performance or a country's economic conditions. Exhibit 14.2 shows the trend in various foreign currency values over time. Most foreign currencies strengthened against the dollar in the late 1970s, weakened during the early 1980s, and began to strengthen again in the mid-1980s. Since then, the trends have been erratic. Foreign currencies have frequently strengthened when their interest rates were high relative to the U.S. interest rate (such as in the early 1990s). The trends in European currency values are somewhat similar. Periods of increased foreign currency values reflect a weak dollar, while periods of decreased foreign currency values reflect a strong dollar.

FOREIGN EXCHANGE DERIVATIVES

Foreign exchange derivatives can be used to speculate on future exchange rate movements or to hedge anticipated cash inflows or outflows in a given foreign currency. As foreign security markets have been more accessible, institutional investors have increased their international investments, which has increased their exposure to exchange rate risk. Some institutional investors use foreign

EXHIBIT 14.2 Exchange Rate Movements of Various Currencies

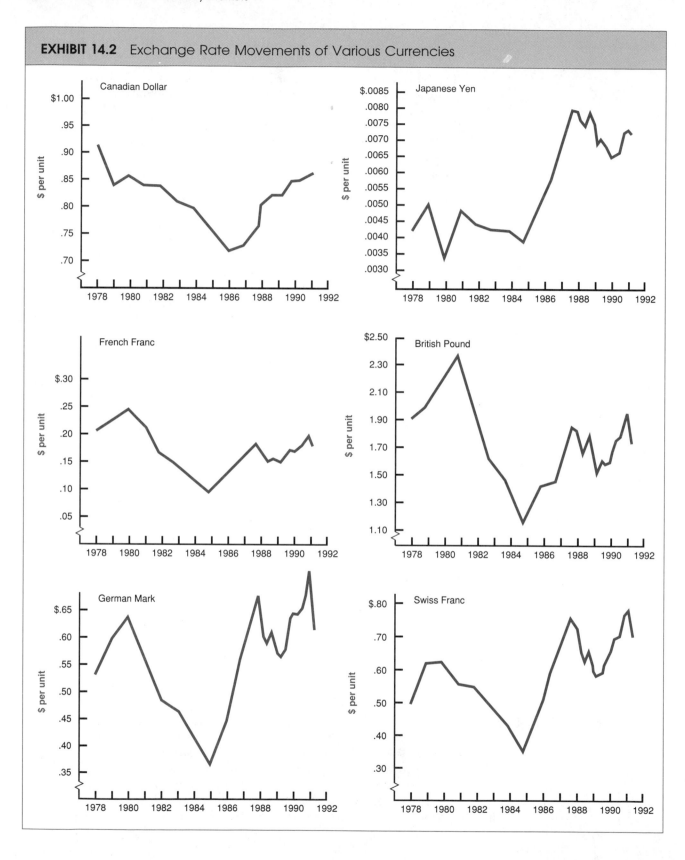

exchange derivatives to hedge their exposure. The most popular foreign exchange derivatives are forward contracts, currency futures contracts, currency swaps, and currency options contracts.

Forward Contracts

Forward contracts are contracts typically negotiated with a commercial bank that allow one to purchase or sell a specified amount of a particular foreign currency at a specified exchange rate on a specified future date. There is a **forward market** that facilitates the trading of forward contracts. This market is not in one visible place, but is essentially a telecommunications network in which large commercial banks match participants who wish to buy a currency forward with other participants who wish to sell a currency forward.

Many of the commercial banks that offer foreign exchange on a spot basis also offer forward transactions for the widely traded currencies. By enabling a corporation to lock in the price to be paid for a foreign currency, forward purchases can hedge the corporation's risk that the currency's value may appreciate over time. For example, consider a U.S. insurance company that planned to invest about $20 million in French stocks two months from now. Because the French stocks are denominated in francs, the amount of stock that can be purchased is dependent on the French franc's value at the time of the purchase. If the company is concerned that the franc will appreciate by the time of the purchase, it could buy francs forward to lock in the exchange rate.

A corporation receiving payments denominated in a particular foreign currency in the future could lock in the price at which the currency could be sold by selling that currency forward. For example, consider a U.S. pension fund that plans to liquidate its holdings of British stocks in six months, but anticipates that the British pound will depreciate by that time. The pension fund could insulate its future transaction from exchange rate risk by negotiating a forward contract to sell British pounds six months forward. In this way, the British pounds received when liquidating the stocks can be converted to dollars at the exchange rate specified in the forward contract.

The large banks that accommodate requests for forward contracts are buying forward from some firms and selling forward to others for a given date. They profit from the difference between the bid price at which they buy a currency forward and the slightly higher ask price at which they sell that currency forward. If a bank's forward purchase and sale contracts do not even out for a given date, the bank is exposed to exchange rate risk. Consider a U.S. bank that has contracts committed to selling DM100 million and purchasing DM150 million 90 days from now. The bank will receive DM50 million more than it sells. An increase in the mark value 90 days from now would be advantageous, but if the mark depreciates, the bank would be adversely affected by its exposure to the exchange rate risk.

The forward rate of a currency will sometimes exceed the existing spot rate, thereby exhibiting a premium. At other times, it will be below the spot rate, exhibiting a discount. Forward contracts are sometimes referred to in terms of their percentage premium or discount rather than their actual rate. For example, assume that the spot rate (SR) of the German mark is $.50 while the 180-day ($n = 180$) forward rate ($FR$) is $.51. The forward rate premium would be

$$\text{Forward Rate Premium} = \frac{FR - SR}{SR} \times \frac{360}{n}$$

$$= \frac{\$.51 - \$.50}{\$.50} \times \frac{360}{180}$$

$$= 4\%$$

This premium simply reflects the percentage by which the forward rate exceeds the spot rate on an annualized basis.

Currency Futures Contracts

An alternative to the forward contract is a currency futures contract, which is a standardized contract that specifies an amount of a particular currency to be exchanged on a specified date and at a specified exchange rate. A firm can purchase a futures contract to hedge payables in a foreign currency by locking in the price at which it could purchase that specific currency at a particular point in time. To hedge receivables denominated in a foreign currency, it could sell futures, thereby locking in the price at which it could sell that currency. A futures contract represents a standard number of units, as shown in Exhibit 14.3. Currency futures contracts also have specific maturity (or "settlement") dates from which the firm must choose.

Futures contracts differ from forward contracts in that they are standardized, whereas forward contracts can specify whatever amount and maturity date the firm desires. Forward contracts have this flexibility because they are negotiated with commercial banks rather than on a trading floor.

Currency Swaps

A currency swap is an agreement that allows one to periodically swap one currency for another at specified exchange rates. It essentially represents a series of forward contracts. Commercial banks facilitate currency swaps by serving as the intermediary that links two parties with opposite needs. Alternatively, commercial banks may be willing to take the position counter to that desired by a particular party. In such a case, they expose themselves to exchange rate risk unless the position they have assumed will offset existing exposure.

Currency Options Contracts

Another instrument used for hedging is the currency option. Its primary advantage over forward and futures contracts is that it provides a right rather than an obligation to purchase or sell a particular currency at a specified price within a given period.

A currency call option provides the right to purchase a particular currency at a specified price (called the exercise price) within a specified period. This type of option can be used to hedge future cash payments denominated in a foreign currency. If the spot rate remains below the exercise price, the option would not be exercised, because the firm could purchase the foreign currency at a lower cost in the spot market. However, options can be obtained only for a fee (or premium), so there is a cost to a firm hedging with options, even if the options are not exercised.

EXHIBIT 14.3	Foreign Currencies for Which Futures Contracts Are Available (on the Chicago Mercantile Exchange)

CURRENCY	NUMBER OF FOREIGN CURRENCY UNITS PER CONTRACT
Australian dollar	100,000
British pound	62,500
Canadian dollar	100,000
German mark	125,000
Japanese yen	12,500,000
Swiss franc	125,000

A put option provides the right to sell a particular currency at a specified price (exercise price) within a specified period. If the spot rate remains above the exercise price, the option would not be exercised, because the firm could sell the foreign currency at a higher price in the spot market. Conversely, if the spot rate is below the exercise price at the time the foreign currency is received, the firm could exercise its put option.

When deciding whether to use the forward, futures, or options contracts for hedging, the following characteristics of each contract should be considered. First, if the firm requires a tailor-made hedge that cannot be matched by existing futures contracts, a forward contract may be preferred. Otherwise, forward and futures contracts should generate somewhat similar results.

The choice of either an obligation type of contract (forward or futures) or an options contract depends on the expected trend of the spot rate. If the currency denominating payables appreciates, the firm will benefit more from a futures or forward contract than from a call option contract. The call option contract requires an up-front fee, but it is a wiser choice when the firm is less certain of the future direction of a currency. The call option can hedge the firm against possible appreciation but still allow the firm to ignore the contract and use the spot market if the currency depreciates. Put options may be preferred over futures or forward contracts for hedging receivables when future currency movements may have a favorable effect on the firm.

Use of Foreign Exchange Derivatives for Speculating

The forward, currency futures, and currency options markets may be used for not only hedging but speculating as well. For example, a speculator who expects the German marks to appreciate could consider any of these strategies:

1. Purchase marks forward and, when received, sell them in the spot market.
2. Purchase futures contracts on marks; when the marks are received, sell them in the spot market.
3. Purchase call options on marks; at some point before the expiration date, when the spot rate exceeds the exercise price, exercise the call option and then sell the marks received in the spot market.

Conversely, a speculator who expects the mark to depreciate could consider any of these strategies:

1. Sell marks forward and then purchase them in the spot market just before fulfilling the forward obligation.
2. Sell futures contracts on marks; purchase marks in the spot market just before fulfilling the futures obligation.
3. Purchase put options on marks; at some point before the expiration date, when the spot rate is less than the exercise price, purchase marks in the spot market and then exercise the put option.

SPECULATING WITH CURRENCY FUTURES. As an example of speculating with currency futures, consider the following information:

- Spot rate of British pound is $1.56 per pound.
- Price of futures contract is $1.57 per pound.
- Expectation of pound's spot rate as of maturity date of the futures contract is $1.63 per pound.

Given that the future spot rate is expected to be higher than the futures price, you could buy currency futures. You would receive pounds on the maturity date for $1.57. If your expectations are correct, you would then sell the pounds for $.06 more per unit than you paid for them (assuming that you sold the pounds at that time).

The risk of your speculative strategy is that the pound may decline rather than increase in value. If it declines to $1.55 by the maturity date, you would have sold the pounds for $.02 less per unit than what you paid.

To account for uncertainty, speculators may develop a probability distribution for the future spot rate:

FUTURE SPOT RATE OF BRITISH POUND	PROBABILITY
$1.50	10%
1.59	20
1.63	50
1.66	20

This probability distribution suggests that four outcomes are possible. For each possible outcome, the anticipated gain or loss can be determined:

POSSIBLE OUTCOME FOR FUTURE SPOT RATE	PROBABILITY	GAIN OR LOSS PER UNIT
$1.50	10%	− $.07
1.59	20	.02
1.63	50	.06
1.66	20	.09

This analysis measures the probability and potential magnitude of a loss from the speculative strategy.

SPECULATING WITH CURRENCY OPTIONS.   Consider the information from the previous example and assume that a British call option is available with an exercise price of $1.57 and a premium of $.03 per unit. Recall that your best guess of the future spot rate was $1.63. If your guess is correct, you will earn $.06 per unit on the difference between what you paid (the exercise price of $1.57) and what you could sell a pound for ($1.63). After the premium paid for the option ($.03 per unit) is deducted, the net gain is $.03 per unit.

The risk of purchasing this option is that the pound's value might decline over time. If so, you will be unable to exercise the option, and your loss will be the premium paid for it. To assess the risk involved, a probability distribution could be developed. In Exhibit 14.4, the probability distribution from the previous example is applied here. The distribution of net gains from the strategy is shown in the sixth column.

Speculators should always compare the potential gains from currency options and currency futures contracts to determine which type of contract (if any) to trade. It is possible for two speculators to have similar expectations about potential gains from both types of contracts yet, because they have different degrees of risk aversion, prefer different types of contracts.

INTERNATIONAL ARBITRAGE

Exchange rates in the foreign exchange market are market determined. If they become misaligned, various forms of arbitrage will occur, forcing realignment. Common examples of international arbitrage follow.

Locational Arbitrage

Suppose the exchange rates of the mark quoted by two banks differ, as shown in Exhibit 14.5. The ask quote is higher than the bid quote to reflect transaction costs charged by each bank. Because Baltimore Bank is asking $.499 for marks

EXHIBIT 14.4   Estimating Speculative Gains from Options Using a Probability Distribution

(1)	(2)	(3)	(4)	(5)	(6)
Possible Outcome for Future Spot Rate	Probability	Will the Option Be Exercised Based on This Outcome?	Gain per Unit from Exercising Option	Premium Paid per Unit for the Option	Net Gain or Loss per Unit
$1.50	10%	No	—	$.03	− $.03
1.59	20	Yes	$.02	.03	− .01
1.63	50	Yes	.06	.03	.03
1.66	30	Yes	.09	.03	.06

USING *THE WALL STREET JOURNAL*

WSJ

FOREIGN EXCHANGE DERIVATIVES

The Wall Street Journal (WSJ) provides the following information related to foreign exchange derivatives on a daily basis:

- Forward rates for six different currencies.
- Price quotations on currency futures contracts for six different currencies.
- Price quotations on options on currency futures.
- Cross-exchange rates, or the exchange rates between non-U.S. currencies.
- A section called "Foreign Exchange" that provides reasons for recent exchange rate movements and suggests how exchange rates may change in the future.

- Price quotations on currency options for six major currencies. For each currency, several different exercise (or strike) prices are available. Each row represents a particular exercise price (in first column) and expiration date (in second column). The volume of contracts traded and the premium per unit for currency call options are disclosed in columns 3 and 4. Volume and premium information for currency put options is disclosed in the last two columns.

SOURCE: *The Wall Street Journal*, August 8, 1994, P. C14. Reprinted by permission of *The Wall Street Journal*, © 1994 Dow Jones & Company, Inc. All rights reserved worldwide.

OPTIONS
PHILADELPHIA EXCHANGE

		Calls Vol. Last		Puts Vol. Last	
DMark				**63.36**	
62,500 German Mark EOM-European style.					
63	Aug	100	0.66	100	0.67
Australian Dollar				**74.33**	
50,000 Australian Dollars-cents per unit.					
69	Dec	...	...	3	0.25
72	Sep	...	...	5	0.25
73	Aug	...	...	4	0.06
73	Sep	...	...	3	0.45
74	Aug	...	...	20	0.32
British Pound				**154.35**	
31,250 British Pounds-European Style.					
160	Dec	100	1.25	...	...
31,250 British Pounds-cents per unit.					
150	Sep	...	...	10	0.43
150	Dec	...	...	32	1.80
152½	Aug	...	...	10	0.08
152½	Sep	1	2.60	88	0.98
155	Aug	96	0.36	...	...
157½	Dec	6	1.85	...	...
British Pound-GMark				**243.77**	
31,250 British Pound-German Mark cross.					
244	Aug	...	...	32	0.64
244	Sep	32	2.10	32	2.06
31,250 British Pound-German mark EOM.					
240	Sep	...	...	100	0.96
244	Sep	100	2.70	...	...
250	Sep	100	0.70	...	...
Canadian Dollar				**72.09**	
50,000 Canadian Dollars-cents per unit.					
72	Aug	18	0.24	...	...
72½	Sep	...	...	20	0.88
GMark-JYen				**63.56**	
62,500 GMark-JYen cross EOM.					
63½	Aug	1	0.57	2	0.61
German Mark				**63.36**	
62,500 German Marks EOM-cents per unit.					
62½	Aug	3	0.85	3	0.48

		Calls Vol. Last		Puts Vol. Last	
62,500 German Marks-European Style.					
62½	Aug	...	...	15	0.14
63	Aug	...	...	10	0.44
63½	Aug	10	0.18	...	...
62,500 German Marks-cents per unit.					
59	Dec	...	...	2	0.40
60½	Sep	...	...	100	0.17
61	Sep	...	...	4	0.21
61	Dec	...	...	32	0.91
61½	Aug	...	...	260	0.05
61½	Sep	...	...	1	0.32
62	Aug	...	...	130	0.06
62	Sep	10	1.45	258	0.47
62	Dec	...	...	229	1.17
62½	Aug	18	0.84	97	0.17
62½	Sep	...	...	5	0.68
63	Aug	306	0.50	805	0.26
63	Sep	1	1.10	11	0.84
63	Dec	2	1.70	7	1.58
63½	Aug	693	0.26	10	0.51
63½	Sep	...	...	75	1.00
64	Aug	2197	0.15	...	...
64	Sep	211	0.67	5	1.45
65	Dec	35	1.06	...	...
65½	Aug	...	...	10	2.38
65½	Sep	143	0.21	...	...
Japanese Yen				**99.77**	
6,250,000 Japanese Yen EOM-100ths of a cent per unit.					
100	Aug	4	0.76	...	...
103	Aug	20	0.17	...	...
6,250,000 Japanese Yen EOM.					
98½	Sep	15	1.43	20	0.56
6,250,000 Japanese Yen-100ths of a cent per unit.					
96½	Sep	5	3.36	15	0.38
97	Sep	...	...	10	0.39
97	Dec	...	...	15	1.24

		Calls Vol. Last		Puts Vol. Last	
98	Aug	...	...	10	0.16
98½	Aug	...	...	10	0.25
99	Aug	...	...	14	0.21
99	Sep	...	...	1	1.02
99	Dec	...	...	40	2.03
99½	Sep	...	...	5	1.31
100	Aug	60	0.36	60	0.86
100	Sep	11	1.19	5	1.51
100½	Aug	...	...	10	1.12
100½	Sep	...	...	2	1.55
101	Aug	40	0.17	15	1.76
101	Sep	...	...	1	2.24
101½	Aug	...	...	10	2.28
102	Aug	...	...	1	2.51
104½	Sep	40	0.23	...	...
6,250,000 Japanese Yen-European Style.					
101	Sep	90	0.81	...	...
Swiss Franc				**75.10**	
62,500 Swiss Francs EOM.					
73½	Aug	...	...	5	0.32
62,500 Swiss Francs-European Style.					
75	Sep	...	...	80	1.37
75	Dec	...	...	32	2.28
75½	Sep	32	0.77	...	...
62,500 Swiss Francs-cents per unit.					
69	Dec	...	...	6	0.31
72	Sep	...	...	22	0.30
73	Aug	...	...	40	0.05
73	Sep	5	2.07	...	...
73	Dec	...	...	25	1.28
74	Aug	7	0.98	...	...
74	Sep	...	...	1	0.92
74½	Aug	4	0.74	...	...
74½	Sep	...	...	28	1.00
75	Aug	...	...	9	0.51
75	Sep	32	0.97	22	1.18
78	Sep	22	0.25	...	...
Call Vol 5,408			Open Int ... 580,506		
Put Vol 3,391			Open Int ... 447,972		

and Sacramento Bank is willing to pay (bid) $.500 for marks, an institution could execute **locational arbitrage.** That is, it could achieve a risk-free return without tying funds up for any length of time by buying marks at one location (Baltimore Bank) and simultaneously selling them to the other location (Sacramento Bank).

As locational arbitrage is executed, Baltimore Bank will begin to raise its ask price on marks in response to the strong demand. In addition, Sacramento Bank will begin to lower its bid price in response to its excess supply of marks recently received. Once the ask price of Baltimore Bank is at least as high as the bid price by Sacramento Bank, locational arbitrage will no longer be possible. Because some financial institutions (particularly the foreign exchange departments of commercial banks) watch for locational arbitrage opportunities, any discrepancy in exchange rates among locations should quickly be alleviated.

Covered Interest Arbitrage

The coexistence of international money markets and forward markets forces a special relationship between a forward rate premium and the interest rate differential of two countries, known as **interest rate parity.** The equation for interest rate parity can be written as

$$p = \frac{(1 + i_h)}{(1 + i_f)} - 1$$

where

p = forward premium of foreign currency

i_h = home country interest rate

i_f = foreign interest rate

For example, assume that the spot rate of the German mark is $.50, the one-year U.S. interest rate is 9 percent, and the one-year German interest rate is 6 percent. Under conditions of interest rate parity, the forward premium of the mark would be

$$p = \frac{(1 + 9\%)}{(1 + 6\%)} - 1$$

$$\approx 2.8\%$$

This means that the forward rate of the mark would be about $.514, to reflect a 2.8 percent premium above the spot rate. When one reviews the equation for interest rate parity, the following relationship is obvious. If the interest rate is lower in the foreign country than in the home country, the forward rate of the

EXHIBIT 14.5 Bank Quotes Used for Locational Arbitrage Example

	BID RATE ON MARKS	ASK RATE ON MARKS
Sacramento Bank	$.500	$.507
Baltimore Bank	$.491	$.499

foreign currency will have a premium. In the opposite situation, it will have a discount.

Interest rate parity suggests that the forward rate premium (or discount) should be about equal to the differential in interest rates between the countries of concern. To illustrate this relationship, assume that both the spot rate and one-year forward rate of the Canadian dollar was $.80. Also assume that the Canadian interest rate was 10 percent, while the U.S. interest rate was 8 percent. U.S. investors could take advantage of the higher Canadian interest rate without being exposed to exchange rate risk by executing **covered interest arbitrage.** Specifically, they would exchange U.S. dollars for Canadian dollars and invest at the rate of 10 percent. They would simultaneously sell Canadian dollars one year forward. Because they are able to purchase and sell Canadian dollars for the same price, their return is the 10 percent interest earned on their investment.

As the U.S. investors demand Canadian dollars in the spot market while selling Canadian dollars forward, they place upward pressure on the spot rate and downward pressure on the one-year forward rate of the Canadian dollar. Thus, the Canadian dollar's forward rate will exhibit a discount. Once the discount becomes large enough, the interest rate advantage in Canada will be offset. What U.S. investors gain on the higher Canadian interest rate is offset by having to buy Canadian dollars at a higher (spot) rate than the selling (forward) rate. Consequently, covered interest arbitrage will no longer generate a return that is any higher for U.S. investors than an alternative investment within the United States. Once the forward discount (or premium) offsets the interest rate differential in this manner, interest rate parity exists.

We can use the interest rate parity equation to determine the forward discount that the Canadian dollar must exhibit to offset the interest rate differential:

$$p = \frac{(i + i_h)}{(1 + i_f)} - 1$$

$$= \frac{(1 + 8\%)}{(1 + 10\%)} - 1$$

$$\approx -1.82\%$$

If the forward rate is lower than the spot rate by 1.82 percent, the interest rate is offset, and covered interest arbitrage would yield a return to U.S. investors similar to the U.S. interest rate.

The existence of interest rate parity prevents investors from earning higher returns from covered interest arbitrate than can be earned in the United States. Yet, international investing may still be feasible if the investing firm does not simultaneously cover in the forward market. Of course, failure to do so usually exposes the firm to exchange rate risk; if the currency denominating the investment depreciates over the investment horizon, the return on the investment is reduced.

INSTITUTIONAL USE OF FOREIGN EXCHANGE MARKETS

The manner by which financial institutions utilize the foreign exchange market and foreign exchange derivatives is summarized in Exhibit 14.6. The degree of

EXHIBIT 14.6 Institutional Use of Foreign Exchange Markets

TYPE OF FINANCIAL INSTITUTION	USES OF FOREIGN EXCHANGE MARKETS
Commercial banks	■ Serve as financial intermediaries in the foreign exchange market by buying or selling currencies to accommodate customers. ■ Speculate on foreign currency movements by taking long positions in some currencies and short positions in others. ■ Provide forward contracts to customers. ■ Some commercial banks offer currency options to customers; these options can be tailored to a customer's specific needs, unlike the standardized currency options traded on an exchange.
International mutual funds	■ Use foreign exchange markets to exchange currencies when reconstructing their portfolios. ■ Use foreign exchange derivatives to hedge a portion of their exposure.
Brokerage firms and investment banking firms	■ Some brokerage firms and investment banking firms engage in foreign security transactions for their customers or for their own accounts.
Insurance companies	■ Use foreign exchange markets when exchanging currencies for their international operations. ■ Use foreign exchange markets when purchasing foreign securities for their investment portfolio or when selling foreign securities. ■ Use foreign exchange derivatives to hedge a portion of their exposure.
Pension funds	■ Require foreign exchange of currencies when investing in foreign securities for their stock or bond portfolios. ■ Use foreign exchange derivatives to hedge a portion of their exposure.

international investment by financial institutions is influenced by potential return, risk, and government regulations. Commercial banks use international lending as their primary form of international investing. Mutual funds, pension funds, and insurance companies purchase foreign securities. In recent years, technology has reduced information costs and other transaction costs associated with purchasing foreign securities, prompting an increase in institutional purchases of foreign securities. Consequently, the financial institutions are increasing their use of the foreign exchange markets to exchange currencies. They are also increasing their use of foreign exchange derivatives to hedge their investments in foreign securities.

SUMMARY

- Exchange rates are influenced by differential inflation rates, differential interest rates, and government intervention. There is upward pressure on a foreign currency's value when its home country has relatively low inflation, or relatively high interest rates. Governments can place upward pressure on a currency by purchasing that currency in the foreign exchange market (by exchanging other currencies held in reserve for that currency). Alternatively, they can place downward pressure on a currency by selling that currency in the foreign exchange market in exchange for other currencies.

- Various foreign exchange derivatives are used to hedge exchange rate risk. Forward contracts can be purchased to hedge future payables or sold to hedge future receivables in a foreign currency. Currency futures contracts can be used in a manner similar to forward contracts to hedge payables or receivables in a foreign currency. Currency swaps can be used to lock in the exchange rate of a foreign currency to be received or purchased at a future point in time. Currency call options can be purchased to hedge future payables in a foreign currency, while currency put options can be purchased to hedge future receivables in a foreign currency. Currency options offer more flexibility than the other foreign exchange derivatives, but require a premium to be paid for them.

- Foreign exchange derivatives can be used to speculate on expected exchange rate movements. When speculators expect a foreign currency to appreciate, they could lock in the exchange rate at which they may purchase that currency by purchasing forward contracts, futures contracts, or call options on that currency. When speculators expect a currency to depreciate, they could lock in the exchange rate at which they may sell that currency by selling forward contracts or futures contracts on that currency. They could also purchase put options on that currency.

QUESTIONS

1. Explain the exchange rate system that existed during the 1950s and 1960s. How did the Smithsonian Agreement in 1971 revise it? How does today's exchange rate system differ?

2. Explain the difference between a freely floating system and a dirty float. Which type is more representative of the United States?

3. Assume that France places a quota on goods imported from the United States and the United States does not plan to retaliate. How could this affect the value of the French franc? Explain.

4. Assume that stocks in Great Britain become very attractive to U.S. investors. How could this affect the value of the British pound? Explain.

5. Assume that Germany suddenly experiences high and unexpected inflation. How would this affect the value of the German mark according to purchasing power parity (PPP) theory?

6. Assume that Switzerland has a very strong economy, placing upward pressure on both inflation and interest rates. Explain how these conditions could place pressure on the value of the Swiss franc and determine whether the franc's value will rise or fall.

7. The Bank of Japan desires to decrease the value of the Japanese yen against the dollar. How could it use direct intervention to do this?

8. When would a commercial bank take a short position in a foreign currency? A long position?

9. Seattle Bank was long in German marks and short in Canadian dollars. Explain a possible future scenario that could adversely affect the bank's performance.

10. How does a weak dollar affect U.S. inflation? Explain.

11. Explain how foreign exchange derivatives could be used by U.S. speculators to speculate on the expected appreciation of the Japanese yen.

12. Assume a horizontal yield curve exists. How do you think the yield curve would be affected if foreign investors of short-term securities and long-term securities suddenly anticipate that the value of the dollar will strengthen? (Refer back to a discussion of the yield curve in Chapter 4 if it would help develop your opinion.)

PROBLEMS

1. Assume the following information:

	INTERBANK INTEREST RATE	SPOT RATE	EXPECTED SPOT RATE IN 5 DAYS
Canadian dollars	6%	$ .80	$ .79
British pounds	7%	$1.50	$1.52

   Explain how Minnesota Bank could speculate, based on this information, by taking a short position in one currency and a long position in the other. What would be the gain if expectations come true, assuming that the bank could borrow one million units of either currency?

2. Assume that a U.S. firm issues three-year notes in Germany with a par value of 60 million marks and a 6 percent annual coupon rate, priced at par. The forecasted exchange rate of the mark is $.50 at the end of Year 1, $.53 at the end of Year 2, and $.57 at the end of Year 3. Estimate the dollar cash flows needed to cover these payments.

3. Using the following information, determine the probability distribution of per-unit gains from selling in French franc (FF) futures:

   - Spot rate of FF is $.10
   - Price of FF futures per unit is $.102.

- Your expectation of FF spot rate at maturity of futures contract is

POSSIBLE OUTCOME FOR FUTURE SPOT RATE	PROBABILITY
$.09	10%
.095	70%
.11	20%

4. Using the following information, determine the probability distribution of net gains per unit from purchasing a call option on British pounds:

- Spot rate of British pound = $1.45.
- Premium on British pound option = $.04 per unit.
- Exercise price of a British pound option = $1.46.
- Your expectation of British pound spot rate prior to the expiration of option is

POSSIBLE OUTCOME FOR FUTURE SPOT RATE	PROBABILITY
$1.48	30%
1.49	40%
1.52	30%

5. Assume the following exchange rate quotes on British pounds:

	BID	ASK
Orleans Bank	$1.46	$1.47
Kansas Bank	1.48	1.49

Explain how locational arbitrage would occur. Also explain why this arbitrage will realign the exchange rates.

6. Assume the following information:

British pound spot rate = $1.58
British pound one-year forward rate = $1.58
British one-year interest rate = 11%
U.S. one-year interest rate = 9%

Explain how covered interest arbitrage could be used by U.S. investors to lock in a higher yield than 9%. What would be their yield? As covered interest arbitrage occurs, explain how the spot and forward rates of the pound would change.

7. Assume the following information:

French one-year interest rate = 15%
U.S. one-year interest rate = 11%

If interest rate parity exists, what would be the forward premium or discount on the French franc's forward rate? Would covered interest arbitrage be more profitable to U.S. investors than investing at home? Explain.

Project

1. **Assessing Exchange Rate Movements**
    Determine how a particular currency's value has changed against the dollar over the past six months. Offer an explanation for the general trend in this currency over the past six months.

Chicago Merc Roiled by Dollar-Propping

Jeffrey Taylor, Chicago

The concerted effort by the Federal Reserve and other central banks to prop up the sagging U.S. dollar has wreaked havoc in the currency pits of the Chicago Mercantile Exchange.

On Monday, for instance, small fortunes were made and lost on the Merc floor in just the first hour after the Fed and central banks in Europe began buying U.S. dollars. It marked the first dollar-support move by the U.S. government since February 1991.

Since Monday, big institutional investors such as banks and commodity funds have been flooding the Merc pits with orders for currency futures and options contracts. Harried traders in multicolored jackets stand on the descending tiers of the pits, some trading for big investors and others trying to scalp profits as contract prices gyrate.

"The market has been wild," says David Silverman, a trader who makes his living buying and selling contracts in the Merc's mark futures pit. "Since the intervention, it's been reacting sharply to any little piece of news it can find."

Until Monday, the dollar's value against European currencies had been sinking steadily for months. The dollar's weakness had, in turn, created a sustained bull market in prices of the Merc's futures and options contracts for the mark, British pound and Swiss franc—contracts that track these currencies' heretofore rising value against the dollar.

The Longs Got Trapped

It was because of this bull market in the Merc currency pits that Monday's unexpected central-bank intervention had such a catastropic effect on futures prices, traders say. As the dollar took off, "Everybody was trying to sell," says Jim Oliff, a floor broker in the British pound futures pit. "There were people who got trapped in long positions—a lot of bloodshed. It looked like sheer panic and it was a bit frightening."

Nowhere was the action hotter than in the mark futures pit. Although news service display boards above the Merc floor had yet to flash the first headlines about the central banks' move, Mr. Silverman and other floor traders became aware of it almost immediately because of a rush of selling in their pit.

Shortly after 9 a.m. Monday, Mr. Silverman says, a floor broker who is known to handle trades for large commodity funds offered to sell 700 mark futures contracts—a huge order that represented about $50 million of marks—at the going market price. Under normal circumstances, brokers bring such big orders to the pit gradually—parceling them out bit by bit so as not to disrupt the market and send prices reeling.

"You know something is up when a customer is trying to sell 700 contracts at once without putting a price limit on," Mr. Silverman says. "This customer was basically saying: 'Sell $50 million worth of German marks and I don't care what price you do it at.' "

Mark Futures Tumble

More big sell orders quickly followed. Within seconds, the prices of mark futures contracts—which had been rising more or less steadily for months—were tumbling in what looked like a death spiral. Happily for Mr. Silverman, he was already holding a short position—a bet that the mark would decline against the dollar. This turned into a highly profitable trade, netting Mr. Silverman a profit that he declines to disclose.

Not all of Mr. Silverman's trades that morning were so lucrative. At one point, thinking that the plunging mark had hit bottom, he bought 20 futures contracts from a floor broker. "The next thing I knew, I was selling the contracts 35 points lower," he said. Each "point" represents a loss or profit of $12.50 a contract; at this rate, Mr. Silverman's trade produced a loss of $8,750 in less than five minutes.

The central banks' intervention had a similar explosive effect in the pit where futures contracts on British pounds are traded. As the pound's value against the dollar plunged, so did futures prices. In the pit, institutional clients began flooding Mr. Oliff, the floor broker, with orders.

Continued

CASE APPLICATION: PANIC IN CURRENCY FUTURES TRADING

Continued

By Monday afternoon, Mr. Oliff had lost his voice from screaming bids and offers at the top of his lungs. For the next two days, he was reduced to using sign language to announce his trades; during an interview yesterday, he spoke in a raspy whisper.

Many futures speculators who do their trading by phone were caught by surprise and had big losses; some others, however, had anticipated the central banks' move.

Kevin Lawrie, vice president, foreign exchange, at Bank of Boston, spent most of Monday protecting the bank's position in global currency markets. Mr. Lawrie also trades currency futures contracts for his personal account, ordering the transaction through a broker who fills them on the Merc floor. "Going into last weekend," he says, "I was long four different currencies" in a wager that the dollar would remain weak.

But "by Monday, the dollar was close to its historic low against the mark" Mr. Lawrie says. "There had been talk the previous week about intervention, so I decided to cut my long positions. I beat the intervention by about 10 minutes and when it happened, I had a good laugh about it."

Since the intervention, trading volume at the Merc has surged. On Monday, for instance, the exchange traded 62,253 mark futures contracts and 34,780 mark options contracts, up sharply from the average daily volume of 44,500 and 20,500 contracts, respectively. On the same day, the trading volume in pound futures and options was 18,599 and 4,640 contracts, respectively, up from average daily volume of 12,700 and 2,500 contracts.

And the lasting effect of Monday's central-bank intervention has been traders' lingering fear that more such moves may be on the way. On Tuesday and again yesterday, the market was extremely sensitive to any news that seemed to signal what the Fed's intentions about the dollar might be.

For example, Fed Chairman Alan Greenspan, testifying before the Senate Banking Committee Tuesday afternoon, roiled the Merc's currency futures pits. Shortly before 3 p.m. EDT close of trading, Mr. Greenspan expressed his view that the dollar's weakness didn't benefit the U.S. economy—contradicting the beliefs of some economists who feel that a weak dollar can help narrow the trade deficit by encouraging U.S. exports. Moments after Mr. Greenspan's remark, Mr. Oliff says, "we had a whole new wave of selling" in the pound futures pit.

SOURCE: *The Wall Street Journal,* July 23, 1992, p. C1. Reprinted by permission of *The Wall Street Journal,* © 1992 Dow Jones & Company, Inc. All rights reserved worldwide.

QUESTIONS

1. Explain the logic of how central bank intervention caused sheer panic for currency futures traders with long positions.

2. Explain the concern caused when a floor broker was willing to sell 700 mark futures contracts (representing a value of about $50 million of marks) at the going market rate. What might this action signal to other brokers?

3. Explain why speculators with short (sell) positions could benefit as a result of the central bank intervention.

4. Some traders with long (buy) positions may have responded immediately to the central bank intervention by selling futures contracts. Why would some speculators with long positions leave their positions unchanged or even increase their positions by purchasing more futures contracts in response to the central bank intervention?

REFERENCES

Adler, Michael, and Bruce Lehmann. "Deviations from Purchasing Power Parity in the Long Run." *Journal of Finance* (December 1983): 1471–1487.

Bodurtha, James N., Jr., and George R. Courtadon. "Efficiency Tests of the Foreign Currency Options Market." *Journal of Finance* (March 1986): 151–161.

Fama, Eugene. "Forward and Spot Exchange Rates." *Journal of Monetary Economics* (November 1984): 319–383.

Hakkio, Craig. "Does the Exchange Rate Follow a Random Walk? A Monte Carlo Study of Four Tests for a Random Walk." *Journal of International Economics* (June 1986): 221–230.

Hilliard, Jimmy E., Jeff Madura, and Alan L. Tucker. "Currency Option Pricing with Stochastic Domestic and Foreign Interest Rates." *Journal of Financial and Quantitative Analysis* (June 1991): 139–151.

Kroner, Kenneth F., and Jahangir Sultan. "Time-Varying Distributions and Dynamic Hedging with Foreign Currency Futures." *Journal of Financial and Quantitative Analysis* (December 1993): 535–551.

Stockman, Alan. "Recent Issues in the Theory of Flexible Exchange Rates: A Review Article." *Journal of Money, Credit, and Banking* (August 1985): 401–410.

Thomas, Lee R. "A Winning Strategy for Currency Futures Speculation." *Journal of Portfolio Management* (Fall 1985): 65–69.

CHOOSING AMONG DERIVATIVE SECURITIES_____

This problem requires an understanding of futures contracts (Chapter 11), options markets (Chapter 12), interest rate swap markets (Chapter 13), and foreign exchange derivative markets (Chapter 14). It also requires an understanding of how economic conditions affect interest rates and security prices (Chapters 2, 3, 4, 8, and 10).

Assume that the United States just experienced a mild recession. As a result, interest rates have declined to their lowest levels in a decade. The U.S. interest rates appear to be influenced more by changes in the demand for funds than in the supply of U.S. savings, because the savings rate does not change much regardless of economic conditions. The yield curve is currently flat. The federal budget deficit has improved lately and is not expected to rise substantially.

The federal government recently decided to reduce personal tax rates significantly for all tax brackets as well as corporate tax rates. The U.S. dollar has just recently weakened. Economies of other countries were somewhat stagnant but have improved in the past quarter. Your assignment is to recommend how various financial institutions should respond to the preceding information.

QUESTIONS

a. A savings institution holds 50 percent of its assets as long-term fixed-rate mortgages. Virtually all of its funds are in the form of short-term deposits. Which of the following strategies would be most appropriate for this institution?

   ▪ Use a fixed-for-floating swap.
   ▪ Use a swap of floating payments for fixed payments.
   ▪ Use a put option on interest rate futures contracts.
   ▪ Remain unhedged.

   Defend your recommendation.

b. An insurance company maintains a large portfolio of U.S. stocks. Which of the following would be most appropriate?

   ▪ Sell stock index futures contracts.
   ▪ Remain unhedged.

Defend your recommendation.

c. A pension fund maintains a large bond portfolio of U.S. bonds. Which of the following would be most appropriate?

- Sell bond index futures.
- Buy bond index futures.
- Remain unhedged.

Defend your recommendation.

d. An international mutual fund sponsored by a U.S. securities firm consists of bonds evenly allocated across the United States, Germany, and the United Kingdom. One of the portfolio managers has decided to hedge all the assets by selling futures on a popular U.S. bond index. The manager has stated that because the fund concentrates only on risk-free Treasury bonds, the only concern is interest rate risk. Assuming that interest rate risk is the only risk of concern, will the hedge described above be effective? Why? Is there any other risk that deserves to be considered? If so, how would you hedge that risk?

PART 5

COMMERCIAL BANKING

The chapters in Part Five focus on commercial banking. Chapter 15 identifies the common sources and uses of funds for commercial banks, while Chapter 16 describes the regulations imposed on sources and uses of funds and other banking operations. Chapter 17 explains how sources and uses of funds are managed by banks to deal with risk. Chapter 18 explains how commercial bank performance can be measured and monitored to assess previous managerial policies. Chapter 19 describes commercial bank regulation, management, and performance from an international perspective.

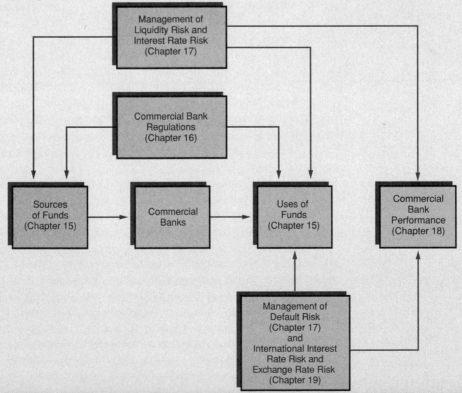

CHAPTER 15

COMMERCIAL BANK SOURCES AND USES OF FUNDS

Commercial banks represent the most important financial intermediary when measured by total assets. Like other financial intermediaries, they perform a critical function of facilitating the flow of funds from surplus units to deficit units.

The specific objectives of this chapter are to:

- describe the most common sources of funds for commercial banks,
- describe the most common uses of funds for commercial banks, and
- describe typical off-balance sheet activities for commercial banks.

BANK SOURCES OF FUNDS

The major sources of commercial bank funds are summarized below:

Deposit accounts

1. Transaction deposits
2. Savings deposits
3. Time deposits
4. Money market deposit accounts

Borrowed funds

1. Federal funds purchased (borrowed)
2. Borrowing from the Federal Reserve banks
3. Repurchase agreements
4. Eurodollar borrowings

Long-term sources of funds

1. Bonds issued by the bank
2. Bank capital

Each source of funds is briefly described in the following subsections.

Transaction Deposits

The **demand deposit account,** or checking account, is offered to customers who desire to write checks against their account. The conventional type of demand deposit account requires a small minimum balance and pays no interest. From the bank's perspective, demand deposit accounts are classified as transaction accounts that provide a source of funds that can be used until withdrawn by customers (as checks are written).

Another type of transaction deposit is the **negotiable order of withdrawal** (NOW) account, which provides checking services as well as interest. As of 1981, commercial banks and other depository institutions throughout the entire country were given the authority to offer them. Because NOW accounts at most financial institutions require a minimum balance beyond what some consumers are willing to maintain in a transaction account, the traditional demand deposit account is still popular.

Savings Deposits

The traditional savings account is the passbook savings account, which does not permit check writing. Until 1986, Regulation Q restricted the interest rate banks could offer on passbook savings with the intent of preventing excessive competition that could cause bank failures. Actually, the ceilings prevented commercial banks from competing for funds during periods of higher interest rates. In 1986, Regulation Q was eliminated. The passbook savings account continues to attract savers with a small amount of funds, as it often has no required minimum balance. Although it legally requires a 30-day written notice by customers to withdraw funds, most banks will allow withdrawals from these accounts on a moment's notice.

Another savings account is the **automatic transfer service** (ATS) account, created in November 1978. It allows customers to maintain an interest-bearing savings account that automatically transfers funds to their checking account when checks are written. Only the amount of funds needed is transferred to the checking account. Thus, the ATS provides interest and check-writing ability to customers. Some ATS accounts were eliminated when the NOW accounts were established.

Time Deposits

A common type of time deposit known as a retail **certificate of deposit** (or retail CD) requires a specified minimum amount of funds to be deposited for a specified period of time. Banks offer a wide variety of CDs to satisfy depositors' needs. Annualized interest rates offered on CDs vary among banks, and even among maturity types within a single bank. An organized secondary market for retail CDs does not exist. Depositors must leave their funds in the bank until the specified maturity or they will normally forgo a portion of their interest as a penalty.

The interest rates on retail CDs have historically been fixed. However, more exotic retail CDs have been offered in recent years. There are bull-market CDs that reward depositors if the market performs well and bear-market CDs that reward depositors if the market performs poorly. These new types of retail CDs typically have a minimum deposit of $1,000 to $5,000. Like the more conventional CDs, they qualify for deposit insurance (assuming that the depository institution of concern is insured). Only time will tell whether these innovative CDs become popular.

Another type of time deposit is the **negotiable CD (NCD),** offered by some large banks to corporations. NCDs are similar to retail CDs in that they require a specified maturity date and a minimum deposit. Their maturities are typically short term, and their minimum deposit requirement is $100,000. A secondary market for NCDs does exist.

The level of large time deposits is much more volatile than that of small time deposits, because investors with large sums of money frequently shift their funds to wherever they can earn higher rates. Small investors do not have as many options as large investors and are less likely to shift in and out of small time deposits.

Money Market Deposit Accounts

The **money market deposit account (MMDA)** was created by a provision of the Garn-St Germain Act of December 1982. It differs from conventional time deposits in that it does not specify a maturity. MMDAs are more liquid than retail CDs from the depositor's point of view. Because banks would prefer to know how long they will have use of a depositor's funds, they normally pay a higher interest rate on CDs. MMDAs differ from NOW accounts in that they have limited check-writing ability (they allow only a limited number of transactions per month), require a larger minimum balance, and offer a higher yield.

The remaining sources of funds to be described are of a nondepository nature. Such sources are necessary when a bank temporarily needs more funds than are being deposited. Some banks use nondepository funds as a permanent source of funds.

Federal Funds Purchased

The federal funds market allows depository institutions to accommodate the short-term liquidity needs of other financial institutions. Federal funds purchased (or borrowed) represent a liability to the borrowing bank and an asset to the lending bank that sells them. Loans in the federal funds market are typically for one to seven days. Such loans can be rolled over so that a series of one-day loans could take place. Yet, the intent of federal funds transactions is to correct short-term fund imbalances experienced by banks. A bank may act as a lender of federal funds on one day and as a borrower shortly thereafter, as its fund balance changes on a daily basis.

The interest rate charged in the federal funds market is called the **federal funds rate.** Like other market interest rates, it moves in reaction to changes in the demand or the supply or both. If many banks have excess funds and few banks are short of funds, the federal funds rate will be low. Conversely, a high demand by many banks to borrow federal funds relative to a small supply of excess funds available at other banks will result in a higher federal funds rate. Whatever rate exists will typically be the same for all banks borrowing in the federal funds market, although a financially troubled bank may have to pay a higher rate to obtain federal funds (to compensate for its higher risk). The federal funds rate is quoted in multiples of one-sixteenth, on an annualized basis (using a 360-day year). Exhibit 15.1 shows that the federal funds rate is generally between .25 percent and 1.00 percent above the Treasury bill rate. The difference normally increases when the perceived risk of banks increases.

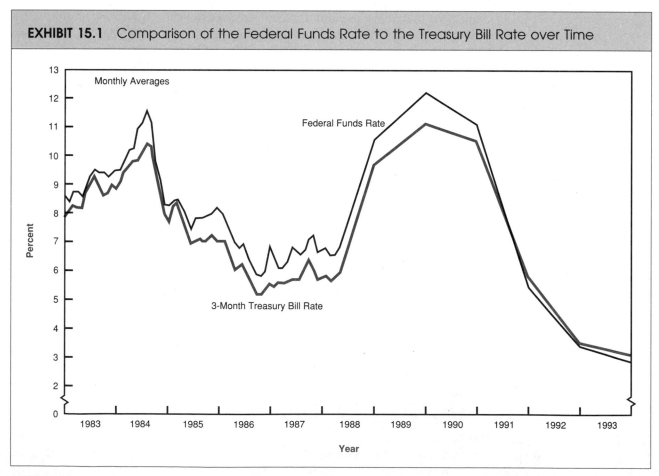

EXHIBIT 15.1 Comparison of the Federal Funds Rate to the Treasury Bill Rate over Time

SOURCE: *Monetary Trends,* Federal Reserve Bank of St. Louis (May 1988); and *Federal Reserve Bulletin.*

The federal funds market is typically most active on Wednesday, because it is the final day of each particular settlement period for which each bank must maintain a specified volume of reserves required by the Fed. Those banks that were short of required reserves on the average over the period must compensate with additional required reserves before the settlement period ends. Large banks frequently need temporary funds and therefore are common borrowers in the federal funds market.

Borrowing from the Federal Reserve Banks

Another temporary source of funds for banks is the Federal Reserve System, which serves as the U.S. central bank. Along with other bank regulators, the Federal Reserve district banks regulate certain activities of banks. Yet, they will also provide short-term loans to banks (as well as to some other depository institutions). This form of borrowing by banks is often referred to as borrowing at the discount window. The interest rate charged on these loans is known as the **discount rate.**

Loans from the discount window are short term, commonly from one day to a few weeks. Banks that wish to borrow at the discount window must first be approved by the Fed before a loan is granted. This is intended to make sure that the bank's need for funds is justified. Like the federal funds market, the discount window is mainly used to resolve a temporary shortage of funds. If a bank needed more permanent sources of funds, it would develop a strategy to increase its level of deposits.

When a bank needs temporary funds, it must decide whether borrowing through the discount window is more feasible than alternative nondepository sources of funds, such as the federal funds market. The federal funds rate is more volatile than the discount rate because it is market determined, as it adjusts to demand and supply conditions on a daily basis. Conversely, the discount rate is set by the Federal Reserve and adjusted only periodically to keep it in line with other market rates (such as the federal funds rate).

Banks commonly borrow in the federal funds market rather than through the discount window, even though the federal funds rate typically exceeds the discount rate. This is because the Fed offers the discount window as a source of funds for banks that experience unanticipated shortages of reserves. If a bank frequently borrows to offset reserve shortages, these shortages should have been anticipated. Such frequent borrowing implies that the commercial bank has a permanent rather than a temporary need for funds and should therefore satisfy this need with a more permanent source of funds. The Fed may disapprove of continuous borrowing by a bank unless there were extenuating circumstances, such as if the bank was experiencing financial problems and could not obtain temporary financing from other financial institutions.

Repurchase Agreements

A **repurchase agreement** (repo) represents the sale of securities by one party to another with an agreement to repurchase the securities at a specified date and price. Banks often use a repo as a source of funds when they expect to need funds for just a few days. They would simply sell some of their government securities (such as their Treasury bills) to a corporation with a temporary excess of funds and buy those securities back shortly thereafter. The government securities involved in the repo transaction serve as collateral for the corporation providing funds to the bank.

Repurchase agreement transactions occur through a telecommunications network connecting large banks, other corporations, government securities dealers, and federal funds brokers. The federal funds brokers match up those firms or dealers who need funds (wish to sell and later repurchase their securities) with those who have excess funds (are willing to purchase securities now and sell them back on a specified date). Transactions are typically in blocks of $1 million. Like the federal funds rate, the yield on repurchase agreements is quoted in multiples of one-sixteenth on an annualized basis (using a 360-day year). The yield on repurchase agreements is slightly less than the federal funds rate at any given point in time, because the funds loaned out are backed by collateral and are therefore less risky.

Eurodollar Borrowings

If a U.S. bank is in need of short-term funds, it may borrow dollars from those banks outside the United States that accept dollar-denominated deposits, or **Eurodollars.** Some of these so-called Eurobanks are foreign banks or foreign branches of U.S. banks that participate in the Eurodollar market by accepting large short-term deposits and making short-term loans in dollars. Because U.S. dollars are widely used as an international medium of exchange, the Eurodollar market is very active. Some U.S. banks commonly obtain short-term funds from Eurobanks.

Bonds Issued by the Bank

Like other corporations, banks own some fixed assets such as land, buildings, and equipment. These assets often have an expected life of 20 years or more and are usually financed with long-term sources of funds, such as through the issuance of bonds. Common purchasers of such bonds are households and various financial institutions, including life insurance companies and pension funds. Banks do not finance with bonds as much as most other corporations, because their fixed assets are less than those of corporations that use industrial equipment and machinery for production. Therefore, they have less of a need for long-term funds.

Bank Capital

Bank capital generally represents funds attained through the issuance of stock or through retaining earnings. Either form has no obligation to pay out funds in the future. This distinguishes bank capital from all the other bank sources of funds that represent a future obligation by the bank to pay out funds. Bank capital as defined here represents the equity or net worth of the bank. Capital can be classified into primary or secondary types. Primary capital results from issuing common or preferred stock or retaining earnings, while secondary capital results from issuing subordinated notes and debentures.

A bank's capital must be sufficient to absorb operating losses in the event that expenses or losses have exceeded revenues, regardless of the reason for the losses. Although long-term bonds are sometimes considered as secondary capital, they are a liability to the bank and therefore do not appropriately cushion against operating losses.

When banks issue new stock, they dilute the ownership of the bank because the proportion of the bank owned by existing shareholders decreases. In addition, the bank's reported earnings per share are reduced when additional shares of stock are issued, unless earnings increase by a greater proportion than the increase in outstanding shares. For these reasons, banks generally attempt to avoid issuing new stock unless absolutely necessary.

Bank regulators are concerned that banks may maintain a lower level of capital than they should and have therefore imposed capital requirements on them. Because capital can absorb losses, a higher level of capital is thought to enhance the bank's safety and may increase the public's confidence in the banking system. In 1981 regulators imposed a minimum primary capital requirement of 5.5 percent of total assets and a minimum total capital requirement of 6 percent of total assets. Because of regulatory pressure, banks have increased their capital ratios in recent years.

In 1988, regulators imposed risk-based new capital requirements that were completely phased in by 1992, in which the required level of capital for each bank was dependent on its risk. Assets with low risk were assigned relatively low weights, while assets with high risk were assigned high weights. The capital level was set as a percentage of the risk-weighted assets. Therefore, riskier banks were subject to higher capital requirements. The same risk-based capital guidelines were imposed in several industrialized countries. Additional details are provided in the following chapter.

Summary of Bank Sources of Funds

Because banks cannot completely dictate the amount of deposits to be received, they may experience a shortage of funds. For this reason, the nondepository sources of funds are useful. To support the acquisition of fixed assets, long-term funds are obtained by either issuing long-term bonds, issuing stock, or retaining a sufficient amount of earnings.

Exhibit 15.2 provides the distribution of fund sources. Transaction and savings deposits make up about half of all bank liabilities. The distribution of bank sources of funds is influenced by bank size. Smaller banks rely more heavily on savings deposits than larger banks. This results from small bank concentration on household savings and therefore on small deposits. Much of this differential is made up in large time deposits (such as NCDs) for very large banks. In addition, the larger banks rely more on short-term borrowings than do small banks. The impact of the differences in composition of fund sources on bank performance is discussed in Chapter 18.

USES OF FUNDS BY BANKS

Having identified the main sources of funds, bank uses of funds can be discussed. The more common uses of funds by banks include

- Cash
- Bank loans
- Investment in securities

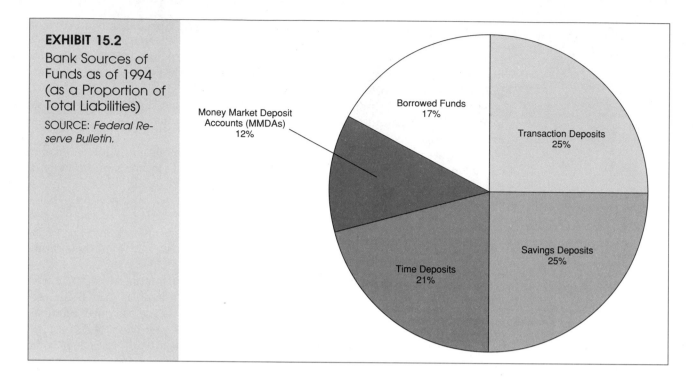

- Federal funds sold (loaned out)
- Repurchase agreements
- Eurodollar loans
- Fixed assets

Cash

Banks are required to hold some cash as reserves because they must abide by reserve requirements enforced by the Federal Reserve. Banks also hold cash to maintain some liquidity and accommodate any withdrawal requests by depositors. Because banks do not earn income from cash, they will hold only as much cash as necessary to maintain a sufficient degree of liquidity. They can tap various sources for temporary funds and therefore are not overly concerned with maintaining excess reserves.

Banks hold cash in their vaults and at their Federal Reserve district bank. Vault cash is useful for accommodating withdrawal requests by customers or for qualifying as required reserves, while cash placed at the Federal Reserve district banks represents the major portion of required reserves. The required reserves are mandated by the Fed because they provide a medium by which the Fed can control the money supply. The required reserves of each bank are dependent on the bank's composition of deposits.

Bank Loans

The main use of bank funds is for loans. The loan amount and maturity can be tailored to the borrower's needs.

TYPES OF BUSINESS LOANS.   A common type of business loan is the **working capital loan** (sometimes called a self-liquidating loan), designed to support ongoing business operations. There is a lag between the point at which a firm needs cash to purchase raw materials used in production and the point at which it receives cash inflows from the sales of finished products. A working capital loan can support the business until sufficient cash inflows are generated. These loans are typically short-term, yet they may be needed by businesses on a frequent basis.

Banks also offer **term loans,** primarily to finance the purchase of fixed assets such as machinery. A term loan involves a specified amount of funds to be loaned out, for a specified period of time, and for a specified purpose. The assets purchased with the borrowed funds may serve as partial or full collateral on the loan. Maturities on term loans commonly range from two to five years and are sometimes as long as ten years.

Because of the long-term nature of a term loan, sufficient documentation is needed to specify any conditions that the borrower must abide by. These conditions, often referred to as **protective covenants,** may specify a maximum level of dividends that the borrower can pay to shareholders per year, require bank approval on some of the borrowing firm's major decisions (such as mergers), and limit the additional debt that the firm can accumulate. Term loans can be amortized so that fixed periodic payments are made by the borrower over the life of the loan. Alternatively, the bank can periodically request interest payments, with the loan principal to be paid off in one lump sum (called a **balloon payment)** at a specified date in the future. This is known as a **bullet loan.** There are also several combinations of these payment methods possible. For example, a portion of the loan may be amortized over the life of the loan, while the remaining portion could be covered with a balloon payment.

As an alternative to providing a term loan, the bank may consider purchasing the assets and leasing them to the firm in need. This method, known as a **direct lease loan,** may be especially appropriate when the firm wishes to avoid further additions of debt on its balance sheet. Because the bank would serve as owner of the assets, it could depreciate the assets over time for tax purposes.

A more flexible financing arrangement provided by banks is the **informal line of credit,** which allows the business to borrow up to a specified amount within a specified period of time. This is useful for firms that may experience a sudden need for funds but do not know precisely when. The interest rate charged on any borrowed funds is typically adjustable in accordance with prevailing market rates. Banks are not legally obligated to provide funds to the business, yet they usually honor the arrangement to avoid harming their reputation.

An alternative financing arrangement to the informal line of credit is the **revolving credit loan,** which obligates the bank to offer up to some specified maximum amount of funds over a specified period of time (typically less than five years). Because the bank is committed to provide funds when requested, it normally charges businesses a commitment fee (of about one-half of one percent) on any unused funds.

The interest rate charged by banks on loans to their most creditworthy customers is known as the **prime rate.** The prime rate is periodically revised by banks in response to changes in market interest rates, which reflect changes in the bank's cost of funds. Thus, the prime rate moves in tandem with the Treasury bill rate. Note that a higher prime rate does not necessarily lead to higher bank profitability. During recessionary periods, the spread between the prime rate and the bank's cost of funds tends to widen, as banks require a greater premium to compensate for the risk of loan default.

LOAN PARTICIPATIONS. Some large corporations wish to borrow an amount of funds that exceeds what any individual bank is willing to provide. Several banks may be willing to pool any available funds they have to accommodate a corporation in what is referred to as a **loan participation.** Although there are various forms of loan participations, the most common form calls for one of the banks to serve as a lead bank by arranging for the documentation, disbursement, and payment structure of the loan. The main role of the other banks is to supply funds to the lead bank which are channeled to the borrower. The borrower may not even realize that much of the funds have been provided by other banks. As interest payments are received, the lead bank passes the payments on to the other participants in proportion to the original loan amounts provided by them. The lead bank receives not only its share of interest payments but also fees for servicing the loan.

The lead bank is expected to ensure that the borrower repays the loan. However, the lead bank is normally not required to guarantee the interest payments. Thus, all participating banks are exposed to default risk.

LOANS SUPPORTING LEVERAGED BUYOUTS. One of the latest fads in commercial banking is financing leveraged buyouts (LBOs). The loan amount provided by a single bank to support an LBO is usually between $15 million and $40 million. The exposure to LBO loans exceeds $1 billion for some large commercial banks. An attractive feature of LBO financing is a relatively high loan rate that can be charged. In addition, some fee income can be generated from the administrative services performed by commercial banks when financing LBOs.

Although LBO financings have generally performed well so far, there is some concern that they will increase the risk of individual banks. Some critics may even suggest the possibility of an LBO debt crisis at some point in the future in which massive rescheduling of loans will be required.

In a sense, financing part of an LBO is no different than financing other privately held businesses. These businesses are highly leveraged and experience cash flow pressure during periods where sales are lower than normal. Their high degree of financial leverage causes cash outflows to be somewhat insensitive to business cycles.

Firms request LBO financing because they perceive the market value of publicly held shares to be too low. The accessibility of these firms to equity funds is favorable because it can serve as a cushion under poor economic conditions. Although these firms would prefer not to go public again during such conditions, they are at least capable of doing so. Banks financing these firms could, as a condition of the loan, require that the firms reissue stock if they experience cash flow problems.

Many firms involved in LBOs represent diversified conglomerates that will be split into various divisions and sold. This may enable banks to spread their lending base by lending to divisions that have been sold. The separation of businesses may result if the sum of the parts appears to be worth more than the whole. Yet, the failure of a single division could be absorbed by a conglomerate company. If the division is independent, its failure is absorbed by its creditors.

A commercial bank's risk may rise as it increases its financing of LBOs. Banks that reduce their more conservative assets to finance LBOs will incur a higher degree of risk. Many LBOs were financed with junk bonds, which suggests a high degree of risk. Thus, banks could be incurring the same risk as if they had purchased junk bonds. However the bank-borrower relationship may allow for more personalized guidance of firms experiencing financial problems. In addition, banks may have first claim to the firm's assets if the firm fails. Thus, these bank loans are considered to be less risky.

Some banks originate the loans designed for LBOs and then sell them to other financial institutions, such as insurance companies, pension funds, and foreign banks. In this way, they can generate fee income by servicing the loans while avoiding the credit risk associated with the loans.

Bank regulators now monitor the amount of bank financing provided to corporate borrowers that will have a relatively high degree of financial leverage. These loans, known as **highly leveraged transactions** (HLTs), are defined by the Federal Reserve as credit that results in a debt-to-asset ratio of at least 75 percent. In other words, the level of debt is at least three times the level of equity. About 60 percent of HLT funds are used to finance LBOs, while some of the funds are used to repurchase only a portion of the outstanding stock. HLTs are usually originated by a large commercial bank, which provides 10 percent to 20 percent of the financing itself. Other financial institutions participate by providing the remaining 80 percent to 90 percent of the funds needed.

COLLATERAL REQUIREMENTS ON BUSINESS LOANS. Commercial banks are increasingly accepting intangible assets (such as patents, brand names, and licenses to franchises and distributorships) as collateral for commercial loans. This change is especially important to service-oriented companies that do not have tangible assets.

LENDER LIABILITY ON BUSINESS LOANS. In recent years, businesses that previously obtained loans from banks are filing lawsuits, claiming that the banks terminated further financing without sufficient notice. These so-called lender liability suits have been prevalent in the farming industry. Some farmers claimed that they were encouraged by banks to borrow, but were cut off from additional financing necessary to make their projects successful and thus lost the land and equipment representing collateral. Lender liability lawsuits have also been filed by companies in other industries, including grocery, clothing, and oil.

TYPES OF CONSUMER LOANS. Commercial banks provide **installment loans** to individuals to finance purchases of cars and household products. These loans require the borrowers to make periodic payments over time.

Banks also provide credit cards to consumers who qualify, enabling purchases of various goods without the customer reapplying for credit on each purchase. A maximum limit is assigned to credit card holders, depending on their income and employment record, and a fixed annual fee is usually charged. This service often involves an agreement with VISA or MasterCard. If consumers pay off the balance each month, they are not normally charged interest. Bank rates on credit card balances are sometimes about double the rate charged on business loans. State regulators can impose **usury laws** that restrict the maximum rate of interest charged by banks, and these usury laws may be applied to credit card loans as well. A federal law requires that banks abide by the usury laws of the state where they are located rather than the state of the consumers. Many states have recently lifted their ceilings on credit card loans.

The process of credit assessment on consumer loan applicants is much easier than on corporate loan applicants. An individual's cash flow is typically simpler and more predictable than corporate cash flow. In addition, the average loan amount to individuals is relatively small, warranting a less detailed credit analysis.

REAL ESTATE LOANS.   Another type of loan provided by banks is the real estate loan. For residential real estate loans, the maturity on a mortgage is typically 15 to 30 years, although shorter-term mortgages with a balloon payment are also common. The loan is backed by the residence purchased. Banks also provide some commercial real estate loans to finance commercial development. Real estate loans by banks generally increased throughout the 1980s. However, in the early 1990s defaults on numerous real estate loans caused banks to reduce these types of loans.

Investment in Securities

Banks purchase Treasury securities as well as securities issued by the agencies of the federal government. Government agency securities can be sold in the secondary market, but the market is not as active as it is for Treasury securities. Furthermore, government agency securities are not a direct obligation of the federal government. Therefore, default risk exists, although it is normally thought to be very low. Banks that are willing to accept the slight possibility of default risk and less liquidity from investing in government agency securities can earn a higher return than on Treasury securities with a similar maturity.

Federal agency securities are commonly issued by federal agencies, such as the Federal Home Loan Mortgage Corporation (called Freddie Mac) and the Federal National Mortgage Association (called Fannie Mae). Funds received by the agencies issuing these securities are used to purchase mortgages from various financial institutions. Such securities can range from one month to 25 years. Unlike interest income of Treasury securities, interest income of federal agency securities is subject to state and local income taxes.

Banks also purchase corporate and municipal securities. Although corporate bonds are subject to default risk, they offer a higher return than Treasury or government agency securities. Municipal bonds exhibit some degree of risk but can also provide an attractive return to banks, especially when considering their after-tax return. The interest income earned from municipal securities is exempt from federal taxation. Banks purchase only **investment-grade securities,** which are rated as "medium quality" or higher by rating agencies.

Exhibit 15.3 shows how the bank allocation of loans versus government securities changes in response to economic conditions. Banks tend to reduce their loans during recessionary periods, as loan demand declines and the perceived risk of potential borrowers rises. As banks reduce their loans, they allocate more funds to government securities. Banks tend to allocate more funds for loans and less funds for government securities during the economic expansions that follow recessions.

Federal Funds Sold

Banks often lend funds in the federal funds market. The funds sold, or lent out, will be returned at the time specified in the loan agreement, with interest. Small

EXHIBIT 15.3 Bank Allocation of Loans Versus Government Securities Over Time

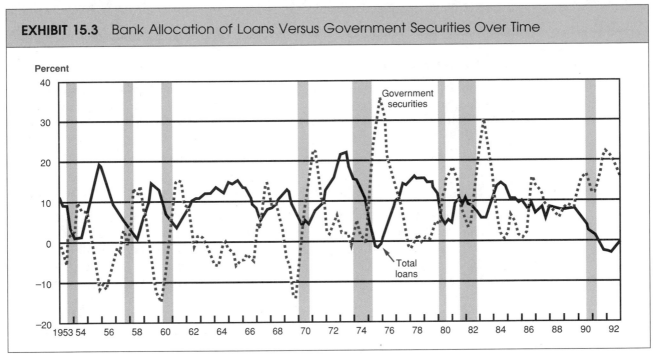

SOURCE: Board of Governors of the Federal Reserve System, Flow of Funds Accounts, and *FRBNY Quarterly Review*/Summer 1993, p. 51.

Note: Shaded areas indicate periods designated recessions by the National Bureau of Economic Research.

banks are common providers of funds in the federal funds market. If the transaction was executed by a broker, the borrower's cost on a federal funds loan is slightly higher than the lender's return, because the federal funds broker matching up the two parties would charge a transaction fee.

Repurchase Agreements

Recall that from the borrower's perspective, the repurchase agreement (repo) transaction involves repurchasing the securities it had previously sold. From a lender's perspective, the repo represents a sale of securities that it had previously purchased. Banks can act as the lender (on a repo) by purchasing a corporation's holdings of Treasury securities and selling them back at a later date. This provides short-term funds to the corporation, and the bank's loan is backed by these securities.

Eurodollar Loans

Branches of U.S. banks located outside the United States and some foreign-owned banks provide dollar-denominated loans to corporations and governments. These so-called **Eurodollar loans** are common because the dollar is frequently used for international transactions. Eurodollar loans are of a short-term nature and denominated in large amounts, such as $1 million or more. Some

U.S. banks may even establish Eurodollar deposits at a foreign bank as a temporary use of funds.

Fixed Assets

Banks must maintain some amount of fixed assets, such as office buildings and land, so that they can conduct their business operations. However, this is not a concern to those bank managers who decide how day-to-day incoming funds shall be used. They will direct these funds into the other types of assets already identified.

Summary of Bank Uses of Funds

The distribution of bank uses of funds is illustrated in Exhibit 15.4. All types of loans make up about 64 percent of bank assets, while all securities make up about 22 percent of bank assets. The distribution of assets per bank varies with the type of bank. For example, smaller banks tend to have a relatively large amount of individual loans and government securities, while larger banks have a higher level of business loans (including loans to foreign firms).

The distribution of bank uses of funds indicates how commercial banks operate. However, in recent years banks have begun providing numerous services that are not indicated on their balance sheet. These services differ distinctly from their traditional operations that focus mostly on the investment of deposited funds. Some of the more popular services offered by banks in recent years include discount brokerage, sales of mutual funds, insurance, and real estate activities. Many large banks are involved in underwriting government and

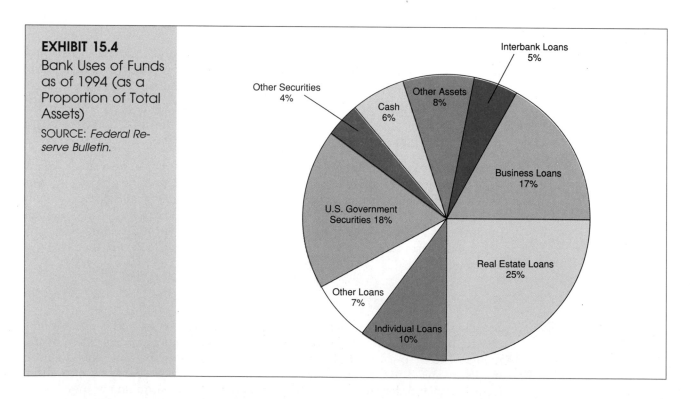

EXHIBIT 15.4

Bank Uses of Funds as of 1994 (as a Proportion of Total Assets)

SOURCE: *Federal Reserve Bulletin.*

Interbank Loans 5%

Other Securities 4%

Other Assets 8%

Cash 6%

Business Loans 17%

U.S. Government Securities 18%

Real Estate Loans 25%

Other Loans 7%

Individual Loans 10%

corporate securities. Some banks also serve as advisers for mergers and acquisitions.

The desire by commercial banks to offer nonbanking services escalated in the early 1990s, when very low interest rates caused depositors to withdraw deposits and invest the proceeds in stocks and bonds. Many banks attempted to retain the business of those depositors by having their subsidiaries offer discount brokerage services or mutual fund services. Thus, even though the funds were withdrawn from the banking operations, they were commonly reinvested in the bank's subsidiaries.

OFF-BALANCE SHEET ACTIVITIES

Banks commonly engage in off-balance sheet activities, which generate fee income without requiring an investment of funds. However, these activities do create a contingent obligation for banks. Some of the more popular off-balance sheet activities are

- Loan commitments
- Standby letters of credit
- Forward contracts
- Swap contracts

Loan Commitments

A **loan commitment** is an obligation by a bank to provide a specified loan amount to a particular firm upon the firm's request. The interest rate and purpose of the loan may also be specified. The bank charges a fee for offering the commitment.

One type of loan commitment is a **note issuance facility** (NIF), in which the bank agrees to purchase the commercial paper of a firm if the firm cannot place its paper in the market at an acceptable interest rate. Although banks earn fees for their commitments, they could experience illiquidity if numerous firms request their loans at the same time.

Standby Letters of Credit

A **standby letter of credit** (SLC) backs a customer's obligation to a third party. If the customer does not meet its obligation, the bank will. The third party may require that the customer obtain an SLC to complete a business transaction. For example, consider a municipality that wants to issue bonds. To ensure that the bonds are easily placed, a bank could provide an SLC that guarantees payment of interest and principal. In essence, the bank uses its credit rating to enhance the perceived safety of the bonds. In return for the bank's guarantee, a fee is charged to the municipality. The bank should be willing to provide SLCs only if the fee received compensates for the possibility that the municipality defaults on its obligation.

Forward Contracts

A forward contract is an agreement between a customer and a bank to exchange one currency for another on a particular future date at a specified exchange rate.

Banks engage in forward contracts with customers because customers desire to hedge their exchange rate risk. For example, a U.S. bank may agree to purchase 5 million German marks in one year from a firm for $0.60 per mark. The bank may simultaneously find another firm that wishes to exchange 5 million marks for dollars in one year. The bank can serve as an intermediary and accommodate both requests, earning a transaction fee for its services. However, it is exposed to the possibility that one of the parties defaults on its obligation.

Swap Contracts

Banks also serve as intermediaries for interest rate swaps, whereby two parties agree to periodically exchange interest payments on a specified notional amount of principal. Once again, the bank receives a transaction fee for its services. If it guarantees payments to both parties, it is exposed to the possibility that one of the parties defaults on its obligation. In such a case, it must assume the role of that party to fulfill the obligation to the other party.

Some banks facilitate currency swaps (for a fee) by finding parties with opposite future currency needs and executing a swap agreement. Currency swaps are somewhat similar to forward contracts, except that they are usually for more distant future dates.

SUMMARY

- The most common sources of commercial bank funds are deposit accounts, borrowed funds, and long-term sources of funds. The common types of deposit accounts are transaction deposits, savings deposits, time deposits, and money market deposit accounts. These accounts vary in terms of liquidity (for the depositor) and the interest rates offered.

  Commercial banks can solve temporary deficiencies in funds by borrowing from other banks (federal funds market), from the Federal Reserve, or from other sources by issuing short-term securities such as repurchase agreements. When banks need long-term funds to support expansion, they may use retained earnings, issue new stock, or issue new bonds.

- The most common uses of funds by commercial banks are bank loans and investment in securities. Banks can use excess funds by providing loans to other banks, or by purchasing short-term securities.

- Banks engage in off-balance sheet activities such as loan commitments, standby letters of credit, forward contracts, and swap contracts. These types of activities generate fees for commercial banks. However, they also reflect commitments by the banks, which can expose them to more risk.

QUESTIONS

1. Create a balance sheet for a typical bank, showing its main liabilities (sources of funds) and assets (uses of funds).

2. What are four major sources of funds for banks?

3. Name two examples of transaction deposits.

4. Briefly explain the automatic transfer service (ATS) account.

5. Compare and contrast the retail CD and the negotiable CD.

6. How does the money market deposit account vary from other bank sources of funds?

7. Define federal funds, federal funds market, and federal funds rate.

8. Who sets the federal funds rate?

9. Why is the federal funds market more active on Wednesday?

10. Explain the use of the federal funds market in facilitating bank operations.

11. Describe the process of borrowing at the discount window. What rate is charged, and who sets it?

12. Why do banks commonly borrow in the federal funds market rather than through the discount window?

13. How does the yield on a repurchase agreement differ from a loan in the federal funds market? Why?

14. What alternatives does a bank have if it needs temporary funds?

15. Why would banks most often issue bonds?

16. What is a bullet loan?

17. Why do banks invest in securities, when loans typically generate a higher return?

18. Is there a formula used to decide a bank's appropriate percentage of each source and use of funds? Explain.

19. Explain the dilemma faced by banks when determining the optimal amount of capital to hold.

20. Use recent issues of a business periodical to determine the federal funds rate and discount rate on a weekly basis over the past month. Compare the volatility of these rates and explain the difference in degree of volatility.

21. Would you expect a bank to pay a lower rate on funds borrowed from repurchase agreements or the federal funds market? Why?

22. Obtain recently quoted interest rates from a business periodical on the bank's main sources and uses of funds. Use these rates along with the average composition of liabilities and assets disclosed in this chapter to estimate the differential between the interest revenue percentage and the interest expense percentage.

23. The level of capital as a percentage of assets for commercial banks was disclosed in this chapter. How do you think this would compare to that of manufacturing corporations? How would you explain this difference?

Losing Ground: Banks' Declining Role in Economy Worries Fed, May Hurt Firms

Kenneth H. Bacon, Washington

The Federal Reserve, which began curing the banking industry's immediate ills two years ago with low interest rates, now is worrying about the patient's long-term health.

In the past 20 years, commercial banks' share of U.S. financial assets has declined to 24.5% from nearly 40%. "The banking industry is becoming irrelevant economically, and it's almost irrelevant politically," says William Isaac, a former chairman of the Federal Deposit Insurance Corp. who now heads Secura Group, a Washington consulting firm. . . .

A Shift in the Risk

With interest rates at the lowest levels in decades, banks' profits are soaring because their cost of funds has declined far more than their returns on loans and investments and because the low rates have bailed out some troubled borrowers. But those rates are also aggravating a long term problem: Investors are seeking higher yields by moving money out of federally insured deposits at banks and thrifts and into uninsured mutual funds. Some experts worry that this trade of security for higher yields could expose depositors to potentially severe losses.

"I think that banks play a fundamentally important role in society that is less well filled by others," says Comptroller of the Currency Eugene Ludwig. "I see a decline in the banking system as a shifting of risk—rather than an elimination of risk—to the public from the government."

At current trends, total investments in mutual funds soon will eclipse the $2 trillion in savings and time deposits at banks and thrift institutions. . . .

Two forces—innovation and regulation—explain banking's decline. Many of the innovations started in the late 1970s, when an inflation-driven surge in interest rates and federal limits on rates banks could pay on deposits drove borrowers and depositors alike away from banks. Money-market mutual funds, banks' sales of home mortgages to the secondary market to collateralize securities and blue-chip corporations' tendency to meet short-term cash needs by selling commercial paper rather than bank loans all took off.

As banks lost their most credit-worthy customers, they began to chase higher returns by lending to riskier borrowers—real-estate developers, Third World nations and corporations scrambling to finance multibillion-dollar buyouts. Charge-offs of bad loans rose steadily throughout the 1980s, and so did bank failures. Meanwhile, mismanaged deregulation nearly destroyed the S&L industry.

The Restrictive 1991 Law

After a decade of deregulation, Congress began to impose new safety rules on depository institutions. Fearing that skyrocketing bank failures were about to drain the Bank Insurance Fund, Congress passed in 1991 a law sharply increasing the scope—and cost—of bank regulation.

When making loans, bankers face capital, documentation and collateralization rules that don't apply to nonbank lenders. In addition, the Fed requires banks to hold noninterest-earning reserves of 10% against checking accounts and other transaction balances. The FDIC imposes a deposit-insurance premium averaging 24.8 cents (up threefold over four years) on each $100 of domestic deposits. One reason money-market mutual funds can pay depositors higher returns than banks can is that they don't face such expenses.

The diversion of money from banks to mutual funds is complicating monetary policy. "The relationship between money and the economy may be undergoing a significant transformation," Mr. Greenspan says. "If this is true, the liabilities of depository institutions will not be as good a gauge of financial conditions as they once were." So, the Fed is trying to devise new, more-useful, money-supply gauges. . . .

Lender of Last Resort

Fed officials deny that the central bank is losing its leverage over the economy. As long as the Fed retains unfettered power to act as lender of last resort, it can provide the liquidity necessary to quell a financial crisis, just as it responded to the 1987 stock-market crash. In 1991, Wall Street firms fought for and won legislation strengthening the Fed's ability to lend directly to troubled brokerage firms.

Continued

CASE APPLICATION: BANK OPERATIONS

Continued

But officials agree that the flow of assets and deposits from the banking system poses a wider range of risks. The Federal Reserve Board is devoting more energy to policing the $7 trillion market in derivatives—the new financial products that link banks, investment firms and corporations in efforts to hedge against changes in interest rates, stock prices, commodity prices and currencies.

One of the fundamental changes that increased saving and investment outside of insured deposits has wrought is the spreading of risk. "Millions of people have branched out from passively holding deposits in banks and thrifts and indirectly owning securities through such intermediaries as private and public pension funds to becoming direct participants, primarily through mutual funds," says Henry Kaufman, a Wall Street economist known for gloomy predictions. He warns that "the household sector may not appreciate all the risks it's taking on, with the result that it may act quite unpredictably if there is a sudden upheaval in the financial markets" that threatens to inflict huge losses in its savings. If this were to happen, he adds, politicians might face pressure to force the Fed to support stock and bond prices.

In fact, however, huge amounts of money didn't flee mutual funds for bank deposits after the Dow Jones Industrial Average plunged 500 points in October 1987. Fidelity Investments and other fund groups found that customers moved money from stock funds to money-market funds within the same family. But it's worth noting that in 1987, mutual-fund holdings totaled just $752 billion, compared with $1.8 trillion today.

A Basic Fed Goal

The Fed's goal is to manage and limit risk, not to eliminate it. Mr. Greenspan believes that Congress went too far with its 1991 law tightening regulation. "If minimizing risks to taxpayers is inter-

preted as minimizing bank failures, then we are very likely to deter banks to an excessive degree from accepting the kinds of risk that create the value of their franchises," he says. "The optimal degree of bank failure is not zero, and, in all likelihood, not even close to zero."

The banking industry is pushing regulatory-relief bills in Congress, arguing that lower costs enable them to make more loans. However, the chairmen of both the House and Senate banking committees oppose weakening the safety and soundness measures that they helped craft in 1991. In addition, the Clinton administration isn't ready to support broad banking legislation this year.

Instead, Mr. Ludwig has launched an effort to week out unnecessary regulations. "Government has layered on banking a mountain of regulations that are often duplicative, superfluous or otherwise wasteful," he says. He notes, for example, that the Office of the Comptroller of the Currency uses seven different definitions of bank capital. "We can maintain safety and soundness while lowering regulatory cost," he says.

Basically, he is studying ways to move away from one-size-fits-all regulation. Strongly capitalized banks and small banks—those that pose the least risk to the financial system—would get more freedom to make loans with reduced paperwork and administrative costs and to offer insurance and other new products. Some of the changes would require legislation.

Besides less regulation, banks want to be unshackled from rules that prevent them from expanding their activities as investment bankers, insurance agents, stockbrokers and mutual-fund salesmen. Expansion into these businesses would enable them to earn more income from commissions and fees, reduce their reliance on volatile interest-rate spreads and help diversify their risks.

But two powerful House Democrats—Banking Committee Chairman

Henry Gonzalez of Texas and Energy and Commerce Chairman John Dingell of Michigan—may stand in the way. They worry that the heavy movement of banks into mutual-fund sales may be confusing consumers about which bank products are insured and which aren't. And nationwide branch banking has been a nonstarter for years.

Bankers are frustrated by their lack of success in winning relief from Congress. The nation "has got a vested interest in keeping the banking industry alive and competitive," says Robert Gillespie, the chairman of Society Corp., a Cleveland bank holding company. "It really isn't in anybody's interest to kill the goose that used to lay the golden egg."

SOURCE: *The Wall Street Journal,* July 9, 1993, p. A1. Reprinted by permission of *The Wall Street Journal,* © Dow Jones & Company, Inc. All rights reserved worldwide.

QUESTIONS

1. Lower interest rates increased bank profitability, but also reduced the amount of funds deposited at banks. Are lower interest rates beneficial to banks?

2. Explain how the withdrawal of bank deposits by households has shifted some risk from banks to households.

3. Explain how banks are at a regulatory disadvantage when competing with some other financial institutions for funds.

4. There is some concern that if business loan demand increased substantially, banks would not be able to accommodate this demand because their funds are limited. Do you think this would cause a major credit crunch in which creditworthy businesses would be unable to obtain loanable funds? Explain.

PROJECT

1. **Examining Changes in a Bank's Financial Structure**
    Your professor will assign you (or your group) a bank or allow you to choose your own bank. Use the most recent annual report of this bank to answer the following questions. (A more thorough analysis of the project can be conducted if the past 10 years are examined, which would require some older annual reports or financial statement data provided by investors' services such as *Moody's Banking and Finance Manual*.)
    a. How has the bank's liability structure changed in recent years? Which major bank liabilities have increased as a percentage of total liabilities? Which major assets have increased as a percentage of total assets? How has the capital ratio changed over recent years?
    b. Has this bank been a net borrower or lender in the federal funds market in recent years?
    c. Based on changes in the bank's financial structure in recent years, do you think the bank's earnings per share will increase or decrease? Do you think the bank's performance will now be more or less sensitive to economic conditions?

    The answers to this project can be used as a foundation for completing the projects in some of the following chapters if you are assigned the same bank.

REFERENCES

Allen, Linda, and Anthony Sauders. "Bank Window Dressing: Theory and Evidence." *Journal of Banking and Finance* (June 1992): 585–623.

Best, Ronald, and Hang Zhang. "Alternative Information Sources and the Information Content of Bank Loans." *Journal of Finance,* (September 1993) 1507–1522.

Brewer, Elijah. "The Risk of Banks Expanding Their Permissible Nonbanking Activities." *Financial Review* (November 1990): 517–538.

Cosimano, Thomas. "Reserve Accounting and Variability in the Federal Funds Market." *Journal of Money, Credit, and Banking* (May 1987): 199–209.

Garcia, Gillian. "The Garn-St Germain Depository Institutions Act of 1982." *Economic Perspectives*, Federal Reserve Bank of Chicago (March–April 1983): 1–31.

Johnson, Sylvester, and Amelia A. Murphy. "Going Off the Balance Sheet." *Economic Review*, Federal Reserve Bank of Atlanta (September/October 1987): 23–35.

ELECTRONIC FUNDS TRANSFER

Electronic funds transfer has facilitated the flow of funds among businesses, households, governments, and financial institutions. The more common forms of electronic funds transfer include automated teller machine transfers, direct deposits or withdrawals of funds, and transfers initiated by telephone.

BANKING TRANSACTIONS

Electronic funds transfer (EFT) has reduced the cost of accepting deposits. Shared automated teller machine networks have been developed to attract deposits without having to construct facilities or hire and train employees. Furthermore, economies of scale are achieved, as the main cost of the networks is fixed.

Another area of banking affected by electronic funds transfer is the automated clearinghouse, a payment mechanism by which institutions transfer funds electronically, substituting for payments by check. The automated clearinghouse not only reduces the costs related to the transportation of paper but also reduces the float involved with check processing, thereby reducing delays in crediting and debiting accounts.

GOVERNMENT TRANSACTIONS

Because of EFT, Social Security payments made by the government can be directly deposited to individuals' accounts. This eliminates much paperwork related to the processing and printing of each check. Government accounting procedures are also more efficient because of direct depositing.

HOUSEHOLD TRANSACTIONS

EFT offers convenience, security, and privacy. Consumers can avoid bank lines and the inconvenience of lost checks. They also have access to funds on days when the bank is closed. Furthermore, they can use the automated clearinghouse to receive direct deposit of Social Security checks and payroll checks. EFT can be used by consumers to make payments as well. For example, funds can be deducted directly from their bank accounts to make payments on automobile loans, home mortgages, or even insurance premiums.

BUSINESS TRANSACTIONS

EFT has been very useful to businesses by providing point-of-sale transactions in which instantaneous transfers of funds are made from the purchaser's account to the seller's account. This reduces the number of transactions by check, credit card, and cash, allowing each retail outlet to reduce its transaction costs. Moreover, the risks involved in accepting checks is eliminated. Because cash need not be handled inside the business, point-of-sale transactions protect against dishonest employees. In addition, the bookkeeping of a retail business with point-of-sale systems is simplified. Easier accountability of sales occurs when an exact record of the sale takes place on a point-of-sale terminal. Because of the lower costs associated with the handling of sales and less risk of embezzlement, retail firms may pass part of their cost savings on to consumers. Therefore, EFT can benefit various sectors at the same time.

Businesses that receive large volumes of cash receipts (such as utilities) use EFT for collection to reduce the processing tasks. Another use of EFT in other types of businesses is the arrangement of direct deposits of salaries and pension contributions into bank accounts. Once again, time and money are saved on the processing. Businesses can also use EFT to consolidate their cash at various bank accounts into a single account at the end of the day.

INTERNATIONAL TRANSACTIONS

International trade often requires payments to corresponding banks, and these payments are made more quickly and efficiently by using the EFT system. It is likely that this system will also be more frequently applied to handle tourism and business travel transactions.

CLEARING AND SETTLEMENT OF PAYMENTS

During the course of a normal day, more than $1 trillion in large-dollar (wholesale) wire transfer payments is exchanged among depository institutions. The electronic funds system allows for a more efficient transfer of these funds. A typical transfer can be described as follows. A firm instructs its depository institution to make payment to another firm by wiring funds from its account to the other firm's account. The depository institution that wired the funds sends the relevant information (name of firms providing and receiving payment and name of depository institution where funds were wired) to the network clearinghouse. This clearinghouse debits the account of the institution that wired the funds and credits the account at the institution receiving the funds.

The settlement of the payment occurs when the clearinghouse notifies the receiving institution that the account is credited. The Federal Reserve System provides settlement services through what is referred to as Fedwire, in which fund transfers occur through reserve accounts of depository institutions at the 12 regional Federal Reserve banks. Many financial institutions have computers linked to the Fedwire so that they can conduct transactions for their corporate customers.

An alternative settlement facility, known as the Clearinghouse Interbank Payments System (CHIPS), is composed of a group of depository institutions that provide settlement services. Payment transfers served by CHIPS are confirmed at the end of the day, when the clearinghouse determines which account balances represent net credit and net debit positions for the day.

CHAPTER 16

BANK REGULATION

Bank regulations are designed to prevent commercial banks from becoming too risky and thus maintain public confidence in the financial system.

The specific objectives of this chapter are to:

- describe the key regulations imposed on commercial banks,
- explain how regulators monitor banks, and
- describe the main provisions of the Federal Deposit Insurance Corporation Improvement Act (FDICIA).

REGULATORY STRUCTURE

The regulatory structure of the banking system in the United States is dramatically different from that of other countries. It is often referred to as the **dual banking system** because it comprises two regulatory systems—federal and state. There are more than 13,000 separately owned commercial banks in the United States, supervised by 3 federal agencies and 50 state agencies. The regulatory structure in other countries is much simpler.

The opening of a commercial bank in the United States requires a charter from either the state or the federal government. A bank that obtains a state charter is referred to as a state bank, while a bank that obtains a federal charter is known as a national bank. The federal charter is issued by the Comptroller of the Currency. An application for a bank charter must be submitted to the proper supervisory agency, should provide evidence of the need for a new bank, and disclose how the bank will be operated. Regulators determine if the bank satisfies general guidelines to qualify for the charter.

State banks may decide whether they would like to be a member of the Federal Reserve System (the Fed). The Fed provides a variety of services for commercial banks and controls the amount of funds within the banking system.

About 35 percent of all banks are members of the Federal Reserve. These banks are generally larger than the norm; their combined deposits make up about 70 percent of all bank deposits.

Before 1980 nonmember banks were subject to reserve requirements enforced by their respective states. Because the Fed's requirements were generally more restrictive than state requirements, Fed members were forced to hold a much greater percentage of their funds as noninterest-bearing reserves. Consequently, many member banks decided to withdraw their membership. Today, both member and nonmember banks can borrow from the Fed, but both are subject to the Fed's reserve requirements. The advantages and disadvantages of being a Fed member bank are not as significant as they once were.

National banks are regulated by the Comptroller of the Currency, while state banks are regulated by their respective state agency. Banks that are members of the Federal Reserve are regulated by the Fed. Banks that are insured by the Federal Deposit Insurance Corporation (FDIC) are also regulated by the FDIC. Because all national banks must be members of the Federal Reserve and all Fed member banks must hold FDIC insurance, national banks are regulated by the Comptroller of the Currency, the Fed, and the FDIC. State banks are regulated by their respective state agency, the Fed (if they are a Fed member), and the FDIC (if they carry insurance from the FDIC).

Because of the regulatory overlap, it has often been argued that a single regulatory agency should be assigned the role of regulating all commercial banks and savings institutions. The momentum for consolidation increased in 1989, as the Financial Institutions Reform, Recovery, and Enforcement Act (FIRREA) was passed. One of the provisions of FIRREA is that commercial banks be allowed to acquire either healthy or failing S&Ls. Prior to the Act, banks could not acquire S&Ls. With the merging of commercial banks and S&Ls resulting from the Act, there is even more rationale for a single regulatory agency that would oversee both industries.

In 1993, the Clinton administration developed a proposal for consolidating the regulation of commercial banks and savings institutions. Based on the proposal, the FDIC would focus on obtaining insurance premiums and closing poorly managed commercial banks. The Fed would focus on monetary policy and would continue to operate the payments system. The Comptroller of the Currency would assume the role of day-to-day regulation for all commercial banks and savings institutions. The proposal was met with some opposition but was a first step in an attempt to reduce regulatory overlap.

REGULATION OF BANK OWNERSHIP

Commercial banks can be independently owned by a holding company. Although some multibank holding companies (owning more than one bank) exist, one-bank holding companies (BHCs) are more common. More banks are owned by holding companies than are owned independently. The popularity of a holding company structure results from the following advantages. In 1970 amendments to the Bank Holding Company Act of 1956 were enacted, allowing BHCs to participate in various nonbanking activities, such as leasing, mortgage banking, and data processing. The ability of BHCs to offer these products provides greater potential for product diversification.

Most states that permit BHC expansion allow BHCs to acquire financial institutions anywhere in the state, so BHCs can diversify geographically without establishing new branches. BHCs also have more flexibility in raising new capital and in repurchasing shares of stock.

There are also some disadvantages of a BHC structure, such as organizational costs (professional and staffing fees) and greater regulatory monitoring. However, the recent popularity in BHC organizations suggests that these disadvantages are usually more than offset by the advantages.

BALANCE SHEET REGULATIONS

In addition to maintaining required reserves, banks are subject to a variety of other regulations on deposit insurance, loans, other assets, and capital. A discussion of these regulations follows.

Regulation of Deposit Insurance

Federal deposit insurance has existed since the creation of the FDIC in 1933 as a response to the bank runs that occurred in the late 1920s and early 1930s. During the 1930–1932 depression period, about 5,100 banks failed, representing more than 20 percent of the existing banks at that time. The initial wave of failures caused depositors to withdraw their deposits from other banks, fearing that failures would spread. Their action actually forced bank failures to spread. If deposit insurance had been available, depositors might not have removed their deposits, and some bank failures might have been avoided.

The specified amount of deposits per person insured by the FDIC has increased from $2,500 in 1933 to $100,000 today. The insured deposits make up 80 percent of all commercial bank balances, as the very large deposit accounts are insured only up to the $100,000 limit. Federal deposit insurance continues to be instrumental in preventing bank runs. Depositors are not so quick to remove their deposits because of a rumor about a bank or the banking system when they realize that their deposits are insured by the federal government.

The pool of funds used to cover insured depositors is now referred to as the **Bank Insurance Fund.** This fund is supported with annual insurance premiums paid by commercial banks. The annual premium ranges from 23¢ to 31¢ per $100 of deposits, depending on the specific bank's financial condition. Until 1991, the riskier banks obtained insurance for their depositors at the same rate as safer banks. Because the riskiest banks were more likely to fail, they were being indirectly subsidized by safer banks. This so-called **moral hazard** problem grew in the late 1980s and early 1990s, as the number of bank failures increased. The FDIC's insurance fund was reduced as a result of the expenses incurred in closing many banks. This prompted bank regulators and Congress to search for a way to discourage banks from taking excessive risk and to replenish the Bank Insurance Fund. As a result of the Federal Deposit Insurance Corporation Improvement Act (FDICIA) of 1991, risk-based deposit insurance premiums were phased in. Consequently, bank insurance premiums were aligned with the risk of banks, thereby removing the moral hazard problem.

Regulation of Loans

As a result of concern about the popularity of highly leveraged loans (for supporting leveraged buyouts and other activities), bank regulators began to monitor the amount of highly leveraged transactions (HLTs). HLTs are commonly defined as those loan transactions in which the borrower's liabilities are valued at more than 75 percent of total assets. Recent annual reports of banks usually disclose the dollar amount of HLTs. In the early 1990s, some commercial banks sold packages of HLTs in the secondary market to reduce the exposure of their loan portfolio to loan losses.

Regulators also monitor the bank's concentration in exposure to debt of foreign countries. Because banks are required by regulators to report significant exposure to foreign debt, investors and creditors have access to more detailed information about the composition of bank loan portfolios.

Banks are restricted to a maximum loan amount of 15 percent of their capital to any single borrower (up to 25 percent if the loan is adequately collateralized). This forces them to diversify their loans to a degree.

Regulation of Other Assets

Banks are not allowed to use borrowed or deposited funds to purchase common stock, although they can manage stock portfolios through trust accounts that are owned by individuals. Banks can invest only in bonds that are investment-grade quality (as measured by a Baa rating or higher by Moody's or a BBB rating or higher by Standard & Poor's). These regulations are intended to prevent banks from taking excessive risks.

Regulation of Capital

Banks are also subject to capital requirements, which forces them to maintain a minimum amount of capital (or equity) as a percentage of total assets. This regulation has been the focus of numerous controversies. In general, banks would prefer to maintain a low amount of capital to boost their return on equity ratio, yet regulators have argued that banks need a sufficient amount of capital to absorb potential operating losses. In this way, the number of bank failures may be reduced, which could enhance the depositor confidence in the banking system.

Minimum capital requirements were imposed on U.S. banks in 1981 by three different regulatory agencies. In 1985, the requirements were made uniform across agencies. Yet, there were still two discrepancies. First, all banks with more than $150 million in assets were subject to the same requirements, even though some banks were taking much more risk than others. Second, banks outside the United States were subject to their respective country's capital requirements. This created an unequal global playing field, because banks with lower capital requirements have a competitive advantage. These banks could achieve an acceptable return on equity with smaller profit margins because of their lower capital level. Thus, they could gain market share by underpricing those competitors that are subject to higher capital requirements.

In 1988, the central banks of 12 countries agreed to uniform capital requirements, which alleviated the discrepancies just discussed. The capital requirements were uniform across countries so that banks from any particular country did not have an unfair advantage. In addition, the specific requirements were dependent on the risk characteristics of each bank. Thus, riskier banks must maintain higher capital levels.

The capital requirements are phased in so that banks deficient in capital would have time to build their capital base. By the end of 1992, banks were required to have a capital ratio of at least 8 percent of risk-weighted assets, with a minimum Tier 1 capital ratio of 4 percent. Tier 1 capital consists mostly of shareholders' equity, retained earnings, and preferred stock, while Tier 2 capital includes loan loss reserves (up to a specified maximum) and subordinated debt.

Assets are weighted according to risk. Very safe assets such as cash are assigned a zero weight, while very risky assets are assigned a 100 percent weight. Because the required capital is set as a percentage of risk-weighted assets, riskier banks are subject to more stringent capital requirements.

OFF-BALANCE SHEET REGULATIONS

Banks offer a variety of off-balance sheet commitments. For example, banks provide letters of credit to back commercial paper issued by corporations. They also act as the intermediary on interest rate swaps and usually guarantee payments over the specified period in the event that one of the parties defaults on its payments.

Various off-balance sheet transactions have become popular because they provide fee income. That is, banks charge a fee for guaranteeing against default of another party and for facilitating transactions between parties. Yet, off-balance sheet transactions also expose the banks to risk. If, during a severe economic downturn, many corporations should default on their commercial paper or on payments specified by interest rate swap agreements, the banks that provided guarantees would incur large losses.

Bank exposure to off-balance sheet activities has become a major concern to regulators. Banks could be riskier than their balance sheets indicate because of these transactions. The risk-based capital requirements are higher for banks that conduct more off-balance sheet activities. In this way, regulators discourage banks from excessive off-balance sheet activities.

INTEREST RATE REGULATIONS

Banks have historically been regulated as to the interest rates they can offer on deposits and charge on some loans. A brief discussion of these regulations follows.

Deposit Rate Regulations

After the Great Depression, during which the banking industry experienced deposit runs, bank regulators took several steps to renew public confidence in the banking system. One of the most significant and controversial steps was

Regulation Q, which placed interest rate ceilings on savings deposits. This was expected to limit the competition for funds by banks and enhance the safety of the banking system.

Exhibit 16.1 illustrates the historical ceiling rate imposed on savings deposits. Until the 1960s, the ceiling was not thought to have a major impact because market-determined rates were typically below it anyway. However, by 1969 market-determined rates were significantly higher. For example, Treasury bill rates were more than 3 percent above the ceiling rate that banks could offer on time deposits.

Even though the ceiling rate on deposits was periodically raised by bank regulators over time, the increase was not large enough to prevent the process of **disintermediation,** whereby savers withdrew bank deposits and invested their funds in alternative investments with market-determined rates. As shown in Exhibit 16.1, the ceiling was periodically raised by one percent or less. This did not keep pace with market rates on Treasury bills, which were as high as 15 percent by 1981, versus a 5.25 percent ceiling on savings accounts at that time.

Throughout the late 1960s and the 1970s, banks argued that they should be allowed to compete on an equal footing for any available funds. Although regulators were not initially willing to remove the deposit rate ceiling on savings deposits, they did allow new financial instruments to be offered by banks in the late 1970s and early 1980s, with market-determined rates. As a result of the

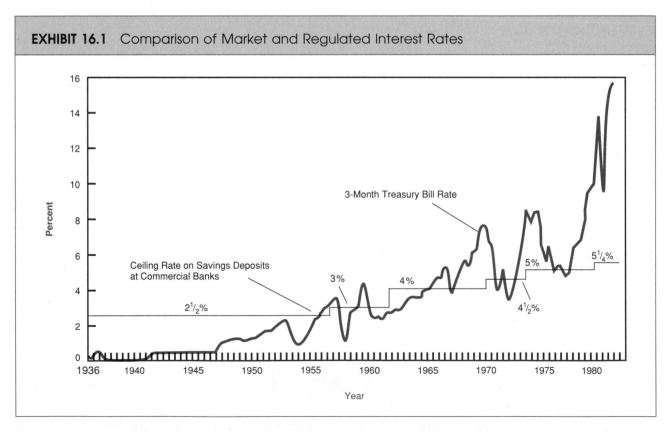

EXHIBIT 16.1 Comparison of Market and Regulated Interest Rates

SOURCE: *Review,* Federal Reserve Bank of St. Louis (December 1981): 4.

Depository Institutions Deregulation and Monetary Control Act (DIDMCA) of 1980, deposit rates were deregulated, and concerns about disintermediation subsided.

Loan Rate Regulations

All consumer loans offered by banks were at one time subject to interest rate ceilings. Each state has the authority to impose usury laws in the effort to keep consumers from being overcharged on loans, although banks argue that competition should automatically prevent overcharging.

When the general level of interest rates exceeded the usury ceilings imposed by some states, banks could not charge a market-determined loan rate on consumer loans, so they began to provide fewer consumer loans. As a result, consumers had difficulty in obtaining loans from banks. Ironically, the ceiling rates imposed on bank loans that were intended to help consumers actually hurt them. Most usury laws have since been eliminated or amended.

GEOGRAPHIC REGULATIONS

Banks have been subject to both intrastate and interstate restrictions that prevented them from entering particular geographic areas.

Intrastate Regulations

The geographic market in which a bank is allowed to establish branches varies among states. States implement one of three branching laws: (1) statewide branching, (2) limited branching, or (3) unit banking (which allows full banking services to be offered only at the home office). Even though they can provide loans in any geographic market they desire, banks subject to intrastate branching restrictions are more limited in their ability to grow, because their growth is determined by the deposits they can attract. Bank holding companies in these states are granted more branching freedom than banks not owned by a holding company. They can own a controlling interest in more than one bank, even if branching is not allowed by the state. They also have flexibility in pursuing nonbanking activities and can raise funds through sales of commercial paper (unlike an individual bank). Most large banks are owned by bank holding companies.

Banks began to set up automatic teller machines (ATMs) across geographic boundaries in the early 1980s. As a result, they can tap other markets for deposits even if they cannot legally establish branches there.

Interstate Regulations

The McFadden Act of 1927 prevented banks from establishing branches across state lines, regardless of their intrastate branching status. The Douglas Amendment to the Bank Holding Company Act of 1956 complemented the McFadden Act by preventing interstate acquisitions of banks by bank holding companies.

Because banks were historically restricted from crossing state lines, no single bank could control the entire market for bank deposits. Thus, geographic restrictions effectively limit the concentration of any bank in the lending business. No single bank can control the entire loan market if it has limited deposit-accepting capabilities. Furthermore, geographic restrictions discourage banks from offering consumer loans or small business loans outside their boundaries. The cost of providing such services long-distance would not allow these banks to be competitive with local banks. For large commercial loans, however, the amount of the loan transaction overshadows the cost of long-distance servicing. Thus, the market for large commercial loans is considered to be nationwide, even with geographic restrictions on branching.

In the past 10 years, there has been a great momentum toward interstate banking. However, the degree of momentum varies across the country because each state established its own interstate laws. As of 1994, 34 states approved nationwide interstate banking. Twenty-one of these states require a reciprocal arrangement, allowing acquisitions by banks residing in those states that would also grant out-of-state acquisitions. The other 13 states do not require a reciprocal arrangement. Fifteen states and the District of Columbia allow acquisitions on a reciprocal basis only by banks residing within a specified region. Exhibit 16.2 distinguishes among the interstate banking rules across states.

Most of the interstate expansion is achieved through bank acquisitions. However, federal guidelines were revised in September 1994, as a banking bill that removed interstate branching restrictions was approved. According to the banking bill, commercial banks are able to open branches nationwide.

Banks were expected to become more efficient as a result, because the provisions have removed requirements that banks maintain separate banking companies in each state that report to bank regulators. Previously, commercial banks operating in multiple states were required to establish separate corporations in each state, with separate boards of directors. Those banks with operations across several states are expected to reduce costs as a result of the banking bill. A study by McKinsey & Co. found that interstate branching could reduce bank reporting costs by $2 billion to $4 billion over a five-year period. Furthermore, the additional savings from reduced costs because of consolidation of operations are expected to be substantially larger than the savings from reduced reporting costs.

Bank customers should benefit not only because of lower costs to banks, but because of convenience. Customer bank accounts shall no longer be restricted to a particular state. Customers could deposit or withdraw funds in their accounts even when they are outside their home state. In fact, customers are now allowed to deposit checks or obtain a loan in any state where the bank has a branch.

ARGUMENTS FOR AND AGAINST NATIONWIDE INTERSTATE BANKING. One of the most widely used arguments in favor of nationwide interstate banking is that it allows banks to grow and more fully achieve a reduction in operating costs per unit of output as output increases. This is commonly referred to as **economies of scale.** If economies of scale could be fully achieved only when banks become very large (through entering new markets), interstate banking could lead to a more efficient banking industry. The strength of this argument depends on whether banks must expand across state lines for economies of scale to be fully realized.

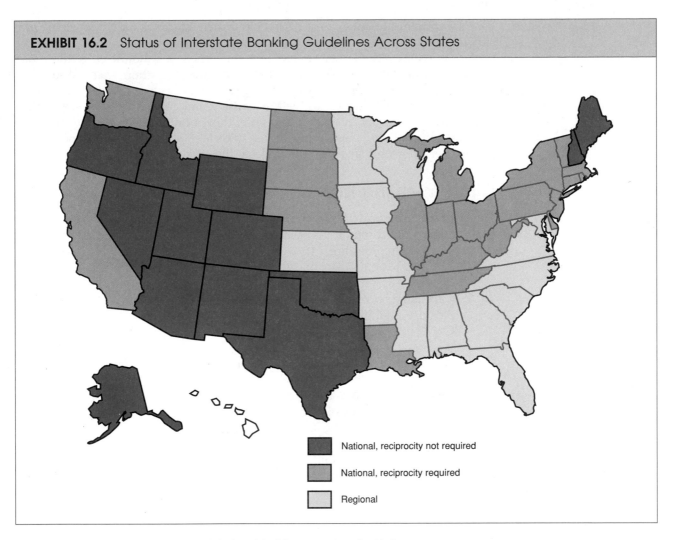

EXHIBIT 16.2 Status of Interstate Banking Guidelines Across States

- National, reciprocity not required
- National, reciprocity required
- Regional

NOTE: Hawaii has not enacted interstate bank holding company legislation.

SOURCE: Financial Structure Section, Division of Research and Statistics, Board of Governors of the Federal Reserve System, *Federal Reserve Bulletin,* December 1993, p. 1078.

A second argument for interstate banking is that it allows banks in stagnant markets to penetrate markets where economic conditions are more favorable. Banks in stagnant areas that enter other markets would improve their performance and reduce the bank failure rate, thus increasing the public's confidence in the banking industry. In addition, banks in all markets are pressured to become efficient as a result of the increased competition.

An extreme argument against nationwide interstate banking is that the ultimate result will be the survival of only a small group of banks. In this event, competition could actually subside, reducing efficiency and consumer satisfaction. It is hard to imagine an industry with more than 13,000 banks converging into just a few banks over time. Furthermore, the Sherman Act and Clayton Act could be enforced to prohibit such a high degree of concentration within the industry.

A second argument against nationwide interstate banking is that small consumers and businesses that are currently served by small banks might not be served as well by the larger banks. This concern was announced by the Small Business Administration when interstate banking legislation was proposed in 1982. There is no evidence, however, that large banks would fail to serve small consumers or small businesses well. Because small consumers and small businesses save or borrow in smaller amounts, they would not be treated the same as large corporations, they would typically receive lower rates on deposits and pay higher rates on loans. Yet, this reflects the current situation.

Circumventing Interstate Barriers

The migration of banks into new areas from which they were previously banned has become quite common in recent years. Some of the more common methods used to cross state lines are

- Qualify as a nonbank bank.
- Capitalize on reciprocal banking arrangements.
- Acquire a failing institution in another state.
- Capitalize on grandfather provisions.

QUALIFY AS A NONBANK BANK.   A depository institution is considered to be a commercial bank if it both accepts demand deposits and provides commercial loans. Thus, a depository institution that provides commercial and consumer loans and offers all types of deposits except demand deposits is not legally defined as a commercial bank. Consequently, it is not subject to regulations enforced by the Bank Holding Company Act of 1956 or the 1970 amendment to the Act. As a second example, a depository institution that provides consumer loans but not commercial loans is also not legally defined as a commercial bank and could therefore escape the related regulations.

There is a fine line between commercial bank operations and the operations of these so-called limited-service banks, consumer banks, loan offices, an so forth that avoid offering either demand deposits or commercial loans. All of these financial institutions are often classified as nonbank banks. Commercial banks have often created such nonbank banks in an effort to cross state lines and enter new markets.

CAPITALIZE ON RECIPROCAL BANKING ARRANGEMENTS.   In recent years, several states have allowed out-of-state banks to enter under a variety of conditions, most commonly the reciprocal banking arrangement, whereby two states agree that their respective banks can cross the state line. In this case, a bank can grow within the two states but is still restricted from entering any other state. An expanded version of this arrangement is a reciprocal agreement among several states. That is, banks in any one of a group of states are allowed to enter other states within that group. Such an arrangement has been implemented in several regions across the U.S.

Each reciprocal arrangement has its own provisions. For example, a state may allow only specific types of depository institutions to enter. Some states may not even require that other states reciprocate with similar permission. The specifics of these arrangements can be quite detailed and may change over time.

ACQUIRE A FAILING INSTITUTION IN ANOTHER STATE. A provision of the Garn-St Germain Act of 1982 allows a depository institution to enter another state if it is acquiring a failing depository institution there (even if a reciprocal arrangement does not exist for that state). The intent is to encourage banks to acquire failing banks so that these failing banks can continue to exist (although under new ownership). In some cases, depository institutions within the state may not be willing to acquire a failing bank nearby, but other out-of-state institutions may. As a result of this law, Citicorp (based in New York) has been able to acquire failing financial institutions in California, Florida, and Illinois.

CAPITALIZE ON GRANDFATHER PROVISIONS. In some cases, banks had previously established themselves in other states through some banking-law loophole or unusual circumstance. Because it might be difficult or unfair to order the bank to discontinue such activities, regulators may allow a grandfather provision permitting those banks to continue such activities but forbidding future attempts by others. For example, 21 bank holding companies were allowed to retain ownership of out-of-state subsidiaries because of a grandfather clause of the Bank Holding Company Act.

REGULATION OF NONBANKING ACTIVITIES

In recent years, banks have attempted to diversify their business beyond conventional banking services. The most widely considered services are related to the securities, insurance, and real estate industries. Banks argue that they can provide these services to consumers at a lower cost and that, by offering a more diversified set of products, they will be less exposed to recessionary business cycles. Thus, their chance of failure is reduced, and the soundness of the banking system would be improved.

Some argue, however, that certain characteristics of banks could give them an unfair advantage over other firms that provide these services. Because there are arguments for and against bank involvement in these services, bank regulators have had difficulty in deciding what services banks should be allowed to offer. They have permitted banks to provide some services in the securities, insurance, and real estate markets, as discussed next.

Bank Provision of Securities Services

The Banking Act of 1933 (better known as the Glass-Steagall Act) stated that banking and securities activities are to be separated. The Act was prompted by problems during the 1929 period when some banks sold some of their poor-quality securities to their trust accounts established for individuals. Some banks were also involved in insider trading, as they used confidential information on firms that had requested loans to buy or sell corporate securities. The Glass-Steagall Act prevents any firm that accepts deposits from underwriting stocks and bonds of corporations. Banks can underwrite general obligation bonds of states and municipalities or purchase and sell securities for their trust accounts. In addition, they can hold investment-grade corporate bonds within their asset portfolio. Yet, they act as a creditor here and not a shareholder.

INTERSTATE BRANCHING LEGISLATION FROM A BANKER'S PERSPECTIVE

The *Wall Street Journal* article below was written by John McCoy, the CEO of Banc One Corp., which has been one of the most profitable banks in the U.S. The article reflects the view of many bank executives.

By John B. McCoy

Congress has its best chance ever to pass legislation phasing in interstate banking and branching. In recent weeks, a key House subcommittee and the full Senate Banking Committee have voted unanimously in favor of this legislation, which also has the support of the Clinton administration.

This show of strong support would usually mean that a bill is well under way to the president's desk. However, there is a long history of important banking bills becoming magnets for extraneous amendments from various interest groups—amendments that ultimately sink the whole package. (This happened most recently in 1991.) With the full House Banking Committee facing a critical vote on the bill today, the real question is: Will Congress permit these extraneous measures to once again sink reforms needed to bring our financial system into the modern world?

There seems to be a strong consensus in Congress that interstate banking legislation should be enacted. Leaders of this congressional effort have pointed to three positive results.

First, interstate banking will be good for consumers and businesses. Interstate banks will pass on cost savings from more efficient operations in the form of lower interest rates on loans. Consumers and businesses will also benefit from the availability of new services, such as more flexible mortgage loans for homeowners and advanced cash-management systems for businesses. In addition, consumers who travel or commute across state lines and businesses that operate in more than one state will see added convenience.

The second benefit of interstate banking legislation is that it will strengthen the banking industry, by giving individual institutions more geographic diversification in their portfolios. And it will allow banks to compete on a level playing field with other players in the financial services industry—such as securities firms and insurance companies—which are already permitted to operate across state lines.

Finally, the legislation will lessen regional economic downturns, such as the one that hit New England several years ago. It is clear that in New England the downturn was made much worse because weakened banks were forced to shrink their loan portfolios as their capital levels fell because of losses. Interstate banking, it is now recognized, would have enabled banks to better withstand regional loan losses and to continue providing credit to job-creating businesses in New England.

Both the House and Senate bills, which are very similar, strike a balance in preserving the competitiveness of banks of all sizes, from small community outfits to giant money centers. The bills also protect the rights of states by enabling them to opt out of the interstate branching system. This careful balance is important not only substantively but also politically. It ensures that the bill will be supported by banks of all sizes and from all states. In the past, interstate banking legislation has been highly controversial, but the industry has now come together to support this approach.

This is a major accomplishment and one that is critical to the future survival of the banking industry. But this careful balance could quickly fall apart if the bill becomes a vehicle for amendments from various interest groups.

Elements of the insurance industry have already tried to add restrictions on bank insurance

continued

POINT OF INTEREST

INTERSTATE BRANCHING LEGISLATION FROM A BANKER'S PERSPECTIVE (Continued)

sales, although that danger seems to have receded, at least in the Senate. The biggest threat in the House comes from community and consumer groups that will reportedly seek amendments requiring banks to provide low-cost services and additional loans in low-income areas. These groups could more productively use their energies to expand the scope of the Community Reinvestment Act—the 1977 law that requires banks to help meet the credit needs of all communities in which they take deposits—to cover all financial service providers, not just banks.

If the community-lending amendments are added to the interstate banking bill, they will be self-defeating. For they will almost certainly consign this bill to the same fate as all recent attempts to modernize our banking system—the legislation will die.

Why? Because most banks, with no interest in branching across state lines, would receive no direct benefits from this legislation. They would surely lobby to kill any bill that imposes new burdens in the form of "community lending" requirements. The American Bankers Association and state associations have said they will oppose an interstate bill with such amendments.

It would be a shame if these amendments kill an opportunity to strengthen American banking. One can only hope that Congress seizes the opportunity to pass a "clean" version of the interstate banking and branching legislation.

Mr. McCoy is chairman and chief executive of Banc One Corp. in Columbus, Ohio.

SOURCE: *The Wall Street Journal,* March 9, 1994, p. A12; Reprinted with permission of *The Wall Street Journal* © 1994, Dow Jones & Company, Inc. All rights reserved worldwide.

The separation of securities activities from banking activities is justified by the potential conflicts of interest that could result. For example, if a bank is allowed to underwrite securities, it could advise its corporate customers to purchase these securities and could threaten to cut off future loans if the customers did not oblige. Furthermore, it might provide loans to customers only if it is understood that a portion of the funds would be used to purchase securities underwritten by the bank.

Banks may suggest that any potential conflicts of interest can be prevented by regulators. Furthermore, banks may have easier access to marketing, technological, and managerial resources and could reduce prices of securities-related services to consumers. In addition, banks could also serve as a financial supermarket where securities activities would be taken care of as well as the normal banking services. This would be an added convenience to customers. Finally, the increased competition could force all firms providing securities activities to be more efficient.

As banks are given more flexibility to offer all types of financial services, they will likely merge their traditional banking operations with firms that provide financial services. Consumers could then purchase bundled services, linking their deposit account, insurance, and brokerage services. Banks that handle corporate deposit accounts would also be able to underwrite stocks and bonds for the corporations, provide advice on corporate restructuring, and help execute mergers and acquisitions.

The separation between banking and securities activities has been blurred, as banks are now allowed to offer discount brokerage services in the securities industry. They can purchase or sell securities for their clients but are not allowed to advise them on which securities to buy or sell. Many banks would like to expand into full-service brokerage services, where advising could also be provided. Of course, this is where the conflict of interest becomes more obvious, as some critics fear that a bank's inside information obtained from corporations applying for loans would be communicated to its brokerage advisory department. Yet, banks could counter that various guidelines could be established to prevent such use of insider information, as is also necessary for brokerage firms.

In June 1986, the Fed ruled that brokerage subsidiaries of bank holding companies can sell mutual funds. In addition, some banks have arranged with financial service firms to establish a mutual fund to be used almost exclusively by bank customers. In this arrangement, often referred to as private label fund, the bank cannot sell shares of the fund but can make its customers aware of it.

In 1989, the Federal Reserve approved debt underwriting applications by J.P. Morgan & Co., Bankers Trust Corporation, Chase Manhattan, and Citicorp. The approval was contingent on two requirements. First, banks had to have sufficient capital to support the subsidiary that would perform the underwriting. Second, they had to be audited to ensure that their management was capable of underwriting debt. The Fed imposed a ceiling on revenues from corporate debt underwriting. The approval set a precedent for applications, and several other banks were also allowed to underwrite corporate debt offerings.

As banks underwrite corporate debt offerings, they can boost their fee income without significantly increasing their asset size. This is especially desirable because of the increased capital requirements imposed in 1988. Although growth in loans automatically causes an increase in the amount of required capital, underwritings can generate cash flow without an increase in required capital.

Banks underwriting corporate debt may also establish better advisory relationships with corporations, which could result in more business in the mergers and acquisitions area. Corporations may be more likely to consider commercial banks that underwrite the debt needed to finance acquisitions when seeking acquisition advice. Furthermore, the underwritings represent a new service offered by banks, which can provide diversification benefits.

Recently, some of the larger U.S. banks such as Chase Manhattan Corp. and Chemical Banking Corp. were applying for approval to underwrite stock offerings for corporations. This would further expand the services banks can offer corporations, along with debt underwriting, foreign exchange services, derivative securities services (such as foreign exchange derivatives and interest rate swaps), and cash management services.

Bank Provision of Insurance Services

As with securities services, banks have also been anxious to offer insurance services. The arguments for and against bank involvement in the insurance industry are quite similar to those regarding involvement in the securities industry. Banks would suggest that they could increase competition in the insurance industry, as they would be able to offer services at a lower cost. They already have facilities and office space and could offer their customers the convenience of one-stop shopping (especially if securities services were also allowed there).

To a limited degree, banks have already participated in insurance activities. Banks involved in some insurance activities before 1971 have grandfathered in their rights to these activities. In addition, banks have entered into cooperative arrangements with insurance companies whereby they sometimes lease space in their buildings for a payment equal to a percentage of sales of the insurance company. Regulatory provisions have become even more confusing as banks in some states have been permitted by state regulators to enter into insurance activities.

Consumers and firms could benefit from one-stop servicing, where all non-bank and bank services could be accommodated. In addition, if bank entrance into nonbank areas would increase efficiency and competition, lower prices could be charged for bank services. Future related regulations will likely aim to enhance customer convenience without giving banks an unfair advantage.

Nonbank Provision of Banking Services

There is a question not only of what services banks should be allowed to provide, but also of what banking services should be allowed by financial institutions other than banks. Some so-called "nonbanks" offer banking services but do not obtain federal insurance on deposits. Consumers might presume that these institutions are federally insured commercial banks. Even when private insurance is obtained by nonbanks, depositors may have a prolonged delay before being reimbursed if the nonbank bank fails. When the nonbank Western Community Money Center of California failed, depositors had to wait six months to get just one-fourth of their funds back from a private insurance company.

Many firms are now offering their own credit cards, and are financing the payments without using banks. This represents a means by which firms are entering a market that was historically dominated by banks. General Electric Financial Services (a subsidiary of the General Electric Company) is an example of a nonbank that competes with commercial banks in various ways. It represents a collection of 22 businesses that provide leasing services, real estate financing, credit cards, insurance services, household loans, and small business loans.

Some securities firms have begun to offer commercial loans. For example CS First Boston originates commercial loans in partnership with Credit Suisse. Merrill Lynch & Co. provides loans to medium and large firms. It sells pieces of these loans to other financial institutions.

How Regulators Monitor Banks

Regulators monitor banks to detect any serious deficiencies that might develop so that they can correct the deficiencies before the bank fails. The more failures they can prevent, the higher the public confidence will be in the banking industry. The evaluation approach used by the FDIC, applied to more than 8,000 state-chartered nonmember banks, is described here. This approach is also used by the Federal Reserve and other regulatory agencies.

The single most common cause of bank failure is poor management. Unfortunately, no reliable measure of poor management exists. Therefore, the FDIC rates banks on the basis of five characteristics, together comprising the CAMEL ratings (so named for the acronym that identifies the five characteristics examined):

- Capital adequacy
- Asset quality
- Management
- Earnings
- Liquidity

Capital Adequacy

Because adequate bank capital is thought by regulators to reduce the risk of the bank, the **capital ratio** (typically defined as capital divided by assets) is determined. Regulators have become increasingly concerned that some banks do not hold enough capital and have increased capital requirements. If banks hold more capital, they can more easily absorb potential losses and are more likely to survive. Banks with higher capital ratios are therefore assigned a higher capital adequacy rating. However, a bank with a relatively high level of capital could fail if the other components of its balance sheet have not been properly managed. Thus, the FDIC must evaluate other characteristics of banks in addition to capital adequacy.

Asset Quality

Each bank makes its own decisions as to how deposited funds should be allocated, and these decisions determine its level of default risk. The FDIC therefore evaluates the quality of the bank's assets.

The difficulty in rating an asset portfolio can be illustrated with the following example. A bank currently has 1,000 loans outstanding to firms in a variety of industries, each loan with specific provisions as to how it is secured (if at all) by the borrower's assets. Some of the loans have short-term maturities, while others are for longer terms. Imagine the task of assigning a rating to this bank's asset quality. Even if all the bank's loan recipients are current on their loan repayment schedules, this does not guarantee that the bank's asset quality deserves a high rating. The economic conditions that have existed during the period of prompt loan repayment may not persist in the future. Thus, an appropriate examination of a bank's asset portfolio should incorporate the portfolio's exposure to potential events (such as a recession). The reason for the regulatory examination is not to grade past performance, but to detect any problem that could cause the bank to fail in the future. Because of the difficulty involved in assigning a rating to a bank's asset portfolio, it is possible that some banks will be rated lower or higher than they deserve.

Management

Each of the characteristics examined relates to the bank's management. Yet, the FDIC specifically rates the bank's management according to administrative skills, the ability to comply with existing regulations, and the ability to cope with a changing environment. The evaluation of this characteristic is clearly subjective.

Earnings

Although the CAMEL ratings are mostly concerned with risk, earnings are very important. Banks fail when their earnings become consistently negative. A commonly used profitability ratio to evaluate banks is **return on assets (ROA)**, defined as earnings after taxes divided by assets. In addition to assessing a bank's earnings over time, it is also useful to compare the bank's earnings with industry earnings. This allows for an evaluation of the bank relative to its competitors.

Liquidity

Some banks commonly obtain funds from some outside sources (such as the discount window or the federal funds market), yet regulators would prefer that banks do not consistently rely on these sources. Such banks are more likely to experience a liquidity crisis whereby they are forced to borrow excessive amounts of funds from outside sources. If existing depositors sense that the bank is experiencing a liquidity problem, they may withdraw their funds, compounding the problem.

Rating Bank Characteristics

Each of the CAMEL characteristics is rated on a 1-to-5 scale, with 1 representing an outstanding rating and 5 a very poor rating. A composite rating is determined as the mean rating of the five characteristics. Banks with a composite rating of 4.0 or more are considered to be problem banks. They are closely monitored, because their risk level is perceived as very high.

The rating system described here is essentially a screening device. Because there are so many banks, regulators do not have the resources to closely monitor each bank on a frequent basis. The rating system identifies what are believed to be problem banks. Over time, some problem banks improve and clear themselves from that "problem list," while others deteriorate further and ultimately fail. Still other banks become new additions on the problem list.

Although examinations by regulators may help detect problems experienced by some banks in time to save them, many problems still go unnoticed, and by the time they are detected, it may be too late to find a remedy. Although an analysis of financial ratios can be useful, the task of assessing a bank is as much an art as it is a science. Subjective opinion must complement objective measurements in order to provide the best possible evaluation of a bank.

The Federal Reserve and Comptroller of the Currency also use systems for detecting bank problems. Although the systems may vary, they all involve the examination of financial ratios that measure a bank's capital adequacy, asset quality, earnings, and liquidity. Because financial ratios measure current or past performance rather than future performance, they do not always detect problems in time to correct them. However, many banks experiencing problems deteriorate slowly over time. These banks may show signs of deterioration in time to search for a solution.

Any system used to detect financial problems may err in one of two ways. It may classify a bank as safe when in fact it is failing or as very risky when in fact it is safe. The first type of mistake is more costly, because some failing banks are not identified in time to help them. To avoid this mistake, bank regulators could lower their benchmark composite rating. However, then there would be many more banks on the problem list, requiring close supervision, and the FDIC would have to spread its limited resources too thin.

Corrective Action by Regulators

When a bank is classified as a problem bank, regulators thoroughly investigate the cause of its deterioration. Corrective action is often necessary. Regulators may more frequently and thoroughly examine such banks and discuss with bank management possible remedies to cure the key problems. For example, regulators may request that a bank boost its capital level or delay its plans to expand. They can require that additional financial information be periodically updated to allow continued monitoring. They have the authority to remove particular officers and directors of a problem bank if this would enhance the bank's performance. They even have the authority to take legal action against a problem bank if the bank does not comply with their suggested remedies. However, such a drastic measure is rare and would not solve the existing problems of the bank.

Any success by the bank regulators in reducing bank failures could increase the public's confidence in the safety of the banking system. However, a possible tradeoff is involved. If banks reduce bank failures by imposing regulations that reduce competition, bank efficiency will be reduced. Perhaps the ideal compromise is for regulators to allow fierce competition but to detect financial problems of banks in time so that they can be cured. In this way, the number of failures within such a competitive environment would be minimized and efficiency achieved without reducing the public's confidence in the banking system.

Funding the Closure of Failing Banks

The Federal Deposit Insurance Corporation (FDIC) is responsible for the closure of failing banks. It must decide whether to liquidate the failed bank's assets or to facilitate the acquisition of that bank by another bank. When liquidating a failed bank, the FDIC draws from its Bank Insurance Fund to reimburse insured depositors. Although the FDIC insures deposits of commercial banks and savings and loan associations, its Bank Insurance Fund is specifically targeted to commercial banks. After reimbursing depositors of the failed bank, the FDIC attempts to sell any marketable assets (such as securities and some loans) of the failed bank. The cost to the FDIC of closing a failed bank is the difference between the reimbursement to depositors and the proceeds received from selling the failed bank's assets.

An alternative solution is for the FDIC to provide some financial support to facilitate another bank's acquisition of the failed bank. The acquiring bank recognizes that the market value of the failed bank's assets is worth less than the failed bank's liabilities. However, it may consider acquiring the failed bank if it is given sufficient funds by the FDIC. The FDIC may be willing to provide funding if its cost is less than the cost of liquidating the failed bank. Whether a failing bank is liquidated or acquired by another bank, it loses its identity.

POINT OF INTEREST

FDIC SUPPORT OF FAILING BANKS

In recent years, some large banks have required financial assistance from the FDIC. First Republic was acquired by NCNB Corporation in July 1988 with financial support from the FDIC. In the same year, First Banc of Texas (with about $11 billion in assets) was rescued by the FDIC. MCorp, another Texas bank with about $15 billion in assets, was also experiencing financial problems. It was acquired by Banc One in 1989 with financial support from the FDIC. In January 1991, the Bank of New England (which in 1990 had as much as $22 billion in assets) was taken over by the FDIC. All deposits, including those over the $100,000 insurance ceiling, were honored. Much of the existing management was retained to continue operations, even though ownership was transferred to the FDIC. The FDIC took control to enhance the safety of deposits, so that a major run on deposits could be prevented. The bank was acquired by Fleet/Norstar in 1991 with financial support from the FDIC.

The FDIC's promise to protect the Bank of New England's deposit accounts beyond the $100,000 insured limit reflects an implicit insurance beyond the limit, which may be intended to prevent runs at other banks by large depositors. Since 1986, all deposits at failed banks with at least $1 billion in assets have been fully reimbursed. Yet, depositors with deposits exceeding this limit at smaller banks have not always received such backing. For example, when Freedom National Bank failed in November 1990, the FDIC reimbursed depositors for 50 percent of the deposits exceeding the $100,000 limit. When Capitol Bank failed in December 1990, the FDIC reimbursed depositors for 45 percent of deposits exceeding the $100,000 limit.

The FDIC uses its reserves accumulated from charging deposit insurance premiums to rescue failing banks. At the beginning of 1991, the FDIC had $9 billion in reserves, versus more than $13 billion in 1989. Because the Bank of New England's failure in January 1991 was expected to require FDIC assistance of about $2.3 billion, that would leave less than $7 billion in reserves. Based on a projected 180 bank failures during 1991, the reserve level would be depleted further. Most of these failures were likely to be on a much smaller scale than the Bank of New England, but would still require some FDIC financial assistance in either liquidating the failed banks or supporting the acquisitions of these banks by other banks.

The most costly rescues of banks are disclosed below:

BANK	LOCATION	ASSETS PRIOR TO FAILURE (IN BILLIONS)	ESTIMATED COST TO FDIC (IN BILLIONS)
First Republic	Texas	$32.9	$2.9
MCorp	Texas	15.4	2.7
Bank of New England	Mass.	22.0	2.3
Continental Illinois	Illinois	33.6	1.1
First City Banc	Texas	11.2	1.0
Texas American	Texas	4.8	.9
N.Y. Banks for Savings	N.Y.	2.8	.7
First National	Texas	.9	.5
First American	Florida	.9	.4
United American	Tennessee	.8	.4
Greenwich Savings	N.Y.	2.5	.4

On November 27, 1991, Congress passed the Federal Deposit Insurance Corporation Improvement Act (FDICIA), which was intended to penalize banks that engage in high-risk activities, and reduce the regulatory costs of closing troubled banks. The more significant provisions of this act were as follows:

1. Regulators were required to act more quickly in forcing banks with inadequate capital to correct the deficiencies. Regulators classify a bank's capital position in one of five categories, ranging from well capitalized to critically undercapitalized. Three of the five categories reflect some deficiency in capital. Any banks that are classified in one of these three categories must meet specific requirements to boost their capital. This provision of the FDICIA forces banks with inadequate capital to correct their deficiencies. Consequently, the regulatory costs of closing the banks that ultimately fail should be reduced. At the time these categories were developed, less than 2 percent of all banks were classified in one of the three lower categories that call for specific corrective action.

2. Regulators were required to close troubled banks more quickly, rather than provide financial support to such banks over extended periods of time. This provision is intended to minimize the losses that may otherwise accumulate if the troubled banks are allowed to remain open.

3. Deposits exceeding the insured limit ($100,000) are not to be covered upon the failure of banks. This provision forces large depositors to consider the risk of a bank before depositing funds there. Because the larger banks typically obtain more funds in the form of large deposits, they will be affected to a greater degree by this provision. In the past, larger banks were perceived to be protected from failure because of the exposure of many uninsured depositors. Because these banks can no longer be protected, their ability to obtain large deposits will be more closely linked with their financial condition. Banks with excessive risk will have to pay higher interest rates (due to a higher risk premium) on large deposits.

4. Deposit insurance premiums were to be based on the risk of banks, rather than being based on the traditional fixed rate. Thus, riskier banks incur higher deposit insurance premiums. The risk-based deposit insurance premiums charged to financial institutions are based on a regulatory rating and the financial institution's capital level, as shown in Exhibit 16.3. The lower the financial institution's rating and the lower the capital level, the higher the annual deposit insurance premium that it must pay.

5. The FDIC was granted the right to borrow $30 billion from the Treasury to cover bank failures, and an additional $45 billion that would be used to finance working capital needs (from the time the FDIC reimburses depositors until it is able to liquidate the assets). The extra funding allows the FDIC more flexibility in the event that its Bank Insurance Fund is depleted, so that it can continue to operate effectively. Without such flexibility, the FDIC could be forced to let troubled banks remain open, if its funding was not adequate to finance the bank closings. Thus, the costs of closing these banks later on would likely be higher. In fact, another objective of the FDICIA was to

EXHIBIT 16.3 Summary of Risk-Based Deposit Insurance Premiums (as of 1993)

REGULATORY RATING	CAPITAL LEVEL	ANNUAL DEPOSIT INSURANCE PREMIUM PER $100 OF DEPOSITS	PROPORTION OF ALL BANKS IN THIS CATEGORY	PROPORTION OF ALL THRIFT INSTITUTIONS IN THIS CATEGORY
A Rating	Well-capitalized	$.23	76%	62%
	Adequate	.26	2%	6%
	Undercapitalized	.29	Nil	Nil
B Rating	Well-capitalized	.26	15%	12%
	Adequate	.29	1%	7%
	Undercapitalized	.30	Nil	2%
C Rating	Well-capitalized	.29	3%	1%
	Adequate	.30	1%	3%
	Undercapitalized	.31	2%	7%

increase within 15 years the Bank Insurance Fund to at least 1.5 percent of all insured deposits.

There are some additional provisions of the FDICIA that complement those described above. The act requires more complete disclosure by commercial banks, which is intended to help detect financial problems at an early stage. This provision can reduce bank losses, and may allow some banks to resolve problems before it is too late. Another provision limits the amount of loans that can be provided by the Fed to undercapitalized institutions. This complements other provisions that enforce capital standards. The FDICIA also requires that regulators enforce standards on real estate loans. This provision is intended to prevent institutions from excessive exposure to the real estate market.

In general, the provisions of the FDICIA attempt to tie a bank's operating costs to its risk level. This is a distinct change from the previous setting in which some costs (such as interest paid on large deposits and insurance premiums) were not linked with the bank's risk. Because FDICIA provisions link costs with risks, banks may be discouraged from taking excessive risks. Thus, bank failures may be reduced, which reduces the costs incurred by the FDIC (and ultimately the taxpayers). Furthermore, the provisions on capital deficiencies and quicker closings of troubled banks can reduce the costs to the FDIC of closing troubled banks.

Perhaps just as significant were the provisions that had been considered over the previous eleven months before passage of the FDICIA but were rejected. These proposed provisions included additional powers for banks in the securities and insurance industries. Banks had lobbied for such powers, contending that they would be able to achieve diversification benefits. Another rejected proposal was nationwide banking, which could have provided economies of scale and geographical diversification benefits for banks. Although the law can enhance the safety of the banking industry, some banks were disappointed that they were not granted additional powers to enter new industries or expand across the nation. Some legislators believed that these provisions could have increased the risk of banks, citing how savings institutions had experienced financial problems because of excessive deregulation. Although provisions for bank expansion across new industries or geographic region were not included in this banking law, those provisions will surely be considered in future legislation.

THE "TOO BIG TO FAIL" ISSUE

Some troubled banks have received preferential treatment by bank regulators. The most obvious example is Continental Illinois Bank, which was rescued by the federal government in 1984. Continental Illinois Bank had experienced serious loan default problems in 1983 and 1984. As of May 1984, its depositors with more than the $100,000 insurable limit began to withdraw their funds. Roughly 75 percent of the time deposits at Continental were in accounts of more than $100,000. The bank's concentration of large accounts was primarily due to its limited ability to obtain additional deposit funds by expanding geographically (because it was subject to unit-banking restrictions). Thus, Continental emphasized large CDs, which were marketed worldwide. Continental normally relied on new deposits to cover any withdrawal requests by old depositors. In May of 1984, though, cash inflows (new deposits) were not sufficient to cover cash outflows (deposit withdrawals). To temporarily correct the cash deficiency, Continental borrowed heavily through the discount window from the Federal Reserve System.

Shareholders also recognized Continental's financial problems. Exhibit 16.4 compares the stock price index movements of Continental to those of other money center banks and the S&P 500. The indexes were designed to be equal as of October 1983. In less than a year, Continental's index declined by more than 80 percent, versus minor declines in the money center bank index and S&P 500 index.

Continental's problems intensified as the remaining depositors began to withdraw their funds. This is a common occurrence for banks that fail. However, unlike most other situations, the bank regulators intervened. During the massive deposit withdrawals in May 1984, the FDIC announced that it would guarantee *all* deposits (and nondeposit liabilities) of Continental, even those beyond the normal $100,000 limit. This was an attempt to prevent further deposit withdrawals until some arrangements could be made to rescue Continental. In July of 1984, the FDIC arranged for a rescue plan whereby it would support Continental through purchasing some of its existing loan commitments and providing capital, with the total support amounting to more than $5 billion. As Continental's performance improved over time, the FDIC received income from selling loans it had assumed, thereby reducing the net cost of the rescue.

During this same time period, other troubled banks were failing without receiving any rescue attempt from the federal government. The reason for the Continental rescue plan was that, as one of the largest banks in the country, Continental's failure could have reduced public confidence in the banking system. Also, the rescue effort was less expensive to the FDIC than dealing with Continental's failure. But even if its direct costs to the FDIC had been higher, the potential indirect costs (such as the possible chain reaction of deposit withdrawals at other large banks) of letting the bank fail could have been too great to risk. Regardless of the reason for the FDIC's rescue, the fact remains that

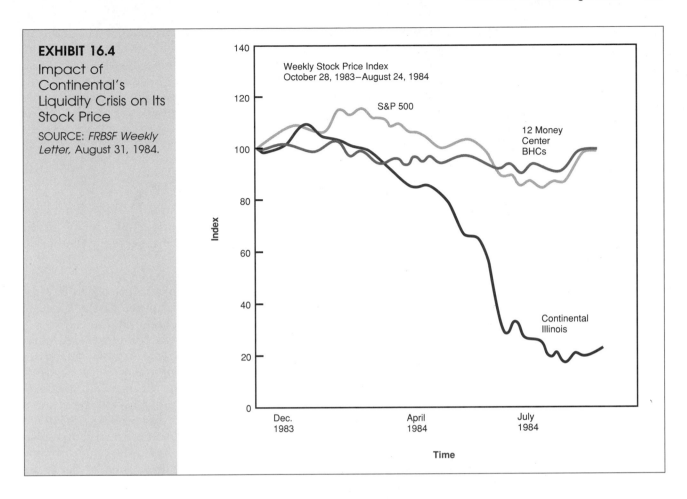

EXHIBIT 16.4

Impact of Continental's Liquidity Crisis on Its Stock Price

SOURCE: *FRBSF Weekly Letter,* August 31, 1984.

Continental Illinois Bank was rescued, while troubled smaller banks were not. This has important implications to the banking industry, identified in the following arguments for and against a government rescue.

Argument for Government Rescue

If the federal government had not intervened and Continental had failed and been liquidated, only the depositors with less than $100,000 would have been assured a full reimbursement. Then depositors with more than $100,000 at other banks could have become more concerned about their risk, and other large banks that were also experiencing serious loan default problems would have been likely candidates for runs on their deposit accounts. Even if other large banks were financially sound, a false rumor could have heightened depositors' worries and caused a run on deposits.

To examine whether depositors may become more concerned about large banks because of one large bank's problems, the spread between the rates on large three-month CDs and those on three-month Treasury bills can be compared during the period of Continental's crisis. The larger the spread, the larger the risk premium required by depositors. The risk premium hovered around 40 to 60 basis points in 1983 and early 1984. In May of 1984, when Continental's problems became widely publicized, the risk premiums of CDs of other large banks increased to more than 100 basis points (one percent), reaching about 190 basis points (1.90 percent) by July. The jump in the spread was likely due to the rumors about Continental. This illustrates how problems at a single large bank could reduce depositors' confidence in all large banks. Therefore, the possibility of a domino effect due to a single large bank's failure seems realistic and supports the FDIC's move to rescue Continental.

Argument Against Government Rescue

A federal government bailout can be expensive. In January 1987 Continental Illinois Bank stated that the FDIC would recover as little as $1.1 billion of the $2.81 billion of troubled loans that it had assumed in 1984, depleting the FDIC's reserve fund.

If the federal government rescues a large bank, it sends a message to the banking industry that large banks will not be allowed to fail. Consequently, large banks may take excessive risks without concern about failure. If risky ventures of a large bank (such as loans to very risky borrowers) pay off, the return will be high. If they do not pay off, the federal government will bail these large banks out. This argument has also been used as a result of the international debt crisis, where large banks with risky loans to less developed countries (LDCs) were aided by U.S. government financial support of the LDCs (increasing the chance that the LDCs would pay the U.S. banks back). If large banks can be ensured that they will be rescued, their shareholders will benefit, because there is limited downside risk. The value of the stock can decline only so far because of a crisis before government intervention will cause investors to have a favorable opinion of the bank and push the stock price back up. Yet, all of the smaller banks are at a disadvantage because the downside risk to their shareholders is much greater. The federal government is unlikely to rescue them should they fail.

Just as deregulation can enhance efficiency, government intervention could reduce efficiency. Large banks would not need to improve their operations to survive because they could count on the government to bail them out. If medium-sized banks felt that they were treated unfairly relative to large banks, they might establish the long-term goal of becoming large enough so that they would also be classified by the FDIC as a bank so big that it cannot be allowed to fail. With the loosening of restrictions on interstate banking, banks have a greater potential for growth. Yet, an objective to grow just to be backed by the federal government may conflict with the optimal size to maximize efficiency. Of course, efficiency would no longer be as critical for banks that have the support of the federal government.

Proposals for Government Rescue

Full agreement may never take place as to whether the federal government should have bailed out Continental. The critical question is how the federal government should react in the future if another large bank is failing. An ideal solution would prevent a run on deposits of other large banks, yet not reward a poorly performing bank with a bailout. One possible solution would be for regulators such as the Federal Reserve and the FDIC to play a greater role in assessing bank financial conditions over time. In this way, they might be able to recognize problems before they become too severe. But there is no guarantee that increased regulatory reviews would have prevented Continental's financial problems. Bankers might suggest that regulators cannot contribute anything beyond what they already know. Thus, the role of a regulator should be more of a police-officer (watching for illegal operations) than a consultant. In addition, increased regulatory reviews would result in an additional cost to the federal government.

SUMMARY

- Banks are regulated on the deposit insurance that they must maintain, the disclosure of their loan composition, the bonds that they are allowed to purchase, the minimum capital level they must maintain, the locations where they can operate, and the services that they can offer. Although capital requirements have become more stringent, regulations on where banks can operate and what services they can offer have been loosened. Most regulations are intended to enhance the safety and soundness of the banking system, without hampering efficiency.

- Bank regulators monitor banks by focusing on five criteria: capital, asset quality, management, earnings, and liquidity. The regulators assign ratings to these criteria to determine whether corrective action is necessary.

- In 1991, the Federal Deposit Insurance Corporation Improvement Act (FDICIA) was passed, which gave regulators the power to act quickly in taking corrective action. Specifically, regulators could force banks with inadequate capital to boost capital levels. Regulators were also required by the act to close troubled banks more quickly.

QUESTIONS

1. Why were member banks withdrawing their Federal Reserve membership in the 1970s? Why did this trend stop in the 1980s?

2. How are banks' balance sheet decisions regulated?

3. Provide examples of off-balance sheet activities. Why are regulators concerned about them?

4. What are usury laws? How can they influence lending decisions of banks?

5. What is disintermediation? How does it relate to bank regulations?

6. Briefly describe the McFadden Act of 1927.

7. Briefly describe the Douglas Amendment to the Bank Holding Company Act of 1956.

8. What led to the establishment of FDIC insurance?

9. Why would commercial banks try to establish nonbank banks?

10. How does the Garn-St Germain Act affect the potential degree of interstate banking?

11. Briefly describe the Glass-Steagall Act.

12. To what extent can banks offer brokerage services?

13. Why might there be a conflict of interest if banks were to offer brokerage services on a full-scale basis?

14. How have banks used leasing to participate in the insurance industry?

15. Describe the main provisions of DIDMCA that relate to deregulation.

16. How did the Garn-St Germain Act allow depository institutions greater flexibility to cross state lines?

17. Explain how the uniform capital requirements in 1988 created a more equal global playing field.

18. Explain how the Financial Institutions Reform, Recovery, and Enforcement Act (FIRREA) would result in increasing integration between the commercial banking industry and the savings institution industry.

19. Describe highly leveraged transactions (HLTs) and explain why bank exposure to HLTs is closely monitored by regulators.

20. Why might banks be even more interested in underwriting corporate debt issues since the higher capital requirements were imposed on them?

21. Explain the moral hazard problem as related to deposit insurance.

22. How do economies of scale in banking relate to the issue of interstate banking?

23. Why did Continental Bank obtain such a high proportion of its funds from large CD accounts?

24. How can the financial problems of one large bank affect the market's risk evaluation of other large banks?

25. Why are bank regulators more concerned with a large bank failure than a small bank failure, aside from the difference in direct cost to the FDIC?

Financial Casualty
U.S. Recession Claims Bank of New England As First Big Victim

Federal Regulators Take Over After Company Warned Of Large Impending Loss
Depositors Rush to Get Funds

Ron Suskind and Kenneth H. Bacon

The recession has claimed its first big banking victim.

Federal regulators yesterday took over Bank of New England Corp., the region's third-largest bank holding company.

The Federal Deposit Insurance Corp. assumed control of Bank of New England, the holding company's $13.2 billion core; Connecticut Bank & Trust Co., which has $7.7 billion in assets, and the $1.1 billion Maine National Bank. As part of the transaction, the FDIC injected $750 million into the banks.

Regulators acted Sunday after anxious depositors mobbed Bank of New England offices to withdraw money in the wake of the bank's announcement Friday that it could lose up to $450 million in the fourth quarter, making it essentially insolvent.

Federal officials hope that their fast response to the first major bank crisis in the current recession will halt the erosion of confidence in the banking system. The arrangement will protect from loss all depositors, even those with accounts exceeding the $100,000 insurance ceiling. The Federal Reserve System, operating through its discount window, announced that it is prepared to lend the banks the money they need to meet their liquidity needs.

Bridge Banks Set Up

After a long weekend of meetings, the Comptroller of the Currency declared the banks insolvent late yesterday. The FDIC became the receiver for the banks and set up a so-called bridge bank for each unit, which the FDIC will run while it works to sell the banks. The FDIC has started negotiating with several potential buyers of the three insolvent institutions. "We have two active bidders, and other well-qualified bidders might apply," said FDIC Chairman William Seidman. "We expect to announce a transaction soon."

Federal regulators hope their approach serves as a model for handling the additional big bank failures that they expect a recession of unknown length and severity to bring. It is a swifter-yet-gentler approach than some federal takeovers of the past. By moving quickly despite the holding company's effort to work out a recapitalization agreement with its bondholders, they hope to preserve the bank's resale value. Yet by leaving management in place, they also hope to minimize the disruption to the bank's operations and to the regional economy. Finally, they hope to set up a rescue plan that ultimately involves both public and private investment. . . .

Urgency Stressed

The failure of the Bank of New England units is the third-largest failure, following that of the $40 billion Continental Illinois Bank & Trust Co., in 1984 and the $32.7 billion First Republic Bancorp. in Texas in 1988.

In acting quickly to address Bank of New England's problems, the FDIC examined a range of options—all involving a cost to the federal government and none of them particularly palatable. The goal was to find "the least-cost, most privately funded" solution that would reduce the potentially huge public cost of a rescue, Mr. Seidman said.

Though no one knows for sure what the cost of rescuing Bank of New England might eventually be, estimates range as high as $3 billion.

Perhaps the most expensive—and therefore a less attractive—option was for the FDIC to simply take over the bank, in a move similar to its 1984 agreement to put $4.5 billion into and assume ownership of the $40 billion Continental Illinois Bank & Trust Co. Since that takeover, the FDIC has sold most of its interest and reduced the cost of the rescue to about $800 million.

William Isaac, then the FDIC chairman and now the head of Secura Group, a bank consulting firm, thinks that this type of transaction could have worked for Bank of New England. In recent weeks, Mr. Seidman and other officials have cited the Continental case as a model of a successful resolution. But Mr. Seidman has also made it clear that he prefers public-private partnerships where possible.

Among the public-private options, the agency considered including in a rescue the holding company's bondholders, who have proposed swapping their debt into stock. That would have sharply

Continued

CASE APPLICATION: REGULATING THE BANK OF NEW ENGLAND'S FAILURE

Continued

reduced debt, cut interest payments by $60 million a year and created $706 million of equity capital.

However, the bondholders' basic condition—some kind of federal assistance that would make a swap feasible—is something of which the FDIC has generally been leery. It wants to protect banks and their depositors, not their owners by giving value to otherwise-worthless securities. "If we were in the business of saving holding companies, we'd be busted," Mr. Seidman said.

As regulators conferred over the weekend, the preferred public-private solution that emerged was to create a so-called bridge bank, with the FDIC holding a majority of the new corporation and the acquiring institution or investor holding a minority. This arrangement would wipe out the stockholders and most lawsuits against the bank. Both the FDIC and acquiring bank would put in capital and, over time, the acquiring group would buy out the FDIC's share.

This was the arrangement Banc One and the FDIC used when they bailed out 20 MCorp banking subsidiaries when the Texas holding company failed in 1989. One advantage of this option is that it can work whether the Bank of New England is sold whole or in parts.

Right now, however, fewer big banks are in a position to take over an institution as large as Bank of New England, the nation's 33rd-largest banking company. Many sound banks, such as NCNB Corp. and Banc One Corp., already are digesting recent acquisitions. Other large banks, such as Citicorp, have their own capital problems. "I don't know if there is anybody big enough to take over Bank of New England now," said William Weber, a banking consultant at Furash & Co. . . .

Federal regulators had to act quickly because of the damage to depositor confidence caused by Bank of New England's announcement on Friday—closely following a financial crisis in Rhode Island. Last Tuesday, Rhode Island Gov. Bruce Sundlun closed 45 banks and credit unions when their private insurer failed, leaving 300,000 accounts uninsured and treating the rest of the region to Depression-era images of police protecting credit unions from irate customers desperate for cash. . . .

Word of Bank of New England's deepening woes spread after it announced the projected $450 million fourth-quarter loss—which would result in a loss for all 1990 of up to $653 million and wipe out the bank's capital (as of Sept. 30) of $255 million. Contributing to the expected loss was a $500 million addition to nonperforming assets, which already total $2.84 billion.

Throughout Friday and into Saturday morning, panicked customers began withdrawing deposits, jamming bank offices and straining the liquidity of the $23 billion bank. So delicate was the situation that Lawrence K. Fish, the bank's chairman, began driving from branch to branch to assure worried customers that their money was safe.

New England is suffering from a now-familiar blight: Free-falling real-estate values cause banks to take huge write-downs on loans, which, in turn, siphon off the cash that banks might otherwise lend. Without available credit, bidders for salable properties disappear, and real-estate values drop further, causing more bank losses, in a self-sustaining cycle. . . .

It is precisely such fast-dropping real-estate values that sunk the Bank of New England. With economists predicting another 12 months of decline for the region's economy, other banks in New England—already struggling under huge portfolios of nonperforming assets—are certain to be writing off even more loans and suffering further losses.

—*Paulette Thomas contributed to this article.*

SOURCE: *The Wall Street Journal,* January 7, 1991, p. A1. Reprinted with permission of *The Wall Street Journal,* © 1991 Dow Jones & Company, Inc. All rights reserved.

QUESTIONS

1. The FDIC could have closed the Bank of New England (BNE) and liquidated the assets instead of assuming temporary control. Explain how closing the bank would have different effects on FDIC costs.

2. Why was it necessary for the Federal Reserve to announce it was prepared to lend BNE funds? Couldn't BNE obtain sufficient funds through deposits or by borrowing in the federal funds market?

3. Why do you think BNE was more exposed to recessionary conditions than other banks?

4. BNE was ultimately acquired by Fleet/Norstar Financial Corp. Why would some banks like Fleet/Norstar have been interested in acquiring BNE, given BNE's poor financial condition?

5. The FDIC could have let BNE attempt to resolve its financial problems on its own before intervening. What are the advantages and disadvantages of giving BNE more time to resolve its problems?

PROJECTS

1. **Assessing the Financial Effects of Deregulation**
   Your professor will assign you (or your group) a bank or allow you to choose one. Use the most recent annual report (along with earlier annual reports if they are available) of the bank to answer the following questions:
   a. Identify any services that the bank now offers as a result of deregulatory provisions in the banking industry.
   b. Identify any changes in the bank's sources and uses of funds that are the result of deregulation.
   c. Identify any services that the bank plans to offer in the future as a result of deregulatory provisions in the banking industry.
   d. Summarize the bank's current status and future regarding the geographic markets it serves.
   e. Do you think the bank has increased its potential performance as a result of how it has reacted to deregulatory provisions? Explain.
   f. Do you think the bank's risk has changed as a result of how it has reacted to deregulatory provisions? Explain.
   g. Do you think this bank will benefit from deregulation? Explain.

2. **Assessing the Interstate Banking Issue**
   a. Obtain the annual report of a commercial bank of your choice or assigned by your professor. From this report, how has the bank operated across state lines? Also, summarize the bank's future planning for growth. Does the bank plan to grow within its headquarters state, in adjacent states, or nationally? How does it plan to enter other states? How do you expect this growth to affect its performance? Why?
   b. Use any related literature from the library to propose a policy for interstate banking. Explain why your policy would be better than alternative policies. (Cite all of your information sources.)

REFERENCES

Besanko, David, and Anjan Thakor. "Banking Deregulation: Allocational Consequences of Relaxing Entry Barriers." *Journal of Banking and Finance* (September 1992): 909–932.

Bundt, Thomas P., Thomas F. Cosimano, and John A. Halloran. "DIDMCA and Bank Market Risk: Theory and Evidence." *Journal of Banking and Finance* (December 1992): 1179–1193.

Dahl, Drew, and Ronald E. Shrieves. "The Impact of Regulation on Bank Equity Infusions." *Journal of Banking and Finance* (December 1990): 1209–1228.

Giammarino, Ronald M., Tracy R. Lewis, and David E. M. Sappington. "An Incentive Approach to Banking Regulation." *Journal of Finance* (September 1993): 1523–1542.

Madura, Jeff, and Alan L. Tucker. "Information Effects of First Republic's Failure." *Applied Financial Economics* (No. 1, 1991): 89–96.

O'Hara, Maureen, and Wayne Shaw. "Deposit Insurance and Wealth Effects: The Value of Being Too Big to Fail." *Journal of Finance* (December 1990): 1587–1600.

Pennacchi, George. "A Re-examination of the Over- (or Under-) Pricing of Deposit Insurance." *Journal of Money, Credit, and Banking* (August 1987): 340–360.

Saunders, Anthony. "Securities Activities of Commercial Banks: The Problem of Conflicts of Interest." *Business Review*, Federal Reserve Bank of Philadelphia (July–August 1985): 17–27.

Wall, Larry D. "Regulation of Banks' Equity Capital." *Economic Review*, Federal Reserve Bank of Atlanta (November 1985): 4–18.

SUMMARY OF THE DIDMCA AND THE GARN-ST GERMAIN ACT

Two of the most important regulatory acts pertaining to the banking industry are the Depository Institutions Deregulation and Monetary Control Act of 1980, and the Garn-St Germain Act of 1982. A discussion of each of these acts follows.

DEREGULATION ACT OF 1980

For many years, discussions by Congress, the regulatory agencies, and depository institutions focused on reducing bank regulations. In 1980 the Depository Institutions Deregulation and Monetary Control Act (DIDMCA) was established to achieve these objectives. The Act contained a wide variety of provisions, but the main ones can be categorized into two categories: (1) those intended to deregulate the banking (and other depository institutions) industry and (2) those intended to improve monetary control. Because this section focuses on deregulation, only the first category of provisions is discussed here.

The DIDMCA was a major force in deregulating the banking industry and increasing competition among banks. Its main deregulatory provisions were

- Phaseout of deposit rate ceilings
- Allowance of checkable deposits for all depository institutions
- New lending flexibility for depository institutions
- Explicit pricing of Fed services

Phaseout of Deposit Rate Ceilings

The interest rate ceilings (enforced by Regulation Q) on time and savings deposits of depository institutions were scheduled to be phased out over time. By April 1986 these ceilings were completely eliminated, allowing banks to make their own decisions on what interest rates to offer for time and savings deposits.

Allowance of Checkable Deposits for All Depository Institutions

The DIDMCA allowed NOW accounts for all depository institutions across all 50 states as of 1981. Although only commercial banks are allowed to offer demand deposits, this advantage was diminished by the DIDMCA ruling. Because NOW accounts normally require a higher minimum balance, they are not suitable for all consumers; however, their ability to pay interest has attracted those who can afford the minimum balance.

New Lending Flexibility for Depository Institutions

The DIDMCA allowed more flexibility for depository institutions to enter into various types of lending. For example, savings and loan associations were allowed to offer a limited amount of commercial and consumer loans. Consequently, competition among depository institutions for consumer and commercial loans increased, and the asset mix of different depository institutions has become more similar over time.

Explicit Pricing of Fed Services

The Federal Reserve had historically provided Fed members with services such as check clearing at no charge. Nonmember banks obtained these services elsewhere. In an effort to improve efficiency in the banking system, the DIDMCA required that the Fed explicitly charge for its services and offer them to any depository institutions that desired them. The reasoning was that if the Fed did not provide these services efficiently, new firms would enter the market and charge a lower price for the services. Thus, the Fed would continue to offer only those services that it could provide efficiently. Of course, it would still retain its regulatory and monetary control powers, regardless of whichever other services it continued or eliminated.

Beyond these deregulatory provisions, the DIDMCA called for an increase in the maximum deposit insurance level from $40,000 to $100,000 per depositor at each given bank to reduce the chances of deposit runs.

Impact of the DIDMCA

Because of the DIDMCA, there has been a shift from conventional demand deposits to NOW accounts. In addition, consumers have shifted funds from the conventional passbook savings accounts to various types of CDs that pay market interest rates. Consequently, banks now pay more for funds than what they would pay if the DIDMCA had not occurred. Also, the DIDMCA has increased competition between depository institutions.

GARN-ST GERMAIN ACT

Banks and other depository institutions were further deregulated in 1982 as a result of the Garn-St Germain Act. The Act came at a time when some depository institutions (especially savings and loan associations) were experiencing severe financial problems. One of its more important provisions permitted depository institutions to offer money market deposit accounts (MMDAs), which have no minimum maturity and no interest ceiling. This account allows for a maximum of six transactions per month (three by check). It is very similar to the traditional accounts offered by **money market mutual funds** (whose main function is to sell shares and pool the funds to purchase short-term securities that offer market-determined rates). Because the MMDA offers savers similar benefits, it allows depository institutions to compete against money market funds in attracting savers' funds.

A second key deregulatory provision of the Garn-St Germain Act permitted depository institutions to acquire failing institutions across geographic boundaries (as mentioned earlier). The intent was to reduce the number of failures that require liquidation, as the chances of finding a potential acquirer for a failing institution are improved when geographic barriers are removed. Also, competition was expected to increase, as depository institutions previously barred from entering specific geographic areas could do so by acquiring failing institutions.

Although the proper degree of deregulation is disputed, consumers appear to have benefited from deregulatory trends in recent years. They now have a greater variety of financial services from which to choose, and the pricing of services is controlled by intense competition.

CHAPTER 17

BANK MANAGEMENT

The performance of any commercial bank depends on the management of the bank's assets, liabilities, and capital. And increased competition has made efficient management necessary for survival.

The specific objectives of this chapter are to:

- describe the underlying goal of bank management,
- explain how banks manage liquidity,
- explain how banks manage interest rate risk,
- explain how banks manage default risk, and
- explain how banks manage capital.

Goal of Bank Management

The underlying goal behind the managerial policies of a bank is to maximize the wealth of the bank's shareholders. Thus, bank managers should make decisions that maximize the price of the bank's stock.

In some cases, managers are tempted to make decisions that are in their own best interests rather than shareholder interests. For example, decisions that result in growth may be intended to increase employee salaries, as larger banks tend to provide more employee compensation. In addition, the compensation to loan officers of a bank may be tied to loan volume, which encourages a loan department to provide loans without concern about risk. These examples suggest that banks can incur agency costs, or costs resulting from managers maximizing their own wealth instead of shareholder wealth. To prevent agency problems, some banks provide stock as compensation to managers. These managers may be more likely to maximize shareholder wealth because they are shareholders as well. Also, if managerial decisions conflict with the intent of maximizing shareholder wealth, the share price will not achieve its maximum. Therefore, the bank may become the takeover target, as other banks perceive it as undervalued, with the potential to improve under their own management. In this way, managers can be disciplined to maximize shareholder wealth.

MANAGING LIQUIDITY

Banks can experience illiquidity when cash outflows (due to deposit withdrawals, loans, etc.) exceed cash inflows (new deposits, loan repayments, etc.). They can resolve any cash deficiency either by creating additional liabilities or by selling assets. Banks have access to various forms of borrowing, such as the federal funds market or the discount window. They also maintain some assets that can be readily sold in the secondary market. The decision on how to obtain funds depends on the situation. If the need for funds is temporary, an increase in short-term liabilities (from the federal funds market or the discount window) may be more appropriate. However, if the need is permanent, a policy for increasing deposits or selling liquid assets may be more appropriate.

Because some assets are more marketable than others in the secondary market, the bank's asset composition can affect its degree of liquidity. At an extreme, banks could ensure sufficient liquidity by using most of their funds to purchase Treasury securities. However, they must also be concerned with achieving a reasonable return on their assets, which often conflicts with the liquidity objective. Although Treasury securities are liquid, their yield is low relative to bank loans and other investment securities. Recent research has shown that high-performance banks are able to maintain relatively low (but sufficient) liquidity. Banks should maintain the level of liquid assets that would satisfy their liquidity needs but use their remaining funds to satisfy their other objectives. As the secondary market for loans has become active, banks are more able to satisfy their liquidity needs with a higher proportion of loans while striving for higher profitability.

Use of Securitization to Boost Liquidity

The ability of banks to securitize assets such as automobile and mortgage loans can enhance a bank's liquidity position. The process of securitization commonly involves the sale of assets by the banks to a trustee, who issues securities that are collateralized by the assets. In turn, the banks may still service the loans but pass through the interest and principal payments received to the investors who purchased the securities. Banks are more liquid as a result of securitization because they effectively convert future cash flows into immediate cash. In most cases, there is a guarantor involved in this process who, for a fee, guarantees future payments to investors who purchased the securities. The loans that collateralize the securities normally exceed the amount of the securities issued or are backed by an additional guarantee from the bank that sells the loans.

MANAGING INTEREST RATE RISK

The composition of a bank's balance sheet will determine how its profitability is influenced by interest rate fluctuations. If a bank expects interest rates to consistently decrease over time, it will consider allocating most of its funds to rate-insensitive assets, such as long-term and medium-term loans (all with fixed rates) as well as long-term securities. These assets will continue to provide the same periodic yield. As interest rates decline, the bank's cost of funds will decrease, and its overall return will increase.

If a bank expects interest rates to consistently increase over time, it will consider allocating most of its funds to rate-sensitive assets such as short-term commercial and consumer loans, long-term loans with floating interest rates, and short-term securities. The short-term instruments will mature soon, so reinvestment will be at a higher rate if interest rates increase. The longer-term instruments will continue to exist, so the bank will benefit from increasing interest rates only if it uses floating rates.

Although banks can construct an asset portfolio that will benefit from a given interest rate movement in the future, there is no guarantee about the direction in which interest rates will move. The chance that rates will move in the opposite direction to what is anticipated represents the bank's exposure to interest rate risk.

A major concern of banks is how interest rate movements will affect performance, particularly earnings. If their liability portfolio and asset portfolio were equally sensitive to interest rate movements, they could maintain a stable spread over time, meaning the difference between the bank's average rate earned on assets minus its average rate paid on liabilities. A more formalized comparison of the bank's interest revenues and expenses is provided by the **net interest margin,** computed as

$$\text{Net Interest Margin} = \frac{\text{Interest revenues} - \text{Interest expenses}}{\text{Assets}}$$

In some cases, net interest margin is defined to include only the earning assets, excluding any assets that do not generate a return to the bank (such as required reserves). Because the rate sensitivity of a bank's liabilities normally does not perfectly match that of the assets, the net interest margin changes over time. The change depends on whether bank assets are more or less sensitive than bank liabilities, the degree of difference in rate sensitivity, and the direction of interest rate movements.

During a period of rising interest rates, a bank's net interest margin will likely decrease if its liabilities are more rate sensitive than its assets, as illustrated in Exhibit 17.1. Under the opposite scenario, where market interest rates are declining over time, rates offered on new bank deposits, as well as those earned on new bank loans, would be affected by the decline in interest rates. Yet, the deposit rates would typically be more sensitive if their turnover is quicker, as illustrated in Exhibit 17.2.

Methods to Assess Interest Rate Risk

Commercial banks that assess their exposure to interest rate movements use the following methods:

- Gap measurement
- Duration measurement
- Regression analysis

EXHIBIT 17.1

Impact of Increasing Interest Rates on a Bank's Net Interest Margin (If the Bank's Liabilities Are More Rate Sensitive Than Its Assets)

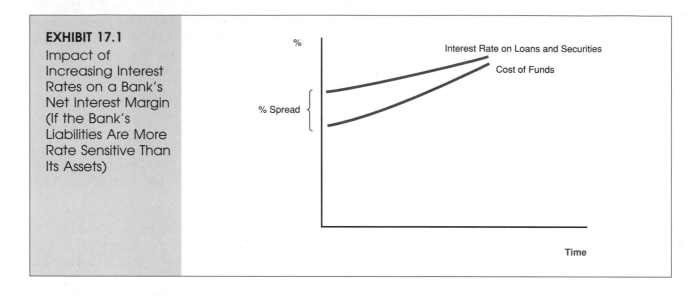

EXHIBIT 17.2

Impact of Decreasing Interest Rates on a Bank's Net Interest Margin (If the Bank's Liabilities Are More Rate Sensitive Than Its Assets)

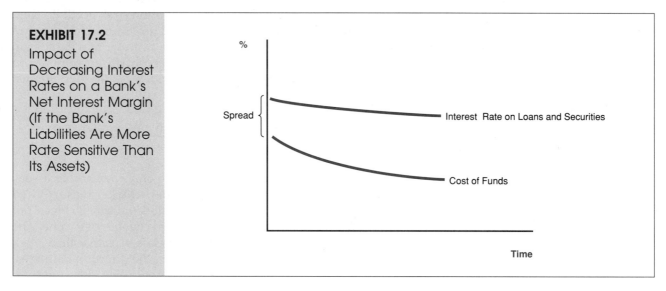

GAP MEASUREMENT.   Banks can attempt to determine their interest rate risk by monitoring their **gap** over time, defined here as

$$\text{Gap} = \text{Rate-sensitive assets} - \text{Rate-sensitive liabilities}$$

An alternative formula is the **gap ratio,** which is measured as volume of rate-sensitive assets divided by rate-sensitive liabilities. A gap of zero (or gap ratio of 1.00) suggests that rate-sensitive assets equal rate-sensitive liabilities, so that net interest margin should not be significantly influenced by interest rate fluctuations. A negative gap (or gap ratio of less than 1.00) suggests that rate-sensitive liabilities exceed rate-sensitive assets. Banks with a negative gap are typically concerned about a potential increase in interest rates, which could reduce their net interest margin.

POINT OF INTEREST

INTEREST RATE GAP ANALYSIS OF NATIONSBANK

Many commercial banks provide a detailed assessment of their interest rate risk in their annual report. For example, the 1993 annual report of NationsBank classifies interest-sensitive assets and liabilities into various categories that represent the time of repricing. This can be used to determine the interest rate gap within each category so that the bank's exposure to interest rate risk can be assessed. The analysis of NationsBank as of December 31, 1993 is summarized in Exhibit A. This exhibit

shows that NationsBank has a negative gap within the 30-day range and 6-month range, but a positive gap within the 3-month and 12-month ranges. Its levels of assets and liabilities classified as nonsensitive or to be repriced beyond 12 months are about equal. NationsBank also takes positions in interest rate swaps and interest rate futures, which can be included in the analysis described above to determine the bank's "adjusted" interest rate gap (as shown in the annual report).

EXHIBIT A Interest Sensitive Assets and Liabilities of NationsBank, Dec. 31, 1993.

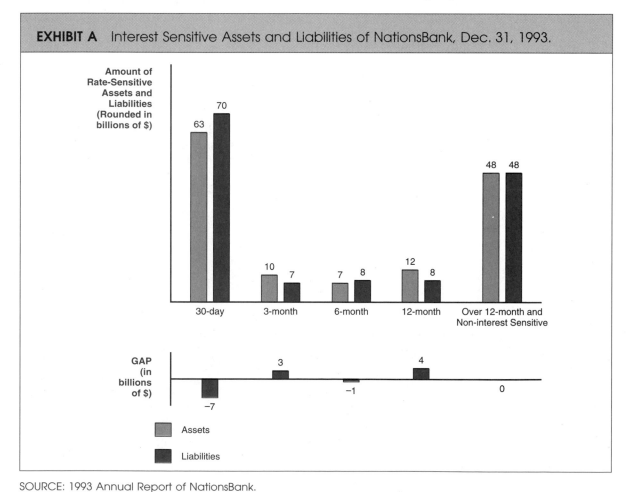

SOURCE: 1993 Annual Report of NationsBank.

Although the gap as described here is an easy method for measuring a bank's interest rate risk, it has limitations. Banks must decide how to classify their liabilities and assets as rate sensitive versus rate insensitive. For example, should a Treasury security with a year to maturity be classified as rate sensitive or rate insensitive? How short must a maturity be to qualify for the rate-sensitive classification?

Each bank may have its own classification system, because there is no perfect measurement of their gap. Whatever system is used, there is a possibility of misinterpreting the gap measurement. Consider a bank that obtains much of its funds by issuing CDs with seven-day and one-month maturities as well as money market deposit accounts (MMDAs). Assume that the bank typically uses these funds to provide loans with a floating rate, adjusted once per year. These sources of funds and uses of funds will likely be classified as rate sensitive. Thus, the gap will be close to zero, implying that the bank is not exposed to interest rate risk. Yet, there is a difference in the *degree* of rate sensitivity between the bank's sources and uses of funds. The rates paid by the bank on its sources of funds would change more frequently than rates earned on its uses of funds. Thus, the bank's net interest margin would likely be reduced during periods of rising interest rates. This reduction would not be detected by the gap measurement.

DURATION MEASUREMENT.   An alternative approach to assess interest rate risk is to measure duration. Some assets or liabilities are more rate sensitive than others, even if the frequency of adjustment and maturity are equal. The value of a 10-year zero-coupon bond is more sensitive to interest rate fluctuations than a 10-year bond that pays coupon payments (as was demonstrated in Chapter 3). Thus, the market value of assets in a bank that invested in zero-coupon bonds would be very susceptible to interest rate movements. The duration measurement can capture these different degrees of sensitivity. In recent years, banks and other financial institutions have used the concept of **duration** to measure the sensitivity of their assets to interest rate movements. There are various measurements for an asset's duration, one of the more common being

$$\text{DUR} = \frac{\sum_{t=1}^{n} \frac{C_t(t)}{(1 + i)^t}}{\sum_{t=1}^{n} \frac{C_t}{(1 + i)^t}}$$

where C_t represents the interest or principal payments of the asset, t is the time at which the payments are provided, and i is the asset's yield to maturity. As an example, a bond with a $1,000 par value offering an 8 percent coupon rate with a yield to maturity of 14 percent and three years to maturity has a duration of

$$\text{DUR} = \frac{\dfrac{\$80(1)}{(1 + .14)^1} + \dfrac{\$80(2)}{(1 + .14)^2} + \dfrac{\$80(3)}{(1 + .14)^3} + \dfrac{\$1,000(3)}{(1 + .14)^3}}{\dfrac{\$80}{(1 + .14)^1} + \dfrac{\$80}{(1 + .14)^2} + \dfrac{\$80}{(1 + .14)^3} + \dfrac{\$1,000}{(1 + .14)^3}}$$

$$= \frac{\$70.18 + \$123.11 + \$161.99 + \$2,024.91}{\$70.18 + \$61.55 + \$54.00 + \$674.97}$$

$$= \frac{\$2{,}380.19}{\$860.70}$$

$$= 2.76$$

For comparison, the duration of a zero-coupon bond with the same 14 percent yield to maturity and three years to maturity has a duration of

$$DUR = \frac{\dfrac{\$0(1)}{(1+.14)^1} + \dfrac{\$0(2)}{(1+.14)^2} + \dfrac{\$0(3)}{(1+.14)^3} + \dfrac{\$1{,}000(3)}{(1+.14)^3}}{\dfrac{\$0}{(1+.14)^1} + \dfrac{\$0}{(1+.14)^2} + \dfrac{\$0}{(1+.14)^3} + \dfrac{\$1{,}000}{(1+.14)^3}}$$

$$= \frac{\$2{,}024.91}{\$674.97}$$

$$= 3.0$$

The duration of the zero-coupon bond is always equal to the bond's maturity, whereas that of a coupon bond is always less than the bond's maturity. Duration essentially converts the coupon bond into a measure that can be compared to the zero-coupon bond. In the preceding example, the zero-coupon bond's duration is 1.087 times the coupon bond's duration (computed as 3.00 divided by 2.76). This implies that the zero-coupon bond is 1.087 times as interest rate sensitive as the coupon bond.

Other things being equal, assets with shorter maturities have shorter durations; also, assets that generate more frequent coupon payments have shorter durations than those that generate less frequent payments. The duration of an asset portfolio is equal to the weighted average of the duration of individual components (the weights measure the proportional market value of each component). Banks and other financial institutions concerned with interest rate risk use duration to compare the rate sensitivity of their entire asset and liability portfolios. They can attempt to create liability durations that conform to their asset duration. Because duration is especially critical for savings and loan associations (S&Ls), a numerical example of measuring the duration of an S&L's entire asset and liability portfolio is provided in Chapter 20.

Although duration is a valuable technique for comparing the rate sensitivity of various securities, its capabilities are limited when applied to assets that can be terminated on a moment's notice. For example, consider a bank that offers a fixed-rate five-year loan that can be paid off early without penalty. If the loan is not paid off early, it is perceived as rate insensitive. Yet, there is the possibility that the loan will be terminated anytime over the five-year period. In this case, the bank would reinvest the funds at a rate dependent on market rates at that time. Thus, the funds used to provide the loan *can* be sensitive to interest rate movements, but the degree of sensitivity depends on when the loan is paid off. In general, loan prepayments are more common when market rates decline, because borrowers refinance by obtaining lower rate loans to pay off existing loans. The point here is that the possibility of prepayment makes it impossible to perfectly match the rate sensitivity of assets and liabilities.

REGRESSION ANALYSIS. The two methods described for assessing interest rate risk are based on the bank's balance sheet composition. An alternative method would be to simply determine how performance has historically been influenced by interest rate movements. To do this, a proxy must be identified for bank performance and for prevailing interest rates, and a model that can estimate the relationship between the proxies must be chosen. A common proxy for performance is return on assets, return on equity, or the percentage change in stock price. A common proxy for interest rates is any market-dominated rate, such as the Treasury bill yield. To determine how performance is affected by interest rates, regression analysis can be applied to historical data. For example, using Treasury bill yields (Y_T) as the interest rate proxy, the S&P 500 stock index as the market return (R_m), and the bank's stock return (R) as the performance proxy, the following regression model could be used:

$$R = B_0 + B_1 R_m + B_2 Y_T + u$$

where R_m is the return on the market, B_0, B_1, and B_2 are regression coefficients, and u is an error term. The regression coefficient B_2 in this model would suggest how the return is affected by interest rate movements. A positive (negative) coefficient would suggest that performance is favorably (adversely) affected by rising interest rates. If the coefficient is not significantly different from zero, this would suggest that the bank's stock returns are insulated from interest rate movements.

Models similar to that described above have been tested for the portfolio of all publicly traded banks to determine whether bank stock levels are affected by interest rate movements. The vast majority of this research has found that bank stock levels are inversely related to interest rate movements (the B_2 coefficient is negative and significant). These results can be attributed to the common imbalance in a bank's rate-sensitive liabilities versus assets. Because banks tend to have a negative gap (their liabilities are more rate sensitive than their assets), rising interest rates reduce bank performance. These results are generalized for the banking industry, and do not apply to every bank.

Because a bank's assets and liabilities are replaced over time, exposure to interest rate risk must be continually reassessed. As exposure changes, the reaction of bank performance to a particular interest rate pattern will change.

Methods to Reduce Interest Rate Risk

Interest rate risk has been monitored by banks since the late 1970s, as interest rate movements have been very volatile. Interest rate risk can be reduced by

- Maturity matching
- Using floating-rate loans
- Using interest rate futures contracts
- Using interest rate swaps

MATURITY MATCHING. One obvious method of reducing interest rate risk is to match each deposit's maturity with an asset of the same maturity. For example, if the bank receives funds for a one-year CD, it could provide a one-year loan or invest in a security with a one-year maturity. Although this strategy would avoid interest rate risk, it could not be effectively implemented. Banks receive a large volume of short-term deposits and would not be able to match up maturities on deposits with the longer loan maturities. Borrowers rarely request funds for a period as short as one month, or even six months. In addition, the deposit amounts are typically small relative to the loan amounts. A bank would have difficulty in combining deposits with a particular maturity to accommodate a loan request with the same maturity.

A recent study by Mitchell found that banks of all sizes have reduced the maturity of their assets since 1979. Thus, even though interest rates were more volatile in the 1980s, banks reduced their exposure to interest rate movements by reducing the difference between their asset and liability maturities.

USING FLOATING-RATE LOANS. An alternative solution is the use of the floating-rate loan, which allows banks to support long-term assets with short-term deposits without overly exposing themselves to interest rate risk. Floating-rate loans cannot, however, completely eliminate the risk. If the cost of funds is changing on a more frequent basis than the rate on assets, the bank's net interest margin is still affected by interest rate fluctuations.

When banks reduce their exposure to interest rate risk by replacing long-term securities with more floating-rate commercial loans, they increase their exposure to default risk, because the commercial loans provided by banks typically have a higher frequency of default than securities held by banks. In addition, bank liquidity risk would increase, because loans are not as marketable as securities.

USING INTEREST RATE FUTURES CONTRACTS. Another method of reducing interest rate risk is to use interest rate futures contracts, which lock in the price at which specified financial instruments can be purchased or sold on a specified future settlement date. For example, there are futures contracts available on CDs. When banks lock in the price at which they can sell CDs for a particular settlement date, this effectively locks in their cost of obtaining these funds. Consequently, their overall cost of future funds is somewhat insulated from interest rate movements.

Exhibit 17.3 illustrates how the use of financial futures contracts can reduce the uncertainty about a bank's net interest margin. The sale of CD futures, for example, reduces the potential adverse effect of rising interest rates on its interest expenses. Yet, it also reduces the potential favorable effect of declining interest rates on its interest expenses. Assuming that the bank initially had more rate-sensitive liabilities, its use of futures would reduce its gap and therefore reduce the impact of interest rates on its net interest margin.

A study by Koppenhaver found evidence that banks whose liabilities are more rate sensitive can benefit considerably from hedging with interest rate futures contracts. This study found that interest rate futures can reduce the variability of profits by as much as 80 percent.

USING INTEREST RATE SWAPS. Commercial banks can hedge interest rate risk by engaging in an interest rate swap, which is an arrangement to exchange periodic cash flows based on specified interest rates. A fixed-for-floating swap allows one party to periodically exchange fixed cash flows for cash flows that are based on prevailing market interest rates.

A bank whose liabilities are more rate sensitive than its assets can swap payments with a fixed interest rate in exchange for payments with a variable

EXHIBIT 17.3

Effect of Financial Futures on the Expected Spread of Banks That Have More Rate-Sensitive Liabilities Than Assets

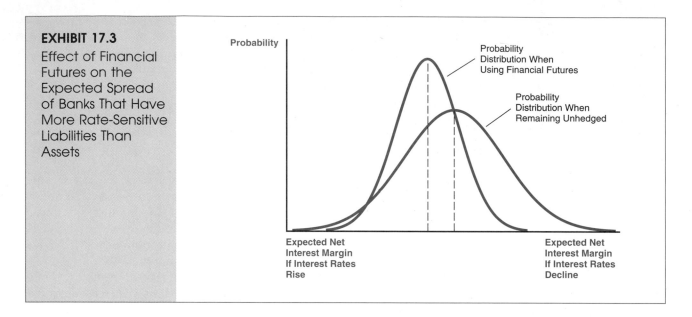

interest rate over a specified period of time. If interest rates rise, the bank benefits because the payments to be received from the swap will increase while its outflow payments are fixed. This can offset the adverse impact of rising interest rates on the bank's net interest margin. In the early 1990s interest rates were unusually low, causing banks such as First Union to take swap positions that protected against a possible increase in interest rates. Chemical Banking Corp. used interest rate swaps to benefit from declining interest rates. By 1993, Chemical became more concerned that interest rates could rise and reduced its exposure to interest rate risk.

An interest rate swap requires another party that is willing to provide variable-rate payments in exchange for fixed-rate payments. Financial institutions that have more rate-sensitive assets than liabilities may be willing to assume such a position, because they could reduce their exposure to interest rate movements in this manner. A financial intermediary is typically needed to match up the two parties that desire an interest rate swap. Some investment banking firms and large commercial banks serve in this role.

MANAGING EXPOSURE TO DEFAULT RISK

Most of a bank's funds are used either to make loans or to purchase debt securities. For either use of funds, the bank is acting as a creditor and is subject to default risk. In this context, default risk refers to the possibility that loans provided by the bank will not be repaid or that securities purchased by the bank will not be honored. The types of loans provided and securities purchased will determine the overall default risk of the asset portfolio.

If a bank wants to minimize default risk, it can use most of its funds to purchase Treasury securities, which are virtually free of default risk. However, these securities may not generate a much higher yield than the average overall cost of obtaining funds. In fact, some bank sources of funds can be more costly to banks than the yield earned on Treasury securities.

At the other extreme, a bank concerned with maximizing its return could use most of its funds for consumer and small business loans. Yet such an asset portfolio would be subject to a high degree of default risk. If economic conditions deteriorate, a relatively large amount of high-risk loans may default.

The ideal objective for managing assets is to simultaneously maximize return on assets and minimize default risk. But, obviously, both objectives cannot be achieved simultaneously. The return on any bank asset depends on the risk involved. Because riskier assets offer higher returns, a bank's strategy to increase its return on assets will typically entail an increase in the overall default risk of its asset portfolio.

Because a bank cannot simultaneously maximize return and minimize default risk, it must compromise. That is, it will select some assets that generate high returns but are subject to a relatively high degree of default risk and also some assets that are very safe but offer a lower rate of return. This way the bank attempts to earn a *reasonable* return on its overall asset portfolio and maintain default risk at a *tolerable* level. What return level is reasonable? What level of default risk is tolerable? There is no consensus on these answers. The actual degree of importance attached to a high return versus low default risk is dependent on the risk-return preferences of a bank's shareholders and managers.

Many banks have increased their credit card business in recent years. Because banks charge higher rates on financing credit card accounts than on most other loans, they can boost their expected return by increasing their credit card business. This is a typical example of increasing default risk in the attempt to increase return. Many banks have become more lenient in their credit standards in order to generate a greater amount of credit card business. Consequently, more undeserving consumers have obtained credit cards, and the delinquency rate has increased. For those banks that were too lenient, the wide spread between the return on credit card loans and the cost of funds has been offset by a high level of bad debt (default) expenses.

The relative default risk incurred by banks can be assessed by comparing the respective compositions of their asset portfolios. However, publicly available information does not provide a complete breakdown on asset composition. We can determine from financial statements the bank's securities as the percentage of total assets and loans as a percentage of total assets. But we are not provided information about the risk levels of loans offered by the bank or of securities purchased. Normally, a higher percentage of loans is perceived as more risky. Nevertheless, a bank with a greater percentage of loans could exhibit less default risk than a bank more heavily concentrated in securities if the former bank's loans are directed to very creditworthy firms while the latter bank's security holdings are somewhat risky.

Over time, economic conditions change and can cause banks to adjust their asset portfolios accordingly. For example, banks generally reduce loans and increase their purchases of low-risk securities during recessionary periods. In addition, they tend to provide a larger than normal volume of loans during an economic upswing.

Measuring Default Risk

An important part of managing default risk is to measure it. This requires a credit assessment of loan applicants. A bank employs a staff of credit analysts to review the financial information of corporations applying for loans. From the review, the staff prepares an evaluation of the firm's creditworthiness. The evaluation should indicate the probability that the firm can meet its loan payments so that a decision can be made as to whether the firm should be granted the loan. If a loan is to be granted, the evaluation can be used to determine the appropriate interest rate. The loan applicants deserving of a loan may be rated on a basis of 1 to 5 (1 being the highest quality), which reflects the degree of default risk. The rating will dictate the premium to be added to the base rate. For example, a rating of 5 may dictate a 2 percent premium above the prime rate, while a rating of 3 may dictate a 1 percent premium. Given the current prime rate along with a rating of the potential borrower, the loan rate can be determined.

Some loans to high-quality (low-risk) customers are commonly offered at rates below the prime rate. This does not necessarily imply that banks have reduced their spread. It may instead imply that the banks have redefined the prime rate to represent the appropriate loan rate for borrowers with a moderate risk rating. Thus, a discount would be attached to the prime rate when determining the loan rate for borrowers with a superior rating.

Each bank has its own formula for setting loan rates. Some banks may use their cost of funds rather than the prime rate as a base. They would attach larger premiums to their base, because the cost of funds will typically be at least 2 percent below the prime rate. Thus, a rating of 3 may translate to a loan rate of "cost of funds + 3 percent" (rather than the 1 percent premium if the prime rate is used as the base).

Diversifying Default Risk

Although all consumer and commercial loans exhibit some default risk, there are methods by which this risk can be managed. Banks should diversify their loans to ensure that their customers are not dependent on a common source of income. For example, a bank in a small farming town that provides consumer loans to farmers and commercial loans to farm equipment manufacturers is highly susceptible to default risk. If the farmers experience a bad growing season because of poor weather conditions, they may be unable to repay their consumer loans. Furthermore, the farm equipment manufacturers would simultaneously experience a drop in sales and may be unable to repay their commercial loans.

This example is one of obvious mismanagement of the loan portfolio. In some cases, the mismanagement may not be so obvious. For example, consider a bank within a city that provides most of its commercial loans to firms in that city and has diversified its loans across various industries to avoid the problem just described. Assume that this city is the home of a large naval base. If for some reason, the servicepeople employed at that base are sent out to sea, the city's firms may not be able to generate sufficient business to repay their loans. This example illustrates how corporate borrowers from different industries but from the same geographic region can be similarly affected by a particular event.

APPLYING PORTFOLIO THEORY TO LOAN PORTFOLIOS. The benefits of proper loan diversification can be recognized when applying portfolio theory to a bank's asset portfolio. The risk of an asset portfolio is sometimes measured as the variability in the portfolio's returns, as this proxy indicates the degree of uncertainty about the portfolio returns. The variance (σ_p^2) of an asset portfolio's returns can be written as:

$$\sigma_p^2 = \sum_{i=1}^{n} \sum_{j=1}^{n} w_i w_j COV(r_i, r_j)$$

for a portfolio of n assets, where w_1 and w_j represent the proportion of funds allocated to the ith and jth assets respectively, and $COV(r_i, r_j)$ represents the covariance between returns of the ith and jth assets. The covariance measures the degree to which the asset returns covary, or move in tandem. Because the covariance of any pair of asset returns is equal to the correlation coefficient between those asset returns (ρ_{ij}) times the standard deviation of each asset's returns (σ_i, σ_j) the portfolio variance can be rewritten as:

$$\sigma_\rho^2 = \sum_{i=1}^{n} \sum_{j=1}^{n} w_i w_j \rho_{ij} \sigma_i \sigma_j$$

From this equation, the portfolio variance is positively related to the correlations between asset returns. If a bank's loans are driven by one particular economic factor (such as real estate prices in a particular region), the returns on the loans will be highly correlated. Thus, the returns of most loans will be high (few loan defaults) under favorable real estate conditions, or poor (many loan defaults) under unfavorable real estate conditions.

To reduce risk, the bank must provide loans whose default risk levels (and therefore returns) are not highly dependent on the regional real estate market. It may consider providing real estate loans outside its main region, but the default risk levels of real estate loans across regions will be correlated if real estate conditions across the regions are correlated. Thus, the bank should consider other types of loans, such as specific commercial loans and consumer loans that are unrelated to real estate conditions. The bank should also consider investing in securities, such as high-quality corporate bonds. However, it should recognize that returns on these types of bonds could be correlated with the returns on some of its loans. That is, defaults on these corporate bonds may be driven by the same economic conditions that cause loan defaults.

When a bank's loans are too heavily concentrated in one particular industry, the bank can reduce its exposure by selling some of those loans in the secondary market. Most loan sales enable the bank originating the loan to continue servicing the loan by collecting payments and monitoring the borrower's collateral. However, the bank that originated the loan is no longer funding the loan, and the loan is therefore removed from the bank's assets. Bank loans are commonly purchased by other banks and some other financial institutions, such as pension funds and insurance companies, and some mutual funds.

The possible benefits from geographic loan diversification can be seen by reviewing the correlations of regional production levels in Exhibit 17.4. A correlation coefficient between production levels was estimated for 12 different districts in the United States. The districts are numbered from 1 (in the Northeast) to 12 (the Far West), moving east to west. Notice from this exhibit that the correlations are generally high for any two districts next to each other (such as the correlation between Districts 1 and 2 = .812). This suggests that the production

EXHIBIT 17.4   Correlations of Production Levels across Federal Reserve Districts

District	DISTRICT										
	2	3	4	5	6	7	8	9	10	11	12
1	.812	.634	.436	.426	.288	.318	.372	.055	−.220	−.312	.133
2		.881	.615	.789	.675	.515	.620	.337	.113	.099	.197
3			.886	.961	.886	.819	.892	.707	.483	.454	.528
4				.873	.797	.975	.960	.851	.633	.607	.821
5					.961	.823	.916	.782	.646	.648	.570
6						.742	.888	.796	.762	.749	.503
7							.945	.850	.622	.629	.847
8								.857	.705	.699	.751
9									.870	.805	.768
10										.937	.640
11											.622

*The variable measured is the deviation in the gross product per capita from the trend over the 1963–1986 period. A high correlation implies that the production level in the two districts is either above the norm or below the norm simultaneously. Each district is a Federal Reserve district.

SOURCE: *New England Economic Review* (May/June 1990): 14.

levels move closely in tandem. Thus, a bank that diversifies its loans within these two districts achieves only limited benefits, because any adverse conditions that cause high default rates could occur in both districts simultaneously. Conversely, production levels in districts that are far away from each other tend to have low correlations. Review the correlations between District 1 and other districts to confirm this.

Because the production level is a measure of economic conditions, it appears that the diversification of loans across districts throughout the United States could achieve significant risk reduction in the loan portfolio. Even if one or two districts experience financial problems in a particular period, the bank exposure to debt of firms in those regions would be limited when using a broad diversification policy. An economic recession would likely have an adverse effect on all districts. However, diversification can still reduce the overall exposure, because some districts may be less susceptible than others to a stagnant economy.

INTERNATIONAL DIVERSIFICATION OF LOANS.   It has sometimes been suggested that a bank can reduce its loan exposure to a recessionary economy by diversifying its loans among countries. For example, a U.S. bank could lend some of its funds to firms or governments in other countries. Therefore, only part of its loan portfolio would be exposed to a U.S. recession. Although this strategy deserves consideration, the international debt crisis in the early 1980s has dampened the desire by banks to implement it. During this crisis, several less developed countries (LDCs) could not repay the loans that were provided to them by U.S. banks. Many of these countries were simultaneously experiencing severe economic problems that were due in part to a worldwide recession in 1982.

EFFECT OF BANK ACQUISITIONS OF NONBANK FIRMS ON BANK RISK

It can be argued that bank acquisitions of nonbank firms (such as insurance, securities, or real estate firms) can diversify the product line and therefore reduce risk. However, a counterargument is that banks are not familiar with nonbank operations and cannot properly manage them. Thus, the risk of banks may increase following the acquisitions of nonbank firms. A recent study by Boyd, Graham, and Hewitt measured how bank risk was affected following acquisitions of nonbanks. Because the results can vary with the type of nonbank, nonbanks were partitioned into three subgroups: insurance firms, securities firms, and real estate firms. The study found that the bank acquisitions of insurance firms can result in lower risk. However, the bank acquisitions of securities firms or real estate firms tend to result in higher risk. These results suggest that risk reduction may only serve as a valid motive for acquiring insurance companies. The acquisitions of securities firms or real estate firms may still be worth considering if the motive is based on potential return rather than on risk reduction.

During this recession, the global demand for LDC exports was substantially reduced. Consequently, the LDC income was not sufficient to repay loans.

The international debt crisis suggests that international diversification of loans among countries does not always prevent the possibility of several simultaneous defaulted loans. The crisis was largely attributed to the similar economic cycles of these countries. If all borrowers around the world are similarly affected by specific events, international diversification of loans is not a viable solution.

In reality, diversifying loans across countries can often reduce the loan portfolio's exposure to any single economy or event. However, if the urge to diversify into geographic regions requires the acceptance of loan applicants with very high risk, the bank is defeating its purpose.

BANK CAPITAL MANAGEMENT

Like other corporations, banks must determine the level of capital that they should maintain. Bank operations are distinctly different from other types of firms because the majority of their assets (such as loans and security holdings) generate more predictable cash flows. Thus, banks can use a much higher degree of financial leverage than other types of firms. The Federal Deposit Insurance Corporation (FDIC), which insures depositors, bears most of the risk in the event of failure. Depositors that are fully insured may not penalize banks for taking excessive risk, which could encourage some banks to use a high degree of financial leverage.

Banks must also consider the minimum capital ratio required by regulators. This minimum could possibly force the bank to maintain more capital than what it believes is optimal. To please shareholders, banks typically attempt to maintain only the amount of capital that is sufficient to support bank operations. If they have too much capital as a result of issuing excessive amounts of stock, each shareholder will receive a smaller proportion of any distributed earnings.

A common measure of the return to the shareholders is the **return on equity** (ROE), measured as

$$\text{ROE} = \frac{\text{Net profit after taxes}}{\text{Equity}}$$

The term *equity* represents the bank's capital. The return on equity can be broken down as follows:

$$\text{ROE} = \text{Return on assets (ROA)} \times \text{Leverage measure}$$

$$\frac{\text{Net profit after taxes}}{\text{Equity}} = \frac{\text{Net profit after taxes}}{\text{Assets}} \times \frac{\text{Assets}}{\text{Equity}}$$

The ratio (assets/equity) is sometimes called the **leverage measure,** because leverage reflects the volume of assets a firm supports with equity. The greater the leverage measure, the greater the amount of assets per dollar's worth of equity. The above breakdown of ROE is useful because it can demonstrate how excessive capital can lower a bank's ROE. Consider two banks called Hilev and Lolev that each has a **return on assets (ROA)** of one percent. Hilev Bank has a leverage measure of 15, while Lolev Bank has a leverage measure of 10. The ROE for each bank is determined as follows:

$$\text{ROE} = \text{ROA} \times \text{leverage measure}$$
$$\text{ROE for Hilev Bank} = 1\% \times 15$$
$$= 15\%$$
$$\text{ROE for Lolev Bank} = 1\% \times 10$$
$$= 10\%$$

Even though each bank's assets are generating a one percent ROA, the ROE of Hilev Bank is much higher, because Hilev Bank is supporting its assets with a smaller proportion of capital. Bank regulators require banks to hold a minimum amount of capital, because capital can be used to absorb losses. Banks, however, generally prefer to hold a relatively low amount of capital for the reasons just expressed.

Because required capital is specified as a proportion of loans (and some other assets), banks can reduce the required level of capital by selling some of their loans in the secondary market. They can still service the loans to generate fee income but would be subject to a lower capital constraint as a result of removing loans from their asset portfolio.

If banks are holding an excessive amount of capital, they can reduce it by distributing a high percentage of their earnings to shareholders (as dividends). Thus, capital management is related to the bank's dividend policy.

A growing bank may need more capital to support construction of new buildings, purchases of office equipment, and so forth. It would therefore need to retain a larger proportion of its earnings than a bank that has no plans for future growth. If the growing bank preferred to provide existing shareholders with a sizable dividend, it would then have to obtain the necessary capital through issuing new stock. This strategy allows the bank to distribute dividends but dilutes proportional ownership of the bank. An obvious tradeoff exists here. The solution is not so obvious. A bank in need of capital must assess the tradeoff involved and enact a policy that it believes will maximize the wealth of shareholders.

MANAGEMENT BASED ON FORECASTS

Some banks will position themselves to significantly benefit from an expected change in the economy. Exhibit 17.5 provides possible policy decisions for four different forecasts and suggests how a bank might react to each. This exhibit is simplified in that it does not consider future economic growth and interest rate movements simultaneously. Furthermore, it does not consider other economic forecasts that would also be considered by banks. However, it illustrates the type of risk-return tradeoff constantly faced by bank managers. For example, if managers expected a strong economy, they could boost earnings by shifting into relatively risky loans and securities that pay a high return. If a strong economy does occur as expected, only a small percentage of the loans and securities will default, and the bank's strategy will result in improved earnings. However, if the bank's forecast turns out to be wrong, its revised asset portfolio will be more susceptible to a weak economy. The bank could be severely damaged during a

EXHIBIT 17.5   Bank Management of Liabilities and Assets Due to Economic Forecasts

ECONOMIC FORECAST BY THE BANKS	APPROPRIATE ADJUSTMENT TO LIABILITY STRUCTURE BASED ON THE FORECAST	APPROPRIATE ADJUSTMENT TO ASSET STRUCTURE BASED ON THE FORECAST	GENERAL ASSESSMENT OF BANK'S ADJUSTED BALANCE SHEET STRUCTURE
1. Strong economy		Concentrate more heavily on loans; reduce holdings of low-risk securities.	Increased potential for stronger earnings; increased exposure of bank earnings to default risk.
2. Weak economy		Concentrate more heavily on risk-free securities and low-risk loans; reduce holdings of risky loans.	Reduced default risk; reduced potential for stronger earnings if the economy does not weaken.
3. Increasing interest rates	Attempt to attract CDs with long-term maturities.	Apply floating-interest rates to loans whenever possible; avoid long-term securities.	Reduced interest rate risk; reduced potential for stronger earnings if interest rates decrease.
4. Decreasing interest rates	Attempt to attract CDs with short-term maturities.	Apply fixed-interest rates to loans whenever possible; concentrate on long-term securities or loans.	Increased potential for stronger earnings; increased interest rate risk.

weak economy, because several borrowers are likely to default on their loans and securities.

Other, more conservative banks could not have been as influenced by an inaccurate forecast of the economy if they maintained a sizable portion of very safe loans and securities. However, if the economy had strengthened as predicted, these banks would not have benefited. The degree to which a bank is willing to revise its balance sheet structure in accordance with economic forecasts depends on the confidence in those forecasts and its willingness to incur risk.

Because the first two forecasts shown in Exhibit 17.5 are on economic growth, they relate to default risk. The last two forecasts are on interest rates and therefore relate to interest rate risk. Banks cannot completely adjust their balance sheet structure in accordance with economic forecasts. For example, they cannot implement a policy of accepting only long-term CDs just because they believe interest rates will rise. Yet, they could attract a greater than normal amount of long-term CDs by offering an attractive interest rate on long-term CDs and advertising this rate to potential depositors.

The bank's balance sheet management will affect its performance (as measured from its income statement) in the following ways. First, its liability structure will influence its interest and noninterest expenses on the income statement. If it obtains a relatively large portion of its funds from conventional demand deposits, interest expenses should be relatively low, while its noninterest expenses (due to check clearing, processing, etc.) should be relatively high. A bank's asset structure can also affect expenses. If a bank maintains a relatively large portion of commercial loans, its noninterest expenses should be high because of the labor cost of assessing the borrower's credit along with loan-processing costs. Yet, banks with the heaviest concentration in commercial loans expect their additional interest revenues to more than offset the additional non-interest expenses incurred. Their strategy would pay off only if they can avoid a sizable number of defaulted loans. Of course, this is the risk they must take in striving for a high return.

Ideally, banks would use an aggressive approach when they can capitalize on favorable economic conditions but insulate themselves during adverse economic conditions. Because economic conditions cannot always be accurately forecasted for several years in advance, there will continue to be defaults on loans by even the well-managed banks. This is a cost of doing business. Banks attempt to use proper diversification so that a domino effect of defaulted loans will not occur within their loan portfolio. Similarly, interest rate movements cannot always be accurately forecasted. Thus, banks should not be overly aggressive in attempting to capitalize on interest rate forecasts. They should assess the sensitivity of their future performance to each possible interest rate scenario that could occur to ensure that their balance sheet is structured to survive any possible scenario.

Bank Restructuring to Manage Risks

Bank operations change in response to changing regulations and economic conditions, and to managerial policies designed to hedge various forms of risk. For example, in recent years banks have attempted to expand across state lines, have diversified their asset portfolios, have boosted their capital ratios, and have ex-

BANK ACQUISITION STRATEGY

Fleet Financial Group is a commercial bank based in Rhode Island that has capitalized on changing economic and regulatory conditions. During the early 1990s, many banks in the New England area experienced financial problems. In fact, Fleet experienced a loss of more than $70 million in 1990. However, Fleet has recovered and grown substantially by acquiring other banks that experienced financial problems. Its strategy has been to acquire bank operations that were similar to its own, so that it could reduce overhead. In this way, Fleet could spread overhead expenses over a larger amount of production, and therefore achieve economies of scale.

In 1991, Fleet acquired the Bank of New England, which was the largest bank in the area and was failing. In 1992, Fleet acquired seven banks, six of which were failing. In 1993 and 1994, Fleet continued its pursuit of banks that had been inefficiently managed in the past. Redundant operations (such as branches in the same location) were eliminated to create cost efficiencies.

Fleet has focused its acquisitions in areas where its prevailing operations are established, because there are more opportunities to remove redundancies. For example, after acquiring the Bank of New England, Fleet cut that bank's overhead costs by $300 million.

Fleet has considered bank acquisitions outside of the New England area, but expects that these acquisitions do not have the same potential for increasing efficiencies. However, growth outside the New England area would allow it to expand its focus on mortgage servicing and investment products. These nontraditional business lines enhanced Fleet's performance during the recession in the early 1990s, when loan demand was weak. Fleet expects its performance to improve even more if and when regulators allow banks to offer more securities services.

SOURCE: "Fast-Moving Fleet Pulls Ahead," *Bank Management*, June 1993, pp. 38–41.

panded their operations into services such as insurance, brokerage, underwriting of securities, and sales of mutual funds. Large changes in bank operations typically require restructuring, which normally must be assessed and approved by the bank's executives and board of directors.

Decisions to restructure are complex because of their effects on customers, shareholders, and employees. A strategic plan to satisfy customers and shareholders will not necessarily satisfy the majority of employees. During the early 1990s, many banks were downsizing their operations because their business declined in response to poor economic conditions. Downsizing forced consolidation of some divisions, and layoffs as well. Although downsizing may be unavoidable in some periods, the plan for restructuring should consider the potential effects on employee morale.

Bank Acquisitions

A common form of bank restructuring is growth through acquisitions of other banks. Growth can be achieved more quickly with acquisitions than by establishing

APPLIED RESEARCH

ARE BANK ACQUISITIONS WORTHWHILE?

Numerous studies have assessed the stock price reaction of banks that acquire other banks. If investors believe that the acquiring bank will benefit from the acquisition, the stock price should rise in response to the acquisition announcement. Most of the related studies have found that the acquiring banks experienced either no reaction or a negative stock price reaction. These results imply that the market does not expect the acquisition to be favorable. One possible explanation is that the acquiring banks will never achieve the expected efficiencies that motivated the acquisition. Second, personnel clashes among the units to be merged could result in high turnover and low morale. Third, the acquiring banks may simply be paying too much for the target banks.

Some recent studies have focused on the stock price reaction of banks that acquire failed banks. As an example, a study by Bertin, Ghazanfari, and Torabzadeh found that the acquiring banks experienced a favorable stock price reaction to these types of acquisitions. Perhaps the more favorable response to these acquisitions is attributed to the subsidy provided by the Federal Deposit Insurance Corporation (FDIC). From the FDIC's perspective, the subsidy may be less than its net payout if the failed bank is liquidated. This study also assessed how the share price reactions across the acquiring banks were affected by firm-specific characteristics. The most interesting finding was that the stock price reaction was higher for acquiring banks that had a higher proportion of outside membership on the board. That is, the announced acquisition was more favorably received for those acquiring banks that had a smaller proportion of their employees (inside members) on the board. This implies that investors may be concerned about an agency problem, in which employees make decisions for themselves rather than for the firm. When a board consists of a higher proportion of employees, there is a greater probability that an acquisition will be undertaken in the interests of those employees rather than the interests of the shareholders.

The studies discussed so far focused on the immediate share price response to announced acquisitions. Another way of determining whether the acquisitions are worthwhile is to measure long-term effects following the acquisitions. A recent study by Madura and Wiant detected adverse share price effects of the acquirer banks over a 36-month period following large acquisitions. This may occur because the price paid for targets is too high, or because the restructuring that occurs after the acquisition results in more costs or fewer benefits than were initially anticipated. The implications of this research are that acquisitions will be more beneficial for banks that use realistic assessments of the efficiencies that can be gained from acquiring potential targets.

new branches. Furthermore, many states do not allow out-of-state banks to establish new branches, but do allow these banks to acquire local banks.

There are several potential advantages of bank acquisitions. First, some banks may be able to achieve economies of scale by acquiring other banks. If the costs of some operations are mostly fixed, an increase in the size of those operations should create efficiencies because the costs in proportion to total assets decline. A related advantage is that bank acquisitions can remove redundant operations. For example, if branches of the acquiring bank are right next to branches of the target bank, some of these branches can be closed without a loss of convenience to customers.

Bank acquisitions can also achieve diversification benefits as the acquirer can offer loans in some new industries. Furthermore, an acquiring bank may have some managerial advantages over a target, which should allow the acquirer to improve the target's performance after the acquisition.

Along with the potential advantages, there are some potential disadvantages associated with bank acquisitions. First, some acquisitions are motivated by highly optimistic projections of the cost efficiencies that will result from combining the operations of the target and acquirer. Thus, the price that an acquirer pays for the target bank can be excessive. Second, there can be significant employee morale problems and high employee turnover following an acquisition, as operations are reorganized.

In general, research has found that the value of the merger between banks exceeds the sum of the individual bank values. However, most of the benefits typically accrue to the target bank, as its share price is bid up substantially at the time of the acquisition. Thus, the target's shareholders benefit from the acquisition more than the acquirer's shareholders.

INTEGRATED BANK MANAGEMENT

Bank management of assets, liabilities, and capital is integrated. A bank's asset growth can be achieved only if it obtains the necessary funds. Furthermore, growth may require an investment in fixed assets (such as additional offices) that will require an accumulation of bank capital. Integration of asset, liability, and capital management ensures that all policies will be consistent with a cohesive set of economic forecasts. An integrated management approach is necessary to manage liquidity risk, interest rate risk, and default risk.

Example

Assume that you are hired as a consultant by Atlanta Bank to evaluate its favorable and unfavorable aspects. Atlanta Bank's balance sheet is disclosed in Exhibit 17.6. A bank's balance sheet can best be evaluated by adjusting the actual dollar amounts of balance sheet components to a percentage of assets. This conversion allows for a comparison of the bank with its competitors. Exhibit 17.7 shows each balance sheet component as a percentage of total assets for Atlanta Bank (derived from Exhibit 17.6). To the right of each bank percentage is the assumed industry average percentage for a sample of banks with a similar amount of assets. For example, the bank's required reserves are 4 percent of assets (same as the industry average), its floating-rate commercial loans are 30 percent of assets (versus an industry average of 20 percent), and so on. The same type of comparison is provided for liabilities and capital on the right side of the exhibit. A comparative analysis relative to the industry can indicate the management style of Atlanta Bank.

It is possible to evaluate the potential level of interest revenues, interest expenses, noninterest revenues, and noninterest expenses for Atlanta Bank relative to the industry. Furthermore, it is possible to assess the bank's exposure to default risk and interest rate risk as compared to the industry.

A summary of Atlanta Bank based on the information in Exhibit 17.7 is provided in Exhibit 17.8. Although its interest expenses are expected to be above the industry average, so are its interest revenues. Thus, it is difficult to determine whether Atlanta Bank's net interest margin will be above or below the industry average. Because it is more heavily concentrated in risky loans and securities, its default risk is higher than the average bank; yet, its interest rate risk is less

EXHIBIT 17.6 Balance Sheet of Atlanta Bank (in Millions of Dollars)

ASSETS			LIABILITIES AND CAPITAL		
Required reserves		$ 400	Demand deposits		$ 500
Commercial loans			NOW accounts		1,200
Floating-rate	3,000		MMDAs		2,000
Fixed-rate	1,100		CDs		
Total		4,100	Short-term	1,500	
Consumer loans		2,500	From 1 to 5 yrs	4,000	
Mortages			Total		5,500
Floating-rate	500		Long-term bonds		200
Fixed-rate	None		CAPITAL		600
Total		500			
Treasury securities					
Short-term	1,000				
Long-term	None				
Total		1,000			
Corporate securities					
High-rated	None				
Moderate-rated	1,000				
Total		1,000			
Municipal securities					
High-rated	None				
Moderate-rated	None				
Total		None			
Fixed assets		500			
TOTAL ASSETS		$10,000	TOTAL LIABILITIES AND CAPITAL		$10,000

because of its relatively high concentration of medium-term CDs and floating-rate loans. A gap measurement of Atlanta Bank can be conducted by first identifying the rate-sensitive liabilities and assets, as follows:

RATE-SENSITIVE ASSETS	AMOUNT (IN MILLIONS)	RATE-SENSITIVE LIABILITIES	AMOUNT (IN MILLIONS)
Floating-rate loans	$3,000	NOW accounts	1,200
Floating-rate mortgages	500	MMDAs	2,000
Short-term Treasury securities	1,000	Short-term CDs	1,500
	4,500		4,700

EXHIBIT 17.7 Comparative Balance Sheet of Atlanta Bank

ASSETS			LIABILITIES AND CAPITAL		
	Percentage of Assets for Atlanta Bank	Average Percentage for Industry		Percentage of Total for Atlanta Bank	Average Percentage for Industry
Required reserves	4%	4%			
Commercial loans			Demand deposits	5%	17%
Floating-rate	30	20	NOW accounts	12	10
Fixed-rate	11	11	MMDAs	20	20
Total	41	31			
Consumer loans	25	20	CDs		
			Short-term	15	35
Mortgages			From 1 to 5 yrs	40	10
Floating-rate	5	7	Total	55	45
Fixed-rate	0	3			
Total	5	10	Long-term bonds	2	2
Treasury securities			CAPITAL	6	6
Short-term	10	7			
Long-term	0	8			
Total	10	15			
Corporate securities					
High-rated	0	5			
Moderate-rated	10	5			
Total	10	10			
Municipal securities					
High-rated	0	3			
Moderate-rated	0	2			
Total	0	5			
Fixed assets	5	5			
TOTAL ASSETS	100%	100%	TOTAL LIABILITIES and CAPITAL	100%	100%

$$\text{Gap} = \$4{,}500 \text{ million} - \$4{,}700 \text{ million}$$

$$= -\$200 \text{ million}$$

$$\text{Gap ratio} = \frac{\$4{,}500 \text{ million}}{\$4{,}700 \text{ million}}$$

$$\approx .957$$

The gap measurements suggest somewhat similar rate sensitivity on both sides of the balance sheet.

The future performance of Atlanta Bank relative to the industry depends on future economic conditions. If interest rates rise, it will be more insulated than other banks. If interest rates fall, other banks will likely benefit to a greater

EXHIBIT 17.8 Evaluation of Atlanta Bank Based on Its Balance Sheet

EXPENSES	MAIN INFLUENTIAL COMPONENTS	EVALUATION OF ATLANTA BANK RELATIVE TO INDUSTRY
Interest expenses	All liabilities except demand deposits.	Higher than industry average because it concentrates more on high-rate deposits than the norm.
Noninterest expenses	Loan volume and checkable deposit volume.	Questionable; its checkable deposit volume is less than the norm, but its loan volume is greater than the norm.
Interest revenues	Volume and composition of loans and securities.	Potentially higher than industry average because its assets are generally riskier than the norm.
Exposure to default risk	Volume and composition of loans and securities.	Higher concentration of loans than industry average; it has a greater percentage of risky assets than the norm.
Exposure to interest rate risk	Maturities on liabilities and assets; use of floating-rate loans.	Lower than the industry average; it has more medium-term liabilities, fewer assets with very long maturities, and more floating-rate loans.

degree. Under conditions of a strong economy, Atlanta Bank would likely benefit more than other banks because of its aggressive lending approach. Conversely, an economic slowdown could cause more loan defaults, and Atlanta Bank would be more susceptible to possible defaults than other banks. This could be confirmed only if more details were provided (such as a more comprehensive breakdown of the balance sheet).

EXAMPLES OF BANK MISMANAGEMENT

Poor bank management will lead to subpar performance or possibly even failure. To illustrate the financial problems that can result, the actual situations for four large well-known banks are summarized below.

Franklin National Bank

Franklin National Bank used an aggressive management approach during the late 1960s and early 1970s. It provided fixed-rate long-term loans to customers with a questionable credit standing. The funds obtained to support these loans were of a short-term nature and therefore were rate sensitive. Overall, the bank had a high exposure to default risk and interest rate risk. As interest rates began to increase, the rate-sensitive liabilities became more expensive while the interest payments received on long-term fixed rate assets were unaffected. In addition, a substantial number of the risky loans defaulted.

In 1973 a deposit run on the bank occurred as the bank's financial problems were realized by the public, subjecting the bank to high liquidity risk. Meanwhile, the bank took speculative positions in foreign exchange in an effort to offset its other losses. Again, the aggressive action backfired as the values of its foreign exchange positions declined, and Franklin National Bank failed in 1974. It has often been suggested that this bank failed because of its foreign exchange dealings. Although this was the final nail in the coffin, other managerial decisions related to default risk and interest rate risk led to its initial problems.

First Pennsylvania Bank

First Pennsylvania Bank used an aggressive management approach over the 1970s. It provided a substantial volume of loans in the early 1970s to customers whose creditworthiness was questionable. The 1974–1975 recession caused massive business failures and led to a high default percentage on its loans. In addition, First Pennsylvania implemented a balance sheet management approach in the mid-1970s that concentrated on rate-sensitive liabilities (short-term deposits) and rate-insensitive assets. Because interest rates increased substantially, the cost of the rate-sensitive liabilities increased, while the interest revenues on rate-insensitive assets were generally unaffected. Financial problems due to these management errors led to a run on deposits (causing high liquidity risk), and the FDIC subsequently intervened to remedy the financial problems and reorganize the bank.

Penn Square Bank

Penn Square Bank used an aggressive lending approach of heavily concentrating on energy-related loans in the late 1970s and early 1980s. These loans were used by corporations to explore and produce various forms of energy. Because of the decline in energy prices in 1981 and 1982, many energy-related ventures no longer appeared feasible. The initially forecasted return on such ventures was based on overly optimistic market prices of energy. In addition, the collateral on these loans was deficient. When borrowers were unable to repay loans, Penn Square commonly "rolled" interest into its existing loans. That is, it would provide a new loan to borrowers that would be used to pay principal and interest on prevailing loans. Then these prevailing loans were recorded as paid rather than overdue (this strategy has also been used by large banks on loans to less developed countries). Penn Square could not afford to roll interest into the growing number of nonperforming loans, and it failed in 1982.

Continental Illinois Bank

Continental Illinois Bank experienced sizable defaults on its loans in the early 1980s. A portion of these defaults were due to loan participations whereby Continental provided loans for energy-related ventures originated by Penn Square Bank. Like the loans made by Penn Square, the loans by Continental in which Penn Square acted as the agent also defaulted. Although Penn Square originated the loans, Continental was held responsible for ensuring that the loan customers were creditworthy. As news of Continental's financial problems became widespread in 1983, those depositors with deposit amounts exceeding the $100,000 insurable limit began to withdraw their funds. Because Continental heavily relied on large depositors for its funds, its deposit level declined dramatically. This liquidity risk compounded Continental's problems, and the FDIC subsequently intervened to rescue the troubled bank.

Bank of New England

The Bank of New England concentrated heavily on real estate loans during a real estate boom in the mid-1980s. However, overbuilding and a reduction in economic growth caused real estate prices to decline. Consequently, many loans provided for the development of commercial real estate defaulted. Although numerous banks in New England were adversely affected by the economic conditions, the Bank of New England was more exposed because of its heavy concentration in real estate loans. It experienced massive losses in 1990 and was acquired by Fleet/Norstar Financial Group Inc. (with some financial support from the FDIC) in 1991.

Implications of Bank Mismanagement

The preceding examples are not meant to imply that banks should always implement ultraconservative strategies. In such a competitive environment, conservative management can cause a bank to fall behind its competitors. However, a proper balance should be maintained. The aggressive lending approaches used by the banks described left the banks severely exposed to default risk. Furthermore, a wide gap between the amount of rate-sensitive liabilities and assets is extremely risky, especially given the volatility of interest rates over time. Banks can provide a moderate amount of high-yielding loans and maintain a moderate gap based on their interest rate forecast without overexposing themselves to the possibility of failure. These examples of bank mismanagement demonstrate the consequences of being overexposed to an inaccurate forecast. Obviously, a correct forecast may have allowed these banks to experience very high performance levels. Yet, the most successful banks over the past several years have not been overly aggressive.

SUMMARY

- The underlying goal of bank management is to maximize the wealth of the bank's shareholders, which implies maximizing the price of the bank's stock.

- Banks manage liquidity by maintaining some liquid assets such as short-term securities, and ensuring easy access to funds (through the federal funds market, or the discount window).

- Banks measure their sensitivity to interest rate movements to assess their exposure to interest rate risk. Common methods of measuring interest rate risk include gap measurement and duration measurement. Some banks use regression analysis to determine the sensitivity of their earnings or stock returns to interest rate movements.

  Banks can reduce their interest rate risk by matching maturities of their assets and liabilities, or by using floating-rate loans to create more rate sensitivity in their assets. Alternatively, they may use interest rate futures contracts or interest rate swaps instead. If they are adversely affected by rising interest rates, they could sell financial futures contracts or engage in a swap of fixed-rate payments for floating-rate payments.

■ Banks manage default risk by carefully assessing the borrowers who apply for loans. They also diversify their loans across borrowers of different regions and industries so that the loan portfolio is not heavily susceptible to financial problems in any single region or industry.

■ Banks attempt to maintain sufficient capital to satisfy regulatory constraints. However, they generally prefer to avoid holding excessive capital because a high level of capital can reduce their return on equity. If banks need to raise capital, they can attempt to retain more earnings (reduce dividends) or issue new stock.

QUESTIONS

1. What is accomplished when a bank integrates its liability management with its asset management?

2. Given the liquidity advantage of holding Treasury bills, why do banks hold only a relatively small portion of their assets as Treasury bills?

3. How do banks resolve illiquidity problems?

4. If a bank expects interest rates to decrease over time, how might it alter the degree of rate sensitivity on its assets and liabilities?

5. List some rate-sensitive assets and some rate-insensitive assets of banks.

6. If a bank is very uncertain about future interest rates, how might it insulate its future performance from future interest rate movements?

7. Define the formula for the net interest margin and explain why it is closely monitored by banks.

8. Assume that a bank expects to attract most of its funds through short-term CDs and would prefer to use most of its funds to provide long-term loans. How could it achieve this and still reduce interest rate risk?

9. According to this chapter, have banks been able to insulate themselves against interest rate movements? Explain.

10. Define a bank's gap and what it attempts to determine. Interpret a negative gap.

11. What are some limitations of measuring a bank's gap?

12. How do banks use the duration measurement?

13. Why do loans that can be prepaid on a moment's notice complicate the bank's assessment of interest rate risk?

14. Can a bank simultaneously maximize return and minimize default risk? If not, what can be done instead?

15. As economic conditions change, how do banks adjust their asset portfolio?

16. In what two ways should a bank properly diversify its loans? Why?

17. Is international diversification of loans a viable solution to default risk? Defend your answer.

18. Do all commercial borrowers receive the same interest rate on loans? Explain.

19. Why might a bank retain some excess earnings rather than distribute them as dividends?

20. If a bank has more rate-sensitive liabilities than rate-sensitive assets, what will happen to its net interest margin during a period of rising interest rates? During a period of declining interest rates?

21. Does the use of floating-rate loans eliminate interest rate risk? Explain.

22. What were the reasons for Franklin National Bank's failure?

Problems

1. Suppose a bank earns $201 million in interest revenue but pays $156 million in interest expense. It also has $800 million in earning assets. What is its net interest margin?

2. If a bank earns $169 million net profit after tax and has $17 billion invested in assets, what is its return on assets?

3. If a bank earns $75 million net profits after tax and has $7.5 billion invested in assets and $600 million equity investment, what is its return on equity?

4. Use the balance sheet for San Diego Bank in Exhibit A and the industry norms in Exhibit B to answer the following questions:
   a. Estimate the gap and the gap ratio and determine how San Diego Bank would be affected by an increase in interest rates over time.
   b. Assess San Diego's default risk. Does it appear high or low relative to the industry? Would San Diego Bank perform better or worse than other banks during a recession?
   c. For any type of bank risk that appears to be higher than the industry, explain how the balance sheet could be restructured to reduce the risk.

EXHIBIT A   Balance Sheet for San Diego Bank (in Millions of Dollars)

ASSETS			LIABILITIES AND CAPITAL		
Required reserves		$ 800	Demand deposits		$ 800
Commercial loans			NOW Accounts		2,500
Floating-rate	None		MMDAs		6,000
Fixed-rate	7,000				
Total		7,000	CDs		
Consumer loans		5,000	Short-term	9,000	
			From 1 to 5 yrs.	None	
Mortgages			Total		9,000
Floating-rate	None		Federal funds		500
Fixed-rate	2,000				
Total		2,000	Long-term bonds		400
Treasury securities			CAPITAL		800
Short-term	None				
Long-term	1,000				
Total		1,000			
Long-term corporate securities					
High-rated	None				
Moderate-rated	2,000				
Total		2,000			
Long-term municipal securities					
High-rated	None				
Moderate-rated	1,700				
Total		1,700			
Fixed assets		500			
TOTAL ASSETS		20,000	TOTAL LIABILITIES AND CAPITAL		20,000

EXHIBIT B   Industry Norms in Percentage Terms

ASSETS		LIABILITIES AND CAPITAL	
Required reserves	4%		
Commercial loans		Demand deposits	17%
Floating-rate	20	NOW accounts	10
Fixed-rate	11	MMDAs	20
Total	31	CDs	
Consumer loans	20	Short-term	35
Mortgages		From 1 to 5 yrs.	10
Floating-rate	7	Total	45
Fixed-rate	3	Long-term bonds	2
Total	10	CAPITAL	6
Treasury securities			
Short-term	7		
Long-term	8		
Total	15		
Long-term corporate securities			
High-rated	5		
Moderate-rated	5		
Total	10		
Long-term municipal securities			
High-rated	3		
Moderate-rated	2		
Total	5		
Fixed assets	5		
TOTAL ASSETS	100%	TOTAL LIABILITIES AND CAPITAL	100%

CASE APPLICATION: HEDGING INTEREST RATE RISK

Many Banks Change Strategies to Manage Rate Risk

Swaps Are Increasingly Used to Protect Margins, Guard Against Fluctuations

Steven Lipin, New York

The interest rate party is mostly over for the banking industry, but banks are beginning to bottle some of the fizz to last another year.

After riding interest rates to 30-year lows and fattening their profits by pushing deposit rates down faster than loan rates, many banks appear to be shifting their strategies to lock in their so-called net interest margins. And they're increasingly managing their profitability with the help of derivative securities such as swap agreements, which allow institutions to exchange a fixed coupon for a floating-rate coupon.

The swap market was developed by big banks and securities firms in the mid-1980s to help corporations manage interest expenses on their debt securities. Now the swaps are increasingly used by big and small banks alike to help manage the risks of fluctuating interest rates.

"We have become more defensive" on the outlook for rates, says Judith Fisher, executive vice president at Huntington National Bank in Columbus, Ohio. In late 1990, the bank had positioned itself to benefit from falling rates by exchanging floating-rate assets for securities that earn a fixed rate. Much like high-yielding bonds, the swaps provided a fixed income stream, widening the bank's profit margins as its borrowing costs fell.

But since the beginning of this year, the main arm of **Huntington Bancshares** Inc. has been engaging in a series of transactions that effectively reduce its susceptibility to rate swings. It is using swaps to lock in funding at a fixed rate, hoping to guarantee against a rise in its borrowing costs. This way, it can retain much of the fat 5.5% net interest margin it enjoyed in the fourth quarter.

"We're locking in some of the income spread and living off of the annuity stream," says Ms. Fisher.

The bank is also reducing its exposure to rising rates by closing out swap contracts while they're still profitable and booking the gains.

There's good reason for Huntington and other banks to take precautionary steps. At a time when the bulk of the industry's bad loan problems have been addressed, the concern now is whether banks are vulnerable to a jump in funding costs without a similar increase in what they earn from the holdings of fixed-rate loans and other assets.

In the late 1970s much of the thrift industry made 30-year mortgages with short-term deposits. When rates skyrocketed, the mismatch, or gap, between assets and liabilities turned into red ink, and helped cause the savings and loan fiasco.

While the outlook for rates does not signal such a mismatch now, an erosion of a bank's profit margins as rates rise is a strong possibility if it does not take steps to hedge itself, analysts say.

"Balance sheet management activities will neutralize the potential negative effects on earnings of the forecast increase in short-term rates," says Thomas H. Hanley, banking analyst at First Boston Corp. He sees more and more banks taking such precautions by using derivatives and extending the maturities on their liabilities, such as certificates of deposit.

"The backup in rates last October motivated a lot of people," says Fred Price, a partner with Sandler, O'Neill & Partners, a bank consulting and brokerage firm. But, he adds, banks still "need a certain amount of interest rate risk to be profitable."

The fear of rising rates is complicated by banks' unusually large holdings of debt securities, which would lose value in a rising rate environment if they were carried at current market value rather than at their purchase price. The accounting industry is pushing for banks to hold much of their securities at market value rather than historical cost.

One way banks are protecting against a decline in the value of investment securities is by selling a Treasury futures contract of the same maturity as the investment. That way, if rates rise and the price of the investment security falls, the bank can offset the loss with the gain from the futures contract.

To be sure, it's impossible to know whether the industry as a whole is becoming less susceptible to rate swings. There is no way to quantify the level of interest rate risk individual banks or the industry as a whole is incurring. The Federal Reserve Board indicated last year

Continued

CASE APPLICATION: HEDGING INTEREST RATE RISK

Continued

that perhaps 20% of the industry was taking excessive risk.

That's one reason why bank regulators have issued proposed rules on including interest rate risk in capital guidelines. In recent months regulators have also been jawboning the industry to avoid taking undue interest rate risks.

Banks appear to be heeding those warnings. Like Huntington, **Chemical Banking** Corp., the nation's third largest bank, had positioned its balance sheet to greatly benefit from falling interest rates, but it changed course at year end. It is not renewing expiring swaps contracts that benefit it as rates fall and expose it to risk if rates rise.

Chemical's balance sheet is now pretty much neutral on the direction of interest rates. Chemical has predicted that this year's net interest income would be stable, and that its four-percentage-point net interest margin would shrink only slightly.

First Union Corp., a Charlotte, N.C., banking company, will receive at least $103 million in guaranteed net interest income this year no matter what happens to interest rates.

The company has a portfolio of swaps and other derivative products purchased in 1991 that yield nearly 6.5%. On the other side of the ledger, the bank has recently locked in borrowing costs, which it has not disclosed, through the use of other derivative products. Although First Union does not stand to gain

as much if rates fall, at least it knows that "we have a certain level of income that's assured," says Ross Annable, manager of the bank's treasury division. First Union's derivatives portfolio—the amount of principal upon which interest is exchanged—has grown to $17 billion, from $7 billion about a year ago.

Bankers say they also like to use swaps because of the low amount of capital needed to establish positions. For example, the purchase of a $100 million security yielding 6% would cost about $4 million in equity capital but balloon the balance sheet by the full $100 million, assuming a capital-to-asset ratio of 4%. A bank could purchase swaps that earn 6% on $100 million, but because no principal is exchanged, a bank would only have to set aside about $20,000. That's for the risk that the other party in the swap agreement won't meet its obligations.

From an accounting standpoint, the derivatives are carried at historical cost, rather than the lower of cost or market value. Yet the risk exposure is virtually identical: Both increase in value when rates fall and lose value when rates rise.

In the capital-intense world of banking, "Why in the world more banks don't look at interest rates swaps to preserve capital, I don't know," says Richard Lodge, senior vice president at Banc One Corp. "It's not an esoteric phenomenon anymore."

While regulators have warned about the hidden or unknown risks in the derivatives market, "the industry believes derivatives are a legitimate and valuable tool for rate risk management," said Ms. Fisher of Huntington.

SOURCE: *The Wall Street Journal,* February 10, 1993. Reprinted with permission of *The Wall Street Journal,* © 1993 Dow Jones & Company, Inc. All rights reserved.

QUESTIONS

1. Explain how banks like Huntington Bancshares Inc. that used interest rate swaps altered their risk-return profile.

2. A bank analyst stated that banks still need some degree of interest rate risk to be profitable. What does this statement mean?

3. First Union's derivatives position grew from $7 billion to $17 billion in one year. Assuming that most of this portfolio represents "fixed-for-floating" interest rate swaps, explain what the change in First Union's position suggests about its interest rate expectations. If First Union suddenly expected interest rates to decline, how might it alter its existing derivatives position?

PROJECT

1. **Assessing a Bank's Managerial Policies**
   Your professor will assign you (or your group) a bank or allow you to choose one. Use the most recent annual report of the bank to answer the following questions. (A more thorough analysis of the project can be conducted if the past 10 years are examined, which would require some previous annual re-

ports or financial statement data provided by investor's services, such as *Moody's Banking and Finance Manual.*)

a. Summarize how the bank manages its liquidity risk (if explained in the annual report).

b. Determine the bank's gap and its gap ratio over recent years. How would the bank's net interest margin be affected if interest rates increase in the future? Explain.

c. If a software regression package is available, determine how the bank's stock returns have been affected by interest rates over time using the model described in the chapter. Interpret the regression results. Based on this regression analysis, how would the bank's net interest margin be affected if interest rates increase in the future? Do these implications coincide with those of part (b)?

d. Summarize the bank's use of floating-rate loans, interest rate futures contracts, or interest rate swaps to manage its interest rate risk.

e. Describe the bank's current status regarding loans to less developed countries. Is it highly exposed? What has it done (if anything) to reduce its exposure to LDC loans?

f. How has the bank's capital ratio changed over time? How will this change affect its risk? How does it affect existing and potential profitability?

g. How will the bank perform if economic conditions are very favorable? Would it be severely affected by a recession? Explain. Based on your projections of interest rates and economic conditions, provide your assessment of the bank. Would you recommend buying or selling stock of this bank? Explain.

REFERENCES

Berger, Allen N., Diana Hancock, and David B. Humphrey. "Bank Efficiency Derived from the Profit Function." *Journal of Banking and Finance* (April 1993): 317–347.

Berger, Allen N., William C. Huner, and Stephen G. Timme. "The Efficiency of Financial Institutions: A Review and Preview of Research Past, Present, and Future." *Journal of Banking and Finance* (April 1993): 221–249.

Bertin, William J., Farrokh Ghazanfari, and Khali M. Torabzadeh. "Failed Bank Acquisitions and Successful Bidders Returns." *Financial Management* (Summer 1989): 93–100.

Booth, James, and Dennis Officer. "Expectations, Interest Rates, and Commercial Bank Stocks." *Journal of Financial Research* (Spring 1985): 51–57.

Boyd, John H., Stanley L. Graham, and R. Shawn Hewitt. "Bank Holding Company Mergers With Nonbank Financial Firms." *Journal of Banking and Finance* (February 1993): 43–63.

Brewer, Elijah. "Relationship between Bank Holding Company Risk and Nonbank Activity." *Journal of Economics and Business* (November 1989): 337–353.

Brewer, Elijah, and G. D. Koppenhaver. "The Impact of Standby Letters of Credit on Bank Risk: A Note." *Journal of Banking and Finance* (December 1992): 1037–1046.

Flannery, Mark J. "How Do Changes in Market Interest Rates Affect Bank Profits?" *Business Review*, Federal Reserve Bank of Philadelphia (September–October 1980): 13–22.

Koppenhaver, G. D. "Selective Hedging of Bank Assets with Treasury Bill Futures Contracts." *Journal of Financial Research* (Summer 1984): 105–119.

Kwast, Myron L. "The Impact of Underwriting and Dealing on Bank Returns and Risks." *Journal of Banking and Finance* (March 1989): 101–125.

Madura, Jeff. "Banking Event Studies: Synthesis and Directions for Future Research." *Review of Research in Banking and Finance* (Spring 1990): 55–82.

Madura, Jeff and Kenneth J. Wiant. "Long-term Effects of Bank Acquisitions." *Journal of Banking and Finance,* forthcoming.

Mester, Loretta, J. "Owners Versus Managers: Who Controls the Bank?" *Business Review,* Federal Reserve Bank of Philadelphia (May/June 1989): 13–23.

Mitchell, Karlyn. "Interest Rate Risk at Commercial Banks: An Empirical Investigation." *Financial Review* (August 1989): 431–455.

_____. "Interest Rate Risk Management at Tenth District Banks." *Economic Review,* Federal Reserve Bank of Kansas City (May 1985): 3–19.

Osborne, Dale K., and Tarek S. Zoher. "Reserve Requirements, Bank Share Prices, and the Uniqueness of Bank Loans." *Journal of Banking and Finance* (August 1992): 799–812.

Whittaker, J. Gregg. "Interest Rate Swaps: Risk and Regulation." *Economic Review,* Federal Reserve Bank of Kansas City (March 1987): 3–13.

STOCK PRICE REACTION TO BANK POLICIES

Bank managers attempt to implement policies that enhance the bank's stock performance. They can assess the market's reaction to previous policies implemented by various banks by performing an event study. If the market reacts favorably, this suggests that the policy is anticipated to improve the bank's performance over time. If the market reacts unfavorably, this implies that the policy is expected to reduce the bank's performance. When there is no market reaction, the policy is expected to have no impact on the bank's performance. A brief explanation of using the event study methodology follows.

Consider the bank policy to cut dividends. One may hypothesize that a dividend cut could be favorably received by the market if the amount representing the reduced dividends is expected to be reinvested by the bank in a manner that will generate high returns in the future. However, an alternative hypothesis is that a dividend cut signals that the bank is expecting poor performance in the future and cannot afford its current dividend payment schedule. To determine how bank share prices are affected, a sample of banks that cut dividends must first be identified. Then the announcement date of each bank's dividend cut must be determined. The announcement date is more important than the actual date in which the dividends are cut, because investors would likely react immediately to the announcement if they react at all.

Daily stock returns for each bank in the sample are compiled for a period before their respective announcement dates (sometimes weekly observations are used instead). This so-called estimation period is used to estimate the bank's beta with the following model:

$$R_{j,t} = B_0 + B_1 R_{m,t} + u_t$$

where
$$R_{j,t} = \text{the bank's return over day } t$$

$$R_{m,t} = \text{the market return over day } t$$

$$B_0 = \text{intercept}$$

$$B_1 = \text{estimated beta of the bank}$$

$$u_t = \text{error term}$$

The length of the estimation period is somewhat subjective, but for our example, assume that it begins 120 days before the announcement date and ends 20 days before the announcement date. Then the expected return of each bank is determined over the so-called examination period, based on the regression coefficients and the actual values of the market return.

For our example, assume that the examination period extended from 19 days before the announcement date until 40 days after the announcement date. The expected return for each observation over this period represents the return on the bank's stock that should have occurred in the absence of any abnormal reaction by the market. By comparing the actual return to the bank's expected return, we can determine whether any abnormal return ($AR_{j,t}$) occurred for the bank during the observation t:

$$AR_{j,t} = R_{j,t} - E(R_{j,t})$$
$$= R_{j,t} - (B_0 + B_1 R_{m,t})$$

The abnormal returns (sometimes called residuals) are estimated for each observation over the examination period. Positive abnormal returns suggest that the actual return is more than it would have been in the absence of any market reaction and therefore that the market reacted favorably. A negative abnormal return implies that the actual return was less than it would have been in the absence of any market reaction and therefore that the market reacted unfavorably.

In some cases, an abnormal return will occur before the announcement date, which suggests that the market anticipated the news before it was officially announced. Because the examination period usually contains some observations before the announcement date, it is possible to detect such an anticipated reaction.

The market reaction to a single bank's policy is not normally considered to be sufficient for making implications about the industry as a whole. For this reason, the procedure described here is replicated for each bank that had a similar announcement. For each day within the examination period, the abnormal returns (or residuals) are consolidated among all banks to estimate an average residual for the portfolio ($AR_{p,t}$):

$$AR_{p,t} = \sum_{j=1}^{n} AR_{j,t} \bigg/ n$$

for all n banks that were examined. The average residual is estimated over each day of the examination period, with specific emphasis around the announcement date. The average residuals, starting on the first day of the examination period, are accumulated over each successive day to determine cumulative average residuals. Because the average residuals for any given observation could differ from zero by chance, they are tested to determine whether they are statistically significant (different from zero). This test provides greater reliability about any implications that are drawn from the analysis.

The analysis described here (or some adaptation of it) has been used to assess the market reaction to a variety of bank managerial policies, such as bank recapitalization plans and the formation of holding companies. It has also been used to assess market reaction to regulatory events, such as the elimination of deposit rate ceilings and intrastate banking regulations. It has even been used to assess market reaction to the international debt crisis. The analysis has also been applied to events affecting other financial institutions, such as brokerage firms, savings institutions, and insurance companies.

SOURCE: Fama, Eugene, Lawrence Fisher, Michael Jensen, and Richard Roll. "The Adjustment of Stock Prices to New Information." *International Economic Review* (February 1969): 1–21; and Madura, Jeff. "Banking Event Studies: Synthesis and Directions for Future Research." *Review of Research in Banking and Finance* (Spring 1990): 55–82.

CHAPTER 18

BANK PERFORMANCE

A commercial bank's performance is examined for various reasons. Bank regulators identify banks that are experiencing severe problems so that they can remedy them. Shareholders need to determine whether they should buy or sell the stock of various banks. Investment analysts must be able to advise prospective investors on which banks to invest in. Furthermore, commercial banks evaluate their own performance over time to determine the outcomes of previous management decisions so that changes can be made where appropriate. Without persistent monitoring of performance, existing problems can remain unnoticed and lead to financial failure in the future.

The specific objectives of this chapter are to:

- compare the performance of banks in different size classifications over recent years, and
- explain how to evaluate the performance of banks based on financial statement data.

PERFORMANCE EVALUATION OF BANKS

Exhibit 18.1 summarizes the performance of all U.S.-chartered insured commercial banks. The characteristics identified in the first column are discussed in order from the top down. Each characteristic is measured as a percentage of assets to control for growth when assessing the changes in each characteristic over time. Exhibit 18.1 serves as a useful reference point for assessing each of the performance proxies discussed throughout this chapter.

EXHIBIT 18.1   Performance Summary of All Insured Commercial Banks, 1981–1993

ITEM	1982	1984	1986	1988	1990	1992	1993
1. Gross interest income	11.36%	10.23%	8.38%	8.95%	9.57%	7.47%	6.86%
2. Gross interest expenses	8.07	6.97	5.10	5.42	6.13	3.57	2.96
3. Net interest income	3.28	3.26	3.28	3.53	3.44	3.90	3.90
4. Noninterest income	.96	1.19	1.40	1.47	1.63	1.95	2.13
5. Loan loss provision	.40	.57	.77	.54	.93	.77	.47
6. Noninterest expenses	2.93	3.05	3.22	3.33	3.45	3.87	3.94
7. Securities gains (losses)	−.06	−.01	.14	.01	.02	.12	.09
8. Income before tax	.85	.83	.82	1.14	.70	1.33	1.72
9. Taxes	.14	.19	.19	.36	.23	.42	.51
10. Net income	.71	.64	.64	.84	.50	.91	1.21
11. Cash dividends provided	.31	.32	.33	.44	.42	.42	.60
12. Retained earnings	.40	.33	.31	.40	.08	.49	.61

SOURCE: *Federal Reserve Bulletin,* various issues.

Interest Income and Expenses

Gross interest income (in Row 1 of Exhibit 18.1) represents interest income generated from all assets. It is affected by market rates and the composition of assets held by banks. As a percentage of assets for all banks in aggregate, it was highest in the early 1980s, when interest rates were at their peak. It was lowest in the early 1990s when interest rates declined.

A comparison of gross interest income levels among four bank size classifications is shown in Exhibit 18.2. The size classifications range from "small" banks (with assets of less than $300 million) to "money center" banks, which are the 10 largest banks that serve money centers such as New York and San Francisco. Exhibit 18.2 shows that since 1987, the gross interest income of money center banks was typically higher than that of other banks, as more of their funds were used for commercial loans (which generate high interest payments).

Gross interest expenses (in Row 2) represent interest paid on deposits and on other borrowed funds (from the federal funds market, discount window, etc.). It is affected by market rates and the composition of liabilities. Since NOW accounts and money market deposit accounts (MMDAs) have become popular, banks have recently attracted a smaller percentage of funds through traditional noninterest-bearing demand deposit accounts. In addition, low interest rate passbook savings accounts have not drawn as much funds because of the alternative CDs available. Because of deregulation, a greater percentage of banks' sources of funds have market-determined interest rates. Gross interest expenses were less in the late 1980s and early 1990s than in the early 1980s for all banks in general because of a decline in market interest rates.

A comparison of gross interest expenses among the four bank size classes is presented in Exhibit 18.3. The interest expense of money center banks is consistently above that of other banks, as money center banks obtain a greater per-

EXHIBIT 18.2 Comparison of Gross Interest Income (as a % of Assets) among Bank Classes

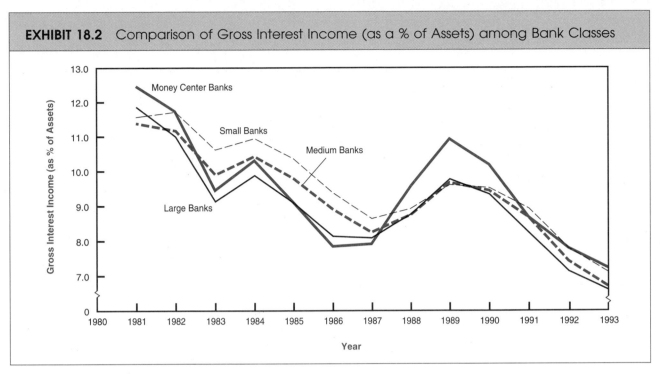

SOURCE: *Federal Reserve Bulletin,* various issues.

centage of their deposits on a wholesale (large-denomination) basis. In contrast, small banks attract significantly more small-denomination deposits from households at the passbook savings rate.

The net interest income (in Row 3) represents the difference between gross interest income and interest expenses, and is measured as a percentage of assets. This measure is commonly referred to as net interest margin. Exhibit 18.1 shows that gross interest income and gross interest expenses have been similarly affected by interest rate movements; therefore, the net interest margin of all banks in aggregate has remained somewhat stable. However, in the early 1990s, when market interest rates declined, interest expenses generally decreased at a faster rate than interest income, allowing for larger net interest margins.

Exhibit 18.4 shows that the net interest margin is consistently highest for the small banks, and lowest for the money center banks. These results are expected, given that the money center banks tend to incur larger interest expenses than the other banks.

Noninterest Income and Expenses

Noninterest income (in Row 4) results from fees charged on services provided, such as lockbox services, banker's acceptances, cashier's checks, and foreign exchange transactions. It has consistently risen over time for all banks in aggregate, as banks are offering more fee-based services than in the past. As banks continue to offer new services (such as insurance or securities services), noninterest income will increase over time.

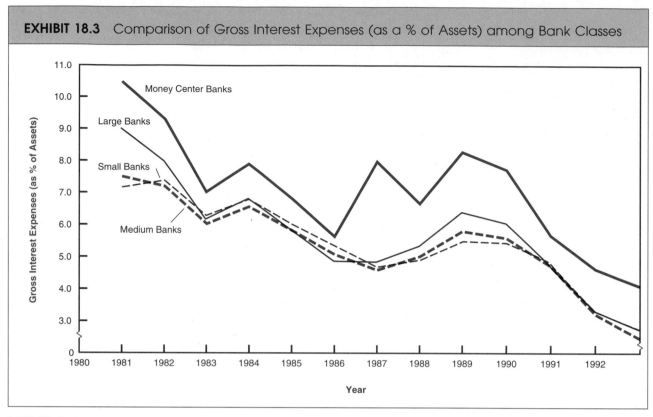

EXHIBIT 18.3 Comparison of Gross Interest Expenses (as a % of Assets) among Bank Classes

SOURCE: *Federal Reserve Bulletin,* various issues.

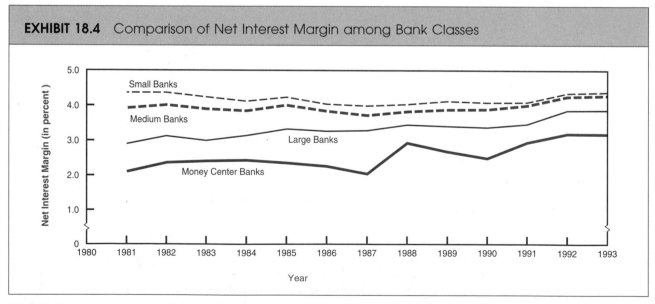

EXHIBIT 18.4 Comparison of Net Interest Margin among Bank Classes

SOURCE: *Federal Reserve Bulletin,* various issues.

EXHIBIT 18.5 Comparison of Noninterest Income (as a % of Assets) among Bank Classes

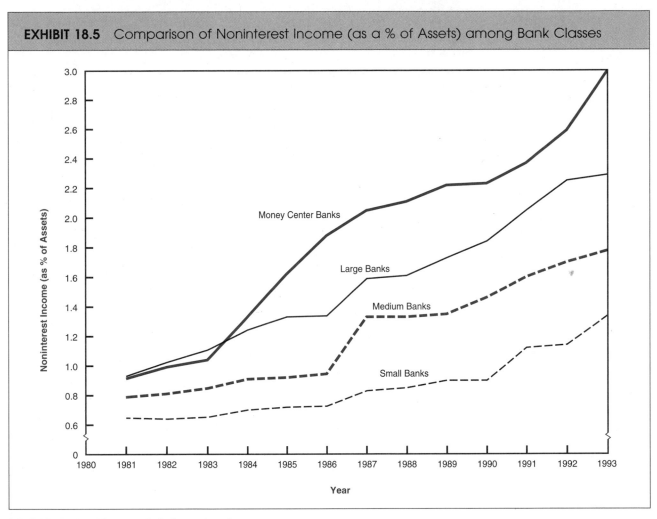

SOURCE: *Federal Reserve Bulletin,* various issues.

Exhibit 18.5 shows that noninterest income is consistently highest for money center banks and lowest for the smallest banks. These differences occur because money center banks provide more services for which they can charge fees. Small banks provide few services that generate noninterest income.

The **loan loss provision** (in Row 5) is a reserve account established by the bank in anticipation of loan losses in the future. It should increase during periods when loan losses are more likely, such as during a recessionary period. In many cases, there is a lagged impact as some borrowers survive the recessionary period but never fully recover from it and subsequently fail. As shown in Exhibit 18.1, the provision for loan losses for all banks in aggregate was much lower in 1981 relative to the other years. The 1982 recession combined with the international debt crisis had an impact on loan losses in the early 1980s. The impact of the international debt crisis continued throughout the entire decade. Money center banks and other large banks boosted their loan loss reserves substantially in 1987 and again in 1989 because of exposure to debt of less developed countries.

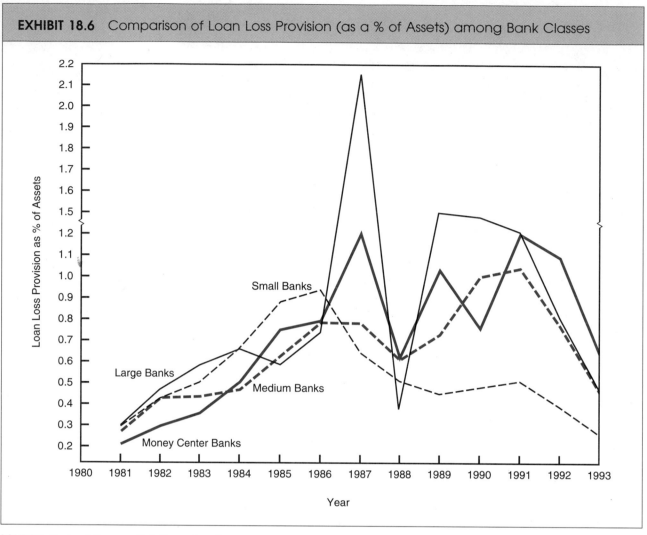

EXHIBIT 18.6 Comparison of Loan Loss Provision (as a % of Assets) among Bank Classes

SOURCE: *Federal Reserve Bulletin,* various issues.

The high level of loan losses in recent years is not solely attributed to the international debt crisis. A large proportion of agricultural loans defaulted throughout the 1980s. In the late 1980s, there was also a high percentage of defaults on real estate loans. For example, the Bank of New England experienced severe financial problems in 1989 and 1990 as a result of nonperforming real estate loans, which led to its failure in 1991.

Exhibit 18.6 shows that the loan loss provision was lower for the money center banks in the early 1980s. However, the international debt crisis caused some money center banks to boost their loan loss reserves in the mid-1980s. The amount of loan loss reserves was high for most banks during the 1992 recession, but declined in 1993.

Noninterest expenses (in Row 6 of Exhibit 18.1) include salaries, office equipment, and other expenses not related to the payment of interest on deposits.

EXHIBIT 18.7   Overview of the Key Components Affecting the ROA (for Banks in Aggregate)

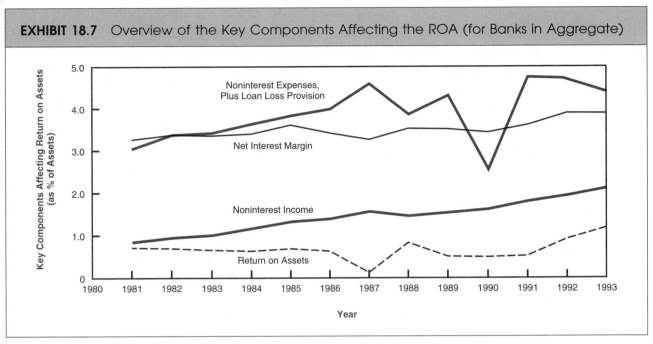

SOURCE: *Federal Reserve Bulletin,* various issues.

These expenses have averaged about 3 percent of total assets for all banks in aggregate, but have increased over time.

Securities gains and losses (in Row 7 of Exhibit 18.1) result from the bank's sale of securities. They have been negligible, when all banks in aggregate are considered. An individual bank's gains and losses might be more significant.

When summing net interest income, noninterest income, and securities gains and subtracting from this sum the provision for loan losses and noninterest expenses, the result is income before tax (in Row 8 of Exhibit 18.1). This income figure decreased over the early 1980s, primarily because of an increase in noninterest expenses and provision for loan losses. In the early 1990s, bank income was enhanced by the increase in noninterest income and in net interest margins.

Return on Assets and Equity

The key income statement item, according to many analysts, is net income (in Row 10 of Exhibit 18.1), which accounts for any taxes paid. The net income figure disclosed in Exhibit 18.1 is measured as a percentage of assets and therefore represents the **return on assets (ROA)**. Fluctuations in the ROA for banks in aggregate can be explained by assessing changes in its components, as shown in Exhibit 18.7. Although the net interest margin has been somewhat stable, the noninterest income has risen over time. However, this has been roughly offset by the combined increase in noninterest expenses and the loan loss provision. The ROA was low in 1987, 1989, and 1990 because of the high level of loan loss reserves, but was unusually high in the early 1990s because of the increase in net interest margins and in noninterest income.

Exhibit 18.8 shows that the ROA for small banks more than doubled that of money center banks in the early 1980s, partially because of the higher net interest margin. Even though small banks continued to have a higher net interest margin in the mid-1980s, their loan loss provision increased at a higher rate. Consequently, their ROA declined significantly. The small and medium-sized banks have consistently had higher ROAs than the money center banks.

Any individual bank's ROA depends on the bank's policy decisions as well as uncontrollable factors relating to the economy and government regulations, as shown in Exhibit 18.9. Gross interest income and expenses are affected by the sources and uses of bank funds and the movements in market interest rates.

Noninterest income is earned on a variety of services, including many new services being offered by banks as some regulatory provisions have been elimi-

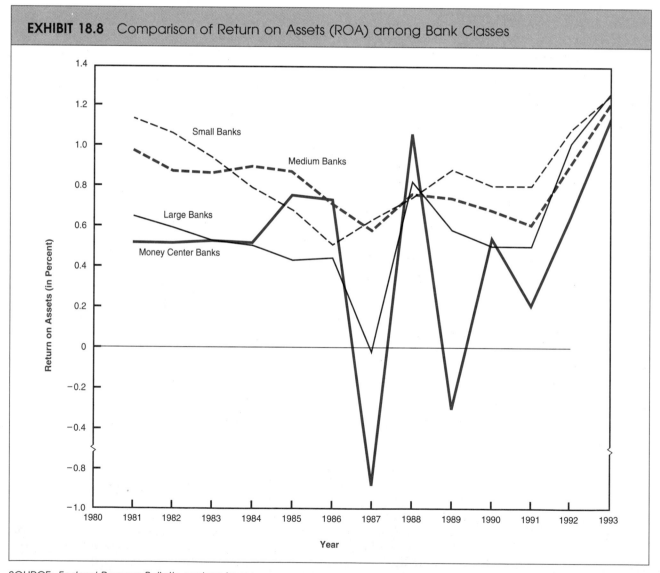

EXHIBIT 18.8 Comparison of Return on Assets (ROA) among Bank Classes

SOURCE: *Federal Reserve Bulletin,* various issues.

nated. Noninterest expenses are partially dependent on personnel costs associated with the credit assessment of loan applications, which in turn are affected by the bank's asset composition (proportion of funds allocated to loans). Noninterest expenses also depend on the liability composition because the handling of small deposits is more time consuming than that of large deposits. Banks offering more nontraditional services will incur higher noninterest expenses, although they expect to offset the higher costs with higher noninterest income. Loan losses depend on the composition of assets (proportion of loans versus securities), the quality of these assets, and the economy. The return on assets is

---

EXHIBIT 18.9 Influence of Bank Policies and Other Factors on a Bank's Income Statement

Income Statement Item as a % of Assets	Bank Policy Decisions Affecting the Income Statement Item	Uncontrollable Factors Affecting the Income Statement Item
(1) Gross interest income	■ Composition of assets ■ Quality of assets ■ Maturity and rate sensitivity of assets ■ Loan pricing policy	■ Economic conditions ■ Market interest rate movements
(2) Gross interest expenses	■ Composition of liabilities ■ Maturities and rate sensitivity of liabilities	■ Market interest rate movements
(3) Net interest margin = (1) − (2)		
(4) Noninterest income	■ Service charges ■ Nontraditional activities	■ Regulatory provisions
(5) Noninterest expenses	■ Composition of assets ■ Composition of liabilities ■ Nontraditional activities ■ Efficiency of personnel ■ Costs of office space and equipment ■ Marketing costs ■ Other costs	■ Inflation
(6) Loan losses	■ Composition of assets ■ Quality of assets ■ Collection department capabilities	■ Economic conditions ■ Market interest rate movements
(7) Pretax return on assets = (3) + (4) − (5) − (6)		
(8) Taxes	■ Tax planning	■ Tax laws
(9) After-tax return on assets = (7) − (8)		
(10) Financial leverage, measured here as (assets/equity)	■ Capital structure policies	■ Capital structure regulations
(11) Return on equity = (9) × (10)		

influenced by all previously mentioned income statement items and therefore by all policies and other factors that affect those items.

The performance characteristics of money center banks differ from small banks because of the differences in their balance sheet composition. For instance, small banks obtain a greater percentage of their funds from traditional demand deposits (at zero percent interest) and small savings accounts (at a relatively low interest rate), while money center banks attract much of their funds through large deposits at a market-determined interest rate. Thus, the net interest margin for money center banks is typically lower than for smaller banks. Consequently, their ROA would likely be lower, unless their noninterest income as a percentage of assets is significantly higher.

An alternative measure of overall bank performance is **return on equity (ROE)**. A bank's ROE is affected by the same income statement items that affect ROA as well as by the bank's degree of financial leverage, as follows:

$$\text{ROE} = \text{ROA} \times \frac{\text{Leverage}}{\text{measure}}$$

$$\frac{\text{Net income}}{\text{Equity capital}} = \frac{\text{Net income}}{\text{Total assets}} \times \frac{\text{Total assets}}{\text{Equity capital}}$$

The leverage measure is simply the inverse of the capital ratio (when only equity counts as capital). The higher the capital ratio is, the lower the leverage measure and the lower the degree of financial leverage.

Exhibit 18.10 shows that in the early 1980s, the ROE was somewhat similar among banks of all classes. Although banks with a greater amount of assets generally experienced a lower ROA during this period (refer to Exhibit 18.8), they had a lower capital ratio (implying a higher degree of financial leverage), offsetting the relatively low ROA.

In the mid-1980s, the ROA of small banks declined. Although it still exceeded that of money center banks, the small banks' relatively high level of equity investment caused their ROE to be significantly lower than that of money center banks as well as other banks. In the mid-1980s, the large banks (except money center banks) experienced the highest ROE, because they improved their ROA and also used a relatively low level of equity capital. Small banks earned the highest ROE in the late 1980s, while large banks earned the highest ROE in the early 1990s.

RISK EVALUATION OF BANKS

In assessing bank performance, risk should not be ignored. However, no consensus measurement exists that would allow for comparison among all banks of various types of risk (such as loan default risk and liquidity risk).

Some analysts measure a firm's risk by its beta, which represents the degree of sensitivity of its stock returns to the returns of the stock market as a whole. Beta is normally measured by the following regression model:

$$R_{j,t} = B_0 + B_1 R_{m,t} + u_t$$

where $R_{j,t}$ = the stock return for the firm of concern in period t

EXHIBIT 18.10 Comparison of Return on Equity among Bank Classes

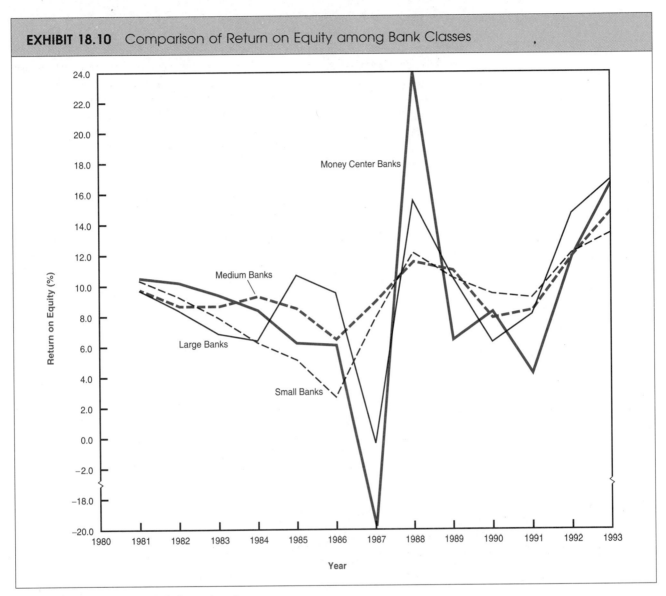

SOURCE: *Federal Reserve Bulletin,* various issues.

$R_{m,t}$ = the return on a stock market index (such as the S&P 500 index) in period t

B_0 = intercept

B_1 = slope coefficient

u_t = error term

The regression model is applied to historical data (usually on a quarterly basis). The regression coefficients B_0 and B_1 are estimated by the regression analysis. The coefficient B_1 is an estimate of beta, because it measures the sensitivity of R_j to R_m. The banks whose stock returns are less vulnerable to economic conditions have relatively low betas. The stock returns of a bank with very conservative management are likely to be less sensitive to stock market movements.

Although the beta reflects sensitivity to market conditions, it ignores any firm-specific characteristics. That is, the beta measures systematic risk but ignores unsystematic risk. A bank's beta will not necessarily remain constant from one period to another. If the bank decides to use more aggressive policies, its beta will likely increase. Its performance and therefore its stock price would become more volatile, because the sensitivity of the bank's stock returns to economic conditions would increase. A higher beta can work for or against the bank, depending on future economic conditions.

HOW TO EVALUATE A BANK'S PERFORMANCE

Up to this point, the discussion of bank performance has mostly focused on the overall industry and different size classifications. Although this information can be beneficial, analysts often need to evaluate an individual bank's performance, in which case financial statements are used. The income and expenses disclosed earlier in Exhibit 18.1 serve as an industry benchmark for evaluating a bank's performance.

Examination of Return on Assets (ROA)

The ROA will usually reveal when a bank's performance is not up to par, but it does not indicate the reason for poor performance. Its components must be evaluated separately. Exhibit 18.11 identifies the factors that affect bank performance as measured by the ROA and ROE. If a bank's ROA is less than desired, the bank is possibly incurring excessive interest expenses. Banks typically know what deposit rate is necessary to attract deposits and therefore are not likely to pay excessive interest. Yet, if all their sources of funds require a market-

EXHIBIT 18.11 Breakdown of Performance Measures

MEASURES OF BANK PERFORMANCE	FINANCIAL CHARACTERISTICS INFLUENCING PERFORMANCE	BANK DECISIONS AFFECTING FINANCIAL CHARACTERISTIC
1) Return on assets (ROA)	Net interest margin	Deposit rate decisions Loan rate decisions Loan losses
	Noninterest revenues	Bank services offered
	Noninterest expenses	Overhead requirements Efficiency Advertising
	Loan losses	Risk level of loans provided
2) Return on equity (ROE)	ROA	See above
	Leverage measure	Capital structure decision

IMPACT OF INTEREST RATES ON BANK PERFORMANCE

Among studies that have examined whether bank performance is affected significantly by interest rate movements, a study by Flannery found the answer to be no. The implication was that banks can effectively insulate themselves against interest rate movements, and these results applied to the entire sample. Of course any bank that did not effectively match the rate sensitivity on both sides of the balance sheet would be affected by interest rate movements.

A study by Scott and Peterson found a significant negative relationship between anticipated (and unanticipated) interest rate movements and bank stock returns, implying that stocks are adversely affected by the market's expectations of rising interest rates. The market apparently believes that commercial bank performance is susceptible to interest rate movements.

The study by Scott and Peterson used the following regression model:

$$R_p = B_0 + B_1 R_m + B_2 i + u$$

where R_p = stock returns of a portfolio of commercial banks

R_m = percentage change in the market index (the S&P 500 Index was used as a proxy)

i = a measure of unexpected interest rate changes (see the article by Scott and Peterson for an explanation of the proxy used for this variable)

B_0 = intercept

B_1 = regression coefficient that measures the sensitivity of stock returns to the market index returns

B_2 = regression coefficient that measures the sensitivity of stock returns to the interest rate movements

u = error term

The coefficient B_1 was estimated to be 0.673 by the regression analysis, suggesting that a one percent change in the market is associated with a 0.673 percent change in the portfolio returns. Thus, the commercial bank stocks were positively correlated with the market. The coefficient B_2 was estimated to be -0.401 by the regression analysis, suggesting that an unexpected one percent increase in interest rates is associated with a 0.401 percent decrease in stock returns of commercial banks. This coefficient was found to be statistically significant. Thus, stock returns on commercial banks were adversely affected by an unexpected increase in interest rates.

Several recent studies found similar results. These results are relevant to managers and investors of commercial banks. Even if interest rates cannot be forecasted with perfect accuracy, investors can use the regression coefficient B_2 to estimate how a bank's stock returns will be affected by a variety of possible interest rate outcomes.

determined rate, that will force relatively high interest expenses. A relatively low ROA could also be due to low interest received on loans and securities because of a bank's being overly conservative with its funds or being locked into fixed rates prior to an increase in market interest rates. High interest expenses and/ or low interest revenues (on a relative basis) will reduce the net interest margin and therefore reduce the ROA.

A relatively low ROA may also result from insufficient noninterest income. Some banks have made a much greater effort than others to offer services that generate fee (noninterest) income. Because a bank's net interest margin is somewhat dictated by interest rate trends and balance sheet composition, many banks attempt to focus on noninterest income in order to boost their ROA.

A bank's ROA can also be damaged by heavy loan losses. Yet, if the bank is too conservative in its attempt to avoid loan losses, its net interest margin will be low (because of the low interest rates received from very safe loans and investments). Because of the obvious trade-off here, banks generally attempt to shift their risk-return preferences according to economic conditions. They may increase their concentration of relatively risky loans during periods of prosperity when they might improve their net interest margin without incurring excessive loan losses. Conversely, they may increase their concentration of relatively low risk (and low-return) investments when economic conditions are less favorable.

Banks with relatively low ROAs often incur excessive noninterest expenses, such as overhead and advertising expenses. Any waste of resources due to inefficiencies can lead to relatively high noninterest expenses.

Example

Consider the information disclosed in Exhibit 18.12 for BankAmerica and the industry over recent years. Because of differences in accounting procedures, the information may not be perfectly comparable. The industry data are based on the class of money center banks. The comparison in Exhibit 18.12 can at least identify some general reasons for the financial problems experienced by BankAmerica.

BankAmerica's income before tax was below the industry norm in the middle and late 1980s. A comparison with the industry figures suggests that BankAmerica's net interest margin and noninterest income were generally higher than the norm. Yet, its loan loss provision has also been higher, even exceeding 2 percent of total assets in 1985. In addition, its noninterest expenses have been consistently higher than the norm. In the early 1990s, BankAmerica had a much higher income than the industry norm, mainly because of its relatively high net interest margin and its relatively low loan loss provision. Exhibit 18.13 provides a separate comparison of each variable to the industry norm over time to confirm the conclusions drawn.

Any particular bank will perform a more thorough evaluation of itself than that shown here. For example, the recent annual reports provided by BankAmerica provide a comprehensive explanation for its subpar performance in recent years, along with a discussion of how it plans to improve its performance over time.

A troubled bank's dividend payout policy should always be examined. Many banks that experience a sharp drop in earnings continue to pay out the same amount of dividends to shareholders as before, perhaps believing that their drop in earnings is just a one-time occurrence. If earnings remain low, though, and dividends are not reduced, the bank's capital will be reduced. However, some banks prefer not to reduce their dividend if possible, because they worry that it might signal to investors (correctly or not) that future earnings will not be sufficient to maintain current dividends.

Information Used in Evaluating Bank Performance

Various investment services can enhance the analysis of a bank's financial statements. Exhibit 18.14 provides an example of an analysis by one well-known service (Value Line) of Citicorp, the holding company of Citibank, the largest bank in the United States. Some of the key performance characteristics discussed

EXHIBIT 18.12   Evaluation of BankAmerica[a]

	1983		1984		1985		1986		1987	
	BA	Industry	BA	Industry	BA	Industry	BA	Industry	BA	Industry
Net interest margin	3.30%	2.40%	3.89%	2.38%	3.94%	2.36%	3.32%	2.28%	3.28%	2.06%
Noninterest income	1.27	1.12	1.54	1.42	2.06	1.75	2.04	2.02	2.04	2.50
Loan loss provision	.62	.36	.83	.50	2.09	.74	1.76	.79	1.97	2.16
Noninterest expenses	3.35	2.34	4.05	2.54	4.24	2.71	3.91	2.96	4.24	3.18
Income before tax[a]	.60	.84	.55	.78	(0.33)	.71	(0.31)	.68	(0.89)	(.70)

	1988		1989		1990		1991		1992	
	BA	Industry	BA	Industry	BA	Industry	BA	Industry	BA	Industry
Net interest margin	3.89%	2.91%	4.07%	2.68%	3.85%	3.31%	4.36%	2.92%	4.75%	3.18%
Noninterest income	1.85	2.11	1.85	2.22	1.93	1.84	2.04	2.37	2.00	2.59
Loan loss provision	.68	.38	.78	1.50	.84	1.17	.69	1.20	.55	1.09
Noninterest expenses	4.07	3.27	3.78	3.42	3.64	3.47	3.62	3.79	3.70	3.83
Income before tax[a]	.99	1.40	1.36	.02	1.30	.54	1.61	.34	1.48	.96

[a]All variables are measured as a percentage of assets. The industry net income before tax also accounts for securities gains and losses.
SOURCE: Bank of America's Annual Reports; and *Federal Reserve Bulletin,* various issues.

in this chapter are included here. The beta of Citicorp is disclosed in the upper left corner of the Value Line analysis. The spreadsheet of financial data includes total assets, net interest income, loan loss provisions, noninterest income, noninterest expenses, and ROA (referred to as "% Earned Total Assets").

The Value Line analysis also measures return on equity (referred to as "% NW to Tot Assets") and the dividend payout ratio (referred to as "% All Dividends to Net Prof."). Furthermore, it provides forecasts of financial ratios and other financial characteristics.

EXHIBIT 18.13 Graphic Comparison of Bank America Expenses and Income to the Industry

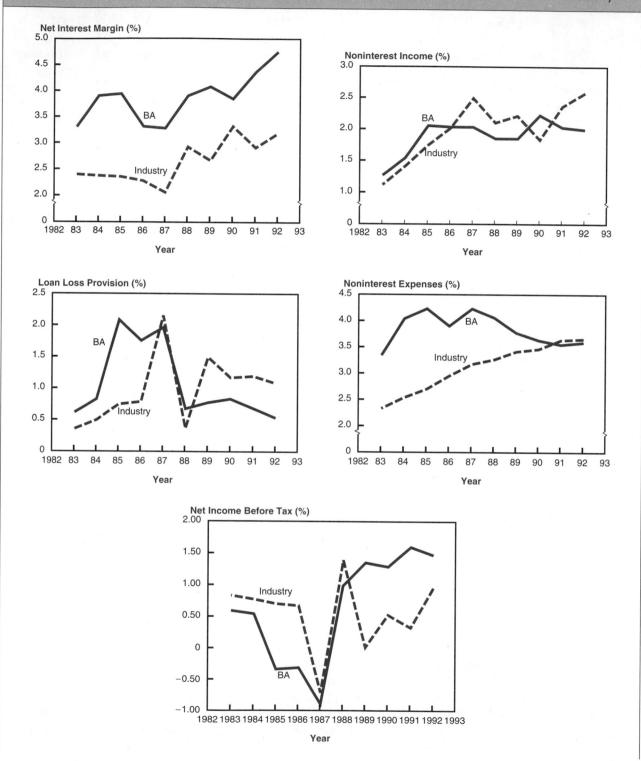

EXHIBIT 18.14   An Analysis of Citicorp's Performance

CITICORP NYSE-CCI

| RECENT PRICE | **36** | P/E RATIO | **9.7** | (Trailing: 12.0 Median: 13.0) | RELATIVE P/E RATIO | **0.58** | DIV'D YLD | **Nil** | VALUE LINE | **2013** |

| | High: | 20.0 | 23.1 | 20.3 | 25.9 | 31.9 | 34.2 | 27.0 | 35.5 | 29.6 | 17.5 | 22.5 | 39.8 | |
| | Low: | 10.8 | 15.3 | 13.7 | 18.4 | 23.4 | 15.9 | 18.0 | 24.6 | 10.8 | 8.5 | 10.4 | 20.5 | |

TIMELINESS 1 Highest
(Relative Price Performance Next 12 Mos.)

SAFETY 3 Average
(Scale: 1 Highest to 5 Lowest)

BETA 1.35 (1.00 = Market)

1996-98 PROJECTIONS

	Price	Gain	Ann'l Total Return
High	70	(+95%)	19%
Low	45	(+25%)	7%

Insider Decisions

	F	M	A	M	J	J	A	S	O
to Buy	0	0	0	0	0	0	1	0	0
Options	1	4	0	5	4	0	3	2	0
to Sell	2	8	0	4	2	0	4	3	1

Institutional Decisions

	1Q'93	2Q'93	3Q'93
to Buy	140	156	165
to Sell	89	101	96
Hld'n(000)	203794	218041	241677

Percent shares traded 12.0 / 8.0 / 4.0

Relative Price Strength

Target Price Range 1996 | 1997 | 1998

10.0 x Earnings p sh

2-for-1 split

Shaded areas indicate recessions

Options: CBOE

1977	1978	1979	1980	1981	1982	1983	1984	1985	1986	1987	1988	1989	1990	1991	1992	1993	1994	© VALUE LINE PUB., INC.	96-98
1.53	1.94	2.18	2.04	2.20	2.80	3.15	3.23	3.56	3.57	d4.26	4.87	1.16	.57	d3.22	1.35	**3.40**	**4.15**	Earnings per sh A	5.75
.53	.58	.65	.71	.78	.86	.94	1.03	1.13	D.92	D1.32	1.45	1.59	1.74	.75	Nil	**Nil**	**.20**	Div'ds Decl'd per sh B	1.00
11.65	13.00	14.52	15.86	17.08	18.92	21.00	22.91	25.31	27.96	22.83	25.93	25.36	24.34	21.22	21.74	**26.00**	**31.15**	Book Value per sh C	51.20
245.63	245.06	247.79	245.27	250.58	254.44	249.15	252.54	258.75	275.23	316.23	319.06	324.74	336.51	346.25	366.49	**380.00**	**390.00**	Common Shs Outst'g F	475.00
8.9	6.1	5.4	5.2	5.6	5.1	6.0	5.3	6.3	7.7	--	4.7	NMF	NMF	--	13.1	Bold figures are Value Line estimates		Avg Ann'l P/E Ratio	10.0
1.17	.83	.78	.69	.68	.56	.51	.49	.51	.52	--	.39	NMF	NMF	--	.79			Relative P/E Ratio	.75
3.9%	4.9%	5.5%	6.7%	6.3%	6.1%	4.9%	6.0%	5.0%	3.4%	5.0%	6.3%	5.3%	8.6%	5.4%				Avg Ann'l Div'd Yield	1.7%

CAPITAL STRUCTURE as of 9/30/93

LT Debt $17623 mill. Due 5 Yrs $14300 mill.
LT Interest $2000 mill.

Pension Liability None

Pfd Stock $3923 mill. Pfd Div'd $312.0 mill.

Common Stock 379,124,000 shs.

						134655	150586	173597	196124	203607	207666	230643	216986	216922	213701	**225000**	**240000**	Total Assets ($mill)	290000
						90283	102707	115264	129206	133467	144992	155383	151857	147636	135851	**136500**	**140000**	Loans ($mill)	175000
						4043.0	4319.0	5446.0	6128.0	6466.0	7605.0	7358.0	7185.0	7265.0	7456.0	**7710**	**8100**	Net Interest Inc ($mill)	9950
						520.0	619.0	1243.0	1825.0	4410.0	1330.0	2521.0	2662.0	3890.0	4146.0	**2630**	**2250**	Loan Loss Prov'n ($mill)	2200
						1808.0	2300.0	3030.0	4272.0	5994.0	5413.0	6394.0	7402.0	7485.0	8165.0	**8240**	**8350**	Noninterest Inc ($mill)	9300
						3757.0	4456.0	5517.0	6875.0	8290.0	8981.0	9698.0	11099	11097	10057	**10185**	**10500**	Noninterest Exp ($mill)	11400
						837.0	890.0	998.0	1058.0	d1138	1698.0	498.0	318.0	d914.0	722.0	**1845**	**2250**	Net Profit ($mill)	3400
						46.8%	42.4%	41.8%	37.8%	--	37.3%	67.5%	61.5%	61.5%	49.1%	**41.0%**	**40.0%**	Income Tax Rate	40.0%
						.62%	.59%	.57%	.54%	NMF	.82%	.22%	.15%	NMF	.34%	**.80%**	**.95%**	% Earned Total Assets	1.15%
						12181	14642	18215	23343	24324	23958	23950	23187	23345	20136	**17600**	**17000**	Long-Term Debt ($mill)	30000
						5811.0	6466.0	7805.0	9100.0	8804.0	9904.0	10116	9769.0	9526.0	11217	**13810**	**16070**	Net Worth ($mill)	28250
						4.3%	4.3%	4.5%	4.6%	4.3%	4.8%	4.4%	4.5%	4.4%	5.2%	**6.0%**	**6.5%**	% N W to Tot Assets	9.5%
						67.0%	68.2%	66.4%	65.9%	65.6%	69.8%	67.4%	70.0%	68.1%	63.6%	**60.5%**	**58.5%**	% Loans to Tot Assets	60.5%
						14.4%	13.8%	12.8%	11.6%	NMF	17.1%	4.9%	3.3%	NMF	6.4%	**13.5%**	**14.0%**	% Earned Net Worth	12.0%
						10.8%	9.9%	9.8%	9.5%	NMF	13.7%	NMF	NMF	NMF	6.4%	**15.5%**	**15.0%**	% Retained to Comm Eq	10.5%
						32%	36%	35%	31%	--	33%	NMF	NMF	NMF	29%	**17%**	**17%**	% All Div'ds to Net Prof	24%

ASSETS ($mill.)

	1991	1992	9/30/93
Loans	147636	135851	135357
Funds Sold	4550	6381	11502
Securities	26777	32141	33687
Other Earning	8259	6550	6828
Other	29700	32778	33933

LIABILITIES($mill.)

Deposits	146475	144175	148546
Funds Borrowed	19174	20014	20326
Long-Term Debt	23345	20136	17623
Net Worth	9526	11217	13419
Other	18402	18159	21393
Total	216922	213701	221307
Loan Loss Resrv.	3308	3859	4260

ANNUAL RATES

of change (per sh)	Past 10 Yrs.	Past 5 Yrs.	Est'd '90-'92 to '96-'98
Loans	3.0%	-1.5%	-3.0%
Earnings	--	--	NMF
Dividends	.5%	-6.0%	3.0%
Book Value	2.5%	-2.5%	10.0%
Total Assets	2.5%	-2.0%	-1.0%

LOANS ($ mill.)

Calendar	Mar.31	Jun.30	Sep.30	Dec.31
1990	155467	154424	155206	151857
1991	151309	146816	148891	147636
1992	144599	144368	144309	135851
1993	133953	135103	135357	136500
1994	137000	137500	138500	140000

EARNINGS PER SHARE A

Calendar	Mar.31	Jun.30	Sep.30	Dec.31	Full Year
1990	.60	.64	.56	d1.26	.57E
1991	.17	d.12	d2.72	d.53	d3.22E
1992	.37	.25	.17	.53	1.35E
1993	.67	.82	.97	.94	3.40
1994	.97	1.01	1.06	1.11	4.15

QUARTERLY DIVIDENDS PAID B

Calendar	Mar.31	Jun.30	Sep.30	Dec.31	Full Year
1989	.37	.405	.405	.405	1.59
1990	.405	.445	.445	.445	1.74
1991	.25	.25	.25	--	.75
1992	--	--	--	--	--
1993	--	--	--	--	--

BUSINESS: Citicorp, the largest banking company in the United States, owns Citibank, N.A. Has more than 3,500 locations in 32 U.S. states, the District of Columbia, and 92 foreign countries. Loan portfolio breakdown at 12/31/92: commercial, government, and lease financing, 40%; consumer, 60%. Net income in 1992: consumer, 38%; commercial, 45%; North American real estate, loss of $1.3 billion; developing country, 17%. Net loan losses, 2.4% of av'g. loans in '92. Loan loss reserve, 3.05% of gross loans as of 9/30/93; nonperforming assets, 9.17% of loans and foreclosed R.E. Has 81,000 employees; 64,000 stockholders. As of 3/93 proxy, insiders own 1.5% of shares. Chairman: J.S. Reed. Inc.: DE. Address: 399 Park Avenue, NY, NY 10043. Telephone: 212-559-1000.

Citicorp appears to be making the transition from a turnaround mode to normal operations. Having completed a two-year plan to strengthen its equity capital base and expand its revenue/non-credit-related expense margin in 1992, the company moved a bit further down the recovery track in 1993. Its core capital-to-assets ratio (viewed by bank regulators as a measure of a bank's financial health) has risen from an acceptable 4.9% to a more comfortable 6%. Its commercial problem assets have declined by over 15% since the end of 1992. The operating margin, which expanded nearly 50% during the 1991-92 turnaround program, has widened another 7% in the first nine months of 1993, helped by strong trading and foreign exchange income. And, though still looking to cut costs where it can, Citi has started investing in promising (mostly consumer and developing country) businesses, in the hopes of reinvigorating revenue growth. The recovery will continue, but at a slower pace, N.A. Revenue growth may not pick up strongly given prospects for only slightly faster economic activity in the year ahead than in 1993, the intense competition (that appears to be worsening daily) in the important credit card business, and the possibility that volatile trading income might not be quite as strong in 1994 as in 1993. Also, Citi's long-term horizons may make keeping investment and advertising spending in line with current revenue growth challenging. And though we look for further declines in Citi's still relatively high level of problem assets to result in lower credit costs, Citi may continue building its loan loss reserve for a few more quarters, which at 78% of its commercial problem loans may be adequate but isn't as high as for peer banks. Several years hence, the geographic diversification of Citi's businesses ought to boost earnings growth. It has built an extensive presence in developing nations where its revenues are growing much faster than in developed economies. Citicorp stock, which has settled back a little since peaking in October, is top-ranked for the year ahead. And we think the dividend on the common stock might be restored in 1994, given the company's improved equity capital ratios.
Theresa Brophy   December 10, 1993

(A) Primary egs until '92; fully-diluted thereafter. In 1977-'82, excl. secur. gains (losses): '82, 9¢. Excl. nonrecurring gains: '82, 9¢; '83, 9¢. Excl. extraordinary gains: '88, 49¢; '90, 42¢; '91, $1.33; '93, 57¢. Next earnings report mid-Jan. (B) Dividend suspended. Last dividend paid August 12, 1991. (C) Incl. intangibles. In '92: $489 mill., $1.33/sh. (D) Only 3 dividend declarations in '86 due to change in timing of declaration dates. (E) Quarterly earnings don't add to total due to change in stock outst'g.(F) In millions, adjusted for stock split.

Company's Financial Strength	B
Stock's Price Stability	30
Price Growth Persistence	20
Earnings Predictability	5

Factual material is obtained from sources believed to be reliable, but the publisher is not responsible for any errors or omissions contained herein. For the confidential use of subscribers. Reprinting, copying, and distribution by permission only. Copyright 1993 by Value Line Publishing, Inc. ® Reg. TM—Value Line, Inc.

To subscribe call 1-800-833-0046.

In addition to the yearly figures disclosed in the spreadsheet, Value Line's analysis provides quarterly loans, earnings, and dividend data. Finally, a brief write-up of the company is presented.

BANK FAILURES

The extreme consequence of poor performance is failure. Exhibit 18.15 illustrates bank failure frequency over time. From 1940 to 1980, there were usually fewer than 20 bank failures per year. But in the late 1980s, there were about 200 failures per year. From 1990 to 1992, the number of failures declined, but was still much larger than in any previous period except the late 1980s. However, in 1993, there were only 43 bank failures, which was a significant improvement.

Reasons for Bank Failure

The cause of failure is often attributed to one or more of the following characteristics. First, fraud within the bank could have existed. Fraud represents a wide range of activities, including embezzlement of funds. Second, a high loan default percentage can lead to failure. Although banks recognize the potential consequence of a high loan default percentage, some continue to fail for this reason anyway. A thorough examination of any bank may show a general emphasis toward a specific industry—such as oil, shipbuilding, aerospace, agriculture, or national defense systems—that makes it vulnerable to a slowdown in that industry (or a related one). Moreover, no matter how well a bank diversifies its loans, its loan portfolio is still susceptible to a recessionary cycle.

A third reason for bank failure is a liquidity crisis. If a rumor of potential failure for a particular bank circulates, depositors may begin to withdraw funds from that bank, even though the bank is insured by the FDIC. The panic can even occur when the rumor is not justified. Under these conditions, a bank may be unable to attract a sufficient amount of new deposits, and its existing deposit accounts will subside. Once deposit withdrawals begin, it is difficult to stop the momentum.

A fourth reason for bank failures is increased competition. Deregulation has made the banking industry more competitive. When banks offer more competitive rates on deposits and loans, the result is a reduced net interest margin, and possibly failure if the margin is not large enough to cover other noninterest expenses and loan losses.

The Office of the Comptroller of the Currency reviewed 162 national banks that failed since 1979 and found the following common characteristics among many of these banks:

- 81 percent of the banks did not have a loan policy or did not closely follow their loan policy.
- 59 percent of the banks did not use an adequate system for identifying problem loans.
- 63 percent did not adequately monitor key bank officers or departments.
- At 57 percent of the banks, major corporate decisions were made by one individual.

EXHIBIT 18.15   Frequency of Bank Failures Over Time

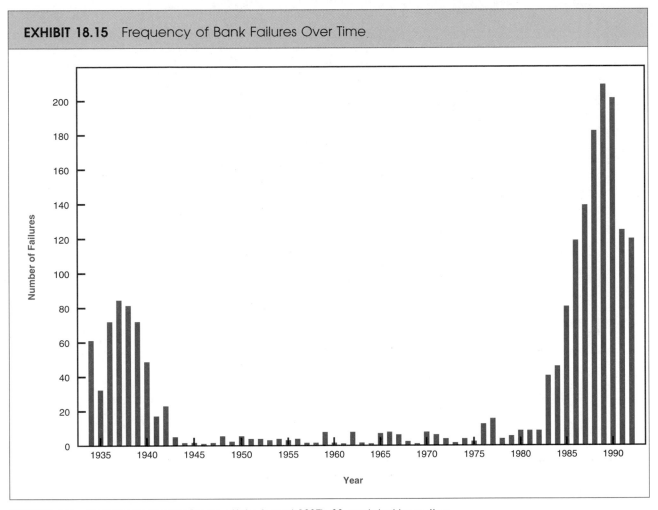

SOURCE: *New England Economic Review* (July–August 1987): 38, updated by author.

Because all of these characteristics are controllable at banks, it appears that many banks failed not because of the environment but because of inadequate management.

SUMMARY

- A bank's performance can be evaluated by comparing its income statement items (as a percentage of total assets) to a control group of other banks with a similar size classification. The return on assets (ROA) of the bank may be compared to that of the control group's mean ROA. Any difference in ROA between the bank and the control group is typically because of differences in net interest margin, loan loss reserves, noninterest income, or noninterest expenses.

   If the bank's net interest margin is relatively low, it either is relying too heavily on deposits with higher interest rates, or is not earning adequate interest on its loans. If the bank is forced to boost loan loss reserves, this suggests that its loan portfolio may be too risky. If its noninterest income is relatively low, the bank is not providing enough services that generate fee income. If the bank's noninterest expenses are relatively high, its cost of operations is excessive. There may be other specific details that make the assessment more complex, but the key problems of a bank can usually be detected with the approach described here.

■ A common measure of a bank's overall performance is its return on assets (ROA). The ROA has consistently been lower for money center banks than other banks. Their relatively low ROA is attributed to a lower net interest income (relatively high interest expenses due to the heavy reliance on large deposits for funds). Loan losses have also been higher for money center banks than other banks. Conversely, small banks have had a relatively high ROA, because of a relatively high net interest margin and a low level of loan loss reserves.

Money center banks have generated more noninterest income than the other banks, but this did not completely offset the relatively poor performance on the items described above.

QUESTIONS

1. How can gross interest income rise while the net interest margin remains somewhat stable for a particular bank?

2. How did deregulation affect gross interest expenses (as a percentage of assets)?

3. What has been the trend in noninterest income in recent years? Explain.

4. How would a bank generate a higher income before tax (as a percentage of assets) when its net interest margin has decreased?

5. Suppose a bank generates net interest margin of 1.50 percent. Based on past experience, would the bank experience a loss or a gain? Explain.

6. Why are large money center banks' net interest margins typically lower than those of smaller banks?

7. What does the beta of a bank indicate?

8. What are some of the more common reasons for a bank to experience a low ROA?

9. Why is it important for banks to have a consistent dividend payout policy, even if they are in trouble?

10. When evaluating a bank, what are some of the key aspects to review?

11. What are some reasons for bank failures identified in this chapter?

12. Assume that SUNY Bank plans to liquidate Treasury security holdings and use the proceeds for small business loans. Explain how the different income statement items would be affected over time as a result of this strategy. Also identify any income statement items that are more difficult to estimate as a result of this strategy.

PROBLEM

1. Hawaii Bank anticipates the following:

   - Loan loss reserves at end of year = 1 percent of assets
   - Gross interest income over the next year = 9 percent of assets
   - Noninterest expenses over the next year = 3 percent of assets
   - Noninterest income over the next year = 1 percent of assets
   - Gross interest expenses over the next year = 5 percent of assets
   - Tax rate on income = 30 percent
   - Capital ratio (defined as capital/assets) at end of year = 5 percent
     a. Forecast Hawaii Bank's net interest margin.
     b. Forecast Hawaii Bank's earnings before taxes as a percent of assets.
     c. Forecast Hawaii Bank's earnings after taxes as a percent of assets.
     d. Forecast Hawaii Bank's return on equity.
     e. Hawaii Bank is considering a shift in its asset structure to reduce its concentration of Treasury bonds and increase its volume of loans to small businesses. Identify each income statement item that would be affected by this strategy and explain whether the forecast for that item would increase or decrease.

Major Banks Are Expected to Report Sharply Higher Profit for 3rd Quarter

Steven Lipin

Major banks are expected to post higher earnings for the third quarter, helped by continued gains in securities and currency trading and a further decline in bad debts.

Expectations for a strong quarter were fueled yesterday by Chemical Banking Corp., which said it will report record earnings for the period. Chemical's shares rose 25 cents a share to close at $45.375 in New York Stock Exchange composite trading, and helped bank stocks continue their recent rally.

Other money-center banks that are expected to report improved results include Citicorp, J.P. Morgan & Co., Chase Manhattan Corp. and Bankers Trust New York Corp.

Analysts said the continued volatility in the European currencies and securities markets is giving banks an opportunity to earn fat profits by selling hedging techniques, such as swaps and options, to clients that want to diversify their risk. Banks also have been posting gains in trading for their own accounts.

"I do expect that we'll see a strong trading quarter pretty much across the board," said Raphael Soifer, banking analyst at Brown Brothers Harriman & Co. "The rest of the revenue will be flattish."

A Chemical spokesman, confirming remarks made by Chairman John McGillicuddy, said the banking company would exceed analysts' estimates of $1.37 a share, driven by strong trading revenue and across-the-board gains in its businesses. In the second quarter, the bank earned a record $1.35 a share. In the year-earlier third quarter Chemical earned 96 cents a share.

Among regional banks, Shawmut National Corp., based in Hartford, Conn., said it will post strong earnings of 70 cents a share because of lower expenses and stronger-than-expected revenue. In addition, nonperforming assets will be down 10% from the second quarter. In the year-earlier third quarter, the bank earned 14 cents a share.

First Boston Corp. is predicting that money-center banks will post an 11% earnings increase from a year earlier while super-regional banks show increases of 28% and regional banks report 26% gains.

"We believe that third-quarter profits for the U.S. commercial banking industry will continue to be characterized by improving fundamentals with respect to asset quality and productivity, as well as modest progress in both lending volumes and revenue growth," First Boston said in a recent report.

Certainly the stock market is expecting another strong quarter. In the third quarter, bank shares were up 3.9%, compared with 1.9% for the Standard & Poor's 500-Stock Index, according to Salomon Brothers.

The driving force behind the industry's continued strong earnings gains is still the decline in provisions for loan losses. Problem loans are on the decline, and many banks are now fully reserved for their bad debts. Net interest margins, a measurement of the profit between rates earned on loans and investments and the cost of borrowing, will continue to shrink gradually from their histori-cally wide levels. Net interest margins narrowed by about 0.07 percentage point in the second quarter.

"Most of the earnings improvement will still come from lower provisions," said Mr. Soifer. "Interest income isn't where it's at when it comes to revenue growth."

There will be revenue gains from some banks, though. Loans outstanding increased in the quarter, with practically all the gains coming from consumer lending, which tends to carry higher interest rates than business loans. In the past six months, bank loans were up $50 billion, driven by increases in credit cards, auto loans and residential mortgages, while delinquencies have fallen.

First Chicago Corp., for one, will likely benefit from the uptick in credit card loans. So will banks in the Southeast and Midwest, where loan growth is strongest.

"Regions which are growing faster than the national economy are acting like it in their loan totals," said Mr. Soifer.

Some analysts, such as Robert Albertson of Goldman, Sachs & Co., argue that there will be a lending recovery—and therefore revenue growth—driven first by consumer lending and then by commercial lending. Commercial loans, though, have yet to pick up, although banks are clearly more willing to extend credit.

Continued

CASE APPLICATION: IMPACT OF ECONOMIC CONDITIONS ON BANK PERFORMANCE

Continued

QUESTIONS

1. What is the underlying reason that would most likely explain the decline in the bad debt at banks?

2. Explain how the volatility in European currencies would affect the profitability of large U.S. banks.

3. Identify the main reasons for improvement in bank performance cited in the article, and offer your opinion on whether each reason is due to improvement in bank efficiency or to some external condition (such as the economy).

4. Within the article, there was a forecast of increased consumer (household) loans. Explain how this forecast can affect the bank income statement items to a different degree than increased loans to large corporations. Which banks should benefit the most from this forecast?

PROJECTS

1. **Assessment of Bank Performance**
   Obtain an investment advisory report (such as Value Line) or annual reports on a commercial bank of your or your group's choice (or one assigned by your professor). Use this information to determine the following:
   a. Is the bank's noninterest income becoming more important over time? Why?
   b. How have the bank's noninterest expenses as a percentage of assets changed over time? Explain why any changes may have occurred.
   c. How have the bank's provisions for loan losses as a percentage of assets changed over recent years? If any significant change occurred, explain why.
   d. Compare the bank's net interest margin to the general level of interest rates over recent years. Explain the relationship you find. The net interest margin is also affected by the bank's sources and uses of funds. Did the bank's net interest margin appear to be affected by any recent changes in sources or uses of funds? Explain.

2. **Impact of Interest Rates on Bank Earnings**
   a. Develop a model that could be used to determine how the return on assets for a particular bank (chosen by you or your professor) is affected by interest rate movements. Include all relevant variables for which data are available.
   b. Test your model to determine how the return on assets was affected by interest rate movements. Do the results support the type of relationship you hypothesized? Explain.
   c. Identify any limitations of your model.
   d. Suggest how you could use your model to forecast a bank's return on assets (ROA) based on projections of any variables that affect ROA.

3. **Estimation of Bank Risk**
   Use historical data to estimate the bank's beta. Does this bank appear to have a relatively high or low level of risk relative to other banks? Explain.

4. **Impact of Interest Rates on Bank Stock Prices**
   a. Develop a model that could be used to determine how the bank's stock returns are affected by interest rate movements. Include all relevant variables for which data are available.
   b. Assume that the bank's returns are thought to be significantly influenced by characteristics that are particularly relevant to the banking industry. Specify a model that could capture this influence.
   c. Apply your model to historical data to determine how the bank's stock returns have been affected by interest rate movements. Do the results support the type of relationship you hypothesized? Explain.
   d. Identify any limitations of your model.

REFERENCES

Berger, Allen N., Diana Hancock, and David B. Humphrey. "Bank Efficiency Derived from the Profit Function." *Journal of Banking and Finance* (April 1993): 317–347.

Black, Harold A., M. Andrew Fields, and Robert L. Schweitzer. "Changes in Interstate Banking: The Impact on Shareholder Wealth." *Journal of Finance* (December 1990): 1663–1672.

Brewer, Elijah, and G. D. Koppenhaver. "The Impact of Standby Letters of Credit on Bank Risk: A Note." *Journal of Banking and Finance* (December 1992): 1037–1046.

Flannery, Mark J. "Interest Rates and Bank Profitability: Additional Evidence." *Journal of Money, Credit, and Banking* (August 1983): 355–362.

Goldberg, Laurence G., Gerald A. Hanweck, and Timothy F. Sugrue. "Differential Impact on Bank Valuation of Interstate Banking Laws." *Journal of Banking and Finance* (December 1992): 1143–1158.

Linder, Jane C., and Dwight B. Crane. "Bank Mergers: Integration and Profitability." *Journal of Financial Services Research* (February 1993): 35–55.

McNulty, James E. "Economies of Scale: A Case Study of the Florida Savings and Loan Industry." *Economic Review*, Federal Reserve Bank of Atlanta (November 1982): 22–30.

O'Hara, Maureen, and Wayne Shaw. "Deposit Insurance and Wealth Effects: The Value of Being Too Big to Fail." *Journal of Finance* (December 1990): 1587–1600.

Osborne, Dale K., and Tarek S. Zoher. "Reserve Requirements, Bank Share Prices, and the Uniqueness of Bank Loans." *Journal of Banking and Finance* (August 1992): 799–55.

Saunders, Anthony, Elizabeth Strock, and Nickolaos Travlos. "Ownership Structure, Deregulation, and Bank Risk Taking." *Journal of Finance* (June 1990): 643–652.

Scott, William L., and Richard L. Peterson, "Interest Rate Risk and Equity Values of Hedged and Unhedged Financial Intermediaries." *Journal of Financial Research* (Winter 1986): 325–329.

Wall, Larry D. "Why Some Banks Are More Profitable Than Others." *Economic Review*, Federal Reserve Bank of Atlanta (September 1983): 42–48.

CHAPTER 19

INTERNATIONAL BANKING

International banking has received more attention in recent years for three reasons. First, banks are increasingly establishing subsidiaries and branches in foreign countries. Second, banking regulations in many countries have loosened, allowing easier entry or access to banking markets. Third, international lending has become a major issue as a result of the international debt crisis that continues to plague many large banks.

The specific objectives of this chapter are to:

- describe key regulations that have reduced competitive advantages of banks in particular countries,
- describe the risks of international banks,
- describe bank solutions to the international debt crisis, and
- describe how banks assess country risk when they consider lending funds to foreign countries.

BANK MIGRATION TO FOREIGN COUNTRIES

Because of historical barriers against interstate banking, some U.S. commercial banks were better able to achieve growth by penetrating foreign markets. It is somewhat ironic that the New York banks historically had branches in Taiwan and Hong Kong but not in New Jersey or Connecticut. If full-fledged interstate banking had been allowed throughout the years, large U.S. commercial banks would probably have concentrated more on the U.S. markets. As it was, international markets were their primary sources of growth. Their international business is normally corporate oriented rather than consumer oriented.

The most common method for U.S. commercial banks to expand is through establishing branches—full-service banking offices that can compete directly with other banks located in a particular area. Attempts by U.S. banks to establish foreign branches are subject to Federal Reserve Board approval. Among the factors considered by the Board are the bank's financial condition and experience in international business.

The U.S. bank presence is larger in the United Kingdom than in any other foreign country. Deposits in foreign branches of U.S. banks are not insured by the FDIC. Commercial banks may also consider establishing agencies, which can provide loans but cannot accept deposits or provide trust services.

Since 1913, **Edge Act corporations** have been established in the U.S. by banks to specialize in international banking and foreign financial transactions. These corporations are not constrained by existing regulations against interstate banking. They can accept deposits and provide loans, as long as these functions are specifically related to international transactions.

During the 1960s and 1970s, numerous banks established subsidiaries in the Eurocurrency market in response to the lack of regulations. The absence of reserve requirements and deposit insurance fees allowed banks to improve their profit margins. In addition, the absence of interest rate ceilings on deposits allowed banks to more aggressively compete for deposits. The Eurocurrency market is currently served by large banks from several different countries. Participating banks accept deposits and offer loans in numerous currencies.

International business allows firms to diversify among various economies so that their performance is less dependent on economic conditions of any single country. This is the motive for many U.S. commercial banks establishing branches around the world. Such international diversification of loans is thought to reduce the impact of a U.S. recession on the risk of U.S. bank loan portfolios. Furthermore, the establishment of branches allows a bank to do business face to face with subsidiaries of U.S.-based multinational corporations. The global expertise of some of the larger U.S. banks distinguishes them from the small and medium banks and enables them to dominate business by attracting the large corporations.

While U.S. banks have entered non-U.S. markets, non-U.S. banks have also entered U.S. markets. Initially, they entered primarily to serve the non-U.S. corporations that set up subsidiaries in the United States. Because this still serves as their primary function, they concentrate on corporate rather than consumer services.

The number of foreign bank offices in the United States has consistently increased over time. More than one-third of all foreign bank offices in the United States are from Japan, Canada, the United Kingdom, and France. Almost half of these offices are located in New York, where many of the foreign-owned corporations conduct business. As an example of non-U.S. bank involvement in the United States, Japanese banks use the U.S. market as a source of funds during periods of tight credit in Japan. Japanese banks also increase their business in the United States when Japanese-U.S. trade increases, which suggests how international banking is dependent on international trade activity.

GLOBAL BANK REGULATIONS

Although the division of regulatory power between the central bank and other regulators varies among countries, each country has a system for monitoring and regulating commercial banks. Most countries also maintain different guidelines for deposit insurance. Differences in regulatory restrictions can allow some banks a competitive advantage in a global banking environment.

Canada's banks tend to be subject to fewer banking regulations than U.S. banks. For instance, Canadian banks can expand throughout Canada, allowing the larger Canadian banks to control much of the market share. Canadian banks are also not as restricted as U.S. banks on investment banking activities, and therefore control much of the Canadian securities industry. Recently, Canadian banks have begun to enter the insurance industry.

European banks tend to have much more freedom than U.S. banks in the offering of investment banking activities such as underwriting corporate securities. In fact, many European branches of U.S. banks provide investment banking services in Europe that would not be allowed in the U.S. European banks have penetrated the insurance industry in recent years by acquiring numerous insurance companies. Many European banks are allowed to invest in stocks.

Japanese commercial banks have some flexibility to provide investment banking services, but not as much as European banks. Perhaps the most obvious difference between Japanese and U.S. bank regulations is that Japanese banks are allowed to use depositor funds to invest in stocks of corporations. Thus, Japanese banks are not only creditors, but are also shareholders of firms. The Japanese government has recently eased banking regulations on interest ceilings and lending activities.

Uniform Global Regulations

The globalization of markets and other financial services is motivated by the standardization of some regulations around the world. Three of the more significant regulatory events allowing for a more competitive global playing field are (1) the International Banking Act, which placed U.S. and foreign banks operating in the United States under the same set of rules, (2) the Single European Act, which placed all European banks operating in Europe under the same set of rules, and (3) the uniform capital adequacy guidelines, which forced banks of 12 industrialized nations to abide by the same minimum capital constraints. A discussion of each of these key events follows.

UNIFORM REGULATIONS FOR BANKS OPERATING IN THE U.S.   A key act related to international banking was the International Banking Act (IBA) of 1978, designed to impose similar regulations across domestic and foreign banks doing business in the United States. Prior to the Act, foreign banks had more flexibility to cross state lines in the United States than U.S.-based banks. The IBA required foreign banks to identify one state as their home state so that they would be regulated like other U.S.-based banks residing in that state. The stock prices of money center banks increased in response to the announcement. Regional banks did not experience a significant stock price reaction. This may have resulted from provisions in the IBA that would allow foreign banks to become more competitive in the United States at the retail level. Such provisions are of more concern to regional banks than wholesale-oriented money center banks and could offset any favorable consequences of other IBA provisions on regional banks.

UNIFORM REGULATIONS ACROSS EUROPE.   One of the most significant events affecting the international banking markets is the Single European Act, which was phased in throughout the European Economic Community (EEC) countries. The following are some of the more relevant provisions of the Act for the banking industry:

- Capital can flow freely throughout Europe.
- Banks can offer a wide variety of lending, leasing, and securities activities in the EEC.
- The regulations regarding competition, mergers, and taxes will be similar throughout the EEC.
- A bank established in any one of the EEC countries has the right to expand into any or all of the other EEC countries.

As a result of the Single European Act, a common market has been established for 12 European countries. One of the key objectives of the Act is to facilitate the free flow of capital across countries in order to enhance financial market efficiency. To this end, the Act eliminated capital controls imposed by individual European countries on services such as deposit taking, lending, leasing, portfolio management advice, and credit references.

European banks are already consolidating across countries. Efficiency in the European banking markets will increase as banks can more easily cross countries without concern about country-specific regulations that prevailed in the past.

Another key provision of the Act is that banks can enter Europe and receive the same banking powers as other banks there. Similar provisions are allowed for non-U.S. banks that enter the United States.

Even some European savings institutions will be affected by more uniform regulations across European countries. Savings institutions throughout Europe are now evolving into full-service institutions, expanding into services such as insurance, brokerage, and mutual fund management.

The European Commission has been empowered to make rules and regulations uniform across member countries. This task becomes very complicated when dealing with goods and services provided by 12 different countries. The commission has switched to a simplified approach where any product approved under one country's national laws can be sold in any other member country. This strategy shifts the burden of regulatory restrictions to the home country of the firm's European headquarters.

Commercial banks in one member country will be able to do business in the other 11 countries without having to conform to country-specific restrictions that previously existed. However, the oligopolistic nature of the industry in some European countries will still represent a significant barrier to foreign banks. The banking industry in France, Great Britain, and Germany is dominated by just a few banks.

UNIFORM CAPITAL ADEQUACY GUIDELINES AROUND THE WORLD. Before 1987, capital standards imposed on banks varied across countries, which allowed some banks to have a comparative global advantage over others. As an example, consider a bank in the United States that is subject to a 6 percent capital ratio that is twice that of a foreign bank. The foreign bank could achieve the same return on equity as the U.S. bank by generating a return on assets that is only one-half that of the U.S. bank. In essence, the foreign bank's leverage measure (assets divided by equity) would be double that of the U.S. bank, which would offset the low return on assets. Given these conditions, foreign banks could accept lower profit margins while still achieving the same return on equity. This affords them a stronger competitive position. In addition, growth is more easily achieved, as a relatively small amount of capital is needed to support an increase in assets.

Some analysts would counter that these advantages are somewhat offset by the higher risk perception of banks having low capital ratios. Yet, if the governments in those countries are more likely to back banks that experience financial problems, banks with low capital may not necessarily be too risky. Therefore, some non-U.S. banks had globally competitive advantages over U.S. banks without being subject to excessive risk. In December 1987, 12 major industrialized countries attempted to resolve the disparity by proposing uniform bank standards. In July 1988, central bank governors of the 12 countries agreed on standardized guidelines. Briefly, capital was classified as either Tier 1 capital (which is primarily retained earnings or funds obtained from issuing stock) or Tier 2 capital (which includes loan loss reserves and some forms of long-term debt). Tier 1 capital must be at least 4 percent of risk-weighted assets. The use of risk weightings on assets implicitly caused a higher capital ratio for riskier assets, because those assets were assigned lower weights. Off-balance sheet items were also accounted for so that banks could not circumvent capital requirements by focusing on services (such as letters of credit and interest rate swaps) that are not explicitly shown on a balance sheet. Even with uniform capital requirements across countries, some analysts may still contend that U.S. banks are at a competitive disadvantage because they are subject to different accounting and tax provisions. Nevertheless, the uniform capital requirements represent significant progress toward a more level global field.

GLOBAL BANK COMPETITION

As the markets for loans and other financial services become more integrated, banks from any given country are recognizing that their main competition may be foreign banks. U.S. banks have always had a competitive advantage in technology, such as devising new products and services. For example, U.S. banks are advanced in their creation of interest rate swaps and currency swaps. They also dominate the market for selling packaged loans.

U.S. BANK EXPANSION IN FOREIGN COUNTRIES. U.S. banks have recently established foreign subsidiaries wherever they expected more foreign expansion by U.S. firms, such as in Southeast Asia and Eastern Europe. In the last few years, expansion has been focused on Latin America. As a result of the North American Free Trade Agreement (NAFTA), several U.S. banks, including Bankers Trust, Chase Manhattan, and Chemical Bank planned to expand their business in Mexico. These banks can help finance the ongoing expansion by U.S-based corporations that are establishing subsidiaries in Mexico. They can also benefit from the increased international trade by offering banker's acceptances, and foreign exchange services. If Mexico's economy strengthens as a result of the NAFTA, these banks will likely offer credit card services and other household services. Because the NAFTA may lead to a broader trade agreement with many Lain American countries, many U.S. banks are also considering expansion throughout these countries.

CITICORP'S GLOBAL OPERATIONS

International banking is not solely concentrated on foreign loans. To illustrate the diversity in international banking services, consider the case of Citicorp. Some of the key services offered by Citicorp to firms around the world include foreign exchange transactions, forecasting, risk management, cross-border trade finance, acquisition finance, cash management services, and local currency funding. Citicorp not only serves large multinational corporations such as Coca Cola, Dow Chemical, IBM, and Sony, but also small firms that need international banking services.

Citicorp is a major participant in the money centers such as London, New York, and Tokyo. Yet, it also does business in smaller cities such as Lima and Taipei. It has also established relations with banks in Eastern Europe so that it can serve its corporate customers that are establishing business there.

Citicorp is abreast of tax and accounting regulations and economic conditions around the world, which allows it to offer related consulting services. It has also established a global account profitability system that tracks revenue and expenses for its clients around the world.

About 40 percent of Citicorp's assets are in countries outside the United States. About 50 percent of its non-U.S. assets are in Europe, the Middle East, or Asia. About 20 percent of the non-U.S. assets are in the Caribbean or in South America. The remaining 30 percent of non-U.S. assets are in Asia or the Pacific Basin. Overall, Citicorp has offices in 93 countries. By spreading itself across the world, Citicorp can typically handle the banking needs of all of a multinational corporation's subsidiaries.

NON-U.S. BANK EXPANSION IN THE U.S.   Non-U.S. banks have been more aggressive in penetrating the U.S. market. Japanese banks have a very significant presence in the United States. They control about 25 percent of the California market. One major reason for their growth is very competitive corporate loans. They also have been known to provide letters of credit for lower fees than those charged by U.S. banks. Another reason for their growth is a relatively low cost of capital, which allows them to take on more ventures that might not be feasible to U.S. banks. Furthermore, the high savings rate of the Japanese banks allows for substantial growth in deposits in Japan, which may then be channeled to support operations in the United States.

Competition for Investment Banking Services

A variety of financial services in addition to loans have become globalized, in which there is competition between financial institutions from numerous countries. Some of the more obvious examples of global participation are in such services as foreign exchange, swaps, and such investment banking services as underwriting and brokerage. Some commercial banks were initially able to offer a complete range of services by establishing subsidiaries in countries with fewer regulations.

One of the most common examples of commercial banks' circumventing regulations by migration to other countries is in the securities industry. In most non-U.S. countries, commercial banks can participate in such securities activities as underwriting and full-service brokerage. In the United States, securities and banking activities continue to be somewhat separated, although commercial banks in the United States have recently been allowed some underwriting and brokerage privileges. Non-U.S. commercial banks are more able to diversify across services products because of fewer regulatory barriers. U.S. banks have attempted to diversify across products by establishing subsidiaries in foreign markets. However, this is an inconvenient approach for smaller banks that would prefer to focus on a region of the United States. In addition, the U.S. restrictions prevent U.S. commercial banks from fully capitalizing on economies of scale in securities activities.

Since 1988, the barriers between securities and traditional banking activities have diminished, allowing U.S. commercial banks to behave more like non-U.S. banks. In 1988, some money center banks in the United States filed applications requesting that specific subsidiaries be allowed to underwrite and deal in corporate debt. In January 1989, the Federal Reserve Board approved the applications contingent on specific requirements, including the requirement that the revenues from debt underwriting be limited to 5 percent of the bank subsidiary's total revenues. The generation of fee income from underwriting has become more desirable since the more stringent capital requirements have been imposed. Underwriting allows banks to boost their revenues without significantly altering their asset size. Therefore, growth into the underwriting business will not necessarily require an increase in the required capital. The underwriting activities by banks could also lead to closer relationships with corporate clients and allow them to facilitate mergers and acquisitions for additional fee income.

IMPACT OF EASTERN EUROPEAN REFORM

The lifting of the Iron Curtain in November 1989 attracted the attention of commercial banks around the world. The privatization of businesses has caused a substantial need for financing. Some of the more obvious ways in which banks can facilitate the trends toward privatization are (1) providing direct loans to businesses, (2) acting as an underwriter on bonds or stock issued by firms in Eastern Europe, (3) providing letters of credit, and (4) providing consulting services on international trade, mergers, and other corporate activities. Although opportunities abound, banks are also wary of the risk. In the past, some banks aggressively pursued loans to Poland, which postponed interest payments in 1982. They aggressively pursued lending to Latin American countries; this activity was followed by numerous debt reschedulings over the 1980s. More recently, some banks have aggressively financed leveraged buyouts and real estate investments, which could also have serious adverse effects.

The deregulatory momentum in Western Europe and Eastern Europe has precipitated strategic responses by commercial banks. Several banks are forming alliances with other banks to provide customers with reciprocal opportunities. Other banks within particular European countries merged as a defensive measure to protect their local business. Some European banks are merging with insurance companies.

Even with the actions just described, the European banking industry will continue to be somewhat fragmented. Cross-border mergers between banks have not been as popular as mergers within countries. With the exception of credit cards, bank services will still be offered on a national basis. Cultural differences between countries will prevent some services from being standardized across countries.

RISKS OF A EUROBANK

Eurobanks, like other commercial banks, must manage their exposure to various types of risk. However, their degree of exposure can differ because of their unique characteristics. The most common types of risk to which Eurobanks are exposed are default, exchange rate, and interest rate risk.

Default Risk

When U.S. banks provide foreign loans, they must often work with less information than they usually have for domestic loans. This is true even when they have branches in the countries where the loans are provided. Regulations in foreign countries pertaining to the method and amount of information disclosure are typically not as strict as in the United States. Even if the bank requests additional information, the industry norms on financial ratios will vary significantly among countries. Thus, banks may be unsure of the proper benchmarks to use when assessing a loan applicant. To deal with this problem, some banks attempt to lend only to the very large corporations that have a global household name. Alternatively, they may concentrate on loans to national governments, who theoretically can use their taxing or money-printing powers to guarantee loan repayment. However, the international debt crisis in the early 1980s proved that loans to national governments are not automatically safe.

The loan portfolio of any given foreign branch of a large U.S. bank is likely to be heavily concentrated in the country where it is located, while the consolidation of all branches may show a widely diversified loan portfolio. If a branch attempts to diversify across countries, it is unable to concentrate on the local area that it knows best. Because loans by each branch are narrowly focused on a particular economy, the performance of each branch can be highly susceptible to that economy. In general, the loan policy of the branch is to diversify loans across industries within the economy, while the overall loan policy of the entire commercial bank is to diversify loans across countries. Both objectives may be achieved if the commercial bank has established branches in various countries.

Exchange Rate Risk

When a bank providing a loan requires that the borrower repay in the currency denominating the loan, it may be able to avoid exchange rate risk. However, some international loans contain a clause that allows repayment in a foreign currency, thus allowing the borrower to avoid exchange rate risk.

In many cases, banks will convert available funds (from recent deposits) to whatever currency corporations want to borrow. Thus, they create an asset denominated in that currency, while the liability (deposits) is denominated in a different currency. If the liability currency appreciates against the asset currency, the bank's profit margin is reduced.

All large banks are exposed to exchange rate risk to some degree. They can attempt to hedge this risk in various ways. For example, consider a U.S. bank that converted dollar deposits into a British pound (£) loan for a British corporation. Assume that the British firm will pay £50,000 in interest per year. The U.S. bank may attempt to engage in forward contracts to sell £50,000 forward for each date in which it will receive those interest payments. That is, it could search for corporations that may wish to purchase £50,000 on the dates of concern.

In reality, a large bank will not hedge every individual transaction but will instead net out the exposure and be concerned only with net exposure. Large banks enter into several international transactions on any given day. Some reflect future cash inflows in a particular currency, while others reflect cash outflows in that currency. The bank's exposure to exchange rate risk is determined by the net cash flow in each currency.

Interest Rate Risk

The performance of commercial banks can be susceptible to interest rate fluctuations regardless of their degree of international business. Yet, the existence of foreign currency balances makes management of interest rate risk even more challenging. The strategy of matching the overall interest rate sensitivity of assets to that of liabilities will not automatically achieve a low degree of interest rate risk. For example, consider a Eurobank that has deposits denominated mostly in marks, while its floating-rate loans are denominated mostly in dollars. Even if the bank matches the average deposit maturity with the average loan maturity, the difference in currency denominations creates interest rate risk. The deposit and loan rates on various currencies depend on the interest rates in those respective countries. Thus, the performance of a bank concentrated in mark deposits and dollar loans will be adversely affected if German interest rates increase and U.S. rates decrease.

Even if the currency mix of a bank's assets is similar to that of its liabilities and overall rate sensitivity of assets and liabilities is similar, interest rate risk may still exist. Consider a bank that has short-term dollar deposits and medium- or long-term fixed-rate mark deposits. Assume that it provides short-term (or adjustable-rate) mark loans and long-term dollar loans. An increase in U.S. rates would reduce the spread on U.S. dollar loans versus deposits, because the dollar liabilities are more rate sensitive than the dollar assets. In addition, an increase in German rates would increase the spread on the mark loans versus deposits, because the mark assets are more rate sensitive than the mark liabilities. This example illustrates that exposure to interest rate risk can be minimized only if the rate sensitivities of assets and liabilities are matched for each currency.

Combining All Types of Risk

When default risk, exchange rate risk, and interest rate risk are considered simultaneously, asset and liability management of a Eurobank becomes very complex. The management of one type of risk can affect exposure to another type. For example, a Eurobank that receives a large amount of French franc deposits may attempt to minimize its exchange rate exposure by calling on those local firms that would most likely need to borrow French francs. The bank is simply attempting to maintain the same currency concentration on both sides of the balance sheet. However, those particular firms may be close to their debt capacity. The bank would therefore need to decide whether to accept a high degree of default risk in order to minimize exchange rate risk. If it decided against channeling these funds to those firms with already high debt, it might be forced to provide loans in some other currency, thereby increasing its exchange rate exposure.

The Eurobank's exposure to various risks can best be understood by considering the typical daily transactions. During any given day, Eurobanks receive deposits in a variety of different currencies, amounts, and maturities and provide loans in various currencies, amounts, and maturities. It is unlikely that even a single deposit will perfectly match a loan request in terms of currency, amount, and maturity. Thus, the bank is constantly converting currencies received as deposits to the type of loans desired, thereby creating a short position in one currency and long position in another. It may also involve the use of short-term deposits to make medium-term loans, exposing the bank to interest rate risk. The Eurobank's exposure to the various forms of risk occurs as it accommodates the precise desires of savers and borrowers. If it is not willing to provide a deposit or loan with the specific currency, amount, and maturity desired by corporations or governments, some other Eurobank will.

INTERNATIONAL DEBT CRISIS

At any given point in time, some countries may be experiencing strong economic growth while others are stagnant. This is a primary reason for limiting the total percentage of loans to any one country. Yet, the 1980 and 1982 recessions affected all countries. To the extent that countries trade with each other, economies are integrated. The stagnant economies in Europe and the United States adversely affected each other in the early 1980s, and exporting volume declined. Furthermore, their demand for exports from less developed countries (LDCs) decreased. Because many LDC economies are highly dependent on their export business, the recession in the United States and Europe had a dramatic impact. In addition, the market price of oil was reduced because of the oil glut at that time. Consequently, the oil-exporting LDCs were generating less revenue than anticipated. As a result of the recession and declining oil prices, borrowers residing in many LDCs (governments and corporations) were not generating enough cash to repay their loans.

The debt problems of the LDCs were adversely affected by the strengthening dollar during the early 1980s. Many of the loans provided to LDCs were denominated in U.S. dollars. As the dollar strengthened, more of the LDCs' currency was needed to make payments. In addition, the interest rates in the early 1980s were at their peak, exceeding 20 percent in 1981. The high market interest rates, combined with the strengthening U.S. dollar, caused the effective (exchange rate-adjusted) interest rate on previous loans to be 30 percent or more.

In August 1982, Mexico's government announced that it was unable to pay on its debt, and several LDCs followed Mexico's lead. This event became known as the international debt crisis (IDC). The effects of the IDC continued throughout the 1980s and into the 1990s. Commercial banks that provided loans to LDCs did not anticipate that several governments would simultaneously announce their inability to repay loans. The situation was intensified by a plea of some of the governments for additional funds to rescue them from economic disaster. This put the bankers on the spot. They were already being criticized for being too aggressive with their lending. Now they were forced to decide between two alternative actions: (1) provide additional loans and incur the risk that these loans as well as previous loans would never be paid back and (2) reject the LDCs' request for additional funds, realizing that the LDCs would then likely be unwilling to repay their existing loans.

The negotiating power of LDCs was enhanced because they, as a group, announced their inability to repay loans. If a single LDC had defaulted, the lending commercial banks would not have been as concerned. However, when several LDCs simultaneously are unable to repay loans, banks are not as willing to write off loans at once. They instead search for a long-term economic rescue plan that may someday allow for repayment.

The commercial banks also had more negotiating power as a group. The LDCs may not be as concerned with threats of a single commercial bank (if certain conditions of the loan agreement are not met), because there are other banks with which the LDCs could do business in the future. But if all lending banks as a group require the LDCs to meet certain conditions, the consequences of not following through are more severe.

Negotiations between the commercial banks, LDCs, and the International Monetary Fund (IMF) were held in 1983. The IMF participated, because one of its main functions is to promote international business. If negotiations between commercial banks and the LDCs had broken down, international trade between the developed countries and the LDCs would have been significantly reduced. In November 1983 the IMF Funding Bill was passed to provide additional funding to those LDCs that could meet specified economic goals. The goals differed for each LDC.

Historically, loan rescheduling allowed for a short-term delay of loan repayments, such as one or two years. This had only a slight impact on the cash flows of lending banks. However, it does not allow the borrowers much time to cure their financial problems. The financial problems of the LDCs were so severe that banks were forced to offer multiyear rescheduling. This strategy offered governments of LDCs a long-term period for curing their financial problems, but also forced the banks to be more patient in receiving their loan repayments.

The ability of debtor nations to cover their debt depends on their ability to export and to attract foreign investment. Since they are unable to attract foreign investment when their existing debt level is perceived to be high, they must rely on exports. Given that many countries have this same goal in mind, they cannot all attain it. Some countries can be net exporters only if others are willing to be net importers.

Reducing Bank Exposure to LDC Debt

Nine money center banks make up more than 60 percent of the total U.S. bank exposure to troubled LDCs. Although the exposure is concentrated within a small group of banks, these nine banks are the largest. The failure of even a single money center bank could potentially result in a panic within the financial system.

To reduce exposure during the international debt crisis, banks utilized the following strategies:

- Selling LDC loans
- Debt-equity swaps
- Boosting loan loss reserves

SELLING LDC LOANS. Many commercial banks in the United States and other countries attempted to sell a portion of their LDC loans in the secondary market. Some Middle Eastern and European banks sold their entire Latin American loan portfolio. Many banks were willing to sell the loans cheaply and incur the loss immediately. The perceived probability of loan repayment can be assessed by reviewing the discounts on LDC loans sold in the secondary market. Exhibit 19.1 shows the market price for which loans to various countries were selling in the secondary loan market as of 1993. The LDC loans were selling for between 50 cents and 89 cents to the dollar, representing discounts from 11 percent to 50 percent.

DEBT-EQUITY SWAPS. An alternative method of reducing exposure to LDC loans is the **debt-equity swap,** in which a bank swaps the debt in exchange for some assets owned by the borrower. As an example, Citicorp swapped claims on Chile's debt in exchange for an equity investment in Chile's gold mining. Chase Manhattan Corporation, First Chicago Corporation, and other banks have exchanged Peruvian debt for Peruvian exports. Many swaps have been conducted through nonbank multinationals. U.S.-based multinationals, including General Electric and Chrysler, purchased LDC loans at a discount in the secondary market and then exchanged the debt for companies or other assets owned by the borrower.

BOOSTING LOAN LOSS RESERVES. Some banks recently reacted to their large LDC debt exposure by increasing their loan loss reserves. Because income is used

---

EXHIBIT 19.1 Secondary Market Price of Loans to Less Developed Countries (as of 1993)

COUNTRY	LOAN PRICE (CENTS PER DOLLAR)
Argentina	60
Brazil	50
Chile	89
Mexico	75
Venezuela	69

SOURCE: *Barrons.*

to build the loan loss reserve account, an increase in reserves causes a reduction in reported earnings. In May 1987, Citicorp announced a $3 billion-dollar increase in loan loss reserves. Over the following months, several other money center and regional banks followed this strategy. These actions signal anticipation that some of the LDC loans will default or that only a portion of the loans will ultimately be repaid.

In September 1989, another round of increases in loan loss reserves began for some money center banks. The most publicized announcement was J.P. Morgan's increase in loan loss reserves by $2 billion, which boosted its loan loss reserve account to match its total LDC debt exposure. The total loan loss reserves at other money center banks only represented between 35 percent and 50 percent of medium- and long-term LDC debt.

Use of the Brady Plan to Reduce LDC Debt Exposure

Over the period from 1985 to 1988 a plan was endorsed as a means of mitigating the LDC debt crisis. The plan was based on voluntary actions by lenders to reduce their exposure. In December 1988 the World bank proposed a gradual implementation of the plan, along with its commitment to provide loans to LDCs in place of bank loans and impose economic reforms on the LDCs. During 1989 the plan gained momentum as the International Monetary Fund signalled its willingness to replace LDC debt maintained by banks. In what then became known as the Brady Plan, negotiations between banks and individual LDCs were encouraged in order to provide banks with the option of having their debt replaced by the World Bank and IMF by trading it in at a discount. In July 1989 banks reached an agreement with Mexico in which they were given the following options: (1) agree to a 35 percent cut in the principal or interest on loans, or (2) grant new loans equal to 25 percent of the Mexican loans. Essentially, the trade-off involved either recognizing losses on previous loans while reducing exposure or increasing investment in LDCs without incurring immediate losses. The agreement could improve Mexico's position because it reduces the amount Mexico owes on existing debt and allows for additional loans from banks. In this way, Mexico may be more able to improve its debt servicing, which would enhance investors' perceptions of Mexican debt maintained by banks. The agreement between banks and Mexico is encouraging because it could pave the way for agreements with other countries.

A dilemma involved in resolving the crisis is that if all banks prefer to discontinue loans to LDCs by writing off all or a portion of existing loans, the LDCs may be unable to secure adequate financing to improve economic conditions. The LDCs' only chance to repay existing loans is by economic reform, which requires more loans. Yet many banks may feel that providing additional loans is like "throwing good money after bad." For this reason, the use of World Bank and IMF funds to assume commercial bank debt at some discounted price could help resolve the ongoing crisis.

Although the impact of the international debt crisis is not over, commercial banks are more prepared to deal with it than they were in the 1980s. The crisis has demonstrated that diversifying loans among foreign countries does not guarantee low risk and that loans for foreign governments are not risk-free. These lessons have changed the long-term planning of commercial banks.

COUNTRY RISK ASSESSMENT

Banks have historically used country risk analysis for measuring the risk of loans to foreign governments. Country risk assessment systems have recently received more attention as a result of the international debt crisis. Those banks that were highly exposed to the loans of the problem LDCs either had a poor country risk assessment system or did not take their assessment seriously. Although each bank has its own unique assessment system, most systems involve identifying factors that influence country risk and then weighting these factors. Some of the factors can be measured in an objective fashion, while others must be measured subjectively. An effective country risk assessment system would signal potential financial problems of a country before they occur, allowing banks to avoid lending to those countries or at least to reduce their existing loan exposure to those countries. Some of the more important factors that affect country risk are:

- Economic indicators
- Debt management
- Political factors
- Structural factors

Short-term and medium-term models of these four aspects can be developed to determine an overall short-term rating for a country and an overall medium-term rating.

Economic Indicators

The economic indicator model evaluates the country's economic environment. Some of the more relevant factors for this model are

- Changes in the consumer price index
- Real growth in gross domestic product
- Current account balance divided by exports

A statistical technique called discriminant analysis can be applied to these and other economic indicators to determine how they influence debt-repayment problems. This analysis creates a function that can be used to assign an overall rating to the country's economic indicators.

Debt Management

The debt management model evaluates a country's ability to manage debt. The more relevant variables for rating debt management include

- Debt service and short-term debt divided by total exports
- Ratio of total debt to gross domestic product
- Short-term debt divided by total debt

Other things being equal, the higher the debt service and short-term debt are relative to exports or to gross domestic product, the higher the probability that a country would experience debt-repayment problems. The ratio of short-term debt to total debt indicates the percentage of debt principal that must be repaid in the near future. A high percentage could cause cash flow problems in the near future. In addition, countries with a high percentage are usually more vulnerable to interest rate movements.

Political Factors

The political rating model is used to measure governmental characteristics and political stability. The political factors (some of which follow) are generally measured subjectively.

- Probability of destabilizing riots or civil unrest
- Probability of increased terrorist activities
- Probability of civil war
- Probability of foreign war
- Probability of government overthrow

Each factor can be assigned a probability ranging from 1 (extremely likely) to 5 (extremely unlikely).

Structural Factors

The structural rating model measures socioeconomic conditions. Some of the more important structural factors are

- Natural resource base
- Human resource base
- Leadership

These factors are also subjectively rated.

Overall Rating

Each of the four models can assign a score between 0 and 100, and the overall rating is determined by weighing the importance of the models. An example of how the overall rating is determined is shown in Exhibit 19.2. Note that a grade is assigned for both the short- and medium-term horizons. The grades for this hypothetical example were higher for the short term. Economic indicators were thought to be more important in the short-term horizon, while the political rating was more important for the medium-term horizon.

The overall numerical grade for each horizon can be converted into a rating based on Standard and Poor's rating system on securities. The country's short-term horizon received a rating of A, while its medium-term horizon received a grade of BBB (see Exhibit 19.3).

Country Risk Ratings

Institutional Investor magazine surveys international bankers to obtain country credit ratings, and discloses the average rating for each country. Recent country risk ratings of various European and Latin American countries are shown in

APPLIED RESEARCH

DISCRIMINANT ANALYSIS FOR IDENTIFYING CHARACTERISTICS THAT AFFECT COUNTRY RISK

Discriminant analysis is useful for identifying factors that are distinctly different between two groups. It has historically been used to identify factors that distinguish (or discriminate) between successful and failing firms. It could even be used to distinguish between good and bad sports teams or between successful and unsuccessful employees of a firm.

As a popular technique for country risk assessment, discriminant analysis attempts to identify factors that distinguish between countries experiencing debt-repayment problems and countries not experiencing such problems. Once these factors are known, they can be closely monitored.

The factors hypothesized to discriminate between two groups must first be identified and then numeri-

cally measurable. The factors are then measured by historical data. Discriminant analysis generates a discriminant function that determines not only which factors distinguish between the two groups but also the type of influence each factor has.

Research by Morgan used discriminant analysis to assess the influence of variables on the likelihood that a country would need to reschedule its loan repayments. Morgan found the following characteristics of countries whose loan payments were rescheduled:

- Their total debt to exports ratio was relatively high.
- Their proportion of floating-rate loans (relative to total loans) was relatively high.
- Their real growth rate in gross domestic product (GDP) was relatively low.

Additional results are provided in the article itself.

Although discriminant analysis is useful for identifying characteristics that distinguish countries that rescheduled loans from those that did not, its accuracy in predicting reschedulings depends on whether those characteristics continue to have a similar impact on reschedulings. For example, using Morgan's results, one would expect that a country with a greater proportion of floating-rate loans would have a higher probability of experiencing loan-repayment problems. However, if interest rates were to decrease in the future, countries with a greater proportion of floating-rate loans might be favorably affected.

EXHIBIT 19.2   Example of Determining Country Risk Ratings

	SHORT-TERM HORIZON			MEDIUM-TERM HORIZON		
	Weight	Grade	Weighted Grade	Weight	Grade	Weighted Grade
Debt management model	.3	80	24	.3	70	21
Economic indicator model	.3	90	27	.2	70	14
Political rating model	.2	60	12	.3	50	15
Structural rating model	.2	75	$\frac{15}{78}$	.2	60	$\frac{12}{62}$

EXHIBIT 19.3	Conversion of a Country's Grade into a Rating	
OVERALL GRADE RATING	**RATING**	
91–100	AAA	Excellent
81–90	AA	
71–80	A	
61–70	BBB	Satisfactory quality, average risk
51–60	BB	
41–50	B	
31–40	CCC	Low quality, high risk
21–30	CC	
11–20	C	
0–10	D	Excessive risk

Exhibit 19.4. In general, the industrialized countries have relatively high ratings, while the ratings in less developed countries in Eastern Europe and Latin America are lower.

SUMMARY

- Recently, key regulations have reduced competitive advantages of banks in particular countries. First, the International Banking Act of 1978 imposed similar regulations across domestic and foreign banks doing business in the U.S. Second, the Single European Act allowed for uniform bank regulations across European countries. Third, uniform capital standards were imposed on banks throughout industrialized countries.

- Banks conducting international business are exposed to default risk on their loans. They are also exposed to exchange rate risk when they convert liabilities denominated in one currency to assets denominated in another currency. They are also exposed to movements in interest rates of any currencies in which they do business (unless the rate sensitivity of the bank's assets and liabilities denominated in each currency are equal).

- Since the international debt crisis, banks with exposure to loans to less developed countries (LDCs) have taken actions to reduce their exposure. These actions include sales of LDC loans, exchanging LDC debt for equity investments in the foreign country, and boosting loan loss reserves.

- When banks consider providing foreign loans, they assess country risk. They measure country risk by assigning ratings to the various indicators of a country's financial and political condition. An overall country risk rating is determined by consolidating these and other indicators.

EXHIBIT 19.4
Country Risk
Ratings Among
Latin American
and European
Countries

SOURCE: *Institutional
Investor,* 1993.

Mexico
46

Venezuela
38

Colombia
40

Ecuador
21

Brazil
28

Peru
15

Paraguay
27

Chile
52

Uruguay
34

Argentina
33

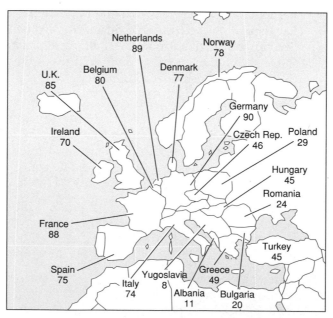

Netherlands
89

Norway
78

U.K.
85

Belgium
80

Denmark
77

Germany
90

Ireland
70

Czech Rep.
46

Poland
29

Hungary
45

Romania
24

France
88

Turkey
45

Spain
75

Yugoslavia
8

Greece
49

Italy
74

Albania
11

Bulgaria
20

QUESTIONS

1. Explain the operations of foreign branches of U.S. banks.

2. What are Edge Act corporations?

3. What was the purpose of the International Banking Act (IBA)?

4. In what ways has the Japanese government recently deregulated its financial markets?

5. Explain how banks become exposed to exchange rate risk.

6. Oregon Bank has branches overseas that concentrate in short-term deposits in dollars and floating-rate loans in British pounds. Because it maintains rate-sensitive assets and liabilities of equal amounts, it believe it has essentially eliminated its interest rate risk. Do you agree? Explain.

7. Dakota Bank has a branch overseas with the following balance sheet characteristics: 50 percent of the liabilities are rate sensitive and denominated in Swiss francs; the remaining 50 percent of liabilities are rate insensitive and are denominated in dollars. With regard to assets, 50 percent of assets are rate sensitive and are denominated in dollars; the remaining 50 percent of assets are rate insensitive and are denominated in Swiss francs. Is the performance of this branch susceptible to interest rate movement? Explain.

8. Why were many LDCs generating less cash flows than they anticipated prior to the international debt crisis?

9. How did the strengthening dollar during the early 1980s affect the ability of LDCs to repay the loans to U.S. banks?

10. Explain why LDCs increased their negotiating power when they joined together to announce their inability to repay loans.

11. Theory suggests that diversification of loans among countries can insulate a bank's loan portfolio from any single event. Yet the international debt crisis devastated the market value of loan portfolios of some large U.S. banks. Does this mean that diversification cannot sufficiently reduce risk? Explain.

12. Identify the four major aspects of a country that are commonly analyzed by country risk assessment systems. How can evaluations of these aspects be used to determine an overall rating for the country?

13. Explain how the Single European Act affects international banking.

14. Explain how the new global capital requirements can discourage banks from taking excessive risk.

15. Explain why Japanese banks have found it feasible to expand even when the expected return on these ventures may not be sufficient for U.S. banks.

16. How may banks facilitate the trend toward privatization in Eastern Europe?

17. Explain how the Brady Plan was intended to deal with the international debt crisis.

CASE APPLICATION: RENEWED LENDING TO LESS DEVELOPED COUNTRIES

'Bridge' Loans to Latin America Rise, But Some Wonder if the Toll Is Too High

Craig Torres, New York

With their scars barely faded from the Latin American lending of years past, big banks are back in the region making temporary "bridge" loans to Latin companies.

Bridge loans picked up a bad name in the U.S. corporate lending market awhile back. They are meant to last a few months quickly replaced with long-term financing. When all works as planned, bridge loans can bring fat fees to lenders and speedy cash to borrowers. But Wall Street will never forget how the 1989 collapse in the junk-bond market turned giant "temporary" bridge loans into bridges to nowhere, generating big write-offs.

Today, the bridge is back, often as a source of upfront cash for junk-rated Latin corporations that are planning bond issues. Bankers Trust New York Corp., Chase Manhattan Corp., Citicorp and J.P. Morgan & Co., as well as foreign banks such as Spain's Banco Santander, all are writing bridge loans to Latin American companies.

A Competitive Tool

In the race to win much-demanded Latin bond offerings today, banks use bridge loans as a competitive tool to differentiate themselves from their rivals at Wall Street investment banks.

Yet the Street doesn't seem envious. "From the standpoint of credit risk, it is not something we've seen as a good business to get into," says Emilio Lamar, managing director at Merrill Lynch &

Co.'s international emerging markets unit. Stephen Dizard, managing director at Salomon Inc.'s Salomon Brothers, adds: "Put simply, we don't do bridge loans to win bond offerings. And I don't think we feel disadvantaged."

A Federal Reserve System official, who declined to be identified, comments, "Some of these bridge loans are incredible, given the track record over the long course of history in Latin America and the recent memory of the 1980s. The Fed official adds, "The appetite for going out and lending extraordinary sums of money to shaky foreign debtors is back."

Bankers acknowledge the risks of bridge lending. Roland Wojewodzki, managing director at J.P. Morgan, says: "We are very cautious." He says J.P. Morgan prefers to write bridge loans only for acquisitions, and only after the bank discerns that the bridge can be repaid out of operating cash, if necessary.

"We have been extremely careful," says Joaquin Avila, managing director at Banco Santander's investment banking unit.

Moody's Investors Service Co. and Standard & Poor's Corp., as a matter of policy, won't rate a company higher than its home country. Chile is the only country in Latin America that has an investment-grade rating from both agencies on its dollar-denominated debt. In effect, billions of dollars in Latin American corporate debt carry a below-investment grade, or "junk" rating. Some companies have investment-grade ratings on debt denominated in local currency, such as Mexican pesos but only a

select few have strong balance sheets and businesses, the agencies say.

Big Demand

High yielding Latin debt is much in demand today. Latin corporations have sold some $25 billion in dollar denominated debt to both mutual funds favored by small investors and institutions during the past year and a half. Several of these debt deals repaid bank bridge loans.

But bull markets in foreign bonds don't last forever. And political risk often is as dangerous as market risk in Latin America.

Chase Manhattan made a $150 million bridge loan to Venezuelan oil company Bariven in advance of a $400 million bond sale in March 1992. But as the bank prepared to sell the bonds, Venezuela plunged into civil turmoil following an attempted coup in February.

The bridge loan was repaid, but Chase ended up holding some of the Bariven 10-year bonds, which by late spring had fallen more than five points, or $50 for each $1,000 face amount.

Bankers Trust wrote a $230 million bridge loan for the working-capital needs of Bariven. A bond sale led by Bankers Trust in December 1991, two months before the coup attempt, repaid the bridge.

It was a timely exit for Bankers Trust. By March 1992, the bonds were down about two points, or $20 for each $1,000 face amount.

Continued

CASE APPLICATION: RENEWED LENDING TO LESS DEVELOPED COUNTRIES

Continued

Bridges to Latin America

Many of the celebrated Latin American bond deals are also financings designed to get banks out of risky bridge loans. Here's a list of some of the bridge loans extended by banks over the past two years, and a comment on the bonds that bailed them out.

COMPANY/ LOCATION	LEAD LENDER	AMOUNT (MILLIONS)	COMMENT
Cemex/ Mexico	Citibank	$1,160	Giant bridge loan helped finance acquisitions by the cement company. Repaid through bond sales including $1 billion bond offering led by J. P. Morgan in June.
Fomsa/ Mexico	J.P. Morgan	1,000	Bridge paid down with asset sales and $325 million bond offering led by Bear Steams, March 1992.
Barivan/ Venezuela	Bankers Trust	230	Bridge loan for oil companys working capital. Repaid with $230 million bond issue December 1991.
Bortven/ Venezuela	Chase Manhattan	160	Bridge financed capital-equipment purchase. Repaid with $400 million bond offering. March 1992.
Astra/ Argentina	Citibank Swiss Bank Banco Santander	100	Cash forwarded to Argentine energy company ahead of $100 million June 1992 bond offering.
Tocpetrol/ Argentina	Chase Manhattan	60	Bridge financed purchase of oil and gas properties from government. Repaid with $60 million bond sale in June.
Vitro/ Mexico	Banco Santander	60	Bridge financed an acquisition. Repaid with $70 million bond issue in October 1992.

QUESTIONS

1. Why do you think Chase Manhattan, J.P. Morgan, Citicorp, and other commercial banks offer bridge loans to less developed countries?

2. Do you believe bridge loans offered by Bankers Trust New York Corp., Citicorp, and other banks to less developed countries (LDCs) are less risky than the loans previously provided to LDCs in the 1970s and 1980s? Explain.

3. Would banks use the same type of country risk analysis for bridge loans to less developed countries that they used for longer term loans to LDCs?

PROJECT

1. Obtain the annual report of a large commercial bank of your choice or assigned by your professor. From the report, how has the bank been involved in international business? Has the bank's involvement in international business improved its overall performance? Explain. Does the bank plan to reduce any of its international operations? (Identify them.) Why? Does it plan to increase any of its international operations? (Identify them.) Why? How should its planned adjustments in international business affect its risk and potential earnings?

REFERENCES

Aharony, Joseph, Anthony Saunders, and Itzhak Swary. "The Effects of the International Banking Act on Domestic Bank Profitability." *Journal of Money, Credit, and Banking* (November 1986): 493–506.

Aliber, Robert Z. "International Banking: A Survey." *Journal of Money, Credit, and Banking* (November 1984): 661–712.

Brewer, Thomas L., and Pietra Rivoli. "Politics and Perceived Country Creditworthiness in International Banking." *Journal of Money, Credit, and Banking* (August 1990): 357–369.

Bruner, Robert F., and John M. Simms, Jr. "The International Debt Crisis and Bank Security Returns in 1982." *Journal of Money, Credit, and Banking* (February 1987): 46–55.

Goldberg, Lawrence G., and Denise Johnson. "The Determinants of U.S. Banking Activity Abroad." *Journal of International Money and Finance* (June 1990): 123–137.

James, Christopher. "Heterogeneous Creditors and the Market Value of Bank LDC Loan Portfolios." *Journal of Monetary Economics* (June 1990): 325–346.

Lee, Suk Hun. "Relative Importance of Political Instability and Economic Variables on Perceived Instability and Economic Variables on Perceived Country Creditworthiness." *Journal of International Business Studies* (Fourth Quarter 1993): 801–812.

Logue, Dennis E., and Pietra Rivoli. "Some Consequences of Banks' LDC Loans: A Note." *Journal of Financial Services Research* (May 1992): 37–47.

Madura, Jeff, and William R. McDaniel. "Market Reaction to Loan Loss Reserve Announcements at Money Center Banks." *Journal of Financial Services Research* (December 1989): 359–369.

Madura, Jeff, Alan L. Tucker, and Emilio Zarruk. "Reaction of Bank Share Prices to the Third-World Debt Reduction Plan." *Journal of Banking and Finance* (September 1992): 853–868.

Morgan, John B. "A New Look at Debt Rescheduling Indicators and Models." *Journal of International Business Studies* (Summer 1986): 37–54.

Schwartz, Eduardo S., and Salvador Zurita. "Sovereign Debt: Optimal Contract, Underinvestment, and Forgiveness." *Journal of Finance* (July 1992): 981–1004.

Waheed, Amjad, and Ike Mathur. "The Effects of Announcements of Bank Lending Agreements on the Market Values of U.S. Banks." *Financial Management* (Spring 1993): 119–127.

FORECASTING BANK PERFORMANCE

This problem requires an understanding of banks' sources and uses of funds (Chapter 15), bank management (Chapter 17), and bank performance (Chapter 18). It also requires the use of spreadsheet software such as LOTUS. The data provided can be input onto a spreadsheet to more easily complete the necessary computations. A conceptual understanding of commercial banking is needed to interpret the computations.

As an analyst of a medium-sized commercial bank, you have been asked to forecast next year's performance. In the month of June you were provided information about the sources and uses of funds for the upcoming year. The bank's sources of funds for the upcoming year are as follows:

SOURCE OF FUNDS	DOLLAR AMOUNT (IN MILLIONS)	INTEREST RATE TO BE OFFERED
Demand deposits	$5,000	0%
Time deposits	2,000	6%
1-Year NCDs	3,000	T-bill rate + 1%
5 Year NCDs	2,500	1-Year NCD rate + 1%

The bank also has $1 billion in capital.

The bank's uses of funds for the upcoming year are as follows:

USE OF FUNDS	DOLLAR AMOUNT (IN MILLIONS)	INTEREST RATE	LOAN LOSS PERCENTAGE
Loans to small businesses	$4,000	T-bill rate + 6%	2%
Loans to large businesses	2,000	T-bill rate + 4%	1%
Consumer loans	3,000	T-bill rate + 7%	4%
Treasury bills	1,000	T-bill rate	0%
Treasury bonds	1,500	T-bill rate + 2%	0%
Corporate bonds	1,100	Treasury bond rate + 2%	0%

The bank also has $900 million in fixed assets. The interest rates on loans to small and large businesses are tied to the Treasury bill rate and will change at the beginning of each new year. The forecasted Treasury bond rate is tied to the future Treasury bill rate, based on the expectation of an upward sloping yield curve that will exist at the beginning of next year. The corporate bond rate is tied to the Treasury bond rate, allowing for a risk premium of 2 percent. Consumer loans will be provided at the beginning of next year, and interest rates will be fixed over the lifetime of the loan. The remaining time to maturity on all assets except Treasury bills exceeds three years. As the one-year Treasury bills mature, the funds are to be reinvested in new one-year Treasury bills (all Treasury bills are to be purchased at the beginning of the year). The bank's loan loss percentage reflects the percentage of bad loans. Assume that no interest will be received on these loans. In addition, assume that this percentage of loans will be accounted for as loan loss reserves (assume that they should be subtracted when determining before-tax income).

The bank has forecasted its noninterest revenues to be $200 million and its noninterest expenses to be $740 million. A tax rate of 34 percent can be applied to the before-tax income in order to estimate after-tax income. The bank has developed the following probability distribution for the one-year Treasury bill rate that will exist as of the beginning of next year:

POSSIBLE T-BILL RATE	PROBABILITY
8%	30%
9	50%
10	20%

a. Using the information provided, determine the probability distribution of return on assets (ROA) for next year by completing the following table:

INTEREST RATE SCENARIO (POSSIBLE T-BILL RATE)	FORECASTED ROA	PROBABILITY
8%		
9		
10		

b. Will the bank's ROA next year be higher or lower if market interest rates are higher (use the T-bill rate as a proxy for market interest rates)? Why? The information provided did not assume any required reserves. Explain how inclusion of required reserves would affect the forecasted interest revenue, ROA, and ROE.

c. The bank is considering a strategy of attempting to attract an extra $1 billion as one-year NCDs to replace $1 billion of five-year NCDs. Develop the probability distribution of ROA based on this strategy:

INTEREST RATE SCENARIO	FORECASTED ROA BASED ON THE STRATEGY OF INCREASING ONE-YR NCDs	PROBABILITY
8%		
9		
10		

d. Is the bank's ROA likely to be higher next year if it uses the strategy of attracting more one-year NCDs?

e. What would be an obvious concern about a strategy of using more one-year NCDs and fewer five-year NCDs beyond the next year?

f. The bank is considering a strategy of using $1 billion to offer additional loans to small businesses instead of purchasing Treasury bills. Using all the original assumptions provided, determine the probability distribution of ROA (assume that noninterest expenses would not be affected by this change in strategy).

INTEREST RATE SCENARIO (POSSIBLE T-BILL RATE)	FORECASTED ROA IF AN EXTRA $1 BILLION IS USED FOR LOANS TO SMALL BUSINESSES	PROBABILITY
8%		
9		
10		

g. Would the bank's ROA likely be higher or lower over the next year if it allocates the extra funds to small business loans?

h. What is the obvious risk of such a strategy beyond the next year?

i. The strategy of attracting more one-year NCDs could affect noninterest expenses and revenues. How would noninterest expenses be affected by the strategy? How would noninterest revenues be affected by the strategy?

j. Now assume that the bank is considering a strategy of increasing its consumer loans by $1 billion instead of using the funds for loans to large businesses. Using this information along with all the original assumptions provided, determine the probability distribution of ROA.

INTEREST RATE SCENARIO (POSSIBLE T-BILL RATE)	POSSIBLE ROA IF AN EXTRA $1 BILLION IS USED FOR CONSUMER LOANS	PROBABILITY
8%		
9		
10		

k. Other than possible changes in the economy that may affect default risk, what key factor will determine whether this strategy is beneficial beyond one year?

l. Now assume that the bank wants to determine how its forecasted return on equity (ROE) next year would be affected if it boosts its capital from $1 billion to $1.2 billion. (The extra capital would not be used to increase interest or noninterest revenues.) Using all the original assumptions provided, complete the following table:

INTEREST RATE SCENARIO (POSSIBLE T-BILL RATE)	FORECASTED ROE IF CAPITAL = $1 BILLION	FORECASTED ROE IF CAPITAL = $1.2 BILLION	PROBABILITY
8%			
9			
10			

Briefly state how the ROE will be affected if the capital level is increased.

PART 6

NONBANK FINANCIAL INSTITUTIONS

The chapters in Part Six cover the key nonbank financial institutions. Each of these chapters is devoted to a particular type of financial institution, with a focus on sources of funds, uses of funds, regulations, management, and recent performance. Each financial institution's interaction with other institutions and participation in financial markets are also emphasized in these chapters.

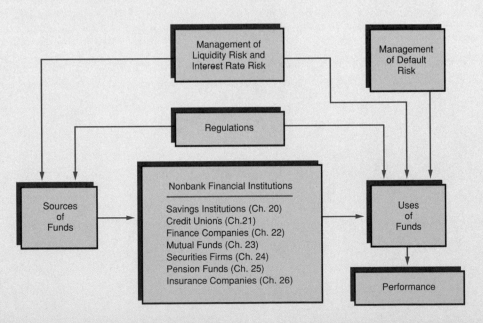

CHAPTER 20

SAVINGS INSTITUTIONS

The term *savings institutions* refers to savings and loan associations and savings banks. These institutions are somewhat similar in that they obtain most of their funds from households and use most of their funds to provide mortgages for households.

The specific objectives of this chapter are to:

- describe the key sources and uses of funds for savings institutions,
- describe the exposure of savings institutions to various types of risk, and
- describe the savings and loan crisis, and the actions taken to resolve the crisis.

BACKGROUND ON SAVINGS INSTITUTIONS

Savings and loan associations (sometimes called S&Ls or savings associations) are the most dominant form of savings institutions, holding in aggregate more than $700 billion of household savings. Roughly 85 percent of them have assets between $25 million and $5 billion. Less than one percent of these associations have assets of more than $5 billion.

S&Ls can be either state or federally chartered. The deposits of federally chartered S&Ls are insured up to $100,000 per depositor. The insuring agency is the Savings Association Insurance Fund (SAIF).

Ownership

S&Ls are classified as either stock owned, or **mutual** (owned by depositors). Although most S&Ls are mutual, many S&Ls shifted their ownership structure from depositors to shareholders through what is known as a **mutual-to-stock conversion.** This conversion allows S&Ls to obtain additional capital by issuing stock.

Beyond having the capability to boost capital, stock-owned institutions also provide their owners with greater potential to benefit from their performance. The dividends and/or stock price of a high-performance institution can grow, thereby providing direct benefits to the shareholders. Conversely, the owners (depositors) of a mutual institution do not directly benefit from high performance. Although they have a pro rata claim to the mutual savings institution's net worth while they maintain deposits there, their claim is eliminated once they close their account.

Because of the difference in owner control, stock-owned institutions are more susceptible to unfriendly takeovers. It is virtually impossible for another firm to take control of a mutual institution, because management generally holds all voting rights. From the owners' perspectives, the stock-owned institution may seem more desirable because the owners may have more influence on managerial decisions.

When a mutual S&L is involved in an acquisition, it first converts to a stock-owned S&L. If it is the acquiring firm, it will then arrange to purchase the existing stock of the institution to be acquired. Conversely, if it is to be acquired, its stock will be purchased by the acquiring institution. This process is often referred to as a **merger-conversion.** Although merger-conversions are relatively new to the industry, they are becoming popular.

Savings Banks

Savings banks have similar characteristics to those of S&Ls. They can be state or federally chartered, although most are start chartered. They can also be mutual or stock owned. Although most savings banks are mutual, there has been an increasing tendency in recent years to convert to stock ownership to have greater access to capital. If a stock-owned savings bank desires to boost capital, it can simply issue more stock.

Savings banks differ from S&Ls in the following ways. While S&Ls are spread across the entire country, savings banks are mainly concentrated along the northeastern portion of the United States. They are not as heavily concentrated in mortgages and have more diversified uses of funds. Although savings banks have had more flexibility in their investing practices than S&Ls, the difference has narrowed over time. In those states where the state regulations imposed on savings banks are very flexible, savings banks will likely continue to offer more diversified services to customers.

Although the differences between savings banks and S&Ls are important, these two types of savings institutions are similar in many respects. The remainder of this chapter discusses savings institutions in general.

SOURCES OF FUNDS

The main sources of funds for savings institutions are deposits, borrowed funds, and capital.

Deposits

Savings institutions obtain most of their funds from a variety of savings and time deposits, including passbook savings, retail CDs, and money market deposit accounts (MMDAs). Before 1978 savings institutions focused primarily on passbook savings accounts. During the early and mid-1970s, disintermediation was common because market interest rates exceeded the passbook savings rate. Because disintermediation reduced the volume of savings at S&Ls, it reduced the amount of mortgage financing available.

In 1981 savings institutions across the country were allowed to offer NOW accounts as a result of the Deregulation Act of 1980 (DIDMCA). This was a major event because they were previously unable to offer checking services. Suddenly, the differences between commercial banks and savings institutions were not so obvious to savers. NOW accounts enabled savings institutions to be perceived as full-service financial institutions.

The creation of MMDAs in 1982 (as a result of the Garn-St Germain Act) allowed savings institutions to offer limited checking combined with a market-determined interest rate and therefore to compete against money market funds. Because these new accounts offered close-to-market interest rates, they were a more expensive source of funds than passbook savings. The new types of deposit accounts have increased the rate sensitivity of savings institution liabilities to interest rate movements.

Like commercial banks, savings institutions were historically unable to offer a rate above a regulatory ceiling on deposits. In 1978 a loosening of regulations allowed them to offer limited types of retail CDs with rates tied to Treasury bills. As a wider variety of retail CDs were allowed in the late 1970s and early 1980s and MMDAs were introduced in 1982, the ceiling rate on passbook savings was no longer as relevant. By 1986, all deposits were free from ceiling rates.

Borrowed Funds

When savings institutions are unable to attract sufficient deposits, they can borrow funds on a short-term basis in the following ways. First, they can borrow funds from other depository institutions that have excess funds in the federal funds market. The interest rate on funds borrowed in this market is referred to as the federal funds rate.

A second source of short-term funds for savings institutions is the Federal Reserve's discount window. The interest rate on funds borrowed from the Fed is referred to as the discount rate.

A third source of short-term funds for savings institutions is a repurchase agreement (repo). A repo allows for the sale of government securities, with a commitment to repurchase those securities shortly thereafter. This essentially reflects a short-term loan to the institution that initially sold the securities until the time at which it buys the securities back.

Capital

The **capital** (or net worth) of a savings institution is primarily composed of retained earnings and funds obtained from issuing stock. During periods when savings institutions are performing well, capital is boosted by additional retained earnings. Capital is commonly used to support ongoing or expanding operations.

Savings institutions are required to maintain a minimum level of capital to cushion against potential losses that could occur and thus help to avoid possible failure. During the early 1980s, losses were common among savings institutions, and the capital levels were reduced. Concerned with the erosion of capital, the regulatory agencies have attempted to tighten requirements.

USES OF FUNDS

The main uses of funds for savings institutions are

- Cash
- Mortgages
- Mortgage-backed securities
- Other securities
- Consumer and commercial loans
- Other uses

Cash

Savings institutions maintain cash to satisfy reserve requirements enforced by the Federal Reserve System and to accommodate withdrawal requests of depositors. In addition, some savings institutions hold correspondent cash balances at other financial institutions in return for various services.

Mortgages

Mortgages are the primary asset of savings institutions. They typically have long-term maturities and can usually be prepaid by borrowers. About 90 percent of the mortgages originated are for homes or multifamily dwellings, while 10 percent are for commercial properties. Mortgages can be sold in the secondary market, although their market value changes in response to interest rate movements, so they are subject to interest rate risk as well as default risk. To protect against interest rate risk, savings institutions use a variety of techniques, discussed later in the chapter. To protect against default risk, the real estate represented by the mortgage serves as collateral.

Mortgage-Backed Securities

To obtain funds, savings institutions commonly issue securities that are backed by mortgages. Other savings institutions with available funds can purchase these securities. The seller may continue to service the mortgages, but it passes on the periodic payments to the purchaser, retaining a small amount as a service fee. The cash flows to these holders of mortgage-backed securities will not necessarily be even over time because the mortgages can be prepaid before their stated maturity.

Other Securities

All savings institutions invest in securities such as Treasury bonds and corporate bonds. Because savings banks are not as heavily concentrated in mortgage loans and mortgage-backed securities, they hold a greater percentage of securities than S&Ls. These securities provide liquidity, as they can quickly be sold in the secondary market if funds are needed. Savings banks are also able to invest in corporate stocks, while S&Ls are not.

S&Ls have also invested in junk bonds. The proportion of funds used to invest in junk bonds varied substantially among S&Ls, as some states imposed limits on this type of investment. As a result of the S&L crisis, regulators prohibited additional investment in junk bonds in 1989.

Consumer and Commercial Loans

Many savings institutions are attempting to increase their consumer loans and commercial loans. As a result of DIDMCA and the Garn-St Germain Act, the lending guidelines for federally chartered savings institutions were loosened. Subsequent to these acts, many state-chartered savings institutions were also granted more lending flexibility by their respective states. Specifically, the acts allowed federally chartered savings institutions to invest up to 30 percent of their assets in nonmortgage loans and securities. A maximum 10 percent of assets can be used to provide non-real estate commercial loans.

Savings institutions have taken advantage of the deregulatory acts by providing corporate and consumer loans with maturities typically ranging between one and four years. Because consumer and corporate loan maturities closely match their liability maturities, savings institutions that reduce their mortgage loan concentration in favor of more corporate and consumer loans will reduce their exposure to interest rate risk. However, their willingness to offer these loans results in some noninterest costs. They must advertise to corporations and consumers that they have now entered this new business, and they must also hire personnel with expertise in these fields. The increased emphasis on corporate and consumer loans can increase their overall degree of default risk. The loss rate on mortgage loans has been significantly lower than the loss rate on credit card loans.

Although savings institutions are now more able to enter the corporate and consumer lending fields, their participation in these fields is still limited by regulators. Thus, mortgages and mortgage-backed securities continue to be their primary assets.

Other Uses of Funds

Savings institutions can provide temporary financing to other institutions through the use of repurchase agreements. In addition, they can lend funds on a short-term basis through the federal funds market. Both methods allow them to efficiently use funds that they will have available for only a short period of time.

POINT OF INTEREST

DEPOSIT RUNS ON OHIO AND MARYLAND SAVINGS INSTITUTIONS

On March 6, 1985, $55 million of depositor withdrawals occurred at Home State Savings Bank of Cincinnati, Ohio. During the next two days, an additional $100 million was withdrawn. The runs on the institution were triggered by unique events growing out of Home State Savings Bank's investments with ESM Government Securities, Inc., a government securities dealer based in Fort Lauderdale, Florida. ESM had made large repurchase agreements with Home State totaling approximately $145 million. Alleged fraudulent dealings of ESM caused their failure, which in turn caused difficulties for Home State.

Deposits at Home State Savings Bank were insured by the Ohio Deposit Guarantee Fund (ODGF), a private fund that insured about 70 state-chartered savings institutions in Ohio. Savings and loan leaders in Ohio originally organized ODGF to provide insurance for institutions considered too small to require or qualify for federal deposit insurance. ODGF was less expensive than federal deposit insurance and enforced fewer restrictions, which led to its popularity. Yet, it could not cover the losses of Home State.

Runs at other Ohio S&Ls insured by ODGF occurred when the Home State closing was announced. Daily deposit withdrawals at seven Cincinnati area institutions ranged from $6 million to $60 million in only four days. These runs occurred only at ODGF-insured institutions.

Several steps were taken to resolve these problems. First, a bill was passed to form a new Savings Association Guarantee Fund, ODGF-II, that was to raise $40 million. A state emergency loan of $50 million was to be combined with this $40 million. As a second step, Ohio's governor, F. Celeste, declared a bank holiday and on March 15, 1985, closed down the savings institutions insured by ODGF.

Another step was a meeting between Ohio bankers and state officials at the Federal Reserve Bank of Cleveland to discuss purchases of ODGF-insured institutions. Because of a lack of information, especially about the quality of assets, proposals for the purchase of any of these institutions could not be completed. Because they were insured by private insurance, they were not required to file financial reports. Forty-four ODGF-insured institutions eventually received full or conditional approval for federal deposit insurance. Twenty-five institutions, including Home State, were merged into or acquired by other institutions.

This same scenario occurred in Maryland in May 1985. Once again, an S&L insured only by private insurance was involved. A run on Maryland S&Ls occurred as a result of news that one of the S&Ls was in financial trouble. Maryland state officials ordered a grand jury to investigate the transactions of alleged fraudulent real estate dealings by the principal owners of the Old Court Savings and Loan Association. In addition, Merrit Commercial Savings and Loan Association was ordered by state regulators to discontinue some of its riskier investment practices.

To circumvent these events in Maryland, Governor Harry Hughes appointed court conservators to run both Old Court and Merritt. He also ordered 100 other privately insured S&Ls in Maryland to limit withdrawals to $1,000 per month per depositor. Legislatures ordered privately insured S&Ls to obtain federal deposit insurance. These events changed deposit insurance regulations in other states. Many states began to require any privately insured S&L to obtain federal insurance.

ALLOCATION OF SOURCES AND USES OF FUNDS

Exhibit 20.1 shows balance sheet information for all savings institutions insured by the SAIF. Mortgages dominate the assets, while savings deposits dominate the liability items. Savings institutions have attempted to diversify their assets and liabilities in recent years. This reflects their effort to depend less on savings deposits as a source of funds and mortgages as a use of funds. Nevertheless, their asset portfolios are not nearly as diversified as those of commercial banks.

REGULATION OF SAVINGS INSTITUTIONS

Savings institutions are regulated at both the state and federal levels. The specific regulator varies with the activity of interest and the type of savings institution involved. For example, the state has some input on various activities of state-chartered savings institutions but not on federally chartered institutions. Supervision and examination powers vary according to whether the savings institution is mutual or stock owned. As is true for the commercial banking industry, the savings institution industry's regulatory structure suffers from overlap. Over time, there may be some consolidation among regulators, or even consolidation with the commercial banking regulators.

Savings institutions have historically been regulated according to their sources and uses of funds (already described in this chapter), the locations where

EXHIBIT 20.1 Balance Sheet Information for S&Ls

	1993	
	Amount in Millions of $	Percentage of Total Assets
Assets		
Mortgages	$490,558	59%
Mortgage-backed securities	122,171	15
Cash and other investment securities	132,210	16
Commercial loans	8,109	1
Consumer loans	36,362	4
Other	41,695	5
Total Assets	$831,105	100
Liabilities and Net Worth		
Savings deposits	$650,045	78%
Borrowed funds	115,107	14
Other liabilities	15,086	2
Net worth	50,867	6
Total liabilities and net worth	$831,105	100

SOURCE: *Federal Reserve Bulletin.*

they could establish branches (geographic regulations), and the products or services offered.

Geographic Regulations

Savings institutions are generally allowed to branch throughout the state, although interstate movement is more restricted. Federally chartered savings institutions are typically prohibited from crossing state lines. State-chartered savings institutions may enter certain states. Interstate mergers involving savings institutions have been allowed when the intent is to save a failing depository institution, as stipulated by the Garn-St Germain Act. Attempts by savings institutions or other financial institutions to enter other states are evaluated on a case-by-case basis. As an example, Citicorp, the largest bank in the United States, was able to acquire failing savings institutions in California, Florida, and Illinois. Even when savings institutions are prohibited from establishing branches in other states, they are allowed to operate automatic teller machines (ATMs) across state lines.

Product Regulations

Savings institutions have diversified not only their asset portfolio in recent years but also the products and services they provide. They have attempted to offer products that were historically offered only by real estate, insurance, or brokerage firms. For example, some savings institutions serve as limited agents for registered brokerage firms and are therefore able to offer their customers access to discount brokerage services. They can introduce the service and provide a toll-free number where trades can be ordered. Some joint ventures also exist, whereby the savings institution will allow a registered broker to offer services on its grounds. The offering of a discount brokerage service and other nontraditional services by savings institutions can attract customers searching for a one-stop shop.

EXPOSURE TO RISK

Like commercial banks, savings institutions are exposed to liquidity risk, default risk, and interest rate risk.

Liquidity Risk

Because savings institutions commonly use short-term liabilities to finance long-term assets, they depend on additional deposits to accommodate withdrawal requests. If new deposits are not sufficient to cover withdrawal requests, these institutions could experience liquidity problems. To remedy this situation, they could obtain funds through repurchase agreements or borrow funds in the federal funds market. Yet, these sources of funds will resolve only a short-term shortage of funds. These sources of funds will not be appropriate if a longer term liquidity problem exists.

An alternative remedy to insufficient liquidity is to sell assets in exchange for cash. Savings institutions can sell their Treasury securities or even some of their mortgages in the secondary market. Although the sale of assets can boost liquidity, it also reduces the size and possibly earnings of S&Ls. Therefore, minor liquidity deficiencies are typically resolved by increasing liabilities rather than selling assets.

Default Risk

Because mortgages represent the primary asset, they are the main reason for default risk at savings institutions. Although Federal Housing Authority (FHA) and Veterans Administration (VA) mortgages originated by savings institutions are insured against default risk, conventional mortgages are not. Private insurance can normally be obtained for conventional mortgages, but savings institutions often incur the risk themselves rather than pay for the insurance. If they perform adequate credit analysis on their potential borrowers and geographically diversify their mortgage loans, they should be able to maintain a low degree of default risk.

Interest Rate Risk

The exposure of savings institutions to interest rate risk has received much attention over the past 15 years, especially during the early 1980s and late 1980s when interest rates increased substantially. Because their assets were mostly rate insensitive while their liabilities were mostly rate sensitive, their spread between interest revenue and interest expenses narrowed when interest rates increased, as shown in Exhibit 20.2. The spread even became negative in the early 1980s.

Like commercial banks, savings institutions commonly measure the gap between their rate-sensitive assets and rate-sensitive liabilities in order to determine their exposure to interest rate risk. However, the gap measurement is dependent on the criteria used to classify assets or liabilities. As an extreme example, a

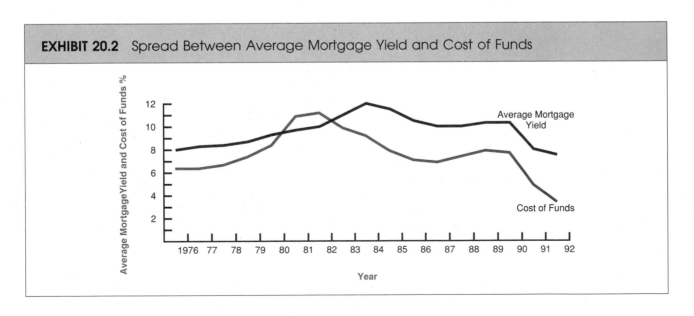

EXHIBIT 20.2 Spread Between Average Mortgage Yield and Cost of Funds

savings institution that obtains most of its funds with two-year CDs and offers 30-year fixed-rate mortgages will have a gap of zero if "rate sensitive" is defined to mean that interest rates are revised at least once a year. Yet, the savings institution will be affected by interest rate changes, as the interest rates on liabilities will be revised more frequently than those of the assets. In this example, the gap measurement is not an accurate indicator of the savings institution's exposure to interest rate risk.

Given the limitations of the gap measurement, some savings institutions may consider measuring the duration of their respective assets and liabilities to determine the imbalance in sensitivity of interest revenue versus expenses to interest rate movements. An example follows.

EXAMPLE OF MEASURING DURATION.   Assume that Tucson Savings Institution (TSI) desires to measure the duration of its assets and liabilities. It first needs to classify each balance sheet component into various maturity categories, as shown in Exhibit 20.3. The rates on most adjustable-rate mortgages are adjusted every year, which is why the amounts under the longer term categories show zero. The average duration for each category is provided below the dollar amount. Some fixed-rate mortgages are classified in the earlier term categories, because they are maturing or will be sold soon. The duration of .91 for adjustable-rate mortgages is a weighted average of their durations, computed as (7,000/ 27,000).30 + (15,000/27,000).80 + (4,000/27,000)1.9 + (1,000/27,000)2.9.

The durations for fixed-rate mortgages and investment securities were computed in a similar manner. The duration for total assets of 2.76 years was computed as a weighted average of the individual assets: (27,000/61,000).91 + (20,000/61,000)5.32 + (14,000/61,000)2.65 = 2.76.

A similar procedure was used to estimate the duration of liabilities. NOW accounts and passbook savings have no specified maturity, but their rate is adjusted less frequently than the rate on MMDAs, which is why MMDAs have a shorter duration. The total liability duration is about .45. TSI's total asset duration is more than six times its liability duration. Its future performance is highly exposed to interest rate movements. Its market value would decrease substantially in response to an increase in interest rates. TSI can reduce its exposure to interest rate risk by reducing its proportion of assets in the long-duration categories.

Computer programs are used by financial institutions to estimate their asset and liability duration and apply sensitivity analysis to proposed balance sheet adjustments. For example, TSI could determine how the asset and liability duration would change if it plans a promotional effort to issue five-year deposits and uses the funds to offer adjustable-rate mortgages.

MANAGEMENT OF INTEREST RATE RISK

Savings institutions have a variety of methods that can be used to manage their interest rate risk, including the use of

- Adjustable-rate mortgages
- Interest rate futures contracts

EXHIBIT 20.3   Duration Schedule for Tucson Savings Institution (Dollar Amounts Are in Thousands)

	RATE READJUSTMENT PERIOD							
Assets	Less Than 6 Months	6 Months to 1 Year	1–3 Years	3–5 Years	5–10 Years	10–20 Years	Over 20 Years	Total
Adjustable-rate mortgages								
Amount ($)	$ 7,000	$15,000	$4,000	$1,000	$ 0	$ 0	$ 0	$27,000
Average duration (yr)	.30	.80	1.90	2.90	0	0	0	.91
Fixed-rate mortgages								
Amount ($)	500	500	1,000	1,000	2,000	10,000	5,000	$20,000
Average duration (yr)	.25	.60	1.80	2.60	4.30	5.50	7.60	5.32
Investment securities								
Amount ($)	2,000	3,000	4,000	2,000	1,000	0	2,000	$14,000
Average duration (yr)	.20	.70	1.70	3.20	5.30	0	8.05	2.65
Total amount ($)	$ 9,500	$18,500	$9,000	$4,000	$3,000	$10,000	$7,000	$61,000
								Asset duration = 2.76
Liabilities								
Fixed-maturity deposits								
Amount ($)	$14,000	$ 9,000	$2,000	$1,000	$ 0	$ 0	$ 0	$26,000
Duration (yr)	.30	.60	1.80	2.80	0	0	0	.62
NOW accounts								
Amount ($)	4,000	0	0	0	0	0	0	$ 4,000
Duration (yr)	.40	0	0	0	0	0	0	.40
MMDAs								
Amount ($)	15,000	0	0	0	0	0	0	$15,000
Duration (yr)	.20	0	0	0	0	0	0	.20
Passbook accounts								
Amount ($)	13,000	0	0	0	0	0	0	$13,000
Duration (yr)	.40	0	0	0	0	0	0	.40
Total amount ($)	$46,000	$ 9,000	$2,000	$1,000	$ 0	$ 0	$ 0	$58,000
								Liability duration = .45

- Interest rate swaps
- Interest rate caps

Adjustable-Rate Mortgages (ARMs)

The interest rates on adjustable-rate mortgages (ARMs) are tied to market-determined rates such as the one-year Treasury bill rate and are periodically adjusted in accordance with the formula stated in the ARM contract. A variety of formulas have been used. ARMs enable savings institutions to maintain a more stable spread between interest revenue and interest expenses.

Although ARMs reduce the adverse impact of rising interest rates, they also reduce the favorable impact of declining interest rates. Suppose a savings institution that obtained most of its funds from short-term deposits used the funds to provide fixed-rate mortgages. If interest rates decline and the savings institution does not hedge its exposure to interest rate risk, the spread will increase. However, if ARMs are used as a hedging strategy, the interest on loans would decrease during a period of declining rates, so the spread would not widen.

The popularity of ARMs has been somewhat erratic. The use of ARMs increased during the 1980s, accounting for 60 percent of mortgages by 1984. The popularity of ARMs diminished in the mid-1980s when interest rates declined but increased again in the late 1980s. Yet, as interest rates declined during the 1990–1993 period, the proportion of ARMs declined again.

ARMs used during the 1970s helped savings institutions perform better but exposed consumers to interest rate risk. Although ARMs typically have a maximum cap limiting the increase in interest rates (such as 2 percent per year and 5 percent over the loan life), the impact on household mortgage payments is still significant. Because some homeowners may prefer fixed-rate mortgages, most savings institutions will continue to offer them and will therefore incur interest rate risk. Thus, additional strategies besides the use of ARMs are necessary to reduce this risk.

Interest Rate Futures Contracts

An interest rate futures contract allows for the purchase of a specific amount of a particular financial security for a specified price at a future point in time. Sellers of futures contracts are obligated to sell the securities for the contract price at the stated future point in time.

Treasury bond futures contracts are used by some savings institutions because the cash flow characteristics of Treasury bonds resemble fixed-rate mortgages. Like mortgages, Treasury bonds offer fixed periodic payments, so their market value moves inversely to interest rate fluctuations. Savings institutions that sell futures contracts on these securities can effectively hedge their fixed-rate mortgages. If interest rates rise, the market value of the securities represented by the futures contract will decrease. Savings institutions would benefit from the difference between the market value at which they can purchase these securities in the future and the futures price at which they will sell the securities. This could offset the reduced spread between their interest revenue and interest expenses during the period of rising interest rates.

Although the concept of using interest rate futures to guard against interest rate risk is simple, the actual application is more complex. It is difficult to perfectly offset the potential reduction in the spread with a futures position.

Interest Rate Swaps

Another strategy for reducing interest rate risk is the interest rate swap, which allows savings institutions to swap fixed-rate payments (an outflow) in exchange for variable-rate payments (an inflow). The fixed-rate outflow payments can be matched against the fixed-rate mortgages held so that a certain spread can be

IMPACT OF INTEREST RATE MOVEMENTS ON STOCK RETURNS OF S&Ls

A recent study by Scott and Peterson assessed the sensitivity of savings and loan associations (S&Ls) to interest rate movements, using the following regression model:

$$R_p = B_0 + B_1 Rm + B_2 i + \mu$$

where R_p = stock returns of a portfolio of savings and loan associations

R_m = percentage change in the market index (the S&P 500 Index was used as a proxy)

i = a measure of unexpected interest rate changes (see the article for an explanation of the proxy used for this variable)

B_0 = intercept

B_1 = regression coefficient that measures the sensitivity of stock returns to the market index returns

B_2 = regression coefficient that measures the sensitivity of stock returns to the interest rate movements

μ = error term

The coefficient B_1 was estimated to be 1.353 by the regression analysis, suggesting that a 1 percent change in the market is associated with a 1.353 percent change in the portfolio returns. Thus, the S&L stocks are positively correlated with the mar-

ket. The coefficient B_2 was estimated to be -3.61, suggesting that an unexpected 1 percent increase in interest rates is associated with a 3.61 percent decrease in stock returns of S&Ls. This coefficient was found to be statistically significant. Thus, stock returns on S&Ls are adversely affected by an unexpected increase in interest rates. Recent related studies have found similar results. The negative coefficient is not surprising, but the magnitude of the coefficient illustrates how highly sensitive the stock returns of S&Ls are to interest rate movements.

achieved. In addition, the variable-rate inflows due to the swap can be matched against the variable cost of funds. In a rising rate environment, the institution's fixed-rate outflow payments from the swap agreement remain fixed, while the variable-rate inflow payments due to the swap increase. This favorable result can partially offset the normally unfavorable impact of rising interest rates on a savings institution's spread. However, an interest rate swap also reduces the favorable impact of declining interest rates. Inflow interest payments decrease, while the outflow interest payments remain the same during a period of declining rates.

Assume that Denver Savings Institution (DSI) has large holdings of 11 percent fixed-rate mortgages. Because its sources of funds are mostly interest rate sensitive, DSI desires to swap fixed-rate payments in exchange for variable-rate payments. It informs Colorado Bank of its situation, because it knows that this bank commonly engages in swap transactions. Colorado Bank searches for a client and finds that Brit Eurobank desires to swap variable-rate dollar payments in exchange for fixed dollar payments. Colorado Bank then develops the swap arrangement illustrated in Exhibit 20.4. DSI will swap fixed-rate payments in exchange for variable-rate payments based on the London Interbank Offer Rate (LIBOR, the rate charged on loans between Eurobanks). Because the variable-rate payments fluctuate with market conditions, DSI's payments received will vary over time. The length of the swap period and the notional amount (the amount to which the interest rates are applied to determine the payments) can be structured to the participant's desires. The financial intermediary conducting the swap charges a fee, such as .1 percent of the notional amount per year. Some financial intermediaries for swaps may act as the counterparty and exchange the payments desired, rather than just match up two parties.

Now assume that the fixed payments to be paid were based on a fixed rate of 9 percent. Also assume that LIBOR is initially 6 percent, and that DSI's cost of funds is equal to LIBOR. Exhibit 20.5 shows how DSI's spread is affected by various possible interest rates when unhedged versus when hedged with an interest rate swap. If LIBOR remains at 6 percent, DSI's spread would be 5 percent if unhedged and only 3 percent when using a swap. However, if LIBOR increases beyond 8 percent, the spread when using the swap exceeds the unhedged spread because the higher cost of funds causes a lower unhedged spread. The swap arrangement would provide DSI with increased payments that offset the higher cost of funds. The advantage of a swap is that it can lock in the spread to be earned on existing assets—or at least reduce the possible variability of the spread.

When interest rates decrease, a savings institution's outflow payments would exceed inflow payments on a swap. However, the spread between the interest rates received on existing mortgages and those paid on deposits should increase, offsetting the net outflow from the swap. During periods of declining interest rates, mortgages are often prepaid, which could result in a net outflow from the swap without any offsetting effect.

Interest Rate Caps

An alternative method of hedging interest rate risk is an interest rate cap, an agreement (for a fee) to receive payments when the interest rate of a particular security or index rises above a specified level during a specified time period. Some commercial banks and brokerage firms offer interest rate caps. The maturity can be tailored to the savings institution's desires. The cap provides compensation during periods of rising interest rates, which can offset the reduction in the spread during such periods.

The fee paid for the caps depends on the terms. The lower the specified ceiling level of an interest cap at a given point in time, the higher the fee (because the probability of receiving compensation is higher). The longer the maturity of an interest rate cap, the higher the fee (for the same reason).

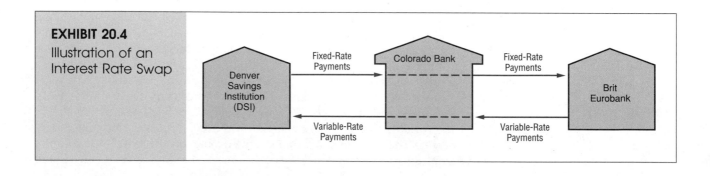

EXHIBIT 20.4
Illustration of an Interest Rate Swap

EXHIBIT 20.5 Comparison of DSI's Spread: Unhedged Versus Hedged

	POSSIBLE LIBOR RATES IN THE FUTURE					
Unhedged Strategy	6%	7%	8%	9%	10%	11%
Average rate on existing mortgages	11%	11%	11%	11%	11%	11%
Average cost of deposits	6	7	8	9	10	11
Spread	5	4	3	2	1	0
Hedging with an Interest Rate Swap						
Fixed interest rate earned on fixed-rate mortgages	11	11	11	11	11	11
Fixed interest rate owed on swap arrangement	9	9	9	9	9	9
Spread on fixed-rate payments	2	2	2	2	2	2
Variable interest rate earned on swap arrangement	7	8	9	10	11	12
Variable interest rate owed on deposits	6	7	8	9	10	11
Spread on variable-rate payments	1	1	1	1	1	1
Combined total spread when using the swap	3	3	3	3	3	3

Conclusions about Interest Rate Risk

During the mid-1980s many savings institutions used the strategies just described to reduce their interest rate risk. Although the strategies described here are useful for reducing interest rate risk, it is virtually impossible to completely eliminate the risk. This is partially because of the potential prepayment on mortgages. Homeowners often pay off their mortgages before maturity without much advance notice to the savings institutions. Consequently, savings institutions do not really know the actual maturity of the mortgages they hold and cannot perfectly match the interest rate sensitivity of their assets and liabilities.

INTERACTION WITH OTHER FINANCIAL INSTITUTIONS

Savings institutions interact with various types of financial institutions, as summarized in Exhibit 20.6. They compete with commercial banks and money market mutual funds to obtain funds as well as with commercial banks and finance

EXHIBIT 20.6 Interaction between Savings Institutions and Other Financial Institutions

TYPE OF FINANCIAL INSTITUTION	INTERACTION WITH SAVINGS INSTITUTIONS
Commercial banks	■ Savings institutions compete with commercial banks in attracting deposits, providing consumer loans, and providing commercial loans. ■ Some savings institutions and commercial banks have merged in recent years. ■ Some savings institutions sell mortgages to commercial banks.
Finance companies	■ Savings institutions compete with finance companies in providing consumer and commercial loans.
Money market mutual funds	■ Savings institutions compete with money market mutual funds in attracting short-term deposits of investors.
Investment companies and brokerage firms	■ Savings institutions often contact investment companies to engage in interest rate swaps and interest rate caps. ■ Savings institutions have made agreements with brokerage services for their customers in order to indirectly offer brokerage services.
Insurance companies	■ Mortgages sold by savings institutions in the secondary market are sometimes purchased by insurance companies.

companies in lending funds. Their hedging of interest rate risk is facilitated by investment companies that act as financial intermediaries for interest rate swaps and caps. Their ability to sell mortgages in the secondary market is enhanced by insurance companies that purchase them.

Many savings institutions have other financial institutions as subsidiaries that provide a variety of services, including consumer finance, trust company, mortgage banking, discount brokerage, and insurance.

PARTICIPATION IN FINANCIAL MARKETS

Savings institutions commonly participate in various financial markets, as summarized in Exhibit 20.7. Mortgage markets provide a source of funds to savings

EXHIBIT 20.7 Participation of Savings Institutions in Financial Markets

FINANCIAL MARKET	PARTICIPATION BY SAVINGS INSTITUTIONS
Money markets	■ Savings institutions compete with other depository institutions for short-term deposits. ■ Some savings institutions issue commercial paper.
Mortgage markets	■ Savings institutions sell mortgages in the secondary market and issue mortgage-backed securities.
Bond markets	■ Savings institutions purchase bonds for their investment portfolios. ■ Savings institutions issue bonds to obtain long-term funds.
Future markets	■ Some savings institutions hedge against interest rate movements by taking positions in interest rate futures.
Options markets	■ Some savings institutions hedge against interest rate movements by purchasing put options on interest rate futures.
Swap markets	■ Some savings institutions hedge against interest rate movements by engaging in interest rate swaps.

institutions that desire to issue mortgage-backed securities or sell their mortgages in the secondary market. Bond markets serve as a use of funds to savings institutions with excess funds and as a source of funds to savings institutions that issue new bonds in the primary market or sell bond holdings in the secondary market. Futures markets and options markets have enabled savings institutions to reduce interest rate risk that results from their investment in mortgages and bonds.

PERFORMANCE OF SAVINGS INSTITUTIONS

The return on assets (ROA) of the savings institutions was relatively stable up to the mid-1970s, as interest rates were somewhat stable during that period. Once interest rates began to fluctuate to a greater degree, so did the ROA of savings institutions. Interest rates rose in the late 1970s and early 1980s. Unprepared for the large increases, many savings institutions experienced substantial losses in 1981 and 1982. The ROA of savings institutions improved in 1983 as market interest rates began to decline, thereby reducing the cost of funds. The improved performance continued throughout the mid-1980s as interest rates remained low. In the late 1980s, many savings institutions experienced severe financial problems that resulted in the savings and loan crisis (discussed in the following section). In the early 1990s, savings institutions performed well in response to declining interest rates.

The underlying factor affecting performance of savings institutions is the spread between the average yield earned on mortgages and the cost of funds, as

APPLIED RESEARCH

ARE THERE ECONOMIES OF SCALE IN THE SAVINGS AND LOAN INDUSTRY?

In recent years there have been several mergers of savings and loan associations. The extent to which the increased size will benefit S&Ls depends partially on whether economies of scale exist. A study by Goldstein, McNulty, and Verbrugge measured the sensitivity of operating costs to output. Operating costs were defined to include salaries and all other operating expenses except interest expenses. The proxy used to measure output was total assets.

(See the article for more specific details about the model used.) The analysis found that economies of scale exist and are more pronounced in the smaller size class, but exist in the medium and larger classes as well. The results suggest that savings and loan associations may achieve greater efficiency through growth, regardless of their size. Because the characteristics of the industry are changing, the impact of growth on efficiency may

change over time. Savings and loan associations have attempted to diversify in recent years in order to behave as full-service financial institutions. Although diversification could reduce their risk, it may also limit their ability to benefit from economies of scale. Perhaps future research will reassess economies of scale in a more recent time period to determine whether today's more diversified S&Ls can increase efficiency through growth.

was illustrated earlier in Exhibit 20.2. The average yield earned on mortgages is less volatile than the cost of funds, because the yields on fixed-rate mortgages are insensitive to interest rate movements. When interest rates rose substantially in the early 1980s, the cost of funds exceeded the average yield earned on mortgages. Conversely, when interest rates declined to very low levels in the early 1990s, the spread became more favorable for savings institutions.

SAVINGS AND LOAN CRISIS

During the late 1980s, numerous S&Ls throughout the United States became insolvent and ultimately failed. To prevent further failures and to restore confidence in S&Ls, the Financial Institutions Reform, Recovery, and Enforcement Act (FIRREA) was implemented by the federal government in 1989. The underlying problems that precipitated the S&L crisis are described here. An explanation of the main provisions of this bailout plan are given, followed by a discussion of the potential impact of the bailout on S&Ls and other financial institutions.

Reasons for Failure

The main reasons for the proliferation of S&L failures were

- Losses on loans and securities
- Fraud
- Illiquidity

LOSSES ON LOANS AND SECURITIES. Just as the international debt crisis was precipitated by unpaid loans, so was the S&L crisis. Many loan defaults occurred

POINT OF INTEREST

EVALUATING THE PERFORMANCE OF SAVINGS INSTITUTIONS

Annual reports are commonly used by investors to evaluate the financial condition of savings institutions. The Value Line Investment Survey provides a summary of financial proxies that measure the performance of savings institutions. An example of the Value Line analysis is shown here for Great Western. The income of savings institutions is measured by the return on assets (referred to as '"% Earned Total Assets") or by the return on equity (referred to as '"% Earned Net Worth"). Each column represents a specific year, so that the changes in performance of the savings institution (as measured by any particular income proxy) can be assessed. The beta of the savings institution is disclosed in the upper left corner. Additional information not shown here is also provided by Value Line.

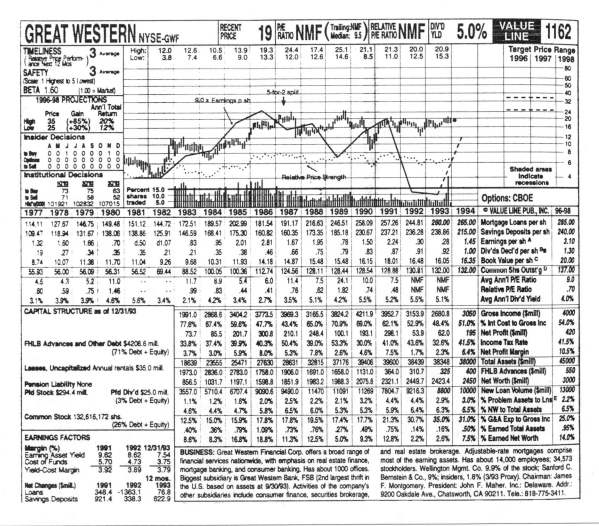

in the Southwest, where economies were devastated by a decline in oil prices. Layoffs in the oil industry resulted, causing a decline in income. Real estate prices dropped dramatically, so that foreclosures on bad real estate loans did not serve as adequate collateral. Although some housing loans defaulted, the major loan losses were in commercial real estate, such as office complexes. S&Ls were forced to assume real estate holdings that were sometimes worth less than half the loan amount originally provided.

S&Ls also experienced losses on their junk bond holdings. For example, Columbia S&L had purchased $4 billion worth of junk bonds. The value of these bonds declined by $1.5 billion as a result of numerous defaults.

FRAUD. Many of the S&Ls experienced financial problems because of various fraudulent activities. One of the most common types of fraud was the use of depositors' funds by managers for their own personal purchases. Following are a few examples of alleged fraud:

- Employees of an S&L in Florida used depositor funds to purchase yachts, helicopters, and fancy cars for themselves and even to sponsor a professional golf tournament. In September 1986 the S&L was bailed out at a cost of more than $1 billion.
- The president of another Florida S&L paid himself $16 million in salary and bonuses over a five-year period and used depositor funds to purchase a yacht for $7 million and art for $29 million.
- An S&L in California invested 80 percent of its funds in junk bonds, currency, and the stock of a firm it planned to acquire. The president of the S&L purchased $750,000 worth of football tickets with depositor funds. He also donated funds to senators, who pressured regulators to terminate their examination of this S&L.
- Presidents of two S&Ls in Illinois made loans to each other with depositor funds. The alleged fraudulent loans were estimated at $30 million.
- Depositor funds of an S&L in Texas were used to pay for the services of a topless dancer and prostitutes for its officers and even some S&L regulators. One regulator was provided with the dancer's companionship and in turn approved the S&L's purchase of three automobile dealerships. The bailout cost was about $1.3 billion.

ILLIQUIDITY. Many S&Ls experienced a cash flow deficiency as a result of loan losses, as the inflows from loan repayments were not sufficient to cover depositor withdrawals. Consequently, they were forced to offer higher interest rates on deposits to attract more funds. This reflects a strategy of borrowing from Peter to pay Paul. As depositors became aware of the S&L crisis, they began to withdraw their savings from S&Ls, which exacerbated the illiquidity problem. Normally, the threat of deposit runs is mitigated by deposit insurance. Depositors were aware, however, that the insuring agency (the Federal Savings and Loan Insurance Corporation, FSLIC) was already experiencing its own liquidity problems, as it provided subsidies to financial institutions willing to acquire failing S&Ls. By April 1988, the net worth of the FSLIC was estimated to be negative $11.6 billion. Media attention about the FSLIC's liquidity problems led to further depositor withdrawals, causing greater liquidity problems for the S&Ls.

Provisions of the FIRREA

Some of the mega-bailouts in California and Texas in 1987 and 1988 provided notes and guarantees but did not boost the capital levels of S&Ls. These bailouts not only heightened concern about the industry but also increased the likelihood of a repeat failure by the S&Ls. Clearly, a more organized bailout plan was needed to restore confidence in the S&L industry. In February 1989, the White House proposed a bill for bailing out S&Ls and enhancing their safety in the future.

The bailout bill was approved by the House of Representatives on August 3, 1989, and received final congressional approval the following day. President Bush signed the bill on August 9. The following is a summary of some of the more relevant provisions of the bailout bill:

- The Federal Savings and Loan Insurance Corporation was terminated. A new insurance agency for S&Ls, called Savings Association Insurance Fund (SAIF), was formed.
- As of January 1990 S&Ls were required to have $1.50 in tangible capital per $100 of deposits, or a 1.5 percent ratio. The ratio was to be increased over time.
- The Federal Home Loan Bank Board (FHLBB), which historically regulated S&Ls, was terminated. The FDIC, current regulator of commercial banks, was assigned the task of regulating S&Ls. The Resolution Trust Corporation was created to deal with insolvent S&Ls.
- The penalties for officers of S&Ls and other financial institutions convicted of fraud were increased.
- S&Ls were required to use 70 percent of their assets for housing loans, up from 60 percent.
- S&Ls were banned in the future from some risky investments, including junk bonds. Those S&Ls holding junk bonds were required to divest them over time.
- Commercial banks were allowed to purchase both failing and healthy S&Ls.

Creation of the RTC

The Resolution Trust Corporation (RTC), was formed. The RTC liquidates an S&L's assets and reimburses depositors or sells the S&L to another financial institution. In the case of liquidation, depositors are reimbursed two days later. The decision of which S&Ls on the list to deal with first is determined by assessing the size, health, and sales potential. Those S&Ls that are more costly to maintain will typically be dealt with first. The RTC executes acquisitions or liquidations of the insolvent S&Ls.

The most popular method for handling failures is the deposit transfer, in which deposits of the failed S&Ls are transferred to an acquiring firm for a fee (called a premium). With this method, the acquiring firm avoids assuming the low-quality assets of the failed S&L.

A less popular method is the acquisition of liabilities and assets of the failed S&L. Some of these assets would be very risky and probably contributed to the failure of the S&L that owned them. Therefore, the acquiring firm will typically purchase these assets at a deep discount.

Another method is a compromise between the aforementioned methods, in which the acquiring firm purchases the liabilities and only the quality assets of the failed S&L. The RTC must dispose of any assets of failed S&Ls that the acquiring firms would not purchase.

Because the RTC was assuming the assets of failed savings institutions, it accumulated large amounts of junk bonds, including those issued by Federated Department Stores, Trump Taj Mahal casino, and RJR Nabisco. Some of the bonds inherited are performing well while others are worthless. Only a few insurance companies held a larger junk bond portfolio. The RTC created a trading desk to sell these bonds in the secondary market.

Several securities firms purchased some of the junk bonds held by the RTC, including Salomon Brothers, Inc., Morgan Stanley & Co., and Merrill Lynch & Co. In addition, some of the junk bonds were purchased at a discount by their initial issuers.

Financing the Bailout

The funds to be spent by the RTC are financed by a variety of sources, including the sale of failed S&L assets, taxpayers, and surviving S&Ls. The RTC sells the assets of failing S&Ls and some assets of the officers who used deposit funds for themselves. The U.S. Treasury borrowed $18.8 billion and provided it to the RTC. The newly created and government-owned Resolution Funding Corporation issues 30-year bonds to help support the RTC. Technically, the bonds are not backed by the government, and therefore the closely monitored budget deficit is not affected by this type of financing. Although this financing circumvents budget deficit numbers, it will make the bailout even more expensive to taxpayers because the interest rate on this type of debt will be slightly higher than on Treasury debt. Financing by a government agency other than the Treasury is more expensive because it is not perceived by potential creditors to be risk free.

S&Ls were required to pay premiums to SAIF of 23 cents per $100 of deposits through 1993, 18 cents per $100 of deposits through 1997, and 15 cents per $100 of deposits thereafter. Although these funds are not to be directly channeled to finance S&L bailouts, they will provide the federal government with additional funds, which may reduce pressure to raise taxes to finance the S&L bailout. Additional costs of the bailout will likely be incurred by taxpayers over time.

Potential Impact of the Bailout

Beyond restoring confidence in the S&L industry, the provisions of the bailout bill carry significant ramifications for risk/return tendencies of S&Ls in the future. As a result of the bill, many S&Ls will be required to maintain a higher minimum level of capital. Some S&Ls will boost their capital by issuing stock. Others will sell assets, because a given level of capital with a smaller book value of assets results in a higher capital ratio. Other S&Ls will simply search for an acquirer, perhaps another S&L or a commercial bank.

The increase in capital requirements is expected to reduce the possibility of fraud by management. Because proportionately more assets will be backed by capital, more shareholders will monitor activities of S&Ls. Furthermore, the additional capital serves as a buffer against loan losses and reduces the likelihood of insolvency. However, the increased capital requirements will not necessarily please all investors. Some shareholders may have preferred S&Ls with less capital, because the higher degree of financial leverage allows the potential for higher returns. In addition, new stock issues have often precipitated an immediate decline in the stock price. If existing shareholders expect S&Ls to boost capital by issuing new stock and anticipate such a price reaction, they may sell any stock of S&Ls that they own.

In addition to boosting capital, S&Ls will be forced to maintain a more conservative asset portfolio. The provisions requiring a higher minimum investment of home mortgages and a liquidation of junk bonds reflect not only less risk but also less potential return. Some critics may suggest that the provisions reflect excessive regulation and limit the potential earning power of S&Ls. Thus, some S&Ls could be less capable of improving their financial condition. In addition, some S&Ls have converted to commercial banks to escape the regulations.

The bailout bill allows commercial banks and other financial institutions to purchase failing *or* healthy S&Ls. Superregional banks have been more aggressive than the larger money center banks because their stocks trade at higher multiples of earnings. They could swap some of their stock in exchange for the S&L stock in order to acquire S&Ls. In addition, superregionals are generally better capitalized than money center banks and can more easily acquire S&Ls while still satisfying minimum capital requirements. Commercial banks that wish to expand geographically or offer diversified services will be most likely to seek acquisitions. Some commercial banks may be enticed by the low share prices of S&Ls relative to their earning power. Under proper management, the acquired S&Ls may improve their performance significantly.

Some healthy S&Ls will acquire some failing S&Ls for the same reason. They perceive the failing S&Ls as undervalued. The deposit bases of these failing S&Ls are sound, but the loan portfolios need to be modified.

Performance Since the FIRREA

Since the FIRREA, savings institutions have generally performed well based on various criteria illustrated in Exhibit 20.8. The mean return on assets (ROA) for savings institutions (see upper left graph of Exhibit 20.8) was negative in 1989 and 1990, nil in 1991, and positive in 1992. The capital ratio of savings institutions (upper right graph of Exhibit 20.8) has consistently increased over this same period. The proportion of savings institutions experiencing negative earnings (lower left graph) declined from more than 30 percent in 1989 to less than 10 percent in 1992. The number of savings institution failures (lower right graph) has declined from 355 in 1990 to 62 in 1992.

The improved performance of savings institutions may be partially attributed to provisions of the FIRREA. In addition, the decline in interest rates enhanced the performance of most savings institutions, because their liabilities are more rate sensitive than their assets.

FUTURE OUTLOOK FOR SAVINGS INSTITUTIONS ⎯⎯⎯⎯⎯⎯⎯⎯⎯⎯⎯⎯⎯⎯

S&Ls may be able to improve performance by increasing their efficiency. Several strategies to increase efficiency deserve to be considered. First, can noninterest

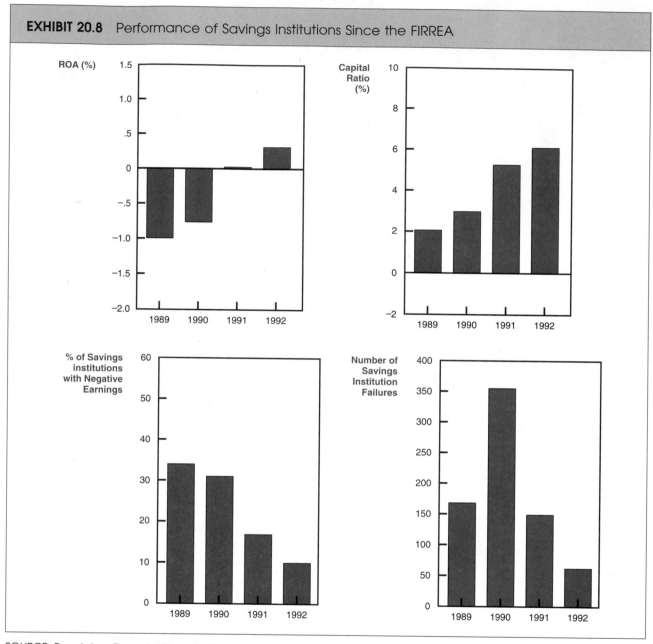

EXHIBIT 20.8 Performance of Savings Institutions Since the FIRREA

SOURCE: Regulatory Financial Reports, *Financial Industry Trends,* 1993, and Resolution Trust Corporation.

expenses be reduced? Salaries tend to comprise a large portion of these expenses. A reorganization of divisions is sometimes used to minimize noninterest expenses. Yet this is not necessarily a short-term solution even if it is effective. Additional costs are incurred for training or adapting to the new structure, and employee turnover tends to be relatively high because of reorganization.

Another strategy to increase efficiency is to divest assets that are being used inefficiently. This not only eliminates some inefficient resources, but also makes it easier for the S&L to meet its capital ratio. By reducing assets and maintaining the same level of capital, the S&L's capital ratio is increased. S&Ls must carefully assess possible divestitures. Some assets that are not "carrying their weight" may be linked to other assets that generate income. For example, a consumer lending division by itself may seem unprofitable, but can indirectly enhance the customer deposit base and mortgage lending volume.

Savings institutions will likely continue to diversify their mix of investments and services over time and therefore reduce their exposure to interest rate risk. However, they must also become accustomed to some new product offerings, thereby increasing their exposure to some other risks. For example, the savings institution's entrance into commercial lending will result in more noninterest expenses and will increase exposure to default risk.

A conflict between diversification and specialization may ensue. An attempt to provide every possible service provides consumers with a one-stop shop and reduces the institution's dependency on the performance of any single service. Yet, a high degree of diversification prevents savings institutions from specializing in the services they do best. Because of deregulation, some services that were previously prohibited are now allowed. As savings institutions experiment with these services over time, they will have to strike a balance between specialization and diversification. That is, they will diversify to a degree but will not offer all possible products at any cost just because they are now allowed to do so.

Because the characteristics vary among savings institutions, what works for one institution may not work for another. Thus, each must choose its own product offerings, geographic markets, and principal customers. The marketing function of savings institutions is likely to become more important in the future as they enter new geographic markets and offer new products—a clear departure from their traditional business of offering more limited products and serving only the local market.

Because savings institutions recognize the up-front costs of offering new products, they may search for ways to participate in some product offerings through an agent. For example, an attempt to enter the corporate lending business requires an experienced credit analysis department. Because of the significant cost of creating such a department, some savings institutions may consider channeling funds through another institution that has a credit analysis department. The institution acting as an agent would likely service the loan and receive a fee for its contribution. This type of loan participation is common in the commercial banking industry.

SAVINGS INSTITUTIONS IN OTHER COUNTRIES

GLOBAL ASPECTS

Savings institutions in non-U.S. countries have not had the severe financial problems experienced by savings institutions in the United States. Their financial characteristics allow them to reduce their susceptibility to economic conditions. For example, Canadian savings institutions typically use short-term mortgages (with the term of one to three years), which are then rolled over. Thus, they can effectively match interest rate sensitivity of mortgages to deposits. The British savings institutions (referred to as building societies) have used variable-rate mortgages since the 1930s, and since the 1960s they rarely even consider offering fixed-rate mortgages. Like Canadian savings institutions, they are not very susceptible to interest rate risk.

Surprisingly, the British building societies are less regulated than U.S. savings institutions. They are not subject to any geographical restrictions, and the rates they charge on mortgages are not subject to regulatory ceilings. British savings institutions do not carry deposit insurance. There are guarantees on deposits up to £20,000 that insure the first 90 percent of deposits for building societies. Because depositors would be directly affected by failures of the British depository institutions, they are more careful to assess the institution's risk. This differs distinctly from the United States, where savings institutions are monitored more closely by regulators than by depositors.

SUMMARY

- The main sources of savings institution funds are deposits and borrowed funds. The main uses of savings institution funds are mortgages, mortgage-backed securities, and other securities.

- Savings institutions are exposed to default risk as a result of their heavy concentration in mortgages, mortgage-backed securities, and other securities. They attempt to diversify their investments to reduce default risk.

  Savings institutions are highly susceptible to interest rate risk, because their asset portfolio is typically less rate sensitive than their liability portfolio. They can reduce their interest rate risk by using interest rate futures contracts, interest rate swaps, or interest rate caps.

- In the late 1980s, many savings institutions experienced heavy losses from loan defaults, adverse interest rate movements, and fraud. These adverse effects led to the savings and loan crisis. In 1989, the FIRREA was passed to resolve the crisis. Specifically, the FIRREA boosted the capital requirements, increased penalties for fraud, and prohibited savings institutions from purchasing junk bonds. It also created the Resolution Trust Company to liquidate assets of failed savings institutions.

QUESTIONS

1. Explain in general terms how savings institutions vary from commercial banks with respect to their sources of funds and uses of funds.

2. What are the alternative forms of ownership of a savings institution?

3. What are some differences between savings banks and savings and loan associations?

4. What are the major sources of funds for savings institutions? Discuss each source of funds.

5. Identify and discuss the main uses of funds for savings institutions.

6. How did the creation of money market deposit accounts influence the savings institutions' overall cost of funds?

7. The allowance of NOW accounts for savings institutions across the nation in 1981 was thought to be a major historical event. Why was this so critical to savings institutions?

8. Discuss the entrance of savings institutions into consumer and commercial lending. What are the potential risks and rewards of this strategy?

9. Describe the liquidity and default risk of savings institutions and discuss how each is managed.

10. What is an adjustable-rate mortgage? Discuss potential advantages such mortgages offer a savings institution.

11. Explain how savings institutions could use interest rate futures to reduce interest rate risk.

12. Explain how savings institutions could use interest rate swaps to reduce interest rate risk. Would savings institutions that used swaps perform better or worse than those that were unhedged during a period of declining interest rates? Explain.

13. What effect did the Depository Institution Deregulation and Monetary Control Act (DIDMCA) of 1980 and the Garn-St Germain Act of 1982 have on savings institutions?

14. Discuss the conflict between diversification and specialization of savings institutions.

15. If market interest rates were expected to decline over time, would an S&L with rate-sensitive liabilities and with a large amount of fixed-rate mortgages perform best by (1) using an interest rate cap, (2) using an interest rate swap, (3) selling financial futures, or (4) remaining unhedged? Explain.

16. Boca Savings & Loan Association has a large portion of 10-year fixed-rate mortgages financed with funds from short-term deposits. It uses the yield curve to assess the market's anticipation of future interest rates. It believes that expectations of future interest rates are the major force in affecting the yield curve. Assume that a downward sloping yield curve exists. Based on this information, should Boca consider engaging in interest rate swaps to hedge its spread? Explain.

17. The following table discloses the interest sensitivity of two S&Ls (dollar amounts are in millions).

INTEREST SENSITIVITY PERIOD				
	Within 1 Year	From 1–5 Years	From 5–10 Years	Over 10 Years
Lawrence S&L				
Interest-earning assets	$ 8,000	$3,000	$7,000	$3,000
Interest-bearing liabilities	11,000	6,000	2,000	1,000
Manhattan S&L				
Interest-earning assets	1,000	1,000	4,000	3,000
Interest-bearing liabilities	2,000	2,000	1,000	1,000

Based on this information only, which S&L's stock price would likely be affected more by a given change in interest rates? Justify your opinion.

18. What were some of the more obvious reasons for the savings and loan crisis?

19. Explain the role of the Resolution Trust Corporation (RTC) as intended by the Financial Institutions Reform, Recovery, and Enforcement Act (FIRREA).

20. Explain how the FIRREA can reduce the perceived risk of savings institutions.

PROBLEM

1. Stetson Savings and Loan Association has forecasted its cost of funds as follows:

YEAR	COST OF FUNDS
1	6%
2	5%
3	7%
4	9%
5	7%

It expects to earn an average rate of 11 percent on its assets over the next five years. It considers engaging in an interest rate swap in which it would swap fixed payments of 10 percent in exchange for variable-rate payments of LIBOR + 1 percent. Assume LIBOR is expected to consistently be one percent above Stetson's cost of funds. Determine the spread to be earned in each year if Stetson uses an interest rate swap to hedge all of its interest rate risk.

Deposit Insurance, Gas on S&L Fire

Robert E. Litan

Nearly three years ago—after virtually all the damage from the savings-and-loan mess had been done—Congress created a bipartisan commission to examine how it came about and how to prevent a similar catastrophe in the future. I was privileged to be apointed to that commission, which released its report this week.

So much has been written about this subject that it may be difficult to overcome the "S&L fatigue" from which the press, the public and policy makers understandably may be suffering.

The popular view of the S&L crisis is that it was created and aggravated by unscrupulous thrift executives, their lawyers, accountants and appraisers, and by venal politicians and regulators who failed to catch the crooks before they could raid the Treasury, which ultimately backed thrift deposits. All that is true, and we say so in our report.

But greedy wrongdoing alone was not the main cause of this crisis. In fact in our work we estimated that fraud accounted for no more than 10% to 15% of total losses. There are more important lessons to be learned—beyond "regulating better the next time"—and they are the focus of our report. At bottom, the S&L debacle was a failure in public policy, one that could have been largely avoided.

To begin to understand why, think of the S&L catastrophe as a giant financial fireball, fueled by gasoline, ignited by several matches, and fanned from the outside by wind gusts of several types.

Dangerous Guarantees

Deposit insurance was the gasoline. Few of the many risks that S&L operators took could have been financed had deposits not been guaranteed by the federal government. Truly uninsured depositors would have been far more careful with their money. They would have insisted on accurate financial data from the institutions, not the phony financial statements encouraged by federal regulatory policy. Simply put, in the absence of insurance, high-risk S&Ls could not have grown.

Like gasoline, deposit insurance still serves a useful purpose, provided it is treated with care and put in a proper container, insulated from sparks or matches. The thrift situation was entirely different.

Until the 1980s, thrifts were required by law to borrow short, lend long—that is, to invest in long-term fixed-rate mortgages funded by deposits with much shorter maturities. Moreover, the interest rates thrifts could pay depositors were subject to a regulatory ceiling.

Both the Hunt and FINE commissions in the mid-1970s pointed out that this structure was an accident waiting to happen. If interest rates soared above the ceilings, depositors would leave. In addition, thrifts were forced to violate what was even then a widely recognized financial principle: that it is prudent to diversify and not to hold virtually all one's assets in one type of financial instrument, in this case mortgages. The recommended solutions were simple: phase out interest-rate ceilings, allow thrifts to extend adjustable-rate mortgages and allow thrifts to invest in other types of loans, like banks.

The commissions were ignored and the accident did happen in the late 1970s and early 1980s. Interest rates rose well into double digits, forcing Congress in 1980 to begin the phase-out of interest-rate ceilings to prevent a massive deposit run to the newly created, unregulated money market funds. But when the ceilings were lifted, thrifts had to pay depositors far higher interest rates than the rates they were stuck collecting on their old fixed-rate mortgages. By 1981, the industry was insolvent by more than $100 million.

Instead of containing the growth of insolvent and undercapitalized thrifts, regulators and Congress threw a series of matches onto the deposit-insurance gasoline.

In particular, regulators gutted capital rules and introduced phony accounting rules, while the number of supervisors was slashed. These actions invited current and new owners of thrifts with nothing to lose (given federal insurance of the deposits) and everything to gain to gamble recklessly. About one-third of the industry then did so, pushing the assets of what was then an insolvent

Continued

CASE APPLICATION: LESSONS FROM THE S&L CRISIS

Continued

industry up by over 50% between 1982 and 1985.

Meanwhile, Congress gave the industry new asset powers that, under the different circumstances of the 1960s and 1970s, they could and would have used in moderation. But in the 1980s, without the supervision and the inhibitions of capital standards, these powers were abused.

Finally, several gusts made the fire grow hotter. The Texas economy collapsed. Tax policy made a mess out of commercial real estate, encouraging too much investment in 1981 and then abruptly pulling the plug in 1986. For years, both the executive branch and Congress failed to give the old thrift insurer (the FSLIC) enough financial water to put out the fire. The job remained undone; the cost grew.

So what are the lessons for the future? If the country wants safe financial gasoline—that is, deposit insurance—it must provide safe containers. To do that, we should gradually move to a system under which deposit insurance is provided only to monetary service companies, or MSCs, that invest in safe, liquid assets that can be readily marked to market, such as obligations of the federal government and quasi-governmental issues (Fannie Mae and Freddie Mac) and highly rated commercial paper. Because their assets would be safe, all the deposits in these monetary service companies would be insured, not just those under $100,000. For the same reason, any

firm—financial or nonfinancial—could own an MSC and integrate that MSC into its overall operations. One single stroke would end the seemingly endless battle over expanded bank powers.

Many will no doubt view the MSC proposal—a variation of which I have advocated in the past—as a radical suggestion. But other commissioners shared the same conclusion, perhaps out of the commonsense view that if the government wants to provide a totally safe investment for individuals, then the government should not also be subject to the risk of future financial configurations.

What would eventually happen to banks and thrifts as we know them today? For starters, there would no longer be separate charters (or separate regulators) for the two types of institutions. Moreover, most institutions themselves would split into two entities, one offering insured deposits (largely checking accounts) with access to the Federal Reserve's payment system, and the other funded by clearly marked, uninsured deposits or commercial paper, just as finance companies like GE Capital are funded today. In the process, bank supervision would be vastly scaled back. The markets would discipline the lenders, and regulators would be required only to check that the MSCs are investing in the permissible safe assets and not lending to parents or affiliates.

QUESTIONS

1. What would happen to the level of deposits at depository institutions if deposit insurance was removed? How might this affect the volume of funds available to households and businesses that borrow from depository institutions? How would the risk premium on loans be affected?

2. The assets of S&Ls grew by more than 50 percent in the early 1980s, which made the S&L crisis of the late 1980s even larger. Explain how the existence of deposit insurance was a key factor in allowing many weak S&Ls to grow.

3. In the early and mid-1990s, interest rates were relatively low. One might argue that S&Ls could experience another crisis, because they continue to offer fixed-rate mortgages, while interest rates had little room to fall and much room to rise. Offer your opinion on whether another S&L crisis may occur.

PROJECTS

1. **Financial Analysis of Savings and Loan Associations**
   Obtain annual reports or investment survey summaries (such as Value Line) for a savings and loan association assigned by your professor (or one of your choice) and answer the following questions:
   a. How has its asset portfolio composition changed in recent years?

    b. How has its liability portfolio composition changed in recent years?

    c. How have the recent changes in asset and liability composition affected the S&L's risk and potential return?

    d. How do you think its performance would be affected by an increase in interest rates? Explain.

    e. Based on the annual report, does the savings and loan association appear to be increasing its nontraditional services? Elaborate.

    f. Has the savings and loan association migrated into other states? If so, how? Is it planning interstate expansion? If so, how?

    g. Has the savings and loan association's performance been better or worse than in previous years? Why?

    h. Has the savings and loan association's noninterest income as a percentage of total assets increased or decreased in recent years? Elaborate.

    i. How has the savings and loan association's net interest margin changed in recent years? Does its net interest margin appear highly influenced by interest rate movements? If so, in what way?

2. Impact of Interest Rate Movements on an S&L's ROA

    a. Develop a model that could be used to determine how the savings and loan association's return on assets (ROA) is affected by interest rate movements. Include all relevant variables for which data are available.

    b. Apply your model to historical data to determine how its return on assets was affected by interest rate movements. Do the results support the type of relationship you hypothesized? Explain.

    c. Identify any limitations of your model.

    d. Suggest how you could use your model to forecast a savings and loan association's return on assets based on projections of any variables that affect ROA.

3. Impact of Interest Rate Movements on an S&L's Stock Returns

    a. Develop a model that could be used to determine how the savings and loan association's stock returns are affected by interest rate movements. Include all relevant variables for which data are available.

    b. Assume that the savings and loan association's returns are thought to be significantly influenced by characteristics particularly relevant to the savings and loan association industry. Specify a model that would capture this influence.

    c. Apply your model to historical data to determine how the savings and loan association's stock returns are affected by interest rate movements. Do the results support the type of relationship you hypothesized? Explain.

    d. Identify any other variables that should be included in the model if the data were available.

REFERENCES

Bae, Sung, C. "Interest Rate Changes and Common Stock Returns of Financial Institutions: Revisited." *Journal of Financial Research* (Spring 1990): 71–79.

Barth, James R., Philip F. Bartholomew, and Michael G. Bradley. "Determinants of Thrift Institution Resolution Costs." *Journal of Finance* (July 1990): 731–754.

Flannery, Mark J., and Christopher M. James. "The Effect of Interest Rate Changes on the Common Stock Returns of Financial Institutions." *Journal of Finance* (September 1984): 1141–1153.

Fraser, Donald R., and James W. Kolari. "The 1982 Depository Institutions Act and Security Returns in the Savings and Loan Industry." *Journal of Financial Research* (Winter 1990): 339–347.

Goldstein, Steven J., James E. McNulty, and James A. Verbrugge. "Scale Economies in the Savings and Loan Industry before Diversification." *Journal of Economics and Business* (August 1987): 199–208.

Gupta, Atul, Richard L. B. Le Compte, and Lalatendu Misra. "FSLIC Assistance and the Wealth Effects of Savings and Loan Acquisitions." *Journal of Monetary Economics* (February 1993): 117–128.

Kane, Edward A. "Principal-Agent Problems in S&L Salvage." *Journal of Finance* (July 1990): 755–764.

LeCompte, Richard L. B., and Stephen Smith. "Changes in the Cost of Intermediation: The Case of Savings and Loans." *Journal of Finance* (September 1990): 1337–1346.

Madura, Jeff., Alan L. Tucker, and Emilio R. Zarruk. "Market Reaction to the Thrift Bailout." *Journal of Banking and Finance* (June 1993): 591–608.

Madura, Jeff, and William C. Weaver. "Hedging Mortgages with Interest Rate Swaps Versus Caps: How to Choose." *Real Estate Finance Journal* (Summer 1987): 90–96.

Mester, Loretta J. "Efficiency in the Savings and Loan Industry." *Journal of Banking and Finance* (April 1993): 267–286.

———. "A Multiproduct Cost Study of Savings and Loans." *Journal of Finance* (June 1987): 423–445.

Pantalone, Colleen C., and Marjorie Platt. "Impact of Acquisitions on Thrift Performance." *Financial Review* (November 1993): 493–522.

Scott, William L., and Richard L. Peterson. "Interest Rate Risk and Equity Values of Hedged and Unhedged Financial Intermediaries." *Journal of Financial Research* (Winter 1986): 325–329.

CHAPTER 21

CREDIT UNIONS

The characteristics of credit unions vary distinctly from those of the other financial institutions discussed so far.

The specific objectives of this chapter are to:

- describe the main sources and uses of credit union funds,
- describe how credit unions are regulated, and
- explain how credit unions are exposed to various forms of risk.

BACKGROUND OF CREDIT UNIONS

Credit unions (CUs) are nonprofit organizations composed of members with a common bond, such as an affiliation with a particular labor union, church, university, or even residential area. About 20 million people are members of a CU. Qualified persons can typically become a member of a CU by depositing $5 or more into an account.

Ownership of Credit Unions

Because CUs do not issue stock, they are technically owned by the depositors. The deposits are called shares, and interest paid on the deposits is called dividends. Because CUs are nonprofit organizations, their income is not taxed. Like savings institutions and commercial banks, CUs can be federally or state-chartered. If the state does not offer a charter, a federal charter is necessary.

Objectives of Credit Unions

Because CUs are owned by members, their objective is to satisfy those members. CUs offer interest on share deposits to members who invest funds. In addition, they provide loans to members who are in need of funds. They are simply acting as an intermediary for the members by repackaging deposits from member savers and providing them to member borrowers. If CUs accumulate earnings, they can use the earnings to either offer higher rates on deposits or reduce rates on loans. Either choice would benefit some members but not others. In many cases, CUs instead use excess earnings for advertising to attract more potential members who qualify for the common bond. Growth can allow CUs to be more diversified and more efficient if economies of scale exist.

Size of Credit Unions

Although a few CUs (such as the Navy Federal CU) have assets of more than $1 billion, most are very small. In aggregate, their assets are much smaller than aggregate assets of commercial banks or savings institutions. They are growing at a faster rate, however. Exhibit 21.1 displays the total asset size of CUs over the past several years, distinguishing between federally and state-chartered CUs. In the late 1970s federally chartered CUs were just slightly ahead of state-chartered ones but later grew at a much higher rate and are now significantly larger than the aggregate size of state-chartered CUs.

A distribution of federally chartered CUs by size is shown in Exhibit 21.2. More than half of them have assets of less than $5 million, and about 70 percent have assets less than $10 million. The large number and small average size of CUs are due to the common bond requirement.

EXHIBIT 21.1 Growth in Credit Union (CU) Assets over Time (in Billions of Dollars)

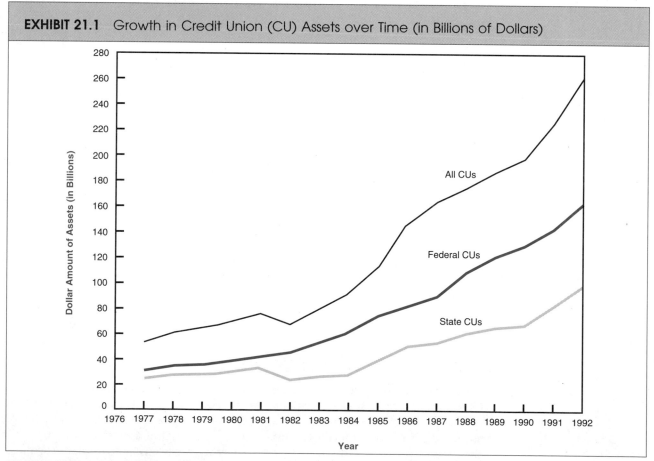

SOURCE: *Federal Reserve Bulletin,* and the NCUA.

EXHIBIT 21.2 Distribution of Federally Chartered Credit
Unions (FCUs)

ASSET SIZE	NUMBER OF FCUs	PERCENTAGE OF TOTAL
Less than $500,000	1,085	13.5%
$500,000 to $1 million	775	9.7
$1 million to $5 million	2,591	32.3
$5 million to $10 million	1,149	14.3
$10 million to $100 million	2,087	26.0
More than $100 million	329	4.1
	8,016	100.0%

SOURCE: NCUA.

Advantages and Disadvantages of Credit Unions

CUs can offer attractive rates to their member savers and borrowers because they are nonprofit and therefore not taxed. In addition, their noninterest expenses are relatively low, because their labor, office, and furniture are often donated or provided at a very low cost through the affiliation that all members have in common.

Some characteristics of CUs can be unfavorable. Their volunteer labor may not have the incentive to manage operations efficiently. In addition, the common bond requirement for membership restricts a given CU from growing beyond the potential size of that particular affiliation. The common bond also limits the ability of CUs to diversify. This is especially true when all members are employees of a particular institution. If that institution imposes labor layoffs, many members may simultaneously experience financial problems and withdraw their share deposits or default on their loans. This could cause the CU to become illiquid at a time when more members need loans to survive the layoff.

Even when the common bond does not represent a particular employer, many CUs are unable to diversify geographically, because all members live in the same area. Thus, an economic slowdown in this area would have an adverse impact on most members. Furthermore, CUs cannot diversify among various products the way that commercial banks and savings institutions do. They are created to serve the members and therefore concentrate heavily on providing loans to members. Finally, in the event that CUs do need funds, they are unable to issue stock because they are owned by depositors rather than shareholders.

SOURCES OF CREDIT UNION FUNDS

CUs obtain most of their funds from share deposits by members. The typical deposit is similar to a passbook savings account deposit at commercial banks or savings institutions, as it has no specified maturity and is insured up to $100,000. CUs also offer share certificates, which provide higher rates than share deposits but require a minimum amount (such as $500) and a specified maturity. The share certificates offered by CUs compete against the retail CDs offered by commercial banks and savings institutions.

In addition to these savings accounts, most CUs also offer checkable accounts called share drafts. These accounts can pay interest and allow an unlimited amount of checks to be written. They normally require a minimum balance to be maintained. Share drafts offered by CUs can compete against the NOW accounts and money market deposit accounts (MMDAs) offered by commercial banks and savings institutions.

If CUs need funds temporarily, they can borrow from other credit unions or from the Central Liquidity Facility (CLF). The CLF acts as a lender for CUs in a manner similar to the Federal Reserve's discount window. The loans are commonly used to accommodate seasonal funding and specialized needs or to boost the liquidity of troubled CUs. Any funds held by the CLF are invested in short-term securities until CUs request additional loans.

The CLF is an emergency lending fund that is part of a much larger internal system called the Corporate Credit Union Network, consisting of the Central Credit Union (a central bank for credit unions) and 42 corporate credit unions. These "credit unions for credit unions" not only provide for short-term liquidity but also offer investment and payment services for credit unions and are important to credit unions' smooth functioning and stability. They provide the funds to capitalize and maintain the CLF.

Exhibit 21.3 shows the percentage distribution of sources of funds of federal CUs. Share drafts became more popular in the early 1990s. The proportion of regular share deposits and share certificates has been somewhat stable in recent years. The proportion of funds obtained through regular share deposits is relatively large compared to the counterpart passbook accounts offered by other depository institutions. This characteristic allows CUs to obtain much of their funds at a relatively low cost.

Exhibit 21.4 shows the average cost to federally chartered CUs of obtaining funds over time. Considering how volatile market interest rates have been, the average cost of funds to CUs has been relatively stable over time. The sensitivity of the cost of funds to interest rate movements has been significantly lower for CUs than for savings institutions or commercial banks, resulting from the greater proportion of passbook deposits at CUs. The rates offered on these accounts have

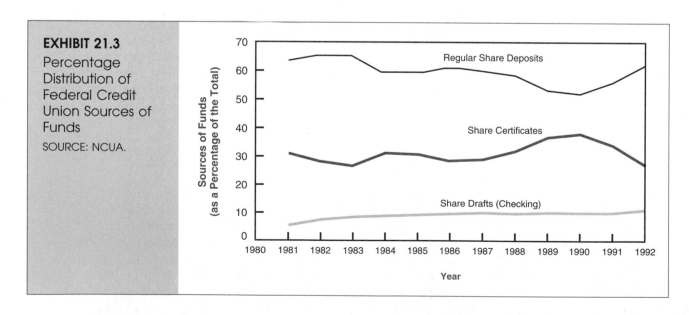

EXHIBIT 21.3

Percentage Distribution of Federal Credit Union Sources of Funds

SOURCE: NCUA.

remained somewhat stable, while rates on CDs and other accounts commonly used by savings institutions and commercial banks move with the market interest rates.

Like other depository institutions, CUs maintain capital. Their primary source of capital is retained earnings. CUs have boosted their capital in recent years, which helps cushion against any future loan losses. Given that CUs tend to use conservative management, their capital ratio is relatively high compared with other depository institutions.

Uses of Credit Union Funds

CUs use the majority of their funds for loans to members. These loans finance automobile, home improvement, or other personal expenses. They are typically secured and carry maturities of five years or less. Some CUs offer long-term mortgage loans, but many prefer to avoid assets with long maturities. In addition to providing loans, CUs purchase government and agency securities to maintain adequate liquidity.

Until recently, rates charged by CUs on loans were constrained by a regulatory ceiling. In the late 1970s and early 1980s, market rates on securities reached the ceiling rates on loans, and the return on relatively risky loans was no higher than the return on high-grade securities. Consequently, CUs restructured their asset portfolio to concentrate on securities in favor of loans. Exhibit 21.5 illustrates the change in CU asset composition over time. Although the ceiling rates were imposed on loans to benefit the borrower, they adversely affected those who were unable to obtain funds because of the CUs' shift from loans to securities. In the early 1990s, the proportion of funds allocated to loans was relatively low, perhaps because of the weak economy at that time.

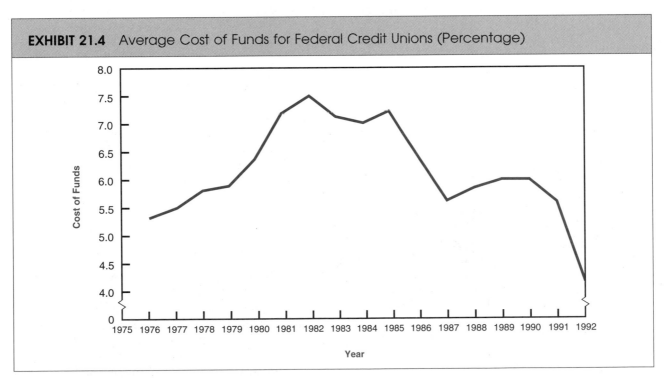

EXHIBIT 21.4 Average Cost of Funds for Federal Credit Unions (Percentage)

SOURCE: Annual Reports of the NCUA.

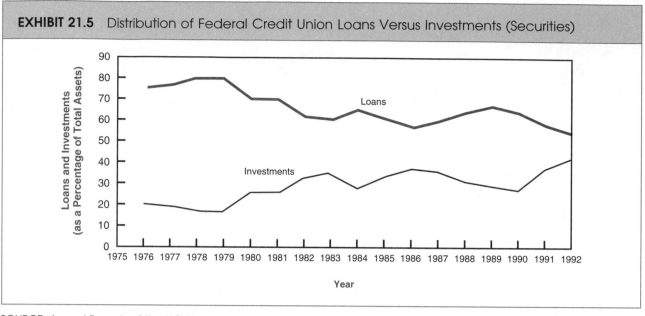

EXHIBIT 21.5   Distribution of Federal Credit Union Loans Versus Investments (Securities)

SOURCE: Annual Reports of the NCUA.

Exhibit 21.6 shows the average yield earned by CUs on loans and investments over time. The yield on loans is generally above that of investments because CUs' investments usually have a relatively low degree of default risk. Because loans dominate the asset portfolio, the overall average yield on assets is more closely tied to the average loan yield. The difference between the average yield on loans and investments has been more pronounced in recent years.

REGULATION OF CREDIT UNIONS

Federal CUs are supervised and regulated by the National Credit Union Administration (NCUA), which is composed of three board members, one of which is distinguished as chairman. The board members are appointed by the president of the United States and confirmed by the Senate. They serve staggered six-year terms. The NCUA participates in the creation of new CUs, as it has the power to grant or revoke charters. It also examines the financial condition of CUs and supervises any liquidations or mergers.

The NCUA has divided the United States into six regions, where its regional offices are responsible for monitoring operations of local CUs. To examine the CUs, the NCUA employs a staff of examiners. All federally chartered CUs as well as those state-chartered CUs applying for federal insurance are examined by the staff. Each CU completes a semiannual call report that provides financial information. This information is first input into a computer by the NCUA examiners to derive financial ratios that measure the financial condition of CUs. The ratios are then compared to an industry norm to detect any significant deviations. Then a summary of the CU, called a Financial Performance Report, is completed to identify any potential problems that deserve special attention in the future.

As part of the assessment of financial condition, examiners of the NCUA classify each CU into a specific risk category, ranging from Code 1 (low risk) to

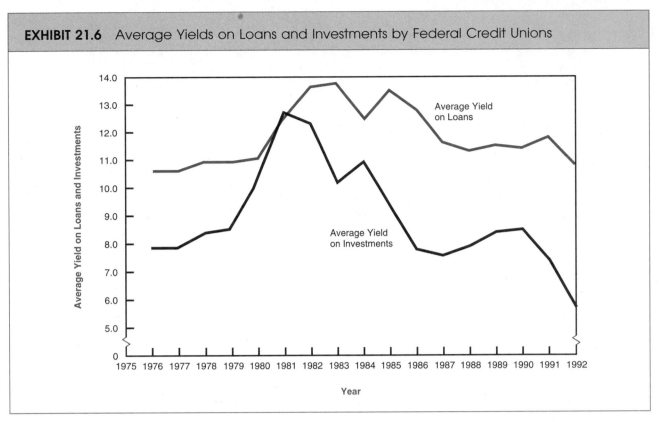

EXHIBIT 21.6 Average Yields on Loans and Investments by Federal Credit Unions

SOURCE: Annual Reports of the NCUA.

Code 5 (high risk). This is intended to serve as an early warning system so that those CUs that are experiencing problems or are in potential danger can be closely monitored in the future. The criteria used to assess risk are capital adequacy, asset quality, management, earnings, and liquidity. The CAMEL system has been used since 1987 and is very similar to the Federal Deposit Insurance Corporation (FDIC) system for tracking the commercial banks it insures. Exhibit 21.7 provides a breakdown of assigned risk ratings among CUs in recent years. Less than 10 percent have been assigned the more risky (4 and 5) ratings in any given year. Although this system will not always correctly classify CUs in their proper risk category, it can at least alert the examiners as to which CUs are experiencing financial problems.

CUs are subject to capital requirements of 8 percent of risk-weighted assets, 4 percent primary capital (such as retained earnings and reserves), and 4 percent secondary capital. CUs are regulated as to the types of services they offer. At one time they were regulated as to the rates they could offer on share deposits or charge on loans, but the Deregulation Act of 1980 led to a phasing out of deposit ceiling rates. In addition, CUs are now able to offer residential loans of any size or maturity and can sell the mortgages they originate.

State-chartered CUs are regulated by their respective states. The degree to which CUs can offer various products and services is influenced by type of charter and by location. In addition to services and rates, loans offered by CUs to officers and directors of CUs also carry certain limitations.

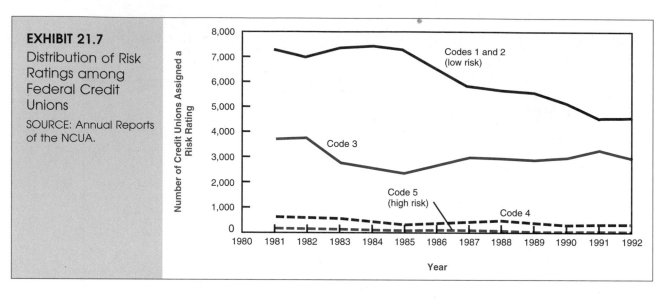

EXHIBIT 21.7

Distribution of Risk Ratings among Federal Credit Unions

SOURCE: Annual Reports of the NCUA.

INSURANCE FOR CREDIT UNIONS

About 90 percent of CUs are insured by the National Credit Union Share Insurance Fund (NCUSIF). They pay an annual insurance premium of one-twelfth of one percent of share deposits. A supplemental premium is added if necessary. Some states require their CUs to be federally insured; others allow insurance to be offered by alternative insurance agencies.

The NCUSIF was created in 1970, without any contributing start-up capital from the U.S. Treasury and Federal Reserve. All federally chartered CUs are required to obtain insurance from the NCUSIF. State-chartered CUs are eligible for NCUSIF insurance only if they meet various guidelines. The maximum insurance per depositor is $100,000.

During the 1970s the NCUSIF's main source of funds was insurance premiums. Because economic conditions were generally favorable, the aggregate insurance premiums received from CUs outweighed payouts to depositors of failing CUs. In the early 1980s, NCUSIF expenses increased, causing the NCUA Board to impose a supplemental insurance premium equal to two-thirds of the normal one-twelfth of one percent premium. In 1983 another supplemental premium, the equal to the normal premium, was assessed. In 1985 the NCUSIF obtained legislation that allowed for capitalized deposits for the fund. Because it had use of these deposits, the NCUSIF waived the normal annual insurance premium in 1985. As of 1993, the total assets of the NCUSIF exceeded $2 billion.

CREDIT UNION EXPOSURE TO RISK

Like other depository institutions, CUs are exposed to liquidity risk, default risk, and interest rate risk. Yet, because their balance sheet structure differs from other institutions, their exposure to each type of risk also differs.

Liquidity Risk

If CUs experience an unanticipated wave of withdrawals without an offsetting amount of new deposits, they could become illiquid. They can borrow from the

Central Liquidity Facility to resolve temporary liquidity problems. However, if the shortage of funds is expected to continue, they need to search for a more permanent cure. Other depository institutions have greater ability to boost deposit levels because they can tap various markets. Although some depository institutions attract deposits from international investors, the potential market for a CU's depositors is much more localized. Because the market is restricted to those consumers who qualify as members, CUs are less capable of quickly generating additional deposits.

Default Risk

Because CUs concentrate on personal loans to their members, their exposure to default risk is primarily derived from those loans. Most of their loans are secured, which reduces the loss to CUs in the event of default. Poor economic conditions can have a significant impact on loan defaults. Some CUs will perform much better than others because of more favorable economic conditions around their area. However, even during favorable economic periods, CUs with very lenient loan policies could experience losses. A common concern of CUs is that their credit analysis on loan applicants might be inadequately conducted by the volunteers they employ, yet the loans provided by CUs do not require elaborate credit analysis because they are consumer oriented.

The performance of CUs is highly dependent on the timeliness of loan repayments. Exhibit 21.8 shows that the delinquency rate for federal credit unions was highest during the 1982 recession but has diminished since then. Loan defaults have remained steady over time.

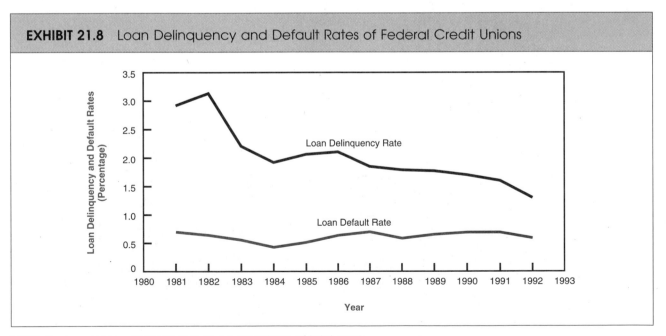

EXHIBIT 21.8 Loan Delinquency and Default Rates of Federal Credit Unions

NOTE: Each variable was measured as a percentage of total assets.
SOURCE: Annual Reports of the NCUA.

Interest Rate Risk

The majority of maturities on consumer loans offered by CUs are short-term, causing their asset portfolio to be rate sensitive. Because their sources of funds are also generally rate sensitive, movements in interest revenues and interest expenses of CUs are highly correlated. Therefore, the spread between interest revenues and interest expenses remains somewhat stable over time, regardless of how interest rates change. CUs are much more insulated from interest rate risk than those savings institutions that are heavily concentrated in fixed-rate mortgages.

PERFORMANCE OF CREDIT UNIONS

As with all depository institutions, the performance of CUs depends largely on the difference between their interest revenues and expenses. Exhibit 21.9 compares the average yield on assets to the average cost of funds for federal credit unions. The difference represents the average interest rate spread of CUs, which has consistently been maintained between 4.1 percent and 5.3 percent. The spread has been quite stable over time because the interest rate sensitivity of CU assets is somewhat similar to that of CU liabilities.

Exhibit 21.10 discloses the number of federally chartered credit unions with negative earnings (losses) over recent years. The high correlation between the delinquent or defaulted loans in Exhibit 21.8 and the CU earnings losses in Ex-

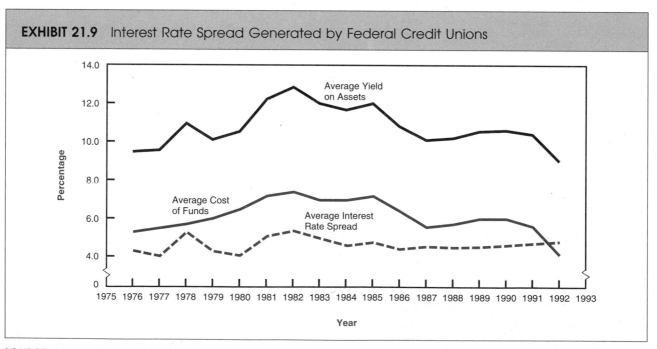

EXHIBIT 21.9   Interest Rate Spread Generated by Federal Credit Unions

SOURCE: Annual Reports of the NCUA.

EXHIBIT 21.10 Number of Federally Chartered Credit Unions (FCUs) That Experienced Losses

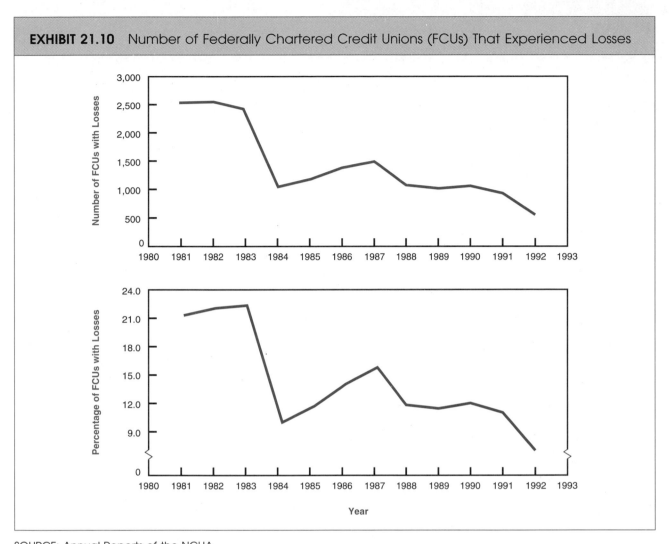

SOURCE: Annual Reports of the NCUA.

hibit 21.10 shows how dependent a CU's overall performance is on its loan portfolio.

If CUs experience economies of scale, growth should be a major objective. A study by Kim found that moderate economies of scale exist for mortgage lending and investment activities of CUs, but diseconomies of scale exist for nonmortgage lending.

To better diversify their services and take greater advantage of economies of scale, there has been an increasing tendency for CUs to merge. Thus, some CUs now allow a person to be from any one of a list of employers, organizations, and so on to qualify as a member. CUs are now also trying to diversify their products by offering traveler's checks, money orders, and sometimes life insurance to their members.

SUMMARY

- Credit unions obtain most of their funds from share deposits by members. If they experience a cash deficiency, they can borrow from other credit unions, or from the Central Liquidity Facility (CLF). They use the majority of their funds for personal loans to members.

- Credit unions are regulated by the National Credit Union Administration (NCUA). The NCUA employs a staff of examiners, who assess the financial condition of credit unions. The examiners classify credit unions into various risk categories, based on capital adequacy, asset quality, management, earnings, and liquidity.

- Credit unions are exposed to liquidity risk because they could experience an unanticipated wave of deposit withdrawals. They are also exposed to default risk as a result of personal loans to members.
  Because the personal loans offered by credit unions are short-term, they are rate sensitive like the liabilities. Thus, the interest rate risk of credit unions is typically less than that of other depository institutions.

QUESTIONS

1. Who are the owners of credit unions?

2. Explain the tax status of credit unions and the reason for that status.

3. What is the typical size range of credit unions? Give reasons for that range.

4. Describe the main sources of funds for credit unions.

5. The average cost of funds to credit unions has been relatively stable even though market interest rates have been volatile. Explain.

6. Why did credit unions increase their emphasis on securities while reducing loans in the early 1980s?

7. Who regulates credit unions? What are their powers?

8. Where do credit unions obtain deposit insurance?

9. Explain how credit union exposure to liquidity risk differs from that of other financial institutions.

10. Explain why credit unions are more insulated from interest rate risk than some other financial institutions.

11. Identify some advantages of credit unions.

12. Identify disadvantages of credit unions that relate to their common bond requirement.

13. How are credit unions diversifying and achieving economies of scale?

CASE APPLICATION: PERFORMANCE OF CREDIT UNIONS

Looking for Better Rates and Lower Fees? Credit Unions Are Favorites These Days

Lynn Asinof

If you're shopping for better interest rates, it can pay to take a look at credit unions.

"Hands down, you best deal is at a credit union rather than at a bank or a thrift institution," says Robert K. Heady, publisher of Bank Rate Monitor, North Palm Beach, Fla. "You are apt to earn more on your savings and save more when you borrow."

Granted, not everyone has access to a credit union, where membership is based on a common bond such as an employer. And a small percentage of credit unions get low financial-health ratings.

But more and more people are finding that expanded services, technical innovation and better rates make credit unions an attractive alternative.

Born in the 1880s in Europe, credit unions are based on the idea that people can pool their money and make loans to one another. Because the credit unions have no shareholders, they don't have to make a profit. They can pass any surplus income to members as increased services or lower fees. That makes it easier for them to beat the competition's rates on both the deposit and lending side.

Currently, for example, credit unions on average are paying about one percentage point more than banks on one-year certificates of deposit and three-quarters of a point more on money-market accounts.

The advantage is even greater for some borrowers, with credit union rates about 1⅓ percentage points lower on a car loan and more than four points less

for a credit card, according to Bank Rate Monitor. The only place where credit unions typically don't beat the competition is mortgages. That is because banks, thrifts and credit unions all sell to the same secondary-market mortgage investors.

Rates vary from credit union to credit union, with higher deposit rates usually found at those seeking cash. Credit unions with lots of money may have particularly attractive loan rates.

The Baltimore Telephone Federal Credit Union, for example, is flush with cash. That means good loan rates, such as the 36-month new car loan of 6.95% with no down payment. But deposits there earn only about the same as at banks and thrifts, with regular savings accounts now at 3.5%.

But even those credit unions that only match market deposit rates may be a better deal if they charge lower account fees.

Credit unions also pride themselves on being consumer friendly. "We have a history of making loans to people that banks and S&Ls would find difficult," says Raymond C. Slade Jr., general manager of the Baltimore Telephone credit union. "There is often a little bit more compassion than there would be with a savings and loan."

Safety has been another attraction. Having refinanced their insurance structure in the early 1980s, credit unions have been "an oasis of stability" amid the turmoil of troubled banks and S&Ls, says Charles W. Filson, president of Callahan & Associates, a Washington-based consultant to the credit union industry.

Credit unions' limited charter—making loans to members—has generally kept them off the shoals of big syndicated real estate loans or Third World lending. The problems that have plagued a lot of our money center banks "really don't apply in the credit union area," says Warren Heller of Veribanc Inc., a Wakefield, Mass., company that rates the safety of financial institutions.

Still, last year's debacle when Rhode Island closed dozens of privately insured credit union underscores the fact that the system isn't problem free. Two of the 50 largest consumer credit unions get "red" ratings from Veribanc for having too little equity, while three get the less severe "yellow" rating.

Some also worry about the large credit unions' limited forays into commercial lending. "They don't have the skills or experience," says Diane Casey, executive director of the Independent Bankers Association of America, who sees this as an area beyond the scope of credit unions' original purpose.

One way for consumers to avoid trouble: "Make sure it is federally insured," says Dennis Gurtz, a Washington financial planner. That means that a depositor is insured for as much as $100,000, the same as with a federally insured bank or savings and loan. Some 95% of all credit unions are now federally insured.

The majority of credit unions are still small: Two-thirds have $5 million or less in assets. But unlike the homey, volunteer-run image that the credit

Continued

CASE APPLICATION: PERFORMANCE OF CREDIT UNIONS

Continued

THE BEST DEAL IN TOWN? A survey of rates this week at banks, thrifts and credit unions showed that credit unions on average pay more for deposits and charge fees for some popular types of credit.

| | DEPOSIT YIELDS | | CREDIT COSTS | |
	MONEY MARKET ACCOUNT	1-YEAR CD	NEW CAR LOANS	CREDIT CARDS
Banks	2.92%	3.33%	9.44%	18.41%
Thrifts	3.12	3.73	9.70	18.48
Credit Unions	3.70	4.30	8.11	14.13

union name evokes, large credit unions today offer practically the same services as banks and thrifts. And it is the large ones that are growing fastest, merging with small credit unions and attracting new members by boosting services.

"In terms of service offerings, there is little difference between a large credit union and a bank," says Jerry Karbon, spokesman for the Credit Union National Association, Madison, Wis. That means everything from checking accounts and automatic teller machines to mortgages and home equity loans. Some credit unions even offer safety deposit boxes, mutual fund investment opportunities and financial planning.

Still, credit unions have strong local roots, typically being located in or near the sponsoring organization. That has made them convenient to, let's say, a person whose credit union is located at his workplace, but not for his mother who lives across town.

But the development of "shared branching"—now taking root in California—could change that. Since credit unions don't compete for customers, they can easily share facilities. By doing

so, they can cost-effectively move the credit union beyond the workplace and onto Main Street, making it more accessible during nonwork hours.

"That would make it more likely you would use it as your primary financial institution," says Bill Hampel, CUNA's chief economist.

Not everyone has the option to choose between a bank or thrift and a credit union. And, as rates do vary among credit unions, they may not want to join the one they have access to.

"Probably about 25% of the adult population is eligible for credit union membership," says Mr. Karbon of CUNA, noting the best way to find a credit union to join is to check with relatives, professional organizations, employers or the state credit union league. But with new rules that make it easier for family members to join and the aggressive expansion of larger credit unions, more people may find they are now eligible.

SOURCE: *The Wall Street Journal,* September 2, 1992, p. C1. Reprinted by permission of *The Wall Street Journal,* © 1992 Dow Jones & Company, Inc. All rights reserved worldwide.

QUESTIONS

1. Explain why credit unions have been more stable than other depository institutions.

2. Explain why the noninterest expenses (after adjusting for size) are smaller for credit unions than other firms.

3. Explain why credit unions can offer lower loan rates to some customers.

4. Some customers could benefit if credit unions offered additional services (including foreign exchange, mutual funds, etc.). What are the possible disadvantages that could be associated with more flexibility in services offered?

REFERENCES

Fried, Harold O., C. A. Knox Lovell, and Philippe Vanden Eeckaut. "Evaluating the Performance of U.S. Credit Unions." *Journal of Banking and Finance* (April 1993): 251–265.

Kim, H. Youn. "Economies of Scale and Economies of Scope in Multiproduct Financial Institutions: Further Evidence from Credit Unions." *Journal of Money, Credit, and Banking* (May 1986): 220–226.

Pearce, Douglas K. "Recent Developments in the Credit Union Industry." *Economic Review,* Federal Reserve Bank of Kansas City (June 1984): 3–19.

CHAPTER 22

FINANCE COMPANIES

All of the financial institutions discussed so far can be classified as depository institutions because they attract most of their funds from depositors. Finance companies differ from these institutions in that their funds obtained are of a nondepository nature. Their main purpose is to provide short- and intermediate-term credit to consumers and businesses. Although other financial institutions provide this service, only the finance company specializes in it. Many finance companies operate with a single office, while others have hundreds of offices across the country, and even in foreign countries. Some finance companies are subsidiaries of bank holding companies, insurance companies, and manufacturing firms. There are even finance companies whose subsidiaries offer insurance or commercial banking services.

The specific objectives of this chapter are to:

- identify the main sources and uses of finance company funds,
- describe how finance companies are exposed to various forms of risk, and
- explain how finance companies interact with other financial institutions.

TYPES OF FINANCE COMPANIES

Until recently, most finance companies could be classified into one of two types. **Consumer finance companies** concentrated on direct loans to consumers, while **sales finance companies** concentrated on purchasing credit contracts from retailers and dealers. The differences in business caused a distinct difference in balance sheet structure. Consumer finance companies provided smaller loans and operated with more offices. Their main source of funds was long-term loans. Sales finance companies provided larger loans and obtained most of their funds by selling commercial paper.

In recent years, both types of finance companies have diversified their sources and uses of funds. Thus, it is difficult to classify most finance companies as a particular type today.

SOURCES OF FINANCE COMPANY FUNDS

The main sources of funds for finance companies are

- Loans from banks
- Commercial paper
- Deposits
- Bonds
- Capital

Loans from Banks

Finance companies commonly borrow from commercial banks and can consistently renew the loans over time. For this reason, bank loans can provide a continual source of funds, although some finance companies use bank loans mainly to accommodate seasonal swings in their business.

Commercial Paper

Although commercial paper is available only for short-term financing, finance companies can continually roll over their issues to create a permanent source of funds. Only the most well-known finance companies, however, have traditionally been able to issue commercial paper to attract funds, because unsecured commercial paper exposes investors to the risk of default. In the past, small or medium-sized finance companies would have had difficulty in placing unsecured commercial paper. In recent years, secured commercial paper has become popular, so more finance companies might have access to funds through this market.

The most well-known finance companies can issue commercial paper through direct placement and thus avoid a transaction fee, lowering their cost of funds. Most companies, however, utilize the services of a commercial paper dealer.

Deposits

Under certain conditions, some states allow finance companies to attract funds by offering customer deposits similar to those of the depository institutions discussed in previous chapters. Although deposits have not been a major source of funds for finance companies, they may become more widely used where legal.

Bonds

Finance companies in need of long-term funds can issue bonds. The choice to attract funds through issuing bonds versus some alternative short-term financing depends on the company's balance sheet structure and its expectations about future interest rates. When the company's assets are less interest rate sensitive than its liabilities and when interest rates are expected to increase, bonds could provide long-term financing at a rate that is completely insulated from rising market rates. If the finance company is confident about projections of rising interest rates, it might consider using the funds obtained from bonds to offer loans with variable interest rates.

Capital

Finance companies can build their capital base by retaining earnings or by issuing stock. As with other financial institutions, capital as a percentage of total assets is maintained at a low level.

Relative Importance of Fund Sources

Exhibit 22.1 shows the average composition of the major sources of funds for finance companies. The amount of commercial paper issued by finance companies has more than doubled over the last 10 years. Finance companies tend to use more long-term debt when interest rates decline to lock in the cost of funds over an extended period of time.

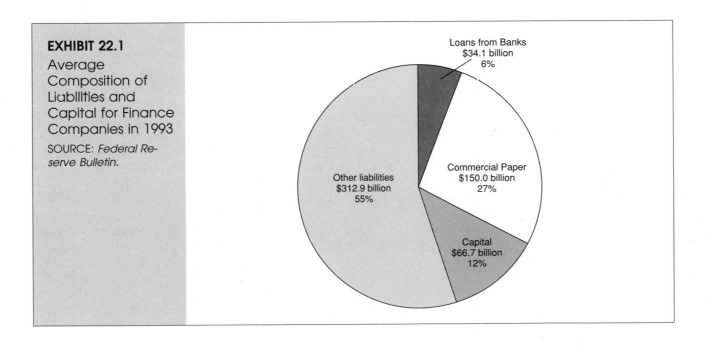

EXHIBIT 22.1

Average Composition of Liabilities and Capital for Finance Companies in 1993

SOURCE: *Federal Reserve Bulletin.*

Loans from Banks
$34.1 billion
6%

Commercial Paper
$150.0 billion
27%

Capital
$66.7 billion
12%

Other liabilities
$312.9 billion
55%

USES OF FINANCE COMPANY FUNDS

Finance companies use funds for

- Consumer loans
- Business loans
- Leasing
- Real estate loans

Each use of funds is described in turn.

Consumer Loans

Consumer loans are extended by finance companies in the form of personal loans. One of the most popular types is the automobile loan offered by a finance company that is owned by a car manufacturer. For example, General Motors Acceptance Corporation (GMAC) finances purchases of automobiles built by General Motors. Ford Motor Company and Chrysler Corporation also have their own finance companies. In recent years, the interest rate offered on such loans has been lower than market rates. Subsidiaries of automobile manufacturers may use unusually low rates to increase automobile sales.

In addition to offering automobile loans, finance companies offer personal loans for home improvement, mobile homes, and a variety of other personal expenses. Personal loans are often secured by a co-signer or by real property. The maturities on personal loans are typically less than five years.

Some finance companies also offer credit card loans through a particular retailer. For example, a retail store may sell products to customers on credit and then sell the credit contract to a finance company. Customers make payments to the finance company under the terms negotiated with the retail store. The finance company is responsible for the initial credit approval and for processing of credit card payments. The retailer can benefit from the finance company's credit allowance through increased sales, while the finance company benefits from the arrangement because of increased business. Finance companies increase their customer base in this way and are accessible for additional financing for those customers who prove to be creditworthy. The specific arrangement between a finance company and retailer can vary.

As a related form of consumer credit, some finance companies offer consumers a credit card that can be used at a variety of retail stores. For example, Beneficial Corporation offers the Bencharge card, which is acceptable at more than 25,000 small stores. In addition, Beneficial has become a large issuer of the premier MasterCards and Visas that offer a credit line of $7,500 to consumers. Their entrance into the credit card business is a useful method for attracting consumer loan applicants. In addition, borrowers with charge cards tend to meet their loan payments so that they can retain the use of their cards.

The main competition in the consumer loan market comes from commercial banks and credit unions. Finance companies have consistently provided more credit to consumers than credit unions have, but they are a distant second to commercial banks. Savings institutions have recently entered this market and are now also considered a major competitor.

Business Loans

In addition to consumer loans, finance companies also provide business (commercial) loans, commonly intended to finance the cash cycle of companies, which is the time from when raw materials are purchased until cash is generated from sales of the finished goods. Such loans are short term but may be renewed, as many companies permanently need financing to support their cash cycle. Business loans are often backed by inventory or accounts receivable.

Some finance companies provide loans to support leveraged buyouts (LBOs). These loans are generally riskier than other business loans but offer a higher expected return. In 1989 and 1990, as some highly leveraged firms experienced financial problems, the exposure to LBO loans received more attention.

Finance companies commonly act as a **factor** for accounts receivable, meaning they purchase a firm's receivables at a discount and are responsible for processing and collecting the balances of these accounts. They would incur any losses due to bad debt. Factoring reduces the processing costs of businesses. It also provides short-term financing, as cash is sent by the finance company to the business prior to the point at which the business would have received funds.

Leasing

Another way finance companies provide financing is by leasing. They purchase machinery or equipment for the purpose of leasing it to businesses that prefer to avoid the additional debt on their balance sheet that purchases would require. This can be important to a business that is already close to debt capacity and is concerned about additional debt adversely affecting its credit rating.

Real Estate Loans

Finance companies offer real estate loans in the form of mortgages on commercial real estate and second mortgages on residential real estate. The offering of second mortgages has become increasingly popular over time. These mortgages are typically secured and historically have a relatively low default rate.

Relative Importance of Uses of Funds

Exhibit 22.2 illustrates the average composition of assets for finance companies. Business loans comprise more than half of finance company assets, on average.

REGULATION OF FINANCE COMPANIES

When finance companies are acting as bank holding companies or are subsidiaries of bank holding companies, they are federally regulated. Otherwise they are regulated by the state. They are subject to a loan ceiling, which places a maximum limit on the loan size. They are also subject to ceiling interest rates on loans provided and to a maximum length on the loan maturity. These regulations are imposed by states, and they vary among states. Because ceiling rates are now sufficiently above market rates, they do not normally interfere with the rate-setting decisions by finance companies.

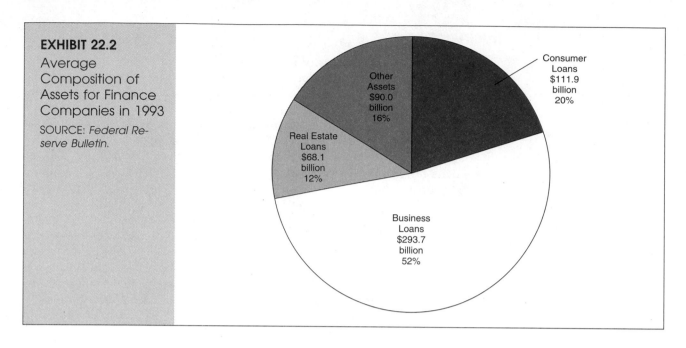

EXHIBIT 22.2
Average Composition of Assets for Finance Companies in 1993

SOURCE: *Federal Reserve Bulletin.*

Other Assets $90.0 billion 16%

Real Estate Loans $68.1 billion 12%

Consumer Loans $111.9 billion 20%

Business Loans $293.7 billion 52%

Finance companies are subject to state regulations on intrastate business. If they plan to set up a new branch, they must convince regulators that it would serve the needs of the people based in that location.

RISKS FACED BY FINANCE COMPANIES

Finance companies, like other financial institutions, are exposed to three types of risks:

- Liquidity risk
- Interest rate risk
- Default risk

Because their characteristics differ from those of other financial institutions, their degree of exposure to each type of risk differs as well.

Liquidity Risk

Finance companies generally do not hold assets that could be easily sold in the secondary market. Thus, if they are in need of funds, they have to borrow. However, their balance sheet structure does not call for much liquidity. Virtually all of their funds are from borrowings rather than deposits anyway. Consequently, they are not susceptible to unexpected deposit withdrawals. Overall, the liquidity risk of finance companies is less than that of other financial institutions.

Interest Rate Risk

Both liability and asset maturities of finance companies are short or intermediate term. Therefore, they are not as susceptible to increasing interest rates as are savings institutions. However, they can still be adversely affected, because their assets are typically not as rate sensitive as their liabilities. They can shorten their average asset life or make greater use of adjustable rates if they wish to reduce their interest rate risk.

Default Risk

Because the majority of a finance company's funds are allocated as loans to consumers and businesses, default risk is a major concern. Customers that borrow from finance companies usually exhibit a moderate degree of risk. The loan delinquency rate of finance companies is typically higher than that of other lending financial institutions. However, their higher average rate charged on loans can possibly more than offset a higher default level. The relative high return and high risk loan characteristics of finance companies can make their performance quite sensitive to prevailing economic conditions.

CAPTIVE FINANCE SUBSIDIARIES

A **captive finance subsidiary (CFS)** is a wholly owned subsidiary whose primary purpose is to finance sales of the parent company's products and services, provide wholesale financing to distributors of the parent company's products, and purchase receivables of the parent company. The actual business practices of a CFS typically include various types of financing apart from just the parent company business. When a captive is formed, an operating agreement is made between the captive and the parent company that includes specific stipulations, such as the type of receivables that qualify for sale to the captive and specific services to be provided by the parent.

The motive to create a CFS can be easily understood by evaluating the automobile industry. Automobile manufacturers were unable to finance dealers' inventories and so had to demand cash from each dealer. Many dealers were unable to sell cars on an installment basis because they needed cash immediately. Banks were the primary source of capital to dealers. However, banks viewed automobiles as luxury items not suitable for bank financing and were not willing to buy the installment plans created from automobile sales. For this reason, the automobile manufacturers became involved in financing.

The most substantial growth in captive finance subsidiaries occurred between 1946 and 1960 as a result of liberalized credit policies and a need to finance growing inventories. By 1960 more than 100 captive finance subsidiaries existed.

There are several advantages to maintaining a CFS. A CFS can be used to finance distributor or dealer inventories until a sale occurs, making production less cyclical for the manufacturer. It can serve as an effective marketing tool by

EVALUATING THE PERFORMANCE OF FINANCE COMPANIES

Annual reports are commonly used by investors to evaluate the financial condition of finance companies. The Value Line Investment Survey provides a summary of financial proxies that measure the performance of finance companies. An example of the Value Line analysis is shown here for Beneficial Corp. The income of finance companies is measured by return on equity, referred to as "% Earned Net Worth." Each column represents a specific year, so that the changes in performance of the finance company (as measured by any particular income proxy) can be assessed. The beta of the finance company is disclosed in the upper left corner.

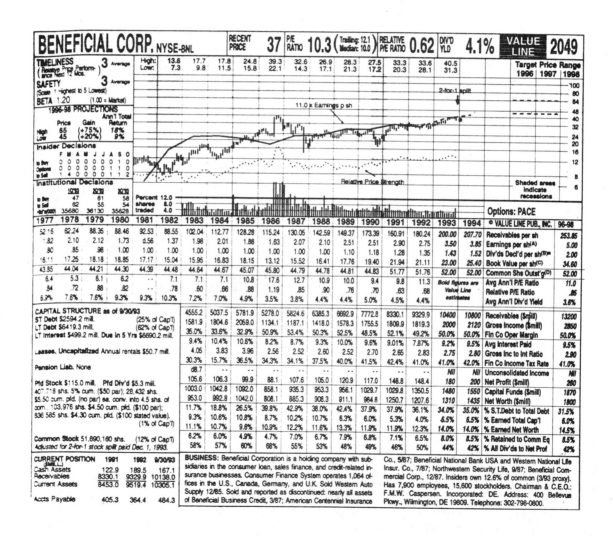

APPLIED RESEARCH

MARKET REACTION TO ESTABLISHMENT OF CAPTIVE FINANCE SUBSIDIARIES

Two possible benefits of a captive finance subsidiary are (1) separating accounts receivable into a subsidiary would increase efficiency and (2) a captive subsidiary can increase a firm's debt capacity. One might argue that in terms of cash flow, liquidity, and profitability, the combined perception of a separated parent and subsidiary should be the same as if there has been no separation. However, the tendency of some firms, such as General Motors

Corporation, Ford Motor Company, Sears Roebuck Corporation, and several other corporations, to establish captive finance subsidiaries suggests that there is a perceived advantage to such a strategy.

A study by Kim, McConnell, and Greenwood assessed the market reaction to the formation of captive finance subsidiaries. Stock returns were abnormally high shortly before the formation, while bond returns were abnormally low. This

implies that shareholders benefited at the expense of bondholders as a result of the anticipated formation of a captive finance company. The reason is that creditors of the newly formed captive finance company will have first claim (ahead of existing bondholders) on the cash flows generated by receivables. Other research on captive finance subsidiaries is reviewed by Fooladi, Roberts, and Viscione.

providing retail financing. It can also be used to finance products leased to others.

A CFS is a profitable operation in itself. Most well-managed finance companies earn 12 percent to 15 percent on their equity capital. A CFS allows a corporation to clearly separate its manufacturing and retailing activities from its financing activities. Therefore, it is less expensive and easier to analyze each segment of the parent company. Also, when lending to a captive finance subsidiary rather than a division of the parent company, the lender need be less concerned with the claims of others. Unlike commercial banks, a CFS has no reserve requirements and no legal prohibitions on how to obtain funds or use funds. Furthermore, a competitive advantage can be gained by a firm with a captive finance subsidiary because sale items such as automobiles and housing may depend on the financing arrangements available.

Captive finance subsidiaries have diversified their financing activities away from just the parent company's product installment plans. General Electric Credit Corporation (GECC) has been the most innovative of all the captive finance subsidiaries. Its financing includes industrial and equipment sales, consumer installment credit, and second mortgage loans on private residences.

The creation of a captive finance subsidiary can affect the debt capacity of the parent company as a whole. Roberts and Viscione evaluated 21 Canadian captive finance subsidiaries, 9 merchandising, and 12 manufacturing companies. The average debt-to-total assets ratios for these firms increased more than the ratios of firms without captives over the time frame of three years before and three years after the formation of the captive. Next, 45 U.S. firms, representing five industries, that formed captive finance subsidiaries were assessed. In each industry, there was a significant increase in the average debt ratios for the three-year period after the captive was formed as compared with the prior three-year period. Both evaluations concluded that a captive finance subsidiary allows more debt. Therefore, firms with captive finance subsidiaries experience increased debt capacity. The credit ratings of bonds issued by the firms that formed captives were unaffected when the firms increased their debt usage.

INTERACTION WITH OTHER FINANCIAL INSTITUTIONS

Finance companies and their subsidiaries often interact with other financial institutions, as summarized in Exhibit 22.3. They are more closely related to commercial banks, savings and loan associations, and credit unions because of their concentration in consumer lending. However, those finance companies with subsidiaries that specialize in other financial services compete with insurance companies and pension plans.

Because finance companies compete with savings institutions in the provision of consumer loans, they are able to increase their market share when savings institutions experience financial problems. Furthermore, some finance companies (such as Household International, Inc.) have acquired savings institutions.

EXHIBIT 22.3   Interaction between Finance Companies and Other Financial Institutions

TYPE OF FINANCIAL INSTITUTION	INTERACTION WITH FINANCE COMPANIES
Commercial banks and savings and loan associations (S&Ls)	■ Finance companies compete with banks and S&Ls for consumer loan business (including credit cards), commercial loans, and leasing. ■ Finance companies obtain loans from commercial banks. ■ Finance companies have acquired some commercial banks. ■ Some finance companies are subsidiaries of commercial banks.
Credit unions	■ Finance companies compete with credit unions for consumer loan business.
Investment banking firms	■ Finance companies issue bonds that are underwritten by investment banking firms.
Pension funds	■ Insurance subsidiaries of finance companies manage pension plans of corporations and therefore compete with pension funds.
Insurance companies	■ Insurance subsidiaries of finance companies compete directly with other insurance companies.

EXHIBIT 22.4	Participation of Finance Companies in Financial Markets

TYPE OF FINANCIAL MARKET	PARTICIPATION BY FINANCE COMPANIES
Money markets	■ Finance companies obtain funds by issuing commercial paper.
Bond markets	■ Finance companies issue bonds as a method of obtaining long-term funds. ■ Subsidiaries of finance companies commonly purchase corporate and Treasury bonds.
Mortgage markets	■ Finance companies purchase real estate and also provide loans to real estate investors. ■ Subsidiaries of finance companies commonly purchase mortgages.
Stock markets	■ Finance companies issue stock to establish a capital base. ■ Subsidiaries of finance companies commonly purchase stocks.
Futures markets	■ Subsidiaries of finance companies that offer insurance-related services sometimes use futures contracts to reduce the sensitivity of their bond portfolio to interest rate movements and also may trade stock index futures to reduce the sensitivity on their stock portfolio to stock market movements.
Options markets	■ Subsidiaries of finance companies that offer insurance-related services sometimes use options contracts to protect against temporary declines in particular stock holdings.
Swap markets	■ Finance companies can engage in interest rate swaps to hedge their exposure to interest rate risk.

Household International, Inc. now has numerous branches of depository institutions across seven states as it continues to diversify its services. Like many other finance companies, Household has become a diversified financial services company.

PARTICIPATION IN FINANCIAL MARKETS

Finance companies utilize various financial markets to manage their operations, as summarized in Exhibit 22.4. The use of financial markets by finance companies for the core business is mainly to obtain funds. However, the subsidiaries of finance companies often utilize financial markets as a method for investing funds or to hedge investment portfolios against interest rate risk or market risk. They may even diversify their financial services in foreign countries. As large finance companies such as Beneficial Corporation expand internationally, they will be better able to use the international bond and commercial paper markets as a source of funds.

Some finance companies have recently acquired insurance companies to enter the insurance business. They have also acquired commercial banks located in various states. In addition, the larger finance companies have diversified into a variety of nonfinancial businesses as well.

MULTINATIONAL FINANCE COMPANIES

Some finance companies are large multinational corporations with subsidiaries in several countries. For example, the consumer finance division of Beneficial Corporation has more than 1,000 offices in the United States, Canada, Germany, and the United Kingdom. U.S.-based finance companies penetrate foreign countries to enter new markets and to reduce their exposure to U.S. economic conditions.

SUMMARY

- The main sources of finance company funds are loans from banks, sales of commercial paper, bonds, and capital. The main uses of finance company funds are consumer loans, business loans, leasing, and real estate loans.

- Finance companies are exposed to default risk, as a result of their consumer loans, business loans, and real estate loans. They are also exposed to liquidity risk, because their assets are not very marketable in the secondary market. They may also be exposed to interest rate risk.

- Finance companies compete with depository institutions (such as commercial banks, savings institutions, and credit unions) that provide loans to consumers and businesses. Many finance companies have insurance subsidiaries that compete directly with other insurance subsidiaries.

QUESTIONS

1. Is the cost of funds obtained by finance companies very sensitive to market interest rate movements? Explain.

2. How are small and medium-sized finance companies able to issue commercial paper?

3. Why do some well-known finance companies directly place their commercial paper?

4. Explain why some finance companies are associated with automobile manufacturers. Why do some of these finance companies offer below-market rates on loans?

5. Describe the major uses of funds by finance companies.

6. Explain how finance companies benefit from offering consumers a credit card.

7. Explain how finance companies provide financing through leasing.

8. What was the historical difference between consumer finance companies and sales finance companies?

9. Explain how the liquidity position of finance companies differs from that of depository institutions such as commercial banks.

10. Explain how the interest rate risk of finance companies differs from that of savings institutions.

11. Explain how the default risk of finance companies differs from that of other lending financial institutions.

12. Explain how finance companies are regulated.

Commercial Finance Firms Have New Rivals in Banks
Realm of Asset-Based Lending Offers Promise of Rich Profits to Competitors

Leslie Scism

Is the party over for commercial finance companies?

Some racked up double-digit growth in loans over the past several years as many commercial banks hunkered down to strengthen capital requirements.

Now, with cleaned-up balance sheets and improved profitability, banks have begun aggressively wooing the finance companies' middle-market customers—companies with annual sales of $1 million to $500 million. Moreover, the stepped-up competition comes at a time when loan demand is growing only slowly.

"It's an awful lot of money chasing deal flow," says Frank Medeiros, a group president for Sanwa Business Credit Corp., a Chicago unit of Japan's **Sanwa Bank** Ltd. Mr. Medeiros is also president of the Commercial Finance Association, a trade group.

For borrowers, the heightened competition is good news because it makes credit more available and lending terms looser. But for the finance companies, the banks' invasion of their turf means less business and potentially smaller profit margins.

Unlike banks, which lend primarily on the strength of a company's cash-flow statement, commercial finance companies generally make loans secured by accounts receivable, inventory, equipment or other property—so-called asset-based loans.

Banks have preferred lending based on cash flow because that means dealing with the most credit-worthy customers.

As a result, companies that are less credit-worthy have had to rely on commercial finance companies, which generally charge more than banks.

Another reason banks have preferred cash-flow lending is that they have been unwilling to develop the nuts-and-bolts knowledge of other industries that is essential to asset-based lending. It's essential because that is what lets a lender properly value the collateral in case the company gets in trouble.

But something has happened at the banks: They've realized that asset-based lending can be a very good business.

At year-end 1992, finance companies' share of commercial and industrial lending was $310 billion, or 34%—up from 30% in 1989, according to Mercer Management Consulting Inc., a business consulting firm.

"Asset-based lenders probably had better opportunities and margins in the last three years than they now do," adds Albert Gamper Jr., a president of CIT Group Holdings Inc., a Livingston, N.J., commercial finance company whose $13.32 billion in assets makes it one of the largest. CIT Group Holdings is a unit of Japan's **Dai-Ichi Kangyo Bank** and **Chemical Banking Corp.**

Casualties in the Field

To be sure, the recession, the sluggish recovery and poor management have left casualties in the commercial finance field; **Westinghouse Electric** Corp. continues to liquidate its finance unit, Westinghouse Credit Corp. The unit was hammered by the collapse of the com-

mercial real estate market and highly leveraged corporate finance deals gone sour.

Nevertheless, the average commercial finance company last year showed 5% to 10% growth in its loan portfolio, industry analysts say. At the same time, write-offs remained low.

"Many finance companies have flourished because they stuck to their own backyards with established credit policies," says Raymond Miller, a Standard & Poor's Corp. director.

Banks have stepped in and out of asset-based lending over the decades, generally eschewing it. Asset-based lending, explains Charles Wendel, a Mercer Management vice president, carries a "blue-collar, rolled-up sleeves image" and requires constant monitoring. Successfull asset-based lenders "are not shy about liquidating because they know how to manage and sell assets," says Nancy Stroker, an analyst with Fitch Investors Services.

But asset-based lending to the middle market does have its attraction, if done right: It can generate "consistently higher spreads and a lot of [monitoring and other] fees that don't occur in unsecured lending," Mr. Wendel says. Typical asset-based spreads today are 2% to 3% above the banks' benchmark prime rate.

In retrenching earlier, banks gave up both secured and unsecured middle-market customers, analysts and commercial finance companies say. In courting them again, some banks seek out the most credit-worthy for partially

Continued

CASE APPLICATION: COMPETITION BETWEEN FINANCE COMPANIES AND COMMERCIAL BANKS

Continued

secured and unsecured loans. But many banks—seeing the profits to be earned—are beefing up asset-based lending units to compete with the finance companies precisely on their terms.

'The Pendulum Has Swung'

''The middle market was ignored for a while by banks, but the pendulum has swung,'' says Donald B. Clark, a vice president at head-hunting firm Paul R. Ray & Co., who has filled four asset-based lending jobs in the Midwest recently.

Indeed, earlier this month Congress Financial Corp. of New York, one of the most established of the asset-based lenders, lost a $4 million deal to be secured by equipment appraised at $5 million. ''Another lender wanted to buy that piece of business so they offered a $7 million loan,'' Barry Kastner, a Congress senior vice president, says, ''On something like that, we wish them well.''

At Congress, a unit of **CoreStates Financial** Corp., Chairman Robert Goldman says his total loan portfolio will grow another 18% this year, but he's bracing for a slowdown in 1994 to 10% growth. Congress now has $1.3 billion in asset-based loan receivables.

Banks aggressively promoting asset-based lending of late include **BankAmerica** Corp.'s Bank of America unit, based in San Francisco. It has an in-house unit wooing the strongest businesses with secured and partially secured deals, says Ronald Tweedy, a Bank of America senior vice president. Meanwhile, BankAmerica Business Credit, an asset-based lending subsidiary inherited through its merger last year with Security Pacific Corp., has generated $246 million worth of middle-market loans over the past eight months, says Linda Chesnut, a BankAmerica Business Credit senior vice president.

Superregional **NationsBank** Corp. of Charlotte, N.C., also has stepped up asset-based lending. Its Business Credit division opened three new lending offices over the last year, bringing the total to a dozen nationwide, and increased its asset-based loan portfolio 15% to $1.4 billion, says Larry Stephens, a NationsBank executive vice president.

Established middle-market asset-based lenders are also getting squeezed by nonbankers. GE Capital Corp., a Stamford, Conn., unit of **General Electric** Co., created an asset-based lending unit last September. The unit's goal is $1 billion in receivables by year end,

says Michael Gaudino, a GE Capital vice president. He says the unit is about ''halfway there.''

SOURCE: *The Wall Street Journal,* June 24, 1993. Reprinted by permission of *The Wall Street Journal,* © 1993 Dow Jones & Company, Inc. All rights reserved worldwide.

QUESTIONS

1. What are the likely factors that motivated commercial banks to lend to firms that normally relied on finance companies for funds?

2. Explain why the risk-return trade-off for finance companies that use asset-based lending typically varies from the commercial banks that focus on loans to the most creditworthy customers.

3. Explain how the criteria to qualify for loans provided by finance companies such as Westinghouse Credit Corp. and GE Capital Corp. vary from the criteria to qualify for bank loans.

PROJECT

1. **Financial Analysis of a Finance Company**
   Obtain an annual report of a finance company assigned by your professor or one of your choice. Based on this report, answer the following questions:
   a. How has the company's asset portfolio composition changed in recent years?
   b. Have the recent changes in asset composition affected the company's risk and potential return?
   c. How do you think the company would be affected by an increase in interest rates? Explain.
   d. Based on its annual report, does the company appear to be increasing its nontraditional services? Elaborate.

REFERENCES

Andrews, Victor L. "Captive Finance Companies." *Harvard Business Review* (July–August 1964): 80–92.

Fooladi, Iraj, Gordon Roberts, and Jerry Viscione. "Captive Finance Subsidiaries, Overview, and Synthesis," *Financial Review* (May 1986): 259–275.

Jensen, Michael, and William Meckling. "Theory of the Firm: Managerial Behavior, Agency Costs, and Ownership Structure." *Journal of Financial Economics* (October 1976): 305–360.

Kim, E. H., John J. McConnell and Paul R. Greenwood. "Capital Structure Rearrangement and Me-First Rules in an Efficient Capital Market." *Journal of Finance* (June 1977): 789–810.

Lewellen, Wilbur G. "Finance Subsidiaries and Corporate Borrowing Capacity." *Financial Management* (Spring 1972): 21–32.

Roberts, Gordon S., and Jerry A. Viscione. "The Captive Finance Company: Solution or Straw Man?" *Credit and Financial Management* (December 1979): 34–35.

———. "Captive Finance Subsidiaries: The Manager's View." *Financial Management* (Spring 1981): 36–42.

CHAPTER 23

MUTUAL FUNDS

A **mutual fund** is an investment company that sells shares representing an interest in a portfolio of securities. Mutual funds have grown substantially in recent years, and are involved in a large proportion of transactions in financial markets.

The specific objectives of this chapter are to:

- explain how characteristics vary among mutual funds,
- describe the various types of stock and bond mutual funds, and
- describe the characteristics of money market funds.

BACKGROUND ON MUTUAL FUNDS

Small investors who purchase securities individually are often unable to diversify because of their limited investment. Mutual funds offer a way by which these investors can diversify. Some mutual funds contain 50 or more securities, and the minimum investment typically ranges from $250 to $2,500. Small investors could not afford to create such a diversified portfolio on their own. Moreover, the mutual fund uses experienced portfolio managers, so investors do not have to manage the portfolio themselves. Finally, some mutual funds offer the investor liquidity, through their willingness to repurchase the investor's shares upon request.

Because of their diversification, management expertise, and liquidity, mutual funds have grown at a rapid pace. There are about 4,000 different mutual funds today, with total assets having increased by more than 12 times the 1979 level. The number of mutual fund shareholder accounts has grown from 9.8 million in 1979 to more than 77 million. The percent of households holding mutual funds has increased from about 6 percent in 1979 to more than 25 percent.

Mutual funds are like depository institutions in that they repackage the proceeds received from individuals to make various types of investments. Yet, the investment in mutual funds is distinctly different from depositing money in a depository institution in that it represents partial ownership, whereas deposits represent a form of credit. Thus, the investors share the gains or losses generated by the mutual fund, while depositors simply receive interest on their deposits. Individual investors view mutual funds as an alternative to depository institutions. In fact, much of the increased investment in mutual funds in the early 1990s came from depository institutions. As interest rates declined in the early 1990s, many individuals withdrew deposits and invested in stock mutual funds and bond mutual funds.

Estimating the Net Asset Value

The **net asset value** (NAV) of a mutual fund indicates the value per share. It is estimated each day by first determining the market value of all securities comprising the mutual fund (any cash would also be accounted for). Any interest or dividends accrued from the mutual fund is added to the market value. Then any expenses are subtracted, and the amount is then divided by the number of shares of the fund outstanding. The reporting of the net asset value of mutual funds is monitored by the Securities and Exchange Commission (SEC). When a mutual fund pays its shareholders dividends, its net asset value declines by the per-share amount of the dividend payout.

Mutual Fund Classifications

Mutual funds are commonly classified as either stock mutual funds, bond mutual funds, or money market mutual funds, depending on the types of securities that they invest. The distribution of investments in these three classes of mutual funds is shown in Exhibit 23.1.

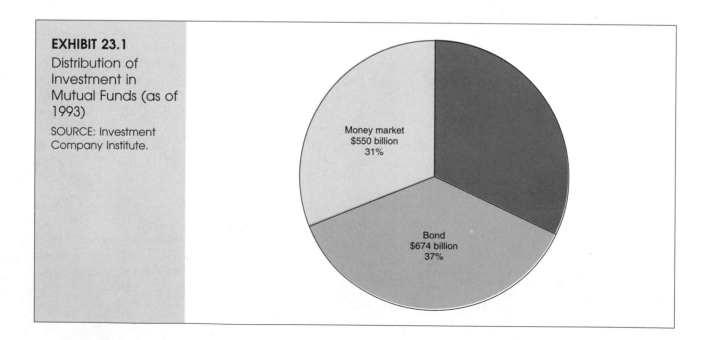

EXHIBIT 23.1
Distribution of Investment in Mutual Funds (as of 1993)

SOURCE: Investment Company Institute.

Money market
$550 billion
31%

Bond
$674 billion
37%

Many investment companies offer a family of mutual funds with as many as 30 different funds so that they can accommodate the diverse preferences of investors. An investor can transfer from one mutual fund to another within the same family.

Management of Mutual Funds

Portfolio managers are hired by the mutual fund to invest in a portfolio of securities that satisfies the desires of investors. A successful portfolio will become attractive to other investors and thus grow over time. To cover managerial expenses, mutual funds charge management fees of typically less than one percent of the total assets per year.

Besides the compensation to portfolio managers, management expenses of a mutual fund include record-keeping and clerical fees. These expenses can be significant, as any given fund may represent ownership by several thousand investors.

Like other portfolio managers, the managers of mutual funds analyze economic and industry trends and forecasts and assess the potential impact of various conditions on companies. They adjust the composition of their portfolio in response to changing economic conditions.

LOAD VERSUS NO-LOAD MUTUAL FUNDS

Mutual funds can be classified as either **load,** meaning there is a sales charge, or **no-load,** meaning funds are promoted strictly by the mutual fund of concern. Load funds are promoted by registered representatives of brokerage firms, who earn a sales charge typically ranging between 3 percent and 8.5 percent. Investors in a load fund pay this charge through the difference between the bid and ask prices of the load funds. Some investors may feel that the sales charge is worthwhile, because a brokerage firm helps determine the type of fund that is appropriate for them. Other investors who feel capable of making their own investment decisions often prefer to invest in no-load funds. Some no-load mutual funds can be purchased through a discount broker for a relatively low fee (such as 1 percent to 2 percent), although investors receive no advice from the discount broker.

In recent years, some small no-load funds have become load funds because they could not attract investors without a large budget to advertise nationally. As a load fund, they will be recommended by various brokers and financial planners, who will earn a commission on any shares sold. Some other no-load funds now charge a fee (called a 12b-1 fee in reference to Securities and Exchange Commission rule 12b-1) to help support advertising expenses. In fact, there are various expenses that can be charged that may not be classified as a load. The fund's expenses are reported in the mutual fund's prospectus in the form of an expense ratio, which is equal to total expenses divided by the NAV.

To illustrate the potential advantage of no-load funds, consider separate $10,000 investments in no-load and load funds. Assuming an 8.5 percent load fee, the actual investment in the load fund is $9,150. If the value of both funds grew by 10 percent per year, the investment in the no-load fund would be worth $2,204 more than the investment in the load fund after 10 years.

OPEN-END VERSUS CLOSED-END FUNDS

Open-end investment funds are willing to repurchase the shares they sell from investors at any time. This is an attractive characteristic, because it offers liquidity to investors. **Closed-end investment funds** do not repurchase the shares they sell. Instead, investors must sell the shares on a stock exchange just like corporate stock. The number of shares sold by a closed-end investment company usually remains fixed, equal to the initial amount issued. When the demand for a particular closed-end mutual fund is strong, the market price may be higher than its net asset value. However, closed-end funds commonly have a market value less than the net asset value. The initial offering of a closed-end fund is normally sold above its net asset value to cover the underwriting commissions earned by investment banking firms.

RETURNS AND RISKS OF MUTUAL FUNDS

Mutual funds can generate returns to their shareholders in three ways. First, they can pass on any earned income (from dividends or coupon payments) as dividend payments to the shareholders. Second, they can pass on capital gains through the sale of securities within the fund. Shareholders can choose either to accept any dividend payments and capital gains distributions or to request that the distributions be reinvested into the fund, thereby representing a purchase of additional shares. A third type of return to shareholders is through mutual fund share price appreciation. As the market value of security holdings increases, the net asset value of the fund increases, and the shareholders benefit when they sell their mutual fund shares.

Although investors in a mutual fund directly benefit from any returns generated by the fund, they are also directly affected if the portfolio generates losses. Because they own the shares of the fund, there is no other group of shareholders to which the fund must be accountable. This differs from commercial banks and stock-owned savings associations, which obtain their deposits from one group of investors and sell shares of stock to another.

STOCK AND BOND MUTUAL FUNDS

Because investors have various objectives, no single portfolio could satisfy everyone. Consequently, a variety of stock and bond mutual funds have been created. The more popular types include

- Growth funds
- Capital appreciation funds
- Income funds
- Growth and income funds
- Tax-free funds
- High-yield (junk bond) funds
- International and global funds
- Asset allocation funds
- Specialty funds

Growth Funds

For investors who desire a high return and are willing to accept a moderate degree of risk, **growth funds** are appropriate. These funds are typically composed of stocks of companies that have not fully matured and are expected to grow at a higher than average rate in the future. The primary objective of a growth fund is to generate an increase in investment value, with less concern about the generation of steady income. Growth funds do not all necessarily share the same degree of risk. Some concentrate on companies that have existed for several years but are still experiencing growth, while others concentrate on relatively young companies.

Capital Appreciation Funds

Also known as aggressive growth funds, **capital appreciation funds** are composed of stocks that have potential for very high growth but may also be unproven. These funds are suited for investors who are more willing to risk a possible loss in value. In response to the rapid changes in the economy, portfolio managers of capital appreciation funds constantly revise the portfolio composition to take full advantage of their expectations. They sometimes even use borrowed money to support their portfolios, thereby using leverage to increase their potential return and risk.

Income Funds

For investors who are mainly concerned with stability of income rather than capital appreciation, **income funds** are appropriate. These funds are usually composed of bonds that offer periodic coupon payments and vary in exposure to risk. Some income funds composed of only corporate bonds are susceptible to default risk, while those composed of only Treasury bonds are not. A third type of income fund contains bonds backed by government agencies, such as the Government National Mortgage Association (called GNMA, or Ginnie Mae). These funds are normally perceived to be less risky than a fund containing corporate bonds. Those income funds exhibiting more default risk will offer a higher potential return, other things being equal.

In addition to being exposed to default risk, income funds are exposed to interest rate risk. Those with a longer average time to maturity are more exposed. Treasury bonds are just as susceptible to interest rate risk as other bonds with similar maturity and coupon characteristics. Some income funds commonly adjust their average maturity in anticipation of market conditions and interest rate movements.

The market values of even the medium-term income funds are quite volatile over time because of their sensitivity to interest rate movements. Thus, income funds are best suited for investors who rely on the fund for periodic income and plan to maintain the fund over a long period of time.

Some income mutual funds use a covered call strategy on a portion of the portfolio. These option income mutual funds invest in stocks and sell call options on those stocks. The premiums received from selling the call options increase the income generated by the mutual funds. However, during bull markets, the stocks on which call options were written must be sold as the options are exercised.

Thus, the mutual funds forgo the potential return that could have been achieved if they were able to retain the shares. Some option income mutual funds write options on only 35 percent to 50 percent of their stock portfolio. This strategy generates less option premium income but reduces the potential amount of stocks that the fund would have to sell if the options were to be exercised.

Growth and Income Funds

For investors who prefer potential for capital appreciation along with some stability in income, a growth and income fund, which contains a unique combination of growth stocks and fixed-income bonds, may be most appropriate. For those funds that emphasize greater investment in growth stocks rather than bonds, there is greater potential for capital appreciation but a lower amount of fixed income generated from the fund.

Tax-Free Funds

High tax bracket investors have historically purchased municipal bonds as a method to avoid taxes. Because these bonds are susceptible to default, a diversified portfolio is desirable. Mutual funds containing municipal bonds allow high tax bracket investors with even small amounts of funds to avoid taxes while maintaining a low degree of default risk. Because municipal bonds typically have long maturities, the market values of tax-free mutual funds are usually exposed to a high degree of interest rate risk. Some of these funds, however, reduce their exposure to interest rate fluctuations by holding only municipal bonds that will mature in the near future.

High-Yield (Junk Bond) Funds

Bond portfolios with at least two-thirds of the bonds rated below Baa by Moodys or BBB by Standard and Poors are available for investors desiring high return and willing to incur high risk. These portfolios are sometimes referred to as high-yield (or junk bond) funds. The bonds held in this portfolio were typically issued by highly leveraged firms. The issuing firm's ability to repay these bonds is very sensitive to economic conditions.

International and Global Funds

In recent years, there has been increasing awareness of foreign securities. Investors historically avoided foreign securities because of the high information costs and transaction costs associated with purchasing them and monitoring their performance. International mutual funds were created to allow foreign investment in securities without incurring these excessive costs.

The returns on international stock mutual funds are affected not only by foreign companies' stock prices but also by the movements of currencies that denominate these stocks. As a foreign currency's value strengthens against the U.S. dollar, the value of the foreign stock as measured in U.S. dollars increases. Thus, U.S. investors can benefit not only from higher stock prices but also from a strengthened foreign currency (against the dollar). Of course, they can also be adversely affected if the foreign currencies denominating the stocks depreciate.

An alternative to the international mutual fund is the global mutual fund, which includes some U.S. stocks within its portfolio. International and global mutual funds have historically comprised stocks from several different countries in order to limit exposure of the portfolio to economic conditions in any single foreign economy. The growth in both types of funds is illustrated in Exhibit 23.2. The asset value of global funds is now more than twice that of international funds.

In recent years some new international mutual funds have been designed to fully benefit from a particular emerging country or continent. Although there is greater potential return from such strategy, there is also greater risk, because the

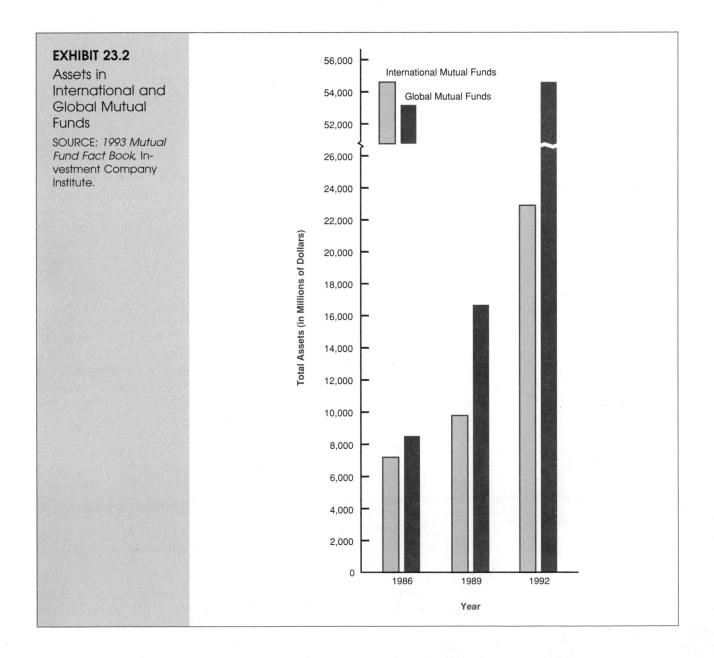

EXHIBIT 23.2

Assets in International and Global Mutual Funds

SOURCE: *1993 Mutual Fund Fact Book,* Investment Company Institute.

entire portfolio value is sensitive to a single economy. For investors who prefer minimum transaction costs, mutual funds have begun to offer index funds. Each of these funds is intended to mirror a stock index of a particular country or group of countries. For example, Vanguard offers a fund representing a European stock index and a Pacific Basin stock index. Because these mutual funds simply attempt to mirror an existing stock index, they avoid the advisory and transaction costs that are common to other mutual funds. International funds are discussed further at the end of this chapter.

Asset Allocation Funds

Asset allocation funds contain a diversity of investments (such as stocks, bonds, and money market securities), and the compositions of these funds are adjusted by the portfolio managers in response to expectations. For example, a given asset allocation fund will tend to concentrate more heavily on bonds if interest rates are expected to decline, or on stocks if a strong stock market performance is expected. These funds may even concentrate on international securities if they forecast favorable economic conditions in foreign countries.

Specialty Funds

Some mutual funds, called specialty funds, represent a group of companies sharing a particular characteristic. For example, there are industry-specific funds such as energy, banking, and high-tech funds. In addition, some funds include only stocks of firms that are likely takeover targets. There are even mutual funds that specialize in options or other commodities, such as precious metals. The risk of specialty funds varies with the particular characteristics of each fund.

GROWTH AND SIZE OF MUTUAL FUNDS

Exhibit 23.3 shows the growth in the number of mutual funds over time. The increasing popularity of bond funds is partially attributed to declining interest rates during the early and mid-1980s, and in the early 1990s, making these funds more attractive than alternative short-term securities. The popularity of stock funds is mainly due to stock market boom periods that occurred over time, along with the relatively low returns offered by alternative short-term securities in some periods. Although net sales (sales minus redemptions) have grown for both types of funds, the growth in bond funds has been much more pronounced.

Exhibit 23.4 shows the distribution of mutual funds according to investment objective. There are more long-term municipal bond funds and growth funds than any other type. Although mutual funds were originally targeted for the more common conservative investors, a variety of funds has recently been created to accommodate all types of investors.

Exhibit 23.5 shows the composition of all mutual fund assets in aggregate. Common stocks dominate, followed by U.S. government bonds and then municipal bonds. Common stocks comprised more than 80 percent of the aggregate asset value of mutual funds in the early 1970s. The percentage has steadily declined, as investment by mutual funds into bonds has increased by a much higher proportion over time. Exhibit 23.6 shows how the relative proportion of three

EXHIBIT 23.3

Number of Stock and Bond Funds over Time

SOURCE: *Mutual Fund Fact Book,* Investment Company Institute, various issues.

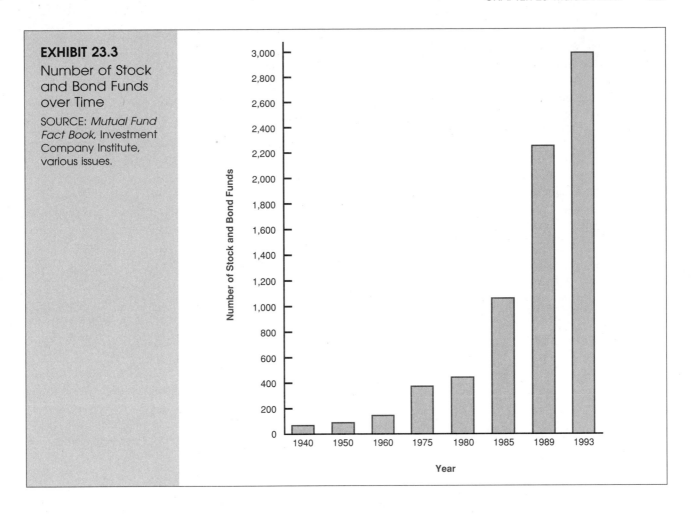

broad categories of mutual funds has changed since 1979. The shift from stocks to bonds is evident.

RELATIVE PERFORMANCE OF MUTUAL FUNDS

The performance of any given mutual fund may be primarily driven by a single economic factor. For example, the performance of growth stock funds may be highly dependent on the stock market's performance (market risk). The performance of any bond mutual fund is highly dependent on interest rate movements (interest rate risk). The performance of any international mutual fund is influenced by the dollar's value (exchange rate risk). When all securities within a given mutual fund are similarly influenced by an underlying economic factor, the fund does not achieve full diversification benefits. For this reason, some investors diversify among different types of mutual funds, so that only a portion of the entire investment is susceptible to a particular type of risk. Diversification among stock mutual funds, bond mutual funds, and international mutual funds can substantially reduce the volatility of returns on the overall investment. The proportion of the entire investment allocated to each type of mutual fund may

EXHIBIT 23.4 Distribution of Stock and Bond Mutual Funds

TYPE OF MUTUAL FUND	NUMBER OF FUNDS OUTSTANDING IN:		TOTAL ASSETS (IN MILLIONS) IN 1992	PERCENTAGE OF TOTAL ASSETS, 1992
	1980	1992		
Aggressive growth	53	233	$24,103	6.7
Growth	137	429	40,992	11.2
Growth and income	77	345	51,535	14.1
Precious metals		32	762	.2
International and global		236	13,562	3.7
Balanced	21	99	11,145	3.0
Income	56	341	38,659	10.6
U.S. government income		257	48,741	13.3
Ginnie Mae		77	27,967	7.7
Corporate bond		71	7,992	2.2
Long-term municipal bond	42	629	54,891	15.1
Global bond		87	13,875	3.8
High-yield bond		89	11,143	3.1
Flexible portfolio		59	5,163	1.4

SOURCE: *1986 Mutual Fund Fact Book;* and *1993 Mutual Fund Fact Book,* Investment Company Institute.

EXHIBIT 23.5

Distribution of Aggregate Mutual Fund Assets

SOURCE: *1993 Mutual Fund Fact Book,* Investment Company Institute.

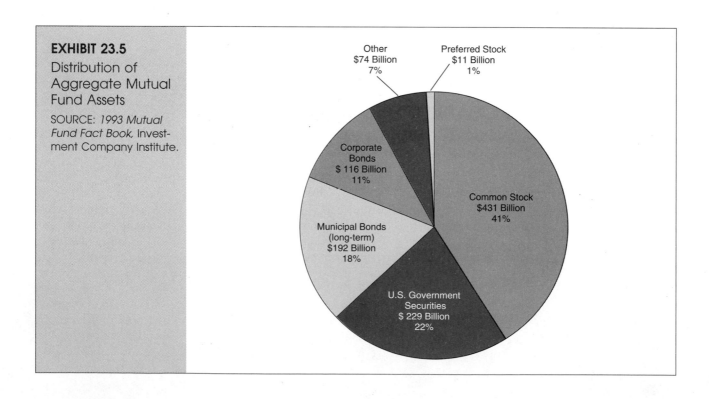

EXHIBIT 23.6 Changes in Distribution of Stock and Bond Mutual Funds

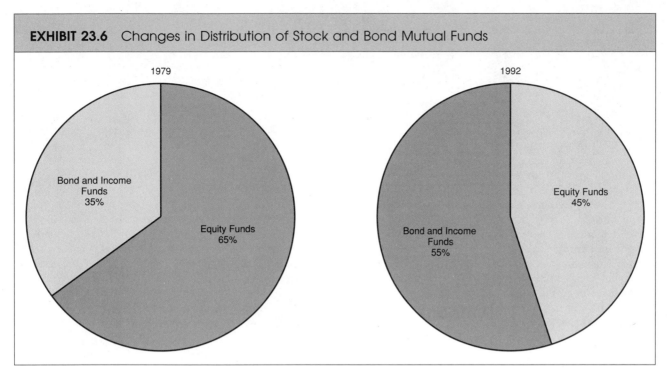

SOURCE: *1993 Mutual Fund Fact Book,* Investment Company Institute.

be based on the forecasts for the underlying factors that affect each fund's value. Yet, constraints could be imposed on the maximum proportion allocated to any type of mutual fund in order to achieve full diversification benefits.

REGULATION AND TAXATION OF MUTUAL FUNDS

Mutual funds must adhere to a variety of federal regulations. They must register with the Securities and Exchange Commission (SEC) and provide a prospectus to interested investors that discloses details about the components of the fund and the risks involved. Mutual funds are also regulated by state laws, many of which attempt to ensure that investors fully understand the fund.

Since July 1993, mutual funds have been required to disclose within the prospectus the names of their portfolio managers and the length of time that they have been employed by the fund in that position. This information is perceived as relevant by many investors, because the performance of mutual funds is highly dependent on its portfolio managers. The past performance of a mutual fund is unlikely to be a reasonable indicator of the future if the portfolio managers leave the fund.

Mutual funds must also disclose their performance record over the past 10 years in comparison to a broad market index. They must also state in the prospectus how their performance was affected by market conditions.

If a mutual fund distributes at least 90 percent of its taxable income to shareholders, it is exempt from taxes on dividends, interest, and capital gains distributed

DO MUTUAL FUNDS BEAT THE MARKET?

A variety of studies (listed in the references for this chapter) have attempted to assess mutual fund performance over time. To measure mutual fund performance solely by return is not a valid test, because it will likely be highly dependent on the performance of the stock and bond markets during the period of concern. An alternative measure of performance is a comparison of the mutual fund return to the return of some index of the market (such as the Dow Jones Industrial Average or Standard and Poor's 500 Index).

A study by Jensen found that mutual funds did not outperform the market in general. A study by Carlson found that mutual funds did not outperform the S&P 500 or NYSE Composite. Carlson also found no relationship between the performance and size of mutual funds and no relationship between the performance and expense ratio of mutual funds. Furthermore, he found that no-load funds outperformed load funds. A study by Klemkosky found that the rank ordering of mutual fund performance over two-year periods was unstable. Thus, the past performance of mutual funds is not necessarily an appropriate indicator of future performance. Although the studies mentioned here are only a small portion of the research on mutual funds, they are somewhat representative.

To appropriately evaluate a mutual fund's performance, risk should also be considered. Even when returns are adjusted to account for risk, mutual funds have, on the average, failed to outperform the market. These results may seem surprising, because the funds are managed by experienced portfolio managers. Yet, many individual stock purchase decisions are also ultimately derived from the so-called expert advice of investment companies that instruct their brokers on what securities to recommend. In addition, advocates of market efficiency would suggest that beyond insider information, market prices should already reflect any good or bad characteristics of each stock, making it difficult to construct a portfolio whose risk-adjusted returns will consistently outperform the market. Even if mutual funds do not outperform the market, they can still be attractive to investors who wish to diversify and who prefer that a portfolio manager make their investment decisions.

to shareholders. The shareholders are, of course, subject to taxation on these forms of income.

BACKGROUND ON MONEY MARKET FUNDS

Money market mutual funds, sometimes called money market funds (MMFs), are portfolios of money market (short-term) instruments constructed and managed by investment companies. The portfolio is divided into shares that are sold to individual investors. Because investors can participate in some MMFs with as little as $1,000, they are able to invest in money market instruments that they could not afford on their own. Most MMFs allow check-writing privileges, although there may be restrictions on the number of checks written per month or on the minimum amount of the check.

MMFs send periodic account statements to their shareholders to update them on any changes in their balance. They also send shareholders periodic updates on any changes in the asset portfolio composition, providing a breakdown of the names of securities and amounts held within the MMF portfolio.

Because the sponsoring investment company is willing to purchase MMFs back at any point in time, investors can liquidate their investment whenever they

USING *THE WALL STREET JOURNAL*

MUTUAL FUND PRICES AND PERFORMANCE

Mutual fund quotations like those shown here are provided in *The Wall Street Journal*. The bold letters represent the sponsoring firms who offer the mutual funds, with the types of funds offered by the firms just below their names. For load mutual funds, the net asset value (NAV) is less than the "offer price" at which the shares of the fund can be purchased. The designation NL in the "offer price" column implies no-load, so that the shares can be purchased at NAV. These mutual funds are open-ended. Closed-end mutual funds are listed separately in *The Wall Street Journal*.

A table of Lipper Indexes is provided on this same page, which compares the performance of different types of mutual funds. This table can be used to determine the types of mutual funds that experienced the highest and lowest returns over the last year.

SOURCE: *The Wall Street Journal,* August 5, 1994, p. C16. Reprinted by permission of *The Wall Street Journal,* © 1994 Dow Jones & Company, Inc. All rights reserved worldwide.

	Inv. Obj.	NAV	Offer Price	NAV Chg.	— Total Return — YTD	39 wks	5 yrs R
AAL Mutual:							
Bond p	BIN	9.68	10.16	...	−3.1	−3.9	+7.7 B
CaGr p	GRO	14.35	15.07	−0.04	−4.1	−3.4	+8.1 D
MuBd p	GLM	10.64	11.17	...	−3.4	−2.6	+7.1 D
SmCoStk p	SML	8.90	9.34	−0.08	−18.0	−14.8	NS ..
Util p	SEC	9.84	10.33	−0.02	NS	NS	NS ..
AARP Invst:							
BalS&B	S&B	14.73	NL	−0.04	NS	NS	NS ..
CaGr	GRO	31.19	NL	−0.18	−8.9	−8.6	+5.3 E
GiniM	BND	14.95	NL	−0.01	−1.8	−1.6	+7.5 D
GthInc	G&I	33.81	NL	−0.17	+4.1	+5.1	+10.6 A
HQ Bd	BND	15.50	NL	−0.01	−3.1	−4.1	+7.7 C
TxFBd	ISM	17.40	NL	...	−3.4	−2.8	+7.4 B
ABT Funds:							
Emrg p	CAP	12.39	13.01	−0.16	−16.4	−11.5	+14.4 A
FL HI	MFL	10.22	10.73	...	−0.9k	+0.2k	NS ..
FL TF	MFL	10.83	11.37	...	−2.5	−1.9	+7.9 B
Gthln p	G&I	10.64	11.17	+0.01	−1.8	−1.0	+4.0 E
Utilln p	SEC	11.44	12.01	...	−7.1	−10.0	+6.3 D
AHA Funds:							
Balan	S&B	11.92	NL	−0.03	−1.4	−0.7	+7.8 D
Full	BND	9.58	NL	−0.01	−2.7	−3.2	+7.9 C
Lim	BST	10.13	NL	...	+0.6	+0.8	+6.8 C
AIM Funds:							
AdjGv p	BST	9.63	9.73	...	+0.3	+0.5	NS ..
Agrsv p	SML	24.29	25.70	−0.14	−0.7	+4.1	+20.7 A
BalB †	S&B	15.34	15.34	−0.06	−4.0	NA	NS ..
Chart p	G&I	8.77	9.28	−0.04	−2.2	−3.5	+10.9 A
Const p	CAP	16.44	17.40	−0.11	−6.1	−1.7	+16.7 A
BalA p	S&B	15.35	16.12	−0.06	−3.5	−4.5	+11.2 A
GoScA p	BND	9.39	9.86	−0.01	−2.4	−2.6	+7.2 D
GrthA p	GRO	10.24	10.84	−0.08	−9.5	−9.0	+4.9 E
GrthB †	GRO	10.17	10.17	−0.08	−10.1	NA	NS ..
HYldA p	BHI	9.33	9.80	...	−1.8	+0.4	+11.2 A
HYldB †	BHI	9.32	9.32	...	−2.2	NA	NS ..

LIPPER INDEXES

Thursday, August 4, 1994

Indexes	Close	Prelim. Prev.	Percentage chg. since Wk ago	Dec. 31
Capital Appreciation .	408.97	− 0.47	+ 1.23	− 5.04
Growth Fund	746.54	− 0.58	+ 1.07	− 2.58
Small Co. Growth	409.69	− 0.49	+ 1.26	− 7.10
Growth & Income	1167.22	− 0.46	+ 1.32	+ 0.53
Equity Income Fd	793.56	− 0.22	+ 1.51	+ 1.00
Science & Tech Fd	313.34	− 0.84	+ 1.53	− 5.09
International Fund '...	495.08	+ 0.07	+ 2.67	+ 4.10
Gold Fund	197.48	+ 1.38	− 0.40	− 9.35
Balanced Fund	852.88	− 0.34	+ 1.10	− 1.24

Source: Lipper Analytical Services, Inc.

Thursday, August 4, 1994

Ranges for investment companies, with daily price data supplied by the National Association of Securities Dealers and performance and cost calculations by Lipper Analytical Services Inc. The NASD requires a mutual fund to have at least 1,000 shareholders or net assets of $25 million before being listed. Detailed explanatory notes appear elsewhere on this page.

desire. In most years, additional sales exceed redemptions, allowing the companies to build their MMF portfolios by purchasing more securities. When redemptions exceed sales, the company accommodates the amount of excessive redemptions by selling some of the assets contained in the MMF portfolios.

Exhibit 23.7 illustrates the growth in assets of MMFs over time. As investors increase their investment in MMFs, the asset level increases. During the 1980s, the total assets of MMFs more than doubled. However, the growth leveled off in the early 1990s when interest rates on short-term securities declined.

PERFORMANCE OF BOND MUTUAL FUNDS

A recent study by Blake, Elton, and Gruber assessed the performance of bond mutual funds. One of the objectives was to determine whether mutual fund managers make better investment decisions than other investors in the bond market. They found that, in general, bond mutual funds underperformed bond indexes. Their general results remain, regardless of the models used for comparing performance. They also determined that bond mutual funds with higher expense ratios generated lower returns. Thus, they recommended that investors select bond mutual funds that have lower expense ratios. Given their results, the authors suggest the creation of additional bond index funds, because these funds can provide bond diversification for small investors without requiring large fees to manage the funds. Overall, bond mutual funds may still appeal to investors, but investors should recognize that the managers of these funds have not been able to outperform the market. This conclusion is only a generalization, as some bond mutual funds experienced very high performance.

The authors also assessed whether past performance of bond mutual funds would serve as an accurate predictor of future performance. They found no conclusive evidence that the past performance of bond mutual funds can serve as a valuable predictor of future performance.

MONEY MARKET FUND CHARACTERISTICS

MMFs can be distinguished from one another and from other mutual funds by the composition, maturity, and risk of their assets. Each of these characteristics is described in the following subsections.

Asset Composition

Exhibit 23.8 shows the composition of money market fund assets in aggregate. Commercial paper dominates and is followed by Treasury securities and repurchase agreements. This composition represents the importance of each type of asset for money market funds overall and does not represent the typical composition of any particular MMF. Each MMF is usually more concentrated in whatever assets reflect its objective. During recessionary periods, the proportion of Treasury bills in MMFs normally increases, while the proportion of the more risky money market securities decreases.

Maturity

Exhibit 23.9 shows the average maturity of MMFs over time. The average maturity is determined by individual asset maturities, weighted according to their relative value. In the mid-1970s, the average maturity was relatively long. As interest rates increased, yields of MMFs were slower to adjust, as the rates on existing assets were fixed. Those MMFs with shorter asset maturities were able to more quickly capitalize on higher interest rates. By the late 1970s the average maturity on MMFs declined to less than half of what it was during the mid-1970s. Thus, most MMFs were in a position to fully benefit from the peak interest

USING *THE WALL STREET JOURNAL*

CLOSED-END MUTUAL FUND QUOTATIONS

Price quotations for closed-end mutual funds are disclosed in *The Wall Street Journal*, as shown here. The funds are partitioned in categories (see the bold headings) such as Specialized Equity Funds, High Yield Bond Funds, and Other Domestic Taxable Bond Funds. For each closed-end mutual fund listed, the net asset value (NAV) is quoted, along with the market price per share and the premium (or discount) of the market price relative to the NAV. Notice that the premiums (or discounts) for some closed-end funds were substantial.

SOURCE: *The Wall Street Journal*, August 1, 1994, p. C25. Reprinted by permission of *The Wall Street Journal*, © 1994 Dow Jones & Company, Inc. All rights reserved worldwide.

CLOSED END FUNDS

Fund Name	Stock Exch	NAV	Market Price	Prem /Disc	52 week Market Return
Adams Express	N	19.31	17³/₈	−10.0	−5.7
Baker Fentress	N	19.37	16¹/₂	−14.8	7.6
Bergstrom Cap	A	94.60	86¹/₂	−8.6	−6.1
Blue Chip Value	N	7.51	6³/₄	−10.1	−12.0
Central Secs	A	18.41	17¹/₈	−7.0	26.2
Charles Allmon	N	10.36	9⁵/₈	−7.1	2.4
Engex	A	9.90	7¹/₂	−24.2	−21.1
Equus II	A	19.07	14¹/₄	−25.3	31.3
Gabelli Equity	N	10.75	11¹/₈	+3.5	15.2
General American	N	23.21	20⁷/₈	−10.1	0.1
Inefficient Mkt	A	N/A	9⁵/₈	N/A	−1.3
Jundt Growth	N	14.17	12⁷/₈	−9.1	−4.2
Liberty All-Star	N	9.78	10¹/₈	+3.5	3.5
Morgan FunShares -c	O	7.32	7¹/₂	+2.4	N/A
Morgan Gr Sm Cap	N	10.96	9¹/₂	−13.3	1.3
NAIC Growth -c	O	10.99	9³/₄	−11.3	−12.5
Royce Value	N	13.29	12³/₈	−6.9	1.7
Salomon SBF	N	14.34	12³/₈	−13.7	7.2
Source Capital	N	39.62	40⁵/₈	+2.5	−8.3
Spectra	O	17.02	14¹/₂	−14.8	13.8
Tri-Continental	N	26.58	22³/₈	−15.8	0.9
Z-Seven	O	16.56	17¹/₄	+4.2	8.9
Zweig	N	10.44	12	+14.9	1.3
Specialized Equity Funds					
Alliance Gl Env	N	11.58	9⁷/₈	−14.7	8.2
C&S Realty	A	8.85	9³/₄	+10.2	9.8
C&S Total Rtn	N	13.61	14	+2.9	N/A
Counsellors Tand	N	15.32	12³/₄	−16.8	−13.3
Delaware Gr Div	N	13.33	13⁵/₈	+2.2	5.5
Delaware Grp Gl	N	13.46	12⁷/₈	−4.3	N/A
Dover Reg Fincl	O	7.21	N/A	N/A	N/A
Duff&Ph Util Inc -a	N	7.76	8¹/₂	+9.5	−11.7
Emer Mkts Infra	N	12.95	11⁷/₈	−8.3	N/A
Emer Mkts Tel	N	21.19	22	+3.8	36.5
First Financial	N	15.50	16	+3.2	42.8
Global Health	N	11.38	9¹/₂	−16.5	−1.8
Global Privat	N	14.09	12¹/₄	−13.1	N/A
H&Q Health Inv	N	15.80	14	−11.4	−14.0
H&Q Life Sci Inv	N	10.20	9¹/₈	−10.5	−19.2
Hampton Utility -c	A	12.12	11³/₄	−3.1	−3.4
Nations Bal Tgt	N	9.48	10	+5.5	N/A
New Age Media	N	12.39	10³/₈	−16.3	N/A
Patriot Glob Dvd	N	12.31	12	−2.5	−8.8
Patriot Pr Dvdll	N	10.28	10¹/₈	−1.5	−9.6
Patriot Pref Dvd	N	12.18	12¹/₈	−0.5	−12.1
Patriot Prem Dvd	N	8.24	8¹/₂	+3.2	−11.4
Patriot Sel Dvd	N	13.43	13¹/₈	−2.3	−18.4
Petroleum & Res	N	30.13	28⁷/₈	−4.2	11.2
Pilgrim Reg Bk	N	12.27	11³/₈	−7.3	11.0
Preferred Inc Op	N	11.76	11³/₈	−3.3	−5.8
Preferred IncMgt	N	13.20	12³/₄	−3.4	−5.4
Preferred Income	N	15.88	15³/₄	−0.8	−4.8
Putnam Divd Inc	N	10.99	10	−9.0	−4.9
Royce Micro-Cap	O	7.45	7	−6.0	N/A
SthEastrn Thrift -c	O	22.10	22¹/₄	+0.7	43.6
Templtn Gl Util	A	14.49	14	−3.4	−0.5
Convertible Sec's. Funds					
Amer Cap Conv	N	22.58	20¹/₄	−10.3	−0.1
Bancroft Conv	A	22.85	23	+0.7	15.2
Castle Conv	A	25.53	22¹/₂	−11.9	−6.2
Ellsworth Conv	A	9.75	8¹/₂	−12.8	−1.6

Fund Name	Stock Exch	NAV	Market Price	Prem /Disc	12 Mo Yield 6/30/94
High Yield Bond Funds					
CIGNA High Inc	N	6.91	7¹/₈	+3.1	13.6
CIM High Yld -a	N	7.42	7³/₄	+4.4	10.5
Colonial Intmdt -a	N	6.42	6³/₄	+5.1	11.2
Corp Hi Yld	N	12.98	13	+0.2	8.5
Corp Hi Yld II	N	12.45	12¹/₈	−2.6	N/A
Franklin Univ -c	N	8.60	7³/₄	−9.9	10.3
High Inc Adv	N	5.58	5⁷/₈	+5.3	11.2
High Inc Adv II	N	6.31	6¹/₄	−1.0	10.8
High Inc Adv III	N	6.71	6⁷/₈	+2.5	11.5
High Yld Income	N	7.31	7⁷/₈	+7.7	11.9
High Yld Plus -a	N	8.07	8	−0.9	10.5
Kemper High Inc	N	8.69	9	−3.6	9.9
Managed High Inc	N	11.34	11	−3.0	10.4
Morgan St Hi Yld -a	N	12.57	13¹/₈	+4.4	N/A
New Amer Hi Inc	N	4.47	4¹/₄	−4.9	14.2
PaineWbr Pr High -f	N	13.76	12³/₈	−10.1	N/A
Prospect St High	N	3.84	3³/₄	−2.3	13.2
Putnam Mgd HiYld	N	13.13	12¹/₈	−7.7	9.7
SB High Inc Opp	N	N/A	11	N/A	N/A
Salomon HIF	N	13.73	13³/₄	+0.1	9.8
Senior Strat Inc	N	9.50	9	−5.3	N/A
USF&G Pacholder -c	A	17.69	18⁵/₈	+5.3	13.3
VanKamp Int Hi	N	5.97	7³/₈	+23.5	12.4
VanKamp Ltd Hi	N	7.95	9¹/₂	+19.5	12.2
Zenix Income	N	6.34	7³/₈	+16.3	11.1
Other Domestic Taxable Bond Funds					
ACM Mgd $	N	10.68	11³/₈	+6.5	N/A
ACM Mgd Income	N	8.19	8³/₄	+6.8	11.9
AIM Strategic	A	9.33	8¹/₈	−12.9	5.3
Alliance Wld $	N	11.26	13¹/₄	+17.7	11.4
Alliance Wld $ 2	N	11.67	12¹/₈	+3.9	N/A
Allmerica Secs	N	11.05	10	−9.5	8.5
Amer Cap Inc	N	7.70	7	−9.1	10.2
Colonial Intrmkt	N	10.79	10¹/₂	−2.7	9.8
Duff&Ph Util Cor	N	13.15	12³/₈	−5.9	10.7
First Boston Inc	N	8.34	7³/₈	−11.6	10.1
First Boston Str	N	9.57	8³/₄	−8.6	10.3
Franklin Mul-Inc -ac	N	9.45	8⁷/₈	−6.1	9.2
Franklin Pr Mat -ac	N	8.70	7⁵/₈	−12.4	7.0
Global Partners	N	11.71	11³/₄	+0.3	N/A
Highlander Inc -c	A	13.42	14¹/₂	+8.0	N/A
J Hancock Income	N	15.79	15¹/₄	−3.4	8.8
J Hancock Invest	N	20.68	20¹/₂	−0.9	8.4
Kemper Multi Mkt	N	10.61	9¹/₂	−10.5	9.8
Kemper Strat Inc	N	13.79	13⁷/₈	+0.6	N/A
Lincoln Income -c	N	12.92	12³/₈	−4.2	12.9
MFS Charter	N	9.82	9	−8.4	7.7
MFS Intmdt	N	7.43	6¹/₂	−12.5	7.7
MFS Multimkt	N	7.11	6¹/₄	−12.1	7.7
MFS Special Val	N	13.83	15	+8.5	2.7
MassMutual Part -a	N	9.05	7⁵/₈	−15.7	8.8
Op Fd Multi-Sec	N	10.30	10³/₈	+0.7	9.4
Putnam Mas Inc	N	8.79	8¹/₄	−6.1	8.9
Putnam Mas Int	N	8.26	7⁵/₈	−7.7	9.1
Putnam Prem Inc	N	8.28	7⁵/₈	−7.9	9.4
Senior Hi Inc	N	9.27	8³/₄	−5.6	8.9
Senior Hi Inc II	N	9.31	8³/₄	−6.0	N/A
Target Income -c	z	10.00	N/A	N/A	N/A
USLife Income	N	9.48	9	−5.1	9.3
Zweig Total Rtn	N	8.41	9	+7.0	10.1

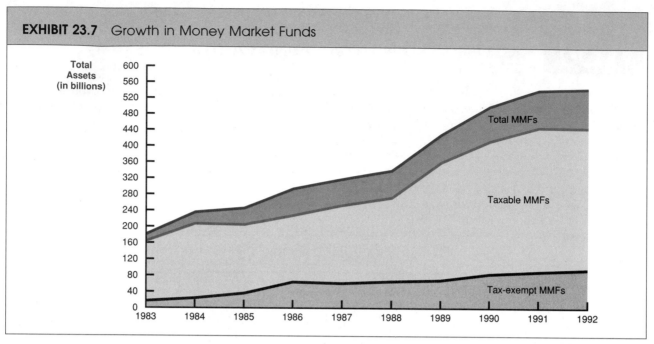

EXHIBIT 23.7   Growth in Money Market Funds

SOURCE: *1993 Mutual Fund Fact Book,* Investment Company Institute.

rates in 1981. The average maturity of money market funds was less volatile during the 1980s than it was in the 1970s. In the early 1990s, the average maturity increased as the annualized yields on money market securities with longer maturities were higher.

Risk

From an investor's perspective, MMFs usually have a low level of default risk. There may be some concern that an economic downturn could cause frequent defaults on commercial paper or that several banking failures could cause defaults on Eurodollar certificates of deposit and banker's acceptances. Yet, these instruments subject to default risk have short-term maturities. Thus, MMFs can quickly shift away from securities issued by any particular corporations that may fail in the near future.

Because MMFs contain instruments with short-term maturities, their market values are not too sensitive to movements in market interest rates (as are mutual funds containing long-term bonds). Although the short-maturity characteristic is sometimes perceived as an advantage, it also causes the returns on money market funds to decline in response to decreasing market interest rates. It is for this reason that some investors choose to invest in a money market fund offered by an investment company that also offers a bond mutual fund. During periods when interest rates are expected to decline, a portion of the investor's funds can be transferred from the money market fund to the bond mutual fund upon the investor's request.

The expected returns on MMFs are low relative to bonds or stocks because of the following factors. First, the default risk of MMFs is normally perceived to

WSJ

USING *THE WALL STREET JOURNAL*

MONEY MARKET FUND QUOTATIONS

Money market fund quotations are provided every Thursday in *The Wall Street Journal,* as shown here. The name of each fund is in the first column. The average term to maturity of the assets contained in each fund is disclosed in the second column. Note that the range varies among funds, but most funds have an average maturity of less than 100 days. The annualized yield for each fund over the last seven days is provided in the third column. These yields are normally comparable to yields on Treasury bills, commercial paper, and other money market securities. The asset level of each fund is disclosed in the fourth column (in millions of dollars). Some money market funds have more than $3 billion in assets.

MONEY MARKET MUTUAL FUNDS

The following quotations, collected by the National Association of Securities Dealers Inc., represent the average of annualized yields and dollar-weighted portfolio maturities ending Wednesday, August 3, 1994. Yields don't include capital gains or losses.

Fund	Avg. Mat.	7Day Yld.	Assets	Fund	Avg. Mat.	7Day Yld.	Assets
AALMny	52	2.97	65	HanvC'sh	53	3.96	798
AARP HQ	27	3.49	336	HanvGov	10	3.88	906
AIM MM C	24	3.55	328	HanvUSTr	12	3.66	1324
AIM MMA	24	3.57	111	HanvTreas	20	3.43	898
AVESTA Tr	66	3.91	23	Harbor	55	3.69	66
AccUSGov	18	3.74	19	HrtgCsh	24	3.72	983
ActAsGv	51	3.78	515	HiMrkDv	35	3.65	318
ActAsMny	55	4.05	4474	HiMrkUS	31	3.52	165
AetnaAdvs	33	4.31	34	HiMrkUST	34	3.39	203
Aetna Sel	33	4.31	153	HilrdGovt	64	3.63	215
AlexBwn	40	3.97	1275	HmestdDly	44	3.71	32
AlxBTr	52	3.66	574	HorznPr	10	4.14	2505
AlgerMM	35	4.28	149	HorznTr	38	4.19	2119
AlliaCpRs	49	3.41	2450	Hummer	26	3.65	150
AliaGvR	41	3.30	2092	IAATrMM	26	3.95	33
AlliMny	48	3.42	1817	IAIMnyMktFd	25	3.72	21
AmAAdTrl	19	4.04	92	IDS CshM	33	3.72	1141
AmAAdMMI	29	4.35	1371	IDS PLA	19	4.05	25
AmCRes	32	3.61	475	IMGLiq	38	3.66	136
AmPerCsh	32	3.85	176	IndCaGv	31	3.34	250
AmPerTrs	19	3.48	141	IndCaMM	42	3.42	312
AmSouth Pr	42	3.85	569	IndOnPr	27	3.92	239
AmSouth US	38	3.54	296	IndOnUS	37	3.71	254
AmbMMF	7	3.94	384	InfnAlGv	44	3.76	41
AmbTreas F	40	3.68	201	InfnCCR Inst	47	4.04	69
AmbTreasl	40	3.53	74	InfCCR	47	3.38	356
AmbMMI	7	3.79	511	InstCsh	25	4.19	414
Amcore Gv	14	3.60	109	InstFd	30	3.50	9
AmAAdMMM	29	4.06	48	InstGov	33	4.16	193
ArchUSTr	42	3.44	2	InvCshTrGv	19	4.06	127
ArchFd	35	3.68	44	InvCshR	30	3.79	701
ArkMnyMkt	34	4.29	242	InvGvtMF	29	3.70	70
ArkUSGovt	25	4.13	370	Invesco	14	4.18	124
ArkUSTrsy	47	3.78	146	InvCshTrTrs	15	4.03	33
AMF St Lq	19	3.74	37	IvyMny	29	3.52	22
AutCsh	40	4.06	1052	JPM InstP	30	4.20	280
AutGvt	31	3.76	2571	JPMInstlTrsy	12	4.15	85
AuGvSvc	33	3.84	420	JanMS Gov	31	3.34	250
AutTreasC	33	3.61	188	JanMS MM	24	3.42	312
BB&T UST Tr	42	3.59	75	JHanCshM	40	3.59	218
BNY Hmltn	31	4.03	344	KemperGvt	27	4.02	704
BT InstCash	15	4.21	858	KemperM	35	4.12	4167
BT InstCshRv	15	4.26	672	KeyLqd	15	3.51	441
BT Inst Trsy	16	3.90	184	KidPeCsh	41	3.85	1770
BT InvCash	15	3.71	152	KidPeGv	45	3.68	306

Fund	Avg. Mat.	7Day Yld.	Assets	Fund	Avg. Mat.	7Day Yld.	Assets
RNC Liq	68	3.92	38	FMMNIn	46	2.73	215
RegisDSI	33	3.78	115	FMCTSvc	57	2.33	206
RemTaxTr	28	3.97	459	FdOHMull	60	2.40	145
RemTreasTr	34	3.68	100	FedTxF c	53	2.60	1217
RemGovtTr	31	3.85	156	FidCapRsMu	29	2.15	122
RenaisGvt	1	3.57	48	FidInTxEx	35	2.82	2408
RenaisMM	13	3.73	321	FidCA	39	2.37	665
ResrveFd Gvt	11	3.35	743	FidCT	53	2.31	308
ReserveFd	35	3.44	1424	FidDlyTE	37	2.41	483
RetirGv	27	3.23	292	FidMA	21	2.20	677
RimcoTrs	61	3.65	109	FidMI	56	2.47	206
RIMCOPrm	58	3.98	391	FidNJ	42	2.29	398
RiverUSGv	40	3.89	145	FidNY	46	2.31	671
RiversdeCap	33	3.28	138	FidOH	47	2.50	287
RdSqMM	28	3.95	689	FidSpCA	40	2.75	1212
RdSqUS	25	3.86	407	FidSpCT	55	2.40	159
RshFGI	44	3.56	552	FidSpNJ	40	2.62	396
Rshmre	25	3.67	22	FidSpNY	45	2.43	535
RydexUSGv	1	3.31	98	FidSpPA	62	2.75	222
SBSF MM	64	3.81	18	FidTxEx	37	2.52	3494
SEICshTrea	41	4.09	69	FidSpMA	22	2.32	352
SEI CsPrB	20	4.01	19	FidSpMu	35	2.75	2356
SEI CsPrC	20	3.79	1	FtInvTax	30	2.18	26
SEI CshGvll	20	4.18	745	FtPraMu	52	2.38	211
SEI CsMM	30	4.41	209	FrkCal	55	2.23	697
SEI CsPr	20	4.31	2302	FrkNYTE	38	2.23	59
SEI LqGv	23	3.87	266	FrkTx c	48	2.22	205
SEI LqPr	21	4.08	1016	Free CA	41	2.34	79
SEI LqTr	19	3.68	1311	FreeTE	49	2.22	268
SEI CsTrllA	28	4.00	408	FtBostInTE	39	2.81	213
SEI CsTrllB	28	3.69	28	FirstUnTFI	74	2.64	421
SITMMkt	21	3.89	17	FirstUnTFT	74	2.94	46
STIPrQuTr	42	3.84	636	FundmentTF	28	1.77	20
STIUSGvTr	30	3.61	240	Gab OC TE	44	2.40	147
STIUSGvIv	30	3.49	37	GalxyTE	61	2.24	279
Safeco f	47	3.83	155	GnTxEx	67	2.47	309
SalomonUST	27	3.60	28	GnCalMu	75	2.62	678
SchbValAdv	47	4.24	2237	GnNYMu	49	2.50	683
Schwabintl	41	4.10	70	GInmdTECsh	57	2.80	218
SchwbRetir	32	3.80	24	GSITNY	48	2.55	67
SchwbGv	45	3.71	1962	GSITCA c	55	2.53	242
SchbMM	48	3.86	10601	GSITDv c	44	2.75	1573
Schb UST	51	3.61	578	GrtHallTF	48	2.35	278
ScudCshIn	41	4.01	1582	HTInsgh	42	2.27	182
Scud UST	60	3.67	372	HanvNY	39	2.11	193
SecurityCsh	26	3.33	48	HanvTF	70	2.43	383
SelectGv	19	3.74	44	HrtgCshMun	63	2.30	220
SeligCsh Gvt	20	3.33	16	HiMrk	66	2.26	52
SeligCshPrA	27	3.57	176	HiMrkCal	63	2.39	149
SentinelUST	40	3.27	72	HorznTE	40	2.64	496
SevnSea f	44	3.99	3228				

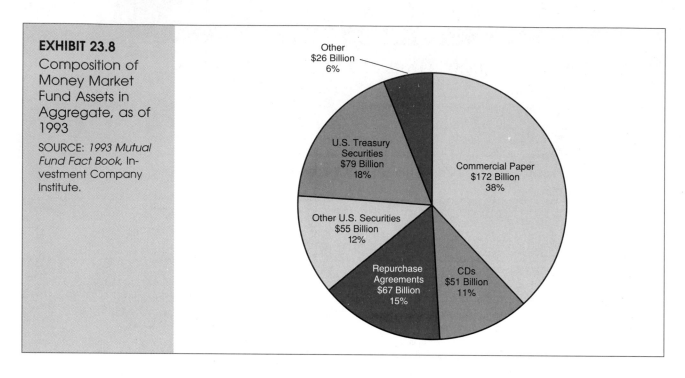

EXHIBIT 23.8

Composition of Money Market Fund Assets in Aggregate, as of 1993

SOURCE: *1993 Mutual Fund Fact Book,* Investment Company Institute.

Other
$26 Billion
6%

U.S. Treasury Securities
$79 Billion
18%

Other U.S. Securities
$55 Billion
12%

Repurchase Agreements
$67 Billion
15%

CDs
$51 Billion
11%

Commercial Paper
$172 Billion
38%

be lower than that of corporate bonds. Second, MMFs have less interest rate risk than bond funds. Third, they consistently generate positive returns over time, whereas bond and stock funds can experience negative returns. Because MMFs are normally characterized as having relatively low risk and low expected return, they are popular among investors who need a conservative investment medium. Furthermore, they provide liquidity with their check-writing privileges.

MANAGEMENT OF MONEY MARKET FUNDS

The role of MMF portfolio managers is to maintain an asset portfolio that satisfies the underlying objective of a fund. If the managers expect a stronger economy, they may replace maturing risk-free securities (Treasury bills) with more commercial paper or CDs. The return on these instruments would be higher yet would not overexpose the fund to default risk. For some MMFs there is very little flexibility in the composition. For example, some MMFs may as a rule maintain a high percentage of their investment in Treasury bills to assure investors that they will continue to refrain from risky securities.

Even if managers are unable to change asset composition of the MMF, they can still influence performance by changing the maturities of the securities they invest in. For example, if managers expect interest rates to increase in the future, they should use funds generated from maturing securities to purchase new securities with shorter maturities. The greater the degree to which a manager adjusts the average maturity of an MMF to capitalize on interest rate expectations,

EXHIBIT 23.9 Weighted Average Maturity of Money Market Fund Assets

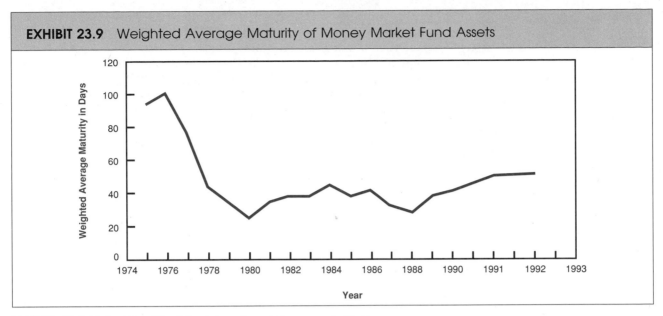

SOURCE: *1993 Mutual Fund Fact Book,* Investment Company Institute.

the greater the reward or penalty. If the expectation turns out to be correct, the MMF will yield relatively high returns, and vice versa.

Although investing individuals and institutions do not manage the portfolio composition or maturity of an MMF, they have a variety of MMFs from which to choose. If they expect a strong economy, they may prefer an MMF that contains securities with some risk that offer higher returns than Treasury bills. If they expect interest rates to increase, they could invest in MMFs with a short average maturity. They are in a sense managing their investment by choosing an MMF with the characteristics they prefer. Some investment companies offer several MMFs, allowing investors to switch from one fund to another based on their expectations of economic conditions.

REGULATION AND TAXATION OF MONEY MARKET FUNDS

As a result of the Securities Act of 1933, sponsoring companies must provide full information on any MMFs they offer. In addition, they must provide potential investors with a current prospectus that describes the fund's investment policies and objectives. The Investment Company Act of 1940 contains numerous restrictions that prevent a conflict of interest by the fund's managers.

Earnings generated by MMFs are generally passed on to the fund's shareholders in the form of interest payments or converted into additional shares. If the fund distributes at least 90 percent of its income to its shareholders, the fund itself is exempt from federal taxation. This tax rule is designed to avoid double taxation. Although the fund can avoid federal taxes on its income, shareholders are subject to taxes on the income they receive, regardless of whether it is in the form of interest payments or additional shares.

In 1991, the Securities and Exchange Commission approved a ruling that less-than-top grade commercial paper can make up no more than 5 percent of a money market fund's assets. In addition, investment in a single issue of top-grade commercial paper was limited to 5 percent of the fund's assets, while investment in a single issue of lesser-grade paper was limited to 1 percent of the fund's assets. These rulings were intended to prevent the potential impact of commercial paper defaults on money market funds.

REAL ESTATE INVESTMENT TRUSTS

A **real estate investment trust (REIT)** (pronounced "reet") is a closed-end mutual fund that invests in real estate or mortgages. Like other mutual funds, REITs allow small investors to participate with a low minimum investment. The funds are pooled to invest in mortgages and in commercial real estate. REITs generate income for shareholders by passing through rents on real estate or interest payments on mortgages. Most existing REITs can be sold on stock exchanges, which allows investors to sell them at any time. The composition of a REIT is determined by its portfolio manager, who is presumed to have expertise in real estate investments. In the early and mid-1970s, many of the mortgages held by REITs defaulted. Consequently, investors' interest in REITs declined. Although the price of a REIT is somewhat influenced by its portfolio composition, it is basically determined by supply and demand. Even if the portfolio has performed well in the past, the REIT's share value may be low if investors are unwilling to invest in it.

REITs can be classified as **equity REITs,** which invest directly in properties, or **mortgage REITs,** which invest in mortgage and construction loans. A third type of REIT, called a hybrid, invests in both properties and mortgages.

Equity REITs are sometimes purchased to hedge against inflation, as rents tend to rise and property values rise with inflation. Their performance varies according to the perceived future value of the real estate held in each portfolio. REITs that have concentrated in potential high-growth properties are expected to generate a higher return than those with a more nationally diversified portfolio. However, they are also susceptible to more risk if the specific locations experience slow growth.

Because mortgage REITs essentially represent a fixed-income portfolio, their market value will be influenced by interest rate movements. As interest rates rise, the market value of mortgages declines, and therefore the demand for mortgage REITs declines. If interest rates are expected to decrease, mortgage REITs become more attractive.

INTERACTION WITH OTHER FINANCIAL INSTITUTIONS

Mutual funds interact with various financial institutions, as described in Exhibit 23.10. They serve as an investment alternative for portfolio managers of financial institutions such as insurance companies and pension funds.

Some mutual funds are subsidiaries of commercial banks. As interest rates declined in the 1990s and investors withdrew deposits from commercial banks, they frequently invested the proceeds in mutual funds sold by subsidiaries of the banks. Some of these subsidiaries are conveniently located on the first floor

---

EXHIBIT 23.10 Interaction between Mutual Funds and Other Financial
Institutions

TYPE OF FINANCIAL INSTITUTION	INTERACTION WITH MUTUAL FUNDS
Commercial banks and savings and loan associations (S&Ls)	■ Money market mutual funds invest in certificates of deposit at banks and S&Ls and in commercial paper issued by bank holding companies. ■ Some commercial banks (such as Security Pacific and Chase Manhattan) have investment company subsidiaries that offer mutual funds. ■ Some stock and bond mutual funds invest in securities issued by banks and S&Ls.
Finance companies	■ Some money market mutual funds invest in commercial paper issued by finance companies. ■ Some stock and bond mutual funds invest in stocks and bonds issued by finance companies.
Securities firms	■ Mutual funds hire securities firms to execute security transactions for them. ■ Some mutual funds own a discount brokerage subsidiary that competes with other securities firms for brokerage services.
Insurance companies	■ Some stock mutual funds invest in stocks issued by insurance companies. ■ Some insurance companies (such as Kemper) have investment company subsidiaries that offer mutual funds. ■ Some insurance companies invest in mutual funds.
Pension funds	■ Pension fund portfolio managers invest in mutual funds.

of the bank, near the area where deposit withdrawals take place. Thus, even if the bank loses some business from deposit withdrawals, its mutual fund subsidiary's business is increased. Furthermore, when investors sell the shares of the mutual fund connected to a bank, they are more likely to deposit the proceeds in the bank.

USE OF FINANCIAL MARKETS

Each type of mutual fund uses a particular financial market, as described in Exhibit 23.11. Because the main function of mutual funds is to invest, all

> **EXHIBIT 23.11** How Mutual Funds Utilize Financial Markets
>
> | TYPE OF MARKET | HOW MUTUAL FUNDS USE THAT MARKET |
> |---|---|
> | Money markets | ■ Money market mutual funds invest in various money market instruments, such as Treasury bills, commercial paper, banker's acceptances, and certificates of deposit. |
> | Bond markets | ■ Some bond mutual funds invest mostly in bonds issued by the U.S. Treasury or a government agency. Others invest in bonds issued by municipalities or firms.
■ Foreign bonds are sometimes included in a bond mutual fund portfolio. |
> | Mortgage markets | ■ Some bond mutual funds invest in bonds issued by the Government National Mortgage Association (GNMA, or "Ginnie Mae"), which uses the proceeds to purchase mortgages that were originated by some financial institutions. |
> | Stock markets | ■ Numerous stock mutual funds include stocks with various degrees of risk and potential return. |
> | Futures markets | ■ Some bond mutual funds may periodically attempt to hedge against interest rate risk by taking positions in interest rate futures contracts. |
> | Options markets | ■ Some stock mutual funds may periodically hedge specific stocks by taking positions in stock options.
■ Some mutual funds take positions in stock options for speculative purposes. |
> | Swap markets | ■ Some bond mutual funds engage in interest rate swaps to hedge interest risk. |

securities markets are commonly used. The futures and options markets are also utilized to hedge against interest rate risk or market risk. Some specialized mutual funds sponsored by Dean Witter, Merrill Lynch, and other securities firms take speculative positions in futures contracts.

GLOBALIZATION THROUGH MUTUAL FUNDS

GLOBAL ASPECTS

International and global mutual funds have facilitated international capital flows and therefore have helped create a global securities market. They can reduce the excessive transaction costs that might be incurred by small investors who attempt to invest in foreign securities on their own. They also increase the degree of integration among stock markets. As international markets become more accessible, the volume of U.S. investment in foreign securities will become more sensitive to events and financial market conditions in those countries.

Mutual funds are popular not only in the United States but in other countries as well. The total assets of mutual funds across countries (translated in U.S.

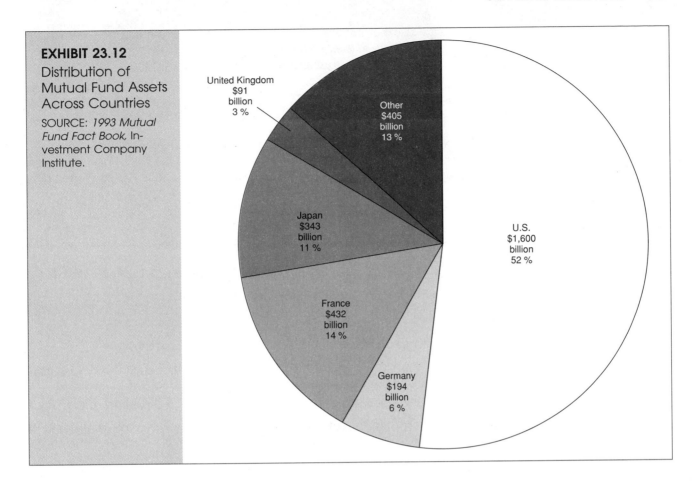

EXHIBIT 23.12

Distribution of Mutual Fund Assets Across Countries

SOURCE: *1993 Mutual Fund Fact Book,* Investment Company Institute.

United Kingdom $91 billion 3%

Other $405 billion 13%

Japan $343 billion 11%

U.S. $1,600 billion 52%

France $432 billion 14%

Germany $194 billion 6%

dollars) are illustrated in Exhibit 23.12. The types of investment companies that sponsor mutual funds vary across countries. Insurance companies are the most common sponsor of mutual funds in the United Kingdom, while banks dominate the sponsorship in France, Germany, and Italy.

European countries have recently agreed to let their respective mutual fund shares be sold across their borders. The shares are under the supervision of their home country but are subject to marketing rules of the countries where they are being marketed. This deregulatory step in Europe may provide the momentum for other countries to do the same.

As a result of the North American Free Trade Agreement (NAFTA), qualified companies will be allowed to sell mutual fund shares in Mexico. Consequently, many U.S. companies that commonly sponsor mutual funds, such as securities firms, commercial banks, and insurance companies, will generate new business in Mexico.

SUMMARY

- Mutual funds can be characterized as load funds (which impose a sales charge) versus no-load funds (which do not impose a sales charge). Mutual funds can also be characterized as open-end investment funds (which are willing to repurchase their shares upon demand), or as closed-end investment funds (which do not repurchase the shares they sell).

- The more common types of mutual funds are capital appreciation funds, growth and income funds, income funds, tax-free funds, high-yield funds, international funds, global funds, asset allocation funds, and specialty funds.

- Money market funds invest in short-term securities, such as commercial paper, repurchase agreements, CDs, and Treasury bills. The expected returns on money market funds are relatively low, but the risk levels of money market funds are also low.

QUESTIONS

1. How do open-end mutual funds differ from closed-end mutual funds?

2. Explain why mutual funds are attractive to small investors.

3. Explain the difference between load and no-load mutual funds.

4. How can mutual funds generate returns to their shareholders?

5. Like the mutual funds, commercial banks and stock-owned savings institutions sell shares, yet proceeds received by mutual funds are used in a different way. Explain.

6. Support or refute the following statement: Investors can avoid all types of risk by purchasing a mutual fund that contains only Treasury bonds.

7. Describe the ideal mutual fund for investors who wish to generate tax-free income and also maintain a low degree of interest rate risk.

8. Explain how changing foreign currency values can affect the performance of international mutual funds.

9. What type of security is dominant when reviewing all stock and bond mutual funds in aggregate?

10. Explain how the income generated by a mutual fund is taxed when it distributes at least 90 percent of its taxable income to shareholders.

11. Have mutual funds outperformed the market, according to recent research? Explain.

12. Would mutual funds be attractive to some investors even if they are not expected to outperform the market? Explain.

13. How do money market funds (MMFs) differ from other types of mutual funds?

14. How can a money market fund accommodate shareholders who wish to sell their shares when the amount of proceeds received from selling new shares is less than the amount needed?

15. Explain the relative risk of the various types of securities that a money market fund may invest in.

16. Is the value of a money market fund or bond fund more susceptible to increasing interest rates? Explain.

17. Which security is dominant when assessing the portfolio of money market funds in aggregate?

18. Explain why diversification across different types of mutual funds is highly recommended.

19. Explain how the income generated by a money market fund is taxed if it distributes at least 90 percent of its income to shareholders.

20. Explain the difference between equity REITs and mortgage REITs. Which type would likely be a better hedge against high inflation? Why?

Hedge Fund Kings Profit Handsomely, Racking Up a 3-Year Winning Streak

Laura Jereski

In the hour it takes other people to browse through the morning newspapers, George Soros's enterprise is earning about $170,000, or 5½ times the average annual income of U.S. households.

It's a bang-up year for Soros Fund Management and the other big investment powerhouses known as hedge funds. Several are finishing the year with investment gains exceeding 70%, before fees.

By tomorrow, when Mr. Soros closes the books on his biggest year ever, his closely held business will have reaped roughly $1.49 billion for the year. (That includes about $612 million from the firm's 15% cut of investment gains, $79 million from an annual management fee and $800 million from investing the businesses's own capital.)

Eat your heart out, Michael Milken. Once, the former junk-bond king stunned investors with his 1987 compensation of $550 million from the late Drexel Burnham Lambert Inc. But a new royalty is sweeping onto Wall Street's center stage: the handful of money managers who run the nation's biggest hedge funds. Thanks to an astounding three-year streak, a half-dozen hedge funds rival the trading prowess of Wall Street's most nimble firms.

Hedge funds are private partnerships that adopt a high-risk investment strategy in pursuit of big returns for a limited number of investors, often based abroad. The word hedge doesn't mean the funds are conservative; it alludes to a strategy of betting on some investments to go up and others to go down, a tactic that at times can help hedge against broad market swings.

The Soros operation leads the pack with about $11 billion under management after recent distributions to investors, up from around $7 billion as the year began, according to Soros watchers. The latest year's gain for Soros-managed funds averaged 73%, before subtracting fees. **Tiger Management** Corp. with Julian Robertson at the helm now runs about $7 billion, thanks to gross returns of 74% this year and a bit of new money; four years ago, the veteran stockpicker ran less than $800 million. Michael Steinhardt manages just under $5 billion today.

These super-hedge funds have become the Titans of high finance. As a result, the men who run them rank among the most powerful, best-compensated executives in the country.

Mr. Robertson's Tiger Management grossed about $640 million in Tiger's share of investment returns plus management fees, based on return figures that the fund shares with its investors. Since most investors reinvest their gains, such bonanzas get piled onto the already-substantial sums the funds wield. Most of the giant hedge funds are closed to new investors.

Stunning returns helped push two newcomers into the limelight: **Omega Advisers,** founded a mere two years ago by Leon Cooperman, the former Goldman Sachs research whiz, now manages

about $3 billion as a result of 73% gross returns this year. Mark Strome in Santa Monica, Calif., started the year with about $200 million; his 140% returns attracted so much new money that he ends the year just shy of $1 billion.

Not only has size not hampered returns, as usually happens, but some investors even argue that the bigger the funds have grown, the better they have been able to perform. "There have been investment opportunities where size has helped," says Antoine Bernheim in New York, who monitors hedge-fund performance as publisher of the U.S. Off-shore Funds Directory.

Once hedge funds stuck to stocks, simultaneously buying and selling similar securities to lock in a gain. No more. As the funds have grown larger, they have started to converge on the same large-scale investments known as "macro" plays.

Increasingly, size forces the funds to gamble on the direction of currencies and interest rates, bets that lend themselves nicely to the kind of high-odds bets hedge-fund managers relish. One manager says he controlled $1 billion of Japanese bonds by paying $14 million in option premiums—less than 1% of his portfolio's funds. Another popular play of the past year, a custom-tailored option on declining French interest rates, gave some managers as much as a 20-to-1 payoff.

Mr. Robertson, a stock picker by training, generated about 40% of his re-

Continued

CASE APPLICATION: PERFORMANCE AND RISK OF HEDGE FUNDS

Continued

turns this year from sophisticated currency and interest-rate bets, including a two-year-old wager on declining short-term Japanese rates.

Similarly, Mr. Steinhardt, also a renowned stockpicker, reaped virtually none of this year's investment gains from the U.S. stock market. Investors say he made impressive returns of about 54% (before subtracting fees) from a combination of futures and foreign bonds.

"The funds often have better access to information, too," says Mr. Bernheim.

For example, former British Prime Minister Margaret Thatcher took a break from promoting her book this year to join several hedge-fund managers, including Mr. Robertson, at an intimate lunch. Likewise, conferences Mr. Soros hosts for his not-for-profit foundations in Europe are attended by cabinet ministers representing countries where he invests, according to a spokeswoman for the not-

for-profit foundation. Neither Mr. Soros nor Mr. Robertson would comment for this article.

"This is a new type of money-management business," says Richard Elden, president of Grosvenor Capital Management, a Chicago-based money manager that invests through hedge funds. Increasingly, hedge funds are staffing up in areas where the founder hasn't any expertise. Incentive-based compensation for these junior staff members can eat up a big slice of the founding manager's take.

SOURCE: *The Wall Street Journal,* May 26, 1993, p. C1. Reprinted by permission of *The Wall Street Journal,* © 1993 Dow Jones & Company, Inc. All rights reserved worldwide.

QUESTIONS

1. How do so-called "hedge funds"

differ from the typical mutual funds?

2. The hedge funds managed by George Soros experienced a 73 percent annual gain (before subtracting fees), which was much higher than the gain for mutual funds in general. Does this imply that the market is inefficient?

3. Explain the apparent relationship between the size and recent performance of hedge funds. Why would a hedge fund (or any mutual fund) restrict growth?

4. Explain how a hedge fund may possibly magnify the potential returns with the use of options. How does this affect the risk?

PROJECTS

1. **Assessing the Risk of a Growth Fund**
   Compare historical returns on a particular growth stock fund against the returns of the S&P 500 Stock Index. Are the fund's returns more or less volatile than that index? Explain why the fund has or has not outperformed the index lately.

2. **Assessing the Performance of an International Fund**
   Evaluate the historical returns on a particular international fund. Explain why that fund has been performing better or worse than most U.S. stocks in recent years.

REFERENCES

Ang, James S., and Jess H. Chua. "Mutual Funds: Different Strokes for Different Folks?" *Journal of Portfolio Management* (Winter 1982): 43–47.

Blake, Christopher R., Edwin J. Elton, and Martin J. Gruber. "The Performance of Bond Funds." *Journal of Business* (July 1993): 371–403.

Carlson, Robert S. "Aggregate Performance of Mutual Funds 1948–1967." *Journal of Financial and Quantitative Analysis* (March 1970): 1–32.

Chang, Eric C., and Wilbur G. Lewellen. "An Arbitrage Pricing Approach to Evaluating Mutual Fund Performance." *Journal of Financial Research* (Spring 1985): 15–30.

———. "Market Timing and Mutual Fund Investment Performance." *Journal of Business* (January 1984): 57–72.

Chen, Nai-Fu, Raymond Kan, and Merton Miller. "Are the Discounts on Closed-end Funds a Sentiment Index?" *Journal of Finance* (June 1993): 791–794.

Grinblatt, Mark, and Sheridan Titman. "The Persistence of Mutual Fund Performance." *Journal of Finance*, December 1992: 1977–1984.

Hendricks, Darryll, Jayendu Patel, and Richard Zeckhauser. "Hot Hands in Mutual Funds: Short-term Persistence of Relative Performance, 1974–1988." *Journal of Finance* (March 1993): 93–130.

Henriksson, Roy D. "Market Timing and Mutual Fund Performance: An Empirical Investigation." *Journal of Business* (January 1984): 75–96.

Jensen, Michael C. "The Performance of Mutual Funds in the Period 1945–1964." *Journal of Finance* (May 1968): 389–416.

Kelmkosky, Robert C. "The Bias in Composite Performance Measures." *Journal of Financial and Quantitative Analysis* (June 1973): 505–5154.

———. "How Consistently Do Managers Manage?" *Journal of Portfolio Management* (Winter 1977): 11–15.

Lehmann, Bruce, and David Modest. "Mutual Fund Performance Evaluation: A Comparison of Benchmarks and Benchmark Comparisons." *Journal of Finance* (June 1987): 233–265.

Madura, Jeff, and John M. Cheney. "Diversifying among Mutual Funds." *AAII Journal* (January 1989): 8–10.

Malkiel, Burton. "The Valuation of Closed-End Investment Company Shares." *Journal of Finance* (June 1977): 847–886.

Veit, E. Theodore, and John M. Cheney. "Are Mutual Funds Market Timers?" *Journal of Portfolio Management* (Winter 1982): 35–42.

CHAPTER 24

SECURITIES FIRMS

Securities firms offer a variety of services, most of which can be classified as investment banking or brokerage. The well-known securities firms such as Merrill Lynch, Salomon Brothers, and Shearson Lehman Hutton have investment banking and brokerage divisions, although their allocation of resources to these divisions may differ. Investment banking focuses on primary market services, such as advising clients about issuing securities and underwriting the securities. Brokerage focuses on secondary market services, such as advising clients on which securities to buy or sell and executing securities transactions.

The specific objectives of this chapter are to:

- describe the key functions of investment banking firms,
- describe the services provided by investment banking firms when they facilitate new stock issues, and
- describe the key functions of brokerage firms.

REGULATION OF SECURITIES FIRMS

The securities industry is regulated by the National Association of Securities Dealers (NASD) and existing securities exchanges. Regulations are imposed to prevent unfair or illegal practices, ensure orderly trading, and address customer complaints. The Securities and Exchange Commission (SEC) regulates the issuance of securities and specifies disclosure rules for the issuers. It also regulates the exchanges and the participating brokerage firms. Whereas the SEC's involvement is based on the establishment of general guidelines, day-to-day regulatory duties are the responsibility of the exchanges or the NASD.

In addition to the SEC, NASD, and exchanges, the Federal Reserve Board has some regulatory influence because it determines the credit limits (margin requirements) on securities purchased. The Securities Investor Protection Corporation (SIPC) offers insurance on cash and securities deposited at brokerage firms and can liquidate failing brokerage firms. The insurance limit is $500,000, including $100,000 against claims on cash. All brokers that are registered with the SEC are assessed premiums by the SIPC, which are used to maintain its insurance fund. In addition to its insurance fund, the SIPC has a $500 million revolving line of credit with a group of banks and can borrow up to $1 billion from the SEC. Because the SIPC boosts investor confidence in the securities industry, economic efficiency is increased, and market concerns are less likely to cause a run on deposits of cash and securities at securities firms.

INVESTMENT BANKING SERVICES

One of the main functions of investment banking firms is raising capital for corporations. These firms originate, structure, and place securities in the capital markets to raise funds for corporations. Their role is primarily as an intermediary rather than as a lender or investor. Therefore, the compensation for raising funds is typically in the form of fees rather than interest income.

Another critical function of investment banking firms is providing advice on mergers and acquisitions. This function is related to raising funds, as many mergers and acquisitions require outside financing, and investment banking firms that are able to raise large amounts of funds in the capital markets are more likely to be chosen as advisors for mergers and acquisitions. A key component of the advisory function is the valuation of a business. Investment banking firms assess the potential value of target firms so that they can advise corporations on whether to merge and on the appropriate price to offer. The valuation process also is used for advising on potential divestitures and on leveraged buyouts. Investment banking firms not only focus on valuation aspects but also help firms with procedural matters regarding the implementation of a merger, acquisition, or divestiture.

In recent years, investment banking firms have loaned their own funds to companies involved in a merger or acquisition. They have even provided equity financing in some cases, whereby they become part owner of the acquired firms.

How Investment Banking Firms Facilitate LBOs

Investment banking firms (IBFs) facilitate leveraged buyouts (LBOs) in three ways. First, they assess the market value of the firm (or division) of concern so that the participants planning to purchase the firm do not pay more than the firm's value. Second, they arrange financing, which involves raising funds and purchasing any common stock outstanding that is held by the public. Finally, they may be retained in an advisory capacity.

A group may not be able to afford an LBO because of constraints on the amount of funds it can borrow. The IBF may therefore consider purchasing a portion of the firm's assets, which provides the group with some financial support. It will either search for an immediate buyer of these assets or maintain the assets over a period of time. If it chooses the latter alternative, it may finance

POINT OF INTEREST

THE DEMISE OF DREXEL

In the 1980s the U.S. corporate structure was influenced by the activities of Michael Milken, a bond trader employed by Drexel Burnham Lambert. Milken was able to support highly leveraged acquisitions by issuing junk bonds for the acquiring firms. He placed junk bonds with institutional investors such as savings institutions, insurance companies, bond mutual funds, and pension funds. He helped to create a takeover binge in the 1980s and to develop a $200 billion market for junk bonds. In 1987 he was paid $550 million as compensation for his services. The issuance of junk bonds was a key source of profit, as Drexel could charge commissions of about 3 or 4 percent of the principal, versus only 1 percent of the principal for higher quality bonds.

In 1989 Drexel paid $650 million in fines after pleading guilty to six counts of mail and securities fraud. Several public sector clients such as municipalities discontinued their relationships with Drexel. In addition, Drexel was having trouble fulfilling its loan commitments in the leveraged buyout of RJR Nabisco.

The value of most junk bonds declined in the fourth quarter of 1989, which may be partially attributed to Drexel's problems and to Moody's downgrade of some debt issued by RJR Nabisco. Over a two-day period, the value of some RJR bonds decreased by 20 percent. In addition, the Financial Institutions Reform, Recovery, and Enforcement Act (FIRREA) of 1989 forced savings and loan associations to divest their junk bond holdings. The decline in the value of junk bonds devastated Drexel because of its large investment in such bonds.

In 1990 Michael Milken pleaded guilty to six felony counts of securities violations, which included cheating some customers and helping others to violate securities law. He was fined $600 million.

In February 1990, Drexel went bankrupt. Just two months before, however, it had paid employees almost $200 million in cash bonuses. The news about Drexel during the late 1980s and early 1990s caused some corporate clients to be skeptical about securities firms.

Looking back, some analysts might say that Milken and his company forced corporations to be more efficient by facilitating leveraged acquisitions of inefficient corporations. The development of the junk bond market was instrumental in this process, yet the process was taken to an extreme by particular individuals, which may have contributed to the bankruptcies of numerous firms that either issued or purchased junk bonds.

---

the purchase by issuing bonds. Its return on this deal is based on the difference between the net cash inflows generated by the assets and the cash outflows resulting from the bond issue. Some IBFs have generated substantial returns on such deals, as the assets were later sold at a much higher price than the purchase price. Yet, the transaction may pose a significant risk to IBFs. First, there is no guarantee that the assets will sell at a premium. Second, IBFs' financing with bonds normally occurs with a lag. IBFs initially borrow short-term until bonds are issued. If interest rates rise prior to the issue date, the cost of long-term financing may be much higher than the IBFs had anticipated. If IBFs engage in more LBO financing activity, their holdings of other assets will increase, and their overall performance will be more susceptible to economic downturns. However, the potential fee income and returns on asset holdings may more than offset this risk.

Merrill Lynch has designed a mutual fund that finances LBOs. The investment in the mutual fund is used mostly to purchase junk bonds of firms that went private. In addition to purchasing junk bonds, the mutual fund provides **bridge loans** for firms which offer temporary financing until junk bonds can be issued. The fund also invests in the equity of some firms.

How Investment Banking Firms Facilitate Arbitrage

Some IBFs also facilitate **arbitrage** activity, which in the securities industry refers to the purchasing of undervalued shares and the resale of these shares for a higher profit. The IBFs work closely with **arbitrage firms** (which are involved in arbitrage) by searching for undervalued firms and raising funds for the arbitrage firms. It is sometimes difficult to distinguish between arbitrage and an LBO because both activities involve an attempt to purchase an undervalued firm, mostly with borrowed funds. Yet, LBOs are commonly executed by management or other employers, who may plan to maintain ownership of a firm. Sometimes arbitrage activity is referred to as a hostile LBO.

One common form of arbitrage would be acquiring a firm and then selling off individual divisions of the firm. This action, called **asset stripping,** was motivated by the perception that the sum of the parts is sometimes greater than the whole. For example, in 1985, Kohlberg, Kravis, and Roberts (KKR) purchased Beatrice for $5.4 billion and then sold the divisions individually. In aggregate, the proceeds of the sales were substantially higher than KKR's investment. IBFs would generate fee income from their advising arbitrage firms as well as receive a commission on the bonds issued to support the arbitrage activity. They would also receive fees from divestitures of divisions. When the raising of funds is not expected to be complete before the acquisition is initiated, the IBFs provide bridge loans. Because the acquisitions are largely financed with borrowed funds, arbitrage firms would essentially pay off their debts with the target's cash flow.

Exhibit 24.1 illustrates the participation of IBFs in an acquisition. Note how many different functions the IBFs may perform for the acquiring firms, all of which generate fees or interest. The IBFs can help finance an acquisition by (1) providing loans to the acquirer, (2) underwriting bonds or stock for the acquirer, and (3) investing their own equity in the acquirer's purchase of the target.

As hostile (uninvited) takeovers became popular, some IBFs offered an advisory service on takeover defense maneuvers. Although these IBFs were financing some hostile takeovers, they were also advising others on defending against hostile takeovers. Some arbitrage firms take positions in targets, just to benefit from the expected takeover by another group. For example, numerous arbitrage firms purchased the stock of UAL Corporation, anticipating an LBO by UAL's management and a resulting increase in the stock price. Some of these firms had invested $40 million or more in UAL and purchased the stock for around $280 per share. In October 1989, financial institutions informed UAL's management that they would not provide the total financing needed to execute the LBO. The stock price plunged to $145 per share within a few weeks after that announcement.

Some attempts at arbitrage failed because target firms were successful at defending against a takeover. However, such defenses were usually expensive. One common defense was for the target firm to buy back the shares held by the arbitrage firm. Because the arbitrage firm may only be willing to sell the shares back at a premium, the target's repurchasing of shares may require massive financing, which could even lower a target's credit rating.

EXHIBIT 24.1 Participation of Investment Banking Firms in an Acquisition

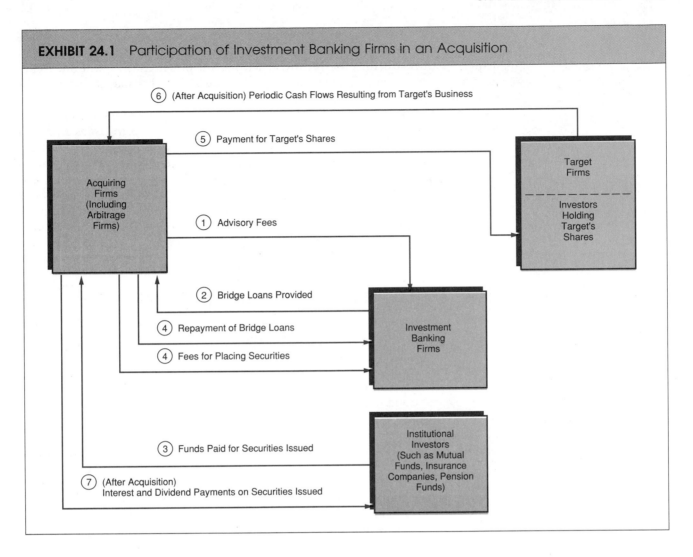

History of Arbitrage Activity

In the early 1980s some arbitrage firms accumulated shares of targets with the expectation that the targets would be willing to buy their shares back at a premium. With this tactic, known as **greenmail,** the arbitrage firms do not anticipate completing a takeover but still profit from the difference between their selling and buying prices on the shares. Some IBFs helped to finance greenmail tactics. The final result of greenmail is that the target is not acquired but incurs a large expense of buying back the stock held by the arbitrage firm. Thus, even though the target has been singled out as being undervalued (possibly as a result of inefficient management), it is still run by the same management.

By the mid-1980s, arbitrage activity was commonly criticized because it often resulted in excessive financial leverage and risk for corporations. In addition, the restructuring of divisions after acquisitions resulted in corporate layoffs. Because some IBFs facilitated arbitrage activity, they were criticized as well. Arbitrage firms and IBFs may counter that arbitrage helps remove managerial inefficiencies. If a firm is not efficiently managed, it should become a target so that an acquirer can restructure the firm to reach its full potential. In addition, shareholders of a target firm can benefit from arbitrage activity because the share price generally rises as the arbitrage firm purchases shares.

Since the late 1980s and early 1990s, the popularity of hostile takeovers has declined in response to several incidents. First, numerous companies that had issued junk bonds were experiencing cash flow problems, so that investors were less willing to provide this type of financing. Second, the bankruptcy of Drexel Burnham Lambert in 1990 reduced the use of junk bond financing, because Drexel was the leading underwriter of junk bonds. Third, savings institutions were required by regulators to phase out their investment in junk bonds. Because they no longer served as a source of funds, it was more difficult to place junk bonds. Fourth, some states began to impose antitakeover provisions to protect local firms.

How IBFs Facilitate New Stock Issues

An IBF acts as an intermediary between a corporation issuing securities and investors by providing the following services:

- Origination
- Underwriting stock
- Distribution of stock
- Advising

ORIGINATION.   When a corporation decides to publicly issue additional stock, it may contact an IBF. The IBF can recommend the appropriate amount of stock to issue, because it can anticipate the amount of stock the market can likely absorb without causing a reduction in the stock price.

Next, the IBF will evaluate the corporation's financial condition to determine the appropriate price for the newly issued stock. If the firm has issued stock to the public before, the price should be the same as the market price on its outstanding stock. If not, the firm's financial characteristics will be compared with other similar firms in the same industry that have stock outstanding to help determine the price at which the stock should be sold.

The issuing corporation then registers with the SEC. All information relevant to the security, as well as the agreement between itself and the IBF, must be provided within the **registration statement,** which is intended to ensure that accurate information is disclosed by the issuing corporation. Some publicly placed securities do not require registration if the issue is very small or sold entirely within a particular state. SEC approval does not guarantee the quality or safety of the securities to be issued; it simply acknowledges that a firm is disclosing accurate information about itself. Included within the required registration information is the **prospectus,** which discloses relevant financial data on the firm and provisions applicable to the security. The prospectus can be issued only after the registration is approved, which typically takes 20 to 40 days.

UNDERWRITING STOCK.   As a result of negotiations between the IBF and an issuing corporation, an **underwriting spread** is determined, which reflects the difference between the price the IBF is willing to pay for stock and the price at which it expects to sell the securities. In essence, the underwriting spread represents a commission to the IBF for selling the stock. The actual commission earned by the IBF depends upon the price at which the stock is sold. The issuing firm is not directly affected by the actual selling price of the stock, if it was guaranteed a certain price by the IBF.

Suppose that Panther Corporation planned to issue 4 million shares of new stock and an IBF guaranteed a selling price of $19 per share, then sold the stock for $20 per share. The underwriting spread earned by the IBF is $1 for every share sold at $20, or 5 percent. The underwriting spread on a percentage basis will average around 3 percent for large issues of stocks and as high as 10 percent or more on small issues.

The original IBF may form an **underwriting syndicate** of IBFs, which are requested to underwrite a portion of the stock. Each participating IBF earns the underwriting spread and assumes the risk for the portion of securities it is assigned. Thus, the risk to the original IBF is reduced to only the stock it is responsible for selling. If the stock sells for a price lower than expected, the original IBF will not be affected as much, because it has allocated much of the responsibility to other IBFs in the syndicate. The original IBF hopes that the other IBFs invited into the syndicate will someday return the favor when they are the original underwriters and need participation from other IBFs. A syndicate may be composed of just a few IBFs, for a relatively small stock issue, or as many as 50 or more for a large issue. The IBFs involved in the most underwriting are Merrill Lynch, Goldman Sachs, First Boston, Shearson Lehman Hutton, Morgan Stanley, and Salomon Brothers.

IBFs may not be willing to act as underwriters for securities issued by relatively risky corporations. Instead, they may offer their best efforts in selling the stock. This results in a **best-efforts agreement,** whereby the IBF does not guarantee a price to the issuing corporation. Although an issuing corporation would normally prefer to have its stock underwritten, it may have to accept a best-efforts agreement if its financial performance is questionable or unproven. In such a case, the issuing corporation bears the risk because it does not receive a guaranteed price from the IBF on the stock to be issued.

DISTRIBUTION OF STOCK. Once all agreements between the issuing firm, the originating IBF, and other participating IBFs are complete and the registration is approved by the SEC, the stock may be sold. The prospectus is distributed to all potential purchasers of the stock, and the issue is advertised to the public. In some cases, the issue sells within hours. However, if the issue does not sell as expected, the underwriting syndicate will likely have to reduce the price to complete the sale. The demand for the stock is somewhat influenced by the sales force involved in selling the stock. Some IBFs participating in a syndicate have brokerage subsidiaries that can sell stock on a retail level. Others may specialize in underwriting but still utilize a group of brokerage firms to sell the newly issued stock. The brokers earn a commission on the amount they sell but do not guarantee a specific amount of sales.

When a corporation publicly places stock, it incurs two types of **flotation costs,** or costs of placing the securities. First, the underwriting spread is paid to the underwriters, who guarantee the issuing firm a set price for the stock. Second, **issue costs** from issuing stock include printing, legal, registration, and accounting expenses. Because these issue costs are not significantly affected by the size of the issue, flotation costs as a percentage of the value of securities issued are lower for larger issues.

ADVISING.   The IBF acts as an advisor throughout the origination stage. Even after the stock is issued, the IBF may continue to provide advice on the timing, amount, and terms of future financing. Included within this advice would be recommendations on the appropriate type of financing (bonds, stocks, or long-term commercial loans).

How IBFs Facilitate New Bond Issues

The IBF's role for placing bonds is somewhat similar to the placement of stock. The four main services of the IBF as related to the placement of bonds are explained in turn.

ORIGINATION.   The IBF may suggest a maximum amount of bonds that should be issued, based on the issuer's characteristics. If the issuer already has a high level of outstanding debt, the issuance of bonds may not be well received by the market, because the issuer's ability to meet the debt payments would be questionable. Consequently, the bonds would need to offer a relatively high yield, which reflects a high cost of borrowing to the issuer.

Next, the coupon rate, the maturity, and other provisions are decided, based on the characteristics of the issuing firm. The asking price on the bonds will be influenced by evaluating market prices of existing bonds that are similar in their degree of risk, term to maturity, and other provisions.

Issuers of bonds must register with the SEC. The registration statement contains information about the bonds to be issued, states the agreement between the IBF and the issuer, and also contains a prospectus with financial information about the issuer.

UNDERWRITING BONDS.   Some issuers of bonds, particularly public utilities, may solicit competitive bids from various IBFs on the price of bonds so as to select the IBF with the highest bid. However, IBFs provide several services to the issuer, so price is not the only consideration. Corporations typically select an IBF based on reputation rather than competitive bids.

Underwriting spreads on newly issued bonds are normally lower than on newly issued stock, because bonds can often be placed in large blocks to financial institutions. Conversely, a stock issue must be segmented into smaller pieces and is more difficult to sell.

As with stocks, the IBF may organize an underwriting syndicate of IBFs to participate in the placement of the bonds. Each IBF assumes a portion of the risk. Of course, the potential income earned by the original IBF is reduced, too. If the IBF is uncomfortable in guaranteeing a price to the issuer, it may offer only a best-efforts agreement rather than underwriting the bonds.

DISTRIBUTION OF BONDS.   Upon SEC approval of registration, a prospectus is distributed to all potential purchasers of the bonds, and the issue is advertised to the public. The asking price on the bonds is normally set at a level that will ensure a sale of the entire issue. The flotation costs generally range from 0.5

percent to 3 percent of the value of bonds issued, which can be significantly lower than the flotation costs of issuing common or preferred stock.

ADVISING. As with the placement of stock, an IBF that places bonds for issuers may serve as an advisor to the issuer even after placement is completed. Most issuers of bonds will need to raise long-term funds in the future and will consider the IBF's advice on the type of securities to issue at that time.

PRIVATE PLACEMENTS OF BONDS. If an issuing corporation knows of a potential purchaser for its entire issue, it might be able to sell its securities directly without offering the bonds to the general public (or using the underwriting services of the IBF). This **private placement** (or direct placement) avoids the underwriting fee. Corporations have been increasingly using private placements. Potential purchasers of securities that are large enough to buy an entire issue include insurance companies, commercial banks, pension funds, and mutual funds. Securities could even be privately placed with two or more of these institutions. A private placement is more common for the issuance of bonds than for stocks.

The price paid for privately placed securities is determined by negotiations between the issuing corporation and the purchaser. Although the IBF is not needed here for underwriting, it may advise the issuing corporation on the appropriate terms of the securities and identify potential purchasers.

The provisions within a privately placed issue can be tailored to the desires of the purchaser, unlike the standardized provisions of a publicly placed issue. A possible disadvantage of a private placement is that the demand may not be as strong as for a publicly placed issue, because only a fraction of the market is targeted. This could force a lower price for the bonds, resulting in a higher cost of financing for the issuing firm.

BROKERAGE SERVICES

Customer requests for brokerage firms to execute securities transactions can usually be classified as one of the following:

- Market orders
- Limit orders
- Short selling

Market Orders

Requests by customers to purchase or sell securities at the market price existing when the order reaches the exchange floor are called **market orders.** In most cases, the actual transaction will occur within an hour from the time of request by the customer, assuming that the request is made while the markets are open.

Limit Orders

Requests by customers to purchase or sell securities at a specified price or better are called **limit orders.** Specialists of an exchange are responsible for monitoring limit orders and executing the transactions in accordance with the limits specified. Some limit orders are cancelled if they are not executed within one day. Other limit orders will remain until they are executed or cancelled by the customer. Some investors order a sale of securities when the price reaches a specified minimum. This is referred to as a **stop-loss order.** If the price were to remain above the specified minimum, the securities would not be sold.

Short Selling

Investors can speculate on expectations of a decline in securities prices by **short selling,** or selling securities that they do not own. For example, an investor who anticipated that the price of Exxon stock would decline could request a short sale of Exxon stock from a broker. The broker would borrow the stock from an inventory of stocks held on margin (from other accounts) and sell it for the investor. The investor is required to deposit funds that reflect the market value of the stock. At some point in the future, the investor would request a purchase of the stock and repay the broker for the stock borrowed. If the stock price declined by the time the investor requested the purchase, the short-sale strategy would generate a positive return. Short sellers are required to reimburse the owners of the stock for any missed dividends.

Full-Service Versus Discount Brokerage Services

Brokerage firms can be classified as either **full-service brokerage firms,** in which information and advice are provided, or **discount brokerage firms,** in which securities transactions are executed upon request. Discount brokerage firms have about 20 percent of retail brokerage business. They are often unable to maintain a long-term relationship with clients, because they provide a service difficult to differentiate from competitors. Full-service brokerage firms provide a more personalized advisory service.

Although discount brokers still concentrate on executing stock transactions, they recently expanded their services to include precious metals, options, and municipal bonds. Some also offer credit cards, cash management accounts, 24-hour phone service, and research reports.

Many discount brokerage firms are owned by large commercial banks, which have historically been prohibited from offering full-service brokerage services. For example, Security Pacific offers a large discount brokerage service. Since 1983 Chase Manhattan Corporation has owned a large discount brokerage firm. Bank America owned Charles Schwab & Company until Schwab bought his company back.

ALLOCATION OF REVENUE SOURCES

Exhibit 24.2 shows the average allocation of revenue sources across securities firms over time. In 1975, commissions (from the brokerage business) made up about 50 percent of the revenue. However, the commission pricing was deregulated in 1975, increasing the competition in brokerage services. In the early 1990s, brokerage commissions comprised only about 20 percent of the revenue of securities firms on average. The largest source of revenue in recent years has

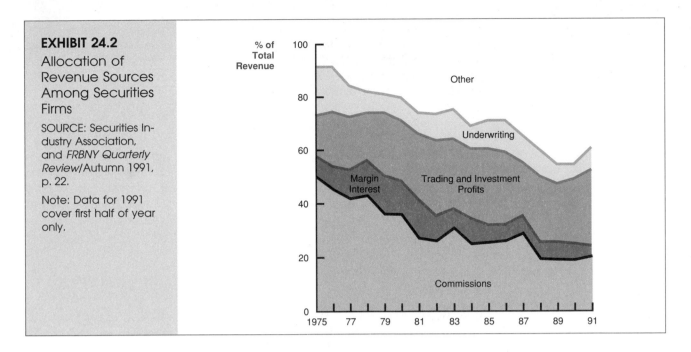

EXHIBIT 24.2

Allocation of Revenue Sources Among Securities Firms

SOURCE: Securities Industry Association, and *FRBNY Quarterly Review*/Autumn 1991, p. 22.

Note: Data for 1991 cover first half of year only.

been trading and investment profits. Underwriting services and margin interest (from providing loans to individual investors) also make up a significant portion of the revenue. The proportion of revenue derived from the "other" category (which includes fees earned on advising and executing acquisitions) has increased over time.

RISK OF SECURITIES FIRMS

The operations conducted by securities firms create exposure to market risk, interest rate risk, credit risk, and exchange rate risk, as explained below.

Market Risk

Securities firms offer many services that are linked to stock market conditions. When stock prices are rising, there is normally a greater volume of stock offerings and secondary market transactions. Because securities firms typically are needed to facilitate these transactions, they benefit from a bullish stock market. Those securities firms that sponsor mutual funds typically benefit from the large investment in mutual funds during a bullish market.

Some securities firms take equity positions in the stocks they underwrite (especially the initial public offerings). They also commonly take a partial equity interest in target firms acquired by their client firms. These firms tend to benefit from a bullish stock market. Acquisitions tend to be more common during favorable stock market conditions. Given their participation in advising and financing acquisitions, securities firms can generate more business under these conditions.

When the stock market is depressed, stock transactions tend to decline, causing a reduction in business for securities firms. Although securities firms have diversified into different services, the demand for many of these services is tied to stock market conditions. Thus, the performance of most securities firms is highly sensitive to the stock market cycles.

Interest Rate Risk

The performance of securities firms can be sensitive to interest rate movements for the following reasons. First, the market values of bonds held as investments by securities firms increase as interest rates decline. Second, lower interest rates can encourage investors to withdraw deposits from depository institutions and invest in the stock market, thereby increasing stock transactions. Thus, the performance of some securities firms will be inversely related to interest rate movements.

Credit Risk

Many securities firms offer bridge loans and other types of credit to corporations. The securities firms are subject to the possibility that these corporations will default on their loans. The probability of default tends to increase during periods when economic conditions deteriorate.

Exchange Rate Risk

Many securities firms have operations in foreign countries. The earnings remitted by foreign subsidiaries are reduced when the foreign currencies weaken against the parent firm's home currency. In addition, the market values of securities maintained as investments and denominated in foreign currencies decline as the currencies weaken against the parent firm's home currency.

INTERACTION WITH OTHER FINANCIAL INSTITUTIONS

Securities firms commonly interact with various types of financial institutions as summarized in Exhibit 24.3. They offer investment advice and execute security transactions for financial institutions that maintain security portfolios. They also compete against those financial institutions that have brokerage subsidiaries. Furthermore, they compete with some commercial banks that have recently been allowed to underwrite securities, and sponsor mutual funds. Because securities firms commonly offer banking and insurance services, while many insurance companies and commercial banks offer securities services, it is sometimes difficult to distinguish among financial institutions. Some savings institutions that experienced financial problems have been acquired by securities firms, and operate as wholly owned subsidiaries.

PARTICIPATION IN FINANCIAL MARKETS

Securities firms participate in all types of financial markets as summarized in Exhibit 24.4. Their investment banking divisions participate in the primary mar-

POINT OF INTEREST

EVALUATING THE PERFORMANCE OF SECURITIES FIRMS

Annual reports are commonly used by investors to evaluate the financial condition of securities firms. The Value Line Investment Survey provides a summary of financial proxies that measure the performance of securities firms. An example of the Value Line analysis is shown here for Merrill Lynch. The income of securities firms is measured by return on equity, referred to as "% Earned Net Worth." Each column represents a specific year, so that the changes in performance of the securities firm (as measured by any particular income proxy) can be assessed. The beta of the securities firm is disclosed in the upper left corner.

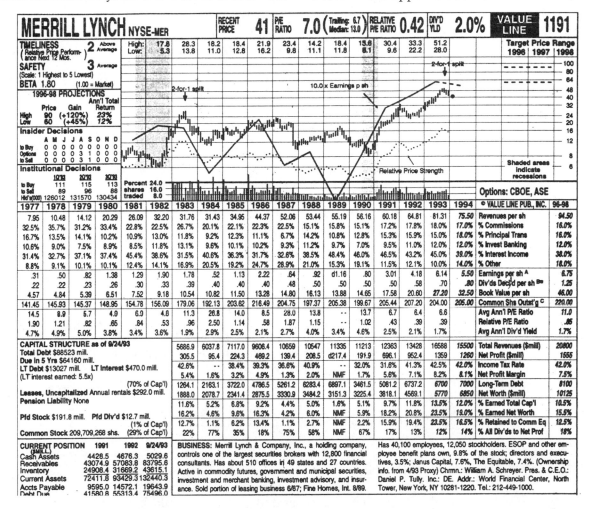

kets by placing newly issued securities, while the brokerage divisions concentrate mostly on executing secondary market transactions for investors. Both the investment banking and brokerage divisions serve as advisors to financial market participants.

EXHIBIT 24.3 Interaction between Securities Firms and Other Financial Institutions

TYPE OF FINANCIAL INSTITUTION	INTERACTION WITH SECURITIES FIRMS
Commercial banks and savings institutions	▪ Securities firms compete with those commercial banks and savings institutions that provide brokerage services. ▪ Those commercial banks that underwrite commercial paper or provide advice on mergers and acquisitions compete directly with securities firms. ▪ In countries other than the U.S., commercial banks and brokerage firms commonly compete, because regulations do not attempt to separate banking and securities activities.
Mutual funds	▪ Securities firms execute trades for mutual funds. ▪ Some mutual funds were organized by securities firms. ▪ Mutual funds purchase newly issued securities that are underwritten by securities firms.
Insurance companies	▪ Securities firms advise portfolio managers of insurance companies on what securities to buy or sell. ▪ Securities firms execute securities transactions for insurance companies. ▪ Securities firms advise portfolio managers of insurance companies on how to hedge against interest rate risk and market risk. ▪ Securities firms underwrite stocks and bonds that are purchased by insurance companies. ▪ Securities firms compete with some insurance companies in the sales of some mutual funds to investors. ▪ Securities firms obtain financing on LBOs from insurance companies. ▪ Some securities firms have acquired, or have merged with insurance companies in order to offer more diversified services (Prudential-Bache is an example).
Pension funds	▪ Securities firms advise pension fund portfolio managers on securities to purchase or sell. ▪ Securities firms execute securities transactions for pension funds. ▪ Securities firms advise pension fund portfolio managers on how to hedge against interest rate risk and market risk. ▪ Pension funds purchase newly issued securities that are underwritten by securities firms.

GLOBALIZATION OF SECURITIES FIRMS

Since 1986 many securities firms have increased their presence in foreign countries. In October 1986 the so-called Big Bang allowed for deregulation in the United Kingdom. With the commission structure competitive instead of fixed, British securities firms recognized that they would have to rely more on other services, as commission income would be reduced by competitive forces. Commercial banks from the United States have established investment banking sub-

EXHIBIT 24.4 Participation of Securities Firms in Financial Markets

TYPE OF FINANCIAL MARKET	PARTICIPATION BY SECURITIES FIRMS
Money markets	■ Some securities firms, such as Merrill Lynch, have created money market mutual funds, which invest in money market securities. ■ Securities firms underwrite commercial paper and purchase short-term securities for their own investment portfolios.
Bond markets	■ Securities firms underwrite bonds in the primary market, advise clients on bonds to purchase or sell, and serve as brokers for bond transactions in the secondary market. ■ Some bond mutual funds have been created by securities firms. ■ Securities firms facilitate mergers, acquisitions, and LBOs by placing bonds for their clients. ■ Securities firms purchase bonds for their own investment portfolios.
Mortgage markets	■ Securities firms place securities that are backed by mortgages for various financial institutions.
Stock markets	■ Securities firms underwrite stocks in the primary market, advise clients on what stocks to purchase or sell, and serve as brokers for stock transactions in the secondary market. ■ Securities firms purchase stocks for their own investment portfolios.
Futures markets	■ Securities firms advise large financial institutions on how to hedge their portfolios with financial futures contracts. ■ Securities firms serve as brokers for financial futures transactions.
Options markets	■ Securities firms advise large financial institutions on how to hedge portfolios with options contracts. ■ Securities firms serve as brokers for options transactions.
Swap markets	■ Some securities firms engage in interest rate swaps to reduce their exposure to interest rate risk. ■ Many securities firms serve as financial intermediaries in swap markets.

COMPETITION BETWEEN SECURITIES FIRMS AND COMMERCIAL BANKS

Commercial banks can compete against securities firms by offering discount brokerage services—for fees typically from 40 percent to 70 percent less than full-service fees. Of course, they still must compete with discount brokerage firms. They can offer such discount services by either acquiring a discount brokerage firm or creating a subsidiary to perform the services. If they opt for the latter course, they face the up-front costs of organizing the operations and training new personnel. In addition, an initial promotional effort is necessary, whereas in an acquisition, the bank could continue to use the acquired firm's name and reputation for the brokerage business.

Still another method is to purchase brokerage services from a registered brokerage firm. In this case, the bank simply acts as an intermediary between customers and the brokerage firm. It normally receives the transactions and communicates the information to the brokerage firm, which executes the transaction. It may even provide customers with a toll-free number that is answered with the name of the bank so that customers will believe the brokerage op-

eration is run by the bank. In this arrangement, the bank promotes the service and receives a portion of the commissions generated—the portion being determined by the degree of work (regarding custodial services, mailing periodic statements, etc.) the bank is responsible for.

The Glass-Steagall Act of 1933 separated the functions of commercial banks and investment banking firms, allowing commercial banks to underwrite general obligation municipal bonds but generally prohibiting them from other securities activities. However, in recent years commercial banks have acquired brokerage subsidiaries and have served in an advisory capacity for mergers and acquisitions. As of 1987, commercial banks were allowed to underwrite commercial paper. Since then, they have not only offered advice on mergers and acquisitions and on private placements of securities but also served as an intermediary for interest rate swaps and currency swaps. In the early 1990s, some commercial banks were allowed to underwrite corporate securities. In these ways, they compete directly with securities firms.

sidiaries overseas, where regulations do not attempt to separate banking and securities activities.

Most large securities firms have established a presence in foreign markets. For example, Morgan Stanley has offices in Frankfurt, London, Melbourne, Sydney, Tokyo, and Zurich. Merrill Lynch has more than 500 offices spread across the United States and numerous other countries. The effort of securities firms to become internationalized is due to the following possible advantages. First, their international presence allows them to place securities in various markets for corporations or governments. Second, some corporations that are heavily involved with international mergers and acquisitions prefer advice from securities firms that have subsidiaries in all potential markets. Third, institutional investors that invest in foreign securities prefer securities firms that can easily handle such transactions.

In recent years, securities firms have expanded their international business by engaging in joint ventures with foreign securities firms. In this way, they penetrate foreign markets, but have a limited stake in each project. Many securities firms have also increased their global presence by facilitating privatizations of firms in foreign markets such as in Latin America and Eastern Europe.

The growth in international securities transactions has created more business for the larger securities firms. For example, many stock offerings are now conducted across numerous countries, as some corporations attempt to achieve global name recognition. In addition, an international stock offering can avoid the downward pressure on the stock's price that might occur if the entire issue is sold in the domestic country. Large securities firms facilitate international stock offerings by creating an international syndicate to place the securities in various countries. Those securities firms that have established a global presence receive most of the requests for international stock offerings.

As a result of the North American Free Trade Agreement (NAFTA), U.S. securities firms have increased their business in Mexico and other Latin American countries. Securities firms will facilitate the increased trading of stocks, bonds, and other securities between the U.S. and Mexico. They will also facilitate the increase in mergers between firms from both countries.

The Japanese government recently allowed foreign securities firms to enter its markets. Merrill Lynch, Morgan Stanley, Goldman Sachs, and other U.S. and non-U.S. securities firms acquired seats on the Tokyo Stock Exchange. The Tokyo Stock Exchange has allowed some non-Japanese firms to acquire a seat on the exchange, including First Boston, Prudential-Bache, and Shearson Lehman Hutton. Yet, there are still explicit and implicit barriers to entry or at least limits on the degree of penetration by non-Japanese firms. Some securities firms complain that restrictions are excessive or vague. Although Japanese securities firms enter other financial markets, non-Japanese securities firms account for a tiny fraction of transactions in the Tokyo Stock Exchange.

Japanese securities firms rely heavily on commissions as their dominant source of revenue, just as U.S. securities firms did in the 1970s. However, because Japanese regulators have recently lowered the commission pricing in phases, Japanese securities firms are attempting to diversify their services. Many Japanese securities firms have entered U.S. markets. For example, Nomura Securities and Daiwa Securities have become primary dealers of U.S. government securities. In addition, other Japanese financial institutions have made large equity investments in U.S. securities firms such as Goldman Sachs, Paine Webber, and Shearson Lehman Hutton.

SUMMARY

- Investment banking firms help corporations raise capital, provide advice on mergers and acquisitions, and may even help finance acquisitions. Some investment banking firms commonly acquire firms and frequently restructure them.

- Investment banking firms facilitate new issues of stock by advising on how much stock the firm can issue, determining the appropriate price for the stock, underwriting the stock, and distributing the stock. New issues of bonds are facilitated by investment banking firms in a somewhat similar manner.

- Brokerage firms can execute securities transactions for their clients by accommodating market orders, limit orders, and short-selling requests. Full-service brokerage firms provide information and advice, and execute the securities transactions desired by their clients. Discount brokers tend to focus exclusively on executing security transactions for their clients.

QUESTIONS

1. Explain the role of the SEC, the NASD, and security exchanges in regulating the securities industry.

2. What is the purpose of the SIPC?

3. Why are investment banks that are more capable of raising funds in the capital markets preferred by corporations that need advising on a proposed acquisition?

4. How do investment banks facilitate leveraged buyouts?

5. Describe the origination process for corporations that are about to issue new stock.

6. Describe the underwriting function of an investment bank.

7. What is the best-efforts agreement?

8. Describe the flotation costs incurred by a corporation that issues stock.

9. Compare flotation costs of issuing bonds with those of issuing stock. Which are higher?

10. Describe a direct placement of bonds. What is an advantage of a private placement? What is a disadvantage?

11. Describe new services recently offered by discount brokers.

12. Explain why securities firms from the United States have expanded into foreign markets.

13. Explain how some investment banking firms (IBFs) facilitate arbitrage activity in the securities industry.

14. What is asset stripping?

15. How have some arbitrage firms attempted to benefit from greenmail tactics?

16. In 1989, regulators required that savings institutions phase out their investments in junk bonds. How do you think this event would possibly affect the cost of financing future acquisitions?

17. Consider a division of Spence, Inc. that experienced a major decline in sales. Assume the corporation prefers not to lay off any employees as a general policy. It is often suggested that these divisions become primary targets to arbitrage firms. Given that the value of a division is the sum of discounted cash flows, explain why the value of this division to the arbitrage firm may exceed the value of this division to Spence, Inc.

18. Why do IBFs typically have some inside information that could affect future stock prices of firms other than their own?

19. Some people have suggested that the popularity of junk bonds in the 1980s indirectly helped to alleviate some inefficiencies in corporate operations. Attempt to explain this indirect influence.

20. Most securities firms experienced poor profit performance after the October 1987 stock market crash. Given what you know about securities firms, offer some possible reasons for reduced profits.

CASE APPLICATION: SECURITIES FIRM RISK

Highly Leveraged Wall Street Gets Rich From Rock-Bottom Short-Term Rates

Michael Siconolfi, New York

What's the secret to Wall Street's record profits?

Sure, stock and bond offerings are sizzling. And individual investors are flocking to the stock market. But it is today's rock-bottom short-term interest rates—and Wall Street's special ability to profit from them—that is giving a powerful kick to the Street's earnings.

Thanks to the unusually large difference between short- and long-term interest rates, big securities firms such as Merrill Lynch & Co., Salomon Inc. and Morgan Stanley Group Inc. are financing huge stockpiles of bonds with inexpensive short-term borrowing. That allows the firms to make money on the difference between the rate they pay to borrow billions of dollars and the higher interest rates they receive on their long-term bond holdings.

How big are these profits? Six big brokerage firms generated a record total $3.19 billion in interest income after expenses in 1992. This "net interest income"—at Merrill, Salomon, Morgan Stanley, Bear Stearns Cos., Paine Webber Group Inc. and American Express Co.'s Shearson Lehman Brothers Inc. unit—is 63% higher than in 1991. And it represents a stunning 76% of the firms' total pretax profit.

"It's easy money as long as it lasts," says Guy Moszkowski, brokerage analyst at Sanford C. Bernstein & Co. In the meantime, he says, brokerage firms have "positioned themselves to catch the pennies from heaven" by significantly boosting their bond holdings and other assets.

Wall Street isn't the only one borrowing heavily in a bid to take advantage of low short-term rates. Individual investors are borrowing more heavily than ever to buy stocks and other investments. They are doing this by borrowing "on margin" from securities firms; margin loans allow investors to borrow cash against stock in their portfolio.

Margin loans outstanding to individual investors recently surged to a record $45.16 billion—surpassing the peak set in the month before the October 1987 stock market crash, according to data tracked by the New York Stock Exchange.

Like commercial banks, securities firms are allowed to highly leverage themselves by borrowing heavily against their equity capital. Today, Wall Street firms are more highly leveraged than ever.

Securities firms are holding a record $26 of assets (bonds and other securities) for every $1 of equity, says the Securities Industry Association, a trade group. Salomon's total assets ballooned 64% to $159 billion at the end of 1992; Merrill's total assets surged 24% to $107 billion.

But there's a risk here. Profits at the nation's securities firms will be severely squeezed if interest rates suddenly surge. If that happens, analysts say, Wall Street's steep leverage will work against it. "This is potentially a risky scenario," says Michael Flanagan, an analyst at Lipper Analytical Securities Corp.

The jump in securities firms' net interest income underscores how significantly the Federal Reserve's push to drive down short-term interest rates has benefited Wall Street.

In addition to boosting brokerage firms' net interest income, falling rates have enabled the companies to nearly double net gains from bond trading from mid-1989 to mid-1992, says the securities trade group. And "because of lower rates, the industry's actual 'dollar bill' for interest (costs) is shrinking back to 1987 levels, despite larger debt, inventory and more revenue," says George Monahan, director of industry studies at the trade group.

Last week, Merrill—the nation's largest securities firm—reported net interest income of $255.6 million for this year's first quarter—a 29% jump from the year-earlier period, and 43% of Merrill's pretax profit. PaineWebber had a 12% increase in net interest income in the first quarter.

Wall Street executives argue that it's misleading in some ways to separate net interest income from the rest of a firm's revenue. They say net interest income is part of the overall activity of Wall Street firms' business, particularly principal trading using a firm's own money.

Wall Street firms also say they take pains to reduce the risk of rising interest rates by hedging their inventories of securities, often by taking offsetting positions through the use of such derivatives as bond futures and options.

Continued

CASE APPLICATION: SECURITIES FIRM RISK

Continued

"We're able to maintain larger inventories because they're hedged," says Herbert M. Allison Jr., Merrill's executive vice president in charge of finance and administration. Thus, he says, Merrill is "not taking huge risks that could cause a reduction in the company's ability to function."

And though a long-term rise in rates would crimp profitability, Mr. Allison says the resulting interest-rate volatility would lead to short-term trading profit. Also, he says, Merrill's inventory of securities is highly liquid, or easily sold if necessary.

Not all firms hedge their inventories so completely, however. At Salomon, for instance, the firm hedges those trading positions executed on behalf of customers. But Salomon's proprietary trading positions for its own account aren't always hedged because the "longer-term proprietary positions are not outright interest-rate bets," says David C. Fisher, Salomon's controller. "Those bets are on various different relationships," including interest-rate and currency changes, and "take a long, long time to come to fruition," he says.

Another factor that has reduced the cost of borrowing funds for many brokerage firms is that their credit ratings have been boosted, as their profits have soared. As Merrill's credit ratings have risen, for instance, its overall borrowing costs have shrunk $25 million a year since early 1991, says Mr. Allison.

The major exception to this is Salomon. Last week, Standard & Poor's Corp. lowered its ratings on about $8 billion of Salomon's long-term debt, citing the wide fluctuations in Salomon's earnings because of its heavy reliance on trading. The ratings downgrade will have "a negative impact" on Salomon's net interest income, says Salomon's Mr. Fisher. "But we don't anticipate that it will be significant."

SOURCE: *The Wall Street Journal,* October 1, 1993, p. C1. Reprinted by permission of *The Wall Street Journal* © 1993, Dow Jones & Company, Inc. All rights reserved worldwide.

QUESTIONS

1. Explain how the performance levels of securities firms such as Merrill Lynch & Co., Salomon Inc., and Morgan Stanley Group Inc. are affected by the yield curve (the relationship between short-term and long-term interest rates).

2. Explain why securities firms such as Merrill Lynch & Co. and others can be adversely affected by rising interest rates.

3. Morgan Stanley, Paine Webber, Merrill Lynch and other securities firms generated large profits during the recent period of low interest rates. However, there was a bullish stock market over this same period. Do you think the high performance was actually attributed to interest rate conditions, stock market conditions, or both? Explain.

PROJECT

1. **Assessing a Securities Firm's Operations**
   Obtain a recent annual report of a securities firm of your choice or one assigned by your professor and answer the following questions:
   a. Describe the securities firm's operations. Does the firm appear to focus on investment banking activities or brokerage activities?
   b. Describe the securities firm's performance in recent years. Offer possible reasons for the change in performance over the past few years.
   c. Has the securities firm expanded into new foreign markets in recent years? If so, why?
   d. Summarize any information offered on the impact of the stock market crash of 1987 on this securities firm.
   e. Does the securities firm plan to diversify into more services in the future or to concentrate on a few key services? Elaborate.

REFERENCES

Brennan, Michael J., and Tarun Chordia. "Brokerage Commission Schedules." *Journal of Finance* (September 1993): 1379–1402.

Chu, Franklin J. "The Myth of Global Investment Banking." *Bankers Magazine* (January–February 1988): 58–61.

Conner, Daryl R., and Byron G. Fiman. "Making the Cultural Transition to Investment Banking." *Bankers Magazine* (January–February 1988): 31–35.

Dyche, David. "Investment Banking: What Do Banks Need to Compete?" *Bankers Magazine* (March–April 1988): 42–46.

Hansen, Robert S., and Paul Torregrosa. "Underwriter Compensation and Corporate Monitoring." *Journal of Finance* (September 1992): 1535–1555.

Saunders, Anthony, and Michael Smirlock. "Intra- and Inter-Industry Effects of Bank Securities Market Activities: The Case of Discount Brokerage." *Journal of Financial and Quantitative Analysis* (December 1987): 467–482.

CHAPTER 25

PENSION FUNDS

Pension funds provide a savings plan for employees that can be used for retirement. They serve a critical function in the United States, where the residents save a smaller percentage of their disposable income than residents of most other developed countries.

The specific objectives of this chapter are to:

- describe the different types of private pension plans,
- describe the pension management styles,
- describe the recent concerns about underfunded pensions, and
- describe the role of the Pension Benefit Guarantee Corporation in enhancing the safety of pension plans.

BACKGROUND ON PENSION FUNDS

Pension plans were used in the late 1800s by the large, regulated transportation companies. By the early 1900s, they were commonly offered by commercial banks, utility companies, mining companies, government agencies, and unions. However, they were severely affected by the Great Depression, as many companies were unable to provide the benefits they promised. Because of substantial layoffs, contributions were low. Consequently, companies tightened their requirements for employees to qualify for a pension and reduced pension benefits. Some even abolished them.

The credibility of pension plans began to develop slowly after the Great Depression. They became especially important during World War II, as the Wage Stabilization Program prevented firms from offering high salaries in the tight labor market, so fringe benefits such as a good pension plan were necessary to attract labor. Then, during the Korean War in the early 1950s, wage and price controls were imposed, again enhancing the appeal of a good pension plan. In the 1960s and 1970s, a broader variety of such plans were created.

All pension funds receive premiums from the employer and/or the employee. In aggregate, most of the contributions come from the employer. Public pension funds can be either state and local, or federal. The most well-known government pension fund is Social Security. In addition to that system, all government employees and almost half of all nongovernment employees participate in other pension funds.

Many public pension plans are funded on a pay-as-you-go basis. At some point, the strategy could cause the future benefits owed to outweigh contributions to an extent that either prevents the pension funds from fulfilling their promises or requires more contributions. This underfunding is potentially dangerous over the long run, as existing employee and employer contributors are essentially supporting previous employees. Some public pension plans have recently attempted to reduce their degree of underfunding.

Private pension plans are created by private agencies, including industrial, labor, service, nonprofit, charitable, and educational organizations. Because some pension funds are so large, they represent major investors in corporate securities.

TYPES OF PRIVATE PENSION PLANS

Private pension funds can be classified by the manner in which contributions are received and benefits are paid. For a **defined-benefit plan,** contributions are dictated by the benefits that will eventually be provided. When the value of pension assets exceeds the current and future benefits owed to employees, companies respond by reducing future contributions. Alternatively, they may distribute the surplus amount to the firm's shareholders rather than the employees. Thus, the management of the pension fund can have a direct impact on shareholders.

As an alternative to the defined benefit plan, a **defined-contribution plan** provides benefits that are determined by the accumulated contributions on the fund's investment performance. This type of plan allows a firm to know with certainty the amount of funds to contribute, whereas that amount is undetermined in the defined-benefit plan. However, the defined-contribution plan provides uncertain benefits to the participants.

As shown in Exhibit 25.1, there are more defined-contribution plans than defined-benefit plans. However, there are more participants in defined-benefit plans, and the aggregate value of assets of defined-benefit plans is greater. New plans allow employees more flexibility to choose what they want. In recent years, the defined-benefit plan has been commonly replaced by the defined-contribution plan. Employees can often decide the pace of their contributions and how their contributions should be invested. Communications from the benefits coordinator to the employees has become much more important, because employees now have more influence on their pension plan contributions and the investment approach used to invest the premiums.

Underfunded Pensions

The future pension obligations of a defined-benefit plan are uncertain because the obligations are stated in terms of fixed payments to retirees. These payments are dependent on salary levels, retirement ages, and life expectancies. Even if the

EXHIBIT 25.1 Participation in Private Pension Plans

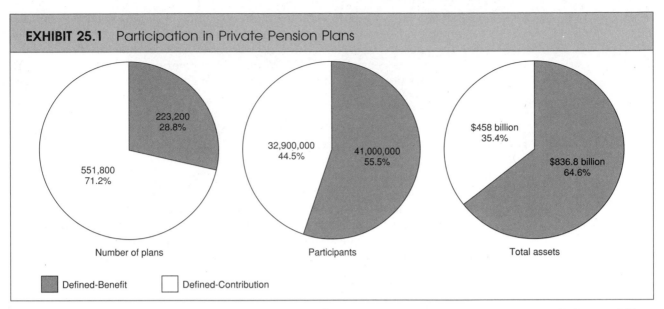

223,200
28.8%

551,800
71.2%

Number of plans

32,900,000
44.5%

41,000,000
55.5%

Participants

$458 billion
35.4%

$836.8 billion
64.6%

Total assets

■ Defined-Benefit   □ Defined-Contribution

SOURCE: Board of Governors of the Federal Reserve System; Flow of Funds Accounts; U.S. Department of Labor; and *New England Economic Review,* Federal Reserve Bank of Boston (November–December 1987): 4.

plan could accurately predict the future payment obligations, it is still unsure of the amount it needs today because of the uncertain rate of return on today's investment. The higher the future return on its investment, the fewer funds that would be needed to be invested today to satisfy future payments.

Many defined-benefit plans have used optimistic projections of the rate of return to be earned on their investments, which creates the appearance that their existing investments are adequate to cover future payment obligations. This allows the corporations to reduce their contributions (an expense) to the plan, which increases its earnings. However, if projected rates of return on the pension funds are overestimated, the pension funds will be underfunded, or inadequate to cover future payment obligations.

Some pension funds have recently made investments that offer high potential returns in order to justify their high projected rates of return. These investments, which include real estate, junk bonds, and international securities, also carry a high degree of risk. Thus, it is possible that some pension plans could be heavily underfunded if these investments perform poorly.

When pension funds become underfunded because of a rate of return projection that turned out to be too optimistic, the corporation will be forced to replenish its underfunded pension fund. To illustrate the impact, consider the case of General Motors, which in 1993 recognized that its projected rate of return of 8.6 percent was overly optimistic. It reduced the projected rate of return to 7.6 percent, which caused the pension fund to be underfunded by about $5 billion. At that time, about one fourth of the pension plans had projected rates of return exceeding 8.6 percent. If most of these pension funds also lower their projected returns, this will result in significant underfunding, which ultimately will reduce their earnings as they replenish their pension funds. Some corporations are placing new stock in their pension fund portfolios. In this way, they are contributing to their pension funds without using up their cash.

As of 1993, the benefit liabilities (future payments owed to employees) total of pension plans was $235 billion, versus $182 billion in assets to pay the benefits. The gap of $53 billion in underfunding was mostly concentrated in a small number of corporate pension plans. More than 70 percent of the gap was due to 50 corporate pension plans, most of which were in the airline, automobile, steel, and tire industries.

PENSION FUND MANAGEMENT

Regardless of the manner in which premiums are contributed, the premiums received must be managed (invested) until needed to pay benefits. Some pension funds attempt to use a **matched funding** strategy in which investment decisions are made with the objective of generating cash flows that match planned outflow payments. An alternative strategy is **projective funding,** which offers managers more flexibility in constructing a pension portfolio that can benefit from expected market and interest rate movements. Some pension fund portfolios may be segmented to satisfy some matched funding, leaving the rest of the portfolio for projective funding.

An informal method of matched funding is to invest in long-term bonds to fund long-term liabilities and intermediate bonds to fund intermediate liabilities. The appeal of matching is the assurance that the future liabilities are covered regardless of market movements. However, matching limits the manager's discretion, allowing only investments that match future payouts. For example, portfolio managers required to use matched funding would need to avoid callable bonds, because these bonds could potentially be retired before maturity. This requirement precludes consideration of many high-yield bonds. In addition, each liability payout may require a separate investment to which it can be perfectly matched, which requires several small investments and increases the pension's transaction costs.

Management of Insured Versus Trust Portfolios

The management of some pensions is performed by life insurance companies. Contributions for such plans, called **insured plans,** are often used to purchase annuity policies so that the life insurance companies can provide benefits to employees upon retirement.

As an alternative, some pension funds are managed by the trust departments of financial institutions. Contributions are invested by the trust, and benefits are paid to employees upon retirement. Although the day-to-day investment decisions of a trust are controlled by the managing institution, the corporation owning the pension normally specifies general guidelines that the institution should follow. These guidelines might include the percentage of the portfolio that should be used for stocks or bonds, a desired minimum rate of return on the overall portfolio, the maximum amount to be invested in real estate, the minimum acceptable quality ratings for bonds, the maximum amount to be invested in any one industry, the average maturity of bonds held in the portfolio, the maximum amount to be invested in options, and the minimum size of companies to invest in.

Corporations may be willing to pay commercial banks to manage their funds because the banks have trust departments that specialize in the management of pension portfolios. Some corporations prefer to split their pension portfolio among the trusts of several different commercial banks. In this way, the overall portfolio is less sensitive to the investment performance of a single trust department. Such an allocation system also allows the corporation to monitor each trust department performance by comparison to the other trust departments.

There is a significant difference between the asset composition of pension portfolios managed by life insurance companies and trusts. Assets managed by insurance companies are designed to create annuities, whereas the assets managed by the trust departments still belong to the corporation. The insurance company becomes legal owner of the assets and is allowed to maintain only a small portion of its assets as equities. Therefore insurance companies concentrate on bonds and mortgages. Conversely, the pension portfolios managed by trusts concentrate on corporate stock.

Pension portfolios managed by trusts offer potentially higher returns than the insured plans and also have a higher degree of risk. The average return of trust plans is much more volatile over time.

Only a small fraction of pension trust funds is used to purchase mortgages. Commercial bank trust departments that manage these trusts are much more acclimated to the trading of stocks and bonds and are not as comfortable with mortgages or mortgage-backed securities. The risk-return characteristics of mortgages and mortgage-backed securities are quite similar to those of Treasury or high-grade corporate bonds. Because trust portfolios already contain these bonds, additional investment in mortgages and mortgage-backed securities may not necessarily reduce the portfolio's interest rate risk.

Some pension funds have begun to invest in leveraged buyouts (LBOs). In fact, about one-fourth of the financing obtained by the well-known Kohlberg, Kravis, and Roberts firm to support LBOs come from pension funds. Because an LBO is mostly financed with borrowed funds, the returns to the business are distributed among a relatively small group of shareholders. Although the potential returns from such an investment are much higher than conventional pension fund investments, the risk is also much higher. There is some question as to whether pension fund portfolio managers should be investing funds in such a risky manner, given that some employees rely on these funds for retirement income. Yet, pension fund managers could argue that the conventional investment in stocks is also subject to considerable risk.

In the late 1980s, some pension fund managers were taking speculative positions in stock options. This strategy would generally not be appropriate for retirement funds because of the high degree of risk involved. Some pension fund managers may have strived for high returns in order to receive higher compensation, even though some of their investments were very risky. As the economy slowed in the early 1990s, pension fund management turned more conservative.

Management of Private Versus Public Pensions

The private pension portfolios are dominated by common stock. Since the early 1980s, credit market instruments other than bonds (such as mortgages) have consistently represented the second largest component, followed by corporate bonds.

Public pension portfolios are somewhat evenly invested in corporate bonds, stock, and other credit instruments. This composition differs significantly from the 1970s and early 1980s, when corporate bonds dominated the portfolios. In comparison to private pension funds, the state and local government pension funds tend to concentrate more on credit market instruments and less on corporate stock. Some state pension funds now prohibit investment in LBOs.

Corporate Control by Pension Funds

Pension funds in aggregate hold a substantial portion of the common stock outstanding in the U.S. These funds are increasingly using their ownership as a means of influencing policies of the corporations whose stock they own. In particular, the California Pension Employees Retirement System (CALPERS) and the New York State Government Retirement Fund have taken active roles in questioning specific policies and suggesting changes to the board of directors at some corporations. Corporate managers consider the requests of pension funds because of the large stake the pension funds have in the corporations. As pension funds exert some corporate control to ensure that the managers and board members serve the best interests of shareholders, they can benefit because of their position as large shareholders.

Management of Interest Rate Risk

Pension fund portfolio managers are very concerned about interest rate risk. If they hold long-term, fixed-rate bonds, the market value of their portfolio will decrease during period when interest rates increase. Some managers periodically hedge against interest rate movements by selling bond futures contracts.

Pension funds that are willing to accept market returns on bonds can purchase bond index portfolios that have been created by investment companies. The bond index portfolio may include investment-grade corporate bonds, Treasury bonds, and U.S. government agency bonds. It does not include the entire set of these bonds but includes enough (200 or so) of them to mirror market performance. Investing in a market portfolio is a passive approach that does not require any analysis of individual bonds. Some pension funds are not willing to accept a totally passive approach, so they compromise by using only a portion of their funds to purchase a bond market portfolio.

Equity portfolio indexes that mirror the stock market are also available for the passive portfolio managers. These index funds have become popular over time, as they avoid transaction costs associated with frequent purchases and sales of individual stocks.

Many portfolio managers periodically sell futures contracts on stock indexes to hedge against market downturns. Portfolio managers of pension funds can obtain various types of insurance to limit the risk of the portfolio. For example, a policy could insure beyond a specified decline (such as 10 percent) in the asset value of a pension fund. This insurance allows managers to use more aggressive investment strategies. The cost of the insurance depends on the provisions of the contract and length of time the portfolio is to be insured.

The pension funds for some companies, such as Lockheed, simply concentrate investment in stocks and bonds and do not employ immunization techniques (to hedge the portfolio against risk). Lockheed has generally focused on highly liquid investments so that the proportion of stocks and bonds within the portfolio can be revised in response to market conditions.

Other pension funds use a more aggressive approach. For example, Eastman Kodak's pension fund portfolio includes real estate, oil and gas, and leveraged

LIFE OF A PENSION FUND PORTFOLIO MANAGER

Managers of pension funds determine the portfolio composition of available funds. They must remain within any guidelines imposed by the sponsoring corporation on a private pension fund or by the government agency of concern on a public pension fund. In some cases, a pension fund is managed by various portfolio managers, each assigned a subset of a portfolio (such as stocks of small companies, long-term bonds).

Managers use a variety of information to make their portfolio decisions. They are overloaded with free, sometimes daily, information from all the major securities firms, which hope that the managers will use their brokerage services when the pension fund portfolio is to be restructured. Given the relatively large trade orders by pension funds, a single trade will normally generate thousands of dollars in commissions to the investment company. Although managers could reduce transaction costs by using a discount brokerage service, they would not receive advice. The advice from full-service securities firms may be in the form of mailed information or even through personal meetings with head advisors of these companies.

Portfolio managers have access to computers to use their time efficiently. Computer terminals show current stock prices of any selected stocks, as well as all news issues and articles that relate to any selected companies. Other terminals are available for screening the entire population of available stocks (to aid selection of those that satisfy a variety of requirements). For example, the portfolio manager may wish to consider investment in companies that can meet specific guidelines on the price/earnings ratio, liquidity ratio, and so on. The terminal can, within seconds, identify the companies that meet these requirements.

The performance of pension fund managers is sometimes assessed on a short-term basis. This creates a dilemma for them, because the nature of the portfolio is to provide long-run benefits to the employees. Consequently, the risk-return preferences of a pension fund's portfolio managers can differ from those of the employees that the pension fund represents, and this may explain the frequent shifting in the portfolio composition of pension funds.

buyouts. General Motors' pension fund portfolio includes venture capital and international securities. The pension fund portfolio of Xerox Corporation includes venture capital and junk bonds. Some pension funds even invest in commodities, futures contracts, and stock options for speculative purposes.

PERFORMANCE EVALUATION OF PENSION PORTFOLIOS

If a manager has the flexibility to adjust the relative proportion of stocks versus bonds, the portfolio performance should be compared to a benchmark that would likely have represented a passive strategy. For example, assume that the general long-run plan is a balance of 60 percent bonds and 40 percent stocks. Also assume that management has decided to create a more bond-intensive portfolio in anticipation of lower interest rates. The risk-adjusted returns on this actively managed portfolio could be compared to a benchmark portfolio composed of 60 percent times a bond index plus 40 percent times a stock index.

Any difference between the performance of the pension portfolio and the benchmark portfolio would result from (1) the manager's shift in relative proportion of bonds versus stocks and (2) the composition of bonds and stocks within their respective portfolios. A pension portfolio could conceivably have stocks that outperform the stock index and bonds that outperform the bond index yet be outperformed by the benchmark portfolio when the shift in the relative bond/stock proportion backfires. In this example, a period of rising interest rates could have caused the pension portfolio to be outperformed by the benchmark portfolio.

In many cases, the performances of stocks and bonds in a pension fund are evaluated separately. Stock portfolio risk is usually measured by the portfolio's beta, or the sensitivity to movements in a stock index (such as the S&P 500). Bond portfolio risk can be measured by the bond portfolio's sensitivity to a bond index or to a particular proxy for interest rates.

Performance of Pension Portfolio Managers

Many pension funds hire several portfolio managers to manage the assets. The general objective of portfolio managers is to make investments that will earn a large enough return to adequately meet future payment obligations. Recent research by the Brookings Institute measured the investment performance of 769 stock portfolios managed by pension portfolio managers over the 1983–1989 period, and found that these portfolios earned 1.3 percent less per year than the S&P 500 index. This implies that for every $1 billion invested, the pension portfolios earn $1.3 million less per year on average. These results do not even consider expenses resulting from hiring portfolio managers and from engaging in securities transactions. Based on the results, pension funds might consider investing in indexed mutual funds, which would perform as well as the market without requiring the pension plan to incur expenses for portfolio management.

PENSION REGULATIONS

The regulations of pension funds vary with the type of plan. For defined-contribution plans, the sponsoring firm's only responsibility is its contributions to the fund. The primary government regulation is the set of Internal Revenue Service tax rules that apply to pension fund income.

Before 1974, private pension funds were criticized for unfair treatment of participants. For example, some pension plans required 25 straight years of continuous service to be vested and thus for participants to qualify for their pension. Any time short of the specified number of years resulted in no pension at all. Another criticism was that some companies were underfunded and consequently unable to provide the benefits promised to employees at the time of retirement.

A third criticism was that most pension plans had committed to a fixed amount of benefits, so that above-average growth of the portfolio value offered no additional pension benefits to employees, while very poor performance could cause benefits to fall short of what was originally promised. Under such conditions, employees would naturally prefer more conservative investment decisions by the portfolio managers.

To resolve these problems, the Employee Retirement Income Security Act (ERISA) of 1974 (also called the Pension Reform Act) was enacted. It requires three vesting schedule options from which a pension fund could choose:

1. One hundred percent vesting after 10 years of service.
2. Graded vesting, with 25 percent vesting after 5 years of service, increasing 5 percent per year over the next 5 years, and then 10 percent vesting over the following 5 years, reaching 100 percent vesting after 15 years.
3. Fifty percent vesting when a participant's age and years of service sum to 45, increasing by 10 percent per year to 100 percent vesting 5 years later.

These options applied to all employees who worked at least 1,000 hours over the previous year and were at least 25 years of age.

The options were revised as of 1989 to shorten the time necessary to become vested. Corporations were required to choose between these vesting options:

1. One hundred percent vesting after 5 years of service.
2. Graded vesting, with 20 percent vesting in the third year, 40 percent in the fourth, 60 percent in the fifth, 80 percent in the sixth, and 100 percent in the seventh year.

Although ERISA's vesting options were revised as shown here, ERISA was responsible for originally specifying the vesting options available to pension funds.

An additional stipulation of ERISA is that any contributions be invested in a prudent manner, meaning that pension funds should concentrate their investments in high-grade securities. Although this was implicitly expected before, ERISA explicitly acknowledges this so-called fiduciary responsibility (monitored by the U.S. Department of Labor) to encourage portfolio managers to serve the interests of the employees rather than themselves. Pension plans can face legal ramifications if they do not oblige.

ERISA also allows employees changing employers to transfer any vested amount into the pension plan of their new employer or to invest it into an **Individual Retirement Account (IRA)**. With either alternative, taxes on the vested amount are still deferred until retirement when the funds become available.

The Pension Benefit Guarantee Corporation

A final result of ERISA was the establishment of the Pension Benefit Guarantee Corporation (PBGC), intended to provide insurance on pension plans. This federally chartered agency guarantees that participants of defined-benefit pension plans will receive their benefits upon retirement. If the pension fund is incapable of fully providing the benefits promised, the PBGC makes up the difference. The PBGC does not receive government support. It is financed by annual premiums, income from assets acquired from terminated pension plans, and income generated by investments. As of 1994, it charged defined-benefit plans an annual insurance premium of $19 for every employee in the plan. It also receives employer-liability payments when an employer terminates its pension plan.

About 40 million Americans, or one-third of the work force, have pension plans insured by the PBGC. As a wholly owned independent government agency, it differs from other federal regulatory agencies in that it has no regulatory powers. Although it has had negative net worth since its creation in 1974, its cash flow has been sufficient to cover current expenses. By 1994, the PBGC's accumulated deficit was about $2.7 billion. Recent terminations of underfunded pension plans of Pan American World Airways and Eastern Airlines required substantial financial support from the PBGC.

The PBGC monitors pension plans periodically to determine whether they can adequately provide the benefits they have guaranteed. If the plan is judged inadequate, it is terminated and the PBGC (or a PBGC appointee) takes control as the fund manager. The PBGC has a claim on part of a firm's net worth if needed to support the underfunded pension assets.

The PBGC's funding requirements depend on all the pension funds it monitors. Because the market values of these funds are similarly susceptible to economic conditions, funding requirements are volatile over time. A poor economic environment will force depressed stock prices and simultaneously reduce the asset values of most pension funds.

When companies experience problems, they often cut their pension contributions to the minimum funding level established by ERISA. In a sense, the funding of pensions becomes a financing source for firms experiencing cash flow problems. Nevertheless, the obligated benefits to be paid out continue to accumulate (on defined-benefit plans). As an example, in 1981 Allis-Chalmers pension plans were more than 60 percent funded. However, the company used minimum funding during the early 1980s, and pension assets declined because of payments to the large retired work force. In 1985, when the PBGC took over, the plan was just 3 percent funded.

The financial burden placed on the PBGC escalated in September 1986, when LTV Corporation terminated one of its pension plans. In January 1987, the PBGC assumed three other LTV pension plans. Not only did this substantially increase the PBGC's accumulated deficit, but it also strained cash flow. Consequently, the PBGC liquidated some of its investments to cover current cash outflows.

To resolve potential funding problems faced by PBGC, various remedies have been considered. Laws have been imposed to prevent the dumping of unfunded liabilities on the PBGC. In 1990 the Supreme Court overruled two lower court decisions, ruling that the PBGC could return the responsibility of the defined benefits to LTV Corporation. This is an important ruling because it places more responsibility with the firms by preventing firms from using the PBGC to support their own obligations.

Self-employed individuals are unable to utilize pension plans offered by other companies, but they can establish their own pension plan, called a Keogh Plan. Contributions of a maximum specified amount can be deposited with a depository institution, life insurance company, or securities firm. These institutions manage Keogh Plans but allow the contributor some discretion as to how the funds should be invested.

Accounting Regulations

Recent accounting rule revisions have allowed companies to more quickly recognize gains and losses. Consequently, the volatility of pension fund returns may increase. Although a thorough discussion of the new rules is beyond the scope of this discussion, it should be noted that the rules could have a significant impact on the portfolio composition of pension funds. Those managers concerned about return volatility may take a more conservative approach to offset the impact of the accounting rule revisions.

The new rules require underfunded pension plans to claim their degree of underfunding as a liability on their balance sheets. This rule is especially relevant to unionized industries that have accommodated collective bargaining requests with the use of pension funds, thereby increasing the degree by which they are underfunded.

Because values of stocks are more volatile than bonds, the asset value of a pension fund composed of stocks is more susceptible to a market downturn. Such a decline could cause underfunding and the subsequent reporting of it on the balance sheet. Consequently, pension funds may attempt to avoid such a possibility by reducing their proportion of stocks.

INTERACTION WITH OTHER FINANCIAL INSTITUTIONS

Exhibit 25.2 illustrates the participation of various financial institutions and markets for managing a pension fund. First, the sponsor corporation decides on a trust pension fund through a commercial bank's trust department or an insured pension fund through an insurance company. The financial institution that is delegated the task of managing the pension fund then receives periodic contributions and invests them. Many investments into the stock, bond, or mortgage market require the brokerage services of securities firms. Managers of pensions instruct securities firms on the type and amount of investment instruments to purchase. In some cases, the financial institutions may bypass securities firms by purchasing a directly placed new issue of bonds or stocks by a corporation. The premiums contributed to pension funds are ultimately used to provide financing for corporations and governments that issue securities. Exhibit 25.3 summarizes the interaction between pension funds and other financial institutions.

PARTICIPATION IN FINANCIAL MARKETS

Because pension fund portfolios are normally dominated by stocks and bonds, the participation of pension fund managers in the stock and bond markets is obvious. Pension fund managers also participate in money and mortgage

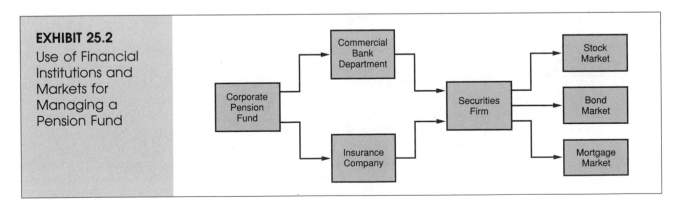

EXHIBIT 25.2

Use of Financial Institutions and Markets for Managing a Pension Fund

EXHIBIT 25.3 Interaction between Pension Funds and Other Financial Institutions

TYPE OF FINANCIAL INSTITUTION	INTERACTION WITH PENSION FUNDS
Commercial banks	■ Commercial banks sometimes manage pension funds. ■ Pension funds commonly purchase commercial loans that are sold by commercial banks in the secondary market.
Insurance companies	■ Insurance companies sometimes create annuities for pension funds.
Mutual funds	■ Some pension funds invest in various mutual funds, which allows them to achieve diversification without incurring excessive transaction costs.
Brokerage firms and investment banking firms	■ Brokerage firms normally execute securities transactions for pension funds. ■ Brokerage firms offer investment advice to pension portfolio managers. ■ Investment banking firms commonly act as advisors on leveraged buyouts in which pension funds participate. ■ Investment banking firms underwrite newly issued stocks and bonds that are purchased by pension funds.

markets to fill out the remainder of their respective portfolios. They sometimes utilize the futures and options markets as well in order to partially insulate their portfolio performance from interest rate and/or stock market movements. Exhibit 25.4 summarizes how pension fund managers participate in various financial markets.

FOREIGN INVESTMENT BY PENSION FUNDS

Several pension funds allocate a portion of their investment to foreign stocks and bonds. Because they are consequently exposed to exchange rate risk, they sometimes use forward contracts, currency futures contracts, and currency options contracts to hedge their exposure. Some pension funds have taken positions in currency futures and options for speculative reasons rather than to hedge exposure. The level of pension fund interest in international investing grew during the early 1990s when the U.S. dollar weakened against major currencies. The exchange rate-adjusted returns on foreign stocks and bonds generally exceeded returns on U.S. securities during this period. Many pension fund portfolios now contain some international securities as a means of effective diversification.

EXHIBIT 25.4 Participation of Pension Funds in Financial Markets

FINANCIAL MARKET	PARTICIPATION BY PENSION FUNDS
Money markets	▪ Pension fund managers maintain a small proportion of liquid money market securities that can be liquidated when they wish to increase investment in stocks, bonds, or other alternatives.
Bond markets	▪ At least 25 percent of a pension fund portfolio is typically allocated to bonds. Portfolios of defined-benefit plans usually have a higher concentration of bonds than defined-contribution plans. Pension fund managers frequently conduct transactions in the bond market.
Mortgage markets	▪ Pension portfolios frequently contain some mortgages, although the relative proportion is low compared with bonds and stocks.
Stock markets	▪ At least 30 percent of a pension fund portfolio is typically allocated to stocks. In general, defined-contribution plans usually have a higher concentration of stocks than defined-benefit plans.
Futures markets	▪ Some pension funds use futures contracts on debt securities and on bond indexes to hedge the exposure of their bond holdings to interest rate risk. In addition, some pension funds use futures on stock indexes to hedge against market risk. Other pension funds use futures contracts for speculative purposes.
Options markets	▪ Some pension funds use stock options to hedge against movements of particular stocks. They may also use options on futures contracts to secure downside protection against stock price movements.
Swap markets	▪ Pension funds commonly engage in interest rate swaps to hedge the exposure of their bond and mortgage portfolios to interest rate risk.

SUMMARY

- For defined-benefit pension plans, the contributions are dictated by the benefits that are specified. For defined-contribution pension plans, the benefits are determined by the accumulated contributions and the returns on the pension fund investments.

- Pension funds can use a matched funding strategy, in which investment decisions are made with the objective of generating cash flows that match planned outflow payments. Alternatively, pension funds can use a projective funding strategy, which attempts to capitalize on expected market or interest rate movements.

- Defined-benefit pension plans of many corporations are significantly under-funded. These corporations may experience cash flow problems in the future as their employees are scheduled to receive retirement benefits.

- The Pension Benefit Guarantee Corporation (PBGC) provides insurance on pension plans. It monitors existing pension plans and has the power to take control of plans that are judged to be inadequate.

QUESTIONS

1. Compare the amount of saving as a percentage of disposable income in the United States to that of other countries. What does this comparison suggest about the importance of pension funds in the U.S.?

2. Why were pension plans adversely affected during the Great Depression?

3. What was the main reason for the growth of pension plans during World War II and during the Korean War?

4. What is the danger of an underfunded pension plan?

5. Describe a defined-benefit pension plan.

6. Describe a defined-contribution plan and explain how it differs from a defined-benefit plan.

7. What type of general guidelines may be specified for a trust that is managing a pension fund?

8. Why do some corporations allocate portions of their pension fund to be managed by different trusts (rather than using a single trust)?

9. Explain the general difference in the composition of pension portfolios managed by trusts versus those managed by insurance companies. Explain why this difference occurs.

10. Explain the risk-return characteristics of a leveraged buyout as a potential investment by pension portfolio managers.

11. Explain a general difference between the portfolio composition of private pension funds and that of public pension funds.

12. How can pension funds reduce their exposure to interest rate risk?

13. What are bond index portfolios, and how are they useful to pension fund managers?

14. How can portfolio managers limit the risk of the pension portfolio, even when they make risky investments?

15. Explain why the objective of the pension fund manager may not necessarily be similar to the objective of employees participating in the pension plan.

16. Identify some common criticisms of private pension plans before 1974 that led to ERISA.

17. Explain how ERISA affected employees who frequently change employers.

18. How have some corporations used their pension plans as a source of funds to finance corporate operations?

19. What is the main purpose of the Pension Benefit Guarantee Corporation (PBGC)?

SEC Challenges Pension-Plan Funding

Laura Jereski, New York

Even some of the healthiest pension plans may soon look a little pale.

The Securities and Exchange Commission is lobbing what amounts to a grenade into the books of many large companies, by effectively challenging whether many corporate pension plans are as fat and happy as they seem.

As a result, a number of companies that today are happily sitting with more assets than they need to meet their pension obligations will lose this cherished "overfunded" status this year, falling into the underfunded realm.

And the corporate fallout will be big.

Some companies will be forced to start making cash contributions to their pension funds once again. Some will show lower earnings. And some will be disclosing the tab they face for pension obligations on their balance sheets for the first time.

"People are sitting up and taking notice because it will mean disclosing larger pension obligations than they have in the past," says Mark Mactas, vice president and actuarial consultant at Towers Perrin in Chicago.

Technically, the SEC is stepping up the pressure by making a stricter application of existing pension-accounting standards. But there's no doubt of the agency's resolve.

Minimizing Obligations

The agency is concerned that many companies have been minimizing their obligations to retirees by using a high assumed interest rate to calculate today's pension liability. To better reflect today's lower-rate climate, the SEC is urging companies to reduce this "discount rate" to about 7%, roughly the current yield on long-term, high-grade corporate bonds.

According to a Goldman, Sachs & Co. study, 307 companies out of 366 surveyed assume a discount rate of 8% or more to calculate pension obligations. These companies will show a higher pension liability if they assume a 7% discount rate.

About 80% of companies with defined-benefit pension plans are currently overfunded. (Defined-benefit plans are the kind where the company promises to pay a certain amount at retirement, rather than setting aside money for an employee to manage for good or ill.) Many have relied on robust stock and bond markets as well as aggressive discount assumptions to avoid putting money into the pension funds. Even though companies use different assumptions for accounting and for funding, the accounting change will make it hard for them to resist the pressure to contribute cash.

Richard Jos, an attorney with Wyatt Co., says he has been pushing clients to start funding again.

"It's a shock to them, because they were so well overfunded during the 1980s," he says. "I'm not going to mince words: They are not happy campers."

Many shareholders won't be either. Lowering the discount rate one percentage point can increase a company's pension liability by between 10% and 25%, depending on the age of the work force and the ratio of current employees to retirees.

Sharp Rise in Underfunding

The SEC's stance will increase the total underfunding of defined-benefit pension plans to $38 billion, from the $18 billion or so that companies currently show on financial statements, according to calculations by the Pension Benefit Guaranty Corp., the government agency that insures private pension plans.

The impact of the SEC's stricture will vary. Many companies with overfunded pension funds have recognized so-called pension income in earnings as a result of quirks in the accounting rules used to calculate annual pension expense. Thanks to pension accounting, **General Electric** Co.'s 1992 net income was $494 million, or 12% higher than it otherwise would have been, according to the Goldman Sachs report. GE, which didn't return calls, used a not-unusual 9% discount-rate assumption. A lower assumption would make that contribution to earnings shrink. (GE and other companies in the table wouldn't necessarily become underfunded.)

Many companies with modest overfunding and high discount assumptions could show a balance sheet liability as a result of the change. **Abbott Laboratories,** for example, enjoys a $293

Continued

CASE APPLICATION: UNDERFUNDED PENSION FUNDS

Continued

Under Pressure Plan sponsors with highest pension income in 1992		
COMPANY	**INCOME ($ MILLIONS)**	**DISCOUNT RATE**
General Electric	$494.0	9.00%
AT&T	441.0	8.00
USX-U.S. Steel	231.0	N.A.
GTE	168.0	8.00
Ameritech	110.5	5.80
U S West	108.4	N.A.
McDonnell Douglas	99.0	9.00
DuPont	83.0	8.50
Rockwell Int'l	54.8	9.00
Unocal	51.0	8.25

N.A. = Not available   SOURCE: *Goldman, Sachs & Co.*

istrants to use discount rates . . . that reflect the current level of interest rates at the next measurement date,'' namely the end of the corporate fiscal year.

SOURCE: *The Wall Street Journal*, November 17, 1993, p. C1. Reprinted by permission of *The Wall Street Journal*, © 1993 Dow Jones & Company, Inc. All rights reserved worldwide.

QUESTIONS

1. Explain the logic behind the statement that companies minimize their pension obligations by assuming a high interest rate to calculate today's pension liability.

2. Explain a reasonable discount rate for determining the current value of the future pension obligations, which determines the level of funds that the pension fund should have available at the current time. (Should the discount rate be based on recent stock returns, recent bond returns, today's long-term Treasury bond yield, today's corporate bond yield, or what?)

3. Consider a company that uses a high rate of return assumption in order to reduce the level of funds needed for its pension fund today. Explain how this assumption may alter the investment strategy of the pension fund portfolio managers.

million surplus in its pension fund due partly to the 9% discount rate the company uses to calculate pension obligations.

But the nastiest shock may come to shareholders of companies that already show a small liability.

''If you have a $15 million liability on your balance sheet because pension assets are $85 million and pension liabilities are $100 million, a one-percentage-point change in the discount rate will almost double the number on the company's balance sheet,'' says Lawrence Bader, a Salomon Brothers vice president. For example, the $161 million unfunded liability **Merck** & Co. shows on its balance sheet will swell when the company lowers its discount rate to 7% from 9%.

The SEC's hard line is coming as a surprise to many companies, consultants say, even though the agency is merely enforcing an accounting standard that has been in effect since 1987. The SEC recently decided to increase pressure on companies to conform to the accounting standard, Financial Accounting Standard 87, after word got out that it was conferring with companies privately.

SEC chief accountant Walter Schuetze addressed a letter for Timothy S. Lucas, director of research at the Financial Accounting Standards Board, in September to emphasize that the SEC ''expects reg-

References

Antler, Jacob, and Yehuda Kahane. "The Gross and Net Replacement Ratios in Designing Pension Schemes and in Financial Planning: The Israeli Experience." *Journal of Risk and Insurance* (June 1987): 283–297.

Arnott, Robert, and Peter L. Bernstein. "The Right Way to Manage Your Pension Fund." *Harvard Business Review* (January–February 1988): 95–102.

Coggin, T. Daniel, Frank J. Fabozzi, and Shafiqur Rahman. "The Investment Performance of U.S. Equity Pension Fund Managers: An Empirical Investigation." *Journal of Finance* (July 1993): 1039–1055.

Ehrlich, Edna E. "Foreign Pension Fund Investments in the United States." *Quarterly Review*, Federal Reserve Bank of New York (Spring 1983): 1–12.

Estrella, Arturo. "Corporate Use of Pension Overfunding." *Quarterly Review*, Federal Reserve Bank of New York (Spring 1984): 17–25.

Hubbard, R. Glenn. "Pension Wealth and Individual Saving." *Journal of Money, Credit, and Banking* (May 1986): 167–178.

Ippolito, Richard A. "The Economic Burden of Corporate Pension Liabilities." *Financial Analysts Journal* (January–February 1986): 22–34.

Mitchell, Mark L., and J. Harold Mulherin. "The Stock Price Response to Pension Terminations and the Relation of Terminations with Corporate Takeovers." *Financial Management* (Autumn 1989): 41–56.

Munnell, Alicia H. "The Current Status of Social Security Financing." *New England Economic Review*, Federal Reserve Bank of Boston (May–June 1983): 46–62.

————. "ERISA—The First Decade: Was the Legislation Consistent with Other National Goals?" *New England Economic Review*, Federal Reserve Bank of Boston (November–December 1984): 44–64.

Sellon, Gordon H. "Changes in Financial Intermediation: The Role of Pension and Mutual Funds." *Economic Review*, Federal Reserve Bank of Kansas City, 3rd Quarter 1992, pp. 53–70.

CHAPTER 26

INSURANCE COMPANIES

Insurance companies serve financial markets by supplying funds to a variety of financial and nonfinancial corporations as well as government agencies.

The specific objectives of this chapter are to:

- describe the different types of life insurance policies,
- describe the main uses of insurance company funds,
- explain the exposure of insurance companies to various forms of risk, and
- describe how insurance companies are regulated.

BACKGROUND

Life insurance companies compensate (provide benefits to) the beneficiary of a policy upon the policyholder's death. They charge policyholders a premium that should reflect the probability of making a payment to the beneficiary as well as the size and timing of the payment. Despite the difficulty of forecasting the life expectancy of a given individual, life insurance companies have historically forecasted with reasonable accuracy the benefits they would have to provide beneficiaries. Because they hold a large portfolio of policies, they use actuarial tables and mortality figures to forecast the percentage of policies that will require compensation over a given period, based on characteristics that would affect this percentage (such as the age distribution of policyholders).

In 1994 there were about 2,000 life insurance companies, classified by either stock or mutual ownership. A stock-owned company is owned by its shareholders, while a mutual life insurance company is owned by its policyholders. About 95 percent of U.S. life insurance companies are stock owned, and in recent years some of the mutual life insurance companies converted to become stock owned. As with the savings institutions industry, a primary reason for the conversions was to gain access to capital through the issuance of stock. The mutual companies are relatively large and make up more than 46 percent of the total assets of all life insurance companies.

TYPES OF LIFE INSURANCE POLICIES

In recent years, a variety of life insurance policies have been offered. Some of the more common types of policies are described here.

Whole Life Insurance

From the perspective of the insured policyholders, **whole life insurance** protects them until death or as long as premiums are promptly paid. In addition, whole life policies provide a form of savings to policyholders. They build a cash value that the policyholder is entitled to even if the policy is cancelled.

From the perspective of the life insurance company, whole life policies generate periodic (typically quarterly or semiannual) premiums that can be invested until the policyholder's death, at which time benefits are paid to the beneficiary. The amount of benefits is typically fixed.

Term Insurance

Term insurance is temporary, providing insurance only over a specified term, and does not build a cash value for policyholders. The premiums paid represent only insurance, not savings. It is, however, significantly less expensive than whole life insurance. Policyholders must compare the cash value of whole life insurance to their additional costs to determine whether it is preferable to term insurance. Those who prefer to invest their savings themselves would likely opt for term insurance.

To accommodate people who need more insurance now than later, decreasing term insurance is available in which the benefits paid to a beneficiary decrease over time. This form of insurance is common for a family with a mortgage. As time passes, the mortgage balance decreases, and the family is more capable of surviving without the breadwinner's earnings. Thus, less compensation would be needed in later years.

Variable Life Insurance

Under **variable life insurance,** the benefits awarded by the life insurance company to a beneficiary vary with the assets backing the policy. Until 1984, the premium payments on variable life insurance were constant over time. However, flexible-premium variable life insurance has been available since 1984, allowing flexibility on the size and timing of payments.

Universal Life Insurance

Universal life insurance combines the features of term and whole-life insurance. It specifies a period of time over which the policy will exist but also builds a cash value for policyholders over time. Interest is accumulated from the cash value until the policyholder uses those funds. Universal life insurance allows flexibility on the size and timing of the premiums, too. The growth in a policy's cash value is dependent on this pace. The premium payment is divided into two portions. The first is used to pay the death benefit identified in the policy and to cover any administrative expenses. The second is used for investments and reflects savings for the policyholder. The Internal Revenue Service forbids the value of these savings from exceeding the policy's death benefits.

Group Plans

Life insurance companies also commonly offer employees of a corporation a **group life policy.** This service has become quite popular and has generated a large volume of business in recent years. It can be distributed at a low cost because of its high volume. Group life coverage now makes up about 40 percent of total life coverage, compared to only 26 percent of total life insurance coverage in 1974.

In recent years, group life insurance has often covered not only the group members but their respective dependents as well. Group policies are most popular for employers and employees. In addition, some unions and professional associations participate in these plans.

PROVISION OF HEALTH CARE INSURANCE

Many insurance companies such as Cigna and Traveler's Insurance have begun to operate **health maintenance organizations** (HMOs), which are intermediaries between purchasers and providers of health care. Employers of a company covered by an HMO are charged an annual fee or premium in return for provision of all medical expenses by a medical staff designated by the HMO. Because health care costs have been frequently underestimated, many HMOs experienced losses in recent years, and some insurance companies have sold their HMOs as a result. The structure of health care insurance is in the process of being reformed.

SOURCES AND USES OF FUNDS

Life insurance companies obtain much of their funds from premiums, as shown in Exhibit 26.1. Total premiums (life plus health insurance) represent about 35 percent of total income. The next most important source of funds is through provision of **annuity plans,** which offer a predetermined amount of retirement income to individuals. The annuity plans have become very popular and now generate proportionately more income to insurance companies than in previous years. The third largest source of funds is investment income, which results from the investment of funds received from premium payments.

The uses of funds by life insurance companies strongly influence their performance. Life insurance companies are major institutional investors. In fact, four of the five largest institutional investors in the United States are in the insurance business. Exhibit 26.2, which displays the assets of life insurance companies,

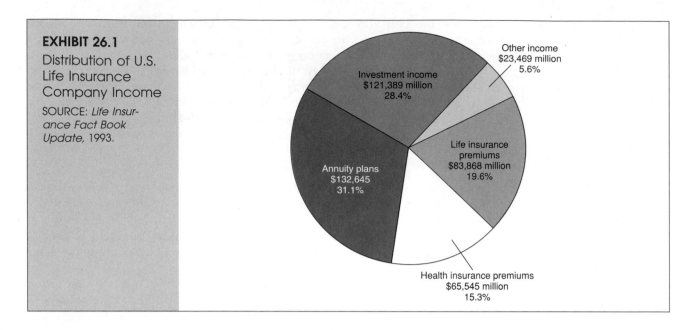

EXHIBIT 26.1

Distribution of U.S. Life Insurance Company Income

SOURCE: *Life Insurance Fact Book Update*, 1993.

indicates how funds have been used. The main assets are described in the following subsections.

Government Securities

Life insurance companies invest in U.S. Treasury securities, state and local government bonds, and foreign bonds. They maintain investment in U.S. Treasury securities because of their safety and liquidity, but also invest in bonds issued by foreign governments in an attempt to enhance return.

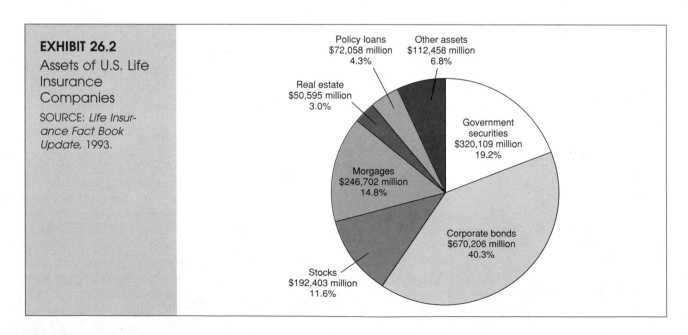

EXHIBIT 26.2

Assets of U.S. Life Insurance Companies

SOURCE: *Life Insurance Fact Book Update*, 1993.

Corporate Securities

Corporate bonds represent the most popular asset of life insurance companies. There is usually a mix between medium- and long-term bonds for cash management and liquidity needs. Although corporate bonds provide a higher yield than government securities, they have a higher degree of default risk. Some insurance companies focus on high-grade corporate bonds, while others invest a portion of their funds in junk bonds.

Because life insurance companies expect to maintain a portion of their long-term securities until maturity, this portion can be somewhat illiquid. Thus, they have the flexibility to obtain some high-yielding, directly placed securities whereby they can directly negotiate the provisions. Because such nonstandardized securities are less liquid, life insurance companies balance their asset portfolio with other more liquid securities. A minor portion of corporate securities are foreign. The foreign holdings typically represent industrialized countries and are therefore considered to have low default risk. Of course, the market values of these foreign bonds would still be susceptible to interest rate and currency fluctuations.

Insurance companies also invest in corporate stocks, although their holdings in stocks are significantly less than their bond holdings. Exhibit 26.3 illustrates the dollar value of bond and stock holdings over time. The dollar value of stock holdings has consistently increased, but not by as much as bond holdings.

The stock market crash of October 1987 affected life insurance companies differently because of differences in the proportion of funds they allocated to stocks. For example, Prudential-Bache Securities Inc. had only about 3 percent of its funds invested in stocks at the time of the crash, lower than most other insurance companies. However, some of its other investments, such as junk bonds (used to finance leveraged buyouts) were adversely affected because the risk perception of investors increased in response to the crash.

Mortgages

Life insurance companies hold all types of mortgages, including one- to four-family, multifamily, commercial, and farm-related. These mortgages are typically originated by another financial institution and then sold to insurance companies in the secondary market. Yet, they are still serviced by the originating financial institution. As shown in Exhibit 26.4, commercial mortgages make up more than 80 percent of total mortgages held by insurance companies. They help to finance shopping centers and office buildings.

Real Estate

Although life insurance companies finance real estate by purchasing mortgages, their return is limited to the mortgage payments, as they are simply acting as a creditor. In an attempt to achieve higher returns, they sometimes purchase the real estate themselves and lease it out for commercial purposes. The ownership of the real estate offers them the opportunity to generate very high returns but also exposes them to greater risk. Real estate values can be volatile over time and can have a significant effect on the market value of a life insurance company's asset portfolio.

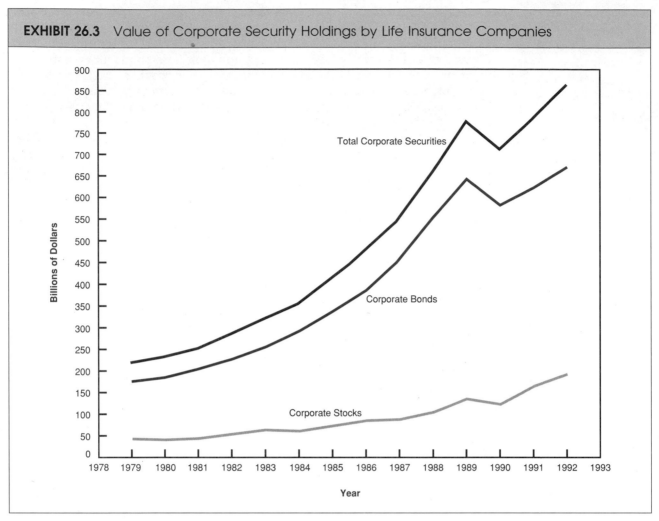

EXHIBIT 26.3 Value of Corporate Security Holdings by Life Insurance Companies

SOURCE: *Federal Reserve Bulletin,* various issues, and *Life Insurance Fact Book Update,* 1993.

Exhibit 26.5 illustrates the dollar value of mortgage and real estate holdings over time. Although investment in both types of assets has grown over time, mortgage holdings continue to be much larger.

Policy Loans

Life insurance companies lend a small portion of their funds to whole-life policyholders (called policy loans). Whole life policyholders can borrow up to their policy's cash value, at a guaranteed rate of interest as stated in their policy over a specified period of time. Other sources of funds for individuals typically do not guarantee an interest rate at which they can borrow. For this reason, policyholders tend to borrow more from life insurance companies during periods of rising interest rates, when alternative forms of borrowing would be more expensive.

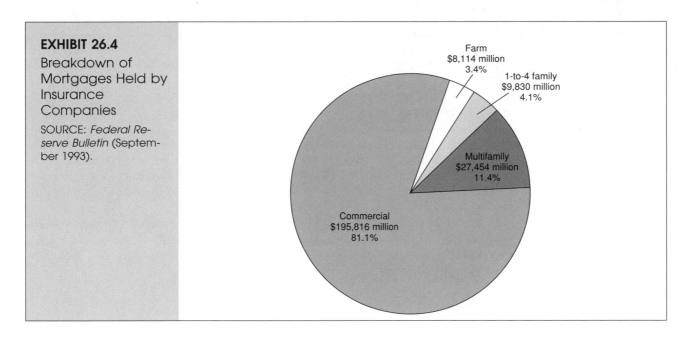

EXHIBIT 26.4

Breakdown of Mortgages Held by Insurance Companies

SOURCE: *Federal Reserve Bulletin* (September 1993).

Farm
$8,114 million
3.4%

1-to-4 family
$9,830 million
4.1%

Multifamily
$27,454 million
11.4%

Commercial
$195,816 million
81.1%

EXHIBIT 26.5 Value of Mortgages and Real Estate Held by Life Insurance Companies

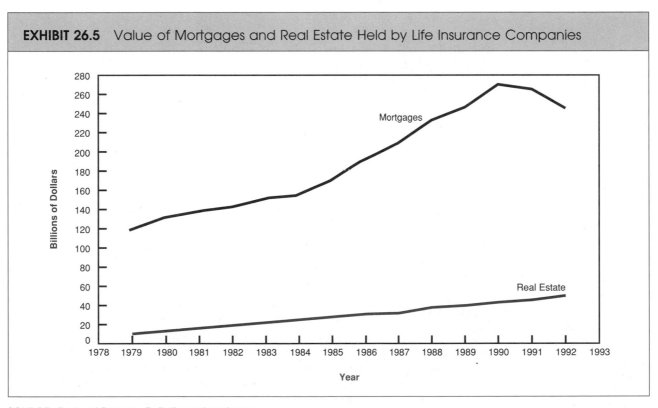

SOURCE: *Federal Reserve Bulletin,* various issues.

EXPOSURE TO RISK

The major types of risk faced by life insurance companies are interest rate risk, default risk, market risk, and liquidity risk.

Interest Rate Risk

Because life insurance companies carry a large amount of fixed-rate long-term securities, the market value of their asset portfolio can be very sensitive to interest rate fluctuations. When interest rates increase, life insurance companies are unable to fully capitalize on these rates, because much of their funds are tied up in long-term bonds.

Life insurance companies have been reducing their average maturity on securities. In addition, they have been investing in long-term assets that offer floating rates, such as commercial mortgages. Both strategies reduce the impact of interest rate movements on the market value of their assets.

Insurance companies have become more aware of their exposure to interest rate risk and more knowledgeable about techniques to hedge the risk, increasingly utilizing futures contracts and interest rate swaps to manage their exposure.

Default Risk

The corporate bonds, mortgages, state and local government securities, and real estate holdings contained in the asset portfolio are subject to default risk. To deal with this risk, some life insurance companies typically invest only in securities assigned a high credit rating. They also diversify among securities issuers so that the repayment problems experienced by any single issuer will have only a minor impact on the overall portfolio. Yet, other insurance companies have invested heavily in risky assets, such as junk bonds. Two large insurance companies, First Executive Corp. and First Capital Corp., were taken over by insurance regulators in 1991 because of losses from investing in junk bonds.

Market Risk

A related risk to life insurance companies is market risk. A good example of market risk is the October 1987 stock market crash, which significantly reduced the market value of stock holdings of life insurance companies. The real estate holdings of insurance companies may be adversely affected by an economic downturn. Some insurance companies became insolvent in the early 1990s as a result of losses on real estate investments.

Liquidity Risk

An additional risk to life insurance companies is liquidity risk. A high frequency of claims at a single point in time could force liquidation of assets at a time when the market value is low, thereby depressing performance. Yet, claims due to death are not likely to occur simultaneously. Life insurance companies can therefore reduce their exposure to this risk by diversifying the age distribution of their customer base. If the customer base becomes unbalanced and is heavily concentrated at the older age group, life insurance companies should increase their proportion of liquid assets to prepare for a higher frequency of claims.

COULD THERE BE AN "INSURANCE COMPANY CRISIS"?

In April 1991, Executive Life Insurance (a subsidiary of First Executive Corporation) failed and was seized by regulators. This was the largest failure in the insurance industry. Sixty-three percent of Executive Life's assets were invested in junk bonds. One week later Executive Life of New York, another subsidiary of First Executive Corporation, was seized by regulators. The majority of its assets were also invested in junk bonds. About 20 percent of the junk bonds held by the parent and its subsidiaries were in default.

Forty-three insurance companies failed in 1989, and another 30 insurance companies failed in 1990. Yet most of these companies were small and did not attract as much attention as First Executive's failure. The problems experienced by First Executive caused some concern about a potential insurance company crisis, similar to the savings and loan crisis a few years earlier. There are some characteristics of insurance companies that make them less susceptible to a string of failures. First, although many insurance companies hold some junk bonds, the average proportion held is 6 percent of assets. Therefore, any possible further declines in the market value of junk bonds affect only a small portion of the asset portfolios maintained by life insurance companies. In addition, some state regulators impose a maximum limit on the proportion of junk bonds that insurance companies can hold and force the companies to set aside more reserves to cover possible losses on the bonds. Insurance companies are not backed by federal insurance, but most states maintain a fund (supported by healthy insurance companies) to back resident policyholders of a failed insurance company. As a result of concerns about the safety of life insurance companies, *more* regulations may be enforced to restore confidence in the industry.

Even though life insurance companies can attempt to balance their age distribution, they are still susceptible to a liquidity deficiency. As interest rates rise, consumers tend to accelerate their voluntary terminations of life insurance and use the funds to make their own investments. Consequently, the cash inflows to life insurance companies are reduced, endangering their liquidity position.

In 1991, financial problems of Mutual Benefit Life Insurance Co. caused policyholders to withdraw $550 million, which created a liquidity deficiency. Most of the withdrawals were from special retirement plans provided by Mutual Benefit for corporations that required periodic corporate contributions. Many corporations transferred their funds to other insurance companies. Because of the liquidity deficiency, Mutual Benefit was seized by insurance regulators. Several insurance companies responded to this event by restructuring their asset portfolios to contain more liquid securities.

ASSET MANAGEMENT

Because life insurance companies tend to receive premiums from policyholders for several years before paying out benefits to a beneficiary, their performance can be significantly affected by asset portfolio management. Like other financial

APPLIED RESEARCH

IMPACT OF UNEXPECTED INTEREST RATE MOVEMENTS ON STOCK RETURNS OF LIFE INSURANCE COMPANIES

A study by Scott and Peterson assessed the sensitivity of life insurance companies to interest rate movements during the 1977–1984 period, using the following regression model:

$$R_p = B_0 + B_1 R_m + B_2 ui + u$$

where R_p = stock returns of a portfolio of life insurance companies

R_m = percentage change in the market index (the S&P 500 Index was used as a proxy)

ui = a measure of unexpected interest rate changes (see the article for an explanation of the proxy used for this variable)

B_0 = intercept

B_1 = regression coefficient that measures the sensitivity of stock returns to the market index returns

B_2 = regression coefficient that measures the sensitivity of stock returns to the interest rate movements

u = error term

The coefficient B_1 was estimated to be 0.793 by the regression analysis, suggesting that a one percent change in the market is associated with a 0.793 percent change in the portfolio returns. Thus, the life insurance stocks are positively correlated with the market. The coefficient B_2 was estimated to be -0.437 by the regression analysis, suggesting that an unexpected one percent increase in interest rates is associated with a 0.437 percent decrease in stock returns of life insurance companies. This coefficient was found to be statistically significant. Thus, stock returns on life insurance companies are adversely affected by an unexpected increase in interest rates. These results are relevant to managers of life insurance companies and investors that consider purchasing stocks of such companies. Even if interest rates cannot be forecasted with perfect accuracy, investors would like to know how a company's stock returns will be affected by a variety of possible interest rate outcomes.

institutions, they adjust their asset portfolio to counter changes in the factors that affect their risk. If they expect a downturn in the economy, they may reduce their holdings of corporate stocks and real estate. If they expect higher interest rates, they may reduce their holdings of fixed-rate bonds and mortgages.

To cope with the existing forms of risk, life insurance companies attempt to balance their portfolio so that any adverse movements in the market value of some assets will be offset by favorable movements in others. For example, under the presumption that interest rates will move in tandem with inflation, life insurance companies can use real estate holdings to partially offset the potential adverse effect of inflation on bonds. When higher inflation causes higher interest rates, the market value of existing bonds decreases. However, the market values of real estate holdings tend to increase with inflation. Conversely, an environment of low or decreasing inflation may cause real estate values to stagnate but nevertheless have a favorable impact on the market value of bonds and mortgages (because interest rates would likely decline). Although such a strategy may be useful, it is much easier to implement on paper than in practice. Because real estate values can fluctuate to a great degree, life insurance companies allocate only a limited amount of funds to real estate. In addition, real estate is less liquid than most other assets.

Many insurance companies are diversifying into other businesses. For example, Traveler's Insurance Corporation and Prudential Bache provide a wide variety of financial products. Such a strategy not only provides diversification but also enables these companies to package products when policyholders desire to cover all these needs at once.

Overall, life insurance companies want to earn a reasonable return while maintaining their risk at a tolerable level. The degree to which they avoid or accept the various forms of risk depends on their degree of risk aversion. Those companies that accept a greater amount of risk in the asset portfolio are likely to generate a higher return. However, if market conditions move in an unexpected manner, they will be more severely damaged than companies that employed a more conservative approach.

PROPERTY AND CASUALTY INSURANCE

Property and casualty (PC) insurance protects against fire, theft, liability, and other events that result in economic or noneconomic damage. Property insurance protects businesses and individuals from the impact of financial risks associated with the ownership of property, such as buildings, automobiles, and other assets. Casualty insurance insures potential liabilities for harm to others as a result of product failure or accidents. PC insurance companies charge policyholders a premium that should reflect the probability of a payout to the insured, and the potential magnitude of the payout.

There are about 3,800 individual PC companies. No single company controls more than 10 percent of the property/casualty insurance market share.

The characteristics of PC insurance are much different from life insurance. First, the policies often last one year or less, as opposed to the long-term or even permanent life insurance policies. Second, PC insurance encompasses a wide variety of activities, ranging from auto insurance to business liability insurance. Life insurance is more focused. Third, future compensation amounts paid on PC insurance are more difficult to forecast than on life insurance. PC compensation depends on a variety of factors, including inflation, trends in terrorism, and the generosity of courts on lawsuits. These factors are difficult to forecast and can vary by areas of the country. Because of the greater uncertainty, PC insurance companies need to maintain a more liquid asset portfolio. Earnings can be quite volatile over time, as the premiums charged may be based on highly overestimated or underestimated compensation.

A unique aspect of the property and casualty insurance industry is its cyclical nature. As interest rates rise, companies tend to lower their rates to acquire more premium dollars to invest. They are hoping losses will hold off long enough to make the cheaper premium profitable through increased investment income. As interest rates decline, the price of insurance will rise to offset decreased investment income. If the timing of the cycle is not predicted well, a company can experience inadequate reserves and a drain on cash. This method of adapting prices to interest rates is called **cash flow underwriting.** It can backfire for companies that focus on what they can earn in the short run and ignore what they will pay out later.

Uses of Funds

The primary uses of funds for non-life (such as PC) insurance companies are illustrated in Exhibit 26.6. Municipal government securities dominate and are followed by Treasury bonds, then by other bonds. The growth of the corporate stock holdings has been more volatile than that of the other components. The most obvious difference in the asset structure of PC companies relative to life insurance companies is the much higher concentration of state and local government securities.

Performance

The performance of PC companies is highly sensitive to weather-related events that cause destruction and to laws on product liability. PC companies experienced poor performance in 1992, which was partially attributed to Hurricane Andrew. The performance is broken down in Exhibit 26.7.

REINSURANCE

Insurance companies commonly obtain **reinsurance,** which effectively allocates a portion of their return and risk to other insurance companies. It is similar to a commercial bank's acting as the lending agent by allowing other banks to participate in the loan. A particular PC insurance company may agree to insure a corporation but spread the risk by inviting other insurance companies to participate. Reinsurance allows a company to write larger policies, because a portion of the risk involved will be assumed by other companies.

The estimated number of companies willing to offer reinsurance has declined significantly because of generous court awards and the difficulty in assessing the

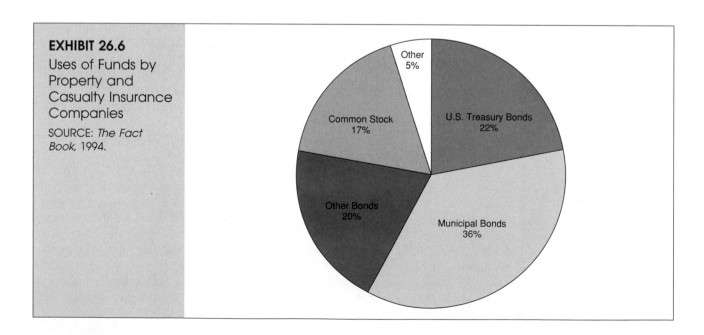

EXHIBIT 26.6
Uses of Funds by Property and Casualty Insurance Companies

SOURCE: *The Fact Book,* 1994.

- Other 5%
- U.S. Treasury Bonds 22%
- Common Stock 17%
- Other Bonds 20%
- Municipal Bonds 36%

EXHIBIT 26.7 Performance of Property & Casualty Insurance Companies, in Aggregate, 1992 (in billions)

Earned premiums	$226.0
Incurred loss	−199.1
Underwriting expenses	−61.5
Policyholder dividends and other items	−2.4
Underwriting gain (loss)	−36.0
Investment income	+33.4
Realized capital gains	+9.9
Income before taxes	+7.4
Taxes	−1.5
Net income	+5.8

SOURCE: *The Fact Book,* 1994.

amount of potential claims. For example, Centennial Insurance Company recently experienced losses of more than $200 million in the reinsurance business as a result of underestimating the amount of potential claims. Reinsurance policies are often described in the insurance industry as "having long tails," which implies that the probability distribution of possible returns on reinsurance is widely dispersed. Although many companies still offer reinsurance, their premiums have substantially increased in recent years. If the desire to offer reinsurance continues to decline, the primary insurers will be less able to "sell off" a portion of the risk they assume when writing policies. Consequently, they will be pressured to more closely evaluate the risk of the policies they write.

REGULATION OF INSURANCE COMPANIES

The insurance industry has been highly regulated by state agencies (called commissioners in some states). Each state attempts to make sure that insurance companies are providing adequate services and also approves the rates insurers may charge. Insurance company agents must be licensed. In addition, the forms used for policies are state approved to avoid misinterpretation of wording.

State regulators also evaluate the asset portfolio of insurance companies to ensure that reasonably safe investments are undertaken and that adequate reserves are maintained to protect policyholders. For example, some states have limited investment in junk bonds to no more than 20 percent of total assets.

The National Association of Insurance Commissioners (NAIC) facilitates cooperation among the various state agencies where an insurance issue is a national concern. It is involved in common reporting issues where it attempts to maintain a degree of uniformity. It also conducts research on insurance issues and participates in legislative discussions.

The Insurance Regulatory Information System (IRIS) has been developed by a committee of state insurance agencies to assist each state's regulatory duties. The IRIS compiles financial statements, lists of insurers, and other relevant information pertaining to the insurance industry. In addition, it assesses the companies' respective financial statements by calculating 11 ratios that are then evaluated by NAIC regulators in order to monitor the financial health of a company. The NAIC provides IRIS assessment results to all state insurance departments that can be used as a basis for comparison when evaluating the financial health of any company. The regulatory duties of state agencies often require a comparison of a particular insurance company to the industry norm. The comparison is conducted to assess one or more financial ratios of a company. Use of the industry norm facilitates the evaluation.

A regulatory system is designed to detect any problems of a company in time to search for a remedy before it deteriorates further. The more commonly used financial ratios assess a variety of relevant characteristics, including

- The ability of the company to absorb either losses or a decline in the market value of its investments
- Return on investment
- Relative size of operating expenses
- Liquidity of the asset portfolio

The objective of monitoring these characteristics is to ensure that insurance companies do not become overly exposed to default risk, interest rate risk, and liquidity risk.

In 1994, the NAIC required that life insurance companies must hold at least 10 times as much capital to back commercial properties and mortgages as the amount required to back A-rated bonds. This requirement represents a form of risk-based capital requirements that are also imposed on commercial banks. The intent is to impose higher capital requirements for life insurance companies that invest in riskier assets.

Regulation of Insurance Rates

In June 1986, the New York state legislature adopted a flex rating regulation, whereby companies could adjust their rates only within limits. To change rates beyond these limits requires approval from the state insurance department. Other states have also begun to set limits on rates. In addition, several states now require that insurance companies provide advance notice of premium changes. Regulators also are requiring full company disclosure of financial information so that they can determine whether premium adjustments are justified.

The regulation of rates is intended to help consumers, yet there is some concern that it will reduce competition and may force insurers to abandon insurance activities that are no longer profitable. The flex rating system may reduce the degree of price cutting, because there would be a limit to percentage price increases later on. This could be beneficial, as price cutting was so severe in the mid-1980s that it devastated the performance of many insurers.

PERFORMANCE EVALUATION OF INSURANCE COMPANIES _____

Some of the more common indicators of an insurance company's performance are quoted in investment service publications such as *Value Line*. A time series assessment of the dollar amount of life insurance and/or property-casualty insurance premiums indicates the growth in the company's insurance business. A time series analysis of investment income can be used to assess the performance

POINT OF INTEREST

EVALUATING THE PERFORMANCE OF INSURANCE COMPANIES

Annual reports are commonly used by investors to evaluate the financial condition of insurance companies. The Value Line Investment Survey provides a summary of financial proxies that measure the performance of insurance companies. An example of the Value Line analysis is shown here for Travelers Corp. The income of insurance companies is measured by the return on equity (referred to as "% Earned Net Worth"). Each column represents a specific year, so that the changes in performance of the savings institution (as measured by any particular income proxy) can be assessed. The beta of the insurance company is disclosed in the upper left corner. Additional information not shown here is also provided by Value Line.

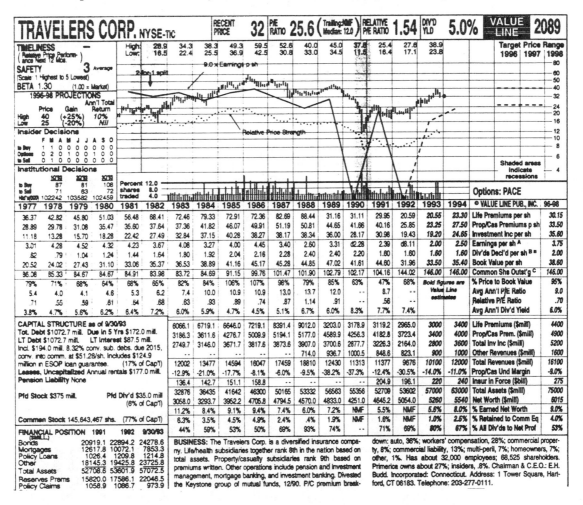

of the company's portfolio managers. However, the dollar amount of investment income is affected by several factors that are not under the control of portfolio managers, such as the amount of funds received as premiums that can be invested in securities, and market interest rates. In addition, a relatively low investment income may result from high concentration in stocks that pay low or no dividends rather than from poor performance.

Because insurance companies have unique characteristics, the financial ratios of other financial institutions are generally not applicable. Liquidity of an insurance company can be measured using the following ratio:

$$\text{Liquidity ratio} = \frac{\text{Invested assets}}{\text{Loss reserves and unearned premium reserves}}$$

The higher the ratio, the more liquid the company. This ratio can be evaluated by comparing it to the industry average.

The profitability of insurance companies is often assessed using the return on net worth (or policyholder's surplus) as a ratio, as follows:

$$\text{Return on net worth} = \frac{\text{Net profit}}{\text{Policyholder's surplus}}$$

Value Line refers to this ratio as "% earned net worth." Net profit consists of underwriting profits, investment income, and realized capital gains. Changes in this ratio over time should be compared to changes in the industry norms, as the norm is quite volatile over time.

The net profit encompasses all income sources and therefore provides only a general measure of profitability. Various financial ratios could be used to focus on a specific source of income. For example, underwriting gains or losses are measured by the net underwriting margin:

$$\text{Net underwriting margin} = \frac{\text{Premium income} - \text{Policy expenses}}{\text{Total assets}}$$

When policy expenses exceed premium income, the net underwriting margin is negative. Yet, as long as other sources of income can offset such a loss, net profit will still be positive.

INTERACTION WITH OTHER FINANCIAL INSTITUTIONS

Insurance companies interact with financial institutions in several ways, as summarized in Exhibit 26.8. They compete in one form or another with all types of financial institutions. As time passes, their penetration in nontraditional markets will likely increase. In addition, other financial institutions will continue to increase their offerings of insurance-related services, so that differences between insurance companies and other financial institutions are diminished. For example, some insurance companies offer certificates of deposit to investors, thereby competing directly with commercial banks for these offerings. In addition, Metropolitan Life Insurance Company recently began to offer a cash management

EXHIBIT 26.8 Interaction between Insurance Companies and Other Financial Institutions

TYPE OF FINANCIAL INSTITUTION	INTERACTION WITH INSURANCE COMPANIES
Commercial banks and savings and loan associations (S&Ls)	■ Insurance companies compete with banks and S&Ls for financing leveraged buyouts. ■ Insurance companies sometimes compete with banks and S&Ls by offering CDs. ■ Insurance companies sometimes compete with banks by offering an account from which checks can be written. ■ Insurance companies merge with banks in order to offer various banking services. ■ Insurance companies face increased competition for insurance-related services as banks and S&Ls attempt to offer such services. ■ Insurance companies commonly purchase loans that were originated by banks.
Finance companies	■ Insurance companies are sometimes acquired by finance companies and maintained as subsidiaries.
Securities firms	■ Insurance companies compete directly with securities firms by offering mutual funds.
Brokerage firms	■ Insurance companies compete directly with brokerage firms by offering securities-related services. ■ Insurance companies compete directly with brokerage firms that offer insurance-related services; many brokerage firms, such as Merrill Lynch, now offer a wide variety of insurance-related services and plan to increase their offerings in the future.
Investment banking firms	■ Insurance companies compete with investment companies for financing leveraged buyouts. ■ Insurance companies commonly purchase stocks and bonds issued by corporations that were underwritten by investment banking firms. ■ Insurance companies issue stock that is underwritten by investment banking firms.
Pension funds	■ Insurance companies offer to manage pension plans for corporations.

account from which checks can be written. Those insurance companies that have merged with brokerage firms (Prudential-Bache Securities Inc. is a prominent example) offer a wide variety of securities-related services. Several insurance companies offer mutual funds to investors. Some state insurance regulators have allowed commercial banks to underwrite and sell insurance, which will result in more intense competition in the insurance industry.

PARTICIPATION IN FINANCIAL MARKETS

The manner by which insurance companies use their funds indicates their form of participation in the various financial markets. Insurance companies are common participants in the stock, bond, and mortgage markets because their asset portfolio is concentrated in these securities. They also use the money markets to purchase short-term securities for liquidity purposes. Although their participation in money markets is less than in capital markets, they have recently increased their holdings of money market instruments such as Treasury bills and commercial paper. Some insurance companies use futures and options markets to hedge the impact of interest rates on bonds and mortgages and to hedge against anticipated movements in stock prices. The participation by insurance companies in the futures, options, and swap markets is generally for risk reduction rather than speculation. Exhibit 26.9 summarizes the manner by which life insurance companies participate in financial markets.

MULTINATIONAL INSURANCE COMPANIES

GLOBAL ASPECTS

Some life insurance companies are multinational corporations with subsidiaries and joint ventures in several countries. They became internationalized as a result of their efforts to penetrate new markets and to serve firms that operate overseas. Insurance companies with some international business may have reduced their exposure to the U.S. economy. However, they must comply with foreign regulations regarding services offered in foreign countries. While differences in regulations among countries increase the information costs of entering foreign markets, they may enable U.S. insurance companies to offer products or services that they could not offer in the United States.

Recently Taiwan, South Korea, and other countries have allowed U.S. insurance companies to establish branches in their countries. In addition, the European countries reduced their barriers to entry. The insurance regulations among European countries have been standardized, which allow insurance companies to more easily expand throughout Europe.

Many U.S. insurance companies have recently established insurance subsidiaries in less developed countries that are underinsured. For example, less than 3 percent of the people in Mexico have life or home insurance, and less than 25 percent have automobile insurance. The lack of a developed insurance market offered much potential to U.S. insurance companies. In addition, the economic growth in Mexico resulting from the North American Free Trade Agreement (NAFTA) was expected to create more demand for commercial insurance.

In many countries, commercial banks and other financial institutions have recently been allowed to offer various insurance services. Thus, the insurance market has become more competitive because of penetration by noninsurance firms, and by foreign insurance companies.

The reinsurance business is enhanced by international participation. U.S. insurance companies earn premiums when assuming specified risks from foreign insurance companies.

Many insurance companies use a portion of their funds to purchase foreign stocks and bonds. The investment in foreign securities is just one more way in which insurance companies can diversify their assets. Some of the foreign bonds

EXHIBIT 26.9 Participation of Insurance Companies in Financial Markets

FINANCIAL MARKET	PARTICIPATION BY INSURANCE COMPANIES
Money markets	■ Insurance companies maintain a portion of their funds in money market securities, such as Treasury bills and commercial paper, to maintain adequate liquidity.
Bond markets	■ Some life insurance company assets and PC insurance company assets are allocated to corporate bond portfolios. ■ Insurance companies frequently purchase bonds that are directly placed, and they are less likely to liquidate these bonds before maturity. ■ Insurance companies also purchase Treasury bonds for their safety and liquidity. ■ Some U.S. insurance companies purchase foreign bonds, primarily issued by Canadian firms.
Mortgage markets	■ Life insurance companies have, in aggregate, allocated some of their assets to a mortgage portfolio. They hold mostly conventional mortgages, as only a small percentage of their mortgages are federally insured. Although PC companies also hold mortgages, their mortgage portfolio represents a smaller percentage of total assets.
Stock markets	■ Life insurance companies have, in aggregate, allocated about 10 percent of their assets to a stock portfolio, while PC companies have allocated about 17 percent of their assets to a stock portfolio. Foreign stocks are often included in their stock portfolios.
Futures markets	■ Some insurance companies sell futures contracts on bonds or a bond market index to hedge their bond and mortgage portfolios against interest rate risk. ■ Some insurance companies take positions in stock market index futures to hedge their stock portfolios against market risk.
Options markets	■ Some insurance companies purchase call options on particular stocks that they plan to purchase in the near future. ■ Some insurance companies also purchase put options or write call options on stocks they own that may experience a temporary decline in price.
Swap markets	■ Insurance companies commonly engage in interest rate swaps to hedge the exposure of their bond and mortgage portfolios to interest rate risk.

purchased are issued by corporations, while others are issued by governments and international agencies. Because insurance companies have increased their investment in foreign securities, they more closely monitor the factors that influence foreign security returns, such as foreign stock market movements, foreign interest rates, and exchange rates.

Insurance companies have invested not only in foreign securities but also in foreign real estate. The majority of foreign real estate purchased by U.S. insurance companies is in Canada.

Although insurance companies have increased their holdings of foreign assets, they have been targeted by foreign companies as takeover candidates. The foreign interest in U.S. insurance companies has grown as a result of the potential loosening of regulations in the insurance industry. At least 20 insurance companies in the United States are owned by firms from Europe or Japan.

SUMMARY

- The most common types of life insurance policies are whole life insurance, term insurance, variable life insurance, and universal life insurance.

- The main uses of life insurance company funds are as investments in government securities, corporate securities, mortgages, and real estate. Property and casualty insurance companies focus on similar types of assets, but maintain a higher concentration in government securities.

- Insurance companies are exposed to interest rate risk, as they tend to maintain large bond portfolios whose values decline when interest rates rise. They are also exposed to default risk and market risk, as a result of their investments in corporate securities, mortgages, stocks, and real estate.

- Insurance companies are regulated by state agencies. Each state approves the rates that insurance companies charge. They also assess the asset portfolios of insurance companies to ensure that the risk of the assets is not excessive.

QUESTIONS

1. How is whole life insurance a form of savings to policyholders?

2. How do whole life and term insurance differ from the perspective of insurance companies? From the perspective of the policyholders?

3. Identify the characteristics of universal life insurance.

4. Explain group life insurance.

5. What are the main assets of life insurance companies? Identify the main categories.

6. How do insurance companies finance real estate?

7. What is a policy loan? When is it popular? Why?

8. What is the main use of funds by life insurance companies?

9. What are two strategies that reduce the impact of changing interest rates on the market value of life insurance companies' assets?

10. What has recent research found with respect to the sensitivity of life insurance equity values to interest rate movements?

11. How do insurance companies manage default risk and liquidity risk?

12. Discuss the liquidity risk experienced by life insurance companies.

13. What purpose do property and casualty (PC) insurance companies serve?

14. Identify the different characteristics of PC insurance as compared to life insurance.

15. Explain the concept of cash flow underwriting.

16. Explain how a life insurance company's asset portfolio may be affected by inflation.

17. What is reinsurance?

18. What is the NAIC, and what is its purpose?

CASE APPLICATION: INSURANCE COMPANY RISK

Seized Insurer's Woes Reflect Perils of CMOs

Laura Jereski

Behind the closed doors of a state courtroom in Atlanta, the fate of a tiny insurer hangs in the balance.

Coastal States Life Insurance Co. was seized in December because Georgia state regulators were alarmed that its liabilities had ballooned with little capital to support them. At the same time, Coastal States was betting on a perilous investment strategy: Of its $128 million in assets, it had invested some $120 million in exotic, highly volatile types of mortgage-backed securities.

Coastal is suing to block the state's seizure. Whatever the destiny of Coastal States, the company's predicament sheds some light on the life-insurance industry's growing appetite for complex and risky mortgage-backed securities. During the past four years, life insurers were able to indulge their craving for the higher-yielding bonds because insurance regulations and accounting standards lagged far behind these sophisticated securities.

Shifting Value

Insurers' holdings of mortgage securities—which are created from pools of home mortgages and backed by government agencies—doubled to $220 billion in the past four years, second only to those of banks, according to Inside Mortgage Securities, a newsletter. About one third is invested in the complex derivative securities known as collateralized mortgage obligations, or CMOs.

These are created by carving up the cash flow from traditional mortgage securities into slices, or "tranches." The value of some CMOs changes drastically with shifts in interest rates.

But regulators are beginning to understand how difficult CMOs can be to value, and just how vague those appraisals can be. Indeed, Coastal States flourished for two years despite regulators' mounting concern, because the insurer could assert it had followed what few rules exist. "For a long time, regulators didn't pay attention to these investments," said Larry Gorski, who heads the National Association of Insurance Commissioners task force on CMOs. "They thought there was no risk associated with them" because of the triple-A credit rating on government-backed mortgage issues, he said.

Regulators' concerns sharpened last year, when some insurance companies reported large, unexpected losses in CMO portfolios. Just as some insurers loaded up on high-yielding junk bonds in the 1980s and later took big losses, regulators now worry that CMOs may present a similar danger for the 1990s.

By the end of this year, the NAIC, which sets standards for state insurance regulators, will put forth new rules that will change how these securities are valued on insurers' books for regulatory purposes, and make it easier to track how erratic the securities' cash flows are likely to be.

But insurers will still be allowed to hold less than 1% of capital against mortgage-backed securities, including CMOs. The government guarantee of the underlying home mortgages make the securities as creditworthy as Treasury debt.

"Coastal States is the benchmark for the new regulations about investments in certain mortgage-backed securities," said Thomas S.Y. Ho, a consultant to the regulators on these complex investments.

During the past two years, Georgia's regulators grew increasingly worried about the fast-growing company's management and its aggressive investment strategy. Coastal's chairman, Ronald C. Guernsey, had been involved with a now-defunct North Carolina insurer whose insolvency could cost that state's guarantee fund as much as $60 million. Mr. Guernsey, who was president of the company's marketing arm, said he had nothing to do with its insolvency.

Regulators fear a demise of Coastal could leave Georgia's state guarantee fund on the hook for $20 million—if the state court allows the insurance commissioner to proceed with the seizure.

"The company has and is being examined," said Charles E. Huff, deputy receiver of the Georgia Insurance Department. The regulators won't comment further because of a gag order placed on all participants in the case by a state judge.

Despite meager capital of $3 million, Coastal States sold about $115 million of single-premium deferred annuities until regulators say they forced it to stop selling in March 1992. To match the high investment rates it promised its annuity holders, which started as high as 11%, Coastal invested nearly all of its assets in two types of mercurial CMOs, whose price and yield change significantly and

Continued

CASE APPLICATION: INSURANCE COMPANY RISK

Continued

unpredictably with fluctuations in interest rates.

Day to Day Risk

"One hundred percent of anything is risky," said Carol Ostapchuk, an examiner in Florida's insurance department. "But with these investments, on any given day you could be insolvent."

Mr. Guernsey, who bought Coastal States in 1990, insists the company did nothing wrong. "We have a situation here where regulators have overstepped their bounds," he said.

Mr. Guernsey set up an insurance agency, FICA Marketing, to sell Coastal States' single-premium deferred annuities. Agents talked up the policies' liberal surrender provisions—the penalties for withdrawing money early—within certain periods, according to a person familiar with the insurer. In reality, policyholders would have to pay surrender charges of up to 14%, more than three times the industry average, to get their money back, say insurance experts. The sales pitch stressed safety. Sales literature featured the Coastal States building, a prominent feature in the Atlanta skyline, even though the life insurer hadn't owned it in years.

In 1990, Coastal States hired Atlantic Portfolio Analytics & Management, an Orlando money-management firm with expertise in the still-new world of mortgage derivatives. Atlantic Portfolio put together a portfolio consisting of two types of CMOs: interest-only strips, which receive only the interest (but no principal) from a pool of underlying mortgages, and inverse floaters, which pay more cash as interest rates fall. Coastal States heightened the leverage of those instruments by borrowing $55 million in reverse repurchase agreements, a practice regulators halted in March 1992.

The mortgage portfolio was supposed to deliver a high yield no matter what direction interest rates went. "It was an asset-liability matching strategy," explained Jon Knight, chief investment officer of Atlantic Portfolio.

That's not quite how things worked out. Currently, the portfolio is about $10 million under water, according to regulators, and everyone involved is pointing fingers.

"I left the portfolio up to them," said Mr. Guernsey.

"This is the portfolio the company wanted," said Mr. Knight.

Here's why the portfolio lost so much value. As interest rates fell during 1991 and 1992, homeowners began refinancing at an unprecedented clip. As a result, the securities in Coastal States' portfolio began paying off far faster than expected as homeowners paid off their old mortgages. Ultimately, the interest-only strips paid down so fast that they returned about $38 million, or barely more than half what the company paid for them.

The inverse floaters that were to have hedged against declining interest rates fared less well than expected, too. Prepayments were so great—as high as 10 times the industry standard "prepayment speed"—that the average life of many securities shortened dramatically, shearing returns to the portfolio.

Yet the company was able to mask its deteriorating financial position, thanks to vague regulatory accounting standards that allowed the company to keep the securities on its books even as they were being paid down. Insurance companies are supposed to estimate the life of their CMOs and put them on the books at a constant yield over that life. The securities must be written down faster only if they are "permanently impaired."

Mr. Guernsey and Atlantic Portfolio picked a prepayment rate so slow that they could amortize the CMOs over 30 years, though most were backed by mortgages with high interest-rate coupons, making them even more susceptible to being refinanced. They also put off recognizing impairment by assuming that prepayments might slow enough for the company to recover its investment. "That was not a good assumption because the company was getting back huge chunks of its future cash flow each month in the form of principal," explained one CMO analyst who examined Coastal's portfolio.

As the portfolio was decaying, the Georgia regulators pressured Coastal to raise additional capital. That set off a scramble for new funds. On June 5, 1992, Mr. Guernsey announced he had closed on a deal to transfer mutual-fund shares valued at $6 million into Coastal States. The securities didn't exist, according to regulators.

SOURCE: *The Wall Street Journal,* May 12, 1993, p. C1. Reprinted by permission of *The Wall Street Journal,* © 1993. Dow Jones & Company, Inc. All rights reserved worldwide.

QUESTIONS

1. Why were the assets of Coastal States Life Insurance Co. considered to be so risky, even though there was a triple-A credit rating on the mortgages backing the securities?

2. Explain why the capital requirements for Coastal were relatively low.

3. How could regulators attempt to discourage insurance companies like Coastal from taking excessive risk?

PROJECT

1. **Financial Assessment of an Insurance Company**
   Obtain annual reports and an investment survey summary (such as *Value Line*) for a particular life insurance company of your choice or one assigned by your professor and answer the following questions:
   a. How has its asset portfolio composition changed in recent years?
   b. Have the recent changes in asset composition affected the company's risk and potential return?
   c. How do you think the company would be affected by an increase in interest rates? Explain.
   d. Based on its recent annual report, does the company appear to be increasing its nontraditional services? Elaborate.

REFERENCES

Cross, Mark, Wallace Davidson III, and John Thornton. "The Impact of a Captive Insurance Company's Formation on a Firm's Value after the Carnation Case." *Journal of Business Research* (August 1987): 329–338.

Haubrich, Joseph G., and Robert G. King. "Banking and Insurance." *Journal of Monetary Economics* (December 1990): 361–386.

Kopcke, Richard W. "The Capitalization and Portfolio Risk of Insurance Companies." *New England Economic Review* (July/August 1992): 43–57.

Mayers, David, and Clifford W. Smith. "Ownership Structure and Control: The Mutualization of Stock Life Insurance Companies." *Journal of Financial Economics* (May 1986): 73–98.

Randall, Richard E., and Richard W. Kopcke. "The Financial Condition and Regulation of Insurance Companies: An Overview." *New England Economic Review* (May/June 1992): 32–43.

Rosenberg, Hilary. "Can Insurers Live with Rate Regulation?" *Institutional Investor* (October 1986): 329–332.

Samson, Dannys, and Howard Thomas. "Linear Models as Aids in Insurance Decision-Making: The Estimation of Automobile Insurance Claims." *Journal of Business Research* (June 1987): 247–256.

Scott, William L., and Richard L. Peterson. "Interest Rate Risk and Equity Values of Hedged and Unhedged Financial Intermediaries." *Journal of Financial Research* (Winter 1986): 325–329.

ASSESSING THE INFLUENCE OF ECONOMIC CONDITIONS ACROSS NONBANK FINANCIAL INSTITUTIONS_____

This problem requires an understanding of the operations and asset compositions of savings institutions (Chapter 20), credit unions (Chapter 21), finance companies (Chapter 22), mutual funds (Chapter 23), securities firms (Chapter 24), and insurance companies (Chapter 26).

As a financial analyst of an investment firm, you have been assigned the task of assessing all nonbank financial institutions. As economic conditions change, it is your job to suggest how each type of financial institution will be affected and which types will be affected the most.

In the past few months, all economic indicators have been signalling the possibility of a recession. Stock prices have already declined as the demand for stocks has decreased significantly. It appears that the pessimistic outlook will last for at least a few months. Economic conditions are already somewhat stagnant but are expected to deteriorate in future months. During that time, firms will not consider mergers, new stock issues, or new bond issues.

An economist at your firm believes that individual investors will overreact to the pessimistic outlook. Once stock prices are low enough, some firms will acquire target firms whose stock appears to be undervalued. In addition, some firms will buy back some of their own stock once they believe it is undervalued. Although these activities have not yet occurred, the economist believes it is only a matter of time.

a. Your strategy is to identify the types of nonbank institutions that will be less adversely affected by the recession. You also want to identify the types of nonbank institutions that are most likely to be undervalued and therefore will perform the best when the demand for stocks increases. So far, the stock prices of all types of nonbank financial institutions have declined by a similar degree. Although it appears that the market is penalizing all of them by the same amount, you believe that the different characteristics should cause some nonbank financial institutions to be affected more than others.

USING LOTUS FOR STATISTICAL ANALYSIS

Financial market participants commonly conduct statistical analysis for analyzing data. This appendix explains some of the more commonly used statistical techniques.

REGRESSION ANALYSIS

Various software packages are available to run regression analysis. The LOTUS package is recommended because of its simplicity. The following example illustrates the ease with which regression analysis can be run.

Assume that a financial institution wishes to measure the relationship between the change in the interest rate in a given period (Δi_t) and the change in the inflation rate in the previous period (ΔI_{t-1}); that is, the financial institution wishes to assess the lagged impact of inflation on interest rates. Assume that the data over the last 20 periods is as follows:

Period	Δi_t	ΔI_{t-1}
1	.50%	.90%
2	.65	.75
3	−.70	−1.20
4	.50	.30
5	.40	.60
6	−.30	−.20
7	.60	.85
8	.75	.45
9	.10	−.05
10	1.10	1.35
11	.90	1.10
12	−.65	−.80
13	−.20	−.35

Period	Δi_t	ΔI_{t-1}
14	.40	.55
15	.30	.40
16	.60	.75
17	−.05	−.10
18	1.30	1.50
19	−.55	−.70
20	.15	.25

Assume the firm applies the following regression model to the data:

$$\Delta i_t = b_0 + b_1 \Delta I_{t-1} + u$$

where Δi_t = change in the interest rate in period t

ΔI_{t-1} = change in the inflation rate in period $t-1$ (the previous period)

b_0 and b_1 = regression coefficients to be estimated by regression analysis

u = error term

In our example, Δi_t is the dependent variable while ΔI_{t-1} is the independent variable. The first step is to input the two columns of data (Columns B and C) into a file using LOTUS. Then, you can perform regression analysis as follows. On the main menu, select *DATA*. This leads to a new menu in which you should select *REGRESSION*. Then, select *X-RANGE* and identify the range of the independent variable (from C2 to C20 in our example). Then select *Y-RANGE* and identify the range of the dependent variable (from B2 to B20 in our example). Then select *OUTPUT* and identify the location on the screen where the output of the regression analysis should be displayed. In our example, E1 would be an appropriate location, which would represent the upper left section of the output. Then, select *GO*, and within a few seconds, the regression analysis will be complete. For our example, the output is as follows:

Regression Output

Constant	.0494
Std Err of Y Est	.1433
R Squared	.9386
No. of Observations	20
Degrees of Freedom	18
X Coefficient(s)	.7577
Std Err of Coef.	.0456

The estimate of the so-called slope coefficient is about .76, which suggests that every one percent change in the inflation rate is associated with a .76 percent change (in the same direction) in the interest rate. The t-statistic is not shown but can be estimated to determine whether the slope coefficient is significantly different than zero. Since the standard error of the slope coefficient is .0456, the t-statistic is $.7577/.0456 = 16.6$, which suggests that there is a significant relationship between Δi_t and ΔI_{t-1}. The R-SQUARED statistic suggests that about 94 percent of the variation in Δi_t is explained by ΔI_{t-1}. The correlation between Δi_t and ΔI_{t-1} can also be measured by the correlation coefficient, which is the square root of the R-SQUARED statistic.

If you had more than one independent variable (multiple regression), you should place the independent variables next to each other in the file. Then, for the X-RANGE, identify this block of data. The output for the regression model will display the coefficient and standard error for each of the independent variables. The t-statistic could be estimated for each independent variable to test for significance. For multiple regression, the R-SQUARED statistic represents the percentage of variation in the dependent variable explained by the model as a whole.

USING REGRESSION ANALYSIS TO FORECAST

The regression results can be used to forecast future values of the dependent variable. In our example, the historical relationship between Δi_t and ΔI_{t-1} can be expressed as:

$$\Delta i_t = b_0 + b_1(\Delta I_{t-1})$$

Assume that last period's change in inflation (ΔI_{t-1}) was one percent. Given the estimated coefficients derived from regression analysis, the forecast for this period's Δi is:

$$\Delta i_t = .0494\% + .7577(1\%)$$

$$= .8071\%$$

There are some obvious limitations that should be recognized when using regression analysis to forecast. First, if other variables that influence the dependent variable are not included in the model, the coefficients derived from the model may be improperly estimated. This can cause inaccurate forecasts. Second, some relationships are contemporaneous rather than lagged, which means that last period's value for ΔI could not be used. Instead, a forecast would have to be derived for ΔI, to use as input for forecasting Δi. If the forecast for ΔI is poor, the forecast for Δi will likely be poor even if the regression model is properly specified.

FINANCIAL DATA BANK[a]

YEAR	BEGINNING OF QUARTER	MEASURES OF MONEY SUPPLY			COMMERCIAL PAPER OUTSTANDING	BANKER'S ACCEPTANCES OUTSTANDING
		M1	M2	M3		
1980	1	$389.0	$1,532.8	$1,785.3	$116.718	$47.780
1980	2	387.6	1,548.0	1,809.2	120.865	50.177
1980	3	394.5	1,609.2	1,865.0	122.259	54.334
1980	4	410.8	1,653.6	1,918.2	122.383	56.610
1981	1	416.1	1,681.7	1,978.2	128.656	54.465
1981	2	433.7	1,738.1	2,044.6	134.229	62.320
1981	3	430.1	1,760.1	2,094.0	151.013	63.721
1981	4	433.0	1,798.8	2,143.3	164.026	66.072
1982	1	448.6	1,840.9	2,204.0	165.118	70.088
1982	2	452.3	1,880.7	2,258.1	171.709	71.128
1982	3	451.3	1,923.4	2,320.2	180.669	72.559
1982	4	468.4	1,968.2	2,382.1	170.253	75.811
1983	1	482.1	2,008.1	2,401.4	165.705	77.529
1983	2	496.5	2,075.1	2,454.5	170.659	70.389
1983	3	514.7	2,127.4	2,508.1	172.199	72.710
1983	4	517.9	2,162.0	2,562.0	175.924	72.902
1984	1	523.0	2,206.2	2,720.5	182.801	73.450
1984	2	535.3	2,242.5	2,709.8	209.535	78.457
1984	3	545.6	2,281.4	2,856.2	221.647	80.957
1984	4	545.5	2,317.2	2,917.3	227.960	75.740
1985	1	562.7	2,398.3	3,020.5	245.322	72.532
1985	2	575.0	2,428.0	3,057.5	255.236	72.825
1985	3	595.8	2,490.2	3,113.6	262.769	68.497
1985	4	611.1	2,533.4	3,179.3	280.930	67.592
1986	1	627.1	2,568.4	3,222.1	302.160	68.205
1986	2	646.1	2,620.9	3,228.3	297.108	66.235
1986	3	676.1	2,699.1	3,375.1	311.435	66.437
1986	4	701.2	2,765.2	3,444.5	329.516	65.920
1987	1	737.6	2,822.0	3,515.7	336.996	65.049
1987	2	750.4	2,838.5	3,540.8	346.769	66.660
1987	3	747.6	2,847.7	3,583.5	348.247	68.495
1987	4	756.6	2,891.1	3,657.7	360.013	71.891
1988	1	758.9	2,925.0	3,686.0	380.475	62.957
1988	2	770.2	2,992.7	3,763.9	406.484	64.112
1988	3	782.3	3,025.9	3,834.9	423.599	64.359
1988	4	783.5	3,037.5	3,868.8	424.160	63.452
1989	1	786.3	3,065.7	3,924.1	471.066	62.212
1989	2	783.2	3,081.3	3,958.1	494.292	64.357
1989	3	777.1	3,117.4	4,002.4	506.095	65.558
1989	4	787.6	3,176.4	4,027.3	507.902	63.660
1990	1	794.7	3,229.1	4,044.7	533.137	60.019
1990	2	807.4	3,271.8	4,065.1	544.481	53.945
1990	3	809.0	3,287.8	4,076.9	545.849	52.006
1990	4	820.1	3,318.8	4,091.7	557.731	52.093
1991	1	826.7	3,332.9	4,126.5	569.378	56.498
1991	2	842.1	3,385.2	4,174.8	542.603	47.086
1991	3	859.6	3,390.5	4,148.5	544.048	44.756
1991	4	879.4	3,398.8	4,146.4	531.886	43.462
1992	1	910.3	3,448.2	4,174.4	533.342	43.112
1992	2	942.9	3,468.2	4,175.7	537.020	39.335
1992	3	960.5	3,462.2	4,163.0	547.242	37.733
1992	4	1,007.2	3,496.5	4,183.3	557.915	37.599
1993	1	1,033.2	3,486.9	4,140.6	542.438	35.995
1993	2	1,043.2	3,474.6	4,142.0	535.966	35.317
1993	3	1,085.3	3,516.8	4,165.1	539.149	33.120
1993	4	1,116.4	3,531.0	4,177.7	550.947	33.069
1994	1	1,133.6	3,571.0	4,230.9	N/A	N/A

DATA SOURCE: Federal Reserve Bulletin, numerous issues.
[a]Dollar amounts are stated in billions.

YEAR	BEGINNING OF QUARTER	PRIME RATE	DISCOUNT RATE (FRB OF NY)	FEDERAL FUNDS RATE	THREE-MONTH COMMERCIAL PAPER RATE (ANNUALIZED)	THREE-MONTH CERTIFICATE OF DEPOSIT RATE (ANNUALIZED)
1980	1	15.25%	12.00%	13.82%	13.04%	13.39%
1980	2	19.77%	13.00%	17.61%	15.78%	16.14%
1980	3	11.48%	11.00%	9.03%	8.41%	8.65%
1980	4	13.79%	11.00%	12.81%	12.52%	12.94%
1981	1	20.16%	13.00%	19.08%	16.58%	17.19%
1981	2	17.15%	13.00%	15.72%	14.56%	15.08%
1981	3	20.39%	14.00%	19.04%	17.00%	17.76%
1981	4	18.45%	14.00%	15.08%	14.85%	15.39%
1982	1	15.75%	12.00%	13.22%	13.09%	13.51%
1982	2	16.50%	12.00%	14.94%	14.06%	14.44%
1982	3	16.26%	12.00%	12.59%	12.94%	13.44%
1982	4	12.52%	10.00%	9.71%	9.20%	9.51%
1983	1	11.16%	8.50%	8.68%	8.17%	8.36%
1983	2	10.50%	8.50%	8.80%	8.53%	8.63%
1983	3	10.50%	8.50%	9.37%	9.25%	9.50%
1983	4	11.00%	8.50%	9.48%	8.99%	9.18%
1984	1	11.00%	8.50%	9.56%	9.20%	9.42%
1984	2	11.93%	8.50%	10.29%	10.18%	10.41%
1984	3	13.00%	9.00%	11.23%	11.19%	11.56%
1984	4	12.58%	9.00%	9.99%	10.12%	10.38%
1985	1	10.61%	8.00%	8.35%	8.03%	8.14%
1985	2	10.50%	8.00%	8.27%	8.37%	8.49%
1985	3	9.50%	7.50%	7.88%	7.56%	7.64%
1985	4	9.50%	7.50%	7.99%	7.80%	7.88%
1986	1	9.50%	7.50%	8.14%	7.71%	7.82%
1986	2	8.83%	7.00%	6.99%	6.60%	6.60%
1986	3	8.16%	6.50%	6.56%	6.33%	6.37%
1986	4	7.50%	5.50%	5.85%	5.68%	5.69%
1987	1	7.50%	5.50%	6.43%	5.84%	5.87%
1987	2	7.75%	5.50%	6.37%	6.45%	6.52%
1987	3	8.25%	5.50%	6.58%	6.65%	6.70%
1987	4	9.07%	6.00%	7.29%	7.89%	8.02%
1988	1	8.75%	6.00%	6.83%	6.87%	6.92%
1988	2	8.50%	6.00%	6.87%	6.86%	6.92%
1988	3	9.29%	6.00%	7.75%	7.82%	7.94%
1988	4	10.00%	6.50%	8.30%	8.24%	8.36%
1989	1	10.50%	6.50%	9.12%	9.04%	9.20%
1989	2	11.50%	7.00%	9.84%	9.81%	9.94%
1989	3	10.98%	7.00%	9.24%	8.68%	8.76%
1989	4	10.50%	7.00%	8.84%	8.53%	8.60%
1990	1	10.11%	7.00%	8.23%	8.10%	8.16%
1990	2	10.00%	7.00%	8.26%	8.30%	8.42%
1990	3	10.00%	7.00%	8.15%	7.99%	8.10%
1990	4	10.00%	7.00%	8.11%	7.98%	8.06%
1991	1	9.52%	6.50%	6.91%	7.10%	7.17%
1991	2	9.00%	5.50%	5.91%	6.07%	6.06%
1991	3	8.50%	5.50%	5.82%	6.05%	5.98%
1991	4	8.00%	5.00%	5.21%	5.35%	5.33%
1992	1	6.50%	3.50%	4.03%	4.07%	4.05%
1992	2	6.50%	3.50%	3.73%	4.04%	4.00%
1992	3	6.00%	3.00%	3.25%	3.44%	3.37%
1992	4	6.00%	3.00%	3.10%	3.30%	3.26%
1993	1	6.00%	3.00%	3.02%	3.25%	3.19%
1993	2	6.00%	3.00%	2.96%	3.14%	3.09%
1993	3	6.00%	3.00%	3.06%	3.20%	3.16%
1993	4	6.00%	3.00%	2.99%	3.26%	3.24%
1994	1	6.00%	3.00%	3.05%	3.19%	3.15%

YEAR	BEGINNING OF QUARTER	THREE-MONTH EURODOLLAR RATE (ANNUALIZED)	THREE-MONTH TREASURY BILL RATE (ANNUALIZED)	ONE-YEAR TREASURY BILL RATE	FIVE-YEAR TREASURY NOTE YIELD
1980	1	14.33%	12.00%	12.06%	10.74%
1980	2	17.81%	13.20%	13.30%	11.84%
1980	3	9.33%	8.06%	8.65%	9.53%
1980	4	13.55%	11.62%	12.49%	11.86%
1981	1	18.07%	15.02%	14.08%	12.77%
1981	2	15.95%	13.69%	14.32%	13.99%
1981	3	18.49%	14.95%	15.72%	14.79%
1981	4	16.34%	13.54%	15.38%	15.41%
1982	1	14.29%	12.28%	14.32%	14.65%
1982	2	15.18%	12.70%	13.98%	14.00%
1982	3	14.37%	11.35%	13.24%	14.07%
1982	4	10.43%	7.71%	9.32%	10.80%
1983	1	8.97%	7.86%	8.62%	10.03%
1983	2	9.23%	8.21%	8.98%	10.03%
1983	3	10.00%	9.08%	10.20%	11.21%
1983	4	9.54%	8.64%	9.81%	11.28%
1984	1	9.78%	8.90%	9.90%	11.37%
1984	2	10.83%	9.69%	10.90%	12.37%
1984	3	12.02%	10.12%	12.03%	13.28%
1984	4	10.77%	9.74%	10.90%	12.06%
1985	1	8.37%	7.76%	9.02%	10.93%
1985	2	8.74%	7.95%	9.14%	11.01%
1985	3	7.89%	7.08%	7.86%	9.70%
1985	4	8.08%	7.16%	8.01%	9.69%
1986	1	8.02%	7.07%	7.73%	8.68%
1986	2	6.80%	6.06%	6.44%	7.05%
1986	3	6.54%	5.83%	6.27%	7.06%
1986	4	5.88%	5.18%	5.72%	6.83%
1987	1	6.10%	5.43%	5.78%	6.64%
1987	2	6.73%	5.64%	6.50%	7.57%
1987	3	6.87%	5.69%	6.68%	8.01%
1987	4	8.29%	6.13%	7.59%	9.08%
1988	1	7.11%	5.81%	6.99%	8.18%
1988	2	7.05%	5.91%	7.01%	8.19%
1988	3	8.09%	6.73%	7.75%	8.66%
1988	4	8.51%	7.34%	8.11%	8.51%
1989	1	9.28%	8.27%	9.05%	9.15%
1989	2	10.04%	8.65%	9.36%	9.30%
1989	3	8.85%	7.88%	7.89%	7.83%
1989	4	8.67%	7.64%	7.99%	7.97%
1990	1	8.22%	7.64%	7.92%	8.12%
1990	2	8.44%	7.77%	8.40%	8.77%
1990	3	8.09%	7.62%	7.94%	8.33%
1990	4	8.06%	7.17%	7.55%	8.51%
1991	1	7.23%	6.22%	6.64%	7.70%
1991	2	6.11%	5.65%	5.85%	7.70%
1991	3	6.01%	5.58%	6.31%	7.91%
1991	4	5.34%	4.99%	5.33%	6.87%
1992	1	4.06%	3.80%	4.15%	6.24%
1992	2	4.05%	3.75%	4.30%	6.78%
1992	3	3.40%	3.21%	3.60%	5.84%
1992	4	3.30%	2.86%	3.30%	5.60%
1993	1	3.22%	3.00%	3.50%	5.83%
1993	2	3.10%	2.87%	3.24%	5.13%
1993	3	3.17%	3.04%	3.47%	5.09%
1993	4	3.26%	3.02%	3.39%	4.71%
1994	1	3.15%	2.98%	3.54%	5.09%

YEAR	BEGINNING OF QUARTER	TEN-YEAR TREASURY BOND YIELD	THIRTY-YEAR TREASURY BOND YIELD	MUNICIPAL BOND YIELDS	
				(Aaa)	(Baa)
1980	1	10.80%	10.60$	6.58%	7.60%
1980	2	11.47%	11.40%	7.95%	9.19%
1980	3	10.25%	10.24%	7.35%	8.46%
1980	4	11.75%	11.59%	8.38%	9.41%
1981	1	12.57%	12.14%	8.98%	9.90%
1981	2	13.68%	13.20%	9.78%	10.85%
1981	3	14.28%	13.59%	10.21%	11.55%
1981	4	15.15%	14.68%	12.05%	13.34%
1982	1	14.59%	14.22%	12.30%	13.95%
1982	2	13.87%	13.37%	11.66%	13.29%
1982	3	13.95%	13.55%	11.47%	13.17%
1982	4	10.91%	11.17%	9.15%	10.66%
1983	1	10.46%	10.63%	9.00%	10.98%
1983	2	10.40%	10.48%	8.28%	9.75%
1983	3	11.38%	11.40%	8.70%	10.06%
1983	4	11.54%	11.58%	8.93%	10.04%
1984	1	11.68%	11.75%	9.00%	10.10%
1984	2	12.63%	12.65%	9.54%	10.30%
1984	3	13.36%	13.21%	10.10%	10.61%
1984	4	12.16%	11.98%	9.72%	10.51%
1985	1	11.38%	11.45%	9.08%	10.16%
1985	2	11.43%	11.47%	8.92%	9.95%
1985	3	10.31%	10.50%	8.34%	9.18%
1985	4	10.24%	10.50%	8.58%	9.54%
1986	1	9.19%	9.40%	7.74%	8.79%
1986	2	7.30%	7.39%	6.81%	7.45%
1986	3	7.30%	7.27%	7.24%	7.95%
1986	4	7.43%	7.70%	6.44%	7.23%
1987	1	7.08%	7.39%	6.12%	6.93%
1987	2	8.02%	8.25%	7.20%	8.29%
1987	3	8.45%	8.64%	7.18%	8.37%
1987	4	9.52%	9.61%	7.90%	8.85%
1988	1	8.67%	8.83%	7.29%	8.12%
1988	2	8.72%	8.95%	7.33%	7.82%
1988	3	9.06%	9.14%	7.50%	7.86%
1988	4	8.80%	8.89%	7.25%	7.72%
1989	1	9.09%	8.93%	7.23%	7.67%
1989	2	9.18%	9.03%	7.37%	7.82%
1989	3	8.02%	8.08%	6.69%	7.17%
1989	4	8.01%	8.00%	6.93%	7.33%
1990	1	8.21%	8.26%	6.81%	7.35%
1990	2	8.79%	8.76%	7.04%	7.43%
1990	3	8.47%	8.50%	6.96%	7.13%
1990	4	8.72%	9.03%	7.23%	7.43%
1991	1	8.09%	8.27%	6.57%	7.17%
1991	2	8.04%	8.21%	6.89%	7.30%
1991	3	8.27%	8.45%	6.82%	7.18%
1991	4	7.53%	7.93%	6.28%	6.70%
1992	1	7.03%	7.58%	6.13%	6.47%
1992	2	7.48%	7.96%	6.36%	6.85%
1992	3	6.84%	7.60%	5.72%	6.10%
1992	4	6.59%	7.53%	6.10%	6.51%
1993	1	6.60%	7.34%	5.91%	6.28%
1993	2	5.97%	6.85%	5.47%	5.88%
1993	3	5.81%	6.63%	5.27%	5.74%
1993	4	5.33%	5.94%	5.13%	5.63%
1994	1	5.75%	6.29%	5.14%	5.60%

YEAR	BEGINNING OF QUARTER	CORPORATE BOND YIELDS				DIVIDEND RATIO ON PREFERRED STOCK	DIVIDEND RATIO ON COMMON STOCK
		(Aaa)	*(Aa)*	*(A)*	*(Baa)*		
1980	1	11.09%	11.56%	11.88%	12.42%	10.14%	5.40%
1980	2	12.04%	13.06%	13.55%	14.19%	11.06%	6.05%
1980	3	11.07%	11.43%	11.95%	12.67%	9.81%	5.20%
1980	4	12.31%	12.68%	13.05%	14.23%	10.64%	4.80%
1981	1	12.81%	13.52%	13.83%	15.03%	11.64%	4.76%
1981	2	13.88%	14.39%	14.82%	15.56%	11.80%	4.84%
1981	3	14.38%	14.79%	15.36%	16.17%	12.43%	5.18%
1981	4	15.40%	15.82%	16.47%	17.11%	13.09%	5.65%
1982	1	15.18%	15.75%	16.19%	17.10%	13.19%	5.95%
1982	2	14.46%	14.90%	15.95%	16.78%	12.90%	5.99%
1982	3	14.61%	15.21%	16.20%	16.80%	13.24%	6.31%
1982	4	12.12%	12.97%	14.34%	14.73%	11.71%	5.12%
1983	1	11.79%	12.35%	13.53%	13.94%	11.23%	4.79%
1983	2	11.51%	12.06%	12.86%	13.29%	10.80%	4.44%
1983	3	12.15%	12.39%	12.99%	13.39%	11.06%	4.21%
1983	4	12.25%	12.49%	12.97%	13.46%	10.97%	4.25%
1984	1	12.20%	12.71%	13.13%	13.65%	11.35%	4.27%
1984	2	12.81%	13.48%	13.77%	14.31%	11.66%	4.64%
1984	3	13.44%	14.12%	14.57%	15.15%	12.13%	4.93%
1984	4	12.63%	13.11%	13.61%	13.94%	11.62%	4.62%
1985	1	12.08%	12.43%	12.80%	13.26%	11.13%	4.51%
1985	2	12.23%	12.69%	13.14%	13.51%	10.75%	4.37%
1985	3	10.97%	11.42%	11.92%	12.43%	9.92%	4.14%
1985	4	11.02%	11.45%	11.94%	12.36%	10.35%	4.28%
1986	1	10.05%	10.46%	11.04%	11.44%	9.85%	3.90%
1986	2	8.79%	9.21%	9.83%	10.19%	8.97%	3.43%
1986	3	8.88%	9.28%	9.76%	10.16%	8.68%	3.41%
1986	4	8.86%	9.33%	9.72%	10.24%	8.17%	3.49%
1987	1	8.36%	8.86%	9.23%	9.72%	7.91%	3.17%
1987	2	8.85%	9.15%	9.36%	10.04%	7.94%	2.99%
1987	3	9.42%	9.64%	10.00%	10.61%	8.25%	2.83%
1987	4	10.52%	10.74%	10.98%	11.62%	8.99%	3.25%
1988	1	9.88%	10.09%	10.43%	11.07%	9.04%	3.66%
1988	2	9.67%	9.86%	10.17%	10.90%	9.19%	3.57%
1988	3	9.96%	10.26%	10.55%	11.11%	9.34%	3.65%
1988	4	9.51%	9.71%	9.99%	10.41%	9.23%	3.61%
1989	1	9.62%	9.81%	10.10%	10.65%	9.31%	3.64%
1989	2	9.79%	9.94%	10.20%	10.61%	9.50%	3.59%
1989	3	8.93%	9.14%	9.42%	9.87%	8.81%	3.38%
1989	4	8.92%	9.19%	9.44%	9.81%	8.85%	3.29%
1990	1	8.99%	9.27%	9.54%	9.94%	8.80%	3.41%
1990	2	9.46%	9.64%	9.89%	10.30%	9.05%	3.51%
1990	3	9.24%	9.47%	9.69%	10.20%	8.94%	3.37%
1990	4	9.53%	9.77%	10.06%	10.74%	9.10%	4.01%
1991	1	9.04%	9.37%	9.61%	10.45%	8.71%	3.82%
1991	2	8.86%	9.12%	9.39%	9.94%	8.43%	3.19%
1991	3	9.00%	9.25%	9.51%	9.89%	8.21%	3.20%
1991	4	8.55%	8.83%	9.08%	9.49%	7.84%	3.14%
1992	1	8.20%	8.51%	8.72%	9.13%	7.54%	2.90%
1992	2	8.33%	8.69%	8.87%	9.21%	7.75%	3.02%
1992	3	8.07%	8.37%	8.49%	8.84%	7.47%	2.97%
1992	4	7.99%	8.32%	8.49%	8.84%	7.22%	3.02%
1993	1	7.91%	8.11%	8.26%	8.67%	7.25%	2.88%
1993	2	7.46%	7.62%	7.80%	8.14%	6.69%	2.76%
1993	3	7.17%	7.35%	7.53%	7.93%	6.89%	2.81%
1993	4	6.67%	6.87%	7.04%	7.31%	6.71%	2.72%
1994	1	6.92%	7.12%	7.30%	7.65%	6.97%	2.69%

YEAR	BEGINNING OF QUARTER	STOCK INDEXES					
		NYSE	INDUSTRIALS	TRANSPORTATION	UTILITY	FINANCIAL	S&P 500
1980	1	63.74	72.67	52.61	37.08	64.22	110.87
1980	2	58.47	66.31	48.62	35.29	57.32	102.97
1980	3	68.56	78.67	59.14	38.77	66.76	119.83
1980	4	75.17	88.00	70.76	38.44	68.29	130.22
1981	1	76.24	89.23	74.43	38.53	70.04	132.97
1981	2	77.60	90.37	80.63	38.34	74.59	134.43
1981	3	74.98	86.64	74.42	38.90	74.97	129.13
1981	4	69.40	78.94	65.65	38.87	72.58	119.81
1982	1	67.91	76.85	62.04	39.30	70.99	117.41
1982	2	66.97	75.59	57.91	39.20	71.44	116.31
1982	3	62.82	71.37	53.40	37.20	64.59	109.38
1982	4	76.10	86.67	66.64	42.67	80.59	132.66
1983	1	83.25	95.37	75.65	45.59	85.66	145.13
1983	2	90.61	104.46	85.26	46.22	99.07	157.71
1983	3	96.74	113.21	92.91	46.61	99.60	166.96
1983	4	96.78	112.87	95.41	48.73	94.79	167.65
1984	1	96.16	112.16	97.98	47.43	95.79	166.39
1984	2	90.67	106.56	83.61	43.86	88.22	157.60
1984	3	87.08	102.29	76.72	44.17	79.03	151.08
1984	4	95.09	110.44	86.82	49.02	92.94	164.82
1985	1	99.11	113.99	94.88	51.95	101.34	171.61
1985	2	104.66	119.93	96.47	55.51	109.39	180.62
1985	3	111.64	126.94	111.67	59.68	114.68	188.31
1985	4	107.57	123.65	103.72	55.84	112.36	186.18
1986	1	120.16	137.13	115.72	62.46	132.36	208.19
1986	2	137.23	157.35	125.92	69.35	154.83	237.97
1986	3	138.32	158.06	112.03	74.20	150.23	240.18
1986	4	136.74	156.56	120.04	73.38	143.89	237.36
1987	1	151.17	175.60	126.61	78.54	153.32	264.51
1987	2	163.88	199.03	137.91	72.74	150.52	289.32
1987	3	174.28	214.12	157.49	74.18	152.27	310.09
1987	4	157.13	189.86	140.95	73.27	137.35	280.16
1988	1	140.55	168.47	121.20	70.01	119.40	250.48
1988	2	148.46	181.01	133.40	69.35	121.66	262.61
1988	3	152.12	184.09	136.49	71.49	129.99	269.05
1988	4	156.36	188.58	141.83	74.19	136.09	277.40
1989	1	160.40	194.62	153.09	75.87	132.26	285.41
1989	2	169.38	204.81	164.32	79.69	143.26	302.25
1989	3	185.15	221.74	179.32	90.40	157.78	331.92
1989	4	192.49	229.40	190.36	94.67	166.55	347.40
1990	1	187.96	225.79	173.67	95.69	150.11	339.97
1990	2	185.61	226.86	173.54	91.92	138.57	338.18
1990	3	196.61	245.86	173.18	89.85	143.11	360.03
1990	4	168.05	208.58	131.99	87.27	108.01	307.12
1991	1	177.95	220.69	145.89	88.59	121.39	325.49
1991	2	207.71	260.16	166.90	92.92	152.64	379.68
1991	3	208.29	262.48	177.15	90.05	151.69	380.23
1991	4	213.10	265.68	187.45	95.25	158.94	386.88
1992	1	229.34	286.62	201.55	99.31	174.50	416.08
1992	2	228.12	286.09	205.53	96.19	174.05	412.56
1992	3	228.17	281.90	198.36	101.18	180.47	415.05
1992	4	226.97	279.70	192.30	101.62	181.36	412.50
1993	1	228.17	292.11	221.00	105.52	203.38	435.40
1993	2	244.72	292.19	237.97	113.78	216.02	443.08
1993	3	247.85	295.34	238.30	116.27	218.89	447.29
1993	4	257.53	306.61	254.04	120.49	228.18	463.90
1994	1	262.11	320.92	278.29	112.67	218.71	472.99

YEAR	BEGINNING OF QUARTER	ASE[b]	NYSE VOLUME (IN MILLIONS)	ASE VOLUME (IN MILLIONS)	GROSS PUBLIC DEBT
1980	1	129.77	52.647	9.363	$ 847.7
1980	2	121.30	32.102	3.428	870.0
1980	3	155.15	46.444	6.195	881.7
1980	4	175.04	44.860	7.087	908.2
1981	1	172.11	45.500	6.024	934.1
1981	2	181.55	54.230	6.339	964.0
1981	3	182.17	43.930	4.374	973.3
1981	4	154.41	46.233	4.233	1,005.0
1982	1	148.25	48.723	4.497	1,038.4
1982	2	135.58	54.119	3.937	1,065.7
1982	3	125.32	54.530	3.611	1,089.6
1982	4	154.37	98.508	7.828	1,142.8
1983	1	180.46	88.463	9.220	1,201.0
1983	2	202.51	89.627	8.576	1,247.9
1983	3	244.03	79.508	8.199	1,326.9
1983	4	233.76	85.445	7.751	1,384.6
1984	1	224.83	105.518	7.167	1,463.7
1984	2	207.66	85.874	5.863	1,512.7
1984	3	192.82	79.156	5.141	1,572.3
1984	4	210.39	91.676	5.587	1,663.0
1985	1	211.82	121.545	9.130	1,710.7
1985	2	229.46	94.387	7.801	1,774.6
1985	3	232.65	87.468	7.275	1,823.1
1985	4	225.00	110.569	7.648	1,945.9
1986	1	245.27	130.872	11.105	1,986.8
1986	2	270.59	146.330	13.503	2,059.3
1986	3	269.93	137.709	10.320	2,125.3
1986	4	257.82	131.155	8.930	2,214.8
1987	1	289.02	192.419	14.755	2,246.7
1987	2	330.65	187.135	14.420	2,309.3
1987	3	348.68	180.356	12.857	2,350.3
1987	4	306.34	227.026	18.173	2,431.7
1988	1	267.29	174.755	9.853	2,487.6
1988	2	300.43	162.518	10.706	2,547.7
1988	3	307.48	166.916	9.938	2,602.3
1988	4	302.83	162.631	9.051	2,684.4
1989	1	316.14	168.193	10.797	2,740.9
1989	2	336.82	131.863	11.529	2,799.7
1989	3	368.52	132.501	11.702	2,857.4
1989	4	383.63	182.394	13.853	2,953.0
1990	1	367.40	172.420	14.831	3,052.0
1990	2	353.32	140.062	13.961	3,143.8
1990	3	359.09	160.490	12.529	3,233.3
1990	4	296.67	159.590	11.294	3,364.8
1991	1	304.08	166.323	10.870	3,465.2
1991	2	365.02	182.510	13.140	3,538.0
1991	3	364.33	157.871	10.883	3,665.3
1991	4	376.82	177.502	13.764	3,801.7
1992	1	409.08	239.903	20.444	3,881.3
1992	2	413.74	226.476	18.126	3,984.7
1992	3	384.07	194.138	10.722	4,064.6
1992	4	371.27	204.787	11.966	4,177.0
1993	1	402.75	266.011	17.184	4,230.6
1993	2	418.54	279.778	15.521	4.352.0
1993	3	434.99	247.574	17.744	4,411.5
1993	4	472.73	280.503	21.279	4,535.7
1994	1	481.14	313.223	19.211	N/A

[b]The ASE halved its index in the third quarter of 1983. The index levels prior to that time were adjusted so that they are comparable to the index levels thereafter.

YEAR	BEGINNING OF QUARTER	MORTGAGE RATE	CONSUMER PRICE INDEX[c]	GROSS NATIONAL PRODUCT
1980	1	12.60%	77.8	$2,520.3
1980	2	13.45%	80.9	2,524.6
1980	3	12.39%	82.7	2,637.3
1980	4	14.38%	84.7	2,730.6
1981	1	14.23%	86.9	2,853.0
1981	2	15.91%	89.1	2,881.0
1981	3	16.76%	91.6	2,956.6
1981	4	17.43%	93.4	2,998.3
1982	1	17.38%	94.3	2,998.4
1982	2	16.31%	94.9	3,045.2
1982	3	16.29%	97.5	3,088.2
1982	4	12.99%	98.2	3,108.2
1983	1	12.87%	97.7	3,170.6
1983	2	12.50%	98.6	3,272.0
1983	3	14.23%	99.9	3,360.3
1983	4	13.23%	101.0	3,436.2
1984	1	13.08%	101.9	3,541.6
1984	2	13.80%	103.1	3,644.7
1984	3	14.58%	104.0	3,695.2
1984	4	13.43%	105.2	3,752.5
1985	1	13.01%	105.5	3,810.6
1985	2	12.97%	106.8	3,853.1
1985	3	12.12%	109.7	4,016.9
1985	4	11.87%	108.6	4,059.3
1986	1	10.78%	109.6	4,115.7
1986	2	9.80%	108.6	4,175.6
1986	3	10.01%	109.5	4,234.3
1986	4	9.80%	110.3	4,268.4
1987	1	8.79%	111.2	4,339.2
1987	2	10.02%	112.7	4,512.0
1987	3	10.38%	113.8	4,598.0
1987	4	10.90%	115.3	4.607.4
1988	1	10.17%	115.7	4,660.9
1988	2	10.46%	117.1	4,823.8
1988	3	10.66%	118.5	4,889.5
1988	4	10.23%	120.2	4,989.9
1989	1	10.69%	121.1	5,116.8
1989	2	10.88%	123.1	5,201.7
1989	3	9.61%	124.4	5.278.9
1989	4	9.73%	125.6	5,289.3
1990	1	10.01%	127.4	5,357.4
1990	2	10.75%	128.9	5,443.3
1990	3	10.11%	130.4	5,514.6
1990	4	10.23%	133.5	5,518.9
1991	1	9.58%	136.3	5,527.3
1991	2	9.61%	135.2	5,612.4
1991	3	9.59%	136.2	5,709.2
1991	4	8.71%	137.4	5,753.3
1992	1	8.72%	138.1	5,840.2
1992	2	8.79%	139.5	5,991.4
1992	3	8.66%	140.5	6,059.5
1992	4	8.08%	141.8	6,194.4
1993	1	8.04%	142.6	6,261.6
1993	2	7.56%	144.0	6,327.6
1993	3	7.51%	144.4	6,395.9
1993	4	7.08%	145.7	6,523.4
1994	1	7.05%	146.2	N/A

[c]The CPI has been measured according to different base indexes over time. This data set has been adjusted to conform to the same base index, so that they are comparable.

GLOSSARY

adjustable-rate mortgage Mortgage that requires payments which adjust periodically according to market interest rates.

American depository receipts (ADRs) Certificates representing ownership of foreign stocks.

annuity Even stream of payments over a given period of time.

annuity plans Plans provided by insurance companies that offer a predetermined amount of retirement income to individuals.

appreciate Increase in the value of a foreign currency.

arbitrage activity In the securities industry, refers to the purchasing of undervalued shares and the resale of these shares for a higher profit.

arbitrage firms (arbitrageurs) Securities firms that capitalize on discrepancies between prices of index futures and stocks.

Arbitrage Pricing Theory (APT) Theory on the pricing of assets, which suggests that stock prices may be driven by a set of factors in addition to the market.

ask price Price at which a broker is willing to sell a specific security.

ask quote Price at which one is willing to sell.

asset stripping A strategy of acquiring a firm, breaking it into divisions, segmenting the divisions, and then selling them separately.

Automatic Transfer Service (ATS) Savings account that allows funds to be transferred to a checking account as checks are written.

balloon-payment mortgage Mortgage that requires payments for a three- to five-year period; at the end of the period, full payment of the principal is required.

banker's acceptance Agreement in which a bank accepts responsibility for a future payment; it is commonly used for international trade transactions.

Bank Holding Company (BHC) Company that owns a commercial bank.

bank insurance fund Reserve fund used by the FDIC to close failing banks; the fund is supported with deposit insurance premiums paid by commercial banks.

basis Difference between the price of a futures contract and the price of the underlying security.

basis risk As applied to interest rate swaps, risk that the index used for an interest rate swap does not move perfectly in tandem with the floating-rate instrument specified in a swap arrangement. As applied to financial futures, risk that the futures prices do not move perfectly in tandem with the assets that are hedged.

best-efforts agreement Arrangement in which the investment banking firm does not guarantee a price on securities to be issued by a corporation, but only states it will give its best effort to sell the securities at a reasonable price.

beta Measured as the covariance between asset returns and market returns divided by the variance of market returns, and represents the sensitivity of an asset's returns to market returns.

bid price   Price at which a broker is willing to buy a specific security.

bid quote   Price at which one is willing to pay.

big bang   Deregulatory event in London in 1986 that allowed investment firms trading in the U.S. and Japan to trade in London, and eliminated the fixed commission structure on securities transactions.

Board of Governors   Composed of seven individual members appointed by the president of the U.S. The roles of the Board are to help regulate commercial banks and control monetary policy.

bond buyer index   Index based on 40 actively traded general obligation and revenue bonds.

bond price elasticity   Sensitivity of bond prices to changes in the required rate of return.

bonds   Debt obligations with long-term maturities issued by governments or corporations.

Brady Plan   Plan endorsed as a means of mitigating the international debt crisis. The plan was based on voluntary bank actions to either forgive a portion of LDC loans or provide additional loans. The specifics of the Plan were to be negotiated with each country separately.

Bretton Woods era   Period from 1944 to 1971, when exchange rates were fixed (maintained within one percent of a specified rate).

bridge loans   Funds provided as temporary financing until other sources of long-term funds can be obtained; these loans are commonly provided by securities firms to firms experiencing leveraged buyouts.

broker   One who executes securities transactions between two parties.

bullet loan   Loan structured so that interest payments and the loan principal are to be paid off in one lump sum at a specified future date.

call feature (call provision)   Provision that allows the initial issuer of bonds to buy back the bonds at a specified price.

call option   Contract that grants the owner the right to purchase a specified financial instrument for a specified price within a specified period of time.

call premium   Difference between the bond's call price and its par value.

callable swap (or swaption)   Swap of fixed-rate payments for floating-rate payments, whereby the party making the fixed payments has the right to terminate the swap prior to maturity.

CAMEL ratings   Characteristics used to rate bank risk.

capital   As related to banks, capital is mainly composed of retained earnings and proceeds received from issuing stock.

capital appreciation funds   Mutual funds composed of stocks of firms that have potential for very high growth, but may be unproven.

capital asset pricing model (CAPM)   Theory that suggests the return of an asset is influenced by the risk-free rate, the market return, and the covariance between asset returns and market returns.

capital markets   Financial markets that facilitate the flow of long-term funds.

capital market securities   Long-term securities, such as bonds, whose maturities are more than one year.

capital ratio   Ratio of capital to assets.

captive finance subsidiary (CFS)   Wholly owned subsidiary of a finance company whose primary purpose is to finance sales of the parent company's products, and purchase receivables of the parent company.

cash flow underwriting   Method by which insurance companies adapt insurance premiums to interest rates.

Central Liquidity Facility (CLF)   Facility that acts as a lender for credit unions to accommodate seasonal funding and specialized needs, or to boost liquidity.

certificate of deposit (CD)   Deposit offered by depository institutions that specifies a maturity, a deposit amount, and an interest rate.

Chattel mortgage bond   Bond that is secured by personal property.

circuit breakers Used to temporarily halt the trading of some securities or contracts on an exchange.

closed-end investment funds Mutual funds that do not repurchase the shares they sell.

collateralized mortgage obligations (CMOs) Represent securities that are backed by mortgages; they are segmented into classes (or tranches) which dictate the timing of the payments.

commercial paper Short-term securities (usually unsecured) issued by well-known creditworthy firms.

commission brokers (floor brokers) Brokers who execute orders for their customers.

common stock Certificate representing partial ownership of a corporation.

Competitive Banking Equality Act Act passed in 1987 that prohibits commercial banks from creating nonbank banks and from offering new insurance, real estate, and securities underwriting services.

consumer finance companies Finance companies that concentrate on direct loans to consumers.

contagion effects Adverse effects of a single firm that become contagious throughout the industry.

convertible bonds Bonds that can be converted into a specified number of the firm's common stock.

convertibility clause Provision that allows investors to convert a bond into a specified number of common stock shares.

corporate bonds Bonds issued by corporations in need of long-term funds.

covered call Sale of a call option to partially cover against the possible decline in the price of a stock that is being held.

covered interest arbitrage Act of capitalizing on higher foreign interest rates while covering the position with a simultaneous forward sale.

credit crunch A period during which banks are less willing to extend credit, which normally results from an increased probability that some borrowers will default on loans.

crowding out effect Potential borrowers, such as corporations and individuals, can be crowded out as a result of excessive borrowing by the Treasury, because limited loanable funds are available to satisfy all borrowers; the interest rates are increased in response to an increased demand for funds, which crowds some potential borrowers out of the market.

currency call option Contract that grants the owner the right to purchase a specified currency for a specified price, within a specified period of time.

currency futures contract Standardized contract that specifies an amount of a particular currency to be exchanged on a specified date and at a specified exchange rate.

currency put option Contract that grants the owner the right to sell a specified currency for a specified price, within a specified period of time.

currency swap An agreement that allows one to periodically swap one currency for another at specified exchange rates; it essentially represents a series of forward contracts.

day traders Traders of financial futures contracts who close out their contracts on the same day that they initiate them.

dealers Securities firms that make a market in specific securities by adjusting their inventories.

debentures Bonds that are backed only by the general credit of the issuing firm.

debt-equity swap An exchange of debt for an equity interest in the debtor's assets.

debt securities Securities that represent credit provided to the initial issuer by the purchaser.

default risk Risk that loans provided or securities purchased will default, so that principal, and/or interest payments, are cut off.

defensive open market operations Implemented to offset the impact of other market conditions that affect the level of reserves.

deficit units Represent individual, corporate, or government units that need to borrow funds.

defined-benefit plan Pension plan in which contributions are dictated by the benefits that will eventually be provided.

defined-contribution plan   Pension plan in which benefits are determined by the accumulated contributions, and on the fund's investment performance.

demand deposit account   Deposit account that offers checking services.

demand-pull inflation   Inflation caused by excess demand for goods.

Depository Institutions Deregulation and Monetary Control Act (DIDMCA)   Act that was intended to deregulate some aspects of the depository institutions industry, such as removing the ceiling interest rates on deposits, and allowing NOW accounts nationwide.

deposit transfer   Procedure of handling failures of savings institutions, in which the deposits of a failing institution are transferred to a healthy depository institution for a fee.

depreciate   Decrease in the value of a foreign currency.

derivative instruments   Instruments created from a previously existing security.

derivative markets   Markets that allow for the buying or selling of derivative securities.

derivatives   Financial contracts whose values are derived from the values of underlying assets.

direct lease loan   Act of purchasing assets and then leasing the assets to a firm.

dirty float   System whereby exchange rates are market-determined without boundaries, but subject to government intervention.

discount bonds   Bonds that sell below their par value.

discount brokerage firms   Brokerage firms that focus on executing transactions.

discount rate   Interest rate charged on loans provided by the Federal Reserve to depository institutions.

disintermediation   Process in which savers transfer funds from intermediaries to alternative investments with market-determined rates.

Dow Jones Industrial Index   Index of stocks of 20 large firms.

dual banking system   Regulatory framework of banking system, composed of federal and state regulators.

duration   Measurement of the life of the bond on a present value basis.

dynamic asset allocation   Switching between risky and low-risk investment positions over time in response to changing expectations.

dynamic open market operations   Implemented to increase or decrease the level of reserves.

economies of scale   Reduction in average cost per unit as the level of output increases.

Edge Act corporations   Corporations established by banks to specialize in international banking and foreign financial transactions.

Employee Retirement Income Security Act (ERISA)   Act that provided three vesting schedule options from which a pension fund could choose. It also stipulated that pension contributions be invested in a prudent manner, and that employees can transfer any vested pension amounts to new employers as they switch employers.

employee stock ownership plans (ESOPs)   Plans to offer periodic contributions of the corporation's stock to participating employees; ESOPs have been used as a means of preventing a takeover.

equity REIT   REIT that invests directly in properties.

equity securities   Securities such as common stock and preferred stock that represent ownership in a business.

equity swap   Swap arrangement involving the exchange of interest payments for payments linked to the degree of change in the stock index.

Eurobanks   Foreign banks or foreign branches of U.S. banks that participate in the Eurodollar market by accepting deposits and making loans denominated in dollars and other foreign currencies.

Euro-commercial paper (Euro-CP)   Securities issued in Europe without the backing of a bank syndicate.

Eurocredit market   Market in which banks provide medium-term loans in foreign currencies.

Eurocurrency market   Market made up of several banks that accept large deposits and provide short-term loans in foreign currencies.

Eurodollars   Large dollar-denominated deposits accepted by banks outside the U.S.

Eurodollar certificate of deposit   Large U.S. dollar deposits in non-U.S. banks.

Eurodollar floating-rate CDs (FRCDs)   Eurodollar CDs with floating interest rates that adjust periodically to the LIBOR.

Eurodollar loans   Short-term loans denominated in dollars provided to corporations and governments by branches of U.S. banks located outside the U.S. and some foreign-owned banks.

Eurodollar market   Market in Europe in which dollars are deposited and loaned for short time periods.

Eurolist   A system that allows investors of one European country to purchase shares of other European countries; the ultimate goal is to allow any publicly traded firm in the European Community to list its stock on all other European stock exchanges without preparing a separate application or a prospectus in the language of each stock exchange.

Euronotes   Notes issued in European markets in bearer form, with short-term maturities.

European Currency Unit (ECU)   Multi-currency unit of account composed of several European currencies, that is used to price some internationally traded goods and securities.

event risk   An increase in the perceived risk of default on bonds resulting from the restructuring of debt or an acquisition.

ex ante real interest rate   Real interest rate that is anticipated (which is equal to the nominal interest rate minus the expected inflation rate).

exchange rate mechanism (ERM)   Arrangement in which many European currency values are pegged to the European Currency Unit (within boundaries), which links the exchange rates between these currencies.

exchange rate risk   Risk that currency values change in a manner that adversely affects future cash flows.

exercise price (or strike price)   Price at which the instrument underlying the option contract can be purchased (in the case of a call option) or sold (in the case of a put option).

ex post real interest rate   Real interest rate that occurred in a previous period (nominal interest rate minus the inflation rate in that period).

extendable swap   Swap of fixed payments for floating payments that contains an extendable feature allowing the party making fixed payments to extend the swap period if desired.

factor   Firm that purchases the accounts receivable at a discount and is responsible for processing and collecting on the balances of these accounts; finance companies commonly have subsidiaries that serve as factors.

Federal Deposit Insurance Corporation (FDIC)   Federal agency that insures the deposits of commercial banks.

federal funds rate   Interest rate charged on loans between depository institutions.

Federal National Mortgage Association (FNMA)   Issues mortgage-backed securities and uses the funds to purchase mortgages.

Federal Open Market Committee (FOMC)   Composed of the seven members of the Board of Governors plus the presidents of five Federal Reserve district banks. The main role of the FOMC is to control monetary policy.

Federal Reserve   Central bank of the U.S.

Federal Reserve district bank   A regional government bank that facilitates operations within the banking system by clearing checks, replacing old currency, providing loans to banks, and conducting research; there are 12 Federal Reserve district banks.

financial futures contract   Standardized agreement to deliver or receive a specified amount of a specified financial instrument at a specified price and date.

Financial Institutions Reform, Recovery, and Enforcement Act (FIRREA)   Act that was intended to enhance the safety of savings institutions; some of the key provisions of the act prevented savings institutions from investing in junk bonds, increased capital requirements, and increased the penalties for fraud.

financial market   Market in which financial assets (or securities) such as stocks and bonds are traded.

first mortgage bond   Bond that has first claim on specified assets as collateral.

Fisher effect   Positive relationship between interest rates and expected inflation.

fixed-rate mortgage   Mortgage that requires payments based on a fixed interest rate.

floor brokers   Individuals who facilitate the trading of stocks on the New York and American stock exchanges by executing transactions for their clients.

floor traders   Members of a futures exchange who trade futures contracts for their own account.

flotation costs   Costs of placing securities.

flow-of-funds accounts   Reports on the amount of funds channeled to and from various sectors.

foreign exchange derivatives   Instruments created to lock in a foreign exchange transaction, such as forward contracts, futures contracts, currency swaps, and currency options contracts.

forward contract   Contract typically negotiated with a commercial bank that allows a customer to purchase or sell a specified amount of a particular foreign currency at a specified exchange rate on a specified future date.

forward market   Market that facilitates the trading of forward contracts; commercial banks serve as intermediaries in the market by matching up participants who wish to buy a currency forward with other participants who wish to sell the currency forward.

forward rate   In the context of term structure of interest rates, is used to represent the market's forecast of the future interest rate. In the context of foreign exchange, is used to represent the exchange rate at which a specified currency can be purchased or sold for a specified future point in time.

forward swap   Involves an exchange of interest payments that does not begin until a specified future point in time.

freely floating system   System whereby exchange rates are market determined, without any government intervention.

full-service brokerage firms   Brokerage firms that provide complete information and advice about securities, in addition to executing transactions.

futures contract   Standardized contract allowing one to purchase or sell a specified amount of a specified instrument (such as a security or currency) for a specified price and at a specified future point in time.

gap   Defined as the rate-sensitive assets minus rate-sensitive liabilities.

gap ratio   Measured as the value of rate-sensitive assets divided by the value of rate-sensitive liabilities.

Garn-St Germain Act   Act passed in 1982 that allowed for the creation of money market deposit accounts (MMDAs), loosened lending guidelines for federally chartered savings institutions, and allowed failing depository institutions to be acquired by other depository institutions outside the state.

general obligation bonds   Bonds which provide payments that are supported by the municipal government's ability to tax.

Glass-Steagall Act   Act in 1933 that separated commercial banking and investment banking activities.

global crowding out   Situation in which excessive government borrowing in one country can cause higher interest rates in other countries.

global junk bonds   Low-quality bonds issued globally by governments and corporations.

Government National Mortgage Association (GNMA)   Agency that guarantees the timely payment of principal and interest to investors who purchase securities backed by mortgages.

graduated-payment mortgage (GPM)   Mortgage that allows borrowers to initially make small payments on the mortgage; the payments are increased on a graduated basis.

greenmail   The accumulation of shares of targets, followed by sales of the shares back to the targets; the targets purchase these shares back (at a premium) to remove the threat of a takeover.

gross interest expense   Represents interest paid on deposits and on other borrowed funds.

gross interest income   Represents interest income generated from all assets.

group life policy   Policy provided to a group of policyholders with some common bond.

growth funds   Mutual funds containing stocks of firms that are expected to grow at a higher than average rate, for investors who are willing to accept a moderate degree of risk.

health maintenance organizations (HMOs)   Intermediaries between purchasers and providers of health care.

hedgers   Take positions in contracts to reduce their exposure to risk.

high-yield funds   Mutual funds composed of bonds that offer high yields (junk bonds) and have a relatively high degree of default risk.

highly leveraged transactions (HLTs)   Credit provided that results in a debt-to-asset ratio of at least 75 percent.

IMF Funding Bill   Bill passed to provide funding to LDCs experiencing problems in repaying their debt.

immunize   The act of insulating a security portfolio from interest rate movements.

impact lag   Lag time between when a policy is implemented by the government and the time at which it has its effect on the economy.

imperfect markets   Markets in which buyers and sellers of securities do not have full access to information, and cannot always break down securities to the precise size they desire.

implementation lag   Lag time between when the government recognizes a problem and the time at which it implements a policy to resolve the problem.

income funds   Mutual funds composed of bonds that offer periodic coupon payments.

indenture   Legal document specifying the rights and obligations of both the issuing firm and the bondholders.

index arbitrage   Act of capitalizing on discrepancies between prices of index futures and stocks.

informal line of credit   Financing arrangement that allows a business to borrow up to a specified amount within a specified period of time.

Initial Public Offering (IPO)   Represents a first-time offering of shares by a specific firm to the public.

installment loans   Loans to individuals to finance purchases of cars and household products.

interest inelastic   Insensitive to interest rates.

interest rate cap   Arrangement that offers a party interest payments in periods when the interest rate on a specific money market instrument exceeds a specified ceiling rate; the payments will be based on the amount by which the interest rate exceeds the ceiling as applied to the notional principal specified in the agreement.

interest rate collar   The purchase of an interest rate cap and the simultaneous sale of an interest rate floor.

interest rate floor   Agreement in which one offers an interest rate payment in periods when the interest rate on a specified money market instrument is below a specified floor rate.

interest rate futures   Financial futures contracts on debt securities such as Treasury bills, notes, or bonds.

interest rate parity   Theory that suggests the forward discount (or premium) is dependent on the interest rate differential between the two countries of concern.

interest rate risk   Risk that an asset will decline in value in response to interest rate movements.

interest rate swap   Arrangement whereby one party exchanges one set of interest payments for another.

international mutual fund   Portfolio of international stocks created and managed by a financial institution; individuals can invest in international stocks by purchasing shares of an international mutual fund.

in the money   Describes a call option whose premium is above the exercise price, or a put option whose premium is below the exercise price.

investment-grade bonds   Bonds that are rated Baa or better by Moody's, and BBB or better by Standard and Poor's.

investment-grade securities   Securities that are rated as "medium" quality or higher by rating agencies.

junk bonds   Corporate bonds that are perceived to have a high degree of risk.

junk commercial paper   Low-rated commercial paper.

Keynesian theory   Theory that suggests how the government can improve economic conditions; as related to monetary policy, the theory explains how money supply can be adjusted to affect interest rates and the economy.

letter of credit   Guarantee by a bank on the financial obligations of a firm that owes payment (usually an importer).

leveraged buyout (LBO)   A buyout of a firm that is financed mostly with debt.

leverage measure   Measure of financial leverage, defined as assets divided by equity.

liquidity   Ability to sell the assets easily without loss of value.

liquidity preference theory   Theory used to explain how changes in the money supply affect interest rates.

liquidity premium theory   Theory that suggests the yield to maturity is higher for illiquid securities, other things being equal.

loan commitment   Obligation by a bank to provide a specified loan amount to a particular firm upon the firm's request.

loan funds   Mutual funds that have a sales charge imposed by brokerage firms who sell the funds.

loan participation   Arrangement in which several banks pool funds to provide a loan to a corporation.

loanable funds theory   Theory that suggests the market interest rate is determined by the factors that control the supply and demand for loanable funds.

locational arbitrage   Arbitrage intended to capitalize on a price (such as foreign exchange rate quote) discrepancy between two locations.

London Interbank Offer Rate (LIBOR)   Interest rate charged on interbank loans.

long hedge   The purchase of financial futures contracts to hedge against the possible decrease in interest rates.

long-term equity anticipations (LEAPs)   Stock options with relatively long-term expiration dates.

low-coupon bonds   Bonds that pay low coupon payments; most of the expected return to investors is attributed to the large discount in the bond's price.

M1   Definition of money supply, composed of currency held by the public plus checking accounts.

M2   Definition of money supply, composed of M1 plus savings accounts, small time deposits, MMDAs, and some other items.

M3   Definition of money supply, composed of M2 plus large time deposits and other items.

margin call   Call from broker to participants in futures contracts (or other investments) that they must increase their margin.

market-makers   Individuals who facilitate the trading of stocks on the NASDAQ by standing ready to buy or sell specific stocks in response to customer orders made through a telecommunications network.

market microstructure   Process by which securities are traded.

market orders   Requests by customers to purchase or sell securities at the market price existing when the order reaches the exchange floor.

market risk Risk that the stock market experiences lower prices in response to adverse economic conditions or pessimistic expectations.

matched funding Strategy in which investment decisions are made with the objective of matching planned outflow payments.

McFadden Act of 1927 Act preventing all banks from establishing branches across state lines.

merger-conversion Procedure used in acquisitions whereby a mutual S&L converts to a stock-owned S&L before either acquiring or being acquired by another firm.

modern quantity theory of money Theory that suggests an increase in the quantity of money leads to a predictable increase in the value of goods produced.

monetarists Economists who advocate a stable low growth in the money supply.

monetizing the debt Act of the Fed's increasing the money supply to offset any increased demand for funds resulting from a larger budget deficit.

money markets Financial markets that facilitate the flow of short-term funds.

money market deposit account (MMDA) Deposit account that pays interest and allows limited checking, and does not specify a maturity.

money market mutual funds Mutual funds that concentrate their investment in money market securities.

money market securities Short-term securities, such as Treasury bills or certificates of deposit, whose maturities are one year or less.

moral hazard problem Refers to the deposit insurance pricing system that existed up until the early 1990s, in which the insurance premiums per $100 of deposits were similar across all commercial banks; this system caused an indirect subsidy from safer banks to risky banks, and encouraged banks to take excessive risk.

mortgage-backed securities Securities backed by mortgages that are commonly sold and purchased by savings institutions.

mortgage pass-through securities Securities issued by a financial institution and backed by a group of mortgages. The mortgage interest and principal are sent to the financial institution, which then transfers the payments to the owners of the mortgage-backed securities after deducting a service fee.

mortgage REIT REIT that invests in mortgage and construction loans.

municipal bond index futures Futures contract allowing for the future purchase or sale of municipal bonds at a specified price.

municipal bonds Debt securities issued by state and local governments, which can usually be classified as either general obligation bonds or revenue bonds.

mutual fund An investment company that sells shares representing an interest in a portfolio of securities.

mutual S&Ls S&Ls that are owned by depositors.

mutual-to-stock conversion Procedure by savings institutions to shift the ownership structure from depositors to shareholders.

National Association of Insurance Commissioners (NAIC) Agency that facilitates cooperation among the various state agencies where an insurance issue is a concern.

National Association of Securities Dealers (NASD) Regulator of the securities industry.

National Association of Securities Dealers Automatic Quotations (NASDAQ) A service for the over-the-counter market that reports immediate price quotations for many of the stocks.

National Credit Union Administration (NCUA) Regulator of credit unions; the NCUA participates in the creation of new CUs, examines the financial condition of CUs, and supervises any liquidations or mergers.

National Credit Union Share Insurance Fund (NCUSIF) Agency that insures deposits at credit unions.

Negotiable Certificate of Deposit (NCD) Deposit accounts with a minimum deposit requirement of $100,000 that require a specified maturity; there is a secondary market for these deposits.

net asset value Financial characteristic used to describe a mutual fund's value per share, estimated as the market value of the securities comprising the mutual fund, plus any accrued interest or dividends, minus any expenses. This value is divided by the number of shares outstanding.

net exposure Used in the context of futures markets, reflects the difference between asset and liability positions.

noise traders Uninformed investors whose buy and sell positions push the stock price away from its fundamental value.

noise trading Theory used to explain that stock prices may deviate from their fundamental values as a result of the buy and sell positions of uninformed investors (called "noise traders"); a market correction may not eliminate the discrepancy if the informed traders are unwilling to capitalize on the discrepancy (because of uncertainty surrounding the stock's fundamental value).

no-load funds Mutual funds that do not have a sales charge, meaning that they are not promoted by brokerage firms.

noninterest expenses Expenses that are unrelated to interest payments on deposits or borrowed funds, such as salaries and office equipment.

noninterest income Income resulting from fees charged or services provided.

note issuance facility Commitment in which a bank agrees to purchase the commercial paper of a firm if the firm cannot place its paper in the market at an acceptable interest rate.

notional principal Value to which interest rates from interest rate swaps are applied to determine the interest payments involved.

NOW accounts Deposit accounts that allow unlimited checking and pay interest.

open-end investment funds Mutual funds that are willing to repurchase the shares they sell from investors at any time.

Open Market Desk Division of the New York Fed district bank that is responsible for conducting open market operations.

open market operations The Fed's buying and selling of government securities (through the Trading Desk).

option premium Price paid for an option contract.

organized exchange Visible marketplace for secondary market transactions.

origination Decisions by a firm (with the help of a securities firm) on how much stock or bonds to issue, the type of stock (or bonds) to be issued, and the price at which the stock (or bonds) should be sold.

out of the money Describes a call option whose premium is below the exercise price, or a put option whose premium is above the exercise price.

over-the-counter (OTC) market Market used to facilitate transactions of securities not listed on organized exchanges.

participation certificates (PCs) Certificates sold by the Federal Home Loan Mortgage Association; the proceeds are used to purchase conventional mortgages from financial institutions.

Pension Benefit Guarantee Corporation (PBGC) Established as a result of the ERISA to provide insurance on pension plans.

perfect markets Markets in which all information about any securities for sale would be freely and continuously available to investors. Furthermore, all securities for sale could be broken down into any size desired by investors, and transaction costs would be nonexistent.

Phillips curve Represents the relationship between unemployment and inflation.

plain vanilla swap Involves the periodic exchange of fixed-rate payments for floating-rate payments.

policy directive Statement provided by the FOMC to the Trading Desk regarding the target money supply range.

portfolio insurance Program trading combined

with the trading of stock index futures to hedge against market movements.

position traders Traders of financial futures contracts who maintain their futures positions for relatively long periods (such as weeks or months) before closing them out.

preemptive rights Priority given to a particular group of people to purchase newly issued stock, before other investors are given the opportunity to purchase the stock.

preferred habitat theory Theory that suggests that although investors and borrowers may normally concentrate on a particular natural maturity market, certain events may cause them to wander from it.

preferred stock Certificate representing partial ownership of a corporation, without significant voting rights; it provides owners dividends, but normally does not provide a share of the firm's profits.

present value interest factor (PVIF) Factor that represents the present value of $1 for a specified period and interest (discount) rate.

present value interest factor of an annuity (PVIFA) Factor that represents the present value of a stream of $1 payments for a specified number of periods and a specified interest (discount) rate.

primary market Market where securities are initially issued.

prime rate Interest rate charged on loans by banks to their most creditworthy customers.

privatization Process of converting government ownership of businesses to private ownership.

program trading The simultaneous buying and selling of a portfolio of at least 15 different stocks valued at more than $1 million.

projective funding Strategy that offers pension fund managers some flexibility in constructing a pension portfolio that can benefit from expected market and interest rate movements.

protective covenants Restrictions enforced by a bond indenture that protects the bondholders from an increase in risk; such restrictions may include limits on the dividends paid, on the salaries paid, and on the additional debt the firm can issue.

purchasing power parity (PPP) Theory that suggests exchange rates adjust, on average, by a percentage that reflects the inflation differential between the two countries of concern.

pure expectations theory Theory suggesting that the shape of the yield curve is determined solely by interest rates.

put option Contract that grants the owner the right to sell a specified financial instrument for a specified price within a specified period of time.

putable swap Swap of fixed-rate payments for floating rate payments whereby the party making floating-rate payments has the right to terminate the swap.

rate-capped swap Swap arrangement involving fixed-rate payments for floating-rate payments, whereby the floating payments are capped.

real estate investment trust (REIT) Closed-end mutual fund that invests in real estate or mortgages.

real estate mortgage conduit (REMIC) Allows financial institutions to sell mortgage assets and issue mortgage-backed securities

real interest rate Nominal interest rate adjusted for inflation.

recognition lag Lag time between when a problem arises and when it is recognized by the government.

registration statement Statement of relevant financial information disclosed by a corporation issuing securities, which is intended to ensure that accurate information is disclosed by the issuing corporation.

Regulation Q Bank regulation that had limited the interest rate banks could pay on deposits.

reinsurance Manner by which insurance companies can allocate a portion of their return and risk to other insurance companies, whereby other companies share in insuring large policies.

repurchase agreement (Repo) Agreement in which a bank (or some other firm) sells some of its government security holdings, with a commitment to purchase those securities back at a later date; this agreement essentially reflects a loan from the time the firm sold the securities until the securities are repurchased.

reserve requirement ratio   Percentage of deposits that commercial banks must maintain as required reserves; this ratio is sometimes used by the Fed as a monetary policy tool.

Resolution Trust Corporation (RTC)   Agency created in 1989 to help bail out failing savings institutions; the RTC liquidates an institution's assets and reimburses depositors or sells the savings institution to another depository institution.

Retail Certificate of Deposit (Retail CD)   Deposit requiring a specific minimum amount of funds to be deposited for a specified period of time.

return on assets (ROA)   Defined as net income divided by assets.

return on equity (ROE)   Defined as net income divided by equity.

revenue bonds   Bonds which provide payments that are supported by the revenue generated by the project.

Reverse Leveraged Buyout (Reverse LBO)   Process of issuing new stock after engaging in a leveraged buyout and improving the firm's performance.

reverse repo   The purchase of securities by one party from another with an agreement to sell them in the future.

revolving credit loan   Financing arrangement that obligates the bank to loan some specified maximum amount of funds over a specified period of time.

S&P 500 Index Futures   Futures contract allowing for the future purchase or sale of the S&P 500 index at a specified price.

sales finance companies   Finance companies that concentrate on purchasing credit contracts from retailers and dealers.

Savings Association Insurance Fund (SAIF)   Insuring agency for S&Ls as of 1989.

secondary market   Market where securities are resold.

secondary stock offering   Represents a new stock offering by a firm that already has stock outstanding.

Securities and Exchange Commission (SEC)   Regulates the issuance of securities disclosure rules for issuers, the exchanges, and participating brokerage firms.

Securities Exchange Act of 1933   Intended to ensure complete disclosure of relevant information on publicly offered securities and prevent fraudulent practices in selling these securities.

Securities Exchange Act of 1934   Intended to ensure complete disclosure of relevant information on securities traded in secondary markets.

securities gains and losses   Bank accounting term that reflects the gains or losses generated from the sale of securities.

Securities Investor Protection Corporation (SIPC)   Offers insurance on cash and securities deposited at brokerage firms.

securitization   Pooling and repackaging of loans into securities, which are sold to investors.

segmented markets theory   Theory that suggests investors and borrowers choose securities with maturities that satisfy their forecasted cash needs.

semistrong-form efficiency   Security prices reflect all public information, including announcements by firms, economic news or events, and political news or events.

shared-appreciation mortgage   Mortgage that allows a home purchaser to pay a below-market interest rate; in return, the lender shares in the appreciation of the home price.

Sharpe index   Measure of risk-adjusted return, defined as the asset's excess mean return beyond the mean risk-free risk, divided by the standard deviation of returns of the asset of concern.

shelf-registration   Registration with SEC in advance of public placement of securities.

short hedge   The sale of financial futures contracts to hedge against the possible increase in interest rates.

short selling   The sale of securities that are borrowed, with the intent of buying those securities to repay what was borrowed.

Single European Act of 1987   Act that called for a reduction in barriers between European countries; this allowed for easier trade and capital flows throughout Europe.

sinking-fund provision   Requirement that the firm retire a specific amount of the bond issue each year.

Smithsonian Agreement   Agreement among major countries to devalue the dollar against some currencies and widen the boundaries around each exchange rate from 1 percent to 2.25 percent.

sovereign risk   As applied to swaps, risk that a country's political conditions could prevent one party in the swap from receiving payments due.

specialists   Individuals who facilitate the trading of stocks on the New York and American stock exchanges by taking positions in specific stocks; they stand ready to buy or sell these stocks on the trading floor.

speculators   Those who take positions to benefit from future price movements.

spot exchange rate   Present exchange rate.

spread   Used to represent the difference between bid and ask quotes. This term is also sometimes used to reflect the difference between the average interest rate earned on assets and the average interest rate paid on liabilities.

Standard & Poors 500 Index   Index of stocks of 500 large firms.

standby letter of credit   Agreement that backs a customer's financial obligation.

stock index futures   Financial futures contracts on stock indexes.

stop-loss order   Order of a sale of a specific security when the price reaches a specified minimum.

strike price (exercise price)   Price at which an option can be exercised.

stripped securities   Securities that are stripped of their coupon payments in order to create two separate types of securities: (1) a principal-only part that pays a future lump-sum, and (2) an interest-only part that pays coupon payments, but no principal.

strips program   Program created by the Treasury in which it exchanges stripped securities for Treasury securities.

strong-form efficiency   Security prices fully reflect all information, including private (insider) information.

subordinated debentures   Debentures that have claims against the firm's assets that are junior to the claims of both mortgage bonds and regular debentures.

surplus units   Individual, business, or government units that have excess funds which can be invested.

swap options (swaptions)   Options on interest rate swaps.

systematic risk   Risk that is attributable to market movements, and cannot be diversified away.

T-bill discount   Percentage by which the price paid for a Treasury bill is less than the par value.

technical analysis   Method of forecasting future stock prices with the use of historical stock price patterns.

term insurance   Temporary insurance over a specified term; the policy does not build a cash value.

term loan   Business loan used to finance the purchase of fixed assets.

term structure of interest rates   Relationship between the term remaining until maturity and the annualized yield of Treasury securities.

theory of rational expectations   Suggests that the public accounts for all existing information when forming its expectations; as applied to monetary policy, it implies that historical effects of money supply growth will be considered when forecasting the effects of prevailing money supply growth.

Trading Desk   Located at the New York Federal Reserve district bank, it is used to carry out orders from the FOMC about open market operations.

Treasury bills   Securities issued by the Treasury that have maturities of one year or less.

Treynor index   Measure of risk-adjusted return, defined as the asset's excess mean return beyond the mean risk-free rate, divided by the beta of the asset of concern.

trustee   Appointed to represent the bondholders in all matters concerning the bond issue.

underwrite   Act of guaranteeing a specific price to the initial issuer of securities.

underwriting spread   Difference between the price at which an investment banking firm expects to sell securities and the price it is willing to pay the issuing firm.

underwriting syndicate   Group of investment banking firms that are required to underwrite a portion of a corporation's newly issued securities.

usury laws   Laws that enforce a maximum interest rate that can be imposed on loans to households.

variable life insurance   Insurance in which benefits awarded by the life insurance company to a beneficiary vary with the assets backing the policy.

variable-rate bonds   Bonds whose coupon rates adjust to market interest rates over time.

weak-form efficiency   Theory that suggests that security prices reflect all market-related data, such as historical security price movements and volume of securities trades.

whole life insurance   Insurance that protects the insured policyholders until death or as long as premiums are promptly paid; the policy builds a cash value that the policyholder is entitled to even if the policy is canceled.

working capital loan   Business loan designed to support ongoing operations, typically for a short-term period.

writer   The seller of an option contract.

yield curve   Curve depicting the relationship between the term remaining until maturity and the annualized yield of Treasury securities.

yield to maturity   Discount rate at which the present value of future payments would equal the security's current price.

zero-coupon bonds   Bonds that have no coupon payments.

zero-coupon for floating swap   Swap arrangement calling for one party to swap a lump-sum payment at maturity in exchange for periodic floating-rate payments.

INDEX

Abnormal return 510
Acquisitions 265–266, 267, 269, 489, 493, 494, 656, 658–659, 665
Active portfolio management strategy 214–215
Actuarial tables 695
Adjustable-rate mortgages (ARMs) 229–230, 572–574
After-tax yield 77–78, 81
Agency costs 267, 475–476
American depository receipts (ADRs) 273
American Stock Exchange (ASE) 4, 255, 256, 259
American-style stock options 320
Amortization schedule 231–233
Annuity 52
Annuity plans 697
Antitakeover provisions 660
Appreciate 396, 403
Arbitrage 307, 405–408, 658–660
Arbitrage firms 658–659
Arbitrage pricing theory 261–262
Arbitrageurs 307
Ask price 201, 256, 392
Ask quote 10, 118
Asset allocation funds 634
Asset quality 458
Asset stripping 658
At the money 319–320

Balance-sheet management 492
Balloon-payment 429, 432
Balloon-payment mortgage 231
Bank capital 422, 426–427, 489–491
Bank charter 443
Bank failures 528–529
Bank Holding Company Act (1956) 444–445, 449
Bank Insurance Fund 445
Bank management 475–500

Bank of New England 500, 517
Bank performance 511–529
Bank policies 509–510, 518
Bank regulation 443–467, 472–474
Bank regulators 444, 536
BankAmerica 524–525
Banker's acceptances 6, 176, 186–187
Banking Act (1933) 453
Basis 299
Basis risk 301, 370–383
Beatrice 658
Before-tax yield 76–78, 81
Beneficial Corporation 614, 618, 622
Beneficiary 695
Best-efforts agreement 661
Beta 260, 261, 283, 509, 520–522, 525, 618, 684
Bid price 201, 256, 392
Bid quote 10
Big Bang 668
Black-Scholes option-pricing model 350–353
Board of Governors 114, 115–116, 121–122, 125
Bond Buyer Index 303
Bond collateral 204
Bond dealers 200
Bond indenture 203
Bond index futures 303–304
Bond issues 662–663
Bond markets 199–220, 579, 621, 648, 669, 687, 689, 712
Bond maturity 47–48, 56, 57–58, 60
Bond mutual funds 628, 630–637
Bond portfolio forecasts 64–66
Bond price forecasts 61–62
Bond ratings 74–75, 212
Bond risk 210–213, 216
Bond valuation 47–53

Bond yield forecasts 62–64
Bond yield interactions 213
Bond yields 62–64, 200, 213
Bonds 199–210, 613, 681
Brady Plan 547
Bretton Woods era 392
Bridge loans 658, 659
Broker 10
Brokerage firms 215, 242, 255, 268, 292, 409, 578, 655–656, 661, 663, 688, 711
Brokerage services 10, 655, 663–664, 670
Brookings Institute 684
Building Societies 587–588
Bullet loan 429
Bundesbank 398
Business loans 615–616

California Pension Employees Retirement System (CALPERS) 682
Call feature 79, 200
Call option 319–324, 330–332, 335, 350–353, 631
Call option premium 325–328
Call premium 82, 204
Call provisions 204
Callable swaps 363–364
CAMEL ratings 458–459, 601
Campeau Corporation 208
Capital 565–566, 613
Capital adequacy 458
Capital appreciation funds 631
Capital asset pricing model 260–261
Capital market securities 4, 6
Capital markets 4
Capital ratio 458, 489, 520, 539, 584, 585–587, 599

Capital requirements 446–447, 584, 601

Caps 229

Captive finance subsidiary 617–620

Cash flow underwriting 705

Casualty insurance 705

Central banks 113, 114, 130–132, 139, 398, 425, 536, 598

Central Liquidity Facility (CLF) 598, 602

Chattel mortgage bond 204

Chicago Board of Trade (CBOT) 292, 294, 303, 311

Chicago Mercantile Exchange (CME) 292, 307, 403

Circuit breakers 7, 307–310

Citicorp 524–525, 527, 540, 546, 547

Clearinghouse Interbank Payments System (CHIPS) 442

Closed-end investment funds 630

Closed-end mutual funds 641

Coastal States Life Insurance Co. 238

Collateral 431, 566

Collaterized mortgage obligations (CMOs) 236, 237–238

Columbia Savings and Loan 208

Commercial bank regulation 443–467

Commercial banks 9, 12–13, 93, 97, 114, 116, 118–119, 185, 188–189, 215, 240–242, 257, 271, 310, 359, 401, 409, 421–436, 484, 512, 578, 612, 614, 620, 622, 646–647, 664, 668, 670, 687–688, 711

Commercial loans 567

Commercial paper 6, 175, 179–183, 612, 613, 644, 646, 670

Commercial paper dealers 181

Commercial paper rates 80, 181

Commercial paper yields 181–183

Commission brokers 292

Commodity Futures Trading Commission (CFTC) 291–292

Common stock 4, 5, 249–251, 681

Comptroller of the Currency 114, 443–444, 459, 528

Consumer finance companies 611–612

Consumer Advisory Council 117

Consumer loans 431–432, 567, 587, 614, 616

Contagion effects 207–208

Continental Illinois Bank 464–467, 499–500

Conventional mortgages 228–229, 237, 571

Conversion feature 208–209

Convertibility clause 79

Convertibility discount 82

Convertible bond 208–210

Corporate bond futures 302

Corporate bonds 6, 81, 199, 203–210, 212, 432, 567, 631, 681, 699

Corporate Credit Union Network 598

Corporate securities 699

Correlation coefficient 487–488

Country risk 548–551

Coupon payment 48–56, 58

Coupon rate 53–56, 59, 200, 201

Covariance 487

Covered call 330–332, 631

Covered interest arbitrage 407–408

Credit crunch 141

Credit risk 234, 371–373, 383, 665, 666

Credit union regulation 601

Credit unions 9, 13, 117, 242, 595–605, 614, 620

Cross-hedging 301–303

Crowding-out effect 35, 158, 161–162

Cumulative provision 251

Currency call option 341, 402

Currency futures contracts 312, 381, 391, 401, 402–403, 404–405, 688

Currency options 341, 391, 401, 402, 405, 688

Currency put option 341

Currency swaps 381–384, 391, 401, 402, 436

Day traders 293

Dealers 10, 183, 184, 186

Debentures 204

Debt-equity swaps 546

Debt management 97–99, 548–550

Debt management model 548–550

Debt securities 5, 73–74

Default risk 74–75, 81, 83, 180, 205, 212–213, 228–229, 234, 236, 432, 458, 484–489, 492, 542, 544, 566, 571, 600, 603, 617, 631, 642, 699, 702

Default risk premium 74, 76, 80–83, 100

Defensive open market operations 120

Deficit units 4, 6, 8, 11–12, 199

Defined-benefit plan 678, 679

Defined-contribution plan 678

Demand deposit account 422, 520

Demand-pull inflation 139

Deposit accounts 421

Deposit rate ceilings 472, 601

Deposit rate regulations 447–448

Deposit runs 568

Depository institutions 8, 12, 116, 121, 124, 125, 127–129, 188, 611, 612, 627–628, 666

Depository Institutions Deregulation and Monetary Control Act (1980) 116, 127–129, 449, 472–473, 565, 567, 601

Depreciate 396, 403

Deregulation 13, 472–474, 512, 528

Derivatives 289, 391

Designated Order Turnaround (DOT) System 258

Direct intervention 397

Direct lease loan 429

Direct placement 663

Dirty float 392

Discount bonds 53

Discount brokerage firms 255, 664

Discount rate 116, 121, 124, 153, 269, 425, 565

Discount window 114, 121, 124, 129, 464, 476, 565, 597

Discriminant analysis 550

Diseconomies of scale 604

Disintermediation 448, 565

Diversification 260, 486–489, 494, 587, 627, 635, 688, 705

Diversifying bond risk 216, 219–220

Divestitures 656

Douglas Amendment to the Bank Holding Company Act of 1956 449

Dow Jones Industrial Average 307–308

Dow Jones Industrial Index 122

Downsizing 493

Drexel Burnham Lambert Inc. 207, 208, 211, 657, 660

Dual banking system 443

Duration 59–61, 477, 480–481, 572–573
Dynamic asset allocation 306, 334–335
Dynamic open market operations 120

Economic indicator model 548, 550
Economies of scale 450, 494, 580, 604
Edge Act corporations 536
Effective yield 194–195
Electronic funds transfer (EFT) 441–442
Employee Retirement Income Security Act (ERISA) 685
Equation of exchange 141
Equilibrium interest rate 29–32
Equity REITs 646
Equity securities 5, 6
Equity swaps 368–370
Estimation period 509–510
Eurobanks 193, 542–544
Eurobond market 217–218
Euro-commercial paper 191, 193–194
Eurocredit market 193
Eurocurrency market 193, 536
Eurodollar borrowings 422, 426
Eurodollar certificates of deposit 191–193, 292
Eurodollar deposit rates 80
Eurodollar deposits 6, 191–193
Eurodollar floating-rate CDs 193
Eurodollar loans 428, 433–434
Eurodollar market 192
Eurodollars 426
Euro-Fed 131
Eurolist 271
Euronotes 191–193
European Commission 538
European Currency Unit (ECU) 393
European Economic Community 131–132, 271, 538
European-style stock options 320
Ex post real interest rate 34
Examination period 509–510
Exchange rate mechanism (ERM) 163–164, 393, 394–395
Exchange rate risk 394–395, 399, 408, 542–544, 665, 666, 688
Exchange rates 100
Exercise price 319, 323, 324,

325–326, 328, 329, 403
Executive Life Insurance 703
Exporter 186–187
Extendable swaps 365–367

Factor 615
Federal Advisory Council 116–117
Federal agency securities 26, 432
Federal budget deficit 158
Federal Deposit Insurance Corporation (FDIC) 444, 445, 457–467, 489, 536, 583, 601
Federal Deposit Insurance Corporation Improvement Act (1991) 445–446, 462
Federal funds 6, 176, 184–185, 422, 423–425, 428, 432–433
Federal funds brokers 185, 426
Federal funds rate 120, 121, 126, 184–185, 424, 426, 565
Federal funds market 120, 184, 423–425, 432–433, 476, 567
Federal Home Loan Bank Board 583
Federal Home Loan Mortgage Association (Freddie Mac) 237, 432
Federal Housing Administration (FHA) 228–229, 236, 237, 511
Federal National Mortgage Association (FNMA; Fannie Mae) 236, 237, 239, 240, 432
Federal Open Market Committee (FOMC) 114, 116–117, 118, 137, 144–145, 149
Federal Reserve Act (1913) 114
Federal Reserve Board 115, 459, 536, 541, 656
Federal Reserve district banks 114–115, 116, 117, 422, 425
Federal Reserve float 125
Federal Reserve System 4, 28, 38, 39, 113–132, 137–161, 398, 425, 442, 443–444, 464, 566
Federal Savings and Loan Insurance Corporation (FSLIC) 582, 583
Fed wire 442
Fee income 435, 541
Finance companies 9–10, 12–13, 189, 215, 242, 257, 359, 578, 611–622, 647, 711
Finance company regulation 615–616

Financial assets 3
Financial futures contract 291–293, 483–484
Financial futures markets 291–312
Financial institutions 8–13, 28, 57, 662
Financial Institutions Reform Recovery and Enforcement Act (FIRREA) 207, 444, 580, 583, 585, 657
Financial leverage 205, 211, 223, 267, 489, 519–520, 585, 659
Financial market efficiency 5, 89
Financial markets 3–12

Gap 477, 478–480, 497, 500, 571–572
Gap ratio 478
Garn-St. Germain Act (1982) 423, 453, 472–474, 565, 567, 570
General Electric Credit Corporation 619
General Electric Financial Services 457
General Motors Acceptance Corporation 614
General obligation bonds 201–202, 303, 453, 670
Getty Oil Company 266
Glass-Steagall Act (1933) 670
Global bank competition 539–541
Global bank regulations 536–539
Global crowding out 161–162
Global futures market 311–312
Global junk bonds 217
Global mortgage markets 242–243
Global mutual funds 632–634, 648–649
Global options market 339–341
Global stock markets 270–276, 648
Global swap markets 380–384
Globex 311
Government agency securities 432, 698
Government intervention 392–393, 397–398, 465–467
Government National Mortgage Association (GNMA; Ginnie Mae) 236–240, 631
Graduated-payment mortgage 232
Grandfather provisions 453
Great Depression 7, 447, 677
Great Western 581
Greenmail 659

Gross interest expenses 512, 518–519
Gross interest income 512, 518–519
Gross national product (GNP) 145
Group life policy 697
Growing-equity mortgage 232, 233
Growth funds 631
Growth and income funds 632
Gulf Corporation 266

Health care insurance 697
Health maintenance organizations (HMOs) 697
Hedge ratio 303
Hedged portfolio 299–300
Hedged position 300
Hedgers 293
Hedging 298–303, 305–306, 330–334, 335, 338–339, 403, 543
Highly leveraged transactions (HLTs) 431, 446
High-yield funds 632
Holiday effect 269
Hostile takeover 658, 660
Hurdle rate 25
Hurricane Andrew 706
Hybrid REIT 646

Illiquidity 476, 582
Immunization techniques 682
Immunize 60
Impact lag 148
Imperfect financial markets 8
Implementation lag 148
Implied standard deviation 353
Importer 186–187
In the money 319–320
Income funds 631–632
Index arbitrage 307
Index funds 634, 682
Indirect intervention 397
Individual Retirement Account (IRA) 685
Inflation rates 33–35, 100, 396–397
Inflationary expectations 210, 212
Informal line of credit 429
Initial margin 292
Initial public offering (IPO) 251–255, 267–268, 269–270, 665
Insider information 269
Insider trading 273
Installment loans 431
Institutional investors 11, 250, 273, 399, 657, 697

Insurance companies 10–11, 12–13, 189, 204, 215, 238, 242, 257, 310, 339–340, 359, 409, 578, 620, 622, 647, 668, 687, 695–713
Insurance company crisis 703
Insurance company performance 708–710
Insurance company regulation 707–708
Insurance rate regulation 708
Insurance Regulatory Information System (IRIS) 707–708
Insured mortgages 228–229
Insured plans 680
Integrated bank management 495–498
Integrated financial markets 100
Interest-inelastic 26
Interest-only classes 238
Interest-only securities 201
Interest rate caps 376–378, 573, 576
Interest rate collars 376, 378–380
Interest rate floors 376, 378
Interest rate futures 292, 293–303, 335, 339, 483, 572, 574
Interest rate parity 407–408
Interest rate regulations 447–449
Interest rate risk 57, 61, 210–212, 229, 234, 236, 355, 357, 370, 476–484, 492, 542–544, 566–567, 571–577, 603–604, 617, 622, 666, 682–683, 702
Interest rate swap 355–376, 436, 483–484, 573–576
Interest rate swap markets 355–384
Interest spread 373–375
Internal Revenue Service (IRS) 684
International arbitrage 405–408
International banking 535–552
International Banking Act (1978) 537
International debt crisis 488–489, 515–516, 535, 542, 544–547
International Monetary Fund (IMF) 545, 547
International Monetary Fund Funding Bill 545
International mutual funds 273, 409, 632–635
Interstate banking 450–452, 454–455, 466, 535, 536
Interstate regulation 449–450
Intrastate regulation 449
Investment banking firms 215, 242,

252, 271, 409, 484, 540–541, 620, 656–663, 688, 711
Investment banking services 655, 656–663
Investment Company Act (1940) 645
Investment-grade bonds 75, 206, 453
Investment-grade securities 432
Iron Curtain 541
Issue costs 661–662

January effect 263, 269
Junk bond funds 632
Junk bond premium 206
Junk bonds 205–208, 431, 567, 582, 584, 585, 657, 660, 699–703
Junk commercial paper 181
Justice Department 200

Keogh Plans 686
Keynesian monetary policy 142
Keynesian theory 137–141, 144
Keynesians 143, 144
Kohlberg Kravis Roberts, Inc. (KKR) 211, 658, 681
Korean War 677–678

Lead bank 430
Leasing 615
Lender liability 431
Less developed countries 466, 488–489, 515, 544–547, 548, 713
Letter of credit 186, 541
Leveraged buyout (LBO) 204–205, 211, 213, 267, 430–431, 446, 615, 656–658, 681, 682
Leverage measure 490, 520, 523
Life insurance companies 241, 680, 695–705
Life insurance policies 696–697
Limit orders 663–664
Limited-service banks 452
Liquidity 4, 5, 74, 75–76, 80–83, 90–91, 93–94, 121, 188, 203, 256, 423, 459, 476, 528, 627
Liquidity premium 82–83, 90–91, 94–95, 100
Liquidity premium theory 90–91
Liquidity ratio 709
Liquidity risk 570–571, 602–603, 616, 702–703
Load 629
Loan ceiling 615

Loan commitments 435
Loan loss provision 512, 515–516,
    517, 519
Loan loss reserves 546–547
Loan participation 430
Loan rate regulations 449
Loanable funds 23–41, 95, 119,
    138–140, 145, 149
Loanable funds theory 23–33, 35
Locals 292
Locational arbitrage 405–407
London Interbank Offer Rate
    (LIBOR) 193, 575–576
London International Financial
    Futures Exchange (LIFFE) 311
Long hedge 301
Long position 398
Long-term equity anticipations
    (LEAPs) 334
Loose-money policy 146
Low-coupon bonds 208
LTV Corporation 686

M1 125–127, 130
M2 125–127, 130
M3 125–127, 130
Maastricht Treaty (1991) 132, 395
Maintenance margin 292
Management fees 629
Margin 250–251, 665
Margin call 250, 292, 308
Marked to market 292
Market correction 263
Market-makers 256, 264, 396
Market microstructure 256
Market orders 663
Market reaction 266, 270, 509–510
Market-related information
    268–269
Market risk 665–666, 702
Market-timers 252
Matched funding 680
Maturity date 200–201
Maturity matching 482–483
McFadden Act (1927) 449–450
Member banks 114–127
Merger-conversion 564
Merrill Lynch 201, 211, 658
Midwest Stock Exchange 255
Milken, Michael 657
Modern quantity theory of money
    142
Monetarist approach 141–143, 145
Monetarists 142–143, 144

Monetary Control Act (1980)
    127–129
Monetary policy 28, 113, 117–125,
    130–132, 137–164
Monetary theory 137–145
Monetizing the debt 158–159
Money center banks 512–519, 541
Money market deposit account
    (MMDA) 125, 421, 423, 565,
    598
Money market fund regulation
    645–646
Money market funds (see Money
    market mutual funds) 13
Money market mutual funds 10,
    125, 189, 473, 578, 628, 638–646
Money market rates 190
Money market securities 4, 6, 10,
    80, 175–189
Money market yields 190
Money markets 4, 155, 175–195,
    579, 621, 648, 669, 689, 712
Money supply 116, 117–129,
    137–145, 149–153
Money supply growth 210
Moodys Investor Service 74–75,
    180, 212, 446, 632
Moral hazard 445
Mortgage-backed securities
    236–240, 566–567
Mortgage banking 235
Mortgage companies 234–235,
    240–241
Mortgage contract 227–228
Mortgage markets 227–243, 579,
    621, 648, 669, 687, 689, 712
Mortgage maturities 230–232
Mortgage pass-through securities
    236
Mortgage rates 230
Mortgage REITs 646
Mortgages 227–234, 566, 567, 569,
    599, 615, 681, 699–701
Multinational insurance companies
    710–713
Multiplier effect 123
Municipal Bond Index (MBI)
    futures 303–304
Municipal bonds 26, 81, 199,
    201–203, 212, 303, 432, 632
Municipal securities 706
Mutual Benefit Life Insurance Co.
    703
Mutual fund regulation 637–638

Mutual funds 10, 12–13, 215, 239,
    242, 257, 310, 339–340,
    627–649, 665, 668, 688
Mutual life insurance companies
    695–696
Mutual savings and loan
    associations 563–564, 569
Mutual-to-stock-conversion 564

National Association of Insurance
    Commissioners (NAIC)
    707–708
National Association of Securities
    Dealers (NASD) 655–656
National Association of Securities
    Dealers Automatic Quotations
    (NASDAQ) 256
National Credit Union
    Administration (NCUA) 601,
    602
National Credit Union Share
    Insurance Fund (NCUSIF)
    601–602
NationsBank 479
Negotiable certificates of deposit
    (NCDs) 6, 176, 183, 187, 423,
    427
Negotiable order of withdrawal
    (NOW) 422, 472, 565, 598
Net asset value 628
Net exposure 301
Net interest margin 477–478,
    483–484, 513, 514, 517–519,
    520, 522
Net present value 24
Net underwriting margin 709–710
New York State Government
    Retirement Fund 682
New York Stock Exchange (NYSE)
    4, 255, 256, 258, 273
Noise traders 263
Noise trading 263
No-load 629
Nominal rate of interest 33–34, 39,
    100
Nonbank 452, 457
Nondepository financial
    institutions 9
Nondiversifiable risk 261
Noninterest expenses 512, 516–517,
    519, 522
Noninterest income 512, 513–515,
    517–519, 520, 522
North American Free Trade

Agreement (NAFTA) 539, 649, 671, 713
Note issuance facility (NIF) 435
NOW accounts 125–126, 129

Off-balance sheet activities 435–436, 447, 539
Off-balance sheet regulation 447
Oil prices 210
Open-end investment funds 630
Open market desk 116
Open market operations 118, 119–120, 124, 130
Option-pricing model 350–353
Option valuation 350–353
Options contracts 258, 320
Options markets 319–341, 579, 621, 648, 669, 689, 712
Organized exchange 4, 255
Origination 660, 662
Out of the money 319–320
Over-the-counter (OTC) market 4, 256, 356
Overpriced stocks 258
Overvalued stock 267–268, 269

Pacific Stock Exchange 255
Par value 48, 53, 56, 178–179
Participating banks 430
Participating certificates 236, 237
Passbook savings account 422, 565, 597
Passive strategy 214–215, 683
Penn Square Bank 499
Pension Benefit Guarantee Corporation 685–686
Pension fund management 680–683
Pension funds 10, 11, 13, 188–189, 204, 215, 257, 310, 339–340, 359, 409, 620, 647, 668, 677–689, 711
Pension Reform Act (1974) 685
Pension regulation 684–687
Perfect financial markets 8
Persian Gulf crisis 210
Phillips curve 145
Plain vanilla swaps 358–361
Policy directive 118
Policy loans 700
Political rating model 549, 550
Portfolio insurance 258
Portfolio performance 683–684
Position traders 293
Preemptive rights 252

Preferred stock 251
Present value interest factor 49–51, 53
Present value interest factor of an annuity 52–55
Primary capital 426, 601
Primary markets 4, 8, 10, 175, 255
Prime rate 429
Principal-only classes 238
Principal-only securities 201
Private pension plans 678–680, 681–682
Private placement 663
Privatization 7
Program trading 258–259, 307
Projective funding 680
Property and casualty insurance 705–707
Property insurance 705
Prospectus 660, 661, 662
Protective covenants 204, 213, 429
Proxy 249–250
Proxy fight 250
Public information 268–269
Public pension funds 678, 681–682
Publicly issued pass-through securities 236, 237
Purchasing power parity (PPP) 396
Pure expectations theory 84–89, 94
Put option 320, 323–325, 330, 332, 335, 403
Put option premium 328–330
Putable swaps 363–365

Quantity theory 141–143

Rate-capped swap 367, 369
Rate-sensitive assets 478–479
Rate-sensitive liabilities 478–479
Real estate investment trusts (REITs) 646
Real estate loans 432, 487, 615–616
Real estate mortgage conduit (REMIC) 240
Real rate of interest 33, 100
Recession 95
Reciprocal banking arrangement 452
Recognition lag 148
Registration statement 660, 662
Regression analysis 39–41, 477, 481–482, 521, 523, 575, 704
Regulation Q 422, 448, 472
Reinsurance 706–707, 713

Repo 183–184, 425, 433, 565
Repo rate 184
Repurchase agreements 6, 119, 176, 183–184, 422, 425–426, 433, 565, 567
Reserve requirement ratio 121–124
Reserve requirements 114, 130, 536, 619
Residential mortgages 227–232, 240, 615
Resolution Trust Corporation (RTC) 583–584
Restructuring 492–495, 659
Retail certificates of deposit 6, 423, 565, 597
Return on assets 459, 490, 517–520, 522–524, 525, 579, 585–586
Return on equity 490, 517, 519–521, 522
Return on net worth 709
Reunification of Germany 36, 38, 195
Revenue bonds 201–202, 303
Reverse repo 184
Reverse leveraged buyout 267–268
Revolving credit loan 429
Reward-to-systematic risk ratio 283, 284–285
Reward-to-variability ratio 283–284
Riding the yield curve 96
Risk-adjusted returns 283–285, 683–684
Risk-averse investors 260
Risk-based capital requirements 427, 447
Risk-based deposit insurance premiums 445–446, 463
Risk-free assets 260
Risk-free rate 82–83, 100, 260, 350–353
RJR Nabisco 211, 213, 657

Sales finance companies 611–612
Salomon Brothers 200
Savings and loan associations (S&Ls) 9, 117, 215, 647, 711
Savings and loan crisis 580–585
Savings Association Insurance Fund (SAIF) 563, 583
Savings banks 9, 117, 257, 359, 563, 564, 566
Savings deposits 421, 422, 427, 520, 565

Savings institution regulation 569–570

Savings institutions (see also Savings and loan associations) 9, 12–13, 93, 189, 207, 240–242, 257, 310, 339–340, 359, 563–588, 614, 660, 668

Second Bank of the United States 113

Second-class CMOs 237–238

Second mortgage 232, 233–234

Secondary capital 426, 601

Secondary markets 4, 6, 7, 8, 96, 114, 175, 178, 179, 187, 199, 202, 203, 249, 255, 432, 546

Secondary mortgage market 229, 234–240

Secondary stock offering 251, 252

Secured commercial paper 612

Securities Act (1933) 7, 645

Securities and Exchange Commission (SEC) 7, 200, 253, 256, 270, 273, 307, 628, 637, 646, 655–656, 660, 662

Securities and Exchange Commission rule 12b-1 629

Securities Exchange Act (1934) 7, 256

Securities firm regulation 655–656

Securities firms 10, 257, 310, 340, 647, 655–671, 687, 711

Securities gains and losses 512, 517

Securities Investor Protection Corporation (SIPC) 656

Securitization 236, 476

Segmented markets theory 91–94

Self-liquidating loan 429

Semistrong-form efficiency 268–269

Settlement date 402

Share certificates 597–598

Share deposits 597–598

Share drafts 598

Shared-appreciation mortgage 234

Sharpe Index 283–284, 285

Shelf-registration 253–255

Short hedge 298–301, 310

Short position 297, 398

Short seller 268, 664

Short-selling 267–268, 663, 664

Singapore International Monetary Exchange (SEMEX) 311

Single European Act (1987) 36, 195, 395, 537–538

Sinking-fund provision 203–204

Smithsonian Agreement 392

Social Security 678

Sovereign risk 372–373, 384

Specialists 256

Specialty funds 634

Speculating 295–297, 332, 335–338, 398–399, 403–405

Speculators 293, 332, 335–337, 341

Spot exchange rate 392

Spread 10, 97, 186, 571, 604

Standard and Poor's 500 Index 304, 305–306

Standard and Poor's Corporation 74–75, 180, 212, 446, 549, 632

Standard deviation 283–284, 350–353, 487

Standard Oil Company of California 266

Standby letters of credit 435

Stock exchange seat 255

Stock exchanges 255–256

Stock index futures 258, 292, 304–310, 335, 339

Stock index options 332–335, 339

Stock issues 660–662

Stock market crash (October 1987) 12, 122, 206–207, 250–251, 258–259, 267, 275, 307, 353, 699, 702

Stock market efficiency 268–270

Stock market integration 273–276

Stock markets 249–276, 621, 648, 669, 689, 712

Stock mutual funds 628, 630–637

Stock option premiums 325–330

Stock options 319–332

Stock performance 283–285

Stock price movements 262–265, 273–274

Stock price reaction 509–510

Stock valuation models 260–262

Stock volatility 258, 265, 305, 353

Stop-loss order 664

Strike price 319

Stripped bonds 201

Stripped securities 201

STRIPS 201

Strong-form efficiency 268–269

Structural rating model 549, 550

Subordinated debentures 204

Superregional banks 585

Surplus units 4, 6, 8, 11–12, 199

Swap contracts 435, 436

Swap options 363

Swap markets 579, 621, 648, 669, 689, 712

Swaptions 363

Tax-exempt bonds 202–203

Tax-free funds 632

Tax Reform Act (1986) 203, 240

Taxable munis 203

Technical analysis 264

Term insurance 696

Term loans 429

Term structure of interest rates 78–79, 84–100

Term to maturity 74, 78–79, 83–100

Texaco Inc. 266

Theory of rational expectations 143–144

Thrift Institutions Advisory Council 117

Tier 1 capital 539

Tier 2 capital 539

Tight-money policy 146, 157

Time deposits 421, 423, 427, 565

Time series analysis 708–709

Too big to fail 464–467

Trading desk 116, 118–119, 125

Trading floor 255–256

Transaction deposit 421, 422, 427

Travelers Corp. 709

Treasury bill auction 176–178

Treasury bill discount 179

Treasury bill futures 294, 302, 335, 574

Treasury bill rates 80, 179, 185, 424, 429

Treasury bill yield 200, 210

Treasury bills 6, 37, 81, 175, 176–179, 188–189, 292

Treasury bond auction 200

Treasury bond futures 294, 302, 335, 574

Treasury bond quotations 200–201

Treasury bond yield 200, 210

Treasury bonds 6, 81, 199–201, 212, 216, 292, 567, 631, 706

Treasury Investment Growth Receipts (TIGRs) 201

Treasury note futures 294, 335

Treasury notes 6, 199–200, 216, 292

Treasury securities 26, 27, 120, 432, 484, 698

Treasury strips 201

Treynor Index 283, 284–285

Trust departments 680–681
Trustee 203

Underfunded pensions 678–680,
    686–687
Underinsured 713
Underpriced stocks 258, 270
Undervalued stock 265–268, 269,
    272, 658
Underwrite 10, 218, 457, 540, 541
Underwriters 271, 457, 661
Underwriting bonds 662
Underwriting risk 218
Underwriting spread 660–661, 662
Underwriting stock 660–661
Unhedged portfolio 300
Unhedged position 300
Uniform capital adequacy
    guidelines 537, 538–539
Uniform global regulations
    537–539

Unit banking 449
Unit trusts 238–239
United Airlines 250
Universal life insurance 696–697
Unsystematic risk 522
U.S. Department of Labor 685
U.S. Treasury 4, 97–99, 176, 199
Usury laws 431

Value Line Inc. 525–528, 581, 618,
    667, 708
Variable life insurance 696
Variable-rate bonds 208
Variance 487
Velocity of money 141–142
Vesting options 685
Veterans Administration (VA)
    228–229, 236, 237, 571
Voting rights 249–250, 251

Wage Stabilization Program 677

Weak-form efficiency 268, 269
Weekend effect 269
Western Community Money
    Center of California 457
Whole life insurance 696
Working capital loan 429
World Bank 547
World War II 677
Writer 319, 341

Yield 73–100
Yield curve 78–79, 84–100
Yield differentials 80–82
Yield on assets 604
Yield on loans 600
Yield to maturity 60, 62–63, 201

Zero-coupon bond 53, 59, 208, 367
Zero-coupon-for-floating swap
    367–368